Praise for the *Handbook of World Englishes*:

"A milestone in the study of World Englishes."

Linguistics

"Bravo! This is an authoritative yet accessible collection of texts by the top scholars in the important new field of world Englishes. It is ideally suited for use as a comprehensive course text of the topic and belongs on the bookshelf of anyone concerned with the teaching and learning of English as a language of wider communication."

Sandra J. Savignon, Pennsylvania State University

"This is a monumental contribution to scholarship and a seminal contribution to the entire field of English language teaching and applied linguistics. I am particularly impressed with the concept of the four diasporas, the wide historical breadth, the international appeal, and the variety of geographical areas considered. It stands alone as the most comprehensive and representative volume and all scholars in languages and linguistics should add it to their reference libraries."

James E. Alatis, Georgetown University

"An indispensable resource for those fascinated or appalled by the global power of English today. Authoritative, accessible chapters unpack the vast panorama of 21st-century world Englishes. Outstanding."

Elizabeth de Kadt, University of KwaZulu-natal, South Africa

"This exceptional volume succeeds in capturing, with an unprecedented array of global voices, the significant theoretical, applied, and pedagogical dimensions related to the phenomenal spread of English worldwide."

Jonathan Webster, City University of Hong Kong

D1567744

Blackwell Handbooks in Linguistics

This outstanding multi-volume series covers all the major subdisciplines within linguistics today and, when complete, will offer a comprehensive survey of linguistics as a whole.

Already published:

The Handbook of Child Language
Edited by Paul Fletcher and Brian MacWhinney

The Handbook of Phonological Theory
Edited by John A. Goldsmith

The Handbook of Contemporary Semantic Theory
Edited by Shalom Lappin

The Handbook of Sociolinguistics
Edited by Florian Coulmas

The Handbook of Phonetic Sciences
Edited by William J. Hardcastle and John Laver

The Handbook of Morphology
Edited by Andrew Spencer and Arnold Zwicky

The Handbook of Japanese Linguistics
Edited by Natsuko Tsujimura

The Handbook of Linguistics
Edited by Mark Aronoff and Janie Rees-Miller

The Handbook of Contemporary Syntactic Theory
Edited by Mark Baltin and Chris Collins

The Handbook of Discourse Analysis
Edited by Deborah Schiffrin, Deborah Tannen, and Heidi E. Hamilton

The Handbook of Language Variation and Change
Edited by J. K. Chambers, Peter Trudgill, and Natalie Schilling-Estes

The Handbook of Historical Linguistics
Edited by Brian D. Joseph and Richard D. Janda

The Handbook of Language and Gender
Edited by Janet Holmes and Miriam Meyerhoff

The Handbook of Second Language Acquisition
Edited by Catherine J. Doughty and Michael H. Long

The Handbook of Bilingualism
Edited by Tej K. Bhatia and William C. Ritchie

The Handbook of Pragmatics
Edited by Laurence R. Horn and Gregory Ward

The Handbook of Applied Linguistics
Edited by Alan Davies and Catherine Elder

The Handbook of Speech Perception
Edited by David B. Pisoni and Robert E. Remez

The Blackwell Companion to Syntax, Volumes I–V
Edited by Martin Everaert and Henk van Riemsdijk

The Handbook of the History of English
Edited by Ans van Kemenade and Bettelou Los

The Handbook of English Linguistics
Edited by Bas Aarts and April McMahon

The Handbook of World Englishes
Edited by Braj B. Kachru; Yamuna Kachru, and Cecil L. Nelson

The Handbook of Educational Linguistics
Edited by Bernard Spolsky and Francis M. Hult

The Handbook of Clinical Linguistics
Edited by Martin J. Ball, Michael R. Perkins, Nicole Müller, and Sara Howard

The Handbook of
World Englishes

Edited by

Braj B. Kachru,
Yamuna Kachru,
Cecil L. Nelson

⊛ **WILEY-BLACKWELL**

A John Wiley & Sons, Ltd., Publication

This edition first published 2009
© 2009 Blackwell Publishing Ltd except for editorial material and organization
© 2009 Braj B. Kachru, Yamuna Kachru, and Cecil L. Nelson

Edition History: Blackwell Publishing Ltd (hardback, 2006)

Blackwell Publishing was acquired by John Wiley & Sons in February 2007. Blackwell's
publishing program has been merged with Wiley's global Scientific, Technical, and
Medical business to form Wiley-Blackwell.

Registered Office
John Wiley & Sons Ltd, The Atrium, Southern Gate, Chichester, West Sussex, PO19 8SQ,
United Kingdom

Editorial Offices
350 Main Street, Malden, MA 02148-5020, USA
9600 Garsington Road, Oxford, OX4 2DQ, UK
The Atrium, Southern Gate, Chichester, West Sussex, PO19 8SQ, UK

For details of our global editorial offices, for customer services, and for information about how
to apply for permission to reuse the copyright material in this book please see our website at
www.wiley.com/wiley-blackwell.

The right of Braj B. Kachru, Yamuna Kachru, and Cecil L. Nelson to be identified as the author
of the editorial material in this work has been asserted in accordance with the Copyright,
Designs and Patents Act 1988.

Wiley also publishes its books in a variety of electronic formats. Some content that appears in
print may not be available in electronic books.

Designations used by companies to distinguish their products are often claimed as trademarks.
All brand names and product names used in this book are trade names, service marks,
trademarks or registered trademarks of their respective owners. The publisher is not associated
with any product or vendor mentioned in this book. This publication is designed to provide
accurate and authoritative information in regard to the subject matter covered. It is sold
on the understanding that the publisher is not engaged in rendering professional services.
If professional advice or other expert assistance is required, the services of a competent
professional should be sought.

Library of Congress Cataloging-in-Publication Data

The handbook of world Englishes / edited by Braj B. Kachru, Yamuna Kachru, Cecil L. Nelson.
   p. cm.
   Includes bibliographical references and index.
ISBN: 978-1-4051-1185-0 (hardback : alk. paper) – ISBN: 978-1-4051-8831-9 (pbk : alk. paper)
   1. English language – Foreign countries. 2. English language – Variation – Foreign countries.
3. English language – Social aspects – Foreign countries. 4. Intercultural communication.
I. Kachru, Braj B. II. Kachru, Yamuna. III. Nelson, Cecil L.

PE2751.H36 2006
427–dc22
                                                                        2005034554
A catalogue record for this book is available from the British Library.

Set in 10/12pt Palatino by Graphicraft Ltd, Hong Kong
Printed and bound in Malaysia by KHL Printing Co. Sdn Bhd

1   2009

Dedicated to
mentors, educators, and researchers
whose contributions have
provided refreshing
visions for our better
understanding of world Englishes

James E. Alatis

Ayọ Bamgboṣe

Maria Lourdes S. Bautista

Anita Desai

John Rupert Firth

Sidney Greenbaum

M. A. K. Halliday

Tom McArthur

C. D. Narasimhaiah

Raja Rao

Larry E. Smith

Edwin Thumboo

Contents

Figures and Tables

Contributors

Michael Aceto, Department of English, East Carolina University, 2201 Bate Building, Greenville, NC 27858-4353, USA. Email: acetom@mail.ecu.edu

John Algeo, University of Georgia, P.O. Box 80206, Athens, GA 30608-0206, USA. Email: JohnAlgeo@aol.com

Ayọ Bamgboṣe, Department of Linguistics and African Languages, University of Ibadan, Ibadan, Nigeria. Email: bamgbose@skannet.com

Robert J. Baumgardner, Department of Literature and Languages, Texas A&M University-Commerce, Commerce, Texas 75429, USA. Email: Robert_Baumgardner@tamu-commerce.edu

Maria Lourdes S. Bautista, Department of English and Applied Linguistics, De La Salle University, P.O. Box 3819, Manila, Philippines 1004. Email: bautistam@dlsu.edu.ph

Margie Berns, Department of English, Purdue University, Heavilon Hall, Room 324, 500 Oval Drive, West Lafayette, IN 47907-2038, USA. Email: berns@purdue.edu

Tej K. Bhatia, Linguistics and Cognitive Sciences, 312 HBC, Syracuse University, Syracuse, New York 13244-1160, USA. Email: tkbhatia@mailbox.syr.edu

Vijay K. Bhatia, Department of English and Communication, Centre for Language Education and Communication Research, City University of Hong Kong, Tat Chee Avenue, KOWLOON, Hong Kong. Email: enbhatia@cityu.edu.hk

Kingsley Bolton, Department of English, Stockholm University, 106 91 Stockholm, Sweden. Email: Kingsley.Bolton@English.su.se

Kimberley Brown, Department of Applied Linguistics, Portland State University, PO Box 751, Portland, OR 97207-0751, USA. Email: brownk@pdx.edu

Fred Davidson, Division of English as an International Language, University of Illinois, 3080 Foreign Language Building, 707 S. Mathews Avenue, Urbana, IL 61801, USA. Email: fgd@uiuc.edu

Daniel R. Davis, Department of Humanities, The University of Michigan–Dearborn, 4901 Evergreen Road, Dearborn, MI 48128-1491, USA Email: davisdr@umd.umich.edu

Pradeep A. Dhillon, Department of Educational Policy Studies, College of Education, University of Illinois, 369, 1310 S. Sixth Street, Champaign, IL 61820, USA. Email: dhillon@uiuc.edu

Wimal Dissanayake, 619 Keolu Drive, Kailua, HI 96734-3927, USA. Email: ddissa@yahoo.com

Fredric Dolezal, P.O. Box 8042, Athens, Georgia 30603, USA. Email: fdolezal@uga.edu

Fiona Douglas, School of English, University of Leeds, Leeds LS2 9JT, UK. Email: f.m.douglas@leeds.ac.uk

Helen Fallon, National University of Ireland Maynooth, Maynooth, Co. Kildare, Ireland. Email: Helen.B.Fallon@may.ie

Ravinder Gargesh, Department of Linguistics, University of Delhi, Delhi-110007, India. Email: rgargesh1@rediffmail.com

Andrew B. Gonzalez, Department of English and Applied Linguistics, De La Salle University, P.O. Box 3819, Manila, Philippines 1004. Email: bautistam@dlsu.edu.ph

M. A. K. Halliday, Unit 14, 133 Sydney Road, Fairlight, NSW 2094, Australia. Email: hasanruqaiya@yahoo.com.au

Nobuyuki Honna, Aoyama Gakuin University, 4-4-25 Shibuya, Shibuya-ku, Tokyo, Japan 150-8366. Email: honna@sipeb.aoyama.ac.jp, nyhonna@ri.aoyama.ac.jp, honna@attglobal.net

Braj B. Kachru, Department of Linguistics, University of Illinois, 4088 Foreign Languages Building, 707 S. Mathews Avenue, Urbana, IL 61801, USA. Email: b-kachru@uiuc.edu

Yamuna Kachru, Department of Linguistics, University of Illinois, 4088 Foreign Languages Building, 707 S. Mathews Avenue, Urbana, IL 61801, USA. Email: ykachru@uiuc.edu

Nkonko M. Kamwangamalu, Department of English, Howard University, 248 Locke Hall, 2441 6th Street N.W., Washington, DC 20059, USA. Email: nkamwangamalu@howard.edu

Scott F. Kiesling, Department of Linguistics, University of Pittsburgh, Pittsburgh, PA 15260, USA. Email: kiesling@pitt.edu

Robert D. King, Departments of Linguistics, Germanic Studies, and Asian Studies, University of Texas, HRHRC 3.318, Austin, TX 78713, USA. Email: rking@mail.utexas.edu

Elizabeth A. Martin, Department of French, University of Illinois at Urbana-Champaign, 2090 Foreign Languages Building, 707 S. Mathews Avenue, Urbana, Illinois 61801, USA. Email: emartin@uiuc.edu

Rajend Mesthrie, Linguistics Section, Department of English, University of Cape Town, Rondebosch, 7707, South Africa. Email: raj@humanities.uct.ac.za

Linda C. Mitchell, Department of English and Comparative Literature, San Jose State University, San Jose, CA 95192-0090, USA. Email: lmitchel@email.sjsu.edu

Marko Modiano, Östermalmsgatan 100, 114 59 Stockholm, Sweden. Email: Marko.Modiano@hig.se

Salikoko S. Mufwene, Department of Linguistics, University of Chicago, 1010 East 59th Street, Chicago, IL 60637, USA. Email: s-mufwene@uchicago.edu

Cecil L. Nelson, Department of Languages, Literatures and Linguistics, Indiana State University, Terre Haute, IN 47809, USA. Email: flcln@isugw.indstate.edu

Gerald Nelson, Department of English Language and Literature, University College London, Gower Street, London WC1E 6BT, UK. Email: g.nelson@ucl.ac.uk

Tope Omoniyi, School of Arts, Roehampton University, Roehampton Lane, London SW15 5PH, UK. Email: T.omoniyi@roehampton.ac.uk

Kanavillil Rajagopalan, Department of Linguistics, Institute of Language Studies, State University at Campinas (UNICAMP), Cidade Universitária "Zeferini Vaz", Distrito de Barão Geraldo, Campinas SP, 13081-970 Brazil. Email: rajagopalan@uol.com.br

Josef Schmied, Chemnitz University of Technology, D-09107 Chemnitz, Germany. Email: josef.schmied@phil.tu-chemnitz.de

Edgar W. Schneider, University of Regensburg, Department of English and American Studies, D-93040 Regensburg, Germany. Email: edgar.schneider @sprachlit.uni-regensburg.de

Larry E. Smith, Christopher, Smith & Associates LLC, 45-301 Akimala Pl. #1070, Kane'ohe, HI 96744-2201, USA. Email: csa@lava.net

Edwin Thumboo, Department of English Language and Literature, National University of Singapore, Block AS5, 7 Arts Link, Singapore 117570. Email: cfahead@nus.edu.sg

Tamara M. Valentine, University of Nevada, Reno, Honors Program MS/112, Reno, NV 89557, USA. Email: tvalenti@unr.edu

Stanley Yunick Van Horn, Intensive English Institute, University of Illinois, 1205 W. Nevada St., Urbana, IL 61801, USA. Email: svanhorn@uiuc.edu

Walt Wolfram, Box 8105, English Department, North Carolina State University, Raleigh, NC 27695-8105, USA. Email: wolfram@social.chass.ncsu.edu

Preface

One might understandably ask, "Why yet another resource volume?" when there is no paucity of reference works for the English language. Such publications are available, with varied orientations, in every genre – companions, encyclopedias, handbooks, and manuals – in almost every part of the English-speaking world.

We had two motivations for initiating this handbook project: First, we thought it important to revisit the proliferation of terminologies and concepts articulating the global uses of Englishes (e.g., *international*, *lingua franca*, *world English*, *global English*) in the post-1950s diffusion and cross-cultural functions and identities of varieties of the language. It has been extensively – and insightfully – argued that all these concepts only partially represent the social, cultural, educational, and attitudinal realities of the presence of Englishes in their worldwide contexts. It is further rightly argued that the multiple and diverse functions of world Englishes in dynamic societies of Asia, Africa, Europe, and the Americas demand theoretical and methodological perspectives that contextualize the varied and increasingly evolving cultural and social characteristics of the language. There is indeed greater emphasis today than in the past on capturing the expanding fusions and hybridizations of linguistic forms and the unprecedented variations in global functions of world Englishes. It is, we believe, appropriate to remind ourselves that the English language has a long history of convergence with and assimilation of other languages. What is new – and not necessarily recognized by all observers – is that the colonial and post-colonial eras opened challenging new doors for contacts with a great variety of distinct linguistic structures and cultures associated with Asian, African, and Native American languages.

Our second set of motivations involved the dynamic global profile of the language, which has drawn the attention of scholars in diverse areas. This interest is evident in studies related to cross-cultural linguistic and literary creativity, language change and convergence, and world Englishes in education, especially in Asian and African contexts. Researchers in these areas will immediately think of that pioneering and insightful undertaking, *The Oxford Companion to the English Language* (1992), edited by Tom McArthur, which brought together selected scholars from all the circles of Englishes. Earlier efforts in this direction, though not with the same encyclopedic range of topics and contributions, include Bailey and Görlach (1982), Smith (1981, 1987), and B. Kachru (1982/1992), to provide just a few examples.

In outlining and designing *The Handbook of World Englishes*, the editors, as expected in any such project, had to face the conflict between practical limitations and larger visions and dreams. This volume is, then, a compromise between an ambitious agenda and the accomplished reality. Our dilemma was very similar to the one that Tom McArthur faced in 1992 (p. vii):

> Liberals would want to be fair to everyone, balancing every viewpoint and counter-viewpoint, until from the point of view of conservatives everything cancelled out everything else.

We finally decided to follow the much-talked-about "middle path" (*madhyama mārga*). The result is *The Handbook of World Englishes* in its present form.

In characterizing this handbook, it might be easier to say what it is actually *not*: it is not an encyclopedia, and it is not a volume of structural descriptions of world varieties of Englishes. A good example of such a work is Kortmann and Schneider (2005). Instead, *The Handbook of World Englishes* is a compendium of selected, thematically integrated topics that brings together multiple theoretical, contextual, and ideological perspectives that may *include* descriptions, but whose primary aim is to provide fresh interpretations of changing identities of users and uses of Englishes across the Three Circles. In this sense, then, we believe that *The Handbook* provides refreshing and, indeed, still hotly debated theoretical and functional constructs of world Englishes. In other words, it locates them in socially relevant and contextually appropriate situations. The contributors of regional profiles (Parts 1–3) were free to present their areas and varieties in terms of what they felt was important to emphasize, in order to provide historical, ideological, and ideational insights for the varieties under discussion.

In realizing our vision for *The Handbook* we are indebted, first, to our contributors, whose cooperation and patience made the volume possible. The editors, of course, bear the responsibility for any limitations of the work. We wish to express our deep gratitude to Larry Smith for his help at every step in the conceptualization of this volume; to Kingsley Bolton for his insight and suggestions; to Stanley Van Horn for his comments on and critique of various points; to Sarah Coleman of Blackwell Publishing for her professional editorial advice and smooth implementation of the editorial process; to Anna Oxbury for copyediting a complex volume with her usual patience and expertise; to Heeyoun Cho, Jamie S. Lee, Wooseung Lee, and Theera Ratitamkul for their assistance in multiple ways at various stages in the completion of the volume; and to the Research Board of the Graduate College of the University of Illinois at Urbana-Champaign for their support. And finally, to our families, who not only tolerated our focusing our time and energies on this extensive and intensive project, often at their expense, but encouraged us at every step with their support and love.

REFERENCES

Bailey, Richard W. and Görlach, Manfred (eds.) (1982) *English as a World Language*. Ann Arbor, MI: University of Michigan Press.

Kachru, Braj B. (ed.) (1982/1992) *The Other Tongue: English across Cultures*. Urbana, IL: University of Illinois Press. 2nd edition 1992.

Kortmann, Bernd and Schneider, Edgar W. (2005) *A Handbook of Varieties of English: A Multimedia Research Tool*. Berlin: Mouton de Gruyter. (Edited together with Kate Burridge, Rajend Mesthrie, and Clive Upton.)

McArthur, Tom (1992) *The Oxford Companion to the English Language*. Oxford: Oxford University Press.

Smith, Larry E. (ed.) (1981) *English for Cross-Cultural Communication*. London: Macmillan.

Smith, Larry E. (ed.) (1987) *Discourse across Cultures: Strategies in World Englishes*. London: Prentice-Hall.

Introduction: The World of World Englishes

BRAJ B. KACHRU, YAMUNA KACHRU, AND CECIL L. NELSON

Introduction

The Handbook of World Englishes presents essentially – but not exclusively – selected critical dimensions of theoretical, ideological, applied and pedagogical constructs related to the unprecedented spread of the English medium in world contexts. The emphasis of the volume's nine parts and forty-two chapters is on exploring and elucidating topics of the following types:

1 the distinctiveness of the sociolinguistic contexts of varieties of Englishes, their diffusion and location in world contexts;
2 the functional ranges and domains in which such varieties are actually used across cultures;
3 the creative processes that determine the distinctiveness of each major variety at various linguistic levels;
4 the relationship of linguistic creativity to acculturation in distinct sociocultural contexts of Asia, Africa and other parts of the English-using world;
5 the distinction between *genetic* and *functional* nativeness, and its theoretical and pragmatic implications;
6 the characteristics of cross-over between canons and canonicities, and devices used for representing such distinctiveness; and
7 attitude-marking love–hate relationships with the medium and their reflections in language policies and language planning in Anglophone societies.

One major aim of *The Handbook of World Englishes* is, then, to represent the cross-cultural and global contextualization of the English language in multiple voices. In this respect, the forty-two invited contributions represent and articulate visions from the major varieties of world Englishes – African, Asian, European, and North and South American.

Structure

The volume is divided into nine parts, and each part comprises thematically appropriate chapters.

Part I: The historical context

The 15 chapters of Part I unfold the spread of English across cultural and linguistic boundaries, roughly following the conceptualization of the Three Circles of English first discussed by Kachru (1985; see also Kachru, 2005: 211–20). In "The Beginnings" (Chapter 1), Robert D. King asks, "how did the English language begin, this supple, economic, subtle instrument of communication, commerce, and belles-lettres that has become de facto and in many institutions and contexts de jure the lingua franca of the world? Where and when was it born?"

In tracing the earliest "growth patterns of English," King follows a tree metaphor. Chapters 2–3 introduce the First Diaspora of the English language, beginning with that of "Wales and Ireland" (Robert D. King). The story of Wales and Ireland is essentially "the first step," "the story of the replacement of one language by another." King warns that "it is almost impossible to resist reaching for military metaphors to give a name to what happened. We talk of a 'conquest' . . . the replacement of one language by another does have points in common with 'conquests' and 'victories'."

The chapter on "English in Scotland" (Fiona Douglas) warns that the title "belies a complex and heterogeneous situation." In the growth of Scottish English, there are, Douglas points out, two strands: first, the development of *Scots*, and later, the development of *Scottish Standard English*, a variety formed in contact with the southern English standard during the eighteenth century.

In the Second Diaspora, "English in North America" (Edgar W. Schneider) "began as the first of Britain's colonial (and later post-colonial) offspring, and it went through the same process of linguistic and cultural appropriation that has shaped the post-colonial varieties." In this respect, then, as Schneider argues, English in North America shares several linguistic processes with varieties of English in, for example, Australia, New Zealand, and South Africa (see also Mufwene, 1996, and 2001: 106, who finds "The same processes in African-American English and other 'disenfranchised Englishes'.").

Chapter 5 discusses the varieties of Englishes in Australia and New Zealand (Scott F. Kiesling). One might ask: Why a single chapter for two distinct varieties in the second diaspora of Englishes? Kiesling appropriately answers this question:

> The relatively short distance from Sydney to Auckland has meant that there has been significant travel and migration between the two since colonization. This intermigration is likely one of the factors that has led them to have similar

ways of speaking. There is thus a very strong linguistic motivation to include them together. Finally, they both were colonized by the British fairly late (Australia in 1788 and New Zealand circa 1840)...[T]here is a logical basis in grouping them together when viewed from historical, geographical, and linguistic viewpoints.

The Third Diaspora transplanted English in new linguistic, cultural and social contexts. It entailed teaching and learning English in multilingual situations with genetically and culturally unrelated African (e.g., Bantu and Niger-Congo), Asian (e.g., Indo-Aryan, Dravidian, and Dardic), and East Asian (e.g., Altaic and Austronesian) language contexts.

In historical terms, these continents opened up fresh linguistic resources for contact and convergence with English, and growth and development of yet more international and regional contact varieties of the language. The result was that new dimensions of linguistic creativity evolved. These aspects of creativity are discussed in detail, with their theoretical and applied implications, in Parts III, IV, VII, and VIII.

The nine chapters grouped under the "Third Diaspora" provide descriptive profiles of the contexts, creativity, and language policies of some selected regions from the third diaspora: South Asia (Ravinder Gargesh), East Asia (Nobuyuki Honna), Southeast Asia (M. Bautista and Andrew Gonzalez), South America (Kanavillil Rajagopalan), South Africa (Nkonko Kamwangamalu), West Africa (Tope Omoniyi), East Africa (Joseph Schmied), the Caribbean (Michael Aceto), and Europe (Marko Modiano).

Chapter 15, "World Englishes Today" (the Fourth Diaspora) provides a penetrating overview of the terminological, functional and theoretical conceptualizations of the current presence of English in its pluralistic world contexts and of its characterization and the constructs of English in world Englishes.

First, Kingsley Bolton explains the "meanings and interpretations" of the term "world Englishes," and the underlying philosophy of a "world Englishes paradigm." A number of "distinct, albeit overlapping, approaches to research (and publications) in the field of 'world Englishes', 'new Englishes', and 'new varieties of English'" are identified and outlined in the following seven approaches: (1) English studies; (2) sociolinguistics (sociology of language, feature-based, Kachruvian, pidgin and creole studies); (3) applied linguistics; (4) lexicographical; (5) the popularizers; (6) critical linguistics; and finally, (7) the futurology approach. This all-embracing survey of the world Englishes "enterprise" shows, as Bolton summarizes it, "a changing disciplinary and discoursal map, marked by a series of paradigm shifts in the last 20 years."

The concluding section considers some points about taking theory to practice – in other words, the implications of such paradigms on applied theory or "applied linguistics." That indeed includes "different understandings of the field of 'applied linguistics'."

Part II: Variational contexts

The first chapter of Part II, "Contact Linguistics and World Englishes" (Rajend Mesthrie), argues for a greater degree of rapprochement between the fields of world Englishes and contact linguistics. The varieties of English in the Outer and Expanding Circles are essentially "contact varieties," with their distinct characteristics of nativization and hybridity, in formal linguistic terms, and in their sociocultural features and identity construction in sociolinguistic terms. The sources for contact and convergence include, argues Mesthrie, the regional dialects of settlers, sailors and soldiers from the Inner Circle, and the first or additional languages of missionaries who were responsible for introducing the teaching of English in diverse contexts. It is claimed that the contribution of the substrate languages notwithstanding, the impact of the superstrate is no less influential than realized earlier in constructs of the varieties in these Circles.

The second chapter, "Varieties of World Englishes" (Kingsley Bolton), high-lights how the concepts *language, variety,* and *variation* are crucial in under-standing the "world Englishes enterprise." Identificational terms such as "varieties of English," "localized varieties of English," "non-native varieties of English," "second language varieties of English," and "new varieties of English" lie at the heart of such a conceptualization. We might, as an aside, add that some of these ideational terms, such as "second language" and "new" varieties are contextually, conceptually, and historically misleading.

In theoretical and pragmatic terms, then, the use of the term "Englishes" emphasizes the autonomy and plurality of the world varieties of the English language. The term "Englishes," Bolton argues, "emphasizes the autonomy and plurality of English languages worldwide." As opposed to this, "the phrase 'varieties of English' suggests heteronomy of such varieties to the common core of 'English'." The "double-voicedness" of such nomenclature (English vs. Englishes) "resonates within the much-cited Bakhtinian distinction between 'centrifugal' and 'centripetal' forces in language change." The chapter locates the term "variety" within the context of world Englishes and "attempts to unravel discussions of the wider theoretical context" in the following sections.

In our understanding of world Englishes and their functional ranges and domains, creoles and pidgins are integral parts of the linguistic ecology. The third chapter, "Pidgins and Creoles" (Salikoko Mufwene), provocatively raises certain conceptual and functional questions about such varieties. Mufwene interrogates the genetic scenario that suggests that creoles evolved from pidgins. He argues that "this genetic scenario is questioned by the colonial history of the territories where these varieties emerged, independent of each other." This chapter addresses three major issues: the nature of pidgins and creoles, the development of creoles, and creolization and general linguistics. Mufwene arrives at the conclusion that "studies of structural aspects of creoles have yet to inform general linguistics beyond the subject matter of time reference and serial verb constructions."

The fourth chapter, "African American English" (Walt Wolfram), discusses the formal linguistic issues concerning African American English. This ethnic dialect has received more scholarly, sociolinguistic, educational, and political attention than any other dialect of English. It has been characterized in many *avataras*, and the discussions have, as Wolfram suggests, "often related to underlying issues of racial politics and ethnic ideologies in American society." The labels for such *avataras* "include: *Negro Dialect, Nonstandard Negro English, Black English, Black English Vernacular, Afro-American English, African American (Vernacular) English, African American Language*," and in recent years, *Ebonics*. This chapter, however, primarily focuses on the "descriptive base" of the variety, "its genesis and its early development," and the change and development it is currently going through.

Part III: Acculturation

The chapters in Part III examine the three major facets of acculturation of world Englishes. Chapter 20, "Written Language, Standard Language, Global Language" (M. A. K. Halliday), provides a larger perspective about how English, along with a small number of other languages in the modern period, has expanded away from local and national to international domains, changing as it moved into different social and cultural contexts. In the evolution of language, critical moments occur when a language is used both as a spoken and written medium, and when it acquires the form of a standard language in what is considered a nation-state. The present reality of the English language, Halliday argues, is that it is acquiring a new identity as the "global language" of the late capitalist world. The chapter discusses some of the consequences of this development. However, Halliday suggests that we have to wait till we realize the long-term effects that globalization has on the English medium.

The two chapters that follow discuss the acculturation of English in terms of specific functional roles in cross-cultural contexts. "Speaking and Writing in World Englishes" (Yamuna Kachru) illustrates the conventions of language and language use in multilingual societies where a number of languages make up the verbal repertoire of speakers/writers. This results in characteristic patterns of language use. The focus of her discussion is on speech acts, cross-cultural speech act research, linguistic politeness, and writing practices.

In Chapter 22, "Genres and Styles in World Englishes," Vijay K. Bhatia brings out the perspectives of register, text-type, and other similar functional criteria to show that genres are motivated by the common concern of highlighting functional variation in a variety of language. The sociolinguistic reality, however, is that all these concepts represent particular ways of identifying functional and formal constructs of a variety of world Englishes. The chapter discusses the distinctions between two frequently used terms, *genre* and *style*. The functional uses of these terms are discussed with reference to world Englishes and liberal vs. conservative genres.

Part IV: Crossing borders

The three chapters of Part IV deal with inclusive issues of acculturation that accrue in the worldwide varieties of English and in the conceptualization of those varieties under one designation, "world Englishes": literary creativity, intelligibility, canonicity and the "culture wars" that arise from territorial allegiances to one or another vision of what "English" is or can be and how it works.

In Chapter 23, "Literary Creativity in World Englishes," Edwin Thumboo argues that "the dynamics of literary creativity . . . are largely generated from within. External influences tend to stimulate rather than confront." The results of this stimulation can be seen in the growth in output and kinds of experimentation in literatures in Englishes across the world. Part of the acculturation of English in various contexts is the addition, subtraction, and expansion of its elements at all levels; another part is its acquisition of new genres and styles. While creative literatures share the medium of English, they retain – and develop – their own identities; as Thumboo concludes: "We ought to treat the new literatures as separate in certain essential aspects despite their sharing of English."

In Chapter 24, "World Englishes and Issues of Intelligibility," Larry E. Smith and Cecil L. Nelson examine one of the central objections of Randolph Quirk and others to recognizing the ongoing development of variation across Englishes, i.e., the "frequently voiced concern . . . that speakers of different varieties of English will soon become unintelligible to one another." The first and most straightforward rejoinder to this apprehension is that one has only to look around the English-using world, historically or in terms of the present day situation, to see that it has always been the case that some English speakers have been at least to some degree unintelligible to other English speakers. The "brogue" of Ocracoke, North Carolina (USA) sounds very different from the English spoken on California's beaches, or on Australia's, for that matter; and there are many mismatches of lexical items across the populations, yet any observer would call all three varieties "English." Having recognized variation, as legitimate observers must, a uniformitarian principle must allow – indeed, make it certain – that the same kinds of variations exist across "non-native" Englishes, institutionalized or not. It remains to document the matches or mismatches, and to investigate the necessary bases of intelligibility, expanded as intelligibility, comprehensibility, and interpretability. As Smith and Nelson conclude, "[S]ince all the evidence shows that most non-Inner-Circle uses of English across the world do not involve Inner-Circle users, more studies of those interactions will continue to reveal what the criteria of intelligibility truly are."

In Chapter 25, "World Englishes and Culture Wars" (Braj B. Kachru), the present diffusion and constructs of and attitudes toward English in the world today are compared to the legendary "Speaking Tree," which awakens in the minds of its beholders "both fear and celebration, aversion and esteem, and indeed agony and ecstasy." Those who see the canon of English literature or of Englishness as relatively fixed, a starting point with distance measured from it to far-flung reduplications of the pattern, are those who view the spread of

English with "fear and aversion," while those who see it from the world Englishes paradigm react to the same data with attitudes of "celebration and esteem." While English is in one sense – cross-culturally – "international," that is a term that Kachru avoids, since there is not *an* English that is uniform in its forms and functions from place to place, from culture to culture. Drawing on the metaphor of Caliban, who was taught speech for the convenience of his master so that they could communicate with one another, but who rejected any allegiance to that speech in no uncertain terms, Kachru writes that the medium of English is shared by all of its users in the three Circles, but that "[t]he *mantras*, the messages and discourses, represent multiple identities and contexts and visions." It is in this "variousness" that English finds its being in the present.

Part V: *Grammar wars and standards*

In all major languages, historical issues related to ideology, attitudes, and standardization have been at the center of the cross-cultural grammar wars. In the case of English, this is reflected, for example, in the anthology of "readings in language, history and cultural identity" entitled *Proper English?* (edited by Tony Crowley, 1991). The readings include papers by John Locke (1690), Jonathan Swift (1712), Samuel Johnson (1747), Thomas Sheridan (1762), James Buchanan (1764), Noah Webster (1789), John Walker (1791), John Pickering (1816), T. Watts (1850), Archbishop R. C. Trench (1851), G. F. Graham (1869), Henry Alfrod (1864), Henry James (1905), Henry Newbolt (1921), Henry Wyld (1934), A. S. C. Ross (1954), Alison Assiter (1983), and John Marenbon (1987). This debate, spread over centuries in the Inner Circle, has still not abated, and yet new constructs of perspectives – ideological, theoretical and methodological – continue to be brought into it.

As an aside, one might add here that earlier examples of such grammar textbooks with loaded ideological, political, and social agendas have a long history. One such example, now from the Outer Circle, is provided by Frances B. Singh (1987). In her pioneering study on pre-Raj and post-Raj South Asia (India), Singh "examines the various connections four grammar books . . . posit between the English language and Indian society." The grammars are by J. Nesfield (1895), L. Tipping (1933), P. C. Wren and H. Martin (1954), and C. D. Sidhu (1976). In her perceptive analysis, Singh first presents Nesfield's agenda in construction of the grammar text:

> The sentences of Nesfield's text propagate the notion of the British supremacy and impose a view of history which justifies colonial rule. It is a view which corresponds to the contemporary conception of English as an imposed foreign language, the language of political domination and synonym for it. (1987: 253)

Second comes the construct of Tipping; his position is:

> . . . that English is to be assimilated to the Indian context. The revised edition of Wren and Martin's grammar follows in the Tipping tradition. English is no longer

seen as something imposed, but as something in the process of being Indianized. (1987: 253)

Finally, comes the grammar of Sidhu which, says Singh, "is radically different from the others":

> It reveals a familiarity with the way life is experienced in India. Sidhu's grammar proves that English language teaching can be taught through and express Indian experiences. (1987: 253)

And Singh rightly concludes that:

> In so doing, the English language becomes the opposite of its historical role: a mode of communication which expresses Indians' consciousness of themselves as citizens of an independent country. (1987: 253)

In this analysis Singh demonstrates the development between the English medium and constructs of the messages. Singh's paper is not part of this handbook, but her insights and analysis, documented briefly here, in this case, in India, are appropriate for our understanding of the strategies and constructs generally used in grammar textbooks.

In Part V, Chapter 26, "Grammar Wars: Seventeenth- and Eighteenth-Century England" (Linda C. Mitchell), outlines how the grammarians of the seventeenth and eighteenth centuries, though claiming to "[protect] the language from corruption . . . were in fact positioning themselves on a cultural battlefield, using linguistics to protest social issues." Mitchell describes four such major battles. First, concerning the status of English vis-à-vis Latin; second, about "good grammar" against "good writing"; third, debate over the nature of "universal grammar"; and, fourth, "how grammar could regulate the speech and therefore power of such marginal groups as foreigners, workers, and the middle class."

In Chapter 27, John Algeo critically outlines the phenomena of grammar wars in the United States, rightly warning us that such wars are not limited to the USA; "The Greeks had a word for it – *logomachia* 'a war about words'." St Paul used that term in his first epistle to Timothy (6:4–5), where he wrote of one who "is puffed up, knowing nothing but doting about questions and disputes of words [*logomachia*], whereof cometh envy, strife, railing, evil surmisings, wrangling of men corrupted in mind and bereft of the truth." One grammar war, following Benjamin Lee Whorf (1956), is "about how we conceptualize words, [it] is to dispute about epistemology – how we know the world. Grammar wars are thus philosophical in their nature, but they have also been linked, more or less closely, with disputes about usage, in the sense of what is genuine, correct or proper language."

These wars result in establishing relationships with sociology and social classes. The two major aspects of such wars are theoretical (or philosophical) and related to usage (or sociological). Algeo's chapter penetratingly discusses multiple dimensions of grammar wars over theory and over usage. In conclusion, he observes: "If we look at the recent history of linguistic theories, it is clear that any equilibrium in logomachia is not likely to last long. In this era of globalization, with rapid advances in information distribution and technology, the intense war over usage is likely to continue. The relative peace of the previous 19 centuries has inexorably given way to new controversies and debates."

Chapter 28, "World Englishes and Descriptive Grammars" (Daniel R. Davis), continues the theme of the paper Davis presented at the International Association for World Englishes conference in Syracuse in 2003, where he reminded us that:

> All discourses about grammar, including teaching, research, and even informal discussion, run certain risks. The comparison of different models suggests the relative nature of grammatical descriptions, thus opening the possibility that the character of the description depends more on the assumptions made in order to construct the object of description than on the reality of the object itself. This theoretical awkwardness must be taken with terminological and bibliographical difficulties of the subject matter.

Davis provides a tentative appraisal of the issues that are encountered in descriptive grammars of world Englishes; these include the roots of the descriptive tradition; the part that varieties of English play in the descriptive grammars of English in the twentieth and early twenty-first centuries; the theoretical difficulties that grammatical description, in particular structuralism, inherits from linguistic theory and their implications on descriptions of world Englishes; recent developments in the description of world Englishes; and, finally, the chapter assesses the potential that grammatical description has in the field of world Englishes.

Part VI: Ideology, identity, and constructs

The three chapters that constitute this part address the strongly articulated debates over ideology, identity, and constructs of the English language. The chapter on "Colonial/Postcolonial Critique: The Challenge from World Englishes" (Pradeep A. Dhillon) considers the function of English "in the construction of colonial, particularly British, discourse and postcolonial critique." The critique and its relevance in relation to world Englishes is discussed in broader theoretical, ideological, and functional contexts, including Orientalism and world Englishes; a return to liberal Humanism; cultural and linguistic complexity; the challenge from world Englishes; world Englishes against Relativism; and beyond Orientalism.

Dhillon essentially argues that "we can find a vivid way of realizing the logic of such an ecological humanism, through the consideration of the nature and use of a particular language – English. This works less as an analogy than as an example, even the epitome, of what is important in cultural coherence and interaction. There is no such thing as a universal language; there are diverse *languages*."

The chapter outlines "the general contours of colonial discourse and postcolonial critique that dominate much of our understanding of the workings of a global language such as English." Dhillon suggests that "world Englishes discourse offers the possibilities of a refinement of liberal international communication in a way that avoids the problems of facile universalist assumptions even as it strives to uncover a deep humanism."

In Chapter 30, "Cultural Studies and Discursive Constructions of World Englishes" (Wimal Dissanayake), it is demonstrated that the relationship between Cultural Studies and English Studies is increasingly drawing the attention of humanistic scholars. It is within that focus that Dissanayake discusses topics such as Cultural Studies and the ontology of world Englishes; world Englishes and transnationalization; world Englishes and the politics of the metaphoric self. In conclusion, Dissanayake suggests selected topics that are "central to the work of Cultural Studies and which could be explored further in terms of the concerns of world Englishes."

In "World Englishes and Gender Identities," Chapter 31, Tamara M. Valentine adopts a socially realistic perspective which has "accepted a gendered approach taking into consideration not only the multilingual contexts but the experiential and attitudinal differences between women and men as language users in the English diasporic contexts." Within this theoretical and methodological backdrop, Valentine discusses the sociolinguistics of world Englishes and gender; gender and power; bilingual women's creativity and the literary canon; and contextualizing gender. In conclusion, Valentine observes:

> Both the study of world Englishes and the study of language and gender have challenged the limits of the traditional approaches, the Western static, monolithic models, and monolingual standards and norms. Their histories are similar in that they both arose from a shift from the existing traditional theoretical, methodological, and pedagogical models to one that accepted linguistic pluralism and multilinguals' creativity; from viewing gender and language as unchanging, homogeneous, and absolute to a more dynamic discussion on function, context, and the social person. Both seek a new direction consistent with an approach that takes into account expanding and connecting boundaries to include the construction of multiple identities and diverse roles and functions, replacing dichotomies of us and them, native and non-native, women and men, and difference and dominance with dimensions of pluralism and expansion of the canon.

Part VII: World Englishes and globalization

The three chapters of Part VII focus on the presence of world Englishes in three cross-cultural and cross-linguistic varieties of the English language in the media (Elizabeth A. Martin), advertising (Tej K. Bhatia), and global commerce (Stanley Yunick Van Horn).

Martin critically summarizes aspects such as research paradigms for the analysis of mass media discourse; media language in terms of power and ideology; linguistic and cultural identities; language attitudes; intelligibility and linguistic innovation; MTV English and legislation; after which, she provides directions for future research.

In "World Englishes in Global Advertising," Bhatia demonstrates that "English is the most favored language of global media and advertising and its use is skyrocketing, creative needs of global advertisers are rarely met by the consideration of global homogeneity and language conformity." Bhatia's focus is on both the users and uses of advertising, in terms of the key issues, approaches, multiple mixing, and the global vs. local paradox. The conclusion is that "in order to gain proper perspectives into the pluralistic nature of world Englishes/global communication and the advertising media, the integration of conceptual, analytical, and experimental frameworks is imperative at the interdisciplinary level."

The chapter "World Englishes and Global Commerce" (Stanley Yunick Van Horn) shows how, "in reality or in myth," the English language is identified as "the" language of worldwide commerce of the present century. These functions are primarily evident in consumer-oriented discourses, i.e., advertising; in market and retail/institutional service encounters; in daily talk at the workplace in a wide social context; and in a wide range of talk that is "the realm of business people and constitute[s] professional identity."

In his analysis, Van Horn prefers a "functionally polymodel" approach of world Englishes, as opposed to a "nativist monomodel" of English, which "differs from prescriptivist models of English in aiming to account for multilinguals' creativity within a linguistic repertoire and within a plural sociolinguistic context." In his discussion, Van Horn surveys several "well-studied" regions (e.g., Asia and Europe), and "lesser-studied" regions (e.g., the Americas, the Middle East, Africa, and Oceania) and their resources for Englishes and business.

In his focus, like that of Valentine on a "socially realistic linguistics," Van Horn demonstrates a relation between topics such as culture and business; culture and Englishes; genre analysis and business letter writing; talking business; meeting and negotiating; world Englishes, commerce, and standards; and ethics and teaching for "specific" purposes.

Part VIII: World Englishes and applied theory

In critiques of applied theories in linguistics, a variety of provocative questions have been raised, particularly about constructs of knowledge and (re)interpretations of knowledge. These discourses are primarily about the conceptual core of methodologies, privileged paradigms, innovations, and constructs of speech communities.[1]

The six chapters in this section address the major issues related to applied theory: language policy and planning (Ayọ Bamgboṣe), teaching world Englishes (Robert J. Baumgardner), models, methods and curriculum (Kimberley Brown), lexicography (Fredric Dolezal), test construction (Fred G. Davidson), and communicative competence (Margie Berns).

As Bamgboṣe mentions, "one reality of language policy discourse in the world today is that it inevitably gravitates toward the role of English." Hence the metaphor of a recurring decimal. It is undeniable that in view of the global presence English has, it has a major part in language education policies. That does not, however, mean that the needs of social justice can be totally ignored or put at the bottom of the list of considerations while planning for languages and their roles in administration, business and commerce, diplomacy, education, law courts, and other domains. Bamgboṣe makes a strong case for extending the scope of language planning "beyond language, and ensuring that it is inclusive, equitable, and ultimately designed to promote the overall cultural and economic development of a country."

Baumgardner presents a brief survey of teaching world Englishes from two perspectives: stand-alone courses at the tertiary level and incorporation of an approach sensitive to plurality of models, and linguistic and cultural hybridity, at all levels of language teaching. The chapter discusses culture in the classroom by looking at case studies of culturally alien material of ELT in specific sociocultural contexts, describes attempts at standardization and language form in world Englishes classrooms in the Inner, Outer, and Expanding Circles, and considers the role of the mother tongue in ELT methodology and the effectiveness of non-native teachers in teaching Englishes. The chapter includes extensive lists of resources in all these areas.

Kimberley Brown's chapter focuses on "how information regarding English language teaching has been conceptualized" and "examines criticisms leveled at such concepts, and suggests what current ways of conceptualizing English language teaching ought to include if the sociolinguistic realities of the spread and functions of English are used as the bases for language planning." She surveys methods and approaches, from audiolingual to constructivist and ecological, and now post-method, and concludes that "attention to a world Englishes perspective in choice of methodology and curriculum design will result in an ecologically sound approach to language education, one that is attentive to the role that shifts in context bring to language education."

Dolezal begins his discussion with the observation that compiling dictionaries of world Englishes is fraught with complexities. He rightly observes that "the tensions inherent in the concept 'Englishes' are not only highlighted when combined with the practical project of compiling a dictionary, but must be answered or attended to, or the compiler will have no systematic method for collecting, describing, and presenting the language." After presenting Susan Butler's discussion of the Australian English dictionary, and the case of the proposed Singaporean English dictionary, he concludes that the history of dictionaries of English, and those of other modern languages, provide appropriate models for world Englishes dictionaries.

Davidson's chapter "explores the relationship of world Englishes and language test development." Large, almost universally administered language tests are not sensitive to the plural nature of world Englishes and its users. He discusses the nature of test items and arriving at them and contrasts norm-based vs. criterion-referenced measurement, and refers to Chalhoub-Deville and Wigglesworth's work involving test raters from the Inner Circle as the kind of research that is needed in the field. Of course, as he suggests, their results may have been different had they included raters from the Outer and Expanding Circles. In his conclusion, Davidson emphasizes that empirical work in language testing must take cognizance of the methodology of test development and research in sociocultural realities in the use of world Englishes.

Berns's chapter on communicative competence, "a well-established construct in explorations of the relationship of language to society and culture," naturally has a great deal of relevance for research on world Englishes. The concept of world Englishes is rooted in the social and functional realities of language users and use of a multi-faceted medium. Berns suggests further avenues of research to illuminate the notion further in the culturally and functionally multiple contexts of world English.

These chapters contextualize the focus of topics within broader interactional perspectives and, we believe, provide first insights for our understanding of applied-theory.

Part IX: Resources on world Englishes

The two chapters in the final part of the volume provide selected research guides for two types of resources on world Englishes: corpus-based methods of linguistic research (Gerald Nelson), and selected references (Helen Fallon), which are "concerned with *comparative* studies of varieties of English" (1992–2004). Nelson's chapter is divided into five sections: electronic corpora; the international corpus of English; corpus-based studies of world Englishes; the international corpus of learner English; and concluding comments on prospects for future research. Fallon's concluding chapter comprises a "select bibliography of comparative studies of world Englishes 1992–2004," journals, and electronic resources.

The primary focus of *The Handbook of World Englishes*, as the above outline indicates, is not to provide mainly structural descriptions of the varieties of Englishes around the world. In this respect, then, this volume is distinct from a variety of research resources that provide descriptions, at various linguistic levels, of major world varieties of Englishes. A recent impressive undertaking in that genre is, just to give one example, *A Handbook of Varieties of English* (2004; in two volumes), edited by Bernd Kortmann and Edgar Schneider, together with Kate Burridge, Rajend Mesthrie, and Clive Upton. The 2,394 pages of these two volumes are supplemented by a CD-Rom – a multimedia reference tool. Another such ambitious initiative, a twelve-volume reference set entitled *World Englishes*, has been announced by Continuum, London, edited by Tometro Hopkins. These volumes, "covering all the regions of the world, celebrate English in all its diversity, and contain chapters on every variety of English . . ." (see also Hickey, 2004).

One terminological explanation is in order: we have used the term "diaspora" in a rather specific sense, as explained in Kachru (1992: 230–1):

> It seems that the original meaning of *diaspora*, which comprises Greek *dia* ('through') and *spora* (seed; in the sense of 'spora seed'), certainly captures the diffusion of English in more senses than one . . . The "seeds" of the language were "spread" in enormously diverse sociocultural environments, and the resultant varieties of the language show this diversity.[2]

In an insightful paper, the literary scholar and poet Edwin Thumboo (1985: 219) provides yet another perspective on this phenomenon in the following words:

> English has its history, culture, and environment, a powerful literary tradition from Chaucer to Ted Hughes, with a connotative reach that does not always apply in the Outer Circle. The denotative provides a substantial common base for all Englishes; the connotative will have to be re-constructed to accord with our individual ecosystems.

In this context, one also thinks of the often used term "borrowing," which literally indicates the intention of return of the "borrowed" item to the source language. That actually is not what happens. This transitory nature of the lexical or grammatical item is further intimated in linguistic units characterized, for example, as *loan words, loan blends, loan shifts,* and *loan translations*. We see such uses of these terms particularly in studies on, for example, historical, comparative, contrastive linguistics, and branches of sociological studies of languages, where "borrowing" and "loan" are traditionally adopted usages.

We believe that the 42 chapters in this handbook provide extensive cross-cultural – and provocative – evidence and arguments to show that the constructs of world Englishes, their histories, their functional ranges, and the architectures of their messages and identities demand paradigm shifts at each linguistic level and indeed in overall understanding of the hybridity of the language. *The Handbook of World Englishes* is, thus, just one further step toward the understanding of this unfolding of the history and contextualization of the world of world Englishes.

NOTES

1 See, e.g., Baugh, 1988; Berns et al., 1998; Bhatt, 2002; Brutt-Griffler, 2002; Canagarajah, 1999; Dendrinos, 1992; B. Kachru, 1988, 1990, 1991, 1996, 2005; Y. Kachru, 1994a, 1994b, 2003; Kumaravadivelu, 2003; Lowenberg, 1992; Nelson, 1985; Parakrama, 1995; Pennycook, 1994/1995, 1998; Phillipson, 1992; Seidlhofer, 2003; Sridhar, 1990, 1994; Tsuda, 1997.

2. For a linguistically insightful discussion of the past and present use of the term "diaspora," see Zgusta (2001: 291–7).

REFERENCES

Baugh, John (1988) Language and race: Some implications for linguistic science. In *Linguistics: The Cambridge Survey. IV Language: The Sociocultural Context*. Edited by F. J. Newmeyer. Cambridge: Cambridge University Press, pp. 64–74.

Berns, Margie et al. (1998) (Re)experiencing hegemony: The linguistic imperialism of Robert Phillipson. *Journal of Applied Linguistics*, **8**(2), 271–82.

Bhatt, Rakesh (2002) Experts, dialects, and discourse. *International Journal of Applied Linguistics*, **12**(1), 74–109.

Brutt-Griffler, Janina (2002) *World English: A Study of Its Development*. Clevedon, UK: Multilingual Matters.

Canagarajah, Suresh (1999) *Resisting Linguistic Imperialism in English Teaching*. Oxford: Oxford University Press.

Crowley, Tony (1991) *Proper English?* London: Routledge.

Dendrinos, Bessie (1992) *The EFL Textbook and Ideology*. Athens, Greece: N. C. Grivas Publications.

Hickey, Raymond (2004) *Legacies of Colonial English: Studies in Transported Dialects*. Cambridge: Cambridge University Press.

Kachru, Braj B. (1985) Standards, codification and sociolinguistic realism: The English language in the Outer Circle. In *English in the World: Teaching and Learning the Language and Literatures*. Edited by Randolph Quirk and Henry G. Widdowson. Cambridge: Cambridge University Press, pp. 11–30.

Kachru, Braj B. (1988) The spread of English and sacred linguistic cows. In *Language Spread and Language Policy: Issues, Implications and Case Studies. Georgetown Round Table on Language and Linguistics 1987*. Edited by Peter H. Lowenberg. Washington, DC: Georgetown University Press, pp. 207–28.

Kachru, Braj B. (1990) World Englishes and applied linguistics. *World Englishes*, **9**(1), 3–20.

Kachru, Braj B. (1991) Liberation linguistics and the Quirk concern. *English Today*, **25**, 7(1), 3–13.

Kachru, Braj B. (1992) The second diaspora of English. In *English in Its Social Contexts: Essays in Historical Sociolinguistics*. Edited by Tim William Machan and Charles T. Scott. New York/Oxford: Oxford University Press, pp. 230–52.

Kachru, Braj B. (1996) World Englishes: Agony and ecstasy. *Journal of Aesthetic Education*, **30**(2), 135–55.

Kachru, Braj B. (2005) *Asian Englishes: Beyond the Canon*. Hong Kong: Hong Kong University Press.

Kachru, Yamuna (1994a) Cross-cultural speech act research and the classroom. In *Pragmatics and Language Learning*. Monograph 5. Edited by Lawrence F. Bouton and Yamuna Kachru. Urbana: University of Illinois, pp. 39–51.

Kachru, Yamuna (1994b) Monolingual bias in SLA research. *TESOL Quarterly*, **28**(4), 795–800.

Kachru, Yamuna (2003) Conventions of politeness in plural societies. In *Anglophone Cultures in South-East Asia: Appropriations, Continuities, Contexts*. Edited by Rüdiger Ahrens, David Parker, Klaus Stierstorfer, and Kowk-Kan Tam. Heidelberg, Germany: Universitätsverlag Winter Heidelberg, pp. 39–53.

Kortmann, Bernd and Schneider, Edgar W. (eds.) (2004) *A Handbook of*

Varieties of English: A Multimedia Reference Tool, 2 vols. Berlin: Mouton de Gruyter.

Kumaravadivelu, B. (2003) *Beyond Methods: Macrostrategies for Language Teaching*. New Haven: Yale University Press.

Lowenberg, Peter H. (1992) Testing English as a world language: Issues in assessing non-native proficiency. In *The Other Tongue*. Edited by Braj B. Kachru. Urbana, IL: University of Illinois Press, pp. 108–24.

Mufwene, Salikoko S. (1996) The legitimate and illegitimate offspring of English. In *World Englishes 2000*. Edited by Larry E. Smith and Michael L. Forman. Honolulu: University of Hawai'i and The East-West Center, pp. 183–203.

Mufwene, Salikoko S. (2001) *The Ecology of Language Evolution*. Cambridge: Cambridge University Press.

Nelson, Cecil L. (1985) My language, your culture: Whose communicative competence? *World Englishes*, 4(2), 243–50. (Also in *The Other Tongue: English across Cultures*. Edited by Braj B. Kachru. Second edition (1992). Urbana, IL: University of Illinois Press, pp. 327–39.)

Nesfield, John C. (1895) *English Grammar Series Book IV: Idiom, Grammar and Synthesis for High Schools*. Calcutta: Macmillan.

Parakrama, Arjun (1995) *De-Hegemonizing Language Standards*. London: Macmillan.

Pennycook, Alastair (1994/1995) *The Cultural Politics of English as an International Language*. New York/London: Longman.

Pennycook, Alastair (1998) *English and the Discourse of Colonialism*. New York: Routledge.

Phillipson, Robert (1992) *Linguistic Imperialism*. Oxford: Oxford University Press.

Seidlhofer, Barbara (2003) *Controversies in Applied Linguistics*. Oxford: Oxford University Press.

Sidhu, Charan D. (1976) *An Intensive Course in English*. New Delhi: Orient Longman.

Singh, Frances B. (1987) Power and politics in the context of grammar books: The example of India. *World Englishes*, 6(3), 195–9.

Sridhar, S. N. (1990) What are applied linguistics? *Studies in the Linguistic Sciences*, 20(2), 165–76.

Sridhar, S. N. (1994) A reality check for SLA theories. *TESOL Quarterly*, 28(4), 800–5.

Thumboo, Edwin (1985) Twin perspectives and multi-ecosystems: Tradition for commonwealth writer. *World Englishes*, 4(2), 213–21.

Tipping, Llewlyn (1933) *Matriculation English Grammar of Modern English Usage*. London: Macmillan.

Tsuda, Yukiko (1997) Hegemony of English vs. ecology of language: Building equality in international communication. In *World Englishes 2000*. Edited by Larry E. Smith and Michael L. Forman. Honolulu: University of Hawai'i and The East-West Center, pp. 21–31.

Wren, P. C. and Martin, H. (1954) *High School English Grammar and Composition*. Revised Edition. New Delhi: S. Chand.

Zgusta, Ladislav (2001) Diaspora: The past in the present. In *Diaspora, Identity, and Language Communities*. Edited by Braj B. Kachru and Cecil L. Nelson. Special issue of *Studies in the Linguistic Sciences*, 31(1), 291–7.

Part I The Historical Context

1 The Beginnings

ROBERT D. KING

1 Introduction

How did the English language begin, this supple, economic, subtle instrument of communication, commerce, and belles lettres that has become de facto and in many institutions and contexts de jure the lingua franca of the world? Where and when was it born? What were the linguistic, historical, and cultural factors that joined to make this language of so small an island so formidable a force in world history?

It is impossible to point to a specific date, a specific place, or a specific person, and say: *that* is when the English language began. The birth of a language is never an event like the birth of a baby, one moment silent and passive residing in a comfortable womb, the next moment crying, flailing, thrashing about – a noisy newcomer to a strange and brave new world. In their origins and spread languages are not unlike trees growing in a dense jungle: the foliage – the varieties of English we can see and hear today: Indian English, Australian English, Singapore English, British English, American English, Irish English – is there plain to see; the roots – the origins – are no longer in sight, long since concealed by generations of accumulations of earth and overgrowth of thick underbrush.

But the growth patterns – to continue, for a moment, the tree metaphor – of languages throughout the world and at all times are so similar as to be virtually universal, and it is the job of the historical linguist to distinguish these patterns in languages and to put together a coherent reconstruction of how a language was born and how it came of age. There is much in the early history of English and its antecedent languages that we do not know and will probably never know for certain, but two centuries of linguistic scholarship have given us a sound basis from which to hazard educated guesses about what happened before we have the written records that are the eyewitness testimony of the early years.

2   Germanic Legacy

English belongs to the Germanic family of languages, whose other members include High German, Low German, Dutch, Faroese, Swedish, Norwegian, Danish, and Icelandic, as well as the oldest attested but now extinct Germanic language, Gothic. Their common ancestral language we call Proto-Germanic, which, unlike the Latin from which the Romance family of languages descend, was never a written language. Both Romance and Germanic belong to the large and important Indo-European family of languages some of whose other members are the languages of northern India (their ancestral tongue Sanskrit, the venerable language of the Hindu scriptures), Persian (usually called Farsi today), the Slavic languages, Greek, Armenian, the Celtic languages (once spoken throughout western and central Europe, now reduced to toeholds in Ireland, Wales, Scotland, and the Brittany peninsula of France).

If the early origins of English are concealed by mists of early history, then doubly so the origins of the Indo-European ancestral tongue. Where the primeval home of the original Indo-European tribe was located and when the language its members spoke was still a single and uniform thing are two vexed questions in historical linguistics, much debated, and both the where and the when are still active topics of research. We probably do not involve ourselves in serious error if we place the age of the Indo-European languages at some 3000 BCE and the primeval home in eastern Europe, just north of the Black Sea in what today is Ukraine. At some point the resources of the region became insufficient to support its population, and groups from the original Indo-European tribe broke off and emigrated east (into Persia and India), north (to Russia and the Baltic regions), and west (to Greece, Italy, western Europe, and the British Isles).

The Germanic tribes had departed the Indo-European primeval home probably by the beginning of the Common Era at the latest. They drifted into western Europe and settled in what today is northern Germany, the Low Countries, and southern Scandinavia. The Baltic Sea, the relatively shallow inland sea that separates Germany and Denmark from Norway and Sweden, was more of a boggy marsh than a sea when the Germanic peoples made this their home, thus easing ingress and movement throughout the area.

The Germanic tribes – Saxons, Angles, Jutes, Frisians – were a roving, restless, aggressive lot like their Indo-European forebears before them, always seeing the other side of rivers, of valleys, of bodies of water as greener, more fertile, more suited to their idea of a proper home than where they were living. This hereditary trait, this restlessness, this urge to sail away and find new lands to conquer, the English later were to display in quantity.

3   The Germanic Presence in England

England at the period in question (roughly 0 BCE/CE plus or minus a hundred years) was anything but a Germanic-language area. The earliest inhabitants of whom we have certain knowledge were the Celts, whose languages survive today in the forms of Irish (the preferred designation today for what still is often called Gaelic), Welsh, and Scots Gaelic. The Romans led by Julius Caesar invaded the island in 55 BCE, but it was almost a century later during the reign of Claudius before they could claim to control even the southern part of the country. The Romans never were able to impose their Latin language on the Celtic substratum to any great degree. People who wanted to get ahead, to become important in Roman Britain, would have learned Latin, as people who have wanted to get ahead anywhere in the world at all times have always had to learn the language of whoever is in charge – it is after all in this way that English gained ascendancy in the countries comprising the British empire. But knowledge of Latin would have been a town and garrison thing. Beyond the walls of the forts, beyond the baths and arenas, the common people continued speaking the Celtic languages that captured, as languages always do, their Celtic identity.

In or around 449 the restless continental Germanic tribes began what we may call the Germanic Conquest of England. The English Channel in good weather is not much of a barrier to even small sailing craft from countries such as Holland, Denmark, Norway, Sweden, and the northern coast of Germany. Already in Roman times bands of Germanic invaders (for whom the conventional name is "Vikings") had been an irritant for the Romans, always grabbing things that did not belong to them, plundering, causing mischief. It was only after Roman rule had become ineffectual against the warriors sailing from the north that Germanic invasion on a large scale could succeed. The Celts, those who did not assimilate to Germanic ways, moved west and south into Cornwall and Wales; Scotland with its hills, wild terrain, and rain remained untamed by both Roman and Saxon.

4   Anglo-Saxon England

Thus came into being an Anglo-Saxon civilization. Its language was Old English (also known as Anglo-Saxon), which we nominally date 450–1150, a fusion language to which various of the Germanic invaders had contributed, most particularly the Saxons from northern Germany. The language of the Saxons who remained behind in northern Germany, Old Saxon, is a good deal more conservative than its wandering cousin Old English, "conservative" in historical linguistic usage meaning "closer to the ancestral language," here Proto-Germanic.

What resemblance did Old English, this rough beast of a language that slouched about in southern England as the legacy of the fusion of Germanic invader-languages, bear to the English of modern times? The answer is: very little. Old English, like the Old Saxon to which it owes most, was a "heavy" language: heavily inflected and richly conjugated, with three genders and four cases, and numerous subclasses of nouns, verbs, and adjectives. Exemplary noun declensions are (dialect variations, of which there were many, are ignored here):

	Masculine 'day'	*Neuter* 'word'	*Feminine* 'gift'
Modern English			
Singular			
Nominative	dæg	word	giefu
Accusative	dæg	word	giefe
Genitive	dæges	wordes	giefe
Dative	dæge	worde	giefe
Plural			
Nominative	dagas	word	giefa
Accusative	dagas	word	giefa
Genitive	daga	worda	giefa
Dative	dagum	wordum	giefum

Compare these declensions with their modern English counterparts, and the greater linguistic complexity of the earlier period is immediately clear: *day/days, word/words, gift/gifts*. The Old English verb conjugations are no less complex in comparison with modern English: where English today has in the present indicative only one marked ending *-(e)s*, in the third-person singular (*goes, tries, kills*), Old English had four. Even the simple, anodyne definite article *the* of modern English required 18 different forms to decline it: three genders in the singular, four cases for the singular and the plural, plus an instrumental case for masculine and neuter singular.

So much for the language. What about the literature it produced? Linguists *qua* linguists are not often disposed to ask about the quality of the literature of these early Germanic languages. That we tend to leave to literary scholars. Our interest focuses more narrowly on forms and phonemes, on scribal errors, on the technical aspects of phonology, morphology, and syntax.

It is just as well that linguists are not always lovers of literature, for the literatures of most of the early Germanic languages are poor things, consisting mostly of bible translations, gospel harmonies (a unified story of Christ's life woven out of the four gospels, used by missionaries), travelers' phrase books (as it were, *How to Say It in Old Saxon*), the odd gloss in a Latin document. Old High German literature (600–1150), for example, which is contemporaneous with Old English, is an inferior thing in comparison with the literature of even its close relative, Old Saxon (*Heliand*), not to mention the further afield Old English. It is vastly inferior to the rich medieval literature of Middle High German (1150–1350) with its courtly epics, its *Nibelungenlied*, its poetry. Old High German literature is not nearly the equal of the slightly later literature of Old Icelandic.

But how different was Old English literature! Its greatest single work was *Beowulf*, a story of heroes and dragons and great deeds still studied today as a classic of world literature. Besides *Beowulf* there is the great war poem *The Battle of Maldon* and numerous religious poems. Under the Anglo-Saxon king Alfred the Great (born 849, reigned 871–899) and due directly to him we have outstanding translations from the Latin of such works as Bede's *Ecclesiastical*

History of the English People and Boethius' *The Consolation of Philosophy*. That a king at that time should have so lofty a mind is remarkable. Even more remarkable, we have every reason to believe that Alfred himself translated these works or at least lent a hand in their translations, this besides making his mark as a gifted military leader and statesman. He initiated the *Anglo-Saxon Chronicle*, which was not completed until two centuries later. A plentiful trove indeed, this body of Old English literature, rich in detail and rich in genius. Because of its existence we are well informed about the social and cultural history of the English peoples at a time when we can see the life of other Germanic peoples only as through a misted glass with many cracks in it, darkness everywhere.

Old English already was disposed toward linguistic hospitality, an openness to the influence of other languages which endures to the present day, welcoming new words from the languages with which it shared territory (Latin, Celtic) and from the languages of influential figures such as warriors and priests who came speaking no English. Many place-names point back to the Celtic linguistic substratum (*Kent, Cornwall, York*) as do words such as *crag* and *bin*. Of far greater importance and extent were borrowings from Latin, earlier from the Latin of Roman conquest, later from the Latin of Christian conquest. From the earlier period we have *camp, mile, pit, cheap, wine,* and many other domestic words so well integrated into English that only an enthusiast would know them not to be originally Germanic. Christianity came to Britain in 597, though it was not to drive out the autochthonous religious traditions until centuries had passed. Its impact on English vocabulary is great: church words such as *bishop, angel, disciple, human, relic,* and *rule*; school words like *school, verse, meter,* and *grammar*; and words not easily categorized such as *elephant, radish, oyster, talent,* and *crisp*.

Scandinavian was the last of the great lexical and grammatical influences on English prior to the Norman Conquest. Vikings had always been sailing to the island. It was not far away, often no more than a few days' sailing, it was attractive and promised wealth and interesting things to steal, and its defenders were usually no match for a boatload of Vikings in battle regalia. According to the *Anglo-Saxon Chronicle* the first major raid occurred in 787. Thereafter incursions from the north occurred without relief until 850. These were raiding parties more interested in plunder and English women than in conquest of territory, but Northmen with more than jewels, girls, and booty on their mind were not far behind. By 1014 the English king had been driven into exile, and England was ruled – though that is surely too strong a word for what must have been a parlous, ephemeral suzerainty – by the Danish king Svein. Most of the invaders settled in the Danelaw, the districts on the northern and eastern coasts of English where the Danish influence was strongest.

The influence of Danish – and other north Germanic languages to a lesser extent, notably Norwegian (Norse) – is vast. Because of their genetic similarities as Germanic languages Old English and Old Danish were not as far apart as English was from Latin or Celtic. The two Germanic languages had similar grammatical structures, declensions, and conjugations, and both may have been mutually intelligible at least in saying the simple things that the buyer and seller of a sheepskin would have to say to conclude a successful transaction. Both had the uniquely Germanic division between strong verbs and weak verbs, the former signaling tense changes by vowel (*sing/sang, ride/rode, eat/ate*), the latter by the addition of a suffix *-ed* (*work/worked, look/looked, sweep/swept*). Though the Romance and Celtic languages have an often daunting array of irregular verbs, only Germanic has the strong/weak division; indeed, no other Indo-European language does. The numerous English place-names in *-by* are Danish in origin: Rugby, Derby, Whitby (the Danish word *by* meant 'farm' or 'town'). Even the word *law* is Scandinavian, and *band, odd, rotten, rugged, die, crawl,* and *scowl* are a small sample of a much larger number of simple-life words borrowed into English from Danish.

5   The French Legacy

In depth and mass of linguistic imprint on the English language, however, all else pales into insignificance in comparison with the French influence that followed upon the Norman Conquest. The Normans were Frenchmen descended from Nordic invaders who had snatched control of pieces of the French coast during the Viking era, much as their cousins had done in England. In 912 the Northmen gained by right of treaty with the king of France the part of France known still today as Normandy. Normans threw themselves into absorbing French culture, military know-how, cuisine, law, and – most importantly for the future history of English – the French language. By the eve of the Norman Conquest Normans were French through and through.

In 1066 the king of England died without an heir. The usual wrangling began, and a second cousin to the deceased king soon announced that he was the rightful successor and was prepared to prove the point by military means if it came to that. This cousin was William, duke of Normandy. William had had a hard childhood, having to overcome the stigma of illegitimacy among much else, and he rose to his dukedom through physical toughness mixed with shrewdness. William made careful preparations for invasion, taking care to cultivate supporters on the English side of the channel (a "Fifth Column"), and in 1066 he sailed with his soldiers across the English Channel, the Channel being very narrow and easy to traverse at this point. It is no accident that the D-Day invasion of June 6, 1944 going the other direction chose the beaches of Normandy to land on.

William and his men landed at Hastings, then as now a town on the Channel not far south of London. The battle did not last long. On Christmas Day, 1066, William was crowned king of England. One of the first effects of the Norman Conquest was the creation of a new French-speaking Norman aristocracy. While William did not complete his conquest for several years to come, a Norman royal court in southeast England came into being almost overnight.

It was not the way in those days to "impose" a language on a conquered people, as the Soviet Union for example imposed Russian on most of its member states. The Normans did not "impose" French, but William's court was French-speaking, and the Normans he had brought with him and who followed spoke French. If, as a speaker of English, you wanted to have dealings with the court, then you had to learn French. If you wanted to sell a pig to the king's kitchen, you had to learn French. If as an aristocrat you decided it would be advantageous to switch your allegiance from Saxon to Norman – this is the stuff of *Robin Hood* and Sir Walter Scott's novel *Ivanhoe* – then you had to learn French. If a Norman fancied a Saxon girl and married her, she would learn French, and so would their children if they wanted to get ahead. The close proximity of France made for a steady stream of fortune-seekers testing the possibilities in this England, which they doubtless regarded as cold, crude, and with not much of interest to eat – not French, in a word. As fortune-seekers are not always respectable members of the aristocracy, French would have been much heard outside the court in the century and a half after 1066.

Two centuries after the Conquest English kings regained power, and the French court was a memory. By the beginning of the fourteenth century English was again the language of the country, but this was a very different kind of English from the English that had preceded the Norman Conquest. It had been profoundly transformed by the course of linguistic evolution and by its fateful encounter with French. It was a far different English from that of *Beowulf*. Alfred would have needed an interpreter. Many of the words with which French had permanently enriched English are from the legal and governing (*legal* and *govern* themselves are French) lexical domains: *crime, criminal, criminality, regal, regental, judge, plea, royal, sue, defend, defendant* – it would be quite impossible to try a case in an English-speaking court anywhere in the world even today without using a French loanword every half minute or so. But not all of what we got from French is abstract and polysyllabic: consider *joy, face, cap, force, war, chase, paint, pay.*

But we got more from the French than individual loanwords. Because those loanwords often came in pairs, for example *críminal/crimináliy, légal/legálity, régent/regéntal, dífficult/difficúlty* (with the acute accent ´ marking the location of main stress in the word), we inherited from French a more complex set of rules for marking word-stress than what we had had before when English vocabulary was more monolithically Germanic. Words from our Germanic heritage, most of them, are monosyllabic, and therefore have a very simple rule for marking stress – stress the only vowel in the word: *gó, cóme, ít, rún, bé, bést, só, stóne, wórd.*

It was not only French that had changed the language so much since Alfred's day. The inexorable force of linguistic change had done its work. By the end of the Middle English period (1150–1500) the language had come to be something not that different from modern English. In nouns for example -*s* had become the only suffix, signifying as it does today either the genitive *day's* or the plural *days*. The multiplicity of unstressed vowels in Old English (the vowels *a, e, u, o* in the final syllables of for example *giefa, giefe, giefum, curon*) had been reduced to a single unstressed -*e*. Of the numerous different forms of the definite article only *the* and *that* have remained. Some strong verbs became weak, some weak verbs strong. The language had become grammatically simpler, especially in its morphology, leaner somehow – and it is this streamlining of the language that later would make it so easy a language to export.

6   Early Modern English

The creation of Early Modern English (or Late Middle English) coincided with the onset of the Age of Discovery. Ships were bigger and better, navigational aids were more reliable, and something in the European *Zeitgeist* demanded exploration. What was the English like that was sent out in search of countries to claim as Britain embarked on its quest to "rule the seas"? It was to begin with a "light" language when compared with Old English, which I earlier described as "heavy." Gone the Indo-Germanic/Germanic complex morphology, gone the Germanic fashions in word compounding and word derivation, gone many of the sounds of Old English (such as the velar fricative [x], spelled *gh* in words such as *light* and *knight*). What remained is what we have today: an English with a preponderance of monosyllabic words, with sounds that are on the whole easy to pronounce or to approximate (though *th* is a stumbling-block for speakers of many languages), a simple morphology, a language mostly free of elite academy-driven notions of correctness. (The *Académie française* regularly issues stern injunctions against using words like *weekend* and *OK*; no ordinary speaker of French pays them the slightest mind. English has never been disposed to put up with such silliness.)

Let us take the English of 1600 as a starting-point. This is a useful date because it was on December 31 of that year that Queen Elizabeth granted a royal charter to a group of merchants for the purpose of exploitation of trade with East and Southeast Asia and India. Although the English East India Company as it was called soon fell into financial difficulty and was never far out of it, it was for a century and a half a major facilitator of the English language. What was the English like that John Company, as the English East India Company was sometimes ironically called in India, exported to these far-off lands?

It would have been richly diverse for one thing. On the lower decks Cockney English would have been well represented along with every conceivable kind of regional English: Yorkshire accents, Devon accents, Welsh accents, Irish accents, Scots accents – even the odd Yankee (American) twang of some poor lout who had been pressed into service. There would have been "r-less" dialects of English alongside "r-ful" dialects. There would be *wery* along with "very" and *vind* beside "wind." "It was 'is to 'ave" would have cheerfully coexisted with "E hain't 'appy." There would be lots of [f] for *th*, *nuffin* for 'nothing' and *wif* for 'with'. There would be speakers for whom *lace* and *lice* rhymed. Words now archaic like *gart* 'caused or made', *sollicker* 'force', and *to fossick* 'to search' would have abounded. Received Pronunciation ("the King's English," "Oxford English," "BBC English") was not a concept at this time, so even the captains and upper-class loungers who fanned out across the world would have had by today's standards huge differences in pronunciation and usage.

And so the stage was set for the triumphant march of the English language to the ends of the earth. The Age of Discovery transformed the world's view of horizon and limitation, as the frigates and brigs and men o'war set out under full sail from this tiny island of England and the Union Jack was planted on alien terrain such as India, Australia, Hong Kong, and America. It is inconceivable that in the minds of these captains and men or those who had sent them lurked even an inkling of what their ultimate and most enduring achievement would be.

They thought they were exploring, trying to find the Northwest Passage, trying to find faster ways to sail to Japan and China. They thought they were going to get rich by locating sources of spices or profiting from the appeal of a new drink like tea. They thought they were claiming some God-forsaken barren island or peninsula for Crown and country forever. Or they were transporting some kind of plant, breadfruit for example, out to a new location to see whether it could be made to grow there as an inexpensive food for slaves to the profit of slave-owners and John Company.

And so they were. They were doing all these things. But little did these empire-warriors know that their one enduring accomplishment would be to make English first among the world's languages – first not in intrinsic worth or beauty or goodness but first in practicality and first as a means of expression for word-gifted people whose first language might be something other than English.

7 Post-Empire English

The British Empire is now gone. The money it made – if indeed it made money for England; Karl Marx thought it did not – is long since gone. The islands and peninsulas where once the Union Jack was proudly planted are now ruled by their own people (if they are inhabited at all). The breadfruit never seemed to find the right kind of soil to prosper in, it never became a profitable crop; besides most of the plants died on the way out. Slave plantations are gone, and so is John Company.

What remains however is infinitely more enduring, chaster and nobler, more of a great thing, than land or plants or possessions. What remains is the English language, a gift to the globe, a "way of speaking, a mouth" to millions of people on this globe, often to people who would not be able to express themselves if not for English. One of the greatest and most underacknowledged gifts of the British Raj to India was English prose style. Not simply narrative prose – after all the *Laws of Manu* were written in Sanskrit prose – but the prose style of the polished English essay, of a Macaulay, of Samuel Johnson's *Idler*, of Edmund Burke or John Stuart Mill. This kind of graceful, spare, ironic prose was something altogether different from the forms of prose in indigenous literature. It was initially foreign to the "cut" of any Indian language, from Sanskrit down to the meanest vernacular. But something about it kindled fire in the Indian mind. By the end it would produce masters of the English language – Rabindranath Tagore, Aurabindo Ghose, Sarvepalli Radhakrishnan and his historian son, Sarvepalli Gopal, Raja Rao, Nirad Chaudhuri, Gandhi, and Jawaharlal Nehru. The English language remains to India after virtually all other traces of the British Raj have decayed and receded from view.

8   Conclusion

What was true of India is true of all the other countries where English once was the language of rule: former British colonies in Africa, Singapore, Hong Kong, Bangladesh, the West Indies, Canada, Australia, New Zealand, and of course America. English is one of the natural means by which gifted writers express themselves in countries once under British rule. And when they write their graceful prose and eloquent poetry, they doubtless do not often stop to reflect on how it came about that it is *English* that is their instrument of choice. And when a Frenchman has dealings with a German or a Swede, when they perforce move into English to do their negotiating, none of them surely thinks back to that day in 449 when Saxons from the north of Germany sailed their ships to southern England and decided to stay there.

"Our beginnings never know our ends," wrote T. S. Eliot. How far we have come from those early days when German and Scandinavian warriors descended on the south of England, unloading their languages along with their weapons of conquest. But as Eliot also wrote, "In my beginning is my end." The dots are not always easy to connect, even for linguists, but connected they are, these dots that take us from Old to Middle to modern English, whose end lies in its beginning.

See also Chapters 15, WORLD ENGLISHES TODAY; 23, LITERARY CREATIVITY IN WORLD ENGLISHES; 25, WORLD ENGLISHES AND CULTURE WARS.

FURTHER READING

Bailey, Richard W. and Robinson, Jay (eds.) (1973) *English as a World Language.* New York: Macmillan.

Bambas, Rudolph C. (1980) *The English Language: Its Origin and History.* Norman, OK: University of Oklahoma Press.

Baugh, Albert C. and Cable, Thomas (1978) *A History of the English People.* 3rd edition. Englewood Cliffs, NJ: Prentice-Hall.

Greenough, James B. and Kittredge, George L. (1961) *Words and Their Ways in English Speech.* New York: Macmillan. Originally published in 1901.

McKay, Janet H. and Cosmos, Spencer (1986) *The Story of English: Study Guide and Reader.* Dubuque, IA: Kendall/Hunt.

Strang, Barbara (1970) *A History of English.* London: Methuen.

Wyld, Henry C. (1936) *A History of Modern Colloquial English.* Oxford: Blackwell.

2 First Steps: Wales and Ireland

ROBERT D. KING

1 Introduction

When we tell the story of the replacement of one language by another, it is almost impossible to resist reaching for military metaphors to give a name to what happened. We talk of a "conquest." We write of the "victory" of the *langue d'oïl* over the *langue d'oc* in the "battle" for what was to become standard French. Vulgar Latin "ceded ground" to Old French as the Middle Ages waned. The French of Quebec has since the 1970s "regained ground" from English in the "battle" of language loyalties in eastern Canada.

Even though this kind of muscular military linguistic usage is vaguely reprehensible in a sober discipline like linguistics, we all talk and write that way because the replacement of one language by another does have points in common with "conquests" and "victories."

2 High and Low Languages

Let us have some terminology first. Linguists use the abbreviations H (for "High") and L (for "Low") to distinguish between two important kinds of usage domain. H is the variety of language used in formal, written, official, ceremonial, solemn, institutional, legal, and other "serious" domains. L is everyday language, spoken in family and other intimate and informal settings. Legal and religious matters – wills, marriage certificates, and contracts, for example – are usually H functions. Farmers arguing about the best kind of dung to spread on their fields will nine times out of ten be conversing in L. H and L can refer to different languages, for example when speaking of the command of Latin over H functions when English was relegated to L functions, as often was the case in medieval English, but they can also refer to variants of the same language so different that mutual intelligibility is complicated (standard French and Creole in Haiti, for example, or standard Arabic and vernacular Arabic most places in the Arab-speaking world). To this latter situation, which is altogether commonplace except in the most literate parts of the world, Charles Ferguson gave the name *diglossia*.

When two languages argue over the same ground, as English and Welsh did in Wales and English and Irish (now the preferred name for the language and not "Gaelic") did in Ireland, for example, what usually ensues is a conflict between the two languages for domain power, for H. One of the two languages comes to be perceived as H, perhaps through force of arms, perhaps because of economic power, perhaps by strength of numbers, perhaps because it is a newcomer language with greater claims to culture and literature or to a more enviable set of social structures and better manners. We then say that the H language "wins," and the L language "loses." The winning language becomes the "superstratum" language, the losing one the "substratum." Whether the substratum language survives or not, it will almost certainly leave traces in the superstratum language.

So when the Indo-Europeans began to move into India through the northwest passes, their language Sanskrit displaced the Dravidian languages on the ground, absorbing them (and their speakers), pushing the Dravidians southward where they and their languages remain today, spoken by several hundred million people. In their earliest contacts the Indo-Europeans were held to be the more advanced of the two peoples, of a higher culture, more developed materially – and thus Sanskrit was H, Dravidian L – at least until the Dravidians established a home in the south of India beyond the reach of Indo-European cavalry and swords where they could sustain themselves and shore up their languages.

Sometimes the L language dies out, sometimes it enters an exiguous phase with an uncertain future, sometimes it rallies and carves out a cultural or geographic niche for itself where it remains safe (as Dravidian did). Almost always the two languages have a mutual influence on each other, though the influence of H on L is always far greater than that of L on H. The story can be repeated thousands of times. It is the story of the spread of English in New Zealand at the expense of Maori; it is the story of the spread of English throughout North America at the expense of the Native American Indian languages. Words from the L language make it into the H language for alien concepts (*canoe, tomahawk, teepee*) and toponyms (*Idaho, Mississippi, Missouri*). Normally the L language is swamped by borrowings from the H language. Today in the Navaho Nation English occupies most H domains, but Navaho remains, however tenuously, the language of intimacy and family warmth (L). In the religious/spiritual domain Navaho preserves an H function in that only Navaho must be spoken in certain religious ceremonies – which demonstrates that the distinction between H and L is not always what it seems to be (as we shall see in the cases of English/Welsh and English/Irish).

Ultimately this is the story of English in Wales and Ireland – the story of battles between languages over which is to be H. The first "conquests" of the English language were of Wales and Ireland. But the use of the metaphor "conquest" is seriously misleading here, precisely because of the confusion of H and L functions among a number of competing languages in the Middle

Ages – Latin, French, Welsh, Irish, and English. We will come to that, but first this story – the story of the spread of English to Wales and Ireland – must be understood against the setting of the general retreat of Celts, of Celtic religion and culture, and of Celtic languages across Europe.

3   The Celts in Europe

At the height of its dominion (nominally circa 400 BCE) the Celtic presence stretched from the British Isles to eastern Europe and Turkey, from a line running just south of Denmark through the middle of Germany down through France and into Italy and Greece. Celtic history thenceforth down to the beginning of the Common Era is one of withdrawal, retraction, and reduction. On the continent the Celts were vanquished by or absorbed into their invaders: Romans, Germans, Slavs, and rough types from Central Asia (Huns, Vandals). In what resembles a cultural/linguistic version of a "last stand," the Celts retreated across the English Channel to the British Isles where they found a refuge at least for a while.

The existence of a Celtic Brittany on the French coast (its language Breton, still spoken today) is deceptive: the Bretons are British Celts who sailed back across the Channel and regained a continental toehold in the fifth century, long after the Celts had been driven from Europe. From the beginning of the Common Era we can distinguish between the two principal linguistic divisions of Celtic: P-Celtic and Q-Celtic, depending on whether the reflexes of Proto-Celtic *k^w are *p* or *kw*. To P-Celtic belong Welsh, Breton, and Cornish (Brittonic), to Q-Celtic Irish, Scots Gaelic, and Manx (Goidelic). The designations "Brittonic" and "Goidelic" are used to refer to these languages before their internal differentiation becomes clear, and that we date approximately to 800 CE.

The Romans led by Julius Caesar invaded England in 55 BCE, but it required almost a century of hard fighting to consolidate their position. They never achieved a really firm control of Britain outside their southeastern base (around what today is London). Linguistically speaking, they never made much of an issue out of imposing their language, Latin, on the Celtic inhabitants outside their immediate domains of power. If you were upwardly mobile, then you learned Latin. Of course. Nor were the Romans disposed to interfere in religious matters as long as that religion did not threaten the Roman state, which Druidism, the major Celtic religion, did not. Contacts between the Welsh and the Romans were extensive, especially among the Welsh ruling classes who of necessity had to come to grips with the fact that the Romans were running things. At this point we must begin to treat the Welsh and Irish situations separately, though they have many features in common. It is primarily a matter of chronology: English came to Wales earlier than it did to Ireland, which because of its island fastness and the barrier of the Irish Sea was quarantined against most English and continental fevers.

Latin influenced the Welsh language during Roman times especially in the area of the lexicon (technically we should speak of "Brittonic" here and reserve "Welsh" for the period after 800), but the linguistic influence became much stronger after Britain was converted to Christianity. By 300 CE the Christian religion was several lengths ahead of the other religions competing in Rome, and the shift to Christianity as the quasi-official religion was symbolically marked when the emperor Constantine converted to Christianity on his deathbed in 337. By 400 the state religion of Rome was Christianity. By the middle of the fourth century England was thoroughly Christianized, at least its ruling and urban classes were, and along with Christianity came monasteries, abbots and bishops, manuscripts, priories, and monks – *and* Latin as the language of high purpose (H), Latin being the official language of the Roman Catholic Church. Probably the Welsh ruling classes were bilingual in both Welsh and Latin, although outside their sphere of influence, in the countryside, one must assume that Welsh alone was the language of the people.

Although Ireland was never under Roman rule, probably owing more to the daunting logistics of attack and Roman fear of dividing forces rather than lack of appetite among the Romans, it became Christian in the fifth century. By tradition Patrick (Saint Patrick), who was born we think in Carlisle, England and was a native speaker most likely of Welsh, converted Ireland between 432 and 461. At a time when most western European males were drinking, raping, stealing, and smashing what they could not carry off, Irish monasteries were a refuge of cultural preservation and learning. This story was the subject of a bestseller by Thomas Cahill, *How the Irish Saved Civilization* (1995), with the subtitle *The Untold Story of Ireland's Heroic Role from the Fall of Rome to the Rise of Medieval Europe*. The language of this cultural preservation was Latin (H), but Irish (L) is what the monks spoke once past the monastery gates.

Thus, by the time the Germanic tribes began their conquest of England (449 CE) the Welsh language and the Irish language were solidly in place – well established as the spoken languages of their respective lands, Wales and Ireland. Both had impressive literatures before the English did. There were poems, stories, narratives, and an opulence of creative writing. Welsh was the language of the law. The *Welsh Lawbooks* are rich in legal vocabulary, but they are stylistically rich as well and therefore are accounted part of the literary tradition of Wales as well as the legal. Social and governing structures were solid, the Welsh nobility being great patrons of Welsh literature and music, even more solid than anything the English had in place prior to the appearance of Alfred the Great. Early Irish literature was rich and varied, studied still today as a glory.

The English language took shape in the period 500–800, a fusion of continental Germanic and Scandinavian components (mainly Old Saxon, the language of northern Germany) and influenced especially in its lexicon by Latin, first because of Roman rule and subsequently because of Christianity. The major external defining event in English linguistic history, however, was the Norman Conquest in 1066, which imposed a French-speaking court and upper class on England. French held sway as the H language for about two centuries and thereafter with declining vigour until the sixteenth century. Borrowings from French, primarily in vocabulary, have left so heavy an imprint on the English language that to the casual observer French and English might well appear more closely related than German and English, even though genetically the opposite is true.

3.1   Celtic and English/The Celts and the English

And now we can turn to the question of the "conquest" of English in Wales and Ireland. Given that the English were aggressive and growing more numerous and powerful all the time, was it not inevitable that their language would displace the principal indigenous Celtic languages – Welsh and Scots Gaelic and then Irish, in time? Does not the most fleeting glance at a map of the British Isles make it glaringly clear that things could have no other outcome? Wales on the western coast of England has no natural defences against determined expansion from southern England, the locus of the English language in medieval times. Nor is Ireland that far away, though the Irish Sea was always a deterrent, and an English invasion of Ireland would have been a much more difficult military operation than a march into Wales. (Though one is bound to reflect on the fact that the Irish Sea would have been a trifling obstacle for the Viking ancestors of the Anglo-Saxons-Normans. Did it discourage the Christian missionaries? No.)

Maps are deceptive things, perhaps most especially so when it comes to illustrating the "power" relationships of languages on the ground: it is hard to map the linguistic battle between H and L. In the early going, let us say to the end of the medieval period, it was not the manifest destiny of the English language to spread throughout the British Isles, geography and appearances to the contrary. Prior to something like 1500 CE it was never a certain thing that English would come to prevail over the strongest indigenous Celtic languages of the region with the largest numbers of speakers and the strongest governing and societal structures – Welsh and Irish. The position of the other Celtic substrate languages such as Cornish and Manx or even Scots Gaelic was never as strong as that of Welsh and Irish nor were their speakers ever as numerous, and so perhaps it was a foregone conclusion that they would succumb under the English invasion. But not Irish and Welsh.

The trouble here lies in the conflicting and often confused "H–L" relationships that obtained among English, Latin, French, Welsh, and Irish in the Middle Ages. Which of these languages was H, which ones were L? The answers are not as clear as one might think. Latin was throughout, both in Wales and Ireland as well as England, one of the H languages and often *the* H language. This was true both during Roman rule and the Christian era. Legal and religious documents were almost always in Latin, and if they appear in one of the other languages it is usually as a translation from Latin.

Beowulf was Germanic to the core, genuinely Old English, as were many other shorter pieces such as *Widsith* and *Deor*, and the great war poems the *Battle of Maldon* and the *Battle of Brunanburh*. These, it must be remembered, were part of the spoken tradition, and while they were being passed down around campfires and through generations English could lay claim to a sort of modified H function, much like Navaho has for ritual purposes.

English may have been the spoken language of the people, but Latin was the unquestioned H language. There was a relatively brief period during which Old English could lay claim to a share of the H prize. This was during the reign of Alfred the Great (871–899). Alfred lamented the decay of the book culture of Old English, and he himself acquired Latin, presumably between battles and other great deeds, in order to spearhead a program of translation into Old English of major works of literature originally written in Latin: Bede's *Ecclesiastical History of the English People*, Pope Gregory's *Pastoral Care*, and Boethius' *The Consolation of Philosophy*. Ælfric and Wulfstan carried on the tradition of Old English prose, but Latin remained the H language.

The Norman Conquest brought French into the picture, and for at least a couple of centuries after 1066 French took command of H functions, in competition with Latin, and English dropped further behind in the race. Welsh and Irish were still largely sovereign in their respective lands, though Wales naturally was more subject to influences from England, from Latin, French, and to a lesser extent at this time, from English. But for most H purposes, in both Wales and Ireland, Latin was the ticket. French had its own set of worries, for the French of the Normans was about to lose the contest for Best French, an award that would shortly go the French of the Ile de France. Geoffrey Chaucer (c.1342–1400) famously made fun of the French of his Prioress in the *Canterbury Tales*:

> And French she spak ful faire and fetisly,
> After the scole of Stratford ate Bowe,
> For French of Paris was to hir unknowe.

4 The Ascendancy of English

And so we have around 1400 a glorious jumble of languages struggling to sort out the H–L relationships in England (Ireland was still on the periphery of the strife). But time, population, trade, transportation, and all else was on the side of English. The old feudal society was in decline, profoundly impacted by the rise of a middle class. Trade and commerce were rising in importance, and they were soon to play a greater role in the resolution of language domains than the Church or the sovereign. English still did not have full control of H functions – total victory would be several centuries coming – but English political control of the country was becoming stronger by the day, and, ultimately more important because more enduring, so was English domination of trade. The language of trade was English, not always and not from the very beginning, but eventually yes, and thus was set the stage for the expansion of the English language into Wales and then Ireland.

By the fifteenth century English had replaced French and Latin as the language of law. Englishmen were writing their wills and their letters in English. The English language thus took command of the H ground, and with a growing population and growing economic power it was now really only a matter of time before Wales would fall to English rule. In 1536, in the reign of Henry VIII, Wales came under English dominion in what is called the Act of Union, a political event that was to have almost immediate linguistic implications. The "Language Clause" of the Act of Union stated:

> All other officers and ministers of the lawe shall proclayme and kepe the sessions courtes hundreds letes Shireves and all other courtes in the Englisshe Tonge . . . And also that frome hensforth no personne or personnes that use the Welsshe speche or langage shall have or enjoy any maner office or fees within the Realme of Englands Wales . . . onles he or they use and exercise the speche or langage of Englisshe.

Welsh was still the spoken language of the vast majority of Welsh, but the speech of the upper classes shifted over time from bilingual in Welsh and English (and/or French) to English. Welsh literature continued to flourish, and in the domain of folk literature the Welsh language continued its H function, but this too gradually passed as the Welsh nobility, traditional patrons of Welsh literature, shifted to English. Welsh was perhaps most tenacious in the Welsh church, and it is no exaggeration to say that the preservation of the Welsh language owes much to its Wesleyan (Methodist) preachers. The 1991 census reported that 18.7 percent of the population of Wales had knowledge of Welsh, though the percentages are much higher in the northern and western counties of Gwynedd and Dyfed – there Welsh exults in a glorious and public victory over the English language, spoken on every street, in every pub, in every intimate occasion of life.

The earliest recorded use of English in Ireland dates from the thirteenth century. Latin and to a lesser degree French occupied most H domains, with Irish commanding L domains throughout the island. English, because of mostly trade-related increased immigration from England, began to make inroads into Ireland beginning in the fourteenth and fifteenth centuries, first showing up in legal documents, town records, and the like. Curiously, in the fourteenth century there is evidence that spoken English among the Anglo-Irish gentry went into decline, with more and more of them adopting Irish as their home language. The Statutes of Kilkenny (1366), written in French, ordained that "every Englishman use the English language, and be named by an English name." It is a linguistic truism that linguistic proclamations like this – "use language X!" – are certain proof that most people are doing the exact opposite – *not* using language X.

In 1541 Henry VIII was proclaimed King of Ireland at the Irish Parliament. Most of the documents associated with this and other acts of Parliament at the time were still in Latin, but other evidence shows clearly that English was encroaching on the H domains of Latin (and French). In swearing loyalty to the new king there is much of a mixture among the Irish lords in doing so in the English and Irish languages. Some lords required an interpreter to put their oath of fealty into English, while others were able to do so in "good Inglisshe."

By no means did English become the spoken language of Ireland overnight just because Ireland was incorporated into the Kingdom of England. It was never on the cards that the victory would be so cheaply earned. It was only in the reigns of Queen Mary and King James I in the sixteenth and early seventeenth centuries that the tide rose dramatically in favor of English. Mary and James instituted the so-called "plantations," here meaning the planting of people – English-speakers – in Ireland, notably the planned settlement of Scots in Ulster, what is today Northern Ireland. Thus were the seeds of conflict laid.

The population mix between Irish and English began then inexorably to shift toward the English, and a census taken in 1659 showed that while Irish was still the majority spoken language in the country English was coming up rapidly, especially in regions such as Ulster and Dublin more accessible from England. Western Ireland remained strongly Irish speaking, and it is in the west that the *Gaeltacht* – the Irish-speaking area – is located today. Successive censuses show a steady decline in numbers of Irish-speakers, and current surveys generally report around 3 percent of the population as native Irish-speaking.

5 Welsh and Irish Englishes

Linguists speak of the "Welsh dialect of English" or the "Irish dialect of English" where normal people would talk about a "Welsh accent" and an "Irish accent." This is of course the universal outcome of the struggle for two languages for control of the H domain: the substratum language percolates upward and leaves its print on the superstratum language. Just so Irish and Welsh on Irish English and Welsh English. Whereas laymen may speak of Irish and Welsh accents as if they were identical throughout the country, to the trained linguistic ear there are subtle differences between different dialects of Irish English and Welsh English.

That is true, but it is also true that there are general characteristics of both varieties of English widely shared throughout each country. I shall enumerate here some of the easiest ones to identify. I must emphasize that there are really quite large regional differences in both Irish and Welsh English, especially in phonology, and when compiling lists like these one runs some risk of being accused of simply listing stereotypes and shibboleths. That is emphatically not my intent here.

5.1   Welsh English

1   A "lilt" or "singsong" intonation usually consisting of a rising-falling contour at the end of utterances in contrast to the falling tone characteristic of RP (standard British English).
2   Loss of initial /h/ (more common in those areas of Wales that are heavily bilingual).
3   Usually no postvocalic /r/.
4   Long vowels in place of diphthongs in such words as *gate* and *go.*
5   /a/ replaces /æ/ as in for example *cat, and, glass,* and *dance.*
6   Three consonants from Welsh but foreign to RP are often present: voiceless /l/ (spelled ll, e.g., *Lloyd*), a strongly trilled apical /r/ as in Scots English, and the velar fricative /x/ (spelled *ch*) mainly in place-names such as *Pentyrch.*
7   *-ing* is generally *-in'.*
8   The final vowel in words like *silly* and *lovely* is a decidedly long monophthong /iː/.
9   The use of *do* to indicate an action regularly performed, e.g., *He do go buyin'* for *He goes buying regularly.*
10   The use of double and even triple negatives: *'E ain't done nothin' to nobody.*
11   Foregrounding, as in *Money they're not short of* or *Goin' down the mine 'e is.*
12   Generalized use of *isn't it?* in tag questions, e.g., *We're 'avin' a party tonight, isn't it?*
13   Use of *There's* for *How* as in *There's lovely* for *How lovely.*
14   Frequent use of *you see* and *look you,* e.g., *We 'ave 'im now, you see* and *Caught a fish, look you, but I let 'im go.*
15   Loanwords direct from Welsh such as *eisteddfod* 'a cultural festival' and *clennig* 'a gift of money'.
16   Common and frequent use of *boyo* from *boy.*

5.2   Irish English

1   Retention of historical /r/ postvocalically in all positions.
2   The use of "clear" /l/ (palatal or alveo-palatal /l/) in all positions (RP has a velar /l/ postvocalically in for example *full* and *fill*).
3   Retention of the contrast between /hw/ and /w/, so that *which* and *whether* are not homophonous with *witch* and *weather.*
4   Monophthongs /eː, oː/ in place of diphthongs /ei, ou/ in for example *face, take, bait* and *goat, go, boat.*
5   Replacement of the voiceless and voiced interdental fricatives (as in for example *thin* and *then*) by stops (*t, d*) and affricates (*tth, ddh*).
6   Retention of vowel distinctions before /r/, so that the vowels of words such as *bird, learn, beard,* and *turn* are contrastive (whereas all but the vowel of *beard* are the same in RP and American English).

7   Neutralization of the contrast of *i* and *e* before *n*, so that for example *pin* and *pen*, *kin* and *Ken*, are homonyms.

8   *-ing* is generally *-in'*.

9   Use of the reflexive pronoun in sentences such as *And it's himself that told me* . . . and *They were payin' no attention to anything at all as long as themselves were well*.

10 The curious matter of the "after perfect": *I'm after doin' it already* and *She understands; she's after havin' children herself* for more standard *I've done it already* and *She understands; she's had children herself*.

11 Loanwords direct from Irish such as *Taosieach* 'Prime Minister'.

12 Non-RP interrogatories such as *Would you be havin' handkerchiefs?* in place of *Do you have handkerchiefs* (for sale)?

6   Conclusion

That brings us to the end of the story of English in Wales and Ireland. What began as a battle between noble languages, fought over a muddled terrain of H and L, of superstratum and substratum, has ended up in a kind of stasis. English is the usual language of discourse in Wales and Ireland, though this is truer of Ireland than of Wales. Welsh and Irish are alive and well in Wales and Ireland, a statement one is more comfortable with in regard to Welsh. Both Welsh and Irish enjoy – now, not a century or less ago – strong governmental support and a touching degree of affection among the Welsh and Irish people as a link to their past and to their identity. How happy it makes the linguist, *this* linguist at least, to walk into a pub in Holyhead (a point of departure for the ferry to Dublin) and hear *everybody* in the pub speaking Welsh, and then to have the bartender switch effortlessly to English to serve the poor outlander who only wants a pint of bitter (and an opportunity to hear Welsh in a totally natural ambience). Such is the easy bliss of the linguist!

Since linguistic "conquest" has so often meant the *extinction* of the substratum language, one is happy to note that the first expansion of the English language did *not* end in complete victory of English. In linguistics, as perhaps in other kinds of warfare, a partial victory is a better outcome than total victory.

See also Chapters 16, Contact Linguistics and World Englishes; 17, Varieties of World Englishes.

NOTE

I wish to expressly acknowledge here my considerable debt in preparing this essay to the two works by Jeffrey Kallen (one his, one a collection edited by him) and Alan Thomas cited in the References. I have not cited every place where I have relied on their careful work because the nature of the current enterprise argues against extensive footnoting, but I want the readership to know how heavily I have profited from the two scholars' work.

REFERENCES

Cahill, Thomas (1995) *How the Irish Saved Civilization: The Untold Story of Ireland's Heroic Role from the Fall of Rome to the Rise of Medieval Europe.* London: Hodder and Stoughton.

Kallen, Jeffrey L. (1994) English in Ireland. In *The Cambridge History of the English Language, vol. 5.* Edited by Robert Burchfield. Cambridge: Cambridge University Press, pp. 148–96.

Kallen, Jeffrey L. (ed.) (1997) *Focus on Ireland* (*Varieties of English Around the World*, General Series, volume 21). Amsterdam/Philadelphia: John Benjamins Publishing Company.

Thomas, Alan R. (1994) English in Wales. In *The Cambridge History of the English Language, vol. 5.* Edited by Robert Burchfield. Cambridge: Cambridge University Press, pp. 94–147.

FURTHER READING

Davies, John (1993) *A History of Wales.* London: Penguin.

James, Simon (1993) *The World of the Celts.* London: Thames and Hudson.

McArthur, Tom (2002) *Oxford Guide to World English.* Oxford: Oxford University Press.

www.gy.com/Society/Ethnicity/Celtic/History (valid 20 October 2004).

www.watson.org/~leigh/celts.html (valid 18 October 2004).

3 English in Scotland

FIONA DOUGLAS

1 Introduction

Scotland maintains its identity as a distinctive country within Britain, and yet it lacks socio-economic and political autonomy. With the Union of the Scottish and English Crowns in 1603, and the Treaty of Union merging the parliaments just over a century later in 1707, Scotland relinquished its independence. For nearly 300 years, Scotland was a stateless nation, until the reinstatement of its own parliament (albeit with limited devolved powers) on July 1, 1999. Scotland did, however, retain its own triumvirate of church, legal, and education systems, and a strong sense of national and cultural identity. In the absence of nationhood, the "imagined community" (Anderson, 1991) is arguably forced to construct its identity from other available resources such as its culture, its history, its distinctive institutions, and its language(s). For Scotland, those languages are Scottish Gaelic (a Celtic language, and therefore outside the remit of this book) and the peculiarly Scottish variety of English described in the following.

The rather simplistic title of this chapter, "English in Scotland," belies a complex and heterogeneous linguistic situation. We can use the term *Scottish English* (SE) to refer to the distinctive localized variety of British English native to Scotland. (It should be noted in passing that I share Hansen's (1997) reservations about the term "British English." I use "British English" to refer to the collective entity that is the Englishes of Scotland, England, Ireland and Wales, and not, as many others (for example, Merriam-Webster, 2005) have done, as an inaccurate synonym for English-English.

2 Historical Development of the Scottish Varieties

In order to explain the development of present day SE, we must consider two key strands: firstly the development of a variety I shall term *Scots* (SC);

and secondly the subsequent development of another Scottish variety, *Scottish Standard English* (SSE), which was the result of contact with the southern English standard during the eighteenth century. What follows is necessarily a summary, and I recommend Jones (1997), Macafee and Aitken (2002), and McClure (1994) as preliminary further reading.

2.1   *Parallel development of cognate varieties*

One of the four Old English dialects, Northumbrian, straddled what is now the Scottish/English border, and was the precursor, not just of SC, but also of modern northern English-English dialects, hence the large number of shared features that can be seen in these varieties to the present day. What we now think of as (British) Standard English developed further south and was based largely on the dialects in the East Midlands area around London and East Anglia. SC and English-English are therefore historically closely related cognate varieties. Given its origins, SC can be linguistically (although perhaps not ideologically) considered a type of "English." (See discussion at 4.1.)

2.2   *Earliest days*

We can trace the earliest days of a language within Scotland that was derived from Old English to 547, when a group of Anglian invaders founded the Kingdom of Bernicia in the area around the present day Scottish–English border. (Similar Germanic invasions were occurring elsewhere in Britain at this time.) Naturally these Anglian invaders brought their language with them. Before that time, Scotland's language and culture had been predominantly Celtic (see McClure, 1994 for further discussion). By the mid-seventh century, the Kingdom of Bernicia had extended further into Scotland to include what is now part of the Scottish Lothians.

2.3   *The impact of Old Norse*

The situation is complicated by the arrival in the eighth century of closely related Germanic language varieties spoken by Viking raiders who began attacking the northern and western isles of Scotland. They eventually settled in Orkney and Shetland, bequeathing the Norwegian variety called *Norn* to the islands, where it was spoken until the eighteenth and nineteenth centuries, respectively. Its influence can still be seen in present day Insular Scots.

Of course, the Vikings also carried out raids south of the border in England, and settled in the "Danelaw" in central England. Because the cognate languages of the Anglo-Saxons and the Viking raiders were mutually comprehensible, some scholars (following Poussa, 1982) have suggested that the linguistic situation that developed in Britain at this time was something akin to creolization, or at least some sort of language mixing leading to the development of a hybrid *Anglo-Scandinavian* variety.

Old Norse (ON) had significant effects on English both north and south of the border, as is evidenced by the adoption of Norse-influenced words at the very heart of the lexicon such as *they*, *their*, and *them*. However, it had an even stronger legacy in Scotland than in England, and many present day SC words were originally ON loanwords and still have cognates in the Scandinavian languages. ON also influenced SC phonology, as is witnessed by the existence of Scots Norse-influenced cognates for words which also exist in English – e.g., *kirk* and *church*; *brig* and *bridge*, *dike* and *ditch*, *skirl* and *shrill*, *skreich* and *shriek*. These pairings are explained by ON having the plosives /k/ and /g/ in environments where Old English had the affricates /ʧ/ and /ʤ/.

2.4   The influence of Norman French

The Norman Conquest in 1066 triggered an influx of Anglo-Norman and Flemish overlords to Scotland, but they were accompanied by a wave of immigrant servants and retainers, particularly from the north of England, causing a significant increase in the use of Anglo-Scandinavian throughout lowland Scotland. Until the twelfth century, the "English" language (or what was to become known as *Scots*) in Scotland was limited largely to the south and south-east, with the areas to the north still dominated by Gaelic. By the fourteenth century, the success of this variety seemed to be assured with a decline in the use of both Norman French and Gaelic.

2.5   The ascendance of Inglis

Over time this Anglo-Scandinavian variety (or *Inglis*, as it was beginning to be known) spread into ever-increasing communicative functions. No longer merely a largely spoken variety, it spread into the written mode and dispersed ever more widely, both geographically and socially. The earliest substantial document we have is Barbour's epic poem *Brus* of 1375, but other documents soon followed, and by 1390 Scottish Acts of Parliament began to be recorded in Inglis rather than Latin. By now, Inglis was the dominant variety for all Scotsmen to the south and east of the Highland line.

During the period from the fifteenth to the early sixteenth centuries SC (now the language of the Scottish court) was the language used in formal registers such as government and administration, and it had an extensive, varied, and rich literature. The varieties north and south of the Scottish/English border were, linguistically speaking, still closely related dialects, but significantly, SC was now being increasingly used in high-status registers. Many of the great Scottish writers such as Henryson, Douglas, and Dunbar date from this period.

2.6   *From* Inglis *to* Scottis *to* Scots

It is worth noting that originally the Scots used the term "Inglis" to refer to the Anglo-Scandinavian varieties spoken both in Scotland and in England, thus bearing testament to their close similarities. It was only in the late fifteenth and early sixteenth centuries that the Scots began to differentiate their variety of this Inglis as *Scottis* – a variety retrospectively termed *Older Scots* by linguists and the precursor of present day SC. (See McClure (1981) for fuller discussion of names for these varieties.) Older Scots is considered to be the period from 1100 to 1700, with Modern Scots beginning in 1700 and persisting to the present day (Robinson, 1985).

2.7   *Increasing Anglicization*

From the mid-sixteenth century onward, SC began to be threatened by increasing Anglicization. The Reformation in 1560 brought with it an English, not Scots, Bible to Scotland, at a time when this was probably the only book owned by many households. The introduction of printing saw a proliferation of imported English-printed books and an accompanying shift towards English norms by many Scottish printers. The Union of the Crowns and the ensuing removal of the Scottish court to London deprived many Scots writers of their patronage (indeed, many of the court poets moved south with the king and Anglicized their verse for an English market), decreased the status of SC, and thus markedly accelerated the Anglicization process. However, although SC was becoming Anglicized in the written mode, it persisted as a clearly distinguishable form in the spoken mode well into the seventeenth century.

With the Treaty of Union in 1707, SC lost political as well as spiritual and social status (Murison, 1979). However, there was some resurgent cultural backlash, with a revival of literary Scots by writers such as Robert Burns and Allan Ramsay and a spate of republishing Scots works of the past. At the same time, many individuals from the Scottish middle and upper classes were trying to eradicate Scotticisms from their writing and speech. Elocution lessons, lists of Scotticisms to be avoided in polite society, and guides on spelling, grammar and pronunciation proliferated (Jones, 1995, 1997). (These developments in Scotland can usefully be considered in the wider British context wherein attempts were being made to *fix* the language in the wake of Johnson's dictionary, and to avoid provincial vulgarisms.) The speech of the aspiring Scottish middle classes was heavily influenced by southern Standard English and this led to the development of a linguistic compromise variety, SSE, which persists to the present day.

As discussed in other chapters in this volume (see also Chapters 4 and 5), SC and SSE were exported around the world from the seventeenth century onward, having significant influences on the language of Ulster (Northern Ireland), the USA, Canada, and Australasia (Montgomery, 2003).

2.8   *Highland English and Gaelic*

Highland English (HE), the variety spoken in the Scottish Highlands and the Western Isles, is a distinctive form of English, influenced mainly by Gaelic rather than Scots, although lowland Scots is beginning to have more of an influence on younger speakers. HE developed much later than SE, as Gaelic was prevalent in the Gaidhealtachd long after it had retreated from other parts of Scotland. HE is therefore derived from Standard English, rather than from Scots. (See McClure, 1994 for a fuller account.) Gaelic persists in pockets in these and a few other areas to the present day, although it no longer has monolingual speakers.

3.0   The Present-Day Scottish-English Linguistic Continuum

Although originating as a linguistic compromise between SC and southern Standard English, SSE now has the status of an autonomous and prestigious language variety (McClure, 1994). SC (the modern reflex of Inglis or Scottis – call it what you will) is now generally regarded as having low prestige (except, arguably, in literary contexts), and persists largely in the speech of the Scottish working classes. And so the linguistic continuum which persists in Scotland to this day was born.

Today *Scottish English* (SE) can be used as a blanket term to cover both regional and social varieties along a linguistic continuum (see Figure 3.1), ranging from SC (sometimes called *Broad Scots* or *Scots dialect*) at one end to SSE (itself a variety of World Standard English) at the other (Aitken, 1979; McArthur, 1979). The SC (or *dense*) end of the continuum is maximally differentiated from Standard English, and the SSE (or *thin*) end minimally so (McClure, 1979). Individuals, taking account of external factors such as context of situation, education, social class, etc., can move along the continuum in either direction, but some individuals will inevitably have a stronger attraction to

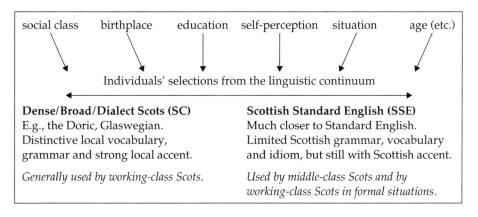

Figure 3.1   The Scottish English linguistic continuum

one pole than the other. Both style-drifting and code-switching are common. In an attempt to make sense of this complex situation, Aitken (1979, 1984a, 1984b) proposed a five-column model of Scottish speech, although, as he notes (1984b: 28), it also has validity as a model for the written mode. Aitken (1984b) also suggests that there are social class differences in the acceptability of certain Scotticisms which do not necessarily correlate with his column divisions.

Whilst notions of maximal and minimal differentiation from Standard English are useful ways of categorizing SE varieties, such an approach encourages us to overlook the many grammatical, lexical, and phonological features which are, and always were, shared by SC and English – the *common core* (see section 5.3). It also implies that SC is a deviant (or nonstandard) form of English which is undoubtedly problematic, but given the current and historical links between these varieties, such comparisons are inevitable.

3.1   Scots

As would be expected, much more variation is found at the SC end of the continuum. As can be seen from the examples given in Figure 3.1, SC is not one homogeneous variety. It includes numerous regional dialects, both urban and rural, and although they share certain common features, some of them are markedly distinct, and indeed are often difficult for people from other parts of Scotland to understand. Conventionally SC dialects are grouped into the following broad geographic areas: *Insular Scots*, *Northern Scots* (and *North-East Scots*), *Central Scots* (*East*, *West*, and *South-West*), *Southern Scots*, *Ulster Scots* (Grant and Murison, 1931–76). A useful map is given by Eagle (2002). We have no firm figures for the number of SC speakers in Scotland, and estimates vary. There was some pressure to include a question to ascertain this in the 2001 Scottish Census, but the request was rejected on the grounds that it would be too difficult to formulate an unambiguous question.

3.2   Scottish Standard English

SSE is used by individuals from all over Scotland, although it may, to some extent, be colored by the features of their local variety. It is the usual variety of the Scottish middle classes, and the variety aimed at by working-class speakers in formal speech situations.

3.3   Written and spoken varieties of Scottish English

The SE continuum applies to both spoken and written varieties, although, as Macafee (1983) notes, the continuum stretches further in either direction for writing than for speech. The written and spoken varieties are not as closely entwined as one might think; for example, much more SC is spoken than is written, and few Scots are practiced writers (or even readers) of SC. Literary Scots bears little resemblance to the spoken Scots one hears, and it is a curious anomaly that those few individuals who do write in SC are usually highly educated and/or middle class – the very people one would least expect to hear using SC in speech. SSE is the language of the Scottish education system, and so, when Scots write in English, their language is largely indistinguishable from other types of British Standard English. I say "largely" as there are two types of Scotticism which are found in Scots' formal written English: "cultural Scotticisms" (Aitken, 1979), which refer to peculiarly Scottish aspects of life, and hence have Scottish labels (e.g., *the Kirk* 'The Church of Scotland'), and what I shall term "formal Scotticisms," such as *outwith* 'outside of' and *uplift* 'collect(ion)'.

Although much usage of SE linguistic features is *covert* (i.e., speakers do not realize it marks them out as Scots), there is also a strong tradition of *overt* usage with people deliberately and knowingly choosing to use Scots linguistic features, often as a way of asserting their Scottish identity (Aitken, 1979, 1984b).

4.0   Problems of Definition, Terminology, and Status

Whilst the concept of the linguistic continuum is useful in explaining the shifting linguistic behavior of many Scots individuals, it glosses over some fundamental ideological issues and linguistic debates. These can be summarized as problems of definition, of terminology, and of status.

4.1   Problems of definition and terminology

One of the key problems associated with studying these varieties is the plethora of terms used by different linguists. As we have seen in section 2, there is a historical component to be considered. However, much of the divergence in the naming strategies adopted is dependent on status and perceptions, i.e., whether individual linguists believe that the most maximally differentiated varieties here (and usually) termed Scots should be considered as forming a separate language or alternatively merely as distinctive dialects of English.

Arguments for separate language status for SC are generally mounted on discussions of its historical development, its strong literary legacy, and because it contains a range of distinctive local dialects. On the other hand, some scholars (e.g., Aitken, 1981a, 1982) have argued that nowadays, in the spoken mode anyway, SC is merely a distinctive national variety of English, and certainly its close association with, and similarities to, other varieties of English would tend to support this view. The argument continues to rumble on and we cannot hope or even attempt to solve it here, but it does have important implications for the status of these varieties.

4.2   *Problems of status*

Attitudes to SE and the status of the individual varieties it encompasses are diverse and often conflicting. On the one hand, SSE is widely regarded as a prestigious national variety of world Englishes. In the spoken mode, SC has covert prestige as a strong in-group identifier for certain social groups. A recent survey showed that a "not too strong" Scottish accent is also perceived as desirable (BBC Voices Survey, 2005). However, Scots are also plagued by linguistic insecurity, and perhaps the majority regard their language as being *bad English* or *slang* rather than *Scots* (Macafee, 1994, 1997; Menzies, 1991; Romaine, 1980). Accounts suggest that historically, some of the blame for these attitudes rests with the Scottish education system. Anecdotal evidence suggests that prejudice against, and ignorance concerning, particular varieties of Scottish English is still rife, even (or indeed, perhaps especially) within Scotland. Most attempts to revive written SC outside the realm of literature are regarded with derision or at best confusion, and perhaps most damagingly of all, such representations of broad SC varieties as do exist, for example, in the media, are usually relegated to domestic, stereotypically Scottish (Burns, haggis, and tartan) or humorous contexts. Much energy has also been expended over the years on the debate of *good* vs. *bad* Scots – where *good* usually translates as rural, conservative and maximally differentiated, and *bad* as urban, innovative and minimally differentiated.

The problematic status of SC has implications for the registers in which its use is considered appropriate. Part of the problem is that SC has no agreed standard form. (*Lallans*, otherwise known as *Plastic/Synthetic Scots*, was a twentieth-century attempt to establish a literary Standard Scots, but it has not been widely adopted.)

The ambiguous status of these varieties also has an impact on how they are regarded within the context of world Englishes. McArthur's (1987) circle of World English places SC on a par with SE as a variety of British English, whereas Görlach's (1990) circle places SE alongside English-English, Welsh English, and Irish English as a variety of British English, but isolates SC outside the circle with varieties such as Anglo-Romani and Tok Pisin, thus emphasizing the discreteness of SC from SE.

5.0   Characteristics of Present-Day Scottish English Varieties

Clearly, it is not possible to give an exhaustive account of the features associated with the range of SE varieties across the continuum. What follows is a brief summary of some of the most important features of SE. It should be noted that some features have varying distributions across the continuum.

5.1   Phonological characteristics

5.1.1   Consonants

The SE consonants are /p b t d k g f θ v ð s z ʃ ʒ x ʍ h ʧ ʤ r l m n ŋ w/ (Stuart-Smith, 2004). The Scottish pronunciation of consonants is largely the same as for most other accents of English. The following features are noted as typical of SE, although, of course, some are shared with other accents.

Perhaps the most obvious distinguishing phonological feature of SE is its rhoticity – i.e., retention of post-vocalic /r/ in words such as *car*. (The precise realization of this phoneme varies and there is some evidence that these realizations are altering (see Stuart-Smith, 2003, 2004; Johnston, 1997 for details). Although this is a feature which strongly marks Scottish speakers out from the majority of British Standard English speakers (note that Irish English retains its rhoticity and there are one or two exceptions in English-English), rhoticity is a feature which is found in some other world Englishes (Abercrombie, 1979), being shared with many but not all varieties of American English and with most varieties of Canadian English (see Chapter 4 in this volume).

Two extra phonemes, the velar fricative /x/ as in *loch*, which is generally realized as /k/ elsewhere in the English-speaking world (except in self-conscious pronunciation of loanwords from Gaelic, Scots, and some other languages), and the voiceless bilabial fricative /ʍ/, which allows Scottish speakers to distinguish easily between *Wales* and *whales*, are found in most Scottish accents. Again, there is some evidence (Johnston, 1997; Macafee, 1983; Stuart-Smith, 2003, 2004) that these traditionally Scottish phonemes may be undergoing erosion or modification for some (especially urban) speakers.

In North-East Scots dialects, <wh> is often pronounced /f/ instead of /ʍ/ giving examples such as *fit* and *fan* instead of *what* and *when*.

T-glottaling (realization of /t/ as [ʔ] is common in SE (as in other accents of English), and has long been a stereotype of Glaswegian speech.

It is thought that there may be some differences in the distribution of voiced and voiceless fricatives compared with some other varieties of English – e.g., *roofs* may be pronounced /rufs/ rather than /ruvz/, and *dwarves* as /dwɔrfs/ instead of /dwɔrvz/.

Stuart-Smith (2004: 63) notes that in SE "the secondary articulation of /l/ tends to be dark in all positions of the word."

5.1.2   Vowels

The vowels within SE are /i ɪ e ɛ a o ɔ ʉ ʌ əi ae oe ʌʉ/ (Stuart-Smith, 2004). SE pronunciation (as with other British English accents) is often compared with that of the British English reference accent Received Pronunciation (RP). (A useful click and play comparison is given by the *Click and Listen Project*, 1997.) SE has fewer vowel contrasts than RP, and a comparison shows differences in vowel distributions in certain words.

SE's retention of post-vocalic /r/ has meant that it maintains certain distinctions not found in varieties of English that have lost post-vocalic /r/, for example, in SE realizations of *soared* /sord/, *sword* /sɔrd/ and *sawed* /sɔd/ (RP, and nearly all English-English accents, have /sɔːd/ for all three).

Most varieties of SE show a three-way distinction between /ɪ/, /ʌ/, and /ɛ/, for example in *pit, putt, and pet*.

Whilst RP has a distinction between *cot* /ɒ/ and *caught* /ɔː/, SE realizes both using the same vowel /ɔ/.

Whilst RP, and most English-English accents distinguish /ʊ/ (a vowel absent from SE) and /uː/ for *pull* and *pool* respectively, SE uses the same vowel /ʉ/ for both.

The Great Vowel Shift did not proceed as far in Scotland as it did in the south (for example, Scots retains the /ʉ/ vowel in words like *hoose* 'house').

Some varieties of English, such as RP, have phonemic vowel length. SE does not. SE does, however, have its own system of context dependent allophonic vowel length, explained by the Scottish Vowel Length Rule (SVLR) which is usually considered to distinguish it from other Englishes. All varieties of SE operate the SVLR to some extent (Aitken, 1981b). The vowels in Scottish pronunciations of *hit* /ɪ/ and *hut* /ʌ/ are always short. (Some commentators, e.g. McMahon (1991, 1994) and Scobbie, Hewlett, and Turk (1999), suggest that /ɛ/ is also short.) In most varieties of SE, the length of the other vowels can be predicted according to their phonetic and morphological conditions using the SVLR. Vowels are long before /r/ and voiced fricatives i.e. /v/, /ð/, /z/, /ʒ/, and also before word or morpheme boundaries; in other environments, they are short. For example, in SE a length distinction can be noted between the vowels in *leaf* [lif] and *leave* [liːv] and *ceased* [sist] and *seized* [siːzd]. However, it should be stressed that the situation is rather complicated. Not all varieties of SE operate the SVLR to the same degree. Scobbie et al. (1999) suggest differences between SC and SSE in its operation and question the vowels affected. McClure (1994) discusses modifications to the implementation of the SVLR in different regional varieties of SC. Agutter (1988) compares SSE with RP and queries whether the SVLR is a defining feature of Scottish speech at all. Clearly more research is required.

5.2   Grammatical, idiomatic and syntactic differences

This is a complex area, and Miller (1993, 2003), Miller and Brown (1982), Macafee (1992), Beal (1997) and Purves (2002) are recommended as further reading.

5.2.1   Morphology

In the written and spoken modes, the past tense and past participle (marked by *-ed* in Standard English) in regular verbs are indicated variously by *-it*, *-d*, and *-t* depending on regional and phonological factors. Present participle endings may be *-in* or *-ing*. The *-and* ending survives in pockets.

SE has a three-way deictic system in demonstratives (*this, that, thon/yon*).

The diminutive suffix *-ie* is common and fairly productive, e.g., *wifie* ('woman', derogatory); *mannie* (NE SC 'man').

Some irregular plurals survive, for example, *een (eyes), shuin (shoes), kye (cows)* – although Miller (2003) suggests many of these are dying out.

5.2.2 Syntax

In SE, the definite article is used in some contexts where Standard English has no determiner, for example, with illnesses (*the cold*), with institutions (*the school, the hospital*), with periods of time (*the day* – today).

5.2.3 The verb phrase

There is some evidence that the SE modal system is also distinctive, with modal auxiliaries having rather different distributions in SE than in other British English varieties.

In both the written and spoken modes we find a characteristic formation of negatives (*-nae* and *-na* enclitic, or freestanding *no* forms), and also distinctive modifications of some modal and auxiliary verbs, e.g., *winna/willna(e)* = *will* + *-na(e)*; *dinna(e)* = *do* + *-na(e)*.

5.3 Distinctive lexis

Because SE shares much of its linguistic heritage with English-English, it is not surprising that these varieties share significant amounts of "common core" vocabulary arising from their shared Old English ancestry, and shared ON and French loanwords. As we have already noted, ON had a greater impact on Scottish varieties, and this can be seen in significant numbers of distinctive SC lexical items. SE also has uniquely Scottish loans from other languages, including a few from Gaelic.

Two further characteristic features of Scots lexis must be mentioned; firstly, that Scottish lexis can be heavily regionalized (e.g., the little finger is *crannie* in the NE but *pinkie* elsewhere in Scotland), and secondly, that SC lacks an agreed spelling system, even though there have been numerous attempts to recommend certain spellings based on criteria such as etymology and phonology. The same word may be spelled in a variety of ways, depending on a range of factors such as the date of the text, its regional origins, or simply the writer's preference, although there are certain spelling conventions which are quite widely used. A recent request that Scottish Language Dictionaries, the charitable body established to develop Scottish lexicography (see SLD, 2002), should produce a dictionary of parliamentary terms for use by the Scottish Parliament may help to encourage "preferred spellings." It is feasible, although by no means uncontroversial, that the institutional acceptance of certain spellings may be enough to trigger the early stages of orthographic standardization.

Much has been written on the erosion of Scots lexis (e.g., Macafee, 2003), and there has undeniably been significant attrition in many semantic areas.

One of the biggest problems has been the lack of generation of Scots vocabulary for technical and learned registers. Thus, in many situations, the language finds itself out of step with the world in which it exists and so we have a seemingly inexorable shift toward integration with the more English end of the continuum. However, that said, the urban SC varieties such as Glaswegian are to some extent lexically innovative, although many purists feel that this is not "true'" or "good" Scots.

For those wishing to investigate Scottish lexis further, primary resources are the well-respected Scots dictionaries such as: *A Dictionary of the Older Scots Tongue (DOST)* (Craigie et al., 1937–2002), which includes the full vocabulary of the language from the twelfth century to 1700 and makes no attempt to restrict entries to specifically Scottish words or senses; *The Scottish National Dictionary (SND)* (Grant and Murison, 1931–76), which covers the period 1700 to the present day and concentrates only on those items which are distinct from Standard English; *The Dictionary of the Scots Language (DSL)* (Rennie, 2004), an online searchable resource combining the data from *DOST* and *SND* (plus supplements); and *The Concise Scots Dictionary (CSD)* (Robinson, 1985), a digest of *SND* and *DOST*.

6   Scottish English: Looking to the Future

What does the future hold for SE? SSE seems secure; the future of Scots may be less so. Scots has always been strongest in literature, but there are now some indications that it could one day once again extend into other domains. Recent years have seen a revival of interest in Scottish language.

In the wake of the new Scottish Parliament we have seen the establishment of a Cross-Party Group for the Scots Language, and attempts to develop an "official public" Scots (Corbett and Douglas, 2003) in McGugan (2003) and Donati et al. (2003). In academia, we have seen the establishment of a significant new research tool, the Scottish Corpus of Texts and Speech (discussed by Douglas, 2003), attempts to set up an Institute for the Languages of Scotland (Carnegie Trust, n.d.), and even academic papers published in SC (e.g., in Kirk and Ó Baoill, 2000–2003). In 2002, the Scottish Arts Council announced it would provide substantial core funding for Scottish Language Dictionaries. In the same year, the Itchy-Coo imprint, "a best-selling, award-winning new imprint which specialises in Scots Language books for children and young people" (Itchy-Coo, n.d.), was established. SC has now been recognized as a "minority language" by the European Bureau for Lesser Used Languages (EBLUL, 2003), something which should improve its status, but activists argue that the UK government has shown little commitment to upholding the treaty for SC.

Modern Scottish writers, such as Irvine Welsh (whose novel *Trainspotting*, later made into a film, received recognition well beyond the Scottish local market) and James Kelman, enjoy huge popularity and/or critical acclaim, and incorporate representations of modern, thin urban SC. In Scottish literature, with one or two exceptions, SC has traditionally been restricted to the "safe" confines of the dialog of selected characters, but, significantly, these writers sometimes also allow it to pervade the wider narrative. Like many others before them, including Burns, they are also playing with the extra stylistic possibilities afforded by the SE linguistic continuum.

And yet, as discussed earlier (in section 5.3), there is ongoing attrition of SC vocabulary, with some linguists (e.g., Macafee, 2003: 51) diagnosing SC as being in "an advanced stage of language death" in much of lowland Scotland. Interestingly, the demise of Scots has been forecast since the eighteenth century (Aitken, 1981a, 1984a) and yet clearly, for the moment, it continues to persist.

So, based on this evidence, what can we predict: will Scots survive in the future, or will it die a slow, painful death? Only time will tell.

See also Chapters 2, First Steps: Wales and Ireland; 17, Varieties of World Englishes.

NOTE

I am grateful to Anthea Fraser Gupta and John Corbett for commenting on an earlier draft of this chapter. All errors remain my own.

REFERENCES

Abercrombie, David (1979) The accents of Standard English in Scotland. In *Languages of Scotland*. Edited by Adam J. Aitken and Tom McArthur. Edinburgh: Chambers, pp. 68–84.

Agutter, Alex (1988) The not-so-Scottish vowel length rule. In *Edinburgh Studies in the English Language*. Edited by John Anderson and Norman Macleod. Edinburgh: John Donald, pp. 120–32.

Aitken, Adam J. (1979) Scottish speech: A historical view with special reference to the Standard English of Scotland. In *Languages of Scotland*. Edited by Adam J. Aitken and Tom McArthur. Edinburgh: Chambers, pp. 85–118.

Aitken, Adam J. (1981a) The good old Scots tongue: Does Scots have an identity? In *Minority Languages Today*. Edited by Einar Haugen, J. Derrick McClure, Derick Thomson, and Adam J. Aitken. Edinburgh: Edinburgh University Press, pp. 72–90.

Aitken, Adam J. (1981b) The Scottish vowel length rule. In *So Meny People Longages and Tonges, Philological Essays in Scots Mediaeval English*. Edited by Michael Benskin and M. L. Samuels. Edinburgh: Published by editors, pp. 131–57.

Aitken, Adam J. (1982) Bad Scots: Some superstitions about Scots speech. *Scottish Language*, **1**, 30–44.

Aitken, Adam J. (1984a) Scots and English in Scotland. In *Language in the British Isles.* Edited by Peter Trudgill. Cambridge: Cambridge University Press, pp. 517–32.

Aitken, Adam J. (1984b) Scottish accents and dialects. In *Language in the British Isles.* Edited by Peter Trudgill. Cambridge: Cambridge University Press, pp. 94–114.

Anderson, Benedict (1991) *Imagined Communities: Reflections on the Origins and Spread of Nationalism.* 2nd edition. London: Verso.

BBC (2005) Voices. (Online.) http://www.bbc.co.uk/voices/. Accessed January 30, 2005.

Beal, Joan (1997) Syntax and morphology. In *The Edinburgh History of the Scots Language.* Edited by Charles Jones. Edinburgh: Edinburgh University Press, pp. 335–77.

Carnegie Trust (n.d.) An institute for the languages of Scotland: Feasibility study. (Online.) http://www.arts.ed.ac.uk/celtscot/institutelanguagesscotland/. Accessed January 30, 2005.

Click and listen (1997) Vowel systems of Scottish English and Standard Southern English. (Online.) Edinburgh: University of Edinburgh. http://www.assets.scotcit.ac.uk/cnl3/systems.htm. Accessed January 30, 2005.

Corbett, John and Douglas, Fiona M. (2003) Scots in the public sphere. In *Towards our Goals in Broadcasting, the Press, the Performing Arts and the Economy: Minority Languages in Northern Ireland, the Republic of Ireland and Scotland.* Edited by John M. Kirk and Dónall P. Ó Baoill. Belfast: Queen's University Belfast Studies in Language, Culture and Politics, pp. 198–210.

Craigie, William, Aitken, Adam J., Stevenson, James A. C., Watson, Harry D., Dareau, Margaret G., and Pike, K. Lorna (eds.) (1937–2002) *A Dictionary of the Older Scottish Tongue (DOST)* (12 vols). Aberdeen: Aberdeen University Press.

Donati, Colin, Hendry, Joy, Robertson, James, and Scott, Paul H. (2003) Scots: A statement of principles: A road forrit for the Scots language in a multilingual Scotland. Edinburgh: The Scots Pairliament Cross-Party Group on the Scots Leid. http://www.scottish.parliament.uk/msp/crossPartyGroups/groups/scots/SoP%20version%202.PDF. Accessed March 18, 2005.

Douglas, Fiona M. (2003) The Scottish corpus of texts and speech: Problems of corpus design. *Literary and Linguistic Computing,* **18**(1), 23–37.

Eagle, Andy (2002) Scots on-line. (Online.) http://www.scots-online.org/grammar/pronunci.htm. Accessed January 30, 2005.

EBLUL (2003) The UK Committee of the European Bureau for Lesser Used Languages. (Online.) http://www.eblul.org.uk/. Accessed January 30, 2005.

Görlach, Manfred (1990) The development of Standard Englishes. In *Studies in the History of the English Language.* Edited by Manfred Görlach. Heidelberg: Carl Winter, pp. 9–64.

Grant, William and Murison, David (eds.) (1931–76) *The Scottish National Dictionary (SND)* (10 vols). Aberdeen: Aberdeen University Press.

Hansen, Klaus (1997) British English and International English: Two debateable terms. In *Englishes around the World, vol. 1.* Edited by Manfred Görlach. Amsterdam/Philadelphia: John Benjamins, pp. 5970.

Itchy-Coo (n.d.) Itchy-Coo: Braw books for bairns o aw ages. (Online.) http://www.itchy-coo.com. Accessed March 16, 2005.

Johnston, Paul (1997) Regional variation. In *The Edinburgh History of the Scots Language*. Edited by Charles Jones. Edinburgh: Edinburgh University Press, pp. 433–515.

Jones, Charles (1995) *A Language Suppressed: The Pronunciation of the Scots Language in the 18th Century*. Edinburgh: John Donald.

Jones, Charles (ed.) (1997) *The Edinburgh History of the Scots Language*. Edinburgh: Edinburgh University Press.

Kirk, John M. and Ó Baoill, Dónall (eds.) (2000–2003) *Belfast Studies in Language, Culture and Politics*. Belfast: Queen's University Belfast.

Macafee, Caroline I. (1983) *Varieties of English around the World: Glasgow*. Amsterdam: John Benjamins.

Macafee, Caroline I. (1992) Characteristics of non-standard grammar in Scotland. (Online.) http://www.abdn.ac.uk/~enl038/grammar.htm. Accessed January 30, 2005.

Macafee, Caroline I. (1994) *Traditional Dialect in the Modern World: A Glasgow Case Study*. Frankfurt am Main: Peter Lang.

Macafee, Caroline I. (1997) Ongoing change in Modern Scots. In *The Edinburgh History of the Scots Language*. Edited by Charles Jones. Edinburgh: Edinburgh University Press, pp. 514–50.

Macafee, Caroline I. (2003) Studying Scots vocabulary. In *The Edinburgh Companion to Scots*. Edited by John Corbett, J. Derrick McClure, and Jane Stuart-Smith, Edinburgh: Edinburgh University Press, pp. 50–71.

Macafee, Caroline I. and Aitken, Adam J. (2002) A history of Scots to 1700. In *A Dictionary of the Older Scottish Tongue, vol. 12*. Edited by William Craigie, Adam J. Aitken, James A. C. Stevenson, Harry D. Watson, Margaret G. Dareau, and K. Lorna Pike. Oxford: Oxford University Press, pp. xxi–clvi.

McArthur, Tom (1979) The status of English in and furth of Scotland. In *Languages of Scotland*. Edited by Adam J. Aitken and Tom McArthur. Edinburgh: Chambers, pp. 50–67.

McArthur, Tom (1987) The English Languages? *English Today*, **11**, 9–13.

McClure, J. Derrick (1979) Scots: Its range of uses. In *Languages of Scotland*. Edited by Adam J. Aitken and Tom McArthur. Edinburgh: Chambers, pp. 26–48.

McClure, J. Derrick (1981) Scottis, Inglis, Suddroun: Language labels and language attitudes. In *Proceedings of the Third International Conference on Scottish Language and Literature*. Edited by Roderick J. Lyall and Felicity Riddy. Stirling: University of Stirling, pp. 52–69. Reproduced in McClure, J. Derrick (1995) *Scots and its Literature*. Amsterdam/Philadelphia: John Benjamins, pp. 44–56.

McClure, J. Derrick (1994) English in Scotland. In *The Cambridge History of the English Language, Volume 5: English in Britain and Overseas, Origin and Development*. Edited by Robert Burchfield. Cambridge: Cambridge University Press, pp. 23–93.

McGugan, Irene (2003) *Inquiry into the Role of Educational and Cultural Policy in Supporting and Developing Gaelic, Scots and Minority Languages in Scotland*. Edinburgh: The Scottish Parliament Education, Culture and Sport Committee.

McMahon, April M. S. (1991) Lexical phonology and sound change: The case of the Scottish Vowel Length Rule. *Journal of Linguistics*, **27**, 29–53.

McMahon, April M. S. (1994) *Understanding Language Change*. Cambridge: Cambridge University Press.

Menzies, Janet (1991) An investigation of attitudes to Scots and Glasgow dialect among secondary school pupils. *Scottish Language*, **10**, 30–46.

Merriam-Webster (2005) *Merriam Webster Online Dictionary*. http://www.m-w.com/. Accessed January 30, 2005.

Miller, Jim (1993) The grammar of Scottish English. In *The Grammar of English Dialects in the British Isles*. Edited by James Milroy and Lesley Milroy. London: Longman, pp. 99–138.

Miller, Jim (2003) Syntax and discourse in modern Scots. In *The Edinburgh Companion to Scots*. Edited by John Corbett, J. Derrick McClure, and Jane Stuart-Smith. Edinburgh: Edinburgh University Press, pp. 72–109.

Miller, Jim and Brown, Keith (1982) Aspects of Scottish English syntax. *English World-Wide*, **3**(1), 3–17.

Montgomery, Michael (2003) The Scots language abroad. In *The Edinburgh Companion to Scots*. Edited by John Corbett, J. Derrick McClure, and Jane Stuart-Smith. Edinburgh: Edinburgh University Press, pp. 233–50.

Murison, David (1979) The historical background. In *Languages of Scotland*. Edited by Adam J. Aitken and Tom McArthur. Edinburgh: Chambers, pp. 2–13.

Poussa, Patricia (1982) The evolution of early standard English: The creolization hypothesis. *Studia Anglica Posnaniensa*, **14**, 69–85.

Purves, David (2002) *A Scots Grammar: Scots Grammar and Usage*. Edinburgh: Saltire Society.

Rennie, Susan C. (ed.) (2004) *The Dictionary of the Scots Language (DSL)*. (Online.) http://www.dsl.ac.uk/dsl/index.html. Accessed January 30, 2005.

Robinson, Mairi (ed.) (1985) *The Concise Scots Dictionary (CSD)*. Edinburgh: Polygon.

Romaine, Suzanne (1980) Stylistic variation and evaluative reactions to speech: Problems in the investigation of linguistic attitudes in Scotland. *Language and Speech*, **23**(3), 213–31.

Scobbie, James, Hewlett, Nigel, and Turk, Alice (1999) Standard English in Edinburgh and Glasgow: The Scottish Vowel Length Rule revealed. In *Urban Voices: Accent Studies in the British Isles*. Edited by Paul Foulkes and Gerard Docherty. London: Arnold, pp. 230–45.

Scottish Corpus of Texts and Speech (n.d.) Scots project. (Online.) www.scottishcorpus.ac.uk. Accessed January 30, 2005.

SLD (2002) Scottish Language Dictionaries. (Online.) http://www.snda.org.uk. Accessed August 1, 2005.

Stuart-Smith, Jane (2003) The phonology of modern urban Scots. In *The Edinburgh Companion to Scots*. Edited by John Corbett, J. Derrick McClure, and Jane Stuart-Smith. Edinburgh: Edinburgh University Press, pp. 110–37.

Stuart-Smith, Jane (2004) The phonology of Scottish English. In *Varieties of English, vol.: Phonology*. Edited by Clive Upton. Berlin: Mouton de Gruyter, pp. 47–67.

FURTHER READING

Corbett, John (1997) *Language and Scottish Literature*. Edinburgh: Edinburgh University Press.

Corbett, John, McClure, J. Derrick, and Stuart-Smith, Jane (2003) A brief history of Scots. In *The Edinburgh Companion to Scots*. Edited by John Corbett, J. Derrick McClure, and Jane Stuart-Smith. Edinburgh: Edinburgh University Press, pp. 1–16.

Görlach, Manfred (1985) *Focus on: Scotland (Varieties of English around the World)*. Amsterdam: John Benjamins.

Macafee, Caroline and Dossena, Marina (ongoing) *A Selected Classified Bibliography of the Scots Language*. (Online.) http://wwwesterni.unibg.it/anglistica/slin/scot-bib.htm. Accessed March 18, 2005.

Macaulay, Ronald K. S. (1997) *Standards and Variation in Urban Speech: Examples from Lowland Scots*. Amsterdam: John Benjamins.

McClure, J. Derrick (1997) *Why Scots Matters*. Edinburgh: Saltire Pamphlets.

Romaine, Suzanne (1982) The English language in Scotland. In *English as a World Language*. Edited by Richard Bailey and Manfred Görlach. Ann Arbor: University of Michigan Press, pp. 56–83.

Tulloch, Graham (1997) Lexis. In *The Edinburgh History of the Scots Language*. Edited by Charles Jones. Edinburgh: Edinburgh University Press, pp. 378–432.

4   English in North America

EDGAR W. SCHNEIDER

1   Introduction

American English is an "Inner-Circle" variety (Kachru, 1985) and one of two major "reference accents" of global English; as such, it is not a prominent topic in the field of world Englishes, which is more concerned with Outer-Circle and Expanding-Circle varieties. However, viewing it in this perspective definitely makes sense, given that centuries ago American English began as the first of Britain's colonial (and later postcolonial) offspring, and it went through the same process of linguistic and cultural appropriation that has shaped other postcolonial varieties (Schneider, 2003, 2007) – it is also a product of the colonial expansion of the British Empire in much the same way as the Englishes of, say, Australia, New Zealand, and South Africa. In comparison with these and other world Englishes, a longer time-depth in association with sociopolitical developments is responsible for its character as a more influential and "stable" variety. On the other hand, a history of in-migration has contributed to a blurring of the distinction between L1 and L2 varieties and the importance of effects of language contact not that much different from "Outer-Circle" and other Englishes. More than others Mufwene (1996, 2001) has emphasized the fact that (white) American English has been shaped by language contact and essentially the same processes as African American English and other "disenfranchised Englishes" (cf. 2001: 106).

2   Settlement History and the Dialectal Diffusion of American English

The distinctive nature and the varieties of English in North America are a product of the continent's settlement history, with individual accents and dialects having resulted from unique mixtures of settlers from different regions of the British Isles and elsewhere and their ways of speaking.[1]

As is well known, the first English-speaking permanent settlers founded the South Atlantic colonies (beginning with Jamestown, Virginia, in 1607) and New England (where the Mayflower landed the Pilgrim Fathers in 1620). Many of them were Puritans and came as religious dissenters, not because of poverty; their region of origin was primarily southern England. For generations these colonies maintained relatively strong political and cultural ties with their mother country, which is why the accents of New England and the South share relatively prominent linguistic features with southern British English, and to some extent with one another. Examples include the non-realization of a postvocalic /r/, which in conservative New England and Southern accents is not pronounced in words like *car*, *card*, *four*, and *fourth*; the retention of /j/ in *tune* or *new*, or the "Boston a."[2] From the original bridgeheads via urban hearths like Boston, Massachusetts, Richmond, Virginia, and then Charleston, South Carolina, such accents got rooted in these regions, in accordance with Mufwene's "Founder Principle" (Mufwene, 2001). Eastern New England has continued this tradition largely to the present day: with important cultural centers and economic prosperity through trade, whaling, and later early industrialization those who had established themselves there saw little reason to leave, so linguistically and culturally the region is somewhat different from the rest of the US. Similarly, a conservative and aristocratic plantation culture with a distinctive accent and culture established itself in the coastal South and expanded along the South Atlantic plains into Georgia. The down side of this culture was the infamous institution of slavery, with Africans having been forced to the region as early as in the late seventeenth century and, in large numbers, throughout the eighteenth and early nineteenth centuries.

Later waves of immigrants in the seventeenth century came through mid-Atlantic ports, where the Quakers had established themselves in Pennsylvania, and their religious tolerance made the location attractive for many newcomers. Unlike the early wave, a majority of them came from northern and western England, Scotland, and also Ireland, and they tended to be of less affluent origins. Hence, very broadly, it can be stated that a mixture of the working-class speech from these regions constituted the basis of colonial mid-Atlantic American speech, which later, after the colonial period, became the basis for the mainstream, inland-northern and western type of American English.

When eighteenth-century immigrants found the best lands along the coast taken and hostile Indians and the earlier presence of the French prevented straight westward movement, settlements spread with a strong south-western bend into the Great Valley of the Appalachian mountains. Many of these settlers were so-called Ulster Scots, labeled Scotch-Irish in the US, who found the landscape, climate and economic possibilities in the mountains familiar and favorable and thus rooted their culture and language features there (with linguistic traces like "positive *anymore*" to be still observed in the region today).

The 1803 Louisiana purchase, followed by the Lewis and Clark expedition, ultimately opened the inland and western parts of the continent for westward expansion and the continuous spread of the region settled by British and European immigrants. A deplorable consequence of this process was the cruel fate of the Native American population, who were continuously driven out of their home lands, decimated, and forcefully relocated. The Great Lakes Area and the Upper Mississippi region were settled predominantly by people from the inland northern parts of the original colonies, from western New England and upstate New York. Throughout much of the nineteenth century new lands further west were being taken, a process advanced by historical events like the building of the transcontinental railroad, the California gold rush of 1848/49, or the admission of Texas to the Union in 1845.

Linguistically, the opening up of the Midwest and West can be character-ized as a continuous and increasing process of mixing and blending of people with different regional origins and of the accents which they brought with them. Dialect contact resulted in koinéization, the emergence of a middle-of-the-road variety in which extreme dialectal forms (which, being used by only a minority, were communicatively inefficient) tended to be rubbed off, so American English has frequently been perceived to be fairly homogeneous – a view which, however, may also be challenged. It is true that along the east coast dialect differences between the various regions are strongest, and the further west we move the less conspicuous speech differences become. On the other hand, scholarship has shown and speakers know that even in the West there are significantly different regional and local speechways.

3   Research History

Research in lexicography, dialect geography, and sociolinguistics in the con-text of English in America has made significant contributions to linguistics in general and is worth recapitulating briefly.

3.1   *Lexicography*

The early American settlers were faced with radically new experiences and objects, and to meet their needs to designate these, they either borrowed or coined new words. By the eighteenth century such "Americanisms" abounded, and lexicographers, most notably the patriotic Noah Webster, began to record and emphasize the lexical distinctiveness of American English – it is interest-ing to see that this "linguistic declaration of independence" followed the political separation of the United States from her British mother country. Webster's influence, in his famous "blue-backed speller" (*The American Spell-ing Book*, first published in 1783), of which 100 million copies were sold during the nineteenth century, and then in his monumental 1828 *American Dictionary of the English Language*, contributed substantially to an awareness and the solidification of such lexical differences, and so for a long time the search for and documentation of Americanisms remained an essential component of the scholarly study of American English. Two mid-twentieth-century scholarly dictionaries epitomize these activities: Craigie and Hulbert (1938–44) document the American vocabulary, understood broadly as things American including British survivals associated with American culture, in the philological fashion of the *OED*, while Mathews (1951) narrowed his definition of Americanisms down to words of American origin only.

Dialect words have been the second major object of American lexicography. The American Dialect Society, founded in 1899, pursued the explicit goal of supporting the compilation of an American Dialect Dictionary equivalent to Joseph Wright's English work, and the realization of that goal was seen in the second half of the last century. Directed by the late Frederic G. Cassidy, the monumental *Dictionary of American Regional English* (*DARE*) project, based upon both a reading program along OED lines and a 50-state lexical dialect survey, now provides systematic coverage of words and expressions which are not in general use in the US, i.e., restricted to certain regions or ethnic groups (Cassidy and Hall, 1985–2002).

3.2   *Dialect geography*

Building upon earlier European dialect atlas models, in the late 1920s an initiative was launched to systematically collect data for a projected "Linguistic Atlas of the United States and Canada," to be directed by Hans Kurath. Because of the vastness of the region and the limitation of resources this project has never materialized as such but was broken down into a series of smaller, regional Linguistic Atlas projects. Methodologically, trained interviewers selected representative informants from regionally scattered localities and recorded their responses to a predetermined questionnaire of some one hundred phonological, lexical, and morphological questions in fine phonetic notation, so that in the end millions of individual responses were put together as maps or lists (cf. Atwood, 1963). By the end of the 1930s, Kurath finished and published the *Linguistic Atlas of New England* (*LANE*), the model project for many to follow, and organized field work along the entire east coast for the *Linguistic Atlas of the Middle and South Atlantic States* (*LAMSAS*), a project whose data have been computerized and are still being analyzed by means of sophisticated statistical methods (cf. Kretzschmar and Schneider, 1996 and recent work by Kretzschmar and others). A series of similar projects followed, to cover almost the entire continent (see Davis, 1983 and the Linguistic Atlas Projects web site us.english.uga.edu). The most recent, and in many ways most modern (using audio recording and computerization technology from the outset) addition is the *Linguistic Atlas of the Gulf States* (*LAGS*; Pederson, 1986–91), which details the South, the most distinctive dialect region of the US.

Based upon lexical data from *LANE* and *LAMSAS*, Kurath (1949) postulated the now classic regional division of American dialects into three main dialect regions (North, Midland, South), with several sub-regions and the general proviso that the distinction is likely to get weaker or disappear the further west one moves. Atwood (1953) and Kurath and McDavid (1961) found this division confirmed on the basis of morphological and phonological data, respectively. Using lexical data from *DARE*, Carver (1987) was the first and only author so far to challenge this three-fold division, arguing instead for a binary distinction into North and South only. However, on closer investigation the differences between both areal classifications are minor, essentially a matter of categorization and conceptualization: Kurath had observed "North Midland" and "South Midland" subdivisions, which in Carver's book resurface as "Lower North" and "Upper South," respectively. Essentially, it seems clear that in terms of regional dialects American English shows two core areas, the North and the South, and a broad transition band in between.

3.3   Sociolinguistics

William Labov's classic study of New York City pronunciation (1966) and other work from that period (cf. Labov, 1972) founded a new sub-discipline of linguistics, the systematic study of sociolinguistic variation and change. Like dialectologists before him (who had already sampled speakers from different social strata), Labov was interested in studying the down-to-earth intricacies of real-life speech, but he was more interested in the social dimension of speech variability and in the theoretical modeling of why languages vary and how this affects language change. He developed new methods and concepts to reach these goals: the tape-recorded "sociolinguistic interview," with free conversation meant to stimulate informants to converse freely and without much effect of the "observer's paradox," in which then the realizations ("variants") of predetermined variables are looked for and interpreted, using quantifying methodology. Typically, the frequency of certain variants is correlated with dimensions like social class, gender, age, and also style. Adopting and developing this methodology, sociolinguists like Labov, Wolfram, Bailey, and many others have since investigated numerous communities across the US, usually interpreting a limited number of variables in the light of specific hypotheses of language variation and change.[3]

Labov and his followers detected and investigated a vigorously ongoing sound change, the "Northern Cities Shift," broadly to be characterized as a clockwise rotation of the short (checked) vowels which is far advanced among young speakers in many inland-northern urban areas (Labov, 1994: 177–201). They carried out a new and large-scale dialect survey project of the entire US known as the "Telsur" ("telephone survey") project with the aim of documenting regional sound systems and sound changes on a broad, national basis. The result of this is a new phonological *Atlas of North American English* (Labov, Ash, and Boberg, 2005), a multimedia product which thoroughly analyzes and exemplifies an immense number of audio data from across the USA. Condensing this wealth of information into a new regional division of American English, Labov basically confirms Kurath's three main areas (with the South expanding more widely into the Midlands than previously assumed) and adds a fourth one, the West. He finds that while the North, the South and the West have fairly homogeneous vowel systems and patterns of change, the Midland is characterized by extreme diversity, a residual region where individual cities have developed dialect patterns of their own.

4   American English and Its Varieties

Typically American English is seen as against British English, and distinguishing features on the levels of phonology, lexis, orthography, and grammar tend to be juxtaposed in list form in many textbooks and other sources (e.g., Strevens, 1972). For example, American versus British choices are reported to include the lexical items *gas* (vs. *petrol*), *fall* (vs. *autumn*), *railroad* (vs. *railway*), etc.; the pronunciations /æ/ (vs. /aː/) in *dance*, *grass*, or *can't*, unrounded /ɑ/ (vs. /ɒ/) in *lot* or *dollar*, and postvocalic /-r/ in *car*, *card*, and so on; on the grammatical level, *have* (vs. *have got*) for possession, *will* (vs. *shall*) for first-person future reference, and a more liberal use of the past (for the present perfect) tense; and spellings like *theater*, *honor*, *recognize*, and *plow* (vs. *theatre*, *honour*, *recognise*, *plough*). Much of this requires qualification and a more careful phrasing, however: not infrequently "American" words or pronunciations exist in Britain as well but are constrained to the status of regional dialect forms, stylistically marked choices, or slightly different usage conditions.[4] Conversely, American innovations are being adopted in British speech as well.

Thus, it is necessary to look into dialects: American English is anything but homogeneous – the notion encompasses not only a rich array of regional forms and some social variation but also, and increasingly so, ethnic varieties shaped by effects of language contact and differential degrees of integration of generations of immigrants into the American mainstream culture.[5]

4.1   *Regional dialects*

Regional dialect differences primarily depend upon different pronunciation patterns and lexical choices. Obviously, the spread of individual forms varies from the strictly local to elements which set off larger dialect regions from adjacent ones. Linguistic Atlas data and publications and many other sources provide ample illustration of such variants; for reasons of space I restrict myself to pointing out some of the best-known characteristics of three large regions. The inland northern region, extending westward from western New England into the Great Lakes area, comes closest to an "unmarked" accent globally perceived as "typically American." The Midlands are essentially a transition region with a small number of features of their own and an increasing number of northern or southern features the further one progresses in the respective direction.

New England pronunciation is most strongly characterized by the lack of a postvocalic /r/ and by a low [a] in words like *bath*, *glass*, or *aunt* (known popularly as the "Boston a"). Conservative dialects from the eastern part of the region maintain a distinction between the vowels in *Mary* ([eː]), *merry* ([ɛ]) and *marry* ([æ]). Lexical items characteristic of the region include *pail* 'bucket', *darning needle* 'dragon fly', *angleworm* 'earthworm', *grinder* 'submarine sandwich', and *rotary* 'traffic circle'.

Southern English, the topic of much recent research (e.g., Nagle and Sanders, 2003), is clearly the most distinctive of all American dialects, also a product of a strong regional identity. Well-known features include the so-called "Southern drawl" (a lengthening and breaking tendency of vowels, as in [ɪə] in *bit*),[6] lack of rhoticity (now recessive), the monophthongization of /aɪ/ (e.g. time [taːm]; generally before voiced consonants and in free position, with regional and social restrictions before voiceless consonants), homophony of mid and high front vowels before nasals (known as *pin/ pen*-merger), the second-person plural pronoun *y'all*, double modals like *might could*, an inceptive future *fixin' to*, and words such as *light bread, pulley bone* 'wishbone', *mosquito hawk* 'dragonfly', *granny woman* 'midwife', or *jackleg* 'unprofessional, dishonest'. It is interesting to see that some traditional features of Southern English are now being given up while new regional shibboleths are emerging. Bailey (1997) claimed that Southern English originated as late as during the post-Reconstruction period after the loss of the Civil War, as a deliberate means of strengthening Southerners' regional identity against outside political dominance.

English as spoken in the West lacks salient characteristics but is regarded as prestigious nationwide. The low back vowels of *lot* and *thought* are merged, and high back vowels as in *goose* or *food* are frequently fronted. Younger California speakers tend to lower their lax front vowels (so *six* sounds like *sex, sex* like *sax*, and *sax* like *socks*; cf. Gordon, 2004). Regional words include borrowings like *canyon* or *corral* and coinages like *parking strip* or *chippie* 'woman considered to have loose morals' (Carver, 1987).

4.2   Social dialects

Numerous sociolinguistic studies from many locations, urban and rural, have yielded insights into some principles governing speech variability and have identified a few robust distributional tendencies. Obviously, the familiar pyramid shape of dialectal variation applies: the higher a speaker's social status, and the more formal a speech situation, the less likely dialectal forms are, and vice versa. Women have widely been found to be leading in linguistic changes, i.e., to adopt and spread linguistic innovations more rapidly than males. While the use of regional words carries no stigma and certain traces of regional accents are acceptable also among upper-class speakers (consider recent US Presidents from the South), nonstandard grammatical phenomena (like multiple negation, the use of *ain't* or preverbal *done*, non-concord copula forms, or nonstandard relativization) are socially stigmatized but hardly regionally diagnostic.

4.3   Ethnic varieties

Immigration has continued to shape the linguistic landscape of the US, and many ethnic varieties are products of language contact, frequently involving language shift on the side of a minority group from an erstwhile ethnic language to the dominant one, English – modifying the latter in this process. The best-known case in point, African American English (AAE), is discussed elsewhere in this volume (Chapter 19).

Relatively little attention has been devoted to the English of Native Americans, which varies from speech with no discernible "accent" to contact varieties (cf. Leap, 1993). Distinctive features seem to lie less in transfer of phonology or grammar (possibly with the exception of some special patterns of tense use) than on the pragmatic level (expressions of respect and politeness, discourse organization, etc.). Lumbee English in North Carolina has been shown to feature distinctive vocabulary (e.g., *ellick* 'coffee', *sorry in the world* 'badly') and grammar (finite *be*, as in *She bes there*, and *I'm* for *I've*, as in *I'm been there*; Wolfram et al., 2002).

Demographic changes and migration effects give special prominence to Hispanic varieties of English. Some work has been done on Puerto Ricans in New York City and very little on Cuban immigrants in Miami, while the "Chicano English" of descendants of Mexican immigrants is fairly well researched (e.g., Fought, 2003; Santa Ana and Bayley, 2004). Characteristic features include some aspects of pronunciation (e.g., strongly monophthongal vowels) and several prosodic phenomena (e.g., a different system of vowel reduction and distinctive intonation contours).

Cajun English is spoken in Louisiana, predominantly by younger speakers who two generations after the language shift from French to English sense a loss of their cultural heritage and have fueled a "Cajun Renaissance." Features include high rates of final consonant deletion (not only in clusters), the monophthongization of diphthongs, lack of aspiration in word-initial stops, and "heavy nasalization," also of consonants (Dubois and Horvath, 2004).

Further linguistic research would also be required concerning the linguistic integration of Asian immigrant groups. Except for some work on Vietnamese English hardly anything has been done in that area.

4.4   Homogeneity and variability, identity and change

Due to the relatively strong degree of mixing, mutual accommodation, and koinéization that occurred during the colonial period and even more strongly in the phase of westward expansion, American English has traditionally been perceived as relatively homogeneous, at least in comparison with British dialects. Based on limited factual evidence, Krapp (1925) coined and the phonetician Kenyon disseminated the notion of "General American," which became popular during the 1930s and can still be found cited in some sources today, to refer to a putatively homogeneous normative type of American English (in practice, it probably meant accents not distinctively New England or Southern). However, dialect geographers like Kurath, Atwood, and others strongly opposed this notion, arguing that there is no nationally uniform standard accent of American English and that on closer investigation American dialects show a great deal of phonetic, lexical, and grammatical variability. This assessment is based on the voluminous Atlas evidence and has been confirmed by works like Frazer (1993), which shows how much variability exists even in the "Heartland," a region where speakers believe that they "have no accent."

Thus, in line with phase 5 as postulated by Schneider (2003, 2007) in the emergence of postcolonial Englishes, American English appears to have transcended the stage of emphasizing homogeneity and proceeded to increasing diversification, both regional and social. In other words, not only culturally but also linguistically the traditional "melting pot" metaphor, assuming that immigrants have been assimilated to join a mainstream culture, is now giving way, if only gradually, to a "salad bowl" conceptualization, in which individual groups remain recognizable through the retention of ethnolinguistic characteristics. This becomes all the more apparent considering the "divergence hypothesis" of AAE (e.g., Bailey and Maynor, 1989) and comparable dissociating trends affecting other ethnic, regional, and social varieties. It is noteworthy that varieties as diverse as AAE, Chicano English, Cajun English, Southern English, and the "brogue" of Ocracoke, North Carolina (Wolfram and Schilling-Estes, 1997) have all been stated to be products of recent strengthening processes of locally or ethnically based group identities.

5   Canadian English

Large-scale English colonization of Canada started as late as the second half of the eighteenth century, when English gained control over the former French colony (a situation which accounts for the country's present-day bilingual status).[7] The British orientation of Canada's early population was strengthened by the influx of loyalists to the Crown during and after the American revolution, and the country has retained strong cultural and political ties with Britain. On the other hand, a strong proportion of Canada's settlers, even more so in the western provinces, has come from the US, and there has never been a way to evade the continuous presence and impact of her large, in some respects dominant, southern neighbor. As a consequence, Canadian English is traditionally described as a mix of British and American features, with the balance between the two varying by region, by generation (an ongoing Americanization has been observed among the young), and by language level (while the pronunciation base is strongly American, the British component is more clearly visible in some vocabulary items and some spelling practices).

However, the post-WWII period has seen the growth of a distinct Canadian identity, mirrored by a small set of uniquely Canadian features (Boberg, 2004). These include the (strongly recessive) word *chesterfield* 'couch', the particle *eh* (inviting approval), and, the most diagnostic of all, the phonetic process of "Canadian Raising," i.e., the pronunciation of /aɪ/ and /aʊ/ with a raised, central onset before voiceless consonants, so that *out* and *bite* sound like [əʊt] and (less generally) [bəɪt].

6   The Growing Impact of American English on Other World Englishes

The vast majority of Outer-Circle world Englishes are products of British colonialism, and traditionally in these countries British English and RP used to be regarded as the linguistic norm and target of education. Only two such varieties are American-derived, namely those of the Philippines and of Liberia. Today, however, an increasing impact of American English on practically all varieties of English around the globe can be observed, manifested in American-influenced lexical choices and also in certain pronunciations.[8] So far the evidence on this phenomenon is largely anecdotal (cf. Crystal, 1997: 138; Jenkins, 2003: 91f.); no systematic and comprehensive studies have been carried out as yet. Thus, we have no firm basis for knowing whether the process is equally strong in different countries or regions. However, it is repeatedly mentioned in passing in scholarly publications, and everybody involved with language use seems to be aware of it. The reasons for this growing impact of American English are also unresearched, though it is possible to make plausible guesses. It may safely be assumed that this increase results from the growing exposure to and the great prestige of American English. Prestige is of course associated with people, so this is a consequence of the dominant role which the United States plays politically and economically in the global context; a certain ambivalence can be sensed here in many contexts (like the spread of American popular culture, the practice of adopting American ways of speaking is taken up by some who, presumably subconsciously, regard this as fashionable and symbolizing high status and an international orientation but it is resisted by others who fear a loss of local identities and traditions).[9] Exposure reflects the global dominance of the American media and music industries, with Hollywood movies being shown and American TV serials being aired (frequently undubbed) on all continents, and it results from the modern facilities for travel and personal contact (tourism, business travel, also student exchange,[10] and, increasingly, the internet).

Of course, the impact of American English on other world Englishes varies from one region to another and is difficult to generalize, but some broader statements can be made. Words travel easily, so the majority of new

Americanisms used elsewhere are from the lexical level. Words which seem to be spreading widely and rapidly include *gas, guy(s), Hi, movie, truck, Santa (Claus),* and *station wagon,* and adolescent slang and fashion terms like *man* as a form of address or *cool* meaning 'very good'. To this may be added older words which have been internationalized so strongly that their American origin may no longer be recognized in many communities, like *radio* (for older British *wireless*), *commute, fan, star, know-how, break even,* or *let's face it* (Gordon and Deverson, 1998: 112). As to pronunciation, rhoticity and "jod-deletion" in words like *new, tune* are widely perceived as "American" and may be adopted for this effect; and for certain words putatively American pronunciations are getting more widespread, e.g., *research* stressed on the first and *primarily* on the second syllable, *schedule* with /sk-/, *lieutenant* with /luː-/, etc. The spelling *center* is clearly preferred over *centre* outside specifically British spheres of influence, and *program* rather than *programme* is also used widely, not only in computing contexts. On the level of syntax, *hopefully* used as a sentence adverbial and patterns like *do you have* seem to be diffusing from the US. American influence can even modify the meaning of words, as in the case of *billion,* which now means 'a thousand million' rather than 'a million million' even in Britain (Peters, 2004: 72).

For Australian English, Taylor (1989; 2001: 324–7) reports some examples and quotes reactions, including fairly emotional and hostile ones, to the perceived "American invasion" of Australian English. Similarly, for New Zealand English, Gordon and Deverson (1998) document and discuss a wide array of Americanisms on different language levels, and divided reactions to them. In the speech of hosts of Singaporean popular radio shows Schneider (1999) observes "a predominantly British pronunciation basis with American features interspersed" (p. 197). The latter include some rhoticity, an unrounded /ɑ/ and a sonorized /t/ in *hottest,* and lexical choices like *figure them out, he's like* 'he says', and *man* as an informal mode of address (*Which movie made you cry, man?* to a female caller). For Nigeria, Soneye (2004), based on the reading and writing of students, finds that despite Nigeria's official British orientation American pronunciation variants are going strong: /skedjuːl/ rather than /ʃedjuːl/ was reported by 45% of all subjects, *tom*[eɪ]*to* rather than *tom*[ɑː]*to* by 70%, *l*[ɪ]*sure* rather than *l*[ɛ]*sure* by 40%, and rhoticity in *car* by 11%. Lower but also notable percentages for American forms are found for spellings (*story/storey* 18%; *draft/draught* 24%; *center/centre* 52%), and the author attests that other American English spellings like *color, honor, theater, inquiry, program, fulfill,* and *jewelry* can also be found in Nigeria.

Hence, it appears that American English is enjoying covert prestige in many countries and communities where British English is promoted as the "official" target norm, also in education. Certainly this has to be taken with a grain of salt and is likely to be sociolinguistically conditioned (preferred among the young, in informal contexts, and in association with certain topics and domains), but the process seems widespread and robust. It deserves more intensive investigation and systematic documentation.

7   Conclusion

As the discussions above have shown, American English is anything but homogeneous; rather, the linguistic landscape of North America displays the kaleidoscope of accents, dialects, and linguistic features associated with both national unity and distinct group identities that characterizes many modern societies. Thus, in a global perspective, it should not be viewed monolithically, as one of two reference varieties as opposed to British English, but rather as a vibrant set of varieties itself, language forms which internally are associated with distinct sociocultural identities and which globally interact with other world Englishes.

See also Chapters 2, FIRST STEPS: WALES AND IRELAND; 3, ENGLISH IN SCOTLAND; 18, PIDGINS AND CREOLES; 19, AFRICAN AMERICAN ENGLISH; 38, WORLD ENGLISHES AND LEXICOGRAPHY; 41, WORLD ENGLISHES AND CORPORA STUDIES.

NOTES

1   For classic and general sources on American English, see Krapp (1925), Marckwardt (1958), Mencken (1963) and titles listed in the Further Readings section. For comprehensive bibliographies of publications on American English up to the early 1990s see Schneider (1984, 1993). For a survey of the history of American English in a world Englishes perspective see ch. 6 in Schneider (2007).

2   Some of these features are now conservative and being given up by the younger generation in these regions, especially in the South, who align themselves linguistically with newly prestigious western accents.

3   For a theoretical introduction, see Chambers (2003); for a methodological discussion, see Milroy and Gordon (2003); for case studies, see contributions to the journal *Language Variation and Change* or the annual NWAVE ("New Ways of Analyzing Variation in English") conference series,

available through the internet and in conference volumes. Substantial theoretical and descriptive harvest is brought home by Labov (1994/2001).

4   Algeo (1989) provides an illuminative and enjoyable case study of the subtlety of the usage distinctions between both varieties.

5   The most comprehensive and systematic survey of the distinctive features of the major varieties of American English available to date is the set of contributions to Schneider et al. (2004) for phonology and Kortmann et al. (2004) for morphosyntax, now united in Schneider (2008).

6   Cf. the local spelling *dawgs* for the University of Georgia football team.

7   Of course, Newfoundland was settled considerably earlier, by Irish and south-western English people, and developed a distinctive English dialect, but within Canada it has very much remained a linguistic enclave.

8   Modiano (1996) argued that in continental Europe this process – a

shift toward American forms starting out from an erstwhile British target orientation – has produced a "Mid-Atlantic English." Simo Bobda (1998) discusses educational consequences of the growing tension between British and American as possible norms, mostly in Outer-Circle countries.

9   Cf. Gordon and Deverson (1998: 108): "However unwelcome the fact is to some, the entire English-speaking world . . . is currently under constant American cultural and linguistic bombardment." Trudgill (1998: 29) cites worries about what he calls the "Americanisation catastrophe."

10   For example, a relatively large and apparently increasing proportion of Singaporean scholars hold PhDs from American rather than British universities.

REFERENCES

Algeo, John (1989) Queueing and other idiosyncracies. *World Englishes*, **8**, 157–63.

Atwood, E. Bagby (1953) *A Survey of Verb Forms in the Eastern United States.* Ann Arbor: University of Michigan Press.

Atwood, E. Bagby (1963) The methods of American dialectology. *Zeitschrift für Mundartforschung*, **30**, 1–29.

Bailey, Guy (1997) When did Southern English begin? In *Englishes around the World, vol. 1: General Studies, British Isles, North America*. Edited by Edgar W. Schneider. Amsterdam, Philadelphia: Benjamins, pp. 255–75.

Bailey, Guy and Maynor, Natalie (1989) The divergence controversy. *American Speech*, **64**, 12–39.

Boberg, Charles (2004) English in Canada: Phonology. In *A Handbook of Varieties of English: A Multimedia Reference Tool, vol. 1: Phonology*. Edited by Edgar W. Schneider, Kate Burridge, Bernd Kortmann, Rajend Mesthrie, and Clive Upton. Berlin/New York: Mouton de Gruyter, pp. 351–65.

Carver, Craig M. (1987) *American Regional Dialects. A Word Geography.* Ann Arbor: University of Michigan Press.

Cassidy, Frederic G. and Hall, Joan (eds.) (1985–2002) *Dictionary of American Regional English, vol. I (A–C); vol. II (D–H); vol. III (I–O; vol. IV (P–Sk)).* Cambridge, MA: Belknap Press for Harvard University Press.

Chambers, Jack K. (2003) *Sociolinguistic Theory.* 2nd edition. Oxford/Malden, MA: Blackwell.

Craigie, William A. and Hulbert, James R. (eds.) (1938–44) *A Dictionary of American English on Historical Principles.* 4 vols. Chicago: University of Chicago Press.

Crystal, David (1997) *English as a Global Language.* Cambridge: Cambridge University Press.

Davis, Lawrence M. (1983) *English Dialectology: An Introduction.* University, AL: University of Alabama Press.

Dubois, Sylvie and Horvath, Barbara (2004) Cajun English: Phonology. In *A Handbook of Varieties of English: A Multimedia Reference Tool, vol. 1: Phonology*. Edited by Edgar W. Schneider, Kate Burridge, Bernd Kortmann, Rajend Mesthrie, and Clive Upton. Berlin/New York: Mouton de Gruyter, pp. 407–16.

Fought, Carmen (2003) *Chicano English in Context*. Houndmills, NY: Palgrave Macmillan.

Frazer, Timothy C. (ed.) (1993) *"Heartland" English: Variation and Transition in the American Midwest*. Tuscaloosa, AL: University of Alabama Press.

Gordon, Elizabeth and Deverson, Tony (1998) *New Zealand English and English in New Zealand*. Auckland: New House.

Gordon, Matthew (2004) The West and Midwest: Phonology. In *A Handbook of Varieties of English: A Multimedia Reference Tool, vol. 1: Phonology*. Edited by Edgar W. Schneider, Kate Burridge, Bernd Kortmann, Rajend Mesthrie, and Clive Upton. Berlin/New York: Mouton de Gruyter, pp. 338–50.

Jenkins, Jennifer (2003) *World Englishes: A Resource Book for Students*. London/New York: Routledge.

Kachru, Braj B. (1985) Standards, codification and sociolinguistic realism: The English language in the outer circle. In *English in the World: Teaching and Learning the Language and Literatures*. Edited by Randolph Quirk and Henry G. Widdowson. Cambridge: Cambridge University Press and The British Council, pp. 11–30.

Kortmann, Bernd, Burridge, Kate, Mesthrie, Rajend, Schneider, Edgar W., and Upton, Clive (eds.) (2004) *A Handbook of Varieties of English: A Multimedia Reference Tool, vol. 2: Morphology and Syntax*. Berlin/New York: Mouton de Gruyter.

Krapp, George P. (1925) *The English Language in America*. 2 vols. New York.

Kretzschmar, William A. and Schneider, Edgar W. (1996) *Introduction to Quantitative Analysis of Linguistic Survey Data: An Atlas by the Numbers*. Thousand Oaks, CA: Sage.

Kurath, Hans (1949) *A Word Geography of the Eastern United States*. Ann Arbor: University of Michigan Press.

Kurath, Hans and McDavid, Raven I. (1961) *The Pronunciation of English in the Atlantic States*. Ann Arbor: University of Michigan Press.

Labov, William (1966) *The Social Stratification of English in New York City*. Washington, DC: Center for Applied Linguistics.

Labov, William (1972) *Sociolinguistic Patterns*. Philadelphia: University of Pennsylvania Press.

Labov, William (1994/2001) *Principles of Linguistic Change, vol. 1: Internal Factors, vol. 2: Social Factors*. Oxford/Malden, MA: Blackwell.

Labov, William, Ash, Sharon, and Boberg, Charles (2005) *Atlas of North American English: Phonetics, Phonology and Sound Change*. Berlin/New York: Mouton de Gruyter.

Leap, William L. (1993) *American Indian English*. Salt Lake City: University of Utah Press.

Marckwardt, Albert H. (1958) *American English*. New York: Oxford University Press.

Mathews, Mitford M. (ed.) (1951) *Dictionary of Americanisms on Historical Principles*. Chicago: University of Chicago Press.

Mencken, H. L. (1963) *The American Language*. One-vol. abridged edition by Raven I. McDavid. New York: Knopf.

Milroy, Lesley and Gordon, Matthew (2003) *Sociolinguistics: Method and Interpretation*. Oxford/Malden, MA: Blackwell.

Modiano, Marko (1996) The Americanization of Euro-English. *World Englishes*, **15**(2), 207–15.

Mufwene, Salikoko S. (1996) The development of American Englishes: Some questions from a creole genesis perspective. In *Focus on the USA*. Edited by Edgar W. Schneider.

Amsterdam/Philadelphia: Benjamins, pp. 231–64.

Mufwene, Salikoko S. (2001) *The Ecology of Language Evolution*. Cambridge: Cambridge University Press.

Nagle, Stephen J. and Sanders, Sara L. (eds.) (2003) *English in the Southern United States*. Cambridge: Cambridge University Press.

Pederson, Lee (1986–91) *Linguistic Atlas of the Gulf States*. 7 vols. Athens, GA: University of Georgia Press.

Peters, Pam (2004) *The Cambridge Guide to English Usage*. Cambridge: Cambridge University Press.

Santa Ana, Otto and Bayley, Robert (2004) Chicano English: Phonology. In *A Handbook of Varieties of English: A Multimedia Reference Tool, vol. 1: Phonology*. Edited by Edgar W. Schneider, Kate Burridge, Bernd Kortmann, Rajend Mesthrie, and Clive Upton. Berlin/New York: Mouton de Gruyter, pp. 417–34.

Schneider, Edgar W. (1984) A bibliography of writings on American and Canadian English (1965–83). In *A Bibliography of Writings on Varieties of English, 1965–1983*. Edited by Wolfgang Viereck, Edgar W. Schneider, and Manfred Görlach. Amsterdam/Philadelphia: Benjamins, pp. 89–223.

Schneider, Edgar W. (1993) Writings on varieties of American and Canadian English. In *A New Bibliography of Writings on Varieties of English 1984–1992/93*. Edited by Beat Glauser, Edgar W. Schneider, and Manfred Görlach. Amsterdam/Philadelphia: Benjamins, pp. 63–124.

Schneider, Edgar W. (1999) Notes on Singaporean English. In *Form, Function and Variation in English: Studies in Honour of Klaus Hansen*. Edited by Uwe Carls and Peter Lucko. Frankfurt: Peter Lang, pp. 193–205.

Schneider, Edgar W. (2003) The dynamics of New Englishes: From identity construction to dialect birth. *Language, 79*, 233–81.

Schneider, Edgar W., Burridge, Kate, Kortmann, Bernd, Mesthrie, Rajend, and Upton, Clive (eds.) (2004) *A Handbook of Varieties of English: A Multimedia Reference Tool, vol. 1: Phonology*. Berlin, New York: Mouton de Gruyter.

Simo Bobda, Augustin (1998) British or American English: Does it matter? *English Today 56*, **14**(4), 13–8.

Soneye, Taiwo (2004) Oral varieties and the vanishing voices: Trends in Nigerians' use of English in the era of globalisation. Manuscript, Obafemi Awolowo University, Ile-Ife.

Strevens, Peter (1972) *British and American English*. London: Collier-Macmillan.

Taylor, Brian (1989) American, British and other foreign influences on Australian English since World War II. In *Australian English: The Language of a New Society*. Edited by Peter Collins and David Blair. St Lucia: University of Queensland Press, pp. 225–54.

Taylor, Brian (2001) Australian English in interaction with other Englishes. In *English in Australia*. Edited by David Blair and Peter Collins. Amsterdam/Philadelphia: Benjamins, pp. 317–40.

Trudgill, Peter (1998) World Englishes: Convergence or divergence? In *The Major Varieties of English: Papers from MAVEN 97*. Edited by Hans Lindquist, Staffan Klintborg, Magnus Levin, and Maria Estling. Växjö: Acta Wexionensia, pp. 29–34.

Wolfram, Walt, Dannenberg, Clare, Knick, Stanley, and Oxendine, Linda (2002) *Fine in the World: Lumbee Language in Time and Place*. Raleigh,

NC: North Carolina State University.

Wolfram, Walt and Schilling-Estes, Natalie (1997) *Hoi Toide on the Outer Banks: The Story of the Ocracoke Brogue*. Chapel Hill, NC: University of North Carolina Press.

FURTHER READING

Algeo, John (ed.) (2001) *The Cambridge History of the English Language, vol. 6: English in North America*. Cambridge: Cambridge University Press.

Francis, W. Nelson (1958) *The Structure of American English*. With a chapter on American English dialects by Raven I. McDavid. New York: Ronald Press.

Preston, Dennis R. (1993) *American Dialect Research*. Amsterdam/ Philadelphia: Benjamins.

Schneider, Edgar W. (ed.) (1996) *Focus on the USA* (Varieties of English Around the World, vol. 16). Amsterdam/Philadelphia: Benjamins.

Schneider, Edgar W. (ed.) (2007) *Postcolonial English*. Cambridge: Cambridge University Press. (Ch. 5: "The emergence of American English").

Schneider, Edgar W. (ed.) (2008) *Varieties of English 1: The Americas and the Caribbean*. Berlin/New York: Mouton de Gruyter.

Tottie, Gunnel (2002) *An Introduction to American English*. Oxford/Malden, MA: Blackwell.

Wolfram, Walt and Schilling-Estes, Natalie (1998) *American English*. Oxford/Malden, MA: Blackwell.

5 English in Australia and New Zealand

SCOTT F. KIESLING

1 Introduction

Besides their obvious geographical proximity, why are New Zealand English (NZE) and Australian English (AusE) the subject of a single entry in this handbook? Speakers and scholars of each variety may feel justifiably slighted that it does not have its own chapter; however, there are reasons to discuss them jointly. The relatively short distance from Sydney to Auckland has meant that there has been significant travel and migration between the two since colonization. This intermigration is likely one of the factors that has led them to have similar ways of speaking. There is thus a very strong linguistic motivation to include them together. Finally, they both were colonized by the British fairly late (Australia in 1788 and New Zealand circa 1840), and thus find themselves at similar stages of development. These colonization dates have also been claimed to be one of the causes of linguistic similarity (Trudgill, 2004; Gordon et al., 2004). This colonization period is shared by South Africa and some other smaller colonies, but these are geographically distant and most arose in very different social and language-contact situations. Certainly each of these two Englishes could fill a chapter of its own in the handbook, but there is a logical basis in grouping them together when viewed from historical, geographical, and linguistic viewpoints.

I will provide brief descriptions of NZE and AusE, including current changes taking place in the linguistic systems of the two varieties. This overview will necessarily be too general for the keenly interested reader; however, it will give someone who has not encountered these Englishes before a basic understanding of the important linguistic and social issues surrounding them. Interested readers are encouraged to explore some of the research cited here for a more in-depth description of both Englishes. In particular, I recommend Gerhard Leitner's (2004a, 2004b) two volumes on AusE. These are broad in scope but detailed and meticulously researched. Moreover, they include important syntheses of previous literature and new ways of thinking about AusE.

Leitner's work is impressive because he has a new way of thinking about the situation of English in Australia. That is, he views the entire linguistic landscape of the country – "habitat" is the term used – rather than a single language, variety, or subsystem of a language. This viewpoint allows him to see the interconnectedness of the different languages and varieties (and peoples) that comprise and have comprised the ways language is used in Australia. He produces a work that is much more faithful to the history and experience of language users and learners in Australia. I cannot do it justice here, so I recommend it to all readers of this handbook as a model for describing the linguistic situation of any English in any country. There is no comparable work for NZE; for the definitive discussion of the development of NZE, I recommend Gordon et al. (2004), which is a fascinating analysis of recordings of very early settlers of New Zealand.

2   Development

No aspect of NZE and AusE studies has yielded more research, and more opinions, than the subject of their origins. That both are colonial varieties, and that the current Englishes are related to the Englishes of settlers from England and other parts of the UK are not in dispute. But the makeup of the original settlers, and the extent of their influence on the subsequent English, is a matter of debate. In addition, because Australia was colonized a little more than a half century before New Zealand, there is a possibility that NZE is derived from, or at least influenced by, the English that formed earlier in New South Wales. I will here give an outline of the important periods in the development of these Englishes, making an effort to represent consensus views and noting where disagreement is still significant. For more complete discussions of these issues, I recommend Gordon et al. (2004), Gordon and Sudbury (2002), Kiesling (2004), Leitner (2004a), and two issues of the *Australian Journal of Linguistics* devoted largely to this question (see Blair and Yallop, 2003). The periods outlined below are based on Mitchell (2003), Leitner (2004a), and Gordon and Sudbury (2002), and are approximate (see also Schneider, 2003).

2.1   Australian settlement and expansion: 1788–1820

Australia was colonized as a penal colony in 1788, and to the extent that a "founder effect" (Mufwene, 1996: 84) has determined the development of AusE, it is this period that is crucial. The founder effect refers to the fact that the first generation of a new dialect has almost overwhelming power to determine what that dialect will be, even with later, large, migration. Gordon et al. (2004) and Leitner (2004a) both show some weaknesses in this view, but in general support the importance of the early settlers. It is generally agreed that most of the settlers from this period came from the southeast of England, and that this numerical advantage gave AusE much of the southeast-of-England character it has today. In addition, Horvath (1985) and Kiesling (2004) argue that Londoners had the kind of control of the linguistic marketplace and social networks that would give them extra advantage even over and above their simple numerical advantage. The lack of more Irish-English (see chapter 2) influence, despite a significant number of Irish settlers, suggests that the prestige and numbers of southeast English varieties played a definitive role in the character of Early AusE.

2.2   *Australian expansion and New Zealand founding: 1820–1850*

By 1820, the Sydney colony had stabilized, and migration was proceeding outward to the west and south. In 1831 the Port Philip (Melbourne) colony was founded, and significant numbers of Sydney settlers moved south to help that colony become established.

In 1840, the official New Zealand colony was established. Its demographic origins are difficult to pinpoint, because even though the influence of the southeast of England is undeniable, this influence could have come from a number of sources at different times (see Gordon et al., 2004: 256). The colony in New Zealand had multiple settlements, with a different mix of varieties in each, and some mobility between them. It is likely, moreover, that the already established early AusE influenced the early NZE.

2.3   *Gold rushes and new migration: 1850–1900*

In both Australia and New Zealand, this period saw two types of events that increased both internal and external migration in the two colonies: gold rushes and an increase in British migration, partially due to policies in England. The gold rushes attracted migrants from all over the world, increasing the diversity of English and other languages in both colonies, and causing significant population movements within them. These population shifts likely had the effect of diluting any incipient dialects that were forming. In both Australia and New Zealand, the increase in English migration may have had a "swamping" effect, damping the strength of the founder effect in both countries (Leitner, 2004c; Gordon et al., 2004: 247–50).

2.4   *Becoming nations: 1900–1960*

During this period, both colonies became de facto nations (Australia, at least, is still technically a colony in 2005). In this period, as shown in Gordon et al. (2004), changes set in motion in earlier periods developed further. However, the linguistic ideology of both nations tended to view the "Received Pronunciation" (RP) standard of England as the norm against which the local Englishes should be compared. This period saw a rising national identity in both colonies, and a linguistic identity to go with it.

2.5 National standard: 1960–present

At the start of this period, an awareness began to emerge that the Englishes in the two nations were national varieties in their own right, and could have their own standards separate from that of England (although this view was not uncontested). The Englishes became the focus of serious scholarship and the development of dictionaries, beginning with the *Macquarie Dictionary* in Australia, codified the local varieties as standards. In this period the linguistic diversity of both nations expanded, with migration from all over the world, but particularly Asia and the South Pacific.

3 Descriptions

NZE and AusE are overwhelmingly similar in most linguistic aspects; they are no more different (if not less different) than the Northern and Southern varieties of the United States. Gordon and Sudbury (2002) provide a useful comparison. Hearers not accustomed to the differences often take one for the other. The most obvious similarity is the vowel system (for acoustic details, see Watson, Harrington, and Evans, 1998). In comparison to most other Englishes, both are characterized by raised short front vowels (/æ/ and /ɛ/), fronting of /u/, the development of an onglide for long high vowels /u/ and /i/, the raising of the nucleus in the diphthongs /aw/ and /ai/, and the monophthongization of /ai/. /oʊ/ in both Englishes exhibits a lowering of the nucleus; in Australia, the glide target is fronted substantially so that /oʊ/ can be heard as /ai/, a change that may also be taking place in New Zealand. Both varieties, except in the Southland dialect in NZE, are "r-less," and exhibit linking/intrusive /r/. /l/-vocalization is present and increasing in both varieties with NZE in the lead (Borowsky and Horvath, 1997; Horvath and Horvath, 2001b). Finally, /t/ can be voiced/flapped intervocalically in both varieties (see Holmes, 1995a, 1995b; Tollfree, 2001). Prosodically, the use of rising intonation on any type of syntactic clause, termed High Rising Terminal (HRT), is noticeable in both AusE and NZE. In both Englishes, the use of this feature seems to be fairly recent, and has been led by Maoris in New Zealand (Britain, 1998; Britain and Newman, 1992) and by non-Anglo-Celtics (Greeks and Italians) in Australia (Guy et al., 1986). Finally, according to Bauer (1994), some lexical items are shared in these two Englishes that are obsolete in England.

3.1 Features distinguishing Australian and New Zealand Englishes

The most distinctive difference between NZE and AusE is in the pronunciation of vowels (see Watson, Harrington, and Evans, 1998). Most prominent is the vowel /ɪ/ as in *bit*, which has taken a different trajectory in Australia and

New Zealand. In Australia, /ɪ/ has been raised and fronted so that it now appears to the front of /i/, and *sit* can easily be mistaken for *seat* by speakers of other varieties of English who have not had experience with the Australian system. The New Zealand /ɪ/ has gone in the opposite direction, centralizing to /ʌ/, so that *sit* will sound more like *sut* (Bell, 1997). The other feature of the phonology of the vowel system of NZE that distinguishes from AusE and all Englishes is the merger of the vowels /ɪə/ and /ɛə/, so that *ear* and *air* sound the same (see Batterham, 2000; Gordon and Maclagan, 1989, 2001; Holmes, 1995b; Maclagan and Gordon, 1996, 2000). In terms of morphosyntax, there is little to distinguish NZE from AusE, and little to distinguish both from other varieties of English. Hundt's (1998) corpus study suggests that AusE and NZE are "virtually indistinguishable" (1998: 139).

One distinctive feature of AusE is the use of some unique hypocoristics and nicknames, for example the use of "Bazza" or "Baz" for "Barry," and the use of an *-o* suffix in place names, such as *Arno* for Arncliffe. The Australian tendency to generally modify names and other terms (such as "arvo" for "afternoon") distinguishes it from other varieties including NZE, and moreover adds to the characterization of the culture as informal. The system is complex but productive and rule-bound, as shown by Simpson (2001).

The lexicon is perhaps the system that displays the most difference both from other varieties of English and between NZE and AusE. These differences are largely because of the incorporation of words from indigenous languages in each country. Most of these words are used for indigenous flora or fauna, as well as for place names.

There has been little in the way of comparison of varieties of any language along the lines of discourse conventions, even though it is in these discourse conventions that many visitors notice differences. I will mention two here, but I am certain that there are others worth discussing. Most such work is often seen as a separate subfield of cross-cultural pragmatics (see Kiesling and Paulston, 2005), but we should not divorce the linguistic system classically defined from norms for speech activities and acts, which are after all just as normative and non-explicitly learned as grammar. The feature of NZE discourse is one that can distinguish a NZE speaker from an AusE speaker, namely the use of the utterance-final particle *eh*, which is used widely in NZE but much less if not at all in AusE (Meyerhoff, 1994; Stubbe and Holmes, 1995; Leitner 2004a: 219). The Australian form is one that I believe has not been mentioned in the literature to date, namely, the norm of how to use *thanks* in a service encounter. In Australia, the service provider will usually name the total due followed by *thanks* ("That'll be two dollars, thanks"). In most other Englishes *thanks* is postponed until the customer offers the money and/or change is given. The fact that this (obvious, from an American's standpoint) difference in discourse routines has not been discussed is emblematic of the lack of discourse studies of English varieties from a cross-cultural pragmatic perspective. This area of study is one that is likely to be fruitful and open to study. Moreover, it is an area that may be more immune to the effects of a global or internationalizing English; as Gumperz (1982) points out, such differences are often maintained even if other linguistic differences are leveled out.

3.2 Sociolinguistic variation in modern NZE and AusE

The descriptions above represent the consensus view of the linguistic characteristics of mainstream NZE and AusE. These characteristics are found to some degree in the speech of all native speakers of these Englishes, and in many cases are encoded in the standardized variety in dictionaries and grammar books. However, as in all Englishes, there is considerable variation among these characteristics, and this variation is not random. Patterns of variation have been found in both varieties based on age, gender, and social class (see Bell and Kuiper, 2000; Holmes, Bell, and Boyce, 1991; Horvath, 1985). In general, the patterns that have been found show that lower classes tend to use the distinguishing features of the Englishes more than the upper classes, who still approximate the RP standard, even though new prestige varieties are developing in both Englishes. In addition, most of the distinguishing features seem to be intensifying, so that younger speakers have more of the distinguishing properties than older speakers (as discussed below, some of these properties are relatively recent developments in both countries). Finally, in terms of gender, most of the patterns found exhibit the patterning generalized by Labov (2001; see also Chambers, 2003), in which women use more new variants in changes from below (so women will use more of the distinguishing properties than men of similar ages and classes). However, as speakers become aware of the features, such as the centralization of /ɪ/ and the *ear-air* merger in NZE, this difference may be reduced or even reversed.

In Australia, Mitchell and Delbridge (1965a, 1965b) developed a three-way continuum of phonetic varieties for Australia, which they termed Broad, General, and Cultivated (henceforth "BGC" when used together). Ever since, observers and linguists in Australia have taken this classification as axiomatic. This unreflective acceptance of the three varieties is so entrenched that corpora of phonetic samples of Australian English take as one of their sampling criteria speakers of Broad, General, and Cultivated, rather than sampling, say, by speaker class, or just attempting to obtain a random sample of Australian English speakers (which would be the most scientifically defensible method). While Mitchell and Delbridge were no doubt talented phoneticians, this three-way organization of variation in Australia has never really been shown using randomly-selected speakers of Australian English and measured using acoustic methods (or even just correlating the auditory methods with acoustic measures). Leitner (2004a: 230) notes that the three-way structure does not hold up in acoustic studies. Although the BGC classification is used productively by Horvath (1985), her description of a factor analysis showed that there were at least four, if not five, recognizable "sociolects" of speakers. Certainly the three categories have linguistic descriptions, but Horvath showed that the characteristics of BGC, do not pattern to form three distinct sociolects. The only conclusion from this finding is that Broad, General, and Cultivated do not describe coherent varieties of Australian English, but phonetic ranges for each sound. Unfortunately, the use of BGC has continued not only in popular press, but in the sociophonetic literature in Australia. Readers are thus advised to approach any study using such terms with trepidation. With that caution noted, there is clearly social variation, mainly along class lines and ethnicity in Australia (although there has been little work after Horvath 1985 that investigates the class distribution of variants in AusE; see Eisikovits, 1989; Kiesling, 2005).

3.3   Varieties of AusE

In Australia, there are mainly two audible – and popularly discussed – English varieties based on the ethnicity of the language users. The first is the English spoken by speakers descended from the aboriginal inhabitants of Australia, the second is the English spoken by non-Anglo-Celtic background Australians, such as Greeks and Italians.

3.3.1   Aboriginal Australian English

Aboriginal AusE (AAusE) developed from Aboriginal contact with English-speaking settlers, contact that began with the earliest days of the first settlement (see Leitner, 2004b and the references there for detailed descriptions and historical background). The early colony and the Aboriginal peoples they contacted developed pidgins for communication, which spread throughout the southeastern part of the continent. In the north, several pidgins such as Chinese Pidgin English developed. Later pidgins developed into two creoles: "Kriol," spoken in Queensland and the Northern Territory, and Torres Strait Creole. AAusE is more clearly a dialect of English – as opposed to a creole – which "is a nationwide vehicle of communication, the most prominent one within the modern Aboriginal language habitat" (Leitner, 2004b: 110). AAusE is identifiable as AusE in many respects, but is different from AusE in linguistic structure, and in norms for use. As is true for African American Vernacular English, the English vs. creole roots of this variety are now impossible to recover completely; it is indisputable that contact was involved, but it is unlikely that the ancestor of AAusE was a creole in the sense that Kriol is. While space here prevents a complete description of these differences (see Harkins, 1994; Leitner, 2004b: 122–38; Malcolm, 2001a, 2001b), some of the most marked features are as follows: In phonology generally, many contrasts – particularly in vowels – tend to be reduced, a simplification common in other contact varieties. There also seem to be prosodic differences, particularly a stress shift to the initial syllable, and the increased use of HRT. In terms of syntax, again the differences from AusE seem to be those of simplification and other contact processes (e.g., copula deletion and possessive -*s* deletion). Features such as the use of distinctive number and definiteness systems and a differential use of pronouns are not necessarily simplification, but are attributable to contact effects. Modern AAusE seems to have very little Aboriginal vocabulary.

The distinctiveness of AAusE is probably most noticeable, however, in the distinctive discourse conventions that seem to have been carried over from Aboriginal cultures. These conventions include lack of eye gaze, "broadcasting" speech, long inter-turn pauses, a strong preference for agreement, and a strong dispreference for individuation. As Eades (1991, 2004) and Walsh (1994) have shown, these differences have a serious detrimental outcome on speech events in which European Australian conventions are dominant, such as courtrooms. They are, nevertheless, the one place in the language where the echoes of ancestors clearly resound, and where AAusE provides a contemporary way for Aboriginal people to preserve some aspects of their culture.

3.3.2 *"Wogspeak"*

The term "wog" was originally a derogatory term for migrants to Australia from non-Anglo-Celtic countries (particularly Southern and Eastern Europe). It has in recent years been refigured as a term used by those groups for themselves, and for them marks the solidarity in their common experiences of migration under less than ideal circumstances. The variety referred to as "wogspeak," which I refer to as "New Australian English" (NAusE) for reasons outlined in Kiesling (2005), is one that is noticed by both those who are purported to speak it and the wider population more generally. It is thus clearly as much a social and ideological construct as a linguistic one.

The ideological basis is illustrated by the fact that this variety is really a furthering of changes in progress in AusE. While it is possible that the features of NAusE are related to contact effects, it is more likely that it arose out of the ways in which these migrants and their children learned English. In other words, the features of NAusE represent advances, or intensifications, of variation present in all varieties of AusE. Horvath (1985) shows that many non-native speakers of AusE have what she termed an "Ethnic Broad" variety, which exaggerates features of the most "Broad" variants. For example, the nucleus of /ai/ is extremely backed and raised. It is unlikely that this backing is due to interlanguage or interference from the ancestral languages, because these features are shared by speakers of different languages, such as Greek, Italian, and Arabic (although at different rates; see Kiesling, 2005). What appears to be happening in NAusE, then, is that migrants are using the existing resources of AusE to help become Australians; perhaps their status as non-native speakers frees them to be more flamboyant with their use of the new language, or their non-native learning causes a kind of "hypervernacularization." In either case, the rise of this variety is at least as likely to be due to issues of identity and ideology as it is to contact effects.

The features commonly cited for NAusE (Horvath, 1985; Clyne, Eisikovits, and Tollfree, 2001; Warren, 2001) include:

rounded front /u/;
/ə/ is realized as [ɛ];
voicing of voiceless stops;
aspiration of /k/;
/θ/ realized as [t] and /ð/ as [d];
/ɪə/ realized as [ijɒ] in words like *here*;
High Rising Terminal (rising final intonation on indicative clauses);
open realization of -*er*, as in *better*, which becomes [bɛɾɒ] (with variation in
    the /t/ as well).

However, there is no complete, corpus-based description of this variety. Kiesling (2001, 2005), and Kiesling and Borowsky (2001) begin such a description; both are based on a corpus of sociolinguistic interviews with Anglo-Celtic, Greek, Italian, Lebanese, and Vietnamese speakers, gathered in Sydney in 1997–8. In both analyses, of -*er* and /u/ respectively, there is some weak evidence of a differentiation from Anglo-Celtic background speakers. However, the strongest and most consistent effect seems to be for speakers of Greek background, who are the most extreme speakers in both cases. I have argued that this result, combined with Horvath's findings, suggest that Greek speakers are leaders in linguistic change in the English of Sydney. However, the patterns so far are still speculative. One of the more intriguing outcomes of the study of -*er* is that there is a strong ethnic differentiation by the duration of the -*er* segment. This result suggests that there may be prosodic contact effects from Greek.

It is clear that the variety known popularly as "wogspeak" is an important identity resource for non-Anglo-Celtic background people in Sydney, particularly those of Middle Eastern and Mediterranean descent. Warren (2001) provides evidence that this variety is not only something that non-Anglo-Celtic people are aware of, but something that they can control and manipulate in different situations.

3.3.3 *Geographic variation*
While it is true that the dialect diversity that exists in the British Isles and in North America makes the diversity in Australia seem unremarkable, there are differences that have been found, and if Schneider's (2003) schema for the development of colonial Englishes is correct, then this uniformity should be beginning to break down. The fact that English has been spoken along Atlantic shores centuries longer than Pacific ones is one possible reason for such differences in dialect diversity, as is the fact that the English input in Australia became mixed in migrations in multiple directions and waves (see Kiesling, 2004).

It is not true that AusE is everywhere the same, however. Pauline Bryant (1995, 1997) has gathered evidence that there are (complex) dialectal differences in lexis, especially between the south-central area of Australia (South Australia including Adelaide), the Southeast of Australia (Victoria and southern New South Wales, including Melbourne), the northeast (Northern NSW including Sydney, and Queensland), and the West (Perth). All dialect areas refer to the heavily-populated coastal areas of Australia, where the vast majority of the population lives. Bradley (1991), Horvath and Horvath, (2001a, 2001b) and Borowsky and Horvath (1997) have shown significant differences in pronunciation, particularly in the use of /æ/ and /a/ in words such as *advance*, *castle*, and *dance*. There is a clear difference in the assignment of word-class of these words regionally, with Melbourne and Sydney almost uniformly using /æ/, Adelaide almost uniformly /a/. All such dialect work suggests that the most significant dialect division is between Adelaide and the southeast (including Melbourne and Sydney, although there are slight differences between them). Further research is needed to determine whether the metropolitan centers of Australia (Adelaide, Brisbane, Melbourne, Perth, and Sydney) are epicenters for changes that are creating further geographic divisions in AusE. Alternatively, what appear to be dialects may be continent-wide changes spreading from one city to another, which will variably maintain the uniformity of AusE in the long term.

3.4   Varieties of NZE

There is some variation in NZE as well; the two clearly identifiable varieties are discussed below.

3.4.1   Maori English

A recognizably different variety of English is spoken by the autochthonous group, the Maori. While there have been occasional references to a Maori English in New Zealand, it is unclear, as in Australia, whether there is a distinct sociolect or whether changes that are taking place in NZE are simply used more by Maori-background people (Bell, 2000; Benton, 1985; Holmes, 1996, 1997; Stubbe and Holmes, 2000). Maori have often been found to use new or vernacular features studied in NZE. For example, they have been found to use more HRT (Britain, 1998; Britain and Newman, 1992; Holmes, Bell, and Boyce, 1991), be ahead in the *ear-air* merger (Gordon and Maclagan, 2001), and use the stereotyped NZE tag *eh* more than Pakeha speakers (Meyerhoff, 1994; Stubbe and Holmes, 1995). Some of the features seem to be the result of contact with the Maori language, such as being less stress-timed than the mainstream NZE (Warren and Britain, 2000) and the non-aspiration of voiceless stops. However, Holmes et al. (1991) show that the category of ethnicity interacts strongly with other social factors in New Zealand, particularly gender. It is clear from this research that a Maori identity is significant in predicting how someone in New Zealand will speak English, but that it by no means determines how that person will speak. In other words, ethnicity in NZE is not the special category it seems to be in Australia (or many other Englishes).

3.4.2   The Southland dialect

Any paleontologists looking at a map of New Zealand would likely immediately predict dialect differences between the two islands, given the barriers to communication between the two. But it turns out that the most significant geographical difference is not (yet) based on this division, but on the early settlement patterns in which settlers of Scottish background settled in the southern area of the south island. The English in this region differs from the rest of New Zealand in that it has a rhotic /r/, although this difference appears to be on the wane, with "Southland" speakers variably rhoticizing /r/, but strongly retaining it in the NURSE lexical set of Wells (1982). Because Gordon et al. (2004) show that the general non-rhotic pronunciation of /r/ in New Zealand was not the overwhelming norm at founding that it is today (see also Sudbury and Hay, 2002), it is possible that this difference simply represents a change in NZE that has taken longest to reach the Southland.

4   Conclusion

I conclude this overview with a focus on changes taking place in these Englishes, and what the future may hold for them. In both varieties we see changes in progress that are causing the Englishes to become more different than the same. The role of ethnicity is important here; in AusE, speakers of Greek and Italian background are leading changes, and in NZE, we find Maori speakers leading changes as well. The most significant changes likely for both Englishes are further internal stratification and differentiation, as regional and social dialects form and intensify in the urban centers in both countries (predicted by Schneider, 2003). In the coming years, the most interesting facts will have to do with features that spread regionally, such as HRT and /l/-vocalization (Horvath and Horvath, 2002), and those that are local, such as the *ear-air* merger in NZE. Finally, as English becomes more and more a language used in Asia, Leitner (2004a) suggests that Australian English will become a regional epicenter of English – i.e., it will form a standard for the regional variety of English in competition with British and American Englishes. It will be those features that are shared by AusE and NZE that are most likely to be included in this regional standard, and it is also likely that in fact, based on the findings of Horvath and Horvath (2001b), NZE will lead in the adoption of those linguistic features that eventually become part of this regional (south)east Asian English.

See also Chapters 17, VARIETIES OF WORLD ENGLISHES; 23, LITERARY CREATIVITY IN WORLD ENGLISHES; 38, WORLD ENGLISHES AND LEXICOGRAPHY; 41, WORLD ENGLISHES AND CORPORA STUDIES.

REFERENCES

Batterham, Margaret (2000) The apparent merger of the front centering diphthongs – EAR and AIR – in New Zealand English. In *New Zealand English*. Edited by Allan Bell and Koenraad Kuiper. Amsterdam: John Benjamins, pp. 111–45.

Bauer, Laurie (1994) English in New Zealand. In *The Cambridge History of the English Language, vol. 5: English in Britain and Overseas: Origins and Development*. Edited by Robert Burchfield. Cambridge: Cambridge University Press, pp. 382–429.

Bell, Allan (1997) The phonetics of fish and chips in New Zealand: Marking national and ethnic identities. *English World-Wide*, **18**(2), 243–70.

Bell, Allan (2000) Maori and Pakeha English: A case study. In *New Zealand English*. Edited by Allan Bell and Koenraad Kuiper. Amsterdam: John Benjamins, pp. 221–48.

Bell, Allan and Kuiper, Koenraad (2000) *New Zealand English*. Amsterdam: John Benjamins.

Benton, Richard A. (1985) Maori, English, and Maori English. In *Cross-Cultural Encounters: Communication and Mis-Communication*. Edited by John Holmes. Melbourne: River Seine Publications, pp. 110–20.

Blair, David and Yallop, Colin (2003) Introduction. *Australian Journal of Linguistics*, **23**(2), 109–10.

Borowsky, Toni and Horvath, Barbara (1997) L-vocalization in Australian English. In *Variation, Change and Phonological Theory*. Edited by Frans Hinskens, Roeland Van Hout, and W. Leo Wetzels. Amsterdam: John Benjamins, pp. 101–23.

Bradley, David (1991) /æ/ and /aː/ in Australian English. In *English around the World: Sociolinguistic Perspectives*. Edited by Jenny Cheshire. Cambridge: Cambridge University Press, pp. 227–34.

Britain, David (1998) Linguistic change in intonation: The use of high-rising terminals in New Zealand English. In *The Sociolinguistics Reader, vol. 1: Multilingualism and Variation*. Edited by Peter Trudgill and Jenny Cheshire. London: Arnold, pp. 213–39.

Britain, David and Newman, John (1992) High rising terminals in New Zealand English. *Journal of the International Phonetic Association*, **22**(1–2), 1–11.

Bryant, Pauline (1995) Regional differences in Australian English. *Australian Language Matters*, **3**(2), 19.

Bryant, Pauline (1997) A dialect survey of the lexicon of Australian English. *English World-Wide*, **18**(2), 211–41.

Chambers, Jack (2003) *Sociolinguistic Theory: Linguistic Variation and its Social Significance*. 2nd edition. Malden, MA: Blackwell.

Clyne, Michael, Eisikovits, Edina, and Tollfree, Laura (2001) Ethnic varieties of Australian English. In *English in Australia*. Edited by David Blair and Peter Collins. Amsterdam: John Benjamins, pp. 223–38.

Eades, Diana (1991) Communicative strategies in Aboriginal English. In *Language in Australia*. Edited by Suzanne Romaine. Cambridge: Cambridge University Press, pp. 84–93.

Eades, Diana (2004) Beyond difference and domination? Intercultural communication in legal contexts. In *Intercultural Discourse and Communication*. Edited by Scott F. Kiesling and Christina Bratt Paulston. Malden, MA: Blackwell, pp. 304–16.

Eisikovits, Edina (1989) Girl talk/boy talk: Sex differences in adolescent speech. In *Australian English*. Edited by Peter Collins and David Blair. St Lucia, Queensland: University of Queensland Press, pp. 35–54.

Gordon, Elizabeth, Campbell, Lyle, Hay, Jennifer, Maclagan, Margaret, Sudbury, Andrea, and Trudgill, Peter (2004) *New Zealand English: Its Origin and Evolution*. Cambridge: Cambridge University Press.

Gordon, Elizabeth and Maclagan, Margaret (1989) Beer and bear, cheer and chair: A longitudinal study of the ear/air contrast in New Zealand English. *Australian Journal of Linguistics*, 9(2), 203–20.

Gordon, Elizabeth and Maclagan, Margaret (2001) "Capturing a sound change": A real time study over 15 years of the NEAR/SQUARE diphthong merger in New Zealand English. *Australian Journal of Linguistics*, 21(2), 215–38.

Gordon, Elizabeth and Sudbury, Andrea (2002) The History of Southern Hemisphere Englishes. In *Alternative Histories of English*. Edited by Richard Watts and Peter Trudgill. New York: Routledge, pp. 67–86.

Gumperz, John (1982) *Discourse Strategies*. New York: Cambridge University Press.

Guy, Gregory, Horvath, Barbara, Vonwiller, Julie, Daisley, Elaine, and Rogers, Inge (1986) An intonational change in progress in Australian English. *Language in Society*, 15(1), 23–51.

Harkins, Jean (1994) *Bridging Two Worlds: Aboriginal English and Crosscultural Understanding*. St Lucia, Queensland: University of Queensland Press.

Holmes, Janet (1995a) Glottal stops in New Zealand English: An analysis of variants of word-final /t/. *Linguistics*, 33(3), 433–63.

Holmes, Janet (1995b) Three chairs for New Zealand English: The EAR/AIR merger. *English Today*, 11(3), 14–18.

Holmes, Janet (1996) Losing voice: Is final /z/ devoicing a feature of Maori English? *World Englishes*, 15(2), 193–205.

Holmes, Janet (1997) Maori and Pakeha English: Some New Zealand social dialect data. *Language in Society*, 26(1), 65–101.

Holmes, Janet, Bell, Allan, and Boyce, Mary (1991) Variation and change in New Zealand English: A social dialect investigation. Project report to the Social Sciences Committee of the Foundation for Research, Science and Technology. Wellington: Victoria University Department of Linguistics.

Horvath, Barbara M. (1985) *Variation in Australian English: The Sociolects of Sydney*. New York: Cambridge University Press.

Horvath, Barbara M. and Horvath, Ronald J. (2001a) A geolinguistics of short A in Australian English. In *English in Australia*. Edited by David Blair and Peter Collins. Amsterdam: John Benjamins, pp. 341–55.

Horvath, Barbara M. and Horvath, Ronald J. (2001b) A multilocality study of a sound change in progress: The case of /l/ vocalization in New Zealand and Australian English. *Language Variation and Change*, 13(1), 37–57.

Horvath, Barbara M. and Horvath, Ronald. J. (2002) The geolinguistics of /l/ vocalization in Australia and New Zealand. *Journal of Sociolinguistics*, 6(3), 319–46.

Hundt, Marianne (1998) *New Zealand English Grammar: Fact or Fiction?* Amsterdam and Philadelphia: John Benjamins.

Kiesling, Scott F. (2001) Australian English and recent migrant groups.

In *English in Australia*. Edited by David Blair and Peter Collins. Amsterdam: John Benjamins, pp. 239–58.

Kiesling, Scott F. (2004) English input to Australia. In *Legacies of Colonial English: Studies in Transported Dialects*. Edited by Raymond Hickey. New York: Cambridge University Press, pp. 418–39.

Kiesling, Scott F. (2005) Variation, style, and stance: Word-final *-er* and ethnicity in Australian English. *English World-Wide*, **26**(1), 1–42.

Kiesling, Scott F. and Borowsky, Toni (2001) The jewel highway to /uw/-fronting in Australia? Paper presented at New Ways of Analyzing Variation Conference, Raleigh, NC.

Kiesling, Scott F. and Paulston, Christina Bratt (eds.) (2005) *Intercultural Discourse and Communication*. Malden, MA: Blackwell.

Labov, William (2001) *Principles of Linguistic Change: Social Factors*. Malden, MA: Blackwell.

Leitner, Gerhard (2004a) *Australia's Many Voices: Australian English – The National Language*. New York: Mouton de Gruyter.

Leitner, Gerhard (2004b) *Australia's Many Voices: Ethnic Englishes, Indigenous and Migrant Languages – Policy and Education*. New York: Mouton de Gruyter.

Leitner, Gerhard (2004c) Beyond Mitchell's views on the history of Australian English. *Australian Journal of Linguistics*, **24**(1), 99–126.

Maclagan, Margaret A. and Gordon, Elizabeth (1996) Out of the AIR and into the EAR: Another view of the New Zealand diphthong merger. *Language Variation and Change*, **8**(1), 125–47.

Maclagan, Margaret A. and Gordon, Elizabeth (2000) The NEAR/SQUARE merger in New Zealand

English. *Asia Pacific Journal of Speech, Language, and Hearing*, **5**(3), 201–7.

Malcolm, Ian (2001a) Aboriginal English: Adopted code of a surviving culture. In *English in Australia*. Edited by David Blair and Peter Collins. Amsterdam: John Benjamins, pp. 201–22.

Malcolm, Ian (2001b) Aboriginal English: From contact variety to social dialect. In *Processes of Language Contact: Case Studies from Australia and the Pacific*. Edited by Jeff Siegel. Montreal: Fides, pp. 123–44.

Meyerhoff, M. (1994) Sounds pretty ethnic, eh? A pragmatic particle in New Zealand English. *Language in Society*, **23**(3), 367–88.

Mitchell, Alexander (2003) The story of Australian English: Users and environment. *Australian Journal of Linguistics*, **23**(2), 111–28.

Mitchell, Alexander and Delbridge, Arthur (1965a) *The Pronunciation of English in Australia*. Sydney: Angus and Robertson.

Mitchell, Alexander and Delbridge, Arthur (1965b) *The Speech of Australian Adolescents*. Sydney: Angus and Robertson.

Mufwene, Salikoko S. (1996) The founder principle in Creole genesis. *Diachronica*, **13**, 81–134.

Schneider, Edgar W. (2003) The dynamics of new Englishes: From identity construction to dialect birth. *Language*, **79**(2), 233–81.

Simpson, Jane (2001) Hypocoristics of place-names in Australian English. In *English in Australia*. David Blair and Peter Collins. Amsterdam: John Benjamins, pp. 89–112.

Stubbe, Maria and Holmes, Janet (1995) You know, eh and other "exasperating expressions": An analysis of social and stylistic variation in the use of pragmatic devices in a sample of New Zealand

English. *Language and Communication*, **15**(1), 63–88.

Stubbe, Maria and Holmes, Janet (2000) Talking Maori or Pakeha in English: Signalling identity in discourse. In *New Zealand English*. Edited by Allan Bell and Koenraad Kuiper. Amsterdam: John Benjamins, pp. 249–78.

Sudbury, Andrea and Hay, Jennifer (2002) The fall and rise of /r/: Rhoticity and /r/ sandhi in early New Zealand English. In *Working Papers in Linguistics: Papers from NWAV 30*. Philadelphia: University of Pennsylvania, pp. 281–95.

Tollfree, Laura (2001) Variation and change in Australian consonants: Reduction of /t/. In *English in Australia*. Edited by David Blair and Peter Collins. Amsterdam: John Benjamins, pp. 45–67.

Trudgill, Peter (2004) *New Dialect Formation: The Inevitability of Colonial Englishes*. Oxford: Oxford University Press.

Walsh, Michael (1994) Interactional styles in the courtroom: An example from Northern Australia. In *Language and the Law*. Edited by John Gibbons. London: Longman, pp. 217–33.

Warren, Jane (2001) "Wogspeak": Transformations of Australian English. In *Stories/Telling: The Woodford Forum*. Edited by Bronwen Levy and Ffion Murphy. Brisbane: University of Queensland Press, pp. 118–33. Originally published 1999 in the *Journal of Australian Studies*, **62**: 86–94.

Warren, Paul and Britain, David (2000) Intonation and prosody in New Zealand English. In *New Zealand English*. Edited by Allan Bell and Koenraad Kuiper. Amsterdam: John Benjamins, pp. 146–72.

Watson, Catherine, Harrington, Jonathan, and Evans, Zoe (1998) An acoustic comparison between New Zealand and Australian English vowels. *Australian Journal of Linguistics*, **18**(2), 185–207.

Wells, John C. (1982) *Accents of English*. Cambridge: Cambridge University Press.

FURTHER READING

Bauer, Laurie (1999) On the origins of the New Zealand English accent. *English World-Wide*, **20**(2), 287–307.

Bauer, Laurie and Bauer, Winifred (2002) Can we watch regional dialects developing in colonial English? The case of New Zealand. *English World-Wide*, **23**(2), 169–93.

Bauer, Laurie and Holmes, Janet (1996) Getting into a flap! /t/ in New Zealand English. *World Englishes*, **15**(1), 115–24.

Bayard, Donn (1999) Getting in a flap or turning off the tap in Dunedin? Stylistic variation in New Zealand English intervocalic (-T-). *English World-Wide*, **20**(1), 125–55.

Bayard, Donn (2000) New Zealand English: Origins, relationships, and prospects. *Moderna Sprak*, **94**(2), 160–6.

Bell, Allan and Holmes, Janet (1990) *New Zealand Ways of Speaking English*. Cleveland, UK: Multilingual Matters.

Bell, Allan and Holmes, Janet (1992) H-droppin': Two sociolinguistic variables in New Zealand English. *Australian Journal of Linguistics*, **12**(2), 223–48.

Blair, David and Collins, Peter (2001) *English in Australia*. Amsterdam: John Benjamins.

Burridge, Kate and Florey, Margaret (2002) "Yeah-no he's a good kid": A discourse analysis of yeah-no in Australian English. *Australian Journal of Linguistics*, **22**(2), 149–71.

Collins, Peter and Blair, David (1989) *Australian English: The Language of a New Society*. St Lucia, Queensland: University of Queensland Press.

Cox, Felicity (1999) Vowel change in Australian English. *Phonetica*, **56**(1–2), 1–27.

Deverson, Tony (1991) New Zealand English lexis: The Maori dimension. *English Today*, **7**(2), 18–25.

Easton, Anita and Bauer, Laurie (2000) An acoustic study of the vowels of New Zealand English. *Australian Journal of Linguistics*, **20**(2), 93–117.

Holmes, Janet (1995) Time for /t/: Initial /t/ in New Zealand English. *Australian Journal of Linguistics*, **15**(2), 127–56.

Holmes, Janet (1999) New Zealand English grammar: Fact or fiction? A corpus-based study in morphosyntactic variation. *English World-Wide*, **20**(2), 328–32.

Kaldor, Susan and Malcolm, Ian (1991) Aboriginal English – an overview. In *Language in Australia*. Edited by Suzanne Romaine. New York: Cambridge University Press, pp. 67–83.

Mühlhäusler, Peter (1991) Overview of the pidgin and creole languages of Australia. In *Language in Australia*. Edited by Suzanne Romaine. New York: Cambridge University Press, pp. 159–73.

Taylor, Brian (1989) A bibliographic survey of 200 years of writings on Australian and New Zealand English and their interaction with migrant and indigenous languages. *Australian Review of Applied Linguistics*, **12**(1), 1–17.

Watson, Catherine I., Maclagan, Margaret, and Harrington, Jonathan (2000) Acoustic evidence for vowel change in New Zealand English. *Language Variation and Change*, **12**(1), 51–68.

6 South Asian Englishes

RAVINDER GARGESH

1 Introduction

In South Asian language policies and planning English has a special place today because of its widespread functions in significant domains of social life, education, and cross-cultural communication (B. Kachru, 1997). It is well en-trenched and perhaps has many more speakers in South Asia than in the USA and the UK combined. Estimates of the number of speakers of English in India alone vary from 333 million (estimate basis 3–5 percent, as per B. Kachru, 1986: 54; see B. Kachru, 2005: 15) to 200 million (estimate basis 20 percent, as per *Encyclopedia Britannica*, 2002: 796 and Crystal, 2003: 50; see also Crystal, 1995) in a population of over a billion people. In addition, there is a large number of speakers of English in the other five countries of the region: Bangladesh, Bhutan, Nepal, Pakistan, and Sri Lanka. In all these countries English is viewed as a language of power and as a means of economic uplift and upward social mobility. Further, the presence of English language for over 200 years in the region has led to the nativization of the language, which is evident in several local varieties of English, collectively referred to as South Asian English (Baumgardner, 1996; B. Kachru, 1984, 2005). The nativization of English has enriched English as well as the indigenous languages through processes of borrowing and coinage of new words and expressions, and through semantic shifts (Baumgardner, 1998: 205–46; B. Kachru, 1983: 66; 1984: 353–83; Mehrotra, 1982: 160–2; K. Sridhar, 1991: 308–18).

English serves as a link language between people of different regions with different mother-tongue backgrounds, and is also the link language among the South Asian countries constituting the South Asian Association for Regional Cooperation (SAARC). Rather than being considered a colonial liability, it is now accepted as an asset in the form of a national and international language representing educational and economic progress.

1.1 *Appropriation and nativization of languages in South Asia*

There is a long tradition of acculturation of non-native languages in South Asia and the appropriation/nativization/acculturation of English is nothing new. The acculturation of Persian led to the development of a non-native Indian variety termed Indian Persian (*Sabk-e-Hindi*), while the acculturation of English has given us labels such as *Indian English*, *Pakistani English*, and *South Asian English* (see, e.g., Baumgardner, 1998: 205–46; S. Das, 1982: 141–9; B. Kachru, 1983: 66; 1984: 353–83; Mehrotra, 1982: 160–2; Nihalani, Tongue, and Hosali, 1979; Rahman, 1990; K. Sridhar, 1991: 308–18; see also Baumgardner, 1987, 1990).

It may be said that in this region the language of intellectual activity has always been different from the local or regional languages; for example, Sanskrit was once the pan-Indian medium, replaced by Persian in the medieval period. The spread of English in South Asia may be considered in the contexts of (1) multilingualism, (2) language policy in education, (3) the use of English in the media, and (4) literary creativity (e.g., as in Rao, 1938/1963). Since India forms the center and is also the dominant region in South Asia, most examples are taken from this region; other regions are mentioned in relevant contexts (see Kachru, 2005).

2 Functions of Languages in a Multilingual Region

Societal bilingualism/multilingualism, as it exists in countries of South Asia, Africa, etc., has begun to be appreciated in the world today. To cite Crystal (2004: 38), "bilingualism/multilingualism, is the normal human condition," for "well over half of the people in the world perhaps two thirds are bilingual." India, for example, has 1,652 mother tongues (1961 census) with a population at present of over a billion people (1,027,015,247 as per the *Census of India 2001*). As a socio-political entity, bilingualism/multilingualism is integrally woven into its cultural fabric. Pandit (1977: 172–3) provides an apt example of functional multilingualism. He describes the language use of an Indian businessman living in a suburb of Bombay (now Mumbai). His mother tongue and home language is a dialect of Gujarati; in the market he uses a familiar variety of Marathi, the state language; at the railway station he speaks the pan-Indian lingua-franca, Hindustani; his language of work is Kachhi, the code of the spice trade; in the evening he watches a film in Hindi or in English and listens to a cricket match commentary on the radio in English. It is clear from this example that in the multilingual speech community of South Asia a whole range of languages, or repertoire, is available to speakers, who choose to use them in their linguistic interaction to perform particular social roles. However, a speaker may not control the full range of the codes of a community's repertoire. What is noteworthy is that different codes perform different social functions, and English has its place in the multilingual space.

2.1   The role of English in multilingual South Asia

The increasing role of English in South Asia is best exemplified by the case of India. A focus on the role of English in the multilingual Indian setting highlights, to borrow Srivastava's (1994) terms, four distinct functions, namely, *auxiliary*, *supplementary*, *complementary*, and *equative*.

In its *auxiliary* function English is used for acquiring knowledge, rather than for communication; in this function English is what is sometimes called a "library language." Learning English for such purposes creates "passive bilinguals." In its *supplementary* function English is used for restricted needs; examples are Indian tourists abroad or tourist guides and taxi drivers in India. In such cases, the use of semi-routinized expressions makes English serve as a "vehicular language." Users of English at this level may be referred to as "unstable bilinguals," with partial competence in the language. In its *complementary* function, English is used along with a first language in well-defined social contexts. In such functions, English serves as a "link language," as when people of Hindi-speaking states communicate with speakers of non-Hindi-speaking states or vice versa. This function creates "stable bilinguals," who have a greater degree of competence than do "unstable bilinguals." In its *equative* function, English is employed as an alternate language in all domains in which a first language is used. This function creates "ambilinguals," as among those educated through the medium of English, or speakers across the world in the Indian Diaspora, the NRIs (Non-Resident Indians) who maintain roots in India, or Indians working for multinational companies.

Most language activity is *need-based social activity*. It is this aspect of necessity that has given rise to pidgin varieties such as Butler English (English for kitchen servants), Babu English (English used by office workers), and the nativized variety of Indian English (see B. Kachru, 2005). Competence in nativized Indian English can be ranked on *a cline of bilingualism* (Kachru, 1965: 393), an ascending scale that begins with the most pidginized variety and ends with an educated variety, with intermediate points with more or less language mixing (Verma, 1973, 1978). Since English today performs prestigious functions in the entire South Asian region, it may be said that there exists a kind of "triglossic" situation within Indian English, in which the language plays the most prominent role in the prestigious domains of education, science, and technology, while the regional standards function at the intermediate level in the domains of education, administration, regional politics and mass media, and the dialects occupy the lowest rung of the linguistic ladder, performing localized interpersonal functions (K. Sridhar, 1989: 149).

Another factor in the positioning of English in South Asia is the "non-conflicting" societal bilingualism prevalent in India. Pattanayak (1990: viii–ix) ascribes this feature to the functional allocation of roles to different languages in the multilingual fabric of the region. Recognition and acceptance of non-conflicting bilingualism reduces the fear of the disappearance of minority languages, since languages co-exist in harmony with distinct functional roles. Crystal (2004: 93) claims that children are born not just with an LAD (Language Acquisition Device), as Chomsky argues, but with an MAD (Multilingual Acquisition Device). Language-acquisition theories tend to focus on the competence of an "ideal" speaker-hearer. A focus on performance led Dell Hymes (1972) to propose the concept of "communicative competence." The bilingual/multilingual situation is a performance-based situation that evinces a complementarity of role for languages. If the bilingual/multilingual situation involves two or more distinct cultures, then we may even extend Hymes' term in order to look at language proficiency from what Oka (2001: 7) calls an "intercultural communicative competence (ICC)" perspective. However, keeping in mind the South Asian situation, it may be better to talk of a "multilingual communicative competence" (see S. Sridhar, 1992).

3 English Language Education

English language education in South Asia has its roots in the colonial history of the region. It arrived in South Asia with the East India Company at the beginning of the seventeenth century, and spread with the growing influence of the Company in the region. The formalization of an English language based education policy on mainland South Asia dates back to Sir Thomas Macaulay's Minute of 1835 (see Aggarwal, 1993: 2–12), which favored a Western mode of education through the medium of English. Intellectual activities before the onset of British Policy had been carried on in Sanskrit and Persian. Wood, however, suggested that "vernacular" languages should also be employed "to teach the far larger classes who are ignorant of, or imperfectly acquainted with English" (quoted by Aggarwal, 1993: 16). This was the beginning of the use of English and the vernacular languages as media of instruction on the subcontinent.

English became the dominant medium for higher intellectual activities with the establishment of the universities of Bombay, Calcutta, and Madras (now Mumbai, Kolkata, and Chennai, respectively) in 1857. The spread of English was so deep-rooted that by the 1920s it had become the language of political discourse. Although a leader like M. K. Gandhi (1869–1948) struggled to create consensus for Hindustani as an acceptable pan-Indian medium of communication, his message to the elite was generally expressed in English. Thus, English was the instrument that various political leaders such as B. G. Tilak, M. A. Jinnah, J. L. Nehru, and C. Rajagopalachari utilized for national awakening and the freedom struggle. By the time of independence it had become the dominant language for education, administration, judiciary, and the Indian media, and it had also created an elite class that was highly proficient in English (see B. Kachru, 2005).

3.1   Current status of English

In 1947 the sub-continent of India was divided into two countries – India and Pakistan (which then included Bangladesh). It is in the larger and more populous India that English has played a more dominant role. When the constitution of India came into force in 1950, Hindi was recognized as the official language of the Union, and English was limited to the role of an Associate Official language for 15 years, i.e., until 1965.

However, people in the non-Hindi-speaking West Bengal and the four South Indian states thought that Hindi as an official language would offer unfair advantage to the people of the north and curtail their upward socio-economic mobility, and so they began to support the retention of English. They did not want Hindi to become the only language for administrative services. Because of the political turmoil in South India in 1963, the then Prime Ministers, first J. L. Nehru and later L. B. Shastri, assured the people of non-Hindi-speaking states that English would continue to be in use beyond 1965. Thus, the Official Language (Amendment) Act 1967 was enacted, and English was designated an "Associate Official Language" with no time limit; it was also expected to serve as a "link language" between the central government and the governments of non-Hindi-speaking states. Since then, the place of English in India has become secure though controversial (Gupta and Kapoor, 1991).

For the development of Indian languages, a Schedule in the Constitution lists 22 mainstream languages. A meeting of the Central Advisory Board of Education was convened in early August 2004. One of the major issues discussed at that meeting was the "inclusion of English in the list of modern Indian languages" (*The Times of India*, August 12, 2004, p. 2). If this status is accorded to English, then the issue of standardization will come up and the study of English will also become far more widespread. At present, on the one hand, "double speak" by politicians throughout South Asia can often be heard against the spread and use of English (with the children of the elite class going to the best of English-medium schools), and on the other hand, the knowledge of English appears to have become imperative, with many business processes being outsourced to India from countries such as the USA. This latter is a compelling development from which there can be no turning back.

3.2   English in pre-university education

The role of English in pre-university (elementary and secondary) education exhibits a more or less similar pattern throughout South Asia. India has the most explicitly stated norms in its educational policy in the multilingual context.

In post-independence India there have been numerous deliberations regarding the teaching of English in the school levels and in higher education. The *Three Language Formula*, first proposed in 1957 and later formalized by an Education Commission (1964–6; see Aggarwal, 1993: 175–93), stipulates that the first language to be studied must be the mother tongue or the regional standard. The second language in Hindi-speaking states will be some other modern Indian language (MIL) or English, and in non-Hindi-speaking states it will be Hindi or English. The third language in Hindi-speaking states will be English or a MIL not studied as the second language, and in non-Hindi-speaking states, English or Hindi, whichever is not studied as the second language.

The implication of this formula was that while the teaching of the first language commenced from class I, the teaching of the second language was recommended from class VI, or at a convenient stage, depending upon the resources of a state. The third language was also recommended to be taught from class VI (for details, see Gargesh, 2002: 191–203). Education is a subject under the control of state governments, hence the actual implementations of the three-language formula vary from state to state. Since no other MIL has as wide a currency as Hindi or English, in practice the Hindi-speaking states have been lukewarm in promoting the study of any regional language of India.

At present there is an increasing trend to begin teaching English as a subject in class or grade I; for example, Delhi, Haryana, and Bihar have begun to teach English as an additional subject from class I starting in 2000, 2002, and 2003, respectively. The state of West Bengal abolished the teaching of English as a second language in 1977, but it has now reintroduced it in the earliest possible class in schools. In fact, providing widespread and effective English-medium education is becoming an election promise as well. The increasing demand for English represents the transformation of a society from an agrarian to an industrial and service-based one, which in turn is in the process of getting linked to the global market.

In Pakistan, English has been a compulsory language at the school level from class VI onwards, as per the recommendations of the Sharif Commission (1959). In the Pakistani provinces of Punjab, Sindh, and more recently in the North West Frontier Province, it is now a compulsory subject from class I onwards (Mansoor, 2004: 351–2). In Bangladesh, the National Committee on Education Policy 1997 recommended that English should be taught from class III onwards and as a compulsory subject in classes IX to XII, with the medium of instruction in all other subjects being Bangla (Shahed, 2001: 25).

3.3   *English in higher education*

The question of the medium of instruction in higher education has been quite contentious in South Asia (Pattanayak, 1981). Initially, the use of English was considered an interim arrangement in all these countries, India subsequently resolved in favor of the use of English in higher education.[1] Although some of the official committees set up to deliberate on the question recommended a quicker switchover from English to Indian languages, others cautioned against haste in this regard. The working group set by the University Grants Commission (UGC) in 1978 made a detailed study of the use of regional languages as media of instruction at different universities and observed that English could not be displaced as the medium of instruction for higher education because regional languages were just not ready to take over its functions.

The working group gave powerful arguments for the retention of English; for example, that English was a highly developed language and was best suited for India's industrial and scientific progress and that English was less divisive because of its neutral character, i.e., a language which all can learn on equal terms. It also noted that English continues to be a status symbol in society and commands prestige in all walks of life.

In Pakistan, it is reported that inadequate attention has been given to problems regarding learners' language difficulties in the English medium and to developing sufficient quality materials in Urdu for higher education. However, as Mansoor (2004: 350) writes: "In all Educational Policies and Reports of Education Commissions and Committees set up in this regard (1957–1998), the official policy with regards to language has been to maintain English as the medium of instruction in Higher Education."

In Bangladesh, following implementation of the Private Universities Act 1990, 55 English-medium private universities have been established, in addition to the 11 existing public universities which employ Bengali as the medium of instruction. Professor Arifa Rahman of Dhaka University regards this as a significant development, since not a single private university has opted for Bengali as the medium of instruction (personal communication).

It may be said, then, that the South Asian region has increasingly accepted English as the medium of instruction. In India, the All India Educational Survey conducted by the National Council of Educational Research and Training (NCERT) showed that the number of languages studied as a school subject decreased from 81 in 1970 to 41 in 1990. The number of languages used as a medium of instruction in school also decreased in the same period, from 47 to 18. It appears that in the age of increasing industrialization, higher science and technical education is available almost solely via English. The educational system reveals a pyramid structure, with the mother tongues forming the base, the regional standards occurring in the middle, and English emerging as the sole language at the top.

The above generalization is true not only of India, but of all the other countries in the region, too. See, however, Pennycook (1994, 2001), Phillipson (1992), Skutnabb-Kangas, Phillipson and Rannut (1994), Spolsky (2004) for issues related to such policies.

4   Toward Standard South Asian English

There is at present no prescribed or defined standard of English in South Asia. Although most speakers consider RP to be the standard variety, the vast majority uses a localized variety, the best known being a variety called Indian English (IE). Some scholars have tried to define a "standard" IE. B. Kachru (1983) defines "standard" IE as the English used by educated Indians. These are the people who institutionalize Indian English through literature, newspapers, journals, radio and TV, and government communications.

It has been mentioned that B. Kachru suggests a *cline of bilingualism*, a scale of different degrees of competence in English in India (see 2.1 above), with three measuring points (1965: 393): (1) the Zero point, i.e. at the bottom point of the cline (e.g., Babu English, Butler English); (2) the Central point, which indicates adequate competence in one or more registers (e.g., English used by civil servants and teachers); and (3) the Ambilingual point, for those users who have native-like competence in English. In addition, there are localized varieties, e.g., Punjabi English, Tamil English, etc. and ethnic varieties, e.g., Anglo-Indian English, Burgher English (Sri Lanka), etc. (McArthur, 1992).

The terms Indian English, Pakistani English, etc. presuppose the study of English as a second language in a bilingual context. The role of mother-tongue interference in the learning of the second language cannot be ignored in a discussion of the nature of IE. B. Kachru suggests that the extent of this interference is closely linked with the cline of bilingualism: "the more interference in a person's English, the lower the person ranks on the cline" (B. Kachru, 1983: 74).

In the 1960s, Bansal (1969) proposed a General Indian (GI) model for IE based on the criterion of international intelligibility. In the process, he rejected some of the widely accepted phonological features of IE, such as the use of dental stops for dental fricatives and voiceless stops without aspiration in the initial position of a stressed syllable. Such concerns with standardization of pronunciation, however, have had no effect in India. The American and Australian pronunciations differ a great deal from that of RP, yet the three varieties, at least in their "educated" form, are mututally intelligible. The same is true of regional variations, e.g., Irish and Scottish within Britain, and ethnic variation, e.g., African American English in the USA. Among speakers of English from the Inner, Outer, and Expanding Circles, phonological intelligibility seems to be a matter of accommodation; different varieties of English exist in harmony in the multilingual mind.

5   Methods and Methodology

South Asia inherited methods of teaching English from its colonial rulers. The teaching of English in the post-1947 era can best be represented by three significant documents from India: The Teaching of English in India (NCERT, 1963), The Study of English in India (Ministry of Education, Govt. of India, 1967), and the CBSE–ELT Project (Central Board of Secondary Education, Delhi, 1997).

5.1   *"The Teaching of English in India" (NCERT, 1963)*

The report prepared by NCERT indicates that initially there was a shift from the grammar-translation method to the "direct method" in India. This resulted in a situation in which grammar ceased to be taught and "oral drills which were devised to replace the teaching of formal grammar and to habituate the learner to correct usage through actual practice were not widely adopted" (NCERT: 20). This teaching approach led to deterioration in the teaching of English. In fact, what remained of the teaching method was "only reading and translation of the text book" (NCERT: 21). It was also noted that poetry was taught to second-language learners in the same way as it was taught to first-language students.

To reform the teaching of English, NCERT recommended that the focus be placed on ensuring comprehension. To make English class interesting, the use of audio-visual aids such as film strips and tape recorders, as well as the proper use of blackboard, flash cards, and wall pictures was recommended. The need for more regional and state institutes for the training of teachers of English was cited. It was felt that pre-service training needed to be re-oriented and in-service training needed to be strengthened (NCERT 32). (See Kumaravadivelu, 2003 on controversies in ELT methods.)

5.2   "The Study of English in India" (Government of India, 1967)

This document, too, was critical of earlier teaching practices. It noted that the syllabus was "heavily weighted on the literature side," that teachers generally "translate English into the regional languages and then drill rules of grammar" (1967: 34, 45). The sentence patterns and other teaching points were now numbered sequentially and graded in terms of difficulty. The report of the Ministry of Education comments that even this approach failed in India because of the teacher's diffidence with reference to spoken English and his or her almost subconscious belief that a second language can only be taught through the grammar-translation method. Predictably, even after about six years of English in vernacular medium schools, Indian students manifested hardly any functional knowledge of English.

The National Policy of Education 1986 and the Programme of Action 1990 were seriously concerned about the improvement of linguistic competencies of school students in all languages, including English. They called for development of text materials, teacher training, research methodology, and infrastructure for language teaching. For issues in teacher education, see Gargesh (2003) and Pattanayak (1997).

5.3   CBSE-ELT Project (1989–97)

The CBSE-ELT project (1989–97) was conducted by the Central Board of Secondary Education (CBSE), Delhi, in collaboration with the College of St Mark and St John, Plymouth, UK, and funded by the Department for International Development (DFID)/Official Development Assistance (ODA) through the British Council Division, New Delhi. The main objective of the project was to improve the teaching and learning of English in classes IX and X with a focus on the development of language skills in communicative situations. The special feature of the project was the intensive involvement of teachers from CBSE schools in all aspects of curriculum development, i.e., designing the syllabus, preparation of text material, creating new testing schemes and sample papers, and creating a training manual for orienting teachers to the new curriculum. The results of the CBSE-ELT project were four books: *Main Course Book*, *Grammar Book*, *Literature Reader*, and *Teacher's Book*. The emphasis was on task-based language learning, and the course design was aimed at developing the communicative competence of students.

The main drawback of the project was that it was planned only for those students who had a good command over the language before they entered class IX. The vast majority of the students continued to study the NCERT textbooks, which, though claimed to be based on the communicative approach, were in fact structural in orientation. After some years of implementation it became clear that most students could not master writing skills well.

5.4   From the twentieth into the twenty-first century

Governments have been at best half-hearted in strengthening the teaching of English in South Asia. The Programme of Action 1990 in India specifically mentioned the need for the NCERT, the Central Institute of English and Foreign Languages (CIEFL), the Regional Institute of English at Bangalore, and the HM Patel Institute of English, Vallabh Vidyanagar, to come together for improving students' language proficiency. Even though there are 11 English Language Teaching Institutes (ELTIs) in the country, the government admits that, despite assistance through the CIEFL, "the ELTIs have not been uniformly effective or dynamic" (http://shikshanic.Nic.in/cd50 years/g/T/V/OTOVOD0.htm – dated 9/14/2003). NCERT revised its own textbooks in 2002–3, though the texts prescribed still do not build communicative skills to a significant degree.

The official language policy in Pakistan has been to encourage the learning of Arabic as the language of religion and Urdu as the medium of instruction for the entire nation. A majority of public schools are Urdu medium; Sindhi and Pashto are confined to their respective regions. However, as the state does not have adequate resources to provide universal education, private institutions are filling in the gap. Madrassas (institutions that impart traditional Qur'anic instruction) are funded and supported by private parties, donations, and religious organizations; the English-medium schools have the backing of civil services and armed forces. Most scientific, technical, and professional education in Pakistan follows the pattern observed in India, i.e., the medium of instruction is English (see T. Rahman, 2004 for a discussion of the current education system in Pakistan).

The official policy in Nepal is to facilitate education through the mother tongue, and various programs are in place to implement that policy. According to the document put out by Ministry of Education and Sports (dated October 2004), Nepal will institute a national Action Plan in primary education between the years 2005 and 2007 that will translate a three-language policy into practice, the three languages being Nepali, a local language, and English.

In Bangladesh, the Ministry of Education, through its implementing bodies such as the National Curriculum and Textbook Board, has over the last few years taken steps to enhance the teaching of English at primary, secondary, and tertiary levels. The latest is the launching of an ambitious English language teaching improvement project (ELTIP) aimed primarily at secondary school level English teaching (A. Rahman, 1998: 28–35).

6   English in the Media

One of the parameters for gauging the spread of English in South Asia is its use in the media, particularly the print and audio-visual media. The Indian scene can be viewed as a representative case.

Abbi, Gupta, and Gargesh (2000) elicited users' perceptions about their own preference for language in newspapers and TV and radio programs. Keeping all three media in mind, the findings revealed that the audience prefers English as the medium for gaining knowledge and information. For entertainment the primary medium is other Indian languages, though there is a growing trend toward enjoying English popular songs, soap operas, and sitcoms among the younger generation in urban India. This appears to be the general trend in South Asia (see Shahed, 2001: 83–4 for Bangladesh).

6.1   *Newspapers*

Newspapers are published in India in about 100 languages that include the 22 principal ones listed in the Eighth Schedule of the constitution; those published in English make up a significant proportion (B. Kachru, 1994). Among all the dailies, for example, the multi-edition *The Times of India*, edited simultaneously from seven cities, has the largest total circulation – 1,695,945 copies – followed by *Malayala Manorama* (eight editions) in Malayalam, with a circulation of 1,132,813, and *Dainik Jagran* (12 editions) in Hindi, with a circulation of 1,122,544 (Government of India, 2000: 21).

In Bangladesh, of the 1,601 registered newspapers countrywide, there are 128 dailies published in Dhaka, of which 11 are in English. Outside Dhaka, there are 6 English dailies out of 233 dailies. The readerships of the three leading English dailies are about 35,000, 21,500 and 20,000, respectively (Shahed, 2001: 54).

The major English language newspapers in Pakistan are *Dawn, Pakistan Times, Muslim, Morning News, Nation, Frontier Post,* and *News International*.

6.2   *Radio*

Radio is the mass medium that has the greatest reach, both geographically and socially, in South Asia.

In India, for entertainment, people mostly listen to their own regional music or to Bollywood film songs. However, news and other information such as debates during Parliament sessions, reviewing the day's proceedings in both the Houses of Parliament, and political commentaries are broadcast in both Hindi and English.

A total of 12 hours and 20 minutes is devoted to news in the Home Service, of which 2 hours and 25 minutes are taken up by 21 news broadcasts in English, while Hindi takes up 2 hours and 30 minutes for 20 news broadcasts. The remaining languages get between 10 and 40 minutes each (Government of India, 2003a).

In Bangladesh, apart from three news bulletins each day and an hour-long program, *Music around The World*, broadcast three times a week, English is hardly used in radio broadcasts.

6.3   *TV* (Doordarshan)

TV (*Doordarshan*) transmission has increased enormously in India since the expansion of television services in India during the Asian Games in 1982. In the National Network, English and Hindi dominate the news component. News in English gets six slots in a day which total 100 minutes, while five slots in Hindi get 100 minutes. The sports channel presents at least 25 percent of its programs in English. The educational programs also have a high percentage of programs in English.

However, private channels such as ESPN, HBO, Star Movies, Star News and Star Sports, Star World, AXN, BBC, CNN, and Discovery provide entertainment and information in various Englishes (Government of India, 2003b).

In Bangladesh, the national TV channel BTV broadcasts English news twice a day and shows English serials twice a week. The two Bangladeshi private channels – Ekushe TV and Channel I – however do not broadcast any news in English, though they present some English serials.

7   Attitudes toward English

The attitude toward English in South Asia is in general favorable. Abbi et al. (2000: 20, 22) gave informants the questions "Given a choice, which language would you like to educate your children in?" and "If you had choice, which language would you choose as a mother tongue?" The responses revealed that while English is overwhelmingly the desired medium of education, it is not desired as a mother tongue. This reinforces the point that English is considered necessary for education and information, whereas the local language or Hindi is preferred for an Indian identity.

Agnihotri and Khanna (1997: 74) in their study of attitudes towards English conclude: "more than 90% informants want some amount of English to be used in teaching at all levels of education." Their study also reveals that one of the major reasons for learning English is the instrumental function: "it is also seen as a means for enhancing social mobility and individual personality" (p. 85). Other interesting findings are that English is regarded as one of the Indian languages by nearly 75 percent of the informants, and that 77 percent believe that progress in science and technology will be hampered without English (p. 90). Regarding attitudes toward English-speaking Indians, more than 60 percent of informants considered them to be sensitive to Indian culture, progressive, and honest. Finally, there is strong parental encouragement of the study of English. The extent of positive attitudes toward English revealed by this research indicates that English is here to stay for quite some time as a valuable tool. Somewhat similar conclusions were reached by Mansoor (2004) for Pakistan and to a lesser degree by Shahed (2001) for Bangladesh.

8   The Variational Range

South Asian English (SAE) represents several varieties of English that have emerged throughout the subcontinent. These varieties manifest themselves in a host of ways through their phonologies, lexicons, syntaxes, and usages.

8.1   *Phonology*

The vowels, consonants, important phonological processes, and major prosodic features of English on the subcontinent have been discussed in Gargesh (2004a: 187–97). These are to a great degree common to SAE. Some significant features related to vowels are as follows:

1   The vowels /e/ and /o/ as in *face* and *goat* are realized as monophthongs, not diphthongs, as in standard British or American English.
2   The opposition between /ʌ/ and /ə/ as in [bʌs] and [bəs], /a/ and /ɔ/, and /ɛ/ and /æ/ is not clear-cut in SAE.

Some features regarding consonants are as follows:

1   The syllable-initial voiceless stops of a stressed syllable are not aspirated.
2   The affricates /ts/ and /dz/ are pronounced as palatal [c] and [j] in SAE.
3   The alveolar [t] and [d] tend to be retroflexed [*certificate* = sərʈɪfɪkeʈ] and *London* = [lənɖən].
4   The interdental fricatives [θ] and [ð] are non-existent and these are articulated as dental aspirated voiceless stop [tʰ] and voiced stop [d], respectively, e.g., *thin* [tʰɪn] and *then* [dɛn]. In South India the alveolar stop [t] is often used for [θ] as in *thought* [tɔt].

Some important phonological processes are:

1   In the northern areas of the subcontinent, the word-initial consonant clusters #sp-, #st-, #sk- are generally broken up. In the eastern part of the

Hindi-Urdu belt a short high prothetic vowel [ɪ] in the word initial position is added, e.g., *speech* [ɪspiːc], *school* [ɪskuːl], while in Punjab and Haryana the low-back untensed svarbhakti (anaptyctic) vowel /ə/ is inserted between the clusters for the same words, e.g., [səpiːc], [səkuːl], etc.

2   The low vowel /ə/ is deleted in relatively light positions, e.g., *dispensary* /dɪs'pɛnsəriː/ = [dɪs'pɛnsriː], *allegory* /ə'lɛɡəriː/ = [ə'lɛɡriː].

SAE generally has its own syllable-timed rhythm, and syllables are uttered with an almost equal prominence. This means that often SAE does not use weak forms of vowels in unstressed positions. Thus a sentence like *I am thinking of you* can be heard as ['aːɪ 'æm 't̪ʰɪŋkɪŋ 'ɔf 'yuː]. Here the first-person singular pronoun, the auxiliary, and the preposition are not realized in short-ened forms such as [aːɪm] or [əv]. Since syllables are articulated more fully, SAE takes relatively more time in articulating similar stretches of the English language than the native varieties.

8.2   Lexicon

But it is in the area of lexicon that the divergence of SAE is most noticeable – words acquire fresh meanings in local contexts. The processes of innovation, compounding, blending, semantic shift, reduplication, etc. in Indian English vocabulary items have been discussed in detail in Hawkins (1986), B. Kachru (1965, 1983), and Nihalani et al. (1979). The same phenomenon in Pakistani and Bangladeshi contexts has been described in Baumgardner (1998: 205–46) and Shahed (2001: 57–60), respectively.

Some examples of the indigenous words introduced into the English lan-guage are units of measurement: *Crore* (10 million) and *lakh* (100,000) are the units used in the *Annual Report* 2002–3 of the Ministry of Human Resource Development, Govternment of India. Goldsmiths, while weighing gold orna-ments, use *ratti:, ma:sha:* (= 8 *ratti:*), *tola:* (= 12 *ma:sha:*) (see Baumgardner, 1998). Most of the units mentioned by Baumgardner and Kennedy (1994) and Gramley (2001: 55–7) for Pakistani English are also in use in Indian English.

Other words of South Asian origin used in SAE are names of food items such as *dosa, idli, vaṛa, roṭi,* etc. In addition, SAE uses innovations such as *finger chips* 'French fries', *full-boiled* and *half-boiled egg* 'hard-' and 'soft-boiled eggs'. Innovative compounds are exemplified by *pen-down-strike, tool-down-strike, driver-cum-salesman, to airlift, to airdash, to chargesheet, to turnturtle,* etc. Some morphemes like +*wa:la:* (signaling ownership or agency), +*hood,* +*ism,* etc. are quite productive, e.g., *policewa:la:, riksha:wa:la:, netahood, goondaism,* etc. English items undergo semantic shift in items such as *four-twenty* 'a swindler' (the penal code 420 defines such crimes); *secular* 'respect for all religions', *communal* 'bigoted' in the context of religion, *trade* 'to exchange' as in "India, Pakistan trade wanted list" (*The Times of India,* August 12, 2004, p. 1).

8.3   Syntax

The syntax of SAE has been described in a number of studies including B. Kachru (1983, 1994), T. Rahman (1990), S. Sridhar (1996), and Bhatt (2004). For instance, the use of complex noun phrases in Indian English reflects the influence of speakers' mother tongues. In Indian contexts they function to concretize a name, e.g., *Metros Operation Control Centre* (the organization that controls the operation of the underground railroad in metropolitan cities). Another feature is the use of present progressive with stative verbs, e.g., *I am having a cold* ('I have a cold'); *Gautam was knowing that he would come* ('Gautam knew that he would come'); *I am loving it* (ad for MacDonald's). B. Kachru (1983: 497–510) points out that articles in IE are used in ways unfamiliar to Inner-Circle varieties, e.g., *the* can occur with proper nouns as in *the Mahatma Gandhi*. Lack of subject-auxiliary inversion is widely attested, e.g., *What you would like to read? When you would like to come?* So is the widespread use of *isn't it* or *no* in tag questions, e.g., *You went there yesterday, isn't it? You went their yesterday, no?* Baumgardner (1987) describes use of noun clause or noun phrase complement constructions in characteristic ways in Pakistani English, e.g., "They were not at all interested in democracy . . . and were only *interested to grab* power at any cost," "Pakistan has no *control to influence* affairs inside Afghanistan," "He *went* to China *for learning* Chinese" (see also Nihalani et al., 1979; Y. Kachru and Nelson, 2006; T. Rahman, 1990).

8.4   Communicative styles

Communicative styles appropriate to South Asian sociocultural context are resorted to in many domains (see B. Kachru, 2003; Y. Kachru, 1987, 1992, 1993, 1999, 2001, 2003; Pandey, 2004). Some examples from matrimonial advertisements, obituaries, product advertisements, and the language of administration follow. Consider the following matrimonial advertisement:

> Convt. prof. Qlfd. Fair bful, Brahmin girl for fair h'some KKB boy, 27/172/, MBA from reputed University with MNC Delhi as International Mkt. Mgr. Send BHP. Write Box No. LUC 510603C *Times of India*, Lucknow-01 (*The Times of India*, August 15, 2004, Matrimonial Section, p. 1).
> [Convt. = convent-educated, prof. Qlfd. = professionally qualified, bful = beautiful, KKB = Kanya Kubja Brahmin, BHP = Biodata, Horoscope, and Photograph]

Many advertisements specifically demand "convent-educated" or "English-speaking" brides, and they mention their caste – here KKB (Kanya Kubja Brahmin) – and most of them, whether settled in India or abroad, ask for BHP (Biodata/Horoscope/Photograph). The Indian ad emphasizes economic solidity and the role of the family is central, for it is the parents who place the ad and act as intermediaries in any ensuing negotiations and the eventual wedding.

Announcements of death are culture specific. *The Times of India* (dated August 10, 2004, p. 4), announces "the sad demise" (sometimes "sudden and untimely demise") of a person whose "pious soul departed for the heavenly abode." This is followed by announcement of a date for "cremation"/"kirtan and ardas for the peace of the departed soul"/"Uthaoni." This is an example of a highly restricted culture-dependent use of a non-native language for naming community-specific rites that is quite unintelligible to a speaker of English outside the Indian culture.

A code mixed style is used in informal talk and in the newspapers. The headline of the *Times of India*, July 21, 2004 was: "PM shatters babus' dreams" (subheading "Officials can't Take Short Leave For Foreign Assignments"). The word "Babus" refers to the bureaucracy. The first sentence of the editorial on page 8 of the *Hindustan Times*, August 4, 2004, reads as "After laboring hard for three days, the BJP's four day Chintan baithak has delivered a mouse." The *Chintan baithak* was a brainstorming session of the BJP (a political party) to take stock of the electoral defeat in the general elections, and the "mouse" refers to the futility of the exercise.

A famous Pepsi ad, "yeh dil mange more," uses the word *more*, which creates interesting ambiguity. In Hindi, a word with identical pronunciation refers to 'peacock', while the English word *more*, coupled with *dil mange* 'heart demands', signals 'greater desire'.

The language of administration also shows characteristic South Asianness. Some examples are: "Minister may like to pass orders," meaning that the file is sent to the minister for his signature; "Submitted for orders," meaning that the Minister has the discretion to approve or reject the proposal; "Please speak," meaning 'come and explain'.

In administrative language, you never write letters, you always *address communications*; you never inform anyone, you always *intimate*; and when you want to know anything you don't say: "Please let me know," you say: *Please enlighten us.*

Politeness in Asian society is a conventionalized phenomenon, which is part of the conversational style of South Asian Englishes (Y. Kachru, 2003). The strategy of maintaining a positive face, i.e., enhancing another's self-esteem, can be seen in the example: *What is your good name, please?* A similar strategy is exhibited through insistence when offering: *Take only this much, just this much* and *Have some more, have some more*. The guest expects this; a request such as *Won't you have more?* would sound negative.

Kinship terms such as *sister, uncle, auntie* are also used for politeness (K. Sridhar, 1991). The honorific suffix *+ji* or *+sahib* attached to names is more deferential than the use of *Mr* or *Mrs*.

IE speakers also at times juxtapose idioms in novel ways, e.g.: "I am in very good health and hope you are in the same boat" (S. Das, 1982: 144; Hawkins,

1986). For more on discourse in varieties of Englishes, see B. Kachru (1992), Smith (1987).

9 Literary Creativity

Creative writing in SAE has gained in stature in recent years. International awards such as the Booker Prize or national ones such as the annual award of the Sahitya Akademi, Delhi, are indications of the increasing appreciation and acceptability of creative writing in SAE.

In present-day bilingual India there are many who write only in English, although it is their second language. Pritish Nandy (1973: 8) in his *Indian Poetry in English Today* declares that English is "a language of our own, yes, an Indian language, in which we can feel deeply, create and convey experiences and responses typically Indian." The poet Kamala Das, for example, is conscious of her Indian multilingualism, for she says:

> I speak three languages, write in
> Two, dream in one.

She answers another objection:

> Don't write in English, they said,
> English is not your mother tongue . . .
> . . . The language I speak
> Becomes mine, its distortions, its queerness
> All mine, mine alone, it is half English, half
> Indian, funny perhaps, but it is honest,
> It is as human as I am human . . .
> . . . It voices my joys, my longings my
>   Hopes . . .
>   (Kamala Das, 1965: 10)

N. Ezekiel in his *Very Indian Poems in Indian English* has created some satirical dramatic monologs in which characters use English at a point somewhere below B. Kachru's central point in the "cline of bilingualism." This is common practice for portrayal of character in IE writing. The example given below exploits the use of the present progressive and the lack of articles, and the rhythm appears to be generated by the accentual-syllable structure that is common to most Indian languages:

> I am standing for peace and non-violence
> Why world is fighting fighting
> Why all people of world
> Are not following Mahatma Gandhi
> I am not simply understanding.
>   (N. Ezekiel, 1989: 237, *The Patriot*)

Contemporary poets and novelists have transcended the colonial past and have entered the postcolonial era in their attitudes and uses of English. Indians have contextualized English as art by making the language look exotic to the Inner Circle through their context-based usages. The appropriations can be seen at times in changing the rhythmic patterns, which may even affect conventional spellings; fusing words; using a more localized lexicon, syntax, and central thematic symbols.

Arundhati Roy, in *The God of Small Things* (1997: 261), captures the rhythm of the speech learnt by heart by the six-year-old Lenin through a differently organized spelling system. Thus, the famous Anthony's speech from Shakespeare occurs as follows:

> I cometoberry Caesar, not to praise him. Theevil that mendoo lives after them,
> The goodisoft interred with their bones.

An example of the English language molded to meet the cultural demands of Indian thought can be seen below:

> . . . take seven steps with him that will make him my ally. (Gauri Deshpande, cited in Chindhade, 2001: 10)

The seven steps in the example are a transcreation of the seven times going around the holy fire that make a Hindu man and woman husband and wife.

The distinct features of creative works of South Asian writers such as the ones mentioned above or writers such as Salman Rushdie, Taslima Nasreen, and Bapsi Sidhwa underscore South Asia's claim not only as a sociolinguistic area (Pandit, 1972), but also as a literary area in a sea of fierce regional and linguistic loyalties. Bengali literature, for instance, is more Bengali than it is South Asian, a fact that applies to other regional South Asian languages as well. But a Bengali who writes in English reaches out to the entire South Asian region. The common feature is that SAE writers nativize their English to the extent that the connotations and semiotics that exist in their local languages are imported into the medium used. Creative writing in SAE is a unique experiment wherein English is the second language of both the writers and their readers. Whereas Beckett and Conrad assimilated to the cultural semiotics of their adopted language, South Asian writers are contributing to the development of new canons in world English literature (see, e.g., Cha'ien, 2004; Dissanayake, 1997; B. Kachru, 2001/2005; Narasimhaiah, 1978; T. Rahman, 1991; S. Sridhar, 1982, among others).

10   Conclusion

English occupies a special place in South Asia, a place unlike that of any indigenous language. Because of institutional and societal support, almost all higher-order activities in the domains of education, commerce, law, and administration have to be negotiated and performed in English (See Rahman, 1990 for Pakistan). The societal and institutional support for English is so strong that it is generally believed that one cannot become a doctor, engineer, lawyer, scientist, pilot, or bureaucrat without proven proficiency in English. And it appears that the functional role of English in South Asia can only increase.

Creative writing shows that English in South Asia has undergone a process of decolonization (B. Kachru, 2005 has extensive bibliographical references). In this context the teaching of English cannot but be influenced by the indigenous character of the other languages which are present. This situation has direct relevance for the development of authentic materials for the teaching of English, given the linguistic, social, and cultural heterogeneity of the region.

The main educational goal in South Asia is to minimize social and economic disparities and inequality of power and to create a positive discrimination in favor of the weak by giving each person an opportunity to learn English. The plural and heterogeneous nature of South Asian society demands that regional autonomy be exercised for developing regionally and culturally specific curricula so that the English language classroom constitutes an important site for initiating indigenous knowledge. In order to achieve this, problems emanating from a gigantic system of education with huge enrolments and not very well prepared teachers will have to be tackled imaginatively. Positive signs are the growing use of television and computer technology for educational purposes and the general awareness among the underprivileged for the need for English education.[2]

See also Chapters 15, WORLD ENGLISHES TODAY; 16, CONTACT LINGUISTICS AND WORLD ENGLISHES; 17, VARIETIES OF WORLD ENGLISHES; 20, WRITTEN LANGUAGE, STANDARD LANGUAGE, GLOBAL LANGUAGE; 23, LITERARY CREATIVITY IN WORLD ENGLISHES; 25, WORLD ENGLISHES AND CULTURE WARS; 36, TEACHING WORLD ENGLISHES; 38, WORLD ENGLISHES AND LEXICOGRAPHY; 41, WORLD ENGLISHES AND CORPORA STUDIES.

NOTES

1   In India various committees, conferences, and commissions have grappled with the question of media of education and examination in higher education. Some important ones need to be mentioned – University Education Commission (1948), the Kunzru Committee appointed by the University Grants Commission (UGC) (1955), National Integration Council (1962), The Education Commission (1964–6), and the UGC's working group on Regional Languages as media of instruction (1978) (see Srivastava, 1994: 178–82).

2   For perspectives on English as a global language, and its teaching, see Gargesh (2004b), Halliday (2003), McKay (2004), Schneider (1997), Smith (1976, 1983), and Widdowson (1997).

REFERENCES

Abbi, Anvita, Gupta, R. S., and Gargesh, Ravinder (2000) A sociolinguistic inquiry into the acceptance level of Hindi as a pan Indian language. New Delhi: ICSSR (Project Report).

Aggarwal, J. C. (1993) *Landmarks in the History of Modern Indian Education.* New Delhi: Vikas Publishing House.

Agnihotri, Ramakant and Khanna, A. L. (1997) *Problematizing English in India.* New Delhi: Sage.

Bansal, Ram Krishana (1969) *The Intelligibility of Indian English.* Hyderabad: CIEFL.

Baumgardner, Robert J. (1987) Using Pakistani newspaper English to teach grammar. *World Englishes,* **6**(3), 241–52.

Baumgardner, Robert J. (1990) The indigenization of English in Pakistan. *English Today,* **6**(1), 59–65.

Baumgardner, Robert J. (ed.) (1996) *South Asian English: Structure, Use and Users.* Urbana and Chicago: University of Illinois Press.

Baumgardner, Robert J. (1998) Word-formation in Pakistani English. *English World-Wide,* **19**, 205–46.

Baumgardner, Robert J. and Kennedy, Audrey E. H. (1994) *Measure for Measure*: Terms of measurement in Pakistani English. *English World-Wide,* **15**(2) 173–93.

Bhatt, Rakesh M. (2004) Indian English: Syntax. In *A Handbook of Varieties of English: Morphology and Syntax.* Edited by Bernd Kortmann, Kate Burridge, Rajend Mesthrie, Edgar W. Schneider, and Clive Upton. Berlin/New York: Mouton de Gruyter, pp. 1016–30.

CBSE (1997) *CBSE-ELT Project: A Report 1989–1997.* Delhi Central Board of Secondary Education. Delhi: CBSE.

Cha'ien, E. N. (2004) *Weird English.* Cambridge MA: Harvard University Press.

Chindhade, Shirish (ed.) (2001) *Five Indian English Poets.* Delhi: Atlantic Publishers.

Crystal, David (1995) *The Cambridge Encyclopedia of the English Language.* Cambridge: Cambridge University Press.

Crystal, David (2003) *English as a Global Language.* 2nd edition. Cambridge: Cambridge University Press.

Crystal, David (2004) *The Language Revolution.* Cambridge: Polity Press.

Das, Kamala (1965) *Summer in Calcutta: Fifty Poems.* New Delhi: Rajinder Paul.

Das, Sisir Kumer (1982) Indian English. In *New Englishes.* Edited by J. Pride. Rowley, MA: Newbury House, pp. 141–9.

Dissanayake, Wimal (1997) Cultural studies and world Englishes. In *World Englishes 2000.* Edited by Larry E. Smith and Michael L. Forman. Honolulu: University of Hawai'i Press, pp. 126–45.

Ezekiel, Nissim (1989) *Collected Poems 1952–1988.* Delhi: Oxford University Press.

Gargesh, Ravinder (2002) English language in school education and print media. In *Linguistic Landscaping in India.* Edited by N. H. Itagi and S. K. Singh. Mysore: CIIL & MGH University, pp. 191–203.

Gargesh, Ravinder (2003) Pre-service and in-service teacher training in India and the classroom. Paper presented at the First Annual Conference of TEEL Asia, held at Busan, South Korea, November 5–7.

Gargesh, Ravinder (2004a) The phonology of English in India. In *Varieties of English: Africa/Southeast*

Asia/India. Edited by Rajend Mesthrie. Berlin: Mouton de Gruyter, pp. 187–97.

Gargesh, Ravinder (2004b) English as an international language: An Indian perspective. Plenary lecture at the Annual Conference of JACET, held at Nagoya, Japan September 5–7.

Government of India (1967) *The Study of English in India*. Delhi: Ministry of Education.

Government of India (2000) *Press in India 2000*. Forty-fourth Annual Report of the Registrar of Newspapers for India. Ministry of Information and Broadcasting, Government of India, New Delhi.

Government of India (2003a) *All India Radio 2003*. New Delhi: Government of India, Prasar Bharati, Director General, AIR.

Government of India (2003b) *Doordarshan India 2003*. New Delhi: Government of India, Prasar Bharati, Director General and Broadcasting Corporation of India. Doordarshan.

Gramley, Stephan (2001) *The Vocabulary of World English*. London: Arnold.

Gupta, R. S. and Kapoor, Kapil (1991) *English in India: Issues and Problems*. Delhi: Academic Foundation.

Halliday, M. A. K. (2003) Written language, standard language, global language. *World Englishes*, **22**(4), 405–18.

Hawkins, P. A. (1986) Supplement of Indian words. In *The Little Oxford Dictionary*. 6th edition. Edited by J. Swannell. Oxford: Clarendon Press.

Hymes, Del (1972) On communicative competence. In *Sociolinguistics*. Edited by John B. Pride and Janet Holmes. Harmondsworth: Penguin, pp. 269–85.

Kachru, Braj B. (1965) The Indianness in Indian English. *Word*, **21**, 391–410.

Kachru, Braj B. (1983) *The Indianization of English: The English Language in*

India. Oxford: Oxford University Press.

Kachru, Braj B. (1984) South Asian English. In *English as a World Language*. Edited by Richard Bailey and Manfred Görlach. Cambridge: Cambridge University Press, pp. 353–836.

Kachru, Braj B. (1986) *The Alchemy of English*. Oxford: Pergamon.

Kachru, Braj B. (ed.) (1992) *The Other Tongue: English Across Cultures*. 2nd edition. Urbana: University of Illinois Press.

Kachru, Braj B. (1994) English in South Asia. In *The Cambridge History of the English Language, vol. 5*. Edited by Robert Burchfield. Cambridge: Cambridge University Press, pp. 497–553.

Kachru, Braj B. (1997) English as an Asian language. In *English is an Asian Language: The Philippine Context*. Edited by M. L. S. Bautista. Manila: Macquarie Library, pp. 1–23.

Kachru, Braj B. (2001) World Englishes and culture wars. In *Ariels: Departures and Returns: Essays for Edwin Thumboo*. Edited by T. C. Kiong, A. Pakir, B. K. Choon, and R. B. H. Crope. Singapore: Oxford University Press, pp. 392–414.

Kachru, Braj B. (2003) On Nativizing *Mantra*: Identity construction in Anglophone Englishes. In *Anglophone Cultures in Southeast Asia: Appropriations, Continuities, Contexts*. Edited by Rüdiger Ahrens, David Parker, Klaus Stierstorfer, and Kowk-Kan Tam. Heidelberg, Germany: Heidelberg University Press, pp. 55–72.

Kachru, Braj B. (2005) *Asian Englishes: Beyond the Canon*. Hong Kong: Hong Kong University Press.

Kachru, Yamuna (1987) Cross-cultural texts, discourse strategies, and discourse interpretation. In *Discourse Across Cultures: Strategies in World*

Englishes. Edited by Larry E. Smith. New York: Prentice-Hall, pp. 87–100.

Kachru, Yamuna (1992) Culture, style and discourse: Expanding poetics of English. In *The Other Tongue: English Across Cultures*. 2nd edition. Edited by Braj B. Kachru. Urbana: University of Illinois Press, pp. 340–52.

Kachru, Yamuna (1993) Social meaning and creativity in Indian English speech acts. In *Language, Communication and Social Meaning*. Edited by James E. Alatis. Georgetown University Round Table Languages and Linguistics, 1992. Washington, DC: Georgetown University Press, pp. 378–87.

Kachru, Yamuna (1999) Culture, context and writing. In *Culture in Second Language Teaching and Learning*. Edited by E. Hinkel. New York: Cambridge University Press, pp. 75–89.

Kachru, Yamuna (2001) Communicative styles in world Englishes. In *Ariels – Departures and Returns: Essays for Edwin Thumboo*. Edited by Tong Chee Kiong and Robbie B. H. Goh. Singapore: Oxford University Press, pp. 267–84.

Kachru, Yamuna (2003) Conventions of politeness in plural societies. In *Anglophone Cultures in South-East Asia: Appropriations, Continuities, Contexts*. Edited by Rüdiger Ahrens, David Parker, Klaus Stierstorfer, and Kowk-Kan Tam. Heidelberg, Germany: Universitätsverlag Winter Heidelberg, pp. 39–53.

Kachru, Yamuna and Nelson, Cecil L. (2006) *World Englishes in Asian Contexts*. Hong Kong: Hong Kong University Press.

Kumaravadivelu, B. (2003) A postmethod perspective on English language teaching. *World Englishes*, **22**(4), 539–50.

Mansoor, S. (2004) TEFL in Pakistan: Emerging issues. *ASIA TEFL*, **1**(1), 349–74.

McArthur, Tom (1992) *The English Languages*. New York: Cambridge University Press.

McKay, Sandra L. (2004) Teaching English as an international language: The role of culture in Asian contexts. *Asia TEFL*, **1**(1), 1–22.

Mehrotra, Raja Ram (1982) Indian English: A sociolinguistic profile. In *New Englishes*. Edited by J. B. Pride. Rowley, MA: Newbury House, pp. 150–73.

NCERT (1963) *The Teaching of English in India*. Delhi: National Council for Educational Research and Training.

Nandy, Pritish (1973) *Indian Poetry in English Today*. New Delhi: Sterling.

Narasimhaiah, C. D. (ed.) (1978) *Awakened Conscience: Studies in Commonwealth Literature*. New Delhi: Sterling.

Nihalani, Paroo, Tongue, R. K., and Hosali, P. (1979) *Indian and British English: A Handbook of Usage and Pronunciation*. Delhi: Oxford University Press.

Oka, Hideo (2001) Second language proficiency from the perspective of bilingualism. Unpublished manuscript.

Pandey, Anita (2004) Culture, gender and identity in cross-cultural personals and matrimonials. *World Englishes*, **23**(3), 403–27.

Pandit, Prabodh B. (1972) *India as a Sociolinguistic Area*. Ganeshkhind: University of Poona Press.

Pandit, Prabodh B. (1977) *Language in a Plural Society*. New Delhi: Devraj.

Pattanayak, Debi Prasana (1981) *Multilingualism and Mother-Tongue Education*. Delhi: Oxford University Press.

Pattanayak, Debi Prasanna (ed.) (1990) *Multilingualism in India*. Clevedon, UK: Multilingual Matters.

Pattanayak, Debi Prasanna (1997) *Language Curriculum for Teacher Educators*. New Delhi: NCTE.

Pennycook, Alastair (1994) *The Cultural Politics of English as an International Language*. London: Longman.

Pennycook, Alastair (2001) *Critical Applied Linguistics: A Critical Introduction*. Mahwah, NJ: Lawrence Erlbaum.

Phillipson, Robert (1992) *Linguistic Imperialism*. Oxford University Press.

Rahman, A. (1998) Perspectives on current uses of English in Bangladesh. *Journal of Institute of Modern Languages*, Issue 1997–1998, 28–35.

Rahman, Tariq (1990) *Pakistani English: The Linguistic Description of a Non-Native Variety of English*. NIPS Monograph Series III. Islamabad: National Institute of Pakistan Studies.

Rahman, Tariq (1991) *A History of Pakistani Literature in English*. Lahore: Vanguard.

Rahman, Tariq (2004) *Denizens of Alien World: A Study of Education, Inequality and Polarization in Pakistan*. Karachi: Oxford University Press.

Rao, Raja (1938/1963) *Kanthapura*. London: Allen and Unwin.

Roy, Arundhati (1997) *The God of Small Things*. New York: Harper Perennial.

Schneider, Edgar W. (ed.) (1977) *Englishes around the World*. Amsterdam: Benjamins.

Shahed, F. H. (2001) English in Bangladesh: A study of urban educated public attitudes. PhD Dissertation, Jawaharlal Nehru University, Delhi.

Skutnabb-Kangas, Tove, Phillipson, Robert, and Rannut, Mart (eds.) (1994) *Linguistic Human Rights: Overcoming Linguistic Discrimination*. New York: Mouton de Gruyter.

Smith, Larry E. (1976) English as an international auxiliary language. *RELC Journal*, **7**(2), 38–53.

Smith, Larry E. (ed.) (1983) *Readings in English as an International Language*. Oxford: Pergamon Press.

Smith, Larry E. (1987) *Discourse Across Cultures: Strategies in World Englishes*. New York: Prentice-Hall.

Spolsky, Bernard (2004) *Language Policy*. Cambridge: Cambridge University Press.

Sridhar, Kamal K. (1989) *English in Indian Bilingualism*. Delhi: Manohar.

Sridhar, Kamal K. (1991) Speech acts in an indigenised variety: Sociocultural values and language variation. In *English around the World: Sociolinguistic Perspectives*. Edited by Jenny Cheshire. Cambridge: Cambridge University Press, pp. 308–18.

Sridhar, S. N. (1982) Non-native English literatures: Context and relevance. In *The Other Tongue: English Across Cultures*. Edited by Braj B. Kachru. Urbana: University of Illinois Press, pp. 291–306.

Sridhar, S. N. (1992) The ecology of bilingual competence: Language interaction in Indigenized varieties of English. *World Englishes*, **11**(2–3), 141–50.

Sridhar, S. N. (1996) Toward a syntax of South Asian English: Defining the lectal range. In *South Asian English: Structure, Use, and Users*. Edited by Robert J. Baumgardner. Urbana: University of Illinois Press, pp. 55–69.

Srivastava, Ravindra Nath (1994) *Applied Linguistics (Studies in Language and Linguistics, vol. 4)*. Delhi: Kalinga Publications.

Verma, Shivendra K. (1973) The Systemicness of Indian English. *ITL Review of Applied Linguistics*, **22**, 1–9.

Verma, Shivendra K. (1978) Syntactic irregularities in Indian English. In *Indian Writing in English.* Edited by R. Mohan. Madras: Orient Longman, pp. 207–20.

Widdowson, Henry (1997) EIL, ESL, EFL: Global issues and local interests. *World Englishes*, **16**(3), 135–46.

FURTHER READING

Bailey, Richard W. (1991) *Images of English: A Cultural History of the Language.* Cambridge: Cambridge University Press.

Baumgardner, Robert J. (ed.) (1996) *South Asian English: Structure, Use and Users.* Urbana and Chicago: University of Illinois Press.

Brutt-Griffler, Janina (2002) *World English: A Study of its Development.* Clevedon, UK: Multilingual Matters.

Dissanayake, Wimal (1985) Towards a decolonized English: South Asian creativity in fiction. *World Englishes*, **4**(2), 233–42.

Graddol, David (1997) *The Future of English?* London: The British Council.

Kachru, Braj B. (1995) Transcultural creativity in world Englishes and literary canons. In *Principles and Practice in Applied Linguistics: Studies in Honor of H. G. Widdowson.* Edited by Guy Cook and Barbara Seidlhofer. Oxford: Oxford University Press, pp. 271–87.

Mehrotra, Arvind Krishna (ed.) (2003) *An Illustrated History of Indian Literature in English.* Delhi: Permanent Black.

Trudgill, Peter and Hannah, Jean (1994) *International English: A Guide to the Varieties of Standard English.* London: Edward Arnold.

7 East Asian Englishes

NOBUYUKI HONNA

1 Introduction

The English language situation in East Asia is being strengthened with a dramatic increase in the number of students learning the language in the whole region. While China witnesses 300 million people toiling at English lessons, Japan has officially activated an English-speaking Japanese development project. Korea and Taiwan are conspicuously committed to strengthening their primary-school English language teaching (ELT) programs. In other parts of Asia where English serves as a language of intranational communication and where ELT spreads and succeeds, national varieties are bound to emerge. Although English is designated as an international (not intranational) language in East Asia, indications are that what amounts to a national variety is developing in each country in this region, too. One cause of this phenomenon can be attributed to the communicative approaches adopted in ELT programs region-wide. Those approaches are meant to put more value on mutual understanding than on simple mimicry and rigid pattern practice. Increased exposure to English-using environments is also expected to make learners aware of varieties, thereby helping them to recognize that they can use English effectively without speaking like a native speaker. This chapter presents a brief description of the current English language situation and ELT innovations while referring to some structural and pragmatic features often noticed in English in East Asia.

2 China

The first contact between English speakers and Chinese on the Chinese mainland occurred in 1637 when four British ships arrived in Macau and Canton on an expeditionary mission. A century later, "Chinese Pidgin English" (which was then called *broken English, jargon, mixed dialect,* or *Canton English*) developed as a lingua franca between natives and foreigners on the coast of South China (Bolton, 2002a: 184–5; see also Bolton, 2002b).

The growth and diffusion of Chinese Pidgin English was enhanced by its extensive usability, advantage of which was taken by Chinese merchants and foreign traders bilaterally. The ban hammered out by the Chinese government on the communication between foreigners and Chinese inhabitants made it extremely difficult for both parties to learn the counterpart's language formally. Those natives who dared to teach the "language of the central flowery nation" to outside "barbarians" were denounced as traitors (Bolton, 2002a: 185). After the first Anglo-Chinese War of 1839–42, Chinese Pidgin English spread to other open port cities including Shanghai, making it an indispensable lingua franca between natives and foreigners and even among Chinese (e.g., compradors) themselves when they spoke different provincial dialects.

After 225 years of international contact, the Treaty of Tientsin of 1862 opened many other places (including inland enclaves) to Western interests of various sorts. Throughout the country, missionaries from the West established schools, where either English was formally taught either as an important subject or adopted as a medium of instruction. By the early twentieth century, there actually developed a social stratification of Chinese English in the continuum of educated and pidgin varieties. The writings by Lin Yutang (1895–1976) and John Wu (1899–1986) represented prominent examples of educated English in China. The missionary influence continued up to the Republican era, subsequent to the overthrow of the Qing dynasty in 1911.

The establishment of the People's Republic of China (PRC) in 1949 brought forth a chain of drastic changes in many domains of life. English disappeared from the school curriculum and Russian became the main foreign language since the new government turned to the USSR for help in its nation-building project (Hu, 2001). After the collapse of the Cultural Revolution (1966–76), English recovered its importance and popularity as the country shifted to modernization and economic development.

2.1   The current English language situation and educational responses

When a Japanese group of college Chinese teachers visited several campuses in major cities to talk with students in Chinese, Chinese students surprised Japanese visitors by greeting them in English. The leader of the Japanese group had to say in English first: "We are Chinese teachers from Japan. Please speak Chinese to us." For many students now, English is recognized as an indispensable language for international exchange and better-paid employment.

A primary school English textbook adopted in Tientsin starts with this preface: "English is usually used at international settings, and it is also a tool to grasp advanced scientific and technological information. In accordance with our country's reform and open-door policies, it is essential that we learn English properly" (Honna, 2000: 104). Thus, the government put a renewed emphasis on English language teaching. While it is introduced at grade 3 in most major cities, English is a very important subject at all levels of formal education. TV and radio stations popularize ELT programs across the country.

The national College English Test (CET) promotes English language learning at the tertiary level. The certificate of CET Band 4/6 has attained such a high social value that a majority of universities adopt the policy of "no CET 4/6 certificate, no graduation diploma," with the result that 6 million students take the tests annually. The China Public English Test System (PETS) also attracts a huge number of learners as more and more business and other organizations use its certificate as an official measure of English language proficiency (Pang, Zhou, and Fu, 2002: 202–3).

2.2   *China English*

At the turn of the twenty-first century, structural and functional studies of Chinese patterns of English blossomed. In those studies (such as Bolton, 2002b, 2003), extensive attempts were made to explore Chinese characteristics of English in the domains of phonology, lexicon, syntax, semantics, pragmatics, and communication styles. The discoveries in these endeavors seem to suggest that Chinese varieties of English are developing. Due to limited space, only a few topics are discussed below.

English language specialists in China tend to refer to local features of English as China English instead of Chinese English (or even Sinicized English) since they claim that the latter characterization sounds derogatory to them, associated with Chinese Pidgin English or Chinglish. To them, China English is an educated variety of English that Chinese speakers of the language are expected to employ at international encounters, expressing their own cultural norms, behavioral patterns, and value systems (Jiang, 2002).

Particularly important is the domain of lexicon. Beside an increasing flood of Chinese words into English in China (such as "guanxi" for relationship or connection), many English phrases have been coined to refer to Chinese ways and experiences of life. Traditional ones include: "Four Books," "Five Classics," "barefoot doctor," "people's commune," "great leap forward," "paper tiger," "ideological remodeling," "reeducation," "reform through physical labor," "red guard," "red rice," "capitalist roader." More recent types are: "one country, two systems," "to replace cadres with new cadres," "the higher authorities have policies and the localities have their countermeasures," "planned commodity economy," "enterprise contracted production system," "vegetable basket project," "safety first and prevention first," "outstanding deeds and advanced persons," "iron bowl of rice," "four modernizations," "one-family-one-child policy," "family contracted responsibility system." *China Daily, Shanghai Daily,* or the *Beijing Today* weekly are full of these expressions.

Since a person's "face" is an enormously important concept related to his/her honor, respect, pride, and identity in China (and most of the oriental world), "face" collocations abound in addition to the ubiquitous "saving/

losing face." Jia (2004) discusses aspects of Chinese "practice of face" and "face negotiation," employing such Chinese-English specific phraseologies as "maintain (strive for) some amount of face," "hold up the Chinese face to the world," "she hasn't showed us the least amount of face," "you shouldn't have given her so much face," "you are simply losing my face," "a Chinese way of giving face to somebody," "have no face (left)," "love (desire) for face," "faceless," "give (grant) me some face," "reject (refuse) face," "rather die to save face," "take my face into consideration," "your face is bigger than mine," "there is no faceless communication," "hierarchical face," "group face," "care for the other's face," etc.

China English accommodates Chinese-based pragmatics. Thus, "I'm not that good. You've overpraised me" is the response to a compliment heard more frequently than "Thank you." Adopting American/British address forms is not a simple matter. "Having been exposed to both Chinese and Western norms," Hong Kong linguist David Li explains, "I often have to undergo a mental struggle in the intercultural workplace before settling on a particular choice . . . I constantly feel that following one set of norms entails violating another" (Li, 2002: 581).

In terms of discourse, the "frame-main" order prevails – in making a request, its reason is stated earlier than its content (Kirkpatrick and Xu, 2002). A similar trend is observed by Jia and Cheng (2002), who characterize Chinese discourse organization as "indirect and inductive" in accordance with the traditional "qi-cheng-zhuan-he" model of rhetorical structuring. For details and ramifications see also Scollon (1991), Scollon, Wong, and Kirkpatrick (2000) and Hu (1999).

These differences can occasionally cause a serious international and intercultural communication problem. Honna, Kirkpatrick, and Gilbert (2001: 16–17) cite a case that was eye-witnessed in Hong Kong prior to its return to China:

> Several years ago, when Hong Kong was still a colony of Britain, I [Kirkpatrick] was sitting in the office of a superintendent of the Hong Kong Police Force. The superintendent was English. In those colonial days, almost all the police officers were expatriates and the sergeants and constables were all locals. I was there because I worked for a company who had been asked to explain the communication problems that were common in the police force at that time.
>
> There was a quiet knock at the door and in came a young Chinese police constable . . .
>
> "Yes?", enquired the superintendent.
>
> "My mother is not very well, sir," started the constable.
>
> "Yes?", repeated the superintendent, a frown appearing on his brow.
>
> "She has to go into hospital, sir," continued the constable.
>
> "So?"
>
> "On Thursday, sir."
>
> The superintendent's frown was replaced by a look of exasperation. "What is it that you want?", he asked sternly.

At this direct question, the constable's face fell and he simply mumbled, "Nothing, sir. It's all right," and turned and left the room.

As soon as the door had closed the superintendent turned to me and said: "You see. A classic case. They can't get to the point."

"So, what would you want him to say?", I asked.

"Well, instead of beating around the bush, he should come straight to the point. He obviously wants some leave so he can look after his mother. He should ask for leave and not waste my time going on about his poor mother."

"You want him to say something like, 'Can I have some leave please, sir?'"

"Yes, exactly," replied the superintendent.

Traditionally, non-native speakers were expected to conform to native speakers' norms of linguistic behavior, because English was broadly considered as an American or a British language. In view of world Englishes, however, these assumptions are increasingly questioned. If English is a multicultural language, it has to be used as such. Honna (2004) argues that restrictive conformism does not meet the requirements of English across cultures and new ways of diversity management should be based on intercultural literacy to be nurtured in language awareness education.

3   Japan

The English language was first introduced into Japan in March, 1600. It was when William Adams, the English pilot of a Dutch ship, reached the western part of the country after a shipwreck. Later renamed as Miura Anjin in the Japanese fashion, he soon acquired Shogun Tokugawa Ieyasu's personal trust and worked as an intermediary between the Japanese ruler and Great Britain's King James I, delivering translated messages back and forth across the seas (Sugimoto, 1999).

However, English did not become a language to be learned by Japanese officials and intellectuals for a long time. Japan allowed foreign relations only with the Dutch as part of its national insulation policy proclaimed in 1635 and upheld until the collapse of the shogunate. In fact, when the shogunate awoke to the deterioration of Dutch influence in world affairs and understood the importance of English as a language for obtaining international information in the early nineteenth century, it was a Dutch trade officer called Jan Cock Bloomhoff (1779–1853) who first taught English language lessons to Japanese samurai and other intellectuals in charge of translation in 1809, using Dutch textbooks and Dutch and Japanese as the languages of instruction (Mozumi, 1989: 89–92).

At the time of Meiji Restoration (1868), Japan's new enlightened leaders came to realize that English would be essential for the country's modernization and development. The Government soon established a national educational system in 1872 and introduced English language teaching in five-year secondary schools, often even in six-year primary schools, in major cities. At the initial stages, reprints of English textbooks brought from the United States and the United Kingdom were used in the teaching of mathematics, physics, chemistry, world geography, world history, or ethics in newly instituted secondary schools. At its dawning period, the Tokyo Imperial University had to employ foreign professors invited from America, Britain, Germany, or France, who offered their lectures in their languages. As depicted in Tsubouchi Shoyo's naturalistic and descriptive novel *The Student Character of the Present Time* (1885–6), there even emerged indications of Japanese and English bilingualism among university students (Ono, 2000). These trends soon subsided as Japanese professors replaced foreign counterparts and English teaching conceded to grammar and translation methods before the close of the Meiji era (1912).

English language teaching was reinvigorated as peace was restored after the end of World War II in 1945. Two years later, the government set up six-year primary school and three-year junior high school education as compulsory, with English introduced nationally as a subject from the first year of the secondary curriculum to continue into the three-year senior high school and then to college. Although it was officially designated as an elective course, almost all schools offered it as a required subject, with English emphasized as an indispensable key to the international community. This approach to ELT continued into the twenty-first century with substantial changes.

3.1   English in Japanese society

Since Japan opened its door to foreign countries, English has always been a very important social issue in Japan. Beside ELT improvements, three prominent issues now include a torrential influx of English words into the Japanese language, arguments for English as a second official language, and corporate responses to English as an international language.

3.1.1   English in Japanese

Perhaps the most remarkable influence which the English language has exerted in Japan is its lexical influx into Japanese (Stanlaw, 2004). Many Japanese consider English "loan words" in Japanese as one of the most important, serious, and grave problems confronting the Japanese language today. The reason is simply that people believe that the influx of a tremendous amount of foreign words into Japanese is an intrusion and will eventually lead to the confusion, corruption, and decay of their national language.

Commentators normally blame those Japanese who resort to "inconsiderate" use of foreign words in a situation where "beautiful, authentic" Japanese ones are available. Letters to the editor's pages of major national newspapers are constantly filled with complaints filed by readers about "excessive use of undecipherable, unnecessary, undesirable, and misleading words" borrowed from English.

In 2003, the National Institute for Japanese Language came up with Japanese substitutes for over a hundred English expressions used in Japanese contexts in an effort to decrease the "thoughtless" dependence on foreign words. The list includes "outsourcing," "action program," "access," "agenda," "assessment," "analyst," and "amenity," to mention just some of the items selected for Japanese translation. Yet, many of the proposed Japanese substitutes may not necessarily work.

There seem to be two major reasons for the difficulties. First, foreign words involve new concepts that are not easy to express in Japanese. Second, foreign words are very often used as euphemisms in Japan; their Japanese renditions would kill the effect and become useless. "Hello Work" (formerly called Public Employment Stabilization Office) and "green car" (Japan Railway's First Class passenger cargo) are cases in point.

These reasons indicate that Japanese people actually need these foreign words for the smooth working of their present-day society. To make sense of the situation, Honna (1995) attempts a systematic analysis of the issues involved in English in Japanese, looking at (1) the Japanization patterns, (2) the role which borrowing plays in modern Japanese society, and (3) the sociolinguistic forces that stimulate the influx of English into Japanese. Oshima (2003) examines the contact process in terms of pidginization and creolization, while Moody and Matsumoto (2003) analyze creative aspects in the use of English in Japanese in terms of "code ambiguation."

3.1.2   Proposal for English as a second official language

Another interesting development is the controversy over a proposal to make English a second official language in Japan, a topic that attracted wide public attention in January 2000. The proposal was included in "The Frontier Within: Individual Empowerment and Better Governance in the New Millennium," a report published by an advisory panel to Prime Minister Keizo Obuchi (Honna and Takeshita, 2003).

The idea of a bilingual policy did not originate with the release of this report. Much earlier, Arinori Mori (1847–89), a prominent statesman, diplomat, and proponent of Western thought and social practices, proposed the abandonment of the Japanese language for English. Yukichi Fukuzawa (1835–1901), an educator, writer, and propagator of Western knowledge, who founded Keio Gijuku (now Keio University), wanted English spread all over Japan. The debate about the use of English, therefore, is not new.

The latest proposal did not make any headway due to the fact that it was simply flown as a trial balloon and it did not show any concrete action programs. Looking back at the proposal now, we may wonder if it is really necessary to have a law that declares English as a second official language in the country. Japanese people and organizations now are becoming more aware than before of the reality of the importance of English as a language of international information, communication, and cooperation.

In some companies, English is already used as a de facto in-house language. In many others, English proficiency, often represented by TOEIC scores, is required as a condition for promotion. For a larger number of Japanese to acquire a working command of English for their own specific purposes, it seems to be much more productive to try to improve ELT programs from a long-range point of view than to plan legal intervention in the use of English in Japanese society. Actually, the proposal caused a great number of repercussions in the nation's renewed efforts for ELT (see 3.2).

3.1.3 Corporate responses to English as an international language

One of the reasons Japanese use to explain their lack of English proficiency is that English is not much needed in Japanese society. Actually, however, in this age of information and communication, Japanese naturally have more actual, immediate, and potential needs for English use in their country than they apparently realize. Internet communication is a good example.

Japan is often referred to as an inscrutable nation. This reputation obviously is caused by the lack of information sent out overseas from Japan. While much is disseminated in Japanese for domestic consumption, little is prepared in English for international audiences. Those abroad who attempt access to English-language websites created by the Japanese government and corporate organizations have often been largely disappointed at not finding what they wished to obtain. Furthermore, overseas observers sometimes find English websites here unrenewed or indecipherable. In reality, those organizations that do not pay careful attention to their English-language websites are most likely to be interpreted as not interested in international perspectives. Marshall McLuhan's axiom that the medium is the message has never been truer than in Japan today.

In view of all this, Honna (2003) suggests that government and business organizations ought to develop concrete and feasible language policies and programs. If their activities attract international interest, they should be asked to distribute information in English as a global language. A working command of English utilized by employees is a great asset of any business firm and public office. Effective in-house training programs will contribute to increased credibility and therefore better evaluation of an organization.

3.2 MEXT initiatives for improved ELT

Although Japan's "English conversation" education industry is said to be worth 2 trillion yen (close to 20 billion US dollars), which is as strong as the country's publication business, Japanese are notorious for their "national" failure to acquire a working command of English. However, in an attempt to meet the increasing trends of globalization and international interdependency in the global village, the Ministry of Education, Culture, Sports, Science and

Technology (MEXT) made public in 2003 an action plan to cultivate "Japanese with English abilities."

The plan calls for the establishment, by the year 2008, of a system to carry out various programs to better Japan's ELT. The Ministry has strongly appealed to the public, local governments, and business and industrial communities for all-out support and cooperation in its initiatives for improved ELT. Starting from 2008, according to the plan, English classes will be mostly conducted in English and teachers will acquire English skills (TOEIC 730) to be able to use the language in the classroom, while 10,000 high school students will study overseas every year and a sizable number of teachers will be sent abroad for advanced ELT training.

The current aim of Japan's ELT in public education is to develop a working command of this global language and nurture international awareness on the part of the students. That is why ELT is often considered as part of a larger endeavor of international awareness education. Theoretically, ELT for this goal is composed of three important elements: (1) understanding other cultures, (2) explaining our own culture, and (3) teaching English as an international language.

Unfortunately, Japan's ELT is inclined to put too much emphasis on reading about foreign cultures, mostly those of the USA and the UK. With a clear understanding of English as an international language for wider communication, it has now become obvious that an end should be put to this practice and a new track be prepared. An increasing number of teachers of English are aware that Japanese people need this additional language to talk about themselves with people from abroad, to explain Japanese customs, and to express their opinions on international occasions. Actually, a change is in sight. New high-school textbooks introduced in 2002 contain more Japanese topics. Emphasis on expressive and explanatory communication skills in ELT has worldwide implications. When Japanese and Vietnamese meet, Japanese will be interested in Vietnam and Vietnamese in Japan. If English is a language for information, we will have to be prepared to give our information in English.

3.3   *Japanese English creativity*

Teachers and students in Japan invariably characterize Japanese English as full of errors, and this evaluation seems to be a common denominator among many corrective books (Petersen, 1988, 1990, for example). Actually, as represented by Takefuta (1982) and Suenobu (2002), most "scientific" studies of Japanese English attempt to discover how deviant Japanese patterns are from American or British standards. When statistically examined, however, utterances that Japanese users of English produce tend to contain fewer grammatical mistakes than widely believed. In a quantitative study of sentences collected from English-language websites created for personal purposes, Miyake (2000) found that the rate of misuse of articles was 4.47 percent, while that of tenses was 2 percent, and those of word order and subject-predicate agreement only 1 percent.

Granted that phonological and syntactic analyses are as important as ever, interesting revelations can emerge from sociocultural approaches as well. Japanese speakers of English are definitely inclined to say "We went to Kyoto by car yesterday" instead of "We drove to Kyoto yesterday," an expression preferred by Americans (Smith, 2003: 92–3). Those Japanese inclinations can be explained by Japanese ways of life. When a friend fails to turn up at a designated place and time for an appointment, a Japanese would say, "I went there. Why didn't you come?" while an American would say, "I was there. Where were you?", a reflection of epistemological differences. Speaking Japanese in English in terms of human relations, Japanese often greet their international acquaintances with, "Oh, I haven't seen you for a long time. Are you OK? You haven't changed. I wanted to see you," instead of "Hi, how are you?" The traditional Japanese rhetorical order of "background-topic-focus" is retained in the English advertisement copy of a sake brand: "The final choice of natural taste/THE REFINED JAPANESE SAKE/ASAHIRAKI."

Japanese English is a set of patterns Japanese speakers of English tend to produce after years of classroom exercise (Honna and Takeshita, 1998); it covers a wide range of proficiency levels and performance varieties. Since non-native speakers commonly look for and settle upon patterns they find easy to handle both structurally and functionally, it will be interesting to identify them descriptively. Although much has been done in the field of phonetics (Takefuta, 1982), little is known about syntactic and semantic inclinations.

A metaphorical explanation may be useful, since it could explain the legitimacy of phrases and expressions, instead of just labeling them ungrammatical and unacceptable. Thus, *This restaurant is delicious* (a sentence Japanese speakers of English often utter) is well understood and generally accepted if the metonomical relation of "restaurant" and "the food served there" is taken into consideration. Actually, the analogy is obvious, given the ubiquity of "he is sharp." Similarly, *Don't put your face* (= head) *out of the window* (a plea a train conductor might make) is simply a case of Japanese localism comparable to "get your butt over here" (an American English order), which is well-formed.

Some of the English-based Japanese coinages can be used as Japanese-originated English. Actually, *walkman*, *karaoke*, *play station*, *case-by-case*, or *forward-looking* have already been received internationally, while *nighter* (bargain), *washlet*, *hot carpet*, or *paper driver* may have a good chance of adoption if appropriately introduced. The use of *my-* as a prefix may have a rough time winning international approval but will be considered a Japanese neologism if resorted to by a sizable number of speakers: "I have two *my-cars*; Did you come here in *my-car*?" The use of *-up/-down* as a suffix could be looked at with more sympathy: "I am on the *image-up* committee of the company; I have a cash flow problem with an *income-down* this year."

4   Korea (Republic of Korea)

In Korea's 120-year history of English language teaching, the 1990s saw enormous changes in all aspects of this endeavor. In 1997, English was formally introduced in primary schools (from 3rd grade up) as a regular and obligatory subject, thereby establishing seamless ELT programs through secondary to tertiary education with a remarkable emphasis on communicative and practical proficiency.

At the same time, some improvements were witnessed in college-level ELT, intended to produce college students who can communicate in English. One such innovation was observed in the English section of the new national College Scholastic Ability Test (CSAT), which all Korean high school graduates are required to take if they wish to go to university. While the similar test of English previously focused on phonological, lexical, and grammatical knowledge, the new examination (first administered in 1993) had the following characteristics: (1) emphasis on communicative competence, (2) introduction of a listening comprehension test, (3) emphasis on fluency over accuracy, (4) emphasis on reading comprehension, and (5) no paper-and-pencil test of pronunciation or spelling (Kwon, 2000: 67–8).

In a larger sense, English became a topic of public debate in 1999, when a Korean industrial association called on the government for the immediate designation of English as the nation's second "public" language. In a forum sponsored by the Korea Center for Free Enterprise on November 2, industrial, political, and intellectual leaders declared unanimously: "When Korean people master English, it will boost Korea's national competitiveness greatly." In explicit support for this drive, some companies were trying to establish English as "the language of all in-house communications" (Yoo, 1999). Actually, since the economic crisis of 1997 in Korea, public awareness of the importance of English has apparently been widened. Concomitantly, contemporary young people, particularly those in business and other professional sections of the society, display stronger readiness than before to use English whenever an opportunity arises.

4.1   English in Korea

The augmented use of English in Korea exerted strong influence on Korean, as is well illustrated by Baik (1994), Lee (1989), and Shim (1994). It also gave rise to Konglish, a coinage that refers to patterns of English Korean students tend to employ. For example, a monthly textbook to go with EBS's *Morning Special* radio program made for ELT carries a section called "MS Konglish Dictionary." Although examples are treated as something to be corrected, they are not presented in a derogatory manner. They cast a reflection of how Korean users are struggling with English in their linguistic and cultural contexts.

Among those on the list in the 2000 June issue (86–7) are: (1) The weather in here is very cold. (2) Isn't he the man who married with my daughter?

(3) I have never studied English nor French. (4) Neither of students are coming. (5) The surgeon who operated the King released new details of his injuries. (6) James and I often have a drink together and quarrel about modern art. (7) Television can be a media for giving information and opinions. (8) Nobody have complained about the noise. (9) She got the job owing to she was the best candidate. (10) I recommend you a walk along the park.

While the employment of a sentence after a preposition in (9) can be regarded as a case of grammatical failure, "quarreling" denoting arguing in (6) may be reflection of Korean semantics. Definitely, most of the other phenomena may be noticed in mother-tongue-influenced basilectal and mesolectal varieties of some Outer- and Expanding-Circle countries. While they are the culminations of cross-linguistic contact and accommodation, it is interesting that they characteristically do not cause communication problems.

4.2 Corpus-based studies of Korean English

An exploratory but nonetheless important work on Korean English is reported in Jung and Min (1999), where analyses are made of the usages of English modals and prepositions based on a corpus of sampled texts from *The Korean Herald*, which is the most widely read English-language newspaper in Korea.

One of the prominent findings in Jung and Min (1999) indicates that *will* and *would* are the most common modals in their data, whereas *shall* (meaning volition and prediction) and *should* (used as a first-person variant of hypothetical epistemic *would*) are found to be almost obsolescent in this English-language newspaper in Korea. Another discovery is that since the Korean language does not have the distinction between *at* and *in* made in English in terms of dimension-type, size, and semantic difference, the grammatical knowledge of Korean may have permeated into the following sentence found in the esteemed newspaper: "The writer is a visiting professor in (instead of at) Korea University" (Jung and Min, 1999: 34–5). A larger-scale corpus study will likely further reveal how English is transplanted in Korean soil.

It is encouraging that Korean-authored articles are used as samples of Korean English in Korea. In Japanese English-language journalism, articles written by Japanese are usually examined and finalized by copy-editors for whom English is a native language. In the same vein, many academic journals prescribe that authors wishing to publish in English should have their articles checked and corrected by native speakers before submission, thus making explicit the presupposition that Japanese English is incorrect.

5 Taiwan (Republic of China)

Maezawa, Honna, and Tan (1990) was a first introduction to English in Taiwan, which depicted its phonological, lexical, syntactic, semantic, pragmatic, and sociolinguistic features. Referring to Chinese linguistic codes, they attempted to explain where such patterns came from: "Please wait until I write this letter well" (meaning 'I'm finished with this letter'); "Now is three o'clock"; "Though I got up early, [zero] was late for school"; "I met the professor [zero] wrote this book"; "Because he was busy, so he didn't come"; "Have you eaten yet?" (as a greeting), etc. A more recent contribution, Chen (2003), explores a wider range of issues extensively. One of her research topics involves comparison of request forms between Taiwanese and American speakers of English. "Since most people in non-native English-speaking countries take English used by native speakers as their learning model and speaking an English close to theirs is regarded as 'good' or 'standard' English in those non-native English-speaking countries (e.g. in Singapore)," she concludes, "Taiwanese or any other English learners certainly can benefit greatly from gaining information on how to interpret and respond to native English speakers appropriately" (p. 154).

5.1   English as a "second semi-official" language

English has been a big issue in Taiwan since President Chen Sui-bian expressed his interest in making English the nation's second official language, highlighting its importance in the light of globalization in 2002. In a well-coordinated move, Premier Yu Shyi-kun promised to make English a "second semi-official" language over a period of six years, while the Minister of Education Huang Jung-tsuen declared he would chair a task force to map out strategic plans (Ko and Yeh, 2002). Different from the similar projects proposed in Japan and Korea, the Taiwan version had government backing from the start. It remains to be seen how the official commitment will be carried out.

   If the policy is ever to be implemented, several problems are to be resolved. For one thing, as Shih (2002) states, it is not clear what a "second semi-official" language means. How widely is English supposed to be used? Do all public servants and government officials need to speak English? Are Taiwanese expected to speak English among themselves on certain occasions? There will have to be a clear-cut definition of the social role to be played by the language. For Shih (2002), another fear is the possibility that the policy might create a two-tier society characterized by the "English divide." "We now see many parents spending a lot of money for their preschool children to learn English," she ponders, "but for those children, whose parents cannot afford to do the same, they will find themselves in the 'inferior' position their first day in school."

6   Conclusion

As trade and cultural relations between the countries in the region grow, the reliance on English for intercultural communication is likely to increase. Asian varieties of English are here to stay, and the claim that *English is an Asian Language* (e.g., Bautista, 1997) may some day apply to East Asia as it does to South and Southeast Asia now.

See also Chapters 4, ENGLISH IN NORTH AMERICA; 15, WORLD ENGLISHES TODAY; 17, VARIETIES OF WORLD ENGLISHES; 33, WORLD ENGLISHES IN GLOBAL ADVERTISING; 34, WORLD ENGLISHES AND GLOBAL COMMERCE; 36, TEACHING WORLD ENGLISHES.

REFERENCES

Baik, Martin Jonghak (1994) Syntactic features of Englishization in Korean. *World Englishes*, **13**(2), 155–66.

Bautista, Ma. Lourdes S. (ed.) (1997) *English Is an Asian Language: The Philippine Context*. Sydney: Macquarie Library.

Bolton, Kingsley (2002a) Chinese Englishes: From Canton jargon to global English. *World Englishes*, **21**(2), 181–99.

Bolton, Kingsley (ed.) (2002b) *Hong Kong English: Autonomy and Creativity*. Hong Kong: Hong Kong University Press.

Bolton, Kingsley (2003) *Chinese Englishes: A Sociolinguistic History*. Cambridge: Cambridge University Press.

Chen, Su-chiao (2003) *The Spread of English in Taiwan*. Taipei: Crane Publishing Co.

Honna, Nobuyuki (1995) English in Japanese society: Language within language. *Journal of Multilingual and Multicultural Development*, **16**(1&2), 45–62.

Honna, Nobuyuki (2000) *Ajiawo Tsunagu Eigo* [English Unites Asia]. Tokyo: ALC Press.

Honna, Nobuyuki (2003) English as a Japanese language for international communication. Lecture given in the web-based lecture series in International Communication, Graduate Department of International Communication, Aoyama Gakuin University.

Honna, Nobuyuki (2004) English as a multicultural language in Asia and intercultural literacy. *Southern Review*, **18**, 1–16.

Honna, Nobuyuki and Takeshita, Yuko (1998) On Japan's propensity for native speaker English: A change in sight. *Asian Englishes*, **1**(1), 117–37.

Honna, Nobuyuki and Takeshita, Yuko (2003) English education in Japan today: The impact of changing policies. In *English Language Teaching in East Asia Today*. Edited by Wah Kam Ho and Ruth Wong. Singapore: Eastern Universities Press, pp. 183–211.

Honna, Nobuyuki, Kirkpatrick, Andy, and Gilbert, Sue (2001) *English across Cultures*. Tokyo: Sanshusha.

Hu, Wenzhong (1999) *Aspects of Intercultural Communication*. Beijing: Foreign Language Teaching and Research Press.

Hu, Wenzhong (2001) A matter of balance: Reflections on China's language policy in education. *Asian Englishes*, **4**(1), 66–79.

Jia, Yuxin (2004) Chinese concept of face and face negotiation involved in conflict resolution. Lecture given in the web-based lecture series in International Communication, Graduate Department of International Communication, Aoyama Gakuin University.

Jia, Yuxin and Cheng, Cheng (2002) Indirectness in Chinese English writing. *Asian Englishes*, **5**(1), 64–74.

Jiang, Yajun (2002) China English: Issues, studies and features. *Asian Englishes*, **5**(2), 4–23.

Jung, Kyutae and Min, Su Jung (1999) Some lexico-grammatical features of Korean English newspapers. *World Englishes*, **18**(2), 23–37.

Kirkpatrick, Andy and Xu, Zhichang (2002) Chinese pragmatic norms and "China English." *World Englishes*, **21**(2), 269–79.

Ko, Shu-ling and Yeh, Lindy (2002) English to be made official. *Taipei Times* (Taiwan), 1 May.

Kwon, Oryang (2000) Korea's English education policy changes in the 1990s: Innovations to gear the nation for the 21st century. *English Teaching*, **55**(1), 47–91.

Lee, Sang-sup (1989) The subversion of Korean: An account of the curious impact of the study of English on the use of Korean. *English Today*, **20**, 34–7.

Li, David C. S. (ed.) (2002) *Discourses in Search of Members: In Honor of Ron Scollon*. Lanham, MD: University Press of America.

Maezawa, Kimie, Honna, Nobuyuki, and Tan, Teichi (1990) English in Taiwan. In *Ajia no Eigo* [Varieties of English in Asia]. Edited by Nobuyuki Honna. Tokyo: Kuroshio Shuppan, pp. 43–67.

Miyake, Hiroko (ed.) (2000) *Nihon Eigo-no Suryouteki Bunseki* [A Quantitative Analysis of Japanese English]. Tokyo: Aoyama Gakuin University.

Moody, Andrew and Matsumoto, Yuko (2003) Don't touch my moustache: Language blending and code ambiguation by two J-Pop artists. *Asian Englishes*, **6**(1), 4–33.

Mozumi, Jitsuo (1989) *Yogo Kyojuhoshi Kenkyu* [A historical study of European language teaching]. Tokyo: Gakubunsha.

Ono, Reiko (2000) The use of English in the Japanese novel *Tosei Shosei Katagi*: The influence of English on Japanese in the late 19th century. *Asian Englishes*, **2**(2), 59–86.

Oshima, Kimie (2003) Gairaigo Usage in Japan: From cultural controversy to a new analytical framework. PhD dissertation, University of Michigan at Ann Arbor.

Pang, Jixian, Zhou, Xing, and Fu, Zheng (2002) English for international trade: China enters the WTO. *World Englishes*, **21**(2), 201–16.

Petersen, Mark (1988) *Nihonjinno Eigo* [Japanese English]. Tokyo: Iwanami Shoten.

Petersen, Mark (1990) *Zoku Nihonjinno Eigo* [Japanese English Revisited]. Tokyo: Iwanami Shoten.

Scollon, Ron (1991) *Eight Legs and Other Elbow: Stance and Structures in Chinese English Compositions*. Banff: International Reading Association.

Scollon, Ron, Wong, Suzanne, and Kirkpatrick, Andy (2000) *Contrastive Discourse in Chinese and English: A Critical Appraisal*. Beijing: Foreign Language Teaching and Research Press.

Shih, Yu-hwei (2002) Improving nation's English skills no easy task. *Taipei Times* (Taiwan), 27 May.

Shim, Rosa Jinyoung (1994) Englishized Korean: Structure, status, and attitudes. *World Englishes*, **13**(2), 225–43.

Smith, Donald (2003) Confessions of a native speaker. *Asian Englishes*, **6**(1), 92–6.

Stanlaw, James (2004) *Japanese English: Language and Culture Contact*. Hong Kong: Hong Kong University Press.

Suenobu, Mineo (2002) *Errorology in English*. Kobe: Yugetsu Shobo.

Sugimoto, Tsutomu (1999) *Nihon Eigo Bunkashi Kenkyu* [A historical study of Japan's English language culture]. Tokyo: Yasaka Shobo.

Takefuta, Yukio (1982) *Nihonjin Eigo-no Kagaku* [The Science of Japanese English]. Tokyo: Kenkyusha.

Yoo, Cheong-mo (1999) Will English as public language boost growth? *The Korea Herald* (Korea), 3 November.

FURTHER READING

Bolton, Kingsley (ed.) (2002b) *Hong Kong English: Autonomy and Creativity.* Hong Kong: Hong Kong University Press.

Bolton, Kingsley (2003) *Chinese Englishes: A Sociolinguistic History.* Cambridge: Cambridge University Press.

Honna, Nobuyuki (2004) English as a multicultural language in Asia and intercultural literacy. *Southern Review*, **18**, 1–16.

Kachru, Braj B. (2005) *Asian Englishes: Beyond the Canon.* Hong Kong: Hong Kong University Press.

Stanlaw, James (2004) *Japanese English: Language and Culture Contact.* Hong Kong: Hong Kong University Press.

8　Southeast Asian Englishes

MARIA LOURDES S. BAUTISTA AND ANDREW B. GONZALEZ

1　Introduction

This chapter describes the current state of new Englishes in countries of Southeast Asia where English is used as a second language, namely, Singapore, Malaysia, and the Philippines (Kachru's Outer Circle) and countries where English is a foreign language, namely, Thailand, Vietnam, and Indonesia (Kachru's Expanding Circle). For the Outer-Circle countries, the description will consist of a sketch of its structure (phonology, lexicon, syntax, and discourse) and the subvarieties within the language; for the Expanding-Circle countries, a few notes will be given on the present status of English as a subject of instruction. The chapter ends with a summary and some theoretical considerations which may pave the way for further research.

2　The Historical and Socio-Political Aspects of English in Southeast Asia

The new Englishes in Southeast Asia emerged from their respective colonial histories. They may, therefore, be collectively referred to as post-imperial Englishes (Fishman et al., 1996). Penang, Malacca, and Singapore constituted the Straits Settlements and were used as trading centers of the British Empire's East India Company. Eventually Singapore fell totally under the British Empire, while the different Malay kingdoms maintained their traditional royal families under the influence of the British Empire. The Straits Settlements became independent from Britain in 1957 and formed the Federation of Malaya. For Singapore, the Federation did not prove advantageous and it seceded from the Federation in 1965 and constituted itself into a city-state. The Federation of Malaya is now Malaysia and has a constitutional monarch with a Prime Minister and a Parliament.

For some time even after independence, until school language policy was changed, ethnic schools for the Chinese, Tamils, and Malays were state-supported in Singapore and Malaysia, where primary education was taught in the ethnic language and English taught as a second language. In secondary school and university, English-taught education became the prevailing mode; Malay, Tamil, and Chinese at the secondary level became marginal, while higher education was totally in English.

Although Singapore recognizes Malay as an official language or symbolic language of identity through its Malay anthem, the dominant language in education and business is English. As the language of education, English has definitely taken over at all levels, with the use of Mandarin, Malay, and Tamil limited to the elementary level. Secondary and tertiary education is in English in Singapore's bid to be a hub of academic excellence in research and in becoming a leader in the region as a knowledge society. English is now acquired as a first language by many Singaporeans.

Malaysia presents an altogether different trajectory. In the interests of national unity and affirmative action for the *bumiputras* (children of the soil), stress is placed on Malay as the national language (Bahasa Malaysia) and the language of instruction at all levels. With the National Language Act of 1976, Malay became the official and only language of government, with future civil servants and university students having to pass advanced examinations in Malay to qualify. A massive effort to translate scholarly works and to encourage the writing of original works and textbooks in Malay was started. The Malaysianization of the medium of instruction was completed by 1983, when it reached university level. English continued to be taught as a subject from Grade 1 to 12.

The Education Act of 1996 reintroduced English as a medium of instruction for technical subjects. In the judgment of the country's leadership, the forging of national unity and identity had been realized, and it was time to undertake the modernization process by bringing back English as a language of science and technology while in no way giving up the concerted program of developing Bahasa Malaysia as a language of intellectual work.

While the younger generation, for the most part, is not competent in English, there is the remnant of the earlier generation that has not given up the use of English; in addition, there is a core of the Malay elite that has continued to study abroad. Moreover, partnerships with British, American, and Australian universities have been started, so that some foreign universities now have campuses in Malaysia or joint programs with local Malaysian universities.

The Philippines became part of the United States colonies, together with Puerto Rico and Cuba, beginning in 1898, and was granted independence in 1946. Under the policy of the American colonial government, the medium of instruction for schools was mandated to be the English language since no local language was discovered widespread and acceptable enough to be the language of instruction. Moreover, there was a Whorfian faith that the English language would better instruct Filipinos in the way of democracy. English was used as the medium of instruction from Grade 1 on, with American teachers recruited from all over the United States to serve in the new system. Gradually, Filipinos took over the teaching of English.

The monolingual English policy was modified when the Tagalog-based national language was proclaimed in 1937, announced for dissemination in 1939, and taught for the first time in schools in Fourth Year high school (the last year in secondary school) and as a required subject for future teachers. The language became an official language in 1941, and its teaching was propagated both during the Japanese Period and subsequently, since Independence, as a subject in all grades from Grade 1 to Fourth Year and subsequently for two semesters in college. It was first used as a medium of instruction for social studies and social sciences in 1974 under the bilingual education scheme of the Department of Education. All other subjects continued to be taught in English.

Philippine official policy has had an ambivalent attitude toward English since the days of nationalistic fervor in the 1970s. The bilingual scheme was a compromise. From 1974 to 1986, the emphasis was on the use of Filipino as a medium of instruction at all levels even in college, at least for some subjects. However, because of the need for an international language in the age of globalization, English has once more taken center stage and is now being emphasized, so much so that there is a return to the use of English even in the social sciences, supposedly the domain of the national language.

3   The Varieties of English in Southeast Asia: Singapore English, Malaysian English, and Philippine English

There are variations in the structural (phonological, lexical, syntactic, discourse) characteristics of these new varieties because of the linguistic substrata or the native languages of those who acquire English as a second language.

However, it is not only in structural features but likewise in social features where variation is found. In other words, there are basilectal, mesolectal, and acrolectal varieties of these languages within the same national community. We suggest the term "edulects" for these socially and economically influenced varieties, since they are the results of certain types of education which are determined by social class but which are transmitted by the teaching and subculture of the school system, especially for the higher income and better educated classes.

Our discussion here of the phonological features is based on the converging analyses of individual listeners, but not on empirical data based on frequency counts and statistically described occurrences. However, with the International Corpus of English database started by Greenbaum (1996) and continued by different Southeast Asian research teams (ICE-Singapore, 2002; ICE-Philippines, 2004; ICE-Malaysia, ongoing), there are oral data which can now be analyzed.

The common factor in these new varieties is the reality that they are spoken as a second language by those who speak genetically unrelated languages. Even if English is learned from childhood, the models for language use – parents and teachers – are second-language speakers of the variety, not native speakers.

Singapore English is influenced by the principal substrate, Baba Malay (the Malay of the Straits Chinese) and Bazaar Malay, and the secondary substrate, assorted southern Chinese languages, mainly Cantonese and Hokkien (Gupta, 1998). Malaysian English shows variations depending on the ethnic roots of the speaker: Malay, Chinese, and Tamil. In the Philippines, the speakers all speak a Philippine-type language which in phonology would be quite similar from one language to another except for the occurrence in some languages of the reflex of the Austronesian pepet (/ə/) and the labiodental fricatives /f/ and /v/.

In describing the linguistic features of these varieties, we realize that it is difficult to identify exactly what we are describing, i.e., there is a continuum of basilect–mesolect–acrolect for each variety. The acrolect, of course, will approach the standard, and the basilect will diverge very radically from it. Perhaps what is being described here is the English used by average, educated Singaporeans, Malaysians, or Filipinos in social situations where they are concerned with communicating ideas and not paying close attention to language.

Bao (1998) has described the phonology of Colloquial Singapore English thus:

1 Stops are unaspirated in all positions.
2 /θ/ becomes /t/ and /ð/ becomes /d/ before a vowel (thin → tin; then → den); /θ/ and /ð/ become /f/ in word-final position (breath → /brɛf/; breathe → /brif/).
3 There is a lack of length contrast and tenseness contrast in vowels.
4 There are no syllabic laterals and nasals.
5 In word-final position, voiced stops become voiceless (/lɛg/ → /lɛk/).

The phonology of Malaysian English has been characterized by Zuraidah (2000, cited by Schneider, 2003/2004, p. 56) as follows:

1 merger of [iː] and [ɪ]: *feel – fill, bead – bid* all have [i];
2 merger of [uː] and [ʊ]: *pool – pull, Luke – look* all have [u];
3 merger of [ɛ] and [æ]: *set – sat, man – men* all have [ɛ];
4 merger of [ɒ] and [ɔ]: *pot – port, cot – caught* all have [ɔ];
5 variant realizations of [ə]: schwa tends to get replaced by a full vowel, the quality of which frequently depends upon orthography;
6 monophthongization of diphthongs: e.g. *coat, load* with [o], *make, steak* with [e];
7 shift in the placement of accents.

Schneider (2003/2004: 56–7) adds the following phonotactic features for Malaysian English:

8   omission of final voiceless stop or its replacement by a glottal stop in monosyllabic words with a CVC structure;

9   reduction of word-final consonant clusters, usually dropping the alveolar stop;

10   replacement of dental fricatives by stops.

Gonzalez and Alberca (1978) have presented the following phonological features for Philippine English:

1   absence of schwa

2   absence of aspiration of stops in all positions;

3   substitution of [a] for [æ], [ɔ] for [o], [ɪ] for [i], [ɛ] for [e];

4   substitution of [s] for [z], [ʃ] for [ʒ], [t] for [θ], [d] for [ð], [p] for [f], [b] for [v];

5   simplification of consonant clusters in final position;

6   syllable-timed, rather than stress-timed, rhythm;

7   shift in placement of accents.

There appears to be a convergence in the phonologies of the Southeast Asian varieties of English – in the merger of vowels, the absence of the schwa, the absence of aspiration of stops, the lack of tenseness of vowels, the substitution of stops for certain fricatives (although the substitution for dental fricatives in word-final position in Colloquial Singapore English stands out), the shift in stress placement, and the syllable-timed rather than stress-timed rhythm.

It would be interesting to examine the differences between the morphophonemic rules of native English and those of the new varieties. More careful analytic phonological research, perhaps aided by new instrumentation in articulatory and acoustic phonetics, as well as careful study of morphophonemic changes, is needed to be able to see these subtle differences explaining "accent."

The most obvious features of the Southeast Asian varieties are the loanwords (different for each society and culture because of the differences in the realia or referents in the culture, e.g., kinship titles, local food terms, indigenous values) and the loan translations, as well as the lack of mastery of idioms and of standard forms of two-word verbs or verb-plus-preposition combinations (two examples from Philippine English: *based from* instead of Standard English *based on*, and *result to* instead of Standard English *result in*, in the speech of even educated speakers). There are likewise changes of meaning from the native language standard of some lexical items; two examples from Singapore English: *stay* is used for permanent or long-term residence (cf. British English, in which *live* is used for permanent residence and *stay* for temporary or short-term residence) and *keep* describes an activity – *I'm going to keep these photos in that drawer* (cf. British English, where *keep* describes a state – *The tools are kept in the shed*) (Wee, 1998). The lexical innovations as well as new collocations have now been gathered in the multi-sourced Macquarie junior dictionaries of Asian English – Delbridge et al. (1999) for Singapore, Malaysian, and Brunei

English, and *Anvil-Macquarie Dictionary of Philippine English for High School* (2000) for Philippine English.

The new area for further exploration, initially brought to notice by Platt and Weber (1980) in their pioneering and often-cited study of Singapore and Malaysian English, is the restructuring going on in the subsystems of the syntax, especially of the verb and the noun phrase, as well as changes in morphology.

Extensive studies have been made of both the Colloquial and Standard subvarieties of Singapore English, perhaps the best studied of the Asian varieties. Alsagoff and Ho (1998: 133ff.), adapting various sources, present the features that differentiate Colloquial Singapore English (the Low Variety which is used in the home and in casual situations and is the native language of children who have learned English from birth) from Standard Singapore English (the High Variety which is used in formal situations, in education, in writing, and is almost identical to Standard English):

- Features connected with the verb:
    1   past tense and present tense not morphologically marked,
    2   copula dropped to describe states,
    3   adverbials preferred to morphological marking of aspect,
    4   progressive aspect marked with *-ing*, sometimes with *still*,
    5   habitual aspect marked with *always*.
- Features connected with the noun:
    6   non-count nouns treated as count,
    7   indefinite article dropped,
    8   relative clause with different word order and *one*.
- Features of sentence structure:
    9   subject and sometimes object dropping (PRO-drop),
    10 conjunction dropping,
    11 use of *or not*,
    12 use of pragmatic particles *lah, ah*,
    13 use of tag question *is it?*

All the characteristics of Standard Singapore English adhere to those of Standard English, except perhaps for the use of *would* for *will* to express politeness, tentativeness, and irrealis aspect ("what is not actually so but may be so").

For informal Malaysian English, the following features have been noted (Schneider, 2003/2004: 57–8):

1   missing noun inflectional endings (mostly the plural *-s* and sometimes the genitive *-s*);
2   missing sentence constituents (object, subject, auxiliary verb, copula, preposition) giving the impression of phrasal "telegraphic" speech;
3   variant complementation patterns following verbs;
4   wrong concord in noun phrases.

Newbrook (1997: 238–40, as cited by Schneider, 2003/2004: 58) mentions three structures in acrolectal Malaysian English:

1 SVO order after *no more, never*;
2 *got* "have" as an auxiliary with bare infinitive;
3 *already* as a completive marker preceding the verb.

Schneider found variable article usage to be widespread, especially noun phrases without specifiers; likewise the absence of the plural marker in constructions involving *one of the* followed by a singular noun.

The restructuring of the syntax of Philippine English has been studied by Gonzalez (1985), Bautista (2000), and Gonzalez, Jambalos, and Romero (2003), and the following have been identified as "perduring" characteristics of the grammar, even among highly educated Filipinos:

1   lack of subject-verb agreement, especially in the presence of an interven-
    ing prepositional phrase or expression;
2   faulty tense-aspect usage including unusual use of verb forms and tenses,
    especially use of the past perfect tense for the simple past or present
    perfect;
3   lack of tense harmony;
4   modals *would* and *could* used for *will* and *can*;
5   adverbial placed at the end of the clause, not between auxiliary and main
    verb;
6   non-idiomatic two- or three-word verbs;
7   variable article usage – missing article where an article is required; an
    article where no article is required;
8   faulty noun subcategorization, including non-pluralization of count nouns
    and pluralization of mass nouns;
9   lack of agreement between pronoun and antecedent;
10 *one of the* followed by singular noun.

Clearly, some of the differences from Standard English usage are common among the three new varieties.

In discourse, the work is just starting. Thanks to breakthroughs in discourse analysis, we are now in a better position to see Asian English discourse patterns set against the largely still Westernized rhetorical patterns taught in English composition classes. It would be fascinating to see if some features of Asian oral literature are finding their way into the fiction and poetry of Southeast Asian authors writing in English. However, at least in Philippine English literature, we have not found transfers of discourse patterns of indigenous epics and poems into contemporary Philippine literature in English, although the referents in Southeast Asian literature (drama and fiction) are clearly indigenous and the behavioral patterns and topics of speeches and turns of phrase of Asian characters are quite different from those of Western characters.

A final comment that has to be made about these Outer-Circle varieties in Southeast Asia is that there are different speaking styles within each community. The style of a formal written speech perhaps exemplifies the growing standard. The colloquial spontaneous variety is clearly different, using intonation patterns from the substratum language and lacking the careful spelling pronunciations of formal speech. But it is still part of the standardizing acrolectal edulectal variety.

In Singapore, the basilectal variety has been captured in situation comedies, in the speech of lower socio-economic status characters on television, and has been described extensively (see Foley et al., 1998). Gupta (1998: 122) makes the point that educated Singaporeans who have mastery of the acrolect use basilectal features in their colloquial speech; she claims that many Singaporean speakers can move at will between Standard English and Colloquial Singapore English.

In Malaysian English, as Asmah (1996) describes it, there is a basilect which is the English of those who have had their education in the medium of Malay, Chinese, or Tamil and have learned English only as a school subject. There is likewise code switching between English and Malay among accomplished bilinguals for rhetorical and accommodation purposes. But among speakers not highly competent in English, code switching is used as a repair strategy.

In the Philippines, code switching between English and the local language is extensively used by urban Filipinos comfortable in both languages. Perhaps code switching in Philippine society can be viewed as the equivalent of the use of basilectal features in Singapore English among educated Singaporeans. There is a basilectal Philippine English and one variant was studied formally by Bautista (1982) in her study of *yaya* (caregiver) English. However, what *yaya* English exhibits is really lack of proficiency in English because of inadequate schooling; it is a restricted code that is highly idiosyncratic and thus far does not seem to show institutionalization or even uniformity.

In any case, when describing indigenous varieties of English, we can no longer speak of these varieties as somehow following one pattern, but, as is the case in all communication codes, there are subvarieties or edulects (depending on the competence from educational training), and future descriptions will have to give more serious consideration to the variation within the variety to be able to extrapolate the directions these new Englishes will take.

4 The Expanding Circle: English in Thailand, Vietnam, and Indonesia

The current language policy of Thailand, Vietnam, and Indonesia is such that the main foreign language being learned is English. There is a similar interest in spreading English in Laos and Cambodia, but the educational system in these countries is in slow revival, and so cannot really make a realistic plan for foreign-language teaching. In Cambodia, French is competing with English because the government of France considers the spread of French as part of its *mission civilizatrice*. Burma, at least in desire, wants to revive English, but the educational system in this country is likewise in a process of restoration. (See Ho, 1998 for a brief description of the English-language teaching situation in Southeast Asia; see Ho and Wong, 2000 for country-specific descriptions of language planning and language-in-education policy in the East Asian countries.)

Among these countries, the one with the longest record of English-language teaching is Thailand, which at one time began the teaching of English as early as Grade 1 in private schools, Grade 3 in university demonstration schools, and Grade 5 in government schools (Wongsothorn, 2000). However, because of a lack of teachers, especially in the rural areas, the policy was changed by postponing the teaching of English to higher grades. In 1996, the curriculum was revised once more, and English is now taught as a subject in Grade 1 to 12. Thus, about 99 percent of Thai students study English at school, but it appears that not very many succeed in acquiring much English proficiency.

Indonesia, a former Dutch colony, used to emphasize the teaching of Dutch (see Alisjahbana, 1990 for a history of English in Indonesia). The movement towards English as a foreign language began at independence, and English is now the main foreign language being learned in Indonesia. English is taught for eight or nine years from primary school (from Grade 4 or 5) through high school (Renandya, 2000). The main objective is to provide reading skills to enable Indonesians to read science-related materials in English. There are institutes (IKIPs) where the teaching of English is systematically taught to future teachers. However, the general consensus is that – for a variety of sociolinguistic and pedagogical reasons – the teaching of English in Indonesian schools has not been successful.

Vietnam has switched from French and Russian to English as the main foreign language to be taught in schools. Under the policy of *doi moi* or economic renovation, English has become a popular foreign language: One survey showed that 90 percent of university students favored English because it would help them improve their work and their lives, and it would facilitate science and technology transfer to Vietnam (Do, 1996). Today, all schools must offer English for all pupils in senior high (Grade 10–12) and, in cities and towns, in lower secondary schools. A pass in the foreign language is compulsory for graduation at Grade 12. However, the country is handicapped by a shortage of trained English teachers and suitable teaching materials and equipment (Goh and Bang, 2000).

5   The Future of English in Southeast Asia

Thus, in Southeast Asia, English is taught either as a foreign language or as a second language, depending on the colonial past of the country. The language is spreading and competence is increasing across wider sections of each society, although as in all teaching of nonnative languages, it is the affluent that have better access to English language tuition than the masses. English competence is an elitist acquisition, depending very much on the quality of schooling and the availability of teaching and learning resources as well as exposure to an international community through tourism, foreign investments, or schooling and employment abroad.

English as a Language of Wider Communication and as a Language of World Knowledge is unprecedented in history in its geographical spread, its appeal, its use, and its cultural influence. Based on the lessons of history, the influence of any language is very much a function of the political hegemony of a conquering or dominant nation. However, language is more conservative and can continue to be influential and in use even if an empire has waned, especially in traditional institutions such as organized religion and worship and in universities. One predicts that the same will be true of English, even long after the American Empire has lost its powers in the future.

In Southeast Asia, the status of English is growing, and its use as a language of education, especially at the tertiary level, and its spread as an international language of commerce, trade, and international relations, are expanding, not contracting. Its place is secure in Singapore, where official language policy and practice are overtly pro-English and where English is perceived to have an equalizing and unifying function. It is in a state of revival in Malaysia, which gave it up for a while in the interests of national unification and nation building. In the Philippines, competence in English is perceived to be diminishing, at least in the impressions of many people; however, the demand for English continues, and there is now a renewed effort to teach it better through improved teacher training and frequent testing with valid instruments. As a foreign language, English continues to dominate the rest of Southeast Asia, even in socialist countries such as Burma and Cambodia.

The future of English, at least for this century and perhaps even in the next, is assured, whatever one's feelings or attitudes may be toward linguistic and perhaps cultural hegemony. There will be forces of standardization in the interests of international communication and mutual intelligibility, aided by electronic means through the mass media, the internet, the mobile phone, and the educational system itself. However, like all languages, English will undergo changes resulting in a diglossic situation, with the higher variety mutually intelligible with other Asian Englishes but with mesolectal and basilectal varieties becoming more distinctive, and perhaps even creating a situation where pidginization may emerge or flourish.

6   Summary, Conclusion, and Theoretical Considerations

We have described the distinctive features of Singapore, Malaysian, and Philippine English as differentiated from their native-language models (British and American English). We have likewise indicated that the changes in the segmental phonological units are quite transparent but that stress, intonation, phonotactics, and morphophonemic processes need further and more detailed and "delicate" (in the Hallidayan sense of the term) study. In the area of the lexicon, neologisms and collocations, as well as loan translations, are likewise discernible and have been "codified" in some dictionaries.

Needing further investigation are descriptions of the restructuring of specific subsystems of the grammars of these new varieties of English, including some of the innovations which may perhaps be described in terms of process rules and perhaps even reordering.

Little has been done in the area of discourse, a field ripe for investigation. Of specific interest to the literary scholar would be the mutual influence of the substratal languages and English on the poetics of each language and in the literature in English emerging from the social situations.

Also needing further study are the uses of these new varieties of English – and their subvarieties – in their respective societies and the emerging patterns of use which present complementarities of functions.

We have also made the observation that these new varieties cannot be studied in isolation as linguistic artifacts, but must be contextualized in their histories and current uses in their societies and in the influences that political, social, and economic factors have on the continued uses of these codes.

Likewise mooted is the need for nuanced methodologies in the investigation of these varieties, beginning with the pivotal question that every field linguist and descriptive linguist must face: Which variety of the language should be described? How many respondents are needed to validate any claims as to distinctive features? Moreover, a description of one variety is insufficient, as all languages show variation in usage because of socio-economic class, level of education (edulect), degree of formality, and other situational and contextual factors. Thanks to modern means of data collection and processing, electronic corpora are now available, frequency counting is made easy, and concordances illustrating uses of certain lexical items and grammatical and discourse features, together with statistical analyses, are easily achievable. The question that must be asked is: What kind of quantitative evidence is needed before any claims can be made that a given feature has become predictable, systemic, or even standardized?

Very brief notes are given of the current state of English as a foreign language in Expanding-Circle countries. No definitive claims can be made about the English language in Indonesia, Thailand, and Vietnam because of the lack of detailed studies thus far, except the assertion that the same problems of descriptive detail and methodology need to be answered to ensure empirical validity for our statements regarding the varieties of English in these countries.

The insights that may be gleaned from the study and its references, which may have later theoretical import or constitute the elements for more vital theory-building, are the realizations that languages change, languages exercise mutual influence on other languages with which they are in contact, and there is transference of influence at all levels (sounds, words, phrases and sentences, discourse patterns, literary patterns). These findings are not new, but they demand integrated treatment. More important is our claim that what is happening is not mere surface borrowing but a restructuring, if these features become systemic and predictable. The challenge is for descriptive linguists to describe such restructuring beyond the traditional contrastive analyses of the applied linguists of the preceding generation. An even greater challenge is to "catch" the drift (Sapir's term) of these restructurings so as to make some predictions about the future designs of these evolving structures within the context of a more rigorous methodology of social analysis.

See also Chapters 15, WORLD ENGLISHES TODAY; 17, VARIETIES OF WORLD ENGLISHES; 20, WRITTEN LANGUAGE, STANDARD LANGUAGE, GLOBAL LANGUAGE; 28, WORLD ENGLISHES AND DESCRIPTIVE GRAMMARS; 34, WORLD ENGLISHES AND GLOBAL COMMERCE; 36, TEACHING WORLD ENGLISHES; 38, WORLD ENGLISHES AND LEXICOGRAPHY; 41, WORLD ENGLISHES AND CORPORA STUDIES.

REFERENCES

Alisjahbana, S. Takdir (1990) The teaching of English in Indonesia. In *Teaching and Learning English Worldwide.* Edited by James Britton, Robert E. Shafer, and Ken Watson. Clevedon/Philadelphia: Multilingual Matters, pp. 315–27.

Alsagoff, Lubna and Ho, Chee Lick (1998) The grammar of Singapore English. In *English in New Cultural Contexts: Reflections from Singapore.* Edited by Joseph A. Foley, Thiru Kandiah, Zhiming Bao, Anthea Fraser Gupta, Lubna Alsagoff, Ho Chee Lick, Lionel Wee, Ismail S. Talib and Wendy Bokhorst-Heng. Singapore: Singapore Institute of Management and Oxford University Press Singapore, pp. 127–51.

Anvil-Macquarie Dictionary of Philippine English for High School (2000) Manila: Anvil Publishing, Inc. and Macquarie Library.

Asmah, Haji Omar (1996) Post-imperial English in Malaysia. In *Post-Imperial English: Status Change in Former British and American Colonies, 1840–1990.* Edited by Joshua A. Fishman, Andrew W. Conrad, and Alma Rubal-Lopez. Berlin: Mouton de Gruyter, pp. 513–33.

Bao, Zhiming (1998) The sounds of Singapore English. In *English in New Cultural Contexts: Reflections from Singapore.* Edited by Joseph A. Foley, Thiru Kandiah, Zhiming Bao, Anthea Fraser Gupta, Lubna Alsagoff, Ho Chee Lick, Lionel Wee, Ismail S. Talib and Wendy Bokhorst-Heng. Singapore: Singapore Institute of Management and Oxford University Press Singapore, pp. 152–74.

Bautista, Ma. Lourdes S. (1982) "Yaya" English. *Philippine Studies*, **30**, 377–94.

Bautista, Ma. Lourdes S. (2000) *Defining Standard Philippine English: Its Status and Grammatical Features.* Manila: De La Salle University Press.

Delbridge, Arthur et al. (eds.) (1999) *Macquarie Junior Dictionary: World English-Asian Context*. NSW: Macquarie Library.

Do, Thinh Huy (1996) Foreign Language Education Policy in Vietnam: The reemergence of English and its impact on higher education. PhD dissertation, University of Southern California.

Fishman, Joshua A., Conrad, Andrew W., and Rubal-Lopez, Alma (eds.) (1996) *Post-imperial English: Status Change in Former British and American Colonies, 1840–1990*. Berlin: Mouton de Gruyter.

Foley, Joseph A., Kandiah, Thiru, Bao, Zhiming, Gupta, Anthea Fraser, Alsagoff, Lubna, Ho Chee Lick, Wee, Lionel, Talib, Ismail S., and Bokhorst-Heng, Wendy (eds.) (1998) *English in New Cultural Contexts: Reflections from Singapore*. Singapore: Singapore Institute of Management and Oxford University Press Singapore.

Goh, Edwin and Bang, Nguyen (2000) Vietnam. In *Language Policies and Language Education: The Impact in East Asian Countries in the Next Decade*. Edited by Wah Kam Ho and Ruth Y. L. Wong. Singapore: Times Academic Press, pp. 321–32.

Gonzalez, Andrew, FSC (1985) *Studies on Philippine English*. Singapore: SEAMEO Regional Language Centre.

Gonzalez, Andrew, FSC and Alberca, Wilfredo L. (1978) *Philippine English of the Mass Media, Preliminary Edition*. Manila: De La Salle University Research Council.

Gonzalez, Andrew, FSC, Jambalos, Thelma, and Romero, Corona S. (2003) *Three Studies on Philippine English across Generations: Towards an Integration and some Implications*. Manila: Linguistic Society of the Philippines.

Greenbaum, Sidney (1996) Introducing ICE. In *Comparing English Worldwide: The International Corpus of English*. Edited by Sidney Greenbaum. Oxford: Oxford University Press, pp. 3–12.

Gupta, Anthea Fraser (1998) The situation of English in Singapore. In *English in New Cultural Contexts: Reflections from Singapore*. Edited by Joseph A. Foley, Thiru Kandiah, Zhiming Bao, Anthea Fraser Gupta, Lubna Alsagoff, Ho Chee Lick, Lionel Wee, Ismail S. Talib, and Wendy Bokhorst-Heng. Singapore: Singapore Institute of Management and Oxford University Press Singapore, pp. 106–26.

Ho, Wah Kam (1998) English language teaching in Southeast Asia: Continuity and change. *Asian Englishes*, **1**(1), 5–30.

Ho, Wah Kam and Wong, Ruth Y. L. (eds.) (2000) *Language Policies and Language Education: The Impact in East Asian Countries in the Next Decade*. Singapore: Times Academic Press.

ICE-Malaysia (ongoing) *International Corpus of English-Malaysia Lexical Corpus*. International Corpus of English Project, University College London.

ICE-Philippines (2004) *International Corpus of English-Philippines Lexical Corpus*, CD-ROM. International Corpus of English Project, University College London.

ICE-Singapore (2002) *International Corpus of English-Singapore Lexical Corpus*, CD-ROM. International Corpus of English Project, University College London.

Newbrook, Mark (1997) Malaysian English: Status, norms, some grammatical and lexical features. In *Englishes Around the World 2 – Caribbean, Africa, Asia, Australasia: Studies in Honour of Manfred Görlach*.

Edited by Edgar W. Schneider. Amsterdam/Philadelphia: John Benjamins, pp. 229–56.

Platt, John and Weber, Heidi (1980) *English in Singapore and Malaysia: Status, Features, Functions*. Kuala Lumpur: Oxford University Press.

Renandya, Willy A. (2000) Indonesia. In *Language Policies and Language Education: The Impact in East Asian Countries in the Next Decade*. Edited by Wah Kam Ho and Ruth Y. L. Wong. Singapore: Times Academic Press, pp. 113–38.

Schneider, Edgar W. (2003/2004) Evolutionary patterns of New Englishes and the special case of Malaysian English. *Asian Englishes*, 6(2), 44–63.

Wee, Lionel (1998) The lexicon of Singapore English. In *English in New Cultural Contexts: Reflections from Singapore*. Edited by Joseph A. Foley,

Thiru Kandiah, Zhiming Bao, Anthea Fraser Gupta, Lubna Alsagoff, Ho Chee Lick, Lionel Wee, Ismail S. Talib, and Wendy Bokhorst-Heng. Singapore: Singapore Institute of Management and Oxford University Press Singapore, pp. 175–200.

Wongsothorn, Achara (2000) Thailand. In *Language Policies and Language Education: The Impact in East Asian Countries in the Next Decade*. Edited by Wah Kam Ho and Ruth Y. L. Wong. Singapore: Times Academic Press, pp. 307–20.

Zuraidah, Mohd Don (2000) Malay + English → a Malay variety of English vowels and accent. In *English Is an Asian Language: The Malaysian Context*. Edited by Mohd Said Halimah and Keat Siew Ng. Kuala Lumpur/Sydney: Persatuan Bahasa Moden Malaysia/Macquarie Library, pp. 35–45.

FURTHER READING

Bautista, Ma. Lourdes S. (ed.) (1997) *English Is an Asian Language: The Philippine Context*. Sydney: Macquarie Library.

Halimah, Moht Said and Ng, Keat Siew (eds.) (2000) *English Is an Asian Language: The Malaysian Context*. Kuala Lumpur/Sydney: Persatuan Bahasa Moden Malaysia/Sydney: Macquarie Library.

Newbrook, Mark (ed.) (1999) *English Is an Asian Language: The Thai Context*. Sydney: Macquarie Library.

These volumes are compilations of selected papers from conferences organized by The Macquarie Library Pty Ltd, and they give an indication of the kinds of current sociolinguistic and pedagogical research on English being done in these three Southeast Asian countries.

Bautista, Ma. Lourdes S. and Bolton, Kingsley (guest eds.) (2004) Special Issue on Philippine English: Tensions and transitions. *World Englishes*, **23**(1).

This collection of articles covers the historical and ideological underpinnings of English in the Philippines and presents linguistic research on Philippine English and studies of Philippine English creative writing.

Gopinathan, S., Pakir, Anne, Ho, Wah Kam, and Saravanan, Vanithamani (eds.) (1998) *Language, Society and Education in Singapore: Trends and*

Issues. Singapore: Times Academic Press.

A state-of-the-art volume containing both historical and empirical perspectives, it has three sections – language in Singapore, language in society, and language in education – and elucidates on the place of English, Mandarin, Malay, and Tamil in Singaporean society. Chapters retained from the 1994 edition have been updated to reflect the current situation.

Llamzon, Teodoro A. (1969) *Standard Filipino English*. Quezon City: Ateneo de Manila University Press.

A groundbreaking monograph, it is perhaps the very first work to describe a new variety of English in Asia. It has an extensive discussion of the phonology of Philippine English and a short sketch of "Filipinisms," English expressions that are not idiomatic in English but instead follow Philippine language structure.

Noss, Richard B. (ed.) (1983) *Varieties of English in Southeast Asia* (Anthology Series 11). Singapore: Singapore University Press for SEAMEO Regional Language Centre.

This anthology contains selected papers from the 1981 RELC seminar and presents theoretical papers on English varieties in general and specific linguistic analyses of Southeast Asian varieties and the pedagogical implications of these analyses.

Platt, John, Weber, Heidi, and Ho, Mian Lian (1984) *The New Englishes*. London: Routledge and Kegan Paul.

This is an excellent introduction to the new varieties of English, beginning with the contexts in which these Englishes have arisen and the criteria for determining whether a variety is a new English or not. It has numerous examples of the phonology, grammar, lexicon, and styles of the new Englishes and ends with a discussion of implications to language education.

Tickoo, Makhan L. (ed.) (1991) *Languages and Standards: Issues, Attitudes and Case Studies* (Anthology Series 26). Singapore: SEAMEO Regional Language Centre.

The issue of standards is the focus of this volume and issues related to theory and pedagogy and issues related to implementation are discussed. The last section of the book presents two papers by Randolph Quirk on the issue of Standard English and two papers by Braj B. Kachru on the case for world Englishes, followed by a note from Quirk and a response from Kachru.

9 South American Englishes

KANAVILLIL RAJAGOPALAN

1 Introduction

South America is a huge continent of vibrant developing nations, an immense land mass, for the most part sparsely populated, rich in rain forests and other natural resources, originally inhabited by native Indians, and, after five centuries that brought successive waves of settlers from Europe, Africa, the Far East and elsewhere, today boasting a truly remarkable and exuberant mosaic of races and cultures. A giant recently awoken from a protracted and debilitating nightmare marked by callous colonial exploitation, followed by agonizing spells of authoritarian military dictatorships, it is today mostly ruled by democratically elected governments. Although still reeling from the burden of gargantuan foreign debts contracted in the past and stringent fiscal and budgetary restraints imposed by the IMF, the World Bank, and the like as a condition for fresh loans, the continent is on the road to steady economic recovery and poised to claim its rightful place in the new post-Berlin Wall world order. This has come about along with a new sense of nationhood and national pride which were conspicuously absent until relatively recently in its 500 plus years of documented history. The following observation by Topik (1992: 408) about the attitude of the early European settlers in Brazil – by far the biggest country in the continent, accounting for just under half of its entire geographical spread as well as population – applies equally well, *mutatis mutandis*, to the rest of the continent:

> Rather than build a "city on a hill" as in Massachusetts, Europeans most commonly sought to unlock the Brazilian treasure chest and imitate Europe. Not until the Modernist movement of the 1920s did writers such as Mario de Andrade, Paulo Prado, Sérgio Buarque de Holanda, and Gilberto Freyre return to stressing the importance of the indigenous roots and the interior as positive contributions to the nationality, rather than as barriers to the creation of a tropical France.

The reference to France is highly significant in the context of any discussion of the growing prestige of English on the continent because until, say, the middle of the twentieth century, French was by far the foreign language most sought after by the upper and middle classes right across the continent (Souza Campos, 1940) and, in many ways, France still serves as the role model and symbol of cultural finesse and sophistication.

1.1   Delimiting South America

The precise extension of the geographical area one refers to as South America depends on whether or not one wants to include in it the group of nations that sometimes falls under the rubric of Central America. As it happens, the term "South America" is ambiguous between a restricted sense in which it is viewed as participating in a three-way distinction among South, Central and North Americas, and a broad sense in which it is claimed to encompass all countries to the south of the United States – thus separating the rich north from the comparatively less well-off south (although glaring disparities in the standard of living both among and within the several nations make any sweeping generalizations far too simplistic).

The term was interpreted in the first sense by the guest editors of a special issue of *World Englishes* who made a point of stressing the linguistic and ethnic diversity in the continent, often unnoticed by the rest of the world, and also the fact that, like Africa, it continues to remain a "forgotten continent" (Berns and Friedrich, 2003). It is also the sense in which the continent is presented by the publishers of World Atlas.com who treat Central America as part of the North American continent (http://www.worldatlas.com/webimage/countrys/sa.htm).

The second sense is what is captured by *The American Heritage Dictionary of the English Language* where the entry on South America reads: "A continent of the southern western Hemisphere southeast of North America between the Atlantic and Pacific oceans. It extends from the Caribbean Sea southward to Cape Horn." In this latter sense, it is roughly coextensive with Latin America, though many countries of the Caribbean do not properly qualify as Latin. Incidentally, this is true also of the restricted sense – Guyana and Suriname are countries where the national/official languages are English and Dutch respectively.

On the other hand, French Guyana, though French-speaking as the name implies and hence unquestionably Latin, is internationally recognized as, not a full-fledged country, but an "overseas department of France" and thus, strictly speaking, a French territory. There is also the disputed territory of Falklands/Malvinas, which remains a British colony to date.

The exact status of Mexico remains somewhat undefined. Both linguistically and culturally, it has close affinities with its neighbors to the south, indeed right down to the far south; yet both geographically and economically it is part of the North American Continent, being one of three countries (alongside the USA and Canada) that are signatories to the North American Free Trade Agreement (NAFTA). A British Council report on the status of English in Mexico begins with the following observation: "Contrary to general belief, Mexico does not form part of either Central or South America. It is, in fact, in North America" (Morris, 2000).

In the final analysis, then, the fuzziness of the term "South America" has to do with the conflict between a linguistic and cultural sense on the one hand and an economically driven geo-political sense on the other.

For the purposes of the present overview, we shall use the term "South America" in the narrower sense, although in view of the pervasive lack of consensus mentioned in the foregoing section, we shall also make passing references to countries like Mexico and Cuba.

2 The Status of English in South America

Made up of 12 sovereign states (Argentina, Bolivia, Brazil, Chile, Colombia, Ecuador, Guyana, Paraguay, Peru, Suriname, Uruguay, and Venezuela) and three major territories (Falkland Islands, French Guyana, and Galapagos Islands), South America is part of the "Expanding Circle" (Kachru, 1985), as far as the status of the English language is concerned. Guyana, where English is the national and official language (alongside a number of indigenous languages as well as Hindi and Urdu, spoken by the descendants of indentured laborers brought from the Indian subcontinent), and the Falklands, where the population of under 5,000, including some 2,000 British military personnel, speaks English, are exceptions to the rule.

Spanish, spoken in 9 of the 12 countries, is overwhelmingly the principal language on the continent, but Portuguese, spoken by roughly 170 million people in Brazil (constituting about half of the estimated 350 million on the continent as a whole), is also a major presence to reckon with. Although most commercial transactions and other exchanges among the different nations generally take place in Spanish and in a makeshift language referred to as "Portuñol," which has been described as "Brazilian Portuguese, versioned to be understood by Spanish speakers" (Amey, in Graddol et al., 1999: 14), English is consolidating itself as the region's principal foreign language, thanks mainly to increasing trade relations with the rest of the world. Referring to the emerging role of English in Argentina, Eayrs (2000) observes: "Traditionally something of a national joke, the importance of English at all levels of Argentine life is now indisputable. Despite the development of Mercosur [the South American common market with Brazil and Argentina as the major players] it is a knowledge of English that middle and upper class Argentines aspire to rather than Portuguese (and in neighboring Brazil the first L2 is English rather than Spanish)." Brazil has recently signed a protocol with South Africa and India with a view to intensifying trade and other countries on the continent are contemplating similar trade agreements both collectively and severally.

The post-World War II years have witnessed a stupendous growth in the demand for learning the English language, widely perceived across the continent to be the key to success and career advancement in the new world order (Alm, 2003; Bohn, 2003; Friedrich, 2003; Ninõ-Murcia, 2003; Velez-Rendon, 2003).

But the spread of English has also set off alarm bells in many sectors of the society at large in many of these countries, often leading to dangerously chauvinistic and xenophobic legislative attempts to curb the advance of English. So what one witnesses at this moment is the presence of two diametrically opposed tendencies: the rising prestige of English as the continent's number one foreign language and a growing suspicion of the implications of the spread of the language. In other words, people's reactions to the advance of English into their daily lives are confused and, at bottom, profoundly ambivalent (Rajagopalan, 2002, 2003). Poised between the Scylla of passive acquiescence and the Charybdis of insurgent chauvinism, ordinary people evince mixed attitudes to the role of English, which many believe is beneficial in the medium or long run, but also detrimental to the survival of local languages and cultures. This means an adequate appreciation of the role played by English in the developing nations of this huge continent is impossible without taking into account the geopolitics of the region as a whole (Busnardo and Braga, 1987).

2.1   The geopolitics of the South American continent

South America has historic ties with the United States, which has jealously guarded its interests in the south. On December 6, 1904, recently reelected and inaugurated US President Theodore Roosevelt unveiled what is referred to as "the Roosevelt corollary to the Monroe doctrine," which claimed in no uncertain terms that "this region was uniquely part of the U.S. sphere of influence" (Horowitz, 1985: 54). In the 1950s, when the Cold War between the US and the then rival superpower USSR kept the world on tenterhooks, US President Dwight Eisenhower and Vice-President Richard Nixon put forward the so-called "domino theory," according to which the moment the first country in a given geographical region fell into the hands of the communists the rest would follow suit in quick succession. Although initially proposed to justify US involvement in Southeast Asia, the theory was soon extended to other parts of the world and, in particular, to Latin America. John F. Kennedy, elected to office in 1960, unflinchingly reiterated the policy of his predecessors and vowed to fight communism at all costs. After the Cuban missile crisis of 1962, the US policy vis-à-vis its neighbors to the south was one of constant vigilance and covert or overt intervention whenever there were signs of local governments falling into the hands of leaders with declared or suspected leftist agendas.

The long tradition of uneasy ties between the north and the south has helped spawn stereotypes that persist today. In the words of Pike (1992):

The lazy greaser asleep under a sombrero and the avaricious gringo with money-stuffed pockets are only two of the negative stereotypes that North Americans and Latin Americans have cherished during several centuries of mutual misunderstanding.

2.2 Lingering suspicions

It should hardly come as a surprise therefore that the prevailing mood amongst the intelligentsia as well as the masses at large in most South American countries today is one of caution and distrust whenever the topic is the establishment of closer links with their powerful neighbor to the north. "The entire continent," writes Brazilian sociologist Emir Sader (2001: A3), referring to talks currently under way for the total elimination of trade tariffs across the Americas and the formation of a common market encompassing the north and the south, "is under threat of becoming a free trade zone for North-American corporations."

2.3 Politics of language and English

As only to be expected, English is caught up in the politics of language as it is currently playing out across the South American continent. Yet even as there is, on the one hand, a growing distrust of English insofar as it is perceived as the most visible sign of US hegemony in the region (Oliveira e Paiva, 1995), on the other hand, there can be no denying either that the English language is very much a coveted asset. A taxi driver in Peru summed up the prevailing mood when he said: *"El ingles en el mundo de hoy es un mal necessário, lo necessitamos sí o sí"* ('English in today's world is a necessary evil, we need it, one way or another'), cited in Ninõ-Murcia, 2003: 142. The insatiable demand for learning English is clearly attested to by the presence of privately owned language schools offering regular and crash courses in English, whose numbers keep growing exponentially (Rajagopalan and Rajagopalan, 2005).

As already pointed out, the role of the English language in many South American countries is best described as ambivalent (Rajagopalan, 2003) – at once loved and loathed. And there can be no denying either that the linguistic issue is but the visible tip of a geopolitical iceberg (Rajagopalan, 2002, 2005b). But one must be careful not to make any direct association between the public perceptions of the role of English in their daily lives and the (often hostile) views entertained by many people in respect of the domineering presence of the United States on the continent. Although British presence is today seen in most of South America as less threatening, a British Council report on Argentina warns: "There would appear to be no residue of anti-British feelings as a result of the 1982 conflict, although one is aware that the wounds are still raw and it is wise to be sensitive" (Eayrs, 2000). But in Chile, where the memories of the alleged role of the CIA in the toppling in 1973 of the Aliende government are still very much alive, there is no generalized resentment against the US, nor does any possibly lingering distrust translate into a rejection of the English language. Quite on the contrary, the overall attitude to English amongst Chileans has been described as "positive" (Angoy, 2000). This is also surprisingly true of Cuba, a Central American country, which has long suffered from a US-led economic stranglehold. In the words of Eastment and Santos (2000), "The revolution of 1959, and the subsequent breakdown of diplomatic relations between Cuba and the USA did not lead to a decrease in the teaching of English. On the contrary, the revolutionary government understood the importance of English as an international language."

3 English up to the Mid Twentieth Century

The history of the presence of the English language in South America may be traced back to 1795 when a Scotsman by the name of Nicholas Vansittart wrote a white paper in which he sketched a plan for taking the continent from Spain, in compensation for the loss of North American colonies. Although initially approved by the British Government, it was soon shelved and ultimately replaced by the "Maitland plan," named after the Scottish Major General, Sir Thomas Maitland, who outlined it. The plan was put into action during the Napoleonic war of 1806. After a series of major setbacks, notably humiliating defeats in the face of stubborn resistance from the populations of Buenos Aires (Argentina) and Monte Video (Uruguay), Britain changed its tactics and began recruiting agents locally and encouraging insurgency from within the colonies themselves. Notable among these recruits was Francisco Miranda, a Venezuelan Freemason who had founded *La Gran Reunion Americana*, a Masonic Lodge based in London and who was very well connected across the continents, having been in contact with influential fellow masons like George Washington, Thomas Jefferson, James Madison, and many of the other founding fathers of (North) America.

   The history of English on the continent is far from uniform across the different countries. Argentina stands apart from the rest in that it maintained very close political and economic ties with Great Britain and there still is (or *was*, until the end of World War II) a socio-economically powerful Anglo-Argentine community, which fostered the language in the country (Graham-Yoll, 1981; Solé-Russinovich, 1995). As reported by Cortes-Conde (2003), with the decline of the British Empire and diminishing influence of Britain in the country, the Anglo communities have been going through excruciating crises of identity. The history of the English language in Uruguay dates back to the "*Invasiones Inglesa*," when the British finally took the city of Montevideo (1806–7) while it was still under Spanish colonial rule. The first printed newspaper in the province (which became independent Uruguay in 1830) was the bilingual *The Southern Star/La Estrella del Sur* (Suárez, 2000). In Brazil, contact with Great Britain in the early nineteenth century was a direct consequence of the looming Napoleonic threat in Europe. King João VI of Portugal was forced to flee Portugal with British naval escort and take refuge in Brazil, then a Portuguese colony. On June 22, 1809, he formally instituted by ordinance the teaching of French and English in public schools in the country.

3.1   The role of English after World War II

The presence of English in South America after World War II is directly related to the emergence of the United States as the most powerful nation in the Western world and, from the collapse of the Berlin Wall on, the only remaining superpower. Earlier, the American Civil War (1861–5) had resulted in droves of disgruntled Confederates emigrating to Latin America to found expatriate enclaves (Hill, 1936). In countries like Brazil (El-Dash and Busnardo, 2001; Rajagopalan, 2002; Walker, 2000), Argentina (Eayrs, 2000; Nielsen, 2003) and Chile (Angoy, 2000) – the continent's major economic and political players – the presence of English is noticeable practically everywhere, from newspaper advertisements to billboards and shop windows. At the other extreme are countries like Colombia (Castro and Garcia, 2000; Velez-Rendon, 2003), Ecuador (Alm, 2003; Barry and Barry, 2000), Peru (Ferreyros, 2000), and Venezuela (Gregson, 2000) where the presence of English is still considerably restricted, although, as in the rest of the continent, expanding rapidly.

4   Current ELT Practices

ELT practices vary considerably from one country to another. Almeida Filho (2003) observes that the year 1930 saw the insertion of Brazil into the select group of countries worldwide that contributed to systematic research on the teaching and learning of languages. Scholars like Carneiro Leão (1935), Junqueira Schmidt (1935), and Chagas (1957) made their presence felt during this period, followed by Mascherpe (1970) and Gomes de Matos (1968, 1970, 1976). The year 1970 saw the adoption of a new policy of language teaching. The Audio-Lingual Method that had until then practically dominated the scene gave way to the Communicative Approach, which steadily gained new adepts after 1978 when a national conference on it was held in Florianópolis. More recently, there has been some talk of critical pedagogy, but its real impact on actual classroom practices is far from clear (Cox and Assis-Peterson, 1999). Also worth special mention in this context is the Brazilian "English for Special Purposes" (ESP) Project spearheaded by Maria Antonieta Alba Celani from 1980 on, in response to the growing demands for a working knowledge of English among students, especially at the university level (Barbara and Scott, 1994; Celani et al., 1988; Gomes de Matos and Pinto, 2000; Holmes, 1989). ESP is also making headway elsewhere in the continent, notably Argentina and Chile (McKay, 2003). See also Stevens and Cunha (2003).

5   Legislation Regarding Schools and Universities

In Brazil, a new law that came into effect in 1996 called *Lei de Diretrizes e Bases da Educação* (Guidelines and Underlying Principles for Education) introduced some major changes to language teaching policies at primary and secondary school levels. Among other things, it decentralized decision-making, transferring power to regional educational authorities. Although this was indeed a welcome step, signaling a sea change from the earlier practice of imposing decisions top down often disregarding regional disparities, the new law also invested local educational authorities with new responsibilities which they were scarcely prepared to assume (Bohn, 2003: 166). The law did not cover foreign language teaching at the university level. Specific recommendations in this regard were finally made available in a Ministry of Education project *Parâmetros Curriculares Nacionais: Língua Estrangeira* (National Curriculum Parameters: Foreign Language).

For reasons already looked into, the English language is more securely ensconced in the Argentinean educational system. Friedrich (2003: 181) points to the emergence of a "semi-institutionalised variety of English" as grounds for endorsing Graddol's claim (Graddol, 1997) that Argentina exemplifies the phenomenon whereby certain Expanding-Circle countries move into the category of Outer-Circle countries.

Chile stands out from the list of the remaining countries in the continent as far as the status of English is concerned. It has been estimated that roughly 10 percent of job advertisements placed in the country's major national newspapers are in English and about 30 percent of the jobs advertised require of potential candidates a working command of English (Angoy, 2000). And the educational system is geared toward attending to the market demand, having already made English a compulsory subject in schools. Although there is a paucity of reliable statistical studies, the penetration of English into the social life of Colombia, South America's third most populous country, may be characterized as modest, a fact that is reflected in the limited presence of the language in school and college curricula.

5.1   *Private language schools*

Right across South America, it is to a large extent privately owned franchise schools and language centers that ensure quality English language teaching. These schools offer courses leading up to internationally recognized examinations such as TOEFL and Cambridge First Certificate and Proficiency etc.

5.2   *Teaching standards*

The quality of English language teaching varies considerably from country to country and, within each country, from urban metropolitan centers to rural areas where, in many cases, people are illiterate and live below the level of poverty.

6   Conclusion, Current Trends, and Prospects

English is today securely established as the continent's number one foreign language. It is in many ways much more than a language; indeed, one might say, it is a commodity around which a powerful fetish is building up. As of now, it is also a powerful divider between the rich minority that has access to education and the vast majority of the peoples who toil under severe conditions of underemployment or downright unemployment. As already pointed out, the exact role of the English language in South America can only be fully appreciated against the backdrop of the highly sensitive geopolitics of the region.

Judging from the way the English language has expanded its presence by leaps and bounds in South America in the past 20 or 30 years, there can be no doubt whatsoever that its future is practically guaranteed for the foreseeable future and probably even beyond. But futurology is always a risky business. Just what the future holds for the continent insofar as the presence of the English language is concerned will depend on a number of imponderables, not the least important of which is the kind of transformation that the language itself may be poised to undergo as a result of its unbridled expansion worldwide (Rajagopalan, 2004, 2005a).

See also Chapters 13, CARIBBEAN ENGLISHES; 17, VARIETIES OF WORLD ENGLISHES; 35, A RECURRING DECIMAL: ENGLISH IN LANGUAGE POLICY AND PLANNING; 36, TEACHING WORLD ENGLISHES; 38, WORLD ENGLISHES AND LEXICOGRAPHY.

REFERENCES

Alm, Cecilia Ovesdotter (2003) English in the Ecuadorean commercial context. *World Englishes*, **22**(2), 143–58.

Almeida Filho, José Carlos Paes de (2003) Ontem e hoje no ensino de línguas no Brasil [Today and yesterday in language teaching in Brazil]. In *Caminhos e Colheita: Ensino e Pesquisa na Área de Inglês no Brasil* [Pathways and Harvest: Teaching and Research in the Field of English in Brazil]. Edited by Cristina Maria Teixeira Stevens and Maria Jandyra Cavalcanti Cunha. Brasília: Editora UnB, pp. 19–34.

Angoy, Patricia (2000) Landmark review of the use of teaching and learning of English in Latin America – Chile. British Council. http:// britishcouncil.org/english/ amerigo/chile.

Barbara, Leila and Scott, Mike (1994) *Reflections on Language Learning:*

In Honour of Antonieta Celani.
Clevedon, UK: Multilingual Matters.

Barry, Ana Maria and Barry, Paul (2000) Landmark review of the use of teaching and learning of English in Latin America – Ecuador. British Council. http://britishcouncil.org/english/amerigo/ecuador.

Berns, Margie and Friedrich, Patricia (2003) Introduction: English in South America, the other forgotten continent. *World Englishes*, **22**(2), 83–90.

Bohn, Hilario I. (2003) The educational role and status of English in Brazil. *World Englishes*, **22**(2), 159–72.

Busnardo, JoAnne and Braga, Denise (1987) Language and power: On the necessity of rethinking English language pedagogy in Brazil. In *Initiatives in Communicative Language Teaching II.* Edited by Sandra Savignon and Margie Berns. New York: Addison-Wesley, pp. 15–32.

Carneiro Leão, Antônio C. L. (1935) *O Ensino de Línguas Vivas* [The Teaching of Live Languages]. São Paulo: Campnhia Editora Nacional.

Castro, Rafael Rey De and Garcia, Diana (2000) Landmark review of the use of teaching and learning of English in Latin America – Colombia. British Council. http://britishcouncil.org/english/amerigo/colombia.

Chagas, Raimundo Valdir (1957) *Didática Especial de Línguas Modernas* [Methodology for the Teaching of Modern Languages]. São Paulo: Editora Nacional.

Celani, Antonieta, Holmes, John, Ramos, Rosinda, and Scott, Mike (1988) *The Brazilian ESP Project: An Evaluation.* São Paulo: Educ.

Cortes-Conde, Florencia (2003) "Who is it that can tell me who I am?" The quest for ethnicity in the Anglo communities of Buenos Aires. *World Englishes*, **22**(2), 103–21.

Cox, Maria Inês Pagliarini and Assis-Peterson, Ana Antônia (1999) Critical pedagogy in ELT: Images of Brazilian teachers of English. *TESOL Quarterly*, **33**(3), 159–77.

Eayrs, Martin (2000) Landmark review of the use of teaching and learning of English in Latin America – Argentina. British Council. http://britishcouncil.org/english/amerigo/argentina.

Eastment, David and Santos, Gilberto Diaz (2000) Landmark review of the use of teaching and learning of English in Latin America – Cuba. British Council. http://www.britishcouncil.org/english/amerigo/cuba/index.htm.

El-Dash, Linda and Busnardo, JoAnne (2001) Brazilian attitudes towards English: Dimensions of status and solidarity. *Journal of Applied Linguistics*, **11**(1), 57–74.

Ferreyros, Pilar (2000) Landmark review of the use of teaching and learning of English in Latin America–Peru. British Council. http://britishcouncil.org/english/amerigo/peru.

Friedrich, Patricia (2003) English in Argentina: Attitudes of MBA students. *World Englishes*, **22**(2), 173–84.

Gomes de Matos, Francisco Cardoso (1968) Foreign language teaching in Brazil. In *Trends in Ibero-American and Caribbean Linguistics.* Edited by Thomas Sebeok. The Hague: Mouton, pp. 468–90.

Gomes de Matos, Francisco Cardoso (1970) *Methodology and Linguistics for the Brazilian Teacher of English.* São Paulo: Pioneira.

Gomes de Matos, Francisco Cardoso (1976) *Lingüística Aplicada ao Ensino de Inglês* [Linguistics Applied to the Teaching of English]. São Paulo: McGraw-Hill.

Gomes de Matos, Francisco Cardoso and Pinto, Abuêndia Padilha (2000) English language education in Brazil: Progress and partnerships. *ESL Magazine*, November/December, pp. 26–8.

Graddol, David (1997) *The Future of English?* London: British Council.

Graddol, David, McArthur, Tom, Flack, David, and Amey, Julian (1999) English around the world. In *English in a Changing World: The AILA Review 13*. Edited by David Graddol and Ulrike H. Meinhof. Amsterdam: John Benjamins, pp. 3–18.

Graham-Yoll, Andrew (1981) *The Forgotten Colony: A History of the English-Speaking Community in Argentina*. London: Hutchison.

Gregson, Mark (2000) Landmark review of the use of teaching and learning of English in Latin America – Venezuela. British Council. http://britishcouncil.org/english/amerigo/venezuela.

Hill, Lawrence F. (1936) *The Confederate Exodus to Latin America*. Austin, TX: Texas State Historical Association.

Holmes, John (1989) Feedback: A systems approach to evaluation and course design. *Working Papers, 21*. São Paulo: CEPRIL.

Horowitz, Irving L. (1985) Latin America, anti-Americanism, and intellectual hubris. In *Anti-Americanism in the Third World*. Edited by Alvin Z. Rubinstein and Donald Smith. New York: Praeger, pp. 49–65.

Junqueira Schmidt, Maria (1935) *O Ensino Científico das Línguas Modernas* [The Teaching of Modern Languages]. Rio de Janeiro: F. Briguiet.

Kachru, Braj B. (1985) Standards, codification, and sociolinguistic realism: The English language in the outer circle. In *English in the World*. Edited by Randolph Quirk and

Henry G. Widdowson. Cambridge: Cambridge University Press, pp. 11–32.

Mascherpe, Mário (1970) *Análise Comparativa dos Sistemas Fonológicos do Inglês e do Português* [Comparative analysis of the phonological systems of English and Portuguese]. Assis, SP: UNESP.

McKay, Sandra (2003) Teaching English as an international language: The Chilean context. *ELT Journal*, **57**(2), 139–48.

Morris, Chris (2000) Landmark review of the use of teaching and learning of English in Latin America – Mexico. British Council. http://www.britishcouncil.org/english/amerigo/mexico/index.htm.

Nielsen, Paul M. (2003) English in Argentina: A sociolinguistic profile. *World Englishes*, **22**(2), 199–209.

Niño-Murcia, Mercedes (2003) "English is like the dollar": Hard currency ideology and the status of English in Peru. *World Englishes*, **22**(2), 121–41.

Oliveira e Paiva, Vera Lúcia Menezes de (1995) Imperialismo lingüístico e identidade cultural: o caso da presença do inglês no Brasil [Linguistic Imperialism and Cultural Identity: The Case of English in Brazil]. *Boletim da ABRALIN*, **17**, 11–19.

Pike, Fredrick B. (1992) *The United States and Latin America: Myths and Stereotypes of Civilization and Nature*. Austin, TX: University of Texas Press.

Rajagopalan, Kanavillil (2002) National languages as flags of allegiance; or the linguistics that failed us: A close at the emergent linguistic chauvinism in Brazil. *Journal of Language and Politics*, **1**(1), 115–47.

Rajagopalan, Kanavillil (2003) The ambivalent role of English in

Brazilian politics. *World Englishes*, 22(2), 91–101.

Rajagopalan, Kanavillil (2004) The concept of "World English" and its implications for ELT. *ELT Journal*, 58(2), 111–17.

Rajagopalan, Kanavillil (2005a) Non-native speaker teachers of English and their anxieties: An experiment in action research. In *Non-Native Language Teachers: Perceptions, Challenges, and Contributions to the Profession*. Edited by Enric Lurda. Boston, MA: Springer, pp. 283–303.

Rajagopalan, Kanavillil (2005b) The language issue in Brazil: When local knowledge clashes with expert knowledge. In *Reclaiming the Local in Language Policy and Practice*. Edited by Suresh Canagarajah. Mahwah, NJ: Lawrence Erlbaum, pp. 99–122.

Rajagopalan, Kanavillil and Rajagopalan, Cristina (2005) The English language in Brazil: A boon or a bane? In *Teaching English to the World*. Edited by George Braine. Mahwah, NJ: Lawrence Erlbaum, pp. 1–10.

Sader, Emir (2001) O Brasil fora da Alca [Brazil out of the FTAA]. *Folha de São Paulo*, 3 April.

Solé-Russinovich, Yolanda (1995) Language, nationalism, and ethnicity in the Américas. *International Journal of the Sociology of Language*, 116, 111–37.

Souza Campos, Ernesto de (1940) *Educação Superior no Brasil* [Higher Education in Brazil]. Rio de Janeiro: Ministério da Educação [Ministry of Education].

Stevens, Cristina Maria Teixaira and Cunha, Maria Jandyra Cavalcanti (eds.) (2003) *Caminhos e Colheita: Ensino e Pesquisa na Área de Inglês no Brasil* [Pathways and Harvest: Teaching and Research in the Field of English in Brazil]. Brasília: Editora UnB.

Suárez, Jorge (2000) Landmark review of the use of teaching and learning of English in Latin America – Uruguay. British Council. http:// britishcouncil.org/english/ amerigo/uruguay.

Topik, Steven C. (1992) History of Brazil. In *Latin America and the Caribbean*. Edited by Paula H. Covington. New York: Greenwood Press, pp. 408–52.

Velez-Rendon, Gloria (2003) English in Colombia: A sociolinguistic profile. *World Englishes*, 22(2), 185–98.

Walker, Sara (2000) Landmark review of the use of teaching and learning of English in Latin America – Brazil. British Council. http:// britishcouncil.org/english/ amerigo/brazil.

FURTHER READING

Gomes de Matos, Francisco (2004) *Criatividade no Ensino de Inglês* [Creativity in the Teaching of English]. São Paulo: Disal.

Berns, Margie and Friedrich, Patricia (2003) Introduction: English in South America, the other forgotten continent. *World Englishes*, 22(2), 83–90.

Nielsen, Paul M. (2003) English in Argentina: A sociolinguistic profile. *World Englishes*, 22(2), 199–209.

Oliveira e Paiva, Vera Lúcia Menezes de (1995) Imperialismo lingüístico e identidade cultural: o caso da presença do inglês no Brasil [Linguistic imperialism and cultural identity: The case of English in Brazil]. *Boletim da ABRALIN*, **17**, 11–19.

Rajagopalan, Kanavillil (forthcoming) Language politics in Latin America. In *Applied Linguistics in Latin America. Special number of AILA Review*. Edited by Kanavillil Rajagopalan. Amsterdam: John Benjamins.

Velez-Rendon, Gloria (2003) English in Colombia: A sociolinguistic profile. *World Englishes*, **22**(2), 185–98.

10 South African Englishes

NKONKO M. KAMWANGAMALU

1 Introduction

For almost half a century, 1948–94, South Africa was known to the rest of the world particularly for its now defunct racist system, *apartheid*, that used language and race as key pillars of its divide-and-rule ideology and whose objective was to ensure the supremacy of whites of Dutch origin, the Afrikaners, over South Africa's black majority population (see Shingler, 1973; Alexander, 1989; Kamwangamalu, 1998). The apartheid system used language to divide, control, rule, and protect white minority privilege and power in all spheres of life – education, economy, politics, the media – at the expense of the black population. The proponents of apartheid believed strongly that races were inherently unequal, and that each racial group had to have its own territorial area within which to develop its unique cultural personality. Drawing on this belief, the architects of apartheid divided South Africa into tribal, language-based homelands for the black population on the one hand, and separate, skin-color-based areas for the Indians, the whites, and the so-called "Coloreds," the people of mixed races (e.g. Kamwangamalu, 2000a). Where people could not be divided on the basis of their skin, as was the case for whites of British and Dutch descent, the Afrikaners, then language, in this case English or Afrikaans, was used as the dividing criterion.

One of the characteristic features of South Africa, which the apartheid system exploited to legitimate its divide-and-rule ideology, is its linguistic diversity. The country has a multiracial population of 40,583,573, speaking at least 25 languages from three major groups: African (e.g., Zulu, Xhosa, Sotho, Venda, etc.), European (English, Afrikaans, Portuguese, German, Italian, etc.), and Asian (Chinese languages, namely Cantonese and Hakka; and Indian languages, e.g., Hindi, Tamil, Gujerati, and Telugu). As a result of the end of apartheid in 1994, 11 of the country's estimated 25 languages were accorded official status. They include English and Afrikaans, formerly and historically the only official languages of what had been considered a bilingual state, and nine African languages, including Ndebele, Pedi, Sotho, Swati, Tsonga, Tswana, Venda, Xhosa, and Zulu.

Constitutionally, the relationship between English and the other official languages of South Africa represents what Clyne (1997) calls symmetrical multilingualism, that is, all the languages have equal status. The reality, however, suggests asymmetrical multilingualism, a relationship in which one at least of the languages, in this case English, has a superior status. According to the 1996 census, Zulu is demographically the most commonly spoken first or home language in South Africa (spoken by 23% of the population), followed by Xhosa (with 18%). Afrikaans (14%) and English (9%), while widely spoken throughout the country, are not as commonly used as home languages as are Zulu, Xhosa, and other indigenous languages (*The People of South Africa Population Census 1996*, 1998). It is within this web of languages that English operates in South Africa. The section that follows traces the history of English in South Africa to provide the background against which the unique position of the language in the country can be understood better (see also Lanham, 1996). The next two sections consider the users and uses of English. The subsequent section discusses South Africans' attitudes towards English and is followed, in conclusion, by a brief discussion of the future of English and its impact on South Africa's indigenous languages.

2   The History of English in South Africa

The history of English in South Africa is discussed comprehensively in a special issue of *World Englishes* (vol. 21(1), 2002), edited by Kamwangamalu. This section reproduces an outline of this history, with additions where necessary. As a background, it is worth noting that prior to the birth of democracy in 1994, South Africa was subjected to three consecutive colonial rules. The country was first colonized by the Dutch from 1652 to 1795, followed by the British from 1795 to 1948, and once again by the Dutch, who by then called themselves Afrikaners, from 1948 until the country liberated itself from apartheid in 1994. For 342 years, Dutch (later Afrikaans) or English was used to divide, control, and rule South Africa and to protect white (Afrikaner or English, depending on which one of the two groups was in power) minority privilege and power in all spheres of life – education, economy, politics – mostly at the expense of the majority black population.

The history of English in South Africa is interwoven with that of Afrikaans, an offspring of Dutch. This history is one of a constant struggle for power; one where, at some point, each language has sought to impose itself over the other (see Kamwangamalu, 2001a: 89). The struggle between English and Afrikaans continues to be aimed, for each language and its (white) speakers, at achieving social, economic, and political control over South Africa. This struggle started in 1795 when British troops invaded what was then the Cape of Good Hope, now Cape Town, and overthrew the Dutch, who had ruled the territory since

1652, to control the strategic sea route between Asia and Europe (Lass, 1995). The British returned the Cape to the Dutch in 1803, but in 1806 they retook control of the territory to prevent it from falling to the French, who had laid claim to Holland during the Napoleonic wars (1805–15). With the territory under their control once more, the British, one of whose primary goals was to replace Dutch with English, embarked on a policy of *Anglicization*. Accordingly, they banned Dutch, which was the official language of the Cape during the Dutch rule (1652–1795), from all spheres of life and imposed the use of English throughout the colony. The British justified the banning of Dutch from the territory on both ideological and religious grounds. Ideologically, the Governor of the Cape, Lord Charles Somerset, conceived it as his honest duty to Anglicize the colonists as soon as possible because:

> they were only a little over thirty thousand in number, and it seemed absurd that such a small body of people should be permitted to perpetuate ideas and customs that were not English in a country that had become part of the British Empire. . . . (Malherbe, 1925: 57)

Religiously, the British authority used what Sundermeier (1975) calls the myth of the Chosen People to justify Anglicization in the colony. One advocate, Cecil Rhodes, wrote:

> Only one race . . . approach God's ideal type, his own Anglo-Saxon race; God's purpose then was to make the Anglo-Saxon race predominant, and the best way to help on God's work and fulfill His purpose in the world was to contribute to the predominance of the Anglo-Saxon race and so bring nearer the reign of justice, liberty and peace. (Sundermeier, 1975: 25)

Anxious to promote English and to further reduce the influence of Dutch, Lord Somerset brought out Scottish Presbyterian ministers to serve in Dutch Reformed churches and Englishmen to teach in country schools (Moodie, 1975: 5; Lanham, 1986: 324). For an extended discussion of the battle over language on religious grounds, see Kamwangamalu (2001b: 380–2). Teachers were expected to use their best efforts to promote Afrikaner acceptance of British rule; and imperial history formed a large part of the curriculum (Warwick, 1980: 351). The British determination to impose Anglicization in the colony and the Afrikaners' resistance against it are, among other factors, said to have contributed to the Anglo-Boer war of 1899–1902, which the British won (e.g., Moodie, 1975). The policy of Anglicization lasted, in theory, until 1910, when the Union of South Africa was formed, thus giving English and Dutch equal status as the co-official languages of the Union. In practice, however, the British never accepted parity between Dutch and English, especially in education. The British government policy, for both political and economic reasons, had laid down that English was a prerequisite for state aid in education (Hartshorne, 1995: 310). Also, according to a British official quoted in Headlam (1931: 514), "the principle of the equality of the two languages [Dutch and English] had consistently been rejected by us [the British] from the first."

The Anglicization policy effectively ended in 1948, when the Afrikaners came into power and introduced *Afrikanerization*. Afrikaans became the main language for the conduct of the business of the state. Although English had the status of co-official language with Afrikaans, Silva (1998: 70) remarks that the apartheid government treated English as a "Cinderella" language. However, in 1953 the apartheid government adopted a controversial language policy, the Bantu Education Act, which brought English back into the limelight. The Act sought to impose Afrikaans as the medium of instruction and reduce the influence of English in black schools. (For more elaborate discussions of the Bantu Education Act, see Kamwangamalu, 1997, 2000b.) The apartheid government's determination to implement this policy and the black pupils' resistance against it led to the bloody Soweto uprisings of June 16, 1976, in which several pupils lost their lives. The aftermath of the Soweto uprisings saw Afrikaans emerge, in the minds of black South Africans, as the language of oppression, and English as the language of liberation (Alexander, 1989). It is against this background of oppression of the black population by the Afrikaners that attitudes toward English, to be discussed later, are to be understood. As Kamwangamalu (1997: 238) observes, it is ironic that one of the most controversial policies of the apartheid era, the Bantu Education Act, had the opposite effect to that desired for it. Despite the fact that in most former British colonies English is often viewed as an interloper, imposed from outside and thus politically suspect (Silva, 1998), English has emerged in South Africa completely untainted by its colonial history (Smit, 1998: 79) because Afrikaans shielded it from that stigma (Silva, 1998: 72). From the time of the Bantu Education Act until the birth of a democratic South Africa in 1994, English has never looked back. Rather, it has become far more hegemonic than any other language in the nation (see, e.g., de Klerk and Barkhuizen, 2001; Webb, 2002; Webb and Kriel, 2000). Following the discussion of the users of English below, I shall explain why English has such a unique, powerful position in South Africa.

3   The Users of English

Kachru (1996) distinguishes three concentric circles in the spread of English. The first, known as the Inner Circle, includes countries where English is used as a native language, among them Australia, Canada, New Zealand, South Africa, the United Kingdom, and the United States of America. The second, the Outer Circle, includes countries where English is an institutionalized variety, that is, is used as an official language. Former British colonies, such as South Africa, India, Nigeria, and Zambia, to list a few, belong in this category. The third, the Expanding Circle, consists of countries where English is used as a performance variety, that is, a foreign language. Some such countries include Japan, China, Argentina, and Rwanda.

In Kachru's framework, it can be stated unequivocally that South Africa belongs simultaneously to two of the proposed three concentric circles of English: the Inner Circle on the one hand, and the Outer Circle on the other. This is because English is used in South Africa as a native language by some, for instance, whites of British descent and the younger generations of South African Indians, and as a second language by others, namely the black population, the older generations of South African Indians, and the whites of Dutch descent, the Afrikaners. Unlike the users of English in other former British or American colonies, who look to Britain or America for a model of English to emulate, especially in education, the users of English in South Africa have a model available in their backyard because of the presence of over a million native speakers of the language. According to the 1996 census, English is spoken as home language by 3,457,467 of South Africans (9%), including 1,711,603 whites (39%), 974,654 Asians (94.4%), 584,101 coloreds (16.4%), and 113,132 Africans (0.4%; *The People of South Africa Population Census 1996*, 1998). Because of its multiple functions as will be discussed later, English receives a lot of support from all the aforementioned constituencies of users, all of whom (both native and non-native) believe that their children's future lies with the global language, English. The language has a wider distribution than most of South Africa's official languages, but the majority of its speakers are concentrated in metropolitan and urban areas. Two of South Africa's nine provinces, Gauteng and KwaZulu Natal, each have more than a million English speakers; these are followed by the Western Cape province with more than half a million speakers.

In South Africa English is not monolithic. It has a wide range of varieties, much as it does in any English-speaking country in the world. Against the background of the apartheid system and the walls it built between communities, clear distinctions can be made between the following varieties: White South African English (SAE), Black SAE, Indian SAE, and Colored SAE. These varieties each have their own standards and sub-varieties. Lanham (1986), for instance, distinguishes three varieties within White SAE: Conservative SAE, Respectable SAE, and Afrikaans English, including its variant, Extreme SAE. The first is associated with whites of British descent; the second with whites of Jewish descent; and the third with whites of Dutch descent. Similarly, recent studies (e.g., van Rooy, 2002; Wissing, 2002) show that each black language community, such as the Zulu, Xhosa, and Tswana, has its own distinct variety of English. South Africa's second-language varieties of English are heavily marked at every level of linguistic structure by the primary languages of their speakers: African languages for Black SAE, Afrikaans for Colored and Afrikaans SAE, and Indian languages for Indian SAE. Concerning the latter, Lanham (1986: 326) remarks that, despite the fact that South African Indians have lost their languages and have shifted to English, their English is characterized by an accent carrying the hallmarks of Indian English elsewhere in the world.

4 The Uses of English

English is highly valued in post-apartheid South Africa and enjoys far more prestige than any other official language, including Afrikaans. Its fortunes date back to the heyday of apartheid, and especially after the Bantu education Act of 1953 and the subsequent Soweto uprising of June 16, 1976, as explained earlier. The language serves all the functions identified in Kachru's (1996: 58) framework: interpersonal, instrumental, regulative, and innovative/imaginative. The interpersonal function refers to the use of English both as a symbol of eliteness and modernity, and as a link language between speakers of various languages in a multilingual society. The instrumental function refers to the use of English in a country's educational system. The regulative function concerns the use of English for the regulation of conduct in such domains as the legal system and the administration. And the imaginative/innovative function entails the use of English in various literary genres.

4.1 The interpersonal function

In South Africa, English provides what Silva (1998: 76) calls "the linguistic glue to bond a [racially, ethnically, and linguistically] diverse and complex society." It is the unmarked language in all inter-racial as well as in most inter-ethnic communication. There is perhaps no clearer evidence of this than in the language use in South Africa's Parliament. Although the Constitution of the Republic of South Africa (1996, section 3(2)) says that all of the 11 official languages must be treated equitably and enjoy parity of esteem, Pandor (1995: 75) observes that in 1994, 87 percent of the speeches made in Parliament were in English; and this is despite the fact that about 80 percent of the members of Parliament are Africans and so are naturally fluent in at least two of the country's nine official indigenous languages in addition to English and Afrikaans. A more recent study by Hibbert (2001) indicates that the percentage of speeches made in English in Parliament has actually increased from 87 percent in 1994 to over 95 percent in 2001. English is not only a link language, but it is also a status symbol. To be educated and be seen as modern goes hand in hand with being able to express oneself in English. As Phaswana (2003: 126) comments on the language practices of South African Parliamentarians, "those who speak in English are said to be well-informed and better educated, while [those] who speak in any African language [are] perceived as uneducated and uncivilized."

4.2 The instrumental function

Against the background of apartheid's language-in-education policies and of the international status of English in particular, the majority of parents (and this includes parents in some sections of the Afrikaans-speaking communities) want their children educated in English-medium schools. English is the medium of instruction at more than 80 percent of South African schools. Currently the country has 22 full-fledged universities and 15 "technikons," tertiary institutions that provide vocational education to supply the labor market with individuals who have particular skills, and technological and practical knowledge in a specific field (Rautenbach, 1992: 358). Most of the technikons and 17 of the universities are English-medium. Five formerly Afrikaans-medium universities have largely become English/Afrikaans-medium to accommodate black students' demand for English-medium education. Since English is the language of power, job opportunities, prestige, and status, it is seen by many as an open sesame by means of which one can achieve unlimited vertical social mobility (Samuels, 1995). As Virasamy (1997) observes, English is the language that some believe "can get you anywhere and everywhere"; it is a language such that, in the words of Slabbert (1994), "if you know [English] you are everything." One who knows English "is everything" because, as Grin (2001: 73) remarks pointedly, even at lower levels of competence, a little English is always associated with higher earnings. Against this backdrop, it is not surprising that when apartheid ended in 1994, and with it school segregation, the country witnessed an influx of black students from the township schools, which use an African language as a medium of instruction for the first three years of elementary education, to formerly white or Indian schools in their quest to be educated, from Grade 1 onward, only through the medium of English (see Kamwangamalu, 2003: 234).

4.3   The regulative function

English plays a central role in the administration of contemporary South Africa. Despite the country's Constitution, English is emerging as the sole language for the conduct of the business of the state. In the current administration, communication between the various organs of the state is exclusively carried out in English. As a matter of fact, Gunning (1997: 7) reports that in their language practices most provincial legislatures use English rather than any other official language. He explains that "politicians seem to prefer English over other languages, practical circumstances dictate its use, [English] is used to avoid confusion, it is the main language of documentation." English is also the language of business, commerce and international trade, science, technology, diplomacy, international communication, the internet, and the media.

Both electronic and print media, perhaps more than any other domains of language use, have accorded English a special status, one that no other language can match. For example, South Africa has three public television channels, SABC1, SABC2, and SABC3 (SABC standing for South Africa Broadcasting Corporation); English has the lion's share of airtime for all three channels. This is evident from Kamwangamalu's (2001c) survey of language practice in the medium of television in South Africa. The study shows that for the period April–June 2001, for instance, South Africa's 11 official languages had a total of 4,664.52 hours to share for all three TV channels. Of that total, broadcasts in English accounted for 3,954.5 hours (85% of the total airtime), while Afrikaans and all nine official African languages had 485 hours (10%) and 226.02 (5%), respectively. About 50 percent of all the programs presented on the SABC are produced locally. Another 50 percent consists of programs imported from overseas, especially from the United Kingdom and the United States. Currently, and this is unlikely to change, most of the programs, both local and imported, are broadcast in English. The same is true for language use in the medium of radio and in the print media. The SABC also has 16 radio stations which broadcast for a combined air time of 300 hours per week to an audience of some 28 million daily listeners. Some 12 private and about 90 community radio stations are also part of the network of radio broadcasting services in South Africa. The majority of these stations broadcast in English (though Afrikaans is also well represented; *South Africa Year Book*, 1999: 470; *Europa World Year Book*, 1999, II: 3227).

   South Africa has 30 major newspapers, including 19 dailies and 11 weeklies. Of all these newspapers, 21 are published exclusively in English and had a combined circulation of 1,936,466 in 1999 (Kamwangamalu, 2001a: 406). The largest daily newspaper in South Africa, the *Sunday Times*, had a circulation of 458,000 copies at that time. Its circulation must have increased by now, since growing numbers of South Africans want English first and foremost; and there are, as de Klerk and Barkhuizen (2001: 113) note, a number of recent studies (Bowerman, 2000; Dyers, 2000) which provide telling evidence of this increase. English prevails not only on television, on the radio and in the print media, but also in the courts, a domain that used to be the preserve of Afrikaans. As a matter of fact, recently the Minister of Justice proposed, and Parliament approved, the idea that English should become the sole language of record in the courts, in order to cut down the costs of keeping record in all the 11 official languages (*The Daily News*, October 20, 2000). Why English? Why not Zulu, Venda, or any of the other official languages? The choice of English again bears testimony to the high esteem in which the language is held in South Africa.

4.4   The innovative/imaginative function

South Africa has produced a large body of creative literature written in English. It is not an overstatement to say that no other language, including Afrikaans, let alone the indigenous African languages, can match the extent of this literature. English has co-existed with South African indigenous languages and Afrikaans for the past two centuries. As a result, the languages have mutually colored one another. There is evidence of Englishization and Africanization or nativization (Gough, 1996; Watermeyer, 1996; Kamwangamalu, 2001d). The former refers to the impact of English on Afrikaans and African languages; and the latter to the impact of African languages and Afrikaans on English. Here I shall present only a few examples of nativization, with a focus on the lexicon.

Several loan words from Afrikaans and the African languages have been integrated into the English lexicon. These words are substantially documented in the *Dictionary of South African English on Historical Principles* edited by Silva et al. (1996). Some of the entries in this dictionary, words which are frequently used in South African newspapers as well as in creative writing, include the following: *indaba* (from Zulu and Xhosa), a serious meeting involving community leaders; *bosberaad* (from Afrikaans), a meeting of leaders at a retreat which is remote from urban centers, intended to provide participants with the chance to focus, undisturbed, on difficult issues; *lekker* (from Afrikaans), cool, better, delicious; *muti* (from Zulu and Xhosa), traditional medicine, magical charm; *lobola* (from Zulu and Xhosa): loosely translated as 'dowry or bride-price'; *braai* (from Afrikaans), barbecue; *mampara* (perhaps from Sotho), waste material, idiot.

Also, there is internal lexical creativity, that is, lexical changes that are taking place within English as a result of social changes, not caused by contact between English and South Africa's indigenous languages (see, e.g., Kamwangamalu, 2001d: 54). The compound "*rainbow-X*," where X can be any English noun, is a case in point. It refers either to the coming together of people from previously segregated communities or to something that affects or benefits these communities. "Rainbow" can combine with any English noun, and this has resulted in compounds such as the following, culled from South African newspapers: *rainbow nation, rainbow complacency, rainbow swimming pool, rainbow gathering*, and *rainbow alienation* (Kamwangamalu, 2001d: 54).

5   South Africans' Attitudes toward English

As a result of the legacy of apartheid, attitudes toward English in South Africa can be described as community-specific. The perennial conflict between English and Afrikaans, discussed earlier, provides the background against which attitudes toward English can be understood better. For the white Afrikaans-speaking community, English has always been characterized as *die vyand se taal*, 'the language of the enemy' (Branford, 1996: 39). For this community, and despite the fact that some of its members acknowledge the instrumental value of English, the language is seen as a serious threat to Afrikaner identity and culture. The Afrikaners' resentment against English has been exacerbated by their fall from power as a result of the demise of apartheid, a fall that has resulted in overwhelming power for English, the de facto current language of rule in post-apartheid South Africa.

Unlike the Afrikaners, since their forebears arrived in South Africa in 1860 as indentured laborers, South African Indians have, for pragmatic reasons, always had positive attitudes toward English. The fact that the Indian community has shifted completely to and is now monolingual in English bears further testimony to its members' attitude toward the language. The black community's attitude toward English has also been positive, as can be recalled from the aftermath of the Soweto uprisings of 1976, an event that entrenched the position of English at the expense of Afrikaans in the black community. Despite the overwhelming support it has in the black community, English has often been considered a double-edged sword (see Kamwangamalu, 2002: 3). Although English provides access to education and job opportunities, it also acts as a barrier to such opportunities for those who do not speak it, or whose English is poor (Branford, 1996: 36). It is an important key to knowledge, science, and technology, but it is increasingly being seen as the major threat to the maintenance of indigenous languages (Masemola and Khan, 2000: 11), as a remnant of colonialism and a cause of cultural alienation (Schmied, 1991: 121), as a vehicle of values not always in harmony with local traditions and beliefs (de Klerk, 1996: 7), and, as wa Thiong'o Ngũgĩ (1993: 35) describes it, as "a language that flourishes on the graveyard of other people's languages."

The following headlines, culled from South African newspapers, attest further to the concerns that the black community has about the increasing spread and hegemony of English, a language that some in the community consider a threat to the very survival of their indigenous African languages:

PROMINENCE OF ENGLISH KILLS AFRICAN LANGUAGES (*Daily News*, Friday, September 24, 1999).
   The New South Africa presides over the death of African languages. Not only are we overseeing the death of African languages, but we are also acting as both executioner and grave-digger. We are truly killing and burying our African languages and the tragedy is that there are very few mourners.

ENGLISH ONSLAUGHT: INDIGENOUS LANGUAGES UNDER THREAT (*Daily News*, Wednesday, December 6, 2000)
   The indigenous languages of South Africa are under tremendous pressure which threatens to literally wipe them off the surface of the linguistic landscape. From the remotest Khoi language of the Kgalakgadi to the pre-eminent Nguni isiZulu tongue in KwaZulu Natal, they all face a common, domineering force – English.

LANGUAGE BARRIER: SOUTH AFRICA HAS 11 LANGUAGES, BUT MANY COULD SOON FACE EXTINCTION, writes Benison Makele (*Sowetan Sunday World*, August 5, 2001)
   People who speak African languages believe that their languages cannot feed them. With more pupils leaving township schools for suburban Model C institutions, concerns have been raised that it might soon be taboo to speak in any African language, especially in the global village.

Only the future will tell whether the hegemony of English can be curbed so that the language can co-exist in harmony, rather than in tension, with its sister official languages in post-apartheid South Africa.

6   Conclusion

This chapter has presented a sociolinguistic profile of English in South Africa. Unlike in other former British colonies, in South Africa English is used both as a native language by the more than a million British who, contrary to what they did in other colonies, never left the country when colonization ended, and as second language by a minority of South Africa's population. Because of its instrumental value and its status as an international language, English is widely held in high esteem in South Africa, both by those who are fluent in it and those who are not. So English has a secure place in South Africa, one that no other official language can match. There are, however, some dissenting voices against English, particularly in the white Afrikaans-speaking community, where it is seen as a threat to Afrikaner culture and identity. Language activists in the black community have also been vocal against the hegemony of English, which they see as contributing to the further marginalization of the indigenous African languages. Notwithstanding all these dissenting voices, it is becoming increasingly apparent, as Vivian de Klerk (1996: 17) remarks pointedly, that "even the strongest opponents of English see to it that their own loved ones master the language."

See also Chapters 11, West African Englishes; 12, East African Englishes; 15, World Englishes Today; 17, Varieties of World Englishes; 23, Literary Creativity in World Englishes; 28, World Englishes and Descriptive Grammars; 32, World Englishes in the Media; 38, World Englishes and Lexicography; 41, World Englishes and Corpora Studies.

REFERENCES

Alexander, Neville (1989) *Language Policy and National Unity in South Africa/ Azania.* Cape Town: Buchu Books.

Bowerman, Sean A. (2000) Linguistic imperialism in South Africa: The unassailable position of English. MA dissertation, University of Cape Town.

Branford, William (1996) English in South African society: A preliminary overview. In *English around the World: Focus on South Africa.* Edited by Vivian de Klerk. Amsterdam: Benjamins, pp. 35–51.

Clyne, Michael (1997) Multilingualism. In *The Handbook of Sociolinguistics.*

Edited by Florian Coulmas. Oxford: Blackwell, pp. 301–14.

Constitution of the Republic of South Africa (1996) Pretoria: Government Printers.

de Klerk, Vivian (1996) Introduction. In *English around the World: Focus on South Africa.* Edited by Vivian de Klerk. Amsterdam: Benjamins, pp. 7–17.

de Klerk, Vivian and Barkhuizen, Gary (2001) Language usage and attitudes in a South African prison: Who calls the shots? *International Journal of the Sociology of Language,* **152**, 97–115.

Dyers, C. (2000) Language, Identity and Nationhood: Language use and attitudes among Xhosa students at the University of the Western Cape, South Africa. PhD dissertation, University of the Western Cape.

Europa World Year Book (1999) London: Europa Publications.

Gough, David (1996) Black English in South Africa. In *English around the World: Focus on South Africa*. Edited by Vivian de Klerk. Amsterdam: Benjamins, pp. 53–77.

Grin, Francois (2001) English as economic value: Facts and fallacies. *World Englishes*, **20**(1), 65–78.

Gunning, E. (1997) Engels voer botoon in provinsies, skuif ander tale uit [English dominates in provinces, edges out other languages]. *Rapport*, 6 April.

Hartshorne, Ken (1995) Language policy in African education: A background to the future. In *Language and Social History: Studies in South African Sociolinguistics*. Edited by Rajend Mesthrie. Cape Town: David Philip, pp. 306–18.

Headlam, Cecil (1931) *The Milner Papers*. London: Cassell.

Hibbert, L. (2001) Changing language practices in parliament in South Africa. Paper presented at the Eighth International Association for World Englishes (IAWE) Conference. University of Potchefstroom, South Africa, 29 November–1 December.

Kachru, Braj B. (1996) Models for non-native Englishes. In *The Other Tongue: English across Cultures*. 2nd edition. Edited by Braj B. Kachru. Delhi: Oxford University Press, pp. 48–74.

Kamwangamalu, Nkonko M. (1997) Multilingualism and education policy in post-apartheid South Africa. *Language Problems and Language Planning*, **21**, 234–53.

Kamwangamalu, Nkonko M. (ed.) (1998) Aspects of Multilingualism in Post-apartheid South Africa. Special issue of *Multilingua*, **17**(2–3).

Kamwangamalu, Nkonko M. (ed.) (2000a) Language and Ethnicity in the New South Africa. Special issue of the *International Journal of the Sociology of Language*, **144**.

Kamwangamalu, Nkonko M. (2000b) A new language policy, old language practices: Status planning for African languages in a multilingual South Africa. *South African Journal of African Languages*, **20**(1), 50–60.

Kamwangamalu, Nkonko M. (2001a) Ethnicity and language crossing in post-apartheid South Africa. *International Journal of the Sociology of Language*, **152**, 75–95.

Kamwangamalu, Nkonko M. (2001b) The language situation in South Africa. *Current Issues in Language Planning*, **2**(4), 361–445.

Kamwangamalu, Nkonko M. (2001c) When 2 + 9 = 1: English and the politics of language planning in a multilingual society, South Africa. The Third Conference on Major Varieties of English (MAVEN). Freiburg, Germany, 6–9 June.

Kamwangamalu, Nkonko M. (2001d) Linguistic and cultural reincarnations of English: A case from Southern Africa. In *The Three Circles of English: Language Specialists Talk about the English Language*. Edited by Edwin Thumboo. Singapore: UniPress, pp. 45–66.

Kamwangamalu, Nkonko M. (ed.) (2002) English in South Africa. Special issue of *World Englishes*, **21**(1).

Kamwangamalu, Nkonko M. (2003) Social change and language shift: South Africa. *Annual Review of Applied Linguistics*, **23**, 225–42.

Lanham, Len W. (1986) English in South Africa. In *English as a World Language*. Edited by Richard W.

Bailey and Manfred Görlach. Ann Arbor: The University of Michigan Press, pp. 324–52.

Lanham, Len W. (1996) A history of English in South Africa. In *English around the World: Focus on South Africa*. Edited by Vivian de Klerk. Amsterdam: Benjamins, pp. 19–34.

Lass, Roger (1995) South African English. In *Language and Social History: Studies in South African Sociolinguistics*. Edited by Rajend Mesthrie. Cape Town: David Philip, pp. 68–88.

Malherbe, Ernst G. (1925) *Education in South Africa (1652–1922)*. Cape Town: Juta.

Masemola, T. and Khan, F. (2000) English onslaught: Indigenous languages under threat. *The Daily News*, 6 December.

Moodie, T. Dunbar (1975) *The Rise of Afrikanerdom: Power, Apartheid, and the Africaner Civil Religion*. Berkeley: University of California Press.

Ngũgĩ, wa Thiong'o (1993) *Moving the Center: The Struggle for Cultural Freedoms*. London: James Currey.

Pandor, Naledi (1995) Constitutional multilingualism: Problems, possibilities, practicalities. *Proceedings of the Fifteenth Annual Conference of the Southern African Applied Linguistics Association (SAALA)*, pp. 57–74.

People of South Africa Population Census 1996 (1998) Pretoria: Government Printers.

Phaswana, Nkhelebeni (2003) Contradiction or affirmation? The South African language policy and the South African national government. In *Black Linguistics: Language, Society, and Politics in Africa and the Americas*. Edited by Sinfree Makoni, Geneva Smitherman, Arnetha Ball, and Arthur Spears. London: Routledge, pp. 117–31.

Rautenbach, W. (1992) The crucial role of technical and vocational education in the restructuring of education in South Africa. In *McGregor's Education Alternatives*. Edited by Robin McGregor and Anne McGregor. Cape Town: Juta, pp. 357–75.

Samuels, John (1995) Multilingualism in the emerging educational dispensation. *Proceedings of the Fifteenth Annual Conference of the Southern African Applied Linguistics Association (SAALA)*, pp. 75–84.

Schmied, Josef (1991) *English in Africa*. London: Longman.

Shingler, John (1973) Education and Political Order in South Africa, 1902–1961. PhD dissertation, Yale University.

Silva, Penny (1998) South African English: Oppressor or liberator? In *The Major Varieties of English*. Edited by Hans Linquist, Staffan Klintborg, Magnus Levin, and Maria Estling. Vaxjo: Vaxjo University Press, pp. 69–92.

Silva, Penny, Dore, Wendy, Mantzel, Dorethea, Muller, Colin, and Wright, Madeleine (eds.) (1996) *A Dictionary of South African English on Historical Principles*. Oxford: Oxford University Press.

Slabbert, Sarah (1994) What is the mother tongue of the Sowetan teenager? And is this the same as home language(s)? *BUA* (formerly *Language Projects Review*), 9(1), 4–7.

Smit, Ute (1998) South African English lexemes for South Africans: A case in point for a developing multicultural standard of English. In *The Major Varieties of English*. Edited by Hans Linquist, Staffan Klintborg, Magnus Levin, and Maria Estling. Vaxjo: Vaxjo University Press, pp. 79–89.

South Africa Population Census 1996 (1998) Pretoria: Statistics South Africa.

South Africa Year Book (1999) Pretoria:
Bureau for Information, Department
of Foreign Affairs.

Sundermeier, Theo (ed.) (1975) *Church
and Nationalism in South Africa*.
Johannesburg: Ravan Press.

Van Rooy, Bertus (2002) Stress placement
in Tswana English: The makings of
a coherent system. *World Englishes*,
21(1), 145–60.

Virasamy, Chrissie (1997) An
investigation into teacher-elicited
Zulu-mother tongue use by Zulu-
speaking pupils in an English-only
classroom. MA thesis, Department
of Linguistics, University of Natal,
Durban, South Africa.

Warwick, Peter (ed.) (1980) *The South
African War: The Anglo-Boer War,
1899–1902*. London: Longman.

Watermeyer, Susan (1996) Afrikaans
English. In *English around the World:
Focus on South Africa*. Edited by
Vivian de Klerk. Amsterdam/
Philadelphia: Benjamins, pp. 99–124.

Webb, Victor (2002) English as a second
language in South Africa's tertiary
institutions: A case study at the
University of Pretoria. *World
Englishes*, **21**(1), 49–61.

Webb, Victor and Kriel, Maria (2000)
Afrikaans and Afrikaner
nationalism. *International Journal
of the Sociology of Language*, **144**,
pp. 19–51.

Wissing, Daan (2002) Black South
African English: A new English?
Observations from a phonetic
viewpoint. *World Englishes*, **21**(1),
pp. 129–44.

FURTHER READING

Branford, William (1996) English in
South African society: A preliminary
overview. In *English around the
World: Focus on South Africa*. Edited
by Vivian de Klerk. Amsterdam:
Benjamins, pp. 35–51.

Gough, David (1996) Black English in
South Africa. In *English around the
World: Focus on South Africa*. Edited
by Vivian de Klerk. Amsterdam:
Benjamins, pp. 53–77.

Kamwangamalu, Nkonko M. (ed.) (2002)
English in South Africa. Special issue
of *World Englishes*, **21**(1).

Lanham, Len W. (1996) A history of
English in South Africa. In *English
around the World: Focus on South
Africa*. Edited by Vivian de Klerk.
Amsterdam: Benjamins,
pp. 19–34.

Lass, Roger (1995) South African
English. In *Language and Social
History: Studies in South African
Sociolinguistics*. Edited by Rajend
Mesthrie. Cape Town: David Philip,
pp. 68–88.

11   West African Englishes

TOPE OMONIYI

1   Introduction

There is a strain of ideological opposition between the two concepts "English in X-Region" (EiX) and "X-Regional Englishes" (X-an E) – as exemplified by "English in West Africa" and the title of this chapter, "West African Englishes." The same strain is noticeable in Ajani's (2001: 1) review of Dakubu (1997) which began thus: "*English in Ghana* (EIG) is a very timely book on the 'new Englishes' and a welcome addition to many of its kind already published for other countries." No doubt both concepts may be a consequence of the same general political experience, i.e. colonization, but they signal different subject positions or perspectives. My first task then is to articulate these different positions, although in doing so, I must stress that neither is a totally exclusive category.

Makoni and Meinhof (2003: 8) identify world Englishes as a paradigm that focuses on "the ways in which English in its spread has been 'indigenized' and appropriated by speakers of African languages," but add less critically that the paradigm "is a way of classifying different varieties of English." In reality, their claim encapsulates what I identify as the two schools of thought on the development of English(es). One is the Manfred Görlach School of English World-Wide (EWW), the focus of which is mainly on varieties' differentiation based on grammatical description. Thus the approach largely adopts a micro-analytical framework. This school overtly or covertly investigates language spread as a periphery phenomenon from an "inquisitive mainstream" perspective and seeks to establish and describe the nature of deviation or difference from "default" native-speaker Englishes (see also Schmied, 1991a and 1991b).

The second is the Kachru School of World Englishes (WE), which perceives the spread and the consequent indigenization and appropriation of English as political and therefore ideologically invested (see B. Kachru, 1986, 1992, 1995,

1996, 1997; Y. Kachru, 1996) in seeking legitimacy for "Other Englishes." The preference here is for a macro-analytical framework that explores contact situations for the sociopolitical relationships they promote and the impact of these on English, indigenous languages, and societies as language users. Thus, a major differentiation between EWW and WE as paradigms is that while the former "retains the trinity of ENL, ESL and EFL," the latter dissolves it. B. Kachru (1997: 66) notes that WE addresses "other vital issues directly concerned with functions, identities, and creativity in Englishes in dynamic socio-cultural and linguistic contexts in practically every English-using part of the world." This differentiation is clearly demonstrated in B. Kachru's (1986: 33) distinction between "English in South Asia" and "South Asian English." According to him, the latter derives its pedigree from institutionalization that performance varieties such as "English in South Asia" lack. This makes Makoni and Meinhof's reference to "a classificatory tool" perhaps more appropriate for EWW and less so for WE.

The same observation goes for Bruthiaux's (2003: 159) and Pennycook's (2003: 513) criticisms of WE as a model. They impose a faulty assessment regime on WE by querying its capacity to achieve outcomes that do not follow logically from the model's objectives. Postcolonial realities and imaginations, and the demands of globalization make West Africa (WA) a unique sociolinguistic context in which both paradigms (WE and EWW) may thrive (cf. Phillipson, 2001, 2004). The WE paradigm fulfils a national desire for colonial closure through associating new and independent status with a recognizable and "autonomous" variety of English toward which all within the boundaries of the nation-state can aspire. The EWW paradigm facilitates the attainment of this desire by codifying such varieties – or at least attracting controversy on the extent to which the identified brand features are peculiar.

Arguably, nativization, indigenization, localization, or however else we choose to describe the process that transforms native into non-native English (or cultivates the latter from the former), may be seen as part of the anti-imperial and anti-colonial apparatus engaged in the pursuit of self-determination and independence in postcolonial societies. Indigenized Englishes served as the major media of elite mobilization for nationalist struggles and decolonization efforts throughout Africa. Thus, from inception, non-native varieties of English as conceptualized in WE were ideologically and politically marked. WE theorizes the periphery from within and is thus invested with an alternative mainstream *tour de force* and scholarship status (cf. B. Kachru, 1996). This is then complemented by the efforts of radical mainstream postcolonial deconstructionists who engage reflexive and reflective research tools in taking the closely related discipline of English Language Teaching to task over what they perceive to be its agenda of sustaining structural imbalance and asymmetry. This model would appear to be the preferred approach for most researchers located at the periphery because it provides an alternative to the hegemonic discourse of the traditional English language teaching and learning diaspora from a Western perspective.

In the rest of this chapter, first, I shall present an overview of the studies of non-native Englishes in WA from John Spencer's edited volume *The English Language in West Africa* (1971) to the more recent edited volume by Lucko, Peter and Wolf, *Studies in African Varieties of English* (2003). This is necessary since claims of the existence of non-native varieties of English in Africa remain steeped in controversy (see, for instance, Ahulu, 1994 and Dolphyne, 1997). Second, I shall identify critical issues around English language usage in WA. In doing this, I shall invoke the sentiments that informed works such as Phillipson (1992), Fishman, Conrad and Rubal-Lopez (1996), Pennycook (1994, 1998, 2000), Canagarajah (1999), and Omoniyi (2003a, 2003b) among others on language issues within social and/or critical theory frameworks. With these considerations in mind, the rest of the discussion is structured broadly into five parts:

- from Spencer (1971) to Lucko et al. (2003), perspective(s) and coverage;
- national varieties of English in WA;
- contemporary social issues around English usage in WA;
- the future of English in WA and the future of WA in English;
- conclusion.

2   From Spencer (1971) to Lucko et al. (2003)

From historical accounts, the English language arrived on the West African coast some time in the sixteenth century after the earliest European explorers had first landed at various ports – Prince Henry the Navigator in Cape Verde in 1444, Sierra Leone in 1460, and Gold Coast in 1471. Spencer (1971: 8) cites Towerson's accounts of his voyages in 1555–7 to the Guinea Coast and the fact that African interpreters were already being sent to Britain for training. Those earliest contacts led to the development of broken language forms, which served as lingua francas in the trade that subsequently developed between the Europeans and the local coastal populations. Arguably, these were the beginnings of the pidgins and creoles that characterize WA today – in Nigeria, Cameroon, Ghana, Sierra Leone, and Liberia. This sociolinguistic intercourse can be said to mark the commencement of Phase One Western occupation and influence if we take a Sapir-Whorfian language, thought, and control perspective. Phase Two may be said to have begun with missionary activities and signaled the start of Western intervention in the cultural lives of the peoples of the region, especially through education. During this phase, the symmetry of the old trading relations was altered with the establishment of structures of dominance such as the Royal Niger Company. Metaphorically, by that act of commercial branding, a natural feature of the West African terrain, the River Niger, was appropriated for the English monarchy. The Berlin Congress of 1884 marked the political formalization of these processes. It is absolutely important to understand the development in this light in order to see how the society was primed for the implantation of colonial languages, especially the English language during and beyond the twentieth century when it became a global political, cultural, and economic enterprise.

2.1 Spencer (1971)

The Spencer volume was a pioneering work, and its title represents its modest focus on identifying West African Englishes by form and function. In their blurb, the publishers claim that "it may be said to inaugurate a new branch of English language studies: the exploration in depth of what is happening to English in areas where, though not a native language, it is widely used for a variety of purposes." They go on to say that "to appreciate the context within which English exists in West Africa requires an understanding of the social, political and educational circumstances of its *implantation and extension*, and the pressures and demands which determine its present growth" (emphasis added). In the foreword to the volume, Randolph Quirk conveyed the sentiment of the times when he described the territory covered in the volume as "this immense conglomeration of exotic cultures, fauna and geophysical wonders," in other words, a spectacle – the quintessential colonial object/subject.

In summary, the volume contains nine articles by the leading researchers of the period. The first paper, by Spencer, discusses the implantation of English in WA, tracing the history of European contact and influence of the various Christian missions on the spread of English. The next two papers, by Bamgboṣe and Boadi, evaluate the role and character of English in Nigeria and Ghana, respectively, especially in education. The next five papers in the volume (Jones, Mafeni, Hancock, Kirk-Green, and Ansre) explore the contact situation and the consequences of contact in specific national contexts – Nigeria, Ghana, etc. The last paper (Young) deals with the subject of language in literary writing. The articles discuss both forms and functions of English in WA.

2.2 Through Lucko et al. (2003)

There have been a few other efforts since Spencer (1971), but many of these have had mostly a national rather than regional coverage. Görlach (1997) presents a collage of English from a variety of discourse genres in Nigeria, including historical documents, newspaper articles, literary texts, and primary research by Jibril (1986), Kujore (1985), and Agheyisi (1988), who distinguishes between "broken," "pidgin," "creole," and "regional standard" forms of English.

Only four other works have claimed to have a regional scope:

1 Bamgboṣe, Banjo, and Thomas (1995), *New Englishes: A West African Perspective*;
2 Görlach, whom John Spencer described as "the leading European authority on the English language diaspora," most of the publications in the *English World-Wide* journal;

3   Bamgboṣe, a special issue of the *International Journal of the Sociology of Language*, The Sociolinguistics of West Africa (2000);
4   Lucko et al., *Studies in African Varieties of English* (2003).

Bamgboṣe's special issue of the *International Journal of the Sociology of Language* is not specifically on the internationalization of English, although some of the papers, especially Banjo's "English in West Africa" (pp. 27–38), address the subject of non-native Englishes. The Lucko et al. volume ambitiously claims a continental scope in its title, but in reality delivers a much narrower focus on four countries: Nigeria, Cameroon, The Gambia, and Sudan, concentrating for the most part on function and description rather than on the sociopolitical life of English in the region. In addition to these works, we can add a long list of theses, dissertations, and academic articles on one non-native national variety of English or another that have been submitted to institutions in WA and around the world.

3   National Varieties of English in WA

"X-Regional English" lends itself more to contexts where a language served as a colonial language prior to independence, hence Cameroonian English, Nigerian English, Ghanaian English, Liberian English, Sierra Leonean English, Gambian English. Ajani (2001) identifies the major focus of these varieties to include models, standards and standardization, norms, descriptive issues, errors, teaching and English language competence among pupils in secondary and tertiary institutions, and so on.

John Singler, whose seminal articles account for a substantial portion of all published work on Liberian English, suggests that non-native national varieties of English constitute a continuum. He notes that "Liberian English, the non-standard English-lexifier speech of Liberia, can be divided into three varieties: Kru Pidgin English . . . Settler English . . . and Vernacular Liberian English" (1997: 205). In another publication, Singler writes, "Liberian English, the range of English from pidgin to standard spoken in Liberia, is characterized by vast variation in the marking of semantically plural nouns" (1991: 545). These subtly contrasting descriptions of Liberian English by the same author exemplify the problem of separating the two concepts "English in West Africa" and "West African Englishes." A selection of published titles from *English World-Wide* further illustrates how fuzzy the distinction is between the two concepts:

1   Nigerian English in political telemarketing (Awonusi, 1998);
2   Eighteenth-century Sierra Leone English: Another exported variety of African American English (Montgomery, 1999);
3   The trilateral process in Cameroon English phonology: Underlying representations and phonological processes in non-native Englishes (Simo Bobda and Chumbow, 1999);

4   Patterns of Nigerian English intonation (Jowitt, 2000);
5   Ghanaianisms: Towards a semantic and a formal classification (Dako, 2001);
6   "First year of nation's return to government of make you talk your own make I talk my own": Anglicism versus pidginization in news translations into Nigerian Pidgin (Deuber, 2002).

On the balance of probability, then, EWW as a paradigm explores micromore than macro-analysis in its focus on form. However, sometimes both analytical approaches may be employed. Bamgboṣe (1997: 19), for instance, describes how newscasters on popular music stations use a strategy of indirectness to add flavor to their news. He argues that "conventions of non-native varieties represent an adaptation of English news reporting to the Yoruba norms in which idioms, proverbs, and indirect references constitute an acceptable style."

4   Contemporary Social Issues around English in WA

The West African sociolinguistic space is now more complex than ever. Earlier research often had an intranational framework and discussed linguistic pluralism in the context of the nation-state. Thus references were to the roles and statuses of all the languages within the territory of a country (see Bamgboṣe, 1991; Gerda, 1993; Omoniyi, 1994; Singler, 1997). Table 11.1 presents an overview of the nature of linguistic pluralism of which English forms a part.

4.1   English and the West African political union

More recently, however, it has become necessary to expand existing frameworks in order to explain how the emerging economic and political union in the region alters the sociolinguistic landscape. Within such a framework, obviously new perspectives are beginning to emerge. Instead of neat packaging according to nation-state boundaries, research now shows that language choice is effected across these boundaries. For example, when Beninois Yoruba parents in Igolo opt for English-medium education for their children and so enroll them in schools in Idiroko on the Nigerian side of the international boundary. Interestingly, therefore, at community and national levels of discourse, choices are being made between English and indigenous languages and between English and French (see Omoniyi, 2004). Whatever the case, the point must be made that several of the languages in the region are transnational. This is achieved either through people moving in search of greater language capital or displacement caused by conflict as refugees search for safe havens, or the historical reason of reuniting with kinsfolk across the arbitrary boundaries put in place during the scramble for and partition of Africa in Berlin in 1884. Table 11.2 presents the distribution of some transnational languages in sub-Saharan Africa.

Table 11.1   Language pluralism in West Africa

Country	Population	No. of languages	Official language(s)
Benin	6.60m	52	French
Burkina	6.90m	72	French
Cameroon	9.60m	253	French/English
C. Verde	0.35m	4	Portuguese
Chad	5.20m	117	French/Arabic
C. d'Ivoire	10.10m	73	French
E. Guinea	0.41m	9	Spanish/French
Gabon	0.82m	38	French
Gambia	0.72m	19	English
Ghana	12.70m	72	English
Guinea	6.10m	28	French
G-Bissau	0.85m	22	Portuguese
Liberia	2.20m	34	English
Mali	7.70m	23	French
Mauritania	1.90m	6	Arabic, Wolof
Niger	6.50m	18	French
Nigeria	97.00m	420	English/French
Sao Tome	0.12m	2	Portuguese
Senegal	6.70m	37	French
S. Leone	3.60m	23	English
Togo	2.70m	42	French

4.2   *Refugee impact on English language spread*

The distribution in Table 11.2 represents the forced contacts created by the arbitrariness of colonial demarcation, which had not taken cognizance of ethnic boundaries. However, the situation today has been made even more complicated by the refugee situation in the region. United Nations High Commission for Refugees (UNHCR) figures for 2003 show that there are about 4.6 million refugees in Africa (UNHCR February 2004). There is no indication of how many of these are in sub-Saharan Africa. There has been no systematic study of the factors that determine the direction of refugee flows, but it is logical to expect that, at least for intra-continental flows in Africa, the pattern will be influenced by access through proximity and the relative ease of adaptation to language and culture.

Kerswill (2006) notes that "in every case of migration, except where a homogeneous group of people moves to an isolated location, language or dialect contact ensues." This situation will be tempered by attitudes, and both Banjo (2000) and Omoniyi (2004) have suggested that there is greater positive attitude toward English in French-speaking countries than there is to French in

Table 11.2 Some of West Africa's transnational languages (figures calculated from Grimes, 2004)

Language	Countries where spoken (population in millions)
Arabic	Chad (0.5), Mauritania (1.6), Nigeria (0.1)
Bande	Guinea (0.05), Liberia (0.07)
Bariba	Benin (0.5), Nigeria (0.1)
English	ESL: Cameroon (nd), Gambia (nd), Ghana (1),* Liberia (L1, 0.07), Nigeria (1),* Sierra Leone (nd); EFL: Francophone states
Ewe	Ghana (1.7), Togo (0.9)
Fon	Benin (1.5), Togo (0.04)
French	Benin (0.2), Burkina Faso (nd), Cameroon (nd), Chad (0.003), Cote d'Ivoire (0.02), Guinea (nd), Mali (0.009), Niger (0.006), Nigeria (nd), Senegal (nd), Togo (0.003)
Fulani/Fulfude/Fuuta Jalon/Pulaar	Benin (0.3), Burkina Faso (0.8), Cameroon (0.7), Chad (0.1), Gambia (0.2), Ghana (0.07), Guinea (2.7), Mali (1.1), Mauritania (0.2), Niger (0.9), Nigeria (7.6), Senegal (2.1), Togo (0.05)
Hausa	Benin (nd), Burkina Faso (nd), Cameroon (0.02), Chad (nd), Ghana (nd), Niger (5), Nigeria (19), Togo (0.01)
Malinke/Maninka	Gambia (0.3), Guinea (2), Mali (0.8), Mauritania (nd), Senegal (0.34), Sierra Leone (0.09)
Mandinka	Gambia (0.4), Senegal (0.54)
Mende	Liberia (0.02), Sierra Leone (1.5)
Pidgin English/ Creole/Krio	Cameroon (2), Liberia (1.5), Nigeria (nd), Sierra Leone (0.5)
Soninke	Cote d'Ivoire (0.01), Gambia (0.06), Guinea (nd), Mali (0.7), Mauritania (0.03), Niger (nd), Senegal (0.17)
Wolof	Gambia (0.15), Guinea (nd), Mali (nd), Mauritania (0.01), Senegal (3.2)
Yoruba	Benin (0.5), Nigeria (19)

Notes: Grouped languages are based on reported similarities and level of mutual intelligibility; * = figures which are presumably modest for their ESL contexts; nd = no data.

English-speaking countries in WA. Table 11.3 gives an idea of the scale of refugee movements as documented by the UNHCR.

Although there are no statistical details of refugee distribution by ethnicity, the degree of multi-ethnicity in the war zones provides a rich basis for conjecture. The real consequence of this lack of data is that it is difficult to characterize the resultant language ecologies and the role that English might play in them. This is a significant development, especially when refugee numbers exceed the population of settlements along the route of flow in some cases.

Table 11.3 Populations of concern to UNHCR end 2002 (*UNHCR Stastistical Yearbook*, 2002)

	Refugees	Asylum seekers	Returned refugees	IDPs[a]	Total population of concern
Benin	5,021	314	–	–	5,335
Burkina F.	457	377	–	–	834
Cameroon	58,288	5,308	–	–	63,596
Chad	33,455	1,034	51	–	34,540
Gabon	13,473	5,663	–	–	19,136
Gambia	12,120	–	–	–	12,120
Ghana	33,515	8,762	–	–	42,277
Guinea	182,163	367	–	–	182,530
Ivory Coast	44,749	1,142	–	100,000	145,891
Liberia	64,956	–	21,901	304,115	390,972
Mauritania	405	12	–	29,917[b]	29,917
Niger	296	44	–	–	340
Nigeria	7,355	30	114	–	7,499
Senegal	20,711	1,928	15	–	22,654
Sierra L	63,494	277	75,978	–	139,749
Togo	12,294	123	–	–	12,417

[a] Internally displaced persons.
[b] 29,500 of these are Malians and Sahrawis.

Perhaps of greater interest are those movements across former Francophone/ Anglophone divides, as is the case between Liberia/Ivory Coast, Liberia/ Guinea, Sierra Leone/Guinea, Nigeria/Cameroon, illustrated in Table 11.4. Of an estimated total of 121,000 Bande in Liberia, 50,000 fled to Guinea as

Table 11.4 Refugees across intra- and intercolonial language boundaries

Donor nation	Refugee numbers and receiving nations							
	Ivory Coast	Ghana	Guinea	Liberia	Mali	Nigeria	Sierra Leone	Gambia
Ivory Coast			2,188	**19,158***				
Liberia	**122,846**	8,865	**82,792**			1,505	10,771	
Sierra Leone		1,998	**95,527**	54,717	**1,415**	2,041		7,734

* Intercolonial figures are in bold type.

refugees. Thus, a substantial percentage of the group has relocated to a new geolinguistic and sociolinguistic environment, with implications that include guaranteed influence on the spread of colonial languages.

These movements over the course of decades of crisis have ramifications beyond the region. For instance, Blommaert (2000: 2) notes that "upon arrival in Belgium and after having stated their desire to obtain asylum, asylum seekers are interviewed by officials, sometimes (but by no means always) assisted by interpreters." In situations such as this, decisions about the genuineness of asylum seekers' cases on the basis of identities suggested by linguistic strains in their speech may be flawed.

5   The Present and Future of English in WA

5.1   The Present

The contemporary relevance of English in the region is ensconced in the language policies of the Anglophone states and the anchorage of the regional economy to a global one for which English remains the most important medium of transaction. The domains of use in the region include:

- administration (local, state and federal governments);
- examinations;
- university entrance;
- job interviews;
- civil service promotion tests;
- aptitude tests;
- education – medium of instruction and curriculum subject; period allocation on school timetables (see Omoniyi, 2003a);
- commerce.

This listing summarizes the link between English language competence, notions of success, and upward social mobility. English has been the major gatekeeper in the attainment of access to higher socio-economic classes in sub-Saharan Africa. The brief of the West African Examinations Council (WAEC) describes it as "the foremost indigenous public examination body in the West African Sub-region" and claims that "The Council has the responsibility of determining examinations required in the public interest in West Africa and to conduct such examinations and to award certificates." The language of this examination is English except for language subjects such as Yoruba, Igbo, Hausa, Ewe, Fulfude, etc., which are tested in the respective languages. The implication of this is that old attitudes that construct English as superior to indigenous languages are sustained by language policy (cf. Adegbija, 1994).

WAEC stipulates the following entry regulations for the West African Secondary Schools Certificate Examinations:

A. Candidates are required to enter and sit for a minimum of eight (8) and a maximum of nine (9) subjects.
These must include the following:

(i)   English Language.
(ii)   Mathematics.
(iii)   At least one Nigerian Language (see footnote).
(iv)   At least one of the following alternative subjects: Physics, Chemistry and Biology.
(v)   At least one of Literature-in-English, History and Geography.
(vi)   Agricultural Science or at least one vocational subject.

These are the core subjects.

It is not insignificant that English Language is the first listed subject. Item (iii) requires candidates to enroll for "at least one Nigerian Language." From an ideological point of view, this ambivalent reference to an un-named language is an indication of the levity with which indigenous language issues are treated. This fact is further affirmed in the following note to the entry regulations for candidates:

> NOTE: The Federal Ministry of Education has given a waiver in respect of Nigerian Languages for the 2003 examination. This implies that candidates' entries are valid with or without a Nigerian language for the period of the waiver.

Statements such as this indicate the continuing relevance of English in the West African region, which is likely to be further enhanced by economic and political union.

5.2   The future

WA as presently politically constituted has two clear traditions – Anglophone and Francophone – of which the region is being discursively divested through the construction of a Union. Banjo (2000) notes two other traditions: dual-heritage nations like Cameroon, and a nation that lacks a colonial history such as Liberia. However, both of the latter still broadly fit under Anglophone/Francophone spheres of influence. I do not share the view expressed by Wolf and Igboanusi (2003: 69), that West African English already exists as a formally recognized regional variety. There is sufficient evidence, however, that it is emergent.

In the last quarter of the twentieth century, efforts intensified to create an economic union in the region, the outcome of which was the Economic Community of West African States (ECOWAS), established in 1975. Its objective was to facilitate economic integration in the region. In 1994, the eight former Francophone states formed the West African Economic and Monetary Union. More recently, regional integration has become an immediate goal redefined along lines of the European Union to include political, social and cultural co-operation. The outcome of this is the establishment of a West African

Parliament and Central Bank, and the Eco as the single currency of the states. This is the context within which any worthwhile evaluation of the future of English in WA must be addressed.

The Sierra Leonean and Liberian troubles lasted more than a decade, and this is a substantial fraction of the lifespan of a generation of West Africans, considering the life expectancy of about 50 for the region (UN, 2005). Also the population of people involved and the duration of the assignments in Sierra Leone and Liberia create an interesting context for the possible emergence of "West African English" as a variety. National varieties such as Nigerian English, Ghanaian English, Sierra Leonean English, and Liberian English are potential "dialects" of West African English. Often, references to this development in the literature of world Englishes have lacked definition and the term has therefore been loosely used. It is invoked as a collectivization of the various national varieties of English that exist within the region.

The global community under the auspices of the United Nations endorsed peace initiatives by ECOWAS with only minimal external human resource support. ECOMOG, the peacekeeping force put together within the region and led by Nigeria, comprised mainly military personnel from Nigeria and Ghana. It will be a while yet before the direct and sustained sociolinguistic impact of these mass deployments becomes obvious, especially in rural locations where the military presence was substantial relative to the civilian population.

The mass displacement of people as a result of these wars has the potential to trigger realignments across the cultural landscape. Guinean refugees are in Sierra Leone and vice versa, Liberian refugees are in Sierra Leone and Ivory Coast and were cited among the precipitators of the 2002 crisis following an attempted military coup d'état in Ivory Coast. The language situation is thus a complex one. At one level, this interpenetration affects non-native varieties of French and English, and at another, the ethnicities that constituted the pre-war nation-states have been modified. Unfortunately, no evidence exists that any critical or systematic study of this language situation has been conducted. The influence is likely to be confined to individual and community levels with no impact on policy at the state level. Where large numbers of people have been involved in the search for safe havens, it is interesting that such demographic changes and the new realities they create are not reflected in national planning.

The new political, economic, and cultural organs put in place in the region, which will be run by personnel from a mix of countries, will create a multilingual context and create a demand for an administrative language. At another level, the age-old competition between La Francophonie and the Anglophone world may be resuscitated. De Swaan (2001) has predicted that the future of the French language diaspora will be determined on the African continent.

6   Conclusion

The distinction I made between EWW and WE in the introduction was intended to demonstrate that the latter, more than the former, entailed a politics that was relevant to life and living in sub-Saharan Africa. It is important to know how West African Englishes came into being and about the processes of their codification, standardization, institutionalization, and usage. But this cannot be a sufficient end in itself. Ultimately, the question we must pose is: "What can we learn about structure and social change in West African societies from West African Englishes?"

The development and use of corpora has produced a sizable portion of the knowledge we have of language use behavior and of social transformation across domains in Inner-Circle societies. Several studies, like Kjellmer's (1986) study of masculine bias in British and American English, have drawn their data from corpora such as the British National Corpus, Survey of English Usage, and the International Corpus of English (ICE). Studies of this kind thus potentially serve as a basis for challenging doctrines and ideology and consequently bringing about social change. Corpora such as the Cameroon Corpus of English (CCE), ICE franchises in WA and others can potentially serve the same purpose in Expanding-Circle societies, but to do that they must be continually updated and not simply serve as data sources for describing varieties. How much of Inner-Circle ideology seeps into Expanding-Circle varieties and, through Whorfian processes, impacts users of any of the West African Englishes remains largely unresearched.

It is a bit premature at the moment to assume the existence of a West African English without an established administrative, political, or cultural community of that description. None of the existing corpora including Lucko et al.'s are vast enough as yet to support that claim. Still, I shall close on a prophetic note about what the future might be for an emerging West African English. Its non-standard or traditional varieties may be characterized by ethnic accents and regional variation, possibly marked by nation-specific vocabulary items. The increasing role of Nigeria as regional "big brother," its dominance in the regional economy, and the spill-over of its population into countries in the region arguably indicate what the future might hold. The growth of digital media technology and the increasing pervasiveness of Nollywood, the Nigerian film industry, which has an estimated annual net income of 45 million US dollars, are added facilitators in the spread and continuing relevance of Nigerian English in sub-Saharan Africa. This sentiment is captured in the vision articulated by B. Kachru (1995: vi) that "The West Africans have over a period of time given English a Nigerian identity."

See also Chapters 10, SOUTH AFRICAN ENGLISHES, 12, EAST AFRICAN ENGLISHES; 13, CARIBBEAN ENGLISHES; 15, WORLD ENGLISHES TODAY; 17, VARIETIES OF WORLD ENGLISHES; 18, PIDGINS AND CREOLES; 23, LITERARY CREATIVITY IN WORLD ENGLISHES; 25, WORLD ENGLISHES AND CULTURE WARS; 35, A RECURRING DECIMAL: ENGLISH IN LANGUAGE POLICY AND PLANNING; 38, WORLD ENGLISHES AND LEXICOGRAPHY; 41, WORLD ENGLISHES AND CORPORA STUDIES.

REFERENCES

Adegbija, Efurosibina (1994) *Language Attitudes in Sub-Saharan Africa: A Sociolinguistic Overview*. Clevedon, UK: Multilingual Matters.

Adegbija, Efurosibina (2003) Idiomatic variation in Nigerian English. In *Studies in African Varieties of English*. Edited by Peter Lucko, Lothar Peter, and Hans-georg Wolf. Frankfurt: Peter Lang, pp. 41–56.

Agheyisi, Rebecca (1988) The standardization of Nigerian Pidgin English. *English World-Wide*, **5**, 211–33.

Ahulu, Samuel (1994) How Ghanaian is Ghanaian English? *English Today*, **38**, 25–9.

Ajani, Temi (2001) Review of *English in Ghana*, edited by Mary E. Kropp Dakubu, Accra: Ghana English Studies Association, 1997. *African Studies Quarterly*, **5**(1). Accessed February 4, 2004 (http://web.africa.ufl.edu/asq/v5/v5i1l.htm).

Awonusi, Victor O. (1998) Nigerian English in political telemarketing. *English World-Wide*, **19**(2), 189–204.

Bamgboṣe, Ayọ (1991) *Language and the Nation: The Language Question in Sub-Saharan Africa*. Edinburgh: Edinburgh University Press.

Bamgboṣe, Ayọ (1997) Non-native Englishes on trial. In *English in Ghana*. Edited by Mary E. Kropp Dakubu. Accra: Ghanaian English Studies Association, pp. 9–19.

Bamgboṣe, Ayọ, Banjo, Ayọ, and Thomas, Andrew (eds.) (1995) *New Englishes: A West African Perspective*. Ibadan: Mosuro.

Banjo, Ayọ (2000) English in West Africa. In Sociolinguistics in West Africa. Special issue of the *International Journal of the Sociology of Language*, **141**, 27–38.

Blommaert, Jan (2000) Analysing African asylum seekers' stories: Scratching the surface. *Working Papers in Urban Language and Literacies*, **14**, 1–32.

Bruthiaux, Paul (2003) Squaring the circles in modeling English worldwide. *International Journal of Applied Linguistics*, **13**(2), 159–78.

Canagarajah, Suresh (1999) *Resisting Linguistic Imperialism in English Teaching*. Oxford: Oxford University Press.

Canagarajah, Suresh A. (2000) Negotiating ideologies through English: Strategies from the periphery. In *Ideology, Politics and Language Policies: Focus on English*. Edited by Thomas Ricento. Amsterdam: John Benjamins, pp. 121–32.

Dako, Kari (2001) Ghanaianisms: Towards a semantic and a formal classification. *English World-Wide*, **22**(1), 23–53.

Dakubu, Mary E. Kropp (ed.) (1997) *English in Ghana*. Accra: Ghana English Studies Association.

Deuber, Dagmar (2002) First year of nation's return to government of make you talk your own make I talk my own: Anglicism versus pidginization in news translations into Nigerian Pidgin. *English World-Wide*, **23**(2), 195–222.

Dolphyne, Florence A. (1997) President's address. In *English in Ghana*. Edited by Mary E. Kropp Dakubu. Accra: The Ghana English Studies Association, pp. 4–7.

Fishman, Joshua A., Conrad, Andrew W., and Rubal-Lopez, Alma (1996) *Post-Imperial English: Status Change in Former British and American Colonies, 1940–1990*. Berlin: Mouton de Gruyter.

Gerda, Mansour (1993) *Multilingualism and Nation Building*. Clevedon, UK: Multilingual Matters.

Görlach, Manfred (1997) *Even More Englishes: Studies 1996–1997*. Amsterdam: John Benjamins.

Grimes, Barbara (2004) *Ethnologue: Languages of the World*. 14th edition. Dallas: SIL.

Jibril, Munzali (1986) Sociolinguistic variation in Nigerian English. *English World-Wide*, **7**, 47–74.

Jowitt, David (2000) Patterns of Nigerian English intonation. *English World-Wide*, **21**(1), 63–80.

Kachru, Braj B. (1986) *The Alchemy of English: The Spread, Functions and Models of Non-native Englishes*. Oxford: Pergamon Press.

Kachru, Braj B. (1992) World Englishes: Approaches, issues and resources. *Language Learning*, **25**(1), 1–14.

Kachru, Braj B. (1995) Foreword. In *New Englishes: A West African Perspective*. Edited by Ayọ Bamgboṣe, Ayọ Banjo, and Andrew Thomas. Ibadan: Mosuro, pp. iii–viii.

Kachru, Braj B. (1996) The paradigms of marginality. *World Englishes*, **15**(3), 241–55.

Kachru, Braj B. (1997) World Englishes and English-using communities. *Annual Review of Applied Linguistics*, **17**, 66–87.

Kachru, Yamuna (1996) Culture, variation, and languages of wider communication: The paradigm gap. In *Linguistics, Language Acquisition and Language Variation: Current Trends and Future Prospects*. Edited by James E. Alatis, Carolyn A. Straehle, Maggie Ronkin, and Brent Gallenberger. Washington, DC: Georgetown University Press, pp. 178–95.

Kerswill, Paul (2006) Migration and language. In *Sociolinguistics/Soziolinguistik: An International Handbook of the Science of Language and Society*. 2nd edition. Edited by Ulrich Ammon, Norbert Dittmar, Klaus J. Mattheier, and Peter

Trudgill. Berlin: Mouton de Gruyter, pp. 2271–2284.

Kjellmer, Göran (1986) "The lesser man": Observations on the role of women in modern English writings. In *Corpus Linguistics II*. Edited by Jan Arts and Willem Meijs. Amsterdam: Rodopi, pp. 163–76.

Kujore, Obafemi (1985) *English Usage: Some Notable Nigerian Variations*. Ibadan: Evans.

Lucko, Peter, Peter, Lothar, and Wolf, Hans-Georg (eds.) (2003) *Studies in African Varieties of English*. Frankfurt: Peter Lang.

Makoni, Sinfree and Meinhof, Ulrike (2003) Introducing applied linguistics in Africa. In *Africa and Applied Linguistics: AILA Review 16*. Edited by Sinfree Makoni and Ulrike Meinhof. Amsterdam: John Benjamins, pp. 1–12.

Montgomery, Michael (1999) Eighteenth-century Sierra Leone English: Another exported variety of African American English. *English World-Wide*, **20**(1), 1–34.

Omoniyi, Tope (1994) Price-tagging child bilingualism: An evaluation of policy and the socio-economic and political implications of commercialization of nursery education in Nigeria. Eric Document Reproduction Service No. ED 365 160. Chicago, IL: Central University.

Omoniyi, Tope (2003a) Language, ideology and politics: A critical appraisal of French as second official language in Nigeria. In *Africa and Applied Linguistics: AILA Review 16*. Edited by Sinfree Makoni and Ulrike Meinhof. Amsterdam: John Benjamins, pp. 13–25.

Omoniyi, Tope (2003b) Local policies and global forces: Multiliteracy and Africa's indigenous languages. *Language Policy*, **2**, 133–51.

Omoniyi, Tope (2004) *The Sociolinguistics of Borderlands: Two Nations, One*

Community. Trenton, NJ: Africa World Press Inc.

Pennycook, Alastair (1994) *The Cultural Politics of English as an International Language*. London: Longman.

Pennycook, Alastair (1998) *English and the Discourses of Colonialism*. London: Routledge.

Pennycook, Alastair (2000) English, politics, ideology: From colonial celebration to postcolonial performativity. In *Ideology, Politics and Language Policies: Focus on English*. Edited by Thomas Ricento. Amsterdam: John Benjamins, pp. 107–20.

Pennycook, Alastair (2003) Global Englishes, Rip Slyme, and performativity. *Journal of Sociolinguistics*, **7**(4), 513–33.

Phillipson, Robert (1992) *Linguistic Imperialism*. Oxford: Oxford University Press.

Phillipson, Robert (2001) English for globalization or for the world's people? *International Review of Education*, **47**(3–4), 185–200.

Phillipson, Robert (2004) English in globalization: three approaches. *Journal of Language, Identity and Education*, **3**(1), 73–84.

Schmied, Josef (1991a) *English in Africa: An Introduction*. London: Longman.

Schmied, Josef (1991b) National and subnational features of Kenyan English. In *English Around the World: Sociolinguistic Perspectives*. Edited by Jenny Cheshire. Cambridge:

Cambridge University Press, pp. 420–34.

Simo Bobda, Augustin and Chumbow, Beban S. (1999) The trilateral process in Cameroon English phonology: Underlying representations and phonological processes in non-native Englishes. *English World-Wide*, **20**(1), 35–65.

Singler, John V. (1991) Copula variation in Liberian Settler English and American Black English. In *Verb Phrase Patterns in Black English and Creole*. Edited by Walter F. Edwards and Donald Winford. Detroit: Wayne State University Press, pp. 129–64.

Singler, John V. (1997) The configuration of Liberia's Englishes. *World Englishes*, **16**(2) 205–31.

Spencer, John (1971) *The English Language in West Africa*. London: Longman.

Swaan, Abram de (2001) *Words of the World: The Global Language System*. Cambridge: Polity Press.

UN (2005) *Human Development Report 2003*. New York: UNDP. http://www.undp.org/hdr2003/indicator/indic_1_1_1.html, accessed January 3, 2006.

Wolf, Hans-Georg and Igboanusi, Herbert (2003) A preliminary comparison of lexical items in Nigerian English and Cameroon English. In *Studies in African Varieties of English*. Edited by Peter Lucko, Lothar Peter, and Hans-Georg Wolf. Frankfurt: Peter Lang, pp. 69–81.

FURTHER READING

Brock-Utne, Birgit (2002) *Language, Democracy and Education in Africa*. Discussion Paper 15. Uppsala: Nordiska Afrikainstitutet.

Mazrui, Alamin (2004) *English in Africa: After the Cold War*. Clevedon, UK: Multilingual Matters.

Mufwene, Salikoko (1994) New Englishes and criteria for naming them. *World Englishes*, **13**, 21–31.

12 East African Englishes

JOSEF SCHMIED

1 Introduction

This survey of East African English (EAfE) focuses on Kenya, Uganda, and Tanzania, which are often seen as the core of East Africa. The varieties of English used there are considered typical ESL varieties, part of the New Englishes and of Kachru's (1986) Outer Circle. The terminology depends more on ideological stance than on "linguistic facts": the "conservative" view emphasizes the common core and acknowledged "standards," the "progressive" view cherishes the diversity of actual usage and the cultural and linguistic innovations. This presentation tries to abstract from some well-known linguistic facts and to leave the interpretations to the readers, their language-political preferences, and attitudes (cf. Chapter 35, this volume).

Kenya, Uganda, and Tanzania share a long, common "Anglophone" background, despite some interesting differences in colonial heritage. They are also characterized by a complex pattern of African first languages (mainly from the Bantu and Nilo-Saharan language families), a common lingua franca (Kiswahili), and a combination of Christian, Islamic and native African religious and cultural beliefs. The East African Community (1967–76, revived in 1997) is a sociopolitical expression of this common heritage.

The neighboring countries in the north – Sudan, Ethiopia, and Somalia – have also experienced some English influences, but they have had their own special histories as well as linguistic and cultural traditions, especially a much more independent development and – in large parts – a more dominant Arabic influence, so that they are usually not considered ESL nations in Kachru's sense. The southern "Anglophone" neighbors – Zambia, Malawi, and Zimbabwe – are often (cf. Schmied, 1996) considered as "Central Africa" or even part of "Southern Africa" since they have been under a dominant impact from the south (including its native speakers of English) for over a century. This influence is engrained in the pronunciation (e.g., the long central vowel tending towards [a.], like girl as [ga.l]) and the lexicon (e.g., the typical SAfE robot for traffic light).

Although many sociolinguistic and linguistic features can also be found in other parts of Africa, EAfE can be distinguished clearly enough from other Englishes and thus justifiably treated as a coherent descriptive entity. A realistic description can only be based on authentic data from the regions, exemplary quotations from individual recorded utterances, a quantified and stratified pattern retrieved from the relevant sections of the International Corpus of English (ICE-EA; cf. Chapter 41 this volume), or a qualified search using internet search engines (Schmied, 2005).

2   Review of the Literature

The scholarly literature on EAfE is still scarce and patchy. There is no introductory volume like Spencer (1971) for West Africa (cf. Chapter 11, this volume). Although the Ford Foundation funded a big sociolinguistic survey of language in Eastern Africa in the late 1960s and early 1970s, the descriptive data published as a result (Polomé and Hill, 1980 for Tanzania; Whiteley, 1974 for Kenya; and Ladefoged, Glick, and Criper, 1971 for Uganda) are relatively limited, especially for English.

Of course, East Africa is covered in the standard surveys of English in Africa (Schmied, 1991a) or of English around the world (Hancock and Angogo in Bailey and Görlach, 1982; Abdulaziz in Cheshire, 1991; Schmied in Kortmann et al., 2004; and contributions in Kachru, 1992). These articles give a good introduction into the sociolinguistic background, including language policies and language attitudes. More detailed studies have been presented on various pronunciation features (Kanyoro, 1991; Schmied, 1991b). Although the availability of data has improved enormously over the last few years, through corpora or selected internet texts from radio stations as well as newspapers (Schmied and Hudson-Ettle, 1996), the systematic description of EAfE has only just started. There are some sophisticated data-based analyses on idiomaticity (Skandera, 2003), on subordination (Hudson-Ettle, 1998), and on prepositions (Mwangi, 2003), all based on the East African part of the International Corpus of English (see below). These corpus texts also come to life in a new text volume with corresponding interpretations (Schmied, forthcoming).

3   The Historical Background

European languages came late to East Africa, as for a long time the colonialists were not particularly interested in this part of Africa; only the Swahili towns on the coast (Kilwa, Zanzibar, Mombasa, Malindi, etc.) were used as stepping stones to the center of the British Empire, India. The last decades of the nineteenth century saw the establishment of British and German colonial power, mainly via Zanzibar. The most famous East African explorers, Livingstone and Stanley (who met at Ujiji in 1871), were accompanied by other explorers and various missionaries: Methodists opened a mission near Mombasa in 1862, Anglicans in Zanzibar in 1863, and Catholics in Bagamoyo in 1868. Ten years later, Christian missionaries moved along the traditional trading route inland through Morogoro and Tabora to Ujiji on Lake Tanganyika. This shows that European intrusion paradoxically followed the established Swahili traditions, including the use of their language, Kiswahili, as a lingua franca. Even the brief German colonial rule in the southern parts of East Africa (from Carl Peter's first "treaties" in 1884 to World War I) did not establish German but Kiswahili in the colony – and laid the foundation for the success of this truly national language in Tanzania later.

After WWI, some differences in colonial administration between Kenya, Uganda, and Tanganyika/Zanzibar can be attributed to the role of the white settlers in Kenya, but a lot of similarities remained, although Tanganyika was only held by the British as a Mandate from the League of Nations. The system of "indirect rule" through African leaders (developed by Lord Luggard in Nigeria) was introduced. In contrast to Rhodesia (especially in present-day Zimbabwe), where the settlers were given self-governance, the primacy of "African interests" was decided in 1923. This is documented in the Land Ordinance Act, which was to secure land rights for Africans and not only Europeans, although over 2000 "settlers" had spread across the country, particularly in the "White Highlands" north of Mount Kenya and east of Mount Elgon. In reality, British rule established a three-class system, with the white colonial officers and settlers at the top, the Indians in the middle, and the black Africans at the bottom.

A system of communication, education, and interethnic exchange developed along the railway and highway lines, with a few ethnic nuclei in fertile areas such as Buganda, Kikuyuland/Mount Kenya, or Chaggaland/Mount Kilimanjaro. The Indians had come to East Africa partly via the Swahili trade in Zanzibar, but mainly as indented laborers for the construction of the railways. They stayed not only in the (railway) administration but also as traders, with their small *dukas* (shops) in the centers, often as "middlemen," who were looked down on by the European settlers and accused of exploitation by the Africans.

Despite the unifying band of British colonial rule, colonial language policy was more complex than is often assumed, as colonial administrations tried to regulate official language use in their territories differently. This usually involved three types of language: the local "tribal" mother tongues, the African lingua franca (mainly Kiswahili, but also Luganda), and English, for local, "intraterritorial" and international communication, respectively. The churches also had an influence on status, attitudes, and usage, not only on church language but also on school language. Even the three British mission societies (the Universities Mission to Central Africa, the Church Mission Society, and the London Mission Society) did not use English for evangelization. Protestant missions in general favored the "language of the people," i.e., the ethnic languages, and also the African lingua franca Kiswahili. The Catholic church was usually more orthodox, supporting not only Latin in its services but also Kiswahili in its preaching. English was established by the colonial rulers only in elitest circles when they tried to regulate communication within the administrative, legal, and education systems. This led to a basically trilingual language policy, with the ethnic "vernacular" for local communication and basic education, Kiswahili in ethnically mixed centers, and English for the highest functions in administration, law, and education.

4   The Sociolinguistic Setting

Today, White East African English is relatively insignificant, although the influence of the early British and South African settlers may have been considerable up to the 1950s. Thus, EAfE is Black African English; it is used "native-like" as the primary language in the home only by highly educated people in mixed marriages and can be described as a socio-educational continuum, since the type of English spoken by Africans depends largely on two factors: (1) their education, i.e., the length and degree of formal education in English; and (2) their social position, i.e., the necessity for and amount of English used in everyday life. Today, of course, English as the international language of science, technology, international development, and communication is also a learner language, but "broken" English or "school English" is usually looked down upon and ridiculed, especially in Kenya, for instance in literature or political campaigns.

Thus the East African Englishes show the characteristic features of New Englishes (cf. Hickey, 2004; Kachru, 1986; Platt, Weber, and Ho, 1984) in background, genesis, and function. This means they are not transmitted directly through native-speaker settlers (instead usage is shaped mainly through their use as media of instruction in school and reinforced outside school) and that they are used in public functions in the national administrational, educational, and legal systems. Interestingly enough though, the term New Englishes is rarely used in East Africa, probably because Standard English (StE), even with EAfE pronunciation or as an (hypothetical) independent East African Standard, is considered more appropriate.

The common cultural background of the three countries accounts for their similar sociolinguistic situation. The major difference is the status of Kiswahili: in Tanzania, it is the true national language, since it is spoken nationwide as a lingua franca, learned in a relatively homogeneous form (sometimes called "Government Swahili") in all primary schools, and used for most national functions, including education in most secondary schools; in Kenya, it is more and more losing its historical connotations with the coast or with lower social positions; in Uganda, however, it is still associated with the military and the "troubled" times of the 1970s and 1980s. These circumstances leave more room for English and the other East African languages in Uganda and Kenya than in Tanzania.

The official status of English in government, parliament, or jurisdiction is not always easy to establish, as laws, regulations, and proclamations since independence over 40 years ago may contradict each other. Whereas English is clearly the language of nationwide politics in Uganda, it is rarely used in those functions in Tanzania; in Kenya, it occupies a middle position.

Knowledge and actual use of English are based on very rough estimates, since no nationwide census data are available and the last language survey was conducted more than 30 years ago. To say, for instance, that English is "spoken" by 30 percent of people in Uganda, 20 percent in Kenya, and only 5 percent in Tanzania may give an indication of the (historical) differences in education, urbanization, modernization, or internationalization, but such statements must be taken with great caution. Since English gives prestige, informants' self-evaluations are unreliable, and results of nationwide proficiency tests for national certificates of education are often disappointing. The fact that universities have started extensive course programs in "Communication Skills" or even explicitly "Remedial English" reveals some of the problems. The discussions can be followed on the Internet, for example in numerous letters to the editors of major national newspapers. The key problem is that English is used as the language of instruction from upper primary school onward (in Uganda and partly in Kenya) and is thus the basis for all further education. The discussion is less about teaching English properly than teaching (other subjects) in English properly.

In all three countries, English is still a result and a symbol of good education and, directly or indirectly, a prerequisite for well-paid jobs with international links in trade and tourism. This is often reflected in popular debates on language attitudes in East Africa.

Attitudes toward EAfE forms are rarely discussed outside scholarly circles. Accepting African forms is hardly ever openly admitted, except regarding pronunciation, where "aping the British" is seen as highly unnatural. Grammar and syntax in particular are considered the glue that holds the diverging Englishes together; and international intelligibility is deemed absolutely essential. Thus, Standard English with African pronunciation may be accepted as an intranational norm, but Ugandan, Kenyan, or Tanzanian English grammar will not be tolerated, at least in the near future. The theoretical British norm in grammar is still upheld in books but rarely used or experienced in use in present-day East Africa (cf. Chapter 28 this volume).

5   Phonology

The features characterizing EAfE can be found at subphonemic, phonemic, and supraphonemic levels. The following description lists examples as well as general tendencies.

Differences at the phonemic level are important because here differences of lexical meaning are maintained. This can be illustrated (and elicited) in minimal pairs like *ram* and *lamb*, *beat* and *bit*, or *show* and *so*. Many Africans do not distinguish clearly in pronunciation between the elements of such pairs, creating a considerable degree of homophony.

Among the consonants, /r/ and /l/ are a particularly infamous pair for many Bantu speakers, both rendered as one and the same, often as an intermediate sound between /loli/ and /rori/ instead of /lori/, for instance. In Kenya the pair is a clear subnational identifier, since even educated Kikuyu clearly tend toward /r/ and the neighboring Embu toward /l/. Occasionally, the sets of voiced and voiceless fricatives around the alveolar ridge /tʃ/, /ʃ/, and /s/, and /dʒ/, /ʒ/, and /z/ are not distinguished clearly, either. Most of these deviations are registered by East Africans as subnational peculiarities. But even phoneme mergers do not endanger the consonant system as a whole, although they may be clearly noticeable. The following examples show three general tendencies for consonants:

1 The merger of /r/ and /l/ is widespread, but still ridiculed.
2 Intrusive or deleted (as a hypercorrect tendency) nasals, especially /n/ before plosives, are common, since some languages like Kikuyu have nasal consonants.
3 English fricatives are generally difficult but particular deviations often restricted to certain ethnic groups.

At the subphonemic level, which is not important for differences in meaning but gives spoken EAfE a particular coloring, an interesting consonant is /r/. As in many English varieties, /r/ is usually only articulated in pre-vocalic positions (i.e., EAfE is non-rhotic, not pronounced in *car*), and its pronunciation varies considerably (it may be rolled or flapped).

A comparison of the English phoneme system with that of most African languages shows that the major differences are not the consonants (although there are fewer consonant combinations), but the small number of vowel contrasts, compared to the extensive English vowel system. Overall, EAfE tends toward a basic five-vowel system. Thus, the vowel system of EAfE is systematically different from StE, vowels tend to merge because the range of the English vowel continuum is not covered by the underlying African systems of, for instance, the Bantu languages. On the whole, three basic generalizations may be made for EAfE vowels:

1 Length differences in vowels are leveled and not contrasted phonemically. This is not only a quantitative but also a qualitative shift, as short vowels in EAfrE are usually longer and more peripheral than in RP, especially /ɪ/ tends toward /iˑ/, /ʊ/ toward /uˑ/, /ɔ/ towards /oˑ/, and /ʌ/ and /æ/ toward /a/.
2 The central vowels /ʌ/, /ɜː/, and /ə/, as in *but*, *bird*, and *a*, are avoided and tend toward half-open or open positions, /a/ and /e/.
3 Diphthongs tend to have only marginal status and to be monophthongized. In the diphthongs /eɪ/ and /aʊ/, the second element is hardly heard in many African Englishes (as in Scotland), thus they almost coincide with

the /eˑ/ and /aˑ/ phonemes. Diphthongs with a longer glide are pre-served, but they are not really pronounced as falling diphthongs, i.e., with less emphasis on the second element than on the first, but rather as double monophthongs (e.g., /ɔɪ/, /aʊ/). All the centering diphthongs (/ɪə, eə, uə/) tend to be pronounced as opening diphthongs or double monoph-thongs (/ɪa, ea, ua/; cf. tendency V2).

Other important features of African English are supraphonemic, i.e., related to phoneme sequences, word stress, intonation, and general rhythmic pat-terns. Consonant clusters are a major phonotactic problem, as many African languages have relatively strict consonant-vowel syllable structures (often CV-CV-CV). Thus, English consonant clusters tend to be dissolved, either by dropping one or some of the consonants involved or by splitting them through the insertion of vowels.

Final consonants are dropped when there are two or more in a sequence, e.g., [neks] for *next* and [hen/han] for *hand*. But this tendency also occurs in native-speaker English, and its frequency in EAfE seems to vary a lot. The general rule appears to be that if plosives are preceded by fricatives, they are dropped in word-final position; if they are preceded by other plosives or occur in non-final position, they are split by vowels inserted between the consonants. Similarly, final vowels are added to closed syllables, i.e., [ɪ] or [ʊ] are inserted, depending on the occurrence of palatal or velar consonants in the environment (e.g., [hosɪpɪtalɪ] for *hospital* or [spɪrɪŋɪ] for *spring*), or on vowel harmony (e.g., in [bʊkʊ] for *book*).

A particularly striking supraphonological feature is the African tendency toward regular stress rhythms. Again, this feature derives partly from the English tendency to maintain the Romance principle of word stress on the penultimate syllable, in contrast to the general Germanic principle of stressing the stem. This complexity leads to differences in word stress between etymo-logically obviously related words when prefixes and suffixes are added; thus, *ad'mire* is not stressed on the same syllable as *admi'ration* and *'admirable*; East Africans are tempted to stress [ad'maɪrabl] and sometimes even [ad'maɪreˑʃen], just like [ad'maɪa].

The most noticeable feature of the speech flow in African Englishes is the tendency toward a stress-timed rather than a syllable-time rhythm. Thus, EAfE tends to give all syllables more or less equal stress and not "cram" up to three unstressed syllables together into one stress unit to create the so-called "weak" forms of Standard British English. This underlying pattern accounts for most of the suprasegmental patterns in EAfE mentioned above (e.g., giving too much articulatory precision to unstressed syllables), and its sometimes unfam-iliar rhythm. These differences may cause misunderstandings in intercultural communication, when EAfE may be misjudged as unfriendly "machine-gun fire" or childish "sing-song." An interesting question is whether syllable-timed English may actually help in communication with Francophone Africans, whose speech is also syllable-timed.

6   Lexicon

The lexicon of EAfE comprises, of course, the core lexicon of StE and specific East Africanisms, which would not be interpreted easily or equally by
the non-initiated, e.g., readers or listeners not familiar with English usage in
East Africa (cf. Chapter 38 this volume). Despite some cultural, especially
sociopolitical, differences among Kenya, Uganda, and Tanzania, the use of
(Kiswahili) loans, the semantic extension of StE lexemes, and idiomatic flexibility are common features.

The geographical range of EAfE lexemes varies a lot. Very old borrowings,
such as *askari, baobab, bwana,* and *safari* have already been incorporated into
general English, and are thus codified in large dictionaries of English, the *Oxford
English Dictionary* with its supplements, for instance. They have entered world
Englishes, and some have even been integrated into other European languages.
They are, however, restricted to African contexts, and thus have a more specific
meaning in general English than in a particular regional English. The most widespread item is perhaps the Kiswahili word *safari*: for Europeans it denotes a
"journey" to see and shoot game, in the old days with a gun, today with a camera,
normally in National Parks; in EAfrE, it retains its more general meaning.

As would be expected, the African environment is inadequately reflected
in the StE lexicon, and is supplemented by African names for characteristic
landscapes, plants or animals. African loans cluster around "African" domains
just as English loans cluster around "European" domains. It is interesting to
see that the semantic expansion of StE lexemes (cf. (3) in the list below) may
create problems of distinction, as in the case of *potatoes*, where Africans often
have to specify *Irish/European potatoes* or *sweet potatoes*. In general, the preferred staple food dish is hardly ever translated: Kenya's/Tanzania's *ugali* is
the same as Uganda's *posho* (from the colonial English *portion*, which was
allocated to workers), the traditional maize dish.

The field of food is probably culture-specific everywhere, but in many
African countries there is a marked contrast between European and African
food (and eating habits) because Europeans in East Africa have tended not
to adopt African food, in contrast to the British in India. Some dishes are
also marked by ethnicity or region, like *irio* and *githeri* for Kikuyu dishes or
vitumbua for coastal rice-cakes. Some are of course clearly imported from Asia,
e.g. *bajia* (an Indian potato dish) and *chai* (tea).

Many African words for kin relations in the intimate family and beyond are
retained in EAfE, especially when used as a form of address. Where African
clothing is still worn it is, of course, referred to with African language names.
African customs have to be rendered in indigenous words (e.g., *lobola* 'bride-
price'), and their uses are governed by local rules of politeness.

An important domain of Africanisms is politics. As African languages
have often played a major role in mobilizing the masses, even before *uhuru*
'independence' was reached, *harambee* ('pulling together') was a national

slogan in Kenya, as were *ujamaa* ('familyhood') and *kujigetemea* ('self-reliance') in Tanzania. It is clear that most of these terms have to be seen in their specific sociopolitical context.

The borderline between code mixing (with two languages overlapping in a sentence or text) and (integrated) loan words can be blurred when, for instance, the Kiswahili locative or directive particle *-ni* is added to a word, as when an officer is *porini* (i.e., 'in the bush' – "up-country," away from the capital or administrative headquarters).

Even if the words used in African English are formally unchanged English words, their meanings may be quite different. Although word usage may depend on the specific linguistic and extralinguistic context, some tendencies can be observed:

1   The level of semantic redundancy tends to be higher in EastAfE than in StE. E.g., a *secret ballot* is considered a tautology ("secret" is semantically included in *ballot*, not in *vote*), *the reason why he came is because* . . . expresses the same meaning in the noun and the conjunct, and *perhaps* is redundant in the context of the modal *may*.
2   Idiomatic expressions are sometimes used in slightly different morphological forms. E.g., *with regards to* combines *with regard to* and *as regards*.
3   English word forms are used in other reference contexts (usually expanded). E.g., having many "brothers" and "sisters" or even "fathers" shows that kinship terms are expanded as reference and address terms; *mother* may refer to the adult female member of the nuclear family or to one of her co-wives or sisters, or any elderly woman from the same village without any blood relation to the speaker.
4   English word forms are confused with similar ones, thus meanings are often expanded. E.g., when *to book* is used like "to hire," *to forget* like "to lose," *to refuse* like "to deny," *to convince* like "to persuade," *to see* like "to look," *to reach* like "to arrive," *arm* like "hand," *guest* like "stranger," *strange* like "foreign," and so on.
5   English word forms are used in other contexts, thus having other collocations and connotations. E.g., fairly general terms are used instead of more specific ones (*an election is done* [cf. "conducted/held"] or *to commit an action* [cf. "crime"]).

However, as has been mentioned above, contexts and style choices constituting idiomaticity form a complex interplay, and this special flavor can only be studied in larger sections of authentic texts. A few examples of typical verb usage from the spoken part of ICE-EA must suffice here:

(1)   I am a matatu driver <u>operating</u> route No. 44 (ICE-EA: S1B065K)

(2)   It is the City Inspectorate who <u>assigns</u> the City Askari. (ICE-EA: S1B066K)

(3)   But he never saw anybody himself; nor anybody <u>alighting</u> from the police m/v go to the house. (ICE-EA: S1BCE07K)

For quantitative comparisons and sample retrievals Internet URLs with the domains .ug, .ke, and .tz can be used (cf. Schmied, 2005). Such a procedure using modern web browsers provides examples of rare cases much more easily nowadays, although the texts have to be evaluated critically, e.g., as to whether they can really be seen as "educated East African English." Country-specific patterns can be distinguished, e.g., Kiswahili address forms like *ndugu* or *mzee* have higher frequencies in Tanzania than in Kenya, and *duka* and *fundi* are less frequent in Uganda, but *sodas* occur in all three East African countries, in contrast to *minerals*, which refer to the same drink in South Africa. *Mitumba* also occurs on .uk web sites, but usually with an explicit explanation in the form of premodifiers or appositions (*the second-hand mitumba* or *mitumba, second-hand clothes*); in South Africa, the term is often used with explicit reference to East Africa.

7   Grammar

The following grammar tendencies are not restricted to EAfE and can also be found in other parts of Africa and beyond, not only in so-called New Englishes but even in some first-language varieties in Britain, America, or Australia. Partly, at least, Englishes all seem to develop in a similar direction, as for instance in terms of simplification and regularization. Frequency, consistency, systematicity, and the developmental, regional, and social distribution of features over various spoken and written text types are a matter for further research, as are implicational hierarchies in frequency and acceptability.

As far as the verb phrase is concerned, the following 12 tendencies may be the most common, even in educated EAfE:

1   Inflectional endings are not always added to the verb, the general, regular and unmarked forms are used instead:

   (4)   K.shs. 33,500/- <u>was</u> [StE were] raised during our pre-wedding. (ICE-EA: S1BCE05K)

2   Complex tenses tend to be avoided. This tendency occurs particularly with the past perfect and conditionals (*It would have been much better if this was done*) and is also common in less formal native-speaker usage. It affects mainly the sequence of tenses taught in school grammar, particularly in the case of subordinate clauses in past contexts and when certain types of modality (especially irrealis) are expressed. Past tense forms are used less frequently to express modality than in StE (as in *I had better* or *If I went . . .*); as this is considered pedantic and typically British, *will* constructions are used instead.

3   Continuous forms (BE + VERB + -*ing* construction) are overused, i.e., not necessarily with StE "progressive" meanings:

   (5)   Some of us may think that women always <u>are having</u> a lot of things to do (ICE-EA: S1BINT13T)

4   Patterns and particles of phrasal/prepositional verbs vary:

   (S6)   . . . to send his driver to <u>pick</u> her at the school for a rendezvous (ICE-EA: W2F029T; for *pick up*)

5   Verb complementation (especially in the case of infinitives and gerunds) varies freely:

   (S7)   he has indicated to want to stop <u>to</u> deliver what he has (ICE-EA: S1B031T; the context makes the meaning 'stop delivering' clear)

As far as noun phrases are concerned, the following features of African English have been found:

6   The use of *-s* plural markers is overgeneralized. This tendency is quite common in New Englishes and most instances are semantically correct, i.e., although they can be seen as collective units, several individual pieces can be distinguished, e.g., with *luggages, furnitures, firewoods,* or *grasses*. Sometimes this tendency conflates more or less subtle semantic differentiations in Standard English, such as between *food – foods, people – peoples*; sometimes it merely regularises (historical) morphological StE irregularities (*fishes*). East African usage basically ignores the grammatical distinction of count vs. non-count nouns, which does not always correspond to the semantic distinction anyway. In StE, plural *-s* is not added to nouns that are considered abstract or collective/mass and thus non-count (*discontents, informations*). But even in StE, some non-countables may occur in the plural in special meanings (e.g., *works*) or in stressed contexts (e.g., *experiences*); thus, differences are often a question of interpretation and frequency.

   (8)   These <u>advices</u> are coming because they've already studied all of us (ICE-EA: S1BINT12T)

7   Articles and other determiners tend to be omitted in front of nouns:

   I am going to church/school > post office as an expansion.

8   Pronouns may be redundant, especially so-called resumptive pronouns:

   (9)   So human being in the first time of his existence <u>he</u> found that he was subjecteded [*sic*] to the work (ICE-EA: S1B004T)

9   Pronouns are not always distinguished by gender. The three possibilities of third-person singular pronouns, *he, she, it* in subject roles and *his, her, its* in possessive roles, are often used indiscriminately, especially when their pronunciation is only distinguished by one consonant, as in the case of *he* and *she*. This can be accounted for as simplification or as interference from mother tongues that do not have sex distinctions in pronouns (e.g., languages that have only one lexical class for animate or human beings in general).

10 Prepositions are underdifferentiated. The most frequent English prepositions *of* and *in* (at the expense of the more special *into*) occur significantly
more frequently in EAfE (cf. Mwangi, 2003), which may be explained as a
"safety strategy"; more specific prepositions (e.g., *off* or *across*) are used
less often. This is sometimes considered underdifferentiation in StE, since
the systems are more complex than they are in African languages. Standard prepositions tend to be chosen (e.g., *in* for *into*) and analogy plays
an important role. Similarly, frequently occurring complex prepositions
(like *because of, according to,* and *due to*) occur more frequently, while less
frequently occurring and even more complex ones (like *in front of, in
favour of, by means of, in the light of*) occur less often.

(10)   many people are just coming <u>in</u> the country. (ICE-EA: S1A018T)

11 Adjective forms tend to be used as adverbs. The unmarked adverbial
form is correct in very few cases in StE (*hard, first, high*), sometimes in
certain contexts or sayings such as *take it easy*, etc.; but such unmarked
forms do occur in EAfE as they do in some American and British English
varieties.

12 Question tags tend to occur in invariant form:

(11)   There we are, <u>isn't it</u>? (ICE-EA: S2B057K)

Finally, word order in EAfE is much more flexible and can be used to
express emphasis and focus more readily than in StE (in this respect it can be
seen as being closer to colloquial spoken English).

8   Discourse

Speakers' intended emphasis is difficult to judge right or wrong and is considered inappropriate only in a few cases. Often, however, the question whether
an unusual construction implies special emphasis or contrast is difficult to
decide.

In contrast to other New Englishes, simple reduplication for emphasis
does not seem to serve this purpose, at least in educated EAfrE. But related
processes do occur, for instance when a stressed reflexive pronoun is placed
in front of a structure and resumed in a personal pronoun afterwards:

(12)   Uh <u>myself</u> uh I am I started working at Muhimbili in nineteen eighty-
seven (ICE-EA: S1B046T)

Topicalization through fronting and a corresponding adjustment of intonation is rare in StE, but common in many English varieties (e.g., Irish). StE has
developed special forms like cleft and pseudo-cleft constructions instead, which
are too complex for second-language speakers.

Similarly, in StE *never* refers to a longer period or adds special emphasis, but occasionally it may simply be used to avoid a complex *to-do* construction with *not*, as in:

(13)   Most Kenyans <u>never</u> hesitate to give generously to help build hospitals, schools, dispensaries. (ICE-EA: W2E018K)

Generally, the presentation of information varies considerably and the perception whether something is marked in discourse or the natural flow varies accordingly, since the optimal choice of a phrase, etc., may depend on many factors.

In African societies that maintain more links with oral tradition than European ones, it is not surprising that some discourse features are culture-specific: they are customarily used, and not really marked for the insider, but are clearly unusual for the European or other outsider. Many such culture-specific discourse features are linked to traditional African social values, including the extended family, an ethnic group, the environment, and customs.

For example, East Africans tend to greet each other elaborately, and if visitors want to make a good impression, they should follow the standard patterns of asking *How is your family, . . . your health, . . . your journey/safari*, and so on (straightforward translations from the Kiswahili *Habari ya watoto, . . . ya afya, . . . ya safari*, etc.), before launching into a direct request. This strategy is considered polite and more appropriate than toning down direct questions with mitigating constructions like *I'm terribly sorry to bother you* or *Would you mind telling me* as in StE, which are considered affected in ordinary conversation and hence not used by East Africans. Again, some code mixing is possible, with handy little words like *sawa* for "okay," *asante* (or intensified *asante sana*) for "thank you," and exclamations like *kumbe* and *kweli* to indicate surprise.

Another East African politeness strategy is to express one's sympathy with some misfortune or unlucky event, e.g., when someone is obviously tired or ill, by inserting *pole* (or intensified *pole sana*) at the beginning, middle, or end of a conversation (not to be confused with *pole pole*, which means 'slowly'). This is often translated as 'I am sorry', but becomes really untranslatable, e.g., when someone stumbles, because its use often implies some fault on the part of the speaker in StE, which is clearly not the case in EAfE (this is why it is clearly marked as an East Africanism <ea> in (14):

(14)   <ea/><u>Pole</u> <ea/><u>sana</u> for what befell you. (ICE-EA: W1B-SK02)

9   Outlook

Since gaining their independence over 40 years ago, East Africans have developed an interesting trifocal language system, where English has the widespread African language Kiswahili as a rival in top language functions in the region (and, through the Organization of African Unity, even across the continent). Although other African languages play a role in subnational communication and influence English pronunciation, East Africa is unique among the English-speaking areas of the world because of this "diglossia," a clear functional co-existence of languages. Interestingly enough, Kiswahili does not threaten English in the area, since its losses in national functions have by far been compensated for by the many international functions of English that have been important for East Africans since their integration into worldwide communication networks over 100 years ago. The occasional heated discussions about standards, usage, functions, and loan words can be seen in the worldwide debate about globalization, and the position of English vis-à-vis (other) African languages can oscillate between complementarity and competition (Mazrui, 2004), but global interpretations should be based on actual evidence and this what this state-of-the-art summary has tried to present. In the long tradition of African multilingualism, English has a promising future in the area, and the knowledge and appreciation of national and regional features will develop and make the diversity of East African Englishes interesting for casual users and specialized researchers alike.

See also Chapters 11, WEST AFRICAN ENGLISHES; 13, CARIBBEAN ENGLISHES; 17, VARIETIES OF WORLD ENGLISHES; 28, WORLD ENGLISHES AND DESCRIPTIVE GRAMMARS; 35, A RECURRING DECIMAL: ENGLISH IN LANGUAGE POLICY AND PLANNING; 38, LEXICOGRAPHY; 41, WORLD ENGLISHES AND CORPORA STUDIES.

REFERENCES

Abdulaziz, Mohamed H. (1991) East Africa (Tanzania and Kenya). In *English around the World: Sociolinguistic Perspectives*. Edited by Jenny Cheshire. Cambridge: Cambridge University Press, pp. 391–401.

Bailey, Richard and Görlach, Manfred (eds.) (1982) *English as a World Language*. Ann Arbor: University of Michigan Press.

Cheshire, Jenny (ed.) (1991) *English around the World: Sociolinguistic Perspectives*. Cambridge: Cambridge University Press.

Hancock, Ian and Angogo, Rachel (1982) English in East Africa. In *English as a World Language*. Edited by Richard Bailey and Manfred Görlach. Ann Arbor: University of Michigan Press, pp. 306–23.

Hickey, Raymond (ed.) (2004) *The Legacy of Colonial English: The Study of Transported Dialects*. Cambridge: Cambridge University Press.

Hudson-Ettle, Diana (1998) Grammatical Subordination Strategies in Differing Text Types in the English Spoken and Written in Kenya. Unpublished PhD dissertation, Chemnitz University of Technology. http://www.tu-chemnitz.de/~dihe.

Kachru, Braj B. (1986) *The Alchemy of English: The Spread, Functions and Models of Non-Native Englishes*. New York: Pergamon Press.

Kachru, Braj B. (ed.) (1992) *The Other Tongue: English across Cultures*. 2nd edition. Urbana, IL: University of Illinois Press.

Kanyoro, Musimbi R. A. (1991) The politics of the English language in Kenya and Tanzania. In *English around the World: Sociolinguistic Perspectives*. Edited by Jenny Cheshire. Cambridge: Cambridge University Press, pp. 402–19.

Kortmann, Bernd and Schneider, Edgar W. (eds.) (2004) *A Handbook of Varieties of English A Multimedia Reference Tool*, 2 vols. Berlin: Mouton de Gruyter.

Ladefoged, Peter, Glick, Ruth, and Criper, Clive (1971) *Language in Uganda*. Nairobi: Oxford University Press.

Mazrui, Alamin M. (2004) *English in Africa: After the Cold War*. Clevedon, UK: Multilingual Matters.

Mwangi, Serah (2003) *Prepositions in Kenyan English: A Corpus-Based Study in Lexico-Grammatical Variation*. Aachen: Shaker Verlag.

Platt, John, Weber, Heidi, and Ho, Mian Lian (1984) *The New Englishes*. London: Routledge and Kegan Paul.

Polomé, Edgar C. and Hill, Charles P. (eds.) (1980) *Language in Tanzania*. Oxford: Oxford University Press.

Schmied, Josef (1991a) *English in Africa*. London: Longman.

Schmied, Josef (1991b) National and subnational features in Kenyan English. In *English around the World: Sociolinguistic Perspectives*. Edited by Jenny Cheshire. Cambridge: Cambridge University Press, pp. 420–32.

Schmied, Josef (1996) English in Zimbabwe, Zambia and Malawi. In *Focus on South Africa*. Edited by Vivian de Klerk. Amsterdam: John Benjamins, pp. 301–21.

Schmied, Josef (2004a) East African English (Kenya, Uganda, Tanzania): phonology. In Bernd Kortmann et al. *A Handbook of Varieties of English, Vol. 1: Phonology*. Edited by Bernd Kortmann et al. Berlin: Mouton de Gruyter, 918–30.

Schmied, Josef (2004b) East African English (Kenya, Uganda, Tanzania): morphology and syntax. In *A Handbook of Varieties of English, Vol. 2: Morphology and Syntax*. Edited by Bernd Kortmann et al. Berlin: Mouton de Gruyter, 929–47.

Schmied, Josef (2005) New ways of analysing ESL on the www with WebCorp and WebPhraseCount. In *The Changing Face of Corpus Linguistics*. Edited by Antoinette Renouf. Amsterdam: Rodopi, pp. 309–24.

Schmied, Josef (forthcoming) *English in East Africa*. John Benjamins: Amsterdam.

Schmied, Josef and Hudson-Ettle, Diana (1996) Analysing the style of East African newspapers in English. *World Englishes*, **15**(1), 103–13.

Skandera, Paul (2003) *Drawing a Map of Africa: Idiom in Kenyan English*. (Language in Performance 26.) Tübingen: Gunter Narr.

Spencer, John (ed.) (1971) *The English Language in West Africa*. London: Longman.

Whiteley, Wilfried H. (ed.) (1974) *Language in Kenya*. Nairobi: Oxford University Press.

FURTHER READING

Abdulaziz, Mohamed H. (1991) East Africa (Tanzania and Kenya). In *English around the World: Sociolinguistic Perspectives*. Edited by Jenny Cheshire. Cambridge: Cambridge University Press, pp. 391–401.

Schmied, Josef (forthcoming) *English in East Africa*. Amsterdam: John Benjamins.

13 Caribbean Englishes

MICHAEL ACETO

1 Introduction

The terms Caribbean Englishes or Restructured Englishes are roughly synonymous with other terms commonly found in the linguistics literature: English creoles, English-derived or English-based creoles, and even dialects of English (Mufwene, 2001). Creolists have never agreed upon a typologically distinct linguistic definition in terms of common structures, features, or processes that demarcate so-called creole languages from non-creole languages (Aceto, 1999a; DeGraff, 1999; Mufwene, 1994, 1996; cf. McWhorter, 1998). This absence of a typological distinction may at first seem troublesome or peculiar, but there is still no precise definition as to what exclusively distinguishes a "dialect" from a "language," yet linguists comfortably use both these terms in a general sense as if they precisely reference specific agreed upon language phenomena in the world. As linguists understand better the social factors surrounding the genesis of most so-called creole languages and the structural features they display, both synchronically and diachronically, it may be more appropriate in some cases to view some of these languages called creoles as simply dialects of their respective lexifiers (e.g., varieties of Bahamian English, Cayman Islands English); in other cases, this approach may be less appropriate (e.g., the creoles of Suriname).

The term "creole" derives more from the sociohistorical circumstances surrounding the genesis and emergence of these restructured varieties than from any single linguistic feature or cluster of features that might eventually prove to be diagnostic of this group of languages. The specifics of this term may vary from region to region in terms of lexical identification, since a creole with an English-derived lexical base is just one possible outcome of linguistic/cultural contact between and among peoples who originally spoke mutually unintelligible languages. That is, there are creoles with French, Spanish, Portuguese, Dutch, Arabic, and African languages (e.g., Kikóngo in Kitúba) as the source of most of the basic morphemes of the language. In fact, in some regions of the

Caribbean, restructured varieties of English co-exist in relatively small, well-defined geographical and cultural spaces (e.g., St Lucia, Carriacou) with chronologically older creoles that do not share the same lexical base (in these cases, French-derived creoles), even if usage of the earlier language appears to be decreasing among the population at large. Furthermore, the social and colonial histories of many creole languages with differing lexical bases are often similar (yet unavoidably different in some cases; see below), and it is here that we might find some common "definition" of what a creole is.

English-derived languages of the Caribbean reveal several sociohistorical factors in common with the emergence of creole languages around the world. These native languages seem to be the result of a disproportionate social/ power relationship in which speakers of one language or, more commonly, a set of languages are dominated socially, economically, and/or militarily by politically (but, crucially, not necessarily numerically) more powerful speakers of another language. In the Americas, this dynamic between relatively more powerful and less powerful peoples was enacted within the crucible of European colonization and the institution of slavery, which forcibly brought immigrants from the west coast of Africa to the Americas. Out of this lopsided power dynamic emerged a new language (whatever term one decides is most appropriate, creole or dialect; see Mufwene, 2001) with many of its basic lexemes derived from the socially more powerful or dominant language. This more powerful language is often called the superstrate and the less powerful one the substrate. (From the perspective of language acquisition/creation, "substrate" can also refer to the language known natively, i.e., below the level of awareness, and "superstrate" to the language not known natively, i.e., above the level of awareness, in terms of a new language to be heard and (re)shaped in some way by speakers trying to make sense of and (re-)organizing this new language data.)

Not all the members of the subordinate group (e.g., West Africans in the Americas) shared the same language. In the Western Hemisphere, many of the ethnic groups represented by West African slaves in specific locations spoke mutually unintelligible languages, which made the emergence of any contact language perhaps crucial for intra-group communication as well as for initiating communication about survival under the control of Europeans. Within the Anglophone context, children born into these multilingual settings grappled with whatever local varieties of English they heard in the mouths of settlers, colonists, and perhaps Africans already familiar with some form of the language from early European contacts in Africa. Children restructured these varieties further, enforcing structural regularity on the second-language varieties they heard being spoken by the adults in their communities, drawing on processes made available through the common human genetic endowment of the language faculty.

What is or is not a linguistic effect derived from the superstrate(s), substrate(s), or common human linguistic processes is a matter of some differing opinions among researchers. It seems uncontroversial that specific words and phonemes can be derived from substrate languages. For example, *dókunu* 'dumpling' is derived from Twi, a language of Ghana (known as the Gold Coast during the colonial period), and is found in several restructured Englishes in the Atlantic region; co-articulated stops such as /kp/ and /gb/ heard in Saramaccan, a mixed English- and Iberian-derived creole of Suriname in northern South America, are also articulated in several languages of West Africa but are conspicuously absent from European languages. However, the source of the creole language's structure or syntax is a subject of some controversy. Some scholars believe it to be related to the structure of the native language(s) originally spoken by the dominated group. This substratist position is a perspective that has dominated creole studies since the 1970s (see Parkvall, 2000 as the latest example of this perspective; see also Holm, 1988–9). Others believe (some of) a creole's structure to be related to features of the regional dialects of the language spoken by the European superordinate group; in the last half of the twentieth century, this perspective has most definitely been a minority voice (for important exceptions see Hancock, 1994; Mufwene, 2001; Niles, 1980; Winford, 2000). Still others insist that a creole language's grammatical structure is related to principles of Universal Grammar as pertaining to first-language acquisition/creation (see Bickerton, 1984, as the most vocal proponent of this view; also DeGraff, 1999), and yet others believe insights from second-language acquisition hold keys to understanding these languages (see Andersen, 1983). These structural issues have not been resolved to anyone's satisfaction (the best multidimensional approach is probably that of DeGraff, 1999) – and this question will certainly not be answered here. The complexity of the question most likely entails that components from all of the above categories have played some role in shaping the "look" or sound of specific creoles or dialects – and, for that matter, of languages everywhere. This observation raises the question again, in the absence of a typologically distinct definition for creoles, as to how these languages are different from any other human language.

2 Where Are Restructured Englishes in the Caribbean Spoken?

Restructured Englishes are spoken along the edges of virtually every major ocean or sea in the world. The reason for this largely geographical distinction is straightforward. Contact between colonizers/settlers speaking regional dialects of British English and subsequently colonized peoples took place via shipping and sailing routes during the period of European expansion and colonialization in the seventeenth through early twentieth centuries. Therefore, contact between English speakers and speakers of non-European languages (e.g., West African languages in the Atlantic region and Oceanic languages in the Pacific region) were often established in coastal areas. Again, in this regard, creole languages are no different from other languages: all natural human languages display the effects of cultural/language contact even if they do not share the social scenario described below as leading to "creolization" (and, again, not all "creoles" share the plantation scenario, either). What makes creole Englishes somewhat unique at this point in history is that they are relatively "new" languages. That is, they are only about 150 to 400 years old, which is young in the life of a language (English and Spanish, for example, are approximately 1,500 and 2,000 years old, respectively).

Dozens of English-derived creoles and dialects are spoken throughout the Americas and on the eastern edges of the Atlantic region in West Africa. Every former British colonial territory in the Caribbean reveals an English language variety spoken today, whether one considers it a creole or a dialect. Many of these languages are distributed across the islands of the Caribbean: Trinidad and Tobago, Grenada, Barbados, St Vincent, St Lucia, Dominica, Montserrat, St Kitts and Nevis, Antigua and Barbuda, Anguila, the Turks and Caicos islands, the various islands of the Bahamas, Jamaica, and the Cayman Islands. The British Virgin Islands of Tortola, Virgin Gorda, Anegada, and Jost Van Dyke contain largely undocumented English varieties. The Dutch Windward Islands of Saba, St Martin, and St Eustatius also reveal English-derived varieties. The languages spoken on the United States Virgin Islands of St Croix, St John, and St Thomas have received little attention from linguists. In many nations largely associated with Spanish as a national language, English-derived restructured varieties have been spoken for more than a century: the Dominican Republic; Providencia and San Andres Islands (politically controlled by Colombia); and the Central American nations of Panama, Costa Rica, Nicaragua, Honduras, and Guatemala. Belize is the only country in Central America in which Creole English is widely spoken (English is the official language). Within the North American mainland, Creole English can be heard in the Gullah-speaking coastal areas of South Carolina and Georgia as well as among their descendants in southern Texas and northern Mexico (as well as among Caribbean immigrant communities in, for example, New York City, Miami, and Harford). Even South America contains English-derived creole speakers of at least four languages in the countries of Suriname and Guyana.

Local names for English-derived varieties may vary. In many locations, speakers may call their language *pidgin* or *creole*, but most simply call their native language *dialect*. Often, unfortunate qualifiers such as *bad*, *raw*, or *flat* (reflecting speaker attitudes) may be used to modify *English*; or they may simply call it *English*. Furthermore, several scholars still insist that all creoles spoken in the Western Hemisphere today derive diachronically from a pidgin on the West Coast of Africa (see McWhorter, 1998 as the most recent example; cf. Bloomfield, 1933); most others view the role of a pidgin in creole genesis as less a prerequisite and more of a variable factor available as the source of some features that would eventually reveal themselves in a particular creole.

3 Different Scenarios for the Emergence of Creoles in the Atlantic Region

Many scholars (e.g., Thomason and Kaufman, 1988) insist that creoles represent a case of broken transmission between the language providing the source of basic lexical material and the subsequent emerging creole or English variety. However, this perspective may be most (and perhaps, in the Western Hemisphere, only) appropriate when considering the English-derived cases for the Surinamese creoles *Sranan*, *Ndyuka*, and *Saramaccan* in which English, as a possible source of ongoing lexical and grammatical influence, was withdrawn from the emerging linguistic matrix when the British exchanged the colony with the Dutch for what was then, in the seventeenth century, New Amsterdam (later renamed "New York"). This description is clearly less accurate and appropriate for the vast majority of restructured Englishes that also bear the name "creole" (e.g., Jamaican, Gullah, Belizean, etc.), where English was established and persisted as an ambient language of power (and thus as one potential source of linguistic influence) before and well after the emergence of the local vernaculars.

In fact, in Creole Studies, rather than considering the Surinamese creoles as exceptional cases of language emergence, these languages are often considered as the baseline against which all Englishes in the Anglophone Atlantic region are measured. Not surprisingly, all other English-derived Atlantic creole languages appear to be lacking in assumed "creole" features in this comparison, despite the fact that no satisfactory typological inventory of creole features has been established within the field. The distorted assumption that all English-derived creoles once looked more like one of the Surinamese creoles (or, from some adjusted theoretical perspectives, so-called "basilectal" Jamaican Creole English) thus ensures that all other Restructured English varieties in the Atlantic region will appear less "creole-like" in comparison, despite the fact that the specific sociohistorical factors that gave rise to the Surinamese creoles are uncontroversially unique in the Americas.

It is likely that comparing the Surinamese creoles to other creoles in the Anglophone Atlantic region has encouraged researchers to perceive "decreolization" as an all-pervasive universal force moving restructured Englishes in a unidirectional manner toward features associated with metropolitan or more standard varieties of English. Any language, creole or otherwise, has options for variation and change unrelated to the pressures of lexically related (even if politically and socially prestigious) metropolitan languages (see Aceto, 1999a). Even if the purported effects of so-called "decreolization" could be rigorously distinguished from what is regular and "normal" diachronic change, which all languages exhibit everywhere (whether they are called "creole" or not), this concept has a tendency to obscure language change that is not derived from contact with metropolitan varieties of English and to discourage research on creole varieties which are considered, from this perspective, to be less "creole-like" and thus less deserving of attention from scholars who identify themselves as creolists. (See Aceto, 2001 for details.)

The slave plantation is often considered the prototypical environment for the emergence of creoles because this colonial context brought together components of a social matrix that seem especially conducive for the emergence and restructuring of these languages. That is, out of the matrix of social factors discussed above in terms of a disproportionate demographic ratio between the socially subordinate (i.e., often slaves, in the Atlantic scenario) and the numerically smaller superordinate group who were the original sources of most European language forms emerged a variety of English that began to be used by African slaves at least initially as a lingua franca and then later as a first language by children born into this context. This general scenario accounts for many of the creole Englishes spoken in the Atlantic region, such as Sranan in Suriname and Jamaican, but it often obscures the likelihood that a range of English-derived varieties may have emerged in any geographical and cultural space where English was spoken as a language of colonial power (see Alleyne, 1971). Furthermore, though most of the participants on the dominated side of the equation were in fact originally slaves in the Americas, not all the languages called creoles, and not even all those varieties with an English-derived lexical base, historically emerged within the context of the slave plantation.

There are several cases of language emergence that resist being neatly classified within the plantation experience, even if some of them are outgrowths and extensions of that same general experience. For example, Barbuda, an island to the north of Antigua in the Eastern Caribbean, was populated with slaves for the explicit function of raising food crops and manufacturing goods to supply plantations on nearby islands such as Antigua (in fact, slaves on Barbuda were often threatened with transfer to plantations on Antigua). These Barbudan slaves often came in contact with no more than a handful of Europeans. In West Africa, Krio in Sierra Leone did not emerge as a plantation creole, nor did Liberian English. The status of Krio is still a subject of some debate, with most scholars insisting it is an import from Jamaica (e.g., Schuchardt, 1883; von Bradshaw, 1965; Hall, 1966; Coomber, 1969; Bauer, 1975; Wilson, 1976; Fyle and Jones, 1980; Boretzky, 1983; see Huber, 2004 who claims an early form of Gullah influenced the formation of Krio), while others (e.g., Hancock, 1986; Aceto, 1999b) maintain that some form of restructured English most likely emerged in the area of the Guinea Coast of West Africa before the arrival of Jamaican immigrants in Sierra Leone in the early nineteenth century (see McWhorter, 2003, who argues that restructured English emerged on the Lower Guinea Coast but *not* the Upper Guinea Coast before the nineteenth century). Nonetheless, the role of immigration and immigrant varieties of English spoken by African slaves and their descendants in the Atlantic region, especially as the descendants of slaves began to move about the Caribbean in search of work in the mostly post-emancipation period, is a topic that has largely been ignored by creolists (except for the case of Krio and perhaps Liberian).

Several of the English-derived creoles spoken in areas and islands of the Caribbean are clearly the result of intra-Caribbean migration. Many of the tens of thousands of speakers in Panama, Costa Rica, Honduras, and Guatemala are the result of English-derived creole-speaking immigrants from Caribbean islands migrating to Central America in search of work in the nineteenth and twentieth centuries (Holm, 1983, 1988–9; Aceto, 1995). In Central America, Belize and the community of Bluefields in Nicaragua appear to be exceptions to this categorization, but neither case falls neatly within the plantation scenario sketched above, either (see Holm, 1983). Winer (1993) demonstrates that the emergence of Trinidadian Creole English in the nineteenth century is the result of immigration by a variety of ethnic groups who already spoke pre-existing and wholly formed creoles and Englishes. Out of this matrix, a new English-derived language variety has emerged.

At least two Surinamese creoles (Ndyuka and Saramaccan) are Maroon creoles that emerged as runaway slaves and rebels formed independent societies in the interior of the country. Maroon languages also emerged in remote mountainous areas of Jamaica, while non-English-lexifier creoles also reveal similar cases (e.g., Palenquero, an Iberian-derived creole of Colombia, is believed to have its roots in a Maroon community; for the Surinamese Maroon creoles, see Smith, 1987; for Jamaican Maroon language, see Bilby, 1983). These creoles may still be considered related to the plantation creole phenomenon since in the Americas many of the new recruits to these independent societies were speakers of or at least familiar with the restructured English emerging on plantations closer to population centers near the coast. However, what makes Maroon languages truly unique (other than the specific matrix of contributing languages in any individual case of language emergence) is that they developed in greater isolation from European influences than languages emerging on plantations.

Other creoles or Englishes are the result of transference of property from one colonial power to another (again, similar to yet crucially different from the Suriname case discussed above). Several former French-held colonial territories in the Caribbean such as St Lucia, Grenada, and Carriacou, where a French-derived creole had earlier emerged, were subsequently transferred to British colonial control in the late eighteenth and early nineteenth centuries. British dominion over these French Creole-speaking islands for the last two centuries has resulted in the emergence of local varieties of English that seem to have been significantly calqued (i.e., translated word-for-word) from the earlier French-derived creole as the functional usage of English expanded more strongly into social domains (e.g., education, government) previously reserved for French or the French-derived creole (see Garrett, 1999, 2003 for the case of St Lucia). These interesting cases of language emergence have largely been ignored by researchers and are only now beginning to be studied (as many cases of non-plantation creoles have similarly been neglected; see Aceto, 2001 for a detailed description of Englishes and creoles in the Western Hemisphere that have received little or no attention from linguists).

Non-Afro-American Anglo-Caribbean varieties – i.e., those English varieties spoken among the descendants of Irish, Scots, and English settlers – have largely been ignored in research paradigms, except for the work of Williams (1985, 1987, 1988, 2003). These English-derived varieties spoken largely by Euro-Caribbeans on Saba, Bequia, the Cayman Islands, Barbados, and Anguilla (see Williams, 2003) may shed light on the English-derived component heard by Africans or Afro-Caribbeans working alongside many of these European immigrants. White indentured servants were often treated socially no differently from African slaves; some of them even joined African-derived Maroon communities (see above).

To sum up: in the Americas, there are Englishes and English-derived creoles that have emerged due to the general colonial plantation experience and its influence, the result of immigration, and/or the result of colonial transference in which the ambient European language of power has been switched. The fact of the matter is that even in the straightforward cases of plantation creoles, such as Sranan in Suriname and Jamaican, the results of all three scenarios have made themselves felt diachronically in a specific geographical location. That is, it would be difficult to find a location in the Anglophone Caribbean that has not been affected by the languages and English varieties spoken by immigrants since emancipation in the nineteenth century and by varieties of the colonial language heard in local metropolitan population centers.

4   Basic Features of Restructured English in the Caribbean

What follows in this section is a brief generalized grammatical and phonological sketch applicable to many English-derived creoles and/or dialects in the Caribbean. Of course, it must be pointed out that all Anglophone creoles spoken in the Caribbean reveal synchronic differences in terms of lexicon, phonology, morphology, and syntax, even if they share many general similarities. Features presented here are not exclusively associated with any specific creole language; that is to say, these features are not, for example, all derived from Jamaican or Guyanese Creole English. This presentation is an abstraction of possible features based on what I have heard spoken in the Caribbean or researched from other sources. The treatment in this section is not in any way intended to be exhaustive. For syntactic features associated with specific creoles, including the Surinamese creoles, readers should consult the survey presented in Hancock (1987); for a discussion of phones and phonemes in Anglophone Atlantic varieties, Wells (1982). The goal of this section is to highlight basic features found in a range of Anglophone Caribbean Englishes.

It is important to remember that the varieties of English that Africans in the Western Hemisphere originally heard were regional, social, and ethnic (e.g., Irish and Scottish) dialects of British English as spoken in the seventeenth through the nineteenth centuries. As Africans and African-descended peoples began to acquire English forms, initially as a second language, they would have heard varieties of English spoken by Europeans and whatever earlier restructured forms they might have encountered on the West African coast or perhaps at slave entrepots in the Caribbean, such as St Eustatius or St Kitts (see Baker and Bruyn, 1998 for references to a scenario in which St Kitts influences emerging Englishes on other islands). Later, as local varieties began to emerge in the decades to follow, slaves would have acquired local varieties as first languages or as native-speaker varieties spoken in the relevant communities by peoples of both African and European descent. Thus, from a diachronic perspective, English-derived Caribbean varieties in general are more British-oriented, at least in their phonologies, though in the last century American and Canadian influence can be expected and documented (e.g., see Van Herk, 2003).

There appear to be some satisfactory reasons for dividing the region of the Caribbean linguistically into geographically designated western and eastern varieties on the basis of comparative phonology and syntax (see Holm, 1988–9: 445; Wells, 1982, 1987; Le Page, 1957–8; Hancock, 1987). However, the grounds for this division are largely abstract and impressionistic, since it is my experience, having done fieldwork in both general locations, that there are few specific features that one may find in one region that absolutely cannot be found in the other. In general, creolists are often comfortable with the highly questionable assumption that earlier varieties of creole languages were monolithic and that contemporary synchronic variation is a more recent (i.e., post-emancipation) phenomenon. However, whether these overlapping patterns represent parallel historical developments or are due to intra-Caribbean migration, especially in the post-emancipation period, is open to debate. As has been made clear in dialect studies over the last 50 years, it is not any specific feature that is diagnostic of a dialect (whether it is a regional, ethnic, or social one), but the bundle of features that are associated with a particular designation. And it is on these grounds that one may find some validity in the motivation for separating Caribbean Englishes into western and eastern varieties. I discuss below features heard in the general Caribbean, while making reference to features believed to be representative of both the eastern and western Caribbean. (The Surinamese creoles are ignored here, since they are largely unintelligible with Anglophone Caribbean varieties spoken outside Suriname.) The data is provided in phonetic symbols within a mostly phonemic presentation.

5 Syntax

5.1 Copula

The verbal complex in Caribbean Englishes has received significant attention from linguists (see Winford, 1993), and the form and distribution of the copula has often been at the center of this discussion. The three basic functions of the copula (attributive, locative, and nominal) are heard in the following forms. Attributive constructions: /ʃi de gud/, /ʃi aarait/ or /ʃi iz gud/, 'she is good, she is doing fine, she is all right'. The verb /de/ or /iz/ is often the copula form in these cases but no overt verb may be realized at all. The locative form is often /de/ as in: /we im de/ or /we im iz/ 'where is he/she/it?' Inversion between the copula and the noun is not required for questions in these languages. Rising intonation often indicates interrogatives. (Furthermore, the question word "where" can take several forms: /we/, /wepaat/, /wiʧpaat/, /wiʧplees/, etc.) The nominal form of the copula displays the following forms: /a/, /iz/, /bi/ and no overt realization at all, e.g., /ʃi a mi sista/, /ʃi iz mi sista/, /ʃi bi mi sista/, /ʃi mi sista/ 'she is my sister.'

5.2   Past tense

The past tense marker, as with most of the overt grammatical markers in creole languages, often occurs as a discrete, free morpheme before the main verb of an utterance. It is common for unmarked non-stative (or dynamic) verbs to have a past interpretation. That is, an utterance such as /mi iit aredi/ could translate as 'I ate already', even though the main verb /iit/ 'eat' is unmarked overtly by any marker. However, both stative and non-stative verbs may be preverbally marked for the past with one of a range of past tense markers. Depending on the context, an utterance may be interpreted as conveying the simple past or what is sometimes called the past perfect. For example, the grammatical information conveyed by /mi iit aredi/ can similarly occur as /mi dʌn iit/ or more generally as /mi bin iit/, /mi woz iit/, /mi di(d) iit/, /mi mi(n) iit/. The latter four utterances would translate as 'I ate' or 'I have eaten', depending on the context. The utterance /mi dʌn iit/ displays the completive marker /dʌn/, which would more closely match 'I already ate/I have already eaten', or 'I'm done eating', 'I done ate already' in other varieties of English.

5.3   Future tense

The preverbal future tense marker is some reflex of either /go/, /a go/, or /goin/ and sometimes /wi/ 'will'. For example, the standard English translation 'they will dance' or 'they are going to dance' will variously correspond to the following utterances: /dem go dans/, /dem wi dans/, /dem gwain dans/, /dem goin dans/, /dem a go dans/, and even /dem wan dans/. In the last instance the future marker *wan* seems to be a grammaticalized form of the verb "want." *Gwain* is often associated with the western Caribbean.

5.4   Progressive aspect

The preverbal markers /de/, /da/, or /a/ and the verbal bound morphological suffix /-in/ are those features most commonly associated with the progressive aspect in Anglophone Caribbean varieties. For example: /di gyal a kaal yu/, /di gyal de kaal yu/, and /di gyal kaalin yu/ all correspond to 'the girl is calling you'.

5.5 Pronouns: subject, object, and possessive

Most of the pronouns below may occur as subject, object, and possessive pronouns with the following exceptions: both /ai/ and /a/ 'I' seem to be only subject pronouns; /ar/ 'her' is an object pronoun with exclusive reference to females; /om/ may refer to 'him, her, it' in object position (its distribution is largely limited to the eastern Caribbean). /(h)ɪm/ indicates males or females or even non-human referents in either subject or object position. The plural pronouns *aayu* and *aawi* are largely heard in the eastern Caribbean, and *unu* is more common in the Western Caribbean.

	Singular	*Plural*
1st	/mi/, /a, ai/ (subject)	/wi, aawi/
2nd	/yu/	/unu, aayu, yaal/
3rd	/(h)i(m)/ 'he, she, it'	/de, dem/
	/(h)i/ 'he, she, it'	
	/ʃi/, /ar/ (object), /om, am/ 'he, she, it' (object)	
	/i(t)/	

The following utterances illustrate that subject, object, and possessive pronouns are often identical in their distribution: /mi gat a saŋ fu unu siŋ/ 'I have a song for you (pl.) to sing', /dem no stie laik dem/ 'they're not like them', /ʃi doz sii ʃi sista evri en da wiik/ 'she sees her sister every weekend' (note the common habitual marker /doz/ is often associated with the eastern Caribbean; many Caribbean Englishes do not overtly mark this distinction; some use /de/ to mark this function (see progressive aspect above)), and /mi mi fait wid om/ 'I fought with him/I have fought with him/her'. The second-person plural pronoun /unu/ is the one pronoun that seems not to be derived from a superstrate source.

5.6 Possession

Possession is marked solely by word order in creoles, rather than by a combination of word order and bound inflectional morphology as is the case in more standard varieties of English, e.g., /mi brada uman de de/ 'My brother's wife/woman is/was there'.

5.7 Infinitival marker

The infinitival marker in many Anglophone Caribbean creoles is often some reflex of "for": /fu/ or /fi/, e.g., /unu ha fu du it/ 'You (pl.) have to do it'. The marker /tu/ associated with other varieties of English is also heard. Some creole constructions not commonly found in metropolitan varieties of English use the form /fu/ or /fi/, e.g., /a fiil fi smuok/ 'I feel like smoking'.

5.8   Pluralization

Pluralization is most often marked by a post-nominal /dem/ rather than a bound inflectional morpheme (the marker can occur in a pre-nominal position as well), unless a number of more than one has already been established previously within the phrase or clause, e.g., /di daag dem/, /di daag an dem/, and /dem daag/ 'the dogs'; cf. /di ʧri daag/ 'the three dogs', which has no plural marker other than the previously established number three. Nouns like "people" and "children," which are not usually pluralized in other varieties of English, are often pluralized in Caribbean Englishes, e.g., /hau di pipl dem trai fi liv/ 'How do the people manage to live?'

5.9   Negation

Negation in most Anglophone Caribbean creoles is designated by a single preverbal negator. This negator is usually some reflex of "no," "not," or "never," e.g., /ʃi no siŋ/, /ʃi na(t) siŋ/, /ʃi neva siŋ/ 'she didn't sing'. It is also possible to find a negator based on auxiliary "don't" or "ain't," e.g., /ʃi duon iit/ or /ʃi en iit/ 'she didn't eat'.

5.10   Serial verbs

One of the most heavily researched areas of Restructured Englishes (though, again, this feature is not structurally diagnostic, since it is also displayed by many non-creole languages) is serial verb constructions (see Winford, 1993). That is, verbs may occur serially with no intervening coordinator or infinitival markers, e.g., /dem gaan iit/ 'they went to eat/they went and ate', /yu wan paas di die wi mi/ 'Do you want to spend the day with me?' Other varieties of English reveal similar serial verb constructions such as "come bring me my food" and "go get my car."

6   Lexicon

An English-derived or -based creole is given that designation because much of its basic lexicon is based upon colonial varieties of English heard in the seventeenth through twentieth centuries. Consequently, many English-derived varieties maintain words that are archaic today in other varieties of English. For example, /krabit/ 'mean, disagreeable' or 'rough, cruel' can be found in several Caribbean Englishes and can be traced to Old English and to usage in Scotland; /fieba/ or *favor* 'to resemble' as in /ʃi fieba you/ 'she resembles you' (this usage of the verb "favor" can also be heard in the American South); and

/beks/ or *vex* 'to anger' as in /wamek yu beks so/ 'Why are you so angry?' are also related to features of older English varieties. *Beg* 'to ask' as in /a wan beg yu wan tiŋ/ 'I want to ask you something' is preserved in most other varieties of English only in the frozen expression "I beg your pardon."

Other words in many creoles reflect the historical usage of language used by sailors. For example, /haal/ transparently derived from "haul" means 'to pull' but seems to be used more frequently in the Caribbean than in other varieties of English, and /gyali/, derived from "the galley or kitchen on a ship," can mean simply 'the kitchen of any household'.

Many African-language-derived words may also be found in the lexicon. Several words found in the Anglophone Caribbean derive from Twi, a language spoken in Ghana on the Lower Guinea Coast (see Aceto, 1999b): /koŋgosa/ 'gossip', /fufu/ 'common food of yam and plantains', /mumu/ 'dull, dumb, silent', /potopoto/ 'mud, muddy'. Other African languages are represented as well: /ʤuk/ 'to stab, poke' or 'to have sex with' appears to be from Fulani, a language spoken in Nigeria and other locations on the Guinea Coast.

The influence of African words can be traced beyond straightforward borrowings. Many English-derived expressions in Caribbean creoles seem to be based upon word-for-word translations or calques from African languages. For example, *big-eye* meaning 'greedy' has a number of correspondences among languages spoken on the Guinea Coast in Africa. *Day-clean* 'daybreak' appears to be another such case.

7 Morphology

It is often claimed that creoles display few if any bound morphemes. McWhorter (1998: 792) qualifies his claim by stating that creole languages rarely have more than one or two inflectional affixes. However, this feature is not diagnostic of any lexifier creole, since non-creole languages (e.g., Chinese languages) also reveal a profound lack of inflectional affixes. At any rate, in the Anglophone Caribbean, bound morphology is illustrated by the following examples: /go/ + /-in/ or /goin/ may function as a future tense marker, e.g., /mi goin iit/ 'I'm going to eat', and a similar combination is found as the progressive aspectual marker when a verb combines with the /-in/ suffix, e.g., /mama kaalin me/ 'mama is calling me'. Many English-derived creoles form comparatives with inflectional affixes and nouns from adjectives through bound derivational and inflectional morphology, e.g., /fas(t) + -a/ 'faster', /wikid + -nis/ 'wickedness', even if many researchers insist these are not features of so-called "deep" or "basilectal" creoles. Many restructured Englishes of the Caribbean have also created phrasal verbs that appear not to be found in contributing British dialects of English or American dialects today, e.g., *kiss up* 'to kiss', *wet up* 'to soak' (cf. with *show up* 'to appear', *cook up* 'to cook' in other dialects of English).

8   Phonology

This section is largely based on Holm (1989–9, vol. 2), Wells (1982), Aceto and Williams (2003), various specific articles referenced below, and the author's own notes from fieldwork whose results have not yet appeared in published articles.

8.1   *Vowels*

Vowel quality in the Caribbean differs from that of the metropolitan varieties of English.

8.1.1   *Long vowels*

The off-glides [ei] and [ou] of metropolitan varieties of English are often not found in the eastern Caribbean, where these sounds most often correspond to [eː] and [oː]. However, recent work by Childs, Reaser, and Wolfram (2003) suggests that in some Bahamian communities the sound [ei] can be heard. In the Leeward Islands, specifically Montserrat (see Wells, 1982: 587), words that historically had long vowels are shortened and they have no off-glides (e.g., [eʲ]), as they do in metropolitan varieties, e.g., /ki/ *key* and /de/ *day*. In many western Caribbean varieties, these same sounds correspond to those with on-glides, e.g., /ie/ and /uo/ as in [fies] *face* and [guot] *goat*. These same vowels can be realized as diphthongs with variants such as [iɛ] and [uɔ].

8.1.2   *Unreduced vowels*

Even in positions not associated with word-final or postvocalic /r/, West Indian varieties of English often display a preference for unreduced vowels, e.g., [abɪlɪtɪ] *ability*, [tawɪl] *towel*, where other dialects of English often display schwa [ə] in the third and second vowel positions respectively. In some dialects of metropolitan English, these word-final segments such as [l] in *towel* or nasals in words like *cotton* may become syllabic consonants. Many varieties in the eastern Caribbean (except for Bajan) have no mid-central vowels, i.e., /ə/ or /ʌ/.

8.1.3   *Other vowels*

The low front vowel /æ/ found in many metropolitan varieties of English in words such as *trap* is often realized further back in the mouth as [a] in the Caribbean, e.g., cat /cæt/ is pronounced as /kyat/ (note the off-glide found after the velar stop /k/ which can also be heard after the voiced segment as in [gyaadin] 'garden'). The /ʌ/ of words like *strut* in metropolitan varieties is backed and close to [ɔ]. However, some varieties of English in the Turks and Caicos Islands (as well as in Bermuda) reveal the presence of [æ].

 Eastern Caribbean English-derived varieties often maintain the difference between sounds in words in metropolitan dialects like the /ɔː/ in *jaw* and the

/aː/ in *jar* (which often has an r-less pronunciation in many varieties but not all, e.g., Bajan). Both sounds have typically merged into /aː/ in the western group.

Words commonly found in all dialects of English often contain different vowels in Caribbean varieties due perhaps to the preservation of older regional British pronunciations that have changed in contemporary forms. For example, *spoil* and *boil* are commonly pronounced as /spail/ and /bail/, especially in the western Caribbean.

8.2 Consonants

Some notable features of the consonants are the following.

8.2.1 Rhoticity

Except for varieties of English in Barbados, and to some degree in Jamaica and Guyana, postvocalic /r/ is often not heard in the Anglophone Caribbean. Bajan English is recognized by its full rhotic nature at all levels of society. Van Herk (2003) states that Bajan is "if anything, more rhotic than North American [Standard English]." This is not the case in other areas, in which full *r*-lessness after vowels (e.g., in Trinidad and the Bahamas) and the variable nature of [r] across a geographical space (e.g., in Guyana) are salient dialect features. In non-rhotic dialects, additional phonemes such as /ea/ (e.g., /nea/ *near*) and /oa/ (e.g., /foa/ *four*) are often created by absence of /r/ after vowels.

8.2.2 /v/–/w/ merger

Many dialects of Caribbean English (e.g., Bahamian, Bermudan, and Vincentian) may alternate [w], [β] (the voiced bilabial fricative), or [ʋ] (the voiced labiodental approximant) for words which in metropolitan varieties begin with [v], e.g., *village* [wɪlɪdʒ]. This feature may be related to component dialect varieties of English heard in the Caribbean in the eighteenth century which contain this same alternation (e.g., Cockney) or possibly to African languages that lacked the /v/ segment. Some Anglophone Caribbean communities may reveal /b/ where metropolitan Anglophone varieties display /v/, e.g., *vex* 'angry' [bɛks], *river* [rɪba], and *love* [lʌb].

8.2.3 Word-initial /h/

In the Leewards (Antigua, St Kitts, Nevis, Montserrat, Anguilla, Barbuda), unlike in Jamaican and other western Caribbean varieties, /h/ is most often *not* dropped from the beginnings of most words. So-called "h-dropping" or word-initial "h-deletion" is common in Jamaica and in the Bahamas as well. H-dropping also occurs in other dialects of English; often British Cockney is cited as the source of *h*-dropping in English-derived Caribbean varieties. In dialects with this feature, which is generally not found in the eastern Caribbean, pairs such as *hair* and *air* are homophonous (both are sometimes [ɪɛr]).

In many Caribbean Englishes, word-initial [h-] does not appear where it would commonly be found in other English varieties, e.g., *whole* [uol], *half* [aaf], but this feature is common in many non-Standard English dialects in Great Britain. On the other hand, words that begin with vowels in many dialects of English often are spoken with a word-initial [h], e.g., *egg* [hɛg], or even [w-], e.g., *ugly* [wogli] in Caribbean varieties.

8.2.4   Nasals

Syllable- or word-final alveolar nasals following /ʌ/ are often velarized or become /ŋ/, e.g., /dʌŋ/ *down*, which often creates new homonyms (e.g., in this case with *dung*). A variant of this type of pronunciation, although likely archaic, is where the preceding vowel becomes nasalized instead of displaying a consonantal segment, e.g., [dɔ̃].

8.2.5   Th-*stopping*

The neutralization of /ð/ and /θ/ as /d/ and /t/, e.g., /tɪŋ/ *thing* and /fada/ *father*, is a common feature of many dialects of Caribbean English as well as in regional, ethnic, and social dialects spoken in North America and Great Britain (which often display reflexes different from those in the Caribbean). This process creates new homonyms in the specific dialects in question. Some of the many examples are: *thin–tin* [tɪn], *faith–fate* [fet], *though–dough* [do], *breathe–breed* [brid].

Neutralization appears to operate particularly readily in the environment preceding an /r/ in an onset consonant cluster: *three–tree* [triː], *through–tru* [truː], though often these segments are realized as palatalized allophones [t͡ʃruː] or [t͡ʃroː]. Sometimes interdental fricatives in metropolitan varieties do not correspond to a stop consonant in Caribbean Englishes. In Kokoy, a variety of creole English spoken in Dominica, where /θ/ occurs in onset consonant clusters in metropolitan varieties with /r/, the output often becomes [f], e.g., *three* [fri], *through* [fru] (Aceto, forthcoming a).

Many speakers of Caribbean Englishes realize interdental fricatives as similarly articulated in metropolitan varieties. In St Eustatius, many speakers, at all levels of society, display interdental segments, while the stop correspondences are still the preference for most speakers (Aceto, forthcoming b). Cutler (2003) makes a similar observation about this feature in the English of Gran Turk Island as does Williams (2003) about some varieties of English spoken in Anguilla.

8.2.6   Consonant cluster reduction

As is typical in many dialects of English around the world, the word-final /t/ segment in consonant clusters preceded by an obstruent is often not realized, e.g., /-ft, -st, -kt/. For example, words such as *left*, *nest*, and *act* are realized as /lɛf/, /nɛs/, and /ak/. Consonant clusters in codas in which /d/ is in the final position are also often not realized in many restructured West Indian Englishes, e.g., /sɛn/ *send* or /bɪl/ *build*.

The reduction of consonant clusters in codas also affects the realization of past tense allomorphs as heard in metropolitan varieties of English, as in *pushed* /puʃt/, *stopped* /stapt/, and *staged* /stedʒd/. The past tense allomorphs [-d], [-t], and [-ɪd] are generally absent in creole varieties of English, but it is difficult to be certain if they always were. However, they are part of the metropolitan speech varieties spoken by many Anglophone Caribbeans today.

Word-final clusters of a nasal and a voiceless consonant are heard in West Indian varieties of English, e.g., [lamp] *lamp*, [tɛnt] *tent*, *tenth* (see description above regarding *th*-stopping), and [baŋk] *bank*. Clusters in codas are also found in combination with liquids (in combination with [l] and [r], if it is a rhotic dialect such as Bajan), e.g., [mɪlk] *milk*, [ʃɛlf] *shelf*, [part] *part*, and [hard] *hard*. Other consonant cluster combinations occur freely such as /ks/, e.g., [aks] *ask*, [baks] *box*, [sɪks] *six*. In some creole Englishes, consonant clusters in onsets or word-initially are dispreferred, e.g., [taːt] *start*, [tan] *stand*, [tap] *stop*.

9 Conclusion

Many of the locations in the Anglophone Caribbean have never even been documented by linguists. Readers may consult Aceto (2001) for a list of underdocumented or undocumented Englishes. This descriptive observation should entice scholars, new and old, into the field to describe these interesting language varieties. Today's synchronic descriptions can help to inform future generations of linguists to accurately compare how, when, where, and perhaps why these languages have changed.

See also Chapters 18, PIDGINS AND CREOLES; 23, LITERARY CREATIVITY IN WORLD ENGLISHES; 28, WORLD ENGLISHES AND DESCRIPTIVE GRAMMARS.

REFERENCES

Aceto, Michael (1995) Variation in a secret creole language of Panama. *Language in Society*, **24**, 537–60.

Aceto, Michael (1999a) Looking beyond decreolization as an explanatory model of language change in Creole-speaking communities. *Journal of Pidgin and Creole Languages*, **14**, 93–119.

Aceto, Michael (1999b) The Gold Coast contribution to the Atlantic English creoles. In *Spreading the Word: The Issue of Diffusion among the Atlantic Creoles*. Westminster Creolistics Series 6. Edited by Magnus Huber and Mikael Parkvall. London: University of Westminster Press, pp. 69–80.

Aceto, Michael (2001) Going back to the beginning: Describing the (nearly) undocumented Anglophone Creoles of the Caribbean. In *Pidgin and Creole Linguistics in the 21st Century*. Edited by Glenn G. Gilbert. New York: Peter Lang, pp. 93–118.

Aceto, Michael (forthcoming a) Kokoy: Dominica's third creole language.

Aceto, Michael (forthcoming b) St Eustatius Creole English: Why did an English-derived creole emerge in a Dutch colony?

Aceto, Michael and Williams, Jeffrey P. (eds.) (2003) *Contact Englishes of the Eastern Caribbean*. Amsterdam: John Benjamins.

Alleyne, Mervyn (1971) Acculturation and the cultural matrix of creolization. In *Pidginization and Creolization of Languages*. Edited by Dell Hymes. Cambridge: Cambridge University Press, pp. 169–86.

Andersen, Roger (ed.) (1983) *Pidginization and Creolization as Language Acquisition*. Rowley, MA: Newbury House.

Baker, Philip and Bruyn, Adrienne (eds.) (1998) *St. Kitts and the Atlantic Creoles: The Texts of Samuel Augustus Mathews in Perspective*. Westminster Creolistics Series 4. London: University of Westminster Press.

Bauer, Anton (1975) Die soziolinguistische Status- und Funktions-Problematik von Reduktionssprachen. Bern: Lang Verlag.

Bickerton, Derek (1984) The language bioprogram hypothesis. *The Behavioral and Brain Sciences*, 7, 173–221.

Bilby, Kenneth M. (1983) How the "older heads" talk: A Jamaican Maroon spirit possession language and its relationship to the creoles of Suriname and Sierra Leone. *New West Indian Guide*, 57, 37–88.

Bloomfield, Leonard (1933) *Language*. New York: Henry Holt and Company.

Boretzky, Norbert (1983) *Kreolsprachen: Substrate und Sprachwandel*. Wiesbaden: Otto Karrassowitz.

Childs, Becky, Reaser, Jeffrey, and Wolfram, Walt (2003) Defining ethnic varieties in the Bahamas: Phonological accommodation in black and white enclave communities. In *Contact Englishes of the Eastern Caribbean*. Edited by Michael Aceto and Jeffrey P. Williams. Amsterdam: John Benjamins, pp. 1–28.

Coomber, Melvin E. A. (1969) A descriptive study of Krio phonology. Unpublished master's thesis, Georgetown University.

Cutler, Cecilia (2003) English in the Turks and Caicos islands: A look at grand Turk. In *Contact Englishes of the Eastern Caribbean*. Edited by Michael Aceto and Jeffrey P. Williams. Amsterdam: John Benjamins, pp. 51–80.

DeGraff, Michel (ed.) (1999) *Language Creation and Language Change: Creolization, Diachrony, and Development*. Cambridge, MA: MIT Press.

Fyle, Clifford and Jones, Eldred (1980) *A Krio–English Dictionary*. Oxford: Oxford University Press.

Garrett, Paul (1999) Language socialization, convergence, and shift in St. Lucia, West Indies. Unpublished doctoral dissertation, New York University.

Garrett, Paul (2003) An English Creole that isn't: On the sociohistorical origins and linguistic classification of the vernacular English in St. Lucia. In *Contact Englishes of the Eastern Caribbean*. Edited by Michael Aceto and Jeffrey P. Williams. Amsterdam: John Benjamins, pp. 155–210.

Hall, Robert A., Jr. (1966) *Pidgin and Creole Languages*. Ithaca: Cornell University Press.

Hancock, Ian (1986) The domestic hypothesis, diffusion and componentiality: An account of Atlantic Anglophone creole origins. In *Substrata versus Universals in Creole Genesis*. Edited by Pieter Muysken and Norval Smith. Amsterdam: John Benjamins, pp. 71–102.

Hancock, Ian (1987) A preliminary classification of the Anglophone Atlantic Creoles with syntactic data from thirty-three representative dialects. In *Pidgin and Creole Languages.* Edited by Glenn G. Gilbert. Honolulu: University of Hawai'i Press, pp. 264–333.

Hancock, Ian (1994) Componentiality and the creole matrix: The Southwest English contribution. In *The Crucible of Carolina: Essays in the Development of Gullah Language and Culture.* Edited by Michael Montgomery. Athens: University of Georgia Press, pp. 95–114.

Holm, John (ed.) (1983) *Central American English.* Varieties of English around the world, T2. Heidelberg: Julius Groos Verlag.

Holm, John (1988–9) *Pidgins and Creoles,* vols 1 and 2. Cambridge: Cambridge University Press.

Huber, Magnus (2004) The Nova Scotia–Sierra Leone connection: New evidence on an early variety of African American Vernacular English in the diaspora. In *Contacts Worldwide: Creoles and Other Linguistic Outputs.* Edited by Geneviève Escure and Armin Schwegler. Amsterdam: John Benjamins, pp. 67–95.

Le Page, Robert B. (1957–8) General outlines of Creole English dialects in the British Caribbean. *Orbis,* **6**, 373–91; **7**, 54–64.

McWhorter, John H. (1998) Identifying the creole prototype: Vindicating a typological class. *Language,* **74**, 788–818.

McWhorter, John H. (2003) The Suriname creoles: Evaluating Afrogensis and genetic relationships. In *Papers in Contact Linguistics.* Edited by Anthony Grant. Bradford: Bradford Studies in Language, Culture and Society, pp. 93–112.

Mufwene, Salikoko S. (1994) On decreolization: The case of Gullah. In *Language and the Social Construction of Identity in Creole Situations.* Edited by Marcyliena Morgan. Center for Afro-American Studies: University of California at Los Angeles, pp. 63–99.

Mufwene, Salikoko S. (1996) The founder principle in creole genesis. *Diachronica,* **12**, 83–134.

Mufwene, Salikoko S. (2001) *The Ecology of Language Evolution.* Cambridge: Cambridge University Press.

Niles, Norma A. (1980) Provincial English Dialects and Barbadian English. Unpublished PhD dissertation, University of Michigan.

Parkvall, Mikael (2000) *Out of Africa: African Influences in the Atlantic Creoles.* London: Battlebridge Publications.

Schuchardt, Hugo (1883) Kreolische Studien X: Ueber das Negerenglisch von Westafrika. Reproduced, translated, and annotated in Glen G. Gilbert (1985) Hugo Schuchardt and the Atlantic Creoles: A newly discovered manuscript, "On the Negro English of West Africa." *American Speech,* **60**, 31–63.

Smith, Norval (1987) The Genesis of the Creole Languages of Surinam. Unpublished PhD dissertation, University of Amsterdam.

Thomason, Sarah G. and Kaufman, Terrence (1988) *Language Contact, Creolization, and Genetic Linguistics.* Berkeley: University of California Press.

Van Herk, Gerard (2003) Barbadian Lects: Beyond Meso. In *Contact Englishes of the Eastern Caribbean.* Edited by Michael Aceto and Jeffrey P. Williams. Amsterdam: John Benjamins, pp. 241–64.

Von Bradshaw, A. T. (1965) Vestiges of Portuguese in the languages of Sierra Leone. *Sierra Leone Language Review,* **4**, 5–37.

Wells, John C. (1982) *Accents of English 3: Beyond the British Isles*. Cambridge: Cambridge University Press.

Wells, John C. (1987) Phonological relationships in Caribbean and West African English. *English World-Wide*, **8**, 61–8.

Williams, Jeffrey P. (1985) Preliminaries to the study of the dialects of white West Indian English. *New West Indian Guide*, **59**, 27–44.

Williams, Jeffrey P. (1987) Anglo-Caribbean English: A Study of Its Sociolinguistic History and the Development of Its Aspectual Markers. Unpublished PhD dissertation, The University of Texas at Austin.

Williams, Jeffrey P. (1988) The development of aspectual markers in Anglo-Caribbean English. *Journal of Pidgin and Creole Languages*, **3**, 245–63.

Williams, Jeffrey P. (2003) The establishment and perpetuation of Anglophone white enclave communities in the Eastern Caribbean: The case of island harbor, Anguilla. In *Contact Englishes of the Eastern Caribbean*. Edited by Michael Aceto and Jeffrey P. Williams. Amsterdam: John Benjamins, pp. 95–119.

Wilson, Ellen Gibson (1976) *The Loyal Blacks*. New York: Putnam's.

Winer, Lise (1993) *Trinidad and Tobago*. Amsterdam: John Benjamins.

Winford, Donald (1993) *Predication in Caribbean English Creoles*. Amsterdam/Philadelphia: John Benjamins.

Winford, Donald (2000) "Intermediate" creoles and degrees of change in creole formation: The case of Bajan. In *Degrees of Restructuring in Creole Languages*. Edited by Ingrid Neumann-Holzschuh and Edgar W. Schneider. Amsterdam: John Benjamins, pp. 215–46.

FURTHER READING

Holm, John (2000) *Introduction to Pidgins and Creoles*. Cambridge: Cambridge University Press.

Holm, John (1988–9) *Pidgins and Creoles*, vols 1 and 2. Cambridge: Cambridge University Press.

Roberts, Peter A. (1988) *West Indians and their Language*. Cambridge: Cambridge University Press.

Roberts, Peter A. (1997) *From Oral to Literate Culture: Colonial Experience in the English West Indies*. Barbados, Jamaica, Trinidad and Tobago: The Press, University of the West Indies.

14   Euro-Englishes

MARKO MODIANO

1   Introduction

The spread of English across European cultures is a complex process, one which is having a profound impact on social, cultural, and political life, as well as on education at all levels. In the words of David Graddol, "No other region has been more affected by the rise of English than Europe" (2001: 47). English is gaining ground at the expense of all other European languages, continues to lay claim to an increasing number of domains, and is considered by many to be a threat to minority languages and cultures (for discussion, see Grin, 1993; Phillipson, 1992; and Skutnabb-Kangas and Phillipson, 1994). This chapter discusses three specific issues which have relevance to the European context.

The first issue involves the inequalities between mainland Europe and the UK when it comes to setting standards for English language teaching (ELT). Mainland European ELT is dependent on the British rendition of the English language because the vast majority of educational materials used in mainland Europe are imported from England. Furthermore, throughout Europe, the British Council operates language-learning services within the framework of Standard British English and the cultural contexts of Britain and the Commonwealth. Thus, how British scholars conceptualize English strongly influences ELT practitioners across Europe. Secondly, there is a focus on the manner in which English is used in mainland Europe as a lingua franca among non-native speakers, giving rise to the concept of "Euro-English." Lastly, there is an examination of the role that English is playing in the European Union (EU). Because English is intimately linked to the future of the Union, the official functions of English within the EU will have considerable impact on the forms and functions of the English language in this part of the world.

English has been studied as a foreign language throughout mainland Europe since the nineteenth century. However, prior to World War II, German – especially in Eastern and Northern Europe – and French were more commonly targeted in foreign language teaching and learning. In the post-war period, English surpassed all other foreign languages in numbers of learners. Official statistics indicate that, prior to the enlargement of 2004, more than 90 percent of all secondary-school pupils were learning English (Eurydice, 2000: 159; see also Berns, 1995 and van Els and Extra, 1987).

Ten countries, the majority of them in Eastern Europe, joined the Union in 2004. Russian had been a required subject in formal education in all Eastern European countries. With the fall of the Soviet Union in the early 1990s, interest in Russian declined, and English became the first foreign language among students in Eastern Europe. There are, moreover, over 55 million native speakers of English in the British Isles. The EU is thus unique in that within its borders there is a substantial community of Inner-Circle first-language speakers producing the lion's share of ELT materials for worldwide distribution, as well as a massive population of non-native speakers receiving compulsory foreign-language education in English.

2   English for Europe

In Britain, many books have been produced which chart the development of English from its origins in England to its current global status (see, for example, Sidney Greenbaum, *The English Language Today*, 1985; Randolph Quirk and Henry Widdowson, *English in the World: Teaching and Learning the Language and Literatures*, 1985; David Crystal, *English as a Global Language*, 1997; and Peter Trudgill and Jean Hannah, *International English*, 2002; (see also Crystal, 2001; and Quirk, 1981)).

Many studies have also been conducted in Britain on the diversity of the language in the context of second-language, pidgin, and creole varieties. Tom McArthur, editor of *English Today* (Cambridge University Press) and of *The Oxford Companion to the English Language* (1992), has for many years been eager to initiate debate on the various ways in which we are coming to terms with the global functions of English. Articles published in *English Today* by writers from all over the world have been instrumental in forming our understanding of English as a language of wider communication. McArthur (1996), in fact, is one of the few editors in Britain eager to publish papers which address developments taking place in mainland Europe. Discussion of English in mainland Europe can also be found in the pages of *World Englishes* (see, for example, Deneire and Goethals, 1997) and *English World-Wide*, an important forum for discussion of world Englishes.

Publishers from Britain, such as Blackwell, Cambridge University Press, Longman, Macmillan, Oxford University Press, and Routledge, with an army of Standard British English grammars, dictionaries, and supplemental materials, provide mainland Europeans with English-language learning supplies. In Germany, Manfred Görlach and Konrad Schröder, who were early editors of *English World-Wide*, promoted a conservative pro-British view of English (for an example of their prescriptivism, see Görlach and Schröder, 1985). However, Standard British English has been seriously challenged by American English for the past 20–30 years (see Decke-Cornill, 2002; and Erling, 2002, for discussion of Germany, and van Essen, 1997 for Holland). Through various forms of media, the American variety of English is impacting the lives of millions of Europeans (see Hilgendorf, 1996, 2001; Martin, 1998, 2002; Modiano, 1996). Within ELT, however, there has been a reluctance to abandon Standard British English in favor of Standard American English as the target variety. The result is that while Standard British English is still the most common platform for ELT in mainland Europe, the attention given to American English and acceptance of American English pronunciation, lexis, and grammar in the school examination processes is increasing, as are efforts to acquire competence in cross-cultural communication (often referred to as *intercultural competence*).

Coinciding with these developments in Europe, traditional ELT platforms have come under attack in Asia and Africa as a result of Braj Kachru's and others' questioning of long-established precepts and practices as they are utilized in the Outer Circle. Kachru's liberation-linguistics perspective on ELT has influenced European ELT, although it has not had the same impact here as it has in many postcolonial communities. Other scholars, including David Crystal, David Graddol, Jennifer Jenkins, Tom McArthur, and Barbara Seidlhofer, have played pivotal roles in liberalization processes for ELT in mainland Europe. Their challenging of traditional perspectives in ELT has opened the door to investigations into how English can operate in a culturally and linguistically complex Europe.

David Crystal has attempted to develop a theoretical basis for coming to terms with new Englishes in the context of diversity and hybridization, something he feels does not necessarily challenge the importance of upholding a traditional standard. Crystal claims that "the need to maintain international intelligibility demands the recognition of a standard variety of English, at the same time as the need to maintain local identity demands the recognition of local varieties of English" (2001: 57). Pedagogy, Crystal insists, must "allow for the complementarity of these two functions of language" (2001: 57). This line of reasoning leads to the notion of *bidialectalism* or even *multidialectalism*, the view that many English language users will have at least two varieties of English at their disposal, one for international forums and one for local purposes.

As to usage in general, Crystal suggests that we abandon the prescriptivist and "absolutist concept" of "correct English" with more liberal "relativistic models" which allow for greater flexibility. Indeed, the standard itself in the British form can now be *normalized*, or in Crystal's words, undergo *dynamic pragmatism*:

> If people in a country increasingly observe their own high-ranking, highly educated people using hybrid forms, if they increasingly hear linguistic diversity

on the World Service of the BBC and other channels, if they find themselves being taught by mother-tongue speakers who themselves reflect current trends in their regionally tinged speech, then who can blame them if they begin to be critical of teaching perspectives which reflect nothing but a parochial past? (Crystal, 2001: 60)

Keeping linguistic diversity at the center of his discussion, Crystal makes it clear that the British dialect will in the years to come have less influence in ELT. Instead, *accommodation* will dominate ELT ideologies. Crystal proposes that "the chief task facing ELT is how to devise pedagogical policies and practices in which the need to maintain an international standard of intelligibility . . . can be made to comfortably exist alongside the need to recognize the importance of international diversity, as a reflection of identity" (2001: 63). This "dynamic linguistic relativism, recognizing as axiomatic the notions of variation and change," Crystal argues, "is the chief challenge facing ELT specialists" (2001: 63). This recognition of the importance of "identity" is directly relevant to the mainland European experience, where emergence of an internationally viable second-language variety of English requires support from the kinds of attitudes that Crystal espouses.

In *The Future of English?* (1997) David Graddol discusses "significant global trends" which he suggests will have an impact on the spread of English in the years to come. Commissioned by the British Council as a component of their *English 2000* initiative, this publication exemplifies the dedication of the British, and especially the British teaching and publishing industries, to supporting English language-learning programs worldwide. (For critiques of British Council policy and initiatives, see Phillipson, 1992.) Graddol's book, which contains relevant information and statistics on the global spread of English, also offers provocative observations. One is made for European youth:

> Non-native forms of English also may acquire identity functions for young people. In Europe, for example, MTV has promoted the use of foreign-language varieties of English as identity markers – a behaviour more usually associated with second-language usage – by employing young presenters with distinctive French, German and Italian English accents, alongside British presenters with regional accents. Such cultural exploitation may indicate that standard, native varieties will be the least influential for the global teenage culture. (1997: 49)

Graddol's reference to "cultural exploitation" suggests a premeditated strategy. It is possible, as well, that MTV's lineup not only indicates the current reluctance to demonstrate near-native proficiency in Standard English, but is more importantly indicative of the movement among mainland Europeans to claim an identity as non-native speakers of the European lingua franca.

Britain, which is the most prolific country in Europe when it comes to the production of scholarly publications which chart and analyze world Englishes, is believed to be the source, at least from a mainland European perspective, of the belief that the British brand of Standard English is the given norm for foreign-language acquisition. Throughout Europe, there are many "non-native" teachers in English studies who are emulating this Anglocentric position. This is one important reason why Europeans have until recently been little concerned with focusing their attention on the actual English of mainland Europeans. Now, with Europe rapidly consolidating into what may one day be defined as a supranational state, it is evident that a *Euro-English* vision of English for mainland Europe may join the ranks of world Englishes (see Jenkins, Modiano, and Seidlhofer, 2001). Thus, when discussing a world Englishes conceptualization of English for Europe, it must be taken into account that those who adhere to prescriptivism based on the virtues of a Standard English are at odds with those who now believe that English is coming into being on its own terms in mainland Europe, much as English has evolved into new varieties in other parts of the world.

3   Critical Stances

Robert Phillipson, the most ardent critic in Europe of English as a global and European lingua franca, published *Linguistic Imperialism* in 1992. In his work there is a great deal of concern for the survival of minority and lesser-used languages, an issue of global relevance, given that so many minority languages are struggling for survival. Linguistic diversity, according to Phillipson and others, is threatened by English, as well as by wide-scale Anglo-Americanization. Western values and practices in a plethora of manifestations, it is argued, are disseminated worldwide in and through the English language. In *English-Only Europe?* (2003), Phillipson has superimposed his theories of linguistic imperialism onto a mainland-European scenario. He argues that measures should be taken to impede the spread of English in the EU at the pan-European as well as at the member-state level (for discussion, see Berns, 1993, 1995; Boyd and Huss, 2001; Coulmas, 1991a, 1991b; Graddol, 2001; and Pool, 1996). Phillipson is supportive of translation and interpretation services, and feels that it is prudent to continue working to ensure that official EU languages are functionally operational at all levels of the Union, both internally as well as locally for EU citizens.

Phillipson's work has strong anti-American undertones. He seems unwilling to reconcile himself to the fact that, for mainland Europeans, British culture and British English can also be experienced as intrusive (apprehension about Anglo-Americanization is a more rational description of the phenomenon). This is demonstrated by Phillipson's lament, "we may be heading for an American English-only Europe" followed by the rhetorical question: "Is this what the citizens and leaders of Europe want?" (2003: 192). Phillipson's aim here is to incite readers to work toward minimizing US influence in Europe. Linguistic Americanization, however, is gaining momentum, and Europeans in general are demonstrating an increasing interest in things American, as well as British. Phillipson's remedy, a call for Esperanto as a solution to the "language problem" in the EU, has not received any noticeable support. Nevertheless, while Phillipson has few followers in Europe who are willing to publicly support his efforts to reduce the role of English in European affairs, his plea that we continue to pay homage to the virtue of the original "official language" policy, delineated in *English-Only Europe?*, is in line with sentiments across Europe. In guaranteeing the rights of each member state to use its language in EU contexts, Europeans seek to protect lesser-used official languages from the encroachment, primarily of English, but also of other major European languages. (Official EU languages such as Danish, Estonian, Finnish, Latvian, and Lithuanian are spoken by less than 1 percent of the population of the EU.)

4 A Postcolonial Perspective for Mainland Europe

In Asian and African communities that have a postcolonial legacy, the criteria for new Englishes are that they are used in education, are not the majority language, have a range of functions, and contain "localized'" or "nativized" features (for discussion, see, e.g., Baumgardner, 1996; Bautista, 1997; Kachru, 1992, 2005; Platt, Weber, and Ho, 1984; Schneider, 1997, among others). A further requirement is that English is used widely within the members of the Outer Circle in addition to its use between them. The production of intellectual properties in these Englishes is seen as further evidence that they have achieved functional second-language-variety status. While there is mounting evidence that these decisive requirements are in the process of being fulfilled for a mainland-European second-language variety of English, the granting of sociolinguistic legitimacy has not yet taken place. Moreover, for speakers of Englishes in developing regions, a postcolonial theoretical position evoked to oppose the hegemony of the West empowers members of such communities in their efforts to form their own sociocultural identities. Mainland Europeans, in the process of creating a pan-European culture in and through English, can also be seen to be on the periphery (to use Phillipson's term). If the standards for the use of the European lingua franca are produced primarily in Britain but also in the United States, what rights and privileges will mainland Europeans have in determining the forms and functions of their lingua franca? English, for them, can act as a form of empowerment.

The linguistic human rights of mainland European non-native speakers of English will require greater attention in the years to come. Up to now, in the literature on the global spread of English, mainland Europeans are defined as foreign-language speakers, and as such are believed to be committed to the acquisition of near-native proficiency in Standard English – most often Standard British English – a teaching and learning regime which leaves little opportunity for mainland Europeans to participate in the development of the language on their own terms.

ELT practitioners across Europe have traditionally been committed to "standard language ideologies," with ideas of prescriptivism and the maintenance of "mutual intelligibility" underpinning foreign-language education (for discussion, see Milroy, 2001). It is widely believed that this is best accomplished by enforcing consistency in Standard English. The standing of British English as the sole target for mainland European ELT (and thus the dominant spoken norm across the continent in formal education), however, is becoming destabilized. Because of this decline in the status and authority of British English, there is now a need to find alternative strategies, not only for ELT, but also for the use of English in other capacities. While it may appear to be the case that the time is now ripe for the acceptance of a local variety of English for mainland Europe, its legitimization, codification, and standardization is proving to be a challenging endeavor.

5   A European Endonormative Model

Barbara Seidlhofer, with her VOICE project based at Vienna University, where a corpus of learners' spoken English, the *Vienna-Oxford ELF Corpus* (The Vienna-Oxford English as Lingua Franca Corpus) is under compilation, is on the front line in the effort to study the way in which mainland non-native speakers are using English in its own right. The ICLE, *International Corpus of Learner English*, a corpus of non-native English, is also available (see Granger, Dagneaux, and Meunier, 2002; Mauranen, 2003). The Cambridge Learner Corpus and the Longman Learners' Corpus, which have been produced to facilitate the acquisition of Standard English, must be differentiated from the work Seidlhofer is conducting in Vienna because Seidlhofer is investigating the successful use of English as a lingua franca without the underlying understanding that language which deviates from native-speaker speech is substandard. Seidlhofer asks whether "there are commonly used constructions, lexical items and sound patterns which are ungrammatical in Standard L1 English but generally unproblematic in ELF [English as a lingua franca] communication?" (2001: 147). In preliminary investigations of the data, Seidlhofer has found that "communicative success comes about despite the fact that there is hardly a turn which is 'correct' or idiomatic by ENL [English as a native language] standards" (2001: 148).

As Seidlhofer notes, "we are witnessing the emergence of an endonormative model of lingua franca English which will increasingly derive its norms of correctness and appropriacy from its own usage rather than that of the UK or the US, or any other 'native speaker' country" (in Jenkins et al., 2001: 15). This line of reasoning can also be traced in the work based on the growing awareness that non-native English-speaking mainland Europeans are primarily using English to communicate with other non-native speakers (see Firth, 1996; House, 1999; James, 2000). A lingua franca perspective is also evident in research on the acquisition of English as a third language (see Cenoz and Jessner, 2000; Knapp and Meierkord, 2002).

While the acceptance of the type of language Seidlhofer is defining as communicatively expedient will not be forthcoming from those who adhere to prescriptivism, the notion that non-native speakers, through their use of the language, are participating in the definition of the language itself is revolutionary. It sets the stage for the kind of paradigm shift which is required for a mainland European second-language variety to come into being. The belief in the wisdom of accommodating non-native speakers in their endeavors to learn English can also be observed in the work of Jenkins; for example, in *The Phonology of English as an International Language* (2000), she presents a case for pronunciation standards and practices for ELT which are not exclusively native-speaker based. In studying the actual communicative contexts of non-native speech where no native speakers are present, Jenkins was able to identify phonological features which proved to be intelligible in lingua franca settings that are not components of Standard English (referred to as the Lingua Franca Core). Here, phonemes which are difficult to master (and indicative of native-speaker speech) can be substituted for by others which, for speakers of various languages, are easier to master. No breakdown in intelligibility was experienced. For example, it was found that the phonemes /θ/ and /ð/ – which are difficult for speakers of many languages – could be substituted for by /f/ and /v/ (Jenkins, 2000: 137–8). Jenkins found, furthermore, that "close approximations to core consonant sounds [are] generally permissible" (2000: 159). Jenkins's thesis is that the teaching and learning of a reduced or simplified core of phonological features that are not disruptive to the communicative act within non-native speaker to non-native speaker contexts aid learners in that they are presented with more easily obtainable goals in the language-learning process. Jenkins explains this in the following manner:

> Once we have identified . . . a phonological core, we will be able to advocate and implement a far more realistic approach to phonology within ELT pedagogy. It will be possible to establish a clearer distinction between learners' productive and receptive phonology, with pronunciation syllabuses no longer being required to embrace large numbers of fine details in an attempt to guide learners to approximate the speech of "native speakers." (2000: 2)

It is possible, moreover, that various aspects of the speech of non-native English users in Europe constitute shared sets of pronunciation challenges which could, through the programs developed by Jenkins, be simplified in ELT. Instead of investing time and resources in an attempt to mimic an idealized native speaker of Standard English, learners can target pronunciation which is easier to learn because it is more attuned to the phonology of their mother tongues, without forfeiting intelligibility. The position that non-native speakers of English no longer need to imitate an idealized Standard English can be seen to be a landmark event in the evolution of European ELT pedagogies and practices.

Modiano (e.g., 2002a) has called for the legitimatization of a mainland European variety of English under the rubric "Euro-English" (see Jenkins et al.,

2001). This work has its basis in the observation that mainland Europeans, to a greater and greater degree, mix features of American and British English (referred to as *Mid-Atlantic English*; see Modiano, 2002a, 2002b), as well as in the tendency for mainland Europeans to interject transferred features into their English usage (for Sweden, for example, see Modiano, 2003). For instance, with the acceptance in many contexts across Europe of the construction *I am coming from Spain* (in response to the question *Where are you from?*), as opposed to Inner-Circle *I come from Spain*, it is suggested that such features be redefined as grammatically correct forms of Euro-English. Moreover, many expressions, proverbs, and idioms prevalent in European languages are crossing over into English in Europe. Instead of stigmatizing such linguistic phenomena, it is suggested that communicatively expedient transference be seen as a resource that enriches the language. While in the work of Seidlhofer and Jenkins it has been possible to envision grammar and pronunciation norms for ELT which oppose traditional notions of English language learning, lexical items, multi-word units, as well as idioms peculiar to mainland European lingua franca English are also relevant to the nativization process. Graddol comments on this development when he suggests that "a new kind of Euro-English may be arising – a variety distinct from the major native-speaker varieties with its own institutionalised forms and norms of usage" (2001: 54).

6   The European Union Context

There is a lack of clear directives on English in the language policies formulated and promoted by the EU. This is perhaps because sensitivity is required when official statements are issued which stipulate how linguistic equality is to be achieved at all levels of the Union. This has not to any noticeable extent hindered English from becoming the *de facto* European lingua franca (see Loonen, 1996; Pool, 1996; and Smith, 1996). In 1958, the Council of Ministers ruled that the official language of all member states should also be deemed to be an official and thus a working language of the Union, and that this right extended to all new members.[1] As a result, translation and interpretation services face a formidable challenge. This difficulty is, nevertheless, alleviated to some extent by the fact that English and French serve as the two main vehicular languages, with English gaining ground in this respect at the expense of French (for discussion of French, see Fosty, 1985; Gehnen, 1991; and Schlossmacher, 1994). This "special status" for English and French is not in line with the basic tenets of the EU, and is an indication of the need to implement practical solutions to what may appear to be nearly insurmountable obstacles.

It would seem to be the case that the rise of English and the ensuing importance of English for the work being conducted in the EU are coming from the citizens of Europe themselves, who are becoming increasingly proficient in the language. Thus, because English is by far the most common foreign language taught in the school systems across Europe, and because those who study

English are succeeding at acquiring impressive levels of proficiency, it is reasonable to assume that this trend, with English gaining on French as the most viable working language of the EU, will continue and even accelerate in the years to come. This order of events challenges the intentions of the Maastricht Treaty and the statutes of the European Charter of Fundamental Rights of the European Union (Article 22) which stipulate the importance of linguistic diversity. Graddol succinctly sums up the EU stance on English in the following terms:

> The Council of Europe's framework has had a significant influence on language curriculum developments in many European countries, but it is more than a mechanism for standardizing the teaching of modern languages. It represents a wider ideological movement to improve citizens' awareness of the multicultural nature of Europe, to encourage a positive attitude towards linguistic diversity, and to promote the learning of several languages. In fact, the Council of Europe's language policy is explicitly to foster large-scale multilingualism (or plurilingualism as it prefers to call it) in Europe. European citizens should ideally learn two languages in addition to their mother tongue. The perceived benefits of such a programme include a better understanding between neighbouring nations, improved mobility of people in work, learning and leisure across language boundaries, and an enhanced sense of shared European identity. (2001: 52)

The official EU directives on language policy exemplify the very dilemma which Europe is now experiencing. On the one hand, there is the clearly stated goal of linguistic multiplicity; on the other hand, we see countless examples of increased English spread. The EU could, by taking a stand on the evolution of English within the European framework, bring some structure to the role which English is to play in the development of Europe. However, without official directives on English and the enforcement which institutional support can provide, the manner in which English is appropriated and utilized in mainland Europe will continue to be defined by private interests, government agencies, educational authorities, and practitioners, with the ensuing diversification of policy and practice which is the case at the current time. Here, it is not unreasonable to claim that the very ideal of imagined sameness for Europe, the goals of *unification* and *integration*, are intimately entwined with Europe's handling of the issue of English, since English is the language in which Europeanization is taking place.

The drive to create a unified Europe, a borderless Eurozone wherein the free exchange of goods, money, people, and services can be conducted without unnecessary bureaucratic interference, is bringing Europeans together. Economic, social, and cultural unification is at the very heart of the European movement. Such intentions suggest that Europeanization, and thus monoculturalization processes, are already set in motion (see Modiano, 2004). At the same time, there is a concerted effort to preserve Europe's cultural and linguistic diversity. The Bureau for Lesser Used Languages is one example, where work is carried out to support moribund and endangered languages.

Within education, the Erasmus, Lingua, and Socrates programs, which promote third-language acquisition through student and teacher exchanges, can also be seen to be tools utilized to ensure the cultural and linguistic pluralism which defines Europe. Yet English continues to spread.

These two forces, the monoculturalization that coincides with the growth of English as the most common supranational language within the EU apparatus as well as in the population at large and efforts based on the belief that the Union will succeed in preserving linguistic diversity, are fundamentally in opposition to one another. Furthermore, not only is the spread of English neutralizing efforts to preserve Europe's rich linguistic multiplicity, the language is at the same time evolving on its own into a culture-specific variety.

One indication of this development into a separate variety is the use of *Eurospeak* or *Eurojargon* within EU institutions. First recognized as a lexical register utilized by Eurocrats, the conceptualization Eurospeak is now becoming much more commonly noticed and cited. Lexical items and multi-word units peculiar to Europe, such as *Brussels* to refer collectively to EU institutions, *Maastricht* to refer to the agreement signed there, *Schengen land* as a term to encompass those countries that have free borders within the EU, *Euro land*, *Euro area*, and *Euro zone* for those countries where the euro has been adopted as the currency, *Eurosceptic* for someone skeptical of European integration, *internal market*, a designation for the EU as a free-trade zone, and *Berlaymont*, a synonym for "red tape," as well as designations such as the "four freedoms" to designate the free movement of goods, money, people, and services across European borders, are regularly used in the EU, but are not commonly understood by users of English unfamiliar with the European context. Indeed, the term *member state* itself, a European invention, says much about how Europeans are molding language to accommodate a new political reality.

These three aspects of language use within the Union – grammar, pronunciation, and lexis – need to be studied more rigorously so that it can be ascertained whether or not it will be possible to codify a second-language variety of English for mainland Europeans. As Seidlhofer notes:

> If "Euro-English" is indeed an emerging variety as a European lingua franca, then it should be possible to describe it systematically, and eventually also to provide a codification which would allow it to be captured in dictionaries and grammars and to be taught, with appropriate teaching materials to support this teaching. (Jenkins et al., 2001: 14)

Eurocrats and elected representatives working in Brussels and elsewhere throughout the Union are not in agreement about the acknowledgment of a specific European variety of English. Within the EU apparatus there is much discussion as to the "quality" of the written and spoken English of non-native speakers working within EU institutions. Manifestations of this concern are the booklet *How to Write Clearly* (published internally by the EU),[2] which encourages clarity in written documentation, and the "Fight the Fog" campaign, which is an attempt to motivate people to accommodate their interlocutors by providing them with easy-to-understand language. These efforts can be seen as responses to the radical language contact taking place in Brussels and Strasbourg, where transference, or what some consider *interference*, is resulting in the acceptance (but often abhorrence) of hybrid forms of language. English is central to these discussions.

7   Conclusion

In the years ahead, conventional accounts of the English language, primarily drawing on the findings of corpus-based empirical research into native-speaker usage, but also by other means, will act as the guidelines promoted in much of the ELT material deployed in settings where Standard English is the educational norm. The movement to downplay the role of English in Europe, and in this process to take measures to safeguard majority, minority, and endangered languages, as well as increased support of the learning of third languages, will continue to counteract the increased spread of English. At the same time, the role that English plays as a medium of cross-cultural communication among Europeans, the ideological and cultural implications of English-language usage, and the processes of identity-building that follow in the wake of unification and integration will result in a growing movement to establish a European second-language variety of English.

With enlargement, official EU work has now become much more linguistically complex. The translation and interpretation services will soon become so bogged down that the call for simplification will almost certainly be heeded. A general belief is that Europe will accept a three-language solution with English, French, and German serving as the working languages of the EU. Even here, it is envisioned by many that English will maintain a dominant position.[3] Young people, because of their interest in English, will accelerate this process. For the teaching of English in schools across the EU, continuing research will support the development of pedagogies which target skill in the use of the language as a medium of communication in culturally and linguistically diverse contexts, as opposed to Anglo-American perspectives which underpin traditional views of the use of the language. Future research will reflect the world Englishes dimension, with increasing numbers of researchers partaking in the effort to study how English is being used by non-native speakers living in mainland Europe. Novel theoretical models and taxonomies need to be constructed for this enterprise. This is because the complexities of European society, which differ radically from postcolonial speech communities, challenge established sociolinguistic precepts utilized in variety-building processes. Empirical studies need to be carried out to document the lexical registers, grammar, and pronunciation of mainland European English, as well as the discourse strategies which distinguish Europeans from others. Such codifying activities can then inform the work which needs to be carried out within the EU to come to terms with the use and status of English as the European lingua franca.

See also Chapters 15, WORLD ENGLISHES TODAY; 17, VARIETIES OF WORLD ENGLISHES; 28, WORLD ENGLISHES AND DESCRIPTIVE GRAMMARS; 40, WORLD ENGLISHES AND COMMUNICATIVE COMPETENCE.

NOTES

1 Until recently, there were 11 official languages: Danish, Dutch, English, French, Finnish, German, Greek, Italian, Portuguese, Spanish, and Swedish. Ten new countries joined the Union in May 2004, raising the number of official languages to 20: Czech, Danish, Dutch, English, Estonian, Finnish, French, German, Greek, Hungarian, Italian, Latvian, Lithuanian, Maltese, Polish, Portuguese, Slovak, Slovenian, Spanish, and Swedish.

2 The booklet, available online at http://europa.eu.int/comm/translation/en/ftfog/booklet/index.htm (the site of the Fight the Fog campaign), has been compiled by Emma Wagner. It is adapted from *The Plain English Guide* by Martin Cutts, Oxford: Oxford University Press, 1996 and *Style: Toward Clarity and Grace* by Joseph M. Williams, Chicago: The University of Chicago Press, 1995.

3 For discussion, see Ammon, 2001; Berns, 1993, 1995; Coulmas, 1991a, 1991b; Deneire and Goethals, 1997; Fettes, 1991; Graddol, 2001; James, 2000; Labrie and Quell, 1997; Modiano, 1998, 1999; Phillipson, 2003; Pool, 1996; and Smith, 1996.

REFERENCES

Ammon, Ulrich (ed.) (2001) *The Dominance of English as a Language of Science: Effects on Other Languages and Language Communities*. Berlin: Mouton de Gruyter.

Baumgardner, Robert (ed.) (1996) *South Asian English: Structures, Use, and Users*. Urbana, IL: University of Illinois Press.

Bautista, Ma. Lourdes S. (ed.) (1997) *English Is an Asian Language: The Philippine Context*. Sydney: Macquarie Library.

Berns, Margie (1993) English in Europe: Language pragmatics or language policy: Language, communication, and social meaning. In *Georgetown University Round Table on Languages and Linguistics 1992: Language, Communication, and Social Meaning*. Edited by James E. Alatis. Washington, DC: Georgetown University Press, pp. 199–207.

Berns, Margie (1995) English in the European Union. *English Today*, **11**(3), 3–11.

Boyd, Sally and Huss, Leena (eds.) (2001) *Managing Multilingualism in a European Nation-State: Challenges for Sweden*. Clevedon, UK: Multilingual Matters.

Cenoz, Jasone and Jessner, Ulrike (eds.) (2000) *English in Europe: The Acquisition of a Third Language*. Clevedon, UK: Multilingual Matters.

Coulmas, Florian (1991a) European integration and the idea of the national language: Ideological roots and economic consequences. In *A Language Policy for the European Community*. Edited by Florian Coulmas. Berlin: Mouton de Gruyter, pp. 1–43.

Coulmas, Florian (ed.) (1991b) *A Language Policy for the European Community*. Berlin: Mouton de Gruyter.

Crystal, David (1997) *English as a Global Language*. Cambridge: Cambridge University Press.

Crystal, David (2001) The future of Englishes. In *Analysing English in a Global Context*. Edited by Anne Burns and Caroline Coffin. London: Routledge, pp. 53–64.

Cutts, Martin (1996) *The Plain English Guide*. Oxford: Oxford University Press.

Decke-Cornill, Helene (2002) "We would have to invent the language we are supposed to teach": The issue of English as a *lingua franca* in language education in Germany. *Language, Culture and Curriculum*, 15(3), 251–63.

Deneire, Marc and Goethals, Michaél (eds.) (1997) Special issue on English in Europe. *World Englishes*, 16(1).

Erling, Elizabeth (2002) "I learn English since ten years": The global English debate and the German university classroom. *English Today*, 18(2), 11–29.

Eurydice (2000) Key data on education in Europe. Brussels: European Commission, D/2000/4008/11.

Fettes, Mark (1991) Europe's Babylon: Towards a single European language? *Esperanto Documents*, 41(A), 1–16.

Firth, Alan (1996) The discursive accomplishment of normality: On "lingua franca" English and conversation analysis. *Journal of Pragmatics*, 26(3), 237–59.

Fosty, Anne (1985) *La langue française dans les institutions communautaires du l'Europe* [The French Language in the Common Institutions of Europe]. Québec: Editeur officiel du Québec.

Gehnen, Marianne (1991) Die Arbeitssprachen in der Kommission der Europäischen Gemeinschaften unter besonderer Berücksichtigung des Französischen [The working languages in the commission of the European Union with special consideration for French]. *Sociolinguistica*, 5, 51–63.

Görlach, Manfred and Schröder, Konrad (1985) Good use in EFL context. In *The English Language Today*. Edited by Sidney Greenbaum. Oxford: Pergamon, pp. 227–32.

Graddol, David (1997) *The Future of English? A Guide to Forecasting the Popularity of the English Language in the 21st Century*. London: The British Council.

Graddol, David (2001) The future of English as a European Language. *The European English Messenger*, 10(2), 47–55.

Granger, Sylviane, Dagneaux, Estelle, and Meunier, Fanny (2002) *The International Corpus of Learner English. Handbook and CD-ROM*. Louvain-la-Neuve: Presses Universitaires de Louvain (http://www.fltr.ucl.ac.be/fltr/germ/etan/cecl/cecl.html).

Greenbaum, Sidney (ed.) (1985) *The English Language Today*. Oxford: Pergamon.

Grin, François (1993) European economic integration and the fate of lesser-used languages. *Language Problems and Language Planning*, 17(2), 101–16.

Hilgendorf, Suzanne K. (1996) The impact of English in Germany. *English Today*, **12**(3), 3–14.

Hilgendorf, Suzanne K. (2001) Language contact, convergence, and attitudes: The case of English in Germany. *Dissertation Abstracts International, Section A: The Humanities and Social Sciences*, **62**(6), 2096.

House, Juliane (1999) Misunderstanding in intercultural communication: Interactions in English as a *lingua franca* and the myth of mutual intelligibility. In *Teaching and Learning English as a Global Language*. Edited by Claus Gnutzmann. Tübingen: Stauffenburg, pp. 73–89.

James, Allan (2000) English as a European lingua franca: Current realities and existing dichotomies. In *English in Europe: The Acquisition of a Third Language*. Edited by Jasone Cenoz and Ulrike Jessner. Clevedon, UK: Multilingual Matters, pp. 22–38.

Jenkins, Jennifer (2000) *The Phonology of English as an International Language*. Oxford: Oxford University Press.

Jenkins, Jennifer, Modiano, Marko and Seidlhofer, Barbara (2001) Euro-English. *English Today*, **17**(4), 13–19.

Kachru, Braj B. (ed.) (1992) *The Other Tongue: English across Cultures*. 2nd edition. Urbana, IL: University of Illinois Press.

Kachru, Braj B. (2005) *Asian Englishes: Beyond the Canon*. Hong Kong: Hong Kong University Press.

Knapp, Karlfried and Meierkord, Christiane (eds.) (2002) *Lingua Franca Communication*. Frankfurt: Peter Lang.

Labrie, Normand and Quell, Carsten (1997) Your language, my language or English? The potential language choice in communication among nationals of the European Union. *World Englishes*, **16**(1), 3–26.

Loonen, Pieter (1996) English in Europe: From timid to tyrannical? *English Today*, **12**(2), 3–9.

Martin, Elizabeth (1998) The use of English in written French advertising: A study of code-switching, code-mixing, and borrowing in a commercial context. *Studies in the Linguistic Sciences*, **28**(1), 159–84.

Martin, Elizabeth (2002) Cultural images and different varieties of English in French television commercials. *English Today*, **18**(4), 8–20.

Mauranen, Anna (2003) The corpus of English as lingua franca in academic settings. *TESOL Quarterly*, **37**(3), 513–27.

McArthur, Tom (ed.) (1992) *The Oxford Companion to the English Language*. Oxford: Oxford University Press.

McArthur, Tom (1996) English in the world and in Europe. In *The English Language in Europe*. Edited by Reinhard Hartmann. Oxford: Intellect, pp. 3–15.

Milroy, James (2001) Language ideologies and the consequences of standardization. *Journal of Sociolinguistics*, **5**(4), 530–55.

Modiano, Marko (1996) The Americanization of Euro-English. *World Englishes*, **15**(2), 207–15.

Modiano, Marko (1998) The emergence of Mid-Atlantic English in the European Union. In *The Major Varieties of English: Papers from MAVEN 97*. Edited by Hans Lindquist, Staffan Klintborg, Magnus Levin, and Maria Estling. Växjö. Sweden: Acta Wexionensia, pp. 241–8.

Modiano, Marko (1999) Cultural pluralism in an English-speaking European Union. In *Dangerous Crossing: Papers on Transgression in Literature and Culture*. Edited by Monica Loeb and Gerald Porter. Umeå, Sweden: Umeå University, pp. 97–103.

Modiano, Marko (ed.) (2002a) *Studies in Mid-Atlantic English.* HS-Institutionens Skriftserie Nr 7. Gävle, Sweden: Högskolan.

Modiano, Marko (2002b) Standardization processes and the Mid-Atlantic English paradigm. In *Standardization: Studies from the Germanic Languages.* Edited by Andrew R. Linn and Nicola McLelland. Amsterdam: John Benjamins, pp. 229–52.

Modiano, Marko (2003) Euro-English: A Swedish perspective. *English Today,* **19**(2), 35–41.

Modiano, Marko (2004) Monoculturalization and language dissemination. *Journal of Language, Identity, and Education,* **3**(3), 215–27.

Phillipson, Robert (1992) *Linguistic Imperialism.* Oxford: Oxford University Press.

Phillipson, Robert (2003) *English-Only Europe? Challenging Language Policy.* London: Routledge.

Platt, John, Weber, Heidi, and Ho, Mian Lian (1984) *The New Englishes.* London: Routledge.

Pool, Jonathan (1996) Optimal language regimes for the European Union. *International Journal for the Sociology of Language,* **121**, 159–79.

Quirk, Randolph (1981) International communication and the concept of nuclear English. In *English for Cross-Cultural Communication.* Edited by Larry Smith. London: Macmillan, pp. 151–65.

Quirk, Randolph and Widdowson, Henry G. (eds.) (1985) *English in the World: Teaching and Learning the Language and Literature.* Cambridge: Cambridge University Press.

Schlossmacher, Michael (1994) Die Arbeitsprachen in den Organen der Europäischen Gemeinschaft. Methoden und Ergebnisse einer empirischen Untersuchung [The working languages of the bodies of the European Union: Methods and results of an empirical study]. In *English only? In Europe, in Europa, en Europe* (Sociolinguistica, 8). Edited by Ulrich Ammon. Tübingen: Niemeyer, pp. 101–23.

Schneider, Edgar W. (ed.) (1997) *Englishes around the World, vol. 2. Caribbean, Africa, Asia, Australasia: Studies in Honour of Manfred Görlach.* Amsterdam: John Benjamins.

Seidlhofer, Barbara (2001) Closing the conceptual gap: The case for a description of English as a lingua franca. *International Journal of Applied Linguistics,* **11**(2), 133–58.

Skutnabb-Kangas, Tove and Phillipson, Robert (eds.) (1994) *Linguistic Human Rights.* Berlin: Mouton de Gruyter.

Smith, Ross (1996) Single market, single currency, single language. *English Today,* **12**, 10–14.

Trudgill, Peter and Hannah, Jean (2002) *International English: A Guide to Varieties of Standard English.* 4th edition. London: Edward Arnold. 1st edition 1982.

van Els, Theo J. M. and Extra, Guss (1987) Foreign and second language teaching in western Europe: A comparative overview of needs, objectives and policies. *Sociolinguistica,* **1**, 100–25.

van Essen, Arthur J. (1997) English in mainland Europe: A Dutch perspective. *World Englishes,* **16**(1), 113–25.

Williams, Joseph M. (1995) *Style: Toward Clarity and Grace.* Chicago: The University of Chicago Press.

FURTHER READING

Ammon, Ulrich and McConnell, Grant (eds.) (2002) *English as an Academic Language in Europe*. Frankfurt: Peter Lang.

Gnutzman, Claus (ed.) (1999) *Teaching and Learning English as a Global Language: Native and Non-Native Perspectives*. Tübingen: Stauffenburg Verlag.

Gunnarson, B.-L. (2001) Swedish, English, French or German: The language situation at Swedish universities. In *The Dominance of English as a Language of Science: Effects on Other Languages and Language Communities*. Edited by Ulrich Ammon. Berlin: Mouton de Gruyter, pp. 287–318.

Murray, Heather and Dingwall, Silvia (2001) The dominance of English at European universities: Switzerland and Sweden compared. In *The Dominance of English as a Language of Science: Effects on Other Languages and Language Communities*. Edited by Ulrich Ammon. Berlin: Mouton de Gruyter, pp. 85–112.

15 World Englishes Today

KINGSLEY BOLTON

1 Introduction

The expression "world Englishes" is capable of a range of meanings and interpretations. In the first sense, perhaps, the term functions as an umbrella label referring to a wide range of differing approaches to the description and analysis of English(es) worldwide. Some scholars, for example, favor a discussion of "world English" in the singular, and also employ terms such as "global English" and "international English," while others adopt the same terms in their plural forms. Indeed, in recent years, a plethora of terminology has come into use, including: English as an international (auxiliary) language, global English(es), international English(es), localized varieties of English, new varieties of English, non-native varieties of English, second-language varieties of English, world English(es), new Englishes, alongside such more traditional terms as ESL (English as a Second Language) and EFL (English as a Foreign Language).

In a second, narrower sense, the term is used to specifically refer to the "new Englishes" found in the Caribbean and in West African and East African societies such as Nigeria and Kenya, and to such Asian Englishes as Hong Kong English, Indian English, Malaysian English, Singaporean English, and Philippine English. Typically studies of this kind focus on the areal characteristics of national or regional Englishes, with an emphasis on the linguistic description of autonomous varieties of Englishes. In a third sense, world Englishes refers to the wide-ranging approach to the study of the English language worldwide particularly associated with Braj B. Kachru and other scholars working in a "world Englishes paradigm." The Kachruvian approach has been characterized by an underlying philosophy that has argued for the importance of inclusivity and pluricentricity in approaches to the linguistics of English worldwide, and involves not merely the description of national and regional varieties, but many other related topics as well, including contact linguistics, creative writing, critical linguistics, discourse analysis, corpus linguistics, lexicography, pedagogy, pidgin and creole studies, and the sociology of language (Bolton, 2002a).

Underlying each of these three broad approaches is an evident concern with monocentrism versus pluricentrism, i.e., one *English* (with all its geographical and social varieties), or multifarious *Englishes* (deserving consideration and recognition as autonomous or semi-autonomous varieties of the language). This tension between the centrifugal and centripetal dynamics of international English(es) also finds expression in discussions of "world English" versus "world Englishes." Butler (1997), for example, writing as lexicographer, claims that in most contexts where English is establishing itself as a "localized" or "new" English "[t]here are two major forces operating at the moment . . . The first is an outside pressure – the sweep of American English through the English-speaking world," which Butler regards as synonymous with *world English*, because "[t]his force provides the words which are present globally in international English and which are usually conveyed around the world by the media" (Butler, 1997: 107). The other dynamic, at the level of *world Englishes*, is "the purely local – the wellspring of local culture and a sense of identity" (p. 109). Thus at the level of lexis, items like *cable TV*, *cyberpunk*, *high five*, and *political correctness* might be identified with "world English," whereas items like *bamboo snake*, *outstation*, *adobo*, and *sari-sari store* would be items found in "world Englishes," more specifically "Asian Englishes."

When Kachru and Smith took over the editorship of the journal *World Language English* in 1985, it was retitled as *World Englishes*, and Kachru and Smith's explanation for this was that *World Englishes* embodies "a new idea, a new credo," for which the plural "Englishes" was significant:

> "Englishes" symbolizes the functional and formal variation in the language, and its international acculturation, for example, in West Africa, in Southern Africa, in East Africa, in South Asia, in Southeast Asia, in the West Indies, in the Philippines, and in the traditional English-using countries: the USA, the UK, Australia, Canada, and New Zealand. The language now belongs to those who use it as their first language, and to those who use it as an additional language, whether in its standard form or in its localized forms. (Kachru and Smith, 1985: 210)

In an early article on this topic, McArthur (1987) postulates a core variety of "World Standard English," which he then contrasts with the wide range of geographical Englishes used worldwide. This contrast between a common core of international "English" and geographically distinctive "Englishes" is currently maintained by a number of other commentators (notably Crystal, 1997).

In the last two decades, there has been a substantial change in approaches to English studies; a paradigm shift that began in the early 1980s. At that time, various branches of linguistics, including English studies, sociolinguistics, and applied linguistics, began to recognize and describe the remarkable spread of English worldwide which was then in progress. Early scholarship in this area included Kachru's *The Other Tongue* (1982) and *The Alchemy of English* (1986), Pride's *New Englishes* (1982), Noss's *Varieties of English in Southeast Asia* (1983), and Platt, Weber, and Ho's *The New Englishes* (1984). The volume edited by Noss included a number of position papers, including one by Llamzon on the "Essential features of new varieties of English." According to Llamzon, new varieties of English are identifiable with reference to four essential sets of features: ecological, historical, sociolinguistic, and cultural (Llamzon, 1983: 100–4). In the last context, Llamzon discusses *cultural features* with reference to creative writing and a local literature in English, arguing that "works by novelists, poets and playwrights have demonstrated that the English language can . . . be used as a vehicle for the transmission of the cultural heritage of Third World countries. The appearance of this body of literary works signals that the transplanted tree has finally reached maturity, and is now beginning to blossom and fructify" (p. 104). The horticultural metaphor also finds expression in his conclusion, where he argues that a "new variety of English may likened . . . to a transplanted tree," which, if properly nurtured "will grow into a healthy and vigorous plant and contribute to the beauty of the international landscape not only by virtue of its lush verdant branches and leaves, but more importantly by its fruits – the literary masterpieces of novels, short stories, poems, dramas and songs of its speakers and writers" (pp. 105–6).

Llamzon's reference to the importance of creative writing and literatures in this context is significant. In many Asian societies, including India, Singapore, and the Philippines, there is a body of creative writing in English that reaches back to the colonial era, and since the early 1980s Commonwealth and postcolonial writers from a range of developing societies have increasingly won acclaim from the international literary world. The emergence of "new Englishes" in the early 1980s thus overlapped with and was influenced by the "new literatures" that were then gaining recognition (see, for example, Hosillos, 1982; King, 1980; Lim, 1984). In the 1980s, such postcolonial creative writing began to attract the interest of both the reading public and academics, and the end of the decade saw the publication of *The Empire Writes Back* (Ashcroft, Griffiths, and Tiffin, 1989). By 1993, the title of their book had been appropriated for a *Time* magazine cover story and feature article, which detailed the successes of the Booker nominees and prize-winners, such as Salman Rushdie and Vikram Seth (both of Indian parentage), as well as Kazuo Ishiguro (of Japanese descent), Timothy Mo (Anglo-Chinese), Michael Ondaatje (Sri Lankan), Ben Okri (Nigerian), and Nobel Prize-winner Derek Walcott (Caribbean). In this article Pico Iyer describes such writers as "transcultural," because "they are addressing an audience as mixed up and eclectic and uprooted as themselves." Iyer argues for "a new postimperial order in which English is the lingua franca," and quotes Robert McCrum to the effect that "There is not one English language anymore, but there are many English languages . . . each of these Englishes is creating its own very special literature, which, because it doesn't feel oppressed by the immensely influential literary tradition in English, is somehow freer" (Iyer, 1993: 53).

The last three decades have seen a rapid growth of interest in the study of the "world Englishes" as well as a number of related fields, however these are glossed: English as an international language, global English(es), international English(es), localized varieties of English, new varieties of English, non-native English, and world English(es), etc. At present there are at least three international academic journals devoted primarily to this branch of linguistics (*English Today*, *English World-Wide*, and *World Englishes*), which have been supplemented by a substantial number of books on the subject. Currently, a number of distinct, albeit overlapping, approaches to research (and publications) in the field of "world English(es)," "new Englishes," and "new varieties of English" may be identified. These include the following (1) the English Studies approach, (2) sociolinguistic approaches (sociology of language, feature-based, Kachruvian, pidgin and creole studies), (3) applied linguistics approaches, (4) lexicographical approaches, (5) the popularizers' approach, (6) critical approaches, and (7) the futurology approach. These are discussed in some detail in the following sections of this chapter.

2   The English Studies Approach

The "English Studies" approach to world Englishes has developed historically from the description of English tradition, which dates back at least to the late nineteenth century and the work of scholars such as Henry Bradley (1845–1923), Otto Jespersen (1860–1943), Daniel Jones (1881–1967), Charles Talbut Onions (1873–1965), Henry Sweet (1845–1912), and Henry Wyld (1870–1945). More recently, this approach may be exemplified by the work of contemporary British linguists, such as Robert Burchfield, David Crystal, Sidney Greenbaum, Tom McArthur, Randolph Quirk, and John Wells.

Randolph Quirk was one of the first in the contemporary period to discuss varieties of English and the notion of "standards" of world English in his 1962 book, *The Use of English*. His *Grammar of Contemporary English* (Quirk et al., 1972) also surveyed varieties of English, although here the aim was to differentiate the "common core" of the language from such classes of variety as "regional," "educational," "social," as well as varieties according to "subject matter," "medium," "attitude," and "interference" (pp. 13–32). Quirk later (1990) assumed the role of a guardian of international "standards" of English and was drawn into a celebrated debate with Braj Kachru on "liberation linguistics," but one obvious irony here is that Quirk seems to have begun his academic life as a "linguistic liberal," with his 1962 essay arguing for tolerance and noting that:

> English is not the prerogative or "possession" of the English . . . Acknowledging this must – as a corollary – involve our questioning the propriety of claiming that the English of one area is more "correct" than the English of another. Certainly, we must realize that there is no single "correct" English, and no single standard of correctness. (Quirk, 1962: 17–18)

Some 20 years on, his 1990 paper was to see him arguing a rather different case, urging overseas teachers of English to keep in constant touch with "native-speaker" norms, and praising the merits of a world "Standard English."

In the mid-1980s, a number of books on world English(es) in the "English studies" tradition were published, including Burchfield's influential *The English Language* (1985), Greenbaum's *The English Language Today* (1985), and Quirk and Widdowson's *English in the World: Teaching and Learning the Language and Literatures* (1985). Each of these attempted to address issues related to the learning and use of English from a global perspective. Burchfield (1985) attracted much attention when he discusses the possible fragmentation of English along the lines earlier seen with Latin:

> The most powerful model of all is the dispersal of speakers of popular forms of Latin in various parts of western Europe and the emergence in the early Middle Ages of languages now known as French, Italian, Spanish, Portuguese, and of subdivision (like Catalan) within these languages, none easily comprehensible to the others . . . English, when first recorded in the eighth century, was already a fissiparous language. It will continue to divide and subdivide, and to exhibit a thousand different faces in the centuries ahead . . . The multifarious forms of English spoken within the British Isles and by native speakers abroad will continue to reshape and restyle themselves in the future. And they will become more and more at variance with the emerging Englishes of Europe and of the rest of the world. (Burchfield, 1985: 160, 173)

Burchfield's comparison of the dispersal of Latin in the Middle Ages with English in the 1980s provides the starting-point for Quirk's (1985) discussion of "The English language in a global context," in which Quirk argues the case for normativity, declaiming at one point that "the fashion of undermining belief in standard English had wrought educational damage in the ENL (English as a native language) countries" and that there is no justification for such an attitude to be "exported" to societies where English has the status of a second or foreign language: "The relatively narrow range of purposes for which the non-native needs to use English (even in ESL countries) is arguably well catered for by a single monochrome standard form that looks as good on paper as it sounds in speech" (Quirk, 1985: 6). By the mid-1980s, it seems that Quirk had transcended the linguistic radicalism of his youth, and that he was anxious to join battle on behalf of both "Standard English" and "standards" of English. His 1985 paper also represents a rehearsal for a later engagement against the forces of "liberation linguistics," an engagement that would pit Quirk in debate against Kachru some five years later in the pages of *English Today*.

Another significant figure in this field since the 1980s has been Tom McArthur, the founding and current editor of *English Today* (from 1985), and the editor of *The Oxford Companion to the English Language* (1992). McArthur's (1987) paper on "The English languages?" sets out part of his theoretical agenda for the study of world Englishes. As the title of the article suggests, the notion of plural Englishes is foregrounded in the discussion, and McArthur asks "If there are by now 'English literatures' can the 'English languages' be far behind?" (McArthur, 1987: 9). Over the two decades, *English Today* has had a substantial impact on the discussion and debate about "English languages" around the world with many articles having a geographical focus (Africa, the Americas, Asia, Europe, etc.), while others have dealt with such issues as corpus linguistics, grammar and usage, history of English, language and gender, and English lexicography worldwide, etc. McArthur has also influenced scholarship on world English(es) greatly with his editorship of *The Oxford Companion to the English Language* (1992), a volume entitled *The English Languages* (1998), and the recently-published *Oxford Guide to World English* (2002).

A third influential figure in the 1980s and 1990s was Manfred Görlach, whose orientation has been described as "the study of varieties of English in a world-wide context" (Schneider, 1997a: 3). Görlach's intellectual lineage was derived of "Anglistik" in the German academic tradition, and he rose to prominence in the field as the founding editor of *English World-Wide*, which began publication in 1980 and publishes a wide range of articles on dialectology, pidgins and creoles, and the sociolinguistics of English throughout the world. Görlach himself has identified his approach as part of "English studies," commenting that: "As a sub-discipline of English Studies, a consideration of English as a world language would provide an ideal opportunity to expand the social, historical and geographical aspects of English Studies and . . . might well serve to enhance the appeal of a traditional and somewhat ageing discipline" (Görlach, 1988: 37–8). Since Görlach's retirement as general editor of *English World-Wide* in 1998, he has been succeeded by Edgar W. Schneider, who has also published widely in this field (e.g., Schneider, 1997a, 1997b).

Others following similar approaches include Quirk's former colleagues on the Survey of English Usage, David Crystal and Sidney Greenbaum. Crystal's early work centered on academically-oriented English studies (e.g., Crystal and Quirk, 1964; Crystal, 1969, 1975), but by the mid-1980s Crystal was moving away from detailed empirical research and embarking on his present career of academic entrepreneur, encyclopedist, broadcaster, and "popularizer" (see section 6 below). Greenbaum's (1985) volume on *The English Language Today* was an important work at the time, and from 1990 until his death in 1996, Greenbaum also directed the International Corpus of English (ICE) research project, which is being run in around 15 countries worldwide (Greenbaum, 1996; Nelson, Wallis, and Aarts, 2002). Other British-based scholars include Wells (1982), Burchfield (1985, 1994), Graddol, Leith, and Swann (1996), and Goodman (Goodman and Graddol, 1996). From the United States, further contributions to the study of varieties of English worldwide have also come from John Algeo (1991), Richard W. Bailey (1991), and Frederic Cassidy (1985).

3   Sociolinguistic Approaches to World Englishes

Sociolinguistic approaches to world English(es) may be regarded as subsuming four types of studies: (1) the sociology of language (Fishman, Cooper, and Conrad, 1977; Fishman, Conrad, and Rubal-Lopez, 1996); (2) "feature-based" approaches to world English(es) (Cheshire, 1991a; Trudgill and Hannah, 2002, etc.); (3) Kachruvian studies (Kachru, 1992, etc.); and (4) pidgin and creole studies (Todd, 1984, etc.).

3.1   The sociology of language

Two books by Joshua A. Fishman and his associates (Fishman, Cooper, and Conrad, 1977 and Fishman, Conrad, and Rubal-Lopez, 1996) have provided sociologically-detailed treatments of "the spread of English" and "post-imperial English" respectively. These studies were published 20 years apart, and the data cited and commentaries given chart a number of developments in the spread of English in the world. The 1977 volume addressed a number of topics, and also attempted to identify the relevant sociopolitical predictors of the use of English in postcolonial societies (former Anglophone colonial status, linguistic diversity, religious composition, and educational and economic development). Fishman also noted that the "international sociolinguistic balance" at that time rested on three factors: (1) the spread of English; (2) the control of English; and (3) the fostering of vernacular languages (Fishman, 1977: 335).

Twenty years later in *Post-Imperial English* Fishman and his colleagues (Fishman et al., 1996) returned to a consideration of some of the same issues. In the first chapter ("Introduction: Some empirical and theoretical issues"), Fishman (1996a) poses three questions: is English "still spreading in the non-English mother tongue world?" (yes); is that continued spread in any way directly orchestrated by, fostered by, or exploitatively beneficial to the English mother tongue world? (to be judged); and, third, are there forces or processes that transcend the English mother tongue world itself and which also contribute to the continued spread and entrenchment of English in non-English mother tongue countries (ditto). Fishman suggests that English is now less "an imperialist tool" and more "a multinational tool":

> Multinationals are pro-multinational rather than pro one or another imperial or national metropolitan center, and English may well be the lingua franca of capitalist exploitation without being the vehicle of imperialism or even neo-imperialism *per se*. Perhaps, just as neo-colonialism has become merely a form of the world capitalist system rather than a form of imperialism itself, so English may need to be re-examined precisely from the point of view of being post-imperial . . . not directly serving purely Anglo-American territorial, economic, or cultural expansion without being post-capitalist in any way? (Fishman, 1996a: 8)

Fishman then goes on to claim that there is evidence to support the view that the world economy has entered a new capitalist phase, which has led to increased living standards globally; that in this new order the growth of English may be not necessarily at the expense of local languages; and that one effect of Anglophone imperialism has been "the rise of local elites and counter-elites who became interested in both English and their local vernaculars in order to communicate with different constituencies." With the end of the cold war, Fishman suggests, our thinking on English should also be "de-ideologized," as it is possible that "the impact of English on cultures and societies throughout the world has been a variable one," not one that can be summarized in "simple moralistic terms" (pp. 9–10).

Partly in response to Phillipson's *Linguistic Imperialism* (1992) (see section 6 below), Fishman also discusses English in the context of economic globalization:

> Economically unifying and homogenizing corporate and multinational forces are increasingly creating a single market into which all societies – former colonial and non-colonial states alike – can be and, indeed, for their own self-interests' sake, usually seek to be integrated. The language of these forces is now most frequently English . . . On the other hand, a similarly powerful trend is occurring in the opposite direction, in the direction of asserting, recognizing, and protecting more local languages, traditions, and identities – even at the state level – than ever before in world history. (Fishman, 1996b: 639)

The former British and American colonies that Fishman surveys are, he asserts, "participating in both trends, in various degrees and with differing priorities"; to characterize the former trend as "the imperialism of English" is both "antiquated" and "erroneous" (p. 639).

3.2   "Feature-based" approaches

In contrast to the sociology of language approach to world Englishes, a "feature-based" approach has typically involved the linguist in identifying and marking statements about the distinctive features of varieties in terms of pronunciation or "accent" (phonology), vocabulary (lexis), or grammar (morphology and syntax). One leading example of this approach is Trudgill and Hannah's *International English* (2002, first edition published 1982) which describes "standard varieties" of English in terms of "differences at the level of phonetics, phonology, grammar and vocabulary" (p. 3). *International English* uses tape-recordings of English speech from Australia, India, Ireland, New Zealand, North America, Scotland, South Africa, Wales, West Africa, and the West Indies. The third edition added an expanded section on creoles, as well as descriptions of Singapore and Philippine English.

However, the merits of an approach based on a notional "standard" have been queried by linguists such as Cheshire, who asserts that:

> Current descriptions, whether of a non-standard dialect, a "new" variety or even
> of a hypothetical international standard variety, are all too often given as lists of
> assorted departures from southern British standard English or from American
> standard English, with no attempt at determining the extent to which the local
> linguistic features function as part of an autonomous system. (Cheshire, 1991b: 7)

In the introduction to her own book on world Englishes, *English Around
the World* (1991a), Cheshire advocates an approach based on empirical sociolinguistic research. The case studies included in this volume usually focus on
the analysis of sociolinguistic variation and many might be more accurately
described as "variation studies" (in the Labovian paradigm) rather than
studies of linguistic features per se. Cheshire argues that in the case of
"second-language" varieties of English, sociolinguistic analysis can answer
the question of where errors stop and where "legitimate features of a local
variety" start (p. 11).

3.3   *The Kachruvian approach*

The work of Braj B. Kachru in this field is of central and enduring importance,
and the influence of the Kachruvian approach to world Englishes (WE)
extends across a range of subdisciplines including applied linguistics, critical
linguistics, descriptive linguistics, discourse analysis, and educational linguistics. Indeed, the coining and promotion of the term "world Englishes" is
chiefly associated with Braj Kachru, Yamuna Kachru, Larry Smith, and a
sizable number of other academics who have adopted a world Englishes
approach to research and teaching in this field. Kachru himself has had an
enormous influence on such work. In addition to his many books and articles
and his editorship of *World Englishes*, Kachru is also responsible for anchor-
ing the annual conferences on world Englishes held by the *International
Association for World Englishes* (IAWE), which provide a forum for research,
discussion, and debate.

Historically, there is general agreement that the study of world Englishes
can be dated from the two conferences on English as a world language that
took place in 1978, one in April at the East-West Center in Hawai'i, and the
second in June–July at the University of Illinois at Urbana-Champaign, and
Braj Kachru played a major role in both conferences (Kachru, 1982; see Smith,
1981). These conferences discussed the sociopolitical contexts of English in
the world; the use of English in former Anglophone colonies; the processes
of "nativization" and "acculturation" in such societies; and the description of
varieties of English (Kachru, 1992: 1). Throughout the 1980s, other conferences
were organized through the auspices of such organizations as IATEFL (International Association for the Teaching of English as a Foreign Language), TESOL
(Teachers of English to Speakers of Other Languages), the Georgetown University Round Table, and the East-West Center, and by the mid-1980s the
term "world Englishes" was gaining currency (Kachru, 1992: 2; Kachru, 1985;

Kachru and Smith, 1988). The justification for the adoption of this term, Kachru argues, is that:

> The term symbolizes the functional and formal variations, divergent sociolinguistic contexts, ranges and varieties of English in creativity, and various types of acculturation in parts of the Western and non-Western world. This concept emphasizes "WE-ness," and not the dichotomy between *us* and *them* (the native and non-native users). (Kachru, 1992: 2)

In Kachru's (1992) survey of "World Englishes: Approaches, issues and resources," he summarizes the study of world Englishes in terms of 11 related and overlapping issues, identified as: the spread and stratification of English; characteristics of the stratification; interactional contexts of world Englishes; implications of the spread; descriptive and prescriptive concerns; the bilingual's creativity and the literary canon; multi-canons of English; the two faces of English: nativization and Englishization; fallacies concerning users and uses; the power and politics of English; and teaching world Englishes (Kachru, 1992: 2). In his discussion of the first issue, "the spread and stratification of English," Kachru argues in favor of the strength of his model of the spread of English in terms of "three concentric circles," the Inner Circle (ENL societies), the Outer Circle (ESL societies), and the Expanding Circle (EFL societies). In the second section on the "characteristics of stratification," Kachru critically examines such sociolinguistic metalanguage as "lect" and "cline," before proceeding to a discussion of the "interactional contexts of world Englishes" and the "implications of the spread" of world Englishes for the Outer and Expanding Circles in linguistic, cultural terms.

The notion of "descriptive and prescriptive concerns" for Kachru involves a critical evaluation of such "sacred cows" of theoretical and applied linguistics as "interference," "interlanguage," "error," "speech community," the "native speaker," and the "ideal speaker-hearer" of English. In addition there are issues linked to questions of the models, norms, and standards for English in the Outer and Expanding Circles. In this context, Kachru distinguishes three types of varieties: First, the *norm-providing* varieties of the Inner Circle, including American English, British English, and the less-preferred varieties of Australian and New Zealand English. Second, the *norm-developing* varieties of the Outer Circle, where the localized (or "endocentric") norm has a well-established linguistic and cultural identity, as in, e.g., Singapore English, Nigerian English, and Indian English. And third, the *norm-dependent* varieties of the Expanding Circle, e.g., as in Korea, Iran, Saudi Arabia, where the norms are external (or "exocentric," i.e., American or British). Two other concerns relate to the identification of "errors" (as opposed to "innovations"), as well as the "variables of intelligibility" in world Englishes.

The issue of "the bilingual's creativity and the literary canon" refers to the existence and development of the "new literatures in English" of Africa, Asia, and the Caribbean, and the extent to which these "contact literatures in English" have undergone *nativization* and *acculturation*. Kachru argues that in South Asia, West Africa, and Southeast Asia, these literatures are thus "both nativised and acculturated" as instanced by the work of the 1986 Nobel Prize winner Wole Soyinka from Nigeria, and Raja Rao of India, and that the issue of the bilingual's creativity is an important area for linguistic, literary, and pedagogical research. The notion of "multi-canon" attempts to accommodate the current sociolinguistic reality in world English where speakers of a wide range of first languages communicate with one another through English, so that, "a speaker of a Bantu language may interact with a speaker of Japanese, a Taiwanese, an Indian, and so on" (Kachru, 1992: 7). As a result English has become acculturated in many "un-English" sociolinguistic contexts, in many African and Asian societies where there is no shared Judeo-Christian or European cultural heritage, or shared literary canon. English then becomes multi-canonical English.

The issue concerning "the two faces of English: nativization and English-ization" focuses on the reciprocal effects of language context: i.e., the effect on English in a localized context (nativization), and the effect on local languages in the same situation (Englishization). Instances of the borrowing of English vocabulary into local languages include Hong Kong, Japan, the Philippines, and many other societies around the world, but Englishization also extends to the level of grammar, as in the adoption of impersonal constructions in Indian languages; or the use of the passive constructions with a "by" equi-valent in Korean, both of which have been traced to English. Finally, in the 1992 article, Kachru notes the pedagogical importance of world Englishes to the teaching of language, literature, and teaching methodology, emphasizing the need for a two-fold paradigm shift:

> First, a paradigm shift in research, teaching, and application of sociolinguistic realities to the functions of English. Second, a shift from frameworks and theories which are essentially appropriate only to monolingual countries. It is indeed essential to recognize that World Englishes represent certain linguistic, cultural and pragmatic realities and pluralism, and that pluralism is now an integral part of World Englishes and literatures written in Englishes. The pluralism of English must be reflected in the approaches, both theoretical and applied, we adopt for understanding this unprecedented linguistic phenomenon. (Kachru, 1992: 11)

Kachru's enthusiasm for the teaching of world Englishes was not shared by everyone in the early 1990s. In a landmark paper, Randolph Quirk, by then Vice-Chancellor of London University, was becoming increasingly worried by what he termed the "half-baked quackery" of English teachers preaching the gospel of "varieties of English," and published a polemical paper taking issue with those he thought to be undermining the importance of Standard English (Quirk, 1990). This involved an attack on the growing study and teaching of "varieties," and was to lead him into a celebrated debate against Kachru.

Central to Quirk's (1990) paper, "Language varieties and standard language" was the distinction between *non-institutionalized* varieties and those varieties that are *institutionalized* (i.e., being fully described and with defined standards). Here he claims that: "Of the latter, there are two: *American English* and *British English*; and there are one or two others with standards rather informally established, notably *Australian English*" (Quirk, 1990: 6). Quirk then argues strongly that the distinction between a "native" variety and a "non-native" variety is crucial, or in his own words "the one that seems to be of the greatest importance educationally and linguistically" (p. 6). He also excludes the possibility that any non-native variety can be institutionalized, asserting that: "I exclude the possibility only because I am not aware of there being any institutionalized non-native varieties." Quirk asserts that "[t]he implications for foreign language teaching are clear: the need for native teacher support and the need for non-native teachers to be in constant touch with the native language," commenting that the research suggested that the "internalizations" of natives were radically different from those of non-natives. He later concludes that "the mass of ordinary native-English speakers have never lost their respect for Standard English, and it needs to be understood abroad too . . . that Standard English is alive and well, its existence and its value alike clearly recognized" (p. 10).

Kachru's (1991) riposte to Quirk, "Liberation linguistics and the Quirk concern," sets out to challenge a number of Quirk's "concerns," arguing (1) "that the recognition of a range of variation for English is a linguistic manifestation of underlying ideological positions"; (2) "that there is confusion of types of linguistic variety"; (3) "that the use of the term 'institutionalized variety' with the non-native varieties of English is inappropriate"; (4) "that there is a recognition of variation within a non-native variety"; (5) "that there is a widely recognized and justified sociolinguistic and pedagogical distinction between ESL and EFL"; (6) "that there is recognition of the 'desirability of non-native norms'" (p. 5). Kachru also questions a number of Quirk's other arguments which are seen as grounded in a rejection of "sociolinguistic realities," and the adoption of a perspective based on monolingual contexts. The actual realities of multilingual societies, Kachru argues, are *linguistic realities, sociolinguistic realities,* and *educational realities* that are quite distinct from those in Britain or North America, and here the core of his arguments is that Quirk ignores the central issue of "sociolinguistic realities" in Outer-Circle societies and fails to specify how he might produce a "pragmatically viable proposal" for the "international codification" of English (pp. 11–12).

3.4 Pidgin and creole studies

There have been periodic discussions in the last 20 years in the field of world Englishes about the relationship between such new Englishes and the study of English-based pidgins and creoles. As the study of world English(es) took off in the 1980s, the specialist journals in the field had to decide on how to deal with pidgin and creole varieties. Görlach (1980: 6) argues that because of the continua that exist in many societies linking pidgins and creoles with standard languages, their study "can therefore with some justification be regarded as being part of English or French or Portuguese studies, as is the study of the respective dialects," citing Krio, Tok Pisin, and Sranan as cases in point. Over the years, Görlach published many such papers on English-based pidgins and creoles, and McArthur's *English Today* has opted for a similar editorial policy, as has the journal *World Englishes*, with at least one special issue devoted to the topic (Mufwene, 1997). Other work in this field includes Todd (1984, 1995) who has commented on the indeterminacy of varieties in pidgin and creole context, noting, for example, in the case of Nigeria that:

> The unidealised truth seems to be . . . that for many speakers in Nigeria it is now extremely difficult, if not impossible, to separate Nigerian English Pidgin from pidginised Nigerian English or anglicized Nigerian Pidgin. Today, in the spoken medium and in the writings of Aik-Imoukhuede, Oyekunle and Saro-Wiwa, we find not compartmentalized English and Pidgin, not even a continuum from basilectal through mesolectal to acrolectal, but a linguistic amalgam where the interinfluencing is so complete that even articulate linguists are not always certain which varieties they are using or why. (Todd, 1995: 37)

It seems clear that "creolistics" overlaps to an extent with the study of world Englishes, although even commentators such as Görlach remain ambivalent on the issue. In a 1996 paper entitled "And is it English?" Görlach discusses the existence of varieties such as code switching, pidgins, creoles, cants, and mixed languages. In the case of pidgins and creoles, Görlach asserts that these are "independent languages on all counts," noting that varieties which are "marginally English" may persist as "one of the more messy facts of life" (p. 171).

4 Applied Linguistics Approaches

One of the first "applied linguistic approaches" to varieties of world Englishes began in the 1960s with the work of Halliday, McIntosh, and Strevens (1964), who sought to apply insights derived from "the linguistic sciences" to the newly-emergent field of applied linguistics, which in Britain and the USA was broadly concerned with theories of language learning, language teaching, and language pedagogy. In section 6 of the book the authors discussed the use of varieties of English around the world, noting that "during the period of colonial rule it seemed totally obvious and immutable that the form of English used by professional people in England was the only conceivable model for use in education overseas" (1964: 292). By the 1960s, they argued, things were very different, and now there was choice available between American, British, Australian, and other regional variants. Thus, they argue (and this has a very contemporary ring) that:

English is no longer the possession of the British, or even the British and the Americans, but an international language which increasing numbers of people adopt for at least some of their purposes . . . In West Africa, in the West Indies, and in Pakistan and India . . . it is no longer accepted by the majority that the English of England, with RP as its accent, are [sic] the only possible models of English to be set before the young. (p. 293)

The publication of the Halliday, McIntosh, and Strevens' book, and the expression of similar viewpoints in other academic papers, prompted Clifford Prator to publish a spirited yet historically misplaced attack on what he called "The British heresy in TESL" (Prator, 1968). This paper is of interest because it pre-dates the Kachru–Quirk debate (see above) by some 20 years; and also because of the fact that some of the issues it raises are still discussed today (see Romaine, 1997). Prator's central argument is that "in a country where English is not spoken natively but is widely used as the medium of instruction, to set up the local variety of English as the ultimate model to be imitated by those learning the language" is "unjustifiable intellectually and not conducive to the best possible results" (Prator, 1968: 459). He identifies seven fallacies associated with the British heresy: (1) that second-language varieties of English can legitimately be equated with mother-tongue varieties; (2) that second-language varieties of English really exist as coherent, homogeneous linguistic systems, describable in the usual way as the speech of an identifiable social group; (3) that a few minor concessions in the type of English taught in schools would tend to or suffice to stabilize the language; (4) that one level of a language, its phonology, can be allowed to change without entailing corresponding changes at other levels; (5) that it would be a simple matter to establish a second-language variety of English as an effective instructional model once it had been clearly identified and described; (6) that students would long be content to study English in a situation in which, as a matter of policy, they were denied access to a native-speaker model; and that (7) granting a second language variety of English official status in a country's schools would lead to its widespread adoption as a mother tongue.

Peter Strevens was one of those singled out for opprobrium by Prator; and it is evidently true that Strevens consistently argued for a varieties-based approach to TESL and TEFL during his academic career (see Strevens, 1977, 1980, 1985). Both his 1977 book *New Orientations in the Teaching of English* and his 1980 volume *Teaching English as an International Language* gave substantial coverage to what he glossed as "localized forms of English" (LFEs), arguing that:

In ESL areas where local L2 forms have developed and where they command public approval it is these forms which constitute the most suitable models for use in schools, certainly more suitable than a British or American L1 model . . . the native speaker of English must accept that English is no longer his possession alone: it belongs to the world, and new forms of English, born of new countries with new communicative needs, should be accepted into the marvelously flexible and adaptable galaxy of "Englishes" which constitute the English language. (Strevens, 1980: 90)

High heresy indeed, but over the next two decades the influence of such heresy was to change the way that many applied linguists would approach their subject, particularly at the level of theory. Thus, throughout the 1980s and 1990s, issues related to world Englishes began to be communicated regularly to an applied linguistics audience through such publications as *The Annual Review of Applied Linguistics, Applied Linguistics, English Language Teaching Journal, TESOL Quarterly,* and other journals in the field.

5   The Lexicographical Approach

The domestic English dictionary traditions as exemplified by Samuel Johnson's (1755) *A Dictionary of the English Language* and J. A. H. Murray's *Oxford English Dictionary* (1884–1928) embodied two principles: (1) the potential of dictionaries for "fixing" and standardizing the language (however unrealistic this might turn out to be); and (2) the identification of a "nucleus" or core of the language, defined according to "Anglicity."

Arguably, the first dictionaries of world Englishes were glossaries produced in the United States at the beginning of the nineteenth century. These included Pickering (1816), Bartlett (1848), etc. Noah Webster, by contrast, was concerned to produce a national dictionary, for reasons partly if not wholly political, because "As an independent nation, our honor requires us to have a system of our own, in language as well as government." Webster further predicted that: "These causes will produce, in a course of time, a language in North America, as different from the future language of England, as the modern Dutch, Danish and Swedish are from the German, or from one another" (1789: 220–3).

His first dictionary appeared early in the nineteenth century (1806), but it was not until 1828 that his major work, *An American Dictionary of the English Language*, was published. In the twentieth century, Webster's was complemented by a number of other works on American English including Craigie and Hulbert (1938–44), Mathews (1951), and a number of dialect dictionaries including Cassidy (1985). Earlier dictionaries of Canadian English include Avis (1967), which has recently been superseded by *The Canadian Oxford Dictionary* (Barber, 1999). Australian lexicography can be traced back to Morris (1898), which was intended as a supplement to the *OED*, and to the list that Lake compiled as a supplement to Webster's (Lake, 1898, cited in Görlach, 1995). It is only in recent years that Australia has had its own "inclusive" national dictionary, *The Macquarie Dictionary*, which was first published in 1981. In 1988, Oxford University Press published *The Australian National Dictionary* (Ramson, 1988), subtitled *A Dictionary of Australianisms on Historical Principles*. In 1997, the *Dictionary of New Zealand English* appeared, edited by Orsman (1997). South Africa has its own dictionary tradition, starting with Pettman (1913), and continuing to the present with Branford (1978), and Silva's *A Dictionary of South African English on Historical Principles* (1998).

India developed its own tradition of glossaries and wordlists, including Whitworth's *An Anglo-Indian Dictionary* (1885) and Yule and Burnell's *Hobson-Jobson: A Glossary of Anglo-Indian Words and Phrases* ([1886] 1969). Later works have included Rao (1954) and Hawkins (1984), but as yet no fully autonomous national dictionary for India or other South Asian societies has appeared. In West Africa, there have been plans for a number of years to complete a *Dictionary of West African English*, but so far this project remains incomplete (Banjo and Young, 1982). For the Caribbean, there is Cassidy and Le Page's *Dictionary of Jamaican English* (1967), and Holm and Shilling's *Dictionary of Bahamian English* (1982), as well as the recent *Dictionary of Caribbean English Usage* (Allsopp, 1996).

Dictionaries are profoundly important for the recognition of world Englishes. As Quirk (1990) has pointed out, it is only when a world variety of English is supported by codification (chiefly expressed through national dictionaries) that one can make a strong claim that such a variety is "institutionalized." Perhaps the best example of this in recent times has been the case of Australia where the *Macquarie Dictionary* has been largely accepted as a "national dictionary" or, in their own words, as "Australia's own." By the 1990s the editors of *Macquarie* had also become activists for the promotion of world Englishes in Asia, and are now planning a dictionary focusing on English in the Asian region with extensive coverage of the vocabularies of the new Englishes of Southeast Asia, particularly those of Hong Kong, Malaysia, Singapore, and the Philippines. Susan Butler, *Macquarie*'s editor, argues that:

> this dictionary will shift attitudes in the region to English. Rather than being seen as an alien language, and a conduit of Western culture, it will be evident that English can also express Asian culture. The flexibility of English, its ability to serve as a vehicle for the expression of local culture, has been one of its great characteristics since it left English shores. (Butler, 1997: 123)

6 The Popularizers

During the 1980s, at the same time as interest in the study of international varieties of English was quickly growing within universities in the West, a number of popular accounts of the spread of English were being published in Britain and North America. The best-known of these was perhaps McCrum, Cran, and MacNeil's *The Story of English* (1986), which was accompanied by the worldwide broadcast of a nine-part BBC documentary on the history of the English language. Although the series and the book were a popular success in both Europe and North America, they provoked a strong reaction from both linguists intolerant of descriptive inaccuracies, and from cultural critics resentful of the perceived triumphalism.

That the charges of triumphalism were somewhat justified seems hard to deny. The first part of the television series, "An English-speaking world," contained such clichés in Robert MacNeil's commentary as "World War II was the finest hour for British English"; "The sun set on the Union Jack, but not on the English language"; and "English, the language of the skies, is now becoming the language of the seven seas"; with the American newspaper pundit William Safire declaiming: "I think it's a glorious language ... it's growing, it's getting more expressive, it's getting more global, getting more accepted around the world." The book, largely authored by McCrum, fiction editor at Faber and Faber and a novelist in his own right, was somewhat more restrained, and McCrum, Cran, and McNeil do at times temper their celebration of English with mention of "[t]he darker, aggressive side of the spread of global English," which includes the elimination of linguistic diversity and "the attack on deep cultural roots" (p. 44), as in Québec. Later they are moved to explain the "peculiar genius" of English which, it emerges, is essentially democratic and freedom-loving:

> Its genius was, and still is, essentially democratic. It has given expression to the voice of freedom from Wat Tyler, to Tom Paine, to Thomas Jefferson, to Edmund Burke, to the Chartists, to Abraham Lincoln, to the Suffragettes, to Winston Churchill, to Martin Luther King. It is well equipped to be a world language, to give voice to the aspirations of the Third World as much as the inter-communication of the First World. (pp. 47–8)

Another eminent popularizer from the late 1980s to the present, has been David Crystal, whose first work in a popular vein was the 1988 Penguin paperback, *The English Language*. This was followed by *The Cambridge Encyclopedia of the English Language* (1995), and *English as a Global Language* (1997), and it was this last work which probably attracted the most criticism. As Crystal himself explains in his introduction, the book was originally prompted by the suggestion of Mauro Mujica, one of the leaders of the US English campaign in the United States. Its aim was to "explain to members of his organization [US English], in a succinct and factual way, and without political bias, why English has achieved such a worldwide status" (1997: ix). Crystal also explains that the report was intended originally for private circulation, but he later decided to rework and expand it into a book for wider circulation. In spite of the fact that the suggestion for the study came from Mujica, Crystal claims that "this book has not been written according to any political agenda," and that he was chiefly concerned to present an account of "the relevant facts and factors" relating to the description of a "world language," the place of English, and the future of English as a global language (1997: x). This slim book is distinguished by a number of arguments, including his assertion that the "remarkable growth" of English is, simply stated, explicable largely in terms of the fact that "it is a language which has repeatedly found itself in the right place at the right time" (1997: 110). In a similar vein, most arguments in Crystal's analysis of the future of "global English" are reducible to the evocative slogan of "having your cake and eating it," a phrase for which Crystal *qua* popularizer appears to have a particular fondness (1997: 138).

The book drew particular flak from Robert Phillipson, who took Crystal to task in a lengthy review in the journal *Applied Linguistics*, charging that the work was "Eurocentric" and "triumphalist," accusations that Crystal countered in a response in the same journal (Phillipson, 1999; Crystal, 2000). By this time, Phillipson had already established himself as one of the leading critical linguists in this field.

7 Critical Linguists

In fact, the discourse on world English(es) changed gear dramatically in 1992 with the publication of Phillipson's book *Linguistic Imperialism*. Whereas the 1980s saw relatively restrained arguments from Kachru and other enthusiasts in the world English(es) "movement" on the need for a paradigm shift in the study of English as an international language, this discourse was formulated according to the game-rules of an essentially Western liberal perspective. Phillipson's arguments, however, represent a harder-edged Marxian, if not Marxist, response to the subject.

At the core of Phillipson's theoretical approach to "linguistic imperialism" are a series of arguments about the political relations between what Phillipson characterizes as the "core English-speaking countries" (Britain, the USA, Canada, Australia, and New Zealand) and the "periphery-English countries" where English either has the status of a second language (e.g., Nigeria, India, Singapore) or is a foreign and "international link language" (e.g., Scandinavia, Japan) (1992: 17). The nature of this relationship, Phillipson argues, is one of structural and systemic inequality, in which the political and economic hegemony of Western Anglophone powers is established or maintained over scores of developing nations, particularly those formerly colonies of European powers. The political and economic power of such nations in the Third World is, moreover, accompanied by "English linguistic imperialism," defined by Phillipson in the following terms:

> A working definition of *English linguistic imperialism is that the dominance of English is asserted and maintained by the establishment and continuous reconstitution of structural and cultural inequalities between English and other languages* . . . English linguistic imperialism is seen as a sub-type of linguicism. (1992: 47, original emphasis)

Finally, Phillipson asks whether ELT can help create "greater linguistic and social equality," and whether "a critical ELT" can help fight linguicism (p. 319). In the final chapter on "Linguistic imperialism and ELT," Phillipson asks who has been responsible for the global spread of English in recent decades, and for the "monolingual and anglocentric" professionalism that has accompanied its teaching worldwide. The "allies in the international promotion of English" were Britain and the USA, but they, or their political leaders and cultural agencies (such as the British Council and United States Information Service (USIS)), have only been partly responsible, as the main force, Phillipson claims, has been structural and he charges that: "The ELT policy-makers themselves, in Center and Periphery, in Ministries of Education, universities, curriculum development centers and the like are part of a hegemonic structure" and that "The structure of academic imperialism has ensured that Center training and expertise have been disseminated worldwide, with change and innovative professionalism tending to be generated by the Center" (p. 305).

Phillipson's book attracted an immense response from applied linguists and sociolinguists. Fishman and Spolsky, two heavyweights active in both disciplines, gave favorable reviews, and *World Englishes* even devoted a special issue to a symposium on the book (Kachru, 1993). Less favorable reviews varied from the "mixed" (McArthur, 1993: 50, "painstaking, fascinating, informative, frustrating but patently well-meant book") to the dismissive (Conrad, 1996: 27, "a kind of toothless Marxism").

Another important theorist and commentator from a critical perspective has been Alastair Pennycook. Pennycook's (1994) *The Cultural Politics of English as an International Language* endorses Phillipson's critique of the role of applied linguistics and ELT in "helping to legitimate the contemporary capitalist order" (1994: 24), and seconds his view that Anglophone countries (Britain and America) have promoted English throughout the world "for economic and political purposes" and "to protect and promote capitalist interests" (p. 22). The final chapter calls for a radical pedagogy, concerned with the creation of "counter-discourses," "insurgent knowledges," "common counter-articulations" so that "critical English language educators" (formerly known as English teachers) join the struggle for "a critical, transformative and listening critical pedagogy through English" (p. 326). Throughout his other writings, Pennycook has sought to advance and refine a critical perspective on both world Englishes and applied linguistics. In his latest book, *Critical Applied Linguistics* (2001), he explains that:

> Critical applied linguistics . . . is more than just a critical dimension added on top of applied linguistics: It involves a constant skepticism, a constant questioning of the normative assumptions of applied linguistics and presents a way of doing applied linguistics that seeks to connect it to questions of gender, class, sexuality, race, ethnicity, culture, identity, politics, ideology and discourse. (Pennycook, 2001: 10)

Both Phillipson and Pennycook have been influential in establishing the agenda for the critical discussion of world English(es) in the last ten years or so. Related work by other authors includes Tollefson (1995, 2002), Eggington and Wren (1997), Holborow (1999), Ricento (2000), and Skutnabb-Kangas (2000).

8   Futurology

Two fairly recent works that have attempted to discuss the future prospects for English in the world are Crystal (1997) and Graddol (1997). Crystal, in the final chapter of *English as a Global Language*, highlights a number of issues related to the "future of global English." The issues he discusses include the anxiety about the mother tongue in societies such as India, the debate about the official English movement in the USA, and the existence and growth of the new Englishes. The first issue he addresses is that of "ownership," noting that "when even the largest English speaking nation, the USA, turns out to have only about 20 percent of the world's English speakers . . . it is plain that no one can now claim sole ownership" of English, and that "[t]his is probably the best way of defining a genuinely global language" (Crystal, 1997: 130). There are those, he continues, especially in Britain, who are "uncomfortable" about this, but they have no alternative:

> Within ten years, there will certainly be more L2 speakers than L1 speakers. Within fifty years, there could be up to 50 percent more. By that time, the only possible concept of ownership will be a global one . . . An inevitable consequence of this development is that the language will become open to the winds of linguistic change in totally unpredictable ways. The spread of English around the world has already demonstrated this, in the emergence of new varieties of English in the different territories where the language has taken root. The change has become a major talking point only since the 1960s, hence the term by which these varieties are often known: "new Englishes." (pp. 130–1)

Instead of fragmented, unintelligible varieties, however, Crystal identifies a new, unifying dialect, that of "World Standard Spoken English" (WSSE), which he now sees developing worldwide:

> People would still have dialects for use within their own country, but when the need came to communicate with people from other countries they would slip into WSSE . . . People who attend international conferences, or who write scripts for an international audience, or who are "talking" on the Internet have probably already felt the pull of this new variety. It takes the form, for example, of consciously avoiding a word or phrase which you know is not going to be understood outside your own country, and of finding an alternative form of expression . . . it is too early to be definite about the way this variety will develop. WSSE is still in its infancy. Indeed, it has hardly yet been born. (pp. 137–8)

Graddol's (1997) *The Future of English?* was commissioned and published by the British Council's English 2000 project, the final section of which is devoted to "English in the future." Graddol identifies two major issues linked to the notion of "world standard English": (1) whether English will fragment into many different languages (the Quirk–Kachru debate); and (2) whether US and

British English will continue to serve as models of correctness, or whether a "new world standard" will emerge. In contrast to Crystal, Graddol rejects world standard English and predicts a "polycentric" future for English standards in the future, presenting a number of analyses of economic and socio-political effects of the spread of English. Graddol's "state-of-the-art" report on English also illustrates the rapid shift in the last 30 years from a focus on "the linguistic" (as in early studies of varieties of English) to an increasing preoccupation with "the extra-linguistic," e.g., the socio-economics of globalization in Graddol, and the Marxism, dependency theory, and postcolonial theorizing of Phillipson and Pennycook.

9   Conclusion

The review of the literature in the preceding section demonstrates just how far the debates and discourses on world English(es) and new Englishes have come since the identification of this topic in sociolinguistics and applied linguistics in the late 1970s and early 1980s. As is indicated above, there are currently a number of overlapping and intersecting approaches to this field of inquiry. What also emerges from this survey, however, is a changing disciplinary and discoursal map, marked by a series of paradigm shifts in the last 20 years. In this final section, we might now pause to consider the implications of such approaches for applied linguistics. The kinds of responses that are possible in this context will depend on a range of factors, including different understandings of the field of "applied linguistics."

For some, applied linguistics has the status of an independent discipline associated with its own body of theory and methodologies, while, for others, it is seen as "mediating" between such parent disciplines as education, linguistics, psychology, sociology, etc. and various forms of problem-solving activities, especially those associated with language learning and language teaching. In this latter context, for example, Widdowson has commented that applied linguistics is "an activity which seeks to identify, within the disciplines concerned with language and learning, those insights and procedures and their effective actualization in practice" (1990: 6, cited in Cook and Seidlhofer, 1995: 8). For the purposes of this short conclusion, I will assume that the term is capable of two broad definitions: in the first sense, as a wide-ranging area of interdisciplinary theory and activity of relevance to such fields as linguistics, psycholinguistics, and sociolinguistics; and in a second sense, as a rather narrower field of activity mainly concerned, following Widdowson, with pedagogic principles and practices.

The significance of world Englishes for applied linguistics in the first and wider sense is profound, challenging the discipline to come to terms with a wide range of issues, descriptive and theoretical, linked to the unprecedented impact of English throughout the world. Current studies suggest that there are now an estimated 375 million users of English in Inner-Circle societies,

375 million in Outer-Circle (ESL) societies, and around 750–1,000 million in the Expanding (EFL) Circle (McArthur, 2001). Other statistics suggest that in Asia alone the number of English users now totals over 600 million people, including over 300 million in India, and over 200 million in China. Virtually every Asian city has an English language newspaper, and many societies in the region also provide English language programs on radio and television. English is also an important pan-Asian lingua franca in the business world, so that, for example, when a factory manager from Vietnam sells garments to a Singaporean merchandiser, the language of choice is usually English. The dominant trend over recent decades is that more and more Asian people are speaking more and more English, and they are speaking it mainly to other Asians (Kachru, 1997b).

The vast majority of teachers of English as a second and foreign language in the world today are "non-native" teachers working in a wide range of settings in Outer-Circle and Expanding-Circle societies. The number of secondary school teachers of English in China alone now totals around 500,000 (Bolton, 2003). In Outer-Circle Asian societies such as Hong Kong, India, Malaysia, Singapore, and the Philippines (as well as a host of African societies), such teachers operate in sociolinguistic contexts where English has established de facto international norms, often at variance with the exonormative targets of traditional teaching materials. In situations such as these, the maintenance of traditional target norms of English proficiency may not only lack realism but may also contribute to the stigmatization of the norms of local users (including teachers and learners), contributing to a "culture of complaint" rather than "a culture of confidence" (Bolton, 2002b).

In addition, the "nativization" of English in many such societies has been accompanied by the "Englishization" of many indigenous languages, leading to complex patterns of contact linguistics, including lexical transfer, code switching and code mixing, and discoursal and syntactic change and accommodation. The interface of English with both local languages and national vernaculars throughout many parts of the world presents applied linguistics (in "sense 1") with a series of challenges: *linguistic* (the description and analysis of language systems), *sociolinguistic* (providing adequate accounts of context and language use), and *psycholinguistic* (in assessing or reformulating extant models of first and second-language acquisition). In this latter context, the notion of "native speaker" has come under increasing scrutiny (Davies, 1991; Singh, 1998).

At the same time, despite the greater recognition accorded to the Englishes of Africa and Asia in the area in recent years, considerable problems for applied linguistics still exist in the area of pedagogic principles and practices (applied linguistics in "sense 2" terms). In many Outer-Circle societies, questions linked to norms and codification are typically unresolved. For example, even though some educationalists in societies such as Hong Kong and the Philippines have started to recognize local norms of educated speech, official attitudes frequently remain ambivalent at best. Attitudes vary considerably from one society to the next, with Filipino teachers often rejecting the imposition of American norms, while Hong Kong teachers continue to express deference to the norms of the "native speaker." Nor is it clear that the official endorsement of "local standards" would necessarily further the world Englishes cause, especially when one considers that varieties are typically caught not taught, and questions of norms and standards are invariably embedded in the particular language cultures and traditions of such societies. One possible innovation that might be considered here, however, is a much-increased provision of courses on "language awareness" (dealing with issues related to world Englishes) for teachers, teacher trainers, and other educators not only in Outer- or Expanding-Circle societies, but also for comparable groups in such Inner-Circle societies as the USA, UK, Australia, Canada, etc. The expanded accessibility of programs of this kind many help to clear the space for new and creative approaches to language education and the teaching of English, in a range of contexts worldwide.

Kachru himself discusses these and related issues in a 1990 paper entitled "World Englishes and applied linguistics," where he notes the limitations of traditional applied linguistics perspectives on world Englishes, suggesting that these had been skewed by the ethnocentrisms of Inner-Circle practitioners, reliance on interlanguage and error analysis frameworks, and misconceptions concerning the sociolinguistic realities of multilingual Outer-Circle societies (Kachru, 1990). A later paper by Kachru and Nelson (1996) goes on to explore the ways in which the world Englishes approach might be adopted within the language classroom, suggesting a number of imaginative strategies that might be employed in teaching Englishes across a variety of educational settings, including multicultural education, the teaching of discourse pragmatics, and the teaching of new literatures in English (see also Kachru, 1997a).

Brown (2000) surveys the resources for research and teaching in the field, and suggests a range of research and applied agendas for world Englishes. At the level of applied linguistics research, these include longitudinal studies of values and attitudes, textual studies in multicultural communities, empirical studies of attitude development and change, and world Englishes-based research on second-language acquisition. Related educational research might then involve comparative classroom-based studies across the three circles (what have elsewhere been dubbed ENL, ESL, and EFL contexts), and the evaluation of learning/teaching materials. Brown also suggests an activist role for world Englishes scholars in organizing conferences, publishing, designing texts and curricular, and playing a leadership role in professional communities worldwide (see also Kachru, 1997a; and Matsuda, 2002).

In the last ten years or so, there has been a growing awareness of the world Englishes paradigm among applied linguists and others in Outer-Circle English-using African and Asian societies. There has also been an evident response to the world Englishes paradigm in many academic circles in the USA, partly in resonance, one speculates, to the relatively high levels of immigration to the United States from Asian societies in recent years, and a nascent awareness of world Englishes in an immigrant context (Lippi-Green, 1997). In other educational settings, such as Europe, with its own crowded ecology of former colonial languages such as French, German, and Spanish, the academic response to the world Englishes paradigm has been mixed.

One particularly acute problem at present remains the center-periphery domination in what has been called "English language industry" (McArthur, 2001) throughout the world. Academic publishing and textbook publishing in both applied linguistics and English language teaching is largely controlled by a small number of publishing houses based in the UK and USA, who rely on a relatively small number of experts for their expertise and professionalism. Historically, however, applied linguistics in both these societies did not arise in a sociopolitical vacuum, but came out of two rather different sets of experiences. In the case of Britain, applied linguistics emerged as a discipline during the 1960s and 1970s when significant numbers of English language specialists were recruited to assist in various educational projects in decolonizing Commonwealth societies. In the USA, in recent decades, the greatest impetus to applied linguistics and TESOL has come from immigrant education and ESL programs in the college and university context. Both approaches seem now to have coalesced around a body of shared practices, professionalism, and theory (see, for example, Candlin and Mercer, 2001; Carter and Nunan, 2001; Kaplan, 2002). Despite what may be the best intentions of Western practitioners to develop an unbiased or at least politically neutral applied linguistics at the level of theory as well as pedagogic principles, it is difficult to ignore the imbalance between the developed and developing world in many of the contexts of English language teaching today. English language teachers in many of the Outer-Circle and Expanding-Circle contexts face difficulties in terms of conditions, facilities, and resources undreamed of in comparable Western institutions. Academics from these societies have parallel difficulties in finding a voice in major journals in the field (although notable exceptions include *English Today* and *World Englishes*), as well as in book production.

In this context, the Kachruvian approach offers a politics that is balanced between the pragmatic recognition of the spread of English(es) and the critical scrutiny of native-speaker ideologies from the Inner Circle. It also affirms the pluricentricity and inclusivity signposted by Kachru and Smith in their first editorial statement for the *World Englishes* journal: "The editorial board considers the native and non-native users of English as equal partners in deliberations on uses of English and its teaching internationally . . . The acronym *WE* therefore aptly symbolizes the underlying philosophy of the journal and the aspirations of the Editorial Board" (Kachru and Smith, 1985: 210). Whether that vision is realizable depends partly on the flow of ideas and insights in at least two directions. A consideration of world Englishes is important to applied linguistics for a range of reasons. Not least because researchers and teachers from Europe and North America may have much to learn from the experiences of the Outer and Expanding Circles, both at levels of theory and description, and in the consideration of pedagogic "principles" and "practice." At an individual level, the English language now plays an important role in the lives of a rapidly increasing proportion of the world's population. From a global perspective, the sociolinguistically complex sites of English-using African and Asian societies are no mere exotic sideshow, but important sites of contact, negotiation, and linguistic and literary creativity. From the perspective of applied linguistics, perhaps the major challenge from world Englishes is how the center–periphery balance might be best redressed, or "re-centered" and "pluricentered." This, however, is likely to be no easy task, given the continuing tendency at present, within both academia and publishing, toward the apparent commodification and homogenization of much of the work in this field, both theoretical and pedagogical.

REFERENCES

Algeo, John (1991) A meditation on the varieties of English. *English Today*, **7**, 3–6.

Allsopp, Richard (1996) *The Dictionary of Caribbean English Usage*. Oxford: Oxford University Press.

Ashcroft, Bill, Griffiths, Gareth, and Tiffin, Helen (1989) *The Empire Writes Back*. London: Routledge.

Avis, Walter S. (1967) *A Dictionary of Canadianisms on Historical Principles*. Toronto: Gage.

Bailey, Richard W. (1991) *Images of English*. Ann Arbor: The University of Michigan Press.

Banjo, Ayọ and Young, Peter (1982) On editing a second-language dictionary: The proposed dictionary of West African English (DWAE). *English World-Wide*, **3**, 87–91.

Barber, Katherine (1999) *The Canadian Oxford Dictionary*. Oxford: Oxford University Press.

Bartlett, John Russell (1848) *Dictionary of Americanisms: A Glossary of Words and Phrases Usually Regarded as Peculiar to the United States*. New York: Bartlett and Welford.

Bolton, Kingsley (2002a) World Englishes: Approaches, issues, and debate. Paper presented at the 11th International Association of World Englishes (IAWE) Conference, University of Illinois at Urbana-Champaign, October 17–20.

Bolton, Kingsley (2002b) Hong Kong English: Autonomy and creativity. In *Hong Kong English: Autonomy and Creativity*. Edited by Kingsley Bolton. Hong Kong: Hong Kong University Press, pp. 1–25.

Bolton, Kingsley (2003) *Chinese Englishes: A Sociolinguistic History*. Cambridge: Cambridge University Press.

Branford, Jean (ed.) (1978) *A Dictionary of South African English*. Oxford: Oxford University Press.

Brown, Kimberley (2000) World Englishes and the classroom: Research and practice agendas for the year 2000. In *The Three Circles of English*. Edited by Edwin Thumboo. Singapore: UniPress, pp. 371–82.

Burchfield, Robert (1985) *The English Language*. Oxford: Oxford University Press.

Burchfield, Robert (1994) *The Cambridge History of the English Language, vol. 5: English in Britain and Overseas: Origin and Development*. Cambridge: Cambridge University Press.

Butler, Susan (1997) Corpus of English in Southeast Asia: Implications for a regional dictionary. In *English is an Asian Language: The Philippine Context*. Edited by Maria Lourdes S.

Bautista. Manila: Macquarie Library, pp. 103–24.

Candlin, Christopher N. and Mercer, Neil (2001) *English Language Teaching in its Social Context*. London: Routledge.

Carter, Ronald and Nunan, David (eds.) (2001) *The Cambridge Guide to Teaching English to Speakers of Other Languages*. Cambridge: Cambridge University Press.

Cassidy, Frederic G. (1985) *Dictionary of American Regional English*. Cambridge, MA: Harvard University Press.

Cassidy, Frederic G. and Le Page, Robert (1967) *Dictionary of Jamaican English*. Cambridge: Cambridge University Press.

Cheshire, Jenny (ed.) (1991a) *English around the World: Sociolinguistic Perspectives*. Cambridge: Cambridge University Press.

Cheshire, Jenny (1991b) Introduction: Sociolinguistics and English around the world. In *English around the World: Sociolinguistic Perspectives*. Edited by Jenny Cheshire. Cambridge: Cambridge University Press, pp. 1–12.

Conrad, Andrew W. (1996) The international role of English: The state of the discussion. In *Post-imperial English*. Edited by Joshua A. Fishman, Andrew W. Conrad, and Alma Rubal-Lopez. Berlin/New York: Mouton de Gruyter, pp. 13–36.

Cook, Guy and Seidlhofer, Barbara (eds.) (1995) *Principles and Practice in Applied Linguistics: Studies in Honour of H. G. Widdowson*. Oxford: Oxford University Press.

Craigie, William A. and Hulbert, James R. (1938–44) *A Dictionary of American English on Historical Principles*. Chicago: University of Chicago Press.

Crystal, David (1969) *Prosodic Systems and Intonation in English*. Cambridge: Cambridge University Press.

Crystal, David (1975) *The English Tone of Voice: Essays in Intonation, Prosody and Paralanguage*. London: Edward Arnold.

Crystal, David (1988) *The English Language*. London: Penguin Books.

Crystal, David (1995) *The Cambridge Encyclopedia of the English Language*. Cambridge: Cambridge University Press.

Crystal, David (1997) *English as a Global Language*. Cambridge: Cambridge University Press.

Crystal, David (2000) On trying to be crystal-clear: A response to Phillipson. *Applied Linguistics*, **21**, 415–23.

Crystal, David and Quirk, Randolph (1964) *Systems of Prosodic and Paralinguistic Features in English*. The Hague: Mouton.

Davies, Alan (1991) *The Native Speaker in Applied Linguistics*. Edinburgh: Edinburgh University Press.

Delbridge, Arthur (ed.) (1981) *The Macquarie Dictionary*. Sydney: Macquarie Dictionary Company Limited.

Eggington, William G. and Wren, Helen (1997) *Language Policy: Dominant English, Pluralist Challenges*. Amsterdam/Canberra: John Benjamins/Language Australia.

Fishman, Joshua A. (1977) English in the context of international societal bilingualism. In *The Spread of English: The Sociology of English as an Additional Language*. Edited by Joshua A. Fishman, Robert L. Cooper, and Andrew W. Conrad. Rowley, MA: Newbury House, pp. 329–36.

Fishman, Joshua A. (1996a) Introduction: Some empirical and theoretical issues. In *Post-Imperial English*. Edited by Joshua A. Fishman, Andrew W. Conrad, and Alma Rubal-Lopez. Berlin/New York: Mouton de Gruyter, pp. 3–12.

Fishman, Joshua A. (1996b) Summary and interpretation: Post-imperial

English 1940–1990. In *Post-Imperial English*. Edited by Joshua A. Fishman, Andrew W. Conrad, and Alma Rubal-Lopez. Berlin/New York: Mouton de Gruyter, pp. 623–41.

Fishman, Joshua A., Conrad, Andrew W., and Rubal-Lopez, Alma (eds.) (1996) *Post-Imperial English*. Berlin/New York: Mouton de Gruyter.

Fishman, Joshua A., Cooper, Robert L., and Conrad, Andrew W. (eds.) (1977) *The Spread of English: The Sociology of English as an Additional Language*. Rowley, MA: Newbury House.

Goodman, Sharon and Graddol, David (eds.) (1996) *Redesigning English: New Texts, New Identities*. London: Routledge.

Görlach, Manfred (1980) Editorial. *English World-Wide*, **1**, 3–7.

Görlach, Manfred (1988) English as a world language: The state of the art. *English World-Wide*, **10**, 279–313.

Görlach, Manfred (ed.) (1995) Dictionaries of transplanted Englishes. In *More Englishes: New Studies in Varieties of English 1988–1994*. Edited by Manfred Görlach. Amsterdam/Philadelphia: John Benjamins, pp. 124–63.

Görlach, Manfred (1996) And is it English? *English World-Wide*, **17**, 153–74.

Graddol, David (1997) *The Future of English?* London: The British Council.

Graddol, David, Leith, Dick, and Swann, Joan (1996) *English: History, Diversity and Change*. London: Routledge.

Greenbaum, Sidney (ed.) (1985) *The English Language Today*. Oxford: Pergamon.

Greenbaum, Sidney (ed.) (1996) *Comparing English Worldwide*. Oxford: Clarendon Press.

Halliday, M. A. K., McIntosh, Angus, and Strevens, Peter (1964) *The Linguistic Sciences and Language Teaching*. London: Longman.

Hawkins, R. E. (1984) *Common Indian Words in English*. Delhi: Oxford University Press.

Holborow, Marnie (1999) *The Politics of English: A Marxist View of Language*. London: Sage.

Holm, John and Shilling, Alison W. (eds.) (1982) *Dictionary of Bahamian English*. Cold Spring, NY: Lexik House.

Hosillos, Lucila (1982) Breaking through the Wayang Screen: Literary interdependence among new literatures in Southeast Asia. In *The Writer's Sense of the Contemporary: Papers in Southeast Asia and Australian Literature*. Edited by Bruce Bennet, Ee Tiang Hong, and Ron Shepherd. Nedlands: Centre for Studies in Australian Literature, University of Western Australia, pp. 59–62.

Iyer, Pico (1993) The empire writes back. *Time*, February, **8**(6), 48–53.

Johnson, Samuel (1755) *A Dictionary of the English Language*. London: Printed by W. Strahan, for J. and P. Knapton.

Kachru, Braj B. (ed.) (1982) *The Other Tongue: English across Cultures*. Urbana, IL: University of Illinois Press.

Kachru, Braj B. (1985) Standards, codification and sociolinguistic realism: The English language in the outer circle. In *English in the World: Teaching and Learning the Language and Literatures*. Edited by Randolph Quirk and Henry G. Widdowson. Cambridge: Cambridge University Press, pp. 11–30.

Kachru, Braj B. (1986) *The Alchemy of English: The Spread, Functions, and Models of Non-Native Englishes*. Oxford: Pergamon.

Kachru, Braj B. (1990) World Englishes and applied linguistics. *Studies in Linguistic Sciences*, **19**, 127–52.

Kachru, Braj B. (1991) Liberation linguistics and the Quirk concern. *English Today*, **25**, 3–13.

Kachru, Braj B. (1992) World Englishes: Approaches, issues and resources. *Language Teaching*, **25**, 1–14.

Kachru, Braj B. (ed.) (1993) Symposium on linguistic imperialism. *World Englishes*, **12**, 335–73.

Kachru, Braj B. (1997a) World Englishes 2000: Resources for research and teaching. In *World Englishes 2000*. Edited by Larry E. Smith and Michael L. Forman. Honolulu: University of Hawai'i Press and the East-West Center, pp. 209–51.

Kachru, Braj B. (1997b) English as an Asian language. In *English is an Asian Language: The Philippine Context*. Edited by Maria Lourdes S. Bautista. Manila: Macquarie Library, pp. 1–23.

Kachru, Braj B. and Nelson, Cecil (1996) World Englishes. In *Sociolinguistics and Language Teaching*. Edited by Sandra L. Mckay and Nancy, H. Hornberger. Cambridge: Cambridge University Press, pp. 71–102.

Kachru, Braj B. and Smith, Larry E. (1985) Editorial. *World Englishes*, **4**, 209–12.

Kachru, Braj B. and Smith, Larry E. (1988) World Englishes: An integrative and cross-cultural journal of WE-ness. In *Robert Maxwell and Pergamon Press: 40 Years' Service to Science, Technology and Education*. Edited by Elisabeth Maxwell. Oxford: Pergamon, pp. 674–8.

Kaplan, Robert (ed.) (2002) *The Oxford Handbook of Applied Linguistics*. New York: Oxford University Press.

King, Bruce (1980) *The New English Literatures: Cultural Nationalism in a Changing World*. London: Macmillan.

Lake, Joshua (1898) *Webster's International Dictionary, Australasian Supplement*. Springfield, MA: G. and C. Merriam.

Lim, Shirley (1984) Gods who fall: Ancestral religions in the new literatures in English from Malaysia and Singapore. *Commonwealth Novel in English*, **3**(1), 39–55.

Lippi-Green, Rosina (1997) *English with an Accent: Language, Ideology, and Discrimination in the United States*. London/New York: Routledge.

Llamzon, Teodoro A. (1983) Essential features of new varieties of English. In *Varieties of English in Southeast Asia*. Edited by Richard B. Noss. Singapore: Singapore University Press, pp. 92–109.

Mathews, Mitford M. (1951) *Dictionary of Americanisms on Historical Principles*. Chicago: University of Chicago Press.

Matsuda, Aya (ed.) (2002) Symposium on world Englishes and teaching English as a foreign language. *World Englishes*, **21**(3), 421–55.

McArthur, Tom (1987) The English languages? *English Today*, **11**, 9–11.

McArthur, Tom (1992) *The Oxford Companion to the English Language*. Oxford: Oxford University Press.

McArthur, Tom (1993) The sins of the fathers. *English Today*, **35**, 9(3), 48–50.

McArthur, Tom (1998) *The English Languages*. Cambridge: Cambridge University Press.

McArthur, Tom (2001) World English and world Englishes: Trends, tensions, varieties, and standards. *Language Teaching*, **34**, 1–20.

McArthur, Tom (2002) *The Oxford Guide to World English*. Oxford: Oxford University Press.

McCrum, Robert, Cran, William, and MacNeil, Robert (1986) *The Story of English*. London: Faber and Faber/ BBC publications.

Morris, Edward E. (1898) *Austral English: A Dictionary of Australasian Words, Phrases and Usage*. London: Macmillan.

Mufwene, Salikoko S. (1997) Introduction: Understanding speech continua. *World Englishes*, **16**, 181–4.

Murray, James A. H. (ed.) (1884–1928) *A New English Dictionary on Historical Principles*. Re-edited and re-titled, *The Oxford English Dictionary* (from 1933). Oxford: Oxford University Press.

Nelson, Gerald, Wallis, Sean and Aarts, Bas (2002) *Exploring Natural Language: Working with the British Component of the International Corpus of English*. Amsterdam: John Benjamins.

Noss, Richard B. (ed.) (1983) *Varieties of English in Southeast Asia*. Singapore: Singapore University Press.

Orsman, Harry (1997) *The Dictionary of New Zealand English: A Dictionary of New Zealandisms on Historical Principles*. Auckland: Oxford University Press.

Pennycook, Alastair (1994) *The Cultural Politics of English as an International Language*. London: Longman.

Pennycook, Alastair (2001) *Critical Applied Linguistics*. Mahwah, NJ: Lawrence Erlbaum.

Pettman, Rev. Charles (1913) *Africanderisms: A Glossary of South African Words and Phrases and of Place and Other Names*. London: Longmans, Green and Co.

Phillipson, Robert (1992) *Linguistic Imperialism*. Oxford: Oxford University Press.

Phillipson, Robert (1999) Linguistic imperialism re-visited – or re-invented: A rejoinder to a review essay. *International Journal of Applied Linguistics*, **9**, 135–42.

Pickering, John (1816) *A Vocabulary or Collection of Words and Phrases which have been Supposed to be Peculiar to the United States of America*. Boston: Cummings and Hilliard.

Platt, John, Weber, Heidi, and Ho, Mian Lian (1984) *The New Englishes*. London: Routledge.

Prator, Clifford (1968) The British heresy in TESL. In *Language Problems of Developing Nations*. Edited by Joshua Fishman, Charles Ferguson, and Jyotirindra Das Gupta. New York: John Wiley, pp. 459–76.

Pride, John B. (1982) *New Englishes*. Rowley, MA: Newbury House.

Quirk, Randolph (1962) *The Use of English*. London: Longman.

Quirk, Randolph (1985) The English language in a global context. In *English in the World: Teaching and Learning the Language and Literatures*. Edited by Randolph Quirk and Henry G. Widdowson. Cambridge: Cambridge University Press, pp. 1–30.

Quirk, Randolph (1990) Language varieties and standard language. *English Today*, **21**, 3–21.

Quirk, Randolph and Widdowson, Henry G. (eds.) (1985) *English in the World: Teaching and Learning the Language and Literatures*. Cambridge: Cambridge University Press.

Quirk, Randolph, Greenbaum, Sidney, Leech, Geoffrey, and Svartivik, Jan (1972) *A Grammar of Contemporary English*. London: Longman.

Ramson, William Stanley (ed.) (1988) *The Australian National Dictionary: A Dictionary of Australianisms on Historical Principles*. Melbourne/Oxford: Oxford University Press.

Rao, G. Subba (1954) *Indian Words in English: A Study in Indo-British Cultural and Linguistic Relations*. Oxford: Clarendon.

Ricento, Thomas (2000) *Ideology, Politics, and Language Politics: Focus on English*. Amesterdam/Philadelphia: John Benjamins.

Romaine, Suzanne (1997) The British heresy in ESL revisited. In *Language and Its Ecology: Essays in Memory of Einar Haugen*. Edited by Ernst H. Jahr. Berlin/New York: Mouton de Gruyter, pp. 417–32.

Schneider, Edgar W. (1997a) Introduction. In *English around the World, vol. 1: General Studies,*

British Isles, North America. Edited by
Edgar W. Schneider. Amsterdam:
John Benjamins, pp. 15–17.

Schneider, Edgar W. (1997b) *Englishes
around the World, vol. 1: General
Studies, British Isles, North America*.
Amsterdam: John Benjamins.

Silva, Penny (1998) *A Dictionary of South
African English on Historical Principles*.
Oxford: Oxford University Press.

Singh, Rajendra (ed.) (1998) *The Native
Speaker: Multilingual Perspectives*.
New Delhi: Sage.

Skutnabb-Kangas, Tove (2000) *Linguistic
Genocide in Education, or Worldwide
Diversity and Human Rights*. Mahwah,
NJ/London: Lawrence Erlbaum.

Smith, Larry E. (ed.) (1981) *English for
Cross-Cultural Communication*.
London: Macmillan.

Strevens, Peter (1977) *New Orientations
in the Teaching of English*. Oxford:
Oxford University Press.

Strevens, Peter (1980) *Teaching English as
an International Language*. Oxford:
Pergamon.

Strevens, Peter (1985) Standards and the
standard language. *English Today*, **2**,
5–8.

Todd, Loreto (1984) *Modern Englishes:
Pidgins and Creoles*. Oxford: Blackwell.

Todd, Loreto (1995) Tracking the homing
pidgin: A millennium report. *English
Today*, **41**, 33–43.

Tollefson, James W. (ed.) (1995) *Power
and Inequality in Language Education*.
Cambridge/New York: Cambridge
University Press.

Tollefson, James W. (ed.) (2002) *Language
Policies in Education: Critical Issues*.

Mahwah, NJ/London: Lawrence
Erlbaum.

Trudgill, Peter and Hannah, Jean (2002)
*International English: A Guide to
Varieties of Standard English*. 4th
edition. London: Edward Arnold.

Webster, Noah (1789) *Dissertations on the
English Language*. Boston: Isaiah
Thomas; facs. Reprinted Menston:
Scolar, 1967.

Webster, Noah (1806) *A Compendious
Dictionary of the English Language*.
Hartford, CN: Sidney's Press for
Hudson & Goodwin and for
Increase Cooke & Co.

Webster, Noah (1828) *An American
Dictionary of the English Language*
(2 vols). New York: S. Converse.
Facsimile reprint, San Francisco:
Foundation for American Christian
Education, 1967.

Wells, John C. (1982) *Accents of English*
(3 vols). Cambridge: Cambridge
University Press.

Whitworth, George C. (1885) *An Anglo-
Indian Dictionary: A Glossary of Indian
Terms Used in English, and of Such
English or Other Non-Indian Terms as
Have Obtained Special Meanings in
India*. London: Kegan Paul, Trench
and Co.

Widdowson, Henry G. (1990) *Aspects of
Language Teaching*. Oxford: Oxford
University Press.

Yule, Henry and Burnell, Arthur C.
([1886] 1969) *Hobson-Jobson: A
Glossary of Anglo-Indian Words and
Phrases*. London: John Murray. New
edition 1903, reprinted 1969,
London: Routledge and Kegan Paul.

FURTHER READING

Smith, Larry E. and Forman, Michael L.
(eds.) (1997) *World Englishes 2000*.
Honolulu: University of Hawai'i
Press and the East-West Center.

Thumboo, Edwin (ed.) (2001) *The Three
Circles of English*. Singapore:
UniPress.

Part II Variational Contexts

16 Contact Linguistics and World Englishes

RAJEND MESTHRIE

1 Introduction

The world Englishes paradigm is most closely associated with the foundational work of Braj Kachru in establishing the field of nativized second-language varieties as a legitimate area of academic study. At the same time, Kachru has taken a proactive applied linguistic stand in fighting for the recognition of these varieties as legitimate in their contexts of use. For Kachru, English in countries such as India or Nigeria has developed its own norms which make it appropriate to its cultural and educational contexts. As a tool of communication within these countries, English has to play a complementary role to that of the local languages in a finely balanced linguistic ecology. The strengths of the Kachruvian approach can be seen in its applicability beyond the realms of the former British empire. It has furnished us with models, schemata, and debates that would appear to apply as well, to varying degrees, to French in Africa, Spanish in the New World, and the rise and fall of Russian in the former Soviet republics.

The successes of the paradigm are clear: world Englishes study is an essential part of the branches of linguistics/sociolinguistics that are characterized by labels like "language spread" and "contact linguistics." In addition, the argument for the legitimation of the varieties and for recognition of their cultural value has made its mark in applied linguistics. The perspective I wish to highlight is that of contact linguistics, with variationist leanings, and a dose of social history. This chapter argues for a greater degree of rapprochement between the fields of world Englishes (or New Englishes) and Contact Linguistics, building on the work of, inter alia, Kachru (1982, 1983), Ho and Platt (1993), and Mufwene (2001). At the same time, it pays attention to certain aspects within the variationist enterprise in sociolinguistics (Labov, 1972 and subsequently).

Four aspects of world Englishes studies await fuller attention:

1 the foundation of New Englishes vis-à-vis the input;
2 establishing a truly comparative data base for linguistic analysis;

3   refining our tools for describing and accounting for variation;
4   describing language shift where it is taking place.

I shall provide brief motivations for (2) to (4), leaving fuller exploration to future research, before focusing in detail on phase (1). Regarding (2), "establishing a truly comparative data base," the foundations have been clearly laid by a number of descriptions of individual varieties in the three journals in the field (*World Englishes*, *English World-Wide*, and *English Today*) and in pioneering dissertations at the University of Illinois (Urbana, Illinois, USA) and elsewhere. These have helped track down recurring similarities as well as idiosyncratic forms in world Englishes, and certain processes such as lectal shifting (the retention of earlier developmental forms for use along stylistic lines, in informal speech or interactions with basilectal speakers). The fact of lectal shifting (see, e.g., Chew, 1995; Platt, 1975) makes it imperative to gather data within similar situations, so that a speaker's baseline can be ascertained and any ensuing stylistic shifts up or down can be tracked. Other sociolinguistic aspects pertaining to "register" are also methodologically important. Comparative work should ideally not mix spoken and written data. Unfortunately, individual case studies do not always adhere to this desideratum. In some cases, analysts are correct in suggesting that certain features from written sources (newspaper articles, students' essays, conversations in a novel) are regular features of the variety concerned. However, writing often has its own conventions, some of which have little connection with features of speech. Newspaper headlines, for example, have their own conventions, such as the deletion of articles, use of present tense or passive without *be*, none of which draws on speech norms. No one says to a friend: *I've got some hot news to tell you – Man bites dog in Illinois*. We rarely have information on the editing process accompanying the written efforts cited in some world Englishes studies. The work of creative writers, particularly, needs to be cited with care, as they are concerned with creating a general effect via language, rather than using constructions with sociolinguistic veracity. Even the best-intentioned authors may be susceptible to linguistic stereotyping or might not be as knowledgable about linguistic norms as they and others believe.

In other instances, even though a piece of creative writing may be written in English, its syntax and discourse patterns may be intended to reflect not the local variety of English, but the first language of the community concerned. Famous examples are Raja Rao's novel *Kanthapura* (1938), and Gabriel Okara's *The Voice* (1970), reflecting, via very creative English, the idioms of Kannada and Ijaw, respectively. But these efforts tell us very little about the spoken English of those communities.

This is not to suggest that written data is unimportant: for earlier periods concerning the genesis of world Englishes, written data may be all that analysts have to go on, and can provide valuable snippets of information for the linguist. Thus, non-literary written sources like ships' logs, court records, missionary diaries, boarding school documents, and the like can be as valuable to the linguist as to the historian. And, obviously, for educational and literacy studies of New Englishes, student writing and revisions are the core material of analysis.

For contemporary studies, though, spoken data is a *sine qua non*, which should ideally be gathered along uniform lines. I suggest that principles well established in variationist sociolinguistics be followed, with modifications as warranted. That is, fieldwork should be undertaken with a reliable judgment sample of the community concerned, culminating in informal tape-recorded interviews. These should stress topics that elicit extended conversation, typically topics centered around local practices and experiences, including possibly Labov's well-known "danger-of-death" module (1972: 92–5). Topics could be of a controversial but not taboo nature. The advantage of the "Labovian" methodology is that it provides comparable data gathered under roughly the same conditions. Some studies of world Englishes have successfully utilized this methodology, at least at the level of data-gathering (Ho and Platt, 1993; Mesthrie, 1992; Sharma, 2002). There is, however, an important caveat, since the aim of urban dialectology is to study the vernacular, i.e. the least formal L1 variety that speakers of a dialect use. The obvious question is whether the same techniques should apply to world Englishes which are not L1s and which are seldom appropriate in the most informal local context. A related question is whether speakers should only use English in a world Englishes interview. It might be sociolinguistically artificial to expect English to be the only language used if the interviewer and interviewee share the same background. Bilingual behavior including mixing and switching should be encouraged where natural and expected. On the other hand, an interviewer who is an outsider may well elicit only English conversation. Overall, there seems to be no reason why the approach by "variationist" interviewers would be inappropriate for world Englishes research, except, perhaps, for "learner" varieties in the Outer Circle. It may well turn out that discussions around school, education, and more "serious topics" like local politics will be more prominent in world Englishes contexts than in urban dialectology.

The data provided in many accounts of world Englishes do not always meet the ideal requirements we would like for formal sociolinguistics. Where a local feature occurs, it is not always clear from the descriptions how frequent it is, which subgroups use it, and what its relations to more standard or colloquial "L1" constructions are. An example of syntactic analysis that I believe lends itself to comparative work is that of Ho and Platt (1993: 30–73) on the Singapore English copula. The work is explicit about its data base (interviews with 150 speakers of Chinese background, of which 100 were selected for study on the grounds of clarity of recording and amount of speech). Several constructions were then isolated for study along descriptive and developmental lines – the copula will serve as an example. Both presence and absence of the copula were charted out in a variety of linguistic contexts per speaker. A Guttman (or implicational) scale was used to show a reliable patterning of data according to the linguistic contexts (__ *Adj*; __ *V + -ing*; __ *Nom*; __ *Loc*, etc.) and the social variables (chiefly educational level). A VARBRUL analysis was performed to ascertain which factors favored deletion above others and which educational groups did so. The implicational scale gives a clear picture of a *panchronic* developmental path. I adapt Saussure's (1966: 95) term here to refer to the way that synchronic variation can be used to make deductions (despite Saussure's disavowal) about diachronic development, in this case the pathways of L2 development. Under certain societal conditions, the (synchronic) pattern outlined by Ho and Platt might prove stable, with fossilization at one end of the continuum. Similar data from other world Englishes (and indeed from a non-Chinese group within Singapore) will verify whether the pathways of copula insertion are the same, whether substrate influence plays a role, or whether variation is random in different world Englishes. The implicational scale model and VARBRUL analysis might also be used to demonstrate (or test) whether there are qualitative differences between Inner- and Outer-Circle varieties in respect of copula variation or other syntactic constructions.

The desideratum of 150 speakers with 100 of them providing extensive, clear data is not likely to be met in EFL settings. But that may change in the globalizing world. Furthermore, since adequate resources may not always be available to support large-scale study in many universities outside the Inner Circle, smaller-scale studies adhering to the same principles could be undertaken, eventually leading to the desideratum of an in-depth, comparable data base. This call does not ignore the existence of corpora, such as ICE (International Corpus of English). Corpora give the researcher the benefit of a wide range of texts (spoken and written) over long periods of time, and can profitably be used to answer specific issues raised in modern dialect description. But for comparative work leading to insights like those provided by an implicational scale, a controlled data base is preferable. A major problem with corpora is that information about speakers is not always forthcoming; nor are details of style, context, etc.

Turning to point (4), it appears that language shift is on the increase worldwide: we are all aware of the alarming statistics on language endangerment. At the moment, some world Englishes that I term "language-shift varieties" are uncommon – South African Indian English (henceforth SAIE), Irish and other Celtic Englishes; possibly Singapore English; Native American (Indian) varieties; Aboriginal Australian varieties; and perhaps Yiddish English in parts of the US (see Mesthrie, 1992: 2–3 for references). There are reports of elites in some Outer-Circle communities shifting to English as sole home language. To some extent this is happening in South Africa; and de Klerk's (2000) research in the eastern Cape shows that it is not just the elites who are voluntarily shifting to English. Is it the case that language shift throws up more variation than does balanced bilingualism? Certainly the greatest variation in world Englishes seems to be reported in Singapore English, Irish English, SAIE, and some varieties of American Indian English. And SAIE certainly shows immensely more variation than its antecedent L2 variety in India. Is it the case that adults involved in the early stages of language shift are the ones who are responsible for the greatest number of innovations, and that children involved in the late stages of language shift (and/or the first post-shift generation) are the ones who act as selectors and stabilizers from this pool of variants? We must leave this topic for future research.

2 Early Contact History

The field of creolistics (or pidgin and creole linguistics) has shown how detailed archival research can illuminate earlier forms of contact languages and offer a firmer foundation against which to test characterizations of creoles and theories of creolization (e.g., Baker, 1995). In particular, the relative contributions of the superstrate, substrate, and universals of one sort or another is an area of intense research and debate in creolistics. Much of the research in world Englishes has been on the transfer from substrates to New Englishes, one of their important characteristics. Yet transfer is not unconstrained. Here, Mufwene's (2001: 18) notion of a "pool of variants" and of subsequent selection from it are useful: "While interacting with each other, speakers contribute features to a **pool** from which they make their selections that can affect the evolutionary trajectory of a language." I suggest that in a contact situation there is a difference between transfer at the early "adding to pool of variants" stage, which is relatively unconstrained, as against the selection stage, which is constrained by principles such as Andersen's (1983) "transfer to somewhere." Andersen proposed that a feature is transferred from L1 to L2 if and only if there is the capacity for such a misgeneralization in the target language itself. At the same time, we have seen that there appear to be universal strategies of simplification and complexification in contact varieties (but this is not the concern of this paper).

As a main focus, I turn to the issue of "input" in world Englishes: the "shape" of the superstrate should not be taken for granted. Many New Englishes are compared to Standard British or US English for reasons of convenience, as we have all done in our research. But such use of modern Standard British English (or sometimes US English) as a sort of metalanguage should not be taken to imply that this is the relevant superstrate for New English study. For historical veracity, we need to keep in mind (1) that standard English of the period of exploration, trade, and colonization was slightly different from English in the twentieth and twenty-first centuries; and (2) that such standard English was not the only input in the formation of New Englishes.

The superstrate was also shaped by sailors, soldiers, adventurers, hunters, divers, tradespeople, indentured workers, plantation owners, overseers, settlers, and schoolteachers. This was, to say the least, a rather varied input, which cautions that the notion of a target language (TL) is an idealization; more often, and certainly outside the classroom, the TL was a varied and "moving" target. It is safe to assume that very few of these introducers of English held MA certificates in TESOL.

A discussion of point (1) above – that standard English of the seventeenth and eighteenth centuries differed from modern Standard British English –

is clearly too great a task to do justice to in this chapter. Instead, by way of exemplification, a few of the main features that were once standard are listed here:

1   unstressed *do:*

(1)   ... Thee 11. day of Iune, the King did anoint the Generall with ritch ointment, and called him his son. (Governors and Assistants of the East India Merchants, 1603)

2   the use of *for to* with infinitives:

(2)   A Billet is a piece of Cleft Wood for to Burn (R. Holme, 1688, cited in the *OED*)

3   the dative of advantage:

(3)   *I got me a servant at Harwich* (Defoe, 1724, cited in Visser, 1963: 630)

4   use of *you was* for singular and *you were* for plural (in the eighteenth century at least).

Some of these may have stabilized in one or another variety of world Englishes, as I suggest in sections 4 and 5. I now turn to less standard superstratal input in the periods of exploration and colonization.

3   Sailors

Bailey and Maynor (1988) carried out a survey of "Ship English," as recorded in the logs of the British Navy between 1631 and 1730, with a view to ascertaining which features of New World Creoles may be attributable to this sociolect. As many of the sailors, including many captains and masters, were not well educated, their written norms do not disguise their speech norms to a very great extent. A fair picture of this sociolect thus emerges. Ship English may not have been an entirely autonomous, monolithic, or stable variety: it must have drawn on non-standard English, regional dialects, and slang. Bailey and Maynor demonstrate how Ship English differed from the standard English of the times in respect of present-tense marking; forms of the verb *be*; past tenses of weak verbs and strong verbs; *a*-prefixing with participles; and so forth. The present tense for verbs used Ø, *-s* and *-th*, but the distribution of these was different from that in the contemporary standard. Bailey and Maynor (1988: 199) found that third-person singular forms are sometimes unmarked:

(4)   the Comondore [sic] who arrived here this Day and seem to be very well pleased.

More common is the occurrence of *-s* on other than third-person singular verbs:

(5)   . . . gross corall Racks [sic] which makes you ride with a short scope.

Such examples give pause for thought even for New English studies, as absence of -*s* is a frequently remarked-upon characteristic of some varieties. Cape Flats English (spoken by people formerly classified "coloured" in and around Cape Town) has a rule that allows -*Ø* for third-person singular verbs and -*s* for third-person plural. Was the inherent variability in the input a contributing factor? Clearly the shape of the superstrate needs to be studied carefully for specific New English varieties. Amongst Bailey and Maynor's examples is an intriguing use of *use to* in a combination with present tense *do* that is reminiscent of a construction in Singapore English:

(6)   in this bay vessels do use to stop for want of a wind.

The use of the present tense (habitual, according to Bailey and Maynor, 1988: 206) *do use* in (6) here implies 'they used to stop and still do'). In Singapore and Malaysia the form *use(d) to* also signifies past habitual tense extending into the present (i.e., non-completive):

(7)   My mother, she use to go to Pulau Tikus market [implying 'she still does so']. (Platt, Weber, and Ho, 1984: 71)

While I do not advocate that all such constructions are necessarily superstratal, I am suggesting caution for a less substratophile interpretation of New English variability.

4   Settlers and Traders

One researcher who does take a conservative view of the New Englishes is Jim Davy (2000). Davy argues that in New English studies it has become common to deduce, falsely, that deviation from modern Standard English is prima facie evidence of linguistic and/or "normic newness." In the field of lexis, he shows from careful use of the *Oxford English Dictionary* (*OED*) that features thought to be unique to parts of Africa have a long history in the UK. Alleged West Africanisms like *how now?*, *not so?*, *trinket* (for 'a precious thing, a jewel'), and *to move with a group* are recorded in the *OED* with British sources, from, respectively, *c*.1838–78, 1606–1978, 1533–1774, and 1697. Another apparent innovation in West African English, including Pidgin, is *beef* for 'cattle, head of cattle'. According to the *OED*, however, this usage was a part of British English up until the nineteenth century (sg. *beef*, pl. *beeves*, for 'any animal of the ox-kind').

Davy conjectures that some syntactic constructions reported as distinctively New English such as single comparatives (e.g., *than* for 'more than' as in *He values his car than his wife*) and use of *be* + *ing* with statives (*I am having a cold*) may turn out to have L1 trajectories, too. To this I would add the form wide-spread in sub-Saharan Africa *can be able*, which was once used by sixteenth- and seventeenth-century authors, including Thomas More, Shakespeare, Congreve, and Dryden (see Visser, 1969: 1738):

(8)   . . . nor al the good words in the world . . . can be able to profyte the man. (Sir Thomas More, 1534)

In order to establish such superstratal continuity convincingly, features must be shown to emanate from the right speakers at the right time. In this vein, Mesthrie and West (1995) undertook a survey of settler English of South Africa of the 1820s, focusing on unpublished archival letters written by new settlers to the governors. As was common, people leaving Britain for the colonies were largely of working-class origins. Their handwriting itself some-times gives a clear indication of their unfamiliarity with the practice of writing; but since problems in the new colony were pressing, they felt the urgency of committing their thoughts in writing to the governor. One such less-than-fully-literate settler (Jeremiah Goldswain, a sawyer from Bucking-hamshire) outdid everyone in keeping a detailed diary, which was eventually published in two volumes (Long, 1946/49). The archival materials give a fasci-nating view of language variation, including the existence of many features which did not survive the process of koineization in South Africa. But several did, including a few that have been mistakenly imputed to subsequent Afrikaans influence, e.g. the adjective with infinitive as in (9):

(9)   The leaves . . . quite capable to withstand even the severest frost.

Mesthrie and West found an unexpectedly large amount of variation in settler speech in South Africa, in which a number of forms usually associated with L2 English were present.

1   Omissions. These included the following: determiners in certain contexts (10–13); prepositions after certain verbs (14–17); possessive *'s* (18–20); and *-s* on third-person singular verbs (21–2):

(10)   in order to procure [Ø] living for my wife and family.

(11)   most probably [Ø] great part of those potatoes are by this time unfit for use.

(12)   this was [Ø] matter of fact.

(13)   could I be permitted here to receive the third of my deposit which [Ø] government proposed to be repaid me on landing.

(14)   He promised him leave to go to Cape Town to complain [Ø] me [Ø] his Excellency.

(15) relative to our colonial passes which were sent from your office [Ø] Cape Town to Grahamstown. [in]

(16) and that the finding [Ø] personal security may not be required. [of]

(17) But on attending at the office this morning I learn with much regret [Ø] your indisposition. [of]

(18) at the Government expence . . .

(19) on hearing of your Lordship design to visit the frontier . . .

(20) which has totally exhausted your Memorialist finances.

(21) your Memorialist humbly hope your Excelency will be so kind . . .

(22) the total impossibility of procuring flour or bread . . . induce your Memorialists . . .

2   *Non-standard morphosyntactic forms.* Those that recur (variably) in the settler corpus are:

(a)   double negation;
(b)   variation in the use of complementizers, especially zero after verbs like *request, expect, state, conceive*, which require an overt complementizer in the standard today;
(c)   use of *is* and *was* with plural subjects; singular form *you was*;
(d)   *have* with third-person singular subjects and *has* with third-person plural subjects;
(e)   use of *-s* endings with verbs following a plural subject;
(f)   plural endings for non-count nouns like *progresses, evidences, sufferings, hopes*.

For further examples, see Mesthrie and West (1995: 127–9).

3   *The dative of advantage.* Amongst syntactic constructions that were once standard is the dative of advantage. This construction survives in Cape Flats English, where it is frequently misdiagnosed by purists as an incorrect use of the reflexive:

(23)   I'm gonna buy me a car.

This construction (also known as the ethical dative in Middle English studies) implies that the action expressed by the verb accrues some advantage to the subject (which was historically in the dative case). Although many of the sentences appear to admit a reinforcive reflexive nuance, this is not always the case, as (24) suggests in another context (L1 Appalachian English):

(24)   I'm gonna write me a letter to my cousin Tom. (Christian, 1991: 16)

Here the writing of the letter accrues some advantage (like personal satisfaction) to the subject: the reflexive interpretation *I'm gonna write myself a letter to my cousin Tom* is inadmissible. Though the dative of advantage is stigmatized today, it was once standard. It was brought to South Africa by a large number of settlers (Mesthrie and West, 1995), who frequently wrote lines like the one in (25) in their reports to the Governor in Cape Town:

(25)   ... your memorialist then built him a house on a spot of Ground. (Mesthrie and West, 1995: 124)

Interestingly, this construction was soon lost in settler speech as people rose in the social world in South Africa, especially after the capital accumulation consequent on the precious metals boom of the 1860s onwards. But before it did so, it stabilized in one L2 variety of the country. A challenge to world Englishes studies is to ascertain why certain superstratal features stabilized in some territories but not others. Is there a reversal of Andersen's 'transfer to somewhere' principle? In reversing this principle to account for retentions like that of the dative of advantage, one might conjecture whether a superstratal feature being jettisoned in the standard will survive better if there is some reinforcement in a prominent substrate language.

In factoring regional dialects into the superstrate, especial attention ought to be paid to varieties like Scots and Irish English. The Scots were influential as schoolteachers in many colonies, whilst the Irish often occupied a lower status as indentured laborers working side-by-side with locals or imported slaves, especially (but not exclusively) in New World contexts – see Rickford (1986: 251). The diffusion of features like *youse* (plural of 'you') in Cape Flats and other Englishes (in the US and Australia) occurred from Irish English. Scottish English is a possible source for items like *to fright for* ('to be afraid of') and *mines* ('mine') in SAIE.

5   Missionaries

Missionaries were a significant presence in most colonies and formed an important linguistic link as introducers of Western education and as early recorders of indigenous languages. As there have been few studies of their own varieties, the default assumption is that they were speakers or proponents of standard English. Mesthrie (1996) shows that, for at least one colony, this assumption is unwarranted for the period when English was first introduced. In the Cape Colony, South Africa, British rule was established first in 1795 and then again in 1806. Missionary and army activity preceded the arrival of a British civilian element by a good 20 years. The first missionaries from the London Missionary Society (LMS) were sent over in 1799 with the aim of converting the local people and introducing Christian and Western concepts via education. What the missionaries lacked in numbers they made up in amount of contact with, influence over, and interest in the local populace ("Hottentots" in the western Cape, Xhosa in the eastern Cape). A survey of the unpublished letters and journals of the first generation of missionaries reveals a surprising number of them to be continental Europeans with little knowledge of English or working-class L1 English speakers with little familiarity with the conventions of literacy and standard English. As an example of the first group, (26) is the opening sentence in the journal of Revd Kayser (born in Saxony, 1800), addressed to his employers at the LMS:

(26)   I hope that you my universal letter, dated the 22nd of June, which our safe arrival in Capetown mentioned, with the extract of my diary, which I the 6th of August too Mr. Beck who embarked with the Ferrie for London delivered have, in safely have recieved. (October 12, 1827)

Clearly Kayser himself was an interlanguage English user who, at the time of his arrival, was so unsure of his English as to resort to a literal translation from his mother tongue (German) in his written English. Although his journals give an indication of improvement in English, he cannot really be said to have mastered it. Yet he started a school for Xhosa children and was its English teacher. (This, from the pupils' perspective, gives a new twist to the term "comprehensible input"!)[1] Kayser was only a slight exception; there were other Dutch and German missionaries laboring in the Cape at this time, whose English varied from mid-interlanguage to close to the TL. Surprisingly, some *English* missionaries also felt uncomfortable in writing English. Missionary work was not always dictated by other-worldly concerns alone. For some, it was a source of employment and an avenue for a better life overseas than as a craftsman with little education in England (Warren, 1967: 11–12). Revd Ayliff, for example, who originally came over as a settler, kept a diary which has been described by its editors, Hewson and van der Riet (1963: 9), as containing "errors in grammar, spelling and punctuation on almost every page, and the use of clichés . . ." Whilst this characterization describes his lack of literacy and literary skills, his diary reveals a great deal of variation between standard and non-standard forms of concord (*was* versus *were*), prepositions, relative pronouns and the like:

(27)   What have I done this last year what have I done doesn't amount to nothing. Can only speak a few words of Dutch instead of being a sufficient master to speak it with Freedom? (Ayliff, 1823, cited in Mesthrie, 1996: 150)

The average English missionary's skill in his native language was superior to that of Ayliff, yet he was not alone in being uncomfortable in the grammatical and discourse conventions of the standard form of the language. It is not yet known whether South Africa's mission field was exceptional in this regard, and if so, why that should be. Preliminary investigation of the repertoires of missionaries elsewhere suggests that in India, whilst some English missionaries were of the working class, this was not widespread (Piggin, c.1984: 34). Of 550 missionaries based in India in the period 1789–1859, Piggin lists 114 as being of the working class (c.1984: 37); on the other hand, he mentions 88 as skilled artisans, mechanics, shop assistants, laborers, etc.:

> The teachers who became missionaries in India then, were drawn from the better educated, professionally conscious, ranks of teachers. Only a few were like Joseph Fletcher who had yet to discover punctuation.

For West Africa, Moorhouse (1973: 324) draws an engaging picture of linguistic diversity in the superstrate, citing a letter from Bishop Towzer:

> "There was Kelleway," he [= Bishop Towzer] wrote home to his sister, "teaching Devonshire of the broadest kind, Sivill the most undoubted Lincolnshire, and Adams indulging in low cockney slang where 'grub' stands habitually for 'food' and 'kid' for 'child.' The effect was that the boys who heard all this jargon were naturally puzzled and, with the exception of a few such sentences like 'O, my Eye' and the like made but a small advance in speaking English."

Such dialect phonology is sometimes claimed to have passed on to the emergent local dialects of English, though it is not clear that they could have been widespread or long-lasting within the "pool of variants." Similar suggestions of dialect input are given by Kirk-Greene (1971) concerning West Africa, and Alexander Kerr (1968), the first principal of Fort Hare College for Black people in South Africa:

> There is ... scope for research into how enduring is the effect of the regional accent of the English teacher on the West African student. Can the trained listener perceive traces of the long line of German and Swiss teachers of English in Ghana and Nigeria? For how long will so many of the Northern Nigerian secretarial grade speak with a Glaswegian intonation acquired from their sole instructor for eleven years? Now comes a new influence. This is the steady flow of American Peace Corps teachers to West African schools, over a thousand in the past few years. (Kirk-Greene, 1971: 129)

> Even the English was variegated according to the school or missionary institution the students had attended. For one could easily distinguish those who had been educated in Presbyterian from those in Anglican or Methodist schools and also from those who had been trained in a French or German environment. The broad vowels and the trilled "r"s of the Scottish missionaries raised no difficulties for me, and when I overheard one of the students reciting "Frriends, Rromans, Countrrymen, lend me your earrs" I was uncertain whether he was "taking me off" or was attempting to speak that brand of English most recently introduced! (Kerr, 1968: 51; cited by Magura, 1984: 56)

Schmied (1991: 11) is more cautious in suggesting that "both the missionaries in the West and the settlers in the South still looked upon England as their model in matters pertaining to the language standard (although most of them did not speak Standard English themselves)." Despite the extreme variability, the missionaries' influence must have been considerable, as they were the ones who converted the locals to Christianity and introduced the use of English. In Mesthrie (1999) I argue that the survival of unstressed *do* in Cape Flats English is most likely to be due to the influence of the continental European missionaries, who used it not only in their preaching styles based on the King James Bible (as in (30)), but in their letters and journals, too:

(28) We did go to the beach yesterday. (contemporary Cape Flats English)

(29) But some did wait till I had finished. (Revd Kayser, 1833)

(30) And they did beat the gold into thin plates. (Exodus 39: 14; King James Bible)

Although unstressed *do* was once standard, it waned in the standard variety from the eighteenth century onwards. It does not occur in the settler corpus of the 1820s, though a more formal perlocutionary legal or affective *do* is used as part of the written style as in *I do declare in the most solemn manner that . . .* The semantics of unstressed *do* in the missionaries' correspondence, on the other hand (highlighting a salient or new VP activity), fits very well with present-day New English norms on the Cape Flats. A reinforcing effect may well be from Afrikaans substrate (McCormick, 1995; Mesthrie, 1999).

6 Soldiers

Among the earliest teachers and propagators of English in the colonies were soldiers. Shivachi (1999) discusses the significance of the King's African Rifles in disseminating a knowledge of English in East Africa in the early twentieth century. In an early attempt to provide education to Indians on some sugar estates in nineteenth-century Natal, discharged soldiers from the Indian army were recruited, since they had acquired some knowledge of an Indian language. This project was soon abandoned, for, as the Superintendent's report of 1880 put it, "their conduct was not such as to command the respect of those among whom their work lay" (Brain, 1983: 205). The role of soldiers as teachers and the status of colonial soldiers' English as a sociolect have still to be investigated. The Indian Army, composed largely of battalions drawing on Hindus, Sikhs, and Muslims from various regions, was involved in the initial conquests that led to the colonization of many South Asian territories such as Malaysia, Burma, etc. What was their role in spreading a local South Asian variety of British English? What was the role of the famous Gurkha battalions in establishing English in their own country (Nepal) and adjacent territories where they fought? And finally, although the officers spoke Standard English (RP at the highest levels), what was the English of the British rank and file like?

7   Teachers

Finally, in characterizing the superstrate via its intermediaries, the teachers (British as well as local) should not be forgotten. An important intermediary of the superstrate was Indian English itself. As one of the earliest colonies and the jewel in the imperial crown, India often supplied English teachers when new Asian colonies were established. This applies at least to Sri Lanka (Kachru, 1983a), Malaysia, and Singapore (Platt and Weber, 1980). Perhaps some New English features were diffused or at least reinforced in this way, notably the following: *by-heart* as a verb (31–2); *alphabets* as a term for 'letters of the alphabet'; *further studies* for 'higher education'; and *tuition(s)* for 'paid tuition outside school hours':

(31)   He by-hearted his work.

(32)   By-hearting should be avoided.

Again, we await more careful sociohistorical work in this area.

8   Conclusion

In this chapter, I have argued that the historical input to individual varieties of world Englishes should not be ignored. This is not intended to diminish the importance of the classroom as the main provider of "input" and as the main site at which world Englishes were forged. There must have been some interplay between pupils' original interlanguages born in the classroom, the informal dialect used by L1 speakers, and the pidgin Englishes (or other "performance varieties") which appeared in many colonized territories. Uncovering information about these early stages and assessing their relative importance is one of the exciting challenges facing world Englishes studies.

NOTE

1   Kayser was assisted in his teaching by his wife, Christina Maria Boehre, and later by his daughter, Charlotte Margaret (born 1829).

REFERENCES

Andersen, Roger (1983) Transfer to somewhere. In *Language Transfer in Language Learning*. Edited by Susan Gass and Larry Selinker. Rowley, MA: Newbury House, pp. 177–201.

Bailey, Guy and Maynor, Natalie (1988) The shape of the superstrate: Morphosyntactic features of Ship English. *English World-Wide*, **9**, 193–212.

Baker, Philip (ed.) (1995) *From Contact to Creole and Beyond*. London: University of Westminster Press.

Brain, Joy B. (1983) *Christian Indians in Natal*. Cape Town: Oxford University Press.

Chew, Phyllis G. L. (1995) Lectal power in Singapore English. *World Englishes*, **14**(2), 163–80.

Christian, Donna (1991) The personal dative in Appalachian English. In *Dialects of English: Studies in Grammatical Variation*. Edited by Peter Trudgill and Jack K. Chambers. London: Longman, pp. 11–19.

Davy, Jim (2000) A conservative view of the New Englishes. Paper presented at the First International Conference on Linguistics in Southern Africa. University of Cape Town, January, pp. 12–14.

de Klerk, Vivian (2000) Language shift in Grahamstown: A case study of selected Xhosa speakers. *International Journal of the Sociology of Language*, **146**, 87–110.

Governors and Assistants of the East India Merchants (1603) *East Indian Trade*. London: Gregg Press.

Hewson, L. A. and van der Reit, F. G. (eds.) (1963) *The Journal of 'Harry Hastings,' Albany Settler*. Grahamstown: Grocott and Sherry.

Ho, Mian Lian and Platt, John T. (1993) *Dynamics of a Contact Continuum*. Oxford: Clarendon.

Kachru, Braj. B. (ed.) (1982) *The Other Tongue: English across Cultures*. Oxford: Pergamon. 2nd edition 1992, Urbana: University of Illinois Press.

Kachru, Braj B. (1983) *The Indianization of English*. New Delhi: Oxford University Press.

Kerr, Alexander (1968) *Fort Hare, 1915–1948: The Evolution of an African College*. Pietermaritzburg: Shuter and Shooter.

Kirk-Greene, Alexander (1971) The influence of West African Languages on English. In *The English Language in West Africa*. Edited by John Spencer. London: Longman. pp. 123–44.

Labov, William (1972) *Sociolinguistic Patterns*. Philadelphia: University of Pennsylvania Press.

Long, Una (ed.) (1946/49) *The Chronicle of Jeremiah Goldswain, Albany Settler 1820* (2 vols). Cape Town: Van Riebeeck Society.

Magura, Benjamin (1984) Style and Meaning in African English. Unpublished PhD dissertation, University of Illinois at Urbana-Champaign. Ann Arbor, MI: University Microfiche International.

McCormick, Kathleen K. (1995) Code-switching, code-mixing and convergence in Cape Town. In *Language and Social History: Studies in South African Sociolinguistics*. Edited by Rajend Mesthrie. Cape Town: David Philip, pp. 193–208.

Mesthrie, Rajend (1992) *English in Language Shift: The History, Structure and Sociolinguistics of South African Indian English*. Cambridge: Cambridge University Press.

Mesthrie, Rajend (1996) Imagint excusations: Missionary English in the nineteenth century Cape Colony, South Africa. *World Englishes*, **15**(2), 135–57.

Mesthrie, Rajend (1999) "Fifty ways to say 'I do'": Tracing the origins of unstressed *do* in Cape Flats English. *South African Journal of Linguistics*, **17**(1), 58–71.

Mesthrie, Rajend and West, Paula (1995) Towards a grammar of Proto South African English. *English World-Wide*, **16**(1), 105–33.

Moorhouse, Geoffrey (1973) *The Missionaries*. London: Eyre Methuen.

Mufwene, Salikoko (2001) *The Ecology of Language Evolution*. Cambridge: Cambridge University Press.

Okara, Gabriel (1970) *The Voice*. London: Heinemann.

Piggin, Stuart (*c.*1984) *Making Evangelical Missionaries 1789–1859*. Abingdon: Sutton Courtenay Press.

Platt, John T. (1975) The Singapore English speech continuum and its basilect "Singlish" as a creoloid. *Anthropological Linguistics*, **17**(7), 363–74.

Platt, John T. and Weber, Heidi (1980) *English in Singapore and Malaysia*. Kuala Lumpur: Oxford University Press.

Platt, John T., Weber, Heidi, and Ho, Mian Lian (1984) *The New Englishes*. London: Routledge.

Rao, Raja (1938) *Kanthapura*. London: George Allen and Unwin.

Rickford, John R. (1986) Social contact and linguistic diffusion. *Language*, **62**(2), 245–89.

Saussure, Ferdinand de (1966) *Course in General Linguistics*. (Edited by Charles Bally and Albert Sechehaye; translated by Wade Baskin.) New York: McGraw-Hill.

Schmied, Josef (1991) *English in Africa: An Introduction*. London: Longman.

Shivachi, Caleb (1999) A Case Study in Language Contact: English, KiSwahili and Luhyia amongst the Luhyia people of Kenya. Unpublished PhD dissertation, University of Cape Town.

Sharma, Devyani (2002) Structural and Social Constraints on Non-Native Varieties of English. Unpublished PhD dissertation, Department of Linguistics, Stanford University.

Visser, F. Th. (1963) *An Historical Syntax of the English Language. Part I: Syntactical Units with One Verb*. Leiden: Brill.

Visser, F. Th. (1969) *An Historical Syntax of the English Language. Part III 1st Half: Syntactical Units with Two Verbs*. Leiden: Brill.

Warren, Max (1967) *Social History and Christian Mission*. London: SCM Press.

FURTHER READING

Appel, Rene and Muysken, Pieter (1987) *Language Contact and Bilingualism*. London: Edward Arnold.

Myers-Scotton, Carol (2002) *Contact Linguistics: Bilingual Encounters and Grammatical Outcomes*. New York: Oxford University Press.

Winford, Donald (2003) *An Introduction to Contact Linguistics*. Malden, MA: Blackwell.

17 Varieties of World Englishes

KINGSLEY BOLTON

1 Introduction

The concepts of language variety and variation lie at the heart of the world Englishes enterprise, not least because many researchers in this field have identified their interests as the study of "varieties of English," "localized varieties of English," "non-native varieties of English," "second-language varieties of English," and "new varieties of English." The issue of linguistic variety is also central to both traditional dialectology and contemporary linguistics, where it is often subsumed into the study of language variation and change.

The notion of world Englishes, in its turn, may be seen as having both a wider and narrower application. The wider application of the concept subsumes very many different approaches to the study of English worldwide (including varieties-based studies) ranging from the Celtic Englishes of Britain, through diverse varieties in the USA, Australia, New Zealand, and Africa to English in Europe and Asia, and also involves the study of discourse and genre in those contexts where English is regarded as a second or foreign language. The narrower application of the term, however, refers to schools of thought closely associated with the Kachruvian approach, many of which are discussed in the other chapters to this volume. Elsewhere (see Chapter 15), I note that research on world Englishes in the wider sense includes at least a dozen distinct approaches, including those of English studies, corpus linguistics, the sociology of language, features-based and dialectological studies, pidgin and creole research, Kachruvian linguistics, lexicographical approaches, popularizer accounts, critical linguistics, and futurological approaches.

In this context, the use of the term "Englishes" consciously emphasizes the autonomy and plurality of English languages worldwide, whereas the phrase "varieties of English" suggests the heteronomy of such varieties to the common core of "English." The "double-voicedness" of such nomenclature (English vs. Englishes) resonates with the much-cited Bahktinian distinction between "centrifugal" and "centripetal" forces in language change. Leaving such tensions aside to begin with, I start by discussing the notion of "variety" within the context of world Englishes, and then attempt to unravel discussions of the wider theoretical context in the later sections of the chapter.

2   Language Varieties and Varieties of English

At first glance, the concept of "varieties" in this context seems useful and unproblematic, as "variety" in the singular is typically defined as a neutral label applicable to many different types of language use, as may be seen in a number of definitions of the term:

> A term used in SOCIOLINGUISTICS and STYLISTICS to refer to any SYSTEM of LINGUISTIC EXPRESSION whose use is governed by SITUATIONAL VARIABLES. In some cases, the situational DISTINCTIVENESS of the LANGUAGE may be easily stated, as in many regional and occupational varieties (e.g., London English, religious English); in other cases, as in studies of social class, the varieties are more difficult to define, involving the intersection of several variables (e.g., sex, age, occupation). Several classifications of language varieties have been proposed, involving such terms as DIALECT, REGISTER, MEDIUM and FIELD. (Crystal, 1997: 408)

> A neutral term used to refer to any kind of language – a *dialect, accent, sociolect, style* or *register* – that a linguist happens to want to discuss as a separate entity for some particular purpose. Such a variety can be very general, such as "American English," or very specific, such as "the lower working-class dialect of the Lower East Side of New York City." (Trudgill, 2003: 139–40)

> We can use "variety" to mean a language, a dialect, an idiolect or an accent; it is a term which encompasses all of these. The term "variety" is an academic term used for any kind of language production, whether we are viewing it as being determined by region, by gender, by social class, by age or by our own inimitable individual characteristics. (Bauer, 2003: 4)

Randolph Quirk in *The Use of English* (1962), was one of the first in the contemporary period to discuss "varieties" of English with reference to the description of English "standards" worldwide. In this early work, Quirk made a plea for linguistic tolerance, arguing that:

> English is not the prerogative or "possession" of the English . . . Acknowledging this must – as a corollary – involve our questioning the propriety of claiming that the English of one area is more "correct" than the English of another. Certainly, we must realise that there is no single "correct" English, and no single *standard* of correctness. (Quirk, 1962: 17–18)[1]

Similar arguments were put forward in the same era by Halliday, McIntosh, and Strevens (1964), who discussed varieties of English in a range of decolonizing contexts. During the colonial era, they noted, "it seemed totally obvious and immutable that the form of English used by professional people in England was the only conceivable model for use in education overseas" (1964: 292). But they argued that by the 1960s an important shift had occurred and that:

> English is no longer the possession of the British, or even the British and the Americans, but ... exists in an increasingly large number of different varieties ... But the most important development of all is seen in the emergence of varieties that are identified with and are specific to particular countries from among the former British colonies. In West Africa, in the West Indies, and in Pakistan and India ... it is no longer accepted by the majority that the English of England, with RP as its accent, are the only possible models of English to be set before the young. (pp. 293–4)

They then went on to discuss the criteria for judging the use of a particular variety as a teaching model, suggesting that there are two major considerations: first, that it is used by a reasonably large number of educated people; and, second, that it is mutually intelligible with other varieties used by educated speakers from other societies. Here they note that "to speak like an Englishman" is by no means the only or obvious target for the foreign learner" (p. 296). Halliday subsequently adopted a varieties framework in a number of his later writings, including Halliday and Hasan (1989) which explores the dichotomy between "dialectal varieties" (dialects) and "diatypic varieties" (registers). Strevens also maintained a strong interest in varieties of English worldwide, arguing for a recognition of "the 'Englishes' which constitute the English language" (Strevens, 1980: 90).

Another important strand that contributed to the studies of "varieties" came out of domestic sociolinguistics. In 1979, Hughes and Trudgill published a volume entitled *English Accents and Dialects* that described varieties of English in the United Kingdom. This was then followed by Trudgill and Hannah's *International English*, which focused on varieties of "standard English" worldwide. In the first edition (1982), these included Australian, New Zealand, South African, Welsh, North American, Scottish, Irish, West Indian, West African, and Indian English. The third edition (1994) added an expanded section on creoles, as well as descriptions of Singapore and Philippine English. The sections dealing with "Inner-Circle" varieties predominate, with some one hundred pages in the latest edition allocated to "native-speaker" varieties, and thirty devoted to creoles and second-language varieties. Cheshire's (1991) *English around the World* extended this features-based approach to include variationist perspectives of the Labovian approach.

3   The Three Circles of Kachru

One particular construct in the Kachruvian paradigm that has been both influential and controversial has been the modeling of English worldwide in terms of the "Three Circles of English" (the "Inner," "Outer," and "Expanding" Circles). The Three Circles model was first published in a 1985 book chapter that came out of a conference held to mark the fiftieth anniversary of the British Council (Kachru, 1985). In this paper, Kachru was concerned to elucidate the sociolinguistics of English "in its international context" with particular reference to postcolonial societies. Here, the model was presented as a "digression" to preface the discussion of issues related to standardization, codification, and linguistic creativity.

The Circles model was intended to represent (1) the *types of spread* of English worldwide, (2) the *patterns of acquisition*, and (3) the *functional domains* in which English is used internationally. The *Inner* Circle of the model referred to those societies where English is the "primary language," i.e., the USA, the UK, Canada, Australia, and New Zealand. The *Outer* Circle was conceived as representing postcolonial Anglophonic contexts, a numerically large and diverse speech community, including such African and Asian societies as Nigeria, Zambia, India, and Singapore. Despite such diversity, the Outer-Circle communities share a number of characteristics, so that typically English is only one of the community languages in what are clearly multilingual societies; and English in such societies usually achieves some degree of official recognition as an official, co-official, legal, or educational language. At the functional level, English is utilized in "un-English cultural contexts," and is used in a very wide range of domains both as an intranational and an international language, and as a language of literary creativity and expression:

> In other words, English has an extended functional *range* in a variety of social, educational, administrative, and literary domains. It also has acquired great *depth* in terms of users at different levels of society. As a result, there is significant variation within such institutionalized varieties. (Kachru, 1985: 13; see also Kachru, 2005: 211–20)

The *Expanding* Circle is defined as comprising those areas where English is an "international language" and traditionally regarded as societies learning English as a Foreign Language (EFL). Nations in the Expanding Circle at this time thus include China, Greece, Indonesia, Israel, Japan, Korea, Saudi Arabia, Taiwan, and the USSR (i.e., the former Soviet Union).

Kachru then went on to note that English was spreading rapidly in non-Western countries, as an "additional language" and "alternative language" in multilingual societies, in response to the demands of modernization and technology, as well as by other sociopolitical and sociolinguistic dynamics. In addition, whereas Inner-Circle societies largely shared common cultural assumptions and similar political systems, the cultural contexts of the other two Circles included such diverse ideologies as Hinduism, Islam, Marxism, and Communism, giving English the potential for "a unique cultural pluralism, and a linguistic heterogeneity and diversity which are unrecorded to this extent in human history" (p. 14).

In a number of other writings, Kachru has expanded on the notions of the "range" and "depth" of English in the Outer and Expanding Circles, establishing a dichotomy between "genetic nativeness" versus "functional nativeness" (Kachru, 1998). Here *range* refers to the functional repertoire of the language in such domains as government, law, business, family, friends, etc.; *depth*, on the other hand, refers to the uses of English available to people at different levels of society, ranging from the elites of business and the professions to lower-level workers, shopkeepers, taxi drivers, etc. Such issues of depth also influence the lectal range of speakers, from basilectal varieties through to the acrolect. A second distinction is that between the *norm-providing* mechanisms of the Inner Circle (including grammars, textbooks, etc.) and the *norm-dependent* (or "norm-accepting") responses of the Expanding-Circle societies, such as China, Japan, etc. The situation in Outer-Circle societies is typically more complex, with a range of possible responses, including efforts to establish local norms. A number of Outer-Circle societies are thus "norm-developing," as in India and the Philippines.

Kachru's conception of the Three Circles has only been one part of his theorization of this field, but it has proved immensely influential. Nevertheless, despite its obvious robustness and utility, some critics have attempted to critique this model on the grounds that it favors standard and "national" varieties, ignores "grey areas," and simplifies discussion of linguistic diversity (Jenkins, 2003: 17–18). Others have argued in favor of the recognition of supranational varieties, including Modiano (1999, and this volume) who has proposed the model of English as an International Language (EIL), which features "centripetal" Circles and bases its description on proficient use of the language rather than the geographical provenance of speakers. A number of these critiques seem misdirected, however, given that Kachru himself anticipated a number of such points 20 years ago, when at the outset he noted that:

> The Outer Circle and the Expanding Circle cannot be viewed as clearly demarcated from each other; they have several shared characteristics, and the status of English in the language policies of such countries changes from time to time. What is an ESL region at one time may become an EFL region at another time or vice versa. (Kachru, 1985: 13–14)

More importantly, such critiques tend to miss the fact that the Circles concept is essentially intended as a historical model that conceptualizes the chronology of the diasporic origins of world Englishes. These diasporas were basically of two types: the first diaspora occurred with transportation of English to settler colonies in Australia, North America, and New Zealand; and the second occurred in British (and occasionally American) administrative colonies in around the globe, and especially in Africa and Asia. These two diasporas created very distinct colonial histories, not least because of the very different demographics of race involved (if, for example, we compare the USA with India). Nevertheless, a number of issues traverse the two diasporic experiences, including questions relating to codification, standardization, and educational norms (Y. Kachru and Nelson, 2006).

It might also be noted that the exponential spread of English since 1985 has continued over the last two decades in ways not entirely anticipated at that earlier date. Today, a list of the major ten English-knowing societies in the world would include not only India but also China (both with estimated populations of English speakers at around 200–300 million). Other Asian societies such as the Philippines (around 52 million speakers) and Japan (around 40 million) are also more visible than in the past; although the spread of English in such societies through education also raises many issues concerning acquisition and "knowing-ness" that are redefining traditional notions of acquisition and proficiency.

4   The Inner-Circle Diaspora

Historically, the transportation of the two external diasporas of English mentioned above were preceded by the spread of English throughout the British Isles to Wales, Scotland, and Ireland, which each have their own particular historics of language contact. In the case of Wales, the political dominance of England was established by two Acts of Union in 1536 and 1542, when Welsh laws and customs were abolished and the English language gained preeminence in law and administration. English was also spread by the establishment of English-speaking townships, and the promotion of English in education. In the late eighteenth century, most of the country was monolingual Welsh, but widespread industrialization and urbanization in the nineteenth century hastened the spread of English. By 1921, 63 percent of Welsh people were monolingual in English, and by 1981 that had risen to around 80 percent of the population (Thomas, 1994: 103). Today, despite its somewhat low academic prestige in Wales (and the ongoing revival of the Welsh language), Welsh English as a distinct variety of the language is being studied by a number of linguists (Coupland and Thomas, 1990; Penhallurick, 1993).

The history of Scottish English is inextricably linked to that of "Scots," whose history as an autonomous Germanic language dates from 1100. While its contemporary usage is restricted to a minority of the rural population, Scots is still seen as forming "the substratum of general English in Scotland" (Aitken, 1992: 899). Scots achieved its greatest prominence in the fifteenth and early sixteenth centuries, but after the Act of Union in 1603, a decline in its prestige and use followed. Throughout the nineteenth century English rapidly gained ground through the expansion of education. Scots gradually lost the status of an autonomous language, and its position as a regional standard was eventually supplanted by that of "Scottish Standard English," "a compromise between London standard English and Scots" (McClure, 1994: 79).

The earliest record of the use of English in Ireland dates from 1250, but English only began to spread significantly after the establishment of Ulster plantation in 1607, which introduced Scots English onto the island. By the early nineteenth century, language shift in Ireland toward English was well underway, a process that has continued to the present with only 3 percent of the population in 1983 claiming a "native-speaker" ability in Irish Gaelic (Kallen, 1994). McArthur currently identifies a range of Irish varieties, including *Hiberno-English*, *Irish English*, and *Ulster English* (2002: 117; see Chapters 2 and 3 in this volume).

The first major variety of English to establish itself outside the British Isles was American English. The earliest American colonies included Jamestown, Virginia (1607) and Plymouth, Massachusetts (1620). Over the following 150 years, 13 colonies emerged along the eastern seaboard, where the majority of settlers were English speakers from various parts of Britain and Ulster. After the United States achieved independence, Noah Webster (1754–1843) gave voice to a brand of linguistic patriotism in his treatise, *Dissertations on the English Language* in 1789, which was followed by his dictionary in 1828. By the nineteenth century, debates on the autonomy of American English had begun. In this era, substantial discussion focused on the merits of "Americanisms" versus standard British usage, while other topics included questions of dialectology, language standardization, immigration, and linguistic borrowings from such sources as Dutch, German, Italian, Yiddish (Davis, 2003). Shortly after World War I, H. L. Mencken published *The American Language* ([1919] 1921), which marked an important stage in the codification of the US variety of English. The study of Canadian English as a distinct system occurred somewhat later (Clarke, 1993).

The other major diasporic varieties of the Inner Circle include Australian English, New Zealand English, and South African English. The first Australian settlers were largely convicts who began to arrive from 1788. By 1840, around 130,000 prisoners had been transported to prisons in Australia from Britain. Most of these early settlers came from London, the Midlands, and Ireland. From the 1840s, they were supplemented by large numbers of "free settlers" who came as farmers and miners. Until 1947, the vast majority of the population were white and of British origin. Today, around 75 percent of Australians are "Anglo-Celtic," 19 percent "other European," and 5 percent Asian, with the aboriginal population accounting for only 1 percent of the total (McArthur, 1992). The British settlement of New Zealand began in 1792 with fishing stations. At first, such settlements were administered from New South Wales. New Zealand became an independent colony in 1840, and after that date many farming settlers established themselves in the country. British settlements in South Africa date from around 1820 in Port Elizabeth. Today, English is the first language of around 10 percent of the population, which includes white people, South Asians, and colored or mixed-race populations (McArthur, 2002: 287–8).

According to Trudgill (2004), the core linguistic characteristics of such Inner-Circle colonial varieties arose out of processes of dialect contact, dialect mixture, and new-dialect formation:

> The Southern Hemisphere Englishes, like colonial varieties of the English language just mentioned, are new and distinctive varieties of the English language which arose as a result of dialect contact, dialect mixture and new-dialect formation. The most important ingredients in the mixture that was to lead the development of these new forms of English were the dialects and accents of the language brought with them by native speakers of English. In Australia, South Africa, New Zealand, and the Falklands, the contact was almost entirely between varieties of English from the British Isles. (Trudgill, 2004: 13)

In the case of Australian English, his argument is that the origins of this variety can be found in the dialects of London, and those of such counties as Essex, Suffolk, Cambridgeshire, Norfolk, etc., to the northeast of the capital. It is likely that Australian English was formed in the speech of those born between 1790 and 1840, and emerged as a "fully-fledged" variety in the speech of children by around 1854. Trudgill estimates that in New Zealand approximately 50 percent of early immigrants were from England, 27 percent from Scotland, and 23 percent from Ireland, that a distinct variety of New Zealand English first developed in the period after 1840, and that by 1905 one finds the first adolescent speakers of New Zealand English. Early South African immigrants came from London, Ireland, Lancashire, Yorkshire, and Scotland. Similarly, South African English was formed by those born between 1820 and 1870, emerging as a "focused variety" by 1885 (2004: 23–4).

5   The Outer-Circle Diaspora

Chronologically, the Englishes and English-based creoles of the Caribbean date from the mid-seventeenth century, in for example Barbados (1627), Jamaica (1655), and Belize (1683; see Chapter 13 in this volume). At around the same time, a British presence also began to be felt in Asia, when British trading posts were established in India from the seventeenth century onwards. Somewhat later, British Malaya developed as a federation of protectorates, from 1786–1896; Singapore became established as a trading port from 1819; and Hong Kong became a crown colony from 1842 onwards. Elsewhere in Asia, the Philippines became a colony of the USA, when Spanish power was overthrown in 1898. Anglophone British colonies in East and West Africa were mainly established somewhat later, from the nineteenth century onwards. These included Gambia (1843), Nigeria (1861), Uganda (1893), Kenya (1920), and present-day Tanzania (1890), Malawi (1907), and Zimbabwe (1923).[2]

Historically, the Outer-Circle diaspora of English has raised a range of issues rather distinct from those of the Inner-Circle societies such as North America and the Southern Hemisphere Englishes of Australia, New Zealand, and South Africa. In the not-so-distant colonial past, such settler colonies were tied to the mother country through close and explicit notions of racial, linguistic, and cultural kinship. As early as 1880, the President of the Statistical

Society of Great Britain was hailing the triumph of the "English speaking race" in North America and elsewhere:

> Of all Western peoples ours is already the most numerous; and when we con-
> template the further spread of the English language over North America
> and Australia, and the habits of order, instincts of self-government, and love
> of liberty which are the inborn characteristics of the Anglo-Saxon race . . . we
> may feel confidence in the future. (Caird, 1880: 571)

In similar vein, at what was arguably close to the height of empire, Charles Wentworth Dilke (1843–1911) published the eighth edition of *Greater Britain* (1885), a personalized account of travels through America, Australia, New Zealand, and a number of Britain's Asian colonies. In Dilke's writing, notions of racial competition and kinship overlap with linguistic commentary, and he draws a basic distinction between the successfully "extirpating" Anglo-Saxon populations of the settler colonies, and those elsewhere in the empire. In his vision of "Greater Britain," the British and Americans are brothers, because (despite the superficial "Latinization" of the English in the USA), "the true moral of America is the vigour of the English race," as "the English in America are absorbing the Germans and the Celts, destroying the Red Indians and checking the advance of the Chinese" (Dilke, 1885: 217). In spite of the immigration of the Germans and Irish and others, Dilke also sees English virtues and the English language at the core of American achievement:

> America is becoming, not English merely, but world-embracing in the variety of
> its type; and, as the English element has given the language and the history to
> that land, America offers the English race the moral dictatorship of the globe, by
> ruling mankind through Saxon institutions and the English tongue. Through
> America England is speaking to the world. (Dilke, 1885: 224)

Elsewhere, Dilke goes on to mention the "thriving" Australian colonies, where "[a] literature is springing up," and a "national character is being grafted upon the good English stock" (p. 381). Although he expresses doubts about "the shape of the Australian mind," Dilke gives his approval to the "burly, bearded, strapping fellows" of New Zealand, who are "physically the perfection of the English race" (p. 289).

The non-settler colonies of Asia and Africa presented a very different set of circumstances. In India, for example, Dilke saw a civilization in decline, blighted by the caste system, poverty, and slavery. In reforming India, he advocated the teaching of English to the general population, arguing that the reform of the "servile condition of the native women" as well as the legal system necessitated such action, and that ultimately the spread of English was necessary for eventual self-rule, asserting that:

> So long as the natives remain ignorant of the English tongue, they remain ignor-
> ant of all the civilization of our time – ignorant alike of political and physical

science, of philosophy and true learning ... English, as the tongue of the ruling race, has the vast advantage that its acquisition by the Hindoos will soon place the government of India in native hands, and thus, gradually relieving us of an almost intolerable burthen will civilize and set free the people of Hindostan. (Dilke, 1885: 224)

But for many imperial theorists, the spread of empire (or English) to non-Anglo-Saxon populations had obvious dangers, not least in the case of India. For example, Edward A. Freeman (1892), then Regius Professor of Modern History at Oxford, made it clear that his notion of the "English-speaking people" was essentially racially determined, and that not all subjects of "the Queen's dominions" qualified for membership:

The English-speaking people and the Queen's dominions are very far from being the same thing. The majority of the Queen's subjects are not English-speaking, and I fancy that the majority of the English-speaking people are not the Queen's subjects. A Confederation of the Queen's dominions, especially if it be called "Imperial," cannot shut out the "Empire" of India; and if that be let in, the European, white, Christian – however we choose to distinguish them – part of Her Majesty's subjects will be a small minority in the confederation. (Freeman, 1892: 46–7)

According to Freeman, then, a true federation of the English-speaking people "must leave out India" and "must take in the United States," although he seems to concede that it would also include "the Negroes" who "are certainly not English, but they are English-speaking" (1892: 46–7).

Brutt-Griffler, in her impressively researched (2002) study of British colonial language planning, argues tellingly that the development of policies for much of the time was a piecemeal and ad hoc affair, guided less by the desire to promote English through linguistic imperialism and more by the desire to run an empire "on the cheap" (Brutt-Griffler, 2002: 86). English-medium instruction was generally favored in Africa and Asia only to the extent that it fostered a locally recruited civil service, or, in some instances, locally trained clerks for commerce. The funding of mass education systems through English, on the American model in the Philippines, was never considered viable or desirable. In fact, Brutt-Griffler argues, the first attempt at establishing a unified policy did not take place until the Advisory Committee on Education in the Colonies met in 1923. The committee's commitment to vernacular education at this time was in essence "a policy of limiting the spread of English to what was minimally necessary to running a colonial empire" (2002: 105).

In many British colonies, too much education and too much English was seen as destabilizing and dangerous, and in many instances the colonial authorities actively sought to restrict access to English-medium schooling, so that the demand for English typically outstripped provision. In the later stages of empire, ideas of "liberty," "social justice," and "socialism" acquired through

Western education also served to gain support for the anti-colonial movement in India and elsewhere (McCully, 1935), leading Brutt-Griffler to claim that:

> Language thereby played a role in the anticolonial struggle that British colonial officials had never envisioned. It became integrally connected to resistance. English in both Asia and Africa began to develop into the common language of the anticolonial struggle, in effect turning the guns of colonial rule against it ... More than individual acts of resistance, in total this anticolonial language policy constituted a concerted drive for the societal acquisition of English. (Brutt-Griffler, 2002: 65)

It seems obvious then that there were basic and substantial differences between the two diasporas of English discussed above. The first external diaspora began in the early seventeenth century, and extended until the mid-nineteenth century, with the development of settler colonies in the United States, Canada, Australia, and New Zealand. This involved the "demographic" spread of English (Quirk, 1988), accompanied by the migration of substantial numbers of colonialists from Britain to such societies. In these new climes, the settlers established themselves as dominant populations (at times through genocide), and English as the "mother tongue" of the majority of the population. A somewhat different pattern developed in the administrative and commercial colonies of the Outer Circle in Asia and Africa, where indigenous languages survived, and bilingual English-using populations came into being. As Brutt-Griffler notes, "[t]he English language spread to Africa and Asia by political and economic means, not demographic ... English never became the language of industry and of the major agricultural districts; instead, it was the language primarily of the colonial administration" (Brutt-Griffler, 2002: 117). While this may have been true in many instances, it was, however, also the case that there were other settings (aside from formal education) for the spread of English, including, in the cases of pidgin and creole varieties, face-to-face interaction with sailors, traders, and plantation owners (Mufwene, 1994).

Whatever the dynamics of colonial Englishes, it seems clear that the most rapid spread of the language has occurred in the postcolonial era, as a consideration of recent demographics shows. In 1962, Quirk estimated the number of "native" speakers of English at around 250 million, compared with 100 million using English as a "second language"; by 1977, Fishman, Cooper, and Rosenbaum give the figure of 300 million for each group; but by 1995, Crystal is arguing that one could then identify 350 million native speakers, around 225 million second-language users, and around 550 million users of English as a foreign language. The overwhelming reason why English spread rapidly from the 1960s until the end of the century is that so many former Anglophone colonies adopted English for use in expanding educational systems during the postcolonial period. In addition, partly as the result of the economic and political power of the USA in the same period, English has also become the most widely taught foreign language in the school systems of Expanding-Circle regions and countries such as Europe, China, and Japan.

Significantly, it is also in the postcolonial period that recognition begins to be accorded to the "new Englishes" of Africa and Asia, so that discussions of varieties of African, Asian, and Caribbean Englishes develop from the 1960s onward, eventually contributing to the discourse of world Englishes and world literatures in English that emerge in the 1980s (Schneider, 2003). Nevertheless, as late as 1990 Quirk is still arguing against what he termed the "half-baked quackery" of the teaching of "varieties of English." Quirk distinguishes between "non-native varieties" (e.g., Indian English, Nigerian English, East African English, etc.) and "native varieties" (including American English, Australian English, British English, etc., as well as such dialects as New England English, Yorkshire English, etc.). In this context, he argues for a distinction between "non-institutionalized" varieties and those that are "institutionalized," in the sense of being fully defined and described, commenting that "[of] the latter, there are two: *American English* and *British English*; and there are one or two others with standards rather informally established, notably *Australian English*" (Quirk, 1990: 6).

The notion of "variety" here serves to bring us back to a consideration of the application of the term itself, and the ways in which linguists have attempted to deal with the concept of variation itself.

6   Varieties and Language Variation

Despite the widely-held acceptance of the term "variety" in sociolinguistics as a neutral, technical term for language description, in fact the label is somewhat indeterminately applied in practice. Hudson, for example, notes that, from a linguistic perspective, non-technical labels such as "languages," "dialects," or "styles" have little consistency, asserting that this leaves us only with the label of variety to refer to "a set of linguistic items with similar social distribution" (Hudson, 1996: 20–1).

After critically reviewing variety-based approaches to language, and the use of such terms as "dialects," "registers," "pidgins and creoles," Hudson registers "essentially negative conclusions" about the use of the term "variety" in sociolinguistics, noting that (1) the borders between varieties of the same type (e.g., one dialect from another) are often blurred; (2) similar problems exist concerning different types of varieties (e.g., languages vs. dialects). For Hudson, the solution thus is to avoid variety "as an analytical or theoretical concept and to focus instead on the individual linguistic item":

> For each item some kind of "social description" is needed, saying roughly who uses it and when: in some cases an item's social description will be unique, whereas in others it may be possible to generalize across a more or less large number of items. The nearest this approach comes to the concept of "variety" is in these sets of items with similar social descriptions, but their characteristics are rather different from those of varieties like languages and dialects. On the other

hand, it is still possible to use terms like "variety" and "language" in an informal way . . . without intending them to be taken seriously as theoretical constructs. (Hudson, 1996: 25–6)

Indeed, today it is noticeable that in many branches of variation study (and sociolinguistics in its most "linguistic" orientation), the inherent problems of such terms are often side-stepped. This is typically done through the adoption of methodologies that focus largely on an item-based approach to linguistic variation, whereby phonological and syntactic (and possibly lexical) variations are correlated against such social variables as age, sex, social class, social network, etc. Within modern urban dialectology, this often obviates the need to make generalized and extensive statements about the dialects of particular regions or localities, as the object of study is defined as a particular linguistic item, or set of items, at the levels of phonology and syntax (Chambers, Trudgill, and Schilling-Estes, 2002).

From a historical perspective, Chambers (1995) reviews the notion of language variation within linguistics, with reference to such sources as the Bible, Locke, Herder, and Jespersen. He then seeks to explain variation not only by reference to such socially embedded variables as social class and identity and such "natural" processes as patterns of regularization, but also by an appeal to language acquisition theory. His argument here is that the acquisition of standard languages requires the suppression of bioprogrammatic "primitive tendencies" toward innovation and variation, so that "we should expect features of the 'innate system' or the 'primitive tendencies' to be richly represented in vernaculars everywhere" (p. 247). Finally, he argues that the "underlying cause" of sociolinguistic variation is "the human instinct to establish and maintain social identity" (p. 250), thus, in sum, Chambers' position seems to appeal to both naturalistic and socially-constructed explanations.

Harris (1998) takes a critical view of the term "dialect," noting that the word, which is derived from the Greek *dialektos*, has a complicated history. *Dialektos* was defined by the Stoics "as an expression (*lexis*)" which is stamped on one people "ethnically and Hellenically" or as "an expression peculiar to some particular region" (Harris, 1998: 84). In examining a number of definitions of the term (as in Bloch, 1948; Crystal, 1985, etc.), Harris suggests that these are broadly of three types. First, there is the "continuum" concept, which involves the recognition of linguistic differences from one region to another. Second, there is the "relational dialect" concept, where "a dialect is conceived of as a particular subvariety of a language" and "a dialect is . . . defined in relation to what a language is." And third, there is the "aggregate dialect" concept which "envisages a dialect as constituted out of the sum total of the linguistic practice of a certain group of individuals" so that "you start off with individuals, and aggregate their linguistic behaviour into dialects" (pp. 86–7). Within modern linguistics, Harris explains, Saussurean theory accords an important role to dialects and subdialects as a unit of analysis:

> Any system of signs, in Saussure's view, had to be the property of a collectivity
> or community, *not* of an individual. So there had to be some level of social
> grouping at which the linguistic system existed; and this level must be, if
> not national, then regional, or even local. That is how and why the dialect
> concept comes to occupy such a crucial role in Saussurean theory. A dialect,
> whether it be of a region, or a locality, or a single village, represents, as it
> were, the basic level at which, in practice, linguistic diversity is reduced to zero.
> (Harris, 1998: 92)

He then argues that the "dialect myth" found in modern linguistics is based
on the supposition that "dialects," however identified, display the high degree of
"linguistic homogeneity" necessary to constitute a Saussurean system of signs,
a supposition easily falsifiable given the fluid nature of language variation.

In contrast, few if any attempts appear to have been made to locate the
adoption of the term "variety" within the discourses of linguistics, although a
cursory survey of the literature shows that the term was in use with reference
to language by the 1880s. For example, Whitney (1880) uses the term in its
modern sense when discussing the diversity of human language, noting that
"[t]he varieties of human speech are without number, and their differences
endless, both in kind and in degree" (pp. 327–8). Another reference to linguistic varieties at around this time is found in H. A. Strong's (1890) translation of Hermann Paul's *Prinzipien der Sprachgeschichte*, which, in one section,
discusses the borderlines between "dialectic varieties" (pp. 27–8), and later
even proceeds to mention the "centrifugal" and "centripetal" dynamics of
language (p. 34).

A much earlier provenance for the use of the term in an academic or scientific sense, however, was the discourse of evolution and natural science.
Darwin, in *On the Origin of Species*, discusses the use of the term "species,"
which he defines as "a set of individuals closely resembling each other," similar
in meaning to "the term variety," which "is given to less distinct and more
fluctuating forms," adding that "[t]he term variety, again, in comparison with
mere individual differences, is also applied arbitrarily, for convenience sake"
(Darwin, 1859: 52). However, further examination suggests that Darwin's use
of both these terms was influenced by the Linnaean taxonomy for biology.
This was established in the *Systema Naturae* (1758) of Carl Linnaeus (1707–78),
where *Varietas* (or "variety") was an individual subspecies within the system
of biological classification known as "the Linnean hierarchy," which in time
also adopted "family" as a unit of analysis (Maggenti, 1989). Around the same
time, Linnaeus also set out one of the earliest classifications of geographical
subspecies of humans (*Americanus Europaeus, Asiaticus*, and *Afer*), while his
contemporary, the Count de Bouffon published an essay entitled "Varieties of
the Human Species" (Marks, 1995).

By the time of Darwin, German comparative linguists such as Franz Bopp,
Jacob Grimm, and August Schleicher were seeking to establish genetic kinship
relationships between languages, and were maintaining that "[t]he kinship of

the different languages may consequently serve, so to speak, as a paradigmatic illustration of the origin of species, for those fields of inquiry which lack, for the present at least, any similar opportunities of observation" (Schleicher, [1869] 1983: 45). Schleicher's views were later challenged by Schuchardt ("the father of creole studies" – Holm, 1988) who advocated a view of language not "as a natural organism, but as social product" (Schuchardt, 1885: 33–5, cited in Seuren, 1998: 97). Whatever the epistemological problems in understanding the origin of the term "variety" in linguistics, the hypothesis that its provenance can be traced through Darwin to Linnaeus seems entirely plausible, given much other linguistic terminology was derived from the developing natural sciences and associated race theories of the nineteenth century (Bolton, 2000).

7   Varieties by Any Other Name

Languages like pidgins and creoles presented a number of problems for comparative linguists, including the notable challenge that such contact languages posed to the "family tree" model of languages associated with Schleicher. In particular, this raised the problem of placing "mixed languages" in such a scheme (Sebba, 1997). Historically, pidgins and creoles were regularly described as "vile jargon," "grotesque gibberish," "baby talk," and, more pointedly, "bastardized jargons" (Bolton, 2000). While modern linguists dismiss such lay opinions as biased and inaccurate, it is also the case that even the language of linguistics relies heavily on the vocabulary of evolution and race, as witnessed by the continuing use of such terms as *monogenesis, polygenesis,* and *hybridization* in contemporary creolistics.

Similar discourses have also permeated discussions of the Englishes of Outer-Circle societies in Africa and Asia. The first-diaspora varieties of America, Australia, and New Zealand have often been regarded (explicitly or implicitly) as branches of a "Greater British" family of English dialects organically and naturalistically related to each other and the wider Germanic family. The "new" Englishes of Asia and Africa have been less comfortably placed at the family table; not least because such varieties are used by speakers of non-Germanic ethnicities in complex multilingual settings and have often had contentious colonial histories. Tellingly, Mufwene (2001) argues that a subtle prejudice still expresses itself in the nomenclature of world Englishes and the use of such terms as "pidgins," "creoles," "non-native," and "indigenized" Englishes. He goes on to assert that, in reality:

> the naming practice of new Englishes has to do more with the racial identity of those who speak them than with how these varieties developed and the extent of their structural deviations . . . The legitimate offspring are roughly those varieties spoken typically by descendants of Europeans around the world, whereas the illegitimate ones are those spoken primarily by populations that have not fully descended from Europeans. (Mufwene, 2001: 107–8)

Throughout the twentieth century, the notion that there was only one variety of "Standard English" (or arguably two) was supported by a standard language ideology associated with traditional approaches to the history of English and an undeconstructed view of English studies in the academy as scholarship on a national language and literary tradition.

One major achievement of world Englishes in the last 30 years or so has been to challenge the previously inviolate authority of Inner-Circle societies in setting or judging the norms of usage in other English-using societies worldwide. In this context, the Circles model of Kachru has had a significant impact:

> Introduced at a time when the duopoly of American and British English was unquestioned and metropolitan attitudes to postcolonial variants often ranged from amused condescension to racist stereotyping . . . the model broke new ground in raising the awareness of dynamic varieties of English with growing populations of speakers and increasingly vibrant media, literatures and popular cultures . . . [T]he very act of pluralizing "English" and encouraging serious debate regarding the nature and role of "New Englishes" denoted both imagination and courage. (Bruthiaux, 2003: 160)

At another level, Algeo (1991) has argued that all language varieties are best regarded as "fictions" in the sense that they are "ordered abstractions" from "unsuppressible" linguistic change; and that such idealizations are completely necessary, "[f]ictions all, but useful ones," as "[t]o describe, to explain, and to predict requires that we suppose there are stable things behind our discourse" (Algeo, 1991: 4).

Thus, in the same way that standard language ideologies are socially and politically constructed, one might also argue that the labels of "Nigerian English," "Kenyan English," "Indian English," and "Hong Kong English" are also fictions, but again extremely useful fictions for the ways in which such labels have contributed to the reconceptualization of English studies in recent decades. Such labels are fictional in the sense that the linguistic description of "national" and "regional" varieties of English around the world typically relies on synoptic and simplified descriptions of linguistic features, lexical, phonological, syntactic, etc. The wider context here, however, is that the recognition of "new varieties" of English has not rested on linguistic criteria alone. Butler (1997), for example, suggests that in addition to a distinctive vocabulary and accent, important defining features of new varieties also include a historical tradition, creative writing, and the existence of reference works of various kinds. Kachru (2005) further explores the cultural turn from postcolonial and literary perspectives in a range of settings in Asia and other parts of the world, discussing the multiple ways in which the world Englishes paradigm has enabled the users of English to increasingly appropriate agency over the language and its linguistic and literary uses. In addition, however, it seems evident that the scope of world Englishes does not and should not limit itself to the areal study of varieties of English worldwide, but encompasses a wide range of other issues as well, including contact linguistics, critical linguistics, discourse analysis, lexicography, literatures in English, pidgin and creole studies, etc. (Bolton, 2005). The indigenization of Englishes in the Outer Circle has also been accompanied by the "Englishization" of languages as a manifestation of linguistic contact, at such levels as vocabulary, grammar, and discourse (Kachru, 2005).

8   The Empire Calls Back

The world Englishes paradigm is not static, and neither are the rapidly-changing realities of language use worldwide. The use of English in Outer- and Expanding-Circle societies continues its rapid spread, while at the same time new patterns of language contact and variety differentiation emerge.

One aspect of this has been the way in which world Englishes have been transported back into Inner-Circle contexts such as Britain and the USA. In the case of the UK, one newspaper report recently claimed that "London is the most linguistically diverse city on earth" (*The Times*, January 22, 2000, p. 8). The same article cited evidence that some 307 languages were spoken by London schoolchildren, and further noted that one third of children came from homes where other languages such as Bengali, Panjabi, Gujarati, Hindi/ Urdu, Turkish, Arabic, and creoles were spoken. The racial and social mix that occurs in such schools throughout London and other British cities is now creating new ethnicities and new patterns of language use, including the "crossing" into creoles and immigrant languages by white British children (Rampton, 1999). Similarly, in the USA, following changes in the immigration laws in the 1960s, there has been substantial immigration to America from the Africa, the Middle East, India, China, and the Philippines, as well as from the Caribbean, and Central and South America. As a result, there has been unease about home languages as well as the various Englishes spoken by immigrant and minority groups (Lippi-Green, 1997).

In other parts of the world, the effects of globalization are being felt in a range of ways. In societies such as India, Singapore, and Hong Kong, increasing numbers of young people may grow up with part of their education in their parents' society, and part, for example, high school and university, in the UK or North America. Such young people are invariably multilingual, and move routinely between Western and Asian societies, typically sampling and mixing both worlds and both cultures as they go. The most visible representatives of such groups include the middle- and upper middle-class sons and daughters of "overseas" *desi* Indian or *hua qiao* Chinese families who acquire an elite education in the best European and US schools. Meanwhile, in the largely publicly funded school systems of Europe, young people are acquiring English at an unprecedented rate as an additional language in education, as well as in less formal domains, such as pop music and computer games.

Within literary studies, the new literatures in English have been the focus of serious literary criticism for some time. Recently, Evelyn Ch'ien's (2004) study of the *Weird English* of such writers as Vladimir Nabokov, Maxine Hong Kingston, Arundhati Roy, Junot Díaz, and Salman Rushdie highlights the ways in which their writing accommodates "multiple loyalties, multiple linguistic commitments, and the multiple anxieties of several histories: the modern and the postmodern self." In this work, Ch'ien notes that the hybridity of such literature finds expression in the "weirding" of the language by these "polycultural" and "polylingual" writers (2004: 249).

Historically, one might argue that one early marker of the "paradigm shift" in world Englishes was when Mencken first presented his rationale for the "American language," and the recognition of an American "variety." In the preface to his classic inquiry, Mencken explained that he had encountered strong resistance, and the consensus of established thought was largely devoted to proving that "no such thing as an American variety of English existed – that the differences I constantly encountered in English and that my English friends encountered in American were chiefly imaginary" (Mencken, [1919] 1921). In Asia, the recognition of new Englishes has been relatively recent, and was largely unanticipated during the colonial period. For example, in 1853, the Revd David O. Allen argued that the prospects for English in India were poor, and that of those then studying the language, "many do not acquire sufficient knowledge for any practical purpose, and only a small part of them learn it thoroughly" (Allen, 1854: 275). Exactly 160 years later, David Crystal is citing statistics to suggest that around 350 million people speak English in India, and that the country is now home to "the largest English-speaking population in the world," whose English is marked by a range of different accents and dialects (Crystal, 2004).

Over the last three decades, work in world Englishes has been able to chart the de-centering and re-centering of English language studies across a variety of fields, including the linguistic, literary, and cultural. At the same time, the double-voicedness of centripetal and centrifugal forces (recalling Bakhtin and Paul) can also be seen in the tension between world Englishes and notions of "international English," "global English," and "world standard English." While the plurality of Englishes highlights the diverse features, functions, and contexts of English worldwide, world "English" in the singular suggests the existence of a transnational standard linked to the power of the USA and UK in particular areas of communication, including computers and international publishing.

McArthur (1997) argues that the notion of a global standard has most reality with reference to print and broadcast media. He thus identifies an "international print standard," an "international media standard," an "international governmental, administrative, and legal standard," an "international commercial and technological standard," and an "international educational standard." Today, no doubt, McArthur would also wish to mention the Microsoft standards that are now programmed into English word-processing software everywhere. He also claims that English "with its print base, is at the end of the 20th century a marked success, serving all humankind as the first high-level global lingua franca" (McArthur, 1997: 16). An alternative view, however, might conceptualize such standards in terms of shared registers or genres of use rather than invariant standardized "varieties."

Another example of "centripetal" tendencies might be identified in the "linguistic outsourcing" currently taking place in India and the Philippines. Currently, the two most important locations for international call centers are located in India and the Philippines. The United States alone lost 250,000 call-center jobs to Asia in the two years from 2001 to 2003 (*CBS News*, 2003), and such centers have become a major new source of employment for educated young people in both those Asian societies. In a recent and controversial article by Susan Sonntag (2003) entitled "The world as India," Sonntag, somewhat naively, eulogizes the industry, the "munificent" salaries, and the work of young Indians in this sector:

> The young people . . . had first to be trained for months, by instructors and by tapes, to acquire a pleasant middle American (not an educated American) accent, and to learn basic American slang . . . so that if the exchange with the client in the United States becomes prolonged, they will not falter with the small talk, and have the means to continue to pass for Americans. (Sonntag, 2003)

Notwithstanding Trivedi's (2003) scathing critique of Sonntag, the issue of linguistic outsourcing and call centers in India does serve to illustrate the changing map of Englishes worldwide.[3] Indeed, one descriptive question raised here is whether we should regard the linguistic behavior of such call-center agents as the adoption of a "native-speaker" or "standard" variety of English. Is this simply an example of "world standard English" asserting its power, or is there an alternative explanation? One possible clue here might be the use of the word "pass" in the quotation from Sonntag where she talks about call-center employees having "the means to continue to pass for Americans." Whatever the linguistic demands or expectations required in such work, the mere (conscious or unwitting) choice of the word *pass* in this context is interesting in itself, resonating as it does with acts of "passing" across the boundaries of gender and race.

The young Asians in call centers in New Delhi or Manila may not have simply acquired a "native-speaker" variety of English in some psycholinguistic sense, but may instead have developed the skill of doing or performing a "native-like variety." The use of such a variety in this context may involve less the use of a particular dialect of language, but more the conscious creation of a linguistic "voice" called forth by context and facilitated by the Asian bilingual's linguistic creativity. Whatever the economic and social realities of such linguistic outsourcing, new contexts such as these will continue to challenge traditional concepts of "dialects" and "varieties." Only 50 years ago, a sociologist like Pieris (1951), based at least for a time in South Asia, was moved to discuss the English-knowing bilingual as a "racial or cultural hybrid, situated on the fringe of two culture as a Marginal Man" (Pieris, 1951: 329). Today, by contrast, multilingualism and what Ch'ien dubs "polyculturalism" seems to speak to the center rather than the margins of contemporary intellectual experience, wherever one is located.

9   Conclusion

In this chapter, I have set out to examine notions of language variety and variation in the context of world Englishes. The early sections of this chapter have discussed the historical diasporas of English, contrasting the histories of such Inner-Circle societies as the USA, Australia, and New Zealand with those of the Outer-Circle postcolonial societies of Africa and Asia. Later sections of the chapter have attempted to unravel the notion of "variety" and "varieties" in the context of language studies. One argument that emerges here is that the likely provenance of "variety" as a technical (or quasi-technical) linguistic term was eighteenth- and nineteenth-century natural science and biology, which, in turn, overlapped with early notions of racial hierarchies. As Mufwene (2001) has pointed out, the naming practices that have been applied to varieties of English have also been affected by the entanglement of racial and linguistic classification. Underlying many of the discussions concerning varieties and variation is a tension between what are seen as the organic qualities of dialects and varieties as the "natural" expression of vital linguistic systems, and the view of languages and language varieties as social and political constructs.

The world Englishes initiative in recognizing and describing the new Englishes of the Caribbean, Africa, and Asia has been partly motivated by a consideration of the local linguistic "facts," and partly by a consideration of the wider cultural and political contexts of language acquisition and use, and the desire to creatively remodel and reconstruct discursive practices. This, in turn, has involved the creative rewriting of discourses toward a recognition of pluralism and multiple possibilities for scholarship. The notion of "varieties" in this context is similarly dynamic, as new contexts, new realities, new discourses, and new varieties continue to emerge. Simultaneously, an awareness of the origins and traditions of the metalanguage, naming practices, and discourses of "varieties of English" has the potential to assist our own conceptualizations and theorizations of this branch of linguistics.

NOTES

1   Quirk's linguistic liberalism is perhaps somewhat ironic here, considering his later stance on such issues (see Quirk, 1990; Kachru, 1991; Davis in this volume).

2   These dates are largely taken from Crystal (1995). Given the complexity of individual colonial histories, they are probably best taken as an approximate guide to events.

3 Trivedi (2003) takes Sonntag to task for her enthusiasm for such call centers, claiming that in this industry "the turnover is rapid, the burn-out is high, and the scars of emotional frustration are deep" and that these "poor young men and women are indeed the cyber-coolies of our global age, working not on sugar plantations but on flickering screens, and lashed into submission through vigilant and punitive monitoring, each slip in accent or lapse in pretence meaning a cut in wages."

REFERENCES

Aitken, Adam J. (1992) Scots. In *The Oxford Companion to the English Language*. Edited by Tom McArthur. Oxford: Oxford University Press, pp. 893–9.

Algeo, John (1991) A mediation of the varieties of English. *English Today*, **27**, 3–6.

Allen, David O. (1854) The state and prospects of the English language in India. *Journal of the American Oriental Society*, **4**, 263–75.

Bauer, Laurie (2003) *An Introduction to International Varieties of English*. Hong Kong: Hong Kong University Press.

Bloch, Bernard (1948) A set of postulates for phonemic analysis. *Language*, **24**, 3–46.

Bolton, Kingsley (2000) Language and hybridization: Pidgin tales from China coast. *Interventions*, **2**(1), 35–52.

Bolton, Kingsley (2005) Where WE stands: Approaches, issues and debate in world Englishes. *World Englishes*, **24**(1), 69–83.

Bruthiaux, Paul (2003) Squaring the Circles: Issues in modeling English worldwide. *International Journal of Applied Linguistics*, **13**(2), 159–78.

Brutt-Griffler, Janina (2002) *World English: A Study of its Development*. Clevedon, UK: Multilingual Matters.

Butler, Susan (1997) Corpus of English in Southeast Asia: Implications for a regional dictionary. In *English Is an Asian Language: The Philippine Context*. Edited by Ma. Lourdes S. Bautista. Manila: Macquarie Library, pp. 103–24.

Caird, James (1880) The inaugural address of James Caird, Esq, CB, FRS, President of the Statistical Society, delivered on Tuesday the 16th of November, 1880. *Journal of the Statistical Society of London*, **43**(4), 559–72.

CBS News (2003) Call center jobs drifting overseas. http://www.cbsnews.com/stories/2003/12/09/national/main587601.shtml. December 9. Accessed January 5, 2005.

Chambers, Jack K. (1995) *Sociolinguistic Theory: Linguistic Variation and Its Social Significance*. Oxford: Blackwell.

Chambers, Jack K., Trudgill, Peter, and Schilling-Estes, Natalie (2002) *The Handbook of Language Variation and Change*. Oxford: Blackwell.

Cheshire, Jenny (ed.) (1991) *English around the World: Sociolinguistic Perspectives*. Cambridge: Cambridge University Press.

Ch'ien, Evelyn N. M. (2004) *Weird English*. Cambridge, MA: Harvard University Press.

Clarke, Sandra (ed.) (1993) *Focus on Canada*. (Volume G11 in the series Varieties of English Around the World.) Amsterdam/Philadelphia: John Benjamins.

Coupland, Nikolas and Thomas, Alan R. (eds.) (1990) *English in Wales:*

Diversity, Conflict and Change. Clevedon, UK: Multilingual Matters.

Crystal, David (1985) How many millions? The statistics of English today. *English Today,* **1**, 7–9.

Crystal, David (1995) *The Cambridge Encyclopedia of the English Language.* Cambridge: Cambridge University Press.

Crystal, David (1997) *English as a Global Language.* Cambridge: Cambridge University Press.

Crystal, David (2004) Subcontinent raises its voice. *Guardian Weekly,* November 19. http://education. guardian.co.uk/tefl/story/ 0,5500,1355064,00.html. Accessed February 18, 2005.

Darwin, Charles (1859) *On the Origin of Species.* London: John Murray. Facsimile edition (1964). Cambridge, MA: Harvard University Press.

Davis, Daniel R. (2003) *The History of World Englishes: North America.* London: Routledge.

Dilke, Charles Wentworth (1885) *Greater Britain: A Record of Travel in English-Speaking Countries.* 3rd edition. London: Macmillan. First published in 1868.

Fishman, Joshua A., Cooper, Robert L., and Rosenbaum, Yehudit (1977) English around the world. In *The Spread of English: The Sociology of English as an Additional Language.* Edited by Joshua A. Fishman, Robert L. Cooper, and Yehudit Rosenbaum. Rowley, MA: Newbury House, pp. 77–107.

Freeman, Edward A. (1892) The physical and political bases of national unity. In *Britannic Confederation.* Edited by Arthur Silva White. London: George Philip and Son, pp. 33–56.

Halliday, Michael A. K. and Hasan, Ruqaiya (1989) *Language, Context, and Text: Aspects of Language in a Social-semiotic Perspective.* Oxford: Oxford University Press.

Halliday, Michael A. K., McIntosh, Angus, and Strevens, Peter (1964) *The Linguistic Sciences and Language Teaching.* London: Longman.

Harris, Roy (1998) The dialect myth. In *Integrational Linguistics: A First Reader.* Edited by Roy Harris and George Wolf. Oxford: Pergamon, pp. 83–95.

Holm, John (1988) *Pidgin and Creoles, volume 1: Theory and Structure.* Cambridge: Cambridge University Press.

Hudson, Richard A. (1996) *Sociolinguistics.* 2nd edition. Cambridge: Cambridge University Press.

Hughes, Arthur and Trudgill, Peter (1979) *English Accents and Dialects.* London: Edward Arnold.

Jenkins, Jennifer (2003) *World Englishes: A Resource Book for Students.* London: Routledge.

Kachru, Braj B. (1985) Standards, codification and sociolinguistic realism: The English language in the Outer Circle. In *English in the World: Teaching and Learning the Language and Literatures.* Edited by Randolph Quirk and Henry G. Widdowson. Cambridge: Cambridge University Press, pp. 11–30.

Kachru, Braj B. (1991) Liberation linguistics and the Quirk concern. *English Today,* **25**, 3–13.

Kachru, Braj B. (1998) English as an Asian language. *Links & Letters,* **5**, 89–108.

Kachru, Braj B. (2005) *Asian Englishes: Beyond the Canon.* Hong Kong: Hong Kong University Press.

Kachru, Yamuna and Nelson, Cecil L. (2006) *World Englishes in Asian Contexts.* Hong Kong: Hong Kong University Press.

Kallen, Jeffrey L. (1994) English in Ireland. In *The Cambridge History of the English Language.* Edited by Robert W. Burchfield. Cambridge:

Cambridge University Press, pp. 148–96, 577–88.

Linnaeus, Carl (1758) *Systema Naturae*. Stockholm: Laurentii Salvii.

Lippi-Green, Rosina (1997) *English with an Accent: Language, Ideology, and Discrimination in the United States*. London/New York: Routledge.

Maggenti, Armand R. (1989) Genus and family: Concepts and natural groupings. *Revue Nématol*, **12**(1), 3–6.

Marks, Jonathan (1995) *Human Biodiversity: Genes, Race and History*. New York: Aldine de Gruyter.

McArthur, Tom (1992) *The Oxford Companion to the English Language*. Oxford: Oxford University Press.

McArthur, Tom (1997) The printed word in the English-speaking world. *English Today*, **49**, 13(1), 10–16.

McArthur, Tom (2002) *The Oxford Guide to World English*. Oxford: Oxford University Press.

McClure, J. Derrick (1994) English in Scotland. In *The Cambridge History of the English Language, vol. 5*. Edited by Robert Burchfield. Cambridge: Cambridge University Press, pp. 23–93.

McCully, Bruce T. (1935) The origins of Indian nationalism according to native writers. *The Journal of Modern History*, **7**(3), 295–314.

Mencken, Henry L. ([1919] 1921) Preface to the first edition. *The American Language: An Inquiry into the Development of English in the United States*. 2nd edition. New York: Alfred A. Knopf, 1921; New York: Bartleby.com, 2002. Accessed January 2005.

Modiano, Marko (1999) Standard English(es) and educational practices for the world's lingua franca. *English Today*, **15**(2), 22–34.

Mufwene, Salikoko S. (1994) New Englishes and criteria for naming them. *World Englishes*, **13**, 21–31.

Mufwene, Salikoko S. (2001) *The Ecology of Language Evolution*. Cambridge: Cambridge University Press.

Paul, Hermann (1886) *Principien der Sprachgeschichte* [Principles of the History of Language]. Halle: Max Niemeyer. Reprinted 1995 by Routledge/Thoemmes Press.

Penhallurick, Rob (1993) Welsh English: A national language? *Dialectologia et Geolinguistica*, **1**, 28–46.

Pieris, Ralph (1951) Bilingualism and cultural marginality. *The British Journal of Sociology*, **2**(4), 328–39.

Quirk, Randolph (1962) *The Use of English*. London: Longman.

Quirk, Randolph (1988) The question of standards in the international use of English. In *Language Spread and Language Policy: Issues, Implications and Case Studies*. Edited by Peter H. Lowenberg. Washington, DC: Georgetown University Press, pp. 229–41.

Quirk, Randolph (1990) Language varieties and standard language. *English Today*, **21**, 3–21.

Rampton, Ben (1999) Sociolinguistics and cultural studies: New ethnicities, liminality and interaction. *Social Semiotics*, **9**(3), 355–73.

Schleicher, August ([1869] 1983) *Darwinism Tested by the Science of Language*. London: John Camden Hotten. In *Linguistics and Evolutionary Theory*. Edited by Konrad Koerner. Amsterdam: John Benjamins.

Schneider, Edgar W. (2003) The dynamics of New Englishes: From identity construction to dialect birth. *Language*, **79**(2), 233–81.

Schuchardt, Hugo (1885) *Ueber die Lautgesetze. Gegen die Junggrammatiker* [On Sound Laws: Against the Neogrammarians]. Berlin: Oppenheim.

Sebba, Mark (1997) *Contact Languages*. Basingstoke: Macmillian.

Seuren, Pieter A. M. (1998) *Western Linguistics: An Historical Introduction.* Oxford: Blackwell.

Sonntag, Susan (2003) The world as India. *Times Literary Supplement,* June 13. Electronic edition. http://www.the-tls.co.uk/. Accessed January 2005.

Strevens, Peter (1980) *Teaching English as an International Language.* Oxford: Pergamon.

Strong, Herbert A. (1890) *Principles of the History of Language* (translation of Hermann Paul's *Prinzipien der Sprachgeschichte*). Reprinted in 1970. College Park, Maryland: McGrath Publishing Company.

Thomas, Alan R. (1994) English in Wales. In *The Cambridge History of the English Language, vol. 5: English in Britain and Overseas: Origins and Development.* Edited by Robert Burchfield. Cambridge: Cambridge University Press, pp. 94–147.

Trivedi, Harish (2003) Cyber-coolies, Hindi and English. *Times Literary Supplement,* June 27. Electronic edition http://www.the-tls.co.uk/. Accessed January 2005.

Trudgill, Peter (2003) *A Glossary of Sociolinguistics.* Edinburgh: Edinburgh University Press.

Trudgill, Peter (2004) *New-Dialect Formation: The Inevitability of Colonial Englishes.* Edinburgh: Edinburgh University Press.

Trudgill, Peter and Hannah, Jean ([1982] 1994) *International English: A Guide to the Varieties of Standard English.* New York: Edward Arnold.

Webster, Noah (1789) *Dissertations on the English Language.* Boston: Isaiah Thomas; facsimile. Reprinted in 1967, Menston: Scolar.

Webster, Noah (1828) *An American Dictionary of the English Language,* 2 vols. New York: S. Converse; facsimile reprint 1967, San Francisco: Foundation for American Christian Education (ADEL).

Whitney, William D. (1880) Logical consistency in views of language. In *Logical Consistency in Views of Language,* **1**(3), 327–43.

FURTHER READING

Bolton, Kingsley and Kachru, Braj B. (2005) *World Englishes: Critical Concepts in Linguistics,* 6 vols. London: Routledge.

Kachru, Braj B. (ed.) (1982) *The Other Tongue: English across Cultures.* Oxford: Pergamon. 2nd edition 1992, Urbana, IL: University of Illinois Press.

Kachru, Braj B. (1986) *The Alchemy of English: The Spread, Functions, and Models of Non-Native Englishes.* Oxford: Pergamon.

Kachru, Yamuna and Nelson, Cecil L. (2006) *World Englishes in Asian Contexts.* Hong Kong: Hong Kong University Press.

Thumboo, Edwin (ed.) (2001) *The Three Circles of English.* Singapore: UniPress.

18 Pidgins and Creoles

SALIKOKO S. MUFWENE

1 Introduction

The title of this chapter, which must be read as a frozen phrase or an idiom of
some sort, is misleading. It suggests that creoles evolved from pidgins, but this
genetic scenario is questioned by the colonial history of the territories where
these varieties emerged, independent of each other, as I show below. Recently,
some creolists have addressed the question of whether, as a group, creoles can
be singled out as a structural type of languages. The answer is negative, even
if one focused on creoles only, or on pidgins. Space limitations prevent me
from developing this position, contra McWhorter (1998), which is discussed in
Mufwene (2000) and DeGraff (2001). Creoles vary as much among themselves
as indigenized Englishes do, taken as a group, and certainly more than the
"native Englishes" of the United Kingdom, North America, and Australia.
They are not genetically related either, because the languages they have evolved
from, misnamed *lexifiers* in creolistics, do not descend from the same parent
language, although these are Indo-European. It is plausible to argue that creoles,
those that have evolved from European languages and that I discuss below,
are new Indo-European language varieties, but this position challenges the
received doctrine in creolistics, which I show to be inconsistent below. In
order for this essay to be both informative and manageable within its space
limits, I focus on what kinds of language varieties creoles and pidgins are,
how they evolved, and some of what is entailed by the position I defend.

2 What Are Pidgins and Creoles?

Strictly speaking, creoles and pidgins are new language varieties which developed out of contacts between colonial non-standard varieties of a European
language and several non-European languages around the Atlantic and in the

Indian and Pacific Oceans in the sixteenth–nineteenth centuries. *Pidgins* typically emerged in trade colonies which developed around trade forts or along trade routes, such as on the coast of West Africa. They are reduced in structures and specialized in functions (typically trade), and initially they served as non-native lingua francas to users who preserved their native vernaculars for their day-to-day interactions. Some pidgins have expanded into regular vernaculars, especially in urban settings, and are called *expanded pidgins*. Examples include Bislama and Tok Pisin (in Melanesia) and Nigerian and Cameroon Pidgin Englishes, which are structurally as complex as *creoles* (based on, for instance, Féral, 1989; Jourdan, 1991). One can certainly argue that the structural complexity of a language variety is ethnographically a function of the communicative functions to which it is put, even as a lingua franca, although from a typological perspective it is difficult to say whether one language is structurally more complex than another, especially whether a language that has complex morphosyntax is also more complex semantically or phonologically.

Creoles are vernaculars that developed in settlement colonies whose primary industry consisted of sugar cane plantations or rice fields and whose majority populations were non-European slaves, in the case of the Atlantic and Indian Ocean, or indentured laborers, in the case of Hawai'i. The latter was colonized by Americans in the nineteenth century, when slavery was being abolished, and did not experience extensive ethnolinguistic mixing, which raises questions about using Hawai'ian Creole English as an exemplar of how creoles developed everywhere. Examples of other creoles include Cape Verdian Criolou (from Portuguese) and Papiamentu in the Netherlands Antilles (apparently Portuguese-based but influenced by Spanish); Haitian, Mauritian, and Seychellois (from French); Gullah in the United States, Jamaican, and Guyanese (all from English); as well as Saramaccan and Sranan in Suriname (both from English, with the former heavily influenced by Portuguese and the latter by Dutch). Note that although Melanesian pidgins are associated with sugar cane plantations, they apparently originated in trade settings and were adopted on the plantations (Keesing, 1988).

The terms *creole* and *pidgin* have also been extended to some other varieties that developed during the same period out of contacts among primarily non-European languages. Examples include Delaware Pidgin, Chinook Jargon, and Mobilian in North America; Sango, (Kikongo-)Kituba, and Lingala in Central Africa, Kinubi in Southern Sudan and in Uganda; and Hiri Motu in Papua New Guinea (Holm, 1989; Smith, 1995). Many of these varieties have historically been designated with the name *jargon*, which is much older in French and English and simply means "a variety unintelligible to the speaker or writer." The term *pidgin* did not arise until the early nineteenth century (Baker and Mühlhäusler, 1990) or perhaps the late eighteenth century (Bolton, 2002). Although it has usually been traced etymologically to the word *business* (as in *business English*), the Cantonese phrase *bei chin* (literally 'pay' or 'give money') seems to be its more probable etymon (Comrie, Matthews, and Polinsky, 1996:

146), partly because of the ecology of its emergence and partly also because it is phonologically more plausible to derive the word from the proposed Cantonese etymon than from the English alternative. Convergence need not be excluded here as an explanation. In the original lay people's naming practice, the term *jargon* was an alternate for *pidgin*.

Although the term must have been taken from China to Melanesia (hence *Tok Pisin*) by sailors and traders in that part of the world, linguists are the ones who have generalized usage of the term, without unfortunately providing operational criteria for the extension to other colonial trade lingua francas. Hall (1966) and Mühlhäusler (1986/1997) argue that pidgins are more stable and jargons are an earlier stage in the "life-cycle" that putatively goes from Jargon, to Pidgin, to Creole, to Post-Creole by progressive structural expansion, stabilization, and closer approximations of the *base language* from which the variety evolved. The fact that the term *pidgin* emerged in Canton, thousands of miles away from the American Iberian colonies where the term *creole* originated in the sixteenth century, should have cast doubt on the scenario that derives creoles from pidgins by a putative process of *nativization* interpreted as (structural expansion through the) acquisition of native speakers. So should the fact that expanded pidgins have equally complex structures developed largely through the agency of adult L2 speakers using it increasingly as a vernacular. The socio-economic histories of the territories where creoles developed speak against the Hall-Mühlhäusler position, to which I return below.

Chaudenson (1992) and Mufwene (1997) argue that creoles developed by *basilectalizing* away from the base language, i.e. by developing a *basilect* – the variety the most different from the *acrolect*, the variety of the upper class. Mufwene (2001) emphasizes that creoles and pidgins developed in separate places, in which Europeans and non-Europeans interacted differently – sporadically in trade colonies but regularly in the initial stages of settlement colonies. The main justification for this position is that plantation settlement colonies typically developed from homestead societies, in which the non-Europeans were minorities and well-integrated and their children spoke the same colonial koinés as the children of European descent. It is only during the later stage of the plantation phase that the basilects, typically identified as creoles, developed by the regular process of gradual divergence from earlier forms of the colonial language.

The term *creole* was originally coined in Iberian colonies, apparently in the sixteenth century, in reference to non-indigenous people born in the American colonies. (See Mufwene, 1997 for references.) It was adopted in metropolitan Spanish, then in French, and later in English by the early seventeenth century. By the second half of the same century, it was generalized to descendants of Africans or Europeans born in Romance colonies. Usage varied from one colony to another. The term was also used as an adjective to characterize plants, animals, and customs typical of the same colonies (Valkhoff, 1966).

Creole may not have applied widely to language varieties until the late eighteenth century, though Arveiller (1963) cites La Courbe's *Premier voyage* (1913:

192), in which it is used for "corrupted Portuguese spoken in Senegal." Such usage may have been initiated by metropolitan Europeans to disfranchise particular colonial varieties of their languages. It is not clear how the term became associated only with vernaculars spoken primarily by descendants of non-Europeans. Nonetheless, speakers of several creoles (or pidgins) actually believe they speak dialects of their lexifiers (Mühlhäusler, 1985; Mufwene, 1988).

Among the earliest claims that creoles developed from pidgins is the following statement in Bloomfield (1933: 474): "when the jargon [i.e., pidgin] has become the only language of the subject group, it is a *creolized language.*" Hall (1962, 1966) reinterpreted this, associating the vernacular function of creoles with nativization. Since then, creoles have been defined inaccurately as "nativized pidgins," i.e., pidgins that have acquired native speakers and have therefore expanded both their structures and functions and have stabilized. Hall then also introduced the pidgin-creole "life-cycle" to which DeCamp (1971) added a "post-creole" stage (see below).

Among the creolists who dispute the above connection is Alleyne (1971), who argues that fossilized inflectional morphology in Haitian Creole (HC) and the like proves that Europeans did not communicate with the Africans in foreigner or baby talk (see below). As noted above, Chaudenson (1979, 1992, 2001, 2003) argues that plantation communities were preceded by homesteads, on which mesolectal approximations of European koinés, rather than pidgins, were spoken by earlier slaves. Like some economic historians, Berlin (1998) observes that in North American colonies creole Blacks spoke the European language fluently. In ads on runaway slaves in British North American colonies, bad English is typically associated with slaves imported as adults from Africa. Diachronic textual evidence also suggests that the basilects developed during the peak growth of plantations (in the eighteenth century for most colonies), when infant mortality was high, life expectancy short, the plantation populations increased primarily by massive importation of labor, and the proportion of fluent speakers of the earlier colonial varieties kept decreasing (Baker and Corne, 1986; Chaudenson, 1992, 2001; Mufwene, 2001).

According to the life-cycle model, as a creole continues to co-exist with its base language, the latter exerts pressure on it to shed some of its "creole features." This developmental hypothesis may be traced back to Schuchardt's (1914) explanation of why African American English (AAE) is structurally closer to North American English than Saramaccan is to English (in the Caribbean?); namely, coexistence with the base language in North America and absence of such continued contact in Suriname. Jespersen (1921) and Bloomfield (1933) anticipated DeCamp (1971), Bickerton (1973), and Rickford (1987) in invoking *decreolization* as "loss of 'creole' features" to account for speech continua in creole communities.

It is in the above context that DeCamp (1971) coined the term *post-creole continuum,* which must be interpreted charitably. If a variety is creole because of the particular sociohistorical ecology of its development (see below), rather than because of its structural peculiarities, it cannot stop being a creole even after some of the features have changed. Besides, basilectal and mesolectal features continue to co-exist in these communities, suggesting that Creole has not died yet. Lalla and D'Costa (1990) present copious data against decreolization in Caribbean English creoles, just as Mufwene (1994) adduces linguistic and non-linguistic arguments against the same process in Gullah. On the other hand, Rickford and Handler (1994) show that in the late eighteenth century, Barbados had a basilect similar to those of other Caribbean islands. It now seems to have vanished. How and why it was lost here but not elsewhere in the Caribbean calls for an explanation.

Closely related to the above issue is the common assumption that creoles are separate languages from their base languages whereas related non-creole colonial offspring of the same European languages are considered as their dialects. Such is the case for the non-standard French varieties spoken in Quebec and Louisiana, as well as on the Caribbean islands of St Barths and St Thomas. Likewise New World non-standard varieties of Spanish and Portuguese are not considered creoles, despite structural similarities which they display with Portuguese creoles. Has the fact that similar varieties are spoken by descendants of both Europeans and Africans in territories where there has been more race hybridization influenced the naming practice? Although not officially acknowledged by creolists, the one obvious criterion behind the naming practice has been to identify as creoles those varieties of European languages which have been appropriated as vernaculars by non-European majorities. There is otherwise no yardstick for measuring structural divergence from the base language, especially since feature composition of the latter was not the same in every relevant contact setting. Besides, contact was a factor in all colonial settings, including those not associated with creoles.

It has also been claimed that creoles have more or less the same structural design (Bickerton, 1981, 1984; Markey, 1982). This position is as disputable as the other, more recent claim that there are creole prototypes from which others deviate in various ways (Thomason, 1997; McWhorter, 1998). The very fact of resorting to a handful of prototypes for the would-be essentialist creole structural category suggests that the vast majority of them do not share the putative set of defining features, hence that the combination of features proposed by McWhorter (1998) cannot be used to single them out as a unique type of language. On the other hand, structural variation among creoles that have evolved from the same base language can be correlated with variation sociohistorical ecologies of their developments (Mufwene, 1997, 2001). The notion of "ecology" includes, among other things, the structural features of the base and substrate languages, the ethnolinguistic makeups of the populations that came in contact, how regularly they interacted across class and ethnic boundaries, and the rates and modes of population growth.

To date the best-known creoles have evolved from English and French. Those of the Atlantic and Indian Ocean are, along with Hawai'ian Creole, those that have informed most theorizing on the development of creoles. While the terms *creole* and *creolization* have been applied often uncritically to various contact-induced language varieties, several distinctions, which are not clearly articulated, have also been proposed in addition to those discussed above, for instance, *koiné, semi-creole, intertwined varieties, foreign workers' varieties* of European languages (e.g., Gastarbeiter Deutsch), and *indigenized varieties* of European languages (e.g., Nigerian and Singaporean Englishes). The denotations and importance of these terms deserve re-examination (Arends, Muysken, and Smith, 1995; Mufwene, 1997, 2001).

3   The Development of Creoles

The central question here is: how did creoles develop? The following hypotheses are the major ones competing today: the substrate, the superstrate, and the universalist hypotheses.

Substratist positions are historically related to the *baby talk hypothesis*, which I have traced back to nineteenth-century French creolists: Bertrand-Bocandé (1849), Baissac (1880), Vinson (1882), and Adam (1883). Putatively, the languages previously spoken by the Africans enslaved on New World and Indian Ocean plantations were the primary reason why the European languages which they appropriated were restructured into creoles. These French creolists assumed African languages to be "primitive," "instinctive," in "natural" state, and simpler than the relevant "cultivated" European languages. Creoles' systems were considered to be reflections of those non-European languages. The baby-talk connection is that, in order to be understood, the Europeans supposedly had to speak to the Africans as to babies, their interpretation of "foreigner talk."

The revival of the substrate hypothesis (without its racist component) has been attributed to Sylvain (1936). Although she recognizes influence from French dialects, she argues that African linguistic influence, especially from the Ewe group of languages, is very significant in Haitian Creole. Unfortunately, she states in the last sentence of her conclusions that this creole is Ewe spoken with a French vocabulary. Over two decades later, Turner (1949) disputed American dialectologists' claim that there was virtually no trace of African languages in AAE and showed phonological and morphosyntactic similarities between Gullah and some West African (especially Kwa) languages. He concluded that "Gullah is indebted to African sources" (p. 254).

Mufwene (1990) identifies three main schools of the substrate hypothesis today. The first, led by Alleyne (1980, 1996) and Holm (1988) is closer to Turner's approach and is marked by what is also its main weakness: invocation of influence from diverse African languages without explaining what kinds of selection principles account for this seemingly random invocation of sources. This criticism is not *ipso facto* an invalidation of substrate influence; it is both a call for a more principled account and a reminder that the nature of such influence must be reassessed (Mufwene, 2001).

The second school has been identified as the *relexification hypothesis*. The proponents of its latest version, Lefebvre (1998) and Lumsden (1999), argue that Haitian is a French relexification of languages of the Ewe-Fon (or Fongbe) group. This account of the development of creoles has been criticized for several basic shortcomings, including the following: (1) its "comparative" approach has not taken into account several features that Haitian (also) shares with non-standard varieties of French; (2) it downplays features which Haitian shares also with several other African languages which were represented in Haiti during the critical stages of its development; (3) it has not shown that the language appropriation strategies associated with relexification are typically used in naturalistic second-language acquisition; and (4) it does not account for those cases where structural options not consistent with those of Ewe-Fon have been selected into Haitian. Moreover, relexificationists assume, disputably, that languages of the Ewe-Fon group are structurally identical and that no competition of influence among them was involved.

The least disputed version of the substrate hypothesis is Keesing's (1988), which shows that substrate languages may impose their structural features on the new, contact-induced varieties if they are typologically homogeneous, with most of them sharing the relevant features. Thus Melanesian pidgins are like (most of) their substrates in having DUAL/PLURAL and INCLUSIVE/EX-CLUSIVE distinctions and in having a transitive marker on the verb. Sankoff and Brown (1976) had shown similar influence with the bracketing of relative clauses with *ia*. However, the pidgins have not inherited all the peculiarities of Melanesian languages. For instance, they do not have their VSO major constituent order, nor do they have much of a numeral classifying system in the combination of *pela* with quantifiers. For an extensive discussion of substrate influence in Atlantic and Indian Ocean creoles, see Muysken and Smith (1986) and Mufwene (1993).

Competing with the above genetic views has been the *dialectologist*, or superstrate, hypothesis, according to which the primary, if not the exclusive, sources of creoles' structural features are the non-standard varieties of their base languages. Speaking of AAE, Krapp (1924) and Kurath (1928), for example, claimed that this variety was an archaic retention of the non-standard speech of low-class whites with whom the African slaves had been in contact. According to them, African substrate influence was limited to some isolated lexical items such as *goober* 'peanut', *gumbo*, and *okra*. It would take until McDavid (1950) and McDavid and McDavid (1951) before allowance was made for limited African grammatical contributions to AAE. D'Eloia (1973) and Schneider (1989) invoke several dialectal English models to rebut Dillard's (1972) thesis that AAVE developed from an erstwhile West African Pidgin English brought over by slaves. Since the late 1980s, Shana Poplack and her associates have shown that AAE shares many features with white non-standard vernaculars in North America and England, thus it has not developed from an erstwhile creole. (See Poplack and Tagliamonte, 2001; Poplack, 1999 for a synthesis.) Because some of the same features are also attested in creoles (Rickford, 1998), we come back to the question of whether most features of creoles did not after all originate in their base languages.

Regarding French creoles, the dialectologist position was first defended by Faine (1937), according to whom Haitian Creole was essentially Norman French. This position was espoused later by Hall (1958: 372), who argues that "the 'basic' relationship of Creole is with seventeenth-century French, with heavy carry-overs or survivals of African linguistic structure (on a more superficial structural level) from the previous language(s) of the earliest speakers of Negro Pidgin French; its 'lexical' relationship is with nineteenth- and twentieth-century French." Chaudenson (1989, 1992) is more accommodating to substrate influence as a factor that accounts for the more extensive structural divergence of creoles from their base languages compared to their non-creole colonial kin.

The *universalist hypotheses*, which stood as strong contenders in the 1980s and 1990s, have forerunners in the nineteenth century. For instance, Adolfo Coelho (1880–6) partly anticipated Bickerton's (1981) *language bioprogram hypothesis* in stating that creoles "owe their origin to the operation of psychological or physiological laws that are everywhere the same, and not to the influence of the former languages of the people among whom these dialects are found." Bickerton pushed things further in claiming that children made creoles by fixing the parameters of these new language varieties in their unmarked, or default, settings as specified in Universal Grammar. To account for cross-creole structural differences, Bickerton (1984: 176–7) invokes a "Pidginization Index" (PI) that includes the following factors: the proportion of the native to non-native speakers during the initial stages of colonization, the duration of the early stage, the rate of increase of the slave population after that initial stage, the kind of social contacts between the native speakers of the base language and the learners, and whether or not the contact between the two groups continued after the formation of the new language variety.

Some nagging questions with Bickerton's position include the following: Is his intuitively sound PI consistent with his creolization qua abrupt pidgin-nativization hypothesis? Is the abrupt creolization hypothesis consistent with the social histories of the territories where classic creoles developed (Mufwene, 1999, 2001)? How can we explain similarities of structures and in complexity between abrupt creoles and expanded pidgins when the stabilization and structural expansion of the latter is not necessarily associated with restructuring by children? Is there convincing evidence for assuming that adult speech is less controlled by Universal Grammar than child language is? How can we account for similarities between abrupt creolization and naturalistic second-language acquisition? Not all creolists who have invoked universalist explanations have made children critical to the emergence of creoles. For instance, Sankoff (1979) and Mühlhäusler (1981) make allowance for Universal Grammar to operate in adults, too.

Few creolists subscribe nowadays to one exclusive genetic account, as evidenced by the contributions to Mufwene (1993). The *complementary hypothesis* (Baker and Corne, 1986; Hancock, 1986; and Mufwene, 1986, 2001) seems to be an adequate alternative, provided we can articulate the ecological conditions under which the competing influences (between the substrate and superstrate languages, and within each group) may converge or prevail upon each other. This position was well anticipated by Schuchardt (1909, 1914) in his accounts of the geneses of Lingua Franca and of Saramaccan. More and more research is now underway uncovering the sociohistorical conditions under which different creoles have developed, for instance, Chaudenson (1979), Baker (1982), Arends (1989, 1995), Corne (1999), and Mufwene (2001).

Still, the future of research on the development of creoles has some problems to overcome. So far knowledge of the colonial non-standard varieties of the European languages remains limited. There are few comprehensive descriptions of creoles' structures – which makes it difficult to determine globally how the competing influences interacted among them and how the features selected from diverse sources became integrated into new systems. Few structural facts have been correlated with the conclusions suggested by the sociohistorical backgrounds of individual creoles. Other issues remain up in the air; for instance, what are the most adequate principles that should help us account for the selection of features into creoles' systems? For developmental issues on creoles and pidgins, the following edited collections are good starting points: Hymes (1971), Valdman (1977), Hill (1979), Muysken and Smith (1986), Mufwene (1993), and Arends et al. (1995). More specific issues may be checked in volumes of the Creole Language Library (John Benjamins) and of Amsterdam Creole Studies, in the *Journal of Pidgin and Creole Languages*, and in *Etudes Créoles*. Several issues of *Pacific Linguistics* also include publications on Melanesian creoles.

4   Creolistics and General Linguistics

There is much more literature on the genesis, sociology, and morphosyntax of PCs than on their phonologies, semantics, and pragmatics. With the exception of time reference (e.g., Michaelis, 1993; Singler, 1990; Schlupp, 1997) and nominal number (see Tagliamonte and Poplack, 1993 for references), studies in semantics and pragmatics are scant. On the other hand, the development of quantitative sociolinguistics owes a lot to research on AAE since the mid-1960s (see, e.g., Labov, 1972) and Caribbean English creoles (e.g., Rickford, 1987). Numerous publications in *American Speech*, *Language in Society*, and *Language Variation and Change* reflect this. There are also several surveys of creolistics today, including the following: Romaine (1988), Holm (1988), Manessy (1994), Arends et al. (1995), and Mühlhäusler (1986/1997). They vary in geographical areas of focus and adequacy. Kouwenberg and Singler (2006) is likely to become a standard reference for several years, with which Chaudenson (2003) and (Mufwene, 2005) will have to compete in regard to their divergence from the received doctrine. DeGraff (2003) will be a forceful deterrent from treating creoles as having exceptional evolutions and a good wakeup call for uniformitarianism. Efforts to bridge research on the development of creoles with that on other contact-based varieties and phenomena (e.g., Mufwene, 2001; Myers-Scotton, 2002; Thomason, 2001; Thomason and Kaufman, 1988; Winford, 2003) are noteworthy.

5   Conclusion

Studies of structural aspects of creoles have yet to inform general linguistics beyond the subject matters of time reference and serial verb constructions. For instance, studies of lectal continua (e.g., Escure, 1997) have had this potential, but little has been done by creolists to show how their findings may apply to other languages. The mixed nature of *mesolects*, those intermediate varieties combining features associated both with the *acrolect* and the *basilect* should have informed general linguistics against the fallacy of assuming monolithic grammatical systems (Labov, 1998; Mufwene, 1992). The notion of "acrolect" deserves rethinking (Irvine, 2004). Creolistics has been bridging with research on grammaticalization, an area that promises to be productive, as evidenced by Kriegel (2003). Andersen (1983) was an important step to consolidate common interests between second-language acquisition and the development of creoles. DeGraff (1999) bridges research on the latter topic with research on (child) language development and on the emergence of sign language. Creolistics can also contribute fruitfully to research on language vitality, including language loss (Mufwene, 2002, 2004).

REFERENCES

Adam, Lucien (1883) *Les Idiomes Négro-Aryens et Malayo-Aryens: Essai D'hybridologie Linguistique* [Negro-Arian and Malay-Arian languages: Essays on Linguistic Hybridization]. Paris: Maisonneuve.

Alleyne, Mervyn C. (1971) Acculturation and the cultural matrix of creolization. In *Pidginization and Creolization of Languages*. Edited by Dell Hymes. Cambridge: Cambridge University Press, pp. 169–86.

Alleyne, Mervyn C. (1980) *Comparative Afro-American: An Historical-Comparative Study of English-Based Afro-American Dialects of the New World*. Ann Arbor: Karoma.

Alleyne, Mervyn C. (1996) *Syntaxe Historique Créole* [Creole Historical Syntax]. Paris: Karthala.

Andersen, Roger (ed.) (1983) *Pidginization and Creolization as Language Acquisition*. Rowley, MA: Newbury House.

Arends, Jacques (1989) Syntactic Developments in Sranan: Creolization as a Gradual Process. PhD dissertation, University of Nijmegen.

Arends, Jacques (ed.) (1995) *The Early Stages of Creolization*. Amsterdam: John Benjamins.

Arends, Jacques, Muysken, Pieter, and Smith, Norval (eds.) (1995) *Pidgins and Creoles: An Introduction*. Amsterdam: John Benjamins.

Arveiller, Raymond (1963) *Contribution à L'étude des Termes de Voyage en Français (1505–1722)* [A Contribution to the Study of Travel Terms in French (1505–1722)]. Paris: D'Artrey.

Baissac, Charles (1880) *Etude sur le Patois Créole Mauricien* [A Study of the Mauritian Creole Patois]. Nancy: Imprimerie Berger-Levrault.

Baker, Philip (1982) The Contribution of Non-Francophone Immigrants to the Lexicon of Mauritian Creole. PhD dissertation, School of Oriental and African Studies, University of London.

Baker, Philip and Corne, Chris (1986) Universals, substrata and the Indian Ocean creoles. In *Substrata versus Universals in Creole Genesis*. Edited by Pieter Muysken and Norval Smith. Amsterdam: John Benjamins, pp. 163–83.

Baker, Philip and Mühlhäusler, Peter (1990) From business to pidgin. *Journal of Asian Pacific Communication*, **1**, 87–115.

Berlin, Ira (1998) *Many Thousands Gone: The First Two Centuries of Slavery in North America*. Cambridge, MA: Harvard University Press.

Bertrand-Bocandé, Emmanuel (1849) Notes sur la Guinée portugaise ou Sénégambie méridionale [Notes on Portuguese Guinea or Senegambia]. *Bulletin de la Société de Géographie*, **12**, 57–93.

Bickerton, Derek (1973) The nature of a creole continuum. *Language*, **49**, 640–69.

Bickerton, Derek (1981) *Roots of Language*. Ann Arbor: Karoma.

Bickerton, Derek (1984) The language bioprogram hypothesis. *Behavioral and Brain Sciences*, **7**, 173–221.

Bloomfield, Leonard (1933) *Language*. New York: Holt, Rinehart and Winston.

Bolton, Kingsley (2002) Chinese Englishes: From Canton jargon to global English. *World Englishes*, **21**(2), 181–99.

Chaudenson, Robert (1979) *Les Créoles Français* [French Creoles]. Paris: Fernand Nathan.

Chaudenson, Robert (1989) *Créoles et Enseignement du Français* [Creoles and the Teaching of French]. Paris: L'Harmattan.

Chaudenson, Robert (1992) *Des Îles, des Hommes, des Langues: Essais sur la Créolisation Linguistique et Culturelle* [About Islands, People, and Languages: Essays on Linguistic and Cultural Creolization]. Paris: L'Harmattan.

Chaudenson, Robert (2001) *Creolization of Language and Culture*. London: Routledge.

Chaudenson, Robert (2003) *La Créolisation: Théorie, Applications, Implications* [Creolization: Theory, Applications, Implications]. Paris: L'Harmattan.

Coelho, F. Adolpho (1880–6) Os dialectos românicos ou neolatinos na Africa, Asia, ae America [Romance dialects or Neo-Latins of Africa, Asia, and America]. *Bolletim da Sociedade de Geografia de Lisboa*, **2**, 129–96 (1880–1); **3**, 451–78 (1882); **6**, 705–55 (1886).

Comrie, Bernard, Matthews, Stephen, and Polinsky, Maria (1996) *The Atlas of Languages: The Origin and Development of Languages throughout the World*. New York: Facts on File.

Corne, Chris (1999) *From French to Creole: The Development of New Vernaculars in the French Colonial World*. London: University of Westminster Press.

DeCamp, David (1971) Toward a generative analysis of a post-creole speech continuum. In *Pidginization and Creolization of Languages*. Edited by Dell Hymes. Cambridge: Cambridge University Press, pp. 349–70.

DeGraff, Michel (ed.) (1999) *Language Creation and Language Change:*

Creolization, Diachrony, and Development. Cambridge, MA: MIT Press.

DeGraff, Michel (2001) On the origin of creoles: A Cartesian critique of Neo-Darwinian linguistics. *Linguistic Typology*, **5**, 213–310.

DeGraff, Michel (2003) Against creole exceptionalism. *Language*, **79**, 391–410.

D'Eloia, Sarah G. (1973) Issues in the analysis of Negro nonstandard English. Review of Dillard (1972). *Journal of English Linguistics*, **7**, 87–106.

Dillard, Joey L. (1972) *Black English: Its History and Usage in the United States.* New York: Random House.

Escure, Geneviève (1997) *Creole and Dialect Continua.* Amsterdam: John Benjamins.

Faine, Jules (1937) *Philologie Créole: Études Historiques et Étymologiques sur la Langue Créole d'Haïti* [Creole Philology: Historical and Etymological Studies on the Creole Language of Haiti]. Port-au-Prince: Imprimerie de l'Etat.

Féral, Carole de (1989) *Pidgin-English du Cameroun* [Pidgin English of Cameroon]. Paris: Peters/SELAF.

Hall, Robert A., Jr. (1958) Creole languages and genetic relationships. *Word*, **14**, 367–73.

Hall, Robert A., Jr. (1962) The life-cycle of pidgin languages. *Lingua*, **11**, 151–6.

Hall, Robert A., Jr. (1966) *Pidgin and Creole Languages.* Ithaca: Cornell University Press.

Hancock, Ian (1986) The domestic hypothesis, diffusion and componentiality: An account of Atlantic Anglophone creole origins. In *Substrata versus Universals in Creole Genesis.* Edited by Pieter Muysken and Norval Smith. Amsterdam: John Benjamins, pp. 71–102.

Hill, Kenneth C. (ed.) (1979) *The Genesis of Language.* Ann Arbor: Karoma.

Holm, John (1988) *Pidgins and Creoles, vol. 1: Theory and Structure.* Cambridge: Cambridge University Press.

Holm, John (1989) *Pidgins and Creoles, vol. 2: Reference Survey.* Cambridge: Cambridge University Press.

Hymes, Dell (ed.) (1971) *Pidginization and Creolization of Languages.* Cambridge: Cambridge University Press.

Irvine, Alison G. (2004) A good command of the English language: Phonological variation in the Jamaican acrolect. *Journal of Pidgin and Creole Languages*, **19**, 41–76.

Jespersen, Otto (1921) *Language: Its Nature, Development and Origin.* New York: W. W. Norton.

Jourdan, Christine (1991) Pidgins and creoles: The blurring of categories. *Annual Review of Anthropology*, **20**, 187–209.

Keesing, Roger M. (1988) *Melanesian Pidgin and the Oceanic Substrate.* Stanford: Stanford University Press.

Kouwenberg, Silvia and Singler, John V. (eds.) (2006) *The Handbook of Pidgin and Creole Studies.* Oxford: Blackwell.

Krapp, George P. (1924) The English of the Negro. *The American Mercury*, **2**, 190–5.

Kriegel, Sibylle (ed.) (2003) *Grammaticalisation et Réanalyse: Approches de la Variation Créole et Française* [Grammaticalization and Reanalysis: Approaches to Variation in Creole and French]. Paris: CNRS Editions.

Kurath, Hans (1928) The origin of dialectal differences in spoken American English. *Modern Philology*, **25**, 385–95.

Labov, William (1972) *Language in the Inner City: Studies in Black English Vernacular.* Philadelphia: University of Pennsylvania Press.

Labov, William (1998) Co-existent systems in African-American vernacular English. In *African-American English: Structure, History, and Use*. Edited by Salikoko S. Mufwene, John R. Rickford, Guy Bailey, and John Baugh. London: Routledge, pp. 110–53.

La Courbe, Michel Jajolet de (1913) *Premier Voyage du Sieur de la Courbe Fait à la Coste d'Afrique en 1685* [Sir de la Courbe's First Voyage to the Coast of Africa in 1685]. Paris: E. Champion.

Lalla, Barbara and D'Costa, Jean (1990) *Language in Exile: Three Hundred Years of Jamaican Creole*. Tuscaloosa, AL: University of Alabama Press.

Lefebvre, Claire (1998) *Creole Genesis and the Acquisition of Grammar: The Case of Haitian Creole*. Cambridge: Cambridge University Press.

Lumsden, John (1999) Language acquisition and creolization. In *Language Creation and Language Change: Creolization, Diachrony, and Development*. Edited by Michel DeGraff. Cambridge, MA: MIT Press, pp. 129–57.

Manessy, Gabriel (1994) *Créoles, Pidgins, Variétés Véhiculaires: Procès et Genèse* [Creoles, Pidgins, and Lingua Francas: Process and Genesis]. Paris: CNRS Editions.

Markey, Thomas L. (1982) Afrikaans: Creole or non-creole? *Zeitschrift fur Dialektologie und Linguistik*, **2**, 169–207.

McDavid, Raven, Jr. (1950) Review of Lorenzo Dow Turner's *Africanisms in the Gullah dialect*. *Language*, **26**, 323–33.

McDavid, Raven, Jr. and McDavid, Virginia (1951) The relationship of the speech of the American Negroes to the speech of whites. *American Speech*, **26**, 3–17.

McWhorter, John H. (1998) Identifying the creole prototype: Vindicating a typological class. *Language*, **74**, 788–818.

Michaelis, Susanne (1993) *Temps et Aspect en Créole Seychellois: Valeurs et Interférences* [Tense and Aspect in the Creole of the Seychelles: Values and Inferences]. Hamburg: Helmut Buske.

Mufwene, Salikoko S. (1986) The universalist and substrate hypotheses complement one another. In *Universals versus Substrate in Creole Genesis*, edited by Pieter Muysken and Norval Smith. Amsterdam: John Benjamins, 129–62.

Mufwene, Salikoko S. (1988) Why study pidgins and creoles? Column. *Journal of Pidgin and Creole Languages*, **3**, 265–76.

Mufwene, Salikoko S. (1990) Transfer and the substrate hypothesis in creolistics. *Studies in Second Language Acquisition*, **12**, 1–23.

Mufwene, Salikoko S. (1992) Why grammars are not monolithic. In *The Joy of Grammar: A Festschrift in Honor of James D. McCawley*. Edited by Diane Brentari, Gary Larson, and Lynn MacLeod. Amsterdam: John Benjamins, pp. 225–50.

Mufwene, Salikoko S. (ed.) (1993) *Africanisms in Afro-American Language Varieties*. Athens: University of Georgia Press.

Mufwene, Salikoko S. (1994) On decreolization: The case of Gullah. In *Language, Loyalty, and Identity in Creole Situations*. Edited by Marcyliena Morgan. Los Angeles: Center for Afro-American Studies, pp. 63–99.

Mufwene, Salikoko S. (1997) Jargons, pidgins, creoles, and koinés: What are they? In *Pidgins and Creoles: Structure and Status*. Edited by Arthur Spears and Donald Winford. Amsterdam: John Benjamins, pp. 35–70.

Mufwene, Salikoko S. (1999) The language bioprogram hypothesis: Hints from Tazie. In *Language Creation and Language Change: Creolization, Diachrony, and Development*. Edited by Michel DeGraff. Cambridge, MA: MIT Press, pp. 95–127.

Mufwene, Salikoko S. (2000) Creolization is a social, not a structural, process. In *Degrees of Restructuring in Creole Languages*. Edited by Ingrid Neumann-Holzschuh and Edgar Schneider. Amsterdam: John Benjamins, pp. 65–84.

Mufwene, Salikoko S. (2001) *The Ecology of Language Evolution*. Cambridge: Cambridge University Press.

Mufwene, Salikoko S. (2002) Colonization, globalization, and the future of languages in the twenty-first century. *MOST Journal on Multicultural Societies*, 4(2), 162–93.

Mufwene, Salikoko S. (2004) Language birth and death. *Annual Review of Anthropology*, **33**, 201–22.

Mufwene, Salikoko S. (2005) *Créoles, Écologie Sociale, Évolution Linguistique* [Creoles, Social Ecology, Language Evolution]. Paris: L'Harmattan.

Mühlhäusler, Peter (1981) The development of the category of number in Tok Pisin. In *Generative Studies on Creole Languages*. Edited by Pieter Muysken. Dordrecht: Foris, pp. 35–84.

Mühlhäusler, Peter (1985) The number of pidgin Englishes in the Pacific. *Papers in Pidgin and Creole Linguistics No. 1: Pacific Linguistics*, **A72**, 25–51.

Mühlhäusler, Peter (1986) *Pidgin and Creole Linguistics*. New York: Blackwell. Revised edition 1997, University of Westminster Press.

Muysken, Pieter and Smith, Norval (eds.) (1986) *Substrata versus Universals in Creole Genesis*. Amsterdam: John Benjamins.

Myers-Scotton, Carol (2002) *Contact Linguistics: Bilingual Encounters and Grammatical Outcomes*. Malden, MA: Blackwell.

Poplack, Shana (ed.) (1999) *The English History of African-American English*. Oxford: Blackwell.

Poplack, Shana and Tagliamonte, Sali (2001) *African American English in the Diaspora*. Malden, MA: Blackwell.

Rickford, John R. (1987) *Dimensions of a Creole Continuum: History, Texts, and Linguistic Analysis of Guyanese Creole*. Stanford: Stanford University Press.

Rickford, John R. (1998) The creole origins of African-American-vernacular English: Evidence from copula absence. In *African-American English: Structure, History, and Use*. Edited by Salikoko S. Mufwene, John R. Rickford, Guy Bailey, and John Baugh. London: Routledge, pp. 154–200.

Rickford, John R. and Handler, Jerome S. (1994) Textual evidence on the nature of early Barbadian speech, 1676–1835. *Journal of Pidgin and Creole Languages*, **9**, 221–55.

Romaine, Suzanne (1988) *Pidgin and Creole Languages*. London: Longman.

Sankoff, Gillian (1979) The genesis of a language. In *The Genesis of Language*. Edited by Kenneth C. Hill. Ann Arbor: Karoma, pp. 23–47.

Sankoff, Gillian and Brown, Penelope (1976) The origins of syntax in discourse: A case study of Tok Pisin relatives. *Language*, **52**, 631–66.

Schlupp, Daniel (1997) *Modalités Prédicatives, Modalités Aspectuelles, et Auxiliaires en Créole* [Predicate Markers, Aspectual Markers, and Auxiliaries in Creole]. Tübingen: Max Niemeyer.

Schneider, Edgar W. (1989) *American Earlier Black English: Morphological and Syntactic Variables*. Tuscaloosa, AL: University of Alabama Press.

Schuchardt, Hugo (1909) Die Lingua
  Franca [Lingua Franca]. *Zeitschrift
  fur Romanische Philologie*, **33**, 441–61.
Schuchardt, Hugo (1914) *Die Sprache der
  Saramakkaneger in Surinam* [The
  Language of the Saramaccan Blacks
  in Surinam]. Amsterdam: Johannes
  Muller.
Singler, John V. (ed.) (1990) *Pidgin and
  Creole Tense-Mood-Aspect Systems*.
  Amsterdam: John Benjamins.
Smith, Norval (1995) An annotated list of
  pidgins, creoles, and mixed
  languages. In *Pidgins and Creoles:
  An Introduction*. Edited by Jacques
  Arends, Pieter Muysken, and Norval
  Smith. Amsterdam: John Benjamins,
  pp. 331–74.
Sylvain, Suzanne (1936) *Le Créole Haïtien:
  Morphologie et Syntaxe* [Haitian
  Creole: Morphology and Syntax].
  Wettern, Belgium: Imprimerie De
  Meester.
Tagliamonte, Sali and Poplack, Shana
  (1993) The zero-marked verb:
  Testing the creole hypothesis. *Journal
  of Pidgin and Creole Languages*, **8**,
  171–206.
Thomason, Sarah G. (1997) A typology
  of contact languages. In *The
  Structure and Status of Pidgins and
  Creoles*. Edited by Arthur K. Spears
  and Donald Winford. Amsterdam:
  John Benjamins, pp. 71–88.
Thomason, Sarah. G. (2001) *Language
  Contact: An Introduction*.
  Washington, DC: Georgetown
  University Press.
Thomason, Sarah G. and Kaufman,
  Terrence (1988) *Language Contact,
  Creolization, and Genetic Linguistics*.
  Berkeley: University of California
  Press.
Turner, Lorenzo Dow (1949) *Africanisms
  in the Gullah Dialect*. Chicago:
  University of Chicago Press.
Valdman, Albert (ed.) (1977) *Pidgin and
  Creole Linguistics*. Bloomington:
  Indiana University Press.
Valkhoff, Marius F. (1966) *Studies in
  Portuguese and Creole: With Special
  Reference to South Africa*.
  Johannesburg: Witwatersrand
  University Press.
Vinson, Julien (1882) Créole. In
  *Dictionnaire des Sciences
  Anthropologiques et Ethnologiques* [A
  Dictionary of Anthropological and
  Ethnological Sciences]. Paris.
Winford, Donald (2003) *An Introduction
  to Contact Linguistics*. Malden, MA:
  Blackwell.

FURTHER READING

Smith, Norval and Veenstra, Tonjes
  (eds.) (2001) *Creolization and Contact*.
  Amsterdam: Benjamins.

19 African American English

WALT WOLFRAM

1 Introduction

In the study of ethnic dialect in the history of English, no dialect has received more attention than African American English. It is by far the most scrutinized dialect of American English (Schneider, 1996), and has now become widely recognized throughout the English-speaking world. Within the last several decades, it has gone through a number of name changes, which include *Negro Dialect*, *Nonstandard Negro English*, *Black English*, *Black English Vernacular*, *Afro-American English*, *African American (Vernacular) English*, *African American Language*, and *Ebonics*. To some extent, these name changes simply have been aligned with changes in naming practices related to the classification of black Americans, but their significance goes deeper than that; in fact, they often relate to underlying issues of racial politics and ethnic ideologies in American society. Though most popularly referred to now as Ebonics, thanks to a widely publicized and highly controversial School Board resolution adopted in Oakland, California, in the late 1990s, most linguists prefer terms such as African American English (AAE) or African American Language because of the strong emotional reactions and racist parodies sometimes engendered by the use of the term Ebonics.

The literature on AAE is vast, and covers a full range of issues – from AAE's origin and early development to its current social capital and educational vulnerability. Its controversial nature is rooted in the fact that the language of black Americans has served as a proxy for wider social and political issues related to the negotiation of racial categories and ethnic identities. This chapter, however, is limited to the linguistic issues related to AAE, including its descriptive base, its genesis and early development, and its current path of change.

2 The Descriptive Base of AAE

The distinctiveness of AAE among the vernacular dialects of American English is an ongoing controversy, though there is little dispute that AAE differs significantly from benchmark European American vernacular varieties in most non-Southern, urban contexts. Given a randomly selected set of audio-recordings whose content contains no culturally identifying material, listeners can accurately identify African American speakers approximately 80 percent of the time (Graff, Labov, and Harris, 1986; Shuy, Baratz, and Wolfram, 1969; Thomas, 2002; Thomas and Reaser, forthcoming). Determining the perceptual basis of this identification, however, is not nearly as straightforward as making the ethnic classification. Linguistically, different levels of language organization may be involved, ranging from minute segmental and suprasegmental phonetic details (Thomas, 2002) to generalized discourse strategies and conversational routines (Smitherman, 1977). Socially, demographic factors such as status, region, and level of education affect listeners' perceptions of ethnic identity, as do interactional factors such as interlocutors and speech setting. Given the array of linguistic, social, and personal variables in identification experiments, different studies may, in fact, show a wide range of reliable ethnic identification. Thus, the ethnicity of some African American speakers in certain contexts may be identified correctly less than 5 percent of the time while other speakers are correctly identified more than 95 percent of the time (Thomas and Reaser, forthcoming).

Region, status, and other sociocultural attributes are also important in determining the structural relationship of AAE to comparable European American vernacular varieties. AAE is rooted historically in Southern-based, rural varieties, so it is structurally more similar to these varieties than it is to its Northern vernacular counterparts, but the development of AAE into a recognized sociocultural variety in the twentieth century has become strongly associated with its use in non-Southern, urban areas.

Though the relationship of African American and European American speech is still not totally resolved after several decades of heated debate, some agreement is emerging. Following is a partial list of prominent phonological and grammatical features of AAE from Wolfram and Schilling-Estes (2006) that are most likely to differentiate AAE from comparable European American vernacular varieties. More extensive lists of the phonological and morphosyntactic traits of AAE (Bailey, 2001; Bailey and Thomas, 1998; Cukor-Avila, 2001; Fasold and Wolfram, 1970; Green, 2002; Labov, 1972; Labov et al., 1968; Rickford, 1999; Thomas, 2001; Wolfram, 1994) may include dozens of phonological and grammatical structures. In addition, there are features on other linguistic levels, including prosodic and pragmatic features, but these have not yet been described in nearly the same detail as phonology and morphosyntax.

Some Distinguishing Features of African American English

(from Wolfram and Schilling-Estes, 2006)

habitual *be* for intermittent activity:
e.g. *Sometimes my ears be itching.*
She don't be usually be there.
absence of copula for contracted forms of *is* and *are*:
e.g. *She nice.*
They acting all strange.
present tense, third-person -*s* absence:
e.g. *she walk* for *she walks*
she raise for *she raises*
possessive -*s* absence:
e.g. *man_ hat* for *man's hat*
Jack_ car for *Jack's car*
general plural -*s* absence:
e.g. *a lot of time* for *a lot of times*
some dog for *some dogs*
remote time stressed *béen* to mark a state or action that began a long time ago and is still relevant:
e.g. *You béen paid your dues a long time ago.*
I béen known him a long time.
simple past tense *had* + Verb:
e.g. *They had went outside and then they had messed up the yard.*
Yesterday, she had fixed the bike and had rode it to school.
ain't for *didn't*:
e.g. *He ain't go there yesterday.*
He ain't do it.
reduction of final consonant clusters when followed by a word beginning with a vowel:
e.g. *lif' up* for *lift up*
bus' up for *bust up*
skr for *str* initial clusters:
e.g. *skreet* for *street*
skraight for *straight*
use of [f] and [v] for final *th*:
e.g. *toof* for *tooth*
smoov for *smooth*

Even with this restricted list, there are important qualifications. In some cases, it is a particular aspect of the phonological or grammatical pattern rather than the general rule that is unique to AAE. Thus, consonant cluster reduction is widespread in English, but in most varieties it only applies when the cluster is followed by a consonant (e.g., *bes' kind*) rather than when followed by a vowel (*bes' en'*). Similarly, we also find plural -*s* absence in some Southern European

American varieties (Montgomery and Hall, 2004; Wolfram, 2003a), but only on quantified measure nouns (e.g., *four mile, five pound*). In other cases, the difference between the patterning of a feature in AAE and in a benchmark European American vernacular variety involves a significant quantitative difference rather than a qualitative one. For example, the absence of the verb *be* for contracted forms of *are* (e.g., *you ugly* for *you're ugly*) is found among Southern European American vernacular speakers, but it is not nearly as frequent as it is in AAE (Cukor-Avila, 2001; Wolfram, 1974).

Debate over the group-exclusiveness of some AAE structures continues despite careful study of the present status of AAE in relation to other varieties. Research by Bailey and Bassett (1986) and Montgomery and Mishoe (1999), for example, shows that finite *be* (e.g., *I be there; They be doing it*) is found in both European American and African American varieties, though its semantic reference is not identical. At the same time, other investigators have suggested that there are additional forms that are unique. For example, Labov (1998) suggests that among the constructions overlooked in earlier descriptions of AAE is resultative *be done*, a sequence of *be* and *done* together in sentences such as *If you love your enemy, they be done eat you alive in this society*; in these types of sentences it indicates a potential action or condition that will lead to some inevitable result.

There are also structures in AAE that appear on the surface to be very much like those in other dialects of English but turn out, upon closer inspection, to have uses or meanings that are unique. These types of structures are called *camouflaged forms* because they bear surface resemblance to constructions found in other varieties of English, but they are used differently. One of these camouflaged constructions is the form *come* in a construction with an *-ing* verb, as in *She **come acting** like she was real mad*. This structure looks like the common English use of the motion verb *come* in structures like *She **came running***, but research indicates that it actually has a special use as a kind of verb auxiliary indicating annoyance or indignation on the part of the speaker (Spears, 1982). The specialized meaning of indignation is apparently unique to AAE. Other camouflaged forms include the progressive use of *steady* in *They be steady running* (Baugh, 1984), the use of *call oneself* with verb *+ing* constructions such as *They call themselves dancing* (Wolfram, 1994), and the use of *ain't* for *didn't* in *He ain't know nothing* (Labov et al., 1968).

Though it is possible to compare structures used by European American and African American speakers on an item-by-item basis, the picture that emerges from this approach does not fully represent the true relationship between AAE and other varieties. The uniqueness of AAE lies more in the particular combination of structures that make up the dialect than it does in a restricted set of potentially unique structures. It is the co-occurrence of grammatical structures such as the absence of various suffixes (possessive, third-person singular, plural *-s*), absence of copula *be*, use of habitual *be*, and so forth, along with a set of phonological characteristics such as consonant cluster reduction, final [f] for *th* (e.g., *baf* for *bath*), postvocalic *r*-lessness, and so forth, that best defines the variety, rather than the subset of unique features. Studies of listener perceptions of ethnic identity certainly support the contention that AAE is distinct from comparable European American vernaculars, but researchers are still investigating how to sort out the precise points of this differentiation. Recent experimental investigation by Thomas and Reaser (forthcoming) suggests that phonetic differences rather than grammatical differences, including differences in vowel pronunciation and voice quality, may have as much to do with the perceptual determination of ethnicity as differences in grammatical structures.

Up to this point, we have discussed AAE as if it were a unitary variety in different regions of the United States. We must, however, admit regional variation in AAE, just as we have to admit regional variation within vernacular European American varieties. Certainly, some of the Northern metropolitan versions of AAE are distinguishable from some of the Southern rural versions, and South Atlantic coastal varieties are different from those found in the Gulf region. While admitting these regional variations, it is also important to point out that one of the most noteworthy aspects of AAE is the common set of features shared across different regions. Features such as habitual *be*, copula absence, inflectional *-s* absence, among a number of other grammatical and phonological structures, are found in locations as distant as Los Angeles, California; New Haven, Connecticut; Austin, Texas; and Meadville, Mississippi, cutting across both urban and rural settings. The foundation of a core set of AAE features, regardless of where it has been studied in the United States, attests to the strong ethnic association and trans-regional dimension of this language variety.

3   The Origin and Early Development of AAE

Hypotheses about the origin and early development of AAE have now gone through several paradigmatic shifts. Four primary hypotheses, in the following chronological sequence, have emerged over the past half century: the Anglicist Hypothesis, the Creolist Hypothesis, the Neo-Anglicist Hypothesis, and the Substrate Hypothesis. Controversy about these positions has not subsided, though most of the controversy now seems to be centered on the last two options.

The Anglicist Hypothesis was initially proposed by prominent American dialectologists such as Hans Kurath (1949) and Raven McDavid (McDavid and McDavid, 1951) in the mid-twentieth century, based on extensive surveys of regional English under the aegis of the Linguistic Atlas of the United States and Canada. Though there were relatively few African Americans included in these surveys, it appeared that older black and white speakers interviewed in the 1930s and 1940s shared many of the same regional features. On this basis, American dialectologists concluded that AAE could be traced to the same sources as earlier European American dialects, the dialects of English spoken in the British Isles. According to this historical scenario, slaves brought a number of different African languages with them when they were transported, but over the course of a couple of generations these were replaced by the English varieties spoken by their regional cohorts, with only a few minor traces of the ancestral languages remaining. As Kurath (1949: 6) put it, "By and large the Southern Negro speaks the language of the white man of his locality or area and of his education."

Under this viewpoint, differences between African American and European American varieties that could not be explained on the basis of regional and social factors were attributed to the preservation of earlier British dialect features. The pursuit of historical evidence to support this position involved the scrutiny of earlier English varieties in the British Isles for features similar to those found in AAE, along with a search for sociohistorical facts that would link speakers of these donor dialects with people of African descent in North America.

The Anglicist Hypothesis was the prevailing position on the origin of AAE until the mid-1960s and 1970s, when the Creolist Hypothesis emerged. According to this hypothesis, AAE developed from a creole language that was fairly widespread in the antebellum South (Bailey, 1965; Stewart, 1967, 1968; Dillard, 1972). This creole was not unique to the mainland South; it showed a number of similarities to well-known English-based creoles in the African diaspora, such as Krio, spoken today in Sierra Leone along the coast of West Africa, as well as English-based creoles of the Caribbean, such as those spoken in Barbados and Jamaica. Creolists maintain that the vestiges of the proto-creole that gave rise to AAE can be found in Gullah, the creole still spoken by some African Americans in the Sea Islands off the coast of South Carolina and Georgia. It is maintained that this creole was fairly widespread among people of African descent on Southern plantations but was not spoken to any extent by whites. As Stewart (1968: 3) put it, "Negro slaves who constituted the field labor force on North American plantations up to the mid-nineteenth century, even many who were born in the New World spoke a variety of English which was in fact a true creole language – differing markedly in grammatical structure from those English dialects which were brought directly from Great Britain." Although not all AAE researchers accepted such a strong interpretation of the Creolist Hypothesis during the 1970s and 1980s, many accepted some version of it. As Fasold (1981: 164) noted, "the creole hypothesis seems most likely to be correct, but it is certainly not so well established as Dillard (1972), for example, would have us to believe."

Contact with other dialects in the US eventually led this creole language to be modified, according to the hypothesis, so that it became more closely aligned with other varieties of English in the process of decreolization, whereby creole features are gradually replaced by non-creole features. However, this process was neither instantaneous nor complete (Fasold, 1976), so that the vestiges of its creole predecessor may still be present in modern AAE. For example, copula absence (e.g., *You ugly*) is a well-known trait of creole languages, so one might maintain that the present-day existence of copula absence in AAE is a vestige of its creole origin. Similar arguments have been made for various types of inflectional -*s* absence (e.g., *Mary go_; Mary_ hat*) (Winford, 1997, 1998), as well as phonological characteristics such as consonant cluster reduction (Wolfram, Childs, and Torbert, 2000). Both the linguistic and social history of blacks in the antebellum South have been cited in support for the creole origin of AAE. J. L. Dillard's book *Black English: Its History and Usage in the United States* (1972) was quite influential in promoting the Creolist Hypothesis, although current creolists (Rickford, 1999; Winford, 1997, 1998) have now engaged in much more rigorous and detailed quantitative analysis in support for this hypothesis than that originally offered by Dillard.

Several new types of data surfaced in the 1980s that called the Creolist Hypothesis into question. New written datasets included the written records of ex-slaves, such as the extensive set of ex-slave narratives collected under the Works Project Administration (WPA) (Bailey, Maynor, and Cukor-Avila, 1991; Schneider, 1989, 1996) in the 1930s; letters written by semiliterate ex-slaves in the mid-1800s (Montgomery and Fuller, 1996; Montgomery, Fuller, and DeMarse, 1993); and other specialized collections of texts, such as the Hyatt texts – an extensive set of interviews conducted with black practitioners of voodoo in the 1930s (Ewers, 1996; Hyatt, 1970–8). All of these records pointed toward the conclusion that earlier AAE was not nearly as distinct from postcolonial European American English varieties as would have been predicted under the Creolist Hypothesis. A limited set of audio recordings of ex-slaves conducted as a part of the WPA in the 1930s (Bailey et al., 1991) also seemed to support this contention.

A different type of data offered in opposition to the Creolist Hypothesis comes from the examination of the varieties of English spoken by black expatriates. For example, in the 1820s a group of blacks migrated from Philadelphia, Pennsylvania, to the peninsula of Samaná in the Dominican Republic, where their descendants continue to live in relative isolation and maintain a relic variety of English (Poplack and Sankoff, 1987; Poplack and Tagliamonte, 1989, 1991, 2001). A significant population of African Americans also migrated from the United States to Canada in the early 1800s, and some of their descendants have preserved a life of relative isolation in Nova Scotia. The examination of the English varieties spoken by blacks in these areas by Poplack and Tagliamonte (Poplack, 1999; Poplack and Tagliamonte, 1991, 1994, 2001) indicates that these insular varieties were quite similar to earlier European American varieties rather than a presumed creole predecessor, thus casting doubt on the Creole Hypothesis.

Close scrutiny of the sociohistorical situation and demographics of the antebellum South (Mufwene, 1996, 2001) has indicated further that the distribution of slaves in the Southeastern Plantation region of the US was not particularly advantageous to the perpetuation of a widespread Plantation Creole, as had been postulated by earlier creolists. In fact, the vast majority of slaves lived on smaller farms with just a few slaves per household rather than on the large, sprawling plantations with large numbers of slaves that are sometimes pictured in popular portrayals of the antebellum South. In fact, over 80 percent of all slaves were associated with families that had fewer than five slaves per household.

The Neo-Anglicist Hypothesis is like the Anglicist Hypothesis in maintaining that earlier, postcolonial African American speech was directly linked to the early British dialects brought to North America. However, the Neo-Anglicist position acknowledges that AAE has since diverged so that it is now quite distinct from contemporary European American vernacular speech. Poplack (1999: 27) asserts that "AAVE [African American Vernacular English] originated as English, but as the African American community solidified, it innovated specific features" so that "contemporary AAVE is the result of evolution, by its own unique, internal logic."

Disputes about the Neo-Anglicist Hypothesis center on the nature of the earlier language contact situation between Africans and Europeans and the general sociohistorical circumstances that framed the speech of earlier African Americans (Rickford, 1997, 1999; Singler, 1998a, 1998b; Winford, 1997, 1998). Research on long-term, historically isolated enclave communities of African Americans in coastal North Carolina (Wolfram and Thomas, 2002) and in Appalachia (Mallinson and Wolfram, 2002; Childs and Mallinson, forthcoming; Mallinson and Childs, forthcoming), for example, suggests that earlier African American speech in some regions converged to a large extent with localized varieties of English spoken by their European American counterparts. In this respect, the data appear to support the traditional Anglicist and Neo-Anglicist hypotheses. But there is also evidence for a durable ethnolinguistic divide that is not generally acknowledged under the Anglicist or Neo-Anglicist positions, giving rise to the Substrate Hypothesis (Wolfram and Thomas, 2002; Wolfram, 2003b). Some of the persistent differences may be attributed to subtle but enduring influence from early contact between Africans and Europeans. For example, structures vulnerable to modification and loss during language contact situations, such as inflectional *-s* on third-person verbs (e.g., *She go*), the copula (e.g., *He ugly*), and word-final consonant clusters (e.g., *lif' up* for *lift up*), distinguished earlier African American speech from that of its regional European American counterparts. Furthermore, these traits persist to this day, despite similarities across varieties with respect to other dialect features. In brief, the Substrate Hypothesis maintains that even though earlier AAE may have incorporated many regional dialect features, enduring substrate effects have consistently distinguished it from other varieties of American English (Wolfram and Thomas, 2002; Wolfram, 2003b). In this respect, the position differs from the Neo-Anglicist position, which argues that earlier AAE was identical to earlier European American English.

Current evidence suggests more regional influence from English speakers than assumed under the Creolist Hypothesis and more durable effects from early language contact situations than assumed under the Anglicist positions, but the issue of regional accommodation and substrate influence continues to be debated. Given the limitations of data, the different local circumstances under which African Americans lived in the antebellum South, and the historical time-depth involved, there will probably always be speculation about the origin and earlier development of AAE.

4   The Development of Contemporary AAE

Questions about the present-day development of AAE have now become as controversial as its earlier history. Though it might be assumed that AAE has gradually been converging with other dialects of English in the century and a half since the Civil War, this view has been strongly challenged. Based on research conducted by Labov and his colleagues in Philadelphia in the mid-1980s (Labov, 1985, 1987; Labov and Harris, 1986) and Bailey and his colleagues (Bailey, 1987; Bailey and Maynor, 1987, 1989), it was concluded that AAE is actually diverging from rather than converging with surrounding vernaculars. As Labov (1985: 1) put it, "their [i.e., African American residents of Philadelphia] speech pattern is developing in its own direction and becoming more different from the speech of whites in the same communities." Studies of urban AAE in the last couple of decades seem to support the contention that some AAE structures are intensifying rather than receding and that new structures are developing (Bailey, 2001; Cukor-Avila, 2001; Dayton, 1996; Labov, 1998). For example, the use of habitual *be* in sentences such as *Sometimes they be playing games* seems to be escalating, to the point of becoming a stereotype of AAE. Similarly, the narrative use of the auxiliary *had* with a past or perfect form of the verb to indicate a simple past tense action, as in *They had went outside and then they had messed up the yard*, seems have arisen more recently and to be on the increase as well (Cukor-Avila, 2001; Rickford and Théberge-Rafal, 1996; Ross, Oetting, and Stapleton, 2004).

The sociological foundation for the so-called divergence hypothesis was based on the social and economic plight of lower-class African Americans – racial isolation brought about by increasing de facto segregation and a widening socio-economic gap between mainstream American society and lower-class minority groups. Perhaps more important than population demographics, however, is the establishment of contemporary cultural and language norms related to African American youth culture that are in opposition to those found in mainstream white culture. The center of African American youth culture today is primarily urban, and many models for behavior, including language, seem to radiate outward from these urban cultural centers.

During the latter half of the twentieth century, a couple of noteworthy sociolinguistic trends have taken place with respect to AAE. First, this variety has taken on an ethnic significance that transcends its regional context. There has also been a growing sense of ethnic identity associated with AAE over the past half-century. This sense of identity is bolstered through a variety of informal and formal social mechanisms that range from community-based social networks to stereotypical media projections of

African American speech (Lippi-Green, 1997). Part of what it means to speak AAE is not only the use of features associated with it, but the avoidance of features associated with regional and standard "white speech." Fordham and Ogbu (1986) note that the adoption of Standard English is at the top of the inventory of prominent behaviors listed by high school students as "acting white." Ethnic identity not only concerns the relations, behaviors, practices, and attitudes of African Americans themselves but also so-called oppositional identity – in other words, how African Americans position themselves with respect to white society.

The question of change in AAE has been addressed in recent years by examining a range of small, rural Southern communities (Carpenter and Hilliard, 2003; Childs and Mallinson, forthcoming; Cukor-Avila, 2001; Mallinson and Childs, forthcoming; Mallinson and Wolfram, 2002; Wolfram and Thomas, 2002) to complement the earlier study of AAE focused on large, urban non-Southern areas (Baugh, 1983; Fasold, 1972; Labov, 1972; Labov et al., 1968; Legum et al., 1971; Wolfram, 1969). Comparative studies of different small Southern communities show several different trajectories rather than a unitary path of change. In the case of one community, Hyde County, a historically isolated community of approximately 2,000 African American residents in coastal North Carolina, we find the movement of African American speech toward a more supra-regional norm (Wolfram and Thomas, 2002; Wolfram, 2003b). Elderly African Americans, who traveled little outside of the region, adopted many of the distinctive dialect traits of the European American dialect of the region while maintaining a core set of AAE features. Over time, however, core AAE features and local dialect features have shown a mirror image in terms of change. Older speakers show moderate levels of core AAE features and extensive local dialect accommodation, while younger speakers show a progressive increase in AAE features and a corresponding loss of local dialect structures. The trajectory of change with respect to the local, Outer Banks dialect features and the core AAE feature in the speech of African Americans of different generational groups in the area, based on our analysis of a number of representative features, is plotted in Figure 19.1 (Wolfram and Thomas, 2002: 200). Speakers are divided into generational groups based on four important sociohistorical periods: speakers who were born and raised in the early twentieth century up through World War I; speakers born and raised between World War I and school integration in the late 1960s; speakers who lived through the early period of school integration as adolescents; and speakers who were born and raised after legalized institutional integration.

From one perspective, the path of change indicated in Figure 19.1 reveals the limited linguistic effects of institutionally mandated integration. From a different vantage point, however, it indicates the growing consciousness of the role of language in the construction of ethnic identity, even in the face of sociopolitical pressure and legal mandates to integrate. Traditional rural dialects like those spoken on the coast of North Carolina now carry strong associations of white, rural speech. In fact, younger African Americans describe

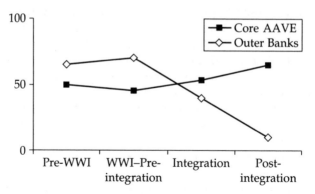

Figure 19.1 Trajectory of language change for African Americans in Hyde County (adapted from Wolfram and Thomas, 2002: 200)

the speech of older Hyde County African Americans as "sounding country" and being "more white" than the speech of younger African Americans. Younger speakers who identify strongly with African American culture contra "white culture" would therefore be inclined to change their speech toward the more generalized version of AAE – and away from the localized dialect norm. An essential ingredient of the contemporary supra-regional norm for AAE is thus the heightened symbolic role of language as an ethnic emblem of African American culture.

A quite different trajectory of change is indicated for a receding Appalachian African American community studied by Mallinson and Wolfram (2002), where only a half-dozen African American residents now remain from a once-stable community of 120 African Americans who lived there from the 1850s through the mid-twentieth century. In this case, we see the recession of core AAE features and the maintenance of the regional features of Appalachian speech. The trajectory of change for the Beech Bottom community is given in Figure 19.2.

A third type of change trajectory, a curvilinear model, is documented for another Southern Appalachian community, Texana (Childs and Mallinson, forthcoming; Mallinson and Childs, forthcoming), a small, stable African American community of approximately 150 African Americans which has existed in the Smoky Mountains for over 150 years. In this case, as shown in Figure 19.3, we see that younger and older speakers indicate relatively low levels of AAE features and high levels of local Appalachian features. At the same time, middle-aged speakers seem to increase their levels of AAE features.

Though middle-aged speakers show more AAE features than their younger and older cohorts, not all middle-aged speakers show this pattern. In fact, Mallinson and Childs (forthcoming) note that this pattern of intensification is restricted to those speakers who have spent time in metropolitan Atlanta, which is a couple of hours away from Texana. This pattern suggests the

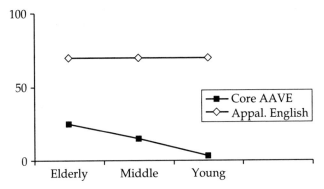

Figure 19.2 Trajectory of language change for Beech Bottom (based on Mallinson and Wolfram, 2002)

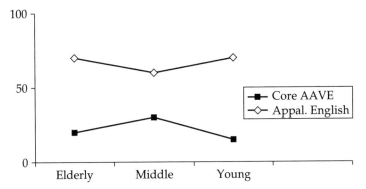

Figure 19.3 Trajectory of language change for Texana (based on Childs and Mallinson, forthcoming)

significance of contact with external, more urban African American populations. It also suggests that group affiliation and cultural orientation may be a factor in the determination of change in AAE, since Mallinson and Childs point to quite differing communities of practice and cultural orientations for middle-aged speakers who indicate more AAE structures.

The comparative study of different rural Southern African American communities shows that there may be alternative trajectories of change with respect to the use of core AAE structures and regional dialect structures, ranging from the intensification of AAE features and the corresponding loss of regionalized features, to the reduction of AAE features and the maintenance of regionalized features. Communities may also indicate a kind of ebb and flow in which core AAE features are intensified or reduced at different periods of time, or among different subgroups and/or individuals within a community.

Factors that affect trajectories of change include the regional setting of the community, community size, the past and present extent of ethnic isolation, significant macro and micro sociohistorical events, patterns of contact with external African American communities, intra-community social divisions, and cultural values within the community. Change in African American speech communities cannot be captured by a unilateral model. Instead, a variety of complex, intersecting factors needs to be considered in describing the present-day course of change in African American speech communities.

5   Conclusion

AAE is a distinct, robust, and stable socio-ethnic dialect of English that is maintaining itself and, in some cases, even intensifying. Though its origin and early development continue to be disputed, it seems apparent that AAE has accommodated itself to host regional varieties of English while maintaining a durable, distinctive substrate that has set it apart in the past and present. Furthermore, a growing sense of linguistic solidarity and identity among African Americans unifies AAE in different locales, though not all local situations follow the path of change. Comparisons of different local situations involving African Americans suggest considerable variation in patterns of change. Furthermore, these differing local situations underscore the significance of the social dynamics and the geographical location of a community in understanding the past and present development of AAE. Original settlement history, community size, local and extra-local social networks, and racial ideologies in American society must all be considered in understanding the course of change in African American speech.

Finally, we must note that AAE is more than a simple assemblage of linguistic structures of the type that we have described here. Linguists and dialectologists have sometimes focused on structural features of grammar and phonology to the exclusion of other traits that might distinguish speech communities. AAE may also encompass culturally significant uses of voice quality and other prosodic features, as well as culturally distinctive pragmatic features such as particular types of conversational routines that include greetings and leave-takings, back channeling, and narrative styles. The soul of AAE does not necessarily reside in the inventory of structural phonological and grammatical traits that have become the obsession of sociolinguistic description over the past few decades, but in its everyday uses of language that encompass the full range of communicative functions and activities.

See also Chapters 11, West African Englishes; 13, Caribbean Englishes; 15, World Englishes Today; 16, Contact Linguistics and World Englishes; 18, Pidgins and Creoles; 21, Speaking and Writing in World Englishes; 25, World Englishes and Culture Wars; 36, Teaching World Englishes.

NOTE

Support for research reported here came from NSF Grants 9910024 and 0236838, and from the William C. Friday Endowment at North Carolina State University.

REFERENCES

Bailey, Beryl (1965) A new perspective in American Negro dialectology. *American Speech*, **11**, 171–7.

Bailey, Guy (1987) Are black and white vernaculars diverging? Papers from the NWAVE 14 panel discussion. *American Speech*, **62**, 32–40.

Bailey, Guy (2001) The relationship between AAVE and White vernaculars in the American South: A sociocultural history and some phonological evidence. In *Sociohistorical and Historical Contexts of African American Vernacular*. Edited by Sonja Lanehart. Philadelphia/Amsterdam: John Benjamins, pp. 53–92.

Bailey, Guy and Bassett, Marvin (1986) Invariant be in the lower South. In *Language Variety in the South: Perspectives in Black and White*. Edited by Michael Montgomery and Guy Bailey. Tuscaloosa: University of Alabama Press, pp. 158–79.

Bailey, Guy and Maynor, Natalie (1987) Decreolization? *Language in Society*, **16**, 449–74.

Bailey, Guy and Maynor, Natalie (1989) The divergence controversy. *American Speech*, **64**, 12–39.

Bailey, Guy and Thomas, Erik (1998) Some aspects of African-American English phonology. In *African American English: Structure, History, and Use*. Edited by Salikoko S. Mufwene, John R. Rickford, Guy Bailey, and John Baugh. London/ New York: Routledge, pp. 85–109.

Bailey, Guy, Maynor, Natalie, and Cukor-Avila, Patricia (eds.) (1991) *The Emergence of Black English*. Philadelphia/Amsterdam: John Benjamins.

Baugh, John (1983) *Black Street Speech: Its History, Structure, and Survival*. Austin: University of Texas Press.

Baugh, John (1984) *Steady*: Progressive aspect in Black Vernacular English. *American Speech*, **59**, 3–12.

Carpenter, Jeannine and Hilliard, Sarah (2003) The lost community of the Outer Banks: African American speech on Roanoke Island. Paper presented at NWAVE 32. Philadelphia: University of Pennsylvania.

Childs, Becky and Mallinson, Christine (forthcoming) African American English in Appalachia: Dialect accommodation and substrate influence. *English World-Wide*.

Cukor-Avila, Patricia (2001) Co-existing grammars: The relationship between the evolution of African American and Southern White Vernacular English in the South. In *Sociocultural and Historical Contexts of African American English*. Edited by Sonja L. Lanehart. Philadelphia/ Amsterdam: John Benjamins, pp. 93–128.

Dayton, Elizabeth (1996) Grammatical Categories of the Verb in African American Vernacular English. PhD dissertation. Philadelphia: University of Pennsylvania.

Dillard, Joey Lee (1972) *Black English: Its History and Usage in the United States.* New York: Random House.

Ewers, Traute (1996) *The Origin of American Black English: Be-Forms in the Hoodoo Texts.* Berlin/New York: Mouton de Gruyter.

Fasold, Ralph W. (1972) *Tense Marking in Black English: A Linguistic and Social Analysis.* Arlington: Center for Applied Linguistics.

Fasold, Ralph W. (1976) One hundred years from syntax to phonology. In *Papers from the Parasession on Diachronic Syntax.* Edited by Sanford Steever, Carle Walker, and Salikoko S. Mufwene. Chicago: Chicago Linguistics Society, pp. 79–87.

Fasold, Ralph W. (1981) The relation between black and white speech in the South. *American Speech,* **56**, 163–89.

Fasold, Ralph W. and Wolfram, Walt (1970) Some linguistic features of Negro dialect. In *Teaching Standard English in the Inner City.* Edited by Ralph W. Fasold and Roger W. Shuy. Washington, DC: Center for Applied Linguistics, pp. 41–86.

Fordham, Signithia and Ogbu, John (1986) Black students' school success: Coping with the burden of "acting white." *Urban Review,* **18**, 176–206.

Graff, David, Labov, William, and Harris, Wendell A. (1986) Testing listeners' reactions to phonological markers of ethnic identity: A new method for sociolinguistic research. In *Diversity and Diachrony.* Edited by David Sankoff. Philadelphia/Amsterdam: John Benjamins, pp. 45–58.

Green, Lisa J. (2002) *African American English: A Linguistic Introduction.* New York: Cambridge University Press.

Hyatt, Harry Middleton (1970–8) *Hoodoo-Conjuration-Witchcraft-Rootwork, vols. 1–5.* Hannibal, MO: Western Publishing Co.

Kurath, Hans (1949) *A Word Geography of the Eastern United States.* Ann Arbor, MI: University of Michigan Press.

Labov, William (1972) *Language in the Inner City: Studies in the Black English Vernacular.* Philadelphia: University of Pennsylvania Press.

Labov, William (1985) The increasing divergence of black and white vernacular: Introduction to the research reports. Unpublished manuscript.

Labov, William (1987) Are black and white vernaculars diverging? Papers from the NWAVE 14 panel discussion. *American Speech,* **62**, 5–12.

Labov, William (1998) Coexistent systems in African-American vernacular English. In *African American English: Structure, History, and Use.* Edited by Salikoko S. Mufwene, John R. Rickford, Guy Bailey, and John Baugh. London/New York: Routledge, pp. 110–53.

Labov, William and Harris, Wendell A. (1986) De facto segregation of black and white vernaculars. In *Diversity and Diachrony.* Edited by David Sankoff. Philadelphia/Amsterdam: John Benjamins, pp. 1–24.

Labov, William, Cohen, Paul, Robins, Clarence, and Lewis, John (1968) *A Study of the Non-Standard English of Negro and Puerto Rican Speakers in New York City.* Washington, DC: United States Office of Education Final Report, Research Project 3288.

Legum, Stanley E., Pfaff, Carole, Tinnie, Gene, and Nichols, Michael (1971) *The Speech of Young Black Children in Los Angeles.* Inglewood: Southwest Regional Laboratory.

Lippi-Green, Rosina (1997) *English with an Accent: Language, Ideology, and Discrimination in the United States.* London/New York: Routledge.

Mallinson, Christine and Childs, Becky (forthcoming) Communities of practice in sociolinguistic description: African women's language in Appalachia. *Penn Working Papers in Linguistics*, **10**.

Mallinson, Christine and Wolfram, Walt (2002) Dialect accommodation in a bi-ethnic mountain enclave community: More evidence on the development of African American Vernacular English. *Language in Society*, **31**, 743–75.

McDavid, Raven I., Jr. and McDavid, Virginia G. (1951) The relationship of the speech of American Negroes to the speech of whites. *American Speech*, **26**, 3–17.

Montgomery, Michael and Fuller, Janet (1996) Verbal -s in 19th-century African-American English. In *Focus on the USA*. Edited by Edgar W. Schneider. Philadelphia/ Amsterdam: John Benjamins, pp. 211–30.

Montgomery, Michael and Hall, Joseph S. (2004) *Dictionary of Smoky Mountain English*. Knoxville: University of Tennessee Press.

Montgomery, Michael and Mishoe, Margaret (1999) "He bes took up with a Yankee girl and moved up North": The verb bes in the Carolinas and its history. *American Speech*, **75**, 240–81.

Montgomery, Michael, Fuller, Janet, and DeMarse, Sharon (1993) The black men has wives and sweet harts [and third-person -s] Jest like the white men: Evidence for verbal -s from written documents on nineteenth-century African-American speech. *Language Variation and Change*, **5**, 335–57.

Mufwene, Salikoko S. (1996) The development of American Englishes: Some questions from a creole genesis perspective. In *Focus on the USA*. Edited by Edgar W. Schneider. Philadelphia/Amsterdam: John Benjamins, pp. 231–64.

Mufwene, Salikoko S. (2001) *The Ecology of Language Evolution*. Cambridge: Cambridge University Press.

Poplack, Shana (ed.) (1999) *The English History of African American English*. Malden/Oxford: Blackwell.

Poplack, Shana and Sankoff, David (1987) The Philadelphia story in the Spanish Caribbean. *American Speech*, **62**, 291–314.

Poplack, Shana and Tagliamonte, Sali (1989) There's no tense like the present: Verbal -s inflection in Early Black English. *Language Variation and Change*, **1**, 47–84.

Poplack, Shana and Tagliamonte, Sali (1991) African-American English in the diaspora: Evidence from old-line Nova Scotians. *Language Variation and Change*, **3**, 301–39.

Poplack, Shana and Tagliamonte, Sali (1994) -S or nothing: Marking the plural in the African American diaspora. *American Speech*, **69**, 227–59.

Poplack, Shana and Tagliamonte, Sali (2001) *African American English in the Diaspora*. Malden/Oxford: Blackwell.

Rickford, John R. (1997) Prior creolization of AAVE? Sociohistorical and textual evidence from the 17th and 18th centuries. *Journal of Sociolinguistics*, **1**, 315–36.

Rickford, John R. (1999) *African American Vernacular English: Features, Evolution and Educational Implications*. Malden/ Oxford: Blackwell.

Rickford, John R. and Théberge-Rafal, Christine (1996) Preterit *had* + V-ed in narratives of African-American preadolescents. *American Speech*, **71**, 227–54.

Ross, Sarah H., Oetting, Janna B., and Stapleton, Beth (2004) Preterite *had* V-ed: A developmental narrative structure of African American English. *American Speech*, **79**, 146–66.

Schneider, Edgar W. (1989) *American Earlier Black English: Morphological and Syntactic Variables*. Tuscaloosa: University of Alabama Press.

Schneider, Edgar W. (ed.) (1996) *Focus on the USA*. Philadelphia/Amsterdam: John Benjamins.

Shuy, Roger, Baratz, Joan C., and Wolfram, Walt (1969) *Sociolinguistic Factors in Speech Identification*. National Institute of Mental Health Research Project MH 15048-01. Washington, DC: Center for Applied Linguistics.

Singler, John V. (1998a) What's not new in AAVE. *American Speech*, **73**, 227–56.

Singler, John V. (1998b) The African-American diaspora: Who were the dispersed? Paper presented at NWAV 27. Athens, GA, October.

Smitherman, Geneva (1977) *Talkin' and Testifyin': The Language of Black America*. Detroit: Wayne State University.

Spears, Arthur K. (1982) The Black English semi-auxiliary *come*. *Language*, **58**, 850–72.

Stewart, William A. (1967) Sociolinguistic factors in the history of American Negro dialects. *The Florida FL Reporter*, **5**(2), 11, 22, 24, 26.

Stewart, William A. (1968) Continuity and change in American Negro dialects. *The Florida FL Reporter*, **6**(2), 14–16, 18, 30.

Thomas, Erik R. (2001) *An Acoustic Analysis of Vowel Variation in New World English*. Publication of the American Dialect Society 85. Durham, NC: Duke University Press.

Thomas, Erik R. (2002) Sociophonetic applications of speech perception experiments. *American Speech*, **77**, 115–47.

Thomas, Erik R. and Reaser, Jeffrey (forthcoming) Delimiting perceptual cues used for the ethnic labeling of African American and European American voices. *Journal of Sociolinguistics*.

Winford, Donald (1997) On the origins of African American Vernacular English – a creolist perspective; Part I: The sociohistorical background. *Diachronica*, **14**, 304–44.

Winford, Donald (1998) On the origins of African American Vernacular English – a creolist perspective; Part II: The features. *Diachronica*, **15**, 99–154.

Wolfram, Walt (1969) *A Linguistic Description of Detroit Negro Speech*. Washington, DC: Center for Applied Linguistics.

Wolfram, Walt (1974) The relationship of Southern White Speech to Vernacular Black English. *Language*, **50**, 498–527.

Wolfram, Walt (1994) The phonology of a socio-cultural variety: The case of African American Vernacular English. In *Child Phonology: Characteristics, Assessment, and Intervention with Special Populations*. Edited by John E. Bernthal and Nicholas W. Bankson. New York: Thieme Medical Publishers, pp. 227–44.

Wolfram, Walt (2003a) Dialect enclaves in the South. In *Language in the New South*. Edited by Stephen Nagle and Sara Sanders. Cambridge: Cambridge University Press, pp. 141–58.

Wolfram, Walt (2003b) Reexamining the development of African American English: Evidence from isolated communities. *Language*, **79**, 282–316.

Wolfram, Walt and Schilling-Estes, Natalie (2006) *American English: Dialects and Variation*. 2nd edition. Oxford: Blackwell.

Wolfram, Walt and Thomas, Erik R. (2002) *The Development of African American English*. Oxford: Blackwell.

Wolfram, Walt, Childs, Becky, and Torbert, Benjamin (2000) Tracing language history through consonant cluster reduction: Evidence from isolated dialects. *Southern Journal of Linguistics*, **24**, 17–40.

FURTHER READING

Mufwene, Salikoko S., Rickford, John R., Bailey, Guy, and Baugh, John (eds.) (1998) *African American English: Structure, History and Use.* New York: Routledge.

Rickford, John R. and Rickford, Russell J. (2000) *Spoken Soul: The Story of Black English.* New York: John Wiley.

Wolfram, Walt and Thomas, Erik R. (2002) *The Development of African American English.* Oxford: Blackwell.

Part III   Acculturation

20 Written Language, Standard Language, Global Language

M. A. K. HALLIDAY

1 Introduction

English, along with a small number of other languages in the modern period, has expanded away from local through national to international domains, changing significantly along the way. But the changes are not simply those that take place in the normal course of the history of a language; other changes come about as a language takes on new cultural, economic, and political responsibilities. Critical moments occur when a language comes to be written as well as spoken, and then when it comes to function as a standard language for some sort of nation-state. In that sociohistorical perspective English is now acquiring a new identity as the global language of the late capitalist world. Some of the consequences of this development are beginning to show; but we have yet to find out what the long-term effects are that arise when a language finds itself globalized.

I myself came from the Inner Circle of Englishes, the OVEs (Old Variety of Englishes) as they are called in South-East Asia; so I would like to start by reminding you that within this circle there are and always have been many different Englishes around (Kachru, 1990). I'm not talking about the relatively recent worldwide varieties – British, North American, South African, Oceanic; but about the old dialects within Britain itself, Northumbrian, Mercian, Wessex, and Kentish at one period in the language's history. As a child I could still hear English rather like this:

> Nobbut t'fireless arth an t'geeable end
> Mark t'spot weear t'Carter family could mend
> An mek onny ilk o' cart,
> Wi' spooaks riven fra' yak, naffs of awm,
> Fellies of esh, grown i' different parts
> O' Swaadil.
>
> (Smith, n.d.)[1]

And although my own speech was nowhere as exotic as that, I was forced at age 7 to make a fairly substantial dialectal shift. And when I moved to Scotland, though I was less than 200 miles from where I grew up, I had problems in understanding the rural talk.

The quote above is North Yorkshire dialect, descended from the speech of the old English kingdom of Northumbria. It wasn't my native speech; but I would have heard it in my great-uncle's dairy, where he made Wensleydale cheese. I grew up in West Yorkshire, where the dialect was Mercian not Northumbrian; but in any case what I spoke was not a dialect of English but an accent – because I grew up in a city, and the city folk had given up the dialect in favor of Standard English. But it was still a local, or at any rate a regional, variety: Standard English with the phonetics, and largely also the phonology, derived from the original dialect. It was far from homogeneous, of course: different people, and the same person on different occasions, would vary between more dialectal and more standard forms.

In other words, the language situation was typical of a European nation-state. Some centuries earlier, in the process – indeed, as part of the process – of England becoming a nation, one English dialect, that of London (which was South-East Mercian, with a dash of Kentish in it), emerged as the bearer of nationhood, to carry the flag, or standard, of the emerging nation. This was now Standard English, although that term was not used until the late eighteenth century; its status took it out of the category of a dialect, and "the dialects" were now defined by opposition to the standard form of the language.

2   Standard Variety of a Language

As we all know, there is no intrinsic value in the various expression features that characterize the standard variety of a language. If the diphthongal vowels of Standard British English are preferred over the monophthongs of the northern tongues, their ascribed value is a result of the standardizing process; in no way can it be a cause of it, and elsewhere – for example in the neighboring nation-state of France – the preference might go exactly the other way. So as linguists we have always insisted that a standard language was just another dialect, but one that happened to be wearing a fancy uniform. But to say that is to leave out the historical basis of language standardization, which has to be understood in terms of the functions that a standard language takes on.

If we take English, and other languages of Western Europe, as prototype (but noting that this is not the only possible route toward supra-national status), the standard language evolves in the context of new demands especially in the areas of commerce, administration, and learning. But these are not simply institutional demands – that is, having to do with the relation between the language and its speakers, or users.[2] They are also systemic – having to do with the nature of the language itself, its total potential for meaning. Of course all these forms of semiotic activity had been going on for a very long time, in

England as in politicized societies everywhere; but in medieval England they were generally conducted in three different languages: commerce in English, administration in French, and learned discourse in Latin; so part of the job of the standard language was to take over and unify all three domains, as well as providing a uniform variety from within English itself. There is an interesting foreshadowing here of what happened much later on, in the colonial period. But over and above all this, there were new meanings to be created; new ways of meaning, in fact, commensurate with the new material conditions (which had in turn arisen from new technology, back to the horse-drawn plough and the movable-rudder sailing boat) and the new modes of production and social and political structures that evolved with them.

When we think of the new resources that develop with the standard language in its construction of the modern nation-state, we usually think first of new vocabulary: exactly in the way that language planners, and planning agencies, conceived of their task of developing national languages in postcolonial nations – their job was to invent new words. Language planners soon came to realize, however, that they needed to establish the principles on which new words should be brought into being, because words do not function as individual elements but always in some systematic paradigmatic relationship one to another. Nobody planned the coining of new vocabulary in the early stages of Standard English; but as it happened there was a principle for making new words already at hand, namely that of switching into another language. This as I mentioned was already a feature of the upper-class reaches of English life, as a result of England having been colonized by the Norman French in the eleventh century; an interesting relic of this multilingual mode of meaning is to be found in common law, where there are a number of triplets, expressions consisting of three words, one native English (Anglo-Saxon), one Norman French, and one Latin, like *stay*, *cease*, and *desist* or *bequeath*, *grant*, and *devise*. Here the words were no doubt intended as synonyms, although the fact that those who framed the laws adopted this practice suggests perhaps they felt each of the words meant something a little different, so that the legal interpretation would be that which was common to all three. But the principle that words of high value, words that carried weight, words of greater force and substance, could be created by borrowing from another language, one that was current among high-standing members of the community, was already present in the culture; and so the registers of the new Standard English, those of administration and centralized authority on the one hand, and those of technology and science on the other, went to Latin as the source of new terminology, building on, strengthening, and expanding a repository that was already there.

3   Sociolinguistic Context and Language

In my title I use the triad "written language, standard language, global language," because I want to consider this relatively new phenomenon of "global

English" in its historical context. I don't mean by this its institutional history, the sociopolitical events which contrived to bring it about; these have been well documented and interpreted by others who are far more competent to do so than I am. Those processes are external to language; whereas what I am looking into are the systemic processes that are going on in the language itself as it moves into these new sociopolitical contexts. So in that sense they are internal processes; but here there is another distinction to be made, because I don't mean the internal processes of sound change and the like – the phono-logical and morpho-syntactic changes that are the province of historical linguistics. These are, prototypically at least, independent of changes in the sociopolitical environment, being located on the plane of expression rather than on the content plane. My concern is with a more functional dimension of a language's history, the sort of history that Kachru opened up for us when he talked of "the Indianization of English" (Kachru, 1983). Historical semantics, and especially semantic field theory, was already pointing the way in this direction, with its interest in changes in the meaning of particular words, and sets of words, in response to changing cultural contexts. I want rather to generalize this notion, focusing on changes in the total meaning potential of a language; seeing this not, however, just as a response to sociopolitical and technological change but rather as an active agent in these historical processes – taking the view that human history is the product of these two fundamental realms of our existence, the material and the semiotic, interacting and inter-penetrating at every level.

4   Standard vs. Global Language

The process of becoming a standard language or national language is some-thing that we can examine historically, looking back on actual cases; and it offers certain analogies with the process of becoming internationalized, or globalized. A standard language is a tongue which has moved beyond its region, to become "national"; it is taken over, as second tongue, by speakers of other dialects, who however retain some features of their regional forms of expression. A global language is a tongue which has moved beyond its nation, to become "international"; it is taken over, as second tongue, by speakers of other languages, who retain some features of their national forms of expres-sion. If its range covers the whole world we may choose to call it "global." A standard language moves into new registers: new spheres of activity, opening up and expanding its meaning potential along the way. A global language does the same – or does it? This is an important question; and if we look at a "standardized" language from this point of view, we can ask in what respects a "globalized" language is, or is not, the same.

   If we start with the development of new vocabulary as the most obvious outward sign of the expansion of the meaning potential, we can characterize what seem to me to be the critical factors in this process by contrasting them with the simple process of inventing new words. We may identify four of these:

1 not just new words, but new word-making principles;
2 not just new words, but new word clusters (lexical sets);
3 not just new words, but new meanings;
4 not just new words, but new registers (functional varieties).

Let me say a little about each of these in turn.

In the first case, the "product" is not a list of words, which is closed, but a set of word-forming principles whose output is open-ended. In English this meant borrowing root forms of words from Latin (and later directly from Greek); and also borrowing the morphological resources for transcategorizing and compounding them.

In the second case, the "product" is not words as isolates but sets of words that are paradigmatically related. There are various possible forms of such a relationship – various dimensions of paradigmatic order; the most fundamental and far-reaching is taxonomic order, whereby one member is either a kind of or a part of another, and this was an important feature of the new standardized English word stock, especially for technology and science.

But, in the third case, the "product" is not the forms as such but the meanings that these forms express: semiotic features, elements, and structures which can be construed by all features of the wording, grammatical as well as lexical. It is this that enables the construction of new forms of knowledge – and also of new forms of authority: those who master the new meanings thereby gain in power.

And so, in the fourth case, the "product" takes the form of modes of discourse, with their own ways of reasoning and arguing, of presenting and marshaling lines of information and control. Standard English took over the registers of administration and learning, and developed discourses which transformed these activities so that they became part of the new "modern" order.

5 Strategies for Making Meaning

All these processes can be seen as ways of opening up, of expanding the semiotic potential that inheres in every language: opening up the creation of new terms; opening up the dimensions along which these terms are organized; opening up the meaning-making resources of the lexicogrammar; opening up the modes of creating and transmitting knowledge, maintaining and strengthening authority. No doubt changes like these are going on in all languages all the time; but at certain historical moments they get speeded up, even to the extent of fundamentally transforming the semiotic power of the language. Speeded up, of course, is a relative term; in English they were able to take place, without any conscious planning, in five to ten generations. If you need to speed them up still further, you create a language-planning agency to intervene in these processes by design.

Taken together, then, these are strategies for making meaning, for expanding the effective meaning potential of a language. Let us call them semogenic strategies. One way of thinking about the evolution of language is that it is a process of the evolution of semogenic strategies. We cannot generally observe this taking place – except in its ontogenic guise: we can watch the semiotic development of children. But the evolution of a standard language does offer the chance of seeing some way into this aspect of linguistic history.

One way of thinking about the effects of these strategies, if we ask in what ways the meaning potential is in fact being opened up, is that they bring new forms of systemic order, adding further dimensions to the language's semantic space. Let me try and clarify what I mean – again, I emphasize that I am talking about what happened in English. Every language will develop relevant semiotic strategies when the moment arises; but how each language does this will depend on a number of circumstances – essentially, on the one hand the ecosocial environment, the material and semiotic processes that are going on around, and on the other hand the character (Sapir's that "certain cut") of the language itself, its ways of meaning and of innovating. What happens will be a product of the impact of these two forces as they appear at that historical moment.

To come back to the most obvious feature, the vast quantity of new words that appeared in the course of the evolution of Standard English. What matters, as I suggested, is not the total number of words, but the resources available for making them, so that the process of word formation becomes open-ended – it has of course been going on ever since. In English, after the Norman invasion (which brought England back into the stream of post-Roman mainland European culture), the source language for most new words was at first Norman French; and then, by an easy transition as the standardization process gained momentum, Latin. So a bug, for example, becomes an insect. Why borrow a word for something already named? – because it is not, in fact, just a synonym. The popular view, among English-speaking children, is that which is embodied in the expression "long words," which means words which are difficult but (therefore) more important. (This seems plausible on iconic grounds: they are longer, so carry more weight. On the other hand in Japanese, where the source of borrowing was Chinese, learned terms tend to be shorter than everyday words.) But the point is that an insect is a more abstract bug. It names a class: a class which can be defined, such that the question "is this (thing, or kind of thing) an insect?" can be definitively answered – whereas you can't really ask about something "is that, or is it not, a bug?" So an insect enters into a systematic taxonomy of living creatures, which can be elaborated by means of derivatives and compounds as such semantic structures become available: we have *insectile, insectarium, insectivore, insecticide,* and so on. Likewise with numerous other Latin terms for familiar objects and phenomena: *ignis* for fire, giving *ignite, ignition, igneous; aqua* for water (*aquatic, aqueous, aquarium, aquifer*); *avis* for bird (*avian, aviary, aviculture* – and cf. *aviation, aviator*), and so on and so on. In all such cases, the Latin word construes some feature of our experience at a more systematic, and in fact systemic, level.

But then as Standard English was evolving, another language came into vogue, namely Greek. Classical Greek learning had been preserved and built on by the Arabs; but for a long time it had been known in western Europe only through Latin translations of a few of its leading scholars such as Aristotle. Greek studies were taken up just at the time when scientific knowledge was expanding and scientific discourse was becoming a significant component in the functional domains of Standard English. So Greek became another source of learned borrowing, made easier by the fact that many of the Latin terms in use had themselves been borrowed (calqued) from Greek in earlier times; Greek words came readily into English alongside those from Latin. Insects in Greek were *entoma* (itself the source of Latin *insecta*); but in English, again, they were not synonymous. The Greek term typically takes the abstraction up to an even higher level; it signifies its status as part of a theory, and therefore as an object of theoretical study: hence terms like *entomic, entomophily*, and, as a branch of knowledge, *entomology*. Likewise *hydro-* for water (*hydrogen, hydrolysis, hydrology*), *ornitho-* for bird (*ornithology*), and so on. Thus the infusion of Greek extended this dimension of semantic space still further, beyond systematic taxonomy into scientific theory. And while over the centuries the distinction has become blurred, and only those interested in language now recognize which elements are from Latin and which from Greek, this vector of the meaning potential, once having been opened up in this way, is still present in the language; moreover it lies behind many of our cultural beliefs and cultural practices (such as education).

Of course Standard English was never the preserve of scholars; learned discourse was only one of its manifestations, though one that was essential to the development of industrial technology. But the status and prestige that accrues to scholarly achievement becomes attached to scholarly language; and since, prior to the emergence of Standard English, Latin itself had been the language of prestige it was no great shift when that status was transferred to a kind of English that sounded like, and was obviously indebted to, Latin. Even the hierarchic distinction between Latin and Greek was carried over into this measure of status: an ophthalmologist is valued as superior to an optician, podiatry is more expensive than pedicure, ethics is a theorized form of morals. Thus latinate (or graecolatinate) discourse in English carries its own loading of prestige; and when this is combined with the authority of Standard English as the discourse of centralized administration what results, not surprisingly, is a language of power: not just in the sense that it possesses enormous power, through its expanded meaning potential, but in another (related) sense, that it gives power to those who control it, and hence serves as a means whereby power structures are put into and maintained in place. We are so surrounded today by these dominant forms of discourse that we scarcely notice them any more; it seems quite natural to be told that this certificate remains the property of the corporation and must be presented on request (. . . still belongs to the body and must be shown when asked for). The internal memoranda of any bureaucratic institution often show up how the power is distributed; while as clients, we know our place when we are told that failure to reconfirm may result in cancelation of your reservations (and even if our reservations have not been canceled, refusal to submit to screening procedures will result in prohibition on entry to the area and prohibition on boarding the aircraft). This has now become the norm, and Anglo-Saxon versions are marked as having very low status: they seem playful, or else merely childish.[3]

English is not alone in turning to a respected foreign language for its highly valued registers of discourse; apart from other European languages, we could cite the examples of Japanese (borrowing from Chinese), Vietnamese (also from Chinese), Thai (from Sanskrit), Urdu (from Persian, which in turn borrowed from Arabic), and the languages of southern India (again from Sanskrit). In these cases, the borrowing was associated not with standardization but with an earlier historical moment, the introduction of writing – or rather, perhaps, the development of written discourse; comparable therefore to the borrowing from Greek into classical Latin rather than that from Latin into English. But they illustrate the same principle: that when a language extends its field of operation, as its speakers, say, adopt a new religion, engage in new types of commerce, or explore new dimensions of knowledge, such changes in the ecosocial functioning of the language will always entail some expansion of its meaning potential. The writing systems that were widely borrowed (the Chinese, the Sanskrit, the Arabic) had themselves, like the Greek alphabet in Europe, been associated with fairly massive semiotic expansions when they first evolved: in religion, philosophy, technology, and also in literature where written genres displaced the earlier highly-valued oral forms.

6   Innovations in Meaning Potential

Since human societies are organized hierarchically, the innovations in meaning potential that are part of these historical processes begin by being the prerogative of a favored few. They will spread, over time, because while the few may struggle to retain their privileged status, the layers of a social hierarchy are typically permeable: castes and classes are not insulated one from another. But there will always be those who are left behind; they become the "marked" category, labeled by some negative term like illiterate or uneducated; and whether or not they aspire to move in to the more highly favored majority – they may or they may not – they are very well aware of their own lack of semiotic power. It was the illiterate peasants, in China in the 1950s, who protested most vigorously against the plan to abandon the charactery in favor of an alphabetic script. They knew that writing was the key to meanings they did not control; and writing meant characters – letters looked rather like a device for keeping them out.

What I am wanting to bring out is that, when a language becomes a written language, and when it becomes a standard language, the change is not merely institutional; it is also systemic. The semogenic power of the language is significantly increased. We might then wonder, if a language becomes a global language, whether the same thing will happen.

There are various historical conditions under which some dialectal variety of a language may emerge as dominant and become "standardized." In England, and in other parts of Europe, this happened as a concomitant of the "birth" of the nation-state. In China, Mandarin evolved as the language of a centralized feudal authority; and its scope was likewise extended, not just in the categories of its users but in the meaning potential of its political, economic, and cultural contexts of use.

So if a language is not just nationalized but internationalized (and let me treat "global" for the moment as the limiting case of being international), what happens then? Is this just an institutional change, with people taking it over as a supra-national second language and living some portion of their lives in it? Or does it create new functions for the language, which then engender new meanings? Is its overall meaning potential increased? And if it is, then in what ways, and who for?

At one level, the answer is obviously yes. One of the first examples of Indian English that Braj Kachru told me about was *flower bed*. This expression, familiar to the Inner Circle as a portion of a garden where flowers are grown (as distinct from the lawns), reappeared in an Indian English context in the sense which they would represent as *marriage bed*. Here "an old expression has taken on a new meaning" – at least for someone who knows Hindi, or who may not know Hindi but can derive the information from the context.

Whenever one language is used to describe settings that are primarily construed in another language, it is bound to take on new meanings, whether it does this by reconstruing old words or by borrowing new ones – as English did, for example, when it came to Australia and talked about bluebottles (jellyfish, not insects) and billabongs. Likewise in contexts of translation: when the Chinese translators of Mao Zedong's works wanted an English equivalent for *zougou*, they sometimes translated it as *lackey* and sometimes calqued it as *running dogs*. Every language enlarges its meaning range when it hosts translations of foreign texts or is used to talk about cultural contexts that are different, and distant, from its own.[4]

But who are the meanings for? Access to them is limited: you have to know the language – English, in the case of *flower beds* and *running dogs*. But access to meanings is always limited, by inequalities in the social structure. Education is designed to increase people's access, and it does so by steering them through these evolutionary changes in turn: first we teach children written language, then teach them standard language (or else both at the same time, depending on the circumstances); and then, perhaps, we may teach them world language.

This is the principle behind the three language policy that has been adopted in a number of countries (and sometimes even implemented, up to a point). It is a reasonable policy, and provided the teachers are trained and the necessary materials are available, children have no great problems in adapting to it. The reason it seldom succeeds is because the resources are not sufficient – or if they are, those who control them are not willing to devote them to education. But a world language could be built into the educational scheme – if it was needed.

But, as language educators know, even with all the necessary resources deployed, the students don't always learn; because they don't perceive a need for what they are learning. This can happen at all stages: some don't see even why they should read and write. The most problematic, in this respect, is a world language. What makes people feel that they need another language? Critically, I think, in all these cases it is what we might call functional complementarity: things can be done with this language – things that they want to do – that cannot be done, or done successfully, without it. That, as we know, is the circumstance in which a global language catches on.

It was also the circumstance in which writing first caught on, and in which standard languages evolve. As our interaction with each other, and with our material environment, comes to be more and more complex, we develop a more and more complex semiotic. One aspect of this process is the technology: first the materials to write on, and tools to write with; then paper and printing; and now electronic keyboards and monitor screens. But equally important were the new ways of meaning that the functional contexts demanded. Writing took the forms of calendar and divination, proclamations, lists of things and of doings, bills of lading, and so on. Standard languages brought new semiotic strategies for administration and learning. And when we look into the grammar that provided the motive power for these strategies, in the history of English, one feature stands out as critical: namely grammatical metaphor. Grammatical metaphor opens up a new dimension of semantic space (Halliday, 1998).

Grammatical metaphor is what turns *move* into *motion*, *resist* into *resistance*, *fail* into *failure*, *long* into *length*, *can* into *possible*, and *so* ('therefore') into *cause* (verb or noun). It is metaphor because it involves cross-coupling between semantics and lexicogrammar: an expression is being used to mean something that has usually been meant by something else. (Better: a meaning that has usually been realized in one way is now being realized in another.) It is grammatical because what is being cross-coupled is not a word (that is, not a lexical item, or "lexeme") but a class: a noun is doing the job of a verb or adjective, an adjective that of a modal verb, a verb is doing the job that has been done by a conjunction. And there are others.

It is this process, or rather this set of processes, that leads to wordings such as:

> Even though the fracture of glass can be a dramatic event, many failures are preceded by the slow extension of existing cracks.

It also gives us the kind of warnings that I quoted earlier – but also may be used to offer reassurances:

> Excellent safe face drying can be achieved by the same action as water was applied by regular wiping with warm hands during drying cycle.

and even in the publicity for a pop star:

> He also credits his former big size with much of his career success.

But it is in scientific writing that grammatical metaphor is most consistently exploited, because there it is functional at a critical level: you cannot develop a scientific theory without it. It reaches its most concentrated state in scientific abstracts, because it enables the meanings to be densely packed:

> Endocrine testings confirmed clinical anterior hypopituitarism. Post-traumatic hypopituitarism may follow injury to the hypothalamus, the pituitary stalk or the pituitary itself. The normal thyroid stimulating hormone response to thyrotropin releasing hormone . . . is in favour of a hypothalamic lesion. (Lim, Ang, and Ngim, 1990)

But such a density would be dysfunctional in other registers of science; these require a less viscous flow of meaning, which is brought about by the oscillation between more metaphoric and more congruent states in the wording.

Grammatical metaphor plays two crucial roles in scientific discourse. One is to carry forward the argument by packaging what has gone before so that it serves as logical foundation for what follows: for example as cause in a chain of cause and effect. The other is to raise the argument to a theoretical level by construing not just individual technical terms but terminologies, sets of terms related in taxonomic order.[5] Both of these principles are illustrated in a sequence such as the following:

> . . . from 1950 to 1980, severe contamination from acid rain resulted in a drop in pH – from about 5.5 to 4.5 – which represented a tenfold increase in the acidity of the lake water. This acidification was caused mainly by the burning of coal containing high levels of sulphur . . . (Stigliani and Salamons, 1993: xii)

Consider the word *acidification*. On the one hand it "packages" the preceding story about acid rain lowering the pH value (hydrogen ion concentration) in the water of the lake, which means making the water more acid; on the other hand it forms part of a theoretical construct which includes terms such as *contamination* and *pH-value*, as well as other items in the surrounding discourse like *atmospheric sulphuric acid* and *buffering capacity of the soil*. These are linked by relational terms *resulted in*, *represented*, *was caused by*. Somebody burned coal, so the water became acid: two processes, linked by a conjunctive relation. But in the text, the processes have turned into things – that is the canonical meaning of a noun; and the conjunctive relation between them has become a verb – that is, has turned into a process.

What is happening here is that the grammar is creating virtual phenomena, phenomena which exist purely on the semiotic plane. This is achieved by a process of semantic junction, whereby two category meanings combine. Acidic is a quality of water, or of some other liquid; when this is nominalized, as *acidity* ('being acidic') or as *acidification* ('becoming acidic'), since the category meaning of noun is a thing, or entity, the effect is of a semantic junction between quality and thing. The quality construed by the adjective *acidic* has been transformed, or metaphorized, into a thing, a virtual entity which can be observed, measured and reasoned about. Likewise "so, therefore" is a conjunctive relation between processes; when it is construed by a verb, as *causes* or *is caused by*, since the category meaning of verb is a process, there is again a semantic junction: the (causal) relation construed congruently by a conjunction, like *so* or *therefore*, has been metaphorized into a process – a virtual process, which can be located in time, negated and so on. It is the creation of these virtual phenomena, by the cross-coupling of grammatical categories with semantic features, that makes scientific discourse, and in fact scientific theory, possible.

Scientists like grammatical metaphor; their lives, or at least their livelihoods, depend on it. Poets, and other creative writers, prefer metaphor in its traditional guise – lexical metaphor. Here it is one word for another, not one class for another. But the same kind of semantic junction takes place, as rhetoricians and stylists have always recognized. So when Edwin Thumboo writes:

> ... the Lord, whose other hand dispenses the dew
> Of sleep on Saul's army ...
>   (cited from Webster, 2001)

we recognize that dew and sleep are fused into a new thing, a virtual dew – one that is also medicinal, since it can be dispensed. This metaphoric potential is an inherent feature of human (post-infancy) language, because a language is a stratified semiotic, in which meaning and wording can be decoupled, and recoupled in new alignments. What the scientific imagination did was to combine these two fundamental resources of language: transcategorizing (deriving one word class from another, like *maker* from *make*, *hairy* from *hair*) and metaphorizing (cross-coupling of semantics and grammar). This process began in classical times, with the written languages of the ancient world (and the iron age technologies, which transformed material substances in somewhat analogous ways); but it was brought to a higher level in the standard languages of the modern period. As far as I know, every language of science has followed the same route, reconstruing the human experience by exploiting the potential for metaphor in its grammar.

7   Translation as a Process of Metaphor

Translation is also, as often pointed out, a process of metaphor: not a proto-type, since it is a second order semiotic activity, but perhaps the limiting case. To return for a moment to the flower bed: when this term is used in Indian English, does it bring about a comparable semantic junction? In other words, is *flower bed* just a new expression for an old meaning, or is it creating a new meaning, a marriage bed which is also a virtual bed of flowers – aided (though somewhat subverted) by the British (or Inner-Circle) English *bed of roses*? (Subverted because *bed of roses* is usually used in the context of a negative, such as *a marriage bed is no bed of roses*.)

By itself, one instance is of little significance. But if a whole culture cares to be represented in a language other than its own (that is, other than that with which it co-evolved), has this now become a different language? Not just different from what it was (so much is clear), but different from either of its progenitors? Is Nigerian English just a rewording of the semantic system of Yoruba and other Nigerian languages, or is it a distinct semiotic, a metaphoric junction of two different semiotic styles? If the latter, then it embodies a new, and different, construal of the human condition.[6]

It is important to ask this question, I think, in the light of our previous history – our semohistory, or history of meaning. The transitions that I have been considering – into written language, into standard language – were, in effect, reconstruals (that is, semiotic reconstructions) of human experience, concomitant with the increasing complexity of our interaction with the eco-social environment. We may think of these as new functional demands on language brought about by advances in technology – which is how I myself used to think about them. But I think that was wrong. Rather, the semiotic and the material are two facets of a single historical process, neither of them driving the other, but neither of them able to take place independently. Writing came with settlement, and a certain level of political organization and materials technology. What I have loosely called standardization came with a more centralized structure of authority and a higher level of technological achievement – in Europe, with the machine age, the technology of power. (In each case, vernaculars persist but do not share in the reconstruction.) So is it to be predicted that the technology of the electronic age, the technology of information, will be accompanied by a comparable reconstrual of experience?

We can see that discourses are changing. Electronic text tends to lessen the distance between the spoken and the written mode; it develops features and patterns of its own, part written part spoken and part perhaps unlike either. Text can be a mix of aural and visual channels, together with components from other, non-verbal modalities. But what we don't know yet – or at least what I don't know – is how far these factors affect the meanings that are being construed. One feature we can begin to observe seems to be a move back (but perhaps really a move forward) to more congruent ways of meaning, at least in the discourses of technology and science (nicely symbolized by the reinvention of biology as life science, geology as earth science); note also the Plain English movement in government and the law. The standard language may be revisiting its origins in everyday speech.

8   English as Global and International Language

At the same time, the "globe" that provides the context for global English is for the moment at least a world in which the voices of international capitalism, with their triumphalist rhetoric about the failure of people's first attempt to design something humane, have learnt to exploit all the semogenic strategies that give language its enormous power. For corporations it comes as a bonus, inherited from colonial days, that the language of convenience in so many international (and even intranational) contexts is none other than English. But it is naive to imagine that if the United Nations had decreed, back in 1950, that some other language – say Esperanto, or even Malay or Korean – was to be adopted as a world language, the global situation would have been any different: whatever language was adopted would soon have been primed to function as a medium of corporate power. In that case English would have continued to serve – as French does today – as a highly-valued international language in certain cultural regions and with certain clearly defined spheres of activity.

The way it has turned out, English has become a world language in both senses of the term, international and global: international, as a medium of literary and other forms of cultural life in (mainly) countries of the former British Empire; global, as the co-genitor of the new technological age, the age of information. So those who are able to exploit it, whether to sell goods and services or to sell ideas, wield a very considerable power. Many people would like to resist this dominance of English. The strategic response would seem to be: do away with English. Don't teach it, or do anything to perpetuate its standing in the community. But most serious thinkers believe that that won't now work: English is too deeply entrenched, and if people are deprived of the chance of learning it they are the ones who suffer. That was not the case 50 years ago, when English was just one international language among many, and it may well not be the case 50 years from now; but for the moment that is how it is. It seems that if you want to resist the exploitative power of English, you have to use English to do it.[7]

9   Conclusion

It is important, I think, to distinguish these two aspects, the international and the global, even though they obviously overlap. English has been expanding along both trajectories: globally, as English; internationally, as Englishes. Both of these expansions involve what I have called semogenic strategies: ways of creating new meanings that are open-ended, like the various forms of metaphor, lexical and grammatical. But they differ. International English has expanded by becoming world Englishes, evolving so as to adapt to the meanings of other cultures. Global English has expanded – has become "global" – by taking over, or being taken over by, the new information technology, which means everything from email and the internet to mass media advertising, news reporting, and all the other forms of political and commercial propaganda. And the two seem not to have really mixed. Infotechnology seems still to be dominated by the English of the Inner Circle; under pressure, of course, but not seriously challenged, perhaps because the pressures have no coherent pattern or direction. If the Englishes of the Outer Circle had more impact on the global scene, those who monopolize the media would no longer automatically also monopolize the meanings. If African and Asian varieties of English are not simply vehicles for their regional cultures but also their communities' means of access to a culture that is already in effect global, those who speak and write these varieties are not constrained to be only consumers of the meanings of others; they can be creators of meanings, contributors to a global English which is also at the same time international. Meanings get reshaped, not by decree but through ongoing interaction in the semiotic contexts of daily life; and these have now become global contexts, even if those who participate in them are still only a fraction of the total population of the globe. Rather than trying to fight off global English, which at present seems to be rather a quixotic venture, those who seek to resist its baleful impact might do better to concentrate on transforming it, reshaping its meanings, and its meaning potential, in the way that the communities in the Outer Circle have already shown it can be done.

See also Chapters 15, WORLD ENGLISHES TODAY; 17, VARIETIES OF WORLD ENGLISHES; 23, LITERARY CREATIVITY IN WORLD ENGLISHES; 25, WORLD ENGLISHES AND CULTURE WARS; 34, WORLD ENGLISHES AND GLOBAL COMMERCE; 38, WORLD ENGLISHES AND LEXICOGRAPHY.

NOTES

1 nobbut 'only', ilk 'kind', yak 'oak', naffs 'hubs', awm 'elm', fellies, 'felloes, rims', esh 'ash', Swaadil 'Swaledale'.

2 I follow here the very useful concept of "institutional linguistics" as defined many years ago by Trevor Hill (1958).

3 The technological and the bureaucratic modes of discourse may of course be combined; cf. Lemke, 1990; Thibault, 1991.

4 For the concept of semantic distance see Hasan, 1984.

5 These two motifs are brought out by detailed analysis of scientific texts; cf. Halliday and Martin, 1993.

6 For views on the operation of English in an "Outer-Circle" environment (in this case Singapore), see Foley et al., 1998.

7 See for example Kandiah, 2001; Pennycook, 2001.

REFERENCES

Foley, Joseph A., Kandiah, Thiru, Zhiming, Bao, Gupta, Anthea Fraser, Alsagoff, Lubna, Lick, Ho Chee, Wee, Lionel, Talib, Ismail S., and Bokhorst-Heng, Wendy (1998) *English in New Cultural Contexts: Reflections from Singapore*. Singapore: Oxford University Press.

Halliday, M. A. K. (1998) Things and relations: Regrammaticizing experience as technical knowledge. In *Reading Science: Critical and Functional Perspectives on Discourses of Science*. Edited by James R. Martin and Robert Veel. London/New York: Routledge, pp. 185–235.

Halliday, M. A. K. and Martin, James R. (1993) *Writing Science: Literacy and Discursive Power*. London/Washington, DC: Falmer Press.

Hasan, Ruqaiya (1984) Ways of saying: Ways of meaning. In *The Semiotics of Culture and Language, vol. 1*. Edited by Robin P. Fawcett, M. A. K. Halliday, Sydney M. Lamb, and Adam Makkai. London: Frances Pinter, pp. 105–62. Reprinted in *Ways of Saying: Ways of Meaning: Selected Papers of Ruqaiya Hasan*. Edited by Carmel Cloran, David Butt, and Geoffrey Williams. London: Cassell, pp. 191–242.

Hill, Trevor (1958) Institutional linguistics. *Orbis*, **7**, 441–5.

Kachru, Braj B. (1983) The *Indianization of English: The English Language in India*. Delhi: Oxford University Press.

Kachru, Braj B. (1990) World Englishes and applied linguistics. *World Englishes*, **9**(1), 3–20.

Kandiah, Thiru (2001) Whose meanings? Probing the dialectics of English as a global language. In *Ariels: Departures and Returns: Essays for Edwin Thumboo*. Edited by Tong Chee Kiong, Anne Pakir, Ban Kah Choon, and Robbie B. H. Goh. Singapore: Oxford University Press, pp. 102–21.

Lemke, Jay L. (1990) Technical discourse and technocratic ideology. In *Learning, Keeping and Using Language: Selected Papers from the 8th World Congress of Applied Linguistics, vol. 2*. Edited by M. A. K. Halliday, John Gibbons, and Howard Nicholas. Amsterdam: Benjamins, pp. 435–60.

Lim, H. S., Ang, B. K., and Ngim, R. C. K. (1990) Hypopituitarism following head injury: A case report. *Academy of Medicine Singapore Annals*, **19**(6), 851–5.

Pennycook, Alistair (2001) English in the world/the world in English. In *Analysing English in a Global Context: A Reader*. Edited by Anne Burns and Caroline Coffin. London: Routledge, pp. 78–89.

Smith, Jane H. (n.d.) Redundancy. *Yorkshire Dialect Society Summer Bulletin*.

Stigliani, William and Salomons, Wim (1993) Our fathers' toxic sins. *New Scientist*, **1903**(11), xii.

Thibault, Paul J. (1991) Grammar, technocracy and the noun: Technocratic values and cognitive linguistics. In *Functional and Systemic Linguistics: Approaches and Uses*. Edited by Eija Ventola. Berlin/New York: Mouton de Gruyter, pp. 281–306.

Webster, Jonathan J. (2001) Thumboo's David. In *Ariels: Departures and Returns: Essays for Edwin Thumboo*. Edited by Tong Chee Kiong, Anne Pakir, Ban Kah Choon, and Robbie B. H. Goh. Singapore: Oxford University Press, pp. 75–88.

FURTHER READING

Halliday, M. A. K. (1998) Things and relations: Regrammaticizing experience as technical knowledge. In *Reading Science: Critical and Functional Perspectives on Discourses of Science*. Edited by James R. Martin and Robert Veel. London/New York: Routledge, pp. 185–235.

Hasan, Ruqaiya (1984) Ways of saying: Ways of meaning. In *The Semiotics of Culture and Language, vol. 1*. Edited by Robin P. Fawcett, M. A. K. Halliday, Sydney M. Lamb, and Adam Makkai. London: Frances Pinter, pp. 105–62. Reprinted in *Ways of Saying: Ways of Meaning: Selected Papers of Ruqaiya Hasan*. Edited by Carmel Cloran, David Butt, and Geoffrey Williams. London: Cassell, pp. 191–242.

Kachru, Braj B. (1990) World Englishes and applied linguistics. *World Englishes*, **9**(1), 3–20.

Kandiah, Thiru (2001) Whose meanings? Probing the dialectics of English as a global language. In *Ariels: Departures and Returns: Essays for Edwin Thumboo*. Edited by Tong Chee Kiong, Anne Pakir, Ban Kah Choon, and Robbie B. H. Goh. Singapore: Oxford University Press, pp. 102–21.

Lemke, Jay L. (1990) Technical discourse and technocratic ideology. In *Learning, Keeping and Using Language: Selected Papers from the 8th World Congress of Applied Linguistics, vol. 2*. Edited by M. A. K. Halliday, John Gibbons, and Howard Nicholas. Amsterdam: Benjamins, pp. 435–60.

21 Speaking and Writing in World Englishes

YAMUNA KACHRU

1 Introduction

English is used in the three Circles for various purposes – as a home language and a medium of education, in professions, media, diplomacy, trade, commerce, and literary creativity. For achieving success in all these areas of activity, users of English have to perform various acts through the language, such as imparting information, negotiating, persuading, agreeing, disagreeing, demanding, apologizing, etc., in different contexts. These "speech acts" (Austin, 1962; Searle, 1969), are performed in the spoken mode in face-to-face interaction; they are also performed in the written mode using strategies and conventions different from those in speech (see, e.g., Reynolds, 1993). This chapter examines the ways in which interlocutors from different Circles of English speak and write English to express their meanings to each other using a shared medium with different sociocultural conventions of language use and different cultural messages (B. Kachru, 2002); it reviews research in speech acts, politeness, conversation analysis, and cross-cultural rhetoric. The conventions differ across varieties because all users of English in the Outer and Expanding Circles are bi-/multilingual. The different messages come from cultural values of the communities and conventions of language use, largely based on concepts of polite and appropriate behavior. The topic of cultural values is beyond the scope of this chapter; what is in focus is the conventions of language and language use.

2 Speech Acts

Although there is a large body of research available on speech acts across languages, not much has as yet been published comparing speech acts across varieties. A beginning has been made in a few studies, e.g., Adegbija (1989), Bailey (2000), Y. Kachru (1998), Kang (2003), Morgan (1998), Silva (1998), and

Sridhar (1991). Studies in conversation analysis, business and commercial negotiations, and professional encounters also give insights into how acts are performed through speech (e.g., Firth, 1995; Stubbe and Holmes, 1999). A number of studies have compared conventions of conversation across cultures, and some have examined how such conventions are reflected in interaction among participants from different groups within the same or across different Circles of English (Firth, 1995; Liao, 1997; Meyerhoff, 1999; Rampton, 1998; Stubbe and Holmes, 1999; among others). There still is a need to investigate whether there are culture-specific speech acts that are not shared across languages and cultures, e.g., the speech acts of *signifying* and *marking* in African American English (Mitchell-Kernan, 1972).

2.1 Cross-cultural speech act research

Research on cross-cultural speech acts of the past three decades has raised serious questions about the universal applicability of several theoretical notions of pragmatics (Green, 1989; Levinson, 1983), including speech acts themselves (Searle, 1969), Gricean maxims (Grice, 1975), and politeness principles (Brown and Levinson, 1987). Unlike in theoretical discussions, where an implicit assumption is made that speech acts refer to the same social acts in all cultures. Fraser, Rintell, and Walters (1980: 78) explicitly claim that, although languages may differ as to how and when speech acts are to be performed, every language "makes available to the user the same basic set of speech acts . . . the same set of strategies – semantic formulas – for performing a given speech act." In contrast, Wierzbicka (1985) claims that speech genres and speech acts are not comparable across languages and cultures; Wolfson, Marmor, and Jones (1989) suggest that "just as different cultures divide the color spectrum into noncorresponding overlapping terms, so the repertoire of speech acts for each culture is differently organized" (p. 180). Matsumoto (1988, 1989) questions the adequacy of the theoretical notions of conversational implicature as proposed by Grice and "face" as postulated by Brown and Levinson (1987) to account for the politeness phenomena in Japanese conversational interactions. Wetzel (1988) concludes that the notion of "power" as discussed in Brown and Gilman (1960) is culturally bound, and therefore not applicable to a discussion of verbal interaction in Japanese. Y. Kachru (2003) argues that the cooperative principle, the politeness principle, rules of politeness, and politeness strategies operate differently across speech communities, and also that they operate quite differently in various social situations among diverse social classes within the same speech community (see Blum-Kulka and Kasper, 1990; Y. Kachru, 1998; Matsumoto, 1988, 1989; Silva, 1998, 2000; Sridhar, 1991; among others). Meyerhoff (1999) asserts that positive and negative politeness are not scalar opposites, but two sides of the same coin.

The problems in the applicability of the speech act theory in the analysis of conversation have been identified in Schegloff (1988) and Schmidt (1983), who point out the limited applicability of the theory because of its inability to handle the sequentiality and temporality of conversational exchanges. More-over, since speech act theory is based on speaker intentions, it neglects the crucial role that interactions between speakers and hearers play in conversa-tions. Furthermore, such research has utilized only a limited range of vari-ables, e.g., those of social distance and dominance (Blum-Kulka, House, and Kasper, 1989), and even those are not well defined (Rose, 1992). Additionally, Y. Kachru (1998) points out that the notions of *Distance* and *Imposition* are too simplistic to be applicable across cultures.

As regards the data for empirical research on speech acts, only a limited number of studies have employed an ethnographic method of observation and analysis of utterances produced in real-life interactions. Some empirical studies that do utilize such data are those on compliments in American English by Manes and Wolfson (1981), compliments in American compared with South African English by Herbert (1989), invitations in American English by Wolfson et al. (1983), requests in Hebrew by Blum-Kulka, Danet, and Gherson (1985), apologies in Bislama in Vanuatu by Meyerhoff (1999) and in New Zealand English by Holmes (1990), and politeness strategies in Korean and African American service encounters in Los Angeles by Bailey (2000). The bulk of speech act research, including cross-cultural investigations, has been conducted using either role play or written questionnaires that direct the par-ticipants to perform discourse-completion tasks. Furthermore, only a limited range of speech acts have been researched, the most commonly studied ones being requests and apologies, as in Blum-Kulka et al. (1989), Y. Kachru (1998), Silva (1998, 2000), and Sridhar (1991), among others.

In spite of the limitations mentioned above, the available research on speech acts, conversation analysis, and verbal encounters in various contexts has yielded valuable understanding of the interactions of sociocultural values, conventions and of language use, and linguistic structure within and across communities. These insights are worth recapitulating and building upon for further understanding of how world Englishes are used across languages and cultures.

2.2   *Linguistic politeness*

One of the main reasons cultures differ in the conventions of their language use in real-life situations is to be found in consideration of politeness. Polite-ness in using language to do things in the Western context has generally been discussed in term of discourse strategies. A number of major Asian languages such as Hindi, Japanese, Korean, and Thai, however, have grammaticized devices at the phonological, morphological, lexical and syntactic levels, in addition to discourse strategies, to signal respectful and polite verbal behavior.

One of the grammatical phenomena described in detail in the grammars of languages such as Hindi and Korean, among others, are the sets of honorific pronouns, verbal endings, and lexical sets that indicate respect for specific addressees or referents.[1] What makes the systems complex is that choice from one set constrains the choices from other sets. For instance, honorific pronouns do not co-occur with non-honorific endings and, similarly, non-honorific pronouns do not co-occur with honorific endings. In addition, an honorific or non-honorific context also determines choices from the lexicon, i.e., which nouns and verbs may or may not be used. Examples of parallel items from the honorific and non-honorific sets of grammatical and lexical items are given in (1–3) below:[2]

(1) Grammatical choices: Hindi

	Honorific	Non-honorific/ Familiar	Intimate
Second-person pronoun	*āp*	*tum*	*tū*
Present imperfect ending	*-E hẽ*	*-E ho*	*-A hai*

Choices from the honorific and non-honorific set are constrained such that the following arrays are ungrammatical:

(2) **āp V-A hɛ*
*tum V-A hɛ
*āp V-E ho[3]
*tū V-E ho
*tum/tū V-E hẽ

(3) Lexical choices: Korean (Hwang, 1990)

Honorific	Plain	Gloss	
Cinci	*pap*	'meal'	
Sengham	*ilum*	'name'	
Capswu-si-ta	*mek-ta*	'to eat'	**meku-si-ta*
Cwumwu-si-ta	*ca-ta*	'to sleep'	**ca-si-ta*

The complexities of such honorific versus non-honorific systems have been described in detail in works such as Martin (1964, Japanese and Korean), Moeran (1988, Japanese), Hwang (1990, Korean), Y. Kachru (1980, Hindi), Srivastava and Pandit (1988, Hindi), and Singh (1989, Maithili).

In fact, it has been suggested for both Japanese and Korean that the relevant concepts for linguistic interaction may be *discernment* (Ide, 1989) and *deference* (Hwang, 1990), respectively. Discernment refers to "the almost automatic observation of socially-agreed-upon rules" (Hill et al., 1986) that characterizes Japanese verbal and non-verbal behavior. Deference has been defined as "power as a social fact, established a priori by the differential positions of individuals or groups within the social structure" (Treichler et al., 1984: 65). Although the two concepts are defined differently, one in social behavioral terms and the other in ideological terms, their linguistic manifestations take the same form: grammaticization of honorific forms.

Politeness, on the other hand, is defined in terms of cognitive psychological notions of self-images of speakers and addressees.[4] This dichotomy, however, is problematic. As the descriptions of polite verbal behavior in Matsumoto (1988) and Moeran (1988), among others, suggest, both discernment/deference and politeness are useful concepts in discussing Asian polite behavior. (They are equally applicable to the African context.) It is, however, noteworthy that whereas discernment/deference has been lexicalized and grammaticized in languages such as Hindi, Japanese, Korean, Thai, and many others, strategies of politeness in all languages generally make use of choices from within the general lexical and grammatical devices available to speakers, even in the absence of such forms. What this means is that a number of languages have a complex dual system of signaling politeness, based both on devices to indicate discernment/deference and on strategies to express politeness.

Compared to the systems of languages such as Hindi, Japanese, and Korean, the English language seems much simpler and more egalitarian, as it does not have systemic choices based on discernment/deference, but only strategies based on politeness considerations.

2.2.1 Discernment/deference and politeness in speech

The framework suggested in Brown and Levinson (1987) makes crucial use of the concept of face. It posits two aspects of politeness in verbal interaction, positive face (presentational) and negative face (avoidance). Positive face indicates a want or need to be desirable to others; therefore, it functions as a strategy of friendliness or camaraderie. Negative face indicates a want or need not to be impeded by others; therefore, it functions as a distancing strategy of formality. All members of a speech community use positive and negative politeness strategies to save, maintain, and enhance face. Brown and Levinson (1987) describe a number of strategies and their linguistic realizations that maintain and enhance positive and negative face of interlocutors in conversation.

In Brown and Levinson's (1987) framework, all potential verbal and non-verbal communicative acts are characterized as face-threatening acts (FTAs). Some acts threaten the interlocutors' positive face, others their negative face. For instance, criticism, disagreement, expression of violent emotions, irreverence, bringing bad news, raising divisive topics (e.g., politics, religion), non-cooperation in an activity (such as interruptions in talk), and use of address terms in initial encounters threaten the hearers' positive face. Orders, requests, suggestions, advice, reminders, threats, warnings, offers, promises, compliments, and expressions of strong emotion toward hearers threaten their negative face. Apologies, acceptance of compliments, breakdown of physical control (e.g., stumbling, falling), self-humiliation, confession, and lack of control over emotion (e.g., laughter, tears) threaten speakers' positive face. Expressing thanks, acceptance of hearers' thanks, excuses, accepting offers, responses to hearers' faux pas, and unwilling promises and offers threaten their negative face (Brown and Levinson, 1987: 65–8).

This characterization of FTAs does not take into account the tension between the two systems of discernment/deference and politeness in Asian languages, nor does it recognize the complexities introduced by speaker–addressee interactions. For instance, in the scheme suggested above, several interaction strategies will be considered face-threatening in Western contexts, whereas they would be perceived as face-enhancing in Asian contexts.

In the Japanese context (Matsumoto, 1988), for example, there are conventionalized expressions for showing deference which do not constitute a negative politeness strategy of minimizing an imposition on an addressee's action, as Brown and Levinson would suggest. One such expression – *doozo yoroshiku* – is translatable as 'I ask you to please treat me well/take care of me.' This phrase is used when the speaker is introduced to someone; it is an expression of the desire on the part of the speaker that the ensuing relationship between the two parties be a good one. A speaker may choose to say this not only for him-/herself, but also on behalf of someone closely related to the speaker, e.g., his/her wife/husband, son, daughter, etc. Using an exactly similar expression, not only for oneself but also on behalf of one's children or relatives or intimate friends, is common in India, too. Such expressions are used to enhance the addressee's face, and enhancing someone's face is a positive politeness strategy, although the direct request sounds like an imposition – an FTA – in a Western context.

These systems are now undergoing changes under the influence of English in some sections of Asian societies. Conversely, as is natural in any language-contact situation, the varieties of English used in Asian societies have assimilated some of the deference strategies of the languages of those cultures. This phenomenon of bi-directional accommodation of politeness strategies is worth serious investigation. Examples of such convergence in conversations and in written texts in world Englishes are discussed below.

Valentine (1995) describes a co-existent agreement-disagreement pattern which is unfamiliar to other English speakers in interactions between women speaking Indian English. According to Valentine (1995), utterances in which both partial agreement-disagreement are expressed are more acceptable if the sequence of expression is *Yes, but* . . . It is unexpected in other varieties of English to have a sequence such as *No* . . . *but yeah*, which does occur in Indian English data (pp. 243–4):

(4) fA: Do you think it [wife abuse] is common?
     fB: In India? In rural families this is common.
     fC: **No, it's common**. Very much common even in very literate families.

The female addressee B responds by agreeing with the interviewer, A's, question. The other participant in the conversation, C, first says no, but then agrees by saying, *it's common*.

This pattern is a familiar one to Hindi speakers, who not infrequently start by saying *na* . . . 'no', but then go on to express agreement.[5]

Young (1982: 76) points out the different rhetorical strategies of interaction between American and Chinese interlocutors in professional settings by citing the following example. After a talk given by a Chinese visiting professor of nutrition from Beijing, an American in the audience raised a question. The following exchange took place:

(5) Post-lecture discussion session
American: How does the Nutritional Institute decide what topics to study? How do you decide what topic to do research on?
Chinese: **Because**, now, period get change. It's different from past time. In past time, we emphasize how to solve practical problems. Nutrition must know how to solve some deficiency diseases. In our country, we have some nutritional diseases, such as x, y, z. But, now it is important that we must do some basic research. *So, we must take into account fundamental problems. We must concentrate our research to study some fundamental research.*

Inner-Circle listeners and readers of the transcription of this exchange would feel frustrated as they process a series of statements that do not seem to answer the question. The Chinese professor is, of course, following a rhetorical strategy that he is familiar with, in which one must first provide the background, which generally consists of the history of the endeavor, and then slowly unfold the main point of what one is trying to convey. The linkers in bold face above, the *because* and the *so*, are the markers of these transitions; the statement (given in italics) which constitutes the answer-as-such to the question comes at the end. Inner-Circle speakers would, particularly in a formal academic context, be much more likely to *begin* such a response with the "straightforward" or "direct" answer.

Young (1982) analyzes a number of examples of this pattern of interaction in settings related to business and finance; many of these contain both the linkers, and most of them contain *so* to mark the transition to the crux of the matter, as exemplified in (5) above.

In non-academic professional contexts, too, Englishes differ in the strategies they follow to convey meanings; e.g., Liao (1997: 107–8) cites the data in (6) to show how bosses convey their dissatisfaction to their employees for substandard job performance in American (AmE) and Taiwanese Englishes (TE):

(6) Boss telling employee his/her job performance is unsatisfactory (pp. 105–8):
AmE: I am concerned about your performance.
I have been extremely concerned about your work performance lately.
I don't feel that you're working to your full potential.
TE: I don't like your performance.
I am not pleased with your performance.
I am not satisfied with your performance.

The author observes that 50 percent of AmE speakers give constructive instructions to employees to improve their job performance, while over 50 percent of TE speakers do not do so.

2.2.2 Silence as speech act

While discussing speech acts and conversation, it is easy to forget that silence, as well as speech, has an important place in interaction. For instance, Nwoye (1985) describes the most appropriate strategy for conveying condolences in the Igbo community of Nigeria. According to him, the most appropriate way of expressing sympathy to the bereaved following a loved one's death is to leave them alone for at least four days, then visit them by going straight to them in their home, stand before them for a short time, and sit down for a while with other mourners in silence. When the visitors feel they have stayed long enough, they again stand in front of the bereaved so that their presence is noted, then leave as silently as they came. In this case, not saying anything says everything: that the mourner shares the grief of the bereaved family and sympathizes with them. In Igbo society, it is felt to be inappropriate to increase the bereaved people's sorrow by talking about the loss of their loved one. Obviously, silence has a different meaning in the Igbo context than it does in Anglo-American, European, or Asian contexts (see Tannen and Saville-Troike 1985 for different perspectives on silence as a code).

Thus, what may seem superficially to be taciturnity or unwillingness to engage with an interlocutor in intercultural conversational exchanges may have other explanations across various Englishes, as discussed in Bailey's (2000) study of Korean retailers' interactions with their African American customers. The African Americans feel that the Korean store owners' unwillingness to engage in small talk reveals a lack of respect for them as black people. The Korean retailers, for their part, feel that the exuberant speaking style of African American customers during business encounters shows a lack of "education," in the sense of conforming to appropriate social behavior. Neither group of participants is aware of the sociocultural norms of interaction of the other; the Korean immigrants are not familiar with the convention of small talk (light-hearted remarks about weather or current affairs, etc., which signals involvement for the African Americans, and the African Americans have no knowledge of the Koreans' idea of serious, taciturn behavior being a sign of well-brought-up, appropriately socialized adults expressing deference toward their interlocutors).

The examples above illustrate the linguistic and sociocultural factors that are responsible for acculturation of Englishes in different regions and for giving conversations a different "flavor" in the Outer and Expanding Circles. One good source of sensitizing speakers of one variety to conventions of other varieties is to encourage familiarity with English literatures (see Nelson, 1991; Chapters 22 and 24 in this volume), and performances (plays, music) and audio-visual media (films, TV; see Chapters 32 and 33 in this volume).

In addition to overarching conventions, minor variations in the uses of single words or particles carry great import. For example, the semantic extensions of items such as "sorry" (Meyerhoff, 1999), "OK" (Adegbija and Bello, 2001), and "no" (Valentine, 1995), or the introduction of discourse markers from indigenous sources, such as *eh* in New Zealand English (Meyerhoff, 1994) and *meh, la,* and *know* in Malaysian-Singapore English (Ler, 2001; Pakir, 1992; Wee, 2003; Wong, 2004), are context-specific; interpretation of such items becomes essential for ensuring success in verbal interaction across the three Circles.

3   Rhetorical Strategies in Writing

Rhetorical strategies are also motivated by considerations of sociocultural appropriateness (Y. Kachru, 1999). A study by Kamimura and Oi (1998) illustrates this assertion. The study investigates rhetorical appeals, diction, and cultural influences in the writings of Japanese college students and American high school seniors who wrote essays on their opinions of capital punishment. The findings were that: (1) American student writers generally offered thesis statements at the beginnings of their essays, supported them with details, and summarized their positions and support at the end. (2) The Japanese writers typically used one of two other patterns, either specific-to-general, with a thesis statement at the end of the essay, or with no thesis offered. The US writers maintained consistent positions, while the Japanese writers tended to present both sides of the argument. (3) Forty-six of fifty-five "appeals" or bases for persuasion by US writers (83.6%) were identified as "rational," compared with thirty-six of fifty-five (65.5%) used by the Japanese. Only nine US appeals (16.4%) were "affective," compared with nineteen (34.6%) of the Japanese appeals. The Japanese writers showed a stronger tendency to try to evoke empathy in the reader's mind, in contrast to the Americans' assertive stances and use of reasoning. (4) The US writers tended toward expressions that emphasized the importance of their arguments by using modal verbs and other elements, e.g., *should/must, totally, no doubt, the* + superlative structures. In contrast, the Japanese writers used "softening" or "downgrading" devices, such as *I think, perhaps, sad, sorrow.*

Thus, though the students used the same medium – the English language – their messages were quite different. The American students presented rational arguments in a linear fashion, the Japanese writers evoked empathy and tried to present both the perspectives with regard to capital punishment.

Such rhetorical differences are not only a feature of student writing, they surface in other genres widely used by English-using communities at large as well, as is illustrated in the fragments of sales letters written by American, British, and Indian firms in (7–9) below (Frank, 1988). The letters were sent to the same recipient, a native speaker of American English, by companies in India (7), Britain (8), and the US (9) which were engaged in the publication of "Who's Who Directories" (Frank, 1988: 26):

(7)   We come back upon the correspondence resting with the inclusion of your biographical note in the forthcoming volume of our "Biography

International" and thank you much indeed for your esteemed cooperation in sending to us the same.

(8) Your name has been put forward for biographical and pictorial inclusion
in the Twelfth Edition of Men of Achievement, and you are respectfully
invited to complete the questionnaire overleaf and return it to our editors
so that they can prepare your detailed biography and send you a type-
script for proofing.

(9) Enclosed is a copy of your sketch as it appears in the 44th edition.
Please proofread it carefully. Make any necessary additions and cor-
rections. Then, even if no changes are needed, sign the sketch where
indicated and return it to me *within the next 15 days.*

Comparisons among these fragments are instructive. The long sentence in
(7) may seem overly complicated to Inner-Circle readers, whose expectations
are satisfied by a simple statement such as "Thank you for your response to
our invitation." The notion of "high style" in the Indian context, however,
would not be fulfilled by such "bald" statements. In the American style of
writing (9), it is appropriate to use direct imperatives with the conventional
politeness marker *please*; in the British style (8), however, more indirect
request strategies are considered appropriate, e.g., *you are . . . invited*, and an
extra marker of politeness, *respectfully*, is used. In the Indian letter, *thank you* is
followed by two intensifying expressions, *much* and *indeed*, and a modifier,
esteemed, is used before *cooperation* to express an extremely deferential attitude
toward the addressee. One other noticeable feature is the linking of the two
clauses with *and*; to an Inner-Circle reader, it appears strange to introduce the
two unrelated episodes – the correspondence regarding a biographical note
with the addressee and expression of gratitude by the writer of the letter – in
this manner. From the Indian point of view, the reference to the correspondence implies receipt of a biographical note from the addressee, for which an
expression of thanks is appropriate, and the two events are thus related.

Research in textual rhetoric suggests that Asian traditions of writing have
not included what has been characterized as "essay-text literacy." Essay-text
literacy is a relatively recent development in the Anglo-American tradition
of rhetoric also, and is characterized by a heavy emphasis on explicit,
decontextualized, impersonal language (Gee, 1986). While the Western tradition of writing has evolved during the past half-century, in part as a result
of technological innovations, modernization of non-Western societies has happened as a result of contact with the West, and English has been the most
salient instrument of this contact. There is a wealth of material available on
linguistic socialization, literacy, bilingualism, and language acquisition that
points to the fact that bilinguals have access to unique and specific linguistic
configurations that are different from those of monolinguals in either language in their repertoires, in the same way that a hurdler is neither a sprinter
nor a high jumper but something completely different, as Grosjean (1989) puts

it. Bilingual and multilingual scholars have adopted and adapted the literacy practices of the Anglocentric West, including those of "essay-text literacy," with adaptations to their own cultural practices. The following (10–11) are examples of such adaptation. The passages are from formal letters of request, the first (10) written by an Indian man to a female addressee asking for some information, and the second (11) by a Japanese male to a non-Japanese male addressee asking for permission to use some material.

(10)   Letter from an Indian scholar (male) to an Indian addressee (female)
       Madam,
       . . .
       Now coming to the crux of the matter . . . I request you *very humbly to enlighten me* of the following points.
       . . .
       So, *with folded hands* I request you to help me by supplying the *needed* information and names of any devotees and fans of E. I am writing to B.S. today. *If you want anything from my side just let me know.* Waiting *very anxiously* for your reply,

                                                                   Yours sincerely,

(11)   Letter from a director of a medical institute (male) to an academic addressee (male)
       Dear Mr. X,
       Explanations of Kangri of Kashmir are written in some medical books in Japan and we know it literary [sic], but there is almost no people practically booking [sic] at the real Kangri. I would like to use to demonstrate Kangri while teaching in postgraduate medical students as well as for researchers working on Kangri cancer.
       I wrote to Consulate General of India, [City], Japan, so Mr. Y sent me your writing [Title of Book] with figure of Kangri, [Date]. I would like to have your permission to reproduce the figure of Kangri to my writing.
       Of course, I will explain the reproduction from your text.
       Your kind consideration on this matter will be greatly appreciated.
                                                                          Sincerely,

Whereas (10) follows the conventions of Indian letter writing, (11) is more like a direct request written in an Anglo-American context.[6] This is to be expected, given the biliterate competence of highly educated professionals in Asia. They develop differentiated literacy skills and are able to use them in contextually sensitive ways. Since the first letter was written by an Indian to another Indian, it follows the Indian politeness strategies of prefacing the request by some general observations, and ends with an offer to reciprocate the anticipated favor. The second, however, was in English for someone in an English-speaking country and follows Anglo-American norms of letters of request, including stating the request in direct terms and not using the kinds of affective elements that (10) exhibits.

Such adaptations and accommodations, however, do not mean that all Outer- and Expanding-Circle academics are happy to conform to the expectations of ELT professionals and follow "the straight-edged geometry of Western rhetoric" (Lisle and Mano, 1997: 16). The Western classical rhetorical triangle which isolates speaker, message, and audience does not make as much sense to people from cultures in which oral traditions remains strong (Lisle and Mano, 1997: 18). The digressions that the ELT professionals find so distressing in non-Anglocentric writing have their sources in the oral-literate continua of other traditions. This, however, is a topic that deserves a more detailed discussion than is possible here.

It is reasonable to suggest that considerations of politeness also figure in the generic structure of academic writing in non-Inner-Circle contexts. In creative literature, the synthesis of oral and literate traditions and strategies of drawing in the audience have produced spectacular results in, for example, African, Indian, and Southeast Asian English writing (B. Kachru, 1992, 2005), and writing in English by recent immigrants in the Inner Circle. Such breakthroughs in academic publishing are possible only if the gatekeepers of the industry shed some of their prejudices. The relationship of scientific or academic discourse to the generic structure of that discourse is not organic; it is based on conventions. As Y. Kachru (1997) has shown, mathematical problems can be posed in verse and so can philosophical arguments, as they were in the Indian tradition of scholarship (see Dhillon, 1998).

Y. Kachru (1997: 61–2) identifies four features of non-Inner-Circle writing. The first is indirectness, as illustrated by Kamimura and Oi's (1998) study discussed above. The Japanese students preferred to present both sides of the argument. The Indian tradition of deliberative essay (Y. Kachru, 1997) also advises writers to present all sides of an argument so that readers may be led to arriving at a well-reasoned conclusion themselves. Secondly, non-Western writers are said to tend toward a "high style," employing "stylistic embellishments, quotations, idioms and metaphors." Thirdly, extensive quotation from previous work is highly valued, whereas mere "appeal to authority" is not considered strong argumentation in the West. Such citations are used not only for the purposes of the argument directly, but because "[i]t is considered good manners to acknowledge one's gratitude and display one's respect for predecessors." Finally, while a stereotypical Western evaluation of non-Western work is to label it derivative and un-original, Y. Kachru observes (1997: 62) that "it is a misconception to think that originality necessarily lies in novelty." She cites the Indian tradition of written commentaries on previous philosophical and literary works, which form traditions in their own right and are valued as "original" works. In fact, the best of the commentaries use the earlier works as points of departure and propose their own ideas and arguments to augment, elucidate or critique aspects of the originals. As Moore (1967: 8) observes about the rich commentary literature of ancient India:

It produces, in the guise of mere commentaries, a wide variety of points of view – at times virtually new systems – that reveal the originality and creativity of mind and thought possessed by these commentators, many of whom are commentators only in what might be called the polite sense of the word.

Consideration of politeness in writing is illustrated by a study (Taylor and Chen, 1991) that compared introductions to scientific papers written by three groups of physical scientists: Anglo-Americans writing in English, Chinese writing in English, and Chinese writing in Chinese. The study revealed several significant differences between the Anglo-American and Chinese texts. One is the Chinese preference for a simple instead of elaborated structure for introductions, and another is lack of critical reviews of literature, irrespective of whether the Chinese-produced texts were written in Chinese or in English. The Anglo-American introductions were 1.7 times longer than the Chinese introductions on average, almost 50 percent of the Chinese introductions opted out of any critical review of literature, and the Chinese texts had almost 57 percent fewer references than the American texts. The authors rule out a developmental explanation of shorter introductions and the missing reviews of literature and paucity of references. That is to say, it was not the case that the Chinese scientists had less competence in the English language. Instead, Taylor and Chen suggest that "the Chinese scholars find it less acceptable to identify by name and to summarize the works of others whom they will then proceed to 'expose,' as it were" (p. 331). Such a treatment of their predecessors is contrary to the Chinese notions of politeness in writing.

It is not the case that the characteristics noted above are attested only in Asian regions. In Arabic rhetoric, verbal artistry and emotional impact are the primary measures of persuasive power: rhythm, sound, repetition, and emphatic assertion carry more weight than factual evidence, and organization may depend more on metaphor and association than on linear logic (Lisle and Mano, 1997: 17). This analysis is supported by Sa'adeddin (1989), who makes a distinction between two different modes of text development: aural and visual (pp. 38–9). The former is characterized by recurrent and plain lexis, exaggeration, repetition of syntactic structures, loose packaging of information, a lack of apparent coherence, etc. – that is, a style that signals informality and solidarity, highly valued in the Arabic tradition. The visual mode, on the other hand, has the features of linearization, progressive development of a thesis, logical coherence, and syntactic cohesiveness, all of which are highly valued in the Western tradition.

Similarly, indirection and circumlocutory rhetoric are a part of African discourse strategies, as well. "By 'stalking' the issues, a speaker demonstrates skill and arouses hearers' interest. The person who gets directly to the issues is said to have little imagination and even less flair for rhetorical style" (Asante, 1987: 51).

In addition to the sorts of cultural preferences mentioned above, research has shown that not all languages and cultures share the text types described or posited in English (Y. Kachru, 2001). For instance, recipes and instruction manuals for manufacturing, weaving, sewing, knitting, etc., are not familiar text types in many cultures, even those with long traditions of literacy (e.g., South Asia).

4 Conclusion

The concepts of speech acts, rhetorical strategies, conversational organization, politeness, and the strategies that manifest politeness are not the same in pluralistic societies as they are in the kind of idealized monolingual, monocultural society assumed in theoretical discussions on these topics. In the contexts of the Outer and Expanding Circles, contact between English and local languages has, on the one hand, resulted in nativization of English, and on the other, in Englishization of indigenous languages. As a result of linguistic and cultural contacts, traditional ways of expressing respect and intimacy are changing, even though they are not resulting in complete Anglicization of Asian or African societies. The kinds of data from these plural societies discussed in this chapter point to a greater need for fresh thinking on the theoretical concepts of speech acts, rhetoric, and politeness, and more empirical research on how Englishes are used across nations for various purposes, including literary creativity.

See also Chapters 15, WORLD ENGLISHES TODAY; 17, VARIETIES OF WORLD ENGLISHES; 22, GENRES AND STYLES IN WORLD ENGLISHES; 23, LITERARY CREATIVITY IN WORLD ENGLISHES; 24, WORLD ENGLISHES AND ISSUES OF INTELLIGIBILITY; 31, WORLD ENGLISHES AND GENDER IDENTITIES.

NOTES

1 The Japanese system is different from those of other languages in that pronouns are usually left out and the verb forms differ along the axis of address and the axis of reference. For a concise description of details of Japanese honorific language use, see Moeran (1988).

2 In consideration of space constraints, I am citing only the second-person pronominal forms and endings; parallel systematic choices are made in the other persons as well. I have followed the following transcription convention: *A/E* denote stem endings that change for gender and number agreement between *ā/e/ī/ī̃*. The choice of the honorific or non-honorific forms depends on the Indian notions of *maryādā* 'limit or constraint, i.e., the bounds within which one acts' and *lihāj* 'consideration, deference' (Y. Kachru, 1992).

3 The form *āp V-e ho* is possible in some colloquial varieties of Western Hindi, e.g., as spoken in Delhi and the Panjab. It is, however, not acceptable in Eastern Hindi, formal style, and in written Hindi.

4   There is by no means agreement on how to define politeness. Researchers are still struggling with the primitives that are necessary and sufficient to theorize about polite linguistic behavior. For detailed discussions, see Watts, Ide, and Ehlich (1992).

5   The genesis of this pattern, which needs further investigation, may be in the use of *na* as the preferred tag-element in Hindi, as in the following (the superscripted *h* represents aspiration, i.e., *tʰ* is an aspirated dental plosive):

āp ne kahā tʰā na ki āp usse mile tʰe?
You had said you saw him, didn't you?

In South Asian English, the use of *no?* and *isn't it?* as tags has been noted in existing literature, e.g., in B. Kachru (1986: 40).

6   The notable features are the following; the term "Dear" is not used in addressing the recipient, as the male writer does not feel comfortable in using that word, which is also a term of endearment, for the unfamiliar and higher-status female addressee; the phrases *very humbly* and *with folded hands* signal humility, a very important consideration in polite behavior; the phrases *enlighten me* and *needed information* indicate the preference for formal, "high" style, and the offer *If you want anything from my side just let me know* is to signal solidarity on the basis of shared nationality as well as politeness in suggesting reciprocity (see Y. Kachru, 1997, 2003 for more detailed discussions).

REFERENCES

Adegbija, Efurosibina (1989) A comparative study of politeness phenomena in Nigerian English, Yoruba and Ogori. *Multilingua*, 8(1), 57–80.

Adegbija, Efurosibina and Bello, Janet (2001) The semantics of "okay" (OK) in Nigerian English. *World Englishes*, 20(1), 89–98.

Asante, Milefi Kete (1987) *The Afrocentric Idea*. Philadelphia, PA: Temple University Press.

Austin, John L. (1962) *How to Do Things with Words*. Cambridge, MA: Harvard University Press.

Bailey, Benjamin (2000) Communicative behavior and conflict between African-American customers and Korean immigrant retailers in Los Angeles. *Discourse and Society*, 11(1), 86–108.

Blum-Kulka, Shoshana and Kasper, Gabriele (eds.) (1990) *Politeness*. (*Journal of Pragmatics*, 14(2).)

Blum-Kulka, Shoshana, Danet, Brenda, and Gherson, Rimona (1985) The language of requesting in Israeli society. In *Language and Social Situation*. Edited by J. Forgas. New York: Springer Verlag, pp. 113–41.

Blum-Kulka, Shoshana, House, Juliane, and Kasper, Gabriele (eds.) (1989) *Cross-Cultural Pragmatics: Requests and Apologies*. Norwood, NJ: Ablex.

Brown, Penelope and Levinson, Stephen C. (1987) *Politeness: Some Universals in Language Usage*. Cambridge: Cambridge University Press.

Brown, Roger and Gilman, Albert (1960) The pronouns of power and solidarity. In *Style in Language*. Edited by T. A. Sebeok. Cambridge, MA: MIT Press, pp. 253–76.

Dhillon, Pradeep (1998) Literary form and philosophical argument in premodern texts. In *Dialogue and Universalism*, **11–12**, 131–41.

Firth, Alan (ed.) (1995) *The Discourse of Negotiation: Studies of Language in the Workplace*. Oxford: Pergamon.

Frank, Jane (1988) Miscommunication across cultures: The case of marketing in Indian English. *World Englishes*, **7**(1), 25–36.

Fraser, Bruce, Rintell, Ellen, and Walters, Joel (1980) An approach to conducting research on the acquisition of pragmatic competence in a second language. In *Discourse Analysis in Second Language Research*. Edited by Diane Larsen-Freeman. Rowley, MA: Newbury House, pp. 75–91.

Gee, James Paul (1986) Orality and literacy: From *The Savage Mind* to *Ways with Words*. *TESOL Quarterly*, **20**, 719–46.

Green, Georgia M. (1989) *Pragmatics and Natural Language Understanding*. Hillsdale, NJ: Lawrence Erlbaum.

Grice, H. Paul (1975) Logic and conversation. In *Syntax and Semantics 7: Speech Acts*. Edited by Peter Cole and Jerry Morgan. New York: Academic Press, pp. 41–58.

Grosjean, François (1989) Neurolinguists, beware! The bilingual is not two monolinguals in one person. *Brain and Language*, **36**, 3–15.

Herbert, Robert K. (1989) The ethnography of compliments and compliment responses: A contrastive sketch. In *Contrastive Pragmatics*. Edited by Wieslaw Olesky. Amsterdam: John Benjamins, pp. 3–35.

Hill, Beverly, Ide, Sachiko, Ikuta, Shoko, Kawasaki, Akiko, and Ogino, Tsunao (1986) Universals in linguistic politeness: Quantitative evidence from Japanese and American English. *Journal of Pragmatics*, **10**, 347–71.

Holmes, Janet (1990) Apologies in New Zealand English. *Language in Society*, **19**(2), 155–99.

Hwang, Juck-Ryoon (1990) "Deference" versus "politeness" in Korean speech. *International Journal of the Sociology of Language*, **82**, 41–55.

Ide, Sachiko (1989) Formal forms and discernment: Neglected aspects of linguistic politeness. *Multilingua*, **8**(2), 223–48.

Kachru, Braj B. (1986) *The Alchemy of English: The Spread, Functions and Models of Non-native Englishes*. Oxford: Pergamon Press. (South Asian edition, New Delhi: Oxford University Press, 1989; US edition, Urbana: University of Illinois Press, 1990.)

Kachru, Braj B. (1992) Meaning in deviation: Toward understanding non-native English texts. In *The Other Tongue: English across Cultures*. Edited by Braj B. Kachru. Urbana: University of Illinois Press, pp. 301–26.

Kachru, Braj B. (2002) On nativizing *Mantra*: Identity construction in Anglophone Englishes. In *Anglophone Cultures in Southeast Asia: Appropriations, Continuities, Contexts*. Edited by Rüdiger Ahrens, David Parker, Klaus Stierstorfer, and Kowk-Kan Tam. Heidelberg, Germany: Heidelberg University Press, pp. 55–72.

Kachru, Braj B. (2005) *Asian Englishes: Beyond the Canon*. Hong Kong: Hong Kong University Press.

Kachru, Yamuna (1980) *Aspects of Hindi Grammar*. New Delhi: Manohar Publications.

Kachru, Yamuna (1992) Speech act in the other tongue: An integrated approach to cross-cultural research. In *The Extended Family: English in Global Bilingualism*. Edited by Larry E. Smith and S. N. Sridhar (special issue of *World Englishes*, **11**(2–3)), 235–40.

Kachru, Yamuna (1997) Culture and argumentative writing in world Englishes. In *World Englishes 2000.* Edited by Larry E. Smith and Michael L. Forman. Honolulu: University of Hawai'i Press, pp. 48–67.

Kachru, Yamuna (1998) Culture and speech acts: Evidence from Indian and Singaporean English. *Studies in the Linguistic Sciences*, **28**, 79–98.

Kachru, Yamuna (1999) Culture, context and writing. In *Culture in Second Language Teaching and Learning.* Edited by Eli Hinkel. Cambridge: Cambridge University Press, pp. 75–89.

Kachru, Yamuna (2001) World Englishes and rhetoric across cultures. *Asian Englishes: An International Journal of the Sociolinguistics of English in Asia/ Pacific*, **4**(2), 54–71.

Kachru, Yamuna (2003) Conventions of politeness in plural societies. In *Anglophone Cultures in South-East Asia: Appropriations, Continuities, Contexts.* Edited by Rüdiger Ahrens, David Parker, Klaus Stierstorfer, and Kowk-Kan Tam. Heidelberg, Germany: Heidelberg University Press, pp. 39–53.

Kamimura, Takeo and Oi, Kyoko (1998) Argumentative strategies in American and Japanese English. *World Englishes*, **17**(3), 307–23.

Kang, M. Agnes (2003) Negotiating conflict within the constraints of social hierarchies in Korean American discourse. *Journal of Sociolinguistics*, **7**(3), 299–320.

Ler, Soon Lay Vivien (2001) The interpretation of the discourse particle *Meh* in Singapore colloquial English. *Journal of Asian Englishes*, **4**(2), 4–23.

Levinson, Stephen C. (1983) *Pragmatics.* Cambridge: Cambridge University Press.

Liao, Chao-Chih (1997) *Comparing Directives: American English, Mandarin and Taiwanese English.* Taipei: Crane Publishing Co.

Lisle, Bonnie and Mano, Sandra (1997) Embracing the multicultural rhetoric. In *Writing in Multicultural Settings.* Edited by Carol Severino, Juan C. Guerra, and Johnnella E. Butler. New York: The Modern Language Association of America, pp. 12–26.

Manes, Joan and Wolfson, Nessa (1981) The compliment formula. In *Conversational Routines.* Edited by Florian Coulmas. The Hague: Mouton, pp. 115–32.

Martin, Samuel E. (1964) Speech levels in Japan and Korea. In *Language in Culture and Society.* Edited by Del Hymes. New York: Harper and Row, pp. 407–14.

Matsumoto, Yoshiko (1988) Reexamination of the universality of face: Politeness phenomena in Japanese. *Journal of Pragmatics*, **12**, 403–26.

Matsumoto, Yoshiko (1989) Politeness and conversational universals: Observations from Japanese. *Multilingua*, **8**, 207–21.

Meyerhoff, Miriam (1994) Sounds pretty ethnic, Eh? A pragmatic particle in New Zealand English. *Language in Society*, **23**(3), 367–88.

Meyerhoff, Miriam (1999) Sorry in the pacific: Defining communities, defining practices. *Language in Society*, **28**(2), 225–38.

Mitchell-Kernan, Claudia (1972) Signifying, loud-talking, and marking. In *Rappin' and Styling' Out: Communication in Urban Black America.* Edited by Thomas Kochman. Urbana: University of Illinois Press, pp. 315–35.

Moeran, Brian (1988) Japanese language and society. *Journal of Pragmatics*, **12**, 427–43.

Moore, Charles (ed.) (1967) *The Japanese Mind: Essentials of Japanese Philosophy and Culture*. Honolulu: The University Press of Hawai'i.

Morgan, Marcyliena (1998) More than a mood or an attitude: Discourse and verbal genres in African-American culture. In *African-American English: Structure, History and Use*. Edited by Salikoko S. Mufwene, John R. Rickford, Guy Bailey, and John Baugh. New York: Routledge, pp. 251–81.

Nelson, Cecil L. (1991) New Englishes, new discourses: New speech acts. *World Englishes*, **10**(3), 317–24.

Nwoye, Gregory O. (1985) Eloquent silence among the Igbo of Nigeria. In *Perspectives on Silence*. Edited by Deborah Tannen and Muriel Saville-Troike. Norwood, NJ: Ablex, pp. 185–91.

Pakir, Anne (1992) Dictionary entries for discourse particles. In *Words in a Cultural Context*. Proceedings of the Lexicography Workshop, Singapore. Edited by Anne Pakir. Singapore: UniPress, pp. 143–52.

Rampton, Ben (1998) Language crossing and the redefinition of reality. In *Codeswitching in Conversation*. Edited by Peter Auer. London: Routledge, pp. 290–317.

Reynolds, Dudley W. (1993) Illocutionary acts across languages: Editorializing in Egyptian English. *World Englishes*, **12**(1), 35–46.

Rose, Kenneth R. (1992) Method and Scope in Cross Cultural Speech Act Research: A contrastive study of requests in Japanese and English. PhD dissertation, University of Illinois, Urbana-Champaign.

Sa'adeddin, Mohammed Akram A. M. (1989) Text development and Arabic-English negative interference. *Applied Linguistics*, **10**, 36–51.

Schegloff, Emanuel A. (1988) Presequences and indirection: Applying speech act theory to ordinary conversation. *Journal of Pragmatics*, **12**, 55–62.

Schmidt, Richard W. (1983) Interaction, acculturation, and the acquisition of communicative competence: A case study of an adult. In *Sociolinguistics and Language Acquisition*. Edited by Nessa Wolfson and Eliot Judd. New York: Newbury House, pp. 137–74.

Searle, John R. (1969) *Speech Acts: An Essay in the Philosophy of Language*. Cambridge: Cambridge University Press.

Silva, Rosangela S. (1998) Pragmatic Competence and Transfer Abilities: Native and Non-Native Speakers of Portuguese. PhD dissertation, University of Illinois, Urbana-Champaign.

Silva, Rosangela S. (2000) Pragmatics, bilingualism, and the native speaker. *Language and Communication*, **20**, 161–78.

Singh, Udaya Narayana (1989) How to honor someone in Maithili. *International Journal of the Sociology of Language*, **75**, 87–107.

Sridhar, Kamal K. (1991) Speech acts in an indigenized variety: Sociocultural values and language variation. In *English around the World: Sociolinguistic Perspectives*. Edited by Jenny Cheshire. Cambridge: Cambridge University Press, pp. 308–18.

Srivastava, Ravindra Nath and Pandit, Ira (1988) The pragmatic basis of syntactic structures and the politeness hierarchy in Hindi. *Journal of Pragmatics*, **12**(2), 185–205.

Stubbe, Maria and Holmes, Janet (1999) Talking Maori or Pakeha in English: Signaling identity in discourse. In *New Zealand English*. Edited by Alan Bell and Koenraad Kuiper. Amsterdam: John Benjamins, pp. 249–78.

Tannen, Deborah and Saville-Troike, Muriel (eds.) (1985) *Perspectives on Silence*. Norwood, NJ: Ablex.

Taylor, G. and Chen, T. (1991) Linguistic, cultural and subcultural issues in contrastive discourse analysis: Anglo-American and Chinese scientific texts. *Applied Linguistics*, **12**, 319–36.

Treichler, Paula A., Frankel, Richard M., Kramarae, Cheris, Zoppi, Kathleen, and Beckman, Howard B. (1984) Problems and problems: Power relationships in a medical encounter. In *Language and Power*. Edited by Cheris Kramarae. Beverly Hills, CA: Sage, pp. 62–88.

Valentine, Tamara (1995) Agreeing and disagreeing in Indian English discourse: Implications for language teaching. In *Language and Culture in Multilingual Societies: Viewpoints and Visions*. Edited by Makhan L. Tickoo. Anthology Series 36, Singapore: SEAMEO Regional Language Center, pp. 227–50.

Watts, Richard J., Ide, Sachiko and Ehlich, Konrad (eds.) (1992) *Politeness in Language: Studies in Its History, Theory, and Practice*. Berlin: Mouton de Gruyter.

Wee, Lionel (2003) The birth of a particle: *Know* in colloquial Singapore English. *World Englishes*, **22**(1), 5–13.

Wetzel, Patricia J. (1988) Are "powerless" communication strategies the Japanese norm? *Language in Society*, **17**(4), 555–64.

Wierzbicka, Anna (1985) Different cultures, different languages, different speech acts: Polish vs. English. *Journal of Pragmatics*, **9**, 145–78.

Wolfson, Nessa, D'Amico-Reisner, Lynne, and Huber, Lisa (1983) How to arrange for social commitments in American English: The invitation. In *Sociolinguistics and Language Acquisition*. Edited by Nessa Wolfson and Elliot Judd. Rowley, MA: Newbury House, pp. 116–28.

Wolfson, Nessa, Marmor, T., and Jones, S. (1989) Problems in the comparison of speech acts across cultures. In *Cross-Cultural Pragmatics: Requests and Apologies*. Edited by Shoshana Blum-Kulka, Juliane House, and Gabriele Kasper. Norwood, NJ: Ablex, pp. 174–96.

Wong, Jock (2004) The particles of Singapore English: A semantic and cultural interpretation. *Journal of Pragmatics*, **36**(4), 739–93.

Young, Linda Wai Ling (1982) Inscrutability revisited. In *Language and Social Identity*. Edited by J. J. Gumperz. Cambridge: Cambridge University Press, pp. 72–84.

FURTHER READING

Berman, Laine (1998) *Speaking through the Silence: Narratives, Social Conventions, and Power in Java*. New York: Oxford University Press.

Cherry, Roger D. (1988) Politeness in written persuasion. *Journal of Pragmatics*, **12**(1), 63–81.

Hayashi, Reiko (1996) *Cognition, Empathy, and Interaction: Floor Management of English and Japanese Conversation*. Norwood, NJ: Ablex.

Kachru, Yamuna and Larry E. Smith (2008) *Cultures, Contexts, and World Englishes*. New York: Routledge.

Mesthrie, Rajend and Rakesh M. Bhatt (2008) *World Englishes: The Study of*

New Linguistic Varieties. Cambridge University Press.

Salih, Mahmoud and Hussein, Abdul-Fattah (1998) English and Arabic oath speech acts. *Interface,* **12**(2), 113–24.

Schiffrin, Deborah (1994) *Approaches to Discourse.* Oxford: Blackwell.

Valentine, Tamara M. (1992) The nativizing of gender: Speech acts in the new Englishes literatures. *World Englishes,* **11**(2–3), 259–70.

Valentine, Tamara M. (1996) Politeness models in Indian English. *Revista de Lenguas para Fines Específicos,* **3**, 279–300.

Yamada, Haru (1992) *American and Japanese Business Discourse: A Comparison of Interactional Styles.* Norwood, NJ: Ablex.

22 Genres and Styles in World Englishes

VIJAY K. BHATIA

1 Introduction

Genre, register, style, text-type, and a number of similar concepts seem to have been motivated by a common concern to highlight functional variation in the use of language; however, in spite of this shared concern, they are conceptualized, discussed, and used in applied and sociolinguistic literature somewhat differently. Each one of these concepts represents a particular way of identifying functional discourse on the basis of typically shared characteristics within that category; however, at the same time, each category is also used to identify variation across other members of the same category. News report as a genre, for instance, is identified on the basis of "generic integrity" (Bhatia, 1993, 1994) which most news reports represent, but at the same time, news report as a genre can also be used to distinguish variation in language use by comparing it with other genres, such as editorials, film reviews, or letters to the editor, even if they are located in the same newspaper. The same is true of registers, text-types, and styles. World Englishes, in a similar manner, indicate integrity within a particular variety as well as variation across varieties. Most speakers of Singaporean English, for instance, will have a number of common features that will identify and establish Singaporean English as a variety in its own right, but this variety, at the same time, will be different in a number of other ways from other Englishes, such as Indian English, Nigerian English, or Australian English. Most of these concepts thus are motivated by a shared understanding of integrity and identity on the one hand, and variation, or creativity, on the other. In this chapter I would like to explore the dual complexity of some of these interesting concepts by looking at a diversity of examples from real-life discourse contexts. In doing so I would also like to devote some attention to the motivations for such variations in discourse, both in terms of the use of text-internal resources, such as lexico-grammatical features available and allowable in specific relevant contexts, and also in terms of text-external resources and constraints operating on these discourses, such as the rhetorical context, the communicative purpose, the sociocultural action that individual discourses tend to serve. However, before undertaking such a task, I would like to clarify some of these concepts by offering in brief my own perceptions of these terms.

2   Genre

Genres are instances of situated linguistic behavior in institutionalized academic, professional, or other social settings, whether defined in terms of "typifications of rhetorical action," as in Miller (1984), "regularities of staged, goal oriented social processes," as in Martin (1993), or "consistency of communicative purposes," as in Swales (1990) and Bhatia (1993). Genre theory, in spite of these seemingly different perceptions, approaches, and orientations, covers considerable common ground. Genre is viewed as an instance of language use in a conventionalized social setting requiring an appropriate response to a specific set of communicative goals of a disciplinary or social institution, and thus giving rise to stable structural forms by imposing constraints on the use of lexico-grammatical as well as discoursal resources. Although genres are primarily identified on the basis of text-external factors, such as rhetorical context, communicative purpose, rhetorical strategies, sociocultural and other institutional constraints, etc., text-internal factors, such as lexico-grammatical resources, discourse organization patterns, etc., often serve as insightful indicators, and hence are given considerable prominence. Besides, although genres tend to be conventionalized communicative events, they are "dynamic rhetorical structures" which enjoy a certain degree of natural propensity for innovation, and are often "manipulated according to conditions of use" (Berkenkotter and Huckin, 1995).

Emphasis on conventions and propensity for innovation, these two features of genre theory may appear to be contradictory in character, in that one tends to view genre as rhetorically stable textual activity, having its own "generic integrity" (Bhatia, 1993), whereas the other assigns genre a natural propensity for innovation that is often exploited by experienced writers to create new forms in order to respond to novel rhetorical contexts. However, as we know, situations may not always recur exactly in the same way; that is, a person may be required to respond to a somewhat changing socio-cognitive need, thus encouraging him to negotiate his response in the light of recognizable or established conventions. It is also possible that he may decide to communicate "private intentions" within the rhetorical context of a "socially recognized communicative purpose" (Bhatia, 1993), which might encourage established members of a professional community to exploit generic resources to negotiate individual responses to recurring and novel rhetorical situations. Or it is also possible that he may consciously introduce variations in the use of lexico-grammar, rhetorical strategies, or discourse patterns (Bhatia, 1996) to indicate his creative ability to establish his own individual identity, or to achieve a specific effect. However, such liberties, innovations, creativities, exploitations are often realized within rather than outside the generic boundaries. The nature of genre manipulation is therefore invariably realized within the broad limits of specific generic boundaries. Any drastic disregard for these generic conventions leads to opting out of the genre and is noticed by the concerned "discourse community" (Swales, 1990) as odd. However, one can see the tension between "generic integrity" and "generic creativity" (Bhatia, 2002) here which is highlighted in some of the following assertions:

- Genres are associated with typical textualizations, yet experienced and established members of professional communities exploit them to create new forms.
- Although genres represent more or less conventionalized use of linguistic resources, it is possible to bring in creativity in linguistic expressions to represent subtle changes in style to convey private, organizational, personal identities, attitudes, intentions, and perceptions.
- Genres serve typical socially recognized communicative purposes; however, they can be exploited or appropriated to bring "adjustments" in communicative objectives creating opportunities for mixing, embedding, and bending of genres.

These are some of the relevant issues for us, as we reconsider typically identifiable and largely differentiated instances of genres, focusing on variations, not only in the use of language in different contexts, but also, perhaps more importantly, in the way these variations might represent differences in the experiences, aspirations, attitudes, and belief systems of speakers of world Englishes. As we may expect, there are likely to be regularities of various kind, in the use of lexico-grammatical, discoursal, and generic resources; there will be recurrence of rhetorical situations, though not exactly in the same form or manner; there will also be expert and well-established users of language from specific disciplinary cultures who would like to exploit, appropriate, and even bend generic conventions and expectations in order to be creatively effective or innovative in their use of language. However, before we discuss these issues any further, I would like to bring in the role of style variations in the shaping of these genres.

3   Style

Whereas genre as a category is often identified predominantly in terms of text-external factors, style is generally defined in terms of text-internal factors, especially in relation to two parameters: a typically individual use of language, or a typically functional use of language, sometimes configured in terms of contextual factors of field, mode, and tenor of discourse. In the second sense, it is also called register, as in Halliday, McIntosh, and Strevens

(1964), whereas some prefer to call it style, as in Crystal and Davy (1969). However, it is possible to see a considerable degree of overlap in these two terms. In this chapter, I would like to distinguish variation in language use in both these senses: style to refer to an individual's use of language, as for instance, when one refers to E. M. Forster's or Hemingway's style; and register to refer to a functional use of language to suit a particular configuration of contextual factors of field, mode, and tenor of discourse (B. Kachru, 1992b). The primary motivation for considering these two together is the fact that both of them are primarily identified in terms of text-internal factors, such as the use of lexico-grammar, or sometimes discourse structures, typically used by a genre writer.

However, when we compare the two concepts, especially the way they are identified, we find an interesting and somewhat confusing contrast. Genres, as we have seen in the preceding sections, are primarily defined in terms of text-external factors, but they also have text-internal indicators, such as the typical use of lexico-grammatical, discourse moves or cognitive structuring. Styles are primarily defined in terms of text-internal features distinguished either in terms of an individual's use of language (Jane Austen's style), or any specific register-sensitive use of language (conversational style, or legal style). Registers, in this respect, come close to style; although viewed in terms of specific configurations of contextual factors such as field, mode, and tenor of discourse, they are also essentially analyzed in terms of typical uses of lexico-grammatical features, with some attention to either discourse patterns, or text-external factors such as participants, communicative purposes, activity-type, etc. The main distinction, in my view, between genre and style, then is the degree of attention paid to text-external or text-internal features. This also underpins another crucial distinction between linguistic forms and communicative values that linguistic forms take on in real life discourse. Genre focuses more on the communicative values, whereas style pays more attention to linguistic form, although both of them are crucial to our understanding of variation in language use. I think this distinction is fundamentally crucial to our understanding of variations in genre and style, which also explains why genres are recognized, shared, owned, maintained, and even policed by discourse or professional communities, whereas styles are often more centrally associated with individual writers.

4 World Englishes

World Englishes, in a similar manner, are viewed in terms of text-internal characteristics of language use by individuals, though they are also conceptualized in terms of text-external perceptions of the world we live in. Like styles, world Englishes are also reflections of individual uses of language though motivated by sociocultural differences in perceptions and attitudes. Since both styles and world Englishes share the use of text-internal resources with genre, any creative change in or innovative use of allowable lexico-grammar will also bring in some degree of creativity in the genre construction and interpretation. Differences in style, or variations due to world Englishes, thus have the potential to create significant differences in genres too. However, so long as genres are identified in text-external factors, changes in lexico-grammar are less likely to bring in substantive variations in the perception of generic integrity, although it is true that such changes or creative variations in lexico-grammar may bring in interesting variations in style. Besides, there may be a number of other factors that influence variation in genres and style in the context of world Englishes, one of which is the nature of the individual genre in question, whether it is liberal, and hence more versatile in accepting creativity, or conservative and rigid in allowable use of lexico-grammatical resources. Let me give more substance to such constraints on variation.

5   Liberal vs. Conservative Genres

In the analysis of variation in genres and styles, especially in the context of world Englishes, an important role is played by the inherent nature of the individual genres in question. Genres seem to form a continuum, at one end of which we may find extremely conservative discourse forms, e.g., legal contracts, legislative statements, and statutes (Bhatia, 1982), and at the other end, we may see exceptionally liberal forms of discourse, both fictional, such as literary genres, and non-fictional, such as advertising. The behavior of many of these standardized genres in respect of their propensity for variation and innovation, including creativity, appropriation, and exploitation, largely depends on the extent to which individual genres may allow variations in the use of text-internal features of language use, such as lexico-grammar, discourse structuring, and perhaps rhetorical strategies, and the extent to which they may allow variation in text-external features without changing the nature of linguistic behavior. In order to ensure that these constraints are respected, we often find social gate-keeping procedures that tend to maintain generic integrity and style, more in professional and institutional discourses than in literary and social genres. In much of academic publishing in English one can see all forms of editorial control by established publishing houses to maintain generic integrity as well as house styles. In some respects, authors are, whether consciously or unconsciously, influenced by what they read, particularly in academic contexts, which is seen as a natural process of initiation into a specific discourse community. This in itself is an essential process of acquisition of genre knowledge, which is a crucial influence on genre construction and interpretation. Over and above that, reviewers and editors play a significant role in curbing individual freedom of innovation (Bhatia, 1997). Unfortunately, such constraints often translate in terms of conformity to largely Western and native English norms, thereby constraining variation, creativity, and innovation in language use, especially motivated by variations in world Englishes.

These factors are important contributors to the maintenance of generic integrity in most conventional genres.

In most of the literary genres, which are primarily identified in terms of their formal characteristics, creativity and innovation in the use of linguistic form are viewed as a great virtue, whereas in most conservative genres, such as legislative documents, variation in linguistic resources is certainly detrimental to the maintenance of unambiguity, clarity, precision and all-inclusiveness, and hence viewed as a serious problem (Bhatia, 1993). Genres such as advertising and a number of other promotional documents have traditionally been considered conventional, but are increasingly being seen as more and more liberal in their use of linguistic resources, including rhetorical strategies. Interesting from the point of view of variation in the use of English will be what Swales (1996) refers to as "occluded" genres, which invariably escape "the overarching dominance of anglophone nativespeakerism" (Swales, 1997: 381). To illustrate some of these processes and their effects, let me consider examples from a range of discourses, some highly conventionalized, both professional and institutional, and others less so. I would like to begin with one of the most conservative forms of discourse, that is, legal texts. Here are four examples of arbitration clauses, constructed and recommended in four different countries: India, the UK, China, and Japan. All four of them represent the same genre, but are written and used in different countries.

(1)   Any dispute or difference whatsoever arising between the parties out of or relating to the construction, meaning, scope, operation or effect of this contract, or the validity or the breach thereof shall be settled by arbitration in accordance with the Rules of Arbitration of the Indian Council of Arbitration and the award made in pursuance thereof shall be binding on the parties.

(The Indian Council of Arbitration)

(2)   Any dispute arising out of or in connection with this contract, including any question regarding its existence, validity or termination, shall be referred to and finally resolved by arbitration under the LCIA Rules, which Rules are deemed to be incorporated by reference into this clause.

(London Court of International Arbitration)

(3)   Any dispute arising from or in connection with this Contract shall be submitted to China International Economic and Trade Arbitration Commission for arbitration which shall be conducted in accordance with the Commission's arbitration rules in effect at the time of applying for arbitration. The arbitral award is final and binding upon both parties.

(China International Economic and Trade Arbitration Commission)

(4)   All disputes, controversies or differences which may arise between the parties hereto, out of or in relation to or in connection with this

Agreement shall be finally settled by arbitration in (name of city) in accordance with the Commercial Arbitration Rules of The Japan Commercial Arbitration Association.

(The Japan Commercial Arbitration Association)

These four arbitration clauses from different countries appear to be perfect examples of a single genre, highly conventionalized not only in terms of their use of lexico-grammatical resources to bring in a relevant degree of specificity, unambiguity, and clarity of expression, typical of legal statements, but also in terms of their conformity to the typical use of lexico-grammatical resources. The only significant difference one may find in these different and yet overlapping versions lies in the varying degrees of specificity and control, which are the functions of the individual legal systems, rather than any other factor. They represent the most conservative genre and are written in the same legal style, and are exceptionally similar in text-external as well as text-internal factors. It is possible that they may have been copied from the same source, as often happens in this area of language use. The gate keeping is essentially the function of the legal culture prevalent in these contexts, though differences in legal systems sometimes bring in interesting variations.

Literary works, on the other side of the liberal/conservative divide, present a contrast to what I have referred to as legislative frozen genres, and literature in world Englishes is full of instances of creativity that one can see in different literary genres (see B. Kachru, 1990, 1992a; Canagarajah, 1994; Lowry, 1992; Osakwe, 1999; etc., to name only a few). Instead of repeating what has been clearly and convincingly demonstrated in published studies, I would like to focus on another closely related genre, which also allows sufficient scope for creativity, which is the film review genre. Let me take up three reviews of the same film, *Something's Gotta Give*; the first written by a native English-speaking film critic, the second by a Singaporean critic, and the third by an Indian film critic. The three writers seem to be very familiar with the genre, and hence in terms of text-external factors the three reviews are very similar. However, in terms of text-internal factors, the three appear to be very different. They talk about the same film, but in the way they describe people and characters, the way they talk about the plot, their descriptions of events and character relationships, there appears to be little in common. The styles are also very different. Let me illustrate this by taking two extracts from each one, first where the three writers introduce the main character Harry Sanborn, played by Jack Nicholson, and then the way they close the review.

(5)   Mr. Nicholson plays Harry Sanborn, a rich, 62-year-old bachelor who has devoted his life to philosophy: the Playboy Philosophy, circa 1966. Harry prides himself on never having dated a woman over 30, and at the start of the movie his babe of the moment is Erica's daughter, Marin (Amanda Peet) . . . "Something's Gotta Give," true to form, does not really depart from the genial, sentimental formulas of its genre. Some of the

jokes are flat, and some scenes that should sparkle with screwball effervescence sputter instead. But what Ms. Meyers lacks in inventiveness she makes up for in generosity, to the actors and therefore to the audience.
(http://movies2.nytimes.com/mem/movies/review.html)

(6) Nancy Meyers' new romantic comedy brings together gramps and his woman in the form of my favourite sleazebag Jack Nicholson and the gorgeous Diane Keaton, who team up for two hours of fun, laughter and romance in the movie. Harry (Nicholson) is an aged music-industry exec who dates younger women like Marin (Amanda) who are no older than 30 . . . Something's Gotta Give stands out from the run-of-the-mill romantic comedy for its story line as well as the performances by its lead characters.
(http://straitstimes.asia1.com.sg/showbiz/reviews)

(7) Look at the two carefully contrasted species of the male gender. While Nicholson playing a 63-year old flirt who sleeps only with women under 30 is, in one word incorrigible, Reeves as the gentle doctor who treats Nicholson's heart attack, is everything that a woman WANTS a man to be . . . The film is too cute to be real. But it has some truly enchanting moments of yearning and longing. It also dares to laugh in the face of death. Nicholson's heart attack is handled with such rare humour, you tend to forgive the excess optimism of the film's basic premise.
(http://movies.indiatimes.com)

The three reviews, based on impressions of the same film, are similar as generic constructs, though they are very different in terms of their use of lexico-grammatical resources, so much so that they hardly appear to be talking the same way about the same thing. That is where one can clearly see the tension between "generic integrity" on the one hand, and "generic creativity" on the other. In other words, one can appreciate fully the distinction between genre and style so richly displayed in these examples, which was completely lost in the earlier legal examples. In the context of world Englishes, one can see an interesting tension between "conformity" to native English on the one hand, and "non-native creativity" on the other. Example (5) makes use of typical American humor in *his babe of the moment, some scenes that should sparkle with screwball effervescence sputter instead.* The Singaporean extract (6) is an attempt to conform to the expectations of the native English audience by using American slang expressions such as *gramps and his woman, my favourite sleazebag Jack Nicholson and the gorgeous Diane Keaton, the run-of-the-mill romantic comedy,* some even outdated in the US. There is a typical Singaporean touch as well in the use of abbreviated forms, as in *gramps* and *exec.* The Indian one (7), in contrast to these, brings in descriptions colored by the traditions reminiscent of the oriental culture, such as *species of the male gender, a 63-year old flirt, in one word incorrigible, everything that a woman WANTS a man to be, truly enchanting moments of yearning and longing, to laugh in the face of death.* Instead of using *dates* as in the other two, it makes use of *sleeps*, which is consistent with expectations in Indian culture, though things seem to be changing now. Similarly, *63-year old flirt* is preferred to *the playboy* in (5) and *sleazebag* in (6). One can see how style can be manipulated in two different directions depending on the background and intentions of the author, either toward conformity to native language and culture, as in (6), or toward one's own culture (7), which seems to be an attempt to translate Hollywood to almost Bollywood style. This creativity in style takes an even more interesting bilingual turn in the review of the Bollywood film "Masti," as the focus is on Indian audiences:

(8)   Having tasted the proverbial sourness in shaadi ka laddo, the three gear up to do some masti and decide that the only way to spice up their lives is to seek to excitement outside home. So the trio begins on their wacky and hilarious adventure to taste the forbidden fruit of an adulterous relation.

This one introduces another factor to our discussion, that is, the intended audience, which in earlier movie reviews was predominantly native English or upper-middle-class non-native English speaking, well versed in English language and culture. As compared with those, in the last one from a review of Bollywood movie the audience consists primarily of Hindi movie enthusiasts, very much familiar with Bollywood culture, who are familiar with interpretations of expressions such as "shadi ka laddo," "masti" (appropriated from the title of the movie, but used as a verb in the review), mixed with more modern native English colloquial expressions such as "spice up" and "wacky ... adventure." The interesting point here is that experienced and expert writers often have a choice between conformity to native English expectations, or creativity in the use of non-native English or bilingual expressions, and sometimes the choice is made on the basis of assumed audience characteristics and expectations.

Let me now take my third set of examples, which come from a discourse which appears to occupy a place somewhere in between these two extremes, that is, cooking recipes. The three examples are from Indonesia, Britain, and India:

(9)   *Nasi Gurih (Fragrant Rice)*
Put the coconut milk with all the flavourings and spices and salt into a large saucepan with a well-fitting lid, and bring slowly to the boil, uncovered. Stir in the rice and return to the boil, then turn heat very low, cover and steam for 20 minutes. Uncover, fork the rice very lightly from around sides of pan, mixing in any coconut milk that has not been absorbed, and replace lid for 5 minutes. Serve hot with fried chicken or curries and hot sambals.

(Solomon, 1976: 76)

(10) *Spicy Rice*

To make Spice Bag, place peppercorns, black onion seeds, cumin seeds, chillies, cinnamon, cardamom pods, ginger and bay leaves in the centre of the piece of muslin. Draw up corners and tie securely.

Place water in a large saucepan and bring it to boil. Stir in rice, lemon juice and salt to taste. Add Spice Bag and bring back to boil, then reduce heat to low, cover and simmer for 12–15 minutes or until rice is cooked.

(Blackley, 1993: 41)

(11) *Perfect Rice*

Begin by warming the frying pan over a medium heat, then add the oil and the onions and let them cook for 3–4 minutes, until lightly brown. Next stir in the rice – there's no need to wash it – and turn the grains over in the pan so they become lightly coated and glistening with oil. Then add the boiling water, along with the salt, stir once only, then cover with the lid. Turn the heat to its very lowest setting and let the rice cook gently for exactly 15 minutes. Don't remove the lid and don't stir the rice during cooking because this is what will break the grains and release their starch, which makes the rice sticky.

After 15 minutes, tilt the pan to check that no liquid is left; if there is, pop it back on the heat for another minute. When there is no water left in the pan, take the pan off the heat, remove the lid and cover with a clean tea cloth for 5–10 minutes before serving, then transfer the rice to a warm serving dish and fluff it lightly with a fork before it goes to the table.

(Smith, 1998: 200)

The three recipes are written by speakers of three different Englishes, the Indonesian, the Indian, and the British. Although the recipes in all three cases come from primarily non-native contexts, the audience in each case appears to be international, which encourages writers toward conformity to native English expressions, such as *flavourings and spices, fork the rice, mixing in any coconut milk that has not been absorbed, Spice Bag, the centre of the piece of muslin, draw up corners and tie securely*. Most of these expressions will be considered alien to those who are natives of the place where the dish originates. In the case of Delia Smith, who is demonstrating an Indian dish to a mainly British audience, you find an interesting variation in the form of explanations for a number of apparently unfamiliar processes, such as *Don't remove the lid and don't stir the rice during cooking because this is what will break the grains and release their starch, which makes the rice sticky*. In contrast to this, consider the following recipe from India for an Indian audience:

(12) *Semolina Laddu*

    i.   Fry semolina in ghee, in a karahi to a pink colour on a medium to slow flame.

    ii.   Mash and roast khoya lightly.
    iii.   Prepare a 2 string syrup with the sugar and water.
    iv.   Mix together all the ingredients. Keep covered for 15 minutes.
    v.   Shape the mixture into round balls or laddus with moist hands.

(Parmar, 1994: 57)

Semolina Laddu is an Indian dish and the recipe is addressed to a predomin-antly Indian audience. Look at the brevity of instructions, with the bilingual mix of terms such as *ghee, karahi, khoya, 2-string syrup, laddu,* which are as-sumed to be understood.

Let me move on to a sports event, that is, reporting on the day's play in cricket. The two texts I have chosen are both from the same website *Wisden Cricinfo* (April 13, 2004), but the first one is part of a report by the Indian writer Amit Varma on an India–Pakistan match, whereas the second one is by Andrew Miller on an England–West Indies match:

(13)   In a dramatic day's play, India, after taking charge of the match, let the advantage slip a bit. First, after the Indian bowlers had reduced Pakistan to 137 for 8, a gutsy 49 by Mohammad Sami helped them to a respectable 224. Then, Virender Sehwag was out off the first ball of the Indian innings, though the Indians avoided further loss, ending the day on 23 for 1.

(The Wisden Bulletin by Amit Varma)

(14)   After being roasted in the Caribbean sun for two-and-a-half days, England's batsmen suffered a prolonged dizzy spell on the third even-ing in Antigua, slumping to 98 for 5 before Andrew Flintoff and the debutant Geraint Jones applied the cold towels with a soothing 73-run partnership.

(The Wisden Bulletin by Andrew Miller)

The two reports are typical of the genre of cricket reporting and both of them, irrespective of the fact that they are written by two different authors who speak two different varieties of English, seem to serve a similar communic-ative purpose and use similar rhetorical structuring. These are the opening paragraphs of the reports; hence, as opening moves, they are quite similar. However, there are elements of creativity brought in by way of variation in individual styles. The Indian writer typically views the match as a battle-ground, which is consistent with the history of prolonged rivalry, often lead-ing to animosity, between the two countries. In the case of the second one, the use of expressions such as *being roasted in the Caribbean sun, suffered a prolonged dizzy spell, the debutant Geraint Jones applied the cold towels with a soothing 73-run partnership* seems to add quite a bit of spicy explanation to the writer's percep-tions of the day's play. The second one is a typical reaction from a writer for whom the suffering in the extreme temperature is as bad as doing badly in the game. In this respect, the Indian opening paragraph seems to be relatively more factual in comparison. But these are differences in style, motivated by different sociocultural experiences of the writers and expressed in their own typical styles of reporting in their specific varieties of English. In spoken commentary, one can notice a greater variation in individual styles, as we see in the following brief extracts from the program "Straight Drive" on Ten Sports concerning the India–Pakistan cricket series. In response to the host Sanjay's question on the performance of the two teams, the two specialists, one from India (Navjot Sidhu) and the other from Pakistan (Ramiz Raja), respond in the same genre but in their individual speech styles:

(15) Sidhu: I think if you want me to place any odds in this situation I think it's 85 in favour of Pakistan and 50 in favour of India . . . make no mistake . . . you see when India has batted well . . . when they've had starts when the top order has clicked . . . it's a different ball game altogether . . . even your bowling comes up to that mark and suddenly your Indian team looks a different unit altogether but when the top order hasn't really clicked for India it's been a dismal cause . . . a hopeless cause . . . but then hope is putting your faith to work when doubting would be easier Sanjay . . . India has got Pakistan in a position where they've started to believe their doubts and doubt their belief . . . now if you give the opposition the impression that you're on the defensive you're looking out for a draw . . . then you are dead meat . . . troubles are like babies, the more you nurse them the more they grow . . .

(16) R. Raja: I think Sanjay Pakistan can end up in being in a lot of problem if they are to chase a lead of 150 or 200 to win the game and I say this because remember their one two and three are all newcomers . . . Yousef Youhana has played well . . . there's every chance he'll fail . . . Inzamanul-haq is also due for a failure . . . so if they can pick up two three earlier wickets who knows . . . I mean India can still come back in this game . . .

As one can see, the two specialists, in trying to answer the same question, not only react differently, but also use very different lexico-grammatical resources to establish their individual identities in what they say and how they say it, especially Sidhu's attempt to generalize or summarize in terms of metaphorical language, sometimes using clichés, but often very creatively, resonating what Y. Kachru (1992: 342) refers to as "the culture of sound," in the use of *it's a different ball game altogether . . . a dismal cause . . . a hopeless cause . . . but then hope is putting your faith to work when doubting would be easier . . . they've started to believe their doubts and doubt their belief . . . if you give the opposition the impression that you're on the defensive . . . you are dead meat . . . troubles are like babies, the more you nurse them the more they grow.* It is so full of Sidhu's own personal style, creatively carved, put together in the form of his unique selection of lexico-grammatical resources. Yet still, it is considered part of the genre. On the other hand, Ramiz Raja answers the same question within the structure of the same genre, but in a very matter of fact, precise, and clear manner. Both are working within the constraints of the genres, but their style features present an interesting contrast: one constructs his discourse in the true Anglophonic, direct, matter of fact rhetorical structuring tradition, whereas the other resorts to his Indian rhetorical style to carve out a unique identity for himself in response to the same question (Y. Kachru, 1997). The two speakers make different choices, one toward conformity with the norms, the other toward creativity in his use of language.

6   Conclusion

In the preceding sections, I have made an attempt to clarify some of the confusion surrounding the perception and use of genre and style in the context of world Englishes. It was pointed out that genre and style, which have often been defined variously by different people in different contexts, share a large area of common ground, which can be effectively used to distinguish variations of different kinds in language use in the context of world Englishes. The two concepts of genre and style are different from each other in terms of their reliance on text-external factors that determine a genre, but are very similar when they are characterized by text-internal influences. Variation in the use of English, which is also primarily perceived as a function of lexico-grammatical choices, socioculturally appropriate discoursal patterns, and preferences in the effective use of rhetorical strategies, influences and, to a large extent, determines both the style and the genre in different ways: style more substantially, especially when we consider individual style, but less so when we consider functional style, and hence more marginally when we consider genres.

We also considered genres on a liberal–conservative continuum. Most professional and institutionalized genres are relatively on the more conservative side, and hence are more constrained in terms of creativity and innovation, partly because there are gate-keeping mechanisms operating in most of these socially constructed genres (Goodrich, 1987; Bazerman, 1994). Besides, academic and professional genres are also used for academic promotions and international visibility, and hence two kinds of additional constraints operate on them. Firstly, most writers like to publish in international journals, and secondly, they take extra care to make their publications conformative to the expectations of native-speaking Anglophone rhetorical traditions. As compared with professional genres, literary or social genres allow greater flexibility to experienced and established writers, who often exploit the versatility of generic constructs to introduce creativity in the use of lexico-grammatical resources of their own specific national varieties of English, keeping in mind their concern to create a unique identity for themselves in their work, sociocultural experiences, attitudes, perceptions, and styles.

Finally, we also find that this process of genre construction has two sides to it. One expects conformity in the construction and interpretation of genres and the other encourages versatility in genre construction by allowing writers to exploit generic conventions to be more innovative. There is very little scope for variation in text-external considerations; one can find immense scope for variation in the use of text-internal resources, including some flexibility in the use of rhetorical strategies and discourse structuring but considerably more in the use of lexico-grammatical features. So genre writers, in principle, have two broad choices, either to follow the path of orthodoxy or that of creativity. Some conservatively follow the safe path by submitting to established generic conventions to fulfil their communicative objectives, and hence stay with the dominant discourse community, whereas others take a more innovative attitude and exploit available generic resources to create an identity of their own through their innovative practices in genre construction. However, all these creative processes and innovations are constrained by several factors, some of which include the nature of the genre in question, the intended audience, the place of publication, the gate-keeping constraints on specific genres, and the "private intention" that the author may have to use his product to fulfil a very specific objective.

To sum up, genre, style, and world Englishes are interesting concepts and all three of them give freedom to language users to construct their identities through various choices, which are not free-for-all kinds of choices; they are restricted choices, controlled by forces that operate both text-internally as well as text-externally. Most importantly, they operate within the confines of a specific genre, rather than outside it. Genre, in this respect, is like a game with its own rules, conventions, and expectations. One may take a certain degree of freedom to bend these conventions, use them creatively within broad expectations of the members of the concerned discourse community, but the moment one takes these innovations too far outside the genre boundaries, it is seen as opting out of the genre and hence viewed as odd by language users, both within a particular variety or within a particular type of world English.

See also Chapters 21, SPEAKING AND WRITING IN WORLD ENGLISHES; 23, LITERARY CREATIVITY IN WORLD ENGLISHES; 25, WORLD ENGLISHES AND CULTURE WARS; 31, WORLD ENGLISHES AND GENDER IDENTITIES; 33, WORLD ENGLISHES IN GLOBAL ADVERTISING; 34, WORLD ENGLISHES AND GLOBAL COMMERCE.

REFERENCES

Bazerman, Charles (1994) Systems of genres and the enhancement of social intentions. In *Genre and New Rhetoric*. Edited by Aviva Freedman and Peter Medway. London: Taylor and Francis, pp. 79–101.

Berkenkotter, Carol and Huckin, Thomas N. (1995) *Genre Knowledge in*

Disciplinary Communication-Cognition/ Culture/Power. Hillsdale, NJ: Lawrence Erlbaum.

Bhatia, Vijay K. (1982) An Investigation into Formal and Functional Characteristics of Qualifications in Legislative Writing and Its Application to English for Academic Legal Purposes. PhD dissertation, University of Aston in Birmingham, UK.

Bhatia, Vijay K. (1993) *Analysing Genre: Language Use in Professional Settings*. London: Longman.

Bhatia, Vijay K. (1994) Generic integrity in professional discourse. In *Text and Talk in Professional Contexts*. Edited by Britt-Louise Gunnarsson, Per Linell, and Bengt Nordberg. Uppsala, Sweden: ASLA, pp. 61–76.

Bhatia, Vijay K. (1996) Nativization of job applications in South Asia. In *South Asian English: Structure, Use and Users*. Edited by Robert J. Baumgardner. Urbana: University of Illinois Press, pp. 158–73.

Bhatia, Vijay K. (1997) Power and politics of genre. *World Englishes*, **16**(3), 359–72.

Bhatia, Vijay K. (2002) Professional discourse: Towards a multidimensional approach and shared practice. In *Research and Practice in Professional Discourse*. Edited by C. N. Candlin. Hong Kong: City University of Hong Kong Press, pp. 39–60.

Blackley, Meera (1993) *Indian Home Cooking*. NSW: AJB Fairfax Press Publication.

Canagarajah, A. Suresh (1994) Competing discourses in Sri Lankan English poetry. *World Englishes*, **13**(3), 361–76.

Crystal, David and Davy, Derek (1969) *Investigating English Style*. Longman: London.

Goodrich, Peter (1987) *Legal Discourse*. London: Macmillan.

Halliday, M. A. K., McIntosh, Angus, and Strevens, Peter (1964) *The Linguistic Sciences and Language Teaching*. London: Longman.

Kachru, Braj B. (1990) *The Alchemy of English: The Spread, Functions, and Models of Non-Native Englishes*. Urbana: University of Illinois Press. 1st edition 1986, Oxford: Pergamon Press.

Kachru, Braj B. (1992a) Meaning in deviation: Toward understanding non-native English texts. In *The Other Tongue: English across Cultures*. Edited by Braj B. Kachru. Urbana: University of Illinois Press, pp. 301–26.

Kachru, Braj B. (ed.) (1992b) *The Other Tongue: English across Cultures*. Urbana: University of Illinois Press. 1st edition 1982.

Kachru, Yamuna (1992) Culture, style, and discourse: Expanding noetics of English. In *The Other Tongue: English across Cultures*. Edited by Braj B. Kachru. Urbana: University of Illinois Press, pp. 340–52.

Kachru, Yamuna (1997) Cultural meaning and contrastive rhetoric in English education. *World Englishes*, **16**(3), 337–50.

Lowry, Ann (1992) Style range in new English literatures. In *The Other Tongue: English across Cultures*. Edited by Braj B. Kachru. Urbana: University of Illinois Press, pp. 283–98.

Martin, James R. (1993) A contextual theory of language. In *The Powers of Literacy: A Genre Approach to Teaching Writing*. Pittsburgh: University of Pittsburgh Press, pp. 116–36.

Miller, Carolyn R. (1984) Genre as social action. *Quarterly Journal of Speech*, **70**, 157–78. Also published 1994 in *Genre and the New Rhetoric*. Edited by A. Freedman and P. Medway. London: Taylor and Francis, pp. 23–42.

Osakwe, Mabel I. (1999) Wole Soyinka's poetry as bilingual creativity. *World Englishes*, **18**(1), 63–77.

Parmar, Pramila (1994) *Mithai: A Collection of Traditional Indian Sweets*. New Delhi: UBS Publishers' Distributors Ltd.

Smith, Delia (1998) *Delia's How to Cook Book One*. London: BBC.

Solomon, Charmaine (1976) *Charmaine Solomon: The Complete Asian Cookbook*. Sydney: Lansdowne.

Swales, John M. (1990) *Genre Analysis: English in Academic and Research Settings*. Cambridge: Cambridge University Press.

Swales, John M. (1996) Occluded genres in the academy: The case of submission letter. In *Academic Writing: Intercultural and Textual Issues*. Edited by Eliza Ventola. Amsterdam: John Benjamins, pp. 45–58.

Swales, John M. (1997) English as *Tyrannosaurus rex*. *World Englishes*, **16**(3), 373–82.

FURTHER READING

Bhatia, Vijay K. (1993) *Analysing Genre: Language Use in Professional Settings*. London: Longman.

Swales, John M. (1990) *Genre Analysis: English in Academic and Research Settings*. Cambridge: Cambridge University Press.

Part IV Crossing Borders

23 Literary Creativity in World Englishes

EDWIN THUMBOO

1 Introduction

Every culture has a literature, whether broadly or narrowly defined, written or oral or both. Each is supported by the relatively deep homogeneity provided by *satu negeri, satu bangsa, satu ugama, satu bahasa*.[1] Within this singularity of a relatively firm political, cultural unity, virtually all aspects of social life become common through slow evolution that provides, moreover, a high degree of linguistic sharing and predictability. In social and other relationships, cause and effect lie within somewhat narrow but familiar parameters. Moreover, the dynamics of literary creativity, as in other major areas of cultural and other substantive activities, are largely generated from within. External influences tend to stimulate rather than confront. An instance of this would be the influence of the Imagist Movement on both Chinese and Indonesian literature.

In the already complex instance of monocultures – as broadly defined by one language, one people, and one religion – structures overlap, extend, at times contradict and compete to create specific and general tensions. But each culture retains its distinctive semiotic system; each occupies the same space–time continuum; each is gripped by the forces of national development; each is exposed to penetration through the formal and informal political, economic, social, and educational context that often pushes a policy of monolingualism.

In these circumstances, language and literature have a special place. As Halliday (1978: 2) points out:

> There are two fundamental aspects to the social reality that is encoded in language: to paraphrase Lévi-Strauss, it is both "good to think" and "good to eat." Language expresses and symbolizes this dual aspect in its semantic system, which is organized around the twin motifs of reflection and action – language as a means of reflecting on things, and language as a means of acting on things. The former is the "ideational" component of meaning; the latter is the "interpersonal" – one can act *symbolically* only on persons, not on objects.

A social reality (or a "culture") is itself an edifice of meanings – a semiotic construct. In this perspective, language is one of the semiotic systems that constitute a culture; one that is distinctive in that it also serves as an encoding system for many (though not all) of the others.

This in summary terms is what is intended by the formulation "language as social semiotic." It means interpreting language within a sociocultural context, in which the culture itself is interpreted in semiotic terms – as an information system, if that terminology is preferred.

That participants are able to "predict" with advantage assumes a language in common, extensively embedded in the personal and social realities through its role in "reflection and action." A sufficient history of usage is implied, one that does not overlap other semiotic systems and subsystems that would introduce new religions, philosophies, myths, and other components that form the cultural semiotic. The literary dimension involves *satu bahasa* and its literature. Language is therefore both instrument and repository. It has a power within culture, society, and environment.

Like all centers of power, languages tend to perpetuate themselves, projecting a practical and intellectual assertiveness, which is seen at its most potent in the development of colonialism/imperialism. When colonies are formed, it is not merely peoples confronting each other: their cultures and their languages are involved, with the more powerful suppressing the lesser. Those are the dynamics behind the emergence of Spanish, Portuguese, English, and French as international languages.[2]

This internationalization of languages, as illustrated by English, occurs in a variety of contexts generated between the impact of colonialism on the one hand, and the response of the colonized cultures on the other. There are two facets to this, far less interlinked than such terms as "postcolonial" would suggest. For reasons of expediency and good management, colonial powers sought to maintain the same policies for all colonies. There was, in this sense, a kind of colonial homogeneity that contributed to its hegemony and identity. It is remarkable to see the extent to which the same texts, songs, educational methods were practised in every part of the British Empire. On the other hand, the politics and subsequent history of former colonies tend to break away from that homogenized hegemony in an attempt to recover national shape, rhythm, and identity, the uniqueness of the pre-colonial – and in some cases, colonial – inheritance. While it anticipates what is to follow, this accounts for the various Englishes that have emerged in Asia (see Kachru, 2005 and Bolton, 2002). Kachru has been the main driving force in the study of global Englishes by providing a theoretical framework and the major mapping that has led to the opening up and development of this very important field. His recent book, *Asian Englishes: Beyond the Canon* (2005), is a major contribution to that growing body of analysis which we need for the field to develop. Bolton's work on English in Hong Kong has done much to raise this interesting field of study. It is recovery of both the individual and the national self, whose uniqueness makes for difference that should not be elided by generalizations, such as "Asian English," rather than "Asian Englishes."

2 The Spread of English

The English language and its literature moved toward multiplicity in three broad sweeps, to (1) Scotland, Wales, and Ireland; (2) North America, Australia, New Zealand, and South Africa; (3) Asia, Africa, the West Indies, the Pacific, and other geographical pockets. Important for my present purpose, in this rough chronology of some five hundred years, are the generalized factors distinguishing each movement. In the first, the language spread by arms, politics, and culture, as part of an assimilative process, through rearranged fiefdoms, principalities, and kingdoms, of Anglo-Saxon–Norman hegemonies over Celts. The Irish, for instance, have hardly had difficulty with the English language – only with the English regime. And lest we forget, at the setting of the sun, the greatest English wits have been Irish. Moreover, the differences were part of a symbiotic relationship arising from a large measure of shared culture, if not shared politics.

In the second movement, language and culture spread as English speakers spread. Major institutions of identity were transferred, at times replicated, and grew. Strong, constant contact with England, at times paradoxical, maintained bonds that survived such varied and chronologically separate happenings as the American War of Independence, the Boer War, the reaction in Australia and New Zealand when Britain joined the EEC, and South Africa's expulsion from the Commonwealth. I do not propose that the historical and contemporary relationships among these nations are simple. John Steed, Rambo, and Crocodile Dundee reflect three unique masculine discourses beneath whose gesture and dress lie complex psychosociolinguistic variables and distillations; they are interesting, but in no way threatening to the deep structures held in common by the Anglo cultural combine.

It is the third movement that provides my subject. British expansion overseas had its origins chiefly in trade – new markets for manufacture and fresh sources of cheap raw material. Responding to internal political, economic, and industrial hungers and to competition among European powers, trade gradually mutated into a sustained colonialism. Britain, with the largest muster of dominions and colonies, proved the most successful; English, introduced to facilitate administration and commerce, became transplanted in every colony. Without exception, it remained to flourish variously as national language, official language, or auxiliary language for technology, science, regional and international finance, and education. English links communities, ethnic groups, national regions, and nations within regions such as ASEAN (the Association of Southeast Asian Nations), the West Indies, and the Pacific Islands. It is at the heart of programs to modernize and performs a mixture of roles supported by governments and ambitious parents.

The complex background of the new literatures is manifest in the following divisions of the third movement. First, there are nations that claim long and elaborate written and oral literary traditions; e.g., India, Sri Lanka, and Malaysia. Second are those that possess powerful, sophisticated oral traditions; e.g.,

Nigeria, Ghana, Kenya, Papua New Guinea, and Samoa. Third, there are areas created by colonial needs, such as Singapore, with a population drawn substantially from the surrounding Malay sultanates, South China, South India, Jaffna in Sri Lanka, and Hadramant; and the West Indies, mainly populated by Africans with East Indians and a smaller number of Chinese, with the Indians as bilinguals and a variety of English as the sole language for the others. There is also a fourth category – and perhaps a fifth, if we were to separate out Black North America – areas where the Anglo culture and/or power dominates indigenous peoples; e.g., the Maoris in New Zealand and the Zulus in Africa.

3   Broadening Perspectives

Despite the fact that the literatures that developed from the spread of English started to gather momentum only in the last 50 years, there is enough in terms of text and context to require that we take a more open view as regards their description and assessment. Difference has not always been given the force it deserves.

More than for the writer who inhabits one language, one culture, and one literary tradition, the writer's situation in the new literatures is open to compulsions revealed by the array of forces at work in a multilingual, multicultural, multiliterary society. As implied earlier, where the language goes, the criticism and its key assumptions tend to follow.

Moreover, terms are rendered unsatisfactory by the rapid, extensive, complicated, and still continuing spread of English, which has outstripped the perspectives, concepts, and terminology that sought to describe and assess it. A substantive question concerns orientation. While positions differ and theories/hypotheses compete, the body of scholarly work on language is now steadily augmented by research findings about and from "non-native" varieties and bases. Similar developments are occurring in the study of the literatures. Criticism still assumes a one-language, one-literature equation: varieties of a language lead to varieties of a literature. That is definitely not the case with English. There is obvious concession in the label "new literatures in English," a label predictably interim. When did American literature emerge as such? We have Australian literature (and a dictionary of Australian English) and New Zealand literature defined by criticism, fuelled chiefly from within, alert to elements – linguistic, attitudinal – that nourish an ethos. Moreover, "new literatures" itself seems a misnomer when applied to India, where the creativity predates Macaulay's Minute of 1835. Nor is "second tongue" accurate, as a majority of the writers wield English as their first language. Nor is "contact literature" a firmly suitable alternative. The literature in English only *starts* as contact literature because, after it acquires body, momentum, and contemporary preoccupation, its "contact" character becomes historical, part of origins. Given the fact that there is a substantial body of literature in most of the former colonies, there is no reason why we cannot say Indian Literature in English, Nigerian Literature in English, Jamaican Literature in English, Philippine Literature in English, Sri Lankan Literature in English, Singapore Literature in English, etc. This will do away with both the covert assumptions and the inaccuracies of a phrase such as "postcolonial," which is historically inaccurate and open to the suspicion of encoding and perpetuating that link between former metropolitan centers and former colonies, which is no longer there.

4   The Response to English

It should be patent even from these brief examples that two of the many factors influencing literary creativity have special importance. Firstly, the last 50 years, during which the literatures in Englishes emerged, have been a period of rapid change, connected with the internal dynamics of nations, as well as rapid globalization. In both English has played an increasing role. The first has meant rapid shifts in the themes that engage writers. With the exception of India, the first generation of writers by and large wrote about the need to reconstruct society, for a society to explain itself to itself, focus around themes of disengagement from the colonial past.

The writer – dramatist and novelist more than poet – must create a suitable English-language semiotic system in a non-English social reality. Powerful elements of culture and attitude come with the language. Present as part of the colonial inheritance, they are maintained, even strengthened, by the formal study of English and the international culture of the mass media, especially television. In order to explore and carry a new social reality, English has to be uncluttered, freed from certain habitual associations; it must develop a new verbal playfulness, new rhythms, additions to its metaphorical and symbolic reach to explain and amplify feelings and ideas about literature and life and cater to the claims of the imagination. The innovations can be as broad, declared, and sustained as Gabriel Okara's *The Voice* (see Thumboo, 1986 for a discussion) or as subtle as Raja Rao's short story *The Cow of the Barricades* or Okot p'Bitek's *Song of Lawino*. The need to innovate is inevitable because it is connected to reorienting the language to express a set of perceptions, a vision faithful to the collective but varied experience and aspirations of a people.

Unless we identify and connect these and other preoccupations, it would be difficult to see in perspective the impulses behind the emergence of the new literatures in English. First are the reasons for writing. These include explaining society to itself, reconstructing the past, exploring the binding of diverse peoples and cultures with the idea of commonality, and giving imaginative expression to the array of forces fashioning society. Other attendant themes include the effect of political and moral corruption – catastrophes played out in the lives of ordinary men and women – or the ambiguous changes wrought by modernization. In a very real sense, themes have often chosen writers, a phenomenon neatly summed up by Nadine Gordimer (1973: 11): "Black writers choose their plots, characters and literary styles; their themes choose them. By this I mean that themes are statements or questions arising from the nature of the society in which the writer finds himself immersed, and the quality of the life around him. In this sense the writer is the voice of the people beyond any glib political connotations of the phrase." Gordimer's remarks pertain to South Africa, where apartheid perpetuated the worst features of a colonial regime hardened by the fact that the colonizers are themselves white natives. The blacks there lived under an unremitting oppression so extensive that black poets cannot help but feel its tragic intensity, as revealed in Stanley Motjuwadi's *White Lies* (Royston, 1973: 12). Motjuwadi's passion, in less intense form, can be found in the earlier phase of most new literatures, in variations of themes from those touching on racism, political suppression, and economic exploitation to those about snobbery and intellectual inequality.

5   Impulses behind the New English Writing

In these literatures there is an attempt to restore dignity, to re-establish the self, and to compensate for deprivation and depersonalization. The Australian aboriginal novelist and poet Cohn Johnson (1985) says, "Creative writers like myself can re-decipher and reinterpret mythology, legends and stories, to a certain extent modernise it or give it relevance and have that tradition going from the 'dreaming' of the beginning to 1983 and onwards. That is where we will link up again with what has been lost somewhat by relying on alien forms of literature" (Breitinger and Sander, 1985: 2). Such connections between writer and society, almost compelled by a reading of contemporary events, are often sanctioned by tradition. It is not unusual for the artist to see himself as a medium, a shaping conduit. Kofi Awoonor, whose poem-novel *This Earth My Brother* remains among the most profound explorations of individual psyche and society, describes a role that Hoggart (1982) and others, bred by a different intellectual, aesthetic climate, would possibly find strange. The artist lives in a society where "forms and motifs already exist in an assimilated time and world construct, and so he serves only as the instrument of transforming these into an artistic whole based on his own imaginative and cognitive world, a world which exists and has meaning only within the larger world. He is not a visionary artist, per se, like the European artist who projects into space and time structures which simply were not there before. There is no otherness locked in the private psyche of his vision" (Awoonor, 1976: 166). Although the artist, his function especially, was not always this tightly circumscribed, firm conventions generally governed the choice and treatment of subjects. Nonetheless, it provides for a sharp contrast to Hoggart's writer – partly of and partly out of society, and of a culture not "formally organised." In third movement paradigms, the writer is moved by a sense of the contemporary that converts into powerful injunctions.

Nor is the dissimilarity confined to conceptions of the artist's role. Perceptions of the world as physical construct likewise differ. While making it clear that she is generalizing, Kamala Markandaya (1973: 22) states that for the West "the earth was created for man: an assumption that seems to be used, consciously or unconsciously, to justify almost any kind of assault upon the animal kingdom and upon the systems of the earth itself." I have had occasion to suggest that prior to the mid-nineteenth century – later, if we exclude Japan – there was a broad contrast between European and Asian attitudes to scientific discoveries. Asia did not fully exploit their practical value, while Europe did, mainly because Asia went more fully into metaphysics while Europe delved predominantly into physics. I find it intriguing to speculate on whether the fact that Europe was dominated for so long by one religion which, despite schisms, allowed a fairly stable view of man and his universe, of man and God, of the separation of the sacred from the secular, encouraged a concomitant scientific spirit and method. Did such earlier centers of scientific inquiry as Egypt and Greece lose the capacity because new religions and fundamentally disruptive new worldviews broke their continuities?

Physics and metaphysics: Markandaya's own background urges that "everything exists in its own right" (1973: 22). She goes on to say that while she does not import that perception directly into her work, nonetheless it seeps in. The sacredness of the Earth – in a Blakean sense, interestingly enough – and the conviction that it is the source of life are to be found in almost all her novels. The conviction generates a kind of fortitude embodied, for instance, in Rukmini in *Nectar in a Sieve*, as well as in *The Coffer Dams*, where the Europeans find "tropical" nature discomforting although the "natives" are fully at home. Without an understanding of the vision behind notions of the luminous, the cosmic, the nature of human beings and their place in the universe, our perceptions would be impoverished.

For many writers the establishment of a refurbished, complete self and society, with history and a sense of recovered dignity, was a primary function. Elechi Amadi's *The Concubines*, Ngũgĩ's *The River Between*, and Achebe's *Things Fall Apart* have for their themes the imaginative reconstruction of life in traditional society either before or at the time when the force of the white man was felt. *The Concubines* and *Things Fall Apart* are essential to a sense of continuity through the values embodied in the past and for images of the complex humanity that marked traditional life before the coming of the white man. As Albert Wendt put it, "The imagination must explore with love, honesty, wisdom, compassion; writers must write with *aroha/aloha/alofa/ loloma*, respecting the people they are writing about, people who may view the void differently and who, like all other human beings, live through the pores of their flesh and mind and bone, who suffer, laugh, cry, copulate and die" (1982: 123).

6   The Writer and the Milieu

The writer has interests, values, and a vision of life constructed out of satisfactions and dissatisfactions with his immediate situation and its larger milieu. The milieu – whose possible complexity is limited only by the semiotic systems referred to earlier as defining the total content of society – provides an inheritance that is simultaneously a constraint and a challenge. On the one hand are the forces of conformity, which are powerfully conservative; on the other are the impulses of an international culture, strongly "Western" and riding upon the global jet-stream of American English. To maintain tradition and to modernize are seen either as a dilemma or a challenge whose dialects impinge upon and revise the notions of life and its contexts. Reorientations and retrievals apart, modernization means, among other things, the creation of new intellectual reflexes, the enlargement of freedoms, the creation of a new order for the betterment of both individual and society. The emergence from colonization involves at least four freedoms. The political is in some ways the most clear-cut, though the routes to it have been various. Brunei was granted independence without a fuss; Kenya had to fight a bloody war. Next comes economic freedom, a difficult task, but one to be accomplished in some measure if a nation is to have stability. It requires planning, sustained effort, and non-corrupt governments, all of which are not always in sufficient evidence. The third freedom requires internal all-round strength – political, economic, social, and cultural – to maintain independence, to be able to withstand the more ambiguous pressures exerted by power blocs. Finally, there is psychological independence, which is perhaps the hardest to achieve.

Figure 23.1 reflects the situation of the writer in any one of the world Englishes. The assumption is that he is bicultural, therefore part of a con-

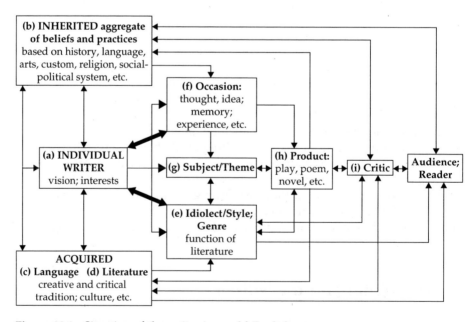

Figure 23.1   Situation of the writer in world Englishes

tinuum that has roots in his own culture as well as what comes with English, which I would prefer to call his main language, as distinguished from his other languages. I have divided the diagram into nine items, excluding *audience/reader*, to represent the following:

(a) Both *vision* and *interest* depend on her background, personal history, formative influences, point of view, agenda of interests, dominant themes, choice of genre. These, in turn, are influenced by

(b) which constitutes his shaping *inheritance* as transmitted through the determinants ranging from folkways to myths, religion, national history politics, social structures and values, etc. These are transmitted through both formal and informal institutions that shape his society. Given his vocation, (a) and (b) are intimately connected with

(c) and (d), which have both the *acquired* that is associated with English and its literatures, and the other, which the writer has inherited under (b). If she is an Indian of Tamil origin, for example, she may be familiar with the *Kurunthokai* and use some of its conventions and techniques, as well as the distinction it makes between personal and public poetry. Those who are familiar with Bahasa Melayu may be able to recreate, to utilize, some of the internal delicacies of the *pantun* in quatrains they write in English. Moreover, as part of creating their own idiolect, and adding through their work to the evolving tradition of writing in English, they could use similes and metaphors based on their other language(s). Both should not be seen as monumental, adding to the surface texture of a poem. They are explorations and restatements with the metaphors commanding the greater directness and complexity. Similes compare, metaphors fuse ideas, experiences. Those familiar with Okara's *The Voice* will recall how he exploits the praise poem structure to add both drama and texture to his narrative. Examples can be multiplied and it is here that the writer's creativity, her ingenuity, shows. And in this, she adds to the reach of English, and in ways that may enable the instruction of her creativity to travel. This leads to

(e) the writer's orchestration of language, where the indigenization of English, the genre he is using, and how his sense of the function of literature informs the way he organizes and directs the discourse. That, of course, is linked to

(f) where she brings as much as possible of her experience, memory, etc. to help deepen and elaborate the discourse,

(g) giving the best articulation to realize

(h) the play, poem, or novel.

(i) The point has been made that the writer is at the same time his own *critic*, and brings all from (a) to (f) to bear upon that act of creation, of investing his text with as much power and articulation as possible.

The boldest arrows suggest the flow of self-instruction and experience that helps the writer acquire confidence, maturity, new directions, change of priorities, technique, and so on. The best illustration of this is when we compare the early to the later W. B. Yeats, or see the progress in Ngũgĩ wa Thiong'o's novels from *Weep Not, Child* (1964) to *Devil on the Cross* (1980).

Including *audience/reader* is merely to raise the question of how much of the writer, in terms of (a) to (f), should we know if we are to try best to understand her before assessing her work. The point of course is, how much preparation does one need to understand Shakespeare, or James Joyce, or C. J. Koch's *The Year of Living Dangerously*?

Given the forces at work in his situation, the writer's interest, expectations, and response to the riddles and enigmas of this society translate into essential notions about life and contacts. As Gordimer has noted, the writer's themes have chosen them. These themes are connected with what I have elsewhere described (1984: 24) as a series of grammars the chief of which comprise "interests" and "motives":

> The sets of interests which accrue constitute what may be described as a grammar for living, one governing action, thought, the way we view events and experiences.
>
> Like anyone else, the writer is subject to the same process but with two notable differences. The first is that the grammar of his interests nourishes a deeper, more personalised grammar of motives – to borrow Kenneth Burke's phrase – generated by and connected to the demands of his vocation. The grammar links life and art and is partly inherited, partly made, augmented, and modified by him. When we identify cardinal influences, primal vision, key themes or structural, metaphorical, and imagistic traits or sources of iconography and the assemblage of their elements that give singularity to a writer's work, we are in fact mapping this narrower, specialised grammar. These features have to do with technique and substance. Technique derives from and returns to sources in his basic or adopted literary tradition or traditions. The second concerns contacts between the writer as individual and the total environment of which he is a part. But as both individual and environment alter, so does the grammar whose pattern is forged, after all, by the organic interplay between self and society.

I consider these grammars essential to an appropriate orientation for the study of new literatures in English, for it is precisely the absence of such orientation (and not a lack of intelligence) that leads to confident but misleading criticism and discussion. The grammars alter, in response to changes in society and in the individual, in writer and reader. The writer's dilemma is whether to maintain a consistency or to run the risk of apparent contradictions. Faint hearts do not found literatures or new varieties of languages. Such grammar formation is not new to English. American, Australian, and New Zealand literature share a great deal with English literature and with each other; they are linked by deep-rooted religions and by philosophical, scientific, intellectual, and other traditions. The new literatures are seldom, if ever, linked to the same extent.

They share the language, the major genres, and certain creative strategies – such as those deriving from oral narrative – and critical practices. Their literary ecology, if inclusive, is shaped by the literary traditions of their other languages. The literature in English in India, in Nigeria, in Singapore, is part of Indian, Nigerian, and Singaporean literature. The writer is formed by two worlds, at times belonging to richly complicated multiliterary eco-systems (see Thumboo, 1985). He has twin perspectives, one established by English, the language of his creativity, the other by his mother tongue and its associated literature or literatures. It is worth remembering that the literary system of Europe that T. S. Eliot outlined in "Tradition and the individual talent" – especially the specific lines of descent from Homer, through Virgil and Dante, down to the national literatures – has counterparts in other literary ecosystems. In India, for instance, there are Sanskrit texts and the great epics.

Moreover, historical parallels arise in the writer's reshaping of English and her material, subject, and themes. There is the case of Anglo-Irish literature, one of whose dominant figures, W. B. Yeats, I see as a Third World poet of a special kind. Familiarity with the growth of American English and American literature, or with specific topics such as sociopolitical themes, in, say, recent Arabic and Israeli literature or the frame of nationalism in French Canadian fiction, would certainly create a fuller sense of the issues taken up in the new literatures. One must look at them from within, on their own terms, through a paradigm that is flexible yet structured enough to power reorientations.

Each language harbors its own logic, its own system of latent and manifest content. English is no exception. Its prestige originally made it attractive to the indigenous ruling/upper class; they were the first bilinguals who knew a foreign language. Siblings and children benefited through an earlier start and the higher status enjoyed by their families. English became a second language and, in some cases, a first language. Here is Lewis Nkosi's experience: "I was reading an incredible amount, reading always badly without discipline; reading sometimes for the sheer beauty of the language. I walked about the streets of the bustling noisy city with new English words clicking like coins in the pockets of my mind; I tried them out on each passing scene, relishing their power to describe and apprehend experience" (quoted in Alvarez-Pereyre, 1984: 5–6).

One feels the excitement in discovering the ability to name things and experiences, and to apply words to give some order, thus setting up a personal semiotic system. That modifying ability engages what Markandaya has called the cortex – that part of the mind, mysterious and not fully known, that enables the person to become a writer, broadly similar to the capacity that Coleridge described as the primary imagination. While Markandaya sees culture, ethos, and roots as being powerful, fundamental, and self-sustaining, what really matters is the "extraordinary cortex that exists in all of us, a cortex that, as it were, governs morality and the sensibility of creation, and like anything else can be cultivated or neglected" (1973: 15–16).

Such a cortex, revealed through the power of its metaphors and images, is essential both to the writer's development and to the reshaping of English in new environments. It is behind the creation of idiolect. It helps the writer negotiate between the demands of two traditions, one inherited, the other brought by English and its great literature. Its new users feel impelled to adapt, to orchestrate a thrust reflecting everyday realities as well as the nuances of its new home. Yet that undertaking cannot always be embarked upon easily. There are those who, like Parthasarathy, feel comfortable in English and (in his case) less so in Tamil, a fact that set up "painful but nevertheless fruitful tension with regard to poetry" (1973: 27).

This challenge confronts almost every bi- or multilingual writer. His bilingualism is one of three broad types – proficient, powerful, or limited; his position in this cline is not static, because quite often one language gains dominance. A bilingual person has at least two language universes, and each language works with its own linguistic circuits. How the two associate depends on whether the languages as neighbors inhabit the same space and time and can bend to serve creative purposes.

7   Multilingual Context and Linguistic Innovations

Language in a sense determines not only consciousness but also one's perception of reality. This suggests a kind of linguistic determinism close to that proposed by Whorf's *Mirror of Language*, from which it follows that speakers or users of different languages possess different patterns of thought. The Whorfian hypothesis has taken hard or soft forms. The soft form is useful especially in its suggestions that there is a tendency for the individual to think along avenues that have been defined by the whole of language. Scope for initiative and variation allows the proficient bilingual to bring into his creative language (in this case, English) some of the strategies and other resources of his native language and its literature. It also provides for the possibility that the proficient bilingual has a sharper perception of reality because she is bifocal.

Be that as it may, the search for idiom and idiolect is ongoing. What F. W. Bateson (1934; quoted in Wellek and Warren, 1955: 177) said about the changing language of poetry would apply to the language of literature as a whole: "the age's imprint in a poem is not to be traced to the poet but to the language. The real history of poetry is, I believe, the history of the changes in the kind of language in which successive poems have been written. And it is these changes of language only that are due to the pressures of social and intellectual tendencies."

There is one notable difference between these changes in a monolingual situation and in a bilingual or multilingual situation. When we talk about the spread of English, we usually have in mind its spread to countries. What is more important at the micro level is its spread *within* so-called second-language areas. The learning of English is at a premium, both as a foreign language and as a second language. In Singapore, for instance, it is the medium of instruction throughout the educational system. The model adopted seeks to reflect an International Standard English close to British English. But the writer's innovations in order to create an idiolect quite often do not follow the general drift of the language as it is promoted educationally. This generalization must be modified to take into account the genre in which the writer works. As a rule, poetry is acrolectal, although there are instances where basilect is used. In drama the characters speak or ruminate in the lect appropriate to their intellectual and social background. Fiction claims a larger number of registers. Even with the first-person narrative we can assume that if the narrator is an acrolectal speaker, it would be possible for him to narrate across the lectal range of the world depicted. Many writers are concurrently attempting to evolve their own idiolect.

Whatever their stance, their choice of genre, their choice of material, writers portray individuals and the warp and woof of society. At times their writing consists chiefly of their own reactions to and seekings about life, in a language that is simultaneously a private and a public possession. Language is the chief medium of consciousness, the instrument through which the external world is received, analyzed, and internalized; it is the instrument of creativity, of reaching out. It mediates upon the flow between the writer and her social reality. Creativity pushes her beyond mere description – meaning as it is – to assemble new meanings that capture the temper, the quintessential flavor of the times, linking generations and roving among decades. The writer takes her substance from the unique, the perennial, and the temporary, the buoyant and the ordinary – which may prove unexpectedly unique to others. She examines the surface and deep structures of her material and themes, exploring in a single moment the vocabulary of understanding and expression, inventing in order to extend the depth and power of both. English for the writer is a language that gives and a language that receives.

Yet the work has to be done if we are to increase our understanding of the back-, middle-, and foreground to the new literatures in English. Although they may write in English, virtually all writers of these literatures are bilingual, bicultural, and (for those in multicultural societies) touched by more than two semiotic systems. The result of that search for an idiolect is a verbal edifice that is under constant enlargement and modification, responding to shifts in the grammars of motives and interests. The edifice has two main doors: one to the world of English, dominated by its linguistic and literary systems; the other to the systems (linguistic, literary, social, philosophical) of the social reality or realities the writer inhabits.

8 New Contexts for English

Questions about language dominate part of the social reality. The place of English, especially as a bridge between ethnic groups, as modernizing, as a creative instrument, forms a set of concerns inevitably reflected in the new literatures. Colonial and postcolonial politics are involved, as are ethnic rivalries and suspicions; the implications of caste and class, of being "educated" and "less educated." Life is always firmly behind language and literature. Each character, whether partially or fully developed, is a pool of consciousness, of understanding and ignorance, of darkness and light, of enlightenment and prejudice. The difficulty is not merely one of an appropriate lect. It extends to forming a lectal range that can reflect a multilingual or bilingual situation. The following passage from Achebe's *Arrow of God* is exemplary. The Igbo Unachukwa uses fractured English when speaking to an Englishman; yet when he speaks to a fellow Igbo, the English must improve, as we are to assume that his Igbo is at least good:

> "Dat man wan axe master queshon."
> "No questions."
> "Yassah." He turned to Nweke. "The white man says he did not leave his house this morning to come and answer your questions."

In order to sustain the impression of the shift from English to Igbo, *queshon* becomes *questions*.

While we are concerned here with creativity in English, it should be noted that the problems are equally present for those who use "indigenous" languages such as Tagalog, Bengali, and Malay, or other migrant languages, of which Tamil and Mandarin in Singapore and Malaysia would be instances. The human situation is complicated by bi- and trilingual, polydialectal factors, not so much for the individual participants as for those who wish to grasp the whole. The writer is concerned to articulate his interest, his vision, and the themes ensuing therefrom. When he reads contemporaries and predecessors, whether in the original or in translation, his motives differ from those of a critic; it is part instruction, part nourishment. If he essays criticism, the practice is informed by writerly insights. The frame of reference for the critic is significantly broader, for while he may be engaged with a particular text or writer, his very role implies a concern with a literature or literatures. He is concerned, in varying degrees, with periods, with movements, with judging writers, preferring one to another and providing grounds for his preferences. His view combines a sense of the contemporary and a sense of the past, the writer with the production of the literature. The writer installs his vision in his work; the critic considers this vision as well as that of other writers. In the context of African literatures in English, it means no less than finding a frame for discussing and evaluating the works of, say, Kofi Awoonor, Chinua Achebe,

Gabriel Okara, Elechi Amadi, Ngũgĩ wa Thiong'o, Okot p'Bitek. Extend the list to include the Anglophone writers in Heinemann's African Writers series – then Indian, West Indian, Southeast Asian, and South Pacific literatures in English, not to mention their links with "indigenous" literary traditions – and you have a fair conception of the critical tasks. For each writer there is perception and performance, active and passive stance ranging from a feel for the larger political and social realities to the specifics of individual thought and feeling.

Criticism is simultaneously a generalizing and a specifying activity. There is the tempting assumption that a work is to some degree characteristic, that its distinctiveness can be accounted for within the prevailing semiotic systems. Moreover, a work that demonstrably cuts against the grain, however powerfully disturbing (Joyce's *Ulysses* is an obvious example), can be accommodated; it does not bring in the context of another linguistic-literary semiotic system. The literature and its language continue to change through revolution and evolution. Donne, Dryden, Fielding, Wordsworth, Eliot, Joyce, and Yeats were innovators, major figures who opened up new possibilities of language and structure that influenced their contemporaries. Thus the revolution settles down to an evolution, establishing a mode, a period. It makes for a degree of acceptable generalization in which the discussion of text or issue has force beyond the specific occasion. Instances are the metaphysical conceit or the theory and practice of Augustan poetic diction. Continuities of literary history encourage the emergence of a critical tradition vigilant of the literature in the language.

The situation is radically dissimilar within the new literatures. They have variety best understood in terms of origins, antecedents, and contemporaneity, attempting to retain much that is traditional in various spheres of life and yet wishing to incorporate change. For the writer, every attempt is a new beginning whose relevance is best judged retrospectively, as the means for judgment are themselves being formed. Innovations are not calculated to alter or refurbish a creative tradition; rather, the tradition, in some instances barely discernible, is emerging. Robust as well as lesser talents are equally in search of creative means, of shaping vision. The overall frame within which specific as well as more general studies can profitably proceed will incorporate a number of foci to sharpen our response. The first focus is for linguistic and literary studies to link up wherever possible, and so avoid what Quirk (1974: 65), referring to the study of Old, Middle, and contemporary English literature, described as "a dichotomy between the relatively modern writings that can be 'appreciated' (these are called 'literature') and the relatively early writings that cannot be (and these are called 'language')." The danger would arise from the divergence in the varieties of English that have resulted from the formal and informal adoption of English within a polity where writers have quite different mother tongues, to the greater divergence between the clines of English in, say, the West Indies, the Philippines, and India. Literature draws upon the full stretch of language. While the standard educated varieties are mutually intelligible in a substantial way, the pidgins and creoles have a local habitation and a name.

9 Models for the Spread of English

The two most recent models for the spread of English are proposed by Kachru and Quirk. They raise important issues whose full implications for nations in the third movement will emerge increasingly from theoretical and applied research. But comprehensive, sustained language surveys require substantial funds and specialists. Language is power.[3] Given limited resources and unlimited needs, governments of third-movement nations are forced into pragmatism, a formula of priorities. The concentration on language in education stresses its practical value, which is quite rightly paramount. Fortunately, scholarly enterprise, however modest in isolation, has a cumulative effect. The study of language and the application of linguistic concepts and methods have contributed to the greater definition of our understanding. An increasing number of texts have attracted stylistic/linguistic analysis. Emmanuel Njara (1982), for instance, has done very useful work on a selection of African novels. And Winfred Lehmann's treatment, sensitive, discriminating, and precise, of Raja Rao's short story "The Cow of the Barricades" both enriches and structures our understanding, linking the linguistic and literary interest. Lehmann's

> presentation proposes within a model of communication three strata; a phonological, a grammatical, and a semiological. Assuming these strata, a text linguist interprets the linguistic material relating the physical phenomena or articulatory and auditory mechanisms using sound waves with the communication situation, including the referential realm, the culture, the language, the social setting and the participation of communicator and audience. These distinctions already make up a rich area for analysis by the text linguist and literary critic. But the three strata provide grounds for added richness. In each of these linguistic strata there are sub-strata with their own elements; the elements are interrelated by means of the formulae known in linguistic study as rules. For illustration I list the seven sub-strata in the grammatical stratum. Beginning with the largest entity these sub-strata are: discourse, paragraph, sentence, clause, phrase, word and the smallest segment of grammatical form, the morpheme. Exploring the treatment of these substrata and of their characteristic elements by a poet might well occupy any literary critic. Phrased differently, the exploration of such well-identified arrays corresponds to the literary critic's task: making explicit the characteristics of their critical procedures in "der Kunst des Lesens – the art of reading." (n.d.: 20–1)

Such analysis via strata and substrata will, as Lehmann suggests, make "explicit the characteristics of critical procedures." The other point apposite to the general thrust of what I have been saying is that while the procedures have been applied to native-based English literatures, they have yet to be systematically employed in the study of new literatures. Starts have been made, but they do not always take into account "the referential realm, the culture, the language, the social setting and the participation of communicator and audience"; i.e., the social reality *and* the constituting genetic/semiotic systems. And where they do, there remain problems of balance between the emphases on each realm.

The network of issues connected with criticism of and creation in the new literatures is endless. It metamorphoses as life and language move. But two further suggestions may provide a useful concluding note. The first concerns the formation of an idiolect; the second, critical approaches. Quarrying into English – or any language – to secure an inwardness sufficient to manage irony, pun, paradox, specific rhythms, striking metaphor, intricate patterns of images, and shades of meaning is never easy. Moreover, the process of formulation is not always conscious. The writer judges as her own critic, but what she judges is both consciously and unconsciously formulated. The mind has its secret thesaurus in which words long unused emerge aptly. The general process includes using language to explore and define an idea, a feeling; the contrary state is an idea, a feeling in search of words. For the writer in the third movement the challenge is complicated by a bilingual, bicultural inheritance. Concepts, the link between custom, behavior, the cosmos, and language as posited by the mother tongue often cannot move across into English. Achebe did not see this as representing a serious problem, but others have. Perhaps it depends on one's experience with English, with the conception of creativity's demands in a polydialectal situation. Writers as geographically dispersed as Edith Tiempo (Philippines), Derek Walcott (Jamaica), and Gabriel Okara (Nigeria) have thought it necessary to bend English to achieve satisfactory statement (see Thumboo, 1986: 253–4). Acts of translation and transcreation mark their creativity, though in this case critical judgments do not possess an original text as benchmark. Nonetheless, the methods of translation, especially those used in English and indigenous languages and covering work in both directions, are useful, if we keep in mind the essential spirit of freedom noted as far back as John Dryden's introduction to Ovid's *Epistles* (1680):

> All translation, I suppose, may be reduced to these three heads. First, that of metaphrase, or turning an author word by word, and line by line, from one language into another. The second way is that of paraphrase, or translation with latitude, where the author is kept in view by the translator, so as never to be lost, but his words are not so strictly followed as his sense, and that too is admitted to be amplified, but not altered. The third way is that of imitation, where the translator (if now he has not lost that name) assumes the liberty not only to vary from the words and sense, but to forsake them both as he sees occasion; and taking only some general hints from the original, to run division on the groundwork, as he pleases.

That new literatures are at least bicultural formations – in which English and its literary inheritance are common – has not been sufficiently realized, except by those who belong to the social reality or one that is comparable. This has led, among other things, to the feeling in certain quarters that criticism from the outside, the mother-tongue bases especially, remains metropolitan centered and, at times, imperial. The sense of distance, of minimal sympathy was never a widespread sentiment in the Anglo diaspora. The coming of age of their literatures was not traumatic: their social realities were offshoots, grafts. The new literatures, which belong to ex-colonies, are a different case altogether.

Nor have critics belonging to the third movement been innocent of misinterpreting works that rest on their own or other social realities. But greater difficulties are faced by those from outside these realities. Some have worked through these; their work shows that without that grasp, inappropriate assumptions or questionable points of departure may misdirect attention. The most potent sin is the tacit assumption that as they use English, or a variety of it, the new literatures are an extension of English literature, and that its critical practice ought to cope with these fledglings comfortably. This is hardly the case when put to the test. Where the criticism has been illuminating, we find reorientations that take into account the contexts of the work.

10   Conclusion

We ought to treat the new literatures as separate in certain essential aspects despite their sharing of English. Moreover, they are – with the exception of West Indian English writing – but one of two, three, or more literatures within the social reality. The focus on English should be balanced by the realization that the literature in it is part of a national literary system upon which its survival and growth depend. Such are the complexities to be unravelled so that the methods of comparative literature may be adopted with profit. The justification strengthens as we move into each literature and discover its distinctiveness, its unique place in a possible whole. Provided that the comparative spirit is sensitively attentive and exploratory, its methods will take us further toward understanding and judging new literatures, individually and as a group, how they relate to each other and to mother-tongue-based literatures, and whether we can ultimately attempt an overview of all literatures in English.

I have sought to suggest what historical and contemporary forces lie behind the emergence and shaping of the new literatures in English, and possible ways of looking at them. The preoccupation with theme, with linguistic and literary resources within and in response to main and subordinate social realities, is by no means exhaustive. This chapter is a plea for constructive understanding as a prelude to literary judgment. There are no conclusions, only beginnings. The urging of more sharply focused and informed criticism of the individual literatures must resist irredentist impulses. Collectively, such criticism should form part of a common enterprise that will, over the long term and especially if it combines literary and linguistic studies, bring about a clear, richer sense of how English has not only spread but also brought forth new literatures upon which the sun will never set.

See also Chapters 3, ENGLISH IN SCOTLAND; 6, SOUTH ASIAN ENGLISHES; 8, SOUTHEAST ASIAN ENGLISHES; 15, WORLD ENGLISHES TODAY; 17, VARIETIES OF WORLD ENGLISHES; 25, WORLD ENGLISHES AND CULTURE WARS; 29, COLONIAL/ POSTCOLONIAL CRITIQUE: THE CHALLENGE FROM WORLD ENGLISHES; 30, CULTURAL STUDIES AND DISCURSIVE CONSTRUCTIONS OF WORLD ENGLISHES; 31, WORLD ENGLISHES AND GENDER IDENTITIES.

NOTES

This chapter is a revised and updated version of a paper that first appeared as "The literary dimension of the spread of English," Chapter 14 (pp. 255–82) in *The Other Tongue: English across Cultures*, 2nd edition, edited by Braj B. Kachru, Urbana: University of Illinois Press, 1992.

1   When translated from the original Malay into English, this slogan becomes 'One land, one people, one religion, one language.'
2   That Dutch failed to make the cut would make an interesting case study of the dynamics involved in the internationalization of a language. It is worth noting that languages can settle and take root in circumstances outside the colonial paradigm, as for instance, Hokkien in Malacca that led to the emergence of Peranakan Malay with interesting and instructive adjustments to their respective semiotic systems.
3   See *World Englishes*, **5**(2–3) (1986), which is devoted to papers given at a 1986 conference on "The Power of English: Cross-Cultural Dimensions in Literature and Media," East-West Center, Honolulu.

REFERENCES

Alvarez-Pereyre, Jacques (1984) *The Poetry of Commitment in South Africa*. London: Heinemann.

Awoonor, Kofi (1976) Tradition and continuity in African literature. In *Exile and Tradition: Studies in African and Caribbean Literature*. Edited by Rowland Smith. Dalhousie: Daihousie University Press, pp. 166–72.

Bolton, Kingsley (ed.) (2002) *Hong Kong English: Autonomy and Creativity*. Hong Kong: Hong Kong University Press.

Breitinger, Eckhard and Sander, Reinhard (eds.) (1985) *Studies in Commonwealth Literature*. Tübingen: Gunter Narr Verlag.

Gordimer, Nadine (1973) *The Black Interpreters: Notes on African Writing*. Johannesburg: SPROCAS/ RAVAN.

Halliday, M. A. K. (1978) *Language as Social Semiotic: The Social*

Interpretation of Language and Meaning. London: Arnold.

Hoggart, Richard (1982) *An English Temper: Essays on Education, Culture and Communication.* London: Chatto.

Kachru, Braj B. (2005) *Asian Englishes: Beyond the Canon.* Hong Kong: Hong Kong University Press.

Lehmann, Winfred (n.d.) Literature and linguistics: Text linguistics. In *English, Its Complementary Role in India.* Edited by C. D. Narasimhaiah and C. N. Srinath. Mysore: Dhvanyaloka, pp. 18–29.

Markandaya, Kamala (1973) One pair of eyes: Some random reflections. *The Literary Criterion,* **11**(1), 14–25.

Njara, Emmanuel (1982) *Stylistic Criticism and the African Novel.* London: Heinemann.

Parthasarathy, R. (1973) The Indian writer's problems: Poet in search of a language. *The Literary Criterion,* **11**(1), 126–9.

Quirk, Randolph (1974) *The Linguist and the English Language.* London: Arnold.

Royston, Robert (ed.) (1973) *Black Poets in South Africa.* London: Heinemann.

Thumboo, Edwin (1984) The writer and society: Some Third World reminders. *Solidarity,* **99**, 24–32.

Thumboo, Edwin (1985) Twin perspectives and multi-ecosystems: Tradition for a Commonwealth writer. *World Englishes,* **4**(2), 213–21.

Thumboo, Edwin (1986) Language as power: Gabriel Okara's *The Voice* as a paradigm. *World Englishes,* **5**(2/3), 249–64.

Wellek, René and Warren, Austin (1955) *Theory of Literature.* London: Jonathan Cape.

Wendt, Albert (1982) Towards a new Oceania. In *Writers in East-West Encounter: New Cultural Bearings.* Edted by Guy Amirthanayagam. London: Macmillan, pp. 202–15.

FURTHER READING

Abad, Gemino H. (2004) Filipino poetry in English: A native clearing. *World Englishes,* **23**(1), 169–81.

Achebe, Chinua (1964) *Arrow of God.* London: Heinemann.

Achebe, Chinua (1969) *A Man of the People.* London: Heinemann.

Baker, Wendy (2001) Gender and bilinguals' creativity. *World Englishes,* **20**(3), 321–39.

Baker, Wendy and Eggington, William G. (1999) Bilingual creativity, multidimensional analysis, and World Englishes. *World Englishes,* **18**(3), 343–58.

Barzun, Jacques (1989) The paradoxes of creativity. *The American Scholar,* **58**, 337–51.

Bateson, Frederick W. (1961) *English Poetry and the English Language.*

2nd edition. New York: Russell. (3rd edition, Oxford: Clarendon, 1973.)

Baumgardner, Robert J. (ed.) (1996) *South Asian English: Structure, Use, and Users.* Urbana: University of Illinois Press.

Brathwaite, Edward K. (2000) Nation language. In *The Routledge Language and Cultural Theory Reader.* Edited by Lucy Burke, Tony Crowley, and Alan Girvin. London: Routledge, pp. 310–31.

Chinweizu (1983) Decolonising the wind. *South* (January), 19–21.

Das, Kamala (1973) *The Old Playhouse and Other Poems.* New Delhi: Orient Longman.

Dembo, L. S. (ed.) (1968) *Criticism: Speculative and Analytical Essays.* Madison: University of Wisconsin Press.

Dissanayake, Wimal (1989) Purism, language, and creativity: The Sri Lankan experience. In *The Politics of Language Purism*. Edited by Bjorn H. Jernudd and Michael J. Shapire. Berlin: Mouton de Gruyter, pp. 185–96.

Dissanayake, Wimal (1998) Questing self: The four voices in *The Serpent and the Rope*. *World Literature Today: A Literary Quarterly of the University of Oklahoma*, **62**(4), 598–602.

Dissanayake, Wimal and Nichter, Mimi (1987) Native sensibility and literary discourse. In *Discourse across Cultures: Strategies in World Englishes*. Edited by Larry E. Smith. New York; Prentice-Hall, pp. 114–22.

Ee Tiang Hong (1976) *Myths for a Wilderness*. Singapore: Heinemann.

Egejuru, Phanuel Akubueze (1978) *Black Writers/White Audience: A Critical Approach to African Literature*. New York: Exposition Press.

Ezekiel, Nissim (1976) *Hymns in Darkness*. New Delhi: Oxford University Press.

Feinberg, Barry (ed.) (1974) *Poets to the People*. London: Allen Unwin. (2nd edition, London: Heinemann, 1980.)

Forster, E. M. (1924) *A Passage to India*. Abinger edition, London: Arnold, 1978.

Frost, Robert (1971) Education by poetry: A meditative monologue. In *The Play of Language*. Edited by Leonard F. Dean, Walker Gibson, and Kenneth G. Wilson. New York: Oxford University Press, pp. 383–92.

Gonzalez, Andrew (1987) Poetic imperialism or indigenous creativity? Philippine literature in English. In *Discourse across Cultures: Strategies in World Englishes*. Edited by Larry E. Smith. New York: Prentice-Hall, pp. 141–56.

Grimm, Reinhold (1986) Identity and difference: On comparative studies

within a single language. *Profession* (MLA), 28–9.

Gupta, A. F. (2004) Review of Hong Kong English: Autonomy and creativity (special issue of *World Englishes*). *Journal of Sociolinguistics*, **8**(2), 279–83.

Gupta, A. F. (2004) Review of Hong Kong English: Autonomy and creativity (special issue of *World Englishes*). *Journal of Sociolinguistics*, **8**(1), 146–50.

Hodge, Robert (1988) Halliday and the stylistics of creativity. In *Functions of Style*. Edited by David Birch and Michael O'Toole. London/New York: Pinter, pp. 142–56.

Hoggart, Richard (1982) *An English Temper: Essays on Education, Culture and Communication*. London: Chatto.

Huxley, Elspeth (1957) *The Red Rock Wilderness*. London: Chatto.

Huxley, Elspeth (1962) *On the Edge of the Rift*. New York: Morrow.

Huxley, Elspeth (1968) *White Man's Country*. 2 vols. London: Chatto.

Johnson, Cohn (1985) Interview with Cohn Johnson. In *Studies in Commonwealth Literature*. Edited by Eckhard Breitinger and Sander Reinhard. Tübingen: Gunter Narr Verlag, pp. 11–14.

Kachru, Braj B. (1985) Standards, codification and sociolinguistic realism: The English language in the Outer Circle. In *English in the World: Teaching and Learning the Language and Literatures*. Edited by Randolph Quirk and Henry G. Widdowson. Cambridge: Cambridge University Press, pp. 11–30.

Kachru, Braj B. (1987) The bilingual's creativity: Discoursal and stylistic strategies in contact literatures in English. In *Discourse across Cultures: Strategies in World Englishes*. Edited by Larry E. Smith. New York; Prentice-Hall, pp. 125–40.

Kachru, Braj B. (1988) Toward expanding the English canon: Raja Rao's 1938 credo for creativity. *World Literature Today: A Literary Quarterly of the University of Oklahoma*, **62**(4), 582–6.

Kachru, Braj B. (1992) Cultural contact and literary creativity in a multilingual society. In *Dimensions of Sociolinguistics in South Asia: Papers in Memory of Gerald Kelly*. Edited by Edward C. Dimock, Jr., Braj B. Kachru, and Bh. Krishnamurti. New Delhi: Oxford and IBH Publishing, pp. 149–59.

Kavanagh, Robert Mshengu (1985) *Theatre and Cultural Struggle in South Africa*. London: Zed Books.

Keim, Curtis A. and Keim, Karen R. (1982) Literary creativity in Anglophone Cameroon. *Research in African Literatures*, **13**(2), 216–22.

Lauture, D. (1986) The gift of creativity. *Black American Literature Forum*, **20**, 252.

MacIntyre, Ernest (1991) Creativity from alienation. In *Perceiving Other Worlds*. Edited by Edwin Thumboo. Singapore: Times Academic Press for UniPress, pp. 377–85.

Njara, Emmanuel (1982) *Stylistic Criticism and the African Novel*. London: Heinemann.

Nkosi, Lewis (1981) *Tasks and Masks: Themes and Styles of African Literature*. Harlow: Longman.

Nkosi, Lewis (1983) *Home and Exile and other Selections*. Harlow: Longman.

Nwoga, Donatus Ibe (1990) Bilingualism and literary creativity: An African perspective on literature in English, In *Literature(s) in English: New Perspectives*. Edited by Wolfgang Zach. Frankfurt am Main/New York: Peter Lang, pp. 95–108.

Okara, Gabriel (1963) African speech . . . English words. *Transitions*, **10**(3), 13–18.

Osakwe, Mable (1999) Wole Soyinka's poetry as bilingual's creativity. *World Englishes*, **18**(1), 63–77.

Parthasarathy, R. (1977) *Rough Passage*. Delhi: Oxford University Press.

Parthasarathy, R. (1982) Whoring after English gods. In *Writers in East–West Encounter: New Cultural Bearings*. Edited by Guy Amirthanayagam. London: Macmillan, p. 64.

Quirk, Randolph and Widdowson, Henry G. (eds.) (1985) *English in the World: Teaching and Learning the Language and Literatures*. Cambridge: Cambridge University Press.

Ramanujan, A. K. (trans.) (1967) *Interior Landscapes: Love Poems from a Classical Tamil Anthology*. Bloomington: Indiana University Press.

Ramanujan, A. K. (1982) Parables and commonplaces. In *Writers in East–West Encounter: New Cultural Bearings*. Edited by Guy Amirthanayagam. London: Macmillan, p. 139.

Rao, Raja (1971) *Kanthapura*. Delhi: Orient Paperbacks.

Ricoeur, Paul (2000) The creativity of language (1981). In *Routledge Language and Cultural Theory Reader*. Edited by Lucy Burke, Tony Crowley, and Alan Girvin. New York: Routledge, pp. 340–4.

Salleh, Muhammad Haji (1977) *Tradition and Change in Contemporary Malay-Indonesian Poetry*. Kuala Lumpur: Penerbit Universiti Kebangsaan Malaysia.

Schilling-Estes, Natalie (2000) Redrawing ethnic dividing lines through linguistic creativity. *American Speech*, **75**(4), 357–9.

Soyinka, Wole (1965) *The Interpreters*. London: Andre Deutsch.

Sweetser, Eve E. (1992) English metaphors for language: Motivations, conventions, and creativity. *Poetics Today*, **13**(4), 705–24.

Talib, Ismail S. (2002) *The Language of Postcolonial Literatures: An Introduction*. London/New York: Routledge.

Tawake, Sandra (2003) Bilinguals' creativity: Patricia Grace and Maori cultural context. *World Englishes*, **22**(1), 45–54.

Thumboo, Edwin (1985) Twin perspectives and multi-ecosystems: Tradition for a Commonwealth writer. *World Englishes*, **4**(2), 213–21.

Thumboo, Edwin (1987) New literatures in English: Imperative for a comparative approach. Paper delivered at Conference on Literature in English: New Perspectives, Graz, Austria, April 21–4.

Walcott, Derek (1972) What the twilight says: An overture. In *Dream on Monkey Mountain, and Other Plays*. London: J. Cape, pp. 9–10.

Webster, Jonathan (1998) The poet's language: Foregrounding in Edwin Thumboo's *Gods Can Die*. *World Englishes*, **17**(3), 359–68.

Webster, Jonathan (1999) Thumboo's *David*. In *Ariels: Departures and Returns: A Festschrift for Edwin Thumboo*. Edited by Tong Chee Kiong, Ban Kah Choon, Anne Pakir, and Robbie B. H. Goh. Singapore: Oxford University Press, pp. 71–83.

Webster, Jonathan (forthcoming) *Analysis of "Conjunction" in Continuing Discourse on Language: A Functional Perspective*. London: Equinox Publishing.

Widdowson, Henry G. (1997) EIL, ESL, EFL: Global issues and local interests. *World Englishes*, **16**(1), 135–46.

Wong Kan Seng (1987) Minister of Community Development, Republic of Singapore. Speech, Annual Cultural Awards Presentation. Singapore, February 10.

Zhang, H. (2002) Bilingual creativity in Chinese English: Ha Jin's "In the Pond." *World Englishes*, **21**(2), 305–15.

24 World Englishes and Issues of Intelligibility

LARRY E. SMITH AND
CECIL L. NELSON

1 Introduction

In recorded history, the present global spread and use of English is unparalleled (see discussions in Kachru, 1986; Quirk and Widdowson, 1985; Smith, 1983; Strevens, 1982). Crystal (1985) estimated that as many as two billion people have some ability in English. Alatis and Straehle (1997) cited a USIA estimate of 700 million users of native and non-native English, and also refer to English being "the most commonly used language at international conferences"; they also cite a British Council number of two billion users of English "with some awareness" of the language. Numbers cited and calculated by Kachru (2005: 14–15 and 205–7) indicate that English users in India and China alone number 533 million, a population of users "larger than the total [number of English speakers] of the USA, the UK and Canada." Whoever's figures are accepted, it is certain that the users of English in the Outer and Expanding Circles outnumber those in the Inner Circle.[1] With such spread of the language, a frequently voiced concern is the possibility that speakers of different varieties of English will soon become unintelligible to one another (see Chapter 17 in this volume). Bansal 1969 is an example of an early attempt to address this question. Citing Halliday, McIntosh, and Strevens (1964), Bansal wrote that "a very sensible view" was "that imported forms of English should be excluded [from consideration 'for use as an educational model'] and mutual intelligibility should be attained by adopting 'standard English grammar and lexis,' and keeping 'the number of phonological units . . . close to those of other educated accents'" (Bansal, 1969: 13). Van der Walt (2000: 173) wrote that "The assumption that South Africans run the risk of becoming incomprehensible internationally was the motivation for [her study]."

In facing this question from a sociolinguistically realistic point of view, however, it must be kept in mind that for at least the last two hundred years there have been native English-speaking people in some parts of the world who have not been intelligible to other English-speaking people in other parts of the world.

Such is a natural phenomenon when any language becomes so widespread. It is not something that is "going to happen" but something that has happened already and will continue to occur. It is unnecessary for every user of English to be intelligible to every other user of English. Our speech and writing in English needs to be intelligible to those with whom we wish to communicate in English. For example, there may be many people in India who use English frequently among themselves and who are not intelligible to English-speaking Filipinos who also frequently use English among themselves; members of these two groups may not, as yet, have felt the need (or had the opportunity) to communicate with one another. These Indians and Filipinos may use English to communicate only with fellow countrymen and have little or no difficulty in doing so. If that is so, neither group needs to be concerned about its international intelligibility. Of course, there are many Indians and many Filipinos who use English to interact internationally, and they are the ones who must be concerned about mutual intelligibility.

2 Defining "Intelligibility"

Perhaps the concern about intelligibility can be rephrased in the following way: In international situations where people wish to communicate with one another in English, how intelligible are speakers of different national varieties? With the global spread of English, is the problem of understanding across cultures likely to increase in frequency?

Elsewhere (e.g., Smith and Nelson, 1985), it has been argued that those who have traditionally been called "native speakers" are not the sole judges of what is intelligible, nor are they always more intelligible than "non-native" speakers (see, e.g., Nelson, 1992; Smith and Rafiqzad, 1979). The greater the familiarity speakers, native or non-native, have with a variety of English, the more likely it is that they will understand and be understood by members of that speech community. Understanding is not solely speaker- or listener-centered, but is interactional between speaker and listener.

Understanding, or "intelligibility" in a broad sense, should be divided into three categories which make it accessible for examination and analysis in more specific terms:

1 intelligibility: word/utterance recognition;
2 comprehensibility: word/utterance meaning (locutionary force);
3 interpretability: meaning behind word/utterance (illocutionary force).

Smith and Christopher (2001: 92–3) present an interactional scenario which will serve to explicate these three components. An Australian woman is reported to have been having a conversation in English with a taxi driver in Istanbul. Things were going well "until she asked [the driver] to turn off the interior light": the driver refused "sharply." Since her request seemed innocuous to the passenger, and since a mutual compatibility in English had been established by the preceding conversation, she thought there had been a simple failure of *intelligibility* or *comprehensibility* – that the driver had misheard or misunderstood some part of her utterance – so she repeated it, only to receive a "near-hostile" negative response and marked silence until the end of the trip, which terminated in the driver "almost [snatching] the fare from her and [driving] away rapidly."

The failure of the interaction turned on a mismatch of *interpretations* of the female passenger's utterance: she just wanted the light turned off, for whatever reason of comfort, or perhaps she simply thought it did not need to be on; the driver was not only culturally but legally bound not to allow himself to be in "a dark and confined space" with a woman. Smith and Christopher speculate that he may have been "shocked" by her request, which may have led to his responding as he did. Smith and Christopher write:

> The whole uncomfortable situation might have been avoided if the Australian had . . . [said], for example: "Do you always leave the interior light on when you drive?" Probably the driver would have replied: "I must leave it on, that is the law." Another source of information may be a *mediator*, an independent third party familiar with [both cultures involved]. (p. 93)

This example shows that successful communication in English is not assured by the participants exhibiting good pronunciation – the focus of so much attention in ESL and EFL teaching and learning – or even good lexis and grammar; utterances have pragmatic effects which cannot be interpreted without situational, social, and cultural awareness. These three categories – intelligibility, comprehensibility, and interpretability – may be thought of as degrees of understanding on a continuum of complexity of variables, from phonological to pragmatic, with *intelligibility* being lowest and *interpretability* being highest.

3   A Study of the Three Components

The remainder of this chapter reports on a study carried out by Smith (1992) designed to help determine: (1) what differences, if any, there are in the intelligibility, comprehensibility, and interpretability of selected taped material of nine national varieties; (2) how familiarity of topic and familiarity of national variety influence the listener's understanding of these varieties; and (3) whether the language proficiency of the speaker and/or listener influences the intelligibility, comprehensibility, and interpretability of these varieties. For this study, the nine national varieties, represented on tape, were spoken by educated speakers (at the graduate level at the University of Hawaii) from China, India, Indonesia, Japan, Papua New Guinea, the Philippines, Taiwan, the United Kingdom, and the United States. The tests of intelligibility, comprehensibility, and interpretability based on these recordings were administered to three different groups of native and non-native educated users of English.

To test assumptions concerning the effects of proficiency in English and familiarity with topic and speech variety on understanding (intelligibility, comprehensibility, and interpretability), it was desirable to have both native and non-native educated English users as subjects. These subjects exhibited a range in their degrees of proficiency in English and in their familiarity with the content of the selections, as well as in their familiarity with the national variety of English being used by the speakers. The three groups were composed of: (1) non-native speakers, (2) native speakers, and (3) mixed non-native and native speakers.

Group 1: Non-native Speakers This group was made up of ten non-native English speakers from Japan whose English proficiency ranged from scores of 375 to 600 on the TOEFL test; four were students in the Hawai'i English Language Program (HELP) at the University of Hawai'i and six were students at the Japan-America Institute of Management Science (JAIMS) in Honolulu. Subjects in this group were familiar with the Japanese variety of English, as well as with the content of the Japanese speaker's presentation of "Forms of Address" (i.e., how Japanese address non-Japanese in English at international meetings). Since they had studied English for at least ten years and were students in the United States, they were also somewhat familiar with the American and British varieties of English and with the content of the US and British speakers' presentations on "Forms of Address" (i.e., how British and Americans address outsiders in English at international meetings). However, these subjects were not familiar with any of the other speech varieties or with the topic of forms of address used in the other countries.

Group 2: Native Speakers This group was made up of ten native speakers of American English who were undergraduate students at the University of Hawai'i. All were quite familiar with the American English used by the American speaker on the tape, as well as with the content of her presentation. They were not totally familiar with any other of the speech varieties on the tapes but had had greater exposure to the Japanese and Filipino varieties than to any of the others. They knew little about forms of address in any country other than the United States.

Group 3: Mixed This group was composed of one native and eight non-native speakers, one each from Burma, China, Indonesia, Japan, Korea, the Philippines, Thailand, and the United States. Each of these people was fully fluent in English (having scored above 600 on the TOEFL test). As East-West Center graduate students, they had all become familiar with several different national varieties of English. They were also familiar to some extent with the forms of address used in different countries because of their interactions at the East-West Center with people from many parts of the world.

All three groups were balanced for age, sex, and educational background. The subjects with the lower TOEFL scores were highly intelligent and well educated, but they had not had much experience of interacting in English.

3.1   Test materials and procedures

In order to have educated English speakers of the nine national varieties interacting with one another, graduate and postgraduate students at the University of Hawai'i who were fluent in English were chosen to produce the listening passages. The speakers were asked to explain to an interactor who was of another national variety the forms of address used by people from the speaker's country when they addressed outsiders in English. The respondent was, in each case, a person whom the speaker did not know and who knew little about, but was interested in, the speaker's country. The respondent was instructed, in the speaker's presence, to listen to the speaker, interrupt with questions of clarification when necessary, and give evidence of understanding the speaker by paraphrasing the important points the speaker made. The speaker was instructed to make sure the respondent understood how people in his/her country would address an outsider in English, for example, at international meetings both inside and outside his/her country.

Both speakers and respondents were told that the language in the recording session was to be informal but real. That is, they were to speak to each other as peers in an informal situation; they were not to pretend that they were other people or that the setting was another place. They were to recognize and accept the fact that they were two people in a recording studio at the East-West Center in Honolulu. They were instructed that the conversation should stop once the speaker was satisfied that the respondent understood what the speaker had said about the topic. The interactors were told that they could make notes but that neither was to read directly from the notes. The sessions were unrehearsed, and lasted from 20 to 40 minutes. The tapes of these sessions were edited down to ten minutes of conversation which could be used as material for the comprehensibility and interpretability tests.

For the intelligibility test, the subjects heard a part of the conversation which was not used as part of the edited ten-minute presentation. This was done so that the subjects would not hear any part of the conversation twice. In addition to the conversations with speakers of the nine national varieties mentioned above, one tape involving a speaker from Burma and a respondent from Thailand was also made to use in a demonstration of the testing procedure for all three subject groups.

Although no formal attempt was made to evaluate the difficulty level of the interactions, all were judged to be approximately equal in that (1) both speaker and respondent were fully proficient in English and believed themselves to be educated speakers of their national variety of English, (2) each person spoke clearly, and (3) the number of embedded sentences and the speed of delivery were approximately the same for all interactions. Of course, the setting and topic were always the same, and technical jargon was never used. In each case, if the speaker was male the respondent was female, and vice versa, so that on each tape both sexes were represented.

Three types of test questions were developed. A cloze procedure was used to test intelligibility (word/utterance recognition). Multiple-choice questions were written to test comprehensibility (word/utterance meaning). Subjects were asked to paraphrase a small portion of the conversation they had heard in order to test their level of interpretability (meaning behind word/utterance). The test questions and directions were recorded by the same speaker.

3.2 The tests

Each testing session began with the researcher saying to each of the three subject groups that he was doing a study on the degrees of understanding of different national varieties of English and that he appreciated the subjects' willingness to cooperate. They were assured that the results of the tests would have no effect on their academic work, but they were encouraged to do their best. The trial test was introduced, and the subjects were told that they could ask any question about the procedure during the sample test.

Each subject group then listened to the tape about forms of address in Burma and filled out the sample test items for the cloze procedure (*intelligibility*), multiple choice test (*comprehensibility*), and paraphrasing (*interpretability*). After the sample test, the subjects filled out the more subjective questionnaire (see Appendix), and they had the opportunity to ask questions about it. On that form, they were asked to state such things as (1) how easy/difficult it was for them to understand the speaker and respondent; (2) how much of the total conversation they had understood; (3) the nationalities of the speaker and the respondent; and (4) the English proficiency level of the speaker and the respondent.

Subjects then went on to the test proper. For each of the five paired recordings, each subject group first listened to the ten-minute conversation, with the respondent asking questions and paraphrasing the important points. At the end of each conversation, the subjects were given a test which consisted of (1) a cloze procedure of a passage with ten blanks (one at every seventh word) to be filled in as they listened, phrase by phrase, to a part of the original, longer conversation that they had not heard before; (2) three multiple-choice questions based on the ten-minute conversation that they had heard; and (3) three phrases taken from the ten-minute interaction they were to paraphrase according to their interpretation of the meanings of the phrases in the conversation. This system was followed for each of the five paired recordings. That is, (1) the subjects heard a tape about a country; (2) the subjects were tested on that country; (3) the subjects heard the next tape about another country; (4) the subjects were tested on that country. This continued until all five paired recordings had been heard and tested. The order of the five pairs of taped conversations was different for each subject group, to insure that any practice effect was balanced across varieties.

All of the tests to the three subject groups were administered on separate days within a two-month period (October and November 1986). Identical playback equipment was used for each group, always in quiet surroundings. The tests were all graded by the same individual within a few days after they were completed and given to the researcher for analysis.

3.3   Results and discussion

Tables 24.1, 24.2, and 24.3 present the tabulated results of the three parts of the test for each of the three groups. The speakers that the subjects heard are listed in alphabetical order (with respondents in parentheses) by country on the left side of each table. In each case, the percentage listed is the percentage of subjects in that group which answered 60 percent or more of the test items correctly. For example, from Table 24.1 we learn that, when listening to the speaker from the United Kingdom interacting with her respondent from Papua New Guinea, 70 percent of the non-native subjects got 60 percent or more of the intelligibility test items correct, whereas 100 percent of the native-speaker subjects and 100 percent of the mixed subjects got 60 percent or more of the intelligibility items correct.

The results tabulated in Tables 24.1, 24.2, and 24.3 show that all three subject groups did best on the test of intelligibility. All of the native subjects, all of the mixed subjects, and 92 percent of the non-native subjects got 60 percent or more of the intelligibility test items correct. It appears that all of the interactions were highly intelligible to the three subject groups, but that the most intelligible were those with the speakers from Japan (respondent from China), India (respondent from the Philippines), and the United States (respondent from Indonesia). The pair with the speaker from China and respondent from

Table 24.1   Intelligibility: subjects scoring 60 percent and above (NNS = non-native speaker; NS = native speaker)

Speaker (respondent)	NNS: 10, all from Japan	NS: 10, all from US	Mixed: 9 (1 NS and 8 NNS, each from a different country)	Average %
China (Taiwan)	90	100	100	97
India (Philippines)	100	100	100	100
Japan (China)	100	100	100	100
United Kingdom (Papua New Guinea)	70	100	100	90
United States (Indonesia)	100	100	100	100
Average	92	100	100	

Table 24.2 Comprehensibility: subjects scoring 60 percent and above

Speaker (respondent)	NNS (10)	NS (10)	Mixed (9)	Average %
China (Taiwan)	40	80	60	60
India (Philippines)	40	90	60	63
Japan (China)	80	80	70	77
United Kingdom (Papua New Guinea)	90	100	100	97
United States (Indonesia)	60	60	60	60
Average	62	82	70	

Table 24.3 Interpretability: subjects scoring 60 percent and above

Speaker	NNS (10)	NS (10)	Mixed (9)	Average %
China (Taiwan)	40	60	89	63
India (Philippines)	10	40	78	43
Japan (China)	40	60	89	63
United Kingdom (Papua New Guinea)	10	50	89	50
United States (Indonesia)	30	40	100	57
Average	26	50	89	

Taiwan and the pair with the speaker from the United Kingdom and respondent from Papua New Guinea were rated as somewhat less intelligible across the groups. Language proficiency may have made a difference in the results of the intelligibility test, but being a native speaker was not shown to be a deciding factor, since the mixed group – with eight non-natives and one native speaker – performed equally well on the test.

Table 24.2, concerning comprehensibility (word/utterance meaning), shows that the averages for all three groups were lower; 62 percent of the non-native subjects, 82 percent of the native subjects, and 70 percent of the mixed subjects got 60 percent or more of the comprehensibility test items. The speaker from the United Kingdom and her respondent from Papua New Guinea were the most comprehensible, with 90 percent of the non-native group getting 60 percent or more of the test items correct, and all of the native group and all of the mixed group doing the same. This is interesting, because this is the pair that was the least intelligible. This result shows that, as demonstrated in the Australian–Turkish example above, the components of overall intelligibility or understanding are not necessarily dependent on one another in any specific case. It is also noteworthy that the Japanese speaker with the Chinese respondent was the second most comprehensible pair, with the pairs from India–Philippines, US–Indonesia, and China–Taiwan being rated about equally in difficulty for comprehensibility.

A priori, all of the subject groups might have been expected to comprehend the tapes about forms of address in the United States and the one about forms of address in the United Kingdom more easily than the others because all the non-native members of each group had studied English for at least ten years and had learned a great deal of cultural information about both countries. In other words, they knew the topic and were also somewhat familiar with each of these Inner-Circle speech varieties. The Japanese group and the American group were expected to comprehend the tapes about forms of address in their respective countries more easily, since obviously they knew the information upon which the test for their country was based. A possible reason why the subjects failed to do this is that, although new information was given on each tape, the general topic was the same. This may explain why familiarity with topic was not a major factor in the subjects' ability to comprehend the interactions. If the topics had been Noh theater, nuclear physics, or anything else besides forms of address, the effects of familiarity with the topic might have been greater.

Examination of the subjective questionnaires for each pair of interactors brought out other information which offered another possible explanation for the surprising lack of effect of topic-familiarity. In both cases dealing with the American and Japanese subjects listening to a speaker from their country interacting with a respondent from another country, the responses of the subjects to the respondents may have been a factor. All of the native-speaker subjects (i.e., the Americans) responded that they could easily understand the American speaker, but only 30 percent said that they could easily understand the respondent, who was from Indonesia. Sixty percent of the non-native group (i.e., the Japanese) responded that they could easily understand the Japanese speaker, but 70 percent said that they had some difficulty with the respondent, who was from China. Their difficulty in understanding the respondent (e.g., "accent too heavy") may have caused them comprehensibility problems with the overall conversation.

Table 24.3 provides some further insightful information. It is evident that the mixed subjects (one native and eight non-natives, each from a different country) who had the greatest familiarity with different speech varieties were best able to interpret correctly the interactions of the five pairs of interactors. Twenty-six percent of the non-native speakers, 50 percent of the native speakers, and 89 percent of the mixed subjects were correct on 60 percent or more of the interpretability test items. The mixed subject group was better on all five pairs than were the native or non-native subject groups. This is an important finding, which shows that interpretability is at the core of communication and is more important than mere intelligibility or even comprehensibility.

This part of the study offers supporting evidence that familiarity with several different English varieties makes it easier to interpret cross-cultural communication in English. No doubt this facility is influenced by the fact that familiarity with different speech varieties also involves an awareness of cultural differences and some knowledge of various specific cultures. This is not to say that proficiency in the language itself is unimportant; the mixed group was fully fluent in English, although not at the native-speaker level, except for one person. Additional evidence that proficiency is important is the fact that the native-speaker subject group was better at interpreting all five interactions than was the less proficient non-native subject group. The non-native and native subject groups found the China–Taiwan and the Japan–China pairs easiest to interpret, and all three subject groups found the India–Philippines pair the most difficult to interpret. Only the mixed group found the US–Indonesia pair the easiest to interpret, perhaps because the mixed-group members were the only ones familiar with many varieties of English. The native-speaker group and the non-native-speaker group were not familiar with the Indonesian speech variety, and this may have been a factor in their inability to interpret the US–Indonesia interaction correctly.

Other responses from the subjective questionnaires were also of interest. Table 24.4 shows the percentage of each subject group that thought they understood 60 percent or more of the conversations between the five sets of interactors. The mixed group of subjects, who were most familiar with different national varieties of English, had the most confidence in their ability to understand the conversations. All of the native-speaker subject group thought they understood the US–Indonesia pair, and 90 percent of the non-native subject group (i.e., the Japanese) thought that they understood the Japan–China pair. Familiarity with topic and familiarity with at least one of the speech varieties being used in a conversation apparently cause listeners to believe that they understand most of what they hear.

Table 24.4 Percentage of subject groups that thought they understood 60 percent or more of the conversations between the five sets of interactors

Speaker (respondent)	NNS (10)	NS (10)	Mixed (9)
China (Taiwan)	30	100	100
India (Philippines)	10	90	100
Japan (China)	90	90	100
United Kingdom (Papua New Guinea)	30	90	100
United States (Indonesia)	40	100	100

Table 24.5 Percentage of subjects making accurate guesses as to the nationalities of the pairs in the conversations

Speaker (respondent)	NNS (10)	NS (10)	Mixed (9)
China	50	100	100
(Taiwan)*	70	60	100
India	20	90	100
(Philippines)*	60	100	100
Japan	90	100	100
(China)*	80	100	100
United Kingdom	70	70	89
(Papua New Guinea)*	10	20	100
United States	90	80	100
(Indonesia)*	0	0	10

* The country of origin was actually mentioned on the tape.

Table 24.5 shows the percentages of subjects making accurate guesses as to the nationalities of the pairs of speakers in the conversations. Again, the mixed subject group was best, followed by the native-speaker group and the non-native speakers.

It was surprising, however, that even though five of the ten interactors on the tapes identified themselves as nationals of a particular country, only the mixed group identified their nationalities accurately. (It was not surprising that few subjects recognized the Indonesian speaker, since they had been exposed to so few Indonesians. It would almost certainly have been the same for the person from Papua New Guinea if he had not identified himself.) Another surprise was that the native-speaker subject group was not as able to correctly identify their fellow American as the non-native group or the mixed group was. The native-speaker subjects were better able to identify the nationalities of the interactors from China, Japan, India, and the Philippines than they were the speaker from the United States. The non-native subject group identified the speakers from Japan most easily and identified speakers from the United States more easily than they did speakers from the United Kingdom. Native speakers of English may be surprised to learn of the native-speaker subject group's low percentage of accuracy, and non-native speakers may be equally surprised to see the non-native subject group's high degree of accuracy. The mixed subject group did well and, except for the Indonesian respondent, seemed confident in their responses. Speakers from all Circles of English perhaps will be surprised that the mixed group did not guess the British person's nationality with greater accuracy.

Responses to two other items on the questionnaire deserve comment. The questions dealt with the subjects' perceptions of the interactors' level of education and proficiency in English. The questions were identical except that number 7 was about the presenter and number 8 was about the respondent (see Appendix). The question was, "Based on what you heard, it seems that the presenter/respondent is (check as many as you wish): highly educated/ educated/not well educated/a native English speaker/a non-native English speaker/a speaker of Standard English/a speaker of non-Standard English."

Table 24.6 gives the tabulated results. First, a great majority of the subjects perceived the interactors to be in one of the top two categories, educated or highly educated. A small percentage (10%) of the non-native-speaker subjects thought the speaker from India was not well educated, and an equally small percentage (10%) of the native-speaker subjects thought the respondents from Papua New Guinea and Indonesia were not well educated. Subjects in the mixed group thought all of the speakers and respondents were highly educated or educated.

Second, all three subject groups did well in correctly identifying the interactors as native or non-native English speakers. The majority were accurate in every case except one: 60 percent of the native-speaker subjects guessed that the respondent from Papua New Guinea was a native speaker of English. In spite of this, the native-speaker group was able to label correctly more of the interactors as native or non-native than either of the other two subject groups, with the mixed group a close second.

What is most interesting about Table 24.6 is the final listing, which concerns the subjects' perceptions about whether the interactors were using Standard or non-Standard English. Most of the native-speaker subject group and the non-native-speaker subject group thought that everyone they heard used Standard English. The only exceptions were the speakers from India and Japan. Fifty percent of the non-native subject group thought the speaker from India used non-Standard English. The native-speaker subject group was equally divided about the speakers from India and Japan in that 40 percent thought they used Standard English and 40 percent thought they used non-Standard. It is heartening, from the world Englishes perspective, to learn that many native and non-native speakers of English would label most educated speakers of non-native English as users of Standard English. The mixed subject group was more critical and seemed to have a stricter criterion for Standard English: 33 percent of this group thought that the speaker from the United States used non-Standard English. One might assume that many non-native speakers and certainly most native speakers would label people who were clearly non-native users as speakers of non-Standard English. It seems clear, however, that non-native English speakers need not be indistinguishable from native speakers in order to be judged as using Standard English.

These results easily support the interpretation that it is possible for Standard English to be spoken with many different accents. This is one of the very positive results of the vast spread of English across the globe.

Table 24.6 Subjects' perceptions of interactors' level of education and proficiency in English

Countries of interactors	HE/E/NWE %	NS/NNS %	SE/NSE %
NNS (10):			
China	50/50/0	20/80	50/10*
Taiwan	30/70/0	10/70*	50/20*
India	30/60/10	0/100	30/50*
Philippines	50/50/0	30/70	50/30*
Japan	40/60/0	20/70*	60/30*
China	40/60/0	10/90	80/0*
United Kingdom	40/60/0	70/20*	50/30*
Papua New Guinea	50/40/0*	40/50*	40/20*
United States	50/50/0	80/20	70/20*
Indonesia	10/90/0	40/60	50/30*
NS (10):			
China	70/30/0	0/100	70/10*
Taiwan	40/60/0	30/70	50/20*
India	10/90/0	20/80	40/40*
Philippines	10/90/0	0/100	50/30*
Japan	10/90/0	0/100	40/40*
China	0/100/0	0/100	70/10*
United Kingdom	50/50/0	90/10	70/0*
Papua New Guinea	20/70/10	60/40	60/20*
United States	40/40/0*	100/0	80/0*
Indonesia	20/60/10*	20/80	60/30*
Mixed (9):			
China	67/33/0	0/100	78/22
Taiwan	33/67/0	0/100	22/78
India	56/44/0	33/67	67/33
Philippines	56/44/0	22/78	67/33
Japan	11/89/0	0/100	11/89
China	22/78/0	0/100	50/50
United Kingdom	56/44/0	89/11	89/11
Papua New Guinea	22/78/0	33/67	33/67
United States	44/56/0	78/22	67/33
Indonesia	11/89/0	11/89	11/89

Key: HE = Highly educated; NNS = Non-native speaker of English; E = Educated; SE = Standard English; NWE = Not well educated; NSE = Non-Standard English; NS = Native speaker of English; * = Some subjects did not reply.

4   Conclusion

In order to determine whether the spread of English is creating greater problems of understanding across cultures, this study was done with three types of subject groups (non-native, native, and mixed) involving nine different national varieties. Understanding was divided into three elements: intelligibility, comprehensibility, and interpretability. Evidence supports the position that there are major differences among intelligibility, comprehensibility, and interpretability as defined in the study. Intelligibility (word/utterance recognition) is easier than comprehensibility (word/utterance meaning) or interpretability (meaning behind word/utterance). Being able to do well with one component does not ensure that one will do well with the others. Having familiarity with the information presented did not seem to affect any of the three groups, but those subjects having a greater familiarity with different varieties of English performed better on the tests of interpretability than did those who lacked such familiarity. Being familiar with topic and speech variety did affect the subjects' self-perceptions of how well they had understood. Language proficiency does influence intelligibility, comprehensibility, and interpretability, but it seems to be most important for comprehensibility. It is a striking result of this investigation that native speakers (from Britain and the United States) were *not* found to be the most easily understood, nor were they, as subjects, the best able to understand the different varieties of English. Thus, being a native speaker does not seem to be as important as being fluent in English and familiar with several different national varieties. These results indicate that the increasing number of varieties of English need not increase the problems of understanding across cultures, if users of English develop some familiarity with them.

Intelligibility has been a paradigmatic area of argument for those concerned about the cross-variety acceptability of varieties of English since before the days of the term and concept of world Englishes. When Outer- and Expanding-Circle varieties (as we now think of them) are observed by some commentators in the Inner Circle, such as Quirk (1985), to cite a well-known exemplar, concerns about imperfect learning are raised, and give rise to appeals to "interlanguage" and the righteousness of models. When those varieties are under scrutiny by some people, including policy-makers, teachers and linguists, in their own Circles, similar apprehensions may arise: "Is our English serviceable enough for interaction in a world market?" (see, e.g., Bansal, 1969 and Nihalani, Tongue, and Hosali, 1979). The work presented here shows that the rash response of attempting to teach and learn an Inner-Circle variety in the Outer and Expanding Circles is, besides being a losing proposition, not a cogent answer, since not even all Inner-Circle varieties of English are mutually intelligible with one another. More research of the kind reported on in this chapter and, for example, by van der Walt (2000) is needed, if these theoretical and pedagogical questions are to be directed usefully. Further investigations across varieties within the Inner Circle could help dispel the "us vs. them" mindset. And since all the evidence shows that most non-Inner-Circle uses of English across the world do not involve Inner-Circle users, more studies of those interactions will continue to reveal what the criteria of intelligibility truly are.

See also Chapters 15, World Englishes Today; 17, Varieties of World Englishes; 21, Speaking and Writing in World Englishes; 23, Literary Creativity in World Englishes; 25, World Englishes and Culture Wars.

NOTES

The core of this chapter is a revised version of Smith (1992), used by permission.

1   Although various writers in world Englishes, including Ferguson (1982) and Paikeday (1985), have presented cogent arguments against employing the "native/non-native" division, the terms are convenient for the exposition of this presentation, and so we will use that distinction in this chapter.

REFERENCES

Alatis, James and Straehle, Carolyn A. (1997) The universe of English: Imperialism, chauvinism, and paranoia. In *World Englishes 2000*. Edited by Larry E. Smith and Michael L. Forman. Honolulu: University of Hawai'i Press, pp. 1–20.

Bansal, R. K. (1969) *The Intelligibility of Indian English: Measurements of the Intelligibility of Connected Speech, and Sentence and Word Material, Presented to Listeners of Different Nationalities.* Hyderadbad: Central Institute of English.

Crystal, David (1985) How many millions? The statistics of English today. *English Today*, 1, 7–9.

Ferguson, Charles A. (1982) Foreword. In *The Other Tongue: English across Cultures.* Edited by Braj B. Kachru. Urbana: University of Illinois Press,

pp. vii–xi. (Reprinted in the 2nd edition, 1992, pp. xiii–xvii.)

Halliday, M. A. K., McIntosh, Angus, and Strevens, Peter (1964) *The Linguistic Sciences and Language Teaching.* London: Longmans, Green.

Kachru, Braj B. (1986) *The Alchemy of English: The Spread, Models and Functions of Non-Native Englishes.* Oxford: Pergamon Press. (Reprinted 1990, Urbana: University of Illinois Press.)

Kachru, Braj B. (2005) *Asian Englishes: Beyond the Canon.* Hong Kong: Hong Kong University Press.

Nelson, Cecil L. (1992) My language, your culture: Whose communicative competence? In *The Other Tongue: English across Cultures.* 2nd edition. Edited by Braj B. Kachru. Urbana:

University of Illinois Press,
pp. 327–39.

Nihalani, Paroo, Tongue, R. K., and
Hosali, P. (1979) *Indian and British
English: A Handbook of Usage and
Pronunciation*. Delhi: Oxford
University Press. (2nd edition, with
Jonathan Crowther, 2004.)

Paikeday, Thomas M. (1985) *The Native
Speaker is Dead!* Toronto: Paikeday
Publishing.

Quirk, Randolph (1985) The English language in a global context. In *English
in the World: Teaching and Learning
the Language and Literatures*. Edited
by Randolph Quirk and Henry G.
Widdowson. Cambridge: Cambridge
University Press, pp. 1–30.

Quirk, Randolph and Widdowson,
Henry G. (eds.) (1985) *English in the
World: Teaching and Learning the
Language and Literatures*. Cambridge:
Cambridge University Press.

Smith, Larry E. (ed.) (1983) *Readings in
English as an International Language*.
Oxford: Pergamon Press.

Smith, Larry E. (1992) Spread of English
and issues of intelligibility. In *The
Other Tongue: English across Cultures*.
2nd edition. Edited by Braj B.

Kachru. Urbana: University of
Illinois Press, pp. 75–90.

Smith, Larry E. and Christopher,
Elizabeth (2001) "Why can't they
understand me when I speak
English so clearly?" In *The Three
Circles of English*. Edited by Edwin
Thumboo. Singapore: UniPress, pp.
91–100.

Smith, Larry E. and Nelson, Cecil L.
(1985) International intelligibility of
English: Directions and resources.
World Englishes, **3**, 333–42.

Smith, Larry E. and Rafiqzad, Khalilullah
(1979) English for cross-cultural
communication: The question of
intelligibility. *TESOL Quarterly*,
13(3), pp. 371–80. (Reprinted 1983 in
*Readings in English as an International
Language*. Edited by Larry E. Smith.
Oxford: Pergamon Press, pp. 49–58.)

Strevens, Peter (1982) World English and
the world's Englishes, or, whose
language is it, anyway? *Journal of
the Royal Society of Arts*, **5311**,
418–31.

van der Walt, Christa (2000) The
international comprehensibility of
varieties of South African English.
World Englishes, **19**(2), 139–262.

FURTHER READING

Berns, Margie (1990) *Contexts of
Competence: Social and Cultural
Considerations in Communicative
Language Teaching*. New York:
Plenum.

Candlin, Christopher H. (1982) English
as an international language:
Intelligibility vs. interpretability.
In *Notes on a Theme: English for
International Communication*. Edited
by C. J. Brumfit. Oxford: Pergamon
Press, pp. 95–8.

Catford, John (1950) Intelligibility.
English Language Teaching, **1**,
7–15.

Ch'ien, Evelyn Nien-Ming (2004) *Weird
English*. Cambridge, MA: Harvard
University Press.

Coppieters, Rene (1987) Competence
differences between native and
near-native speakers. *Language*,
63, 544–73.

Kachru, Braj B. (1982) Meaning in
deviation: Toward understanding

non-native English texts. In *The Other Tongue: English across Cultures*. Edited by Braj B. Kachru. Urbana: University of Illinois Press, pp. 325–50.

Kachru, Yamuna (1993) Social meaning and creativity in Indian English. In *Language, Communication and Social Meaning*. Georgetown University Monograph Series on Languages and Linguistics 1992. Edited by James E. Alatis. Washington, DC: Georgetown University Press, pp. 378–87.

Matsuura, Hiroko, Chiba, Reiko, and Fujieda, Miho (1999) Intelligibility and comprehensibility of American and Irish Englishes in Japan. *World Englishes*, **18**(1), 49–62.

Nelson, Cecil L. (1982) Intelligibility and non-native varieties of English. In *The Other Tongue: English across Cultures*. Edited by Braj B. Kachru. Urbana: University of Illinois Press, pp. 58–73.

Nelson, Cecil L. (2001) Intelligibility and creativity in world English literatures. In *The Three Circles of English*. Edited by Edwin Thumboo. Singapore: UniPress, pp. 35–44.

Seidlhofer, Barbara (2001) Closing a conceptual gap: The case for a description of English as a lingua franca. *International Journal of Applied Linguistics*, **11**(2), 133–58.

Smith, Larry E. and Bisazza, John (1982) The comprehensibility of three varieties of English for college students in seven countries. *Language Learning*, **32**, 259–70.

Appendix

Directions: Answer the following questions by putting a check mark (✓) in the appropriate space provided, according to how you feel about the taped material that you have just heard.

1. Could you understand what the presenter said?
   easily : with some difficulty : with great difficulty : not at all
2. Could you understand what the respondent said?
   easily : with some difficulty : with great difficulty : not at all
3. How much of the conversation did you understand?
   90%> : 75%–89% : 1%–74% : 50%–60% : 34%–49% : <33%
4. Did you have difficulty understanding the conversation?
   Yes _____ No _____ If Yes, check the appropriate reasons.
   (You may check as many as you wish.)
   _____ I could not understand the meaning of what was said.
   _____ One or both speakers spoke too quickly.
   _____ The accent of the presenter was too heavy.
   _____ The accent of the respondent was too heavy.
   _____ Other (please write) _____
5. What is the presenter's nationality? _____
6. What is the respondent's nationality? _____

7. Based on what you heard, it seems that the presenter is (check as many as you wish):
   highly educated _____ educated _____ not well educated _____
   a native English speaker _____   a non-native English speaker _____
   a speaker of Standard English _____ a speaker of non-Standard English _____
8. Based on what you heard, it seems that the respondent is (check as many as you wish):
   highly educated _____ educated _____ not well educated _____
   a native English speaker _____   a non-native English speaker _____
   a speaker of Standard English _____ a speaker of non-Standard English _____

25 World Englishes and Culture Wars

BRAJ B. KACHRU

1 Introduction

This chapter addresses two issues that continue to be debated internationally about the presence of the English language in the global context: one of celebration and triumphalism, and the other of the use of the language as part of the arsenal in what have been termed civilizational "culture wars."

The spread of English is characterized in subtle and sometimes not-so-subtle tones as a triumphalistic march of the language, that has gained global currency over other major languages (see, e.g., Crystal, 1997, and later, and for another perspective, see Kachru, 1986 and 2005). It is now generally recognized that the Hydra-like language has many heads, representing diverse cultures and linguistic identities. English represents the legendary status of the "Speaking Tree."[1] This legend goes back at least four millennia, to the period of Alexander the Great. It is said that the great warrior king was taken in India "to an oracular tree which could answer questions in the language of any [one] who addressed it" (Lannoy, 1971: xxv).

The tree was unmatched, says the legend – its trunk was made of snakes and animal heads, and its branches "bore fruit like beautiful women, who sang the praises of the Sun and Moon" (Lannoy, 1971: xxv). The tree acquired a special status in the Islamic tradition and in Mughal miniature paintings, and is called in that tradition the Waqwaq Tree – the Speaking Tree. The Waqwaq Tree is viewed both with feelings of awe and attraction, and there are versions of this legend in other cultures, too. The metaphor of the Speaking Tree, therefore, represents both fear and celebration, aversion and esteem, and, indeed, agony and ecstasy (see., e.g., Kachru, 1996c).

The trunk of the English language tree – the Inner Circle (e.g., the UK, the USA, Australia) – continues to evoke reactions of suspicion, of conspiracies, and of mistrust.[2] There continues to be a lingering Trojan-horse association with the language and its managers, not only in Asia and Africa, but even in the UK and the USA.

There is, however, another reality that has haltingly, but certainly, emerged since the 1950s. After a long and agonizing wait, the branches of the Waqwaq Tree are bearing delectable fruit: accessibility to a variety of methetic functions through the language, in a shared medium of pluralistic identities. It is in this sense of multiplicity and pluralism that English has become a global "access" language. What Salman Rushdie says of his much-discussed *The Satanic Verses* (1991[1988]: 394) is actually true, by extension, of world Englishes: they stand for "change-by-fusion, change-by-conjoining. It is a love song to our mongrel selves. It actually is a celebration of syncretism."

This takes me to the first part of the title – the concept *world Englishes*.[3] This concept entails a distinction between language as a *medium* and language as a *message*. The medium refers to the *form* of language – its phonology, morphology, and syntax – and the message embodies the functions in which the medium is used. There are, indeed, a variety of underlying theoretical, functional, pragmatic, and methodological reasons that demand this pluralization of the language – Englishes and not English (see, e.g., Kachru, 1994b; see also Ch'ien, 2004; McArthur, 1998 and 2001; and Chapters 15, 17, and 30 in this volume).[4]

The concept world Englishes, then, emphasizes the pluricentricity of the language and its cross-cultural reincarnations. This conceptualization about the functions and multi-identities of English, therefore, has become a loaded weapon for those who view the spread of the language exclusively in terms of the celebration of the Judeo-Christian *mantras* of the language – the view that the "global," "international," and "world" presence of the language is essentially a victory of what is perceived as a monocultural Western medium, and that the language is the English-using West's weapon in the clash of civilizations.[5] That view, as I will discuss below, does not represent the current global state of the language or the multiple identities English has created across cultures.

These discourses of global triumph of the language need serious re-evaluation in terms of functional pragmatism – especially that of multiple canonicity in Englishes, British, North American, African, and Asian, as is reflected and discussed in various chapters in this volume. In other words, what we need is a conceptualization of world Englishes in a framework of pluricentricity and distinct cultural canon-formation.

The issue of canonicity is critical here, since canons, as Kermode (1979, cited in Altieri, 1990: 22) perceptively reminds us, are essentially "strategic constructs by which societies maintain their own interests." And canons also provide two types of control: first, in terms of the control over the texts that "a culture takes seriously," and second, in terms of the authority "over the methods of interpretation that establish the meaning of serious."

The "loose canons" of English, to use the term of Henry Gates, Jr. (1992), have yet to acquire this control, because the major paradigms in English studies – literary or linguistic – have not initiated any meaningful discussion of the global presence of English from this perspective – the perspective that the cultural identities and their *interpretations* have also become pluralistic.[6]

In the discourse on English outside the Inner Circle, reference is frequently made to Caliban – both as a symbol and as a metaphor. So now let me bring Caliban into this discussion. I shall decontextualize Caliban from its territorial contexts of colonized human beings in a part of the Western hemisphere. Whatever happened on that island symbolizes what has happened in the colonized world, irrespective of languages and cultures. In all colonial contexts, Caliban is assigned a space by control and submission. Caliban is told:

> I pitied thee,
> Took pains to make thee speak, taught thee each
> hour
> One thing or other: . . .
> I endowed thy purposes
> With words that made them known.

And Caliban answers:

> You taught me language, and my profit on't
> Is I know how to curse. The red plague rid you
> For learning me your language! (*The Tempest*, I.ii)

This metaphor, then, is central to these ongoing, vibrant, provocative, and often acrimonious debates about the canons which are at the linguistic and literary peripheries and continue to be associated with Caliban's curse. The users of such canons, as Salman Rushdie warns us, are:

> kept strictly apart, like squabbling children, or sexually incompatible pandas, or, perhaps, like unstable, fissile materials whose union might cause explosions. (1991: 61)

The debates about these Calibans' voices, their statuses, and the locations of such voices within the canonicity of Englishes has become increasingly articulate. The questions these voices raise in West and East Africa, South and East Asia, in the Philippines, and even in the USA and UK are not unrelated to the broader debate on "opening of the borders" and "loose canons." These are significant linguistic, attitudinal, and ideological questions.

When Levine (1996) addressed this question of canons, he was essentially providing counter-arguments to Bloom (1987) and a string of books by D'Souza (1991), Bennett (1992), and Bernstein (1994), to name just four authors who articulate a need to guard the borders of the Western canon. The concerns of Bloom and D'Souza are not necessarily related to Caliban's uncontrollable tongue, nor are they directly related to my discussion in this chapter. Rather, it is the underlying conceptualizations basic to these two approaches, to canon and canonicity, to language and language "ownership" and identities, that are relevant here.

This, then, takes me to the second part of my title: the ongoing "culture wars" of our times and the agendas for the new millennium. In these culture wars, we see that language – the English language – is now a major issue. It has indeed become a vital weapon for articulating various positions and visions.

The issues in this debate touch us – all of us – as members of the English-using speech communities, irrespective of the variety of world Englishes we use or the speech fellowship of English we identify with. These speech fellow-ships of English cover all the continents, all major cultures, and almost all major geographical groups.

It is in that diverse, cross-cultural sense that English is *international*. I have avoided the term *international language* with English. The term "international" used with "English" is misleading in more than one sense: it signals an *international* English in terms of acceptance, proficiency, functions, norms, pragmatic utility, and creativity. That actually is far from true – that is not the current international functional profile of the English language and never was.[7]

2 Cassandras of English

The English language is now the most sought-after medium for initiating and accelerating global bilingualism and multilingualism. This crossover across borders has brought various strands of hybridity and pluralism to the language. The need, then, is for the reconstruction and rethinking of what such hybridization and pluralism imply with reference to creativity in the language and its functions, and our conceptualization of the presence of English language in world contexts.

And now, at the dawn of a new millennium, this reconstruction of English has taken several forms, and more Cassandras have appeared on the scene, with their messages and visions of the doom and decay of English. This sooth-sayer's enterprise has developed into a variety of genres. The Cassandras' sociolinguistic speculations about English are based on what they see in their ideological crystal balls for now, and beyond the end of the millennium, in which English is vigorously being related exclusively to Western civilization and to the conflicts in the "remaking of world order." In their view, the major concerns about the English language are varied. I will, however, discuss just two such concerns to illustrate my point.

2.1 *Demographic shrinking and decline*

The first concern has to do with what is perceived by some as the demographic shrinking of the English language. This concern is quite contrary to the current statistical profile of the language, and to the increasing worldwide perception that the juggernaut of English is rolling over cultures and languages – both major and minor – across the world. One example of Cassandra's cry about the decline of English is provided by Bailey (1987), who argues that:

popular journalism, and academic inquiry have all conspired to obscure a remarkable basic fact . . . [that] . . . *English, too, is declining in proportional numbers of speakers and in the range of its users.* [Emphasis added]

Bailey's concern for the decline in the numbers of users and the functional range of English is based on five phenomena. These are:

First, the initiatives to "foster multilingualism" in the USA, UK, and Australia;
Second, the efforts – in the USA and internationally – in linking "mother, mother tongue, and motherland" as "persuasive arguments" to declare that languages other than English will better serve *democratic* and *economic* goals" (1987: 6);
Third, the national language policy reversals and reassessments that entail shifts toward languages other than English (e.g., in Malaysia, the Philippines, and Singapore);
Fourth, the "cultural resistance to English in East and West Africa;
And *fifth*, the increasing "pluricentricity of English": that is, the multiple centers in Asia and Africa where the language has developed institutionalized norms (see also Bailey, 1996).

Bailey, of course, is not the first Cassandra of the language and certainly will not be the last. The latest articulation of this view comes from Samuel P. Huntington, a distinguished Harvard political scientist, in his provocative and much-discussed book *The Clash of Civilizations and the Remaking of World Order* (1996a). A more accessible, and somewhat alarming, summary of the book appeared in *Foreign Affairs* (1996b), with the sweet-and-sour title "The West unique, not universal."

The parts that specifically interest me relate to the English language. I do, however, share Huntington's broader concern when he says that:

In recent years Westerners have reassured themselves and irritated others by expounding the notion that the culture of the West is and ought to be the culture of the world. (1996b: 28)

In Huntington's view, as he says, "[t]his conceit manifests itself in two forms. One is the Coca-colonization thesis . . . The other has to do with modernization." And he believes that:

Both these project the image of an emerging homogeneous, universally Western world – and both are to varying degrees misguided, arrogant, false, and dangerous. (p. 28)

Huntington provides the profiles of speakers of major languages (in terms of percentages of the world's population) given in Table 25.1. This profile leads him to two conclusions relevant to English:

First, "that significant declines occurred in the population of people speaking English, French, German, Russian, and Japanese" (1996a: 60);

Second, "that a language foreign to 92 percent of the people in the world cannot be the world's language" (1996a: 60).

Table 25.1 Speakers of major languages (in percentages)

	1958	1970	1980	1992
Arabic	2.7	2.9	3.3	3.5
Bengali	2.7	2.9	3.2	3.2
English	9.8	9.1	8.7	7.6
Hindi	5.2	5.3	5.3	6.4
Mandarin	15.6	16.6	15.8	15.2
Russian	5.5	5.6	6.0	4.9
Spanish	5.0	5.2	5.5	6.1

2.2 *Severing the umbilical cord*

The second concern I will discuss relates to yet another type of perceived decay – the "decay" of the language as it is appropriated by the Anglophone African and Asian countries, who are, as it were, severing their umbilical cords from the Inner Circle, or the original native-English-speaking countries, and thus are making English a culturally pluralistic world language. This appropriation, in the Cassandras' view, colors the language in a variety of ways – linguistic, literary, and ideological – rendering it alien to its occidental "owners." Even worse, they believe a *hybrid English* is becoming institutionalized and recognized as a viable vehicle for African and Asian norms for linguistic innovation and creativity.

Yet another expression of the concern over this phenomenon is an Epilogue entitled "Alice's unvisited" by Felipe Fernández-Armesto (1995). In his peep into Futurology, Fernández-Armesto's regret is that communications have been unable to "homogenize culture." A most "surprising example" of this, according to him, is that of the English language:

which, until recently, was widely hailed or feared as the world medium of the future; in fact, in defiance of the predicted effects of global broadcasting, *the English of the English-speaking world is breaking up into mutually unintelligible tongues, as happened with Latin in the dark ages.* (1995: 730, emphasis added)

This, for Fernández-Armesto, is not a reassuring future, and his pessimistic interpretation of the horoscope of English is that:

Krio, Pidgin, and Negerengels are already unintelligible to speakers of other forms of post-English. The street patois of African-American communities has to be translated for residents of neighbouring streets. The specialized jargon of communication on the Internet is a hieratic code, professed to exclude outsiders. Copy editors and authors on either side of the Atlantic sometimes keenly feel the width of the ocean. (1995: 730–1)

This agony is identical to Bailey's earlier concern when he saw "English at its twilight." The metaphor "twilight" is like a double-edged sword which can be a harbinger of "bright morning" for the English language, or can be frightening and murky to the tower-builders at Babel (1990: 84).[8]

One has to agree, however, with Huntington's (1996b: 62) more forthright and pragmatically correct observation when he says that:

> The people who speak English throughout the world also increasingly speak different Englishes. English is indigenized and takes on local colorations which distinguish it from British or American English and which, at the extreme, make these Englishes almost unintelligible one to the other, as is also the case with varieties of Chinese.

That English has been "indigenized" is certainly true; but that "these Englishes" have, therefore, become functionally "almost unintelligible one to the other" is certainly empirically doubtful (see, e.g., Smith 1992 and later, see Chapter 24 in this volume). In terms of functional and pragmatic uses of the English language, what actually happens is that English is used effectively for "thinking globally," and used, by choice, "to live locally" – thus establishing a pragmatic link between the two identities – global and local.[9]

I do not intend to respond to each point raised by Bailey and Huntington in this chapter. One major argument, however, must be addressed here, and that is Huntington's assertion that a language which is not used by "92 percent of the people" is not entitled to the label *world language*.

There are four problems with Huntington's assumption. The first relates to the total estimated percentage of English users. Recent estimates of users of English worldwide vary from 1 billion to 2 billion. If we take the lower number, then out of the 6.5 billion people in the world (United Nation's report, February 24, 2005), 18 percent use English. If we take the higher number, the percentage of English users jumps to 36 percent. Whichever figure is used, the important point is that the users of English in the Outer and Expanding Circles outnumber the users in the Inner Circle. Huntington does not, for whatever reason, address that vital point of global English. This disparity is an unparalleled linguistic phenomenon with a number of theoretical, methodological, pedagogical, and indeed ideological, implications (see, e.g., Thumboo, 2001).

The second point is that the demographic profile of English across cultures is distinctly different from that of Mandarin, Hindi, and Spanish (see Table 25.1 above) – some of the competing languages listed by Huntington. The English language has developed a unique functional range and unprecedented identities on every continent, both in terms of the functional range of the medium and its societal depth. In India today, an estimated figure for

Table 25.2 Functional domains of English

Function	Inner Circle	Outer Circle	Expanding Circle
Access Code	+	+	+
Advertising	+	+	+
Corporate trade	+	+	+
Development	+	+	+
Government	+	+	
Linguistic impact	+	+	+
Literary creativity	+	+	+
Literary renaissance	+	+	+
News broadcasting	+	+	+
Newspapers	+	+	+
Scientific higher education	+	+	+
Scientific research	+	+	+
Social interaction	+	+	+

English users is about 333 million, and there are over 200 million students enrolled in English programs in China.[10] It is a reality that the sun has already set on the Empire but does not set on the users of English.

The third point is that Huntington and Bailey – to name just two commentators – do not make a distinction between the comparative functional domains of languages and their mere numbers of speakers: They do not rank languages either in terms of their *range* of functions (what one can do with a language) or in terms of their social *penetration* (how deep the language use is in the social hierarchy), particularly in what are generally labeled "non-native" contexts of the English language.

The functional domains of English across the Three Circles are as in Table 25.2: as mentioned earlier, the Inner Circle represents countries such as the US, Britain, and Australia, where English is widely used as a first language; the Outer Circle represents countries such as India, Nigeria, and Singapore where English is institutionalized; and the Expanding Circle represents countries such as China, Japan, and Korea where the diffusion of English has come about relatively recently; however, the social acceptability and social penetration of English is fast increasing (see, e.g., Kachru, 1992, 2005).

Now, if we compare this overwhelming range and depth with other languages of wider communication, e.g., Mandarin, Hindi, Spanish, Arabic, and so on, it will be readily apparent that no other language comes close to English in number of domains of use or in penetration to various social levels. This is clearly reflected in varieties that have developed within a variety, as in Singapore, Nigeria, and India, to give just three examples.

The fourth point relates to the life of English in the post-imperial period. Bailey, for example, says that in Malaysia, the Philippines, and Singapore, there are language policy *reassessments* toward languages other than English. This statement is only partially correct. In fact, the direction of the reassessments are in favor of English. In Malaysia in the 1990s, for example, the reversal of the national pro-Bahasa-Malaysia language policy toward favoring English indicates "compromise over its cultural convictions" (*The Economist*, January 15, 1994):

> "There would have been riots over this ten years ago," says Rustum Sani, a leading member of the pro-Bahasa lobby . . . Dr. Mahathir, ever the pragmatist, has said *that English is necessary if the country is to stay competitive.* [Emphasis added]

Malaysia's senior educator, Asmah Haji Omar, puts this pragmatism in the right cultural context when she says:

> Attitudes toward English have changed most significantly among the Malays. English is looked at *as an entity which can be separated from English culture.* This is evident in the urging *"to learn English but not to ape the Western [meaning Anglo-American] culture."* (Omar, 1996: 532, emphasis added)

In the Republic of Singapore, English always had the status of a dominant language. Now English is gradually being elevated to the status of *first* language by the younger generation. They do not hesitate to consider English their "mother tongue" (see Kachru, 2005: 239–343).

In the Philippines, the debate about English is also vibrant. A venerable English writer of the Philippines, Francisco Sionil José, says that "English has not colonized us but we have colonized the language," by using it as an exponent of the Philippine culture. There is a new revival, and a fresh awakening, about the use of a liberated English in the Philippines (see Bautista, 1997 [1996] and Bautista and Bolton, 2004).

The message here is that statistics and the numerical profiles provide some indicators about *visible* language and educational policies but tell us almost nothing about what have been called *invisible* policies, about attitudes, and about identities.[11] The invisible trade in and spread of the English language is extensive and has developed into a multi-billion-dollar industry, under the characterization of "the ELT Empire" (Butler, 1996), ELT meaning "English Language Teaching."

3   Medium (*Mādhyama*) vs. Message (*Mantra*)

In the perceptions outlined above there is an underlying concern about Caliban's linguistic curse: the way Caliban contextualizes and recreates the medium. In its new incarnations, English has become a repertoire of culturally specific African and Asian messages (*mantras*). It is true that this distinction has existed from the pre-imperial period. But now, in the post-imperial period, it is being articulated more vigorously.

The pluralism of the message is partly indicative of crossovers from what is perceived as the "center" of English. It is with reference to the center that the peripheries traditionally were defined. Formation of pluralism is a shift, then, from the Judeo-Christian and Western identities of the English language toward its African, Asian, and African American visions. In these multiple identities of the language, the pluralism of world Englishes – the *mādhyama*, the medium – is shared by us, all of us, as members of the world Englishes community. The *mantras*, the messages and discourses, represent multiple identities and contexts and visions. The *mantras* are diverse, cross-cultural, and represent a wide range of conventions. It is precisely in this sense that the medium has indeed gained international diffusion; it has broken the traditional boundaries associated with the language.

When we use epithets such as *global, international,* and *universal* with English, we are not talking of homogeneity and uniformity. We should not. The messages have to be learnt, acquired, absorbed, and appreciated within the appropriate cultural contexts of the *mantras*. The medium provides a variety of shifting cultural "grids" through which users gain access to the multiple canons of the language: American, British, West African, East African, South Asian, East Asian, and so on.[12]

4   Exponents of Multiple Canonicity

The multiple canonicity of world Englishes manifests itself in many subtle ways: formal and attitudinal, one overlapping with the other, and in turn, each contributing to distinct canons with one shared thread – that of the medium (*mantra*). The divergence and crossovers of these varieties of English are of the following types:

1   *identification specific to a variety* (e.g., Nigerian English, Singaporean English);
2   *acculturation of the variety* (e.g., reflection of sociocultural, religious, and interactional contexts);
3   *institutionalization of discourse strategies, speech acts, and genres*;
4   *recontextualization of icons of identity* (e.g., relating creativity to local literary and cultural traditions (*paramparā*); and
5   *alteration of textual texture* (e.g., by embedding devices of "mixing" etc.).

In these shifts and crossovers, the boundaries of the center, as embodied in the language, are permeable. The periphery increasingly comes into the foreground.

These crossovers result in a reconstruction of the language in "accord with our individual ecosystems," as Edwin Thumboo sees it (1985). The attempt here is to establish a relationship between formal characteristics of a text

– that is, its linguistic texture – and the contexts in which the language that constitutes that text functions.

Such crossovers entail recognition of three realities:

> *First*, that the medium is shared by two distinct types of speech communities: those that perceive themselves as monolingual and those that are *multilingual* and *multicultural* (see section 8 below);
> *Second*, that there is a long tradition of distinct literary and/or oral traditions and mythologies associated with these communities; and
> *Third*, that they represent distinct repertoires of stylistic and literary creativity.

5   Toward a Historiography of Canonicity

The historiography of canonicity of Englishes in Asia and Africa, indeed in all the peripheries, has yet to be written in any serious sense. The peripheries have traditionally been ignored by literary historians. A recent example of such neglect is *The Cambridge History of the English Language, vol. 5*, devoted to "English in Britain and Overseas." The planning of the volume, we are told, began in 1984, and the volume was ultimately published in 1994. The introduction tells us that:

> It was the notable lack of professional scholarship at the time on the English of African countries such as Kenya, Nigeria, Tanzania, and so on . . . that led to the exclusion of these varieties [from the volume]. (Burchfield, 1994: 4)

The editor, the late Robert Burchfield, patronizingly assures us that "their turn will come one day . . ." It is worth noting, however, that the volume edited by Bailey and Görlach, published over a decade earlier, in 1982, found no such "lack of professional scholarship." Bailey and Görlach were able to include surveys on English in East, West, and South Africa. In the same year, in putting together an edited volume, *The Other Tongue*, I had no problem in obtaining a scholarly survey of the Africanization of English and another study on Kenyan English. The moral seems to be "seek and you will find." In contrast, the don't-look-and-you-won't-find attitude is also evident in many scholarly books meant to assess "the state of the English language."

One such book in particular comes to mind, perhaps because of its title: *The State of the Language*. This book, edited by Leonard Michaels and Christopher Ricks, was published in 1988, and had a 1990 edition by the same editors with the names reversed. The latest edition, the jacket tells us, provides *new observations, objections, angers, bemusements, hilarities, perplexities, revelations, prognostications, and warnings for the 1990s*. The learned editors apparently, however, did not find any aspects of English language use in Africa and Asia which would characterize the state of the English language or literature in these ways.

These two volumes, Burchfield (1994) and Michaels and Ricks (1988/1990), are the results of projects initiated by the English-Speaking Union, San Francisco, and the publication of the 1990 volume was, we are told, "supported by a generous grant from the George Frederick Jewett Foundation." The omissions made in these volumes are clear indicators of the persistent attitudes toward Caliban's creativity (see also Kachru, 1992: 1–15, particularly pp. 2–3, and Kachru, 2005, chapters 7 and 8).

The stirrings for canonicity in world Englishes have a long history. These issues of identity and innovations in creativity are not extensions of the "liberation theology" of the 1960s, resulting in articulation of "liberation linguistics," as is sometimes argued in the literature.[13] Nor did this institutionalization begin with the "Rushdiesque language" or "Rushdie's technique." In reality, the "hybrid form" and "radical linguistic operation" (Langeland, 1996: 16) associated with Rushdie follows in the tradition of much earlier linguistic innovations and creativity in African and Asian English.

The earliest conceptualizations of indigenization go back to the 1870s. Later reformulations, and more specific characterizations, began after the 1930s. We see characterizations of African Englishes in the writings of Nigeria's Chinua Achebe, T. M. Aluko, Buchi Emecheta, Amos Tutuola, and, of course, Wole Soyinka; in Kenya's Ngũgĩ wa Thiong'o; in Somali's Nurudin Farah; in India's Raja Rao, Mulk Raj Anand, Anita Desai, and R. K. Narayan; and in a long list of writers from Malaysia, the Philippines, Singapore, and Sri Lanka.

In South Asia, the first well-articulated conceptualization of such a crossover – linguistic and contextual – was presented in 1937 (published in 1938) by Raja Rao, in his novel *Kanthapura*. However, Rao's was not the first attempt to bring the South Asian voice to English. In a novel entitled *Bengal Peasant Life*, published in 1874, Lal Behari Day almost apologetically presents the dilemma in contextualizing English in Bengal:

> Gentle reader, allow me here to make one remark. You perceive that Badan and Alanga speak better English than most uneducated English peasants; they speak almost like educated ladies and gentlemen, without any provincialisms. But how could I have avoided this defect in my history? If I had translated their talk into the Somersetshire or the Yorkshire dialect, I should have turned them into English, and not Bengali, peasants. You will, therefore, please overlook this grave though unavoidable fault in this authentic narrative. (cited in B. Kachru, 1982: 368)

6 Approaches for Redefining Identities

The shift from the norms of the center has been slow and gradual. And the approaches for establishing linguistic and literary identities adopted by each writer, in each region, and each linguistic group are not identical. One sees several major approaches for establishing local literary and linguistic identities for English.

6.1   Ritualistic and metaphysical

In this approach, there is no Caliban's sting, no Caliban saying "You taught me language, and my profit on 't / Is I know how to curse."

In *Kanthapura*, Rao provides five perspectives to authenticate the crossover of English in the South Asian context in terms of the following:

1   the relationship between the medium (*mādhyama*) and the message (*mantra*);
2   reconceptualization of the contextual appropriateness of English as a medium of creativity;
3   the relevance of hybridity and creative vision and innovation;
4   the relevance of language variety, linguistic appropriateness, and identity (Thumboo, 1970);
5   stylistic transcreation, cultural discourse, and their relationships with local *paramparā* (Kachru, 1998c: 66–7).

In his often-cited "Author's Foreword" of just 461 words, Rao did not sing the song of linguistic liberation for his innovative and nativized style or his Kannadization and Sanskritization of English. He argued on the basis of convergence, cohesion, and assimilation of the language, and thus brought English within the mainstream of India's linguistic and cultural traditions – *paramparā*. And in a later paper, "The Caste of English" (Rao, 1978), as I have discussed elsewhere (Kachru, 1998c), Rao placed English on the same elevated pedestal of Truth on which Indians have traditionally kept Sanskrit ("The Perfected Language") for thousands of years. He said that:

> Truth ... is not the monopoly of the Sanskrit language. Truth can use any language ... and so long as the English language is universal, it will always remain Indian. (1978: 421)

Rao brings to the discourse on English a certain mystique; he even involves the gods in his approach to English:

> We in India welcome everything outlandish and offer it the gods, who taste it, masticate it, and give it back to us as prasadam ['offerings to the gods returned to man sanctified']. When our English will have come to that maturity it might still achieve its own nationhood. Till then it will be like Anglo-Norman, neither French nor English, an historical incident in the growth of culture. (1988: 95)

And Rao responds to India's linguistic chauvinism by declaring English "of our caste, our creed and of our tradition." This is a subtle and sensitive way of including the language within the canon. His statement has a symbolic meaning too; it is like performing the initiation, the *samskāra*, of the English language, and putting around it the symbol of initiation, "the sacred thread."

6.2   Strategic linguistic weapon

This second approach to English views the colonial medium as a strategic "linguistic blade," to be used as an effective weapon and turned back on the colonizer. The most passionate and skillful articulation of this position is by Wole Soyinka. Soyinka recognizes that in the sociolinguistic context of Africa, English plays "unaccustomed roles" as "a new medium of communication," in "a new organic series of mores, social goals, relationships, universal aware-ness – all of which go into the creation of a new culture." And what did the African people do with this colonial weapon? Soyinka answers:

> Black people twisted the linguistic blade in the hands of the traditional cultural castrator and carved new concepts onto the flesh of white supremacy. (Soyinka, 1988: 88)

The result, says Soyinka, is: "the conversion of the enslaving medium into an insurgent weapon." The medium now has a message: it is an *African* message. Thus, on the African continent, the English language was put to a "revolution-ary use" by writers such as Nkrumah and Nelson Mandela. And, Soyinka continues (1988: 88):

> The customary linguistic usage was rejected outright and a new, raw, urgent and revolutionary syntax was given to this medium which had become the greatest single repository of racist concepts.

This is a different path than the one adopted by Ngũgĩ, who considers English a racist language and abandons the medium (see Ngũgĩ, 1981).

6.3   Contrastive pragmatism

The third approach to English was lucidly articulated by Chinua Achebe in 1965. Achebe provides a cogent argument for the stylistic Africanization and acculturation of English by explaining how he approaches the use of English in a contrastive way. He compares the *Africanized* and *non-Africanized* versions of creativity and then, contrasting the two styles, he argues (Achebe, 1965):

> the material is the same. But the form of the one is in character [of the Africanized style], the other is not. It is largely a matter of instinct but judgment comes into it too.

And Okara (1964: 137) conveys an identical message when he says that:

> from a word, a group of words, a sentence and even a name in any African language one can glean the social norms, attitudes and values of a people.

Despite their different attitudes and positions on the acculturation of English, these three approaches converge in their underlying unity. In all these approaches, one fundamental motive is shared, and that is to move away from the Western canons of power and control – away from the putative center – and design yet another path for creativity in Asian and African English, and to use the medium for their *mantra*.

The tradition of such bilinguals' creativity is not new in multilingual cultures. Crossovers to another medium have been an integral part of such societies, for example in literary creativity and in discourses on philosophic, epistemological, and religious topics. There has always been yet another language, yet another code, yet another style for such universes of discourse: Sanskrit for three thousand or more years and Persian after the thirteenth century in South Asia, and the High varieties of dominant regional languages such as Arabic, Greek, Tamil, Bengali, and Kashmiri. The newness is in the extension of this tradition of creativity to a Western medium – a medium that has recent colonial associations and presumed external centers of power and control. All these approaches are means of working toward redefining the medium and contextualizing English in yet other sociocultural and linguistic contexts.

The metaphor of Caliban applies to other voices in English – not only to African and Asian and to other canonicities and formal experimentation. When Henry Louis Gates, Jr. uses the term "loose canons" he is actually talking of such voices, such canons and of multiple identities of English. Gates warns us:

> Cultural pluralism is not, of course, everyone's cup of tea. Vulgar cultural nationalists – like Allan Bloom or Leonard Jeffries – correctly identify it as the enemy. (1992: xvi)

And he continues:

> These polemicists thrive on absolute partitions: between "civilization" and "barbarism," between "black" and "white," between a thousand versions of Us and Them.

But for us – some of us – Gates is reassuring when he says that "[the polemicists] are whistling in the wind."

7   "The Outward Sign of Inward Fires"

One might then ask what, in this context, are the outward signs of these "inward fires"? The liberated creativity of English in Africa and Asia has resulted in two major responses from the West.

One response views this creativity and stirrings for canonicity in ideological terms as "liberation linguistics" — as loaded "liberation theology," as mentioned above.[14] The second response considers such creativity to be an indicator of what may be called "de-homogenizing creativity" – creativity that is not contributing to "homogenizing cultures." To Fernández-Armesto (1995: 730):[15]

> communications seem to be unable to homogenize culture; the most surprising example is that of the English language, which, until recently, was widely hailed or feared as the world medium of the future.

In Fernández-Armesto's view there is only one space for English, and only one representation – one cultural definition – of the medium (see also Fishman, 1998–9).

That is not all. This creativity and articulation of cultural, linguistic, and regional identities is additionally viewed as a *"managed and revolutionary shift from English to something more local"* (Bailey, 1990: 86, emphasis added). It is presented almost as a linguistic conspiracy. In this context, Bailey gives the example of Emeka Oreke-Ezigbo, who defends Nigerian Pidgin as:

> a partial, viable, flexible language distilled in the alembic of our native sensibility and human experience. (Bailey, 1990: 86)

This discussion reminds one of the recent controversy over Ebonics in the USA, which soon ceased to be a sociolinguistic issue and became almost entirely a political issue. In Bailey's view, the decay of English has yet another dimension: he makes a distinction between English for "outward-looking aspirations" and English for "inward-looking patriotism." And he mourns that "English as a purely mental instrument of human expression is dying" (1990: 86). The concern is about local identities of English – the African, the Asian, and so on – and its acculturation. These are, then, some of the "language-coming-apart" hypotheses.

The constructs of literary creativity in world Englishes in the Outer Circle (particularly in Africa and Asia) in terms of "de-homogenizing creativity" and "managed and revolutionary shift" have not quite abated.

In distinguishing between "thoroughly developed countries" and "emergent economies," Randolph Quirk provides yet another defining construct against what he earlier termed "liberation linguistics" (see Kachru, 1994a). In his paper "Getting their clause into English" (2001), Quirk's concern is for utilitarian functions of English in global contexts so that it can provide "a major service to all countries on earth" (p. 7). In his view:

> it is the people in this vast third world whose need for English is the greatest. Their claws must be firmly in it for all the reasons that obtain in rich countries.

And he elaborates on this assertion that:

> To this end, their medium must be largely standard English – the "largely" mitigated by *a judicious tincture of the exotic*: enough (but only just enough) to

engage interest abroad: thus, for example, *mammachi, papachi, (Ammu) kutty* in Arundhati Roy's Booker-Prize novel of 1997. (Quirk, 2001: 7; emphasis added)

What Quirk proposes for the Outer and Expanding Circles to meet these functional ends is "an English as nearly as possible indistinguishable from that in the rest of English-speaking commerce and officialdom" (p. 7). In 2003, Quirk further elaborates the concept of Standard English when he says:

> What is new in this late-twentieth-century movement is the danger, as some see it, of an erosion of the very idea of a standard language uniting a polity. This is of particular concern insofar as it applies to English-speaking countries, because of the world-wide reliance upon English and the concomitant assumption that English has reliable and universally recognized standards. (pp. 13–14)

Concluding his paper, Quirk emphasizes that:

> if English (or any other language) is to achieve the wide currency, the expressive effectiveness, the indisputable comprehensibility, and anything like the sheer staying power of Latin, it is the duty of those of us in linguistics to do more than just stand back and observe. *No one, after all, is better placed to mount rational argument (strongly laced with realpolitik) toward the goal of ensuring that a powerful Standard English is taught and sustained world-wide.* (p. 15, emphasis added)

And, for yet another perspective on standards and norms of world Englishes, see Evelyn Nien-Ming Ch'ien's *Weird English* (2004), for a voice not identical to that of Quirk. The *weirdization* of English, Ch'ien tells us, is characterized by the following features (2004: 11):

1   Weirding deprives English of its dominance and allows other languages to enjoy the same status.
2   Weird English expresses aesthetic adventurousness at the price of sacrificing rules.
3   Weird English is derived from non-native English.
4   The rhythms and structure of orthodox English alone are not enough to express the diasporic cultures that speak it.

In this paradigm we have yet another construct of Englishes for this ongoing debate.

8   The War of Cultures and Canons

What I have said above provides just an overview of the major strands of the ideological and power-related issues that are central to the debates on culture wars. But this is just the tip of the proverbial iceberg of world Englishes. There are two other issues that deserve our attention and provide some explanation for current attitudes toward Caliban's creativity.

The first issue concerns our sociolinguistic conceptualization of the architects of the canon; our view of who comprises the speech community of English, the strands that constitute the canon, and our notion of who can initiate changes and modifications in the canon. In other words, the questions are: What establishes the foundation of the canon? And who are the makers of the canon? It is by answering these questions in certain ways that we establish the territory of canonicity.

The second issue, of course, relates to the economics of English – English as a commodity, with immense value in the international language market. Those with *ownership* of the commodity want to safeguard it and preserve it in terms of pounds and dollars.

The sociolinguistic issues relate to the linguistic, literary, and attitudinal sacred cows in the culture of the speech community. These attitudes ultimately shape our beliefs about what constitutes a harmonious, cohesive, integrated, and motivated speech community. In the case of English, these attitudes determine how we view multilinguality or biliguality, individual and social bilingualism, and, indeed, multilinguals' literary creativity (see Kachru, 1988).

When we talk of creativity in world Englishes, particularly in Asia and Africa, we are talking of the world of creativity, in which our concepts are essentially based on various types and levels of hybridity, both linguistic and cultural. We are talking of the type of hybridity in which African and Asian interculturalism and linguistic innovations and experimentation play a vital role. This type of hybridity is in conflict with the traditional conceptualization of canons. There seem to be three reasons for being suspicious of the acquired hybridity of world Englishes. The first reason relates to the *type of diversity* introduced in the text by, for example, Asian and African writers. The second reason is the traditional *negative attitudes* toward bilingualism and pluralism in Western societies. The third reason, as Lefevere (1990: 24) says, is the "monolingualization of literary history by Romantic historiographers."

This negativity toward diversity and bilingualism has been abundantly expressed in earlier research on bilingualism, specifically in the USA, the UK, and Australia.[16] These negative views come from a wide range of social scientists and humanists, and they are expressed in several ways, including assertions such as:

1 that pluralistic societies are complex and their descriptions present explanatory complexities;
2 that homogeneity and uniformity need to be emphasized in linguistic and cultural descriptions;
3 that diversity – social, cultural, and linguistic – essentially leads to chaos;
4 that bilingual groups are marginal and problem generating;
5 that bi/multilingualism retards economic growth; and
6 that bilingualism has serious negative implications for educational progress.

This is indeed a long list of significant problem areas, which have raised questions that have resulted in acrimonious debates in the USA and elsewhere. I will not go into that digression. One must, however, ask: what are the implications of such perceptions regarding bilingualism for our attitudes toward bilinguals' creativity? Foster (1970: 7) argues that:

> we have all been brought up to believe that each language has its mystery and its soul, and that these are very sacred things, in whose name indeed much blood has been shed.

Lefevere (1990) brings to this discussion yet another perspective, that of the *monolingualization* of literary history as an ideological and identity tool of the state. He points out the emphasis by Romantic historiographers on "creating 'national' literatures preferably as *uncontaminated as possible by foreign influences*" (1990: 24; emphasis added).

In this conceptualization, then, African and Asian creativity is not only essentially "contaminated" and contextually "foreign" to the perceived tradition of the "Western canon," it is also threatening to that canon. And equally crucial to the debates on multilinguals' creativity is the generally held view that literary creativity is primarily carried out in one's *mother* tongue – and creativity in another language is an exception, in the sense that it is contrary to the norm. This view is not uncommon in the scholarly community. Let me give here two examples of such views: one from a social scientist, Edward Shills, and the second from a linguist, David Crystal. Shills (1988: 560) believes that:

> The national language of literary creation is almost always the language of the author's original nationality.

The exceptions Shills thinks of are:

> Conrad, and, at a lower level, Nabokov and Koestler, Apollonaire and Julien Green.

Even if we accept his assessment of Nabokov and the others, it is clear that Shills did not look beyond Europe. If he had, he might have changed his mind. And Crystal (cited in Paikeday, 1985: 66–7), says that:

> it is quite unclear what to make of cases like Nabokov and the others George Steiner (*Extraterritorial Papers*) talks about as having no native language.

Crystal obviously considers these writers to be "marginal cases."

The assertions of Shills and Crystal clearly reflect attitudes about multilinguals' creativity. The distinction Crystal makes between a *native* and a *non-native* speaker is based on "the fact that there are some topics that they [non-native speakers] are 'comfortable' discussing in their first language.

'I couldn't make love in English,' said one man [a non-native speaker] to me."
In reality, the facts are quite the opposite; creativity in English is no exception
to multilingual language-users' creativity in many other languages. The list of
writers and their languages is long, and such resourcefulness has an impressive tradition in South and East Asia, in East and West Africa, and, indeed,
also in Europe.

In linguistic paradigms, too, bilinguality and bilinguals' creativity are
still on the periphery. For example, describing the grammars of bilinguals
is considered extremely complicated; the emphasis is on homogeneity and
uniformity. In 1950, Haugen articulated this concern when, discussing bilingualism in general and the bilingual as a person, he said:

> the subject was for many years markedly neglected in this country [the USA],
> and we might say that both popularly and scientifically, bilingualism was in
> disrepute. Just as the bilingual himself often was a marginal personality, so the
> study of his behavior was a marginal scientific pursuit. (p. 272)

It is true that in recent years we as professionals have begun to ask questions and propose solutions for the complex issues concerning the forms and
functions of world Englishes, and have done exciting research on various
aspects of bi- and multilingualism. However, we are still hesitant to cross the
threshold and face the complexities of multilinguals' language behavior and
the impact of that data on our hypotheses and our attitudes. We are reluctant
to modify, reformulate, revisit, and reassess our favorite paradigms. The result
of this attitude disinclination is the marginalization of the multiple voices
heard in world Englishes.

9 Conclusion

What we see, then, is that in creativity in world Englishes we have "the interplay of diverse voices," as Dissanayake puts it (1989: xvi). We have multiple
cultural visions, discourses, and linguistic experimentation. We have an
unparalleled multicultural resource through one medium with many *mantras*;
we have to ask ourselves how to make use of it. And this concern raises
important theoretical, methodological, ideological and pedagogical questions.

In looking at the global contexts of world Englishes, we need a perspective
of "variousness," as I have argued in the context of the mythology associated
with the teaching of English (see Kachru, 1995). Perhaps Geertz (1983: 234) has
a message for us when, addressing anthropological researchers, he says that
"the world is a various place" in many ways:

> various between lawyers and anthropologists, various between Muslims and
> Hindus, various between little tradition and great, various between colonial thens
> and nationalist nows . . .

And, Geertz continues:

> much is to be gained, scientifically and otherwise, by confronting that grand actuality rather than wishing it away in a haze of forceless generalities and false comforts.

The need now is to recognize the "variousness" of world Englishes and ask the right questions of the Speaking Tree. It means seeking answers for the "curatorial" and "normative" functions of canon, to use Altieri's words (1990: 33). These are the types of questions we must ask if we do not want to continue walling up the world visions – including African and Asian – in this unique cultural and linguistic resource of our times, world Englishes.

As a closing word, I cannot resist the impulse to quote once more from the eminent American linguist James H. Sledd (1914–2003), who in one of his last publications wrote (Sledd, 1993: 275, cited in Kachru, 2005: 256):

> If English, rightly or wrongly, is to remain preeminent among world languages, it has to be various. It exists in the minds of its multifarious users, and its varieties mark differences among people and their multifarious purposes. Variation in English remains, and has indeed increased, despite centuries of effort to stamp it out. Its longevity results from its utility.

That, as I have concluded elsewhere, is indeed the heart of the matter.

See also Chapters 15, WORLD ENGLISHES TODAY; 17, VARIETIES OF WORLD ENGLISHES; 20, WRITTEN LANGUAGE, STANDARD LANGUAGE, GLOBAL LANGUAGE; 21, SPEAKING AND WRITING IN WORLD ENGLISHES; 22, GENRES AND STYLES IN WORLD ENGLISHES; 23, LITERARY CREATIVITY IN WORLD ENGLISHES; 29, COLONIAL/POSTCOLONIAL CRITIQUE: THE CHALLENGE FROM WORLD ENGLISHES; 30, CULTURAL STUDIES AND DISCURSIVE CONSTRUCTIONS OF WORLD ENGLISHES; 31, WORLD ENGLISHES AND GENDER IDENTITIES.

NOTES

This chapter is a substantially updated and expanded version of several points discussed in some of my earlier papers, particularly Kachru (1994a, 1994b, 1996a, 1996b). A version of this chapter has appeared in *Ariels: Departures and Returns: Essays for Edwin Thumboo*, edited by Tong Chee Klong, Anne Pakir, Ban Kah Choon, and Robbie B. H. Goh (2001), Singapore: Oxford University Press. An earlier version was presented as a Sir Edward Youde Memorial Fund Lecture on November 30, 1998, at the University of Hong Kong.

1 See Kachru (1994b).
2 See, e.g., Fettes (1991), Fishman et al. (1996), Kachru (1996a and 1998a), and Pütz (1995).
3 For a state-of-the-art survey of the history and conceptualization of world Englishes, and a selected list

of annotated references on this topic for research and teaching, see Kachru (1998a).

4   See, for example, Bautista (1997 [1996]) for the Asianization of English. See also Burchfield (1994), Butler (1996), Cheshire (1991), and Kachru (1992) for extensive references on cross-cultural and cross-linguistic functions and identities of world Englishes.

5   It is, of course, an oversimplification to use cover terms in combining the Judeo-Christian traditions, and to claim that Western tradition is monolithic and all Western countries share one tradition. Taken literally or strictly, that would be a broad and uninsightful generalization.

6   See, e.g., Kachru (1996a) for a detailed discussion and relevant references.

7   I believe that the much-abused term "lingua franca" is also misleading – and functionally inappropriate – when used for the sociolinguistic profile of world Englishes. I have discussed this point in Kachru (1996b).

8   I have responded to some of these issues in Kachru (1996a).

9   This observation has been made by Indian critic and educator C. D. Narasimhaiah (1991: viii).

10   My earlier figure of over 60 million users of English in India is already out of date. A survey by *India Today*, Delhi (August 18, 1997), shows that "contrary to the [Indian] census myth that English is the language of a microscopic minority, the poll indicates that almost one in every three Indians claims to understand English, although less than 20 percent are confident of speaking it."

The estimated population of India is 1 billion: There are, then, almost 333 million Indians who understand English, and almost 200 million who have some spoken competence in the language. India's English-using speech community is estimated to be numerically equal to the total population of the USA, the UK, and Canada. The total English-using populations of India and China add up to 533 million. For China, see Yong and Campbell (1995); see also Kachru (1998b).

11   For example, by Edwin Thumboo and Anne Pakir in the context of Singapore.

12   For further discussion of this topic, see papers in Hardgrave (1998).

13   See discussion in Kachru (1998c).

14   For different perspectives on the major issues and attitudes, particularly on "liberation linguistics," see papers in Tickoo (1991, especially section 3).

15   Note, for example, Fishman's concern about "strong regional *idiosyncrasies* that English acquires" (emphasis added) in contexts where English is used as an additional language.

16   See Kachru (1996a), especially section 2, "Paradigm Myopia" (p. 242).

REFERENCES

Achebe, Chinua (1965) English and the African writer. *Transition*, 4(18), 27–30. Also in Ali A. Mazrui (1975) *The Political Sociology of the English Language: An African Perspective*. The Hague: Mouton, pp. 216–23.

Altieri, James (1990) *Canons and Consequences: Reflections on the Ethical*

Force of Imaginative Ideals. Evanston, IL: Northwestern University Press.

Bailey, Richard W. (1987) Resistance to the spread of English. Paper presented at Georgetown University Round Table, March 1987 (manuscript).

Bailey, Richard W. (1990) English at its twilight. In *The State of the Language*. Edited by Christopher Ricks and Leonard Michaels. Berkeley: University of California Press, pp. 83–94.

Bailey, Richard W. (1996) Attitudes toward English: The future of English in South Asia. In *South Asian English: Structure, Use, and Users*. Edited by Robert J. Baumgardner. Urbana, IL: University of Illinois Press, pp. 40–52.

Bailey, Richard W. and Görlach, Manfred (eds.) (1982) *English as a World Language*. Ann Arbor, MI: University of Michigan Press.

Bautista, Ma. Lourdes S. (ed.) (1997 [1996]) *English Is an Asian Language: The Philippine Context*. Sydney: Macquarie Library.

Bautista, Ma. Lourdes S. and Bolton, Kingsley (2004) (eds.) *World Englishes*, **23**(1), special issue: Philippine English: Tensions and Transitions.

Bennett, William J. (1992) *The De-valuing of America: The Fight for Our Culture and Our Children*. New York: Summit Books.

Bernstein, Richard (1994) *Dictatorship of Virtue: Multiculturalism, and the Battle for American Future*. New York: A. A. Knopf.

Bloom, Allan (1987) *The Closing of the American Mind: How Higher Education has Failed Democracy and Impoverished the Souls of Today's Students*. New York: Simon and Schuster.

Burchfield, Robert (ed.) (1994) *The Cambridge History of the English Language, vol. 5: English in Britain and Overseas: Origins and Developments*. Cambridge: Cambridge University Press.

Butler, Susan (1996) World Englishes in an Asian context: The Macquarie dictionary project. *World Englishes*, **15**(3), 347–57.

Cheshire, Jenny (ed.) (1991) *English around the World: Sociolinguistic Perspectives*. Cambridge: Cambridge University Press.

Ch'ien, Evelyn Nien-Ming (2004) *Weird English*. Cambridge, MA: Harvard University Press.

Crystal, David (1997) *English as a Global Language*. Cambridge: Cambridge University Press.

Day, Lal Behari (1874 [1913]) *Bengal Peasant Life*. 2nd edition. London: Macmillan.

Dissanayake, Wimal (1989) Introduction: Literary history, narrative, and culture. Perplexities of meaning. In *Literary History, Narrative and Culture: Selected Conference Papers*. Edited by Wimal Dissanayake and Steven Bradbury. Honolulu: University of Hawai'i Press.

D'souza, Dinesh (1991) *Illiberal Education: The Politics of Race and Sex on Campus*. New York: The Free Press.

Fernández-Armesto, Felipe (1995) *Millennium: A History of the Last Thousand Years*. New York: Scribner.

Fettes, Mark (1991) Europe's Babylon: Towards a single European language? *History of European Ideas*, **13**, 201–13.

Fishman, Joshua A. (1998–9) The new linguistic order. *Foreign Policy*, **113**, 26–40.

Fishman, Joshua A., Conrad, Andrew W., and Rubal-Lopez, Alma (eds.) (1996) *Post-Imperial English: Status Change in Former British and American Colonies, 1940–1990*. Berlin/New York: Mouton de Gruyter.

Foster, Leonard (1970) *The Poet's Tongues: Multilingualism in Literature* (The de Carle Lectures at the University of Otago 1968). Cambridge: Cambridge University Press (in association with University of Otago Press).

Gates, Henry Louis, Jr. (1992) *Loose Canons: Notes on the Culture Wars.* New York: Oxford University Press.

Geertz, Clifford (1983) *Local Knowledge.* New York: Basic Books.

Hardgrave, Robert L., Jr. (ed.) (1998) *Word as Mantra: The Art of Raja Rao.* New Delhi: Katha.

Haugen, Einar (1950) Problems of bilingualism. *Lingua*, **2–3**, 271–90.

Huntington, Samuel P. (1996a) *The Clash of Civilizations and the Remaking of World Order.* New York: Simon and Schuster.

Huntington, Samuel P. (1996b) The West unique, not universal. *Foreign Affairs*, **75**(6), 28–46.

Kachru, Braj B. (1982) South Asian English. In *English as a World Language*. Edited by Richard W. Bailey and Manfred Görlach. Ann Arbor: University of Michigan Press, pp. 353–83.

Kachru, Braj B. (1986) *The Alchemy of English: The Spread, Functions, and Models of Non-native Englishes.* Oxford: Pergamon Press. Reprinted 1990, University of Illinois Press.

Kachru, Braj B. (1988) The spread of English and sacred linguistic cows. In *Language Spread and Language Policy: Issues, Implications and Case Studies*. Edited by Peter H. Lowenberg. Georgetown University Round Table on Language and Linguistics 1987. Washington, DC: Georgetown University Press, pp. 207–28.

Kachru, Braj B. (ed.) (1992) *The Other Tongue: English across Cultures.* Urbana, IL: University of Illinois Press.

Kachru, Braj B. (1994a) Liberation linguistics and the Quirk concern. *English Today*, **25**, 7(1), 3–13.

Kachru, Braj B. (1994b) The speaking tree: A medium of plural canons. In *Educational Linguistics, Cross-cultural Communication, and Global Independence*. Edited by James Alatis. Georgetown University Round Table on Language and Linguistics 1994. Washington, DC: Georgetown University Press, pp. 6–22.

Kachru, Braj B. (1995) Teaching world Englishes without myths. In *INTELEC '94: International English Language Education Conference, National and International Challenges and Responses*. Edited by Saran K. Gill. et al. Bangi, Malaysia: Pusat Bahasa Universiti Kebangsaan, pp. 1–19.

Kachru, Braj B. (1996a) The paradigms of marginality. *World Englishes*, **15**(3), 241–55.

Kachru, Braj B. (1996b) English as lingua franca. In *Contact Linguistics: An International Handbook of Contemporary Research*. Edited by Hans Goebl, Peter H. Nelde, Zdenek Stary, and Wolfgang Wölck. Berlin/New York: Walter de Gruyter, pp. 906–13.

Kachru, Braj B. (1996c) World Englishes: Agony and ecstasy. *Journal of Aesthetic Education*, **30**(2), 135–55.

Kachru, Braj B. (1998a) World Englishes 2000: Resources for research and teaching. In *World Englishes 2000*. Edited by Larry E. Smith and Michael L. Forman. Honolulu: University of Hawai'i Press, pp. 209–51.

Kachru, Braj B. (1998b) English as an Asian language. *Links and Letters 5*. Bellaterra (Barcelona): Universitat Autonoma de Barcelona: Servi de Publications, pp. 89–198.

Kachru, Braj B. (1998c) Raja Rao: Mādhyama and mantra. In *Word as*

Mantra: The Art of Raja Rao. Edited by Robert L. Hardgrave, Jr. New Delhi: Katha, in association with the Center for Asian Studies, the University of Texas at Austin, pp. 60–87.

Kachru, Braj B. (2005) *Asian Englishes: Beyond the Canon.* Hong Kong: Hong Kong University Press.

Kermode, Frank (1979) Institutional control of interpretation. *Salmagundi,* **43**, 72–86.

Langeland, Agnes Scott (1996) Rushdie's language: An analysis of how Salman Rushdie destabilizes the Western bias in English. *English Today,* **12**(1), 16–22.

Lannoy, Richard (1971) *The Speaking Tree: A Study of Indian Culture and Society.* New York: Oxford University Press.

Lefevere, Andre (1990) Translation: Its genealogy in the West. In *Translation: History and Culture.* Edited by Susan Bassnett and Andre Lefevere. London/New York: Pinter Publishers, pp. 4–28.

Levine, Lawrence W. (1996) *The Opening of the American Mind: Canons, Culture, and History.* Boston: Beacon Press.

McArthur, Tom (1998) *The English Languages.* Cambridge: Cambridge University Press.

McArthur, Tom (2001) World English and world Englishes: Trends, tensions, varieties, and standards. *Language Teaching: The International Abstracting Journal for Language Teachers, Educators and Researchers,* **34**, 1–20.

Michaels, Leonard and Ricks, Christopher (eds.) (1988) *The State of the Language.* Berkeley: University of California Press. (2nd edition 1990.)

Narasimhaiah, C. D. (1991) *N for Nobody: Autobiography of an English Teacher.* Delhi: B. R. Publishing Corporation.

Ngũgĩ, wa Thiong'o (1981) *Writers in Politics.* London: Heinemann.

Okara, Gabriel (1964) *The Voice.* London: Heinemann.

Omar, Asmah Haji (1996) Imperial English in Malaysia. In *Post-Imperial English: Status Change in Former British and American Colonies 1940–1990.* Edited by Joshua A. Fishman, Andrew W. Conrad, and Alma Rubal-Lopez. Berlin: Mouton de Gruyter, pp. 513–33.

Paikeday, Thomas M. (1985) *The Native Speaker Is Dead!* Toronto/New York: Paikeday Publishing.

Pütz, Martin (ed.) (1995) *Discrimination through Language in Africa? Perspectives on the Namibian Experience.* Berlin/New York: Mouton de Gruyter.

Quirk, Randolph (2001) Getting their clause into English. *Concord,* winter, 7–8.

Quirk, Randolph (2003) From Latin to English. *The Use of English,* **55**(1), 7–15.

Rao, Raja (1938 [1963, 1974]) *Kanthapura.* London: Allen and Unwin.

Rao, Raja (1978) The caste of English. In *Awakened Conscience: Studies on Commonwealth Literature.* Edited by C. D. Narasimhaiah. Delhi: Sterling Publishers, pp. 420–2.

Rao, Raja (1988) *The Chessmaster and His Moves.* Delhi: Vision Books.

Rushdie, Salman (1991 [1988]) *The Satanic Verses.* London and New York: Viking.

Rushdie, Salman (1991) *Imaginary Homelands: Essays and Criticism.* New York: Viking.

Shills, Edward (1988) Citizen of the world: Nirad C. Chaudhuri. *The American Scholar,* Autumn, 549–73.

Sledd, James H. (1993) Standard English and the study of variation: "It all be done for a purpose." In *Language Variation in North American English: Research and Teaching.* Edited by A. Wayne Glowka and Donald M. Lance. New York: Modern

Language Association of America, pp. 275–81.

Smith, Larry E. (1992) Spread of English and issues of intelligibility. In *The Other Tongue: English across Cultures*. 2nd edition. Edited by Braj B. Kachru. Urbana, IL: University of Illinois Press, pp. 75–90.

Soyinka, Wole (1988) *Art, Dialogue and Outrage: Essays on Literature and Culture*. New York: Pantheon Books.

Thumboo, Edwin (1970) Malaysian poetry: Two examples of sensibility and style. In *National Identity*. Edited by Kenneth L. Goodwin. London and Melbourne: Heinemann Educational Books, pp. 187–96.

Thumboo, Edwin (1985) Twin perspectives and multi-ecosystems: Traditions for a commonwealth writer. *World Englishes*, **4**(2), 213–22.

Thumboo, Edwin (ed.) (2001) *The Three Circles of English: Language Specialists Talk about the English Language*. Singapore: UniPress and the Center for the Arts, National University of Singapore.

Tickoo, Makhan L. (ed.) (1991) *Language and Standards: Issues, Attitudes, Case Studies*. Anthology series 26. Singapore: SEAMEO Regional Language Centre.

Yong, Zhao and Campbell, Keith P. (1995) English in China. *World Englishes*, **14**(3), 377–90.

FURTHER READING

Bolton, Kingsley (ed.) (2002) *Hong Kong English Autonomy and Creativity*. Hong Kong: Hong Kong University Press.

Bolton, Kingsley (2003) *English in China*. Cambridge: Cambridge University Press.

Bolton, Kingsley and Kachru, Braj B. (eds.) (2006) *World Englishes: Critical Concepts in Linguistics*, 6 vols. London/New York: Routledge.

Brutt-Griffler, Janina (2002) *World Englishes: A Study of Its Development*. Clevedon, UK: Multilingual Matters.

Canagarajah, Suresh (1999) *Resisting Linguistic Imperialism in English Teaching*. Oxford: Oxford University Press.

Potter, Russell (1995) *Spectacular Vernaculars*. Binghamton, NY: State University of New York Press.

Kachru, Braj B. (2008) "World Englishes in world contexts." In *A Companion to the History of the English Language*. Edited by Haruko Momma and Michael Matto. Oxford: Blackwell.

Thumboo, Edwin (ed.) (2001) *The Three Circles of English: Language Specialists Talk about the English Language*. Singapore: UniPress and the Center for the Arts, National University of Singapore.

Part V Grammar Wars and Standards

26 Grammar Wars: Seventeenth- and Eighteenth-Century England

LINDA C. MITCHELL

1 Introduction

Although seventeenth- and eighteenth-century English grammarians claimed to be correcting errors in grammar and protecting the language from corruption, they were in fact positioning themselves on a cultural battlefield, using linguistics to protest social issues. As a result, English grammar affected, and was affected by, such factors as race and gender. Several major battles in these cultural wars will be described. The first battle regards the status of English vis-à-vis Latin. Grammarians debated how successfully Latin models could be used to teach, legitimate, or standardize English, resulting in long-lived tensions between prescriptive and descriptive grammars. A second battle pitted "good grammar" against "good writing" as some grammarians insisted that all writing be grammatically correct, while others emphasized style and eloquence. A prolonged third battle was over the nature of "universal grammar." Seventeenth-century grammarians could not agree on a language scheme, whereas eighteenth-century grammarians tried instead to identify universal systems that could be applied to English. In a fourth battle, grammarians debated how grammar could regulate the speech and therefore power of such marginal groups as foreigners, women, and the middle class.

2 The Status of English vis-à-vis Latin

By mid-seventeenth century the status of English as the language of the educated centered on at least three issues: to learn Latin or English grammar first, to recognize the merits of English, and to use Latin to legitimize English.

2.1   Latin or English?

Grammarians debated whether students should learn Latin or English grammar first. Thomas Farnaby makes a case in the preface of *Systema Grammaticum* (1641) for Latin to be taught in Latin because the elements of English models are not transferable and because bilingual translations make schoolboys lazy.[1] The case for teaching in the vernacular met with resistance by those still committed to classical learning, such as John Milton (1669). Still, the number of grammarians focusing on the mother tongue first and Latin second grew in number. Pedagogues argued convincingly that the vernacular should be taught as a way to prepare students to learn Latin. Against the pedagogy of Farnaby, Charles Hoole sets up a bilingual text in *Latine Grammar* (1651) with English models on the left side of the page and Latin models on the right side. John Wallis takes the position in *Grammatica Lingua Anglicanae* (1653) that English should not be forced to conform to Latin. He claims that earlier grammarians (e.g., Alexander Gill, *Logonomia Anglica*, 1619 and Ben Jonson, *English Grammar*, 1640) have sacrificed "understanding; for all of them have forced our tongue too much into the pattern of Latin" (Praefatio). Wallis asks, "Why should we introduce a fictitious and quite foolish collection of Cases, Genders, Moods and Tenses, without any need, and for which there is no reason in the basis of the language itself?" (Praefatio). Jeremiah Wharton in *English Grammar* (1654) maintains that a student who learns English grammar first and then transfers the knowledge to Latin will be accurate in both languages (p. A5v). The use of analogy, or the transfer of knowledge, forms the basis of Elisha Coles's *Syncrisis* (1675b) and A. Lane's *A Rational and Speedy Method Attaining to the Latin Tongue* (1695). In the eighteenth century, grammarians like John Clarke and Richard Johnson are still complaining about the emphasis on Latin.

2.2   The merits of English

Although Latin was the language of the educated in the early part of the seventeenth century, grammarians continued to build the credibility of the vernacular, especially as national identity was increasingly being defined by the mother tongue. George Snell contends in *The Right Teaching of Useful Knowledge* (1649) that knowing English will "bee a verie excellent and useful skil" (p. 28). Even though Joseph Aickin acknowledges in *English Grammar* (1693) that rules are not codified, he maintains that "in reality the English Tongue is far more copious than [Latin]" (p. A3v). Henry Care disagrees with the assumption "that none can write true English, but such as have been taught Latine" (1699: A1v). In *Tutor to True English* (1699) Care argues for learning English because when parents "take their sons out of Latin school and make them Apprentices to Mechanic Arts, Shop-keeping, and the like, all their petty Acquirements vanish through disuse, and quickly forgot" (p. A1v). And the author of *The Pleasing Instructor* (1756) complains that grammarians are too dependent on Latin models to teach English.

2.3 Latin to standardize English

Since Latin grammars had been available for centuries, textbook authors naturally copied the grammatical categories of Latin grammarians and applied them to English grammar in hopes of bringing consistency to the English language. Although Latin models of grammar did not always apply to English, grammarians forced them to fit English anyway. Moreover, the illogical practice of forcing models of Latin rules of grammar onto the non-Latinate grammar of English has persisted into the twentieth century. A reasonable explanation for this logical and illogical use of models may lie in how rigorously they were applied to language. Grammarians in the seventeenth century, for instance, may have applied English models to Latin only when they fit. They were not enslaved to forcing rules of English grammar onto Latin because Latin was already a codified language, and English models were merely a teaching aid to explain Latin grammar. However, when grammarians wanted to standardize English, they looked to Latin models as a way to codify grammar rules. George Snell explains in *The Right Teaching of Useful Knowledge* (1649) that grammarians were responsible for getting language to a "fixed and immutable state," one that would not go "out of date" (p. 40). He agrees that Latin proves useful if one "can applie the Ruels of His Latine Grammar to maintain the rights of his English speech" (p. 30).

By the early eighteenth century, Latin was no longer required to do business, and grammarians were rethinking their pedagogy for teaching both English and Latin grammar. Latin instruction did not necessarily mean classical studies, and subjects formerly required – like imitation and translation – might not be offered at all. English grammar was taught for the purpose of learning the vernacular, and Latin models were more frequently used to settle disputes over matters of usage. Even though the application of Latin models to English was often illogical, and even though the models forced a Germanic language into a Latin framework, pedagogues accepted the Latin models of grammar more readily than they did the English models.[2] By using Latinate forms, George Fisher attempts to codify orthography in *The New Spelling Book* (1700). Fisher was characteristic of the grammarians who thought that if they could standardize spelling, they could fix the English language and its rules. However, he discovered that no one could control the many variations of spelling in spite of using the most polished of Latin models to arrive at the correct forms.[3] Richard Brown made a similar attempt in *English School Reformed* (1701). Grammarians had yet to censure specific errors and to formulate rules for correctness; moreover, they still had not sorted problems of custom and usage. Anxiety over what seemed the uncertain state of English was expressed by Jonathan Swift in *Proposal for Correcting, Improving, and Ascertaining the English Tongue* (1712). Richard Johnson rigorously applied the models of Latin, whether they fit English or not, in *Grammatical Commentaries* (1706).

By the second half of the eighteenth century, Latin models were supporting prescriptive English grammar. We do not have to search too far to find examples of the way Latin distorted English grammar. For instance, the centuries-old double negative "I don't want nothing" became stigmatized because it did not conform to the Latin pattern which would translate "I don't want anything." Grammarians declared the double negative incorrect and illiterate. In a *Short Introduction to English Grammar* (1762), prescriptive grammarian Bishop Lowth goes back to ancient Latin rules in an attempt to fix the English language. He cites the rule using a *to be* verb: "The Verb to Be has always a Nominative Case after it; as, it was I" (p. 111). Once considered correct for centuries, *It's me* was now considered incorrect since the Latin construction *ego sum* made use of the subject form of the pronoun, *ego* rather than the object form *me*. It is an issue still hotly debated today. Joseph Priestley, a descriptivist, believed that language cannot be fixed. In *Rudiments of English Grammar* (1761) he writes that the "best forms of speech will, in time, establish themselves by their own superior excellence" (p. vii). Priestley followed a more liberal practice of rules and custom than did Lowth.

The two centuries were filled with controversy over how to codify and standardize the English language. The practice of using Latin models to decide rules in English is still done today.

3   "Good Writing" versus "Good Grammar"

As school grammars began to include rhetoric in the seventeenth century, grammarians debated whether to privilege "correctness" or eloquence and style. Some grammars tried to emphasize both grammar and style, such as Ralph Johnson's *Scholars Guide* (1665), Guy Miège's *English Grammar* (1688), and Charles Gildon's *Grammar of the English Tongue* (1712). In *English Grammar* (1712) Michael Maittaire admits that "the work is yet but half done" by knowing grammar; writing is the other significant part (p. 228). John Collyer, however, shocks fellow grammarians when he states in *The General Principles of Grammar* (1735) that it is acceptable to break rules of grammar for the sake of good writing: "Sometimes we are obliged to transgress, to avoid the concurrence of certain rough words, which will not admit of conjunction, and another disposition frequently renders them harmonious" (p. 102). Grammarians complained frequently that school grammars had an excess of grammar rules and a shortage of writing instruction, but they did not succeed in remedying the problem. In *A Treatise on Education* (1743) James Barclay claims that writing will be improved with "rules concerning the justness of expression . . . the force and harmony of certain phrases, the proper meaning of words, their connection one with another, and the necessary skill of placing them all in regular order" (p. 66). Barclay, however, privileges grammar when he rules out *I shall now proceed to examine* in favor of *I proceed to examine* and when he recommends getting rid of adverbs like *really, indeed, surely, perhaps, at the same time* (p. 69).

Grammarians tried balance grammar and style. In *Practical English Grammar* (1750) Ann Fisher contends that those who learn grammar from rote or custom will not so easily be able to transfer the knowledge with "Propriety or Elegance" (p. iv), yet someone "unacquainted with grammar will be unable to express himself properly" (p. vi). Following a similar philosophy to Fisher, Joseph Priestley in *Rudiments of English-Grammar* (1761) includes examples of composition "from our most celebrated writers, for the exemplification both of the rules of Grammar, and of the Observations on Style" (p. 65). He uses short sentences for "illustrating the fundamental rules of grammar," and long, complex sentences for showing "particularly those in which the natural construction hath been made to give place to the harmony of style" (p. 65).

Since grammarians had long argued that learning Latin grammar improved composition, a bond between writing and grammar was already assumed. Edward Leedes's *More English Examples Turned into Latin* (1726) is one of the first publications to include correction exercises in a grammar text. Another publication to follow the practice of bad exercises was Ann Fisher's *New Grammar* (1757). This illogical exercise could hardly have reinforced skills in grammar: "That no wimen can be handsom by the sorses of seaters alone, any more then she can be wittey Onley by the Help of speach" (p. 131). Bishop Robert Lowth followed with "bad exercises" to correct in *A Short Introduction to English Grammar* (1762). Daniel Fenning argues in *A New Grammar of the English Language* (1771) that "examples of bad English . . . may have a very bad effect. They are more likely to perplex a young Scholar, and to confirm an old one in error, than to direct the judgment of the one, or correct the bad habit of the other" (p. vi). Fenning suggests that schoolmasters turn to student writing for examples of bad grammar and "false Construction" because students will "frequently err against every rule of syntax" (p. vii). Fenning points out, "a child will attend more carefully to the correction of an error made by himself, than to the correction of one made by another" (p. vii). "Bad" sentence exercises for Joshua Story in *Introduction to English Grammar* (1783) supports one view that if students saw the incorrect sentence, they would remember the correct version in both the written and spoken word. Grammarians have yet to prove whether correcting grammar in isolation will have a direct correlation to writing.

4   The Battle for a "Universal Grammar"

A variety of schemes for universal language and universal grammar were introduced in the seventeenth century. Promoters of the schemes argued that a common language would also fulfill the perceived need of restoring man to pre-Babel times. Grammarians who supported a common language in the seventeenth century argued that it would help the spread of religion, promote commerce in foreign countries, and bring scientists together. Eighteenth-century grammarians continued to use the term "universal grammar," but elaborate schemes of the seventeenth century became the rational, practical grammars of the eighteenth century.

4.1 *Repairing Babel*

At first, grammarians wanted to return to the language of Adam, as it is described in the eighth chapter of Genesis when all the earth was "of one language and one speech." Some grammarians argued for the merits of such languages as Latin, Hebrew, and Chinese, while others maintained that the answer to finding a universal grammar was to create an artificial one. In creating these languages, grammarians tried to construct what they thought would be the most functional system with the least ambiguity. Language planners insisted that a language be harmonious and that it signify the thing each word represented in the natural world. Each word was to incorporate the complex and abstract meanings of an idea. All these projects used the same grammatical principles, even though they built widely varying models of language.[4] Some of these languages consisted of bizarre numerical combinations, difficult musical notes, or confusing symbols.[5] Borrowing from Descartes's theory of innatism, they argued that learning a new language would simply be a matter of knowledge recovery.

Francis Lodowyck, author of *A Common Writing* (1647), is credited with the first published project of universal character and language. In it, Lodowyck creates an artificial language made up of signs, which, he argues, is a hieroglyphical representation of words that people can learn and communicate universally. His artificial language attempts to be an "expression or outward presentation of the mind" (p. 21). As one would expect, Lodowyck's language scheme was not adopted as an international language because his method proved to be awkward and impractical. In *The Universal Character* (1657), Cave Beck creates an artificial language, one that is mostly an application of Latinate grammar, but based on a numerical system he believed to be superior to other symbolic schemes. Beck claims that his scheme can be learned in "two Hours space," "be Spoken as well as Written," and will increase communication in commerce and religion (pp. A7r–A7v). Beck rejected obtuse, confusing symbols presented by symbolic writing and hieroglyphs. He instead chose a universal character of arithmetical numbers, hoping to bring order to his world, to simplify language by using symbols that are sequential and universal, and also to improve defects in spoken languages (p. A8r). He complains about the "evils" of learning Latin, but one might note that he has stayed with the Latin tradition in syntax and with the traditional rules of tenses, moods, and cases (p. A7v). As was the case with other universal language proponents, Beck did not recognize the inadequacies of his system.

Some grammarians rejected artificial, nonsense language schemes and chose instead a system constructed from "real" character, that is, a system built from elements, symbols, and numbers of an existing language. Language planners envisioned grammar as an organic entity capable of remaining rational, sensible, and systemized. George Dalgarno and John Wilkins went beyond Beck's and Lodowyck's ideas of simply inventing symbols that stood for words. Dalgarno and Wilkins viewed language rationally and philosophically, and promoted systems that would force order on reality by setting up formulas to show shades of meaning. They began by combining meaningful units of characters to create a universal language. Next, they set up categories to organize words by genera, species, and specific differences, using properties of the "real character" to form letters and words. Dalgarno and Wilkins shared with their contemporaries a conviction that if they could symbolize the order of things and notions (how the world is organized) in a universal language they would have a greater understanding of their world. In *Ars Signorum* (1661) George Dalgarno's scheme may also be viewed as a philosophical language in that he sets up a system of classification as a rational means of ordering the universe, claiming that his "universal character and new Rational language" is superior to other systems of shorthand. Language planner John Wilkins approached his language scheme in a more scientific manner than his contemporaries. In *Essay Towards a Real Character* (1668) Wilkins develops a universal character and philosophical language with more forethought as to the linguistic way it worked. He intended to devise a universal language that one could use to observe the world and make sense out of it in a theoretical context (p. 289).[6] Wilkins did not recognize that his system was difficult to use and that the rigidity of his system did not allow for many changes with the passage of time. However, he eventually became known as the father of modern linguistics.

Although these grammarians were trying to invent a language that would visually represent the world, they instead created limited worlds. Dalgarno's and Wilkins's classifications, for instance, remained symbols of what they called reality and did not move beyond superficial categories. Both grammarians had intended for their universal language systems to be complete and functional, but that did not happen because their characters were not capable of breaking down the complex concepts into easily understandable units. Instead, these systems confused the listener and frustrated the speaker. Another failure in a universal language was Samuel Botley's *Maximo in Minimo* (1674), a system of symbolical characters that proposed to teach the art of memory and simplified syntax.[7] Universal language schemes had appeared earlier, but the time was ripe in the seventeenth century for them to gain attention. It was also a time to prove their inadequacies in practical use. Toward the end of the seventeenth century, universal grammar and universal language projects shifted in focus to that of comparing the similarities of languages and of looking at the rationale or philosophy of language. In *Syncrisis* (1675b) Elisha Coles has already recognized the approaching eighteenth-century view of universal grammar, and his grammar text marks a shift from universal language of invented character to a universal language of similarities.

4.2   *Universal grammar and practical grammars*

Eighteenth-century grammarians continued to use the term "universal grammar," but the more elaborate universal grammar schemes of the seventeenth century became the rational, practical grammars of the eighteenth century. Grammarians no longer used the term to describe speculative systems but rather to describe language itself. To these eighteenth-century grammarians, universality meant combining the more traditional categories of the parts of speech, like nouns and verbs, with the philosophical rationale to represent universal language constants. They thought of universal grammar in terms of analogies among languages, as a tool they would attempt to use to determine a doctrine of correctness. The vernacular did not have the voice of authority that Latin had carried with it, but if similar linguistic elements could be found in another language, then analogy could be used to determine what was correct. One of the earliest examples of the eighteenth-century concept of a "rational" or "universal" grammar to appear in England appears as early as 1695 in A. Lane's *A Rational and Speedy Method of Attaining the Latine Tongue*. The work is the first to put forward a system of grammar based on the vernacular rather than on Latin, an interesting early, but controversial, claim that English has the qualities of a universal tongue.

From about 1700 to 1750, activity in the field of universal grammar was no longer as much concerned with the creation of a new language as it was with the philosophical basis of language. Grammarians such as Richard Johnson in *Grammatical Commentaries* (1706) continued to argue the merits of Latin as "a Universal Language" because it is "common to Learned Men of all Countries" (pp. A1v–A2r). Universal language to him emphasized how different grammars were constructed with similar rules of logic, not based on the linguistic ontology of corresponding categories that we see in the seventeenth century (p. A2r). A major work on universal grammar is James Harris's *Hermes: A Philosophical Enquiry concerning Universal Grammar* (1751). Harris takes each part of grammar from the basic word unit to the sentence and analyzes it in a philosophical way, explaining how each thing relates to its universe (p. 2). Language follows a universal principle: "that Words must of necessity be Symbols" and consequently that "all Language is founded in compact, and not in Nature" (p. 337). Harris sees "Language [as] a kind of Picture of the Universe" (p. 330), where words symbolize general ideas (p. 341). In *Lingua Britannica Reformata* (1749), however, Benjamin Martin disagrees with the analogy principle and focuses on speech and linguistics, not so much on grammar and logic. He claims that as long as language is in a "mutable and fluctuating state," it cannot be fixed to a standard "purity and perfection" (p. 111). Martin was one of the few to recognize that using custom to dictate rules may produce some awkward, clumsy language. By the middle of the eighteenth century, grammarians were arguing for a doctrine of correctness based on analogy, or the common principles in a general system. In *The Royal*

Universal British Grammar (1754) Daniel Farro claims, a "doctrine of correctness" is reached through observing the elements of various grammars and then deciding what the consistent rule is. Farro writes, "If all languages share the same substantial Notion of Beings, Actions, and Passions," then English is "universal" (p. xv).

Joseph Priestley's *The Rudiments of English Grammar* (1761) marks a shift in the emphasis of the universal language debate. In the second half of the eighteenth century, controversies over grammar came to a focus on the establishment of a codified, standardized grammar. Gone were the debates over finding Adam's original language or converting the world to a newly devised language scheme. Priestley and his fellow linguists were not tracing language to the original tongue, but methodically looking at the changes in language itself. Priestley did not believe in a "divine alphabet" and claimed instead that human speech comes about naturally. Priestley was, however, sympathetic to constructing a "philosophical language, which should be adequate to all the purposes of speech, and be without those superfluities, defects, and ambiguities, either in words or structure" (p. 297). The most rational plan for this project, according to Priestley, was that of John Wallis. But the universal languages of Dr Wallis's time, the mid-seventeenth century, were no longer fashionable. Controversies over grammar in the eighteenth century centered on how the definition of universal grammar had changed, that is, on what elements grammarians thought most languages possess. Grammarians increasingly used universal grammar as a means of dealing with other language issues. In *Short Introduction to English Grammar* (1762) Bishop Robert Lowth, unlike earlier grammarians, focuses on accuracy or practice (words as words), not theory (words as ideas) as a way of repairing the state of grammar. As a prescriptivist, he wanted to use universal grammar to establish a doctrine of correctness through the use of analogy (p. 1). Universal grammar, he explains, "must be done with reference to some language already known; in which the terms are to be explained, and the rules exemplified" (1767, pp. viii–ix). The belief that analogy could establish rules of grammar gained the support of most grammarians by the end of the eighteenth century.

An interesting and surprising anomaly in the latter part of the eighteenth century is Rowland Jones's attempt to revive an interest in a universal language that was characteristic of the seventeenth century. In *Circles of Gomer* (1771) Jones presents a type of system not seen since Wilkins and Lodowyck. In *Hieroglyfic* (1768) he experiments with a universal grammar of primitive or "original" language. Jones's text should not be considered as merely a creative endeavor or a late attempt to repair Babel, but should instead be viewed as a text following eighteenth-century rational and philosophical principles. His effort at the universal language came too late to be taken seriously, but it does demonstrate another attempt for a means of codifying the English language in the eighteenth century. Toward the end of the eighteenth century, many grammarians continued to examine universal grammar from philosophical and rational perspectives.

As the eighteenth century came to a close, the prevailing kind of universal grammar promoted by grammarians such as Lowth and Farro supported the codification of English and, consequently prescriptivism. Historians of the English language have long canonized Lowth as being a central, founding father of grammar books. This assertion is problematic because Lowth needs to be understood not in isolation, but in the context of his period. He comes after a century of discussion about universal language, and reaps the benefits of his predecessors. His grammar book is a result of many decades of successes and failures, of experimentation and controversy by those who came before him.

5   Grammarians and Marginal Groups

Grammarians also had the power to create, assign, and reinforce identities for marginal social groups, such as foreigners, women, and the middle class. When grammarians assigned identities to marginal groups, they reinforced their designated status.

5.1   *Foreigners and national identity*

To prove they accepted their new country and its customs, foreigners had to learn English properly before they could be assured of mobility. Requiring foreigners to learn to speak English properly, then, was a means by which the British imposed a moral and national identity on the new residents.[8] Grammarians also insisted that foreigners acknowledge that English was a superior, global language. As early as 1582, Richard Mulcaster notes in *The First Part of the Elementarie* that foreigners should learn English because "Our tung doth serve to so manie uses, bycause it is conversant with so manie peple, and so well acquainted with so manie matters, in so sundrie kindes of dealing" (preface). In his posthumously published *English Grammar* (1640), Ben Jonson tells foreigners, "The profit of Grammar is great to Strangers, who are to live in communion and commerce with us."

Throughout the seventeenth century, as foreigners were learning the "mother tongue," grammarians worried that foreigners would corrupt the newly enfranchised English language. Jeremiah Wharton counsels foreigners to use his *English Grammar* (1654) because it "will bee the most certain Guide, that ever yet was existant" (pp. A6r–A6v). Guy Miège, an immigrant himself, wrote *English Grammar* (1688) because he wanted to preserve the purity of English and to help foreigners to speak correctly.[9] Miège claims that foreigners who used to resist learning English as an "Insular Speech" with "groundless prejudice" are now admirers of the language, especially since he has provided help for them (p. 6). However, Miège warns both native speakers and foreigners not to incorporate any more foreign words into English: "now the English is come to so great Perfection, now 'tis grown so very Copious and Significant, by the Accession of the Quintessence and Life of other Tongues, 'twere to be wished that a Stop were put to this unbounded Way of Naturalizing foreign Words" (p. A9).

It was an unsettling idea that foreigners might not speak the language; worse yet that they might not accept all aspects of British culture. Some grammarians insisted that foreigners be able to read the Bible in English, as we see in John Wallis's *Grammatica Linguae Anglicanae* (1653) (pp. A6–A7). In a book designed for foreigners, *A New English Grammar* (1662), James Howell tells any new resident that he must know English if he is to live or work in England (pp. 3–4). Christopher Cooper is even more specific in *Grammatica Linguae Anglicanae* (1685) when he cites four reasons for foreigners to learn English: to practice their trades, to communicate, to understand the culture, and to be knowledgeable in art and science (preface). Joseph Aickin complains in his *English Grammar* (1693) that foreigners are slow to learn English, and "the true cause" is their not understanding grammar (A2v). Like Aickin, A. Lane makes the same complaint in *A Key to the Art of Letters* (1700) that foreigners are slow to learn English, and he lays out the easiest methods for learning the vernacular. James Greenwood's *Essay Towards a Practical English Grammar* (1722) is another example of a grammarian who specifically tries to assist foreigners in learning English (p. 28). However, John Rice's *Introduction to the Art of Reading* (1765) specifically makes the point that foreigners should learn the "Idiomatical Order of its Words in common Discourse and simple Narration" (p. 358).

Insisting that foreigners learn English as part of accepting their new country is surprising for a time when the vernacular was just acquiring its own identity. English traders, after all, did not accord the same privilege to people in other countries, but instead demanded that foreigners conduct business in English, even in their own countries.

5.2 *Women*

Discussions in seventeenth- and eighteenth-century grammar books tell us to what extent learning was considered appropriate for females. Women were thought to be mentally and physically incapable of taking on rigorous academic tasks. A woman's responsibility in society was to be a good wife and mother. Sometimes authors even thought that women possessed the same diminished intellectual capacity as children. Females were allowed to learn only enough to stay within their social spheres, and going beyond those limits was considered morally reprehensible. Since grammar was a subject partially within those limits, grammar books helped regulate the moral identity of women.

The widely held view expressed by authors in the introductions to their textbooks was that females did not have the strength or intellect to pursue advanced studies. Richard Mulcaster claims in *The First Part of the Elementarie* (1582) that because men govern, education "most properly belonged to them" (p. 18). He advises that women should be limited in what they learn, but vocational training of men was to be "without restriction either as regards subject-matter or method" (pp. 52–3). Mulcaster states that girls have a natural weakness: "their brains be not so charged as boys," and "like [an] empty cask they make the greater noise." The learned woman's proper place in society was thought to be where she would do the least harm. Samuel Hartlib cautions in *The True and Readie Way to Learne the Latine Tongue* (1653) that education might make women dangerously attractive, lest they become "objects of lust and snares unto young Gentlemen" (p. 21). Their education should "fit them for the true end of their life in a Christian Commonwealth, to become modest, discreet, and industrious house-keepers" (p. 21). In *The Academy of Eloquence* (1654), Thomas Blount also weighs in on the subservient position of women: "Women, being of one and the self same substance with man, are what man is, only so much more imperfect, as they are created the weaker vessels" (p. 101). He puts women in two categories: saints or evil doers (p. 103). The evil doers "are Horseleeches, which draw blood from the veins of a House and State, where they exercise their power. They are Syrens of the earth, which cause shipwracks without water" (p. 113).

Even reformer Johann Amos Comenius, in spite of his progressive plans for educational reform, assumed that a woman's proper social role was to serve in a male-dominated world. He argues in *The Reformed School* (1642) that females should learn to become "carefull housewives, loving towards their husbands and their children when God shall call them to be married" (p. 38). Women, Comenius claims, do not need to satisfy their "natural tendency to curiosity," but should develop "sincerity and contentedness" in order to "accomplish womanly tasks" (p. 68). The pictures and language in Comenius's *Orbis Sensualium Pictus* (1659) are male dominated, except for a few domestic scenes. For example, men are interacting at school, work, church, and social occasions, but women are limited to domestic scenes in the roles of wives, mothers, or other caretakers.

There were almost no female voices to support women except authors like Bathsua Makin. In *An Essay to Revive the Antient Education of Gentlewomen* (1674), she condemns the "barbarous custom to breed women low" and the belief that "women are not endued with such reason as men, nor capable of improvement by education" (p. 3). Makin complains that "[a] learned woman is thought to be a comet that bodes mischief whenever it appears" (p. 3). She reports that male authors believe that to offer women a liberal education is "to deface the image of God in man," and it will make women "so high and men so low, [that] like fire in the house top it will set the whole world in a flame."

Grammarians remained steadfast in their vision of women as saints or sinners. William Mather sets restrictions for females in his *Young Man's Companion* (1695). He sees a wife as one "Linked to us [husbands] by such Obligations of Love and Duty" and "wholly Assigned to her Husband, on whom she solely depends" (p. 212). He even goes so far to say, "many Women are to blame" for leading men astray: "The Gorgeous Attire of Women do make Men more dissolute, careless, and bent to Lust, and other Evils . . . namely when they build wide Windows for their Breasts, and give their Eyes liberty to wander; the high Towers (or whorish Attire above their fore-heads) the frizzled Hair, and especially the wanton Eye, and Lascivious or Shameless Countenance are the forerunners of Adultery" (pp. 214–15). "Lest [a wife] incur the name of a Harebrain" (p. 215), Mather argues, she is one who "meddleth only with her Household Affairs, that loveth her Husbands Bed, and keepeth her Tongue quiet" (p. 215). And some grammarians like Lane in *Key to the Art of Letters* (1700) focus on perceived physical limitations, that young women have been discouraged from learning because of their "tender Constitution not being able to endure those rugged and thorny Difficulties in the Methods hitherto practiced" (p. xvi). Michael Maittaire argues in *English Grammar* (1712) that too "much effort is put into caring for females," "in the variety of breeding, some for the feet, some for the hands, others for the voice" (p. v). He, however, relents somewhat and admits that it is "cruelty or ignorance, to debar [females] from the accomplishments of speech and Understanding; as if that Sex was . . . weak and defective in its Head and Brains" (pp. v–vi). In *The Pleasing Instructor* (1756), the anonymous author complains that grammar is "too much out of Fashion, especially among the Ladies" (p. vii), and they "feel an Entanglement" and are "blind to the Beauties and Idioms of Language" because they are "left lame in their Learning" (p. ix). One of the obstacles is that "they are mostly put to Sewing or similar Articles, under the Care of some Mistress, who is perhaps either utterly incapable of assisting them in the Pursuit of Knowledge, or who, from a Crudity of Scholars, [has no] Time to point out or explain to them" (p. ix). The author, however, does not "mean to recommend Reading at the Expence of Sewing" (p. ix).

One of few defenses of women comes from James Buchanan. He laments in *The British Grammar* (1761) that "the Fair Sex have been in general so shamefully neglected with regard to a proper English Education" (p. xxix). He wonders why "Many of them, by the unthinking Part of the Males, are considered and treated rather as Dolls, than as intelligent social Beings" (p. xxix). Buchanan argues that women "are not inferior to the other Sex, yet due Care is not always taken to cultivate their Understandings, to impress their Minds with solid Principles, and replenish them with useful Knowledge" (p. xxix). His statements about the education of females are surprisingly strong, even for 1761. He asks why a female should "be cruelly deprived" of not being able to attain the "Capacity of expressing herself with Fluency and Accuracy in speaking or writing her Mother tongue" (p. xxix). Fathers should, he states, "be embracing every Opportunity of enlarging their [females'] Minds, and improving those Talents which the God of Nature has conferred upon them" (p. xxx). Still, Buchanan drifts back into what is appropriate for women when he states that if men take care of "these more beautiful Pledges," they will "become dutiful Children, good Wives, good Mothers, good Friends, ornamental to their Sex, and, in their several Stations, useful Members to the Community" (p. xxxi).

One female who transcended the moral and emotional identity assigned to her was Ann Fisher. Fisher went against the convention of what was appropriate for her to learn, and she wrote and published *New Grammar* (1757). Authorship was a man's territory, so much so that if a woman wrote a book, the gender of her name might be disguised in order to sell the text.

Thus, grammar books prescribed what was appropriate for women to learn, what they were to do with that learning, and how they were to conduct themselves.

5.3   *The middle class, grammar, and religion*

Foreigners and women had an identity imposed upon them, but the middle class generated its own identity through morals and literacy. The upper class already had its identity of being respectable and literate, but members of the middle class had to find learning situations where their children could acquire the necessary skills to advance. A logical place for the schoolmaster to teach middle-class children language and religion was in grammar books, because all students had to take grammar.

Some educational reformers took the position that grammar and religion were inseparable in the classroom. In *The Reformed School* (1642) Johann Amos Comenius lays out a plan where school children will be taught "Godliness, wherein every day they are to be exercised, by prayers, reading of the word, catecheticall Institutions, and other exercises subordinate unto the life of Christianity" (p. 41). George Snell leads "the learner to the sacred Scriptures, and to the Grammar for English" in *The Right Teaching of Useful Knowledge* (1649) (p. 26). The idea that a man is as good as his word or that a person with good grammar is a good person takes root in texts such as those of Elisha Coles. He provides the opportunity to learn morals from reading selections in the Bible or translating Latin through reading Bible stories. Coles emphasizes Protestant doctrine through pictures of Biblical themes in *Syncrisis . . . Learning Latin: By comparing it with English Together with the Holy History of Scripture-War* (1675b). In *Nolens Volens* (1675a), Coles teaches grammar and scripture with "the Youths Visible Bible."

Besides the connection of grammar and Protestant doctrine, grammarians also linked grammar and moral character. Edward Leedes, in *New English Examples Turned into Latin* (1685), maintains that good scholars make good men (preface) and provides exercises to reinforce that concept. In *English Examples of Latin Syntaxis* (1686) William Walker uses "smart Moral and Prudential Sentences" because "Learning without Religion" may save time, but it makes men the "more desperately debauched, and the more mischievously wicked" (preface). To make a student a better Christian, Thomas Tryon includes proverbs, moral training essays, and a catechism in the *Compleat School-Master* (1700). Some grammarians ventured more radical opinions in their texts. Richard Johnson admonishes learned men in *Grammatical*

Commentaries (1706) because they have not learned Latin and therefore missed their chance at furthering their religious crusade against Catholicism: "The eager Desire of converting Roman Catholicks, which has appear'd for so many Years, wou'd in all likelihood have been much more furthered by this means" (pp. B1v–B2r). One of the strongest statements about religion in a grammar text appears in *The English Scholar Compleat* (1706). The unknown author blames any faults one has "chiefly upon the Papists" and plans "to expose their horrid, erroneous, ridiculous and base Religion, and to beget an early inbred Abhorrency and Aversion to it in the Children" he teaches (p. A4v). Jonathan Swift also sees a connection between language and religion. He argues in *Proposal for Correcting, Improving, and Ascertaining the English Tongue* (1712) that "if it were not for the Bible and Common Prayer Book in the vulgar Tongue, we should hardly be able to understand any Thing that was written among us an hundred Years ago" (p. 32). For keeping standards, he claims, "those Books being perpetually read in Churches have proved a kind of Standard for Language, especially to the common People" (p. 32). And, he praises the "Translators of the Bible" because they were "Masters of an English Style much fitter for that Work, than any we see in our present Writings" (p. 33).

Grammarians continued to connect grammar and religion in the classroom well into the eighteenth century. In *English Exercises for School-Boys To Translate into Latin* (1719) John Garretson introduces "useful admonitions relating to the Duty of Children towards God, or Man, or themselves, because [children] can never have Principles of Virtue or Prudence suggested to them too soon" (p. A5r). Thomas Dilworth needs to be highlighted because he is even more aggressive about using religion to teach grammar in *A New Guide to the English Tongue* (1740, 1751). He recognizes the concern for the "Salvation of Souls" in educating children and for saving "so many poor Creatures from the Slavery of Sin and Satan" (p. iii). He attempts to "save these little Ones from utter Destruction" through the "Protestant Religion [which] is herein gloriously discovered by those Principles of that best constituted Church, as professed in the Church of England, which You cause to be taught, and in grafted in the tender Age of Your Pupils" (p. iii). In the preface he claims that with the Reformation "Ignorance has gradually vanished at the increase of Learning amongst us, who take the Word of God for a Lantern to our Feet" (p. iv). His religious position is deeply rooted in education: "Since the Sunshine of the Gospel of Jesus Christ has risen amongst us: since we are loosed from the Bands of Ignorance and Superstition; since every Protestant believes it to be his Duty to promote Christian Knowledge; certainly it will be confessed, that all Improvement in Learning ought to be in encouraged" (p. iv). He reminds the reader of what Solomon said: "Train up a Child in the Way he should go, and he will not depart from it" (p. iv).

Grammar and moral character played a large role in the self-generated identity of the middle classes. A significant element of this moral identity was literacy which was partially defined as the absence of corrupt language. One of the first ways of protecting themselves from deteriorating language was to empower the language police of the seventeenth and eighteenth centuries. Grammarians like A. Lane (1700) and Richard Johnson (1706) monitored changes in usage, while Jonathan Swift (1712) and Samuel Johnson (1747) tried to no avail to fix the English language. Lane even goes so far as to say in *A Key to the Art of Letters* (1700) that grammar is a necessity because it "polishes and perfects those noble Faculties of Reason and Speech, by which Men are distinguished from Brutes" (p. vii). The middle class was not secure with vague rules or changing usage; they wanted consistency so that they would not make mistakes. The upper-class student, in contrast, came from a privileged background where he had learned rules and followed them when he chose to do so. A student from the lower ranks had to work at learning rules and acquiring refinement. He would be entering a world where knowledge of literature, elocution, and logic had little value and was seldom used. He learned to read and write among hoards of other students who were all struggling to learn practical skills they would use later as apprentices. For the working class, refinement remained a distant, rich relative on the educational family tree. The working class, instead, strove for literacy.

Members of the middle class also chose to define literacy and morality for themselves by battling colloquialism, incorrectness, and archaism. By determining the criteria by which refined speech was to be judged, they hoped to avoid the stigma of incorrect usage, outdated forms, and substandard language. For example, they rejected "power-coding," that is, indicating through speech another person's social status. They adopted the use of the *you* of the mannered upper-class people rather than the *thou* of working-class people. The rejection of a term of inequality marked the desire of the rising classes to have a more democratic voice. What is interesting in this shift is that the middle classes did not designate any distance from the lower classes, perhaps reacting to an egalitarian ethic. The rejection of *thou* was also a safeguard from offending people. With the increasing material status of some middle-class entrepreneurs, one did not want to risk using a lower-status term of address to someone of higher socio-economic standing.

In the eighteenth century, members of the middle class became more aggressive in creating criteria for what they perceived to be a literate person. Thomas Dilworth's *A New Guide to the English Tongue* (1740), for example, was intended "to enable such as are intended to rise no higher, to write their Mother-Tongue intelligibly, and according to the Rules of Grammar" so they could read *The Spectator* and *The Tatler*, not "Grubstreet Papers, idle Pamphlets, lewd Plays, filthy Songs" (pp. 8–9). The rising classes did not want to be branded by using the kind of uneducated language that Moll Flanders spoke.

Other pedagogues reinforced the connection of grammar to morals and literacy. It became evident to the middle classes that knowing grammar and reading had some status attached to it. The ability to acquire books and to read them added a degree of status to the middle-class home. Authors quickly realized the profit in such books as Isaac Watts's *Art of Reading and Writing* (1721). John Clarke observes in *Essay upon Study* (1731) that reading liberates or makes a person independent in thought and action "As their Business in the World, is to guide and govern their fellow-Cityzens" (p. 228). In *A Treatise on Education* (1743) James Barclay claims that boys who learn the mother tongue will be able to "observe the beauty of the moral world and the whole rational creation" (p. 219). Few grammarians stressed in their texts that being literate and moral also meant understanding the words and comprehending the meaning. John Rice argues in *An Introduction to the Art of Reading* (1765) that it is possible that a person can look at a word and pronounce it correctly, yet he may have no comprehension of the meaning nor be able to read it.

Grammar texts communicated to foreigners that they had to learn the English vernacular in order to prove that they accepted their new country and its customs. Through the act of learning the English language, foreigners were allowed to assume the national identity. The texts also defined how much knowledge was appropriate for women so that they would not stray into territory reserved for men. If women went beyond the intellectual limits allowed them, they were learning too much and they risked being "immoral." Moreover, grammar books instructed the aspiring classes in morals and literacy. Whereas the grammarians assigned an identity to foreigners and females, the aspiring classes generated their own. The middle classes used grammar books to teach the skills they thought were important in building a strong national identity: reading, writing, and speaking correctly. They also encoded other values like honesty, hard work, and morals. Within the context and purposes set by grammarians, grammar books served these many functions for the marginal groups like foreigners, women, and the lower classes.

6 Conclusion

In the seventeenth and eighteenth centuries, battles were fought in the name of grammar, but often battles were really about other issues like correctness, gender, politics, religion, and class. Even today, grammar may be perceived to be a boring subject, yet an attack on one's language is considered an attack on family, culture, and race. It is this element that makes grammar a challenging, yet exciting subject.

See also Chapters 1, THE BEGINNINGS; 2, FIRST STEPS: WALES AND IRELAND; 3, ENGLISH IN SCOTLAND; 25, WORLD ENGLISHES AND CULTURE WARS; 27, GRAMMAR WARS: THE UNITED STATES; 31, WORLD ENGLISHES AND GENDER IDENTITIES.

NOTES

1　A "model of grammar" refers to a grammatical construction in one language that can be used as an analogy to teach a similar construction in another language.

2　Lane (1695) was already making this argument, preface.

3　Several earlier grammarians had tried spelling reform as a way to standardize the vernacular: Bullokar (1586); Gill (1619); Butler (1633).

4　For early schemes on writing, see Knowlson (1975), pp. 44–64.

5　Besnier (1675) invented a system based on musical notes designed to be used to learn languages. He states in *Reunion of Languages* that one can master all languages by knowing one. Besnier's two aims in the book are to show that a student learns grammar when "an accord between several languages makes them attainable by comparison" and when languages are founded upon reason, pp. 23–5.

6　Knowlson (1975) has an extended discussion on Wilkins's methodology, pp. 98–107.

7　Other books that deserve mention are Theophilus Metcalfe's *Short Writing* (1645); John Farthing's *Short-Writing Shortened* (1684); Elisha Coles's *The Newest, Plainest, and Best Short-hand* (1674); and George Ridpath's *Short-Hand Yet Shorter* (1687).

8　For discussions on foreigners learning the English language, see Padley (1985); Poldauf (1948); Webster (1974).

9　Vivian Salmon states, "The teaching of English to foreigners was therefore largely responsible for the outstanding development of phonetics which charactereized seventeenth-century England" (1996: 21).

REFERENCES

Aickin, Joseph (1693) *English Grammar*. London.

Barclay, James (1743) *A Treatise on Education*. Edinburgh.

Beck, Cave (1657) *The Universal Character*. London.

Besnier, Pierre (1675) *A Philosophical Essay for the Reunion of the Languages*. Oxford.

Blount, Thomas (1654) *The Academy of Eloquence*. London.

Botley, Samuel (1674?) *Maximum in Minimo*. London.

Brown, Richard (1701) *English School Reformed*. London.

Buchanan, James (1761) *The British Grammar*. London.

Bullokar, John (1698) *An English Expositor*. London.

Butler, Charles (1634) *The English Grammar*. Oxford.

Care, Henry (1699) *Tutor to True English*. London.

Clarke, John (1731) *Essay upon Study*. London.

Clarke, John (1736) *An Essay Upon the Education of Youth in Grammar-schools*. Dublin.

Clarke, John (1740) *An Introduction to the Making of Latin*. London.

Coles, Elisha (1647) *The Newest, Plainest, and the Shortest Short-Hand*. London.

Coles, Elisha (1675a) *Nolens Volens*. London.

Coles, Elisha (1675b) *Syncrisis*. London.

Collyer, John (1735) *The General Principles of Grammar*. London.

Comenius, Johann Amos (1642) *The Reformed School*. London.

Comenius, Johann Amos (1659) *Orbis Sensualium Pictus*. Translated by Charles Hoole. London.

Cooper, Christopher (1685) *Grammatica Linguae Anglicanae*. London.

Dalgarno, George (1661) *Ars Signorum*. London.

Dilworth, Thomas (1740, 1751) *A New Guide to the English Tongue*. London.

The English Scholar Compleat (1706) London.

Farnaby, Thomas (1641) *Systema Grammaticum*. London.

Farro, Daniel (1754) *The Royal Universal British Grammar*. London.

Farthing, John (1684) *Short-Writing Shortened*. London.

Fenning, Daniel (1771) *A New Grammar of the English Language*. London.

Fisher, Ann (1750) *Practical English Grammar*. London.

Fisher, Ann (1757) *New Grammar*. London.

Fisher, George (1700) *The New Spelling Book*. London.

Garretson, John (1719) *English Exercises for School-Boys to Translate into Latin*. London.

Gildon, Charles (1712) *Grammar of the English Tongue*. London.

Gill, Alexander (1619) *Logonomia Anglica*. London.

Greenwood, James (1722) *Essay Towards a Practical English Grammar*. London.

Harris, James (1751) *Hermes: A Philosophical Enquiry concerning Universal Grammar*. London.

Hartlib, Samuel (1653) *The True and Readie Way to Learne the Latine Tongue*. London.

Hoole, Charles (1651) *Latine Grammar*. London.

Howell, James (1662) *A New English Grammar*. London.

Knowlson, James (1975) *Universal Language Schemes in England and France 1600–1800*. Toronto and Buffalo: University of Toronto Press.

Johnson, Ralph (1665) *Scholars Guide*. London.

Johnson, Richard (1706) *Grammatical Commentaries*. London.

Johnson, Samuel (1747) *The Plan of a Dictionary of the English Language*. London.

Jones, Rowland (1768) *Hieroglyfic*. London.

Jones, Rowland (1771) *Circles of Gomer*. London.

Jonson, Ben (1640) *English Grammar*. London.

Lane, A. (1695) *A Rational and Speedy Method of Attaining the Latine Tongue*. London.

Lane, A. (1700) *Key to the Art of Letters*. London.

Leedes, Edward (1685) *New English Examples Turned into Latin*. London.

Leedes, Edward (1726) *More English Examples Turned into Latin*. London.

Lodowyck, Francis (1647) *A Common Writing*. Oxford.

Lowth, Bishop Robert (1762) *Short Introduction to English Grammar*. London.

Maittaire, Michael (1712) *English Grammar*. London.

Makin, Bathsua (1674) *An Essay to Revive the Antient Education of Gentlewomen*. London.

Martin, Benjamin (1749) *Lingua Britannica Reformata*. London.

Mather, William (1695) *Young Man's Companion*. London.

Metcalfe, Theophilus (1645) *Short Writing*. London.

Miège, Guy (1688) *English Grammar*. London.

Milton, John (1669) *Accedence Commenc't Grammar*. London.

Mulcaster, Richard (1582) *The First Part of the Elementarie*. London.

Padley, George A. (1985) *Grammatical Theory in Western Europe: 1500–1700: Trends in Vernacular Grammar I*. Cambridge: Cambridge University Press.

The Pleasing Instructor (1756) London.

Poldauf, Ivan (1948) *On the History of Some Problems of English Grammar Before 1800*. Prague: Facultas philosophica Universitatis Carolinae Pragensis 55. Reprinted 1961.

Priestley, Joseph (1761) *The Rudiments of English Grammar*. London.

Rice, John (1765) *An Introduction to the Art of Reading*. London.

Ridpath, George (1687) *Short-Hand Yet Shorter*. London.

Salmon, Vivian (1996) Effort and achievement in seventeenth-century British linguistics. In *Language and Society in Early Modern England: Selected essays, 1982–1994*. Amsterdam: John Benjamins, pp. 3–29.

Snell, George (1649) *The Right Teaching of Useful Knowledge*. London.

Story, Joshua (1783) *Introduction to English Grammar*. London.

Swift, Jonathan (1712) *Proposal for Correcting, Improving, and Ascertaining the English Tongue*. London.

Tryon, Thomas (1700) *The Compleat School-Master*. London.

Walker, William (1686) *English Examples of Latin Syntaxis*. London.

Wallis, John (1653) *Grammatica Lingua Anglicanae*. London.

Watts, Isaac (1721) *Art of Reading and Writing*. London.

Webster, Charles (ed.) (1974) *The Intellectual Revolution of the 17th Century*. London: Routledge.

Wharton, Jeremiah (1654) *English Grammar*. London.

Wilkins, John (1668) *Essay Towards a Real Character*. London.

FURTHER READING

Adolph, Robert (1968) *The Rise of Modern Prose Style*. Cambridge, MA: MIT Press.

Amussen, Susan D. (1988) *An Ordered Society: Gender and Class in Early Modern England*. Oxford: Blackwell.

Brekle, Herbert E. (1975) The seventeenth century. In *Current Trends in Linguistics: Historiography of Linguistics 13*. Edited by Thomas A. Sebeok. The Hague: Mouton, pp. 277–382.

Bryan, William Frank (1923) Notes on the founders of prescriptive English grammar. In *Manly Anniversary Studies*. Edited by John M. Manly. Chicago: University of Chicago Press, pp. 383–93.

Cannon, G. H. (1979) English grammars of the seventeenth and eighteenth centuries. *Semiotica*, **26**, 121–49.

Clauss, Sidonie (1982) John Wilkins' *Essay Towards a Real Character*: Its place in the seventeenth-century episteme. *Journal of the History of Ideas*, **43**, 531–53.

Cohen, Murray (1977) *Sensible Words: Linguistic Practice in England 1640–1785*. Baltimore: Johns Hopkins University Press.

Constantinescu, Ilinca (1974) John Wallis (1616–1703): A reappraisal of his contribution to the study of English. *Historiographia Linguistica*, **1**, 297–311.

DeMott, Benjamin (1958) The sources and development of John Wilkins' philosophical language. *Journal of English and Germanic Philology*, **57**, 1–13.

Emsley, B. (1933) James Buchanan and the eighteenth century regulation of English usage. *PMLA*, **48**, 1154–66.

Finegan, Edward (1992) Style and standardization in England: 1700–1900. In *English in its Social Contexts: Essays in Historical Sociolinguistics*.

Edited by Tim W. Machan and Charles T. Scott. New York: Oxford University Press, pp. 102–30.

Houston, Robert A. (1988) *Literacy in Early Modern Europe: Culture and Education 1500–1800*. New York: Longman.

Jones, Richard F. (1953 [1974]) *Triumph of the English Language*. Stanford: Stanford University Press.

Joseph, John E. (1987) *Eloquence and Power: Rise of Language Standards and Standard Languages*. London: Francis Pinter.

Kennedy, A. G. (1926) Authorship of the British grammar. *Modern Language Notes*, **41**, 388–91.

Knowles, Gerry (1997) *A Cultural History of the English Language*. Arnold: New York.

Lass, Roger (ed.) (1999) *The Cambridge History of the English Language 1476–1776, vol. 3*. Cambridge: Cambridge University Press.

Law, V. (1975) The grammatical tradition and the rise of the vernaculars. In *Current Trends in Linguistics: Historiography of Linguistics 13*. Edited by Thomas A. Sebeok. The Hague: Mouton, pp. 231–75.

Leith, Dick (1983) *A Social History of English*. London: Routledge.

Leonard, Sterling A. (1929 [1962]) *The Doctrine of Correctness in English Usage, 1700–1800*. New York: Russell and Russell.

Michael, Ian (1970) *English Grammatical Categories and the Tradition to 1800*. Cambridge: Cambridge University Press.

Michael, Ian (1987) *The Teaching of English: From the Sixteenth Century to 1870*. Cambridge: Cambridge University Press.

Milroy, James and Milroy, Lesley (1985) *Authority in Language: Investigating Language Prescription and Standardization*. London: Routledge.

Mitchell, Linda C. (2001) *Grammar Wars: Language as Cultural Battlefield in Seventeenth and Eighteenth Century England*. Aldershot, UK: Ashgate.

Murphy, James J. (1990) *A Short History of Writing Instruction: From Ancient Greece to Twentieth-Century America*. Davis, CA: Hermagoras Press.

O'Day, Rosemary (1982) *Education and Society 1500–1800: The Social Foundations of Education in Early Modern Britain*. New York: Longman.

Padley, George A. (1988) *Grammatical Theory in Western Europe: 1500–1700: Trends in Vernacular Grammar II*. Cambridge: Cambridge University Press.

Salmon, Vivian (1979) *The Study of Language in Seventeenth-Century England*. Amsterdam: John Benjamins.

Slaughter, Mary M. (1982). *Universal Languages and Scientific Taxonomy in the Seventeenth Century*. Cambridge: Cambridge University Press.

Sugg, R. S., Jr. (1964) The mood of eighteenth-century English grammar. *Philological Quarterly*, **43**, 239–52.

Tucker, Susie I. (1961) *English Examined: Two Centuries of Comment on the Mother-Tongue*. Cambridge: Cambridge University Press.

Vincent, William A. L. (1969) *The Grammar Schools: Their Continuing Tradition, 1660–1714*. London: Cox and Wyman.

Vorlat, Emma (1975) *Development of English Grammatical Theory: 1586–1737*. Leuven: Leuven University Press.

Watson, Foster (1908, [1968]) *The English Grammar Schools to 1660: Their Curriculum and Practice*. London: Frank Cass.

Wrightson, Keith (1982) *English Society 1580–1680*. London: Hutchinson.

27 Grammar Wars: The United States

JOHN ALGEO

1 Introduction

Grammar war is not a new phenomenon, nor has it been limited to the United States. The Greeks had a word for it – *logomachia* 'a war about words'. St Paul used that term in his first epistle to Timothy (6.4–5), where he wrote of one who "is puffed up, knowing nothing but doting about questionings and disputes of words [*logomachia*], whereof cometh envy, strife, railing, evil surmisings, wrangling of men corrupted in mind and bereft of the truth." In the anglicized form *logomachy*, it has been used in English since 1569 (according to the *Oxford English Dictionary*). The usual sense is 'an argument that is about words rather than things', but because that is what most grammatical disputes are, they have their place in the ancient, if not honorable, tradition of the logomachy.

Logomachy, including grammar wars, is not limited to unimportant arguments about words, however. Words are powerful things, and disputes about them can have significant, indeed catastrophic, results. Because *logos* means 'word, reason, order', arguments about words may be arguments about the perception of order in society or, for that matter, in the cosmos.

To dispute about words is to dispute about how we conceptualize the world around us, as Benjamin Lee Whorf (1956) pointed out long ago. To dispute about grammar, that is, about how we conceptualize words, is to dispute about epistemology – how we know the world. Grammar wars are thus philosophical in their nature, but they have also been linked, more or less closely, with disputes about usage, in the sense of what is genuine, correct, or proper language. And usage disputes, in their turn, are often linked, again more or less closely, with sociology, specifically views concerning social classes. So grammar wars have these two major aspects: theoretical (or philosophical) and usage (or sociological).

2 Grammar Wars over Theory

The history of grammar wars over theory illustrates the evolutionary pattern called "punctuated equilibrium," co-identified by Niles Eldredge and Stephen Jay Gould (1972) and popularized by the latter. This pattern sees evolution not as a slow, continuous process, but rather as consisting of long periods of stability ("equilibria") that are "punctuated" by events of relatively sudden and rapid change. In the case of the Western grammar wars, the equilibrium lasted for a couple of millennia, beginning with the Alexandrian Dionysius Thrax in the first century BC and extending through the nineteenth and early twentieth centuries. That equilibrium included a number of fluctuations, but they did not disturb or seriously modify the approach to grammar study that was established by Thrax in Alexandria during its heyday as an intellectual center of the Western world and that continued until the nineteenth century. Thus American grammar wars entered the traditional grammatical equilibrium late in its history.

The traditional equilibrium focused grammatical study on written language (hence the term *grammar* from Greek *grammatikē* 'the study of letters'). The main purpose of grammar was to assist in the interpretation of literature (which was also a matter of letters, from Latin *litteratura* 'writing, learning'). Its major categories were defined philosophically ("A noun is the name of a person, place, or thing," etc.). The orientation of grammar was pedagogical, that is, its purpose was to teach someone how to use language. The main subject of grammar was the word – its identity and relationship to other words.

The earliest study of grammar in America is continuous with that in Britain. However, early on, new directions developed in the New World, some of which were parallel with those of the motherland, but others not so. The history of English grammar in America can be seen as consisting of several major phases, defined by scholarly approaches to the subject (Algeo, 1986 approaches the subject from a more pedagogical standpoint).

2.1 Latinate and nativist grammars

In the first phase, American English grammar was solidly in the Latinate tradition. In early works of the phase, an opposition appeared between (1) descriptions that imposed Latin categories on English and (2) nativist ones that presented English on its own terms. An example of Latin-bound grammar is Thomas Dilworth's *A New Guide to the English Tongue*, first published in London in 1740, but soon and often reprinted in America. It describes the morphology of the English noun as consisting of six cases: nominative "A Book," genitive "Of a Book," dative "To a Book," accusative "The Book," vocative "O Book!" and ablative "From a Book." An example of nativist grammar is John Ash's *Grammatical Institutes* (1760), another British work that became popular in America. The acme of the nativist works is Goold Brown's

The Grammar of English Grammars, which was published in 1851, underwent ten editions, and continued to be reprinted at least until the end of the century. Its thousand-plus pages are a compendium of the tradition, offering rules to be memorized, sentences to be parsed word by word, and "false syntax" (i.e., errors) to be corrected.

2.2   *Word-focused and clause-focused grammars*

Despite the opposition between Latinate and nativist grammars, they agreed in being pedagogically oriented and word-focused. In a second phase, the pedagogical emphasis continued, but word-focused grammar was replaced by clause-focused grammar. The latter is less concerned with individual words – their parts of speech and inflectional characteristics – and more concerned instead with types of constructions (sentences, clauses, and phrases) and their functional components (subjects, objects, heads, and modifiers), often displayed by diagrams of various sorts. Examples of clause-focused grammars are S. W. Clark's *A Practical Grammar* (1847), which diagrammed sentences by writing their components in cartouche-shaped balloons linked together in various ways, and Alonzo Reed and Brainerd Kellogg's *Higher Lessons in English* (1877), which introduced a style of sentence diagramming still used today. Clause-focused grammar became the standard on both sides of the Atlantic, reaching its acme in the scholarly-traditional *A Comprehensive Grammar of English* (1985) by Randolph Quirk et al. That work belongs essentially to the clause-focused approach of grammatical description though it lacks diagrams of syntactic structure and is vastly improved by a thorough grounding in data and an incorporation of insights from the later structural and transformational phases.

2.3   *Historical, dialectal, and variation linguistics*

Clause-focused grammars, like the earlier word-focused ones, were synchronic in their orientation and were concerned primarily with the standard language, whether in Britain or in America. Their development, however, coincided roughly with that of a new phase in language study: historical and dialectal linguistics. These disciplines, both originally motivated by diachronic interests, emphasized variation over time and space but returned to a primary focus on the word – its phonology, semantics, and morphology – rather than on syntax (at least until relatively recent times).

Historical and dialectal studies were more narrowly academic in their constituency, rather than broadly pedagogical or popular. They both had an Old Curiosity Shop appeal to the general public, but that was incidental to the interests of the scholars who pursued the studies. Well-grounded popular presentations of their results have been made (for example, John McWhorter, 2003, *The Power of Babel*), but for the most part their domain is academia. Only a few scholarly works in the area can also be appreciated by general readers;

one of those is Frederic Cassidy and Joan Hall's (1985–) *Dictionary of American Regional English*.

By the later twentieth century, however, variation study became more concerned with language differences of a social nature: urban versus rural, class and gender correlations, first- versus second- or foreign-language varieties, and so on. William Labov's work beginning in 1966 redirected American interests to urban and sociological linguistics. For international English, Braj Kachru is the central figure for defining the types of English found around the world (Thumboo, 2001, *Three Circles of English*). Those expanded concerns had implications for both pedagogy and the wider social context. The study of language variation over time, space, and social groups ultimately proved to be a significant change because it increased scholarly knowledge, affected teaching, and contributed to a change in social awareness about the meaning of linguistic and hence other forms of cultural variation. It also prepared the way for theoretical developments that were to follow.

2.4   *Structuralism: Descriptive and generative*

In the twentieth century, the grammatical tradition received a still stronger challenge from scholarly study – the rise of structuralism in two principal forms: descriptive and generative. These two forms were sharply different in one respect. Descriptive structuralism in the tradition of Ferdinand de Saussure – including such American practitioners as Leonard Bloomfield, Charles Carpenter Fries, Kenneth Pike, Charles Hockett, George Trager, Henry Lee Smith, Jr., and many anthropological linguists – started with a corpus and aimed at a grammatical description of its system. Generative structuralism, in the tradition of Chomsky and his followers – including Chomsky's own developing theories – aimed at a set of rules that would not merely describe the system of a given corpus but would predict or define all possible utterances of that system and would do so in terms of universal principles of language (e.g., Chomsky, 2002).

Descriptive structuralists were free to have recourse to various "hocus-pocus" descriptive techniques as long as they accounted adequately for the corpus; their descriptions could be regarded as convenient fictions. The emphasis of the generativists on "explanatory" adequacy (especially in its later, minimalist, variety), implied that they were committed to finding *the* correct account, one that corresponded to the reality behind surface appearance. Generative theory is often equated with transformationalism, but the latter is simply a technique proposed by Harris (1951), which can be used either descriptively (as a hocus-pocus device) or generatively (as an aspect of universal grammar).

The aim of generative grammar – to predict all possible utterances of a given language – was attacked by Charles Hockett in *The State of the Art* (1968). In that work, Hockett argued that the generative aim presupposes a language to be a well-defined system, like chess (with which language has often been compared) – a mental reality for which the physical system is useful but unnecessary. But in fact every language is an ill-defined system, like sandlot baseball. That is, it is a system whose rules are constantly changing, as some players manage to convince other players to handle the physical system as they prefer. An ill-defined system, like sandlot baseball or language, cannot be defined generatively because its margins are unclear and constantly shifting. The best you can do with an ill-defined system is to describe what its users generally accept as part of it and generally regard as not part of it. The quest for what the language really is, is chimerical.

Despite their differences, Bloomfieldian and Chomskyan linguistics (to identify them with their two most prominent American exponents) have enough in common to justify both being called "structuralism," as they are concerned with describing or predicting grammatical structures in formal terms. They – together with historical, dialectal, and social variation studies – were a major punctuation in the traditional grammatical equilibrium. The tradition concerned itself primarily with writing and literature; the new theories, whenever possible, preferred speech and everyday language. The tradition was philosophical and semantic in its approach; the new theories aspired to scientific and formal approaches. The tradition's main concern was teaching people how to use language; the new theories were concerned with understanding how language works. The tradition was primarily lexical in focus; the new theories were primarily systematic.

Efforts were made to present the issues of structuralism, both descriptive and generative, to the general public and to adapt them for use in the classroom. Classroom efforts were notable but also notably unsuccessful. Among successful efforts to communicate with the general educated public are the works of Steven Pinker (e.g., Pinker, 1994, 1999).

A major grammar war was thus the conflict between traditional grammar, principally European in its origin, and structural grammar as it developed (or, in the case of generative theory, originated) in America. Although there are still echoes of this war in the subsequent conflicts dealt with below, it was settled in favor of structuralism. The distinguished scholarly traditional grammars that continue have simply absorbed much of the structuralist agenda, while omitting its more abstruse formalisms.

The grammar war between descriptive and generative structuralism, however, was not so much settled as stalemated. For linguists interested in grammatical theory, one or another of its varieties has clearly won the day. But for linguists interested in other pursuits (dialectology, lexicography, social variation, first- or second-language acquisition, literary analysis, and so on), the dispute became largely irrelevant because neither formalism proved to be particularly useful for their purposes. Consequently, the field of language study has divided into two camps: one pursuing generative theoretical concerns and the other pursuing data-oriented concerns and using whatever approach is helpful for those concerns, but often with relatively little attention to the underlying theory. The result is not a new grammar war, but a grammar détente in which each side uses the work of the other when it is useful but regards the other side as otherwise uninteresting.

3 Grammar Wars over Usage

The grammar wars that have been most fiercely fought and that have most engaged the attention of the public have been usage wars. These are by no means unrelated to the earlier disputes, but have a life of their own. Traditional grammar, especially in its Latinate form, tended to look on correctness in usage as an absolute. Historical linguistics, dialectology, variation studies, and descriptive structuralism, by their very natures, all adopted a relativist approach to usage. The theoretical stance of generative structuralism is implicitly absolutist, but the practice of most generativists has been relativistic, except for a tendency to declare structures "grammatical" or "ungrammatical," sometimes it seems merely on the basis of the declarer's usage. Thus the earlier theoretical grammar wars set the scene for a usage war that pitted "purists" against "relativists" (each term being used by the other as a slur).

The usage wars have been fought on several fronts: (1) purism versus relativism or maintaining the standard versus recognizing linguistic diversity (of which the great battle was the flap at the publication of *Webster's Third New International Dictionary*); (2) ethnocentrism versus multiculturalism in educational practice (of which the great battle was a call for "back to basics" versus the students' right to their own language); (3) official English versus non-English languages (of which the great battle was the move in many states and on the national scene to establish English as the only official language of the United States versus requiring the use of other languages in communities where they are prominent); and (4) the gender war over the generic use of masculine forms versus sex-neutral language as well as the struggle about how to name minorities. All of these fronts share a concern over preserving historical norms versus reforming practices to suit changing circumstances – the conservative versus liberal axis. One is tempted to agree with Private Willis of the Grenadier Guards, who sings Sir William Gilbert's lyrics in *Iolanthe*:

> I often think it's comical
> How Nature always does contrive
> That every boy and every gal
> That's born into the world alive
> Is either a little Liberal
> Or else a little Conservative!

3.1 Purism and relativism

The purism-versus-relativism war raged during the twentieth century. Purism is concerned with an inventory of usages that were identified as shibboleths, some as early as the eighteenth century. That inventory of shibboleths has been augmented over the past three hundred years, but many of its items have persevered, and its spirit has never faltered (Algeo, 1977). The earliest study seeking to establish the facts of usage objectively, which thus inaugurated the relativist opposition to purism, was J. Lesslie Hall's *English Usage* (1917). It was followed from the 1930s onward by a series of usage works based, not on the writer's opinion or on previous usage guides (though works of that ilk also abounded), but on studies of actual use. An impressive, because extensive and thorough, example of such works is Ward Gilman's *Merriam-Webster's Dictionary of English Usage* (1994).

The purism-versus-relativism war reached a sort of climax with the publication of Philip Gove's *Webster's Third New International Dictionary* (1961). That work, based on the best linguistic and lexicographical principles of its day, reported facts of usage for the most part unfiltered by the editor's personal judgment. For example, it recorded of the shibboleth *ain't*: "though disapproved by many and more common in less educated speech, used orally in most parts of the U.S. by many cultivated speakers, esp. in the phrase *ain't I.*" That comment was based on extensive evidence, although the cultivated speakers were doubtless rather conservative (though not in the purist sense) and old-fashioned, as the usage in question was upper-class standard in the eighteenth century before it acquired its negative status as a shibboleth. *Webster's Third* was received with outraged reviews in many periodicals. The history of the flap over *Webster's Third* was recorded at the time by James Sledd and Wilma Ebbitt in *Dictionaries and That Dictionary* (1962). The history of the making of the dictionary and of its reception was later told in detail by Herbert Morton in *The Story of "Webster's Third"* (1994).

3.2 Ethnocentrism and multiculturalism: Back to the basics and the students' right

A conflict between ethnocentrism and multiculturalism was the natural consequence of applying the concerns of purism versus relativism to the cultural context, especially of education. Each side of that war has something to be said for it and something to be said against it. There is much to be said for placing the historical ethnic traditions of the nation at the center of education; but there is also much to be said against confining education to a single ethnic tradition. Similarly, there is much to be said for educating children and the public to the fact that cultures vary in many and interesting ways and that such variation exists, not only in exotic places around the globe, but in most communities in America; but there is also much to be said against fragmenting cultural education so greatly that the traditions underlying American democracy are lost. A *via media* is needed.

Applied to education, the idea that correctness is relative to a context and that variation is normal in language was misunderstood by purists as a lack of standards and an "anything goes" attitude. It was also similarly misunderstood by some who embraced the idea. The result was that some of Private Willis's "little Liberals" denied the existence of a standard language, apparently ironically agreeing with the purists that, if uniformity is lacking, a standard cannot exist. The result was a position that came to be known as "The Students' Right" (to their own language), in a 1972 resolution of the Executive Committee of the Conference on College Composition and Communication (available at www.english.wayne.edu/writing/dialect/studentsrights.html):

> We affirm the students' right to their own patterns and varieties of language – the dialects of their nurture or whatever dialects in which they find their own identity and style. Language scholars long ago denied that the myth of a standard American dialect has any validity. The claim that any one dialect is unacceptable amounts to an attempt of one social group to exert its dominance over another. Such a claim leads to false advice for speakers and writers, and immoral advice for humans. A nation proud of its diverse heritage and its cultural and racial variety will preserve its heritage of dialects. We affirm strongly that teachers must have the experiences and training that will enable them to respect diversity and uphold the right of students to their own language.

At its best, the "Students' Right" statement aimed at educating teachers and everyone in the realities of language: that no variety is inherently better or worse than any other, that varieties are linked with social structures, and that one's native variety is part of one's identity. At its worst, it was interpreted as prohibiting teachers from the "linguistic imperialism" of teaching standard English to students whose native variety was nonstandard, and it denied the right of a prestige variety to exist.

The controversy is far from resolved, as indicated by a number of Georgetown University Round Table papers published as *Language in Our Time* (Alatis and Tan, 2001: 253–313). The controversy over teaching in African American English (under the name "Ebonics") sparked a controversy parallel to that over teaching recent immigrants' children in their native language (also covered in the volume just cited, especially pages 111–48). A crucial difference, however, is that, despite some claims to the contrary, African Americans speak a variety of English. Consequently, bilingual education, with respect to non-English languages, has stronger support from professionals than does the Ebonics movement.

The direct response to the "Students' Right" movement was to ignore it and to continue teaching the sort of English that English teachers had always taught. However, there was also an indirect response directed toward the curriculum in general. It was the Back to Basics movement, which rejected "frills" in education, including the sort of human social engineering implicit in the "Students' Right" movement, in favor of the traditional focus on the three Rs. The on-line *Oxford English Dictionary* defines the term *back to (the) basics* as "a catch-phrase applied (freq. attrib.) to a movement or enthusiasm for a return to the fundamental principles in education, etc., or to policies reflecting this." Its citations are from the mid 1970s onward, such as the following from the *National Observer* (January 8, 1977): "The current 'back to basics' movement, the campaign to give the highest priority to the teaching of the fundamentals of reading, writing, and arithmetic." The *Oxford English Dictionary*'s first citation in 1975, however, applies the term to churches rather than schools, and the expression has become extraordinarily popular, with a positive application to a wide variety of subjects, from agriculture to zoology, as evidenced by a Google search that generates millions of results for the phrase.

3.3   Ethnocentrism and multiculturalism: Official English and non-English languages

Another aspect of ethnocentrism and multiculturalism is the war between the promoters of Official English and those who oppose it. It is difficult to find objective and nonpartisan treatments of the subject. A reasonably dispassionate one is *Nativism Reborn?* (1955) by Raymond Tatalovich. The Official English movement, whose main organization was US English (established in 1983), seems to have been a response to pressure by local ethnic communities for multilingual education and government services. Although America has seen repeated waves of immigrants, the Hispanic influx of recent years was exceptional in size and concentration, and it was among this group that the pressure began.

The proponents of Official English see it as promoting cultural continuity and national unity. Its opponents brand it as xenophobic, anti-immigration, and racially or culturally biased, a charge that may apply to some of its advocates, but hardly to all, such as to Senator S. I. Hayakawa, who in 1981 proposed in the American Congress a constitutional amendment to establish English as the official language of the United States (Hayakawa, 1985).

The academic response has been strongly in opposition to Official English. Dennis Baron in *The English-Only Question* (1990) places the movement in its historical context while arguing strongly against it. An even more one-sided presentation of the question is R. D. González and I. Melis's *Language Ideologies: Critical Perspectives on the Official English Movement* (2000–1).

3.4   Generic masculine and sex-neutral language: Terms for minorities

At one time, the primary linguistic taboos were on terms for sexual activities and excretion. Today they are on terms for gender and minority status. The gender issue is particularly that of sexist language, the generic use of words deemed to be masculine in reference. The minority-status issue concerns a variety of factors, especially race and ethnicity.

The widespread concern to avoid offensive terms has resulted in a successful effort to engineer the language. Publishers have adopted strict codes to avoid offensive terms, and much colloquial use has also been affected. Those who waged this war have clearly won. And it is noteworthy that those who would normally bristle at any suggestion of censorship determinedly censor language in this respect. It has become not only permissible but obligatory to control such use of words. The Modern Language Association's Commission on the Status of Women in the Profession produced a guide, *Language, Gender, and Professional Writing*, by Francine Frank and Paula Treichler, which ends thus (1989: 278): "The use of nonsexist language is . . . the only linguistic choice that enables us . . . to be responsible members of our profession."

Marilyn Schwartz, on behalf of a task force of the Association of American University Presses, produced *Guidelines for Bias-free Writing* (1995), which covered five areas of new taboos: (1) gender, (2) race, ethnicity, citizenry and nationality, and religion, (3) disabilities and medical conditions, (4) sexual orientation, and (5) age. The following advice is notable under the heading of sexual orientation (p. 86): "Instead of *husband, wife,* or *spouse,* writers are encouraged to use the more inclusive terms [*partner, companion,* etc.] . . . instead of marriage, they may employ terms such as *committed relationship* or *primary relationship.*"

A problem is that terms recommended as inoffensive may turn out also be offensive. One person's euphemism is another's dysphemism. One aged professor was known to complain, "You can call me a dirty old man, but not a senior citizen."

3.5 Usage and politics

Usage wars are disputes over the best way to phrase an idea. But they are not therefore superficial. A notable example is the work of George Lakoff, who departed from Chomsky's formalism to emphasize the connection between worldview and language expression in a theory of cognitive linguistics. Lakoff's position is that both our thought process and our language are fundamentally metaphorical (Lakoff and Johnson, 1980; Lakoff, 1987). Because the metaphors that underlie the way we think and talk are largely unconscious, they are extremely powerful.

To explain the success of right-wing politicians in recent US elections, Lakoff analyzed the metaphorical basis of their discourse and subsequently proposed that, to be successful at the polls, politicians on the left must "frame" their discourse in equally evocative metaphorical terms. His handbook of political usage, *Don't Think of an Elephant! Know Your Values and Frame the Debate* (2004) has become a vade mecum for many liberals. If Lakoff is right, metaphor trumps logic by tapping into the deepest level of our minds. And thus usage wars are not about etiquette but about ethos.

4 Conclusion

If we look at the recent history of linguistic theories, it is clear that any equilibrium in logomachia is not likely to last very long. In this era of globalization with rapid advances in information distribution and technology, the intense war over usage is likely to continue. The relative peace of the previous 19 centuries has inexorably given way to new controversies and debates, as well as to new applications of usage study in civil concerns.

See also Chapters 17, VARIETIES OF WORLD ENGLISHES; 20, WRITTEN LANGUAGE, STANDARD LANGUAGE, GLOBAL LANGUAGE; 26, GRAMMAR WARS: SEVENTEENTH- AND EIGHTEENTH-CENTURY ENGLAND; 28, WORLD ENGLISHES AND DESCRIPTIVE GRAMMARS.

REFERENCES

Alatis, James E. and Tan, Ai-Hui (eds.) (2001) *Language in Our Time: Bilingual Education and Official English, Ebonics and Standard English, Immigration and the Unz Initiative.* Baltimore, MD: Georgetown University Press.

Algeo, John (1977) Grammatical usage: Modern shibboleths. In *James B. McMillan: Essays in Linguistics by His Friends and Colleagues.* Edited by James C. Raymond and I. Willis Russell. University, AL: University of Alabama Press, pp. 53–71.

Algeo, John (1986) A grammatical dialectic. In *The English Reference Grammar: Language and Linguistics, Writers and Readers.* Edited by Gerhard Leitner. Tübingen: Max Niemeyer, pp. 307–33.

Ash, John (1760) *Grammatical Institutes; or, Grammar, Adapted to the Genius of the English Tongue.* Worcester: Printed by R. Lewis.

Baron, Dennis (1990) *The English-Only Question: An Official Language for Americans?* New Haven: Yale University Press.

Brown, Goold (1851) *The Grammar of English Grammars, with an Introduction Historical and Critical.* New York: Samuel S. and William Wood.

Cassidy, Frederic G. and Hall, Joan Houston (eds.) (1985–) *Dictionary of American Regional English,* vol. 1–. Cambridge, MA: Belknap.

Chomsky, Noam (2002) *On Nature and Language.* Edited by Adriana Belletti and Luigi Rizzi. Cambridge: Cambridge University Press.

Clark, Stephen Watkins (1847) *A Practical Grammar: In Which Words, Phrases, and Sentences Are Classified According to Their Offices, and Their Various Relations to Each Other: Illustrated by a Complete System of Diagrams.* New York: A. S. Barnes.

Dilworth, Thomas (1740) *A New Guide to the English Tongue.* London: Hodgson.

Eldredge, Niles and Gould, Stephen Jay (1972) Punctuated equilibria: An alternative to phyletic gradualism. In *Models in Paleobiology.* Edited by T. J. M. Schopf. San Francisco, CA: Freeman, Cooper, pp. 82–115.

Frank, Francine Wattman and Treichler, Paula A. (1989) *Language, Gender, and Professional Writing: Theoretical Approaches and Guidelines for Nonsexist Usage.* New York: Commission on the Status of Women in the Profession, Modern Language Association of America.

Gilman, Ward E. (ed.) (1994) *Merriam-Webster's Dictionary of English Usage*. Springfield, MA: Merriam-Webster.

González, Roseann Dueñas and Melis, Ildikó (eds.) (2000–1) *Language Ideologies: Critical Perspectives on the Official English Movement*, 2 vols. Urbana, IL: National Council of Teachers of English; Mahwah, NJ: Erlbaum.

Gove, Philip Babcock (1961) *Webster's Third New International Dictionary of the English Language*. Springfield, MA: Merriam-Webster.

Hall, J. Lesslie (1917) *English Usage: Studies in the History and Uses of English Words and Phrases*. Chicago: Scott, Foresman.

Harris, Zellig S. (1951) *Methods in Structural Linguistics*. Chicago: University of Chicago Press.

Hayakawa, S. I. (1985) *The English Language Amendment: One Nation . . . Indivisible?* Washington, DC: Washington Institute for Values in Public Policy.

Hockett, Charles F. (1968) *The State of the Art*. The Hague: Mouton.

Labov, William (1966) *The Social Stratification of English in New York City*. Washington, DC: Center for Applied Linguistics.

Lakoff, George (1987) *Women, Fire, and Dangerous Things: What Categories Reveal about the Mind*. Chicago: University of Chicago Press.

Lakoff, George (2004) *Don't Think of an Elephant! Know Your Values and Frame the Debate: The Essential Guide for Progressives*. Foreword by Howard Dean. White River Junction, VT: Chelsea Green, 2004.

Lakoff, George and Johnson, Mark (1980) *Metaphors We Live By*. Chicago: University of Chicago Press.

McWhorter, John H. (2003) *The Power of Babel: A Natural History of Language*. New York: HarperCollins, Perennial.

Morton, Herbert C. (1994) *The Story of "Webster's Third": Philip Gove's Controversial Dictionary and Its Critics*. New York: Cambridge University Press.

Pinker, Steven (1994) *The Language Instinct*. New York: Morrow.

Pinker, Steven (1999) *Words and Rules: The Ingredients of Language*. New York: Basic Books.

Quirk, Randolph, Greenbaum, Sidney, Leech, Geoffrey, and Svartvik, Jan (1985) *A Comprehensive Grammar of English*. London: Longman.

Reed, Alonzo and Kellogg, Brainerd (1877) *Higher Lessons in English: A Work on English Grammar and Composition, in Which the Science of the Language Is Made Tributary to the Art of Expression*. New York: Clark and Maynard.

Schwartz, Marilyn (1995) *Guidelines for Bias-free Writing*. Bloomington, IN: Indiana University Press.

Sledd, James and Ebbitt, Wilma R. (1962) *Dictionaries and **That** Dictionary*. Chicago: Scott, Foresman.

Tatalovich, Raymond (1955) *Nativism Reborn? The Official English Language Movement and the American States*. Lexington, KY: University Press of Kentucky.

Thumboo, Edwin (ed.) (2001) *The Three Circles of English: Language Specialists Talk about the English Language*. Singapore: UniPress.

Whorf, Benjamin Lee (1956) *Language, Thought, and Reality*. Edited by John B. Carroll. Cambridge, MA: Technology Press of the Massachusetts Institute of Technology.

FURTHER READING

Newmeyer, Frederick J. (1983) *Grammatical Theory, Its Limits and Its Possibilities*. Chicago: University of Chicago.

Robins, Robert Henry (1997) *A Short History of Linguistics*. 4th edition. London: Longman.

Whitney, William Dwight (1833) *The Life and Growth of Language: An Outline of Linguistic Science*. London: H. S. King, 1875; New York: Appleton, 1892.

28 World Englishes and Descriptive Grammars

DANIEL R. DAVIS

1 Introduction

There has been significant progress in the grammatical description of varieties of English in the past 25 years (see Schneider, 2003: 234). Specific grammatical descriptions play an important role in the recognition of different English languages, and demarcate a distinct stage in the history of the grammatical tradition. Nevertheless, the writing of these descriptions comes at a cost. They depend on assumptions drawn from various areas of linguistics and language study, and these assumptions limit the uses to which these descriptions can be put.

This chapter is inspired by the integrational linguistic approach set forth in Harris (1998), and draws upon the work of sociolinguists James Milroy, Lesley Milroy, and Deborah Cameron. The chapter is integrationist in its commitment to the assumption that current grammatical description, both in form and intent, owes a great deal to the general cultural background, the historical contexts, intellectual issues, and philosophical discourses of the English languages. Even the most basic grammatical terms are set within an intellectual tradition, and have political implications: There is no such thing as a value-free description. This approach speaks to the experiences of those using, encountering, and analyzing world Englishes and varieties of English. Milroy and Milroy (1999) explore the importance that social networks and grammatical traditions have for social attitudes toward grammar, and Cameron (1995) draws out the political conditions and social implications of public discourse about grammar and related forms of what she terms "verbal hygiene." These three sociolinguists have therefore called into question the supposed irrelevance of language prescription in linguistics.

2 Descriptive Grammar in Prescriptive and Historical Linguistic Traditions

Traditional prescriptive grammars of English reveal surprising openness to the question of varieties. Wallis (1972 [1653]: 108–13 [xxv–xxvii]) clearly intends to describe the language for the benefit of both foreign learners and native speakers, and finds that accounts of English based too closely on Latin models are not suitable for this purpose (see Michael, 1970: 164–5 and 495–6). This emphasis on description suggests the possibility of an empirical approach to the language of the community, and allows for the adaptation of terminology to reflect linguistic difference. Wallis nonetheless chooses to retain Latin terminology, a decision reflected in the terminology of descriptive grammar today. Kirkham (1833: 59, 63) questions the usefulness of his own prescriptive rules and allows that both singular and plural agreement work equally well with collective nouns, while arguing that incorrect agreement sounds "harsh." Even a traditional and explicitly prescriptive grammar, in the right hands, is open to the problem of variation. Milroy and Milroy (1999: 30) define standardization as the suppression of optional variation, and trace the development of this ideology in British and American culture from the seventeenth to twentieth centuries. Prescription is awarding prestige to one variant. Implicit in this is the descriptive act of recognizing that (given the analytical framework of the parts of speech) several variants exist.

In the late nineteenth and early twentieth century, historical linguistics and dialectology offered a basis for descriptive grammar tied to a social and historical conception of linguistic correctness. Even in the prescriptive and normative context of a school grammar, historical linguist H. C. Wyld (1925: 8–13, 205–6) defines grammar as the facts of a spoken language, places this in a community setting, and allows for variation across and within communities. His conception of the English language is explicitly pluricentric, and he recognizes the role of social and historical change in reconfiguring the standard and literary forms of the language (1925: 220). His examples, however, are confined to British English dialects. Jespersen (1933: 16) mentions subdivisions of English, including geographical (Scottish, Irish, American) and social. Like Wyld, he defines descriptive grammar empirically (1933: 19–20), "what is actually said and written by the speakers of the language investigated . . . lead[ing] to a scientific understanding of the rules followed instinctively by speakers and writers."

This calls to mind Saussurean structuralism, in that language is situated in the community and recognized to be in a state of variation from one individual to another, and from one community to another. Nevertheless, this variable data is analyzed in order to derive an abstract set of rules (a language structure) followed by language users. It is ironic that traditional prescriptivism depending on descriptivist assumptions has been supplanted by a descriptivism assuming an underlying unity (see J. Milroy, 1999, for extensive analysis of the impact of standardization on linguistic description). This replacement has serious consequences for the representation of variation in descriptive grammar. As Harris says:

> The situation in which an established descriptive format devised for one particular purpose is taken over and adapted to serve some new and quite different purpose is a situation fraught with potential errors and inconsistencies of all kinds. (Harris, 1981: 54)

3   World Englishes in Late Twentieth-Century Descriptive Grammars

Descriptive grammars draw heavily on the prescriptive tradition for their terminology and method. They are arranged on a traditional framework of the parts of speech, refined with the use of structuralist discovery method (see Biber et al. 1999: viii and 4 for confirmation of this, although the corpus-based approach of this grammar admits context of use into the foundation of the grammar and gives it greater sociolinguistic value). The various frameworks of syntactic theory are not usually part of these descriptions, but rather use these descriptions as the basis for theory. Henry (2002: 267) discusses the way in which syntactic theory is for the most part predicated on assumptions that rule out variation.

Although Quirk et al. (1985, hereafter termed "the Quirk grammar" unless specific page reference is given) discuss the possibility of grammatical variation in world Englishes in their introduction, the main body of this work adheres to the familiar pattern of presenting a core English with two equally prestigious varieties, each acceptable within its own regional monopoly. The index cites 150 sections or notes referring to American English constructions, and 136 sections or notes referring to British English constructions. No other varieties appear in the index with constructions, except for "non-standard" with 26 constructions, and "regional" with 35 entries (not restricted to constructions). This is out of a total of 1,450 sections, and one might infer that approximately 9–10 percent of the sections of the grammar deal with variation between American and British English (Görlach, 1991: 25), while only 2–3 percent of the sections of the grammar deal with other varieties, including non-standard varieties.

It should be recalled that the Quirk grammar is not a direct reflection of the English language in its entirety, but rather represents a notional "Standard English." To take a convenient example, Quirk et al. (1985: 1247–9) discuss the non-personal relative pronouns *which, that,* and "zero," but make no mention of the non-standard relative markers *what* or *as.* Therefore, although it is "descriptive," the Quirk grammar cannot itself be used as evidence for the common core, as it excludes many non-standard forms by definition. These forms may equally merit representation within a very different "core." In addition, this section-counting method does not indicate the comparative frequency of variable constructions, nor how these frequencies vary according to register. Finally, the market for the grammar is quite clearly those users in search of an authoritative treatment, a description of what correct English is, that may be used prescriptively to say what is not correct English. Non-standard forms and "regional" varieties are not in this picture, except insofar as forms encountered by learners must be explained (thus the account of relative pronouns, but also of the royal *we* and non-standard *us* "Give us a job"; Quirk et al., 1985: 351).

Successors to the Quirk grammar conform to this pattern, for reasons of market, purpose, and methodology. Large-scale descriptive grammars reflect the concerns of language learners, the publishing industry, and language specialists. Although both the *Longman Grammar* and the *Cambridge Grammar* identify their target audience as linguists (Biber et al., 1999: 45–6 and Huddleston and Pullum, 2002: xv), the size and expense of these works suggest that a large part of their market must be libraries in need of reference grammars. Like the Quirk grammar, they are consulted in order to find sanction for particular forms and usages. One cannot ignore the prescriptive power of a good description (see Marenbon, 1987, cited in Cameron, 1995: 10).

The Longman grammar (Biber et al., 1999: 17–20, 25–6) is based on a 40-million-word corpus of British and American English, and deals extensively with differences between American and British varieties, but also with differences between registers (conversation, fiction, newspaper language, and academic prose). Frequencies are given, making it possible to discern levels of normative agreement in different registers (see also Biber, 1988). An entire chapter is devoted to the grammar of conversation (pp. 1038–125), with a small section devoted to non-standard forms. The text asserts that most variation occurs in the area of morphosyntax, and that syntax is largely variation-free, with the multiple negative and double comparative illustrated by "AmE" (p. 1125). Non-standard forms are mentioned in the text, as in the discussion of non-standard relative markers *what* and *as* (p. 608). Reliance on the LSWE (Longman Spoken and Written English) corpus of British and American texts and conversations, which makes possible the frequency statements, also rules out discussion of world Englishes, although the authors direct readers to the International Corpus of English project (p. 1133, n. 1). The Cambridge grammar (Huddleston and Pullum, 2002) incorporates some reference to different varieties of English, although the emphasis is on syntactic structure derived from acceptability judgments. This has the effect of limiting serious consideration of varieties. For example, in the discussion of relative clauses there is no mention of non-standard forms, and the goal is to describe the patterning of the standard relative pronouns and to identify the syntactic structures necessary to account for integrated and supplementary relative clauses (Huddleston and Pullum, 2002: 1059–61).

4 Theoretical Problems Inherited from Structuralism

Kachru (1992: 304) identifies Quirk et al. (1972) as the moment of recognition for world Englishes. Quirk et al. (1972) arrive at this recognition in the course of defining their object of study. The text uses the concept of a common core of English as a foundation for Standard English, which in turn is defined as the usage of the educated. On the basis of an analogy with taxonomy and intra-species variation (the dog features or "dogness" of dogs embodied in different varieties of dog), the authors argue that "we need to see a common core or nucleus that we call 'English' being realized only in the different actual varieties of the language that we hear or read" (1972: 13). The empirical condition for the common core is that there are common grammatical features in all varieties of English:

> The fact that in this figure the "common core" dominates all the varieties means that, however esoteric or remote a variety may be, it has running through it a set of grammatical and other characteristics that are present in all others. It is presumably this fact that justifies the application of the name "English" to all the varieties. (Quirk et al., 1972: 14)

The logic of this passage, that there must be a common core shared by all varieties of English, and that this core consists in grammatical features, raises a number of difficulties (see Kachru, 1986: 83). Even if one accepts the premise that a common core is necessary in order to found a taxonomy of animals or languages, it is not clear that such a taxonomy is the purpose of a descriptive grammar of English. If it were, the grammar would have to contain information about the features of all varieties of English, and of other languages and their varieties historically related to varying degrees (and even after this work the linguistic features would merely suggest rather than confirm relationships). This information is to be found in a historical and comparative grammar.

In Quirk et al. (1985: 16), the core is no longer explained, but merely asserted, and it no longer "dominates" – "A COMMON CORE or nucleus is present in all the varieties so that, however esoteric a variety may be . . ." Still, the last sentence of the paragraph remains, "justifies the application of the name 'English' to all of the varieties" (1985: 16). The core has been called into existence in order to define the descriptive object of study, much as *langue* or the language system, also defined as a commonality, has been constructed as the object of study in Saussurean linguistics: "it is something which is in each individual, but which is none the less common to all" (Saussure, 1983: 38).

Quirk et al. (1985: 15) define Standard English from within this core, as the "supra-national" usage of the educated, standing in opposition to the uneducated speech more closely aligned with the regional dialects. Like the core,

Standard English is defined in opposition to variation, in terms of what is common to all educated speakers:

> What we are calling national standards should be seen as distinct from the Standard English which we have been discussing and which we should think of as being "supra-national," embracing what is common to all ... there are two national standards that are overwhelmingly predominant both in the number of distinctive usages and in the degree to which these distinctions are 'institutionalized': American English and British English. Grammatical differences are few and the most conspicuous are widely known to speakers of both national standards. (Quirk et al., 1972: 17)

This quotation highlights problems with the core, and with the notion of Standard English. Having first defined the core and the standard negatively, that is, as not containing any linguistic features not present in all varieties (or all varieties used by educated speakers in the case of the Standard), it becomes necessary to identify two national standards used by educated speakers in their respective societies, precisely because these varieties do contain distinctive features which are institutionalized (that is, which are accorded the status of a standard). "One for all and all for one," has been replaced by, "All animals are created equal, but some animals are more equal than others." Quirk et al. (1972) are required by their argument to say that Standard English is different from the national standards. Otherwise, they must either insist that either American English or British English is not Standard English (leaving the other the winner on the world stage) or admit that English has split into at least two standards. The compromise position which they take is to hypothesize a Standard English of shared common linguistic features, which manifests itself in British and American contexts (most obviously publishing) as two separate national standards, each of which has additional features authorized as standard by the institutions of the respective society.

And this brings us to the moment of recognition of which Kachru tells us. Quirk et al. (1972) say:

> At the opposite extreme are interference varieties that are so widespread in a community and of such long standing that they may be thought stable and adequate enough to be institutionalized and regarded as varieties of English in their own right rather than stages on the way to a more native-like English. There is active debate on these issues in India, Pakistan and several African countries, where efficient and fairly stable varieties of English are prominent in educated use at the highest political and professional level. (p. 26)

Having defined community acceptance and support (institutionalization) as a way to explain the existence of nationalized British and American standard English alongside Standard English, there is no way to shut the door on any variety which can show distinctive features and institutionalization in the context of a nation (or perhaps a clearly demarcated community).

Although the Quirk grammar does not follow through on this statement (opting instead for a common-core model with ad hoc recognition of British and American differences), the stage is set for the variationist treatments of the early 1980s.

5 Variationist Treatments of Grammar

As we have seen, the problem with the Quirk grammar is that specific discussion of variant forms of grammar is limited to standardized varieties of British and American English. Space in such a large grammar is clearly at a premium, but one would be forgiven for assuming that these two varieties are the only ones sufficiently standardized to merit the attention of students and scholars. Variationist treatments of the early 1980s, including Bailey and Görlach (1982), Trudgill and Hannah (1982), and Platt, Weber, and Ho (1984), sought to correct this assumption by demonstrating the linguistic distinctiveness and social institutionalization of varieties of English.

Bailey and Görlach (1982) consists of a number of chapters by different contributors, each devoted to a particular variety of English. Each variety is treated in terms of its external history, linguistic features, and other sociolinguistically important or relevant aspects. The treatments of linguistic features are concise and tend to emphasize phonology and lexis (vocabulary). The purpose of the book is to trace the origin and institutionalization of target varieties, with an eye toward accounting for plurality by means of a social historical frame of reference.

Platt, Weber, and Ho (1984) organize their text around levels of analysis and grammatical constructions, which are then compared across varieties. This plan is somewhat more convenient for examining grammatical features found in more than one form of English, with separate chapters on variation in the noun phrase, variation in the verb phrase, semantic change grouped with derivational morphology, and syntax at the sentence level. The authors' aim is to present both the unity and diversity of the new Englishes (non-native varieties) in particular, and their treatment of grammatical features contributes to the establishment of unity.

Trudgill and Hannah (1982) do not attempt to treat, except incidentally, the social history and institutional contexts of different varieties of English. Instead they focus on linguistic features, using a terminology and organization reminiscent of the Quirk grammar. The book groups historically related and linguistically similar varieties into chapters, and within chapters proceeds according to levels of linguistic analysis. The effect is striking: each "standard" variety is awarded a section which lists the features distinguishing it from nearby varieties, and from the most closely related "major" variety, either English English or American English. The text thus fulfills the project suggested by the Quirk grammar's compromise: Englishes that have proven themselves to have educated speakers are given thorough delineation in terms of their features. This arrangement speaks to use by English language learners and teachers, who want to identify the varieties they encounter, adapt their usage toward a particular standard variety, and possibly make allowances for the diverse English language backgrounds of other speakers (see Hundt, 1998: 142). Recent editions have expanded the treatment of West Indian Englishes and creoles, African Englishes, Asian Englishes, and lesser-known Englishes.

The problems of Trudgill and Hannah (1982) are far outweighed by its utility. Nevertheless, they illustrate the difficulties in applying a descriptive approach to varieties of English. First, the text divides the world into English English and American English sectors. This is not justifiable from variationist or historical linguistic perspectives, nor does it reflect, except in the crudest political terms, the complex histories of English around the world. Second, the dividing up of the English language into standardized varieties tends to fall into national stereotyping of varieties. Statements of linguistic features are generalized broadly throughout a national area, and the inclusion of a particular variety amounts to the recognition of those varieties that have made the grade either through having an educated population or an army and a navy. Within this view, Canada and Singapore make the grade (in the third edition, 1994), but Martha's Vineyard, or Ocracoke, or Hong Kong, do not. Trudgill has in his more recent work taken pains to correct this impression (see Trudgill, 2002). Saint Helena thus receives increasing attention in the third and fourth editions, and the Miskito Coast is discussed in the fourth edition (Trudgill and Hannah, 1994: 119, and 2002: 118–19). African-American English awkwardly holds the same status as dialects of American English until the fourth edition, when it is discussed in the context of post-creoles (Trudgill and Hannah, 2002: 112). The point is not that the inclusion or exclusion of a particular variety is incorrect, but rather that the attempt to describe "standard" varieties must of necessity lead to a great deal of exclusion on non-linguistic grounds. Third, despite frequent cross-referencing, the compression of the book does not allow for recognizing the complexity of grammatical patterning, particularly overlaps in usage between certain British varieties and certain American varieties, and standard/non-standard variation (for example, when British non-standard usage resembles American standard, or vice versa). Changes made in successive editions show that the authors are aware of these shortcomings and have tried to ameliorate them. The problems derive from the Quirk grammar compromise and from the attempt to merge the function of a descriptive grammar with the representation of variation found in a historical and comparative grammar. Although new varieties are recognized and given license to exist (an improvement on the practice of the Quirk grammar), they are described in a way that can give rise to false impressions. An uncritical reader could well develop the following misconceptions: that world Englishes are derivative of British and American English, that they are arrayed as a sphere of particularized satellites diverging from the two dominant core varieties, and that national sovereignty alone authorizes linguistic variation.

This set of views can be traced in the reluctance of descriptions of world Englishes to admit the possibility of profound grammatical variation. It is almost as if to admit divergence from the norm would be a national disgrace and grounds for ejection from the commonwealth of the English language. The following set of comments from entries in McArthur (1992) give a sense of this:

African English	"The discussion of syntax tends to centre on deviation from standard English rather than a consideration of distinctively AfrE forms." (pp. 21–2)
Australian English	"There are no syntactic features that distinguish standard AusE from standard BrE, or indeed any major non-standard features not also found in Britain, but there are many distinctive words and phrases." (p. 92)
Canadian English	"Where CanE differs grammatically from BrE it tends to agree with AmE. However . . . Canadians are often more aware of both usages than Americans." (p. 181)
Indian English	"There is great variety in syntax, from native-speaker fluency (the acrolect) to a weak command of many constructions (the basilect)." (p. 506)
Anglo-Irish	"Standard Anglo-Irish is close to the standard BrE varieties. Non-standard Anglo-Irish syntax has six features also found outside Ireland." (p. 68)
New Zealand English	"Standard NZE is to all intents and purposes the same as standard BrE." (p. 696)
Pakistani English	"Distinctive grammatical features relate to uses of the verb, article, relative clause, preposition, and adjective and verb complementation, all shared with IndE. Features of the indigenous languages influence use of English and code-mixing and code-switching are common, including among the highly educated." (p. 742)

Syntax as a topic seems to require linguists to assert that the variety they are describing has a standardized form which does not deviate from standardized forms of British or American English. Only Indian English and Pakistani English are described as allowing variation in grammar. One might assume that this table reports directly on the nature of the varieties in question, but again, the pressure of the same ideologies and approaches that inform the Quirk grammar cannot be ruled out of consideration.

How do the ideologies in question define descriptive grammar with respect to varieties? First, there is the pressure to be included in (literate) "Standard English"; this leads to the "commonwealth" statement that the grammar of the variety in question does not diverge from Standard (British or American) English. Second, there is nationalist pressure to identify a few characteristics that establish national identity. Third, when incontrovertibly profound grammatical variation is encountered, as in pidgins and creoles, the variety in question is reclassified as outside of "English." As Quirk et al. (1985: 28) state, "It is a matter of debate, and to some extent politics, whether these should be regarded as falling within the orbit of the English language." (Compare Mühlhäusler, 1996: 99–103, on the politics of labeling pidgin languages.)

6   Recent Developments in the Grammatical Description of World Englishes

The grammatical description of world Englishes over the past 20 years has seen the convergence of techniques of data analysis from several fields. These include: socio-historical linguistics, the development of register-specific (spoken vs. written) analysis of syntactic patterning, the detailed description of non-standardized varieties, the application of sociolinguistic methodology to the grammatical variation in world Englishes, and the development of the International Corpus of English (ICE).

Romaine (1982) establishes a method for sociohistorical linguistics with reference to variable relative markers in Middle Scots, showing that the sociolinguistic study of syntactic change requires the use of corpora. Denison (1998) gives a thorough discussion of syntactic change during the present-day period, using a descriptive terminology similar to the Quirk grammar. He makes impressive use of corpora and casts the widest possible net for non-standard forms. His discussion of relative clauses includes mention of genitive *that's* ("the house that's roof was damaged") and non-standard *as* and *but* (". . . not one of the children but was relieved to find that . . .") (Denison, 1998: 279–82). This chapter is an important resource for those who would require evidence for grammatical variation omitted from the present-day syntactic and descriptive accounts.

Miller and Weinert (1998: 75–6, 397) demonstrate on the basis of cross-linguistic data that the syntax of spoken and written language differ from one another significantly. They introduce the concept of *magnasyntax* to refer to the heavily-documented morphology and syntax of the written English tradition (p. 377). This work interprets the difference between spoken and written, but also standardized and non-standardized varieties, as a function of register and degree of analytical focus.

A range of recent studies employ various perspectives to undertake the serious systematic description of non-standard English morphology and syntax, including Henry (1995) on the syntax of Belfast English, Wales (1996) on personal pronouns, and Anderwald (2002) on negation. These studies combine theoretical sophistication with a critical attention to detailed grammatical description. Cheshire and Stein (1997) theorize the differences between the syntax of standardized and non-standardized varieties in terms of sociolinguistic function. Their contributors include valuable descriptive detail regarding the morphology and syntax of less-standardized varieties (see Seppänen, 1997, on the genitive of English relative pronouns, and Wright, 1997, on second-person plural pronouns).

The chapters in Cheshire (1991) apply sociolinguistic methodology to many instances of grammatical variation in world Englishes. Mesthrie (1991: 464–7) illustrates the descriptive inclusiveness of this method in his analysis of relative clauses in South African Indian English, including near-relatives ("You get carpenters, they talk to you so sweet"), correlatives ("Which one haven' got lid, I threw them away"), contact (zero-subject) relatives, relatives with a resumptive pronoun, and other non-standard relative pronouns, including *what*. Mesthrie's data indicate that younger middle-class females seemed to be leading assimilation to the standard (Mesthrie, 1991: 472).

Hundt (1998) assesses the degree of independence of New Zealand English language norms, using American, British, and New Zealand corpora to compare a list of morphological, syntactic, and lexico-grammatical variables. She tests numerous generalizations about the specific grammatical features of New Zealand English, and adopts a pluricentric model to trace similarities with Australian, American, and British varieties. Her balanced conclusion recognizes the contingency of the notion of "a variety," while arguing that the data support a grammatical distinction between New Zealand English and these other varieties.

Gisborne (2002) undertakes a similarly open-ended grammatical description while examining the contribution of relative clauses to the definition of Hong Kong English as a discrete system. He lists six types of relative clause: contact relatives, participial relatives with a relative marker, where-relatives with a directional as well as locative sense, the omission of prepositions, resumptive pronouns, and the absence of restrictive/non-restrictive contrast, and then considers the second type of relative in the context of the morphosyntactic feature system of Hong Kong English, using examples from ICE-HK. Gisborne's approach suggests that a sensitive application of an analytical framework to language data can result in a description which balances system and variation. He does not define Hong Kong English by the over-generalization of one variable feature, nor does he ignore this variation in order to conform to the prestigious systematicity of another form of English. Cautious description of this sort will be extremely important in realizing the full potential of linguistic corpora in describing world Englishes.

The most promising development in the descriptive grammar of world Englishes is the use of corpus linguistics in connection with the ICE, introduced and explained in Greenbaum (1996). Meyer (2002: 46–53) presents the methodology of corpus linguistics, in particular discussing the emphasis that corpora place on native vs. non-native speakers, and the role of editors in shaping newspaper English in different varieties. He notes the problems that corpora have in reflecting sociolinguistic variation, especially dialect differences. Nelson, Wallis, and Aarts (2002) lists recent research on British English using the ICE-GB corpus. The grammatical model conforms to the Quirk grammar's categories with some modification, and the text makes reference to the differences between this model and Government and Binding theory. Hundt (1998: 130) warns that the application of statistical tools on corpora is not useful for the discovery of grammatical differences between varieties. ICE will prove invaluable as a testing ground for grammatical and variational hypotheses, but the quality of these will still depend on the ingenuity of linguists. A good deal of ingenuity and careful description is to be found in the monumental study of the morphology and syntax of varieties of English in Kortmann et al. (2004).

7   Conclusion: Potential for the Grammatical Description of World Englishes

Language descriptions will continue to benefit from advances in the size, complexity, and refinement of linguistic corpora. However, these must be used with care, as they reflect language attitudes within national education systems, publishing industries, and media. Descriptive grammars will continue to be a flashpoint, as they are accorded prescriptive weight by their consumers. They can embody resistance to nationalist hegemony and traditionalist doctrine. On the one hand, they can be symbols of vibrant national literature, media, and intellectual life, and on the other, they can be a narrow nationalist stereotype, a betrayal of the richness and complexity of language heritage, language variation, and the negotiation and renegotiation of identities inherent in language. Language users and linguists would do well to allow this dialectic to inform their language practices.

See also Chapters 17, Varieties of World Englishes; 20, Written Language, Standard Language, Global Language; 26, Grammar Wars: Seventeenth- and Eighteenth-Century England; 27, Grammar Wars: The United States; 36, Teaching World Englishes.

REFERENCES

Anderwald, Lieselotte (2002) *Negation in Non-Standard British English: Gaps, Regularizations and Asymmetries*. London/New York: Routledge.

Bailey, Richard W. and Görlach, Manfred (1982) *English as a World Language*. Ann Arbor: University of Michigan Press.

Biber, Douglas (1988) *Variation across Speech and Writing*. Cambridge: Cambridge University Press.

Biber, Douglas, Johansson, Stig, Leech, Geoffrey, Conrad, Susan, and Finegan, Edward (1999) *Longman Grammar of Spoken and Written English*. Harlow, Essex: Pearson Education.

Cameron, Deborah (1995) *Verbal Hygiene.* London: Routledge.

Cheshire, Jenny (ed.) (1991) *English around the World: Sociolinguistic Perspectives.* Cambridge: Cambridge University Press.

Cheshire, Jenny and Stein, Dieter (eds.) (1997) *Taming the Vernacular: From Dialect to Written Standard Language.* London/New York: Longman.

Denison, David (1998) Syntax. In *The Cambridge History of the English Language, vol. 4: 1776–1997.* Edited by Suzanne Romaine. Cambridge: Cambridge University Press, pp. 92–329.

Gisborne, Nik (2002) Relative clauses in Hong Kong English. In *Hong Kong English: Autonomy and Creativity.* Edited by Kingsley Bolton. Hong Kong: Hong Kong University Press, pp. 141–60.

Görlach, Manfred (1991) English as a world language: The state of the art. In *Englishes. Studies in Varieties of English 1984–1988.* Amsterdam/ Philadelphia: John Benjamins. Originally published 1988 in *English World-Wide, 9,* 1–32.

Greenbaum, Sidney (ed.) (1996) *Comparing English Worldwide: The International Corpus of English.* Oxford: Oxford University Press.

Harris, Roy (1981) *The Language Myth.* London: Duckworth.

Harris, Roy (1998) *Introduction to Integrational Linguistics.* Oxford: Pergamon (Elsevier Science).

Henry, Alison (1995) *Belfast English and Standard English: Dialect Variation and Parameter Setting.* Oxford: Oxford University Press.

Henry, Alison (2002) Variation and syntactic theory. In *The Handbook of Language Variation and Change.* Edited by J. K. Chambers, Peter Trudgill, and Natalie Schilling-Estes. Oxford/Malden, MA: Blackwell, pp. 267–82.

Huddleston, Rodney and Pullum, Geoffrey K. (2002) *The Cambridge Grammar of the English Language.* Cambridge: Cambridge University Press.

Hundt, Marianne (1998) *New Zealand English Grammar: Fact or Fiction? A Corpus-Based Study in Morphosyntactic Variation.* Amsterdam/Philadelphia: John Benjamins.

Jespersen, Otto (1933) *Essentials of English Grammar.* London: George Allen and Unwin.

Kachru, Braj B. (1986) *The Alchemy of English: The Spread, Functions and Models of Non-Native Englishes.* Oxford: Pergamon.

Kachru, Braj B. (1992) Meaning in deviation: Toward understanding non-native English texts. In *The Other Tongue: English across Cultures.* 2nd edition. Edited by Braj B. Kachru. Urbana: University of Illinois Press, pp. 301–26.

Kirkham, Samuel (1833) *English Grammar in Familiar Lectures; Accompanied by a Compendium Embracing a New Systematick Order of Parsing, a New System of Punctuation, Exercises in False Syntax, and a System of Philosophical Grammar in Notes: To Which Are Added, an Appendix, and a Key to the Exercises Designed for the Use of Schools and Private Learners.* 26th edition. New York: M'Elrath, Bangs, and Herbert.

Kortmann, Bernd, Burridge, Kate, Mesthrie, Rajend, Schneider, Edgar W., and Upton, Clive (2004) *A Handbook of Varieties of English, vol. 2: Morphology and Syntax.* Berlin/New York: Mouton de Gruyter.

Marenbon, John (1987) *English Our English: The New Orthodoxy Examined.* London: Centre for Policy Studies.

McArthur, Tom (ed.) (1992) *The Oxford Companion to the English Language.* Oxford: Oxford University Press.

522   *Daniel R. Davis*

Mesthrie, Rajend (1991) Syntactic variation in South African Indian English: The relative clause. In *English around the World: Sociolinguistic Perspectives*. Edited by Jenny Cheshire. Cambridge: Cambridge University Press, pp. 446–61.

Meyer, Charles F. (2002) *English Corpus Linguistics: An Introduction*. Cambridge: Cambridge University Press.

Michael, Ian (1970) *English Grammatical Categories and the Tradition to 1800*. Cambridge: Cambridge University Press.

Miller, Jim and Weinert, Regina (1998) *Spontaneous Spoken Language: Syntax and Discourse*. Oxford: Oxford University Press.

Milroy, James (1999) The consequences of standardisation in descriptive linguistics. In *Standard English: The Widening Debate*. Edited by Tony Bex and Richard J. Watts. London/New York: Routledge, pp. 16–39.

Milroy, James and Milroy, Lesley (1999) *Authority in Language: Investigating Standard English*. 3rd edition. London/New York: Routledge.

Mühlhäusler, Peter (1996) *Linguistic Ecology: Language Change and Linguistic Imperialism in the Pacific Region*. London/New York: Routledge.

Nelson, Gerald, Wallis, Sean, and Aarts, Bas (2002) *Exploring Natural Language: Working with the British Component of the International Corpus of English*. Amsterdam/Philadelphia: John Benjamins.

Platt, John, Weber, Heidi and Ho, Mian Lian (1984) *The New Englishes*. London: Routledge and Kegan Paul.

Quirk, Randolph, Greenbaum, Sidney, Leech, Geoffrey, and Svartvik, Jan (1972) *A Grammar of Contemporary English*. London: Longman.

Quirk, Randolph, Greenbaum, Sidney, Leech, Geoffrey, and Svartvik, Jan (1985) *A Comprehensive Grammar of the English Language*. London/New York: Longman.

Romaine, Suzanne (1982) *Socio-Historical Linguistics: Its Status and Methodology*. Cambridge: Cambridge University Press.

Saussure, Ferdinand de (1983) *Course in General Linguistics*. Translated by Roy Harris. London: Duckworth. (Originally published 1916.)

Schneider, Edgar W. (2003) The dynamics of new Englishes: From identity construction to dialect birth. *Language*, **79**(2), 233–81.

Seppänen, Aimo (1997) The genitives of the relative pronouns in present-day English. In *Taming the Vernacular: From Dialect to Written Standard Language*. Edited by Jenny Cheshire and Dieter Stein. London and New York: Longman, pp. 152–69.

Trudgill, Peter (2002) The history of the lesser-known varieties of English. In *Alternative Histories of English*. Edited by Richard Watts and Peter Trudgill. London/New York: Routledge, pp. 29–44.

Trudgill, Peter and Hannah, Jean (1982) *International English: A Guide to Varieties of Standard English*. 2nd edition 1985. 3rd edition 1994. 4th edition 2002. London: Edward Arnold.

Wales, Katie (1996) *Personal Pronouns in Present-Day English*. Cambridge: Cambridge University Press.

Wallis, John (1972) *Grammar of the English Language with an Introductory Grammatico-Physical Treatise on Speech, or on the Formation of All Speech Sounds*. Translated by J. A. Kemp. London: Longman. (Originally published 1653.)

Wright, Susan (1997) "Ah'm going for to give youse a story today": Remarks on second person plural pronouns in Englishes. In *Taming the Vernacular: From Dialect to*

Written Standard Language. Edited
by Jenny Cheshire and Dieter Stein.
London/New York: Longman,
pp. 170–84.

Wyld, Henry Cecil. (1925) *Elementary
Lessons in English Grammar*. Oxford:
Oxford University Press. (Preface
dated 1909.)

FURTHER READING

Aarts, Bas and Meyer, Charles F. (eds.)
(1995) *The Verb in Contemporary
English: Theory and Description*.
Cambridge: Cambridge University
Press.

Aceto, Michael and Williams, Jeffrey P.
(eds.) (2003) *Contact Englishes of the
Eastern Caribbean*. Amsterdam/
Philadelphia: John Benjamins.

Banjo, Ayọ (1997) Aspects of the syntax
of Nigerian English. In *Englishes
around the World: Studies in Honour
of Manfred Görlach, vol. 2: Caribbean,
Africa, Asia, Australasia*. Edited by
Edgar W. Schneider. Amsterdam/
Philadelphia: John Benjamins,
pp. 85–96.

Bauer, Laurie (2002) *An Introduction to
International Varieties of English*.
Edinburgh: Edinburgh University
Press.

Bautista, Ma. Lourdes S. (2000) *Defining
Standard Philippine English: Its Status
and Grammatical Features*. Manila:
De La Salle University Press.

Bell, Allan and Kuiper, Koenraad (eds.)
(2000) *New Zealand English*.
Amsterdam/Philadelphia: John
Benjamins.

Blair, David and Collins, Peter (eds.)
(2001) *English in Australia*.
Amsterdam/Philadelphia: John
Benjamins.

Cassidy, Frederic G. (1971) *Jamaica Talk:
Three Hundred Years of the English
Language in Jamaica*. 2nd edition.
Basingstoke: Macmillan. (1st edition,
1961.)

Corbett, John, McClure, J. Derrick, and
Stuart-Smith, Jane (eds.) (2003) *The
Edinburgh Companion to Scots*.
Edinburgh: Edinburgh University
Press.

Dannenberg, Clare J. (2002) *Sociolinguistic
Constructs of Ethnic Identity: The
Syntactic Delineation of an American
Indian English*. Publication of the
American Dialect Society no. 87.
Durham, NC: Duke University Press
for the American Dialect Society.

De Klerk, Vivian (ed.) (1996) *Focus on
South Africa*. Amsterdam/
Philadelphia: John Benjamins.

Filppula, Markku (1999) *The Grammar of
Irish English: Language in Hibernian
Style*. London/New York:
Routledge.

Görlach, Manfred (1991) *Introduction to
Early Modern English*. Cambridge:
Cambridge University Press.
(Original work published 1978.)

Ho, Mian-Lian and Platt, John (1993)
*Dynamics of a Contact Continuum:
Singaporean English*. Oxford:
Oxford University Press.

Holm, John (1997) Passive-like
constructions in English-based and
other creoles. In *Englishes around the
World: Studies in Honour of Manfred
Görlach. Vol. 1: General studies, British
Isles, North America*. Edited by Edgar
W. Schneider. Amsterdam/
Philadelphia: John Benjamins,
pp. 71–86.

Jones, Charles (ed.) (1997) *The Edinburgh
History of the Scots Language*.
Edinburgh: Edinburgh University
Press.

Jones, Charles (2002) *The English
Language in Scotland: An Introduction*

to Scots. East Linton, Scotland: Tuckwell.

Kandiah, Thiru (1996) Syntactic "deletion" in Lankan English: Learning from a new variety of English about—. In *South Asian English: Structure, Use, and Users*. Edited by Robert J. Baumgardner. Urbana: University of Illinois Press, pp. 104–23.

Kytö, Merja (1991) *Variation and Diachrony, with Early American English in Focus: Studies on CAN/MAY and SHALL/WILL*. University of Bamberg Studies in English Linguistics 28. Frankfurt am Main: Peter Lang.

Lindquist, Hans, Klintborg, Staffan, Levin, Magnus, and Estling, Maria (eds.) (1998) *The Major Varieties of English: Papers from MAVEN 97, Växjö 20–22 November 1997*. Acta Wexionensia Humaniora Humanities no. 1 1998. Växjö, Sweden: Växjö University.

Mehrotra, Raja Ram (1997) Negation in Indian Pidgin English. In *Englishes around the World: Studies in Honour of Manfred Görlach. Vol. 2: Caribbean, Africa, Asia, Australasia*. Edited by Edgar W. Schneider. Amsterdam/Philadelphia: John Benjamins, pp. 213–18.

Mesthrie, Rajend (1997) A sociolinguistic study of topicalisation phenomena in South African Black English. In *Englishes around the World: Studies in Honour of Manfred Görlach. Vol. 2: Caribbean, Africa, Asia, Australasia*. Edited by Edgar W. Schneider. Amsterdam/Philadelphia: John Benjamins, pp. 119–40.

Milroy, James and Milroy, Lesley (eds.) (1993) *Real English: The Grammar of English Dialects in the British Isles*. London: Longman.

Mufwene, Salikoko S., Rickford, John R., Bailey, Guy, and Baugh, John (eds.)
(1998) *African-American English: Structure, History, and Use*. London/New York: Routledge.

Mühlhäusler, Peter (1997) Grammatical properties of Milne Bay English and their sources. In *Englishes around the World: Studies in Honour of Manfred Görlach. Vol. 2: Caribbean, Africa, Asia, Australasia*. Edited by Edgar W. Schneider. Amsterdam/Philadelphia: John Benjamins, pp. 219–28.

Nagle, Stephen J. and Sanders, Sara L. (eds.) (2003) *English in the Southern United States*. Cambridge: Cambridge University Press.

Newbrook, Mark (ed.) (1987) *Aspects of the Syntax of Educated Singaporean English*. Frankfurt am Main: Peter Lang.

Newbrook, Mark (1997) Malaysian English: Status, norms, some grammatical and lexical features. In *Englishes around the World: Studies in Honour of Manfred Görlach. Vol. 2: Caribbean, Africa, Asia, Australasia*. Edited by Edgar W. Schneider. Amsterdam/Philadelphia: John Benjamins, pp. 229–56.

O'Neil, Wayne (1993) Nicaraguan English in history. In *Historical Linguistics: Problems and Perspectives*. Edited by Charles Jones. London/New York: Longman, pp. 279–318.

Ooi, Vincent B. Y. (ed.) (2001) *Evolving Identities: The English Language in Singapore and Malaysia*. Singapore: Times Academic Press.

Quirk, Randolph (1995) *Grammatical and Lexical Variance in English*. London/New York: Longman.

Sand, Andrea (1998) First findings from ICE-Jamaica: The verb phrase. In *Explorations in Corpus Linguistics*. Edited by Antoinette Renouf. Amsterdam/Atlanta, GA: Rodopi, pp. 201–16.

Schmied, Josef J. (1991) *English in Africa: An Introduction*. London/New York: Longman.

Schneider, Edgar W. (1989) *American Earlier Black English: Morphological and Syntactic Variables*. Tuscaloosa/London: University of Alabama Press. (Originally published 1981.)

Todd, Loreto (1999) *Green English: Ireland's Influence on the English Language*. Dublin: O'Brien.

Trudgill, Peter (ed.) (1984) *Language in the British Isles*. Cambridge: Cambridge University Press.

Trudgill, Peter and Chambers, J. K. (eds.) (1991) *English Dialects: Studies in Grammatical Variation*. London: Longman.

Wolfram, Walt and Schilling-Estes, Natalie (2006) *American English: Dialects and Variation*. 2nd edition. Oxford: Blackwell.

Part VI Ideology, Identity, and Constructs

29 Colonial/Postcolonial Critique: The Challenge from World Englishes

PRADEEP A. DHILLON

1 Introduction

The terms "colonial discourse" and "postcolonial critique" have long histories, and scholars disagree about exactly what they mean. I shall say more about this later, but I begin by asking the reader to rely on his or her intuitive understanding of the words and consider territories, citizens, and the legitimizing processes and modes of State governance. What is their relationship? What role does language play in the establishment, maintenance, and shifts in the relationship? The focus of this chapter will be to consider the role of English in the construction of colonial, particularly British, discourse and postcolonial critique. However, it is important to remember that both these processes can be found in various parts of the world at various times in human history. In other words, colonialism was not a unique invention of the European states as they rose to global power over the last five hundred years nor is its critique limited to the contemporary literary world. Rather, its logic can be traced in the establishment of the Greek nation-state, the ambitions of Genghis Khan as he rode out of the Mongolian steppes, and the expansive impulses of the Hindu kings of Vijayanagara, just as its critique can be found in Heraclitus, Euripides, and Ibn-Batuta. However, the systematic study of European, particularly British, colonialism served to establish a secure analytic place for colonial discourse in contemporary humanisitic discourse where it has provided a tool for critical epistemology and political action over the past few decades.

2 Colonial Discourse and Postcolonial Critique

The *Oxford English Dictionary* defines the term "colonialism" as:

> a settlement in a new country ... a body of people who settle in a new locality,
> forming a community subject to, or connected with, their parent state; the

community so formed, consisting of the original settlers and their descendants and successors, as long as the connection with the parent state is kept up.

In other words, when citizens of one state travel to, and then establish domicile in another, where they live and work for much of their lives, all the while maintaining a relationship with their state of citizenship, they become part of the colonial process. Large enough numbers participating in such a relocation over a period of time effect identifiable social, cultural and political changes. In the event that the values of the out group become the valorized systems of knowledge and behavior, incorporating and subordinating local knowledge and culture, such groups are said to have established a colony of the parent state.

The recognition that the places to which settlers relocated were already populated by groups of people who enjoyed long-standing cultural traditions keeps this definition from being merely descriptive of the movement of a group of people to distant lands. These colonized places had populations with languages and cultural traditions, often going back thousands of years. In Ania Loomba's words (1998: 1):

> [The definition of colonialism] quite remarkably, avoids any reference to people other than the colonizers, people who might already have been living in those places where colonies were established.

The absence of a mention of indigenous populations in the definition signals two important aspects in the study of colonialism. First, it elides the sometimes benign, but all too often violent encounters between cultures that disrupted, changed, and in some cases even erased the cultural traditions of the peoples who already inhabited these places. In other words, an important aspect of this process is that the two states that are brought together by these processes bear unequal power in relation to each other. The changes mentioned above, then, are not simply the effects of time and travel but are brought about by instruments of economic and political power. Thus, by the middle of the nineteenth century, we find European settlers, and armies, educational, and judicial institutions in various parts of the globe where they had reshaped not only the physical but also the cultural, linguistic, and psychological landscapes in deep and abiding ways. One of the aims colonial discourse sets itself is to recover the experience of these encounters. Second, the elision of local peoples, language, and culture marks the definition itself as part of the dominant discourse which postcolonial critique seeks to note and correct. Thus, we move from colonialism to its representations – the area of colonial discourse proper, in which historical, literary, and anthropological texts with sensitivity to difference and the pragmatics of meaning and colonial critique and literary resistance developed. That such research was undertaken primarily in English and within English departments is one of the curious ironies of this development.

Without tracing the influence of such thought on the humanities in general, let me simply identify as the locus classicus of studies of colonial difference Edward Said's *Orientalism* (1978). This publication is considered the foundational text for the field of colonial discourse and postcolonial studies. It claims this position primarily because of the way Said spatially extends Michel Foucault's insights about the nature and role of critique in the formation of liberal political institutions of the West and to embrace international relations by making the world a text. Thus, *Orientalism* as critique constitutes a particularly efficacious historical and historiographical site to think through issues of the colonial discourse and "difference" as it relates to world Englishes. In this essay, in addition to providing an overview of the field, I argue that the study of world Englishes takes us beyond *Orientalism* and entails refiguring the notion of "culture." I examine the continuing importance of humanistic thought – though of a deeper sort – in a global context that has shifted from being "after colonialism" into one that reflects the linguistic struggles, albeit of speakers of varieties of English, within a global democratic society.

3 Orientalism and World Englishes

The publication of *Orientalism* marked a paradigm shift in thinking about the relationship between the West and the non-Western world. Edward Said sought to untangle the ways in which Western political, literary, and scholarly representations of the Middle East were inflected by political power. The crisis of representation that Said's intervention engaged had been brewing for some time. In different ways, the humanities had already begun the task of demonstrating the Western assumptions underlying humanism. Harnessing continental poststructuralist theories, liberation politics constituted a major move that gave opponents of the established literary canon enormous critical power. Here, precisely, *Orientalism* had its greatest impact. It provided a dramatic example of how Michel Foucault's ideas could be brought to bear upon the representation of non-Western languages, cultures, and societies in European thought. Said demonstrated the ways in which Western discourse linked to power, rested on racist stereotypes, and continually reproduced itself. In naming this discourse "Orientalism," Said coupled his critique of European discourse to issues of representation generally. In the process, he made it available to all who had been seeking an effective means of intellectually opposing the canon in its various disciplinary manifestations.

More broadly, the critique of orientalism is a manifestation of the crisis in late twentieth-century Western humanism in both its Enlightenment and modernist forms. As an outgrowth of poststructuralism, the critique of orientalism intersects with the broad intellectual movement contesting the homogeneity and essentialism which Enlightenment humanist values was said to assume. As a discourse of power, it is argued, orientalism, like other forms of knowledge, constrained and inflected the ways in which the object of its vision, in this case the non-Western other, was perceived and represented. Such representations, it was argued, became the facts that drove policies and policy makers. Thus, through the work of American intellectuals on behalf of minority cultures within the United States and internationally, French poststructuralist thought has been transformed from a brahmanical discourse into a tool of cultural critique and empowerment.

A central point of departure for Said, Foucault, and those inspired by them has been understanding the Enlightenment as a moment of epistemological rupture and Enlightenment thought as a discourse of power as well as a scientific discourse. In this view, the desire for knowledge about the non-Western Other was fatally flawed from its inception by the desire for power over non-Western worlds. Thus, orientalism may be defined as the discourse of power by which imperialism rationalized itself to itself, justifying its domination while distorting its image of the other. The strength of this approach was that it helped make sense of how racism systematically obscured European understandings and representations of colonized peoples. At a stroke, the legacy of colonial science was repositioned in the intellectual field along with contemporary forms of knowledge about the non-West. In retrospect, we can see that two important intellectual operations were involved. First, as already mentioned, was Foucault's re-vision of Enlightenment science as generating a series of "othering" discourses and thus deeply invested in the project of control. Here his work on institutions like the prison, the school, the medical clinic, and the madhouse provided instances of how knowledge and power were fused in Enlightenment thought and practice to discipline and order subject populations (Foucault, 1965 [1961], 1973 [1963], 1979 [1975]).

A second operation involved revealing the supremacist implications of the Enlightenment idea of progress. Some who follow Said argue that such an inflection of Enlightenment thought when applied to colonial arenas took such a particularly virulent form that it must be viewed separately from the metropolitan centers. Others who also follow Said contend that while supremacist ideology was imbricated in Enlightenment discourse, qualitative differences in the colonial sphere did not add up to differences in kind (Prochaska, 1990, 1996). In this view, Europe alone was invested with agency; its historical role was to awaken classical societies and civilizations from their supposed torpor.

The central idea here is that Said's substitution of Foucaultian power/knowledge for Marxist ideology transformed the intellectual field of Oriental studies and Colonialism by pitching the discussion in a new way (Spivak, 1988). The advantage for Said in adopting Foucault's methodology was the rigor it lent his contextual analysis of discourse as omnipotent – and how it enabled him to weld text/knowledge and context/power together (Said, 1978). Nevertheless, the disadvantage of using Foucault was that Said painted himself into a polemical corner. It is at this point that I wish to enter the debate in a bid to break out of the impasse between "us" and "them" occasioned by the analyses inspired by Foucault and Said. Such an impasse is problematic for the making of policies that simultaneously take Said's concerns seriously while refusing the radical separations, from the macro- to the micro-levels of international engagements, his theory entails.

Ironically, in seeking to develop such an approach toward policy making, we have to return to Western liberal thought and some of its central ideas. In so doing, we attempt to work toward finishing the humanistic project of the Enlightenment, as suggested by Franz Fanon, rather than rejecting it by building societies that bear the weight of the concerns of all through a responsibility toward all.

4   A Return to Liberal Humanism

Liberalism comprises the core values of "justice," "freedom," and "equality." What remains unstated in much of liberal discourse is the ways in which these values are understood, for it is clear that these are not the sole preserve of the liberal. Indeed, it is doubt about liberal construal of these terms and their metaphysical underpinnings that lies at the heart of problems with liberal multilingual education. It is often proposed that the most salient of the values of justice, freedom, and equality in this respect is equality. However, taking an explicitly Kantian view on this, one could argue that none of the values stand on its own or provides anything but the thinnest of procedures for justice and equality without the humanistic value of respect – the treatment of others as ends in themselves rather than as means to an end – operating as a regulative ideal. For the liberal, manifest individual or cultural differences signal an underlying humanity that is common to all. It is in this respect that we are equal. It is in virtue of such humanism that all should be treated as ends in themselves rather than as means to an end. Above all, it is on the basis of this that concern with human rights, including linguistic rights, has become so prominent a feature of contemporary global politics.

If the idea of a common humanity received its most powerful expression in the modern world in the thought of the Enlightenment, it is the substantive forms of European expansion that elicited the strongest reactions against it. Most relevant for international educational policies is the kind of relativism that has frequently been evident in the refusal of cultural groups to be judged by or to live by standards alien to them. Thus, when we consider the varieties of English spoken around the world, we can expect an increasing insistence on maintaining accents and syntactic constructions tied to particular ways of life not only in spoken English but also in written English. A focus on the varieties of English used throughout the world with increasingly robust literary traditions reminds us that, regardless of difference, we are bound by a global language.

A degree of cultural relativism has been brought to the fore in many respects in discussions of international language and education. The field of world Englishes finds much resonance with the trends in Foucauldian-inspired colonial discourse, but with an important difference: tied by a single language, the discourse does not run the risk of falling into relativism. Furthermore, the Foucauldian-inspired line of thinking, including colonial and postcolonial discourse, is limited by its somewhat promiscuous and gleeful drawing on the supposed loss of certainty in ethics and epistemology. I do not propose to rehearse these relativistic arguments here. Rather I want to consider reactions against such cultural relativism from two principal sources.

On the one hand, these reactions concern individual linguistic rights and welfare; on the other, a commitment to gender equity. Concern for linguistic groups' rights to fairness and respect might lead to the suppression of the rights of individuals and subgroups. The welfare and cultural integrity of the larger group is often offered as a reason for overriding individual concerns regarding respect and equality. These latter rights, it is argued, are ascribed a lower priority because they might weaken the momentum of a movement that seeks to promote its political and cultural ends within an environment of global inequity. Feminists, for example Susan Okin, have been increasingly insistent in pointing out that the search for democratic international education might present a problem for gender equity (Okin et al., 1999), a worry shared by feminist philosophers (Nussbaum, 2000) and postcolonial theorists alike (Spivak, 1999). Meanwhile, some contemporary approaches to the politics of international language education, as represented, for example, by Ella Shohat, refuse this hierarchy of priorities. One way to ease the tension between, on the one hand, concerns for individual linguistic rights and gender equity and, on the other, respect for different cultures is by addressing the idea of cultural integrity itself on which much of colonial discourse and critique rests, and to which I now turn.

5   Cultural and Lingusitic Complexity

The dominant approach to a critique of international language education, increasingly carried on in English, and based on Edward Said's concept of "orientalism," keeps in focus the very many ways – from the psychological through the linguistic to the legal – that individuals are excluded from full participation within national and international cultures. This is solely because of their membership of linguistic groups formed along such lines of difference as race, class, nation, region, and gender. The main concern in these discussions is about the demands for equity among diverse users of English in the classroom, the curriculum, and wider society. It is often assumed in such discourse that references to culture point to collective group identity and that membership of groups determines personal identity. In this view, culture is not merely a set of settled practices constitutive of people and their beliefs and preferences, but rather takes on a mystical force in the making of the self. This view rests on the assumption that there is an undeniable link between an individual and a culture, and that there is individual moral value to be derived from the recognition of such a link. Such a view of identity depends on and draws moral force from a certain notion of authenticity based less on an individual's characteristics and agency than on her belonging to a particular people (Taylor, 1991, 1992). Theoretically, this way of thinking is at odds with one of the key insights that motivates poststructural/postcolonial/feminist thought, and that is the refusal of any discourse that rests on "essentializing the Other."

More importantly, in the struggle to remove the continuing valorization of a variety of English, namely the dialect achieved either by birth into the British upper classes or through an upper-class British education, this way of thinking reproduces this prejudice. This is because its very articulation depends on taking the standpoint of the users of what is called "standard English." Staying within the domain of poststructural theory, shifting perspectives would let us see the West, and our varying use of English, in non-essentialist ways that would render international relationships with some of the complexity and nuance they rightly deserve.

Furthermore, the idea that culture determines identity makes the concept of culture interchangeable with quasi-biological and highly problematic concepts of "race," "gender," and "ethnicity." These concepts are fiercely contested within nationalist contexts such as can be found in the United States, but grow ever more unstable when placed in an international or global context. Stereotypes regarding the abilities of individuals and practices of discrimination are generated from such a collapse between the concepts of "identity" and "culture" as also an unreflective identity politics. In other words, the danger of taking such a deterministic view of culture in relation to the individual is that it yields quite easily to moral, and even political, practices that can be protected from internal and external criticism. We would do well to remember instances of fascism in modern history that depended precisely on such a linkage.

The discipline of anthropology, even in its most nuanced practices, has contributed largely to this way of thinking about culture. However, responding to some of the more voluble and hence visible of these, it is well to keep in mind what we have learned from anthropologists such as Lila Abu-Lughod, Renato Rosaldo, Michael Taussig, and George Marcus, literary and cultural theorists such as Mary Louise Pratt, sociologists such as Anthony King, and historians like Fernand Braudel, Janet Abu-Lughod, and Antoinette Burton. Cultures, they argue, are not hermetically sealed. Cultures have always exerted mutual influence. Such mutual influence is noted even under conditions of colonialism and the even more extreme conditions of slavery, where the colonizing and enslaving culture changes even as it effects changes on the cultures of groups that are brought under its power – as for example in the architectural form of the bungalow and the influence of jazz. Think also of the library of Alexandria and the gardens of the Alhambra in evaluating the claims for theories that assert the uniqueness of individuals, groups, and cultures. Such reflection places in doubt the claim to uniqueness that drives much of the academic discussion of politics at the national and international levels despite the poststructural leanings of its proponents.

6   The Challenge from World Englishes

It is important to note that the Kachruvian approach to making sense of the global distribution and use of English presupposes just such a sophisticated understanding of the complexity of cultural interaction. That is, it is worth noting that the concept of "world Englishes" embraces difference without losing the force of that which has come to be globally shared. Its discourse, under the influence of Braj Kachru, recognizes:

> the importance of inclusivity and pluricentrity in approaches to the linguistics of English worldwide, and involves not merely the description of national and regional varieties, but many other related topics as well, including contact linguistics, creative writing, critical linguistics, discourse analysis, corpus linguistics, lexicography, pedagogy, pidgin and Creole studies, and the sociology of language. (Bolton, 2004a: 367–8)

That is, the world Englishes approach recognizes the hegemony that lurks under the spread of language through institutions of power. At the same time, however, it does not deny the creativity that allows for human agency even under the most difficult situations (Bolton, 2004a, 2004b; Dhillon, 2001).

Furthermore, non-relativistic approaches to the study of language and culture which remain sensitive to difference show us that we can no longer claim that we are going through a new condition within the world economy. What is new, however, is that for the first time world economy has a truly global scope. Moreover, the effects of this shift in international relations are quickly and deeply noticeable under contemporary conditions of the density and speed in travel and communication technologies, as they are also in the near universalization of media like radio and television – much of which takes place in American English, with local responses offered in the many varieties of English. In other words, recent conditions of globalization have folded regional economies into the global economy, making it difficult to maintain a strict distinction between core and peripheral regions of the world economy as geographically bounded. World Englishes discourse undercuts the notions of culture and cultural relativism which form the cornerstone of the critique of universal human values on which Edward Said's *Orientalism* rests.

The concept of world Englishes also undercuts the claim that the global spread of a language, such as English, or of a specific variety, such as American English, would necessarily effect the homogenization of language use. The linguistic phenomena captured by the term world Englishes speak no doubt to the language that is shared, but speak with as much force to the ways in which varieties have developed in response to specific life-worlds. The concept captures the creativity with which humans take up the linguistic resources they find in their environment to enable the development and growth of their own projects. This is true regardless of the historical processes through which cultural elements, such as language, have found their way into their environments. Colonial discourse, with its focus on groups and the asymmetrical distribution of power between cultures, misses human agency as a response to these hegemonic processes, while the concept of "world Englishes" highlights it.

Furthermore, concern for the welfare of subgroups (or individuals) within marginalized groups in a global context suggests that the prevailing discourse on international education and linguistic diversity takes cultural groups to be both undifferentiated and hermetically sealed. That is, most discussions of cultural diversity rest on an idealized view of culture.

Michele Moody-Adams (1997) argues that (1) an idealization of group cultures can be found in the discourse of both those outside a group as well as those who are members; and (2) that the idealization of cultural groups often turns on making a distinction between "modern" and "traditional" cultures. The former are taken to be dynamic, differentiated, and open-ended, and the latter stagnant and closed. Thus, we see arguments for teaching language skills to Chinese students in a manner that would enable more imaginative, creative, and independent approaches to language learning even as researchers note the parsimony of the Chinese morpho-phonetic system. What is overlooked is that despite the "poverty" of the notational system of the language, the Chinese are able to do all the things that users of language anywhere do: even opera! To have to make an argument for creativity in this and other similar cases is to ignore the Kantian arguments for creativity as a faculty of human nature and to fall into a view of creativity that ascribes special powers to certain individuals or groups and a prejudiced logic to an unfolding world history.

Even when not tied to a Hegelian view of world history, notions of "traditional" cultures suggest that their members have holistic systems of meaning tied to a seamless web of beliefs and lead either to an unreflective universalistic metaphysics of meaning, as for Michael Katz, or to a defeatist relativism, such as that suggested by W. O. Quine (Dhillon, 2001). This is not to say that there have been no attempts to break this division between "us" and "them" within liberalism. Perhaps the most valiant of these is Bernard Williams's argument to break down this distinction "because cultures constantly meet one another and exchange and modify practices," and so it is implausible that "social practices might come forward with a certificate saying that they belonged to a genuinely different culture" (2005 [1985]: 158). Moody-Adams makes a similar point when she argues that there is no conception more mystical or unreflective than the doctrine of cultural integration, along with its usual companion, the assumption that beliefs and values of "traditional" or "primitive" societies must be *more* integrated than those of any other (Moody-Adams, 1997: 53).

7   World Englishes against Relativism

The point is that an appreciation of complexity as we find in the discussion of varieties of English in the world Englishes discourse undermines relativism.

Relativist positions are inadmissible on this account since they rest on taking languages and cultures as being bounded and homogeneous. It has not been noted enough that "traditional" cultures are varied, and differentiated. Mary Midgely takes the example of the Samurai practice in medieval Japan of testing a new sword's worth – its ability to cut a person in half – on random passersby. While such a practice seems abhorrent to us from a modern standpoint – as it also must to contemporary members of Japanese society – there is no reason for us to think that the practice was universally accepted by medieval Japanese culture. Ignoring cultural differentiation would lead us to the uncomfortable conclusion that the random passersby, and their families, would not have objected to the morality of the practice. Medieval Japanese culture, Midgely goes on to remind us, was a contentious, troubled time in Japanese history (Midgely, 1991).

Let us consider the use of technologies like amniocentesis in deciding which pregnancy is to be terminated. Embedded in patriarchal practices, these decisions would overwhelmingly favor male fetuses. In both these cases, a relativist view, one that relies on an undifferentiated and bounded view of culture, would miss the criticisms of these practices by Japanese historians of modern sensibility and Indian feminists informed by Western theories of gender oppression and equity. The relativist view would also miss indigenous criticisms of such practices such as those against gender inequity, as can be found in early sixteenth-century Sikh thought. Located as they often are within institutions of power, even the most well-intentioned of theorists can miss the irony of the subtle hegemony such relativistic arguments lead them to enact. In sum, that this kind of mutual cultural influence happens does not necessarily destroy the relativist's worry that there is no neutral ground outside particular cultures upon which to judge the worth of a linguistic variety or culture. What it does do is weaken the belief that a culture's values are determined and to be judged exclusively from within since neither language nor culture is as tidily sealed as the relativist might have thought.

Surely, the relativist might argue, it is difficult to deny that there are some practices so alien from our standpoint and yet so accepted within a certain culture with which we can have only "notional" confrontations. Thus, we can imagine varieties of English recognized as English by local users of the language which would not be recognized as such by English speakers elsewhere. When looked at both more closely and within a global context from the perspective of cultural complexity, somewhat different explanations begin to suggest themselves. The individual cases are quite different in the extent to which they take the interests of those directly affected into account. However, when a speaker of Indian English uses a construction like "I am going to go," he is readily understood by other speakers of Indian English. Meanwhile, speakers of other forms of English might find it difficult to parse such a sentence. Nevertheless, there is: (1) the recognition of such an utterance as a sentence of English regardless of the difficulties in parsing; and (2) the possibility that some other speakers of English will be critical and correct the construction.

Finally, when these practices are followed within liberal-Western democracies, as long as they are not disruptive to communication, they are tolerated with ease. The criticisms tend to come only from those preoccupied either with linguistic purity or with an unreflective commitment to linguistic rights and critique of linguistic hegemony. The use of varieties of English around the world is worthy of reflection to take colonial discourse beyond the polarized judgments of universal or relativist points offered by critiques of "orientalism." Such reflection draws our attention to several presuppositional aspects of our inquiry.

First, we acknowledge not only that cultures are not bounded but also that they are internally differentiated. Furthermore, the recognition that languages and cultures are not bounded suggests we treat the absence of criticism, even the celebration, of local linguistic practice with some reserve in order to yield explanations and descriptions of greater subtlety and responsibility than even Bernard Williams's idea of "notional" confrontation or relativism at a distance suggests. Postcolonial feminist theorists, such as Gayatri Spivak and Lata Mani have shown how the practice of *sati* sharply increased as a result of the outlawing of such practices under British colonial rule (Mani, 1998; Spivak, 1988). These theorists argue that the increase in instances of *sati* (a traditional practice of a widow immolating herself on her husband's funeral pyre in medieval India) was a retaliatory reaction within a context of unequal power relations. Separating a concern for the welfare of women from concerns regarding cultural equity, they point out that such contestations were often played out on the female body. It seems to me that one could make a similar argument for the extreme enactment of local varieties of English, such as the African American English movement which emerged in the late eighties and through the nineties of the last century. At the very least, the taking up of such arguments based on the recognition of the relationality between language varieties and the complexity of cultures would indicate that we look at how the practices of judgment tied to power might result in an increase in practices that make the already educationally vulnerable even more so. The implication is that the persistence, even intensification and celebration, of such practices is arguably tied to the permeability and relationality of languages and cultures within national and international contexts rather than their isolation and difference, however ironic this may be to the well-intentioned critic of universalism (Dhillon, 1996).

8 Beyond *Orientalism*

In other words, relativistic views of linguistic and cultural practices, both "Western" and "non-Western" alike, that rest on a division between "us" and "them" need to be examined further, and world Englishes discourse offers us an excellent site to pursue such a line of research. The urgent motivation to undertake such an examination of relativism that much of colonial discourse compels us to take from a critical global standpoint would be twofold. First, we would be called on to scrutinize positions ever more closely in order to determine whether any unacknowledged sense of moral supremacy lurks within such a relativism. Second, we would need to educate ourselves more thoroughly in the traditions whose practices are in question in order to find ways of making alliances with members of such a culture who uphold conservative values. We would do so in order to make the lives of women, members of subgroups, and others who are vulnerable a little easier, perhaps even less dangerous. That is, we would be acting thus for reasons of a universal democratic humanity.

Contemporary critical discourse demands of us, whether we are looking at instances that generate moral alienation in a global or local context, that we question whether our criticisms of Muslim, Christian, Hindu values, European, even secular values, are in any way implicated in practices that violate our deepest humanistic commitments (Shohat and Stam, 1994). Alastair Pennycook, writing much more baldly, adopts and refines H. G. Widdowson's distinction between critical and hypocritical discourse within the field of world Englishes and lays out four hypocritical positions that critical discourse must avoid (2004: 802–3). These are the hypocritical denial of (1) ethical responsibility; (2) political responsibility; (3) intellectual responsibility; and (4) social and cultural responsibility.

A critique along these lines would demand that we familiarize ourselves with linguistic traditions varying in their respect for the moral systems that guide linguistic action. While it might be held that such values are precisely the concern of anthropology and sociolinguistics, these fields are characteristically vulnerable to the kinds of criticism Wittgenstein makes in his remarks on Frazer's *Golden Bough*: the anthropologist approaches the practices of the tribe from within an unquestioned commitment to a certain metaphysics. Thus, even liberal and Marxist criticisms can be shown to have their roots in a Western metaphysics (e.g. Foucault, 1979; MacIntyre, 1985). What we need is a deeper conception of the part that the practice plays in the life of the community, which operates both locally and globally, of a ritual or symbolic function that such critical approaches are apt to occlude. It is only through taking a more completely moral – even religious – point of view that we can hope to better evaluate instances that call for judgment across cultures without a too facile recourse to relativism as a critique of universalism, irrespective of how well intentioned such a turning might be. The concerns for international communication raised by relativism addressed in this essay are not to be taken as arguments for any kind of absolutism. Rather, these concerns call for closer investigation of relativist positions from the perspective of World Englishes.

This epistemological turn is what we might call a "deep humanism." When offered as a regulative ideal for the work of international communication – an ideal that remains vigilant against the encroachment of dogmatism – it enfolds both the mechanisms of criticisms that remain alert to the many ways in which we stray from this ideal through notions of supremacy derived from identifications with nation, region, class, race, gender, sexuality, and so on. In other words, even the most abrasive of criticisms would find a place within such international communication when motivated by a commitment to the Kingdom of ends. Criticisms of English as a global language driven by resentment of colonialism or nostalgia for a lost tradition – regardless of their source – might be more difficult to justify. As Ella Shohat (1998) reminds us, critical international communication has moved, from an anticolonial, orientalist, stance to the more complex postcolonial position that can find expression within fully liberal national and international institutions (Dhillon, 1996).

I have argued that we can find a vivid way of realizing the logic of such an ecological humanism through the consideration of the nature and use of a particular language – English. This works less as an analogy than as an example, even the epitome, of what is important in cultural coherence and interaction. There is no such thing as a universal language; there are diverse *languages*. Still, these are neither unchanging nor unaffected by each other, and while precise translation between them may sometimes be difficult, use is seldom a problem (Dhillon, 2001). Furthermore, contemporary concepts of intertextuality suggest something of the inevitably global nature of our lives.

Perhaps no contemporary philosopher captures the ethics reflecting the deep humanism of this idea as well as Thoreau did in the nineteenth century: Thoreau called for a kind of multilingualism that is very helpful in relation to universalism. This is not something that a nation like the United States, for example, has to learn – as some simpler strands of Saidian criticisms might imply. Rather these resources are already available to us. Take for example the following passage from Thoreau's *Walden Pond*:

> Those who have not learned to read the ancient classics in the language in which they were written must have a very imperfect knowledge of the history of the human race; for it is remarkable that no transcript of them has ever been made into the modern tongue, unless our civilization itself may be regarded as such a transcript . . . That age will be rich indeed when those relics which we call Classics, and the still older and more than classic but even less known Scriptures of the nations, shall have further accumulated, when the Vaticans shall be filled with the Vedas and Zendavestas and Bibles, with Homers, and Dantes, and Shakespeares, and all the centuries to come shall have successively deposited their trophies in the forum of the world. By such a pile we may hope to scale heaven at last. (cited in Cavell, 1992: 6)

Extending this metaphor to include traditions other than those mentioned by Thoreau, we could resist a reductive view of identity. Thus, we would leave open the possibility of a critical collectivity. We are enabled then to reflect on, and deeply value, the diverse languages and cultures that are present and have contributed toward the making of a certain "tradition" or "civilization," as also the relations between them. The arguments of responsibly critical international communication brought to bear on issues of regional, national, and sub-national identifications would enable the forging of robust new linguistic and cultural identities that are not based on exclusionary practices tied to reductive identifications endorsed by nostalgia or resentment.

I have attempted to present here the general contours of the colonial discourse and postcolonial critique that dominate much of our understanding of the workings of a global language such as English. I have suggested that world Englishes discourse offers the possibilities of a refinement of liberal international communication in a way that avoids the problems of facile universalist assumptions even as it strives to uncover a deep humanism. The work of rendering such an approach non-anthropomorphic remains to be done. It is my judgment that liberal international communication, as offered by the recognition of geographically dispersed varieties of a language understood in the light of this deep humanism, will require of educators and language policy makers the highest exercise of practical reason.

NOTE

1   The following works have provided valuable insights for this chapter: Abu-Lughod (1999), Bonnell and Hunt (1999), Bourdieu (1977, 1993 [1984]), Braudel (1984), Chatterjee (1993), Clifford (1988), Derrida (1976 [1967]), Dhillon (1999), Fauconnier and Turner (2003), Foucault (1970 [1966], 1972 [1969]), Geertz (1988), Grabar (1978), Kachru (1990), King (1995), Obeyeskere (1992), Pratt (1986), Sahlins (1995), Said (1983), Sewell (1999), and Williams and Chrisman (1994).

REFERENCES

Abu-Lughod, Janet (ed.) (1999) *Sociology for the Twenty-first Century: Continuities and Cutting Edges.* Chicago: University of Chicago Press.

Bolton, Kingsley (2004a) World Englishes. In *The Handbook of Applied Linguistics.* Edited by Alan Davies and Catherine Elder. Oxford: Blackwell, pp. 367–96.

Bolton, Kingsley (2004b) *Hong Kong English: Autonomy and Creativity.* Hong Kong: Hong Kong University Press.

Bonnell, Victoria E. and Hunt, Lynn (eds.) (1999) *Beyond the Cultural*

Turn. Berkeley: University of California Press.

Bourdieu, Pierre (1977) *Outline of a Theory of Practice.* New York: Cambridge University Press.

Bourdieu, Pierre (1993 [1984]) *Sociology in Question.* Thousand Oaks, CA: Sage.

Braudel, Fernand (1984) *Civilization and Capitalism, 15th–18th Century.* New York: Harper and Row.

Cavell, Stanley (1992) *The Senses of Walden.* Chicago: University of Chicago Press.

Chatterjee, Partha (1993) *The Nation and Its Fragments: Colonial and*

Postcolonial Histories. Princeton: Princeton University Press.

Clifford, James (1988) *The Predicament of Culture*. Cambridge, MA: Harvard University Press.

Derrida, Jacques (1976 [1967]) *Of Grammatology*. Baltimore: Johns Hopkins University Press.

Dhillon, Pradeep A. (1996) Unhomely readings of philosophy's fictions. *Thesis Eleven*, **44**, 87–9.

Dhillon, Pradeep A. (1999) (Dis)locating thoughts: Where do the birds go after the last sky? In *Critical Theories in Education: Changing Terrains of Knowledge and Politics*. Edited by Tom Popkewitz and Lynn Fendler. New York: Routledge, pp. 191–207.

Dhillon, Pradeep A. (2001) The longest way home: Language and philosophy in diaspora. *Studies in the Linguistic Sciences*, **31**(1), 181–92.

Fauconnier, Gilles and Turner, Mark (2003) *The Way We Think: Conceptual Blending and the Mind's Hidden Complexities*. New York: Basic Books.

Foucault, Michel (1965 [1961]) *Madness and Civilization: A History of Insanity in the Age of Reason*. New York: Random House.

Foucault, Michel (1970 [1966]) *The Order of Things: An Archeology of the Human Sciences*. New York: Random House.

Foucault, Michel (1972 [1969]) *The Archeology of Knowledge*. New York: Random House.

Foucault, Michel (1973 [1963]) *The Birth of the Clinic: An Archeology of Medical Perception*. New York: Random House.

Foucault, Michel (1979 [1975]) *Discipline and Punish: The Birth of the Prison*. New York: Random House.

Geertz, Clifford (1988) Being there, writing here. *Harper's Magazine*, March.

Grabar, Oleg (1978) *The Alhambra*. Cambridge: Harvard University Press.

Kachru, Yamuna (1990) Context, creativity, and style: Strategies in Raja Rao's novels. In *Word and Mantra: The Art of Raja Rao*. Edited by Robert Hardgrave, Jr. New Delhi: Katha in association with the University of Texas, Austin, pp. 88–117.

King, Anthony, D. (1995) *The Bungalow: The Production of a Global Culture*. Oxford: Oxford University Press.

Loomba, Ania (1998) *Colonialism/ Postcolonialism*. London: Routledge.

MacIntyre, Alisdair (1985) *Marxism and Christianity*. South Bend: University of Notre Dame Press.

Mani, Lata (1998) *Contentious Traditions: The Debate on Sati in Colonial India*. Berkeley: University of California Press.

Midgely, Mary (1981) *Heart and Mind; The Varieties of Moral Experience*. New York: St Martin's Press.

Midgely, Mary (1991) *Can't We Make Moral Judgments?* New York: St Martin's Press.

Moody-Adams, Michele (1997) *Fieldwork in Familiar Places: Morality, Culture, and Philosophy*. Cambridge, MA: Harvard University Press.

Nussbaum, Martha (2000) *Women in Development*. Cambridge: Cambridge University Press.

Obeyeskere, Gananath (1992) *The Apotheosis of Captain Cook: European Mythmaking in the Pacific*. Princeton: Princeton University Press.

Okin, Susan M., Cohen, Joshua, Howard, Mathew, and Nussbaum, Martha (eds.) (1999) *Is Multiculturalism Bad for Women?* Princeton, NJ: Princeton University Press.

Pennycook, Alastair (2004) Critical applied linguistics. In *The Handbook of Applied Linguistics*. Edited by Alan Davies and Catherine Elder. Oxford: Blackwell, pp. 784–807.

Pratt, Mary Louise (1986) Fieldwork in common places. In *Writing Culture*:

544 *Pradeep A. Dhillon*

The Poetics and Politics of Ethnography. Edited by James Clifford and George E. Marcus. Berkeley: University of California Press.

Prochaska, David (1990) *Making Algeria French: Colonialism in Bône.* New York: Cambridge University Press.

Prochaska, David (1996) History as literature, literature as history: Cagayous of Algiers. *American Historical Review*, **101**, 670–711.

Sahlins, Marshall (1995) *How "Natives" Think: About Captain Cook, For Example.* Chicago: University of Chicago Press.

Said, Edward (1978) *Orientalism.* New York: Random House.

Said, Edward (1983) *The World, the Text and the Critic.* Cambridge, MA: Harvard University Press.

Sewell, William (1999) The Concept(s) of Culture. In *Beyond the Cultural Turn.* Edited by Victoria E. Bonnell and Lynn Hunt. Berkeley: University of California Press, pp. 35–61.

Shohat, Ella (ed.) (1998) *Talking Visions: Multicultural Feminism in a Transnational Age.* Cambridge, MA: MIT Press.

Shohat, Ella and Stam, Robert (1994) *Unthinking Eurocentricism: Multiculturalism in the Media.* London/New York: Routledge.

Spivak, Gayatri (1988) Can the Subaltern speak? In *Marxism and the Interpretation of Culture.* Edited by Cary Nelson and Larry Grossberg. Urbana: University of Illinois Press, pp. 271–313.

Spivak, Gayatri (1999) *A Critique of Postcolonial Reason: Toward a History of the Vanishing Present*, Cambridge, MA: Harvard University Press.

Taylor, Charles (1991) *The Ethics of Authencity.* Cambridge, MA: Harvard University Press.

Taylor, Charles (1992) *Multiculturalism and "The Politics of Recognition."* Edited by Amy Gutmann. Princeton: Princeton University Press.

Williams, Bernard (2005 [1985]) *Ethics and the Limits of Philosophy,* Cambridge, MA: Harvard University Press.

Williams, Patrick and Chrisman, Laura (eds.) (1994) *Colonial Discourse and Postcolonial Theory: A Reader.* New York: Columbia University Press.

FURTHER READING

Bartolovich, Crystal and Lazarus, Neil (eds.) (2002) *Marxism, Modernity, and Postcolonial Studies.* Cambridge: Cambridge University Press.

Kachru, Braj. B. (2005) *Asian Englishes: Beyond the Canon.* Hong Kong: Hong Kong University Press.

Masten, Jeffrey (ed.) (1997) *Language Machines: Technologies of Literary and Cultural Production.* London: Routledge.

Mohanty, Chandra Talpade (2003) *Feminism without Borders: Decolonizing Theory, Practicing Solidarity.* Durham, NC: Duke University Press.

30 Cultural Studies and Discursive Constructions of World Englishes

WIMAL DISSANAYAKE

1 Introduction

The relationship between Cultural Studies and English Studies is increasingly attracting the attention of scholars in the humanities. It is a relationship that is potentially fruitful, but at the same time fraught with tensions and perils. In this chapter, I wish to reflect on the relationship between Cultural Studies and world Englishes and suggest some topics that merit further exploration.

Cultural Studies has been described in diverse ways. According to Raymond Williams, the word "culture" is one of the two or three most complicated words in the English language. Hence, it is hardly surprising that Cultural Studies has been defined in so many different ways. For example, it has been characterized as an "interdisciplinary, transdisciplinary, and sometimes counter-disciplinary field that operates in the tensions between its tendencies to embrace both a broad anthropological and a more narrowly humanistic concept of culture" (Grossberg, Nelson, and Treichler, 1992). The authors of this statement make the point that unlike traditional anthropology, Cultural Studies has emerged from the explorations into modern industrial societies. In terms of methodologies, Cultural Studies is typically interpretive and evaluative. In contradiction to traditional evaluations, it rejects as untenable the exclusive equation of culture with high culture and emphasizes the need to study all available forms of cultural production in relation to the prevalent cultural practices and social institutions.

Writers maintain that Cultural Studies should be committed to the study of the entire range of a society's arts, beliefs, institutions, and processes. The journal *Cultural Critique*, which in many ways represents this new thinking on the study of culture, states in its prospectus that the publication is concerned with "culture" in the most inclusive sense of the term, as at once a material and discursive human practice. Thus, the goal of *Cultural Critique* may be formulated most comprehensively as the examination of received values, institutions, practices, and discourses in terms of their economic, political, social, and aesthetic genealogies, constitutions, and effects. These statements embody the general orientation of this mode of investigation.

Cultural Studies draws on a plurality of established academic disciplines including literary studies, anthropology, philosophy, communication, media studies, sociology, and feminist studies. However, it seeks to transcend the boundaries of these disciplines and bring about a reconfiguration of thought. It does not confine itself to a single methodology and draws freely upon the resources of, for example, poststructuralism, postmodernism, hermeneutics, new historicism, Marxism, and semiotics. Cultural Studies bears the signatures of many modern theorists, such as Raymond Williams, Clifford Geertz, Jacques Derrida, Michel Foucault, Jacques Lacan, Roland Barthes, Pierre Bourdieu, Julia Kristeva, Jean Baudrillard, Homi Bhabha, and Edward Said. It attaches no privileged significance to a single subject or methodology. Moreover, the emphasis of Cultural Studies seems to differ in various countries in keeping with their dominant interests and perspectives. For example, John Frow and Meaghan Morris maintain that Australian work in Cultural Studies is less concerned with philosophical and abstract issues than with specific issues in concrete situations with a political resonance.

2   Cultural Studies and Other Disciplines

Cultural Studies, it needs to be borne in mind, has very important links with the study of literature. Cultural Studies as we know it today grew largely out of the work of the Center for Contemporary Cultural Studies at Birmingham, England, established in 1964. Two of the prominent scholars closely associated with Cultural Studies in Britain, Richard Hoggart and Raymond Williams, came out of literary studies. The last 15 years or so have witnessed a literary turn in the human sciences, most notably in the United States, Canada, and Australia; this literary turn in the human sciences has had a profound impact on the growth of Cultural Studies. Today, literary theory has come to dominate the intellectual landscape of these countries as never before, shaping a variety of academic disciplines ranging from anthropology to legal studies.

In anthropology, a discipline closely related to modern Cultural Studies, the influence of literary theory is unmistakable, especially in the work of younger scholars. Anthropological texts, like literary texts, are seen as constructed texts and not transparent descriptions. Therefore, understandably, questions of rhetoric and textuality have assumed a significance and compelling power hitherto unseen in meta-anthropology. Literary style and figurality are regarded not as external embellishments but as vital components of meaning in the representation of other cultures and ways of life. As James Clifford (1988) has remarked, the writing and reading of ethnography are over-determined by numerous forces that lie beyond the control of an author or an interpretive community. Contingencies of language, rhetoric, ideology, and power need to be openly and honestly confronted in the process.

Modern anthropologists – or at least a significant number among them – subscribe to the notion that ethnographies are essentially rhetorical performances that have as their aim the narrating of a convincing story. They see these stories as producing an important body of cultural knowledge through encounters of Self and Other. It is by now generally accepted that cultural redescriptions are historically contingent and contestable, and that a focus on the modes of textual production themselves opens useful pathways to understanding the fundamental dilemmas of anthropology. Questions related to the notions of epistemology, authenticity, ethnographic authority, and rewriting the other can be analyzed usefully only by placing language, tropes, and constructedness of ethnography at the center of discussions in the way that literary theorists do. What the literary turn in anthropology has succeeded in emphasizing is the fact that cultural redescription is fundamentally an interpretive process closely associated with the dynamics of writing.

The older and widely prevalent view that ethnography is a transparent form of documentation has rightly been discarded in favor of the view that it is a form of writing where figurality and narration are central, and that epistemology and rhetoric are indissolubly linked. As Paul Rainbow (1986: 244) observes:

> the self-consciousness of style, rhetoric, and dialectic in the production of anthropological texts should lead us to a finer awareness of other, more imaginative ways to write.

George Marcus and Michael Fischer, in their influential book, *Anthropology as Cultural Critique* (1986), point out that "While we do not presume to do the work of literary scholars in our treatment of recent texts, an understanding of the controversial importance of literary awareness of anthropological rhetoric has clearly informed our characterization of present trends."

These same trends can be discerned in the field of history. Up until recent times, history was regarded primarily as a domain of inquiry with a positivistic outlook. The task of the historian was taken to be the accurate and dispassionate reporting of events that had taken place in the past. This view still persists as the dominant credo in the field. However, thanks in large part to the efforts of metahistorians such as Hayden White and Dominick LaCapra, who are clearly influenced by various facets of contemporary literary theory, an alternative mode of historical interrogation has been opened up. This expansion is generating a great measure of interest among younger scholars and is rapidly gaining momentum. This newer approach to historiography foregrounds the problematics of representation, in the way that contemporary literary theory does, and emphasizes the pivotal role of language, strategies of textual production and narrativization in the redescription of reality. White (1973: 51) remarks:

> Theorists of historiography generally agree that all historical narratives contain an irreducible and inexpungeable element of interpretation.

The historian has to interpret his materials in order to construct the moving pattern of images in which the form of the historical process is to be mirrored. This is because the historical record is both too full and too sparse. On the one hand, there are always more facts in the record than the historian can possibly include in his narrative representation of a given segment of the historical process, and so the historian must "interpret" his data by excluding certain facts from his account of some event or complex of events as irrelevant to his narrative purpose. On the other hand, in his efforts to reconstruct "what happened" in any given period of history, the historian inevitably must include in his narrative an account of some event or complex of events for which the facts that would permit a plausible explanation of its occurrence are lacking. This means that historians must "interpret" their materials by filling in the gaps in their information on inferential or speculative grounds. A historical narrative is thus necessarily a mixture of adequately explained events, a congeries of established and inferred fact, at once a representation that is an interpretation and an interpretation that passes for an explanation of the whole process mirrored in the narrative.

It is White's conviction that interpretation in history consists of the generation of plot structures for a sequence of actions or events so that their nature as an understandable process is exhibited by their figurality as a story of a particular kind, a sequence of events that one historian may emplot as tragedy, another may emplot as romance or comedy. Drawing on the formulations of Northrop Frye and Roman Jakobson, White has elaborated this idea in detail in his writings. He states unequivocally the importance of literary theory in the writing of history. According to White (1973: 99):

> History as a discipline is in bad shape today because it has lost sight of its origins in the literary imagination. In the interest of appearing scientific and objective, it has repressed and denied to itself its own greatest source of strength and renewal.

White, LaCapra, and others like them who espouse a literature-inspired historiography are not asserting that historical events and fictional events are of the same type. What they are pointing to is the question of representation through language and the similar ways in which narratives are organized in literary and historical works.

Philosophy, as it has been taught up until recent times, paid very little attention to the way philosophical texts are linguistically constructed, and the centrality of writing and figurality in the textual production of philosophical works was neglected. This resulted in a logocentric bias which tended to equate speech, consciousness, and truth as self-presence. Philosophers such as Jacques Derrida have maintained that Western philosophers from Plato to Hegel ignored tropes and rhetorical strategies that are crucial to the construction of any verbal text, philosophical or otherwise. Deconstructive philosophers have forcefully underlined this deficiency.

This is, of course, not to suggest that such sentiments were not expressed in earlier times before the emergence of deconstructive philosophers in the 1960s. Nietzsche (1986: 46), who in many ways is a forerunner of this mode of interrogation, says that truth is:

> A mobile army of metaphors, metonyms, and anthropomorphisms – in short, a sum of human relations, which have been enhanced, transposed, and embellished poetically and rhetorically, and which after long use seem firm, canonical, and obligatory to a people: truths are illusions about which one has forgotten that this is what they are.

However, it needs to be noted that it is with the writings of Derrida and others like him who have had a profound influence on modern literary theory that this approach to philosophical inquiry began to win widespread acceptance.

The work of literary theorists such as the late Paul de Man, who was considerably influenced by Derrida, puts into circulation the view that philosophical texts should be treated as literary texts. De Man (1978: 115) observed, "philosophy turns out to be an endless reflection on its own destruction at the hands of literature." He calls attention to the centrality of rhetoric and figurality in the constitution of philosophical texts. Traditionally, philosophers have deemed conceptual analysis to be the proper domain of philosophy, and close reading and topological analysis as that of literary studies. But what philosophers like Derrida and literary critics like de Man point out is that epistemology and rhetoric are inextricably linked.

The writings of Richard Rorty, whom Harold Bloom has described as the most interesting philosopher in the world today, are extremely important in this regard. His works, including *Philosophy and the Mirror of Nature*, *Consequences of Pragmatism*, and *Contingency, Irony and Solidarity*, have given rise to many productive and forward-looking philosophical discussions. Rorty, who can be usefully described as an anti-foundationalist and pragmatic philosopher, is unambiguously critical of the efforts to construct a systematic philosophy that valorizes the notion that the task of philosophy is to discover authentic foundations and arrive at universal truths and that philosophy as a mode of human inquiry can transcend the dictates of history. It is his judgment that this is a futile undertaking and that philosophers should see their charge as one of conversation and not of investigation. Rorty, much in the manner of modern-day literary theorists, emphasizes the need to re-understand the intricate workings of language and rhetoric in the construction of philosophical texts and the complex ways in which philosophical language games arise and disappear.

Our access to reality is conditioned by language, the specific historical moment and what counts as knowledge. Hence, the often-stated claim by philosophers that philosophy adjudicates between truth and non-truth is questionable. From the seventeenth century onwards in Western philosophy, the idea of representation has been central to any discussion of philosophy. The mind was regarded as a mirror that reflected reality, and knowledge as that which dealt with those reflections. The task of philosophy was to design strategies by which this body of knowledge could be extracted. Rorty discards this view. He finds efforts to discover the correspondence between language and the world futile and counterproductive. His aim is to refashion philosophy as a mode of conversation with culture, and to him, questions of language and historicity are crucial. In *Philosophy and the Mirror of Nature*, Rorty maintains that the search for knowledge and epistemological certitude so prized by mainstream philosophers has always been a victim of its own figurality: "It is pictures rather than propositions, metaphors rather than statements, which determine our philosophical convictions" (1979: 90). His conviction that philosophy is a form of cultural conversation which is best conceived as a form of writing has a great deal in common with contemporary literary theory.

Rorty does not draw only on modern literary theory but also finds novelists far more illuminating and helpful than philosophers when it comes to the exploration of individual fulfillment and social solidarity that he sees as the task of philosophical discourse. For example, he compares the novelist Milan Kundera and the philosopher Martin Heidegger, two writers he admires. He regards both of them as seeking to challenge the Western metaphysical tradition that tries to delineate the unitary pattern that underlies apparent diversity. However, according to Rorty, there is a substantial difference between the two of them as they go about their task. As Heidegger sees it, the counterforce to metaphysics is the openness to "being," a state of mind that can be attained more easily in peasant communities that have not been subject to the transforming power of technology, and where customs are relatively stable. As Rorty (1989: 19) says, "Heidegger's utopia is pastoral, a sparsely populated valley in the mountain, a valley in which life is given shape by its relationship to the primordial Fourfold – earth, sky, man, and gods. Kundera's utopia is carnivalesque, Dickensian, a crowd of eccentrics rejoicing in each other's idiosyncrasies, curious for novelty rather than nostalgic for primordiality." It is evident that Rorty finds Kundera's approach far more relevant than Heidegger's for modern times.

I have, so far, briefly touched on the disciplines of anthropology, history, and philosophy to reinforce the point that the literary turn in humanities and social sciences has a profound impact. One can, with equal justification, examine such diverse fields as political science, feminist studies, religious studies, architecture, cultural geography, and law to demonstrate the growing impact of literary theory. The main point, as far as the objective of this chapter is concerned, is to recognize the formative influence of literary theory in the growth of Cultural Studies. And as Cultural Studies expands and claims newer territories for exploration, the field of literary studies, too, has to take stock of itself and redefine itself in the light of the thematics and protocols of analysis of Cultural Studies.

Cultural Studies and Discursive Constructions of World Englishes

3   Cultural Studies and the Ontology of World Englishes

Cultural Studies is a rapidly expanding field of investigation that is unafraid of drawing on the conceptualities of diverse theorists as it seeks to confront and investigate cultural realities. The concept of power and genealogy of Foucault, demystification of mythologies of Barthes, rhetorical readings of texts propounded by Derrida, thick descriptions of Geertz, linguistic constructions of the self and the nature of the imaginary enunciated by Lacan, the nature and conditions of postmodern knowledge of Lyotard, the cultural materialism of Raymond Williams, the subjectivity of women as foregrounded by Judith Butler and Gayatri Chakravorty Spivak, and the Orientalism of Said, to mention but a few focuses and writers, have been assimilated into the fabric of Cultural Studies. In this chapter, I focus on a few topics that find repeated and productive articulation in modern Cultural Studies and underline their importance in our attempts to understanding the complex ontology of world Englishes.

The concept of power, along with the notion of ideology, is pivotal to many innovative works of scholarship associated with Cultural Studies. With the writings of Michel Foucault, the idea of power received a newer inflection, one that has been instrumental in spawning much useful cultural research. In Foucault's hands, the concept of power became something omnipresent and not only repressive but also productive. In terms of the theme of this chapter, the relationship between power and discourse is most significant. Foucault (1972: 10) said that "in any society the production of discourse is at once controlled, selected, organized and redistributed according to a number of procedures whose role is to avert its powers and its dangers, to master the unpredictable event." This line of approach has important implications for the study of world Englishes.

The significance of the concepts of power and ideology in the understanding of the nature of world Englishes has been pointed out by a number of scholars in recent times. In several seminal essays, Braj Kachru (1986, 1992, 2003, 2005) has alerted us to the need to pay greater attention to questions of power and ideology. Robert Phillipson (1992) has focused on the contemporary phenomenon of English as a world language and a dominant force, paying close attention to power and ideology. The promotion of English as a world language by dominant powers and its imbrication with foreign policy is an aspect that attracts Phillipson's attention. Gauri Viswanathan (1989) explains how the discipline of English came into its own in an age of colonialism, and asserts that any purposeful discussion of the growth of English must come to terms with the imperial mission of educating and civilizing colonial subjects in the arts and letters of England.

There are a number of subthemes connected to power, ideology and language that need to be explored in greater depth. The diverse ways in which creative writers – poets, novelists, dramatists – seek to subvert the English language in a gesture of defiance and self-assertion deserve careful consideration. The complex and multivalent relationship between linguistic imperialism and the new literatures in English offers us interesting insights into the way in which power and ideology work. Salman Rushdie (1982b: 7) made the comment that:

> Language, like much else in the newly independent societies, needs to be decolonized, to be made in other images, if those of us who use it from positions outside Anglo-Saxon cultures are to be more than "Uncle Toms". And it is this endeavor that gives the new literatures of Africa, the Caribbean, and India much of their present vitality and excitement.

How are the producers of new literatures in English rising to this challenge? How are their efforts connected to questions of power and ideology? Passages from two well-known novels will help to make this connection clear. The first is from Raja Rao's *Kanthapura* and the second from Salman Rushdie's *The Satanic Verses*:

> The rains have come, the fine, first-footing rains that skip over the bronze mountain, tiptoe the crags, and leaping into the valley, go splashing and wind-swung, a winnowed pour, and the coconuts and betel-nuts and the cardamom plants choke with it and hiss back. And there, there it comes over the Bebbur Hill and the Kanthur Hill and begins to paw upon the tiles, and the cattle come running home, their ears stretched back, and the drover lurches behind some bel-tree or papal-tree, and people leave their querns and rush to the courtyard, and turning towards the Kenchamma Temple send forth a prayer, saying, "There, there, the rains have come, Kenchamma; may our houses be white as silver," and the lightning flashes and the thunder stirs the tiles, and children rush to the gutter-slabs to sail paper boats down to Kashi. (Rao, 1963: 156)

> O, my shoes are Japanese, Gibreel sang, translating the old song into English in semi-conscious deference to the uprushing host-nation. These trousers English, if you please. On my head, red Russian hat; my heart's Indian for all that. The clouds were bubbling up towards them, and perhaps it was on account of that great mystification of cumulus and cumulo-nimbus, the mighty rolling thunderhead standing like hammers in the dawn, or perhaps it was the singing (the one busy performing, the other booing the performance), or their blast-delirium that spread them foreknowledge of the imminent . . . but for whatever reason, the two men, Gibreelsaldin Farishtachamcha, condemned to their endless but also ending angelicdevilish fall, did not become aware of the moment at which the process of their transmutation began. (Rushdie, 1989)

In these two passages, we find boldly defiant uses of the English language. In the first excerpt, Raja Rao has used creatively the speech rhythms of Kannada to recreate a characteristically South Indian experience (see Kachru, 2005: 137–54). In the second, Rushdie deploys English audaciously, along with Indian intertextualities (the reference to the famous song in Raj Kapoor's popular film *Sri 420*) to communicate a distinctively non-Western experience. Now, are these writers victims of English linguistic imperialism? Or are they strategically extending the range, tonalities, and discursivities of English? Are they, in their different ways, subverting from within the colonizing ambitions of English? These and related questions demand careful answers. The topic of power and ideology, then, is one that can prove to be extremely productive in exploring the nature and significance of world Englishes.

The concept of the public sphere that figures so prominently in the writings of proponents of Cultural Studies is one that can be utilized productively into explorations of the efficacies and impacts of world Englishes. The German social philosopher Jürgen Habermas (1989), in his book *The Structural Transformation of the Public Sphere*, foregrounded a set of forces and institutions that emerged in the late seventeenth and eighteenth centuries in Europe that he regards as crucial to the understanding of democratic societies. He terms these forces and institutions the bourgeois public sphere.

The most noteworthy facet of this formulation, in the opinion of Habermas, is the feasibility of separating the political dimensions from both the state and civil society and promoting a critical and questioning perspective on both domains. The bourgeois public sphere, according to Habermas, is central to a proper understanding of the democratic social transformation that occurred in Europe in the eighteenth century, and to the consequent rise of the nation-state. In his view, the institutionalized public sphere not only constitutes a nexus of interests and a site of contestation and oppositionality between state and society, but also a practice of rational-critical discourse on topics and issues that relate to politics in the larger and more inclusive sense of the term. Both social scientists and humanists have employed this concept in their research, at times taking Habermas to task for his limitations and blind-spots, with remarkable results. English, it needs hardly be mentioned, is used, whether in Nigeria or Hong Kong or Pakistan, by the elite who wield considerable power in society. The creative writers from non-Western countries who use English as their preferred and privileged medium of communication are for the most part from the upper crust of society and have the potential for exercising a significant influence on social tides. Hence, the concept of the public sphere can be deployed very fruitfully by commentators and researchers in world Englishes.

Gayatri Chakravorty Spivak (1993), in a remarkably perceptive essay on R. K. Narayan's novel *The Guide*, demonstrates how new literatures in English could be usefully examined in terms of the public sphere. In this essay, Spivak explores a multiplicity of dimensions in Narayan's text including his use of English in relation to Indian languages, his use of "devadasis" (temple dancers) as a vehicle for his narrative about a male protagonist and the ensuing questions of female subjectivity in an androcentric society, the class implications of the institution of devadasis, and the way that the novel, an elitist text in English, was transformed into a popular text, a Bombay film. Through her analysis, Spivak has demonstrated the importance of examining English creative writings from Asia, Africa, and the Caribbean in terms of the public sphere. By situating these writings in the public sphere as a means of teasing out the complex layers of meaning embedded in them, we can attain a deeper understanding of such works.

Another informative example is this poem by the Indian poet A. K. Ramanujan (1997), *Invisible Bodies*:

> Turning the corner of the street
> he found three newborn puppies
> in a gutter with a mother curled
> around them.
>
> Turning the corner of the street
> she found a newborn naked baby
> male, battered, dead in a manhole
> with no mother around.
>
> Turning the corner of the street
> the boy stepped on the junkie
> lying in the alley, covered with flies,
> a dog sniffing his crotch.
>
> Just any day, not only after a riot,
> even among the gamboges maples of fall
> streets are full of bodies, invisible
> to the girl under the twirling parasol.

The author has sought to place this poem, which is built on the juxtaposition of visibility and invisibility, with all its critical interrogations, within the public sphere, as a way of enforcing his theme. The way world Englishes and their concomitant creative writings relate to the Habermasian public sphere is another area that could be fruitfully explored as we strive to attain a better and more nuanced understanding of the dynamics of world Englishes. The two topics referred to so far in this chapter – power and the public sphere – are, of course, interconnected in challenging ways.

Another topic that merits closer investigation is the relationship between English writings and indigenous writings in a given cultural or national setting. In countries like India or Malaysia or Hong Kong, literary works are being produced in English as well as in the national indigenous languages. Hence, an investigation of the relationship that exists between writings produced in English and other languages can yield interesting results and open up newer avenues of inquiry. In a recent essay, Salman Rushdie (1997: 50) makes the following observation with regard to the Indian literary scene:

> The prose writing – both fiction and nonfiction – created in this period by Indian writers working in English is proving to be a stronger and more important body of work than most of what has been produced in the eighteen "recognized"

languages of India, the so-called "vernacular languages," during the same time; and, indeed, this new, and still burgeoning, "Indo-Anglican" literature represents perhaps the most valuable contribution India has yet made to the world of books. The true Indian literature of the first postcolonial half century has been made in the language the British left behind.

Not everyone, of course, would agree with Rushdie's assessment. However, it is an indisputable fact that during the past 15 years or so, a number of distinguished Indian writers of fiction have emerged who have generated a great measure of interest beyond India. Among them, Salman Rushdie himself, as well as Vikram Seth, Amitav Ghosh, Rohinton Mistry, Vikram Chandra, Arundhati Roy, Shashi Tharoor, Amit Chaudhuri, and Kiran Desai deserve special mention.

How the works of authors writing in English relate thematically, stylistically, and in terms of social vision to the corpus of indigenous writing is an area of investigation that could engender interesting insights. How do these two sets of writers confront the imperatives of postcoloniality and articulate their different understandings? How can we make use of one set of writing to interrogate the other, given the fact that they both grew out of the same historical conjuncture and cultural geography? This has also great implications for the teaching of non-native English writings. In an essay that discusses the writings of Rudyard Kipling, Nadine Gordimer, Hanif Kureshi, Rabindranath Tagore, Mahashweta Devi, and Binodini Devi, Gayatri Chakravorty Spivak (1993), proceeding from the premise that the goal of teaching literature is epistemic in that the aim is to transform the way in which objects of knowledge are constructed, remarks:

> in the post-colonial context, the teaching of English literature can become critical only if it is intimately yoked to the teaching of the literary or cultural production in the mother tongue(s). In that persistently asymmetrical intimacy, the topics of language learning, in its various forms, can become a particularly productive site.

Here the English writings produced by speakers of English in Asia and Africa can play a very significant and productive role. Situated as these writings are between two cultural worlds, two thought worlds, the pedagogic function alluded to in Spivak's essay can be usefully accomplished by investigating them deeply, paying close attention to the shifts between cultural registers and the tensions of interlingual dynamics. The special value of world Englishes and their attendant creative writings in linguistic and literary pedagogy has as yet not received its due share of scholarly attention.

4   World Englishes and Transnationalization

That world Englishes, the object as well as the concept, emerged as a consequence of the complex processes of globalization and transnationalization is abundantly clear. Hence, any ontological and epistemological analysis demands that the writings associated with world Englishes be situated at the interface between the global and the local. One of the defining features of the modern world is the increasingly complex and multifaceted interaction of localism and globalism. Clearly, this process has been going on for centuries, but its velocity has risen dramatically during the past half-century. This interaction produces remarkable changes in the spaces of economics, politics, and culture as newer forms of capital, largely originating in the West, enforce their local visibilities and inflect historically sedimented practices in unforeseen ways. How symbolic forms and ways of associating with Western capitalism are transformed, localized, and legitimized in the Third World countries in relation to their historical narratives and changing lifeworlds is at the heart of the discourse of localism. This is a discourse that advocates of Cultural Studies have found to be of very great interest.

World Englishes presents us with a vibrant site where cultural articulations of the mutual embeddedness of the local and the global are given comprehensible shape. A fruitful way of apprehending the dialectic between the local and the global is through the production of newer localities. When we explore the imbricated narratives of the local and the global, what we are doing, in point of fact, is to focus on the production of the local and its ever-changing contours in response to the imperatives of the global. The local is never static; its boundaries, both spatial and temporal, are subject to constant change. It is characterized by a web of power plays, agnostic interests, pluralized histories, battles over polysemous signs, and asymmetrical exchanges. The local is constantly transforming itself as it seeks to reach beyond itself and engage the translocal. What is interesting about world Englishes is that they foreground and give figurality to these processes in compelling interesting ways. The well-known anthropologist Clifford Geertz (1983) is surely right when he underlines the need in social understanding and cultural redescription for a continual dialectical tacking between the most local of local details and the most global of global structures in such a way as to bring them into simultaneous view. Deleuze and Guatarri (1986) focus on this phenomenon when they refer to "deterritorialization," where the production of the local is inflected by the nexus of activities taking place elsewhere. What is interesting about the emerging body of writing associated with world Englishes is that it makes available a semiotic space for the articulation of the global imaginary and its formation within the phenomenology of the local.

We are living at a moment in history when the local and the global are complicated in unanticipated ways. As a consequence of the phenomenal growth of science and technology, and of the unprecedented proliferation of media and communication, the world is shrinking as never before. And this very shrinkage, paradoxically enough, has had the effect of spawning local narratives and projects with added vigor. As Wilson and Dissanayake (1996) have observed, a new world-space of cultural products and national representations which are simultaneously becoming more globalized as a consequence of capitalism moving across borders and more localized, fragmented into contestatory enclaves of difference, coalition, and resistance in everyday life has come into play. The interface of global forces, images, codes, sites, technologies of transformationalization with those of local communities, tactics, symbolic strategies that would confront and challenge them in the production of locality and the making of everyday space is one of the distinctive phenomena of contemporary society. The evolving corpus of writing linked to world Englishes provides us with narratives, repertoires of images, and conceptualities that enable us to make greater sense of this interanimation of the local and the global.

If we pause to examine the novels and short stories of younger Indian writers such as Arundhati Roy and Ardashri Vakil, we perceive this local–global interplay not only in the experiences selected for contextualization but in the very sensibility that shapes the language that is used to write about them. For example, the following short passage from Arundhati Roy's *The God of Small Things* (1997: 8) bears this out:

> During the funeral service, Rachel watched a small black bat climb up Baby Kochamma's expensive funeral sari with gently clinging curled claws. When it reached the place between her sari and her blouse, her bare midriff, Baby Kochamma screamed and hit the air with her hymnbook, the singing stopped for a "What is it? What happened?" and for a Furrywhirring and a Sariflapping.

The interplay between the local and the global and the production of newer localities are important in understanding the creative writings associated with the new literatures in English. This interplay also refocuses attention on the vexed question of nationhood. The new writings in English stand in a complex and angular relationship to nationhood and postcoloniality in view of the fact that they employ the ambiguous bequest – the language – of the colonial masters. At the same time, they display their desire to move away from the parochialism and chauvinism of nationalists. In the works of Salman Rushdie, Rohinton Mistry, Shashi Tharoor, Amitav Ghosh, Arundhati Roy, to take just a few examples from India, we see the production of counter-narratives of nation and the desire to destabilize the ideological strategies by means of which imagined communities are given essentialist identities. The monochromatic homogeneity of the nation-state and its legitimating metanarratives begin to be fissured when writers like these strive to enunciate the hopes and experiences and modes of being of linguistic, ethnic, and religious minorities. By these means, they open up a representational space from which the hegemonic discourse of the nation-state can be purposefully challenged and the ideas of cosmopolitanism and cultural difference can be profitably foregrounded. The discourse of localism and globalism, then, is a topic that clearly invites further exploration in terms of the intentionalities and trajectories of development of new writings in English.

5   World Englishes, Politics of Culture, and Metaphoric Self

Cultural Studies and politics of culture are inseparably linked. How objects of culture are produced, how they are studied, and the institutional settings and processes that facilitate those explorations are imbricated with politics. As a matter of fact, one of the readily identifiable influences of modern Cultural Studies has been this politicization, and the concomitant desire to challenge the hegemonic power of the nation-state, multinational corporations, mainstream and entrenched scholarship. Investigations into world Englishes demand that we pay closer attention to this dimension as well. Our inquiries into the works of world Englishes will benefit greatly by delving more deeply into these imbricated issues.

This political analysis has to take place against the backdrop of colonialism and imperialism. After all, the spread of English in Asia, Africa, and the Caribbean is traceable to these phenomena. And the class from which many of the writers of English in the Third World descend is one that was privileged under colonial rule. John Updike (1997: 156) says that English writers from countries like India, where they write against a background of native tongues and traditions that are repressed in the creative effort, risk being enlisted in a foreign, if not enemy, camp, that of the colonizer. Therefore, questions of politics of culture, politics of social location, imperialism, and colonialism have to be brought into our discussions of world Englishes. For example, Frantz Fanon (1965: 210) said that "Colonialism is not satisfied merely with holding a people in its grip and emptying the native's brain of all form and content. By a kind of perverted logic, it turns the past of the people, and distorts, disfigures and destroys it." If this is so, what is the role of writers in English in Asia and Africa as public intellectuals addressing not only the body of indigenous readers but also the world outside? How have they confronted and repossessed their respective histories? How have they fared so far? These are questions that are as urgent as they are recondite, and they merit deeper study.

Creative writers associated with world Englishes can most often be described as metaphorical selves. In *After Virtue*, a book that played a central role in restoring ethics to the center of philosophical discourse, Alasdair MacIntyre (1981) remarks that selfhood resides in the unity of narration. This is, no doubt, a very productive line of approach. MacIntyre, however, does not explore the question of language, which enters so persistently into this equation – as becomes evident when we pause to examine the works of novelists linked to world Englishes who have sought to create a selfhood for themselves through fiction.

Whether we examine the fictional writings of older novelists like Raja Rao, R. K. Narayan, Chinua Achebe, Wole Soyinka, Amos Tutola, G. V. Desani, and Albert Wendt, or of relatively younger writers like Salman Rushdie, Rohinton

Mistry, Amitav Ghosh, Shashi Tharoor, Arundhati Roy, M. G. Vassanji, Mongane Serote, and Catherine Lim, the complex relationship between self, narrative, and language becomes evident. These writers are seeking to gain entrance to their multifaceted subjectivities by "decolonizing" the English language and the sedimented consciousness that goes with it. Many of them regard the English language as the repressive instrument of a hegemonic colonial discourse. They wish to emancipate themselves from its clutches by probing deeper and deeper into their historical pasts, cultural heritages, and the intricacies of the present moment. Through these means, they seek to confront their protean selfhoods. What is interesting is that these writers are striving to accomplish this liberation through the very language that has in the past shackled them to what can be characterized as an ambiguous colonial legacy.

These writers are constantly crossing and recrossing boundaries both topographical and linguistic so as to capture the complex dynamics of the present historical conjuncture and cultural moment. Some of them move back and forth between home and exile, at times interchanging their ontologies. They are exiled from home but at home in the language that over-determines the exilic experience, and their identities are shaped in the tensional interstices of two cultures. This liminality, in-betweenness, appears to be a vital maker of postcolonial spaces; writers like Rushdie and Ghosh and Mistry are seeking to textualize its inner trajectories, and the aesthetics of linguistic migrations are vital to a proper understanding of their work. In view of these considerations, these writers may be characterized as "metaphoric selves" with subversive intents. The term "metaphoric self" has two senses here. First, *metaphor*, in its original sense derived from Greek, denoted the act of "carrying across." What these writers are attempting to do is to carry themselves from one cultural topography to another. The word "translation," with which the word "metaphor" shares a common area of meaning, is important in this regard, in that the act of cultural translation is important to their efforts. Second, these writers are seeking to reconstruct and refashion their identities through language, more specifically, through the instrumentality of metaphoricity. Hence, another area of world Englishes that merits closer research attention is what is characterized here as the metaphoric self.

This discussion of metaphoric selves further relates to two important desiderata of Cultural Studies: first, the need to adopt a more complex and nuanced approach to the interplay of Western and non-Western cultures; second, the need to problematize the very notion of culture so as to attain a deeper comprehension of its nature. When we discuss some of the more innovative writers connected to world Englishes in terms of metaphoric selves, it is important to bear in mind the fact that we are not talking of West and the Rest in terms of two essentialized and immutable categories. Rather, they are discursive constructions, representational spaces in which an incessant contestation of meaning is taking place. And, like the West, the non-West is no monolith; there is Africa, Asia, the Pacific, the Caribbean, and so on, and each of them comprises complex entities. Asia, for example, is not unitary or monolithic any more than the West is. Therefore, it is important that we pluralize the West as well as the non-West so that the diverse historicities, temporalities, and ideologies that are inscribed in different cultures that constitute the West and non-West can be understood more usefully. Hence, when we talk of the writers of English in Asia or the Pacific as metaphoric selves, we are not talking of two unconnected entities, whether they are the West and Asia or the West and the Pacific, but of closely connected and mutually constitutive entities. However, the fact is that despite these interlinkages, these are obvious differences, and the cultural spaces and subjective spaces occupied by these writers can only be purposefully understood in terms of the metaphoricity alluded to earlier.

The second important need is to problematize culture, and the works of many of the most innovative writers of English in Africa, the Pacific and the Caribbean, and Asia underline this fact. Their works demonstrate that all cultures are polysemous and impure texts, and that the ever-increasing interdependence of countries makes it imperative that we abandon the notion of cultures as homogeneous and self-contained, and embrace the idea that they are porous, interactive, and dynamic. The notion of culture conceived in terms of symbolic systems located in readily identifiable spaces or territories is being problematized (Dissanayake, 1996). Therefore, as these creative writers rightly point out, instead of searching for authenticities of culture, our critical and interrogatory attention should be directed toward the interactions of cultures with others. The ideas of metaphoric selves as concretized in the writings of the authors of new literatures in English serve to draw attention to this need. What these writers point to is the importance of challenging naturalized and taken-for-granted conceptions of spatialized cultures and of investigating the production of difference within commonly shared cultural spaces.

The crossing and recrossing of cultural boundaries by writers of new literatures of English focus on the question of subject-positions of these writers. From which vantage point do they speak, and to whom? As Asian or African writers functioning as public intellectuals become more and more exposed to Western forces and influences, we need to examine the ways in which they position themselves culturally. Here, concepts such as "hybridity," formulated by cultural critics like Homi Bhabha, can be extremely valuable, if we also bear in mind their limitations. As Bhabha (1989: 67) remarks:

> It seems to me the only place in the world to speak from was at a point whereby contradiction, antagonism, the hybridities of cultural influence, the boundaries of nations were not sublated into some utopian sense of liberation or return the place to speak from was through these incommensurable contradictions within which people survive, are politically active and change.

Bhabha proposed the observation that hybridity can be interpreted as unexplored moments of the history of modernity. It is important that terms like "hybridity," which were once negatively valorized and carried a pejorative freight of meaning, have now been transformed into positively valorized conceptual spaces from which the intricate interactions between the West and Asia or West and Africa can be productively explored.

This notion of hybridity has diverse implications for world Englishes. If we are prepared to pluralize this concept and bring into the equation the asymmetries of power and the play of capital, it could provide us with a fecund theoretical space for mapping the unfolding of world Englishes. Rorty (1991: 51), speaking of Indian and Western texts, makes the observation that "The really important texts are the ones that render our old classifications unsatisfactory and force us to think up new ones." He continues:

> My hunch is that our sense of where to connect up Indian and Western texts will change dramatically when and if people who have read quite a few of both begin to write books that are not clearly identifiable as belonging to any particular genre, and are not clearly identifiable as either Western or Eastern. Consider, as an example, the novels of Salman Rushdie. There is no good answer to the question of whether he is an English or a Pakistani novelist, nor to whether *Shame* is a contribution to political journalism or to mythology, or *The Satanic Verses* a contribution to Islamic thought or to the novel of manners. Rushdie seems to me to be the sort of figure who has read a lot of books coming from the two sides of the world, and is likely to help create a culture within which intellectuals from both sides may meet and communicate.

This hybridity manifests itself most vividly in the prose of writers from the Third World who use English as a vehicle of creative communication. In the following representative passages, hybridity can be seen to go with a sense of new-found freedom and self-confidence.

> From that day onwards, my education became free and my own business. I fought off the hard-clinging feeling of my motherlessness. I studied the daily press, picked up tips from the stray Indian street-dog as well as the finest Perceptor-Sage available in the land. I assumed the style-name H. Hatterr ("H" for the nom de plume "Hindusstaaniwalla" and "Hatterr" the nom de guerre inspired by Rev. the Head's too-large-for-him-hat), and, by and by (autobiographical I, which see), I went completely Indian to an extent few pure non-Indian blood sahib fellers have done. (Desani, 1972: 30)

> The thousand faces of Kariakoo . . . From the quiet and cool, shady and darj inside of the shop you could see them through the rectangular doorframe as on a wide, silent cinema screen: vendors, hawkers, peddlers, askaris, thieves, beggars and other more ordinary pedestrians making their way in the dust and the blinding glare of the heat, in kanzus, msuris, cutoffs, shorts, khaki or white uniform, khangas, frocks, buibuis, frock-pachedis . . . Africans, Asians, Arabs; Hindu, Khoja, Memon, Shamshi, Masai, Makonde, Swahili . . . men and women of different shades and hues and beliefs. The image of quiet, leafy, suburbia impressed on the mind, of Nairobi's Desai Road, cracked in the heat of Dar into a myriad refracting fragments, each a world unto its own. (Vassanji, 1989: 85)

In the back verandah of the History House, as the man they loved was smashed and broken, Mrs. Eapen and Mrs. Rajagopalan, Twin Ambassadors of God-knows-what, learned two new lessons.

> Lesson Number One:
> Blood barely shows on a Black man. (Dum dum)
> And
> Lesson Number Two:
> It smells though,
> Sicksweet.
> Like old roses on a breeze. (Dum dum)
>
> "Madiyo" one of History's Agents asked
> "Madi aayirikkum" another replied.
> Enough?
> Enough.

They stepped away from him. Craftsmen assessing their work. Seeking aesthetic distance. Their Work, abandoned by God and History, by Marx, by Man, by Woman and (in the hours to come) by children, lay folded on the floor. He was semi-conscious, but wasn't moving. (Roy, 1997: 293)

It has been two whole days since Padma stormed out of my life. For two days, her place at the vat of mango kasaundy has been taken by another woman – also thick of waist, also hairy of forearm; but, in my eyes, no replacement at all! – while my own dung-lotus has vanished into I don't know where. A balance has been upset; I feel cracks widening down the length of my body; because suddenly I am alone, without my necessary ear, and it isn't enough. I am seized by a sudden fit of anger: why should I be so unreasonably treated by my one disciple? Other men have recited stories before me; other men are not so impetuously abandoned. When Valmiki, the author of the Ramayana, dictated his masterpiece to elephant-headed Ganesh, did the god walk out on him halfway? He certainly did not. (Note that, despite my Muslim background, I'm enough of a Bombayite to be well up in Hindu stories, and actually I'm very fond of the image of the trunk-nosed, flap-eared, Ganesh solemnly taking dictation!) (Rushdie, 1982b: 177)

These excerpts display hybridity and self-confidence in bending the English language for the purposes the authors have in mind. The passage above by Rushdie, which is taken from *Midnight's Children*, and, indeed, that entire book, foregrounds some of the characteristics that I have been referring to. In this novel, the author has succeeded in pulling together a great deal of history, fabulation, folklore, wit and humor, and social and political analysis to produce a portrait of India that is many-sided and intricate in a way that those writers who are imprisoned within commonly established colonial discursivities could not hope to achieve.

Rushdie aims to challenge and subvert the ruling colonial discourses and their attendant signifying practices using a number of semiotic and representational strategies. First, he deploys the English language with a self-assured irreverence, a calculated iconoclasm that has the effect of exploding the cultural containment and domestication that had been in place for so long. He writes against the deeply ingrained stereotypes perpetuated by the colonizers by artfully manipulating English and thereby decolonizing it. Second, like Chinua Achebe before him, but in a more purposive way, he has mined the repertoires of techniques and styles associated with oral narrative. Literary critics have rightly drawn attention to certain parallelisms and commonalities of interest between Rushdie and Gunther Grass, Garcia Marquez, and Laurence Sterne; however, they have not adequately recognized the importance of oral narratives in his art of story-telling. By imaginatively utilizing traditional narrative forms, Rushdie is able to reappropriate and repossess fictional discourse that had come under the influence of regimes of colonial authority. Third, in his fiction, Rushdie succeeds in refocusing on the idea of literature as performance – witty, humorous, fantastic, and interactive. As a consequence of the distinctive line of development of English fiction and the ways in which it assumed the role of containing the cultural Other within its narrative discourses, the idea of performativity which is at the base of traditional Indian narrative lost its hold on popular imagination. Rushdie sought to reinvigorate this aspect in his stories, as Raja Rao had done earlier in *Kanthapura*. The art of oral narrative and the idea of performance are closely linked, and Rushdie (1991: 48) makes the following observation:

> Listening to this man reminded me of the shape of the oral narrative. It's not linear. An oral narrative does not go from the beginning to the middle to the end of the story. It goes in great swoops, it goes in spirals or in loops, it every so often reiterates something that happened earlier to remind you, and then takes off again, sometimes summarizes itself, it frequently digresses off into something that the story-teller appears just to have thought of, then it comes back to the main thrust of the narrative . . . It seemed to me in fact that it was very far from being random or chaotic, and that the oral narrative had developed this shape over a long period, not because story-tellers were lacking organization, but because the shape conformed very exactly to the shape in which people liked to listen, that in fact the first and the only rule of the story-teller is to hold his audience; if you don't hold them, they will get up and walk away. So everything that the story-teller does is designed to keep the people listening most intently.

It is to Rushdie's credit that he has succeeded in recapturing some of these auditory imperatives in his art of written narrative.

Fourth, Salman Rushdie, in contradistinction to a writer like Naipaul, makes a conscious and determined effort to draw on the inherited storehouse of traditional imaginative and speculative formulations – myths, fables, allegories, cosmologies. In his hands, this move becomes an instrumentality at the service of enlarging the discursive boundaries of English fictional narration and unsettling some of the restrictive colonial signifying practices. The final outcome of these efforts is to engender, in the memorable words of Nietzsche, a "rival will," and a newer cultural space wherein the ontological complexities of the Other could be given nuanced and forceful articulation. All these distinguishing features of his writing can and should be understood in relation to his imaginative and bold use of language. His works of fiction are important in the ways in which he clears a path out of the restrictive and distorting influences of colonial discourse by devising and putting into circulation newer rhetorical and representational strategies. Rushdie has been able to destabilize existing codifying schemes and signifying practices, thereby shifting the reference point in the binary analytic of colonial discourse. This aspect of the work of Rushdie as well as of the other newer novelists writing in English in the Third World deserves careful scrutiny.

6   Conclusion

In this chapter, I have sought to suggest a few topics that are central to the work of Cultural Studies and which could be explored further in terms of the concerns of world Englishes. Clearly, my list is more suggestive than exhaustive, and one can add more topics to it. As we go about this task, it is important to bear in mind a distinction between two types of cultural reading: expository reading and interventionist reading. In expository reading, careful attention is paid to the elucidation of themes, styles, forms, techniques, and so on, but without any intention to subvert the analytical framework within which analysts have operated for so long. In interventionist readings, on the other hand, there is an attempt at self-empowerment, subverting the ruling analytical protocols, bringing out the play of ideology, and explicating the ways in which textual production is intimately linked to institutional determinations. In our explorations into world Englishes, what we need to promote is perceptive interventionist readings which would have the salutary effect of reshaping the current literary and intellectual discourses which bear the imprint of colonial hegemony.

World Englishes as a discursive construct is a topic that is increasingly generating interest among practitioners of Cultural Studies. The work already done constitutes a significant achievement. However, much more needs to be done in investigating some of the issues that contribute to our better understanding of Cultural Studies. In this regard, I wish to identify a few areas that merit further analysis. Some of these have already been opened up in current studies in world Englishes.

1   What is the nature of the politics of world Englishes, if any?
2   How can the ambiguous colonial legacy of English be made into an instrument of self-liberation?
3   How can the new literatures in English overturn the colonial heritage even as they use the very instrument and medium of repression for this purpose?
4   How do issues of bilingual creativity impact world Englishes?
5   What is the relationship between English writing and the body of work produced in other, indigenous languages?

6 How do scholars of world Englishes press into service such contemporary cultural theories as deconstructionism and poststructuralism?
7 How is the increasing spread of the internet influencing English as an international language?
8 What are the new pedagogical issues related to the teaching of world Englishes?
9 How do current formulations related to hybridity and border-crossing impact the study of world Englishes?
10 How can we tap into indigenous conceptualizations of cultural analysis to further the work of scholars of world Englishes?

See also Chapters 25, WORLD ENGLISHES AND CULTURE WARS; 29, COLONIAL/ POSTCOLONIAL CRITIQUE: THE CHALLENGE FROM WORLD ENGLISHES; 31, WORLD ENGLISHES AND GENDER IDENTITIES.

REFERENCES

Bhabha, Homi (1989) Location, intervention, incommensurability: A conversation with Homi Bhabha. *Emergences*, **1**, 63–88.

Clifford, James (1988) *The Predicament of Culture*. Cambridge, MA: Harvard University Press.

De Man, Paul (1978) *Allegories of Reading*. New Haven: Yale University Press.

Deleuze, Gilles and Guattari, Felix (1986) *Kafka: Toward a Minor Literature*. Minneapolis: University of Minnesota Press.

Desani, Govindas (1972) *All About H. Hatterr*. New York: Lanver Books.

Dissanayake, Wimal (1996) *Narratives of Agency: Self-making in China, India and Japan*. Minneapolis: University of Minnesota Press.

Fanon, Frantz (1965) *The Wretched of the Earth*. New York: Grove Press.

Foucault, Michel (1972) *The Archaeology of the Earth*. New York: Grove Press.

Geertz, Clifford (1983) *Local Knowledge: Further Essays in Interpretive Anthropology*. New York: Basic Books.

Grossberg, Lawrence, Nelson, Cary, and Treicher, Paula (1992) *Cultural Studies*. New York: Routledge.

Habermas, Jürgen (1989) *The Structural Transformation of the Public Sphere*. Cambridge, MA: MIT Press.

Kachru, Braj B. (1986) The power and politics of English. *World Englishes*, 5(2/3), 121–40.

Kachru, Braj B. (1992) Why applied linguistics leaks. Plenary talk at the American Association for Applied Linguistics, Seattle, Washington, February 28–March 2.

Kachru, Braj B. (2003) On nativizing mantra: Identity construction in Anglophone Englishes. In *Anglophone Cultures in Southeast Asia: Appropriations, Continuities, Contexts*. Edited by Rüdiger Ahrens, David Parker, Klaus Stierstorfer, and Kwok-Kan Tam. Heidelberg: Universitätsverlag Winter, pp. 55–72.

Kachru, Braj B. (2005) *Asian Englishes: Beyond the Canon*. Hong Kong: Hong Kong University Press.

MacIntyre, Alasdair (1981) *After Virtue*. Notre Dame: University of Notre Dame Press.

Marcus, George and Fischer, Michael (1986) *Anthropology as Cultural Critique*. Chicago: University of Chicago Press.

Nietzsche, Friedrich (1986) *The Portable Nietzsche*. New York: Viking Press.

Phillipson, Robert (1992) *Linguistic Imperialism*. Oxford: Oxford University Press.

Rainbow, Paul (1986) Representations are social facts: Modernity and postmodernity in anthropology. In *Writing Culture: The Poetics and Politics of Ethnography*. Edited by James Clifford and George E. Marcus. Berkeley: University of California Press, pp. 224–61.

Ramanujan, A. K. (1997) Invisible Bodies. *The New Yorker*, June 23 and 30.

Rao, Raja (1963) *Kanthapura*. New York: New Directions.

Rorty, Richard (1979) *Philosophy and the Mirror of Nature*. Princeton: Princeton University Press.

Rorty, Richard (1989) *Contingency, Irony and Solidarity*. New York: Cambridge University Press.

Rorty, Richard (1991) *Cultural Otherness: Correspondence with Richard Rorty*. Edited by Anindita N. Balslev. New Delhi: Munshiram Manoharlal, p. 51.

Roy, Arundhati (1997) *The God of Small Things*. New York: Random House.

Rushdie, Salman (1982a) The Empire writes back with a vengeance, *The Times of London*, July 3, p. 8.

Rushdie, Salman (1982b) *Midnight's Children*. New York: Avon Books.

Rushdie, Salman (1989) *The Satanic Verses*. New York: Viking Penguin.

Rushdie, Salman (1991) *Imaginary Homelands*. London: Granta Books.

Rushdie, Salman (1997) Damme, this is the oriental scene for you. *The New Yorker*, June 23 and 30, p. 156.

Spivak, Gayatri Chakravorty (1993) How to teach a "culturally different" book. In *Colonial Discourse/Post-Colonial Theory*. Edited by Francis Barker, Peter Hulme, and Margaret Iverson. Manchester: Manchester University Press, pp. 126–50.

Updike, John (1997) A review of *The God of Small Things*. *The New Yorker*. June 23 and 30, 156.

Vassanji, Moyez (1989) *The Gunny Sack*. Oxford: Heinemann International.

Viswanathan, Gauri. (1989) *The Masks of Conquest*. New York: Columbia University Press.

White, Hayden (1973) *Metahistory: The Historical Imagination in Nineteenth-Century Europe*. Baltimore: The Johns Hopkins University Press.

Wilson, Rob and Dissanayake, Wimal (1996) *Global/Local: Cultural Production and the Transnational Imaginary*. Durham, NC: Duke University Press.

FURTHER READING

Dissanayake, Wimal (1996) *Narratives of Agency: Self-making in China, India and Japan*. Minneapolis: University of Minnesota Press.

Kachru, Braj B. (1986) The power and politics of English. *World Englishes*, 5(2/3), 121–40.

Kachru, Braj B. (2005) *Asian Englishes: Beyond the Canon*. Hong Kong: Hong Kong University Press, Part III.

Quirk, Randolph and Widdowson, Henry G. (eds.) (1985) *English in the World: Teaching and Learning the Language and Literatures*. Cambridge: Cambridge University Press.

Williams, Raymond (1976) *Keywords*. London: Fontana.

Wilson, Rob and Dissanayake, Wimal (1996) *Global/Local: Cultural Production and the Transnational Imaginary*. Durham, NC: Duke University Press.

31 World Englishes and Gender Identities

TAMARA M. VALENTINE

1 Introduction

In the 1960s, when Braj B. Kachru introduced the notion of the "Indianization of Indian English," the early seeds of the study of world Englishes (WE) were sown (Kachru, 1965). By the 1980s, moving from describing the linguistic features in the non-native varieties of English in the previous decade, the use of the term "world Englishes" became associated with "the functional and formal variations, divergent sociolinguistic contexts, ranges and varieties of English in creativity and various types of acculturation in parts of the Western and non-Western world" (Kachru, 1997: 212). The study of world Englishes emphasized interdisciplinary and integrative approaches and different methodologies aimed to capture both the universal essence of WE-ness as well as the distinct regional and social identities of different Englishes. The fluidity within the world Englishes framework allowed new approaches to bend and sway with the many expressions of English around the world. Inherent in this global, pluralistic perspective was the view that the English language represented many distinct native cultural identities or "cultural emblems" (Kachru, 2000: 18), and central to this perspective was the need to continually and critically re-evaluate the existing traditional theoretical, methodological, and pedagogical models that often had been rigid and conservative in scope.

Today, within the world Englishes paradigm, linguistic pluralism is the accepted norm; multiple identities in creativity are viewed as meaningful constructions; and language, power, and ideology are integral in understanding the changing roles and functions of English around the world. Terms such as pluricentrism, bilinguals' creativity, liberation linguistics, language diasporas, multi-norms, concentric circles, non-native literatures, transcreativity, and multi-canonicity attest to the many expressions and manifestations of the global lingua franca. However, amidst all the consideration paid to the pluricentric nature of English, multilinguals' creativity, and linguistic ideologies, a review of the literature demonstrates the minimal attention paid to the multiple identities that exist within societies and to the construction of social identities in the postcolonial multilingual communities of English users. Only recently has world Englishes addressed the interplay between language and the social variables of gender, ethnicity, and class in multilingual societies, identifying issues related to postcolonial experiences, and the conceptualization of social identities as an ongoing process of construction within the contexts of the spread of English. Since the guiding principle of the Kachruvian model is a socially realistic approach to world Englishes, it seems only natural for the study of world Englishes to advocate inclusivity and incorporate social identity in general and gender identity specifically into its theoretical and applied research areas in the Outer and Expanding Circles of world Englishes.

Like the research in world Englishes, research on language and gender has been troubled by the many preconceptions and presuppositions about power and language, issues of diversity and equality, dichotomies of dominance and difference, and binary models. Within the past decade the study of world Englishes has slowly accepted a gendered approach taking into consideration not only the multilingual contexts but the experiential and attitudinal differences between women and men as language users in the English diasporic contexts. Establishing bilingual women's creativity as one of the "various strands of pluralism" in the spread of English, this paper looks at the research in world Englishes that examines the influence of gender in multilingual English-speaking communities in the postcolonial contexts addressing the issues of the pluricentric nature of English, the nature of power in the spread of English, and multilinguals' creativity in the world Englishes.

2   The Sociolinguistics of World Englishes and Gender

An integral part of world Englishes and the postcolonial experience is the notion of pluralism to refer to the multiple faces and facets of English and its speakers in the global spread of Englishization. As Kachru (1986a) states in *The Alchemy of English*, "the legacy of colonial Englishes has resulted in the existence of several transplanted varieties of English having distinct linguistic ecologies – their own contexts of function and usage." The pluralization of the term "English," alone, to "Englishes," "New Englishes," "non-native Englishes," and "world Englishes," symbolizes the multiple dimensions to the spread of English: formal and functional variation, divergent sociolinguistic, historical, and literary contexts and domains, and varying degrees of penetration in different non-Western societal contexts; multiple centers of reference for norms and standards; the wide spectrum of linguistic, sociolinguistic, discoursal, and literary creativities; the range of proficiencies and attitudes; the multiple forms of linguistic beliefs and practices representing the multilinguals' realities; and the construction of various multicultural identities associated with English. The sociolinguistic reality in world Englishes is that as a result of the acculturation of English in new sociolinguistic environments, the traditional dichotomy between native and non-native English is no longer meaningful, but now is replaced by the "socially realistic" study of world Englishes. Traditional theoretical and methodological frameworks have been replaced with an emphasis on language variation, linguistic pluralism and diversity, and multilingualism. And the shift of the linguistic center to account for the repertoire of cultural pluralism and to accommodate the sociolinguistic reality has led to the increasing power of English both globally and locally (Crystal, 1997; Kachru, 1982, 1986a, 1996; Smith, 1981, 1987; Thumboo, 2001).

An extension to the world Englishes paradigm is its potential for pluricentricity. Rather than a monocentric language model, the pluricentric approach challenges the idealized notion of the native English speaker and the monolingual, monocultural Anglocentric identity. It views the English language as several interacting centers, with each center interacting and interreacting with the others. Within the Kachruvian model, pluricentrism is visualized as three concentric circles. Others such as Yasukata Yano (2001) argue that in order to indicate the looseness, openness, and internationality of the boundaries among the many English varieties, the world Englishes can be depicted as a bundle of circles of equal size. The pluricentric models are designed to express both the global and local identities of speech communities, the international and intranational forms and functions of world Englishes, the intersecting and overlapping boundaries, and the evolving social identities of its speakers.

When we look at the research dealing with women in plurilingual settings in postcolonial contexts, we look at the work done on multilingual communities of English users and on the relationship between women and language policy and practice. As a result of the long-term contact of English with other languages in multilingual and multicultural contexts, the varieties of world Englishes, most of which share a history of a colonial past, acquired "multicultural identities and pluricentricity" (Kachru, 1992). One consequence of this phenomenon of Englishization is the impact that the process of colonialism has had on the histories of the countries and on its participants who belong to the communities of bilingual English users. What has not been seriously explored, however, is that when the creation of new non-Western cultural identities emerged regionally, so did multiple social identities of English and varying degrees of identification and involvement with the world language. With the increased use of English, the values and attitudes that are associated with language choice shift, particularly in terms of their relation to the native culture and local languages. The study of world Englishes argues that we have taken a sanitized view of language for too long; consequently, world Englishes is beginning to fill the longstanding "ungendered" accounts with "gendered" accounts in language study, hoping to gain a greater understanding of the ways in which social identity is constructed in different speech communities as English spreads around the globe. Studies show that women and men hold different feelings toward and relationships to languages of power. Gender does make a difference in language choice and in the construction of identity.

3   World Englishes, Gender, and Power

Shared by both the feminist study of language and the study of world Englishes is the notion of power. Whether we talk about economic power, political power, colonial power, ideological power, the power of language, the power of knowledge, or the power of nature, all these manifestations of power have the following in common: the position and capacity to control and manipulate linguistically, psychologically, and sociopolitically (Kachru, 1986c). The power of English involves issues related to the ideological, cultural, and elitist power of English, and it globally shows up in many ways. David Crystal (1997) suggests that English has become a global language as a result of the political power, economic power, and cultural power of its people who are associated with the control of knowledge and the prestige the language acquired as a result of its use in various functions and domains. According to Kachru, the more important the domains, the more "powerful" the language becomes. A manifestation of the power of English derives from its great range of roles and functions, and widespread use which elevates its importance in many societies. The politics and power of world Englishes is closely linked to what has been termed linguistic imperialism or the promotion of English through covert means. For linguist Robert Phillipson (1992) or Gikuyu writer Ngũgĩ wa Thiong'o (1981), English linguistic imperialism is a multi-faceted phenomenon which has economic, political, military, cultural, social, and communicative dimensions and the use of English is the means for effecting "unequal resource and power allocation" (Phillipson, 1992: 318). Therefore, English is linked to the struggle for gender equity and the construction of social identity (Valentine, 1993).

"Language is a fundamental site of struggle for postcolonial discourse because the colonial process itself begins in language. The control over language by the imperial center – whether achieved by displacing native languages, by installing itself as a 'standard' against other variants which are constituted as 'impurities', or by planting the language of empire in a new place – remains the most potent instrument of cultural control. Language provides the terms by which reality is constituted" (Ashcroft, Griffiths, and Tiffin, 1995: 283). Hence, gendering language is one way of perpetuating power hierarchies in world societies and of contributing to certain types of inequality.

In the tradition of gender studies, researchers studying language are generally sensitive to the power of language. Feminist theory is founded on the premise of male power, and its aim is to explain the various structures that underlie the systematic oppression of women in the world (Cameron, 1985).

The primary focus on power, gender, and language began in the mid 1970s when sociolinguistics in general and women's studies in particular raised awareness of how language shaped the understanding of the world and women's place within it, focusing primarily on the population of white middle-class monolingual English-speaking women. Efforts were underway to debunk the political agenda of "keeping women in their place" and to expose gender bias and male domination in the form and function of language. The quantitative sociolinguistic studies of William Labov (1972) in New York and Peter Trudgill (1972) in Norwich at the time attempted to quantify selected linguistic features and correlate them with the social category of sex; they concluded that women's language reflected their conservative nature, status consciousness, linguistic insecurity, and hypersensitivity to social norms – assumptions still unshakable in studies on language and gender. Seen as forming part of the language and gender "canon," these early studies provided the foundation for critiquing power in society.

By the 1980s, the notion of gender inequity was replaced by the power-based view that women's language was a function of the existing power relationship between women and men (Fishman, 1983; Lakoff, 1975; Zimmerman and West, 1975). An alternative to viewing power as restriction of freedom and as the ability to control and dominate was to view power as exercised equally across speakers and as shared between the genders (Tannen, 1990). Today, however, the scope of language and gender studies has broadened substantially to include multilingual communities, postcolonial contexts, and diglossic linguistic situations, applying interdisciplinary perspectives, methods, and approaches – a similar history and vision to that of the study of world Englishes. The latest phase of language and gender studies has expanded its boundaries to include femaleness and maleness as social constructions with language helping to constitute gender within the contexts of global and local multilinguistic contexts. This nature of power is explored in some of the studies devoted to examining bilingual women's relationships to English within the world contexts.

Women's relationship to language is different from that of men's. Women's access to the dominant languages is affected by various economic, gender, and familial pressures that do not affect men to the same degree. For example, Stella Mascarenhas-Keyes (1994) finds that in India, Catholic Goan women play a major role in the marginalization and displacement of the mother tongue Konkani and in promoting the dominant Western languages, Portuguese and English. The legacy of Portuguese colonialism and the modern-day emphasis on women's social roles as teachers, writers, and progressive mothers have propelled women to act more favorably toward the prestigious Western languages and varieties. As mothers and as advocates for education, these women are reshaping the linguistic face of their Goan families and community by furthering the spread of English and other non-Indian languages at the expense of native language maintenance, leading to the possible loss of the minority regional Indian languages.

In contrast, as in many speech communities worldwide, minority language maintenance is defined or controlled by women of the community and their actions. In the Indian village of Totagadde in Karnataka, Helen Ullrich (1992) finds that maintaining the vernacular caste dialect, Havyaka, is the sole domain of the women who speak the variety amongst themselves in the community; women transmit the home language to their children by childrearing, social networking, and family stability. Although the women consider themselves "linguistically limited," they understand the economic advantage, the professional importance, and the social significance of being multilingual in English, Hindi, or Kannada. By promoting multilingualism in their community, these women offer greater economic opportunities to their children as well as claiming the opportunity to enhance their own self-image and strengthen their social standing in the community. In the tradition of William Labov and Peter Trudgill, these women are gaining social status through linguistic means. For the identity they construct through their use of language and actions are related to the nature of power. Women are influencing the choice of language by increasing the formal and functional ranges of English for wider communication.

4   Bilingual Women's Creativity and World Englishes

Within the interactional contexts of world Englishes, the term bilinguals' creativity is used for "those creative linguistic processes which are the result of competence in two or more languages" (Kachru, 1986b: 20). Bilinguals' creativity in world Englishes refers to the productive linguistic processes at different linguistic and discoursal levels capturing the total linguistic repertoire available to the bilingual with reference to her speech community. Several studies on bilinguals' creativity have convincingly demonstrated the range of functional and pragmatic uses in the world Englishes. According to Jean D'souza (1988: 160), language style and strategy is constrained by the *grammar of culture* or the acceptable linguistic possibilities of behavior within a particular culture. For the grammar of culture affects and influences the use of language and is in turn affected by language.

The sociolinguistic dimension of bilinguals' creativity views the process of creativity in terms of acculturation and nativization of the use of English in the Outer Circle, recognizing the language types of discourse strategies and stylistic innovations, speech acts, code mixing and code switching, and genre analysis. By manipulating her linguistic resources in language use, the multilingual English user generates new meanings to capture the bilingual and bicultural competences, developing new linguistic forms and functions in both spoken and written discourse.

Contributing to the body of literature exploring issues of world Englishes and gender, Elizabeth de Kadt's recent research on the current spread of

English in KwaZulu-Natal, South Africa, examines gender identities through English. Her work addresses the range of student attitudes toward English (1993) and how gender is one of the factors impacting the construction of gender identities of young multilingual Zulu speakers as feminine or masculine in urban and rural contexts (2002a). She finds that teenage girls in the rural community accept their role in the perpetuation of traditional gender identities. Zulu English-speaking girls act as guardians of the culture and of the mother tongue Zulu by internalizing the concept of the higher status accorded to boys in Zulu society; the more frequent use of English in more contexts by males, then, is one means of expressing the dominant male status. In contrast, in the urban community where there is a strong awareness of gender equity, all speakers feel that English is a more desirable and important language than Zulu. That females claim to use English in more contexts and domains than males demonstrates that the use of English enhances the female self-image and strengthens the female social status in the community. At an early age, gender attitudes toward language and language choice are forming.

In studies examining the pragmatic aspect of politeness in the world Englishes context, speakers are clearly gendering speech acts. In the discourse of English-speaking male and female Zulu students, Busayo Ige and Elizabeth de Kadt (2002) and de Kadt (2002b) find that politeness plays a role in the construction of gender identities among Zulu men and women when speaking English. English, being both a symbol and vehicle of the increasing heterogeneity among Zulu speakers, carries with it the dominant Western values system. However, it is the female speaker who uses English more than the male speaker. Interestingly, English is viewed by both genders as being more polite and respectful than Zulu. Where the dominant male perspective on politeness conforms with the expectations and norms of the Zulu culture, the female speakers show a shift of identity from their Zulu culture. Zulu women avoid transferring their constructed identity as Zulu women when interacting with non-Zulus. These women seek to construct an identity more Western-oriented by using the English language. This phenomenon demonstrates how the changing roles of males and females are negotiated in the modern Zulu society of South Africa.

Within the Hindu sector of the South African Indian English-speaking community, Bharuthram and de Kadt (2003) show how politeness is gendered in English; conforming to the community values of politeness, speakers use the speech acts of requests and apologies to signal the subordinate societal position of women; the act of rejecting these expectations signals a challenge to the traditional cultural norms. The results show that women produce more indirect requests and use more mitigating supportive linguistic moves in English. Men perceive a need to be more polite toward women than toward men; women use indirect requests more frequently toward other women than toward men. Moreover, young girls, too, are more invested in politeness work than boys. The authors conclude that women are expected to be more polite and so indeed seek to be more polite by using English.

In these English-using multilingual situations, women play a primary role in initiating and furthering linguistic change in their local communities and in negotiating gender identity. Language choice is linked to cultural identity, women's place in society, their community networking, their self image, and their attitudes toward the languages. As in most studies on bilingual women (Burton, Dyson, and Ardener, 1994), the second or third language is often the language of a dominant group associated with power, prestige, and access to economic benefits. These English-speaking bilingual women, then, within their local communities may position themselves as both guardians of their mother tongues and innovators of language change. The strength of the status of English in world communities, for example, is based in part on the choices women make to meet the needs of their speech communities and to achieve the desired results of a better future for themselves, their families, and their social groups. With English fast becoming the language of necessity around the world, women as primary language caretakers are advancing the progress of English, which in turn helps it to gain acceptance and merit alongside the regional, caste, and vernacular dialects, both in private and in public environments. Studies on bilingual women who cross borders between languages, such as Kathryn Remlinger's work (1994) on South Asian women's linguistic role in new American English settings and Viv Edwards and Savita Katbamna's study (1988) on wedding songs among British Gujarati women illustrate the phenomenon of women as "keepers" of language and culture when they cross geographic and linguistic boundaries. It is clear that women play a key role in the transmission of the English language in world contexts and in constructing new identities.

4.1   Bilingual women's creativity and the literary canon

Expanding the scope of bilinguals' creativity in world Englishes to include gender and discourse, a few studies show how gender may function as one of the means of shaping linguistic pluralism and diversity. My work, for example, on gender-specific speech functions in spoken and written discourse of Indian English (Valentine, 1988, 1995), on discourse markers in spoken and written Indian English (1991), and on discourse types in African English and Indian English creative writings (1992) illustrates the expanding sociocultural dimensions of English use to include gender as one of the factors impacting the spread of English. Given the centrality of speech acts to discourse as well as speakers' and users' sensitivity to sociocultural factors, differences in the use of speech acts by women and men are observable among the varieties of world Englishes. I provide evidence from samples of both natural speech and from conversation in novels and short stories to show aspects of English language use most revealing of nativizing gender: forms of address and reference, abuses and insults, indirectness, politeness patterns, and other discoursal differences in the use of questions, discoursal flow, organization of discourse, and topic selection. Shukla and Khare (1994) also find that the authors of Indian English writings transfer the social context of gender in India to the extent that the sociocultural patterns, notions, and ideas operating in India are reflected in a specialized Indianized variety for female and male speakers in cross-sex conversation – female characters use more polite forms than male characters do in Indian English fiction. Such studies help to refine the definition of bilinguals' creativity to include gender as an essential exponent of the institutionalization of pluralism.

Examining the linguistic and stylistic aspects in the fiction writing of world Englishes and the influence of gender on writing styles, Wendy Baker and William G. Eggington (1999) investigate bilinguals' creativity in several world English literatures written in Indian, West African, Britain, Anglo-American, and Mexican American varieties of English. Baker (2001) specifically looks at works written by male and female authors, a corpus representing the Inner Circle and Outer Circle of English. Among other results, Baker finds that gender differences are related to the culture of the writer. For example, texts written by West African men, Mexican American men, and Indian men display marked differences in literary styles from those written by West African women, Mexican American women, and Indian women. That female writers may have a different perception of the function of creative writing is illustrated in the differences between male and female writings based on five dimensions: involved vs. informational production, narrative vs. non-narrative concerns, explicit versus situation-dependent reference, overt expression of persuasions, and abstract versus non-abstract information. Baker's work certainly expands the understanding of bilinguals' creativity to include the influence of gender on the Englishizing process.

Valentine (2001a, 2001b), too, examines the relationship between gender and the spread of English with special reference to bilingual women from the multilingual settings of South Asia, identifying three cultural communities of practice: the communities of women as writers, the communities of women in their local settings, and the communities of women crossing borders and transplanting English to new cultural environments. Women in these contexts are constructing new identities as writers, linguistic guardians, linguistic innovators, and transmitters of cultural and linguistic norms and values. Further, Valentine (2004) identifies four categories of gender identity that the writings in multilingual English users fall into: universalization, linguistic muteness, creative empowerment, and linguistic defiance. Linguistic resistances take many forms: some writers challenge the dominant ideologies others conform to dominant thought. In either resistance, these postcolonial writers adapt the colonial language to local needs, thus, as Kachru suggests, sometimes appropriating the language as a subversive strategy.

In a very powerful piece, Chinese-Malaysian writer Shirley Geok-Lin Lim (1990) reflects on the colonial writing experience. Lim examines the subject of self and the contemporary Asian woman writer of English. Accepting that the body of creative literature published in the twentieth century by Asian women is still small, she approaches the English works of early Indian poets Toru Dutt and Sarojini Naidu, Indian novelists Kamala Das and Gauri Deshpande, Filipino writers Paz Marquez Benitiz, Edith Tiempo, and Linda Ty-Casper, and Southeast Asian writers such as herself from a feminist perspective, arguing that Asian women writers are marginalized by gender and by their choice of writing in English. Filipino women writers, too, attest to the factors influencing their writing and to their struggles of writing in the other tongue (Manlapaz, 2004). It is clear that the spread of English is not a neutral affair; those who gain access to English may gain access to increased power but, simultaneously, their choice of English condemns them to a new cultural oppressiveness. Such language variation produces culturally distinctive writing in multilinguistic societies.

5   Contextualizing Gender Further

In the cultural and linguistic systems of the many varieties of English, English is used in a number of rhetorical and literary contexts to reflect diverse linguistic genres, situational contexts, participant and role relationships, functional domains, and conversational styles. Raj Ram Mehrotra (1998), Kachru's extensive work, and others illustrate highly contextualized, cultural-specific English interactions by providing evidence of nativization in reference to the caste and class hierarchies, regional attitudes, ethnic and gender identities, and family structures in Asian and African contexts, considering matrimonial advertisements, announcements of death, personal letters, and other forms of written media in South Asian English and African English.

Rukmini Bhaya Nair (1991) demonstrates how English has become acculturated in the "un-English sociolinguistic" context of Indian matrimonial newspaper advertisements. Nair deconstructs gender in the cross-cultural context of the matrimonial advertisement, illustrating how the matrimonial advertisements in English newspapers across India contextualize gender. By embedding social ideologies and cultural presuppositions, this form of discourse, the Indian matrimonial, helps to perpetuate the native ideology of gender. By publishing matrimonials in English, the language associated with the elite colonialism, a highly specialized, distinct discourse type has developed. Gender roles and the social institutions of matchmaking, marriage, and family organization are recreated through the use of the English language.

Anita Pandey (2004), too, examines world Englishes in the diasporic context of the English used in personals and matrimonials in newspapers from the United States and from publications targeted at Indians in the United States. Not only are there certain distinctive pragmatic, discoursal, syntactic, and lexical features distinct in each advertisement, but the creative aspect varies circle to circle. In her cross-cultural analysis of gender and identity she explains the contextual differences in gendered language usage, most particularly the use of culture-specific terms, in the strong gender roles, relations, and expectations within the South Asian speech communities. The gender relations and expectations are embedded in the culturally specific context of marriage and English matrimonials.

6   Conclusion

Neglected in the past, issues related to world Englishes and gender have recently become a focus of many studies. Much of the research that I mention above addresses questions of linguistic pluralism, multiple identities, language and power, and gendered world Englishes, e.g., Elizabeth de Kadt's work on gender and usage patterns of English in South Africa, Wendy Baker's research on gender and bilinguals' creativity in world English literatures, my work on English discourse in South Asian contexts, and the multiple expressions of new selves in the works of creative women. Although these authors have contributed significantly to the study of cross-cultural English and gender variation, their discussions tap only the surface. The notion of gendered Englishes goes beyond these ideas as some studies attest: Susan Frenck's (1998) *World Englishes* symposium on linguistic creativity in lesbian, gay male, bisexual, and transgendered discourse draws attention to language variation within and across genders; the ambitious TEaGirl research project (2004) investigates Transcultural Englishes and Gender-Inclusive Reform of Language in the Englishes used in Singapore, Hong Kong, and the Philippines.

Both the study of world Englishes and the study of language and gender have challenged the limits of traditional approaches, Western static, monolithic models, and monolingual standards and norms. Their histories are similar in that they both arose from a shift from the existing traditional theoretical, methodological, and pedagogical models to one that accepted linguistic pluralism and multilinguals' creativity, from viewing gender and language as unchanging, homogeneous, and absolute to a more dynamic discussion on function, context, and the social person. Both seek a new direction consistent with an approach that takes into account expanding and connecting boundaries to include the construction of multiple identities and diverse roles and functions, replacing dichotomies of us and them, native and non-native, women and men, and difference and dominance with dimensions of pluralism and expansion of the canon. It is only natural, then, that world Englishes establish bilingual women's creativity as one of the "various strands of pluralism" in the spread of English.

See also Chapters 21, SPEAKING AND WRITING IN WORLD ENGLISHES; 29, COLONIAL/POSTCOLONIAL CRITIQUE: THE CHALLENGE FROM WORLD ENGLISHES; 30, CULTURAL STUDIES AND DISCURSIVE CONSTRUCTIONS OF WORLD ENGLISHES.

REFERENCES

Ashcroft, Bill, Griffiths, Gareth, and Tiffin, Helen (eds.) (1995) *The Post-Colonial Studies Reader*. London: Routledge.

Baker, Wendy (2001) Gender and bilinguals' creativity. *World Englishes*, **26**(3), 321–39.

Baker, Wendy and Eggington, William G. (1999) Bilingual creativity, multidimensional analysis, and world Englishes. *World Englishes*, **18**(3), 343–57.

Bharuthram, Sharita and de Kadt, Elizabeth (2003) The value placed on politeness by men and women in the Hindu sector of the South African Indian English speaking community. *Southern African Linguistics and Applied Language Studies*, **21**(3), 87–102.

Burton, Pauline, Dyson, Ketaki Kushari, and Ardener, Shirley (eds.) (1994) *Bilingual Women*. Oxford: Berg.

Cameron, Deborah (1985) *Feminism and Linguistic Theory*. London: Routledge. Revised 2nd edition, 1992.

Crystal, David (1997) *English as a Global Language*. Cambridge: Cambridge University Press.

De Kadt, Elizabeth (1993) Attitudes towards English in South Africa. *World Englishes*, **12**(3), 311–24.

De Kadt, Elizabeth (2002a) Challenging gender identities through English. IAWE Conference 2002, University of Illinois, Urbana, October 17–20.

De Kadt, Elizabeth (2002b) Gender and usage patterns of English in South African urban and rural contexts. *World Englishes*, **21**(1), 83–97.

D'souza, Jean (1988) Interactional strategies in South Asian languages: Their implications for teaching English internationally. *World Englishes*, **7**(2), 159–71.

Edwards, Viv and Katbamna, Savita (1988) The wedding songs of British Gujarati women. In *Women in Their Speech Communities*. Edited by Jennifer Coates and Deborah Cameron. New York: Longman, pp. 158–74.

Fishman, Pamela (1983) Interaction: The work women do. In *Language, Gender, and Society*. Edited by Barrie Thorne, Cheris Kramarae, and Nancy Henley. Rowley, MA: Newbury House, pp. 89–102.

Frenck, Susan (1998) Symposium on linguistic creativity in LGBT discourse: Introduction. *World Englishes*, **17**(2), 187–90.

Ige, Busayo and de Kadt, Elizabeth (2002) Gendering politeness: Zulu speakers of English at the University of Natal, Durban. *Southern African Linguistics and Applied Language Studies*, **20**, 147–61.

Kachru, Braj B. (1965) The Indianness in Indian English. *Word*, **21**, 391–410.

Kachru, Braj B. (ed.) (1982) *The Other Tongue: English across Cultures*. Urbana, IL: University of Illinois Press. 2nd edition 1992.

Kachru, Braj B. (1986a) *The Alchemy of English: The Spread, Functions, and Models of Non-Native Englishes*. Oxford: Pergamon Press. Reprinted 1990, Urbana: University of Illinois Press.

Kachru, Braj B. (1986b) The bilinguals' creativity. *Annual Review of Applied Linguistics*, **6**, 20–33.

Kachru, Braj B. (1986c) The power and politics of English. *World Englishes*, **5**(2/3), 121–40.

Kachru, Braj B. (1992) World Englishes: Approaches, issues and resources. *Language Teaching*, **25**, 1–14.

Kachru, Braj B. (1996) The paradigms of marginality. *World Englishes*, **15**(3), 241–55.

Kachru, Braj B. (1997) World Englishes 2000: Resources for research and teaching. In *World Englishes 2000*. Edited by Larry E. Smith and Michael L. Forman. Honolulu: University of Hawai'i and the East-West Center, pp. 209–51.

Kachru, Braj B. (2000) Asia's Englishes and world Englishes. *English Today*, **16**(1), 17–22.

Labov, William (1972) *Sociolinguistic Patterns*. Philadelphia: University of Pennsylvania Press.

Lakoff, Robin (1975) *Language and Woman's Place*. NY: Harper and Row.

Lim, Shirley Geok-Lin (1990) Semiotics, and experience, and the material self: An inquiry into the subject of the contemporary Asian woman writer. *World Englishes*, **9**(2), 175–91.

Manlapaz, Edna Zapanta (2004) Filipino women writers in English. *World Englishes*, **23**(1), 183–91.

Mascarenhas-Keyes, Stella (1994) Language as diaspora: The use of Portuguese, English and Konkani by Catholic Goan women. In *Bilingual Women*. Edited by Pauline Burton, Ketaki Kushari Dyson, and Shirley Ardener. Oxford: Berg, pp. 149–66.

Mehrotra, Raj Ram (ed.) (1998) *Indian English: Texts and Interpretation*. Philadelphia: John Benjamins.

Nair, Rukmini Bhaya (1991) Critique of deconstructing gender in a cross-cultural context: The matrimonial advertisement as a discourse. Fifth Annual International Conference on Pragmatics and Language Learning, Parasession: Approaches to the Study of Gender and Language, University of Illinois at Urbana-Champaign, April 4–6.

Ngũgĩ wa Thiong'o (1981) *Decolonising the Mind: The Politics of Language in African Literature*. Portsmouth, NH: Heinemann.

Pandey, Anita (2004) Culture, gender, and identity in cross-cultural personals and matrimonials. *World Englishes*, **23**(3), 403–28.

Phillipson, Robert (1992) *Linguistic Imperialism*. Oxford: Oxford University Press.

Remlinger, Kathryn (1994) Language choice and use: Influences of setting and gender. In *Differences that Make a Difference*. Edited by Lynn H. Turner and Helen M. Slerk. Westport, CT: Bergin and Garvey, pp. 163–73.

Shukla, Hira L. and Khare, Asha (1994) Gender and politeness codes in Indian fiction. In *Indianisation of English Language and Literature*. Edited by Ram Shankar Pathak. New Delhi: Bahri Publications, pp. 145–50.

Smith, Larry E. (ed.) (1981) *English for Cross-Cultural Communication*. London: Macmillan.

Smith, Larry E. (ed.) (1987) *Discourse across Cultures: Strategies in World Englishes*. New York: Prentice-Hall.

Tannen, Deborah (1990) *You Just Don't Understand: Women and Men in Conversation*. New York: William Morrow.

TEaGirl (2004) Transcultural Englishes and Gender-Inclusive Reform of Language. The University of Western Australia, www.teagirl.arts.uwa.edu.au.

Thumboo, Edwin (ed.) (2001) *The Three Circles of English*. Singapore: Unipress Centre for the Arts, National University of Singapore.

Trudgill, Peter (1972) Sex, covert prestige and linguistic change in the urban British English of Norwich. *Language in Society*, **1**, 179–95.

Ullrich, Helen (1992) Sociolinguistic change in language attitudes: A Karnataka village study. In *Dimensions of Sociolinguistics in South Asia*. Edited by Edward C. Dimock, Braj B. Kachru, and Bh. Krishnamurti. New Delhi: Oxford and IBH Publishing Co., pp. 113–27.

Valentine, Tamara (1988) Developing discourse types in non-native English texts: Strategies of gender in Hindi and Indian English. *World Englishes*, **7**(2), 143–58.

Valentine, Tamara (1991) Getting the message across: Discourse markers in spoken Indian English. *World Englishes*, **10**(3), 325–34.

Valentine, Tamara (1992) The nativizing of gender: Speech acts in the new Englishes literatures. In *The Extended Family: English in Global Bilingualism: Studies in Honor of Braj B. Kachru*. Edited by Larry Smith and S. N. Sridhar. New York: Pergamon.

Valentine, Tamara (1993) Linguistic imperialism: The feminist perspective. *World Englishes*, **12**(3), 361–5.

Valentine, Tamara (1995) Agreeing and disagreeing in Indian English discourse: Implications for language teaching. In *Issues and Attitudes: An Anthology of Invited Papers*. Edited by Makhan L. Tickoo. Singapore: SEAMEO Regional Language Centre, pp. 227–50.

Valentine, Tamara (2001a) Women and the other tongue. In *The Three Circles of English: Language Specialists Talk about the English Language*. Edited by Edwin Thumboo. Singapore: Unipress National University of Singapore, pp. 143–58.

Valentine, Tamara (2001b) Reconstructing identities and gender in discourse: English transplanted. In *Diaspora, Identity, and Language Communities, Studies in the Linguistic Sciences*, **31**(1) (Spring). Edited by Braj B. Kachru and Cecil L. Nelson. Urbana, IL: University of Illinois, pp. 193–212.

Valentine, Tamara (2004) Rattling the gilded cage: Bilingual South Asian women write. ACS Women's/ Gender Studies, Gender Acts! Activism: History, Theory and Practice, Furman University, Greenville, SC, March 26–7.

Yano, Yasukata (2001) World Englishes in 2000 and beyond. *World Englishes*, **20**(2), 119–31.

Zimmerman, Don and West, Candace (1975) Sex roles, interruptions and silences in conversation. In *Language and Sex: Difference and Dominance*. Edited by Barrie Thorne and Nancy Henley. Rowley, MA: Newbury House, pp. 105–29.

FURTHER READING

Holmes, Janet (1998) Signalling gender identity through speech. *Moderna Sprak*, **92**(2), 122–8.

Walters, Keith (1996) Gender, identity, and the political economy of language: Anglophone wives in Tunisia. *Language in Society*, **25**(4), 515–55.

Part VII World Englishes and Globalization

32 World Englishes in the Media

ELIZABETH A. MARTIN

1 Introduction

Most of the research on world Englishes in the media focuses on news discourse (including television and radio news broadcasts, printed news, and sports reporting across media) and advertising. Although almost every region has been the focus of analysis, those areas of the world that have been described in far greater detail in this regard include Asia (e.g., T. Bhatia, 1987, 1992, 2000, 2001a; Gonzalez, 1991; Haarmann, 1984; Hsu, 2001, 2002; Jung, 2001; MacGregor, 2003; Masavisut, Sukwiwat, and Wongmontha, 1986; Min, 2001; Natarajan and Xiaoming, 2003; Takashi, 1990; Upadhyay, 2001; Yuen-Ying, 2002; H. Zhang, 2001; L. Zhang, 2002) and parts of Europe (e.g., Berns, 1988; Birken-Silverman, 1994; Dürmüller, 1994; Hermerén, 1999; Hilgendorf and Martin, 2001; Husband and Chouhan, 1985; Larson, 1990; Martin, 1998; Pavlou, 2002; Schlick, 2003; Vachek, 1986; Truchot, 1990), with some additional analyses of media discourse in Africa (e.g., Leitner and Hesselmann, 1996; Mesthrie, 2002; Norbrook and Ricketts, 1997; Sanders, 2000; Schmied and Hudson-Ettle, 1996) and South America (e.g., Alm, 2003). Much information can be gleaned as well from publications written by those who are best known for placing English in a regional or global context while addressing a wide range of issues, including but not exclusively media-related topics (e.g., Bell and Kuiper, 1999; Bolton, 2002; Cheshire, 1991; Crystal, 1997, 1999; Görlach, 1991, 1998, 2002a, 2002b; Kachru, 1990, 1992; McArthur, 1992; McCrum, Cran, and MacNeil, 1992). Various in-depth analyses of certain genres (V. Bhatia, 1993, 2001) such as news media (e.g., Bell, 1991; Fowler, 1993; van Dijk, 1985a, 1988) and advertising discourse (e.g., Cook, 1992; Geis, 1982; Myers, 1994; Vestergaard and Schrøder, 1985; Tanaka, 1994) have also been extremely useful.

The bulk of the research conducted to date can be grouped by topical focus into the following main categories: power and ideology, linguistic and cultural identities, language attitudes, intelligibility and linguistic innovation, and language planning, with some of the studies addressing several of these topics simultaneously. There have also been a few attempts to explore the impact of technology on the spread of English and the shaping of new varieties (e.g., Baron, 2000) plus the occasional study focusing solely on intelligibility of different varieties of English in the media (e.g., van der Walt, 2000). However, more recent technological advances (text messaging on cell phones, e-mail, chat discourse, the use of MP3 technology for downloading music off the internet, and so forth) have been largely ignored by linguists actively exploring other issues related to world Englishes, receiving only passing comments embedded in broader discussions. This is somewhat unfortunate given the pervasiveness of these phenomena in today's society and therefore warrants further empirical investigation.

2   Approaches to Media Communication Analysis

Research paradigms for the analysis of mass media discourse vary considerably as this chapter will reveal. Methodologies used (both quantitative and qualititative) include critical discourse analysis, mediasemiotics, and corpus-linguistic analysis, as well as content analysis supplemented by interviews with media audiences and/or members of the media industry. There is also a growing body of literature reporting the use of media to elicit audience reactions to specific varieties of English as a means of discounting certain pedagogical models (primarily RP).

Most studies focusing on different varieties of English in the media approach language from a "socially-realistic" perspective (Kachru, 1981). Indeed, much of this research is inspired by the work of pioneers in the field of sociolinguistics who introduced and developed the notion of "context of situation" (e.g., Firth, 1935; Halliday, 1978; Halliday and Hasan, 1985; Hymes, 1972) as well as those known for their work in critical discourse analysis and semiotics (e.g., Barthes, 1964; Bentele, 1985; Fairclough, 1995; Foucault, 1981; van Dijk, 1985b). Some of the media studies reported here have adopted speech act theory (Searle, 1969) while considering the relationship between language and ideology (following, for example, Thompson, 1987 and Fowler, 1993). In addition (as noted by van Dijk, 1985a: 7), the field of ethnography of communication can play a vital role in analyses of media discourse:

> Research in sociolinguistics and the ethnography of communication . . . has shown how practically all features of discourse, as well as those of discourse production and understanding, are systematically related to the many features of the socio-cultural context. This means that we also need detailed ethnographic observations about the production and uses (participation) of communicative events in the media, both for communicative events (e.g., talkshows) "in" the media, as well as those "by" the media, i.e. with media users as participants.

Van Dijk (1985b: 69–93) provides a theoretical framework for the analysis of media based on the "thematic" and "schematic" structures of printed newspaper discourse. Setting aside the "micro-organization" of news discourse (such as its lexicogrammatical, morpho-syntactical, and rhetorical features), van Dijk focuses rather on "the formal representation of the global *content* of a text or dialogue" as well as "the overall *form* of a discourse" (van Dijk, 1985b: 71):

> A "pure" structural analysis is a rather irrelevant theoretical exercise as long as we cannot relate textual structures with those of the cognitive and socio-cultural contexts of news production and reception. The development of linguistics and discourse analysis in the 1970s has shown, indeed, that a "context-free" approach to language, for instance in the construction of formal grammars, is one-sided at best and certainly empirically inadequate. Of course, the same holds for the analysis of news discourse.

In his study of public broadcast and printed news in Hong Kong, Scollon (1997) demonstrates "the ambiguity of power in news discourse." Using Goffman's (1981) communicative roles (author, animator, and principal) as a point of reference, Scollon provides a useful framework for the analysis of "discursive power" in the media, examining in detail the following (Scollon, 1997: 384):

1 "the power to command animation and authorship";
2 "the power to give and deny voice"; and
3 "the power to frame discursive events."

Scollon notes, for instance, that bylining practices must be interpreted within the sociocultural context in which they operate. Indeed, whereas attributing a story to a well-known reporter may be flattering in North America (and add a certain prestige to the article), in China it may also be a form of repression as journalists are often clearly identified in the media so that they may be held accountable should the government find the story offensive or otherwise unacceptable (Scollon, 1997: 387).

Altheide (1985) provides fascinating details regarding the choice of programming on American TV networks. Conceding that "TV production leads the audience to confirm certain points of view" (1985: 45), Altheide notes as well that "visual emphasis has a major impact on news content" (1985: 112) and provides numerous examples of pertinent news stories from around the world that were covered by the Associated Press only to be ignored by American television networks such as ABC, CBS, and NBC due to a lack of videotaped footage (see Altheide, 1985: 116–17).

Exploring another media genre, Vestergaard and Schrøder (1985: 16–18) describe the language of advertising from a functional perspective. According to this communication model (based to a large extent on speech act theory, e.g., Searle, 1969), language performs *expressive, directive, informational, metalingual, interactional, contextual,* and/or *poetic* functions, depending on the communicative situation. Inspired by the pioneering work of Geoffrey Leech (1966) on advertising, among others, Vestergaard and Schrøder (1985: 15) describe the communicative situation in terms of "code" (both verbal and non-verbal), "channel" (e.g., sound waves for radio and television), and "context" (which they define as "the situation in which addresser and addressee are placed, including the immediately preceding events, [but also] the wider cultural context of the addresser and addressee, and the knowledge which they share about their total situation and their culture").

As for corpus-linguistic analysis, a main source of material/text types has been The International Corpus of English (ICE) (Greenbaum, 1990). One such example can be found in Schmied and Hudson-Ettle (1996), who examine specific grammatical linguistic features (in this case, the distribution of the verbal suffix *-ing* over various East African newspaper text types).

3   Power and Ideology

A recent study on the effect of American cinema on children's attitudes towards minority groups powerfully illustrates the importance of examining media language in terms of power and ideology. Pandey (1997) explores in exquisite detail different varieties of English portrayed in Walt Disney movies directed at children (e.g., *The Jungle Book, 101 Dalmatians, The Lion King*) and notes that there is "a consistent attempt to present speakers of nonstandard varieties of English as powerless proletarians of low cultural and socioeconomic status" (p. iii). Through her in-depth analysis of excerpts from these and other animated films, she provides convincing evidence that, in the Hollywood movie industry, language functions as an ideological tool where "dialectal variations are systematically synthesized with variations in power and moral worth" (p. iii).

In his study of English loan words in Thai print media, Kapper (1986: 17) claims that English is widespread in Thai journalistic discourse and that the favored domains for English (e.g., business and marketing) "suggest social, economic and political motivations" and "a kind of linguistic imperialism":

> Language-exporting countries are those which create a need for their language by being a source of consumer products, technology, "innovation" and sometimes "aid." The result of all this is that countries like Thailand are literally buying into western culture. This is the mechanism which maintains the status of English as a global prestige language. (Kapper, 1986: 17)

Similar observations reverberate elsewhere in the literature. Truchot (1997) claims that remakes of movies originating in the Expanding Circle get more recognition internationally if filmed in English, noting that French film-maker and producer Claude Berri was disappointed that his adaptations of Marcel Pagnol's novels (*Jean de Florette* and *Manon des Sources*, distributed around the world in their original French version with subtitles) were less successful than he had hoped. Truchot (1997: 70) concludes: "The idea that a product reflecting too closely the culture of a particular country, and written in a national language, will not reach an international audience is now largely accepted . . . As a consequence an increasing number of films (and also television programmes, songs) are produced along the lines of so-called international standards largely inspired by those of the USA, and English is their *lingua franca*."

4 Linguistic and Cultural Identities

The debate over linguistic and cultural identities in the media has been approached from several different angles. In addition to Pandey's (1997) study on animated movies mentioned earlier, other scholars have noted the lack of respect for "non-native" varieties of English and the misrepresentation of culture in the media. A very insightful survey of twentieth-century African American language and cultural images in American advertising, for instance, appears in O'Barr (1994: 107–56) along with a discussion of other ethnic minorities in the media. (See also Avraham and First, 2003; Haarmann, 1984; Mufwene, 1993 and 2001.) Another example is provided by T. Bhatia (2001b: 279) who describes how Indians are portrayed "in an overwhelmingly negative light" in American media, leaving the Indian American population feeling "betrayed and exploited":

> Gruesome images left by movies such as "Indiana Jones and the Temple of Doom" do irreparable damage to the perception of Indians by Americans. Their sacred symbols, especially Hindu symbols, are exploited for commercial gains and damage their religious tolerance. Two recent cases in point are Madonna wearing the sacred *Vaishnava Tilak* (which is a symbol of purity) on her forehead, and the Aerosmith album cover that shows distorted and mutilated images of Krishna.

Many Indians worldwide find solace, however, in Bollywood films, which Bhatia describes as "the lifeline of the promotion of the Indian identity," noting that "Indians abroad take this identity, perhaps, much more seriously than Indians in India" (T. Bhatia, 2001b: 282). Gokulsing and Dissanayake (1998: 117) have made similar observations: "Indian popular cinema, particularly through the influence of its music, is producing a different kind of empowerment – its impact on the reconfiguration of diaporic Asians is powerful." One very positive development of the growing international success of Bollywood films has been the celebration of diversity and ethnicity in both the recording industry (e.g., world music) and cinema. An example is the worldwide recognition of an Indian musical genre known as Bhangra. Gokulsing and Dissanayake (1998: 118) report that this form of celebratory folk music was exported to Britain from India by Punjabi immigrants in the 1950s and 1960s and has since evolved into a highly popular dance music mixing several different genres (rap, reggae, house, soul). Indeed, Bhangra is featured in the music soundtracks of many Indian movies that have gained international recognition. As for choice of language for the Bollywood dialog, acclaimed Indian film director Mira Nair, whose movies include *Monsoon Wedding, Kama Sutra, Mississippi Masala,* and *Salaam Bombay!,* notes in a recent interview that, in her films, English is used as merely one form of communication among others so as to imitate as closely as possible the language mixing that occurs in everyday life:

> Like music and costumes, language is also something we play with very much in India. It's very common and totally natural to speak mixing two or three languages: Hindi, English and Punjabi in this case. [In *Monsoon Wedding*] we just went with the absolute honest flow of exactly how we would do it in life . . . to celebrate being from India rather than look upon the west as anything as close to happiness in any way. (Director commentary provided on DVD for *Monsoon Wedding*)

Gill (2000: 85–102) paints a similar picture of linguistic and cultural diversity in her description of Malaysian radio advertisements. Focusing her analysis on the different subvarieties of Malaysian English, she notes that "the English language and how it is employed in radio advertisements in Malaysia plays an integral role in reflecting Malaysian identity" (p. 89). This observation is confirmed by copywriters who emphasize the importance of "understanding the consumer's mind-set" and using local varieties "to create closeness to the audience" (Gill, 2000: 98). Gill observes that in Malaysia, the subvariety of Malaysian English chosen for the ad depends on the target group, the brand image, the function and positioning of text within the ad (opening, main text, final summary), or may simply be used as an attention-getter.

Although studies such as these have done much to dispel cultural stereotypes and clarify the notion of local varieties of English, the misrepresentation of cultural and linguistic identities remains, unfortunately, a recurring theme in the literature on world Englishes in the media. In his book on rural Indian advertising, T. Bhatia (2000) observes that rural consumers are bombarded with Western images and values that do not correspond with the local perceptions, sensibilities and traditions, and highlights various problems associated with the use of English when addressing this audience (e.g., pronunciation of English product names, misinterpreted slogans, irrelevance and lack of appeal, etc.).

Those who study news discourse have also pointed to English as both a marker of globalization and the language most used for international media. Referring to Hong Kong and the media coverage of the 1997 handover from British to Chinese rule, Yuen-Ying (2000: 328) notes "the outside world's dependency on Western sources for news and analysis," claiming that "often these mediated images are distorted and narrowly framed, reinforcing established stereotypes." The author concludes that the solution lies in training local journalists in the art of English-language news reporting "for the global stage" in order to avoid the often misformed observations made by "parachute reporters" (those who only remain a few days in the country for the purposes of reporting a story) and the "typical colonial discourses that often portray Hong Kong before and after the 1997 handover in black and white terms" (Yuen-Ying, 2000: 333). (For additional research on Asian news discourse see Bolton, 2002; V. Bhatia, 2001; Natarajan and Xiaoming, 2003; Scollon, 1997.)

5   Language Attitudes

Some of the research on world Englishes in the media has investigated whether certain audiences favor one variety of English over another in global media discourse. The results of several studies suggest that, through the influence of American films, television programs, and pop music, American English is becoming increasingly attractive (and intelligible) to certain media consumers. Based on a study involving a questionnaire and listening samples of both British and American varieties of English distributed to 760 students, Mobärg (1998) reports that younger audiences in Sweden express a clear preference for American English and strongly favor English rock lyrics over Swedish. They also much prefer the use of subtitles for English-language movies (as opposed to dubbing) (Mobärg 1998: 256–7). One of the author's conclusions is that "the traditional insistence on RP as a model accent in schools does not fully respond to the positive momentum created by the students' being exposed to popular media" (p. 261). Oikonomidis (2003: 56) notes a preference for subtitling English-language movies and television programs in Greece. Martin (2002a) describes different varieties of English in French television advertising.

Sajavaara (1986) also reports attitudinal data regarding English in the media, claiming that for young people in Finland television seems to be a major source of English. Of the 539 students surveyed as part of the Jyväskylä Anglicism Project, a research initiative designed to measure "the impact of English on the Finnish language and Finnish culture," "at least one English-language TV programme was seen by 70 percent of the informants every week" (Sajavaara, 1986: 68–71). This research effort is particularly worth noting, however, in that it measures audience reactions to the use of English in many different media genres, including press news, comic strips, advertisements, job announcements, popular music, television, and translated fiction (p. 70). One of the most interesting findings is that self-reported language attitudes do not necessarily reflect social behavior, even when one is being observed in a controlled research environment. Whereas a very large majority (90%) of the informants claimed that English appearing in Finnish advertisements rendered them "less efficient," they were just as likely to choose "anglicized ads" over those containing only Finnish (p. 75).

6   Intelligibility and Linguistic Innovation

Other attitudinal studies measure audience's reactions to different language varieties in the media while underscoring the notion of intelligibility. Van der Walt (2000) used recordings of television and radio broadcasts to test "the international comprehensibility" of South African English. Varieties included in the study were traditional "White" South African English, Indian English, Cape English, Black English, and Afrikaans English, with 140 study participants in Germany, the Netherlands, Canada, and the USA. She found that although "all varieties of South African English are comprehensible internationally . . . those Englishes spoken by the advantaged white communities ('Traditional White' and 'Afrikaans') and by communities that speak English as a first language ('Traditional White' and 'Indian') receive the most positive responses" (van der Walt, 2000: 145–8).

Myers (1994: 90–104) provides some fascinating examples of language varieties used for special effect in advertising. One strategy consists of writing English text in such as a way as to imitate other varieties. This is achieved by producing a line of nonsensical text (such as a slogan) that, when pronounced by an English-speaker, becomes intelligible, as in: *De woord onder bus es Oranjeboom . . . Not everyone will get it* (British bus poster campaign for the Dutch beer "Oranjeboom"). To illustrate the foregrounding of different varieties of English in advertising, Myers (1994: 98) also shares an ad for Brooks running shoes used in South Africa: "It shows a naked man, his groin covered by pictures of shoes. The text says *'I feel naked without my Brooks.' Mark Page.* This works as a pun only in South Africa, where *brooks* is borrowed from Afrikaans, as slang for shorts." Myers (p. 97) also points out that consumers associate certain concepts with particular varieties of English in advertising and that British ads are notorious for exploiting this technique.

The "cross-fertilization" between different varieties of English as a result of exposure to international media discourse has been noted by many including McArthur (1992: 1025), who writes, "a global market in films, television programmes, and print products . . . has affected national and regional language usages within the English-using world [leading, for example, to] the adoption of Americanisms in the UK and to a lesser extent Briticisms in the US." There are also many studies illustrating the impact of English on other languages. In conducting an in-depth analysis of English borrowings in several copies of Austrian newspapers (*Kleine Zeitung* and *Die Presse*), Viereck (1986) found a greater occurrence of partial substitutions over a ten-year period (1974–1984), suggesting that "the tendency to form compounds in German has increased further under English influence" (1986: 167) and that "in comparison with the sports language in the Federal Republic, Austrian sports terminology has been considerably more influenced by English terms" (p. 171). As for intelligibility, Viereck's results indicate that younger Austrians (aged 18 to 30) and those with the most education were more likely to understand English borrowings in the press. There was also some indication in the data that borrowings introduced most often via aural media such as radio or television were more difficult to parse in their written form.

Another growing body of literature examines language-mixing in advertising with a particular focus on the symbolic functions of English and the tremendous linguistic creativity encountered in advertising copy (e.g., Buamgardner, 2005; T. Bhatia, 1987, 1992, 2001a; Cheshire and Moser, 1994; Hsu, 2002; Kelly-Holmes, 2005; Jung, 2001; Martin, 1998, 2002b, 2006; Pavlou, 2002; Piller, 2003; Takashi, 1990).

7   MTV English

A topic that has received relatively little attention in the research on world Englishes is the public's exposure to English via the recording industry. While many acknowledge the spread of English through pop music and other musical genres, the vast number of varieties of English sung on the radio, television and the internet (not to mention music CDs, music videos, and DVDs) has not been the primary focus of much research to date. McCrum, Cran, and MacNeil (1992: 26) underscore, with fascinating examples, the extent to which English dominates this industry:

> English as the language of international pop music and mass entertainment is a worldwide phenomenon. In 1982, a Spanish punk rock group, called Asfalto (Asphalt), released a disc about learning English, which became a hit. The Swedish group Abba recorded all its numbers in English. Michael Luszynski is a Polish singer who performs almost entirely in English . . . Luszynski notes wryly that a phrase like *"Stysze warkot pociagu nadjedzie na torze"* does not roll as smoothly in a lyric as *"I hear the train a-coming, it's rolling down the line . . ."* (McCrum, Cran, and MacNeil, 1992: 26)

Céline Dion, a famous pop recording artist from Quebec, also markets her music internationally through the medium of English. Indeed, even in France where she can very easily communicate with her audiences in French, television commercials for her latest recordings feature English lyrics and album titles. During a recent television interview on a major French network (TF1), she alludes to the fact that English opens doors to an international career. When asked why she sings in English, she responded: *"Vous savez, comme moi, que la langue anglaise, c'est la langue internationale. Alors, je pense qu'il faut mettre toutes les chances de son côté"* ('You know, as I do, that English is the language for international communication. I feel I should do what's necessary to succeed'; TF1 interview with Patrick Poivre D'Arvor, March 2002. My translation).

Roe and Cammaer (1993) have investigated the impact of music television on adolescents in Flemish provinces of Belgium. Indeed, as they note, this form of mass communication popular among young people is not to be ignored: "Since its inception in 1988, MTV-Europe, The Music Television Channel, has become a significant factor on the European media scene. It now broadcasts non-stop, around the clock, seven days a week, to around 36 million homes in 26 countries" (Roe and Cammaer, 1993: 169). Questionnaire data solicited from 783 area high school students regarding their MTV viewing habits suggest that music videos have totally captivated this segment of the television viewing audience – 42 percent of respondents reported watching MTV at least every other day and 61 percent remained tuned to the channel during commercials. As a result, an overwhelming majority (80 percent) were able to recall a specific brand name featured in MTV advertising, with Coca-Cola, Braun, and Nike topping the list (Roe and Cammaer, 1993: 173; see also Wallace-Whitaker, 1989). The authors also noted audience reactions to English in this "hybrid medium":

> While beamed predominantly at Continental Europe, the dominant language of MTV is English. However, this did not appear to present a problem for most of our respondents: only 29 percent gave negative responses regarding this dominance and only 24 percent stated that they would watch more MTV if more programmes were in Dutch. (Roe and Cammaer, 1993: 173)

8   Legislation

Any discussion of English in the media would be incomplete without some mention of government-led efforts to curb its use in certain contexts. The pervasiveness of English in blockbuster movies, syndicated television programs, music broadcast on radio and other media has, indeed, met with some resistance. A case in point is France, a country that has made repeated attempts to limit the amount of English in the media through official legislation (e.g., 1975 Bas-Lauriol law; 1994 Toubon law). With their long history of language policy aimed at "protecting the French language" (and numerous organizations, starting with the *Académie Française* founded in 1635), the French have been attacking anglicisms since Americans began seriously exporting their products (including Hollywood movies, television programs, and popular music) after World War II. This "cultural invasion" led to the adoption of certain English borrowings and that which French language purists refer to as *Franglais* (or "Frenglish," a mixture parodied by French literary scholar René Etiemble (1964) in his famous book *Parlez-Vous Franglais?*). Soon thereafter came the creation of various organizations funded by the government (e.g., *Haut Comité* pour la défense et l'expansion de la Langue Française, 1966; *Haut Conseil* de la Francophonie, 1984) whose mission was to promote the French language and enforce, to the extent possible, the use of French terms coined by government appointed terminology commissions to replace anglicisms. In more recent years, there has been stricter legislation specifically targeting the media, such as the French language quota for music broadcast on French radio (1994 Pelchat amendment to the Carignon law adopted in 1996) and the 1994 Toubon law (Articles 2 and 12) requiring "equally legible" French translations for all foreign languages appearing in advertisements in print and broadcast media.

A fascinating description of the French crusade against English appears in Nelms-Reyes (1996: 310), who writes "the much ballyhooed cultural objective of the Loi Toubon remains frustrated because the statute as worded is unable to affect the way French is spoken in 'everyday discourse,' which is where a language truly exists." Nevertheless, an organization known as the General Association of French Users, or AGULF (*Association générale des utilisateurs de la langue française*), created in 1976 "to defend the linguistic and cultural patrimony of French speakers" (Nelms-Reyes, 1996: 283–4), has brought several "language offenders" to justice, including the Paris Opera which was cited for "non-use of French" after publishing a five-page program in English for a theatrical production with a much shorter French version (Nelms-Reyes, 1996: 286). Other well-known French court cases include those target-ing the bottled water EVIAN because of the slogan "Fast Drink des Alpes," the cigarette sold under the brand name NEWS by another French company SEITA (both examples appearing in Hausmann, 1986: 93), and the Paris Metropolitan Transit Authority (RATP) which was fined 4,000 francs (appro-ximately $800 at the time) for selling bus and subway tickets written in English (Nelms-Reyes, 1996: 286). (See also Truchot, 1997: 74–5.) It has been clearly demonstrated, however, that members of the media industry in France (advertising agencies in particular) have found ingenious ways of circumventing the legislation, including registering slogans (e.g., Nike's *Just do it*) and expressions (e.g., *airbag*) as trademarks and liberally exploiting English in areas that are not targeted by the Toubon Law (such as product names and jingles) (Martin, 1998).

Another context in which the limits of English have been legally defined is Quebec, where similar legislation (Bill 101, or Charter of the French Language) was passed in 1977. The large English-speaking population in the area of Montreal, however, provided an interesting twist whereby a group known as Alliance Quebec defending English language rights offered financial assistance to several people accused of putting illegal English on shop signs (McArthur, 1992: 833). (Crystal, 1997: 358 provides an example of Welsh nationalists defacing English on road signs as a sign of protest. See also Watson, 1997: 212–30.) The section of the bill targeting shop signs was declared unconstitutional in 1988, after which the Quebec government adopted additional legislation (Bill 178) authorizing English shop signs for inside use only. This new measure became, as McArthur (1992: 833) puts it, "an ordinance mocked by some Anglophones as the 'inside outside' law." (See Robinson, 1998 for in-depth analysis of Canadian language policy and the media; Hausmann, 1986: 99–100 also addresses language legislation in Quebec.)

9   Directions for Future Research

One of the main objectives of world Englishes scholars working on media related issues should be to seek out opportunities to collaborate with members of the media industry and those who conduct media communications research. Much knowledge and insight can be gained through a continual cross-disciplinary dialog of this nature. There is also a general lack of information on audience reactions to different media with most of the research reported thus far involving only "captive audiences" such as students. Whereas audience statistics are readily available, tapping into the attitudes of media consumers has been a somewhat more challenging task, but one well worth pursuing nonetheless. The impact of emerging technologies on everyday discourse has also opened new avenues of research which have yet to be fully explored, creating, in essence, new sub-genres (such as chat, e-mail, and text messaging), all of which are resurfacing as colloquial discourse in other media genres. This gradual reshaping of different varieties of English is all the more intriguing in that these new discourses sometimes defy geographical description due to the global electronic environment in which they exist. Other topics which have received relatively little attention to date include the pedagogical applications of various media (e.g., Baik and Shim, 2002); broader regional varieties (such as the "Euro-English" or "Mid-Atlantic" variety described in Modiano, 1996; see also McArthur, 2003), and the impact of language policy on minority languages in the media. These and other research efforts will help determine whether the media consistently and accurately reflect the "pluricentricity" of English or, on the contrary, largely misrepresent both linguistic and sociocultural reality.

See also Chapters 22, Genres and Styles in World Englishes; 33, World Englishes in Global Advertising; 34, World Englishes and Global Commerce.

REFERENCES

Alm, Cecilia Ovesdotter (2003) English in the Ecuadorian commercial context. *World Englishes*, **22**(2), 143–58.

Altheide, David L. (1985) *Media Power*. London: Sage.

Avraham, Eli and First, Anat (2003) "I buy American": The American image as reflected in Israeli advertising. *Journal of Communication*, **53**(2), 282–99.

Baik, Martin Jonghak and Shim, Rosa Jinyoung (2002) Teaching world Englishes via the Internet. *World Englishes*, **21**(3), 427–30.

Baron, Naomi S. (2000) *Alphabet to email: How Written English Evolved and Where It's Heading*. London: Routledge.

Barthes, Roland (1964) Rhétorique de l'image. *Communications*, **4**, 40–51.

(English translation: Rhetoric of the image. In Roland Barthes (1977), *Image Music Text*. London: Fontana/Collins, pp. 32–51.)

Baumgardner, Robert J. (2005) The visual rhetoric of Mexican signage in English. Paper presented at the Symposium in Rhetoric: Rhetoric and Culture. Texas A&M University – Commerce, February 25.

Bell, Allan (1991) *The Language of News Media*. Oxford: Blackwell.

Bell, Allan and Kuiper, Koenraad (eds.) (1999) *New Zealand English*. Amsterdam: John Benjamins.

Bentele, Günter (1985) Audio-visual analysis and a grammar of presentation forms in news programs: Some mediasemiotic considerations. In *Discourse and Communication: New Approaches to the Analysis of Mass Media Discourse and Communication*. Edited by Teun A. van Dijk. Berlin: Walter de Gruyter, pp. 159–84.

Berns, Margie (1988) The cultural and linguistic context of English in West Germany. *World Englishes*, **7**(1), 37–49.

Bhatia, Tej K. (1987) English in advertising: Multiple mixing and media. *World Englishes*, **6**(1), 33–48.

Bhatia, Tej K. (1992) Discourse functions and pragmatics of mixing: Advertising across cultures. *World Englishes*, **11**(2/3), 195–215.

Bhatia, Tej K. (2000) *Advertising in Rural India: Language, Marketing Communication, and Consumerism*. Tokyo: Institute for the Study of Languages and Cultures of Asia and Africa, Tokyo University of Foreign Studies.

Bhatia, Tej K. (2001a) Language mixing in global advertising. In *The Three Circles of English*. Edited by Edwin Thumboo. Singapore: UniPress, pp. 195–216.

Bhatia, Tej K. (2001b) Media, identity and diaspora: Indians abroad. *Studies in the Linguistic Sciences*, **31**(1), 269–87.

Bhatia, Vijay K. (1993) *Analysing Genre: Language Use in Professional Settings*. London: Longman.

Bhatia, Vijay K. (2001) Shifting paradigms in media discourse. In *The Three Circles of English*. Edited by Edwin Thumboo. Singapore: UniPress, pp. 319–40.

Birken-Silverman, Gabriele (1994) Code-mixing and code-switching in the Corsican media. Network on Code-Switching and Language Contact. Summer School for Code-Switching and Language Contact, 14–17 September. Ljouwert/Leeuwarden, The Netherlands: Fryske Akademy, pp. 29–38.

Bolton, Kingsley (ed.) (2002) *Hong Kong English: Autonomy and Creativity*. Hong Kong: Hong Kong University Press.

Cheshire, Jenny (1991) *English around the World: Sociolinguistic Perspectives*. Cambridge: Cambridge University Press.

Cheshire, Jenny and Moser, Lise-Marie (1994) English as a cultural symbol: The case of advertisements in French-speaking Switzerland. *Journal of Multilingual and Multicultural Development*, **15**(6), 451–69.

Cook, Guy (1992) *The Discourse of Advertising*. London: Routledge.

Crystal, David (1997) *English as a Global Language*. Cambridge: Cambridge University Press.

Crystal, David (1999) *The Cambridge Encyclopedia of the English Language*. Cambridge: Cambridge University Press.

Dürmüller, Urs (1994) Multilingual talk or English only? The Swiss experience. *Sociolinguistica*, **8**, 44–64.

Etiemble, René (1964) *Parlez-Vous Franglais?* Paris: Gallimard.

Fairclough, Norman (1995) *Critical Discourse Analysis: The Critical Study of Language.* London: Longman.

Firth, John R. (1935) The technique of semantics. *Transactions of the Philological Society.* (Reprinted in J. R. Firth (1957) *Papers in Linguistics 1934–1951.* London: Oxford University Press, pp. 7–33.)

Foucault, Michel (1981) *The Archaeology of Knowledge.* New York: Pantheon Books.

Fowler, Roger (1993) *Language in the News: Discourse and Ideology in the Press.* London: Routledge.

Geis, Michael L. (1982) *The Language of Television Advertising.* New York: Academic Press.

Gill, Saran Kaur (2000) *International Communication: English Language Challenges for Malaysia.* Selangor Darul Ehsan: Universiti Putra Malaysia Press.

Goffman, Erving (1981) *Forms of Talk.* Philadephia: University of Pennsylvania Press.

Gokulsing, K. Moti and Dissanayake, Wimal (1998) *Indian Popular Cinema: A Narrative of Cultural Change.* London: Trentham Books.

Gonzalez, Andrew B. (1991) Stylistic shifts in the English of the Philippine print media. In *English around the World: Sociolinguistic Perspectives.* Edited by Jenny Cheshire. Cambridge: Cambridge University Press, pp. 333–63.

Görlach Manfred (1991) *Englishes: Studies in Varieties of English 1984–1988.* Amsterdam: John Benjamins.

Görlach, Manfred (1998) *Even More Englishes.* Amsterdam: John Benjamins.

Görlach, Manfred (2002a) *English in Europe.* Oxford: Oxford University Press.

Görlach, Manfred (2002b) *Still More Englishes.* Amsterdam: John Benjamins.

Greenbaum, Sidney (1990) Standard English and the International Corpus of English. *World Englishes,* 9, 79–83.

Haarmann, Harald (1984) The role of ethnocultural stereotypes and foreign languages in Japanese commercials. *International Journal of the Sociology of Language,* 50, 101–21.

Halliday, M. A. K. (1978) *Language as Social Semiotic.* London: Edward Arnold.

Halliday, M. A. K. and Hasan, Ruquaiya (1985) *Language, Context and Text: Aspects of Language in a Social-Semiotic Perspective.* Oxford: Oxford University Press.

Hausmann, Franz Josef (1986) The influence of the English language on French. In *English in Contact with Other Languages.* Edited by Wolfgang Viereck and Wolf-Dietrich Bald. Budapest: Akademiai Kiado, pp. 79–105.

Hermerén, Lars (1999) *English for Sale: A Study of the Language of Advertising.* Lund, Sweden: Lund University Press.

Hilgendorf, Suzanne and Martin, Elizabeth (2001) English in advertising: Update for France and Germany. In *The Three Circles of English.* Edited by Edwin Thumboo. Singapore: UniPress, pp. 217–40.

Hsu, Jia-Ling (2001) The sources, adapted functions, and the public's subjective evaluation of the Englishization of Mandarin Chinese in Taiwan. In *The Three Circles of English.* Edited by Edwin Thumboo. Singapore: UniPress, pp. 241–56.

Hsu, Jia-Ling (2002) English mixing in advertising in Taiwan: A study of readers' attitudes. Paper presented at the Thirteenth World Congress of

Applied Linguistics, Singapore, December 16–21.

Husband, Charles and Chouhan, Jagdish M. (1985) Local radio in the communication environment of ethnic minorities in Britain. In *Discourse and Communication: New Approaches to the Analysis of Mass Media Discourse and Communication.* Edited by Teun A. van Dijk. Berlin: Walter de Gruyter, pp. 270–94.

Hymes, Dell (1972) Models of the interaction of language and social life. In *Directions in Sociolinguistics: The Ethnography of Communication.* Edited by John J. Gumperz and Dell Hymes. New York: Holt, Rinehart and Winston, pp. 35–71.

Jung, Kyutae (2001) The genre of advertising in Korean: Strategies and "mixing." In *The Three Circles of English.* Edited by Edwin Thumboo. Singapore: UniPress, pp. 257–76.

Kachru, Braj B. (1981) Socially-realistic linguistics: The Firthian tradition. *International Journal of the Sociology of Language,* **31**, 65–89.

Kachru, Braj B. (1990) *The Alchemy of English: The Spread, Functions, and Models of Non-Native Englishes.* Urbana: University of Illinois Press.

Kachru, Braj B. (ed.) (1992) *The Other Tongue: English across Cultures.* Urbana: University of Illinois Press.

Kapper, James (1986) English borrowing in Thai as reflected in Thai journalistic texts. ERIC document No. ED351876.

Kelly-Holmes, Helen (2005) *Advertising as Multilingual Communication.* London: Palgrave Macmillan.

Larson, Ben E. (1990) Present-day influence of English on Swedish as found in Swedish job advertisements. *World Englishes,* **9**(3), 367–9.

Leech, Geoffrey N. (1966) *English in Advertising: A Linguistic Study of Advertising in Great Britain.* London: Longmans, Green and Co.

Leitner, Gerhard and Hesselmann, Markus (1996) "What do you do with a ball in soccer?": Medium, mode, and pluricentricity in soccer reporting. *World Englishes,* **15**(1), 83–102.

MacGregor, Laura (2003) The language of shop signs in Tokyo. *English Today,* 73, **19**(1), 18–23.

Martin, Elizabeth (1998) Code-Mixing and Imaging of America in France: The Genre of Advertising. PhD dissertation, Department of French, University of Illinois at Urbana-Champaign.

Martin, Elizabeth (2002a) Cultural images and different varieties of English in French television commercials. *English Today,* 72, **18**(4), 8–72.

Martin, Elizabeth (2002b) Mixing English in French advertising. *World Englishes,* **21**(3), 375–401.

Martin, Elizabeth (2006) *Marketing Identities through Language: English and Global Imagery in French Advertising.* London: Palgrave Macmillan.

Masavisut, Nitaya, Sukwiwat, Mayuri, and Wongmontha, Seti (1986) The power of the English language in Thai media. *World Englishes,* **5**(2/3), 197–207.

McArthur, Tom (ed.) (1992) *The Oxford Companion to the English Language.* Oxford: Oxford University Press.

McArthur, Tom (2003) World English, Euro-English, Nordic English? *English Today,* 73, **19**(1), 54–8.

McCrum, Robert, Cran, William, and MacNeil, Robert (1992) *The Story of English.* New York: Penguin Books.

Mesthrie, Rajend (2002) Mock languages and symbolic power: The South African radio series *Applesammy and Naidoo. World Englishes,* **21**(1), 99–112.

Min, Su Jung (2001) Constructing ideology: A critical linguistic analysis of the *Korea Herald*. In *The Three Circles of English*. Edited by Edwin Thumboo. Singapore: UniPress, pp. 115–32.

Mobärg, Mats (1998) "Media exposure vs. educational prescription: The case of British and American English in Sweden." In *The Major Varieties of English. Papers from MAVEN 97*. Edited by Hans Lindquist, S. Klintborg, M. Levin, and M. Estling. Växjö: Acta Wexionensia, pp. 249–62.

Modiano, Marko (1996) The Americanization of Euro-English. *World Englishes*, **15**(2), 207–15.

Mufwene, Salikoko S. (1993) *Africanisms in Afro-American Language Varieties*. Athens, GA: University of Georgia Press.

Mufwene, Salikoko S. (2001) English in the black diaspora: Development and identity. *Studies in the Linguistic Sciences*, **31**(1), 51–60.

Myers, Gregg (1994) *Words in Ads*. London: Edward Arnold.

Natarajan, Kalai and Xiaoming, Hao (2003) An Asian voice? A comparative study of Channel News Asia and CNN. *Journal of Communication*, **53**(2), 300–14.

Nelms-Reyes, Loretta (1996) Deal-making on French terms: How France's legislative crusade to purge American terminology from French affects business transactions. *California Western International Law Journal*, **26**, 273–311.

Norbook, Hamish and Ricketts, Keith (1997) Broadcasting and English. In *New Englishes: A West African Perspective*. Edited by Ayọ Bamgboṣe, Ayọ Banjo and Andrew Thomas. Trenton, NJ: Africa World Press, pp. 300–6.

O'Barr, William M. (1994) *Culture and the Ad: Exploring Otherness in the World of Advertising*. Oxford: Westview Press.

Oikonomidis, Agapios (2003) The impact of English in Greece. *English Today*, 74, **19**(2), 55–61.

Pandey, Anjali (1997) Articulating Prejudice: A linguistic perspective on animated movies. Unpublished PhD dissertation, Department of Linguistics, University of Illinois at Urbana-Champaign.

Pavlou, Pavlos (2002) The use of dialectal and foreign language elements in radio commercials in Cyprus. Paper presented at the Thirteenth World Congress of Applied Linguistics, Singapore, December 16–21.

Piller, Ingrid (2003) Advertising as a site of language contact. *Annual Review of Applied Linguistics*, **23**, 170–83.

Robinson, Gertrude J. (1998) *Constructing the Quebec Referendum: French and English Media Voices*. Toronto: University of Toronto Press.

Roe, Keith and Cammaer, Gerda (1993) Delivering the young audience to advertisers: Music television and Flemish youth. *Communications*, **18**(2), 169–76.

Sajavaara, Kari (1986) Aspects of English influence on Finnish. In *English in Contact with Other Languages*. Edited by Wolfgang Viereck and Wolf-Dietrich Bald. Budapest: Akademiai Kiado, pp. 65–77.

Sanders, James (2000) *South Africa and the International Media 1972–1979: A Struggle for Representation*. London: Frank Cass.

Schlick, Maria (2003) The English of shop signs in Europe. *English Today*, 73, **19**(1), 3–11.

Schmied, Josef and Hudson-Ettle, Diana (1996) Analyzing the style of East African newspapers in English. *World Englishes*, **15**(1), 103–13.

Scollon, Ron (1997) Attribution and power in Hong Kong news

discourse. *World Englishes*, **16**(3), 383–93.

Searle, John R. (1969) *Speech Acts*. London: Cambridge University Press.

Takashi, Kyoko (1990) A sociolinguistic analysis of English borrowings in Japanese advertising texts. *World Englishes*, **9**(3), 327–41.

Tanaka, Keiko (1994) *Advertising Language: A Pragmatic Approach to Advertisements in Britain and Japan*. London: Routledge.

Thompson, John B. (1987) Language and ideology: A framework for analysis. *The Sociological Review*, **35**(3), 516–36.

Truchot, Claude (1990) *L'Anglais dans le Monde Contemporain* [English in the Contemporary World]. Paris: Le Robert.

Truchot, Claude (1997) The spread of English: From France to a more general perspective. *World Englishes*, **16**(1), 65–76.

Upadhyay, Shiv R. (2001) Identity and politeness in Nepali print media. *Multilingua*, **20**(4), 331–59.

Vachek, Josef (1986) Some remarks on English loans in Czech sports terminology. In *English in Contact with other Languages*. Edited by Wolfgang Viereck and Wolf-Dietrich Bald. Budapest: Akademiai Kiado, pp. 25–30.

van der Walt, Christa (2000) The international comprehensibility of varieties of South African English. *World Englishes*, **19**(2), 139–53.

van Dijk, Teun A. (ed.) (1985a) *Discourse and Communication: New Approaches to the Analysis of Mass Media Discourse and Communication*. Berlin: Walter de Gruyter.

van Dijk, Teun A. (1985b) Structures of news in the press. In *Discourse and Communication: New Approaches to the Analysis of Mass Media Discourse and Communication*. Edited by Teun A. van Dijk. Berlin: Walter de Gruyter, pp. 69–93.

van Dijk, Teun A. (1988) *News Analysis: Case Studies of International and National News in the Press*. Hillsdale, NJ: Lawrence Erlbaum.

Vestergaard, Torben and Schrøder, Kim (1985) *The Language of Advertising*. Oxford: Blackwell.

Viereck, Karin (1986) The influence of English on Austrian German. In *English in Contact with other Languages*. Edited by Wolfgang Viereck and Wolf-Dietrich Bald. Budapest: Akademiai Kiado, pp. 159–77.

Wallace-Whitaker, Virginia (1989) Awareness of American brand names in the Soviet Union. Paper presented at the annual meeting of the Association for Education in Journalism and Mass Communication, Washington, DC, August 10–13.

Watson, Iarfhlaith (1997) A history of Irish language broadcasting: National ideology, commercial interest and minority rights. In *Media Audiences in Ireland: Power and Cultural Identity*. Edited by Mary J. Kelly and Barbara O'Connor. Dublin: University College Dublin Press, pp. 212–30.

Yuen-Ying, Chan (2000) The English-language media in Hong Kong. *World Englishes*, **19**(3), 323–35.

Yuen-Ying, Chan (2002) The English-language media in Hong Kong. In *Hong Kong English: Autonomy and Creativity*. Edited by Kingsley Bolton. Hong Kong: Hong Kong University Press, pp. 101–15.

Zhang, Hang (2001) An analysis of TV advertising language across cultures. *Studies in the Linguistic Sciences*, **31**(2), 187–211.

Zhang, Lena Liqing (2002) Are they still listening? Reconceptualizing the Chinese audience of the Voice of America in the cyber era. *Journal of Radio Studies*, **9**(2), 317–37.

FURTHER READING

FURTHER READING

FURTHER READING

FURTHER READING

FURTHER READING

FURTHER READING

FURTHER READING

FURTHER READING

FURTHER READING

FURTHER READING

600 *Elizabeth A. Martin*

FURTHER READING

Bhatia, Tej K. (2000) *Advertising in Rural India: Language, Marketing Communication, and Consumerism.* Tokyo: Institute for the Study of Languages and Cultures of Asia and Africa, Tokyo University of Foreign Studies.

Bhatia, Tej K. (2001) Language mixing in global advertising. In *The Three Circles of English.* Edited by Edwin Thumboo. Singapore: UniPress, pp. 195–216.

Gokulsing, K. Moti and Dissanayake, Wimal (1998) *Indian Popular Cinema: A Narrative of Cultural Change.* London: Trentham Books.

Halliday, M. A. K. and Hasan, Ruquaiya (1985) *Language, Context and Text: Aspects of Language in a Social-Semiotic Perspective.* Oxford: Oxford University Press.

Hermerén, Lars (1999) *English for Sale: A Study of the Language of Advertising.* Lund, Sweden: Lund University Press.

Yuen-Ying, Chan (2000) The English-language media in Hong Kong. *World Englishes,* **19**(3), 323–35.

33 World Englishes in Global Advertising

TEJ K. BHATIA

1 Introduction

Theodore Levitt, the Business Guru from Harvard, predicted in the 1980s that "The era of multinational companies customizing their products and advertising . . . is over." The assumption was that in the era of rapid globalization and super-branding, advertising messages all over the globe will conform to extreme homogeneity in terms of the use of language, the display of logo, and the content of the message. English will naturally be the chosen language of global advertisers. Two decades later, although English is the most favored language of global media and advertising and its use is skyrocketing, creative needs of global advertisers are rarely met by the consideration of global homogeneity and language conformity. Thus, with super-branding and hyper-globalization going hand in hand with diversity marketing, the cross-fertilization of world Englishes and other languages in advertising is also becoming more prominent than ever before.

2 English Users and Advertising

Since the pioneering publication of Leech (1966), there has been a proliferation of studies devoted to advertising in English. Following Leech's model, a bulk of linguistic studies concerned themselves with the linguistic and literary devices (phonology, morphology, lexis, borrowings, clause and sentence structure, puns, metaphors, simile, and alliteration, etc.) used by advertisers. Recent works mark a point of departure in a number of ways: (1) *Scope*: In addition to works devoted to advertising in the Anglophone countries – United States, Canada, United Kingdom, and Australia – a body of research devoted to advertising in Asia, European Union, and South America is growing rapidly. In typological terms, following Kachru's Three Concentric Circles model of English users, research since the 1980s has crossed the threshold of the Inner

Circle and has entered into the Outer Circle and the Expanding Circle. (For details about Kachru's model (1981), see Chapter 25 in this volume.) Notable works from the three circles are as follows: Inner Circle – Cook (1992), Forceville (1998), Geis (1982), Goddard (1998), Hermeren (1999), Myers (1999); Outer Circle – Hilgendorf and Martin (2001), Martin (1998, 2002a, 2002b); and Expanding Circle – Haarmann (1984), Hsu (2001), Jung (2001), Lee (2003), MacGregor (2003). The boundary between the Outer and the Expanding Circles becomes rather fluid in the case of European countries. (2) *Context*: The Inner-Circle advertising is grounded in the monolingual context while the advertising from the other two circles capitalizes on the bilingual and multilingual environment of those countries. (3) *Theoretical and Analytical Orientation*: The primary focus of the Inner-Circle studies is the syntactic interface with semantics and pragmatics (Geis, 1982; Vestergaard and Schrøder, 1985), while contact situation is key to Outer- and Expanding-Circle studies. (4) *Discourse Analysis*: The unit of analysis has shifted from sentence level to discourse. (5) *Comparative Studies*: Works such as Tanaka (1994) exemplify a comparative advertising discourse of Inner- and Expanding-Circle English. (6) *Topical focus*: The topics addressed by the research include but are not necessarily limited to the following: Speech Acts, Conversation Maxims, semantic notions (e.g. presupposition, inference, implications), persuasion, manipulation, and deception receive significant attention in Inner-Circle advertising studies; topics such as language mixing, language attitudes, linguistic innovations, group targeting, and domain allocation are the prime focus in the other two circles. Content analysis of ads forms a common core of monolingual and bilingual ads.

Inspired by the sociolinguistic and socio-psychological research on one hand, and globalization and marketing forces on the other, the treatment of the mixing in various linguistic and media forms has gained several new dimensions during the past two decades. This chapter will focus primarily on these two latest trends with special reference to world Englishes.

3   Key Issues

Although a number of issues confront global advertisers (choice of medium, media buying, etc.), from the perspectives of the topic at hand, the following three issues are the main concerns of international advertisers.

3.1   *Standardization versus adaptation*

One of the central concerns of globalization for international advertisers is how to resolve the paradox of globalization and localization (national and regional interests, appeals, affiliations, etc.) in terms of formal and functional linguistic manifestations (see Friedman, 1999; and Berger and Huntington, 2002 on the general and various types of globalizations). This concern has manifested itself in the form of the "standardization" versus "adaptation" debate in international advertising, media, and marketing (see Heileman, 1997; Hite and Fraser, 1988; Kanso, 1991; Kujala and Lehtinen, 1989; Mueller, 1992; Onkvisit and Shaw, 1987; Ryans and Ratz, 1987, among others). Such issues of debate include: Should logo, colors, and other iconic representations be subjected to monolithic norms or should they be adapted to regional norms, tastes and sensitivities? Should models/actors in an ad represent a fused style with universal appeal or mark specific Western and non-Western identities? These dichotomies are driven by the consideration of the standardization versus adaptation issue.

3.2 Language choice and language attitude

The linguistic aspect of the standardization versus adaptation debate is the question of the most suitable linguistic vehicle for globalization and customization. There is no doubt that the question of language choice is practically resolved. English is the choice of global advertisers and marketers. English has effectively dethroned its competitor languages, such as French and Russian, and continues to do so with more vigor and dynamics, thus becoming the single most important language of globalization. Indeed a cursory examination of world advertising reveals that ad writers and marketers either consciously or unconsciously subscribe to bilingualism. English is viewed as the most suitable linguistic tool for promoting global bilingualism.

Although the language choice is settled, the question of which variety of English is appropriate is still very much alive. English is undergoing dynamic changes in the process of engendering and shaping global market discourse; this has important ramifications for international advertising media and marketing on one hand and world Englishes on the other.

3.3 Audience reach and modality choice

One of the serious challenges that confront international advertisers is how to tap "new emergent hot markets" in international business, dubbed B2-4B (Business to 4 Billion). The hot new market is the 4 billion people worldwide. With the saturation of traditional urban and domestic markets, marketers are in search of new markets. Rural and semi-rural areas in countries such as India, China, and Brazil are potential "hot markets." The urgent problem for advertisers then is how to reach the target new consumers, who are linguistically and geographically dispersed. How do you reach a target audience which lives in 637,000 villages and speaks scores of officially recognized different languages? The simple solution is to make use of conventional mass media (television, radio, and print). However, the reach of conventional media is limited in a number of ways due to the skyrocketing cost; geographical, linguistic, and social barriers; and limited or lack of reach (signal towers and frequent power failures) of electronic media in some parts of the world. This issue requires an unconventional approach to modes of communication and message transmission. Bhatia (2000) details non-conventional mediua (e.g., wall advertising, video van and other such non-conventional advertising forms) which are used by global advertisers in India and other developing countries to reach the new audience. The issue of local language choice and/or national/ world varieties of Englishes in unconventional media gives a new perspective on the overall debate on standardization versus adaptation.

4   Approaches

In addition to the linguistic and semantic/pragmatic approaches, theoretical and analytical frameworks for advertising analysis are as diverse as fields concerned with the interaction of language and society: sociolinguistics (Halliday, 1978; Kachru, 1981; Labov, 1972), ethnography of speaking (Hymes, 1974), sociology of language (Fishman, 1972), critical discourse analysis (van Dijk, 1985), semiotics (Barthes, 1984; Foucault, 1981), speech accommodation (Giles, Coupland, and Coupland, 1991), language and ideology (Fowler, 1993; Thompson, 1978), communication (Myers, 1999), among others. See Bhatia (2000: 108–19) and Chapter 32 in this volume for details.

Analytical tools include content analysis, ANOVA, chi-square, frequency table, t-test, and regression analysis.

On methodological grounds, both qualitative and quantitative techniques are employed. Data collection methods include random sampling, judgmental sampling, nonprobability sampling, and stratified random sampling drawn from both conventional and non-conventional advertising. In addition to interview and survey methods, experimental techniques are also employed. Experimental techniques have been the salient feature of psycholinguistic aspects of advertising research. See Samiee and Jeong (1994) for details. The main concern of psycholinguistic research is to address issues pertaining to memory and product name recall. In recent years, this type of research has begun to align itself with the multilingual nature of advertising.

5   Multiple Mixing and World Englishes

Based on the pattern of advertising outside the Anglophone world, Piller (2003) notes that advertising functions as a site for language contact. Advertising, for instance, can be seen as an intrinsically mixed medium – a mixture of written–spoken forms, text–image mixing, music, etc. In terms of language mixing, even Inner-Circle advertising shows some openness to language mixing. The addition of a few diacritics and phonological/syntactic adaptations lends monolingual ads the flavor of French, German, or other European languages (e.g., L'Eggs, el Cheapo, Norishe). Besides this low-level cosmetic mixing, the more frequent and dominant trend in global advertising is the "high-level" fusion which manifests itself in the following four ways:

- mixing of world Englishes,
- mixing of world English accents,
- mixing of English with other languages,
- mixing of English with non-Roman scripts.

5.1 Mixing of world Englishes

The influence of British and American advertising on global advertising is so significant that Inner-Circle Englishes seem to be exercising a "melting pot" effect on global Englishes. In addition to the common lexicon (drawn from fashion, entertainment, beverages, food, sports, music, and other sources of popular culture), the use of structures such as a string of noun phrases (*Oak Wood Furniture Express*), negative structures (*no hassle, no payment,* etc.), and discourse styles (e.g., informationalization, promotional discourse, "cold call" scripting; see Goodman and Graddol, 1996: 141–57) reflect the important ways in which the qualitative aspects of global advertising are undergoing homogenization (see Bhatia and Ritchie, 2004 for more details). Nevertheless, it would be premature to claim that the influence of Inner-Circle Englishes is unidirectional (i.e., from the Inner Circle to the Outer and Expanding Circles). Linguistic innovations outside the UK, Canada, and the United States have left a lasting influence on native-English-speaking advertising. The bi-directional accommodation and mutually-feeding relationship of global Englishes is the salient feature of international advertising, as shown in Figure 33.1.

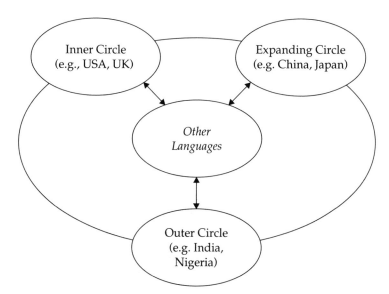

Figure 33.1 World Englishes and language mixing: contact and convergence

5.2   *Product naming and world Englishes*

Nowhere is the pattern of mixing world Englishes more obvious than in the area of product naming. The success story of the Walkman (invented by Japanese advertisers) is a case in point. Although it was met with great skepticism initially in the native-English-speaking world, its innovative appeal silenced puritans and skeptics. Now it has become not only a part of the global English lexicon, but also a model of a very productive strategy in product naming in international advertising.

What is even more interesting is that so pressing is the need for product naming through English that, a little more a decade ago, the Japanese Ministry of Trade and Industry (MITI) determined that there were not enough names for the hundreds of soft drinks being produced in Japan. To fill this gap, the emergency use of non-sense English-sounding words (McKeldin, 1994: 71) such as *posmic, Cham-pe,* was approved by the government. It is no accident the choice of language for filling such a gap was English.

In the non-English-speaking world, product naming and company naming is the domain for which English is the most favored language. Bhatia (1987: 35) shows that English performs an overwhelming function in product naming. Based on the analysis of more than 1,200 advertisements primarily in Hindi that were printed between 1975 and 1985, the study revealed that more than 90 percent of the advertisements analyzed carried a product name in English. It is also true even of products for the rural market where familiarity with and literacy in English are minimal. The following leading soap/detergent brand names current in India are drawn overwhelmingly from English: Arial, Cinthol, Det, Gnat, Lux, Lifebuoy, Magic, Bonus, Liril, Margo, Palmolive, Rexona, Sunlight, Surf, Wheel, Marvel, Crowing Glory, and Ponds. The two notable exception are Nirma and Hamam. Meraj (1993: 224) shows a similar trend in Urdu advertising in Pakistan. Her sample reveals that English product names account for 70 percent of the ads while only 9 percent of product names were drawn from Urdu. The remaining 21 percent were mixed product names (English + Urdu) such as *Chanda Battery Cell, Good Luck Haleem,* and *National Kheer.* The same trend is widely attested in Russia and other European countries. Thonus (1991) identifies ten different structural types of English-Portugese hybrid product/business names.

In Japan and Korea, English product names qualified with English first-person possessive pronouns (e.g., *my juice, my car*) are quite frequent. The possessive pronoun can be further subjected to the process of reduplication (e.g., *MyMy Workman*).

While Inner-Circle English is enriching other Englishes, it is in turn being enriched by product names drawn from other languages: *Nike* (Greek), *Volvo* (Latin), *Samsara* (Sanskrit), and *Nokia* (Finnish). The mutually feeding relationship among the world Englishes and other languages is shown in Figure 33.1.

5.3 Mixing of world English accents

The incidence of accent mixing in global advertising ranges from standard to non-standard accents at national and international levels. In television commercials from the Inner Circle, the mixing of local/regional accents is utilized not only to generate local appeals and identities but also to render socio-psychological effects such as trustworthiness of the product advertised and sincerity on the part of advertisers/actors. A case in point is the use of a Southern accent in US advertising. In global advertising, on the other hand, a wide variety of national/European accents are employed to render the international appeal of the product. For example, McDonald's does not exclusively rely on standard British or American English accents to invoke the international branding of its product and company. According to Piller (2003: 177), "it seems that some of the major brands may actually be moving away from the exclusive use of English. At the time of writing, McDonald's, for instance, is running an advertising campaign in Australia that features a commercial set in Italy, with characters using a few Italian words and manifesting a heavy Italian accent in English." Such a move is crucial for global indexing as opposed to asserting either British or American identity. Due to the overt phonetic component, the ethno-cultural stereotypes are marked often by means of world English accents. For instance, images of holy men, immigrant cab drivers, or food items (curry) often invite the use of an Indian accent in English. Similarly, a black English accent marks black Urban US ghettos. On the power and ideology of world English accents, see Chapter 32 in this volume.

5.4 English mixing in non-English advertising

In contrast with the use of symbolic or mocking use of foreign languages in Inner-Circle English advertising, the qualitative and quantitative pattern of mixing with English in non-Inner-Circle English advertising is significantly different. Bhatia and Ritchie (2004: 530–4) show that beside product names, the use of English has found its way into the structural domains of advertising, such as attention-getters, company logo or name, packing and labeling, pricing, slogans, and even the main body of the text. The acquisition of such domains signifies the power of English in Outer- and Expanding-Circle advertising.

Based on cross-linguistic study of advertising, Bhatia (1992, 2001) showed that the mixing with English is a near-universal tendency. Subsequent studies further confirm this claim. Martin (1998, 1999) shows in her study of more than 4,000 French television commercials and print ads that English is widely used. The increasing use of English is particularly notable in cosmetic and beauty-product advertising in France. Given the international status of French, the linguistic rivalry between French and English, together with the linguistic attitudes of French speakers and the French academy, it is particularly surprising to find English in a domain in which French has asserted its supremacy, authority, and international status for centuries. Attention-getters also favor the use of English over French. Expressions such as *advanced cream, extra help makeup, multi-protection* are being steadily used not only as attention-getters but also in the body of French advertisements in the context of offering explanations for the merits of the product in question (Bhatia, 1992). The same pattern is emerging with more vigor than ever before in Asian (see Japan: Takashi, 1990, 1992; Wilkerson, 1997; Korea: Jung, 2001, Lee, 2003; Taiwan: Hsu, 2001) and other European countries (Switzerland: Cheshire and Moser, 1994; Spain: Aldea, 1987; France and Germany: Hilgendorf and Martin, 2001; Russia: Ustinova, 2001).

In considering the quantitative aspects, what is the proportion of English language material in non-English advertisements? According to a Dutch study of television commercials, one-third of the commercials on Dutch television contain English words (Gerritsen et al., 2000). Based on the analysis of 658 German commercials broadcast in 1999, Pillar (2001) shows that 73.4 percent made use of a language other than German, with English having a major share of the pie. Bajko (1999) concludes that the use of English became dominant in the 1990s in German advertising (Piller, 2003: 174).

In short, mixing with English is not only near-universal, but is rapidly on the increase in quantitative as well as qualitative terms since globalization became the marketing mantra.

6   Laws and Regulations

To restrain the use of English in advertising, some countries have in place regulatory statutes. A case in point is the Toubon Law in France which came into effect in 1994. Articles 2 and 12 of this law aim at restricting the use of English in the French media. Article 12 requires any foreign language words in advertising to be accompanied by their corresponding equivalents in French with the following condition: the equivalents in French must be as legible, audible, or intelligible as the foreign language version (Martin, 1998). The law safeguards the use of French against English in French media and advertising. The newly independent countries of the former Soviet Union have similar regulations in place. In countries such as Lithuania and Armenia, government regulations include language police, who play a crucial role in confining the influx of English.

7   World Englishes in Roman Scripts and Language Attitudes

The extent of English usage in global advertising is greater than meets the eye. In Asian and European countries, it is a common practice to write English lexical items in non-Roman scripts such as Hangul (Korea), Katakana (Japan), Devanagari, Gurmukhi or scores of other Indic language scripts, and Arabic (India, Pakistan or Arabic-speaking countries). Of course, Roman and non-Roman script mixing is also a common sight. Clearly, such ads are aimed at consumers who may not be fluent or even literate in English. On the surface, this might appear to be counter-intuitive and counter-productive. However at the deeper level, this practice is reflective of the underlying assumption or unconscious planning on the part of national or international advertisers who expect their readers to be somewhat bilingual in English. This is in agreement with their conception of the global citizen: in order to be a global citizen, some knowledge of English is a prerequisite.

Not only is English, with or without Roman letters, introduced, but an attempt is also made not to deprive consumers of the meaning and pronunciation of English phrases by employing strategies such as paraphrasing or translating English expressions into local script. How does one introduce English in countries such as Japan where the incidence of bilingualism with English is perhaps less than one percent? Consider the ad in Figure 33.2. Notice that

Figure 33.2   English expression and its pronunciation guide in katakana

Table 33.1   Script mixing in global advertising: functions

Covert	Overt
• Bilingualism through English • Positive linguistic attitudes toward English	• Mixing of native and non-native Englishes • Paraphrasing, reiteration, puns, other stylistic functions • Structural accommodation • Linguistic accommodation

right above the English expression (Final Stage Premium) is printed a pronunciation guide for Japanese consumers in the Katakana script.

What is interesting about such practices is that not only does script mixing and English mixing in non-Roman scripts set the stage for bilingualism, but it also provides a fertile ground for the mixing of native and non-native Englishes. For instance, the pronunciation guide in the Japanese ad adapts the target English expression with CVCV-type phonological adaptation. The main functions of script mixing are summarized in Table 33.1.

8   Determinants and Functions of World Englishes

The quantitative and qualitative pattern of use of English worldwide has added yet another, but invisible, dimension to English which can be termed the "mystique factor." English mixing is not motivated by low-level considerations such as borrowings, i.e., the use of English to fill a lexical gap in the host language. After all, is there a language in the world which lacks an English equivalent of words such as *new*, *design*, or *juice*? The use of English is motivated by the deeper, creative desires on the part of advertisers (see Martin, 1998, 1999 on the perception of English as a powerful creative tool on the part of French advertisers and copywriters). English is considered to be a "cool" language capable of rendering audience identity (as international, modern, rational, objective, ethno-cultural stereotypes etc.) and appeal of the product (as standard, American or British). For more details see Bhatia and Ritchie (2004).

In addition to rendering the socio-psychological features and indexing identities, mixing with English performs other literary and psycholinguistic functions such as rhyming (*Trentenaire On Air* – a French radio station ad), reduplication (*MyMy Workman* in a Korean ad), puns (*must* with two meanings: English *must* and Hindi *must* 'crazy'), humor, slogans (changing value system: a slogan such as "Freedom is my birth right" aimed at gender equality and empowerment). These functions have immense psycholinguistic power since they play important roles in product recall and information primacy effects. These are special effects and creative meanings which advertisers strive for. Creativity through English enables them to conquer the negative social evaluation of mixing.

8.1 Creativity or deception?

The aim of an ad is to inform and persuade consumers to buy a product. But these two aims do not carry equal weight. In the process of persuading consumers ads sometimes go overboard, either intentionally or unintentionally. Therefore, the boundary between creativity and deception becomes blurred. Holbrook (1978) and Shimp (1983) distinguish between factual and evaluative advertising. Factual advertising refers to factual claims in a real-world situation, like pricing, packing, and product attributes. The truth-value or validity of factual advertising claims can easily be assessed. In contrast, evaluative advertising refers to what is called in the advertising register, "Puffery." Puffery, or evaluative advertising, refers to those aspects of advertising that make advertising more like an art. It makes subjective claims that can neither be empirically proved nor disproved. The use of English for deceptive purposes is no longer limited to the Anglophone countries. With English quickly becoming the near-universal language of product naming, and the forces of globalization (top-down and bottom-up) at work, English is leading in the race of global deception. Consider the case of rural India, where English has become a powerful weapon of deliberate deception. Even leading brand name products such as *Lifebuoy* and *Boroline* are not spared. Relying heavily on the copied logos and other visual signs, deceptive marketers change a letter of the product name in English and deceive villagers into thinking that they are buying a brand name product. *Lifebuoy* is spelled as *Lifeboy* and *Boroline* as *Boriline* to cheat the unsuspecting villager. Such problems are not unique to rural India; the growing role of deception involving English product names is an increasingly pervasive phenomenon.

9 Globalization: Resolving the Global vs. Local Paradox

As pointed out earlier, as urban markets reach the point of saturation and conventional advertising loses its punch, international marketers turn to the new and emerging semi-urban and rural markets of Asia, Africa, and South America. This trend marks the process of globalization from the bottom up which calls for a new approach to marketing communication and innovative ways of reaching the potential four billion consumers. Although mass media are very popular around the globe, the search for unconventional ways to send commercial messages is gaining prominence. In many countries of Asia and Africa, wall advertising/painting is quite popular not only with local/

Table 33.2 Models of globalization: competitive and cooperative

Model	Approach	Language/Script	Text
Competitive	Either/or	One	Monolingual
Cooperative	Mixed	Two or more	Bilingual or multilingual

regional/national advertisers but also international advertisers. What might appear to be graffiti to a Western eye, wall advertising, is a very powerful form of reaching rural audiences (see Bhatia, 2000 for more details on the structure, power, and reach of this media modality). This section will discuss globalization with special reference to this media modality to demonstrate the scope and magnitude of the impact of world Englishes in global advertising.

What is intriguing to observe is that advertisers, either unconsciously or by design, have developed two distinct models of globalization in relation to localization, which, in turn, govern their linguistic representational strategies and linguistic choices. These views can be characterized as "competitive" and "cooperative." The two divergent views naturally lead to two distinct underlying linguistic representational strategies in global advertising: the competitive view leads to language segregation, whereas the cooperative view yields language mixing. Language segregation is the natural outcome of the perception of globalization and localization as oppositions, while language integration is the consequence of the perceived accommodation between the two. The perceived models of globalization and its linguistic renderings are summarized in Table 33.2. Based on these two models, three distinct patterns are evident in advertising worldwide. The first two patterns lend themselves to language separation.

9.1   Think global and act global

This pattern is carried out by means of English only, preferably by native varieties of English in Roman letters. The global brands which subscribe to this type of advertising are Coke, Pepsi, Nike, etc. Not only top-down, but even bottom-up globalization reflects this approach. Following the standardization model of international advertising, Coke and Pepsi display their brands both in non-conventional and conventional media forms. Global advertisers have begun to paint walls in rural India so vigorously that no standing structure is spared. Two years ago when Coke and Pepsi ads appeared painted on rocks on the 33-mile stretch of the road between Manali and Rohtang Pass in the ecologically sensitive areas of the Himalayan region of India, environmental groups (including earth scientists) filed a legal suit against these companies, charging them with violation of the Forest Conservation Act of India (see Bagla, 2002).

9.2   Think local and act local

On the opposite side from the think-global-and-act-global ads fall the think-local-and-act-local type of ads. These ads strive for hyper-localization through local languages and indigenous scripts and illustrate the strategy of glocalization through language mixing.

Some ads depart from the exclusive "think global and act global" strategy and make room for globalization by way of bridging with localization. Reaching the masses by means of local languages and scripts paves the way for a safe and less risky globalization appeal. Although the approaches are overtly mutually exclusive both in conceptual and linguistic terms, the localization-to-globalization gap is bridged primarily by nonlinguistic means – either by sharing logographic properties of the product or by maintaining the common color scheme.

Rather than relying on visual cues and an indirect approach, some ads rely on content-sensitive means to induce some degree of globalization. A case in point is the ad for *Aral engine oil*, a German product (Figure 33.3).

(1)   araal – jarmanii   kaa   nambar   ek   injan   aail.
       Aral   Germany   of   number   one   engine   oil.
       'Aral – the number one German engine oil.'

Figure 33.3   Bridging the global vs. local divide

The message has a topic-comment structure. The topic, *Aral* (the product name) is separated from the comment – *the number one German engine oil* – by the slight, rising wall dividing the two portions of the wall. The entire ad is in the Devanagari script and the grammatical markers are those of Hindi. The suggestion of global appeal is brought about by the content of the comment structure. The affiliation part contains information about the Germanic association of the product, and the evaluation part reveals that the product is the number one product.

Rather than pitting global appeals against local or satisfying themselves with minimal content (as in the standardized ads displaying one word – Coke, Pepsi), the unmarked pattern, both on qualitative and quantitative grounds, in global advertising is that advertisers break the barriers posed by linguistic segregation and attempt to integrate the globalization and localization themes by integrating the participating linguistic systems and their scripts. This is an optimization strategy which subscribes to the "think and act both global and local at the same time" approach, which renders optimization in the strength and appeal of their messages. One of the outcomes of this strategy is the increased use of Inner-Circle Englishes together with national and local brands of Englishes, on the one hand, and the creation of their own modes and standards of mixing English, on the other. *Staba* stands for Starbucks Coffee in Japan, MacDonald's is called either *Mac* (Tokyo area) or *Macdo* (in the western areas such as Osaka and Nagoya). The process of globalization from the bottom up has opened the flood-gates of English in those remote parts of the world which were earlier out of the reach of English.

9.3   *Cross-cultural translations and intelligibility*

Cross-cultural translations are another salient feature of globalization. The question of appropriateness and acceptance of world Englishes in advertising figures prominently in two contexts: cross-cultural translational mishaps and intelligibility of Inner-Circle English commercials for Outer- and Expanding-Circle consumers. Translation mishaps/blunders and product failure within and outside the English-speaking countries have been the major concern of cross-cultural advertising on the part of global advertisers, media practitioners, and marketers. When the Scandinavian makers of the Electrolux vacuum cleaner wanted to promote their product in the USA, they used the following slogan: "Nothing sucks like an Electrolux." The negative connotation of the verb "sucks" in American English did not add to the success of the product. The same is true of Japanese product names such as *Calpis Water*, and *Pocari Sweat*: they are perfectly acceptable lexical innovations for Japanese consumers, but it is not the case for markets of the Inner-Circle English regions. In India, *Eveready Torch* is an acceptable product name of a flashlight, but for the speakers of American English, it flashes the picture of arson, aggression, and violence. A chilled beer is written as "Child Bear" in an Indian shop. A sign "sex shop" for a shop in China is not a taboo; such stores sell herbal tea or other general health products (vitamins, etc.). However, such names highlight the problems of intelligibility and lexical semantic asymmetries between the world varieties of Englishes. Hence, some studies, such as those by Gerritsen et al. (2000) are concerned with the comprehension of Inner-Circle English commercials on the part of Dutch consumers.

The use of foreign languages and non-Inner-Circle Englishes in ads aimed at Inner-Circle consumers has also had its own share of problems which range from complaints of the editors about ungrammatical use of English to incomprehensible content causing emotive reactions such as ads being "too foreign" and "too annoying." While the ads exploit the good, the bad and the ugly of "foreignness" or "otherness," as Kelley-Holms (2005) shows, the main function of such usage is to exploit national stereotypes (e.g., Germans as mechanical and thorough; Indians as mystic). Starbucks' product names such as *taazo cay* (use of Rajashthani Hindi and Gujarati) and sizes (e.g., Spanish and Italian: *grande*) optimize the appeal of the message while appropriately highlighting the multilingual context of English in the Inner Circle.

10 Conclusion

International advertising and media is a fertile ground for the mixing of world Englishes, on one hand, and the mixing of English and other languages on the other. Contrary to the expectations and predictions of market gurus and proponents of the "Standardization" strategy, even in the age of super-branding and hyper-globalization, international advertising does not exclusively favor the use of Inner-Circle English and its accents. Language mixing in general and the mixing of world Englishes in particular is an unwritten law of international advertising which enables international advertisers to optimize the strength and the appeal of their message in terms of audience identity construction, product branding, and socio-psychological rendering of both audience and products.

11 Future Directions for Research

In order to tap the conscious and unconscious knowledge which plays a critical role in the creation of ads, it is imperative to understand the complex process in the making of an ad. How do features of market research and product positioning map onto an ad copy? How is an ad adapted or created cross-culturally in the age of hyper-globalization by making visual and linguistic choices? In order to answer these questions and gain insights into the process of standardization and/or adaptation of cross-cultural ads, interdisciplinary research and dialog among the users of world Englishes and international advertisers is needed. Marketing research on the linguistic aspects (including the use of English) suffers from conceptual and analytical oversimplification (e.g., the treatment of English mixing as loans), which interdisciplinary research can rectify. Research on the use of world Englishes in non-conventional media, audience reaction and attitudes toward non-conventional media and world Englishes is still in the infant stage. In order to gain proper perspectives into the pluralistic nature of world Englishes/global communication and the advertising media, the integration of conceptual, analytical, and experimental frameworks is imperative at the interdisciplinary level.

See also Chapters 22, Genres and Styles in World Englishes; 32, World Englishes and the Media; 34, World Englishes and Global Commerce.

REFERENCES

Aldea, Santiago (1987) Funcion del prestamo en el discurso propagandistico [The function of loans in advertising discourse]. *Miscelanea*, **8**, 5–19.

Bagla, Pallava (2002) Coke, Pepsi under fire for painting rocks in India. http://news.nationalgeographic.com. August 28.

Bajko, István Zsigmond (1999) Fremdworter in der deutshen Werbesprache am Beispiel zweier Slogankorpora [Foreign words in German advertising language, exemplified by two corpora of slogans]. *Moderna Sprak*, **93**, 161–71.

Barthes, Roland (1984) *Image Music Text, Translated and Selected from the French 1961–71*. Translated by Sherley Heath. London: Fontana.

Berger, Pete L. and Huntington, Samuel P. (2002) *Many Globalizations: Cultural Diversity in the Contemporary World*. Oxford: Oxford University Press.

Bhatia, Tej K. (1987) English in advertising: Multiple mixing and media. *World Englishes*, **6**(1), 33–48.

Bhatia, Tej K. (1992) Discourse functions and pragmatics of mixing: Advertising across cultures. *World Englishes*, **11**(2–3), 195–215.

Bhatia, Tej K. (2000) *Advertising in Rural India: Language, Marketing Communication, and Consumerism*. Tokyo: Tokyo Press.

Bhatia, Tej K. (2001) Language mixing in global advertising. In *The Three Circles of English*. Edited by Edwin Thumboo. Singapore: Singapore University Press, pp. 195–215.

Bhatia, Tej K. and Ritchie, William C. (2004) Bilingualism in global media and advertising. In *The Handbook of Bilingualism*. Edited by Tej K. Bhatia and William C. Ritchie. Oxford: Blackwell, pp. 513–46.

Cheshire, Jenny and Moser, Lise-Marie (1994) English as a cultural symbol: The case of advertisements in French-speaking Switzerland. *Journal of Multilingual and Multicultural Development*, **15**, 451–69.

Cook, Guy (1992) *The Discourse of Advertising*. London: Routledge.

Fishman, Joshua (1972) *The Sociology of Language: An Interdisciplinary Social Science Approach to Language in Society*. Rowley, MA: Newbury House.

Forceville, Charles (1998) *Pictorial Metaphor in Advertising*. London: Routledge.

Foucault, Michel (1981) *The Archaeology of Knowledge*. New York: Pantheon Books.

Fowler, Roger (1993) *Language in the News: Discourse and Ideology in the Press*. London: Routledge.

Friedman, Thomas (1999) *The Lexus and the Olive Tree*. New York: Farrar, Straus, Giroux.

Geis, Michael L. (1982) *The Language of Television Advertising*. New York: Academic Press.

Gerritsen, Marinel, Korzilius, Hubert, van Meurs, Frank, and Gijsbers, Inge (2000) English in Dutch commercials: Not understood and not appreciated. *Journal of Advertising Research*, July–August, 17–31.

Giles, Howard, Coupland, Nikolas, and Coupland, Justine (1991) Accommodation theory: Communication, context and consequences. In *Contexts of Accommodation: Developments in Applied Sociolinguistics*. Edited by Howard Giles, Justine Coupland, Nikolas Coupland, Keith Oatley, and Antony Manstead. Cambridge: Cambridge University Press, pp. 1–68.

Goddard, Angela (1998) *The Language of Advertising*. London: Routledge.

Goodman, Sharon and Graddol, David (eds.) (1996) *Redesigning English: New Texts, New Identities*. London: Routledge.

Haarmann, Harold (1984) The role of ethnocultural stereotypes and foreign languages in Japanese commercials. *International Journal of the Sociology of Language*, **50**, 101–2.

Halliday, M. A. K. (1978) *Language as Social Semiotic: The Social Interpretation of Language and Meaning*. Baltimore: University Park Press.

Heileman, John (1997) Annals of advertising: All Europeans are not alike. *The New Yorker*, April 28/May 5, pp. 174–81.

Hermeren, Lars (1999) *English for Sale: A Study of the Language of Advertising*. Lund, Sweden: Lund University Press.

Hilgendorf, Suzanne and Martin, Elizabeth (2001) English in advertising: Update for France and Germany. In *The Three Circles of English*. Edited by Edwin Thumboo. Singapore: Singapore University Press, pp. 217–40.

Hite, Robert E. and Fraser, Cynthia (1988) International advertising strategies. *Journal of Advertising Research*, **28**(5), 9–17.

Holbrook, Morris B. (1978) Beyond attitude structure: Toward the information determinants of attitudes. *Journal of Marketing Research*, **15**, 546–56.

Hsu, Jia-Ling (2001) The sources, adapted functions, and the public's subjective evaluation of the Englishization of Mandrin Chinese in Taiwan. In *The Three Circles of English*. Edited by Edwin Thumboo. Singapore: Singapore University Press, pp. 241–56.

Hymes, Dell (1974) *Foundations in Sociolinguistics: An Ethnographic Approach*. Philadelphia, PA: University of Pennsylvania Press.

Jung, Kyutae (2001) The genre of advertising in Korean: Strategies and "Mixing." In *The Three Circles of English*. Edited by Edwin Thumboo. Singapore: Singapore University Press, pp. 257–75.

Kachru, Braj B. (1981) Socially-realistic linguistics: The Firthian tradition. *International Journal of the Sociology of Language*, **31**, 65–89.

Kanso, Ali (1991) The use of advertising agencies from foreign markets: Decentralized decisions and localized approaches? *International Journal of Advertising*, **10**, 129–36.

Kelly-Holms, Helen (2005) *Advertising as Multilingual Communication*. New York: Palgrave Macmillan.

Kujala, Ari and Lehtinen, Uolevi (1989) A new structural method for analyzing linguistic significance in market communications. *International Journal of Advertising*, **8**, 219–36.

Labov, William (1972) *Sociolinguistic Patterns*. Philadelphia, PA: University of Pennsylvania Press.

Lee, Jamie (2003) Linguistic constructions of modernity: Korean-English mixing in TV commercial. Manuscript.

Leech, Geoffrey N. (1966) *English in Advertising: A Linguistic Study of Advertising in Great Britain*. London: Longmans, Green and Co.

MacGregor, Laura (2003) The language of shop signs in Tokyo. *English Today*, **73**, 19 (1), 18–23.

Martin, Elizabeth (1998) Code-Mixing and Imaging of America in France: The genre of advertising. PhD dissertation, University of Illinois at Urbana-Champaign.

Martin, Elizabeth (1999) The politics of English in France: Creative strategies for using English in French television commercials despite legal restrictions. Paper presented at the Fifth International Conference on World Englishes, University of Illinois, November 5–7.

Martin, Elizabeth (2002a) Cultural images and different varieties of English in French television commercials. *English Today*, **18**(4), 8–72.

Martin, Elizabeth (2002b) Mixing English in French advertising. *World Englishes*, **21**(3), 375–401.

McKeldin, Caroline (1994) *Japanese Jive: Wacky and Wonderful Products from Japan*. New York: Tengu Books.

Meraj, Shaheen (1993) The use of English in Urdu advertising in Pakistan. In *The English Language in Pakistan*. Edited by Robert J. Baumgardner.

Karachi: Oxford University Press, pp. 221–52.

Mueller, Barbara (1992) Standardization vs. specialization: An examination of westernization in Japanese advertising. *Journal of Advertising Research*, **1**, 15–24.

Myers, Greg (1999) *Ad Worlds: Brands, Media, Audiences*. London: Edward Arnold.

Onkvisit, Sak and Shaw, John (1987) Standardized international advertising: A review and critical evaluation of theoretical and empirical evidence. *Columbia Journal of World Business*, Fall, 43–55.

Piller, Ingrid (2001) Identity constructions in multilingual advertising. *Language in Society*, **30**, 153–86.

Piller, Ingrid (2003) Advertising as a site of language contact. *Annual Review of Applied Linguistics*, **23**, 170–83.

Ryans, John K. and Ratz, David G. (1987) Advertising standardization: A re-examination. *International Journal of Advertising*, **6**, 145–58.

Samiee, Saeed and Jeong, Insik (1994) Cross-cultural research in advertising: An assessment of methodologies. *Journal of the Academy of Marketing Science*, **22**(3), 205–17.

Shimp, Terence A. (1983) Evaluative verbal content and deception in advertising. In *Information Processing Research in Advertising*. Edited by Richard J. Harris. Hillsdale, NJ: Lawrence Erlbaum, pp. 195–216.

Takashi, Kyoko (1990) A sociolinguistic analysis of English borrowings in Japanese advertising texts. *World Englishes*, **9**, 327–41.

Takashi, Kyoko (1992) Language and desired identity in contemporary Japan. *Journal of Asian Pacific Communication*, **3**, 133–44.

Tanaka, Keiko (1994) *Advertising Language: A Pragmatic Approach to*

Advertisements in Britain and Japan. London: Routledge.

Thompson, John (1978) Language and ideology: A framework for analysis. *The Sociological Review*, **35**(3), 516–36.

Thonus, Terese (1991) Englishization of business names in Brazil. *World Englishes*, **10**(1), 65–74.

Ustinova, Irena (2001) English in Russian Advertising. PhD dissertation, Syracuse University.

van Dijk, Teun (1985) *Discourse and Communication: New Approaches to the Analysis of Mass Media Discourse and Communication.* Berlin: Walter de Gruyter.

Vestergaard, Torben and Schrøder, Kim (1985) *The Language of Advertising.* Oxford: Blackwell.

Wilkerson, Kyoto T. (1997) Japanese bilingual brand names. *English Today*, **13**, 12–16.

FURTHER READING

Bhatia, Tej K. (2001) Language mixing in global advertising. In *The Three Circles of English*. Edited by Edwin Thumboo. Singapore: Singapore University Press, pp. 195–215.

Bhatia, Tej K. and Ritchie, William C. (2004) Bilingualism in global media and advertising. In *The Handbook of Bilingualism*. Edited by Tej K. Bhatia and William C. Ritchie. Oxford: Blackwell, pp. 513–46.

Bhatia, Tej K. (2007) *Marketing and Advertising in Rural India*. New Delhi: Macmillan.

Hilgendorf, Suzanne and Martin, Elizabeth (2001) English in advertising: Update for France and Germany. In *The Three Circles of English*. Edited by Edwin Thumboo. Singapore: Singapore University Press, pp. 217–40.

Martin, Elizabeth (2002) Mixing English in French advertising. *World Englishes*, **21**(3), 375–401.

Martin, Elizabeth (2006) *Marketing Identities through Language: English and Global Imagery in French Advertising*. New York: Palgrave Macmillan.

Meraj, Shaheen (1993) The use of English in Urdu advertising in Pakistan. In *The English Language in Pakistan*. Edited by Robert J. Baumgardner. Karachi: Oxford University Press, pp. 221–52.

Tanaka, Keiko (1994) *Advertising Language: A Pragmatic Approach to Advertisements in Britain and Japan*. London: Routledge.

Wilkerson, Kyoto T. (1997) Japanese bilingual brand names. *English Today*, **13**, 12–16.

34 World Englishes and Global Commerce

STANLEY YUNICK VAN HORN

1 Introduction

In his perceptive and influential study, the anthropologist Bronislaw Malinowski (1884–1942) described the Trobriand Islanders in a way perhaps apt for human kind as a whole: "The whole of tribal life is permeated by a constant give and take" (Malinowski, 1922: 167). Give and take in commerce is critical to survival, success, and enrichment, and, for many, English plays an increasing role in it. At the same time, language itself is a symbolic good with its own principles of give and take.

English is identified, however much in reality or in myth, as "the" language of worldwide commerce of the twenty-first century – with an attending implicit model of a single international standard. More or less well-meaning and more or less profitably, English language textbooks for business prescribe "best practice." In doing so, they frequently subscribe to a single native-speaker recipe for linguistic success, which B. Kachru has termed a "nativist mono-model" of English – standing in contradistinction to a "functionalist polymodel" of world Englishes (1990: 7). Studies in world Englishes differ from prescriptivist models of English in aiming to account for multilinguals' creativity within a linguistic repertoire and within a plural sociolinguistic context, (see e.g., B. Kachru, 1986/1990, 1990, 1992a, 1992b, 2005; Bolton, 2004).

The functions of English and Englishes in the world marketplace are many: in consumer-oriented discourses such as advertising (surveyed by T. Bhatia in Chapter 33 of this volume, and thus excluded here), in market and retail/institutional service encounters (e.g., Clark and Pinch, 1994; Ventola, 1987), in daily talk at the workplace at various societal levels (e.g., Clyne, 1994), and in various forms of talk which are the realm of business people and constitute professional identity (e.g., Bargiela-Chiappinini and Harris, 1997a; Holmes, Stubbe, and Vine, 1999).

The sociolinguistic literature on professional discourse in English which has emerged in the last two decades is largely made up of *cross-cultural studies* (where data is collected from separate languages and communities and compared; e.g., Bargiela-Chiappini and Harris, 1997a; Hampden-Turner and Trompenaars, 1993; Yamada, 1992, 1996, 1997; Yli-Jokipii, 1994, 1998; many papers in Bargiela-Chiappini and Nickerson, 1999 and in Bargiela-Chiappini and Harris, 1997b) and *intercultural studies* (where data is collected from the coming-together of members of separate languages and cultures; e.g., Clyne, 1994; Firth, 1990, 1991, 1995a, 1995b, 1996; Garcez, 1993; Gumperz, 1992; Marriott, 1995). The advantages of cross-cultural and intercultural studies are that the sociolinguistic processes at work in professional discourse are made more explicit through comparison. Such work forms an important platform for beginning to describe and explain the contexts, repertoires, and creativity in English in business.

The risks in cross-cultural and intercultural comparative work, however, are that units of analysis may be culturally biased, that descriptions of linguistic products and activities may or may not be suitable for comparison, and that linguistic actors may appear as stereotypes. Potential shortcomings, such as the danger of under-noticing non-Western cultural contexts and language patterns, have been discussed by Y. Kachru (e.g., 1992, 1996, 1997; and Y. Kachru and Nelson, 2006). Important caveats in doing contrastive discourse work, with specific reference to professional discourse, have similarly been noted by Scollon and Scollon (2001). Early, pioneering work in cross-cultural pragmatics (see e.g., Blum-Kulka, House, and Kasper, 1989) showed some degree of sensitivity to notions of sociolinguistic context in comparing speech acts (such as apologies, requests, etc.), and some later work in this area has begun to examine linguistic and cultural aspects of context in conversation (Kasper, 2001). The inaugural issue of the journal *Intercultural Pragmatics* (published by Mouton de Gruyter, 2004) addresses a variety of theoretical issues in this field of study. While these concerns are not always or often brought specifically to bear on business genres, they are essential to balanced comparisons of Englishes in business.

This survey of world Englishes and global commerce may read as something of a double-edged research agenda. On the one hand, there has been limited recent work on Outer- and Expanding-Circle varieties of Englishes in commercial and professional domains of use, and so the epistemologically distinct intercultural and cross-cultural studies on professional discourse may stamp out territory for expanding the empirical and theoretical framework of world Englishes. On the other hand, cross-cultural and intercultural studies rarely devote serious attention to multilingual creativity in either intranational or international arenas. A dialog between the world Englishes framework and this growing literature on professional discourse will serve the greater understanding of the pluricentric evolution and uses of English in business.

2   English and Professional Discourse in the Outer and Expanding Circles

Notwithstanding the global consumption of business English tests and courses and textbooks, there has been only modest growth in empirical research on the uses of English in commerce worldwide. A main barrier to research in business discourse is the proprietary and private nature of, and therefore restricted access to, writing and speaking inside corporations. A significant exception to this trend has been a burst of research activity on professional discourse in Europe since the 1990s, an indication of interest in (and funding for) research on language in business contexts, alongside a willingness of some European firms to grant access to linguists for research. Studies in various global regions and general resources on Englishes and business are surveyed here.

2.1   Asia

Because of the vitality and importance of Asia in global commerce, the use of English in business in Japan, Korea, China, South Asia, and Southeast Asia is the source of comment and curiosity – but is less often the subject of peer-reviewed research. Scholarly journals focusing on uses of English in this region such as *Asian Englishes: An International Journal of the Sociolinguistics of English in Asia/Pacific* (published by ALC Press Inc.; established in 1998) and the *Journal of Asian Pacific Communication* (published by John Benjamins; established in 1990) have not yet seen business contexts as a main focus. A general picture of how English is used within and between corporations and between corporations and consumers is yet to emerge.

Japan has long been the focus of cross-cultural and intercultural studies, probably because of longstanding Western trade interests there and educational ties to the United States and Australia. Connor (1988) examines exchanges of letters in English between American and Japanese business partners. Morrow (1995) discusses language training within a Japanese corporation. Marriott (1997) discusses intercultural meetings and negotiation between Australians and Japanese. Yamada (1992, 1996, 1997) extensively analyses Japanese business meetings in comparison to American business meetings. Jones (1995) similarly discusses negotiation in Japanese meetings. Yotsukura (2003) describes Japanese business telephone interactions, with a view to applying concepts cross-culturally. Relatively absent are world Englishes studies on the use of English in Japanese business, aside from advertising strategies, which have been broadly documented (Stanlaw, 2004).

English is an important language of corporate business in South Asia and often the preferred language of international business. The Japan-India Business Cooperation Committee (see www.jcci.or.jp) has noted that Indian information technology specialists push for wider acceptance of English in contracts and daily work despite pressure to use more Japanese in working with Japanese clients. Academic studies of such contexts are severely limited; most research has been conducted in public domains.

Early work of John Gumperz in the 1970s and 1980s (revisited, e.g., 1992) examined intercultural gate-keeping encounters and service encounters between South Asians and Britons. V. Bhatia (1996) more recently outlines the nativization of job applications within South Asia. T. Bhatia examines English and language mixing in rural advertising (2000, and Chapter 33 this volume). Hartford and Mahboob (2004) examine letters of complaint and general complaints in letters to the editor in South Asian varieties of English and in Urdu.

Grundy (1998) examines parallel memos in Chinese and English in a Hong Kong bank. Bilbow (1997) compares Hong Kong Chinese and British employees in impression management strategies in requesting and giving directives. Pang, Xhou, and Fu (2002) present a survey of attitudes toward English as China is joining the World Trade Organization. In the Singaporean context, Chew (1997) examines cultural difference and problematic participation in job interviews.

In the Malaysian context, Gill (1999) and Nair-Venugopal (2000a, 2000b, 2003) outline discourse practices and varietal features of Malaysian English in the workplace. Nair-Venugopal (2000a) is the only monograph in a world Englishes framework on discourse in business. This volume includes discussion of lexical choices, style shifting, local forms of linguistic accommodation, and code choice/mixing including English in the professional workplace in Malaysia.

While research on varieties of English in Korea and in Southeast Asia outside Malaysia has seen some recent attention on the whole, research on English in commerce is not widely available. One study of Korean business letters in English is Park, Dillon, and Mitchell (1998).

2.2   Europe

In the European context, there is a notable spike in interest in the use of English as language of wider communication in business, both within and across national borders, which is perhaps in part attributable to the expansion of and developments in the European Union. A few studies describe intranational uses of English for business, in the Netherlands (Nickerson, 1999a, 2000; Van Nus, 1999) and Finland (Louhiala-Salminen, 1996).

At the same time, there is broad interest in cross-cultural and cross-linguistic comparisons. Yli-Jokipii (1994, 1998) provides a detailed cross-linguistic analysis of British, American, and Finnish business letters. Bargiela-Chiappini (1999) compares the business culture of Italy and the UK as expressed in human resources trade magazines. Bargiela-Chiappini and Harris (1997a) provide a monograph-length cross-cultural comparison of business meetings in the UK and Italy. Gavioli (1997) contrasts Italian service encounters with British ones.

These studies exist alongside many other cross-cultural comparisons of Spanish-Danish, Norwegian-German, etc. Work on central and eastern Europe is yet to develop.

2.3   Lesser-studied regions: The Americas, the Middle East, Africa, Oceania

A main source of data on Englishes in Latin America is a special issue of the journal *World Englishes* (vol. 22, no. 2, 2003); papers on language in business schools in Argentina (Friedrich, 2003) and in commerce and advertising in Ecuador (Alm, 2003) appear in that issue.

Research on English in Brazil shows a variety of interests: analyses of meetings (Perez de Souza e Silva, 1994), advertising (Friedrich, 2002), and intercultural negotiation (Garcez, 1993), and a survey of the use of English in various spoken and written genres (Barbara et al., 1996).

In the Middle East, English teaching materials for commercial areas such as banking and finance are common. One well-illustrated analysis of business letter-writing in English in the Middle East is Al-Khatib (2001). Other studies include examination of data on code switching in the United Arab Emirates (Khuwaileh, 2003) and the use of English by business students in Kuwait (Dehrab, 2002).

Among studies of language and business in Africa are an analysis of workplace lexicon in Nigeria (Alabi, 2000), language choice and use in the engineering workplace in South Africa (Hill and Van Zyl, 2002), and complaint and application letters in Cameroon (Nkemleke, 2004).

One study of English in advertising in Oceania is Romaine's (1997) discussion of Pidgin English Advertising in New Guinea. In New Zealand and Australia, studies of workplace English for immigrant workers are a main focus for language and business (e.g., Brown and Lewis, 2003 for New Zealand; Clyne, 1994 for Australia).

2.4   Additional resources

In addition to published research on Englishes in global commerce, there are international conferences and organizations that focus on language and business. The Association for Business Communication (www.businesscommunication.org), established in 1935, has regional conferences in North America, Asia, and Europe and publishes two journals, *The Journal of Business Communication* (with a theoretical focus), and *Business Communication Quarterly* (with a pedagogical focus). An additional journal is *The Journal of Language for International Business* (Thunderbird, the Garvin School of International Management in Arizona, USA).

A younger European conference is the "Languages and Business" Conference on Languages and International Business Communication (www.sprachenberuf.com). Other associations and journals with focus on language and applied linguistics which do not focus on business and commerce in themselves but which may have papers of interest to business include: the journal *English for Specific Purposes* (Elsevier); the journal *World Englishes* (Blackwell); the meetings of the International Association for World Englishes; the International Association of Applied Linguistics (AILA); and its North American affiliate, the American Association of Applied Linguistics (AAAL).

3 Culture, Business Culture, and Englishes

A non-trivial concern for a "socially realistic linguistics" (Kachru, 1981) is the carefully drawn interrelationships between language, contexts of situation, and context of culture. An understanding of the language in contexts of commerce requires an investigation of ways in which varieties of language create, reflect, and reproduce cultural systems.

Business professionals are deeply interested in cultural points of view and may be willing to pay for consultants or at least for advice in mass-market books, in order to feel more confident about making a deal in another land. Of some influence have been the business and culture theories of Hall (outlined in Campbell, 1998), Hofstede (1980, 2001), Hampden-Turner and Trompenaars (1993, 2000), and Trompenaars (1994). These culture theories are largely based on psychological and sociological questionnaires. Hampden-Turner and Trompenaars elicited responses to various business "dilemmas" to test the values of business people in different countries. With provocative concepts like "How to create wealth from conflicting values" (Hampden-Turner and Trompenaars, 2000), cultural differences are presented as exploitable assets for all.

The question arises: to what extent, if any, are the supposed cultural principles present in a way that can be shown empirically to operate in linguistic interaction? A number of studies attempt to make the connection between culture and language behavior. Niemeier, Campbell, and Dirven (1998) and Bargiela-Chiappini and Harris (1997b) attempt to relate a cultural concept with linguistic variation in business contexts. For example, Grundy (1998) examines Confucian values and how they play out in a memo in Chinese in a Hong Kong firm in contrast to a parallel memo in English. Mulholland (1997) draws on folk perceptions of Korean difference and identity (such as the business "warrior") in her discussion of business interaction between Koreans and English speakers. Both of these sample studies attempt to relate national or regional culture to linguistic practice in business.

A few studies attempt to identify sociolinguistic behaviors of narrower business cultures. Bargiela-Chiappini (1999) uses a sort of register analysis to identify operative categories in human resources trade journals in Italy and the UK. Pogner (1999) examines different national norms toward the amount of specification and audience-design required in technical engineering documents as they line up with bureaucratic practices and industry relations.

A few studies address the slippery notion of "corporate culture" in multi-national corporations (e.g., Nickerson, 2000; Louhiala-Salminen, 2002) and suggest that, for some routine interactions, corporate culture is significant in socializing employees into local norms for formality or informality in inter-actions, and that the national and ethnic origins of the employees play a lesser role in communicative patterns within the multinationals.

Constructs of national business cultures and national business styles must be examined critically in a situated linguistics analysis. If they even exist, they may prove not to play into a particular context at all. Work on business communication and culture must move beyond correlational hypotheses and come to a thorough-going analysis of text and context.

4   Genre Analysis and Business Letter Writing

Sociolinguistic work on business writing draws mainly from the resources of register and genre analysis. Genre analysis assembles insights from register analysis in relating functions of text to context, and superimposes a set of relations among sociocultural categories and rhetorical and interactional moves within a text. Genre analysis highlights the importance of rhetorical purposes and discourse community in attributing meaning to text. Swales (1981, 1986, 1990) is generally recognized as a main mind behind this incarnation of theory of text and context. V. Bhatia (1993) continued to develop this framework and has extended the application of genre analysis to examination of varieties of English (1997, and Chapter 33 in this volume). For an overview of register analysis and genre analysis, see Yunick (1997).

In genre analysis, the notion of *discourse community* is central, as members of a discourse community have a largely shared set of norms for language use and interpretation. Through socialization, the discourse community provides norms for the application of strategies and for constraints in a culturally de-fined type of language production. In examining text, genre analysis aims to explicate purposes achieved through strategic choices of moves, and how the moves themselves are built up by strategic lexico-grammatical choices. A poten-tial pitfall in carrying out genre analysis is that discourse communities may be assumed to exist where they have not been demonstrated to exist, thereby imputing norms in recipe fashion to various communities to which they might not apply. It has nonetheless provided a productive starting point for research.

An important line of genre analysis research for business was inspired by V. Bhatia's 1993 monograph detailing promotional (sales) letters. Several works on promotional letters (Van Nus, 1999), request letters (Yli-Jokipii, 1994, 1998), faxes (Akar and Louhiala-Salminen, 1999), and eventually email (Gimenez, 2000; Mulholland, 1999; Nickerson, 1999a) emerged. More complex and embedded genres, such as bids (Barbara and Scott, 1999), letters of negotiation (dos Santos, 2002), and bureaucratic technical documents (Pogner, 1999) have also been described.

As business correspondence is transactional and interpersonal, and as many of its rhetorical moves correspond to speech acts (apologies, requests, etc.), analyses such as those of Nickerson (1999b, 2000) and Yli-Jokipii (1994, 1998) also draw on politeness theory (Brown and Levinson, 1987) as an added textual-analysis tool. They analyze, for example, how social distance and relative imposition affect the variety and combination of politeness strategies (mitigators, "off record expressions," etc.) in letters.

In a cross-cultural comparison of American, British, and Finnish letters of request, Yli-Jokipii (1994, 1998) outlines how the distinct grammatical resources of Finnish and English work differently in terms of face maintenance. Yli-Jokipii also observes that there generally appears to be a smaller amount of register variation in Finnish request letters when compared to those in English (and also in British when compared to American).

These analyses point to the essential work of examining and integrating the layers of language from lexico-grammatical resources to discourse strategies, in order to achieve a balanced interpretation of something so relatively simple as a business letter. Y. Kachru (1992: 239) also provides a reminder that speech act theories and politeness sometimes fall short of accounting for verbal interaction, and ethnography of communication may at times be needed for a complete picture. Business letters, while not poetry, are fundamentally creative, and their interpretation cannot necessarily be taken for granted if resources and strategies are not shared.

The recognition of specific cultural patterning of lexico-grammatical and discourse resources has long been noted in a world Englishes framework. For example, the resources of English may be patterned with South Asian politeness strategies to achieve a "high prose" style of letter writing that contrasts significantly with Inner-Circle letters. In terms of the intercultural impact, Y. Kachru (1996: 190) notes that "adverse reactions to [the South Asian 'high' prose style] are well documented" and remarks that reactions to US/UK letters within South Asia may be similarly adverse.

It is a further research question to what extent and in what domains the high prose style continues to operate in South Asia. It is perhaps unlikely that it is used to create professional identity in memos and email messages in an IT or marketing firm. An empirically based update on business writing in South Asia might be revealing of the evolution of English and of the linguistic exponents of a South Asian "professional identity" as put forth in writing. V. Bhatia's (1996) description of the nativization of job applications and Hartford and Mahboob's (2004) description of letters of complaint in South Asia are two such investigations in that direction.

Works of genre analysis, cross-culturally, cross-linguistically and in specific varieties of English, have begun to spell out important textual and contextual dimensions in business writing. V. Bhatia (1997) draws attention to the creative power of genres, in the ability to flout the conventions and mix generic features, and to the politics of genres' inclusive and exclusive functions. Genre analysis may be used as an interpretive tool for understanding variation (as in

V. Bhatia, 2004, and Chapter 22 in this volume, with respect to film reviews), including variation across varieties of Englishes.

5   Talking Business: Meeting and Negotiating

Meetings and negotiations are two types of spoken language vital to commerce: meetings are central to meaning-making and relationship-maintenance, and negotiations are vital in producing change that may mean growth and profit.

5.1   *Meetings*

Bargiela-Chiappini and Harris (1997a: 7) assert that "meetings are the essence of many if not most organizations; in fact, one could argue that they *are the organizations themselves*" (emphasis original). Meetings as a form of social encounter have sometimes been of interest to conversation and discourse analysts (e.g., Cuff and Sharrock, 1985) and are a prime location for the investigation of an internal "corporate culture" and of how national cultures and Englishes play into the construction of that corporate culture.

Bargiela-Chiappini and Harris (1997a) detail the organization and social structures which emerge in a series of Italian and British business meetings in a British-Italian venture, and compare them cross-culturally. They found that the two groups were much more similar than different, although thematic progression and topic management seemed to be slightly more distributed in the British meetings than in the Italian meetings. They discuss other cross-cultural (and, through interview data, intercultural) observations more informally.

Yamada (1992, 1996, 1997) analyzes the distribution of topic and turns in Japanese meetings and compares them with meetings in US settings. Among Yamada's cross-cultural findings are that: turns are more evenly distributed in number in Japanese meetings; American meetings are more agenda-driven; Japanese meetings have an initial sounding-out phase which is lacking in American meetings.

5.2   *Negotiation*

Within business contexts, "negotiation" may have a variety of meanings, from simply trying to get a desired something to settling on terms to make a deal. For an attempted definition of negotiation in discourse, see Wagner (1995). A school of European researchers has been generating research on negotiation for over a decade. Charles (Charles, 1996; Lampi, 1986),[1] presents a two-tiered model of business negotiation based on her research in the UK, analyzing how different discourse strategies are used at different phases of negotiation. Stalper (1992) analyzes cross-cultural business phone negotiations, finding that business calls are more "matter of fact" than ordinary calls, in that repairs may not be carried out and that important topics may be resumed out of sequence without the normally requisite facework. Firth (1990, 1995a, 1995b, 1996) similarly analyzed intercultural business negotiations on the telephone and corroborated Stalper's finding that repair sequences were often abandoned in the endeavor to get the work done. In 1995, two anthologies, Firth (1995c) and Ehlich and Wagner (1995), appeared, presenting a variety of additional work on negotiation in the European context.

Much of the work on negotiation takes on the advantages and the constraints of ethnomethodology and a conversation analysis methodology (see Markee, 2000 for overview). Ethnomethodology and conversation analysis aim to uncover organizing social categories in talk through scrutiny of the sequential organization. Practitioners of conversation analysis are strict in refusing to assign interpretation to talk other than that warranted by the sequential organization of turns.

These tools were brought from the realm of the study of everyday conversation to institutional discourses in law and medicine in the 1980s and early 1990s, and eventually to business and administrative realms. (See Geluykens and Pelsmaekers, 1999, for a substantial bibliography of earlier work in professional discourses of a variety of types; for earlier references and typology, see Couture, 1992.)

While a strict conversation analysis perspective has not yet been applied to negotiation encounters outside the European school or within a world Englishes framework, more broadly defined discourse analyses have been applied to world Englishes data, often focusing on code switching, code mixing, and style/lectal shifting in fictional (e.g., Y. Kachru, 1989; Lee, 2004; Osakwe, 1999; Pandey, 1995; Tawake, 2003; Vaid, 1980; Zhang, 2003) and natural data (see Banu and Sussex, 2001; Bolton, 2002; Bwenge, 2003; Dako, 2002; Jung and Min, 1999; Kang, 2003; Kouega, 2003; Ngom, 2002). So far, this work has not been extended to analysis of cultural discourses of business (with the notable exception of Nair-Venugopal, 2000a).

6 World Englishes, Commerce, and Standards

In the business realm, as elsewhere, the tension between cravings for a single standard exist alongside recognition of variety in language form and function. Bolton (2004), Brutt-Griffler (2002), and others have identified "centripetal and centrifugal" forces at play in English and the tension between more apparently static concepts such as "World English" and more apparently dynamic ones such as "world Englishes." In business practices, English use is increasing intranationally and internationally, and both forces of control and creativity are at work. The Englishes of business are of necessity global, local, and "glocal" (see Chapter 33, this volume, for a fleshing out of these terms).

In times of rapid technological and social change, cravings for a global standard are often voiced. Business texts and manuals are usually available to feed and fuel this desire. Multinational firms also put some store in a general standard for employees in business English skills by accepting or requiring documentation such as the Cambridge Business English Certificate (BEC). The BEC is offered in various locations worldwide, at British Council offices and elsewhere. BEC criteria below are excerpted from http://www.britishcouncil.org/india/india-exams/india-exams-3/india-exams-english-test-listings/india-exams-bec.htm.

BEC Preliminary
Prepares candidates to interact effectively while carrying out routine business transactions, for e.g. speaking to clients over the telephone, writing brief letters, making appointments.

BEC Vantage
Assesses how candidates can conduct and take part in meetings and teleconferences using skills of negotiation to put across a point of view. Ability to draft letters, memos, minutes of meetings and topics for presentation using appropriate business vocabulary and format.

BEC Higher
Assesses proficiency in the use of English for making presentations, negotiating effectively in the promotion of products and services, and in engaging in extended conversations with clients at meetings and seminars.

On the one hand, these BEC benchmarks are general enough to allow for varieties of English. On the other hand, some of the elements of even the Preliminary certificate (such as "speaking to clients over the telephone") show potential for variation in politeness strategies within and across varieties. It is thus an open question whether the BEC has adopted a mono-model in order to evaluate, or whether it can still fill the need of business people for credentials while working within a polymodel of English.

Voices for centripetal forces of English, both descriptive and standard-imposing, have been emerging from Europe in the last decade. Firth (1990, 1996) describes a de facto, functioning "lingua franca" English in Europe, which accomplishes linguistic interaction without some of the complete set of conversational inferencing strategies found in established varieties. Firth (1990) goes on to wonder whether there can exist such a thing as a pan-cultural international negotiator. Seidlhofer (2001) also calls for a description of English as a lingua franca.

Brutt-Griffler (2002) goes a step further, to posit a model where mother-tongue varieties and macro-acquisitional varieties (i.e., Outer- and Expanding-Circle varieties) begin to converge: World English. Brutt-Griffler does not claim that a World English has arrived, only that it might arrive, a "domain in which national distinctions dissolve" (2002: 181). This is a qualitatively different assertion from the question of pan-national strategies for managing complexity and ambiguity in overlapping but not necessarily convergent systems. For the time being, there is no solid empirical evidence that a convergent standard, alongside multiple varieties, is on its way soon.

Some global executives would like to see one global norm for the ease of promotion and distribution of products. Sless (1999) examines the mass production of "personalized" letters. Global businesses would also be happy to be able to apply customer service telephone scripts worldwide, although Shaw et al. (2004) show the reactions to telephone scripts vary to some degree cross-culturally.

Some of the strongest voices in favor of standards come from technical disciplines and international organizations who operate under the assumption that a simpler language is a clearer language. Among industries who have standards for simplified language are maritime and aviation industries, which are concerned about potentially fatal consequences of miscommunication. A few studies representing these have appeared in *World Englishes*: Johnson (1999) and Sampson and Zhao (2003) on maritime communication, and Tajima (2004) on aviation.

In the 1980s, the European aerospace industry developed Simplified English, loosely based on notions developed by semanticists I. A. Richards and C. K. Ogden's Basic English (Ogden and Richards, 1923; Richards, 1943; Ogden, 1930, 1931), with limited vocabulary and grammar and the enforcement of monosemy of words. Simplified English, along with data-mining procedures to add lexical sets, has been used to generate basic manuals and instructions of various kinds. Varieties of simplified English have been proposed by those who would promote a universal brand of English, including Quirk's (1981) nuclear English with emphasis on simplified syntax.

Alongside these proponents of universals have been scholars who recognize and legitimate variation in language. A general response to these notions of universals appears in B. Kachru (1987, 1991, 2005). In contrast to the idea of a simplified word semantics, studies of varieties of English present patterns of lexical shift and innovation. Melchers and Shaw (2003) outline lexical variation in world Englishes and present tautonyms (same name, different meaning in different varieties) and heteronyms (different names in different varieties for one denotation). English in commerce, as in other domains, provides a context for examining the spread and evolution of English.

While the commercial desire for standards is great, the concurrent needs of serving and selling to consumers are another important force, in some ways centripetal and in some ways centrifugal. In global, regional, and local advertising and marketing, enormous amounts of money and time are invested in order to get the right message to reach customers through the creative (and manipulative) use of images, sound, and language, often with concurrent elements global and some highly particularized (see Chapter 33, this volume; Martin, 2002).

Alongside the need to maintain a consistent technical vocabulary and advertise, businesses also want to maintain a positive relationship with clients and customers and will consider adapting their service, and sometimes language, to meet clients' needs. Linguistically, this may come in the form of symbolic accommodation. For example, the aerospace industry (particularly in Europe) uses a bureaucratic "incapacitated passenger" designation, borrowed from an old, legalistic maritime term. This designation is used on a form for passengers with medical needs, both to accommodate them and to evaluate whether they will be permitted to fly. However, in customer-oriented documents, customers are told to contact the airline about "special needs" or "additional needs" or requiring "special assistance." These terms exist alongside the more general "disability" and "disabled." No one is called "incapacitated" outright in, e.g., the USA.

A "toy" register analysis of 20 airlines websites, visited September 2004, showed an interesting distribution of these lexical items. A majority of airlines did tailor their homepages to customers by the use of "special needs," "additional needs," or "special assistance." Among these airlines were United Airlines (US), British Airways, Qantas (Australia), Swiss International Air, Singapore Airlines, Korean Airlines, and Thai Airways, and, with variations, Air Canada used "special services" and "service for people with disabilities."

Air India had both a section for "special needs" and a statement about "incapacitated passengers" in the baggage allowance (wheelchair) section. Air France used "disabled travelers." KLM (Netherlands) used "physically challenged passengers" and "disabled passengers." Northwest (USA) used "customers with disabilities." Other airlines did not use "needs" at all and exclusively referred directly to "incapacitated passengers." These included Malaysia Air, Air Philippines, Air Garuda (Indonesia), Tarom (Rumania), and Turkish Airlines.

In a highly coordinated endeavor such as the airline industry, competing needs have spawned parallel terms. From a mere "toy" analysis, these terms appear to have spread in different patterns to various organizations. Factors in varying diffusion could be multiple. Perhaps "incapacitated" was not viewed as face-threatening in some places as it was in others. Perhaps, and quite likely, some places relied on computer-assisted generation (such as with Simplified English) of their websites that uniformly insisted on the European technical term. And perhaps some airlines have not perceived a need to communicate the customer service function in English or have not appropriated the English customer service jargon, whether intentionally or not.

Commercial activity, even at its most coordinated, seems as likely to generate a plurality of terms along with its plurality of purposes, in this case technical versus customer service terms, as to encourage convergence. Companies at the same time show a great similarity in their customer service language. As regards expanding varieties of English, it is not clear in which ways industrial and commercial networks will or will not create shared norms.

Terminological differences and shifting purposes are expected in a world where things and concepts are constantly being created. Perhaps newer to the scene is that terminological banks, databases, templates, and simple algorithms may be used to generate documents for public consumption on the internet.

While these documents do not exhibit ordinary linguistic creativity, their auto-mated output might be accidentally exploited for human creative purposes. In the lexicon of world Englishes, an analysis of registers and genres of use in commercial activity may contribute to a broader understanding of shifting paradigms of meanings in word sets.

7 Ethics and Teaching for "Specific" Purposes

A polycentric model for English has not only theoretical but also ethical impli-cations for language teaching and training. Early English for Specific Purposes (ESP) materials in the 1970s and 1980s commonly emphasized vocabulary development and correctness of expression in "English for banking," "English for engineers," "English for aviation," and so on. B. Kachru (1986a, 2005) challenged the validity of teaching a mono-model of ESP, asserting that it was based on a faulty understanding of linguistic needs and was therefore an inappropriate and overly prescriptive pedagogy.

By the 1990s, however, the methodological tide turned toward task-based language learning and apprenticeship models of language education for spe-cific purposes. Practitioners of ESP have acknowledged the risk of teaching language skills which do not match real-word requirements and have begun to encourage instructors to do ethnographic projects and organize courses that would engage learners in tasks which begin their socialization into pro-fessional practices (e.g., Boswood and Marriott, 1994). Proponents of genre analysis in the teaching of reading and writing also present alternatives to mono-model thinking and encourage learners to "destabilize" their notions of genre (Johns, 2002). Other ESP practitioners have dedicated their careers to advocating that English language teacher training involve exposure to polymodels of English (Baumgardner and Brown, 2003).

8 Conclusion

As the depth and range of English expands in various commercial contexts around the world, it is likely that the hunger for prescriptive mono-norms will continue to re-surface and that the temptation will arise to ignore and obscure the richness and variety of language practices in use. As the power and pol-itics of English (Kachru, 1986b) play out in the commercial sphere, there will surely be prescription-texts which cater to the desire for norms, and at the same time there will also be teachers and trainers who promote creativity and awareness of varied contexts and discourses. The educational endeavor can only benefit from continued research on varieties of professional discourse and cultural ways of speaking and writing.

See also Chapters 22, GENRES AND STYLES IN WORLD ENGLISHES; 32, WORLD ENGLISHES AND THE MEDIA; 33, WORLD ENGLISHES AND GLOBAL ADVERTISING.

NOTE

1   Lampi and Charles are one and the same.

REFERENCES

Akar, Didar and Louhiala-Salminen, Leena (1999) Towards a new genre: A comparative study of business faxes. In *Writing Business: Genres, Media and Discourses*. Edited by Francesca Bargiela-Chiappini and Catherine Nickerson. Essex: Longman, pp. 207–26.

Alabi, Victoria A. (2000) Semantics of occupational lexis in Nigerian English. *World Englishes*, **19**(1), 107–12.

Al-Khatib, Mahmoud (2001) The pragmatics of letter-writing. *World Englishes*, **20**(2), 179–200.

Alm, Cecilia Ovesdotter (2003). English in the Ecuadorian commercial context. *World Englishes*, **22**(2), 143–58.

Bakhtin, Mikhail M. (1986) *Speech Genres and Other Late Essays*. Austin: University of Texas Press.

Banu, Rahela and Sussex, Roland (2001) Code-switching in Bangladesh. *English Today*, **17**(2), 51–61.

Barbara, Leila, Celiani, M., Antonieta A., Collins, Heloisa, and Scott, Mike (1996) A survey of communication patterns in the Brazilian business context. *English for Specific Purposes*, **15**(1), 57–71.

Barbara, Leila and Scott, Mike (1999) Homing in on a genre: Invitations for bids. In *Writing Business: Genres, Media and Discourses*. Edited by Francesca Bargiela-Chiappini and Catherine Nickerson. Essex: Longman, pp. 227–54.

Bargiela-Chiappini, Francesca (1999) Meaning creating and genre across cultures: Human resource management magazines in Britain and Italy. In *Writing Business: Genres, Media and Discourses*. Edited by Francesca Bargiela-Chiappini and Catherine Nickerson. Essex: Longman, pp. 129–52.

Bargiela-Chiappini, Francesca and Harris, Sandra J. (1997a) *Managing Language: The Discourse of Corporate Meetings*. Amsterdam: John Benjamins.

Bargiela-Chiappini, Francesa and Harris Sandra (eds.) (1997b) *The Languages of Business: An International Perspective*. Edinburgh: Edinburgh University Press.

Bargiela-Chiappini, Francesca and Nickerson, Catherine (eds.) (1999) *Writing Business: Genres, Media and Discourses*. Essex: Longman.

Baumgardner, Robert J. and Brown, Kimberley (2003) World Englishes: Ethics and pedagogy. *World Englishes*, **22**(3), 245–51.

Bhatia, Tej K. (2000) *Advertising in Rural India: Language, Marketing, Communication and Consumerism*. Tokyo: Tokyo Press.

Bhatia, Vijay K. (1993) *Analysing Genre: Language Use in Professional Settings*. London: Longman.

Bhatia, Vijay K. (1996) Nativization of job applications in South Asia. In *South Asian English: Structure, Use and Users*. Edited by Robert J. Baumgardner. Urbana: University of Illinois Press, pp. 158–73.

Bhatia, Vijay K. (1997) The power and politics of genre. *World Englishes*, **16**(3), 359–71.

Bhatia, Vijay K. (2004) *Worlds of Written Discourse*. London: Continuum.

Bilbow, Grahame T. (1997) Spoken discourse in the multicultural workplace in Hong Kong: Applying a model of discourse as "impression management." In *The Languages of Business: An International Perspective.* Edited by Francesca Bargiela-Chiappini and Sandra Harris. Edinburgh: Edinburgh University Press, pp. 21–48.

Blum-Kulka, Shoshana, House, Juliana, and Kasper, Gabriela (1989) Investigating cross-cultural pragmatics: An introductory overview. In *Cross-Cultural Pragmatics: Requests and Apologies.* Edited by Shoshana Blum-Kulka, Juliane House, and Gabriele Kasper. Norwood: Ablex, pp. 1–34.

Bolton, Kingsley (2002) *Hong Kong English: Autonomy and Creativity.* Hong Kong: Hong Kong University Press.

Bolton, Kingsley (2004) World Englishes. In *The Handbook of Applied Linguistics.* Edited by Alan Davies and Catherine Elder, Malden, MA: Blackwell, pp. 367–96.

Boswood, Tim and Marriott, Alison (1994) Ethnography for specific purposes: Teaching and training in parallel. *English for Specific Purposes*, **13**(1), 3–21.

Brown, Penelope and Levinson, Stephen C. (1987) *Politeness: Some Universals in Language Usage.* Cambridge: Cambridge University Press.

Brown, T. Pascal and Lewis, Marilyn (2003) An ESP project: Analysis of an authentic workplace conversation. *English for Specific Purposes*, **22**(1), 93–8.

Brutt-Griffler, Janina (2002) *World English, A Study of its Development.* Clevedon, UK: Multilingual Matters.

Bwenge, Charles Muttabazi (2003) Codeswitching in Political Discourse in Tanzania: A case study of parliamentary proceedings. PhD dissertation, University of Virginia.

Campbell, Charles P. (1998) Rhetorical ethos: A bridge between high context and low context cultures? In *The Cultural Context in Business Communication.* Edited by Susanne Niemeier, Charles P. Campbell, and René Dirven. Amsterdam: John Benjamins, pp. 31–47.

Charles, Mirjaliisa (1996) Business negotiations: Interdependence between business discourse and business relationships. *English for Specific Purposes*, **15**(1), 19–36.

Chew, Phyllis Ghim-Lian (1997) Generic power at the gate. *World Englishes*, **16**(3), 395–405.

Clark, Colin and Pinch, Trevor (1994) The interactional study of exchange relationships: An analysis of patter merchants at work on street markets. In *Higgling: Transactors and their Markets in the History of Economics. Annual Supplement to vol. 26 History of Political Economy.* Edited by Neil De Marchi and Mary S. Morgan. Durham, NC: Duke University Press, pp. 370–400.

Clyne, Michael (1994) *Inter-Cultural Communication at Work.* Cambridge: Cambridge University Press.

Connor, Ulla (1988) A contrastive study of persuasive business correspondence: American and Japanese. In *Global Implications for Business Communications: Theory, Technology and Practice. Proceedings of the 53rd National and 15th International Convention of the Association for Business Communication.* Edited by Sam J. Bruno. Houston: School of Business and Public Administration, University of Houston-Clear Lake, pp. 57–72.

Couture, Barbara (1992) Categorizing professional discourse: Engineering, administrative and technical/professional writing. *Journal of Business and Technical Communication*, 6(7), 5–37.

Cuff, E. C. and Sharrock, Wes W. (1985) Meetings. In *The Handbook of Discourse Analysis, vol. 3: Discourse and Dialogue*. Edited by Teun van Dijk. London: Academic Press, pp. 149–59.

Dako, Kari (2002) Code-switching and lexical borrowing: Which is what in Ghanian English? *English Today*, 18(3), 4–54.

Dehrab, Badrieh Ahmeed (2002) A Study of Code-Switching in Four English for Specific Purposes Classrooms at the College of Business Studies in Kuwait. PhD dissertation, The Ohio State University.

Ehlich, Konrad and Wagner, Johannes (eds.) (1995) *The Discourse of Business Negotiation*. Berlin: Mouton de Gruyter.

Firth, Alan (1990) "Lingua franca" negotiations: Towards an interactional approach. *World Englishes*, 9(3), 269–80.

Firth, Alan (1991) Discourse at Work: Negotiating by telex, fax and phone. PhD dissertation. Aalborg University.

Firth, Alan (1995a) Talking for a change: Commodity negotiating by telephone. In *The Discourse of Negotiation: Studies of Language in the Workplace*. Edited by Alan Firth. Oxford: Pergamon, pp. 183–222.

Firth, Alan (1995b) Telenegotiation and sense-making in the "virtual market-place." In *The Discourse of Business Negotiation*. Edited by Konrad Ehlich and Johannes Wagner. Berlin: Mouton de Gruyter, pp. 127–49.

Firth, Alan (ed.) (1995c) *The Discourse of Negotiation: Studies of Language in the Workplace*. Oxford: Pergamon.

Firth, Alan (1996) The discursive accomplishment of normality: on "lingua franca" English and conversation analysis. *Journal of Pragmatics*, 26, 237–59.

Friedrich, Patricia (2002) English in advertising and brand naming: Sociolinguistic considerations and the case of Brazil. *English Today*, 18(3), 21–8.

Friedrich, Patricia (2003) English in Argentina: Attitudes of MBA students. *World Englishes*, 22(2), 173–84.

Garcez, Pedro de Moraes (1993) Point-making styles in cross-cultural business negotiation: A microethnographic study. *English for Specific Purposes*, 12, 103–20.

Gavioli, Laura (1997) Bookshop service encounters in English and Italian: Notes on the achievement of information and advice. In *The Languages of Business: An International Perspective*. Edited by Francesca Bargiela-Chiappini and Sandra Harris. Edinburgh: Edinburgh University Press, pp. 136–58.

Geluykens, Ronald and Pelsmaekers, Katja (1999) Bibliography of professional discourse, 1987–1999. In *Discourse in Professional Contexts*. Edited by Ronald Geluykens and Katja Pelsmaekers. Muenchen: Lincom Europa, pp. 23–78.

Gill, Saran Kaur (1999) Standards and emerging linguistic realities in the Malaysian workplace. *World Englishes*, 18(2), 215–31.

Gimenez, Julio C. (2000) Business e-mail communication: Some emerging tendencies in register. *English for Specific Purposes*, 19, 237–51.

Grundy, Peter (1998) Parallel texts and diverging cultures in Hong Kong: Implications for intercultural communication. In *The Cultural Context in Business Communication*.

Edited by Susanne Niemeier, Charles P. Campbell, and René Dirven. Amsterdam: John Benjamins, pp. 167–83.

Gumperz, John J. (1992) Interviewing in intercultural situations. In *Talk at Work: Interaction in Institutional Settings*. Edited by Paul Drew and John Heritage. Cambridge: Cambridge University Press, pp. 302–27.

Hampden-Turner, Charles and Trompenaars, Alfons (1993) *The Seven Cultures of Capitalism: Value Systems for Creating Wealth in the United States, Japan, Germany, France, Sweden and the Netherlands*. New York: Doubleday.

Hampden-Turner, Charles and Trompenaars, Alfons (2000) *Building Cross-Cultural Competence: How to Create Wealth from Conflicting Values*. New Haven: Yale University Press.

Hartford, Beverly and Mahboob, Ahmar (2004) Models of discourse in the letter of complaint. *World Englishes*, **23**(4), 585–600.

Hill, Pat and Van Zyl, Susan (2002) English and multilingualism in the South African workplace. *World Englishes*, **21**(1), 23–35.

Hofstede, Geert H. (1980) *Culture's Consequences: International Differences in Work-Related Values*. Beverly Hills: Sage.

Hofstede, Geert H. (2001) *Culture's Consequences: Comparing Values, Institutions and Organizations across Nations*. Thousand Oaks, CA: Sage.

Holmes, Janet, Stubbe, Maria, and Vine, Bernadette (1999) Constructing professional identity: "Doing power" in policy units. In *Talk, Work and Institutional Order: Discourse in Medical, Mediation and Management Settings*. Edited by Srikant Sarangi and Celia Roberts. Berlin: Mouton de Gruyter, pp. 351–85.

Johns, Ann M. (2002) Destabilizing and enriching students' genre theories. In *Genre in the Classroom: Multiple Perspectives*. Edited by Ann M. Johns. Mahwah, NJ: Lawrence Erlbaum, pp. 237–46.

Johnson, Barry (1999) English in the Global Maritime Distress and Safety System. *World Englishes*, **18**(2), 145–57.

Jones, Kimberly (1995) Masked negotiation in a Japanese work setting. In *The Discourse of Negotiation: Studies of Language in the Workplace*. Edited by Alan Firth. Oxford: Pergamon, pp. 141–58.

Jung, Kyutae and Min, Su Jung (1999) Some lexico-grammatical features of Korean English newspapers. *World Englishes*, **18**(1), 23–37.

Kachru, Braj B. (1981) "Socially realistic linguistics": The Firthian tradition. *International Journal of the Society of Languages*, **31**, 65–89.

Kachru, Braj B. (1986a) ESP and non-native varieties of English: Toward a paradigm shift. *Studies in the Linguistic Sciences*, **16**(1), 13–34.

Kachru, Braj B. (1986b) The power and politics of English. *World Englishes*, **5**(2/3), 121–40.

Kachru, Braj B. (1986/1990) *The Alchemy of English: The Spread, Functions and Models of Non-Native Englishes*. Urbana: University of Illinois Press.

Kachru, Braj B. (1987) The spread of English and sacred linguistic cows. In *GURT '87: Language Spread and Language Policy: Issues, Implications and Case Studies. Proceedings of the Georgetown University Round Table on Languages and Linguistics*. Edited by Peter Lowenberg. Washington, DC: Georgetown University Press, pp. 207–28.

Kachru, Braj B. (1990) World Englishes and applied linguistics. *World Englishes*, **9**(1), 3–20.

Kachru, Braj B. (1991) Liberation linguistics and the Quirk concern. *English Today*, **7**(1), 3–13.

Kachru, Braj B. (1992a) World Englishes: Approaches, issues and resources. *Language Teaching*, **25**(1), 1–14.

Kachru, Braj B. (1992b) Models for non-native Englishes. In *The Other Tongue: English across Cultures*. Edited by Braj B. Kachru. 2nd edition. Urbana: University of Illinois Press, pp. 48–74.

Kachru, Braj B. (2005) *Asian Englishes: Beyound the Canon*. Hong Kong: Hong Kong University Press.

Kachru, Yamuna (1989) Code-mixing, style repertoire and language variation: English in Hindi poetic creativity. *World Englishes*, **8**(3), 311–19.

Kachru, Yamuna (1992) Speech acts in the other tongue: An integrated approach to cross-cultural research. *World Englishes*, **11**(2/3), 235–40.

Kachru, Yamuna (1996) Culture, variation, and languages of wider communication: The paradigm gap. *Georgetown University Round Table on Languages and Linguistics 1996*. Washington, DC: Georgetown University Press, pp. 178–95.

Kachru, Yamuna (1997) Cultural meaning and contrastive rhetoric in English education. *World Englishes*, **16**(3), 337–50.

Kachru, Yamuna and Nelson, Cecil (2006) *World Englishes in Asian Contexts*. Hong Kong: Hong Kong University Press.

Kang, M. Agnes (2003) Negotiating conflict within the constraints of social hierarchies in Korean American discourse. *Journal of Sociolinguistics*, **7**(3), 299–320.

Kasper, Gabriela (2001) Four perspectives on L2 pragmatic development. *Applied Linguistics*, **22**(4), 502–30.

Khuwaileh, Abdullah A. (2003) Code switching and multilingualism in a small multi-ethnic group society (UAE). *The Journal of Language for International Business*, **14**(2), 32–49.

Kouega, Jean-Paul (2003) Camfranglais: A novel slang in Cameroon schools. *English Today*, **19**(2), 23–9.

Lampi, Mirjaliisa (1986) *Linguistic Components of Strategy in Business Negotiations*. Helsinki: Helsingin Kauppakorkeakoulun Kuvalaitos.

Lee, Jamie Shinhee (2004) Linguistic hybridization in K-pop: Discourse of self-assertion and resistance. *World Englishes*, **23**(3), 429–50.

Louhiala-Salminen, Leena (1996) The business communication classroom vs. reality: What should we teach today? *English for Specific Purposes*, **15**(1), 37–51.

Louhiala-Salminen, Leena (2002) The fly's perspective: Discourse in the daily routine of a business manager. *English for Specific Purposes*, **21**(3), 211–31.

Malinowski, Bronislaw (1922) *Argonauts of the Western Pacific*. London: Routledge.

Markee, Numa (2000) *Conversation Analysis*. Mahwah, NJ: Lawrence Erlbaum.

Marriott, Helen E. (1995) "Deviations" in an intercultural business negotiation. In *The Discourse of Negotiation: Studies of Language in the Workplace*. Edited by Alan Firth. Oxford: Pergamon, pp. 247–68.

Marriott, Helen (1997) Australian-Japanese business interaction: Some features of language and cultural context. In *The Languages of Business: An International Perspective*. Edited by Francesca Bargiela-Chiappini and Sandra Harris. Edinburgh: Edinburgh University Press, pp. 49–71.

Martin, Elizabeth (2002) Mixing English in French advertising. *World Englishes*, **21**(3), 375–401.

Melchers, Gunnel and Shaw, Philip (2003) *World Englishes: An Introduction*. London: Arnold.

Morrow, Phillip R. (1995) English in a Japanese company: The case of Toshiba. *World Englishes*, **14**(1), 87–98.

Mulholland, Joan (1997) The Asian connection: Business requests and acknowledgments. In *The Languages of Business: An International Perspective*. Edited by Francesca Bargiela-Chiappini and Sandra Harris. Edinburgh: Edinburgh University Press, pp 94–114.

Mulholland, Joan (1999) E-mail: Uses, issues and problems in an institutional setting. In *Writing Business: Genres, Media and Discourses*. Edited by Francesca Bargiela-Chiappini and Catherine Nickerson. Essex: Longman, pp. 57–84.

Nair-Venugopal, Shanta (2000a) *Language Choice and Communication in Malaysian Business*. Bangi: Penerbit Universiti Kebangsaan Malaysia.

Nair-Venugopal, Shanta (2000b) English, identity and the Malaysian workplace. *World Englishes*, **19**(2), 205–13.

Nair-Venugopal, Shanta (2003) Malaysian English, normativity and workplace English. *World Englishes*, **22**(1), 15–29.

Ngom, Fallou (2002) Sociolinguistic variables in the Senegalese satirical newspaper *Le Cafard Libéré*. *The French Review*, **75**(5), 914–24.

Nickerson, Catherine (1999a) The use of English in electronic mail in a multinational corporation. In *Writing Business: Genres, Media and Discourses*. Edited by Francesca Bargiela-Chiappini and Catherine Nickerson. Essex: Longman, pp. 35–56.

Nickerson, Catherine (1999b) The use of politeness strategies in business letters written by native speakers of English. In *Discourse in Professional Contexts*. Edited by Ronald Geluykens and Katja Pelsmaekers. Muenchen: Lincom Europa, pp. 127–42.

Nickerson, Catherine (2000) *Playing the Corporate Language Game: An Investigation of the Genres and Discourse Strategies Used by Dutch Writers Working in Multinational Corporations*. Amsterdam: Rodopi.

Niemeier, Susanne, Campbell, Charles P., and Dirven, René (eds.) (1998) *The Cultural Context in Business Communication*. Amsterdam: John Benjamins.

Nkemleke, Daniel (2004) Job applications and students' complaint letters in Cameroon. *World Englishes*, **23**(4), pp. 601–11.

Ogden, Charles Kay (1930) *Basic English: A General Introduction with Rules and Grammar*, London: Paul Treber and Co.

Ogden, Charles Kay (1931) *Debabelization: With a Survey of Contemporary Opinion on the Problem of a Universal Language*. London: K. Paul, Trench, Trubner and Co.

Ogden, Charles K. and Richards, Ivor A. (1923) *The Meaning of Meaning: A Study of the Influence of Language upon Thought and of the Science of Symbolism*. London: K. Paul, Trench, Trubner and Co.

Osakwe, Mabel I. (1999) Wole Soyinka's poetry as bilingual's creativity. *World Englishes*, **18**(1), 63–77.

Pandey, Anita (1995) The pragmatics of code alternation in Nigerian English. *Studies in the Linguistic Sciences*, **25**(1), 75–115.

Pang, Jixian, Xhou, Xing, and Fu, Zheng (2002) English for international trade: China enters the WTO. *World Englishes*, **21**(2), 210–16.

Park, Mi Young, Dillion, W. Tracy, and Mitchell, Kenneth L. (1998) Korean business letters: Strategies for effective complaints in cross-cultural communication. *The Journal of Business Communication*, **35**(3), 328–45.

Pérez de Souza e Silva, Maria Cecilia (1994) The analysis of verbal interaction: A meeting. In *Reflections on Language Learning*. Edited by Leila Barbara and Mike Scott. Clevedon, UK: Multilingual Matters, pp. 195–203.

Pogner, Karl-Heinz (1999) Discourse community, culture and interaction: On writing by consulting engineers. In *Writing Business: Genres, Media and Discourses*. Edited by Francesca Bargiela-Chiappini and Catherine Nickerson. Essex: Longman, pp. 101–27.

Quirk, Randolf (1981) International communication and the concept of nuclear English. In *English for Cross-Cultural Communication*. Edited by Larry E. Smith. Hong Kong: Macmillan, pp. 151–65.

Richards, Ivor A. (1943) *Basic English and its Uses*. New York: W. W. Norton and Company.

Romaine, Suzanne (1997) Pidgin English advertising. In *Sociolinguistics: A Reader*. Edited by Nikolas Coupland and Adam Jaworski. New York: St Martin's Press, pp. 353–60.

Sampson, Helen and Zhao, Minghua (2003) Multilingual crews: Communication and the operation of ships. *World Englishes*, **22**(1), 31–43.

Santos, V. B. M. Pinto dos (2002) Genre analysis of business letters of negotiation. *English for Specific Purposes*, **21**, 167–99.

Scollon, Ron and Scollon, Suzanne Wong (2001) *Intercultural Communication*. 2nd edition. Oxford: Blackwell.

Seidlhofer, Barbara (2001) Closing the conceptual gap: The case for a description of English as a lingua franca. *International Journal of Applied Linguistics*, **11**(2), 133–58.

Shaw, Philip, Gillaerts, Paul, Jacobs, Everett, Palermo, Ofelia, Shinohara, Midori, and Verckens, J. Piet (2004) Genres across cultures: Types of acceptability variation. *World Englishes*, **23**(3), 385–401.

Sless, David (1999) The mass production of unique letters. In *Writing Business: Genres, Media and Discourses*. Edited by Francesca Bargiela-Chiappini and Catherine Nickerson. Essex: Longman, pp. 85–98.

Stalper, Judith (1992) Between matter-of-factness and politeness. In *Politeness in Language: Studies in its History, Theory and Practice*. Edited by Richard J. Watts, Schiko Ide, and Konrad Ehlich. Berlin: Mouton de Greyter, pp. 219–30.

Stanlaw, James (2004) *Japanese English: Language and Culture Contact*. Hong Kong: Hong Kong University Press.

Swales, John M. (1981) *Aspects of Article Introductions*. Aston ESP Research Report, 1. Birmingham, UK: University of Aston in Birmingham.

Swales, John M. (1986) A genre-based approach to language across the curriculum. In *Language across the Curriculum*. Edited by Makhan L. Tickoo. Singapore: SEAMEO Regional Language Centre, pp. 10–22.

Swales, John M. (1990) *Genre Analysis: English in Academic and Research Settings*. Cambridge: Cambridge University Press.

Tajima, Atsushi (2004) Fatal miscommunication: English in aviation safety. *World Englishes*, **23**(3), 451–70.

Tawake, Sandra (2003) Bilinguals' creativity: Patricia Grace and Maori cultural context. *World Englishes*, **22**(1), 45–54.

Trompenaars, Alfons (1994) *Riding the Waves of Culture: Understanding*

Diversity in Global Business. Burr
Ridge, IL: Irwin Professional
Publishing.
Vaid, Jyotsna (1980) The form and
functions of code mixing in Indian
films: The case of Hindi and
English. *Indian Linguistics*, **41**(1),
37–44.
Van Nus, Miriam (1999) "Can we count
on your bookings of potatoes to
Madeira?" Corporate context and
discourse practices in direct sales
letters. In *Writing Business: Genres,
Media and Discourses.* Edited by
Francesca Bargiela-Chiappini and
Catherine Nickerson. Essex:
Longman, pp. 181–205.
Ventola, Eija (1987) *The Structure of Social
Interaction: A Systemic Approach to
the Semiotics of Service Encounters.*
London: Frances Pinter.
Wagner, Johannes (1995) What makes
discourse a negotiation? In *The
Discourse of Business Negotiation.*
Edited by Konrad Ehlich and
Johannes Wagner. Berlin: Mouton
de Gruyter, pp. 9–36.
Yamada, Haru (1992) *American and
Japanese Business Discourse: A
Comparison of Interactional Styles.*
Norwood, NJ: Ablex.
Yamada, Haru (1996) *Players of a
Different Game: American and Japanese
Communication in Contrast.* Oxford:
Oxford University Press.

Yamada, Haru (1997) Organisation in
American and Japanese meetings:
Talk vs. relationship. In *The
Languages of Business: An
International Perspective.* Edited by
Francesca Bargiela-Chiappini and
Sandra Harris. Edinburgh:
Edinburgh University Press,
pp. 117–35.
Yli-Jokipii, Hilkka (1994) *Requests in
Professional Discourse. A Cross-
Cultural Study of British, American
and Finnish Business Writing.*
Helsinki: Suomaliainen
Tiedeakatemia.
Yli-Jokipii, Hilkka (1998) Power and
distance as cultural and contextual
elements of Finnish and English
business writing. In *The Cultural
Context in Business Communication.*
Edited by Susanne Niemeier,
Charles P. Campbell, and René
Dirven. Amsterdam: John
Benjamins, pp. 121–44.
Yotsukura, Lindsay Amthor (2003)
*Negotiating Moves: Problem
Presentation and Resolution in Japanese
Business Discourse.* Amsterdam:
Elsevier.
Yunick, Stanley (1997) Genres, registers
and sociolinguistics. *World Englishes*,
16(3), 321–36.
Zhang, Hang (2003) Bilingual creativity
in Chinese English; Ha Jin's "In the
Pond." *World Englishes*, **21**(2), 305–15.

FURTHER READING

Bargiela-Chiappini, Francesca and
Harris, Sandra J. (1997a) *Managing
Language: The Discourse of Corporate
Meetings.* Amsterdam: John
Benjamins.
Bargiela-Chiappini, Francesca and
Nickerson, Catherine (eds.) (1999)
*Writing Business: Genres, Media and
Discourses.* Essex: Longman.

Ehlich, Konrad and Wagner, Johannes
(eds.) (1995) *The Discourse of
Business Negotiation.* Berlin:
Mouton de Gruyter.
Nair-Venugopal, Shanta (2000a)
*Language Choice and Communication
in Malaysian Business.* Bangi:
Penerbit Universiti Kebangsaan
Malaysia.

Yamada, Haru (1992) *American and Japanese Business Discourse: A Comparison of Interactional Styles.* Norwood, NJ: Ablex.

Yli-Jokipii, Hilkka (1994) *Requests in Professional Discourse: A Cross-Cultural Study of British, American and Finnish Business Writing.* Helsinki: Suomaliainen Tiedeakatemia.

Part VIII World Englishes and Applied Theory

35 A Recurring Decimal: English in Language Policy and Planning

AYỌ BAMGBOṢE

1 Introduction

Language policy is sometimes overt in terms of pronouncements, laws, regulations, constitutional provisions, and a series of measures by governmental and non-governmental organizations and agencies. Quite often, however, language policy is covert and can only be inferred from observed practices. Whether overt or covert, language policy is ever present, and, by implication, so is language planning, irrespective of number, status, size, geographical spread, and power of the languages in a country.

One reality of language policy discourse in the world today is that it inevitably gravitates toward the role of English. This is regardless of whether such discourse relates to any of Kachru's categories of Inner, Outer, and Expanding Circles. It is, of course, entirely understandable that English should loom large in language policy in Inner-Circle countries, such as the USA, Britain, and Australia. However, even in countries of the other Circles, language policy discourse eventually ends up either as a discussion of the position and role of other languages in relation to English or vice versa. To this extent, English is always present – in the words of Pennycook (1994: 4), "It seems to turn up everywhere." My metaphor for this ubiquitous presence is *a recurring decimal*. Try dividing 10 by 3 and you end up with 3.33333 *ad infinitum*. There will always be a decimal 3, no matter how long you go on. This recurring decimal is very much like the way English recurs in language policy discourse.

2 Recurrence of English in Language Policy Discourse

The prominence that a language has in language policy may be due to a number of factors, such as population, prestige, status, functionality, and nationalism.

English shares all these factors in different countries, and may in fact have more than one of the factors in the same country. In Inner-Circle countries, where English is the first language of the majority of the population, all factors are involved. Consequently, any language policy must take as its point of departure the centrality of English. The issues that arise in such countries have more to do with what role should be given to minority languages (for example, in education), and how immigrants are to be integrated into the larger society (Herriman, 1996; Herriman and Burnaby, 1996; Ozolins and Clyne, 2001; Ricento, 1996; Thompson, Fleming, and Byram, 1996). Status planning decisions in such countries have nothing to do with "what language?" but perhaps with "what dialect of English in addition to the standard dialect?" This is particularly important in the case of divergent and/or stigmatized dialects such as Black English. Needless to say, prestige, status, and functionality are to be assumed where English is the first language of the overwhelming majority of the population. Given the entrenched position of the language, it may be thought that nationalism will play no part in the promotion of English, but such is its force that there are people who advocate an English-only policy, in the mistaken belief that it will ensure national unity and identity in the utopian context of a "melting pot" (Dicker, 2000: 50–2).

In Outer-Circle countries, where English was implanted as a result of colonial rule, only a minority of the population may be said to be proficient in English. Statistics of estimates of L2 speakers in such countries are no more than "guesstimates." For example, Crystal (1997: 59) credits Nigeria with 43 million speakers of English out of a population of 95 million. As someone who is professionally involved in language studies in Nigeria, I do not know where these millions of speakers are to be found. It is truer to say that in Nigeria, as in all other former British colonies, English remains a minority, but powerful, language used by an elite. Given the fact that literacy in English is acquired through formal education, and that a sizable percentage of children have no access to formal education, it is not surprising that the English-using population is not a large one. However, what English lacks in numbers, it makes up for in prestige, status, and functionality. Hence, language policy discourse in these countries revolves around its role as an official language, whether any other language can share this role at the national level, allocation of functions (particularly in education), when English should be introduced in schools, and what models of English should be aimed at in ELT.

Even when there is emphasis on languages and cultures indigenous to a country, such is the dominance of English that such discussion is carried out by reference to English. The acronym LOTE, standing for *Languages other than English*, which has been popularized in Australia, makes good sense in the context of a predominantly English-using country. However, when it is used for languages whose populations of speakers are far larger than that of English, all it shows is the dominance of English in language policy discourse. While, in Outer-Circle countries, the functionality of English is recognized and accepted, nationalism does not feature as justification for promoting English, even by the English-using elite. That is why most African countries that make English their official language refrain from according it the status of a national language as well. All the same, English is a constant feature of language policy in these countries.

In Expanding-Circle countries, English lacks a strong population base, it is not likely to have any official status, nor is the push for it born of any nationalistic considerations. Yet it has enormous prestige, mainly on account of its instrumental value. Although the role of English varies from its use in certain domains (such as tourism) to institutionalized entrenchment in the educational system, what all these countries have in common is the learning and using of English as a foreign language. What has accelerated the use of English in Expanding-Circle countries is the impact of globalization. Nowhere is this trend more evident than in Europe, where English is said to have become almost a lingua franca in, e.g., Scandinavia and the Netherlands, and is the "preferred first foreign language taught in schools" in virtually all of Europe (Hoffmann, 1998: 145–6). In Switzerland, French Swiss are said to be more attracted to English than to German, while German Swiss also tend to favor English over French as a second language (Dicker, 1996: 224). Even in the countries of the European Union, which has an official policy of 11 official languages for conducting its business, as Phillipson (2001: 7) remarks, "the rhetoric of equality of the official 11 languages is hollow" since "there is a pecking order of languages, and . . . English has the sharpest beak." Hence, even in countries in which English is a foreign language, it still features prominently in language policy discourse.

3   Choice and the Hegemony of English

The dominance of English in language policy is often presented as the effect of a deliberate choice. English has been found useful and functional; it opens doors to knowledge and technological advancement, and it is the language of globalization *par excellence*. In the case of most Outer-Circle countries, it is the one language that serves as a lingua franca in a complex multilingual situation. Hence, it is only natural that it should be given a significant role in educational and general language policy. In a survey of post-imperial English in 20 countries (including the European Union, which was treated as one unit), it was found that English was widely used in several domains, including education, the media, science, technology, commerce and industry, and informal social contacts. Based on this data, Fishman (1996: 639) concluded that "the socioeconomic factors that are behind the spread of English are now indigenous in most countries of the world and part and parcel of daily life and social stratification."

While Fishman's conclusion may serve as a rebuttal of extreme views of linguistic imperialism (cf. Phillipson, 1992), it fails to "problematize the notion of choice" (Pennycook, 1994: 12). Is the choice of English a free choice or are there constraints that make the choice inevitable? In the 20 case studies of post-imperial English, only three – Nigeria, Papua New Guinea, and Puerto Rico, as documented by Bamgboṣe (1996), Oladejo (1996), and Ramirez-Gonzalez and Torres-Gonzalez (1996), respectively – specifically allow for the possibility that the dominance of English may have been constrained by factors other than free choice. If a country has had a long history of contact with English, if in the multilingual situation it is the only link language among speakers of different languages, and if contacts with other countries through trade, industry, and higher education are in English, it does not require a clairvoyant to predict that English is bound to occupy a central role in the language policy of the country in question. What is true of a single country is also true of the demand for English in the world at large. Hence, one cannot but agree with Pennycook (1994: 74), when he says, "given the broader inequitable relationships in the world, people have little choice but to demand access to English."

The problem of choice, or lack of it, is perhaps more evident when applied to individuals. It would appear that because of the enormous advantages which knowledge of English confers, people deliberately demand and opt for it. For example, there are prospects of better jobs and upward social mobility, particularly in countries where English is an official language. On the face of it, this argument makes sense in light of investments that people make sending their children to English-medium schools, hiring private English tutors, going abroad for special courses in English, etc. A closer examination, however, reveals that it is not so much *wanting* to learn English because of the advantages it confers (though there is undoubtedly an element of this) as *needing* to learn it, because not learning English is not really a choice. While writing this paper, I listened to a news item about a candidate for the post of Secretary-General of the Organization of Oil Producing and Exporting Countries (OPEC). As this candidate does not speak English, but only Spanish, it was said that his chances of being elected were slim. For such a position, English is a requirement, not merely an advantage. Can anyone imagine a candidate for the post of Secretary-General of the United Nations organization who does not speak English, in addition to whatever other languages he or she may speak?

Major constraints on free choice are historical, economic, and bureaucratic. Attention has been drawn to the fact that the logic of postcolonial policy is maintenance rather than change. While post-independence governments appear to be making language policy, most of the time they are only perpetuating colonial language policy (Bamgboṣe, 1991, 2000). This inheritance situation has meant a futile struggle between change and continuity, with the latter usually gaining the upper hand. In practically all African countries colonized by Britain, English remains an official or co-official language. Attempts to promote the use of any other language as national or official have resulted either in failure or only limited success. The South African experience is instructive in this regard. While there has been a determined effort to empower languages other than English and Afrikaans by entrenching nine African languages in the Constitution and making supplementary provisions for their use in the legislature, education, and broadcasting, such is the hold of the past on the present that English has remained dominant in most domains (Alexander, 2001: 361–2; Bernsten, 2001; de Klerk and Barkhuizen, 2002: 11; Kamwangamalu, 1997: 244; McLean and McCormick, 1996: 329; Reagan, 2001: 63). The influence of the historical factor is such that status planning, as far as English is concerned, is a predetermined choice, for it is no exaggeration to say that once you go for English, it will always be English. In turn, each variety of English is itself determined by historical factors, as shown in the case of South Africa, where the recognized varieties of English are Traditional White English, which can be traced to the first-language speakers, and a series of second-language varieties, including Afrikaans English, South African Indian English, Cape/Colored English, and South African Black English, with each variety identified with an original indigenous or settler group (Bernsten, 2001: 226).

A major constraint in the choice of language is its economic power. Under normal circumstances, it is unlikely that a student would choose to learn a language that does not offer the prospect of a good job or social advancement. This explains why measures to promote indigenous languages have often been singularly unsuccessful, as knowledge of such languages generally does not confer any appreciable economic advantages. Although it has been suggested that in countries such as Japan, where English is not used for internal purposes, thus the language is "not a central basis for deciding who has access to economic resources and political power" (Tollefson, 2000: 13), it is still the case that English is prestigious, particularly in international business relations and communication. In other countries, where English is used for internal purposes, it is a major determinant of position and power. Why, in the name of giving a head start to their children, do some parents insist on their learning English starting in kindergarten or speaking English at home, even when English is not the language of the community? Their idea is to position the children for a good education and prospects of economic advancement. What is true of choices made for children is also true of choices made by adults. They are constrained by the hope of expected economic prospects and rewards.

Most policy decisions on language status are bureaucratic in three senses. First, they are taken by government or quasi-government bodies. Second, their implementation depends on rules and regulations made by bureaucrats. Third, the officials responsible for decision-making are members of the elite that have a vested interest in maintaining the role and status of English. The question of who makes policy (Cooper, 1989) is a non-trivial one, as it affects what policies are made. Given the tendency for "elite closure" (Myers-Scotton, 1990), the consumers of policy tend to be those who have no leverage on, nor input into, policy-making. The result is that, for them, there is really no choice, as they can only abide by laid-down-policy. If, as is usually the case, such policy is oriented toward English, the hegemony of English is further enhanced.

4 Effect of the Hegemony of English

The hegemony of English may be said to be beneficial on the one hand and detrimental on the other. When one considers its communicative and instrumental function, its role as lingua franca in many countries, and its global reach (which further enhances the concept of a shrinking world), it is easy to see why the spread of English is often viewed as "natural, neutral and beneficial" (Pennycook, 1994: 7, 9, 11, 141) – a claim that is increasingly being disputed (see Phillipson, 1992; Pennycook, 1994; Skuttnabb-Kangas, 2000; Tollefson, 2000). In the contexts of Outer-Circle countries, where English is largely acquired through formal education, the detrimental effects of the hegemony of English can be seen in social stratification, exclusion, and problems associated with education and literacy, status of languages other than English, and language rights.

Inherent in the way English is propagated is the emergence of an educated elite. It so happens that this elite is privileged in terms of access to positions, power, and influence. And it is a self-perpetuating elite, since it ensures that the opportunities it has are transferred to its offspring, particularly in terms of privileged education. The situation described for the Philippines by Tollefson (2000: 14–15) is true of virtually all Outer-Circle countries:

- English proficiency is a major criterion for access to higher education and to jobs;
- a dual system of education is in place such that children of the elite attend well-funded and well-staffed private schools, while children from poor families attend overcrowded and poorly staffed public schools;
- although the medium of education is English in both public and private schools, the quality of instruction in the latter is superior and the products of the private schools end up with greater proficiency in English;
- the differential in English proficiency means a better chance of the elite getting more lucrative jobs and thus being able to send children to private schools.

Since those who make policy are most certainly likely to be drawn from the ranks of the elite, a situation arises in which policy and practice are self-reinforcing and constitute the entrenchment of a self-perpetuating social class. This elite has a vested interest in maintaining the hegemony of English, since it gives its members an overwhelming advantage in terms of access to jobs, social status, and power. Hence, it does all it can through the educational system to maintain its privileged position and to reproduce itself (Dua, 1996: 3; Rubagumya, 1991: 76).

Whenever there is a privileged class, there is bound to be an element of exclusion. This is amply illustrated in the dual education system just mentioned, which separates those who have superior proficiency in English from those that do not. There are other categories of those excluded, such as those who have not had the opportunity of formal education or who have had such education but in a medium other than English. In a situation in which English is an official language, lack of familiarity with it "constitutes one of the greatest impediments in a country, affecting as it does, access to education, public services, jobs, political positions, and effective functioning in a society." English thus becomes "a bar between those who can participate using the official language and those who cannot" (Bamgbose, 2000: 2, 11). Consequently, those likely to benefit from the policy are "[c]ertainly not the poor" or economically disadvantaged (Brock-Utne, 2001: 115). Also in the category of the excluded are those who have imperfect mastery of English. Although they pretend to be able to participate, they are, in fact, functionally excluded since they do not function adequately, but admitting their inadequacy would involve loss of job or loss of face (Bamgbose, 2000: 11). Where a language has been empowered to function alongside English in certain domains, such as in politics, the basis for participation may be widened. For example, in the wake of the adoption of Swahili as a national language in Tanzania and Kenya, certain politicians became more relevant as a result of their competence in the language. An even more interesting case, reported by Canagarajah (1999), is the emergence of a monolingual Tamil-speaking elite in the Tamil-controlled areas of Sri Lanka. Given that the leadership of the military regime in control there is largely monolingual, a new elite has emerged that has control of political power. This elite exists side by side with an older elite that is bilingual in English and Tamil and dominates the economy and the professions. Hence, there is an awareness of "parallel elites." But even in this situation, it is reported that English is still perceived as "a class marker (i.e., the language of the educated and rich)" (Canagarajah, 1999: 29).

In a multilingual situation in which English is not the first language but is the medium of learning and teaching in schools, it has been repeatedly observed that a significant percentage of pupils repeat classes, drop out before the end of the elementary education cycle, or fail to obtain the required school-leaving certification. Although several factors, including teacher competence, learning environment, teaching materials and other facilities, financial capability of parents, and community support may affect success or failure in schools, the fact is that the medium of instruction is also a significant factor. Given the prevailing attitude that English-medium education is best, it is not surprising that parents opt for it in the belief that the earlier a child is exposed to instruction in English, the better will be its chances of success in higher cycles of education. What is often lost sight of is that conditions for the teaching of English are usually unsatisfactory. Hence, length of instruction in English does not automatically translate into greater competence and more effective education. In other words, "longer" does not always mean "better." Although the alternative of bilingual education is often ignored, the reality is that it offers a more promising approach in a multilingual situation. Rather than having an English-only medium at the elementary level, which is terminal for most children in many African countries, it is much better to have a combination of the child's first language and English as languages of instruction. Even if the child then fails to complete its primary education or completes it without the required certification, there will be another language in which it may be said to be literate.

What is true of basic education is also true of adult literacy. Given an estimated illiteracy population of 854 million in the less developed regions of the world in 2000, eradication of illiteracy is understandably a major preoccupation of developing countries. It is reported that "[o]f the twenty-three countries with estimated illiteracy rates higher than 50% today, fifteen are located in sub-Saharan Africa and five in Southern Asia" (UNESCO, 2000: 37). Needless to say, eradication of illiteracy can hardly be achieved unless literacy education is conducted in a language that adult learners already speak either as a first language or a language of the immediate community. Attempts to carry out mass literacy campaigns in an official language which is not the mother tongue of adult learners have usually been difficult or unsuccessful (UNESCO, 1992: 23). Hence, should English be used as the language of literacy, it would hardly make a dent in the war against illiteracy.

In status planning, one consequence of making a language an official language is the status it confers on the language and its speakers. The official language becomes dominant and other languages become disadvantaged and policies affecting such official languages "affect the viability and stability of other languages used in the community" (Herriman and Burnaby, 1996: 9). For example, as an official language, in many African countries, English holds a dominant position over other languages. Some will even say, with a touch of exaggeration, that "English poses a direct threat to the very existence of other languages" (Pennycook, 1994: 14) or to "the country's linguistic and cultural diversity" (Webb, 1996: 176). Where there have been attempts to break away from the colonial tradition and adopt a language other than English as an official language, such is the force of the dominance of English that new policies have only been partially successful. A good example of this is Swahili in Tanzania, which does not function beyond the primary school level as a language of instruction.

In a country such as South Africa, where nine African languages are recognized as co-official languages with English and Afrikaans, such is the dominance of English that, compared with English-medium education, education in an African language does not confer any visible benefits, either in terms of social mobility or better economic prospects (Alexander, 2001: 361; Kamwangamalu, 1997: 245). Consequently, there is a rush to enroll in English-medium schools, with the result that loyalty to the mother tongue by the younger generation is weakening and competence in the mother tongue is decreasing (de Klerk, 1999: 319). Although it has been suggested that "neither Afrikaans nor most of the indigenous African languages are in any immediate danger," the point has also been made that "language shift towards English is clearly taking place at an accelerated rate, and the number of spheres in which languages other than English can be used is rapidly declining" (Reagan, 2001: 63). In Europe, where there are well-entrenched national languages, it is said that "in particular, the popularity of English is also a looming threat" (Dicker, 1996: 227).

In discussions of the hegemony of English, the case for the use of other languages is often presented in terms of linguistic human rights. The focus is mainly on minority languages and the need to preserve them. Hence, there are grassroots language revival movements to promote the use of regional languages in education and the media. In Europe, in particular, there is institutional support by the European Union through the European Bureau for Lesser Used Languages, which finances, among others, projects in Gaelic in Ireland and Frisian in the Netherlands (Dicker, 1996: 227). A language rights approach to language policy is fraught with problems. First, it attributes undue power and influence to international conventions and agreements, which advocates of linguistic rights are fond of invoking. The reality, of course, is that such agreements are often ignored because they are not legally enforceable (Bamgboṣe, 2000: 19). As de Varennes (1999: 117) has pointed out, agreements that have a moral rather than a legal force are "things which governments 'should' do, if they are 'nice', not something they must do." And one may just add that governments are not particularly noted for being nice.

Second, a linguistic human rights approach is idealistic. For example, Article 24 of the Barcelona Declaration of Linguistic Rights states as follows:

> All language communities have the right to decide to what extent their language is to be present, as a vehicular language and as an object of study, at all levels of education within their territory: preschool, primary, secondary, technical and vocational, university, and adult education.

It is simply unrealistic to expect that *all languages* will be used as media of instruction at *all levels* of education. While it is ideal for a child's mother tongue to be used as medium of instruction, in practical terms and in certain situations a language of the immediate community may be a preferred medium. Similarly, in Outer-Circle countries, the language of instruction at secondary and tertiary levels is likely to continue to be English. Third, a linguistic human rights approach limits language choice in cases where, for good reason, parents do not opt for their own mother tongue as a language of instruction in schools for their children. It is this possibility of choice and the making of uninformed choices that is often to blame for the entrenchment of English. Although dominance is presented in anthropomorphic terms as if it is the language itself and not its speakers that is responsible for maintenance and promotion of a language, speakers of other languages are, to some extent, responsible for the hegemony of English, particularly in terms of their attitudes to their own languages. Even when allowance has been made for those factors that encourage the hegemony of English, a family that abandons the mother tongue in favor of English as the medium of communication in the home cannot at the same time complain that its mother tongue has been marginalized in other domains.

5   Broader Issues in the Context of English Hegemony

As most of the studies of world Englishes have been conducted within the frameworks of linguistics sciences, researchers on world Englishes have tended to put the emphasis on descriptive and analytical studies, often complemented by issues of language pedagogy. It has been suggested that more attention has to be paid to "the more macro aspects of English language teaching, which include such political, cultural, and social issues as language policies and their implications for schooling practices" (Hall and Eggington, 2000: 1). This is because language learning cannot be divorced from its "social, cultural and educational contexts" (Pennycook, 1994: 299). Unfortunately, such concerns are either relegated to the pedagogical aspect or presented in a high profile, adversarial or polemic treatise, which tends to give the impression that there is something sinister about the spread of English in the world. This is exemplified in particular by Phillipson (1992) on "Linguistic Imperialism," which provoked a symposium that appeared in *World Englishes* (vol. 12, no. 3, Kachru and Smith, 1993), and has continued to be a topic for discussion in the literature.

The volume titled *New Englishes: A West African Perspective* (Bamgboṣe, Banjo, and Thomas, 1995) is a good example of what has been said above on research in world Englishes. Of the twenty-one chapters in the book, only five deal with general issues of language policy and the context of English language teaching. Apart from two which discuss literature in English, the remaining fourteen are devoted to varieties of English and variety differentiation, indigenization processes, standards and codification (Kachru, 1985), code switching, communicative competence, and corpus research. In my own research, I have concentrated on identification and indexical markers of Nigerian English, registers, endonormative norms, and codification. These issues are no doubt important, and it is right that the emphasis in world Englishes research should initially be on justifying the very existence of world Englishes and their viability. Increasingly, however, I have been drawn to the broader issues of educational failure and the role of English in language policy and planning. In the Nigerian school system, for instance, the following problems have been observed:

- teachers who are themselves poor models of English language teaching;
- children who are made to learn through an English medium from the fourth year of primary education when their English proficiency is still low;
- drop-out rates ranging from 37.4 to 52.7 percent at primary school level;

- lack of readiness for English language tasks expected at the beginning of secondary education;
- carry-over of poor performance in English to end-of-secondary-school examinations, which are marked by failure rates of over 66 percent in English and between 56 and 73 percent in other subjects;
- mass failure in the compulsory University Matriculation Examination English paper, as well as in other subjects;
- poor standard of English among university undergraduates necessitating the requirement of a use of English course.

Several factors may be suggested as contributing to the observed educational problems including curriculum, teacher training, teaching materials, methodology, and examinations, but above all, it is language policy (Akere, 1995; Bamgboṣe, 1992; Mohammed, 1995). Irrespective of whichever factors are the greatest, a situation in which English becomes a barrier has to be seriously addressed. Unfavorable outcomes of the system include: children who are unable to complete primary education because of their inability to cope with subjects being taught in English, students who have to take and retake the English Language paper (without which they cannot gain admission to tertiary institutions), and teachers who reinforce the learning errors of their students by their own poor grammar and pronunciation. All these are instances of educational failure.

6   Implications for Language Policy and Planning

Language policy discourse in relation to English has implications for language planning, particularly with regard to extending its scope beyond language, and ensuring that it is inclusive, equitable, and ultimately designed to promote the overall cultural and economic development of a country. The hegemony of English is a reality that language policy and planning should take account of. Given that English is ever present and needed, how does one formulate policy so that it tries to avoid most of the undesirable effects associated with hegemony? First, it must be recognized that language policy is not about language alone (Herriman and Burnaby, 1996: 13), but that it encompasses sociopolitical and economic issues. For example, some of the problems associated with educational failure can be tackled with better funding, closer attention to institutional structures, and curriculum reform. No matter how desirable language policies may be, unless they are backed by the will to implement them, they cannot have any effect. Hence, implementation should be well articulated, even at the point when policy is being formulated. Allowance should, however, be made for distortions that occur in the process of implementation owing to contrary attitudes and actions of stakeholders affected by a policy. This is what has been referred to as *"un-planned* language planning" (Kachru, 1991: 8; Kaplan and Baldauf, 1997: 297–9).

Second, an effective language policy has to be inclusive, in the sense that it caters not just for a minority, but also for the generality of the population. In relation to English hegemony, what this means is that a multilingual policy is to be preferred to a monolingual one. Even if not all children of school-going age can make the transition to secondary level, a meaningful bilingual educa-tion policy will ensure that those who complete primary education are at least able to absorb and transmit information either in their mother tongue or in a combination of their mother tongue and English.

Third, language policy must be equitable, in that it should minimize the incidence of exclusion, whether in terms of those who have access or who are denied access on grounds of language alone (Bamgboṣe, 2000: 8–16). In this connection, the tendency to marginalize minority languages needs to be firmly resisted, perhaps in terms of positive action. The example of India is instruc-tive in this regard. Article 347 of the 1996 revised Constitution empowers the President to direct that any language spoken in a state be recognized, pro-vided there is a demand by a substantial proportion of the population of the state (Choudhry, 2001: 392). Similarly, if a minority group constitutes at least 60 percent of the total population of a district, the language of that minority group may be recognized as an official language, in addition to the official language of the state (Dua, 1996: 14).

Fourth, language policy is not an end in itself. The rationale for it must be what it can contribute to the overall cultural, human, and socio-economic development of a country (Afolayan, 1984: 1; Bamgboṣe, 2000: 116; Reagan, 1995: 320; Webb, 1996: 186). In this connection, it is not enough to place emphasis on globalization, information and communication technology, and the need for a language of wider communication to the detriment of the first language through which most of the population can participate and make any meaningful contribution to national development.

7 Conclusion

The dominance of English is an inescapable fact that language policy and planning must come to terms with. In so doing, this dominance must be so managed as to produce maximally favorable outcomes. In Outer-Circle coun-tries, in particular, a proper definition of language roles should minimize the incidence of exclusion. Researchers in world Englishes cannot turn a blind eye to the problems of educational failure or unfavorable language policy outcomes. The research activity must contribute to language policy discourse insofar as it relates to the role of English. Such a contribution must be in-formed by an understanding that, although the English language is one major, global and powerful resource in the world today, its role can only be comple-mentary to that of other languages in a multilingual and multicultural context.

See also Chapters 20, WRITTEN LANGUAGE, STANDARD LANGUAGE, GLOBAL LANGUAGE; 30, CULTURAL STUDIES AND DISCURSIVE CONSTRUCTIONS OF WORLD ENGLISHES; 41, WORLD ENGLISHES AND CORPORA STUDIES.

REFERENCES

Afolayan, Adebisi (1984) The English language in Nigerian education as an agent of proper multilingual and multicultural development. *Journal of Multilingual and Multicultural Development*, **5**(1), 1–22.

Akere, Funso (1995) Languages in the curriculum: An assessment of the role of English and other languages in the educational delivery process in Nigeria. In *New Englishes: A West African Perspective*. Edited by Ayọ Bamgboṣe, Ayọ Banjo, and Andy Thomas. Ibadan: Mosuro Publishers for the British Council, pp. 178–99.

Alexander, Neville (2001) Majority and minority languages in South Africa. In *The Other Languages of Europe*. Edited by Guus Extra and Durk Gorter. Clevedon, UK: Multilingual Matters, pp. 355–69.

Bamgboṣe, Ayọ (1991) *Language and the Nation*. Edinburgh: Edinburgh University Press.

Bamgboṣe, Ayọ (1992) *Speaking in Tongues: Implications of Multilingualism for Language Policy in Nigeria*. Kaduna: Nigerian National Merit Award: Award Winners' Lecture.

Bamgboṣe, Ayọ (1996) Post-imperial English in Nigeria 1940–1990. In *Post-Imperial English*. Edited by Joshua A. Fishman, Andrew W. Conrad, and Alma Rubal-Lopez. Berlin: Mouton de Gruyter, pp. 357–72.

Bamgboṣe, Ayọ (2000) *Language and Exclusion*. Hamburg/London: LIT Verlag.

Bamgboṣe, Ayọ, Banjo, Ayọ and Thomas, Andy (eds.) (1995) *New Englishes: A West African Perspective*. Ibadan: Mosuro Publishers for the British Council.

Bernsten, Jan (2001) English in South Africa: Expansion and nativization in concert. *Language Problems and Language Planning*, **25**(3), 219–35.

Brock-Utne, Birgit (2001) Education for all: In whose language? *Oxford Review of Education*, **27**(1), 115–34.

Canagarajah, Suresh (1999) *Resisting Linguistic Imperialism in English Teaching*. Oxford: Oxford University Press.

Choudhry, Amitav (2001) Linguistic minorities in India. In *The Other Languages of Europe*. Edited by Guus Extra and Durk Gorter. Clevedon, UK: Multilingual Matters, pp. 391–406.

Cooper, Robert L. (1989) *Language Planning and Social Change*. New York: Cambridge University Press.

Crystal, David (1997) *English as a Global Language*. Cambridge: Cambridge University Press.

de Klerk, Vivian (1999) Black South African English: Where to from here? *World Englishes*, **8**(3), 311–24.

de Klerk, Vivian and Barkhuizen, Gary (2002) English in the prison services: A case of breaking the law? *World Englishes*, **21**(1), 9–22.

de Varennes, Fernand (1999) The existing rights of minorities in international law. In *Language: A Right and a Resource: Approaching Linguistic Human Rights*. Edited by Miklós

Kontra, Robert Phillipson, Tove Skutnabb-Kangas, and Tibor Várady. Budapest: Central European University Press, pp. 117–46.

Dicker, Susan J. (1996) *Languages in America: A Pluralist View*. Clevedon, UK: Multilingual Matters.

Dicker, Susan J. (2000) Official English and bilingual education: The controversy over language pluralism in U.S. society. In *The Sociopolitics of English Language*. Edited by Joan Kelly Hall and William G. Eggington. Clevedon, UK: Multilingual Matters, pp. 45–66.

Dua, Hans Raj (1996) The politics of language conflict: Implications for language planning and political theory. *Language Problems and Language Planning*, **20**(1), 1–17.

Fishman, Joshua A. (1996) Summary and interpretation: Post-imperial English 1940–1990. In *Post-Imperial English*. Edited by Joshua A. Fishman, Andrew W. Conrad, and Alma Rubal-Lopez. Berlin: Mouton de Gruyter, pp. 623–41.

Hall, Joan Kelly and Eggington, William G. (eds.) (2000) *The Sociopolitics of English Language Teaching*. Clevedon, UK: Multilingual Matters.

Herriman, Michael (1996) Language policy in Australia. In *Language Policies in English-Dominant Countries*. Edited by Michael Herriman and Barbara Burnaby. Clevedon, UK: Multilingual Matters, pp. 35–61.

Herriman, Michael and Burnaby, Barbara (eds.) (1996) *Language Policies in English-Dominant Countries*. Clevedon, UK: Multilingual Matters.

Hoffmann, Charlotte (1998) Luxembourg and the European schools. In *Beyond Bilingualism: Multilingualism and Multilingual Education*. Edited by Jasone Cenoz and Fred Genesee. Clevedon, UK: Multilingual Matters, pp. 143–74.

Kachru, Braj B. (1985) Standards, codification and sociolinguistic realism: The English language in the outer circle. In *English in the World: Teaching and Learning the Language and Literatures*. Edited by Randolph Quirk and Henry G. Widdowson. Cambridge: Cambridge University Press, pp. 11–30.

Kachru, Braj B. (1991) Liberation linguistics and the Quirk concern. *English Today*, **25**, 3–13.

Kachru, Braj B. and Smith, Larry E. (eds.) (1993) Symposium on linguistic imperialism. Special issue of *World Englishes*, **12**(3), 335–91.

Kamwangamalu, Nkonko M. (1997) Multilingualism and education policy in post-apartheid South Africa. *Language Problems and Language Planning*, **21**(3), 234–53.

Kaplan, Robert B. and Baldauf, Richard B., Jr. (1997) *Language Planning: From Practice to Theory*. Clevedon, UK: Multilingual Matters.

McLean, Daryl and McCormick, Kay (1996) English in South Africa 1940–1996. In *Post-Imperial English*. Edited by Joshua A. Fishman, Andrew W. Conrad, and Alma Rubal-Lopez. Berlin: Mouton de Gruyter, pp. 303–37.

Mohammed, Aliyu (1995) Communicative competence acquisition in infelicitous learning environments: The problem with SSS English in Nigeria. In *New Englishes: A West African Perspective*. Edited by Ayọ Bamgboṣe, Ayọ Banjo, and Andy Thomas. Ibadan: Mosuro Publishers for the British Council, pp. 130–52.

Myers-Scotton, Carol M. (1990) Elite closure as boundary maintenance: The case of Africa. In *Language Policy and Political Development*. Edited by Brian Weinstein. Norwood NJ: Ablex, pp. 25–42.

Oladejo, James (1996) English in Papua New Guinea. In *Post-Imperial*

English. Edited by Joshua A. Fishman, Andrew W. Conrad, and Alma Rubal-Lopez. Berlin: Mouton de Gruyter, pp. 589–620.

Ozolins, Uldis and Clyne, Michael (2001) Immigration and language policy in Australia. In *The Other Languages of Europe: Demographic, Sociolinguistic, and Educational Perspectives*. Edited by Guus Extra and Durk Gorter. Clevedon, UK: Multilingual Matters, pp. 371–90.

Pennycook, Alastair (1994) *The Cultural Politics of English as an International Language*. Harlow, UK: Longman.

Phillipson, Robert (1992) *Linguistic Imperialism*. Oxford: Oxford University Press.

Phillipson, Robert (2001) Global English and local language policies: What Denmark needs. *Language Problems and Language Planning*, **25**(1), 1–24.

Ramirez-Gonzalez, Carlos and Torres-Gonzalez, Roame (1996) English under U.S. sovereignty: Ninety-five years of change of the status of English in Puerto Rico. In *Post-Imperial English*. Edited by Joshua A. Fishman, Andrew W. Conrad, and Alma Rubal-Lopez. Berlin: Mouton de Gruyter, pp. 173–204.

Reagan, Timothy (1995) Language planning and language policy in South Africa: A perspective on the future. In *Language and Social History: Studies in South African Sociolinguistics*. Edited by Rajend Mesthrie. Cape Town: David Philip, pp. 319–28.

Reagan, Timothy (2001) The promotion of linguistic diversity in multilingual settings: Policy and reality in post-apartheid South Africa. *Language Problems and Language Planning*, **25**(1), 51–72.

Ricento, Thomas (1996) Language policy in the United States. In *Language Policies in English-Dominant Countries*. Edited by Michael Herriman and Barbara Burnaby. Clevedon, UK: Multilingual Matters, pp. 122–58.

Rubagumya, Casmir M. (1991) Language promotion for educational purposes: The example of Tanzania. *International Review of Education*, **37**(1), 67–85.

Skuttnabb-Kangas, Tove (2000) Linguistic human rights and teachers of English. In *The Sociopolitics of English Language Teaching*. Edited by Joan Kelly Hall and William G. Eggington. Clevedon, UK: Multilingual Matters, pp. 22–44.

Thompson, Linda, Fleming, Michael, and Byram, Michael (1996) Languages and language policy in Britain. In *Language Policies in English-Dominant Countries*. Edited by Michael Herriman and Barbara Burnaby. Clevedon, UK: Multilingual Matters, pp. 99–121.

Tollefson, James W. (2000) Policy and ideology in the spread of English. In *The Sociopolitics of English Language Teaching*. Edited by Joan Kelly Hall and William G. Eggington. Clevedon, UK: Multilingual Matters, pp. 7–21.

UNESCO (1992) *A Literate World*. Paris: Unesco/International Bureau of Education.

UNESCO (2000) *World Education Report 2000*. Paris: UNESCO Publishing.

Webb, Vic (1996) English and language planning in South Africa: The flip-side. In *Focus on South Africa*. Edited by Vivian de Klerk. Amsterdam/Philadelphia: John Benjamins, pp. 175–90.

FURTHER READING

Bokamba, Eyamba (1982) The Africanization of English. In *The Other Tongue: English across Cultures*. Edited by Braj B. Kachru. Urbana, IL: University of Illinois Press, pp. 125–47.

Spencer, John (ed.) (1963) *Language in Africa*. Cambridge: Cambridge University Press.

Spencer, John (1971) *The English Language in West Africa*. London: Longman.

Ubahakwe, E. (ed.) (1979) *Varieties and Functions of English in Nigeria*. Lagos: AUP, in association with the Nigerian Studies Association.

36 Teaching World Englishes

ROBERT J. BAUMGARDNER

1 Introduction

This chapter will briefly survey teaching world Englishes from two perspectives: (1) stand-alone courses in world Englishes at the tertiary level; and (2) English language courses which incorporate a Kachruvian philosophy of language (see, e.g., B. Kachru, 1988 and 1995),[1] that is, a philosophy or perspective which (a) views English as belonging to those who use it, (b) espouses a polymodel (see discussion below) versus a monomodel in the classroom, and (c) recognizes that local contexts shape linguistic evolution. I will not deal with how a world Englishes component can be included in teacher training courses, or with considerations of specific methods, approaches, and materials in the classroom; for that discussion see Chapter 37 in this volume.

2 Courses in World Englishes

In 1985, Braj B. Kachru and Larry E. Smith launched the journal *World Englishes: Journal of English as an International and Intranational Language*, "devoted to the study of the forms and functions of varieties of English, both native and non-native, in diverse cultural and sociolinguistic contexts."[2] Kachru's research and teaching has focused on non-native varieties of English, particularly Indian English since the 1960s (see, e.g., Kachru, 1983) and both Kachru and Smith had been drawing attention to the unprecedented use of English as a world language since the 1970s (Kachru, 1992a and Smith, 1981). The field is now represented not only by *World Englishes* (Blackwell), but also by three other journals – *English Today* (Cambridge University Press), *English World-Wide* (John Benjamins), and *Asian Englishes* (Shirayuri College, Tokyo, Japan). Articles on world Englishes also now appear in other linguistics journals, e.g. *Applied Linguistics*, *Language in Society*, the *RELC (Regional English Language Centre) Journal* (Singapore), and *TESOL Quarterly*. Kachru's ideas have also influenced mainstream second-language acquisition (SLA) theory. A recent textbook on SLA, *Learning New Languages* (Scovel, 2001), includes a lengthy discussion of Kachru's "Three Circles of English" (Kachru, 1992b) and how they must be considered in an informed discussion of SLA.

In a 1988 article (reprinted 1995), Kachru suggested that a course in world Englishes should incorporate the following components: (1) bilinguals' creativity, (2) contact and convergence, (3) cross-cultural discourse, (4) textual competence and interpretation, (5) language acquisition, (6) language attitudes, (7) language in society, and (8) lexicography. For each of these areas, Kachru (1995: 246) urges a "paradigm shift," i.e., that each component should be studied from the perspective of "other" speakers of English, not just that of the so-called "native speakers" of English. As Bolton (2004: 367–8) has written:

> The Kachruvian approach has been characterized by an underlying philosophy that has argued for the importance of inclusivity and pluricentricity in approaches to the linguistics of English worldwide, and involves not merely the discussion of national and regional varieties, but many other related topics as well, including contact linguistics, creative writing, critical linguistics, discourse analysis, corpus linguistics, lexicography, pedagogy, pidgin and creole studies, and the sociology of language.

Kachru (1988, 1997) offers an extensive list of resources for teaching such a course in world Englishes. (See also Brown, 1993 and Brown and Peterson, 1997 for discussions of paradigm shift in world Englishes.) However, the field of world Englishes has developed so quickly that today a wide array of reference works and self-contained instructional materials are available for such a course, which is appropriate for either teacher training or general Applied Linguistics curricula (see Brown, 1993). Following is a select list of sample materials which would be suitable for a course in world Englishes.

Stand-alone world Englishes course books include Brutt-Griffler (2002), Gramley (2001), Jenkins (2003), B. Kachru (1986, 2005), Y. Kachru and Nelson (2006), Melchers and Shaw (2003), and Platt, Weber, and Ho (1984). Texts which concentrate on one particular variety of world Englishes are Bamgboṣe et al. (1997), West Africa; Baumgardner (1993), Pakistan; Baumgardner (1996), South Asia; Bautista (1997) and Bautista and Bolton (2004), the Philippines; Bolton (2002), Hong Kong; Bolton (2003), Hong Kong and China; Crewe (1977), Singapore; Foley (1988), Singapore; Gill (2002), Malaysia; B. Kachru (1983), India; Hartmann (1996), Europe; Llamzon (1969), the Philippines; Mazrui (2004), Africa; Sey (1973), Ghana; Stanlaw (2004), Japan; and Tongue (1974), Singapore and Malaysia. More general texts on English as an international language are Brumfit (1982), Crystal (1997), Fishman, Conrad and Rubal-Lopez (1996), Flaitz (1988), Graddol and Meinhof (1999), B. Kachru (1986), McArthur (1998), McKay (2002), Pennington (1996), Trudgill and Hannah (2002), and Weiner and Smith (1983). World Englishes readings texts include Bailey and Görlach

(1982), B. Kachru (1992a), Pride (1982), and Smith (1981, 1983 and 1987). For specific articles on the teaching of world Englishes see Baumgardner (1987), Baumgardner and Brown (2003), Brown (1993, 1995 and 1997), Friedrich (2002), Görlach (1999), B. Kachru (1988, 1994, 1997 and 2003), and Kachru and Nelson (1996 and 2001). Internet websites, many pedagogical in nature, are devoted to world Englishes; for example, a Google search (May 2004) for "English as an Asian Language" yielded 112 hits.

Courses in World Englishes are offered in the United States at, among others, Eastern Washington University (Spokane), Indiana State University (Terre Haute), Portland State University (Oregon), Purdue University (West Lafayette, Indiana), St John's University (NY City), Syracuse University (NY), the University of Hawai'i at Honolulu, and the University of Illinois at Urbana-Champaign; and outside the United States at Bayero University (Kano, Nigeria), Chukyo University (Nagoya, Japan), Hong Kong University, King's College London (UK), Kingston University (UK), University of Essex (UK), University of Gävle (Sweden), University of Kent (UK), University of Koblenz and Landau (Germany), University of Leeds (UK), University of Luton (UK), University of Magdeburg (Germany), University of Manchester (UK), University of Nottingham (UK), University of Stellenbosch (South Africa), University of Stockholm (Sweden), University of Tamagawa (Tokyo), and Waseda University (Tokyo). A web-based course entitled "Sojourn to world Englishes" is offered by the Open Cyber University of Korea (Baik and Shim, 2002), and from Fall 2005, King's College London will devote an entire MA program to world Englishes (Jennifer Jenkins, 2004, personal communication). Chukyo University (Nagoya, Japan) has recently established a Division of World Englishes as an academic unit (B. Kachru, 2003). According to Brown (1993: 66), "Recent TESOL workshops have [also] included courses in World Englishes . . ." and as an indication of their wide range of influence, Matsuda (2002) suggests using the teaching of world Englishes to promote "international understanding" (see further discussion below).

3 World Englishes in Courses

In this section I will discuss English language courses which are based upon a Kachruvian philosophy of teaching. While all English language courses which represent the social reality of the context in which they are taught fall under the rubric, I will not cover mainstream Standard English language courses or materials, a plethora of information about which is available in the literature (see, e.g., recent British, Canadian, US, or Australian Cambridge University Press, Longman, or Oxford University Press ESL catalogs). I will concentrate first on culture in the classroom; I will then discuss standardization and language form in world Englishes classrooms; finally, I will discuss the role of the mother tongue and the non-native teacher in teaching.

3.1   *Culture in the classroom*

> It wasn't until I read Paulo Freire's work [1997] that I understood that the struggle I had in school . . . was a result of learning the word as separate from the world. (Cadiero-Kaplan, 2004: xvii)

Cadiero-Kaplan's sentiments toward learning to read and write in her US English mother tongue but in Standard English are representative of English language-learning classrooms, both native as well as non-native, throughout the world – learners simply do not see themselves in the texts they are using. What they often see is an alien world of Australian, British, Canadian, or US characters in unfamiliar settings. Textbook writing, needless to say, is a commercial as well as a political enterprise; nonetheless, John Gray and the overseas teachers of English he interviewed in his 2002 study of ESL textbooks "clearly felt the need for what might be called a *glocal* coursebook – something that would give them 'a better fit' and simultaneously connect the world of their students with the world of English" (Gray, 2002: 116).

The underlying issue here is, of course, the position in which the English language finds itself today as an international language. As Smith (1976/1983: 1) noted three decades ago, "English belongs to any country which uses it and may have as wide or as limited a use (either as an international or auxiliary language) as is felt desirable." The role of English is that of the world's lingua franca in a myriad of diverse settings (cf. Widdowson, 1994). More often than not, these diverse settings do not involve a native speaker of English. As B. Kachru (1996: 144) has pointed out: "The elevated status of English across cultures came at a price. Its multicultural identities resulted in deep sociolinguistic shifts." It is precisely these "deep shifts" that make it necessary for teachers of English outside English-speaking countries to infuse local culture into their English language classrooms. English is being learned nowadays in most parts of the world for pragmatic or instrumental reasons rather than for integrative ones. From countries in the Expanding Circle such as Morocco to those in both the Outer Circle such as Sri Lanka and the Inner Circle such as Australia, materials designers, teachers, and learners are appropriating the English language for their own uses.

In Morocco, materials writers opted for a predominantly Moroccan cultural content of a secondary English course because "many Moroccan teachers of English are uncomfortable in the role of presenters of alien cultures with which they may not identify and which they perhaps have not themselves experienced" (Adaskou, Britten, and Fahsi, 1990: 8). As Cunningsworth (1984: 19) has pointed out: "Cultural gaps pose problems to learners of English, particularly where the social, political, or religious differences are great." This is the case for both teachers and learners in predominantly Muslim Morocco: a textbook containing lessons centered around "dating" would be socially and religiously inappropriate. In the northern Sri Lankan city of Jaffna, reports Canagarajah (1999: 87), "the situations represented [in foreign textbooks] – such as commuting by plane, cooking with a microwave, or shopping in department stores – assume an urbanized, Western culture that is still largely alien to rural students, and likely to clash with their traditional values." In Australia, the predominant position of Standard Australian English is being challenged by the indigenized, Outer-Circle English of the country's Malaysian population: "The imperial centre brought English to the distant colonies of the periphery. Now these postcolonial nations not only bring new Englishes to the monolingual Anglophones, but are contesting their power to authorise English and its teaching" (Singh, Kell, and Pandian, 2002: 26).

Rhetorical conventions constitute another area where culture in the classroom is of paramount importance. Canagarajah writes about a dialog used for a role play in a Jaffna classroom in Sri Lanka. In the dialog, a loquacious woman misses her train because she is involved in a conversation with the station agent. "The message indirectly and unintentionally conveyed to students by this passage is that they should value a strictly focused, goal-oriented, utilitarian conversational style, whereas Tamil discourse values the digression and indirection typical of predominantly oral, rural communities" (Canagarajah, 1999: 87). Youmans (2001) reports differences in English usage of polite epistemic modals (*can* and *could*) in the Mexican-American community of East Los Angeles and Anglo visitors to the community, while Y. Kachru discusses the differences in discoursal strategies among multilingual speakers of Indian English: "It is clear that the discourse strategies developed along with the acquisition of Indic languages are discernible in Indian English discourse as well" (1987: 97). In a similar vein, Cunningsworth (1984: 19) recounts the following incident: "I recall from my own experience a case where a Chinese speaker of English was looking after an American professor on a lecture tour of China. After the American's first lecture the Chinese, using a standard formula of politeness in China, told the lecturer that he looked tired and asked him to take a rest. The American interpreted this as a criticism of his performance and was somewhat displeased." Sensitivity to conventions of polite interaction needs more attention in pedagogical materials and practices.

World Englishes in the Expanding and Outer Circles, as well as in varieties other than mainstream Standard English in the Inner Circle, reflect the cultural imprints of those communities that use them. While the classroom is the ideal forum in which to address such innovations, it often turns out to be the site for cultural suppression. As Alptekin and Alptekin (1984: 15) have so incisively pointed out: "Indeed, being at the receiving end of a virtually one-way flow of information from Anglo-American centers, the host country runs the risk of having its own culture totally submerged . . ." Through the recognition of world Englishes within a Kachruvian perspective, no such cultural submersion will occur.

Representative texts in the area of culture in the world Englishes classroom are Block and Cameron (2002), Canagarajah (1999), Candlin and Mercer (2001),

Coleman (1996), García and Otheguy (1989), Hinkel (1999), Kramsch (1993), Smith (1987), and Widdowson (2003). For a discussion of the three types of cultural content in language-teaching materials – target, source, and international – see McKay (2002). Of particular interest also for materials design case studies are two volumes in the British Council ELT Documents series, ELT Documents Special, *Projects in Materials Design* (British Council, 1980) and ELT Documents 116, *Language Teaching Projects for the Third World* (Brumfit, 1983). For a discussion of "critical cultural consciousness" in language learning materials, see Kumaravadivelu (2003). Articles of interest on culture in the classroom include Atkinson (1999), Bowers (1992), Brown (1990), Canagarajah (2001), Cortazzi and Jin (1999), Gray (2002), Y. Kachru (1987 and 1999), Kramsch (1996), Lin (2001), Norton (1997), Prodromou (1988 and 1992), and Strevens (1987).

3.2   *Standardization and form in the classroom*

English English standardization, still an ongoing process, developed over a period of some five hundred years (see, e.g., Bex and Watts, 1999; Trahern, 1989; and Wright, 2000). Other British English varieties, never as prestigious as standard English English, developed, often with concomitant bloodshed (Bailey, 1985), within bilingual contexts of the indigenous Celtic languages of Britain. The first major overseas transplanted variety of Inner-Circle English, American English, struggled initially but finally established its own standard apart from the British model (Finegan, 1980; B. Kachru, 1981). Other overseas colonial transplanted varieties of English, those which developed in Outer-Circle countries such as India, Pakistan, Singapore, and Nigeria, also developed, like Irish, Scottish, and Welsh Standard English, within bilingual, or more often multilingual, contexts of use. Hence, the Englishes that resulted were influenced by a substrate language or languages whose influence manifests itself more at the "indigenously functional" level rather than at the international[3] Standard level (Pakir, 1991: 116). The quandary that speakers of Outer-Circle varieties of English face in terms of a standard is the same one previously faced by speakers of overseas Inner-Circle varieties of English – to accept an exonormative form of the language (usually British) as standard or to recognize an endonormative variety. As Pakir (1991: 109–10) has asserted: "Norm-setter, norm-maker and norm-breaker may all be found in one and the same Singaporean who has been schooled in English from an early age but who speaks several other languages and interacts with speakers of these other languages . . ." The same dilemma is faced by speakers of Expanding-Circle varieties of English who now consider English an international lingua franca (see, e.g., Jenkins, 2000; Modiano, 1999; and Seidlhofer, 1999 and 2001 on emerging Euro-English standards). For further reading on language standards see Chapters 26 and 27 in this volume. For readings on standardization in the Outer Circle see Bautista and Bolton (2004), Gill and Pakir (1999), Tickoo (1991).

The crucible for the question of standards in the Inner, Outer, and Expanding Circles is the classroom – which form of the language should be taught to English language learners? Interestingly, the form that is taught (at least orally) by default is often a localized or dialectally influenced variety, since teachers are sometimes unaware that what they use (and are inadvertently modeling) is not international Standard English. Standards can also change from exonormative to endonormative, i.e., a local variety of English can become more accepted in formal written contexts, e.g. newspapers, as is happening today in Pakistan (Baumgardner, 1995).

Two decades ago, B. Kachru (1983) called for a polymodel versus a monomodel approach to teaching English in world Englishes classrooms:

> In discussing English as an international and intranational language it is difficult to raise the question of choice of model. The local, national, and international uses of English . . . raise questions about the validity of *didactic* models, those which emphasize a *monomodel* approach to the teaching of English. One has to be realistic about such questions and aim at a *dynamic* approach, based on a *polymodel* concept. The choice of a model cannot be separated from the functions of the language. (pp. 238–9)

The use of world Englishes in the classroom is representative of Kachru's idea of the polymodel. In Inner-Circle classrooms, this would entail making students aware of and tolerant of different varieties of world Englishes, including national varieties. Accent and dialect intolerance in the United States has been well documented by Lippi-Green (1997). Jordan (1997), Ortiz (1997), Purcell-Gates (1995), Stavans (2005), and Tan (2005) have written about the linguistic discrimination faced by African Americans, Native Americans, European Americans, Hispanic Americans, and Asian Americans, respectively, in the USA. Kubota (2001) proposes teaching an awareness of world Englishes to native speakers of English in US high schools, and Wolfram, Adger, and Christian (1999) show how local dialects should also be part of English and language arts classes at the elementary and secondary levels.

The 1996–7 Ebonics controversy in Oakland, California represents another attempt to bring world Englishes into the classroom. In essence, the Oakland School Board wanted Oakland teachers to use African American Vernacular English (or Ebonics – see Williams, 1975) to teach Standard US English to African American children. The Board sought funds to educate white and middle-class black teachers about the structure of the dialect so they could use it contrastively with Standard English in the classroom, rather than dismissing Ebonics as corrupted English. Simpkins, Holt, and Simpkins (1977), in their *Bridge* series, espoused a more radical approach than the Oakland contrastive approach; they believed in a bidialectal education approach in which speakers of Ebonics should begin reading in Ebonics and gradually move to Standard English, an idea seen by some in the African American community "as a plot to prevent the schools from teaching the linguistic aspects of the culture of power, thus dooming black children to a permanent outsider caste" (Delpit, 1995: 29). For further reading on African American Vernacular English and the Ebonics controversy, see Baugh (1983, 1999, and 2000), Burling (1973), Delpit and Dowdy (2002), Perry and Delpit (1998), Rickford and Rickford (2000), Smitherman (2000), and Chapter 19 in this volume.

Baumgardner (1987), Friedrich (2002), and Matsuda (2002) exemplify attempts to bring world Englishes into Outer- and Expanding-Circle classrooms. Following Kachru's polymodel concept, Baumgardner used contrastive analysis to teach English complementation to Pakistani university students. In Pakistani English, an indigenized variety, complementation differs from that in Inner-Circle English (at least in informal, spoken form) in a number of ways, for example: *He went to China for learning Chinese* vs. *He went to China to learn Chinese*. Baumgardner (1987) used these differences to raise the awareness of his students (and Pakistani English teachers) to differences between their own local or national variety of English and international English. Both Friedrich (2002) and Matsuda (2002) found that for learners in the Expanding-Circle countries of Argentina, Brazil, and Japan, "English" meant primarily British English (Argentina) or American English (Brazil and Japan). Friedrich (2002: 442) writes: "In all of the questions where naming a variety was called for, only British and American English were mentioned to the detriment of other native varieties and all of the non-native ones." Matsuda (2002: 437), in a similar vein, found that "Quantitative and qualitative analysis of the language varieties, users, and uses of English revealed that the current representation of English in these [Japanese] textbooks focuses almost exclusively on the Inner Circle." Friedrich (2002: 444) concludes that "By bringing awareness to the different varieties of English that the students will encounter and by teaching them to view these varieties as legitimate expressions of a language in constant change and spread, a world Englishes approach can greatly facilitate learning." Matsuda (2002: 438) avers that an understanding of world English may help to promote international understanding: "An incomplete presentation of the English language may . . . lead to confusion or resistance when students are confronted with different types of English users or uses. Students may be shocked by varieties of English that deviate from Inner Circle English, view them as deficient (rather than different), or grow disrespectful to such varieties and users, which seems counter-productive to facilitating international understanding." Whether in Inner-, Outer-, or Expanding-Circle classrooms, students' sensitivity toward the unprecedented spread and diversification of the English language should be one of all teachers' goals.

For further reading on world Englishes in the classroom in the Inner Circle, see Anzaldúa (1997), Brandes and Brewer (1977), Ferguson and Heath (1981), Goldstein (1987), Kaldor (1991), Kalmar (2001), Mundari (1997), Nero (1997), and Trueba (1989). For the Outer Circle, see Gill (1993), Halverson (1966), Kujore (1997), Omodiaogbe (1992), and Peña (1997), and for the Expanding Circle, Erling (2002), Görlach (1999), Hu (2004), Jenkins, Modiano, and Seidlhofer (2001), and Yajun (2003).

3.3   L2 in the classroom and non-native educators

Numerous Western language-teaching methods, in an attempt for SLA to mirror first-language acquisition, forbade the use of the mother tongue in the classroom. *The Direct Method, Audiolingualism*, and some forms of *Communicative Language Teaching* were among those methods that agreed that English was best taught through English. True as this may be, "it does not necessarily follow that English should therefore always be the only language used in every classroom" (Atkinson, 1987: 242). There can be no doubt that second-language acquisition is similar to first-language acquisition; second-language acquisition, however, is also different in a number of ways (Scovel, 2001). One of these is the knowledge that a second-language learner brings to the learning task. Part of that knowledge is the mother tongue, the pedagogical proscription of which Phillipson (1992a) terms the *monolingual fallacy*.

A number of methods favor the use of the mother tongue as a useful tool in the English language learning classroom, namely the venerable *Grammar-Translation Method* as well as newer "designer" methods like *Suggestopedia* and *Community Language Learning*. Ancient Romans learned Greek using a bilingual method "which began informally in the relaxed atmosphere of their homes" (Bowen, Madsen, and Hilferty, 1985: 6).

In contexts where world Englishes are acquired as a second language in schools, in fact, a bilingual approach is the method of preference since, as Sridhar and Sridhar (1992: 103) point out, in such contexts "the goal of SLA is bilingualism." Douglas Walatara's *Reconstruction: An English Technique for an Asian Context* (1974) begins with the mother-tongue (Singhala/Tamil) equivalent of a text to be learned in English, and Michael West used comprehension questions in the vernacular (Bengali) to test vocabulary (Howatt, 1984: 247).

Ironically, a very unorthodox program for language instruction was formulated by Halmuth Schaefer (1963) during the heyday of Audiolingualism, a method known for its use of only the target language in the classroom. Schaefer's program, called "language redundancy," suggested the use of target language words in source language texts in places where the source language was unequivocally redundant, i.e., there was no doubt as to the word which fit into the place where the target language element was inserted. For example, the sentence *A line may be either curvilinear or straight* could be rewritten for English-speaking learners of German as *A line may be either curvilinear oder straight*, where the target language German word *oder* can be inserted, since the English word "or" is redundant. Over time, more and more of the target language is introduced in this way.

Burling (1982) proposed a similar method, which he called "mixed-language," for the teaching of reading and listening comprehension; in this method, target-language words are gradually introduced into a source-language text until learners can read the text entirely in the target language. Morgan and Rinvolucri (1986: 36–7) suggest so-called "two-language texts" (inspired, they note, by works like Anthony Burgess's *A Clockwork Orange*) as a technique in teaching reading. Empirical tests by both Schaefer (1963) and Burling (1982) show that students do indeed make considerable progress in at least the so-called "passive" skills – aural comprehension and reading – by using such methods. (Schaefer even noted improvement in pronunciation.) There have been numerous calls of late from the Inner-Circle English Language Teaching establishment for more use of the mother tongue in the classroom (see, e.g., Atkinson, 1987; Auerbach, 1993; Harbord, 1992; Skutnabb-Kangas, 1981, in fact, considers the use of the mother tongue in the classroom one dimension of linguistic human rights).

An issue related to the *monolingual fallacy* is Phillipson's (1992a: 126) notion of the *native speaker fallacy*, the idea that "native speakers of English are automatically the best teachers of English. By implication, it follows that periphery teachers are second-best, if not expendable for teaching English." If, however, the goal of English teaching is for students to become bilingual, then it follows that the English teacher in Outer- and Expanding-Circle classrooms *must* have a knowledge of both source and target languages. As Richard-Amato (2003: 9) writes: "Because of their experience learning another language, they are generally more aware of helpful strategies, pitfalls to avoid, language learning difficulties, and the personal and social needs of their students." In short, they are more effective teachers to the largest group of English language learners in the world – those in the Outer and Expanding Circles. Finally, this calls into question the time-honored concept of the "native speaker" in linguistics and SLA theory. If native-speaker English is not the goal in the majority of English language learning contexts throughout the world, it is time to re-define the concept of the native speaker. It is time to realize that the goal of second-language acquisition in world Englishes classrooms can be the speech of a proficient user of English in the Outer or Expanding Circle just as well as one in the Inner Circle (see, e.g., Y. Kachru, 1994; Sridhar, 1994).

For further reading on the non-native teacher in the classroom, see Christophersen (1988), Cook (1999), Kramsch (1997), Liu (1999), Medgyes (1992, 1994, and 2001), Phillipson (1992b), Rampton (1990), and Wong (1982). For a revealing discussion of the non-native speaker in the US English classroom, see Braine (1999), and for the debate concerning the concept of the "native speaker," see Davies (1991, 2003, and 2004), Paikeday (1985), and Singh (1998).

4   Conclusion

This chapter presents an overview of the teaching of world Englishes from two perspectives: courses on the varieties at the tertiary level and incorporation of materials from English language courses at various levels in all the Three Circles of English. The resources listed in the references and further reading point to the many aspects of the complex issues involved in this enterprise.

See also Chapters 24, WORLD ENGLISHES AND ISSUES OF INTELLIGIBILITY; 37, MODELS, METHODS AND CURRICULUM FOR ELT PREPARATION; 39, WORLD ENGLISHES AND TEST CONSTRUCTION; 40, WORLD ENGLISHES AND COMMUNICATIVE COMPETENCE.

NOTES

1 I would like to thank Kimberley Brown, Braj B. Kachru, Yamuna Kachru, Jennifer Jenkins, Kingsley Bolton, Barbara Seidlhofer, Larry Smith, and David Belmarez Schultz for information, advice, and encouragement in the writing of this paper; any errors, of course, are my own.

2 *World Englishes* began with volume 4, number 2 (Summer 1985) of the journal *World Language English*, edited by William R. Lee.

3 *International English*, according to Görlach (1999: 13n), is "applicable to syntax and lexis, where it refers to features shared among varieties worldwide, including a few sets of predictable alternates . . ."

REFERENCES

Adaskou, K., Britten, D., and Fahsi, B. (1990) Design decisions on the cultural content of a secondary English course for Morocco. *ELT Journal*, **44**(1), 3–10.

Alptekin, Cem and Alptekin, Margaret (1984) The question of culture: EFL teaching in non-English-speaking countries. *ELT Journal*, **38**(1), 14–20.

Anzaldúa, Gloria (1997) How to tame a wild tongue. In *Living Languages: Contexts for Reading and Writing*. Edited by Nancy Buffington, Marvin Diogenes, and Clyde Moneyhun. Upper Saddle River, NJ: Prentice-Hall, pp. 29–39.

Atkinson, David (1987) The mother tongue in the classroom: A neglected resource? *ELT Journal*, **41**(4), 241–7.

Atkinson, Dwight (1999) TESOL and culture. *TESOL Quarterly*, **33**(4), 625–54.

Auerbach, Elsa (1993) Reexamining English only in the ESL classroom. *TESOL Quarterly*, **27**(1), 9–32.

Baik, Martin Jonghak and Shim, Rosa Jinyoung (2002) Teaching world Englishes via the Internet. *World Englishes*, **21**(3), 427–30.

Bailey, Richard W. (1985) The conquests of English. In *The English Language Today*. Edited by Sidney Greenbaum. Oxford: Pergamon, pp. 9–19.

Bailey, Richard W. and Görlach, Manfred (eds.) (1982) *English as a World Language*. Ann Arbor, MI: University of Michigan Press.

Bamgboṣe, Ayọ, Banjo, Ayọ, and Thomas, Andrew (eds.) (1997) *New Englishes: A West African Perspective*. Trenton, NJ: Africa World Press.

Baugh, John (1983) *Black Street Speech: Its History, Structure and Survival*. Austin: University of Texas Press.

Baugh, John (1999) *Out of the Mouths of Slaves: African American Language and Educational Malpractice*. Austin: University of Texas Press.

Baugh, John (2000) *Beyond Ebonics: Linguistic Pride and Racial Prejudice*. New York: Oxford University Press.

Baumgardner, Robert J. (1987) Utilizing Pakistani newspaper English to teach grammar. *World Englishes*, **6**(3), 241–52. (Also in Baumgardner, 1993.)

Baumgardner, Robert J. (ed.) (1993) *The English Language in Pakistan*. Karachi: Oxford University Press.

Baumgardner, Robert J. (1995) Pakistani English: Acceptability and the norm. *World Englishes*, **14**(2), 261–71.

Baumgardner, Robert J. (ed.) (1996) *South Asian English: Structure, Use, and Users*. Urbana, IL: University of Illinois Press.

Baumgardner, Robert J. and Brown, Kimberley (2003) World Englishes: Ethics and pedagogy. *World Englishes*, **22**(3), 245–51.

Bautista, Ma. Lourdes S. (ed.) (1997) *English as an Asian Language: The Philippine Context*. NSW, Australia: Macquarie Library.

Bautista, Ma. Lourdes S. and Bolton, Kingsley (eds.) (2004) Philippine English: Tensions and transitions. Special issue of *World Englishes*, **23**(1).

Bex, Tony and Watts, Richard J. (eds.) (1999) *Standard English: The Widening Debate*. London: Routledge.

Block, David and Cameron, Deborah (eds.) (2002) *Globalization and Language Teaching*. London: Routledge.

Bolton, Kingsley (ed.) (2002) *Hong Kong English: Autonomy and Creativity*. Hong Kong: Hong Kong University Press.

Bolton, Kingsley (2003) *Chinese Englishes: A Sociolinguistic History*. Cambridge: Cambridge University Press.

Bolton, Kingsley (2004) World Englishes. In *The Handbook of Applied Linguistics*. Edited by Alan Davies and Catherine Elder. Oxford: Blackwell, pp. 367–96.

Bowen, J. Donald, Madsen, Harold, and Hilferty, Ann (1985) *TESOL Techniques and Procedures*. Boston, MA: Heinle and Heinle.

Bowers, Roger (1992) Memories, metaphors, maxims, and myths: Language learning and cultural awareness. *ELT Journal*, **46**(1), 29–38.

Braine, George (1999) *Non-Native Educators in English Language Teaching*. Mahwah, NJ: Lawrence Erlbaum.

Brandes, Paul D. and Brewer, Jeutonne (1977) *Dialect Clash in America: Issues and Answers*. Metuchen, NJ: Scarecrow Press.

British Council (1980) *Projects in Materials Design*. London: The British Council.

Brown, Gillian (1990) Cultural values: The interpretation of discourse. *ELT Journal*, **44**(1), 11–17.

Brown, Kimberley (1993) World Englishes in TESOL programs: An infusion model of curricular innovation. *World Englishes*, **12**(1), 59–73.

Brown, Kimberley (1995) World Englishes: To teach or not to teach. *World Englishes*, **14**(2), 233–45.

Brown, Kimberley (1997) A world language perspective: English, French, and Spanish. In *Beyond Methods: Components of Second Language Teacher Education*. Edited by Kathleen Bardovi-Harlig and Beverly Hartford. New York: McGraw-Hill, pp. 137–51.

Brown, Kimberley and Peterson, Jay (1997) Exploring conceptual frameworks: Framing a world Englishes paradigm. In *World Englishes 2000*. Edited by Larry E. Smith and Michael L. Forman.

Honolulu, HI: University of Hawai'i and East-West Center, pp. 32–47.

Brumfit, Christopher J. (ed.) (1982) *English for International Communication*. Oxford: Pergamon.

Brumfit, Christopher J. (ed.) (1983) *Language Teaching Projects for the Third World* (ELT Documents 116). Oxford: Pergamon.

Brutt-Griffler, Janina (2002) *World English: A Study of Its Development*. Clevedon, UK: Multilingual Matters.

Burling, Robbins (1973) *English in Black and White*. New York: Holt, Rinehart and Winston.

Burling, Robbins (1982) *Sounding Right*. Rowley, MA: Newbury House.

Cadiero-Kaplan, Karen (2004) *The Literacy Curriculum and Bilingual Education: A Critical Examination*. Frankfurt am Main: Peter Lang.

Canagarajah, A. Suresh (1999) *Resisting Linguistic Imperialism in English Teaching*. Oxford: Oxford University Press.

Canagarajah, A. Suresh (2001) Critical ethnography of a Sri Lankan classroom: Ambiguities in student opposition to reproduction through ESOL. In *English Language Teaching in Its Social Contact*. Edited by Christopher N. Candlin and Neil Mercer. London: Routledge, pp. 208–26.

Candlin, Christopher N. and Mercer, Neil (eds.) (2001) *English Language Teaching in Its Social Context*. London: Routledge.

Christophersen, Paul (1988) "Native speakers" and world English. *English Today*, **4**(3), 15–18.

Coleman, Hywel (ed.) (1996) *Society and the Language Classroom*. Cambridge: Cambridge University Press.

Cook, Vivian (1999) Going beyond the native speaker in language teaching. *TESOL Quarterly*, **33**(2), 185–209.

Cortazzi, Martin and Jin, Lixian (1999) Cultural mirrors: Materials and methods in the EFL classroom. In *Culture in Second Language Teaching and Learning*. In Eli Hinkel. Cambridge: Cambridge University Press, pp. 196–219.

Crewe, William J. (ed.) (1977) *The English Language in Singapore*. Singapore: Eastern Universities Press.

Crystal, David (1997) *English as a Global Language*. Cambridge: Cambridge University Press.

Cunningsworth, Alan (1984) *Evaluating and Selecting EFL Teaching Materials*. London: Heinemann.

Davies, Alan (1991) *The Native Speaker in Applied Linguistics*. Edinburgh: Edinburgh University Press.

Davies, Alan (2003) *The Native Speaker: Myth and Reality*. Clevedon, UK: Multilingual Matters.

Davies, Alan (2004) The native speaker in Applied Linguistics. In *The Handbook of Applied Linguistics*. Edited by Alan Davies and Catherine Elder. Oxford: Blackwell, pp. 431–50.

Delpit, Lisa (1995) *Other People's Children*. New York: New Press.

Delpit, Lisa and Dowdy, Joanne Kilgour (eds.) (2002) *The Skin that We Speak: Thoughts on Language and Culture in the Classroom*. New York: New Press.

Erling, Elizabeth (2002) "I learn English since ten years": The global English debate and the German university classroom. *English Today*, **18**(2), 8–13.

Ferguson, Charles A. and Heath, Shirley Brice (eds.) (1981) *Language in the USA*. Cambridge: Cambridge University Press.

Finegan, Edward (1980) *Attitudes toward English Usage: The History of a War of Words*. New York: Teachers College Press.

Fishman, Joshua A., Conrad, Andrew W., and Rubal-Lopez, Alma (eds.) (1996) *Post-Imperial English: Status Change in Former British and*

American Colonies, 1940–1990.
Berlin: Mouton de Gruyter.

Flaitz, Jeffra (1988) *The Ideology of English: French Perceptions of English as a World Language.* Berlin: Mouton de Gruyter.

Foley, Joseph (ed.) (1988) *New Englishes: The Case of Singapore.* Singapore: Singapore University Press.

Freire, Paulo (1997) *Pedagogy of the Oppressed* (Revised 20th-Anniversary edition). New York: Continuum.

Friedrich, Patricia (2002) Teaching world Englishes in two South American countries. *World Englishes,* **21**(3), 441–4.

García, Ofelia and Otheguy, Ricardo (eds.) (1989) *English across Cultures: Cultures across English.* Berlin: Mouton de Gruyter.

Gill, Saran Kaur (1993) Standards and pedagogical norms for teaching English in Malaysia. *World Englishes,* **12**(2), 223–38.

Gill, Saran Kaur (2002) *International Communication: English Language Challenges for Malaysia.* Serdang: Universiti Putra Malaysia Press.

Gill, Saran Kaur and Pakir, Anne (eds.) (1999) Symposium on standards, codification and world Englishes. Special issue of *World Englishes,* **18**(2), 159–289.

Goldstein, Lynn M. (1987) Standard English: The only target for nonnative speakers of English? *TESOL Quarterly,* **21**(3), 417–36.

Görlach, Manfred (1999) Varieties of English and language teaching. In *Native and Non-Native Perspectives. Teaching and Learning English as a Global Language.* Edited by Claus Gnutzmann. Tübingen: Stauffenburg Verlag, pp. 3–21.

Graddol, David and Meinhof, Ulrike H. (eds.) (1999) *English in a Changing World.* Milton Keynes: AILA.

Gramley, Stephan (2001) *The Vocabulary of World English.* London: Arnold.

Gray, John (2002) The global coursebook in English Language Teaching. In *Globalization and Language Teaching.* Edited by David Block and Deborah Cameron. London: Routledge, pp. 151–67.

Halverson, John (1966) Prolegomena to the study of Ceylon English. *University of Ceylon Review,* **24**(1/2), 61–75.

Harbord, John (1992) The use of the mother tongue in the classroom. *ELT Journal,* **46**(4), 350–5.

Hartmann, Reinhard (ed.) (1996) *The English Language in Europe.* Oxford: Intellect.

Hinkel, Eli (ed.) (1999) *Culture in Second Language Teaching and Learning.* Cambridge: Cambridge University Press.

Howatt, Anthony P. R. (1984) *A History of English Language Teaching.* Oxford: Oxford University Press.

Hu, Xiao Qiong (2004) Why China English should stand alongside British, American, and other "world Englishes." *English Today,* **20**(2), 26–33.

Jenkins, Jennifer (2000) *The Phonology of English as an International Language.* Oxford: Oxford University Press.

Jenkins, Jennifer (2003) *World Englishes: A Resource Book for Students.* London: Routledge.

Jenkins, Jennifer, Modiano, Marko, and Seidlhoher, Barbara (2001) Euro-English. *English Today,* **17**(4), 13–19.

Jordan, June (1997) Nobody mean more to me than you and the future life of Willie Jordan. In *Living Languages: Contexts for Reading and Writing.* Edited by Nancy Buffington, Marvin Diogenes, and Clyde Moneyhun. Upper Saddle River, NJ: Prentice-Hall, pp. 194–209.

Kachru, Braj B. (1981) American English and other Englishes. In *Language in the USA.* Edited by Charles A. Ferguson and Shirley Brice Heath.

Cambridge: Cambridge University Press, pp. 21–43.

Kachru, Braj B. (1983) *The Indianization of English: The English Language in India*. Delhi: Oxford University Press.

Kachru, Braj B. (1986) *The Alchemy of English: The Spread, Functions and Models of Non-Native Englishes*. Oxford: Pergamon.

Kachru, Braj B. (1988) Teaching world Englishes. *ERIC/CLL News Bulletin*, **12**(1), 1, 3, 4, 8.

Kachru, Braj B. (ed.) (1992a) *The Other Tongue: English across Cultures*. Urbana, IL: University of Illinois Press. 1st edition 1981.

Kachru, Braj B. (1992b) The second diaspora of English. In *English in Its Social Contexts: Essays in Historical Sociolinguistics*. Edited by Thomas W. Machan and Charles T. Scott. Oxford: Oxford University Press, pp. 230–52.

Kachru, Braj B. (1994) Teaching world Englishes without myths. In *INTELEC '94: Proceedings of the International English Education Conference, Kuala Lampur, Malaysia*. Edited by Saran Kaur Gill, et al. Kuala Lumpur: Language Centre, Universiti Kebangsaan Malaysia, pp. 1–19.

Kachru, Braj B. (1995) World Englishes: Approaches, issues, and resources. In *Readings on Second Language Acquisition*. Edited by H. Douglas Brown and Susan Gonzo. Upper Saddle River, NJ: Prentice-Hall Regents, pp. 229–61.

Kachru, Braj B. (1996) World Englishes: Agony and ecstasy. *Journal of Aesthetic Education*, **30**(2), 135–55.

Kachru, Braj B. (1997) World Englishes 2000: Resources for research and teaching. In *World Englishes 2000*. Edited by Larry E. Smith and Michael L. Forman. Honolulu: University of Hawai'i and East-West Center, pp. 209–51.

Kachru, Braj B. (2003) World Englishes in the Classroom: The Japanese Context. Presented at the Workshop on World Englishes in the Classroom, Chukyo University, Nagoya, Japan, December 7–8.

Kachru, Braj B. (2005) *Asian Englishes: Beyond the Canon*. Hong Kong: Hong Kong University Press.

Kachru, Braj B. and Nelson, Cecil L. (1996) World Englishes. In *Sociolinguistics and Language Teaching*. Edited by Sandra Lee McKay and Nancy H. Hornberger. Cambridge: Cambridge University Press, pp. 71–102.

Kachru, Braj B. and Nelson, Cecil L. (2001) World Englishes. In *Analysing English in a Global Context: A Reader*. Edited by Anne Burns and Caroline Coffin. London: Routledge, pp. 9–25.

Kachru, Yamuna (1987) Cross-cultural texts, discourse strategies and discourse interpretation. In *Discourse across Cultures: Strategies in World Englishes*. Edited by Larry E. Smith. New York: Prentice-Hall, pp. 87–100.

Kachru, Yamuna (1994) Monolingual bias in SLA research. *TESOL Quarterly*, **28**(4), 795–800.

Kachru, Yamuna (1999) Culture, context, and writing. In *Culture in Second Language Teaching and Learning*. Edited by Eli Hinkel. Cambridge: Cambridge University Press, pp. 75–108.

Kachru, Yamuna and Nelson, Cecil L. (2006) *World Englishes in Asian Contexts*. Hong Kong: Hong Kong University Press.

Kaldor, Susan (1991) Standard Australian English as a second language and as a second dialect. In *Languages and Standards: Issues, Attitudes, Case Studies*. Edited by Makhan L. Tickoo. Singapore: SEAMEO Regional Language Centre, pp. 68–85.

Kalmar, Tomás Mario (2001) *Illegal Alphabets and Adult Biliteracy: Latino*

Migrants Crossing the Linguistic Border. Mahwah, NJ: Lawrence Erlbaum.

Kramsch, Claire (1993) *Context and Culture in Language Teaching*. Oxford: Oxford University Press.

Kramsch, Claire (1996) The cultural component of language teaching. *Zeitschrift für Interkulturellen Fremdsprachenunterricht*, **1**. Retrieved 25/3/2004, from http://www.spz.tu-darmstadt.de/projekt_ejournal/jg_01_2/beitrag/kramsch2.htm.

Kramsch, Claire (1997) The privilege of the nonnative speaker. *PMLA*, **112**(3), 359–69.

Kubota, Ryuko (2001) Teaching world Englishes to native speakers of English in the USA. *World Englishes*, **20**(1), 47–64.

Kujore, Obafemi (1997) Whose English? In *New Englishes: A West African Perspective*. Edited by Ayọ Bamgboṣe, Ayọ Banjo, and Andrew Thomas. Trenton, NJ: Africa World Press, pp. 367–80.

Kumaravadivelu, B. (2003) *Beyond Methods: Macrostrategies for Language Teaching*. New Haven, CT: Yale University Press.

Lin, Angel M. Y. (2001) Doing-English-lessons in the reproduction or transformation of social worlds? In *English Language Teaching in Its Social Contact*. Edited by Christopher N. Candlin and Neil Mercer. London: Routledge, pp. 271–86.

Lippi-Green, Rosina (1997) *English with an Accent: Language, Ideology, and Discrimination in the United States*. London: Routledge.

Liu, Jun (1999) Nonnative-English-speaking professionals in TESOL. *TESOL Quarterly*, **33**(1), 85–102.

Llamzon, Teodoro A. (1969) *Standard Filipino English*. Manila: Ateneo University Press.

Matsuda, Aya (2002) "International understanding" through teaching world Englishes. *World Englishes*, **21**(3), 436–40.

Mazrui, Alamin (2004) *English in Africa after the Cold War*. Clevedon, UK: Multilingual Matters.

McArthur, Tom (1998) *The English Languages*. Cambridge: Cambridge University Press.

McKay, Sandra Lee (2002) *Teaching English as an International Language*. Oxford: Oxford University Press.

Medgyes, Péter (1992) Native or non-native: Who's worth more? *ELT Journal*, **46**(4), 340–9.

Medgyes, Péter (1994) *The Non-Native Teacher*. London: Macmillan. (2nd edition 1999, Hueber Verlag.)

Medgyes, Péter (2001) When the teacher is a non-native speaker. In *Teaching English as a Second or Foreign Language*. 3rd edition. Edited by Marianne Celce-Murcia. Boston, MA: Heinle and Heinle, pp. 429–42.

Melchers, Gunnel and Shaw, Philip (2003) *World Englishes: An Introduction*. London: Arnold.

Modiano, Marko (1999) Standard English(es) and educational practices for the world's lingua franca. *English Today*, **15**(4), 3–13.

Morgan, John and Rinvolucri, Mario (1986) *Vocabulary*. Oxford: Oxford University Press.

Mundari, Ingrid (1997) Language as image maker. In *Living Languages: Contexts for Reading and Writing*. Edited by Nancy Buffington, Marvin Diogenes, and Clyde Moneyhun. Upper Saddle River, NJ: Prentice-Hall, pp. 91–6.

Nero, Shondel J. (1997) ESL or EDL? Teaching English to Caribbean English speakers. *TESOL Journal*, **7**(2), 6–10.

Norton, Bonny (1997) Language, identity, and the ownership of English. *TESOL Quarterly*, **31**(3), 409–29.

Omodiaogbe, Sylvester A. (1992) 150 years on: English in the Nigerian school system – past, present, and future. *ELT Journal*, **46**(1), 19–28.

Ortiz, Simon (1997) The language we know. In *Living Languages: Contexts for Reading and Writing*. Edited by Nancy Buffington, Marvin Diogenes, and Clyde Moneyhun. Upper Saddle River, NJ: Prentice-Hall, pp. 40–7.

Paikeday, Thomas M. (1985) *The Native Speaker Is Dead!* Toronto: PPI.

Pakir, Anne (1991) The status of English and the question of "standard" in Singapore: A sociolinguistic perspective. In *Languages and Standards: Issues, Attitudes, Case Studies*. Edited by Makhan L. Tickoo. Singapore: SEAMEO Regional Language Centre, pp. 109–30.

Peña, Phebe S. (1997) Philippine English in the classroom. In *English Is an Asian Language: The Philippine Context*. Edited by Ma. Lourdes S. Bautista. Sydney: Macquarie Library, pp. 87–102.

Pennington, Martha C. (1996) *Phonology in English Language Teaching: An International Approach*. London: Longman.

Perry, Theresa and Delpit, Lisa (eds.) (1998) *The Real Ebonics Debate: Power, Language, and the Education of African-American Children*. Boston, MA: Beacon Press.

Phillipson, Robert (1992a) *Linguistic Imperialism*. Oxford: Oxford University Press.

Phillipson, Robert (1992b) ELT: The native speaker's burden? *ELT Journal*, **46**(1), 12–18.

Platt, John, Weber, Heidi, and Ho, Mian Lian (1984) *The New Englishes*. London: Routledge and Kegan Paul.

Pride, John B. (ed.) (1982) *New Englishes*. Rowley, MA: Newbury House.

Prodromou, Luke (1988) English as cultural action. *ELT Journal*, **42**(2), 73–83.

Prodromou, Luke (1992) What culture? Which culture? Cross-cultural factors in language learning. *ELT Journal*, **46**(1), 39–50.

Purcell-Gates, Victoria (1995) *Other People's Words: The Cycle of Low Literacy*. Cambridge, MA: Harvard University Press.

Rampton, M. B. H. (1990) Displacing the "native speaker": Expertise, affiliation, and inheritance. *ELT Journal*, **44**(2), 97–101.

Richard-Amato, Patricia A. (2003) Participatory language teaching. In *Making It Happen: From Interactive to Participatory Language Teaching: Theory and Practice*. Edited by Patricia A. Richard-Amato. White Plains, NY: Longman, pp. 70–91.

Rickford, John Russell and Rickford, Russell John (2000) *Spoken Soul: The Story of Black English*. New York: John Wiley.

Schaefer, Halmuth H. (1963) A vocabulary program using "language redundancy." *Journal of Programed Instruction*, **2**(3), 9–16.

Scovel, Tom (2001) *Learning New Languages*. Boston, MA: Heinle and Heinle.

Seidlhofer, Barbara (1999) Double standards: Teacher education in the Expanding Circle. *World Englishes*, **18**(2), 233–45.

Seidlhofer, Barbara (2001) Closing the conceptual gap: The case for a description of English as a lingua franca. *International Journal of Applied Linguistics*, **11**(2), 133–58.

Sey, Kofi Abakah (1973) *Ghanaian English*. London: Macmillan.

Simpkins, Gary, Holt, Grace, and Simpkins, Charlesetta (1977) *Bridge: A Cross-Culture Reading Program*. Boston, MA: Houghton Mifflin.

Singh, Michael, Kell, Peter, and Pandian, Ambigapathy (2002) *Appropriating English: Innovation in the Global*

Business of English Language Teaching.
New York: Peter Lang.

Singh, Rajendra (ed.) (1998) *The Native
Speaker: Multilingual Perspectives.*
New Delhi: Sage.

Skutnabb-Kangas, Tove (1981)
*Bilingualism or Not: The Education
of Minorities.* Clevedon, UK:
Multilingual Matters.

Smith, Larry E. (1976) English as an
international auxiliary language.
RELC Journal 7(2). Reprinted 1983 in
*Readings in English as an International
Language.* Edited by Larry E. Smith.
Oxford: Pergamon, pp. 1–5.

Smith, Larry E. (1981) *English for Cross-
Cultural Communication.* London:
Macmillan.

Smith, Larry E. (ed.) (1983) *Readings in
English as an International Language.*
Oxford: Pergamon.

Smith, Larry E. (ed.) (1987) *Discourse
across Cultures: Strategies in World
Englishes.* New York: Prentice-Hall.

Smitherman, Geneva (2000) *Talkin that
Talk: Language, Culture and Education
in African America.* London:
Routledge.

Sridhar, Kamal K. and Sridhar, S. N.
(1992) Bridging the paradigm gap:
Second-language acquisition theory
and indigenized varieties of English.
In *The Other Tongue: English across
Cultures,* 2nd edition. Edited by Braj
B. Kachru. Urbana, IL: University
of Illinois Press, pp. 91–107.

Sridhar, S. N. (1994) A reality check for
SLA theories. *TESOL Quarterly,*
28(4), 800–3.

Stanlaw, James (2004) *Japanese English:
Language and Culture Contact.* Hong
Kong: Hong Kong University Press.

Stavans, Ilan (2005) Spanglish: The
making of a new American
language. In *The New World Reader:
Thinking and Writing about the Global
Community.* Edited by Gilbert H.
Muller. Boston: Houghton Mifflin,
pp. 96–103.

Strevens, Peter (1987) Cultural barriers
to language learning. In *Discourse
across Cultures: Strategies in World
Englishes.* Edited by Larry E. Smith.
New York: Prentice-Hall, pp. 169–
78.

Tan, Amy (2005) Mother tongue. In *The
New World Reader: Thinking and
Writing about the Global Community.*
Edited by Gilbert H. Muller. Boston:
Houghton Mifflin, pp. 78–83.

Tickoo, Makhan L. (1991) Stakeholders
and standards: Englishes for
tomorrow's India. In *Languages and
Standards: Issues, Attitudes, Case
Studies.* Edited by Makhan L. Tickoo.
Singapore: SEAMEO Regional
Language Centre, pp. 131–52.

Tongue, R. K. (1974) *The English of
Singapore and Malaysia.* Singapore:
Eastern Universities Press.

Trahern, Joseph B. (ed.) (1989)
*Standardising English: Essays in
the History of Language Change,*
Tennessee Studies in Literature,
vol. 31. Knoxville: University of
Tennessee.

Trudgill, Peter and Hannah, Jean (2002)
*International English: A Guide to
Varieties of Standard English,*
4th edition. London: Arnold.

Trueba, Henry T. (1989) *Raising Silent
Voices: Educating the Linguistic
Minorities for the 21st Century.*
Boston, MA: Heinle and Heinle.

Walatara, Douglas (1974) *Reconstruction:
An English Technique for an Asian
Context.* Denipitiya, Hunnasgiriya:
P. L. F. de Silva.

Weiner, Eva S. and Smith, Larry E.
(1983) *English as an International
Language: A Writing Approach.*
Oxford: Pergamon.

Widdowson, Henry G. (1994) The
ownership of English. *TESOL
Quarterly,* **28**(2), 377–89.

Widdowson, Henry G. (2003) *Defining
Issues in English Language Teaching.*
Oxford: Oxford University Press.

Williams, Robert L. (ed.) (1975) *Ebonics: The True Language of Black Folks.* St Louis, MI: Robert L. Williams and Associates.

Wolfram, Walt, Adger, Carolyn Temple, and Christian, Donna (1999) *Dialects in Schools and Communities.* Mahwah, NJ: Lawrence Erlbaum.

Wong, Irene (1982) Native-speaker English for the Third World today? In *New Englishes.* Edited by John B. Pride. Rowley, MA: Newbury House, pp. 261–86.

Wright, Laura (2000) *The Development of Standard English 1300–1800: Theories, Descriptions, Conflicts.* Cambridge: Cambridge University Press.

Yajun, Jiang (2003) English as a Chinese language. *English Today,* **19**(2), 3–8.

Youmans, Madeleine (2001) Cross-cultural difference in polite epistemic modal use in American English. *Journal of Multilingual and Multicultural Development,* **22**(1), 57–73.

FURTHER READING

Bolton, Kingsley (2004) World Englishes. In *The Handbook of Applied Linguistics.* Edited by Alan Davies and Catherine Elder. Oxford: Blackwell, pp. 367–96.

Kachru, Braj B. (2005) Part V, Pedagogy. *Asian Englishes: Beyond the Canon.* Hong Kong: Hong Kong University Press, pp. 185–202.

Savignon, Sandra J. (ed.) (2002) *Interpreting Communicative Language Teaching: Contexts and Concerns in Teacher Education.* New Haven, CT: Yale University Press.

Tawake, Sandra (guest ed.) (1995) Symposium on World Englishes in the Classroom. *World Englishes,* **14**(2).

37 Models, Methods, and Curriculum for ELT Preparation

KIMBERLEY BROWN

1 Introduction

There is a tradition of centuries in which language educators have been seeking for the one correct way to teach people languages. Kelly (1976) traced these various methodologies and looked at whether specific languages have been or need to be taught in particular ways. Other authors who have examined the history of English language teaching in various contexts include Howatt (1984), Prabhu (1987), Larson-Freeman (2000), Celce-Murcia (2001), and Knight (2001).

This chapter explores from a historical perspective how information regarding English language teaching has been conceptualized, examines criticisms leveled at such concepts, and suggests what current ways of conceptualizing English language teaching ought to include if the sociolinguistic realities of the spread and functions of English are used as the bases for language planning.

2 Models and Methods

A number of terms are commonly used in discussing models and methods of language teaching. They all imply that it is possible to discover and use "the one best method."

Anthony (1963) treated the relationships among Approaches, Methods, and Techniques. (See also Richards, 1987 and Richards and Rogers, 1986.) Anthony suggested that, at the broadest level, languages are guided in their Approaches by their assumptions dealing with teaching and learning. Following from those are Methods which are consistent with the Approaches, plans for linking theory with practice, and ultimately Techniques for implementation. According to Richards and Rogers (1986: 15), following Anthony: "[M]ethods is the level at which theory is put into practice and at which choices are made about the particular skills to be taught, the content to be taught, and the order in which the content will be presented." Techniques are at the most concrete level; they comprise the activities undertaken by teachers (or learners) to implement Methods. (Methods may be equated with *strategies*, though this term is often used in the literature for teaching activities, and Techniques would then be comparable to *tactics*.)

Kumaravadivelu (2003: 24) suggests that a traditional view of Method is that "it does not refer to what teachers actually do in the classroom; rather it refers to established methods conceptualized and constructed by experts in the field." This description of Method is not unlike A. Hadley's (1993: 481–2) description of curriculum planning:

> curriculum planning involves such things as the setting of goals (for both the whole sequence of instruction and each individual course), the selection of materials and teaching approaches, the design of the testing program and the appropriate use of program-evaluation procedures.

The term "model" is also commonly used. Woodward (1991) uses the term in its broadest sense, to refer to ways pre-service teachers look toward their teachers or trainers for instruction in the way to do something. She states:

> Whatever the questions we might have, we use the giving and following of models in teacher training and language teaching all the time. We talk about providing good phonological models and of approximating texts. (p. 84)

In traditional ELT practices, such models have typically looked toward the native speaker as the ideal speaker-hearer and have not used context as a variable to vary the proposed methodology. Kachru (1983) referred to this as a "monomodel" for teaching. It arises from the Positivist tradition, arguing that there must be a universally agreed-upon definition of the best way to teach. Clarke and Silberstein (2002: 10), for example, write that teachers and teacher educators often believe "good language teaching will always display certain key characteristics . . . [leading inappropriately to] the implicitly mandated reality to which all teachers are expected to aspire."

An examination of various ELT methodologies reveals inconsistent uses of the terms reviewed above, as well as an inconsistent movement from Approach/Model to Method to Curriculum Design to Technique/Implementation (Kelly, 1976). One such example would be what some term "Freirian methodology." Freire, a Brazilian educator most known for his *Pedagogy of the Oppressed* (1972), has deeply influenced a school of professional language educators best represented by Elsa Auerbach and Nina Wallerstein (Auerbach, 1992; Wallerstein, 1983; Auerbach and Wallerstein, 1987), and Timothy Reagan and Terry Osborn (2001), among others. None of these individuals refers to "Freireian methodology." Most consider themselves educators deeply connected to critical theory. Yet students in TESOL Methods classes study Freirean pedagogy the same way they examine Total Physical Response, Communicative

Language Teaching, and the Natural Approach. All are grouped into some broad category that mixes the terms Anthony (1963) has outlined.

For the initial purposes of this chapter, then, the terms "models of ELT teaching" and "approaches to ELT teaching" will be used synonymously. The term "methods" will be used in concurrence per the above discussion with the understanding that, generally, a method is more prescriptive and specific than an approach or model. Finally, the term "curriculum" will be used as defined by Woodward (1991).

Following a brief summary of types of ELT models and methods that have been employed historically and a discussion of the most prevalent ELT curricula, this chapter then explores the criticisms leveled at the models, methods, and curricula.

Most models that English language teachers are familiar with have their origins in what are sometimes termed "Northern" or "developed" countries. From a chronological perspective, they have included the Grammar-Translation Method, the Direct Method, Audiolingualism, "designer methods" such as the Silent Way, Counseling Learning, Suggestopedia, Total Physical Response (TPR), the Language Experience Approach (alternatively termed the Whole Language Approach), the Natural Approach, the Communicative Approach, the Freirian Approach, and what numerous authors, among them H. D. Brown (1980), Celce-Murcia (2001), and Kumaravadivelu (2003), term the "Eclectic Approach." Rich discussions of all of these can be found in Celce-Murcia (2001), Oller and Richard-Amato (1983), Richards and Rodgers (1986), and Stevick (1976).

Grammar-Translation, most popular in the North countries through the 1950s, and to some degree through the following decade in spite of advances in Audiolingualism, involves, as its labels indicates, translation of sentences or passages from one language to another. Students familiarize themselves with a grammar rule in the target language, sometimes contrasting it with the structures that correspond to it in their home language. There is a strong focus on the written language and usually very little spoken production. The method is still used throughout the world; in particular, it remains a frequently adopted methodology for less commonly taught languages.

The Direct Method was developed primarily by the US military as the armed services recognized the need for fluent conversationalists in various languages. In this method, the mother tongue is not used at all. Perhaps the best-known language school around the world that utilized this method was the Berlitz chain.

Audiolingualism was a direct reaction to the two prior methods. It developed from strongly Behaviorist psychological perspectives on language. The emphasis was on accurate spoken production following repetition of models, often in language laboratories. This methodology, quite prevalent in the United States, emerged during the Cold War in response to the need for accurate, spoken fluency in what are sometimes termed "critical languages," i.e., those necessary for national security.

Strong cognitive responses to Audiolingualism followed. A. Hadley (1993) discusses what are sometimes termed the Humanistic methodologies that emerged in response to Audiolingualism. Moskowitz is well known for her work in this area, evidenced in the volume *Caring and Sharing in the Foreign Language Class* (1978). Stevick, in his *Memory, Meaning, and Method* (1976), examines in detail the assumptions behind The Silent Way, Counseling-Learning, and Suggestopedia, three methodologies that emerged during this period. In all three of these latter cases, those who developed the methodologies did not see themselves as linguists or even as professional language educators. To some degree, all these methods were worked out by charismatic individuals who were convinced there was a link between some aspect of another discipline and the manner of teaching which they created.

The Silent Way's Caleb Gattegno believed that students could ultimately focus on accurate production with little intervention from the teacher. The use of color-coded production charts for grammar and pronunciation and of cuisenaire rods, often used as manipulables in language classrooms, further distinguished this method. It was not ever widely used outside Europe, North America, Australia, and New Zealand.

Counseling-Learning was linked to Adlerian and Rogerian psychology, and focused on the role of the teacher as facilitator or translator. It depended on the technology of a tape recorder and a small, safe setting for learners in which they determined for themselves what they wished to say.

Suggestopedia, the final "designer method," was crafted by Bulgarian psychologist G. Lozanov, whose interest in hypnotism and the subconscious led to a strong emphasis on crafting a foundation for learners to be open to new material. This usually involved setting the classroom scene with Baroque music, with rhythms set at roughly that of the human heart, 60 beats per minute. It sometimes involved learners assuming new identities and names in their language classrooms. Because Lozanov was forbidden to leave Bulgaria for more than ten years, there were few professional presentations at international language meetings by those directly involved in the method. Lozanov has since criticized neo-Suggestopedic versions of his original work. As with the Silent Way and Counseling Learning, this method calls for specific props and activities that do not lend themselves easily to use in large classrooms with fixed chairs and set curricula dictated by Ministries of Education. None of these methods has been widely used throughout much of the world because of such constraints.

Yet another method, Total Physical Response, which was quite popular in the 1970s and early 1980s, was designed by James Asher (e.g., 1983). This method depended on students actively moving through a series of commands while listening to but not initially producing language. It is an outgrowth of the Direct Method (e.g., A. Hadley, 1993) and is still often used to frame warm-up activities and beginning-level language study throughout the world. Its link to the Natural Approach (Krashen and Terrell, 1983; Terrell, 1977, 1983) is more generally recognized today than at its inception.

3   Communicative Language Teaching

Berns states that the "term communicative language teaching identifies new pedagogical orientations that have grown out of the realization that knowledge of grammatical forms and structures alone does not adequately prepare learners for effective and appropriate use of the languages they are learning" (1990: 79). Littlewood (1981: 6) looks at four dimensions of speaker skills within this approach: achievement of linguistic competence, understanding of the relationship of linguistic competence to a broader communicative system, self-awareness and flexibility to vary usage if necessary, and an understanding of what is socially appropriate, i.e. "generally acceptable forms."

A. Hadley suggests that Communicative Language Teaching is an approach and not a method. She states that its congruence with "proficiency-goals will depend on the choices made by the program designers and instructors" (1993: 105). Proficiency-based instruction was particularly popular in foreign language teaching in the United States during the decade of the 1990s. In spite of problems with much of the ELT material labeled communicative as discussed below, typical citations of developers of such material include Brumfit and Johnson (1979), Brumfit and Roberts (1983), Finochiaro and Brumfit (1983), Widdowson (1990, 2002), and Wilkins (1976).

Berns has suggested that much of what is termed "communicative" is in fact a set of surface level activities *practicing* communication without actually *engaging in* communication (1990: 87). She suggests that there are weaknesses in the functional-notional approach as defined by Finochiaro and Brumfit, and by Wilkins. These weaknesses become particularly apparent in materials and curriculum: "[Finochiario and Brumfit] do not call attention to the roles that the speaker's cultural background plays in determining the appropriateness of linguistic structures and lexical items selected to realize a function" (1990: 87).

In spite of the observations made by Berns and others (cf. H. D. Brown, 1980) throughout the late 1970s, the Council of Europe worked tirelessly to specify language situations and functions that could be used to identify threshold or proficiency levels in language. The importance of functional linguistics in Europe, unlike in the US, spurred much of this work. Wilkins (1976), closely associated with the Council of Europe, first listed functions and notions for ELT instructors to incorporate in their syllabi. Those functions were based on categories of meaning ranging from semantic-grammatical and modal to communicative function. A functional syllabus would focus on communicative functions. A notional syllabus focuses on using semantics to choose what to incorporate in the syllabus (cf. Berns, 1990 for a more inclusive discussion of these dimensions).

Moving beyond David Wilkins' (1976) proposal of a notional syllabus, van Ek, Alexander, Trim and others (see, e.g., van Ek, 1987) suggested that it was possible to identify for all member-country languages in Europe, including

English, a body of situations or contexts where the target language would be used. It should further be possible to identify all topics, the activities a user could participate in, the functions necessary to complete a transaction, the "general" and "specific" notions (1987: 80) the learners would need to use, and both the forms and level of proficiency of use the learners would demonstrate. The power of the Council to influence the design of language materials and curricula in Europe and around the world for almost two decades is important. Set in a Positivist framework, the assumption of the creators of the Notional-Functional idea was that with care, the right set of researchers and educators working together, and some attention to setting, a universal set of parameters could be outlined for the teaching of English.

Critics of the inflexibility of the Communicative Approach look at "hidden agendas" linked to it (G. Hadley, 2004; Kazmi, 2004), chief among them the notion that promotion of a Communicative Approach linked strongly to ideologies of Western countries and particular notions of modernity, which is not the neutral promotion of a universally appropriate method.

In addition to concerns about the promotion of values, attitudes, and beliefs tied to Inner-Circle countries, these authors also look at the economics of textbook promotion. McKay (2002) examines problems with a universal application of this methodology, drawing attention to conflicts that arise when students are asked to do things in a manner that conflicts with their ideas of appropriate activities, e.g., the question of religion in government in certain states. She also looks at lack of support for use of the mother tongue in the classroom and the marginalization of "local teachers, who at times are asked to implement a methodology that may be in conflict with their own sense of plausibility" (p. 119). Sociopolitical variables, the notion that local conditions could affect varieties of language use, and the notion of ownership of English played no role in this or any other of the methodologies identified so far. Yet these are the primary tenets of a world Englishes perspective that will be discussed below.

Some dimensions of context are used in The Language Experience or Whole Language Approach. Most often used with young children learning their first language, this method has had wide appeal in Australia, New Zealand, and the United States for its emphasis on learners producing language important to them in a non-threatening environment without strong attention to grammar and spelling. Learners' speech is captured by an instructor in written form without initial correction. The Whole Language Approach has been used with adults, particularly with refugees who are encountering resettlement trauma. Two key proponents, Yvonne and David Freeman, revised the title of their original *Whole Language for Second Language Learners* to *ESL/EFL Teaching: Principles for Success* (1998), suggesting that too many teachers, parents, and administrators came to associate the phrase "whole language" with problematic dimensions of language learning. Similarly, they suggest that the phrase "second language learner" does not refer to learners outside what Kachru terms "Inner-Circle" countries. Because of the international applicability of this approach, they now use "ESL/EFL teaching." It is interesting that, even as late as 1998, they did not choose a phrase like "English in a Global Context." As do proponents of Communicative Language Teaching, they have underscored their belief that there are indeed universal principles for successful language learning.

The Natural Approach, based on work by Krashen and Terrell (e.g., 1983), is the method most closely tied to second-language acquisition research. These authors have suggested that an acquisitional environment must be replicated in the classroom in order to promote authentic language use. TPR, described above, follows closely from this same framework. Both ESL and EFL materials were designed in the 1980s to reflect the influence of the Natural Approach. The EFL Materials, titled *New Wave* (Longman) were designed to provide as authentic a context as possible for communication to take place within the four walls of a classroom. Their success is subject to the same lens Berns (1990) applies to other settings when she asks whether the underlying philosophy assumes "the" truth or "a" truth, affected strongly by the sociocultural context and the speakers themselves.

Throughout the 1980s and 1990s, dimensions of teacher and learner reflection were introduced in ELT in many of the North countries. Teacher-preparation texts like those of Schön (1983, 1987) actively promoted teacher awareness of frameworks of activities. Underlying this reflection, however, is an ideology that best methods or practices, while modified through teacher–student negotiation, still exist. This focus is still visible in texts like that of Gebhard and Oprandy (1999).

At the same time, English language teachers attempted to design *functional-notional syllabi, communicative syllabi,* the *Threshold-level syllabus, English for Specific Purposes curriculum, English for Academic Purposes curriculum,* and ultimately the *project-based curriculum* (Nunan, 1989, 1997; Petzold, 2002; Ulichny, 1996; see also Chapter 36 in this volume).

A more recent philosophical influence that has affected the design of curricula but has yet to be strongly reflected in ELT methods sequences is that of Constructivism (cf. Diaz-Rico, 1999; McGroarty, 1998). This term has been used to denote the importance of a negotiation regarding activities between teacher and learner in a particular context (cf. Dantas-Whitney, 2002; Chen, 2003). Within a Constructivist approach, local culture plays a critical role in determining what will be taught and how. Bohn (2003: 169) faults the Brazilian government's unwillingness to use such an approach to provide adequate English and other foreign language instruction to learners:

> Brazilian schools have also been unable to bring into the language classroom the local culture, that is, the set of social meanings, beliefs, values, behaviors, and practices related to the learners' cultures and lives . . . [T]heir mother tongue, their culture, and social identities have not been invited to participate in the construction of new linguistic expression in the new language. Because the local culture has been kept out of schools, children's and adolescents' bodies,

emotions, and imaginative and creative capacities have been likewise kept from the classroom. . . . English teachers . . . have not valued locally and nationally generated research and knowledge on language teaching and education.

In her discussion of problems with notional-functional syllabi, Berns (1990), like Bohn (2003), looks at the absence of attention to learners' cultures. This flaw is actually characteristic of all the approaches cited so far. Berns (1990) suggests that this failure persists because the underlying philosophy of teaching has remained unchanged from the time of Audiolingualism: it remains linked to the idea that there is one appropriate way to teach, control, and assist students in mastering information. Tudor (2003: 3) uses the phrase "technology of teaching" and argues that, despite growing reflectivity and creativity in the domain of ELT, effective results will only occur when the social context at a particular moment is considered.

Like Van Lier (1996), part of Tudor's push is for an Ecological Approach, defined as an exploration of "language teaching and learning within the totality of the lives of the various participants involved, and not as one subpart of their lives which can be examined in isolation" (2003: 40). The Ecological Approach is clearly compatible with Constructivist approaches to language education which rely on the co-construction of knowledge by participants in the language system, i.e., both teachers and learners drawing heavily on biological and social dimensions of local contexts. The importance of the insights of social scientists other than linguists, most particularly Maturana and Varela (1992), has been immeasurable in the development of this approach. Berns and Tudor's consistent attention to both macro-level and micro-level variables, much as a biologist frames his or her micro-level research results within the larger umbrella of the health of the total ecosystem, can be said to be part of the Ecological Approach to language education. Within such an approach, local context becomes particularly important.

4 Methods vs. Post-Methods

Quite separate from the Ecological and Constructivist approaches, but compatible with them, is that of Kumaravadivelu (2003). He suggests that we are no longer in a Methods era, but rather a post-Method era that is characterized by an awareness on the part of researchers and practitioners that we cannot find one best method and that simply knowing what method is effective does not assist people in becoming effective professional language educators. This perspective holds much in common with that of the reflective practitioners of the past two decades, but is most strongly linked to how context calls for shifts in the activities that language educators engage in. Scholars such as Kazmi (2004), Mehrotra (2000), Mohammed (1997), and Pennycook (1989) push for attention to local needs. Haded (1998: 39), e.g., looks at pan-Islamic student needs: "Due to the fact that the needs and perceptions of Muslim students are unique, it is recommended that they be encouraged to create, in collaborative groups, their own problem-solving exercises."

The approaches detailed above call for meaningful communication as defined in a local setting by the language learners and teachers co-creating their syllabi. Awareness of both macro- and micro-level variables affecting teaching and learning are advocated. Most call for reflection on what accounts for success or failure. What is missing is a dimension Qualley terms "reflexivity," defined as a "dialectical engagement with the other" (in Carter and Gradin, 2001: 3). This dialectical dimension draws upon power, equal and unequal, among language learners and teachers. It is the hallmark of critical theorists' writing about language teaching. A growing number of publications, including Phillipson's *Linguistic Imperialism* (1992), Tollefson's *Planning Language, Planning Inequality* (1991), and Pennycook's *The Cultural Politics of English as an International Language* (1994) have built analyses of power into their discussions of Methods and Approaches. Such authors also include Canagarajah (1999), McKay (2002), and Kazmi (2004).

5   World Englishes and Language Teaching

How does a world Englishes framework fit into this plethora of methods- and non-methods-based approaches to language instruction? Kachru (e.g., 1988: 1, 3, 4, 8) has delimited three aspects of a world Englishes theoretic framework or perspective: a belief that there is a "repertoire of models for English" as opposed to one best model; a belief that "the localized innovations [in English] have pragmatic bases"; and a belief that "the English language belongs to all those who use it."

In numerous papers, K. Brown has explored what such a perspective entails in the ELT Methods sequence (1993, 1995, 2002, 2005) and the degree to which current ELT preparatory programs build such perspectives into their curricula. It is evident from her research, as well as that of Vavrus (1991), Morgan and Schwarte (1995), and Grosse (1991), that this framework is rarely introduced as a central component of English language teacher training, particularly in the North countries. This is also evidenced in a recent electronic survey of content of methods courses by Murphy (2005), in which "world Englishes" is not even mentioned as a possible category for inclusion in ELT methods courses.

McKay looks at what she terms a "comprehensive theory of teaching and learning English as an International language" (2002: 125) coupled with a discussion of teaching goals and approaches. Drawing upon Kachru's work, she argues that intelligibility is central to what is taught. She also advocates a focus on the particular domains for which the language is needed, as well as acknowledgment that the zone of contact between speakers calls for cross-cultural pragmatic competence so that the users can actually establish "comity," defined as "friendly relations" (p. 128). She underscores the need for respect for local culture and teacher flexibility in choice of methods to achieve maximum productivity with maximum attention to what she terms "local culture[s] of learning" (p. 128). While she does not explore to what degree teacher trainers or scholars build information about such local cultures into their preparatory programs, other authors lament not only the degree to which local culture has been absent from English language curriculum design (Bohn, 2003), but also what Bohn characterizes as the lack of "locally and nationally generated research and knowledge on language teaching and education" (p. 169).

While McKay espouses what has been described above under a Constructivist Approach to use of a particular method, she does not focus extensively on power differences between those who have crafted the method and those who may employ it. This is the domain of the critical theorists. On a continuum moving from left of center to more left of center, Phillipson (1992) pushes for critical reflection on the power differential between core countries and periphery countries. Supportive of Kachru's calls for recognition of polymodels in language education, Phillipson suggests that Kachru has begun to explore differences in power indirectly; Kazmi (2004) supports this characterization. Pennycook (1994: 74) looks at the degree to which Phillipson writes about power and English as a commodity and asserts that Phillipson has not gone far enough in his analysis, particularly at the micro level. Kazmi likewise criticizes Phillipson for keeping his analysis at a macro level without looking at "the existential reality of people of the developing countries at the microlevel and show[ing] how that reality is altered by the learning and teaching of the English language, and who benefits from that alteration" (p. 3). Canagarajah goes even further, criticizing Phillipson and Pennycook for not drawing heavily enough on scholarship from Outer- or Expanding-Circle countries.

Kazmi suggests that in Kachru's view, all varieties of English "enjoy equal power" (2004: 8), and that he has not been sensitive "to the true modalities of power that continue to function through the use of the English language" (2004: 8). In fact, however, Kachru suggests that all varieties have the potential to wield the level of power necessary at a given time (Kachru, 2005).

6   Conclusion

While it is true that Kachru has focused less on issues of power than the self-styled critical theorists, the world Englishes paradigm has demonstrated the greatest level of adaptability to such notions. Attention to a world Englishes perspective in choice of methodology and curriculum design will result in an ecologically sound approach to language education, one that is attentive to the role that shifts in context bring to language education. At the present time, teacher preparatory programs, particularly in North countries, do not pay enough attention to the role of context. Without a world Englishes framework underlying ELT methods courses, it is unlikely that we will move beyond a focus on technical education or education for limited proficiency.

See also Chapters 36, TEACHING WORLD ENGLISHES; 39, WORLD ENGLISHES AND TEST CONSTRUCTION; 40, WORLD ENGLISHES AND COMMUNICATIVE COMPETENCE.

REFERENCES

Anthony, Edward (1963) Approach, method, and technique. *English Language Teaching*, **17**, 63–7.

Asher, James (1983) Motivating children and adults to acquire a second language. In *Methods that Work*. Edited by John Oller, Jr. and Patricia Richard-Amato. Cambridge, MA: Newbury House, pp. 329–36.

Auerbach, Elsa (1992) *Making Meaning, Making Change: Participatory Curriculum Development for Adult ESL Literacy*. McHenry, IL: Center for Applied Linguistics/Delta Systems.

Auerbach, Elsa and Wallerstein, Nina (1987) *ESL for Action*. New York: Addison Wesley.

Berns, Margie (1990) *Contexts of Competence: Social and Cultural Considerations in Communicative Language Teaching*. New York: Plenum Press.

Bohn, Hilario (2003) The educational role and status of English in Brazil. *World Englishes*, **22**(2), 159–72.

Brown, H. Douglas (1980) *Principles of Language Learning and Teaching*. Englewood Cliffs, NJ: Prentice-Hall.

Brown, Kimberley (1993) World Englishes in TESOL programs: An infusion model of curricular innovation. *World Englishes*, **12**(1), 59–73.

Brown, Kimberley (1995) World Englishes: To teach or not to teach. *World Englishes*, **14**(2), 233–46.

Brown, Kimberley (2002) Ideology and context: World Englishes and EFL teacher training. *World Englishes*, **21**(3), 445–8.

Brown, Kimberley (2005) World Englishes: Pedagogical practices in the TESOL preparatory sequence. In *Case Studies in TESOL Practice Series: Teaching English from a Global Perspective*. Edited by Anne Burns. TESOL.

Brumfit, Christopher and Johnson, Keith (eds.) (1979) *The Communicative Approach to Language Teaching*. Oxford: Oxford University Press.

Brumfit, Christopher and Roberts, John (1983) *A Short Introduction to Language and Language Teaching*. London: Batsford.

Canagarajah, Suresh (1999) *Resisting Linguistic Imperialism in English Teaching*. Oxford: Oxford University Press.

Carter, Duncan and Gradin, Sherrie (2001) *Writing as Reflective Action: A Reader*. New York: Longman.

Celce-Murcia, Marianne (2001) Language teaching approaches: An overview. In *Teaching English as a Second or Foreign Language*. 3rd edition. Edited by Marianne Celce-Murcia. Boston, MA: Heinle and Heinle, pp. 3–11.

Chen, Teresa (2003) Reticence in class and on-line: Two ESL students' experiences with communicative language teaching. *System*, **31**, 259–81.

Clarke, Mark and Silberstein, Sandra (2002) Problems, prescription, and paradoxes in second language teaching. In *Enriching ESOL Pedagogy: Reading and Activities for Engagement, Reflection, and Inquiry*. Edited by Vivian Zamel and Ruth

Spack. Mahwah, NJ: Lawrence Erlbaum Associates, pp. 3–16.

Dantas-Whitney, Maria (2002) Critical reflection in the second language classroom through audio-taped journals. *System*, **30**, 543–55.

Diaz-Rico, Lynne (1999) The postmodern shift: A real revolution in ESOL teaching. *TESOL Matters*, **9**(1), 20.

Finochiaro, Mary and Brumfit, Christopher (1983) *The Functional-Notional Approach: From Theory to Practice*. Oxford: Oxford University Press.

Freeman, Yvonne and Freeman, David (1998) *ESL/EFL Teaching: Principles for Success*. Portsmouth, NH: Heinemann.

Freire, Paulo (1972) *Pedagogy of the Oppressed*. Harmondsworth, UK: Penguin Books.

Gebhard, Jerry G. and Oprandy, Robert (1999) *Language Teaching Awareness: A Guide to Exploring Beliefs and Practices*. Cambridge: Cambridge University Press.

Grosse, Christine Uber (1991) The TESOL methods course. *TESOL Quarterly*, **25**(1), 29–50.

Haded, Mohamed (1998) Focus on the Muslim learner of English: The communicative approach and the teacher's role. *Muslim Education Quarterly*, **16**(1), 30–40.

Hadley, Alice (1993) *Teaching Language in Context*. Boston, MA: Heinle and Heinle.

Hadley, Gregory (2004) ELT and the new world order: Nation building or neo-colonial reconstruction? Retrieved May 1, 2004, from www.tesolislamia.org/articles.html.

Howatt, Anthony P. R. (1984) *A History of English Language Teaching*. Oxford: Oxford University Press.

Kachru, Braj B. (1983) *The Indianization of English: The English Language in India*. New Delhi: Oxford University Press.

Kachru, Braj B. (1988) *ERIC/CLL News Bulletin*. September, **12**(1), 1, 3, 4, 8.

Kachru, Braj B. (2005) *Asian Englishes: Beyond the Canon*. Hong Kong: Hong Kong University Press.

Kazmi, Yadullah (2004) The hidden political agenda of teaching English as an international language. Retrieved May 1, 2004, from http://www.tesolislamia.org/articles.html.

Kelly, Louis (1976) *25 Centuries of Language Teaching*. Rowley, MA: Newbury House.

Knight, Paul (2001) The development of EFL methodology. In *English Language Teaching and Its Social Context: A Reader*. Edited by Christopher Candlin and Neil Mercer. London: Routledge, pp. 147–66.

Krashen, Stephen and Terrell, Tracy (1983) *The Natural Approach: Language Acquisition in the Classroom*. New York/San Francisco: Pergamon Press/Alemany Press.

Kumaravadivelu, B. (2003) *Beyond Methods: Macrostrategies for Language Teaching*. New Haven: Yale University Press.

Larson-Freeman, Diane (2000) *Techniques and Principles in Language Teaching*. 2nd edition. New York: Oxford University Press.

Littlewood, William (1981) *Communicative Language Teaching: An Introduction*. Cambridge: Cambridge University Press.

Maturana, Humberto and Varela, Francisco J. (1992) *The Tree of Knowledge*. Boston, MA: Shambhala.

McGroarty, Mary (1998) Constructive and constructivist challenges for applied linguistics. *Language Learning*, **48**(4), 591–622.

McKay, Sandra (2002) *Teaching English as an International Language*. Oxford: Oxford University Press.

Mehrotra, Raja Ram (2000) Decolonizing English teaching in India. *RELC Journal*, **31**(2), 134–45.

Mohammed, Aliyu (1997) Communicative competence acquisition in infelicitous learning environments. In *New Englishes: A West African Perspective*. Edited by Ayọ Bamgboṣe, Ayọ Banjo, and Andrew Thomas. Trenton, NJ: African World Press, pp. 130–52.

Morgan, Betsy and Schwarte, Barbara (1995) A survey of TESOL methods courses: The sequel. Paper presented at the TESOL International Convention 1995, Long Beach, CA, March.

Moskowitz, Gertrude (1978) *Caring and Sharing in the Foreign Language Class: A Sourcebook on Humanistic Techniques*. Rowley, MA: Newbury House.

Murphy, John and Weigle, Sara Cushing (2005) Survey of the MATESOL methods course. Paper presented at the TESOL International Convention 2005, San Antonio, TX, March.

Nunan, David (1989) *Designing Tasks for the Communicative Classroom*. Cambridge: Cambridge University Press.

Nunan, David (1997) Does learner strategy training make a difference? *Lenguas Modernas*, **24**, 123–42.

Oller, John, Jr. and Richard-Amato, Patricia (eds.) (1983) *Methods that Work: A Smorgasbord of Ideas for Language Teachers*. New York: Newbury House.

Pennycook, Alastair (1989) The concept of method, interested knowledge, and the politics of language teaching. *TESOL Quarterly*, **23**(4), 589–618. Reprinted in *Enriching ESOL Pedagogy* (2002). Edited by Vivian Zamel and Ruth Spack. Mawah, NJ: Lawrence Erlbaum and Associates, pp. 45–72.

Pennycook, Alastair (1994) *The Cultural Politics of English as an International Language*. London: Longman.

Petzold, Ruth (2002) Toward a pedagogical model for ELT. *World Englishes*, **21**(3), 422–6.

Phillipson, Robert (1992) *Linguistic Imperialism*. Oxford: Oxford University Press.

Prabhu, N. (1987) *Second Language Pedagogy*. Oxford: Oxford University Press.

Reagan, Timothy and Osborn, Terry (2001) *The Foreign Language Educator in Society: Toward a Critical Pedagogy*. Mahwah, NJ: Lawrence Erlbaum.

Richards, Jack (1987) Method: Approach, design, and procedure. In *Methodology in TESOL: A Book of Readings*. Edited by Michael Long and Jack Richards. Rowley, MA: Newbury House, pp. 145–57.

Richards, Jack and Rodgers, Theodore (1986) *Approaches and Methods in Language Teaching: A Description and Analysis*. Cambridge: Cambridge University Press.

Schön, Donald (1983) *The Reflective Practitioner: How Professionals Think in Action*. New York: Basic Books.

Schön, Donald (1987) *Educating the Reflective Practitioner: Toward a New Design for Teaching and Learning in the Professions*. San Francisco: Jossey-Bass.

Stevick, Earl (1976) *Memory, Meaning, and Method*. Rowley, MA: Newbury House.

Terrell, Tracy (1977) A natural approach to the acquisition and learning of a language. *Modern Language Journal*, **61**, 325–36.

Terrell, Tracy (1983) The natural approach to language teaching: An update. In *Methods that Work*. Edited by John Oller, Jr. and Patricia Richard-Amato. Rowley, MA: Newbury House, pp. 267–83.

Tollefson, James (1991) *Planning Language, Planning Inequality*. London: Longman.

Tudor, Ian (2003) Learning to live with complexity: Towards an ecological perspective on language teaching. *System*, **31**, 1–12.

Ulichny, Polly (1996) What's in a methodology? In *Teacher Learning in Language Teaching*. Edited by Donald Freeman and Jack Richards. New York: Cambridge University Press, pp. 178–96.

Van Ek, Jan Ate (1987) The threshold level. In *Methodology in TESOL: A Book of Readings*. Edited by Michael Long and Jack Richards. Rowley, MA: Newbury House, pp. 78–85.

Van Lier, Leo (1996) *Interaction in the Language Curriculum: Awareness, Autonomy, and Authenticity*. New York: Longman.

Vavrus, Frances (1991) When paradigms clash: The role of institutionalized varieties in language teacher education. *World Englishes*, **10**(2), 181–96.

Wallerstein, Nina L. (1983) The teaching approach of Paulo Friere. In *Methods that Work*. Edited by John Oller,

Jr. and Patricia Richard-Amato. Cambridge, MA: Newbury House, pp. 190–204.

Widdowson, Henry (1990) *Aspects of Language Teaching*. Oxford: Oxford University Press.

Widdowson, Henry (2002) The ownership of English. In *Enriching ESOL Pedagogy: Readings and Activities for Engagement, Reflection, and Inquiry*. Edited by Vivian Zamel and Ruth Spack. Mahwah, NJ: Lawrence Erlbaum, pp. 381–92. (Also appeared 1994 in *TESOL Quarterly*, **26**(2), 337–89.)

Wilkins, David (1976) *Notional Syllabuses*. Oxford: Oxford University Press.

Woodward, Tessa (1991) *Models and Metaphors in Language Teacher Training: Loop Input and Other Strategies*. Cambridge: Cambridge University Press.

FURTHER READING

Baumgardner, Robert J. and Brown, Kimberley (2003) World Englishes: Ethics and Pedagogy. *World Englishes*, **22**(3), 245–51.

Brown, Kimberley and Peterson, Jay (1997) Exploring conceptual frameworks: Framing a world Englishes paradigm. In *Literary Studies East and West: World Englishes 2000, vol. 14*. Edited by Larry Smith and Michael Forman. Manoa, Hawai'i: University of Hawai'i Press, pp. 32–47.

Kachru, Braj B. (1994) Teaching world Englishes without myths. In

INTELEC '94: Proceedings of the International English Education Conference, Kuala Lampur, Malaysia. Edited by Saran Kaur Gill et al., Kuala Lumpur: Language Centre, Universiti Kebangsaan Malaysia, pp. 1–19.

Tsuda, Yukio (1997) Hegemony of English vs. ecology of language: Building equity in international communication. In *World Englishes 2000*. Edited by Larry E. Smith and Michael Forman. Honolulu: University of Hawai'i Press, pp. 21–31.

38 World Englishes and Lexicography

FREDRIC DOLEZAL

1 Introduction

The compilation of a dictionary of world Englishes is a complex undertaking. All the ideological underpinnings, the tensions inherent in proposing the study of Englishes, the hierarchies of English varieties, and the very concept of the English language itself are revealed when we have to collect, identify, describe, and explain the printed and spoken linguistic evidence. Linguistic, literary, cultural, and even political considerations are brought to the foreground of our research, separately and intertwined, the moment we decide to record and explain the English language of a "community" of speakers (in some cases speakers and writers). The notion of legitimacy for pluralized "Englishes" (see, e.g., Kachru and Kahane, 1995) largely rests upon the presence or absence of an authoritative text called "the dictionary." Because the idea of a dictionary is so firmly rooted, even traditional, within the history of English and its Englishes, there are certain expectations from users, lexicographers, and publishers that theorists and practitioners must observe and negotiate.

There are basic linguistic requirements that all dictionary projects must meet: for instance, in order to look up a word in a language, there must be a codified notion of "word," "phrase," and "clause" for the language being described. In languages that have been spoken, not written, or for which no norms or standards have been laid out, there must first be a comprehensive grammatical analysis of the language in order to determine the shape of words in the language (as a reflection of syntax and morphology). More precisely, there must be well-motivated criteria to establish the canonical form of a word. In the case of underdescribed or undocumented Englishes, the prevailing cultural-lexicographical expectations concerning the paradigms of English word classes are a central, if not exclusionary, influence on the formation of dictionary entry words (usually the canonical forms). Nevertheless, before a comprehensive dictionary of a variety of English can begin, there must be a grammatical description of the individual variety.

2 "Legitimacy" and the Dictionary

Dictionaries confer legitimacy upon a language as a comprehensive concept, or some part of a language, whether we call that register, dialect, lexicon, or vocabulary, to choose some of the more common designations. "Legitimacy" can be understood as a shorthand for identifying and establishing the varieties of Englishes that are used in various locations around the world. English speakers have been accustomed to relying on the dictionary as not just a reference, or look-up tool, but as an authority that tells us whether a certain locution is actually a part of the language: "Is it in the dictionary?" The ordinary speaker relies on the presence or absence of a word or phrase in a dictionary as a marker of legitimacy. The situation may be somewhat different for would-be speakers of English, but the proliferation of learners' dictionaries provides an excellent, if unstated, introduction into the "culture" of English speakers' past and present. In the case before us of lexicography and Englishes, the issue of legitimacy has primary importance.

Finding a word in "the dictionary" gives the user not only information but also *confidence*; when we find the word we are looking for in a dictionary, we are assured that our language usage has been confirmed, even anointed. Given this expectation built upon tradition, it should not be surprising that an individual speaker of an English, that is, one who identifies his or her brand of English with a discernible community of speakers, would gain more confidence and assurance to find a comprehensive dictionary of the speaker's separate and legitimate manner of speaking and writing. She or he would be led to believe that the English he or she speaks is not merely a collection of odd phrases and words scattered throughout a "standard" or "prestige" English dictionary, but a language with its own history and community. A dictionary is not a requirement for a people to recognize themselves as part of a distinct set of English language users, but the presence of such a dictionary would undoubtedly seal the argument for the existence of a separate and equal English.

3 Standards and the Dictionary

The circumstances and attitudes related above find expression in Butler (1997: 285) on selecting South-East Asian words for the third edition of the *Macquarie Dictionary*. Pakir (1997: 175–9), writing about possible descriptions of Singaporean English, elaborates upon ideas found in Butler by questioning the practical relevance of the notion "standards" as the concept has been developed in relation to codifying "traditional Englishes."

> The complexity behind corpus planning factors in Singapore arises from its multilingual situation which involves choice of languages and standards for them,

as well as the influence of contact languages on the emerging variety of English. Although multilingual and multiracial Singapore has a local educated variety of English that is internationally intelligible, this variety has not been codified. (Pakir, 1997: 176–7)

Butler makes the point that an author who "is carried along by the tide of American English" has much more latitude "to parade a swag of words" from her dialect (in this case a writer of the Newfoundland dialect) than a writer "struggling in the small (but lively) tributary of Singaporean English," who, Butler says, "has to argue a case just to use *horn* as a verb" (that is, "horned him loud and long."). Undoubtedly, *swag of words* is underwritten by a dictionary entry.

In these circumstances it does help to be able to say that your words are in a dictionary. That sort of respectability carries weight with editors and publishers in these particular literary difficulties, *and in general has more effect on the public perception of the validity of a variety than many words spent in linguistic theorising.* (Butler, 1997: 285, emphasis added)

4   The Idea of a Dictionary

The idea of a dictionary has such force that the very act of collecting words and phrases and then printing them in alphabetical order with definitions begins to establish another traditional expectation; that is, once a language is distributed and arranged according to the normal practice of lexicography, users of that language develop, or begin to develop, the notion of a *standard*. Once the language appears not in narrative or discursive formats, but as a list of items, we cannot avoid thinking of the language as a set of rules; for ordinary speakers, the idea of "rules" may be expressed as "correctness." Those who make dictionaries often have intentions that may conflict with the expectations of ordinary users. Dictionary makers generally describe their work as describing the language, while users generally look to a dictionary for guidance, thus emphasizing the dictionary as an authoritative arbiter and prescriber of correctness. Dictionaries, whether regional, national or international, influence how the users perceive or understand the standard.

Zgusta (1989: 70–9) describes four kinds of dictionaries and the ways that they attempt to influence the standard:

1   dictionaries that aim at creating a written standard: *standard-creating dictionaries;*
2   dictionaries that try to render the standard more modern: *modernizing dictionaries;*
3   dictionaries that try not only to stop any change in the standard, but even to reverse change, to reintroduce obsolete forms and meanings: *antiquating (or archaizing) dictionaries;*

4   dictionaries that try to describe the existing standard, thereby clarifying it:
    standard descriptive dictionaries.

Zgusta notes that "many [if not most or all] dictionaries are typologically mixed" and that secondarily there are typological variations such that "others can be seen as connected with a cultural, literary, scientific movement, or with some change in society."

How linguistic change is regarded by the dictionary maker underlies the decisions that result in a particular dictionary being of one type or another, or some mix of types. Of central interest to this topic is whether a dictionary of a regional or national variety of English proposes to establish a standard, or whether such a dictionary more narrowly proposes to establish a record of the language. The effect of making decisions concerning standardization and description results in how exclusive or inclusive the vocabulary selected for a dictionary is. Even dictionaries that are intended to record "non-normal" usage, rather than to describe a discrete variety of English, have some influence on standardizing the usages, if for no other reason than the general expectations and attitudes of dictionary users. Dictionaries of regional varieties of English, when compiled, will eventually form their own subcategory of standardizing dictionaries.

5   The Concept "Englishes"

The tensions inherent in the concept "Englishes" are not only highlighted when combined with the practical project of compiling a dictionary, but must be answered or attended to, or the compiler will have no systematic method for collecting, describing, and presenting the language. Thus, the notions "standard," "variety," "regional," etc. do not come pre-defined, but must be given definitions. The linguistic, cultural, and political conditions that are associated with a set of language users provide the linguistic, sociolinguistic, and pragmatic data upon which the lexicographer must devise his principles. The standard variety, and a text produced to exemplify it, does not require such a detailed accounting of education, background, birthplace, travels, or age of a user because the standard comprises all registers and a wide-ranging vocabulary that no one English user can know. How we describe the divide between a standard variety and a regional variety depends largely upon how we account for linguistic change.

Lexicographers and linguists of the present time staunchly and quickly assert the naturalness of languages changing continually. However, the linguistic laity more likely views contemporary change as a falling away from the true, the original, and the pure. Linguistic change has special significance for speakers whose cultural, ethnic, or political identity is largely defined by the variety of language they use. Susan Butler succinctly describes the situation as it is felt by speakers of Australian English (or, *Australian*, as is reported). She has Australians asking (Butler, 2001: 153–4), "Have we kept our hold on our own special language or is it slipping away from us?" and calls our attention to the divide between the coolly scientific calm ("no cause for alarm") and the more ordinary notion that greets linguistic change ("Change in our own lifetime . . . is equated with decay and corruption").

Though Butler does not make this point in particular, the "alarm" associated with "decay and corruption" can be found expressed by language theorists and lexicographers in English literature since at least the seventeenth century. The alarm over losing "identity" reveals more about the attitudes toward language use of people and communities in our own time.

Dictionaries can have an influence on how people make individual decisions on language use; in the case of Englishes that are newly collected and codified, the dictionary compiler can choose just how much "guidance" a dictionary user requires or is seeking. Selection of information (how many varieties outside the standard are listed?) and setting notes and labels for usage have been standard methods for providing a key to norms, standards, and "acceptable" usages. Lexicographers negotiate these difficult decisions by relying on reported usage and matching that with some notion of the needs of the user; this of course begs the question when considering an English that has not been adequately documented. Deciding upon the number and type of usage labels, if any, requires the lexicographer to balance the descriptivist purity of the linguist with the sociolinguistic reality of the dictionary user.

Picking up a dictionary and using it answers a felt need. Dictionary users commonly and quite naturally only look up a word in a dictionary for a particular reason; in fact, many dictionary users consult a dictionary for advice on usage. Beyond any need to identify with one group or another, there is a need to communicate, which gives rise to the need for mutual intelligibility and codification. A dictionary must first answer the communication needs of the users of a language. Rightly or wrongly, many if not most speakers and writers of a language assume that there is "good" usage and "bad" usage.

6   Prescriptivism versus Descriptivism

Linguists sometimes set the issue of usage labeling in the broader question of so-called *prescriptivism* versus *descriptivism*. Because of the pejorative denotation ascribed to *prescriptivism* – and usage labels are considered by some users to be prescriptive notes – dictionary makers are thrown into the arena of considering who decides the norms, standards, and codification within the sociolinguistic reality of the language community being described. Allsopp (1996) in the "Introduction" to the *Dictionary of Caribbean English Usage* provides a succinct account of the questions that need to be answered in a section called "The Need for a Norm." He notes that the *Dictionary of Jamaican*

English, while being an acclaimed "scholarly achievement," does not address the "everyday needs" of a dictionary user of a "national standard language"; in this regional dictionary the appeal is to historical principles, not the intuitions of the native speaker. Allsopp lays out questions concerning how a dictionary that includes the English spoken in 12 independent nations makes judgments about each people's "linguistic entitlement to a national standard":

> What is the right/wrong *national* way to speak? May local or regional usage be *formally* written? By what criteria is acceptability to be judged, and acceptability to whom – Britain, North America, the "international" community, other Caribbean states, teachers? . . . What spellings shall be determined (and by whom) . . . What terms are unparliamentary, libellous, offensive? What *norms*, what *guide* must national examiners and those on the (then emergent) Caribbean Examinations Council observe? (Allsopp, 1996: xix)

In a dictionary usage notes and labels may be just what a dictionary user would like to find; after all, to describe the pragmatic meaning of a word or phrase will always appear prescriptive. People who consult dictionaries do not just want answers to questions, they want authoritative answers. However, we must note that a dictionary that attaches labels (*vulgar, colloquial, dialect*, etc.) without a discussion of how a word is determined to need a label or an explanation of the judgments that underlie the label leaves the decision mostly to the user. On the other hand, a dictionary that supplies usage notes in the form of explanatory discussions that elaborate upon usage labels makes explicit what labels only imply. There are no commonly accepted usage or status labels, so each dictionary compiler decides how much to leave to the user and how much to make explicit. The statement in *A Dictionary of South African English* (Branford, 1980: xxi) that "[n]o scheme could possibly hope to fit this shifting and unstable ground [i.e., the difference between *colloq.* and *slang*]" epitomizes the tentative self-consciousness surrounding labels in dictionaries.

An account of the use of labels in English dictionaries can be found in an article by Frederic Cassidy (1997); there is also a thematic section on dialect labeling in the same volume. The higher the level of "notes" and labels, the more likely it is that a dictionary will be regarded as prescriptive and, perhaps, even engaged in language planning. Usage notes and labels must be understood not only by frequency, or whether supported by few or detailed explanatory notes, but also by the status of the language being documented. Dictionaries for languages that have a well-established standard or norm will normally avoid the more directive use of labels and notes; can an authoritative description of a variety of English language find acceptance among users who do not share perceptions of "correctness," and "good" and "bad" versions of their English? The descriptive and explanatory adequacy of a dictionary does not in itself promote an attitude of legitimacy for the language being described.

7   Standard and Norms

In the case of the lexicography of Englishes, much of what we understand about "standards," "norms," and the like will rely on the various perspectives that have been established for identifying the varieties of Englishes. Kachru's diagram of circles, Inner and Outer, serves as a useful tool when considering standardization and codification (see Kachru, 1985). Any dictionary of an Outer-Circle English must always contend, culturally, commercially, and ideologically, with the long-standing lexicographic traditions of the two recognized global standards, British and American English. The bilingual dictionary tradition must also be regarded as highly influential on the development (or lack) of a world Englishes lexicography; clearly, the development of Englishes and their respective lexicons (and their linguistic systems) can be profitably studied as case studies of language contact.

The scholarly literature on lexicography and world Englishes has increased over the past 20 years, but is still a relatively undeveloped research field. Actual dictionary projects or proposals have been well documented with insightful notes and commentaries by Manfred Görlach in his series of "Englishes" volumes (1991, 1995, 1998); he rightfully questions whether dictionaries of Englishes have either the institutional support or the commercial viability necessary for beginning and finishing the arduous and lengthy tasks associated with dictionary making. Görlach indicates the obstacles:

> to launch such projects requires not only the existence of a norm in the eyes of more than just linguistic experts, but also a belief in such a regional standard among ministries of education and school boards. (1991: 40)

Kachru (1983), in one of the earliest commentaries and surveys on dictionaries for Englishes of the "non-native varieties," including the varieties in South Asia, Southeast Asia, South Africa, and West Africa, makes a case for the importance of cultivating studies of the lexicon and the production of dictionaries; though he too points to the difficulties inherent in any attempted dictionary project:

> One cannot say that research in this area has been neglected purely for lack of interest; other reasons . . . the magnitude of the undertaking . . . time factors and financial implications, naturally discourage scholars. Furthermore, there is the general attitude toward these varieties which has by and large not been conducive to scholarly work in this area. (Kachru, 1983: 188)

In the intervening decades we can see that Kachru's suggestion that the cautious and even hostile attitudes toward nativized varieties of English were undergoing a slow change was correct. As it turns out, the work on dictionaries of the English-as-a-first-language varieties of world Englishes, specifically dictionaries compiled in Australia, New Zealand, Canada, and the Caribbean, has helped promote scholarly work on the non-native varieties of English. To a degree, the compiling of dictionaries of national and regional identity stands as a major argument to the world of standard Englishes that the variety of English being described does indeed exist as a standard variety itself. However, for there to be an acceptance of a variety as something more than a "different" way of speaking the standard, there must be "confidence and consistency" (Nelson, 1992: 336):

> For Indian English to assume an ascendant place in the world, the attitudinal allegiance of the users of Indian English must be such that they can say to themselves and to the world, "I am a speaker of Indian English. I do not aspire to be indistinguishable from a British or American speaker. English as I know it and use it serves my needs."

In this case, a dictionary for Indian English would not establish an identity of "Indianness," but would support the identity and existence of a separate but equal English, that is, Indian English.

We find a passage in the "Introductory Remarks" of *Hobson-Jobson* attributed to "Burnell's fragment of intended introduction" that neatly summarizes prevailing attitudes toward Indianized English. The condescending, even contemptuous, tone joins with the collection of names for local flora, fauna, and cultural artifacts that comprise much of what one might expect to find in a dictionary of localisms and regionalisms, as well as a compilation of exotica:

> Considering the long intercourse with India, it is noteworthy that the additions which have thus accrued to the English language are, from the intellectual standpoint, of no intrinsic value. Nearly all the borrowed words refer to material facts, or to peculiar customs and stages of society, and, though a few of them furnish allusions to the penny-a-liner, they do not represent new ideas. (Yule and Burnell, 1886 [1968]: xxi)

Even with these remarks and comments (among many others) that are jarring to our twenty-first-century sensibilities, the compilers of *Hobson-Jobson*, by hook or by crook, worked within a still recognizable tradition of lexicography: names of flora and fauna and customs constitute much of what we find and expect in dictionaries of Englishes "struggling in a small tributary." The voice of the "native speaker" (though this concept is always fraught with practical and theoretical difficulties) may not be evident in *Hobson-Jobson*, but the compilers supply relatively lengthy encyclopedic information from specialists (leaving aside questions of our retrospective confidence in them) when defining specialist vocabulary (customs, laws, even etymology). Kachru (1983) has this to say in "Toward a Dictionary": "In its methodology, though not in its attitude toward Indian English, *Hobson-Jobson* is a healthy break from the tradition of earlier lexical research on this variety of English" (Kachru, 1983: 172; see also Kachru, 2005a, 2005b).

8 Toward a Theoretical Model

All the same, we also find that even this lexical achievement is limited by lack of an authoritative theoretical model, "but [the earlier lexicographical research] provides a substantial source of data" (Kachru, 1983: 169); the same might be also said of much of the current state of world Englishes lexicography (theory and practice are at a more informed level in our time, but compiling "a substantial source of data" describes much of the value of any lexicographical research). In the same book, Kachru provides a survey of "Earlier Lexicographical Research," with commentary and descriptions of glossaries and dictionaries of South Asian English (Kachru, 1983: 169–77); he also considers lexicographical research of other "minority forms," including African English and Caribbean English.

From the preceding brief sample of attitudes of a bygone era, we can draw lessons that are central to any dictionary project, especially those that would collect, describe, and explain a heretofore undocumented variety of English; a language variety is not the sum of its "exotic" parts. Thus, we note a backing away from the glossary tradition in current dictionaries of world Englishes because "[d]ialect dictionaries tend . . . to over-invest in three particular areas: flora, fauna and the more ephemeral colloquialisms" (Branford, 1980: xvi). From the perspective of accentuating the different, it would almost seem that a variety of English is nothing more than hybrid and substandard word forms, the consequence of contact with another language, that are simply integrated with, or added to, the standard.

An approach that only regards "colorful words," folk taxonomies of flora and fauna, and so-called deviations from the standard, may produce a well-documented, limited vocabulary of a certain group of English speakers, but it will fall short of being a description of the language as used by speakers representing all perceived levels of the language. No matter the size of the community of speakers, any variety of a language will be divisible into subvarieties. Thus, the methods and practice of identification and selection of linguistic items, along with an appreciation of language change, will be an important measure by which one can determine the scope, legitimacy, and authenticity of a dictionary. In this context, Butler (1997: 276) advocates the primary authority of the "native speaker": "we should hold the need for ultimate decisions about inclusion or exclusion in the dictionary to be made by native speakers or we will lose some essential lifeline to truth." She also is quite aware of the limitations of native-speaker intuition; suffice it to say, when describing and explaining an English as "non-native English," we must question the ideology of "the native speaker." The lexicography of world Englishes creates a challenge to redefine, change, or reaffirm commonly held linguistic attitudes and ideas.

9 The Dictionary Tradition of English

The dictionary tradition in English is so strongly and comprehensively developed that we must look at how traditional English lexicography influences, or could influence, dictionaries of Englishes outside the circle of American and British standard Englishes. There is coverage of "outlying" Englishes in the major British and North American dictionaries; however, the coverage is neither systematic nor comprehensive. Nevertheless, any dictionary project regarding a regional or local English will depend on the mass of lexical and syntactic information already available in the standard dictionaries of English. The major dictionaries, which now include dictionaries of Australian English, depend in their turn on any intensive research into vocabulary and grammar of regional and local Englishes. The economic facts have thus far made it more likely that the British, North American, and Australian dictionaries of English will expand their repertoires outside the Inner Circle – alongside of, or in place of, comprehensive regional and local dictionaries. There are already efforts to create international corpora of English(es); as always, the meaning of "international" is open to discussion: in the past "international" meant British, North American, and Australian, but there is now an awareness among publishers that they should expand their definition and thereby expand their markets. The latest international corpora of English are collaborative projects that depend on individuals from a wide range of English-using communities throughout the world collecting and analyzing data from their respective local sources, who then send their findings along to a central databank.

Another source of competition for English dictionary markets is the well-developed tradition of English learners' dictionaries and the related promotion of English as an international language. If the perceived needs of an English-using community are met by one of the "standard" dictionaries of English, or even by learners' dictionaries of English, then there will not be the necessary intellectual, social, or economic demand that would underwrite the time and resources needed to undertake and complete a major dictionary publication. There have even been attempts to internationalize English by reducing the language to the "basics"; the best-known attempt was Charles K. Ogden's Basic English, which still has some adherents some 60 years after its inception. Basic English serves the needs of global communication by simplifying the vocabulary of English for use in scientific, industrial, and commercial transactions that are generally task oriented. Undoubtedly, the idea of a "basic" English levels all Englishes; however, while the effect may be to compete with the growth of regional or local Englishes, it is not inherently a challenge to the use and documentation of any variety of English. One is an (artificial) English designed for specific purposes across all language communities, the others are (natural) ordinary Englishes that develop or "decay" according to the communicative and expressive needs of the users, which may not include complete "mutual intelligibility" with other regional or local Englishes.

At this juncture it will be useful to mention some of the general and specific works on lexicography and world Englishes: for an excellent analysis on the practical and theoretical dimensions of lexicography, especially in the context of "developing" local, national, or regional economies, we recommend a standard of lexicography, Zgusta (1970). The *Macquarie Dictionary* (Delbridge, 1987: 11–42) has a series of insightful articles that explain the theoretical and practical concerns (e.g., needs, pronunciation, vocabulary, history) of constructing a comprehensive dictionary of a national variety of English that will be highly useful for understanding similar lexicography projects of regional and local varieties. Also of high usefulness is the front matter of dictionaries of Canadian English, South African English, Caribbean English, and of Australian and New Zealand English (see the "Further Reading" list below); the idea of "a dictionary upon historical principles" provides the structure for some of the South African, New Zealand, and Australian dictionaries; the *Dictionary of Jamaican English* also stands in this tradition. An English without a "history," that is, with little in the way of historical and reliable documents, will be more likely to effect the approach to Caribbean English, a usage dictionary (see Allsopp, 1996). For an excellent census and commentary on the widest range of dictionaries and projects under the heading of "new" Englishes, there is a series of volumes by Manfred Görlach. He comes to a conclusion in the latest of the series, noting that "no progress" had been reported on a proposed dictionary of West African English, or Singaporean English, nor can "much progress . . . be expected as far as the lexicography of [Indian English] is concerned." Current work on lexicography and the Englishes of Asia may help brighten some future reports on progress. For a general and historical overview, see Görlach (1991: 36–68, "Lexicographical Problems of New Englishes and English-related Pidgin and Creole Languages"; 1995: 124–63, "Dictionaries of Transplanted Englishes"; 1998: 152–86, "Recent Dictionaries of Varieties of English [1997]"). All these volumes have chapters on many of the issues mentioned in this essay. Görlach emphasizes the "scholarly" approach to lexicography, but fairly evaluates "commercial" or "amateur" projects. For a broad understanding of the dictionary projects, attempted, completed, and contemplated, these volumes are a valuable reference tool.

10   Conclusion

The history of English lexicography may provide the most pertinent lessons for the future of the lexicography of world Englishes: the first monolingual English dictionary, published in 1604, was not a comprehensive dictionary of Jacobean English, but a dictionary of "hard words," which relied on bilingual Latin–English dictionaries, glossaries, and books on rhetoric for its selection of vocabulary. Within 60 years there were dictionaries that collected proverbs and dialects found in the British Isles; and soon there were dictionaries of "ordinary" English and slang. Obviously, the expansion and development of early English lexicography relied on available print artifacts (pamphlets, books, newspapers, glossaries, etc.) and on field research; the growth of English lexicography was, not coincidentally, in historical parallel with the growth of English grammars and rhetorics. What has become a publication industry began as authors working on sometimes competing entrepreneurial projects. The language being described, or even prescribed and proscribed, reflects the culture in which a dictionary appears. The expectations of many people that a dictionary provides us with "correctness" and what is "normal" and "standard" and "good" are held fairly closely; the appearance of a dictionary in a language community that looks outward for its standard will meet a reluctant audience unless scholars, well-informed aficionados of the language, and entrepreneurs lay the groundwork of collecting not just data, but collecting and editing what will become, each in their own part, an oral history, a literary canon, and a full-fledged grammar of the language community. Successful English dictionaries are not just reference tools; they are also informative, entertaining, and sometimes irritating books that raise our awareness of language and people and culture.

See also Chapters 20, WRITTEN LANGUAGE, STANDARD LANGUAGE, GLOBAL LANGUAGE; 39, WORLD ENGLISHES AND TEST CONSTRUCTION; 41, WORLD ENGLISHES AND CORPORA STUDIES.

REFERENCES

Allsopp, Richard (ed.) (1996) *Dictionary of Caribbean English Usage*. Oxford: Oxford University Press.

Branford, Jean (1980) *A Dictionary of South African English*. Cape Town: Oxford University Press.

Butler, Susan (1997) Selecting South-East Asian words for an Australian dictionary: How to choose in an English not your own. *Englishes around the World (vol. 2: Caribbean, Africa, Asia, Australia): Studies in Honour of Manfred Görlach*. Edited by Edgar W. Schneider. Amsterdam/ Philadelphia: John Benjamins, pp. 273–86.

Butler, Susan (2001) Australian English: an identity crisis. In *Varieties of English around the World, vol. 26: English in Australia*. Edited by David

Blair and Peter Collins. Amsterdam/ Philadelphia: John Benjamins, pp. 151–62.

Cassidy, Frederic G. (1997) The rise and development of modern labels in English dictionaries. *Dictionaries*, **18**, 97–112.

Delbridge, Arthur (ed.) (1987) *The Macquarie Dictionary*. Chatswood, NSW: Macquarie Library.

Görlach, Manfred (1991) *Varieties of English around the World, vol. 9: Englishes: Studies in Varieties of English 1984–1988*. Amsterdam/ Philadelphia: John Benjamins.

Görlach, Manfred (1995) *Varieties of English around the World, vol. 13: More Englishes: Studies in Varieties of English 1988–1994*. Amsterdam/ Philadelphia: John Benjamins.

Görlach, Manfred (1998) *Varieties of English around the World, vol. 22: Even More Englishes: Studies in Varieties of English 1996–1997.* Amsterdam/Philadelphia: John Benjamins.

Kachru, Braj B. (1983) *The Indianization of English: The English Language in India.* Delhi: Oxford University Press.

Kachru, Braj B. (1985) Standards, codification and sociolinguistic realism: The English language in the outer circle. In *English in the World: Teaching and Learning the Language and Literatures.* Edited by Randolph Quirk and Henry Widdowson. Cambridge: Cambridge University Press, pp. 11–30.

Kachru, Braj B. (2005a) *Asian Englishes: Beyond the Canon.* Hong Kong: Hong Kong University Press.

Kachru, Braj B. (2005b) English in India: A lexicographical perspective. In *Lexicology 2: An International Handbook on the Nature and Structure of Words and Vocabularies.* Edited by Alan Cruse, Franz Hundsnurscher, Michael Job, and Peter Rolf Lutzeier. Berlin: Walter de Gruyter, pp. 1274–9.

Kachru, Braj B. and Henry Kahane (eds.) (1995) *Cultures, Ideologies, and the Dictionary: Studies in Honor of*

Ladislav Zgusta. Tübingen: Max Niemeyer Verlag.

Nelson, Cecil L. (1992) My language, your culture: Whose communicative competence? In *The Other Tongue: English across Cultures.* Edited by Braj B. Kachru. Urbana and Chicago: University of Illinois Press, pp. 327–39.

Pakir, Anne (1997) Standards and codifications for world Englishes. In *World Englishes 2000.* Edited by Larry E. Smith and Michael L. Forman. Honolulu: University of Hawai'i Press, pp. 169–81.

Yule, Henry and Burnell, Arthur C. (1886 [1968]) *Hobson-Jobson: A Glossary of Colloquial Anglo-Indian Words and Phrases, and of Kindred Terms, Etymological, Historical, Geographical and Discursive.* 2nd edition of "New Edition" edited by William Crooke (1903). Delhi: Munshiram Manoharlal.

Zgusta, Ladislav (1970) *The Manual of Lexicography.* The Hague: Mouton.

Zgusta, Ladislav (1989) The role of dictionaries in the genesis and development of the standard. In *Dictionaries: An International Encyclopedia of Lexicography.* Edited by Franz Hausmann, Oskar Reichmann, Herbert E. Wiegand, and Ladislav Zgusta. Berlin: Walter de Gruyter, pp. 70–9.

FURTHER READING

Allsopp, Richard (1972) *Why a Dictionary of Caribbean English Usage?* Barbados: University of West Indies.

Beeton, Douglas Ridley (1975) *A Dictionary of English Usage in South Africa.* Cape Town: Oxford University Press.

Benson, Phil (1997) English dictionary in Asia: Asia in English dictionaries.

In *English Is an Asian Language: The Phillippine Context.* Edited by Maria Lourdes Bautista. Australia: Macquarie Library, pp. 125–40.

Benson, Phil (2000) Hong Kong words: Variation and context. *World Englishes,* **19**(3), 373–80.

Benson, Phil (2002) Hong Kong words: Variation and context. In *Hong Kong*

English: Autonomy and Creativity.
Edited by Kingsley Bolton.
Hong Kong: Hong Kong University
Press, pp. 161–70.

Bernard, John R. L. (1987) Australian
pronunciation. In *The Macquarie
Dictionary.* Edited by Arthur
Delbridge, John Bernard, David
Blair, Pam Peters, and Susan
Butler. Sydney: Macquarie Library,
pp. 18–27.

Blair, David (1987) Words and the
world. In *The Macquarie Dictionary.*
Edited by Arthur Delbridge, John
Bernard, David Blair, Pam Peters,
and Susan Butler. Sydney:
Macquarie Library, pp. 34–6.

Branford, William (1987) *The South
African Pocket Oxford Dictionary.*
Cape Town: Oxford University
Press.

Burchfield, Robert (1986) *The New
Zealand Pocket Oxford Dictionary.*
Auckland: Oxford University Press.

Butler, Susan (1996) World English in an
Asian context: The *Macquarie
Dictionary* project. *World Englishes*,
15(3), 347–57.

Butler, Susan (1997) World English in the
Asian context: Why a dictionary is
important. In *World Englishes 2000.*
Edited by Larry E. Smith and
Michael L. Forman. Honolulu:
University of Hawai'i Press,
pp. 90–125.

Cassidy, Frederic G. and Le Page, Robert
(eds.) (1967) *Dictionary of Jamaican
English.* Cambridge: Cambridge
University Press.

Clark, Manning (1987) Introduction. In
The Macquarie Dictionary. Edited by
Arthur Delbridge, John Bernard,
David Blair, Pam Peters, and Susan
Butler. Sydney: Macquarie Library,
p. 11.

Delbridge, Arthur (1984) *Aussie Talk: The
Macquarie Dictionary of Australian
Colloquialisms.* Sydney: Macquarie
Library.

Delbridge, Arthur (1987) The need for
an Australian dictionary. In *The
Macquarie Dictionary.* Edited by
Arthur Delbridge, John Bernard,
David Blair, Pam Peters, and Susan
Butler. Sydney: Macquarie Library,
pp. 12–16.

Delbridge, Arthur (2001) Lexicography
and national identity: The
Australian experience. *Varieties of
English around the World, vol. 26:
English in Australia.* Edited by David
Blair and Peter Collins. Amsterdam/
Philadelphia: John Benjamins,
pp. 303–16.

Dore, Wendy, Mantzel, Dorothea, Muller,
Colin, and Wright, Madeleine (eds.)
(1996) *A Dictionary of South African
English on Historical Principles.*
Oxford: Oxford University Press.

Greenbaum, Sidney and Nelson, Gerald
(1996) The international corpus of
English (ICE) project. *World
Englishes*, **15**(1), 3–15.

Holm, John A. and Shilling, Alison W.
(1982) *Dictionary of Bahamian English.*
Cold Spring, NY: Lexik House.

Jonsen, Helen (1988) *Kangaroo's
Comments and Wallaby's Words:
The Aussie Word Book.* New York:
Hippocrene.

Mendes, John (1986) *Cote ce Cote la:
Trinidad and Tobago Dictionary.*
Trinidad and Tobago: Superb
Printers.

Mesthrie, Rajend (1992) *A Lexicon of
South African Indian English.* Leeds:
Peepal Tree Press.

Mihalic, Francis (1957) *Grammar and Dictionary of Neo-Melanesian.* Westmead,
NSW: Westmead Printing.

Mondesir, Jones E. (1992) *Dictionary of
St. Lucien Creole.* New York: Mouton
de Gruyter.

Moore, Bruce (ed.) (1999) *The Australian
Oxford Dictionary.* Melbourne:
Oxford University Press.

Nihalani, Paroo, Tongue, R. K., Hosali,
Priya, and Crowther, Jonathan (eds.)

(2004) *Indian and British English: A Handbook of Usage and Pronunciation.* 2nd edition. New Delhi: Oxford University Press.

Ooi, Vincent B. Y. (1997) Analysing the Singapore ICE corpus for lexicographic evidence. In *Corpus-Based Studies in English: Papers from the Seventeenth International Conference on English Language Research on Computerized Corpora, Stockholm, May 15–19, 1996.* Edited by Magnus Ljung. Amsterdam: Rodopi, pp. 245–59.

Orsman, Harry W. (ed.) (1997) *The Dictionary of New Zealand English: A Dictionary of New Zealandisms on Historical Principles.* Auckland, NZ: Oxford University Press.

Orsman, Harry W. (1989) *Heinemann New Zealand Dictionary.* Auckland, NZ: Heinemann Educational.

Ramson, William S. (1987) The vocabulary of Australian English. In *The Macquarie Dictionary.* Edited by Arthur Delbridge, John Bernard, David Blair, Pam Peters, and Susan Butler. Sydney: Macquarie Library, pp. 28–33.

Ramson, William S. (1987) The historical study of Australian English. In *The Macquarie Dictionary.* Edited by Arthur Delbridge, John Bernard, David Blair, Pam Peters, and Susan Butler. New South Wales: Macquarie Library, pp. 37–42.

Ramson, William S. (ed.) (1988) *The Australian National Dictionary: A Dictionary of Australianisms on Historical Principles.* Melbourne: Oxford University Press.

Silva, Penny (1996) Lexicography for South African English. In *Focus on South Africa.* Edited by Vivian de Klerk. Amsterdam: John Benjamins Press, pp. 191–210.

Turner, George W. (ed.) (1984) *The Australian Pocket Oxford Dictionary.* Melbourne: Oxford University Press.

Turner, George W. (ed.) (1987) *The Australian Concise Oxford Dictionary of Current English.* Melbourne: Oxford University Press.

Valls, Lito (1990) *What a Pistarckle!: A Dictionary of Virgin Islands English Creole: New Supplement.* St Johns, Virgin Islands: L. Valls.

Wilkes, Gerald Alfred (1978) *A Dictionary of Australian Colloquialisms.* London: Routledge.

39 World Englishes and Test Construction

FRED DAVIDSON

1 Introduction

This chapter explores the relationship of world Englishes and language test development. To do so, I first review the existing argument that English language testing (in many world settings) ignores rich variation. I then argue that a dominant psychometric variance-based worldview is effectively in control of language tests even in contact situations where world Englishes should be considered; the fundamental problem is not one of Englishes in contact with one another – it is, instead, a matter of item statistics and, more likely, of the manner in which item writers internalize their creative mandates. My chapter endorses heartily an empirical research agenda and closes with an appeal to reach out to our colleagues in the world community of measurement scholars.

2 World Englishes and Language Tests: The Basic Argument

There is a well-established and legitimate concern that large, powerful English language tests are fundamentally disconnected from the insights in analysis of English in the world context. These exams set forth linguistic norms that do not necessarily represent the rich body of English varieties spoken and used in contact situations all over the world. Lowenberg (1993) was among the first to note the phenomenon. Stated in the general form: If an English language test sets items that are scored according to a particular English language norm, and if that test is subsequently used in a setting where some other norm is spoken, then items calibrated in the test target norm will be locally invalid. Lowenberg illustrated how the right answer might be wrong and the wrong might be right.

I am taking care here to avoid the term "bias." Brown (2004) provides an excellent overview of the term, and of its various legal and technical permutations. To call a test item "biased" runs the risk of pejorative attribution of intent, and I am not sure that is the case.[1] I prefer to say that the fundamental problem is one of validity. How can we ensure that the item is measuring the same thing which its designers intended?

Lowenberg (1993), Davies, Hamp-Lyons, and Kemp (2003), and scholars whom they cite provide examples of this phenomenon. I will provide one example here, drawn from my own experiences in English norms. I served in the US Peace Corps in Liberia in the 1970s. Following is a potential English language test item that engages Liberian English norms:

[Imagine that you want to take a few days off from work to attend a family event, such as an important wedding. You explain to your boss that you need to attend the event, and then you say:]

(1)   Please, may I have a few days?

(2)   I beg you, I may take a few days?

(3)   Hey, ya, my man – I can have a few days?

(4)   My friend, can I have a few days?

If this item were used in a North American test of English, the intended "best" answer is probably (1). It is both pragmatically appropriate and syntactically common.[2]

If this item were pre-tested in North America, the item might survive into an operational test, and it would be "keyed" to expect only (1) as the correct response. The item statistics might yield results as expected: students who display strong total scores tend to choose (1) as the correct response. Students with lower total scores might be equally distributed across (2), (3), and (4). The item would be said to "discriminate." The item score would "correlate well" with the total score.

If this item were pre-tested in Liberia, or – arguably – if it were tested in North America with many Liberians in the norming group, it would "bounce." Its item statistics would probably appear quite bizarre. Some of the test-takers most able in Liberian English would pick (2) or possibly (3) or (4). And some might even choose (1).[3] The item would display weak enough statistics that it would not survive the empirical vetting process, and it would be "swept into the dumpster at the end of the production day" (Davidson, 1994: 379). A vibrant and rich set of linguistic constructions, shown in these four choices, would not be testable due to the English varieties spoken by the test-takers on whom the test is normed. That is a frustrating situation, and such frustration is at the core of all the literature on world Englishes and language testing.

Lowenberg's argument, as I phrased it above, is that the right answer becomes wrong and the wrong answer becomes right depending on the match-up of the test norm group with the target testing group. The problem with this Liberian English situation is a bit more muddy. This item would become eliminated from the test because there is no right answer. So long as sufficient Liberian English speakers are part of this item's norm group, the item would be eliminated because it would not discriminate.

That, at least, is the statistical basis of the world Englishes language testing problem. There is a more subtle and far-reaching basis to the problem, one that involves the nature of test construction in a fundamental way.

The Liberian item scenario presumes that the item *does* get all the way to pilot pre-testing, that the test agency *secures* a large enough norm group to include a number of Liberian English speakers, and that these speakers *have not* acquired North American English to a sufficient level to out-think the test and reckon what they are supposed to do. Frankly, this is an unlikely scenario. This is because test developers are constantly seeking ways to pre-think their results. They are trying to out-guess the way that examinees will vary in test performance.

3   The Nature of Variance

Central to all educational and psychological assessment, language testing included, is the notion of variance. A test elicits a sample of behavior, and it is presumed that the test-takers vary in their ability at that behavior. Usually, this sample is an aggregate of a number of behavioral samples.

When the sample is an aggregate, the aggregation is done across a number of individual test items. Each item is scored, and the sum of the scores is used as an estimate of ability, perhaps after first being re-scaled to some common metric to allow comparison to previous versions of the exam. Item scoring can be against a fixed answer key, as when multiple-choice items are used, or it can involve expert judgment, as when short-answer questions are given.[4]

Language tests commonly also employ assessment that is not aggregated. Test-takers might be given an essay exam or an oral task, for which the resulting score is an expert rating of the entire integrative performance. This overall score is often a single number that represents a text statement about examinee ability – such text statements are called a performance band or descripter.[5] Sometimes, a set of numbers results which indicates – in turn – a set of components. An example of the former would be an oral interview placement test, for which the result is simply: into which course should the student enroll? An example of the latter would be the very same test, for the very same purpose, but in addition to a recommended course the exam also gives individual ratings on particular language components (vocabulary, syntax, pragmatics, and so on). These components might prove helpful to the subsequent course teacher in designing lessons.

Any of these language tests functions with a simple premise: language is a skill and people vary in their mastery of it. Furthermore, we presume to be able to sample those skills – be those samples aggregates of individual items or single performances like an oral test – and those samples will spread out the test-takers. Once we spread out the test-takers, we can make decisions about them and utilize that decision information in some meaningful manner – like placement into an instructional sequence.

How did this evolve?

4   The Discovery of Variance

In the mid-1800s, scholars of what would become sociology (and related disciplines) noted that many human phenomena seem to follow predictable statistical trends. Crime, suicide, buying habits, and many other human activities seem to fall out in a bell-shaped distribution, which came to be known as the Normal Curve. By the turn of the century, scholars discovered how to engineer the Normal Curve; that is, they discovered how to pre-test, select, edit, and de-select test items such that the resulting total score distribution achieved a bell shape. This is now an established technology nearing one hundred years of age.[6]

If a phenomenon can be distributed and achieve a normal bell shape, then the amount of data at or below each point on the curve is a known fact.[7] A student whose score is at a certain point on the Normal Curve test has a known rank among peers on whom the test was developed.[8]

Social, economic, political, and educational structures can be established based on the normal curve. A good example is hat size. Hats are available at a wide range of shops, such as department stores, sports stores, even at the kiosks outside of a football game. The hats offered cover a certain range of human head sizes. In the case of one-size-fits-all caps sold at a football kiosk, the adjustable band is intended to fit only a certain range of human head sizes. The majority of humans have head sizes within the central portion of that predictable normally-distributed range. Hat manufacturers have little motivation to make hats at the tails of the curve because people with those head sizes are few in number. There are a some of us – myself included – whose head size regrettably falls outside the range typically displayed by a hat vendor.

But is language ability like hat size?

5   Challenges to Variance

After instructional intervention, we presume that learners will improve. If our intervention is successful, we presume that the learners will not only improve, but that they will *all* improve. A normal curve does not seem logical. We hope that learners will bunch up at the higher end of any test distribution.[9]

This realization was the birth of the only true challenge to the paradigm of norm referenced measurement (NRM): criterion referenced measurement (CRM). A good example of a CRM situation is a driving test. In a behind-the-wheel driving examination, an examiner sits next to the test-taker, who performs such things as: starting the car, backing out of a parking spot, entering traffic, exiting traffic, signaling intentions, controlling speed, using safety features of the vehicle, and so forth. After the driving test has ended, it would not be logical for the examiner to turn to the test-taker and say something like: "Congratulations! You are equal to or better than 85 percent of the drivers whom we examine!" Rank-based decisions seem irrelevant to a driving exam. Some governmental entity – a state or nation – wishes to know: is this person able to drive a car? If the answer is yes, then the person gets a license. If the answer is no, then no license is issued.[10]

When resources are relatively unencumbered, CRM seems to work well. There seem to be enough roadways to accommodate a steady stream of new drivers. On the other hand, language tests frequently operate in systems where the result of the test directs students into some limited resource, like the number of seats available in a university program. Relative decision making is manageable with NRM. The Normal Curve helps to compare results and allocate limited resources. CRM does not work well.

CRM and NRM seem today to co-exist. CRM did not unseat NRM, and indeed, the technology to produce good NRM tests has grown in complexity.[11] It is very difficult to think of a single high-stakes language test that is *not* dominated by normative thinking – at least in a large part. Some high-stakes language tests may claim to be criterion-referenced, and indeed, they may provide thick written descriptions of results.[12]

6 Presumptions about Richness

Testing textbooks often advocate the use of test specifications (see Davidson and Lynch, 2002). A specification is a generative blueprint for test building. From a well-crafted test specification – or "spec" – many equivalent test items can be written. In some systems, the specs might not be written down, or if they are written, experienced test item writers don't consult the specs regularly. Test-writing is often done from the very same source of trusted expertise and well-established knowledge base that is accessed when teachers plan lessons. Educators write test items based on our shared knowledge of what does and does not work. They trust that knowledge.

This trust is important. It is the genesis of "stasis" in an educational assessment system – whether that system relies on NRM tests, on CRM tests, or on NRM tests that yield score profiles of a CRM nature. Stasis is a term borrowed from biological sciences where it refers to the fundamental harmony of plant and animal life in a given region or biosphere.

Tests function to maintain stasis. A placement test is an excellent example. Used year in and year out, it should provide its school administrators with a predictable sense of the number of students requiring a particular level of instruction. Quality instruction attempts to optimize its resources so that predictable strain is achieved. Sudden shifts in demand are cause for all kinds of chaos; for example, a sudden drop in the number of students needing a particular class might mean that the system has over-hired teachers at that level, and it might mean that the system must honor its commitment to pay the teachers even though they will have abnormally small class sizes. The sudden drop is a threat to the stasis of the school.

It seems more likely that linguistic richness is abrogated during test construction rather than sublimated by results from statistical piloting. Testing systems don't have the resources to do extensive piloting of test items, or if they do, then the systems are very careful to test only those items that have a likelihood of surviving and providing the information desired. Test specifications exist to delimit not only what is to be tested, but also (by omission or overt negative guidance) what is *not*.

In most North American ESL institutes, the Liberian item above would not even make it to the pilot stage. Specifications and expert review would presumptively nix it from the mix, early in the preparation of the test soup.

7 New Enquiries and New Dialogs

We are starting to see empirical research on the relationship of English language varieties and test construction, performance, and delivery. One exciting avenue of work is that charted by Chalhoub-Deville and Wigglesworth (2005). They have examined expert-rated test performance across various groups of English language raters: from Australia, Canada, the UK, and the US. They conclude that there was no significant difference in rating student ability dependant on the English variety from which the rater came. This is seminal research, and it cries out for extension into performance by raters from other English varieties. I find myself wondering: would the Chalhoub-Deville and Wigglesworth findings still obtain if the study were replicated with raters from Liberia, from Singapore, and so on? The most significant contribution of their work is that it begins to turn our attention toward empirical data as a driving force in solving the world Englishes/testing issue. Empirical enquiry must continue, and we will begin to understand how data helps answer the question stated so succinctly by Davies et al. (2003): "Whose norms" shall we use? Regardless of our own epistemologies, the *realpolitik* of many large testing companies is that they will act and act most profoundly when confronted with hard, cold numbers.[13]

Empirical work in language testing and world Englishes scholarship is essential. In addition, a new dialog is needed, one that invites our colleagues from educational and psychological measurement onto the stage of enquiry.[14] In this chapter, I have argued that item creation and survival to an operational test is determined by item statistics, and more likely, that it is determined by the archetypal thinking that evolves in a group of test item writers. As their experience grows, as they write more and more items or develop more and more rating prompts, as they encounter more and more evidence from the field of real-world use, they internalize and make instinctful a sense of that-which-works versus that-which-does-not. This phenomenon has an old history, far predating the birth of language testing as a separate academic discipline.[15] It is a phenomenon that goes back nearly a century, to the very early days of normative test construction. I don't think we can solve it entirely on our own. And furthermore, we may be able to make significant contributions back out to the wider world of educational and psychological testing – a world of seekers on much the same quest as ourselves.

See also Chapters 20, WRITTEN LANGUAGE, STANDARD LANGUAGE, GLOBAL LANGUAGE; 28, WORLD ENGLISHES AND DESCRIPTIVE GRAMMARS; 37, MODELS, METHODS AND CURRICULUM FOR ELT PREPARATION; 38, WORLD ENGLISHES AND LEXICOGRAPHY; 41, WORLD ENGLISHES AND CORPORA STUDIES.

NOTES

1   I tend to side with Anne Frank: People are basically good at heart. Years of experience consulting and advising in various test situations have taught me that there is very little true malice at play.

2   I grant that this item is an armchair construction, included in this paper largely for logical reasoning. Walters (2004), in what I believe is the first dissertation to fuse conversation analysis and language testing, points out that tests of pragmatics should reflect better a survey of what is actually said in talk.

3   North American English forms a major part of the Liberian English substrate, because of the historical founding of Liberia's federated nationhood by returned American slaves. Liberian English is also influenced by the Englishes spoken elsewhere in West Africa, and hence, it reflects certain British constructions. Finally, Liberian English shows various features that derive from the different African languages spoken in and near Liberia. For more information on Liberian English, I recommend the "Liberia: Brief Introduction" webpage at the "English in West Africa" website, maintained by Humbolt University in Berlin – an audio sample is available there. The website address is given in my reference list.

4   The Liberian English example presumes a fixed answer key.

5   The recent empirical work by Chalhoub-Deville and Wigglesworth (2005), which I cite in some detail later in this paper, is an example of such an assessment. The measurement derives from aggregated judgments by expert "raters" of student performance, and not from aggregate summation across keyed items.

6   There are a number of wonderful resources on this history, including but not limited to Hacking (1990), Gould (1996), and Lemann (1999). For some discussion of the relationship of variance-controlling tests and eugenics, see Kevles (1995) and especially Black (2003).

7   Philosophers may argue with the use of the word "fact" here. I take it to mean: a repeatedly observed and stable observation.

8   The peers on whom a test is developed are known as a "Norm Group."

9   In statistical parlance, after instruction we hope for a negatively skewed curve. This is a distribution in which the bulk of results are at the upper end, with a tail that drops off to the lower end.

10 I am simplifying this example somewhat. Driving tests are actually "domain-referenced," because the examiner watches a wide range of abilities, which testers call a "domain." "Criterion" is actually a singular noun. In any case, a driving test is not supposed to yield a normative decision.

11 At my university, doctoral students in Educational Psychology who specialize in psychometrics – the "scientific" name of testing – and language testing need a minimum of about five courses in statistics and measurement theory. Several of these are legend in their complexity and difficulty.

12 There is a growing use of "score profiles" in professional testing. The result of the test is not a score, but rather a set of scores on a number of components. Each component is accompanied by a written descrip-tion of expected candidate ability. If the score user – an admitting educational institution, for example – uses the results to rank and compare students, then this kind of testing is CRM-flavored NRM. The CRM flavoring is but a dash of spice if, as often seems to be the case, the score profile is developed by the testing company with full foreknowledge that its user clients will do such rank comparison.

13 An alternative to numerical analysis might be the qualitative study of group dynamics among test developers. Davidson and Lynch (2002: ch. 6) illustrate this approach, albeit with goals other than detection of varietal avoidance in test items and tasks.

14 I believe a good way to start would be a major international conference that reaches out from the world Englishes community to the international community of assessment specialists.

15 Yerkes (1921) is, in my opinion, the crucible of modern variance-driven testing, although work of other scholars and psychologists set the stage (e.g., Binet and Galton – Gould (1996) relates that history, and Hacking (1990) gives the relevant sociological pre-history). Yerkes tells the story of the rollout of the massive US Army's World War I intelligence testing program. Interestingly, the Army program included a test of English as a Foreign Language: the "Linguality" exam (pp. 355–61).

REFERENCES

Black, Edwin (2003) *War against the Weak: Eugenics and America's Campaign to Create a Master Race.* New York: Four Walls Eight Windows.

Brown, James Dean (2004) What do we mean by "bias," "Englishes," "Englishes in testing" and "English language proficiency"? *World Englishes,* **22**(2), 317–19.

Chalhoub-Deville, Micheline and Wigglesworth, Gillian (2005) Rater judgment and English language speaking proficiency. *World Englishes*, **24**(3), 383–92.

Davidson, Fred (1994) The Interlanguage metaphor and language assessment. *World Englishes*, **13**(3), 377–86.

Davidson, Fred and Lynch, Brian K. (2002) *Testcraft: A Teacher's Guide to Writing and Using Language Test Specifications*. New Haven: Yale University Press.

Davies, Alan, Hamp-Lyons, Liz, and Kemp, Charlotte (2003) Whose norms? International proficiency tests in English. *World Englishes*, **22**(4), 571–84.

Gould, Stephen J. (1996) *The Mismeasure of Man* (revised and expanded). New York: W. W. Norton.

Hacking, Ian (1990) *The Taming of Chance*. Cambridge: Cambridge University Press.

Kevles, Daniel J. (1995) *In the Name of Eugenics: Genetics and the Uses of Human Heredity. With a New Preface by the Author*. Cambridge: Harvard University Press.

Lemann, Nicholas (1999) *The Big Test: The Secret History of the American Meritocracy*. New York: Farrar, Straus, and Giroux.

Liberia: Brief Introduction (2004) English in West Africa website. Humbolt University, Berlin. http://www2.hu-berlin.de/angl/WAfr/intro/liberia.html. (Website address verified 25 August 2005; contains an audio sample and an expository text excerpt from: Wolf, Hans-Georg (2001) *English in Cameroon. Contributions to the Sociology of Language 85*. Berlin: Mouton de Gruyter.)

Lowenberg, Peter (1993) Issues of validity in tests of English as world language: Whose standards? *World Englishes*, **12**(1), 95–106.

Walters, F. Scott (2004) An Application of Conversation Analysis to the Development of A Test of Second-Language Pragmatic Competence. PhD dissertation, University of Illinois, Department of Educational Psychology.

Yerkes, Robert M. (ed.) (1921) *Psychological Examining in the United States Army. Memoirs of the National Academy of Sciences, vol. 15*. Washington, DC: US Government Printing Office.

FURTHER READING

Brown, James Dean and Hudson, Thom (2002) *Criterion-Referenced Language Testing*. Cambridge: Cambridge University Press.

Hughes, Arthur (2003) *Testing for Language Teachers*. 2nd edition. Cambridge: Cambridge University Press.

McNamara, Tim (2000) *Language Testing*. Oxford: Oxford University Press.

McNamara, Tim (2004) Language testing. In *The Handbook of Applied Linguistics*. Edited by Alan Davies and Catherine Elder. Oxford: Blackwell, pp. 763–83.

Weigle, Sara Cushing (2002) *Assessing Writing*. Cambridge: Cambridge University Press.

40 World Englishes and Communicative Competence

MARGIE BERNS

1 Introduction

The notion *communicative competence* has proven indispensable to world Englishes (WE) studies because of its attention to the issue of appropriateness in language use. This issue is highly relevant in the context of multiple and diverse settings of the learning and use of English and the attendant nativization of the linguistic code. As each setting is shaped by local cultural and social values, local norms of use develop consistent with these values, norms that specify what, when, where, and how something can be said at all linguistic levels from the phonological to the pragmatic. The determination of what is or is not "normal" cannot be made without accounting for local norms of the users of English in a particular sociocultural setting.

2 Communicative Competence: Sources

Communicative competence is now a well-established construct in explorations of the relationship of language to society and culture. It has been elaborated within two linguistic traditions: American anthropological linguistics, as represented by Dell Hymes (1962, 1972) and his ethnography of communication, and the British tradition of linguistics, as represented by Michael Halliday (1978) and his systemic-functional paradigm. Their contributions, although distinctive, are complementary and inform the use of communicative competence as a theoretical construct in WE studies.

Although Hymes is generally credited with introducing communicative competence as a linguistic construct in the 1970s, J. R. Firth had stressed the importance of the *context of situation* for understanding why language is used as it is some 40 years prior to that. The founder of the British school of linguistics, Firth held that "a piece of speech, a normal complete act of speech, is a pattern of group behavior in which two or more persons participate by means of common verbalizations of the common situational context, and of the experiential contexts of the participants" (1930: 173). Firth's interpretation of context of situation – which can be as broad as a speech community or as narrow as an interpersonal interaction – provides a theoretical orientation for describing the individual communicative competence of each speaker that has evolved in non-native settings. This concept is essential to an understanding of communicative competence in general because it leads to an appreciation of communicative competence "in specific." That is, only through inclusion of context of situation as a parameter for determining what communicative competence means do the pluralistic nature of a language and the independent existence and the dynamic creative processes of non-native varieties come into focus. It is this formulation of the social and cultural bases of communication that influenced Hymes as well as Halliday, and that accounts for their parallel interests in the making of meaning through language.

From Hymes comes the term *communicative competence* itself, which he interpreted as knowledge of sociolinguistic rules that is separate from knowledge of grammatical rules. The necessity of this notion came about in response to his recognition that communication is more than knowing how to create and construct grammatically correct sentences, the view offered by Chomsky which dominated American linguistics at the time (and still does). Rather, he sees communication as also entailing knowledge of how to use language appropriately in ways that are acceptable to other members of the speech community; thus, performance and competence cannot be separated. Communicative competence is what users of a language realize in choosing what to say as well as when and how to say it. And it is the context – cultural as well as social – that influences these features of linguistic performance.

Hymes expresses concern with the integration of linguistic theory into a more general theory of communication and culture: "social life shapes communicative competence and does so from infancy onward. Depending on gender, family, community and religion, children are raised in terms of one configuration of the use and meaning of language rather than another" (1980: vi). Enculturation into a group provides the members of that group a set of linguistic and cultural resources for communication with one another.

From Halliday comes a focus on the role of the social context and the options it presents to language users for "doing things with language," that is, using language to perform communicative functions. The various options a particular context offers he calls *meaning potential*, the choices (phonological, lexical, syntactic, and pragmatic) that language users have available to them when interacting through language. This meaning potential "is inherent in the social system as it is interpreted by the members of this or that subculture" (1978: 90). Thus, a culture's meaning potential has the same origins as a speech community's communicative competence: the social and cultural context in which users of the language make use of their linguistic system to express, interpret, and negotiate meaning between and among one another.

Hymes and Halliday offer views of language based on a relationship between form and function, between culture and language, between society and norms of use. However, their conceptualizations of the means to explain these relationships differ significantly. Halliday's focus is the interpersonal dimension of language and potential as a social construct, while Hymes' intrapersonal orientation is associated with a system of internalized rules of use, that is, communicative competence.

3   Communicative Competence and the World Englishes Paradigm

While Hymes and Halliday were developing their theories of appropriateness and meaning-making in language, Braj Kachru (1976, 1977, 1981) was making the case for recognition of the social realities of the growing use and nativization of English and demand for English instruction around the world, and in Outer-Circle contexts, in particular. This case needed to be made in the face of the unchallenged Anglocentric interpretation of standard, norm, and model that prevailed at the time among Inner-Circle linguists and language specialists. Kachru's argument focused on the need for a new research paradigm to explain the formal and functional variation observed in English as used in such contexts as India, Nigeria, or Singapore. This perspective would de-center the Inner Circle and its norms, standards, and models and shift the focus to the pluricentric realities of English – local, national, or international – and the communicative competences corresponding to the potential purposes, roles, and situations found in these contexts.

Multiple norms for English use – whether spoken or written – as represented by differences in rhetorical and communicative styles problematize a view of communicative competence as a monolithic notion. The concept of acceptability, appropriateness, and intelligibility (i.e., communicative competence) cannot be used independently of the context of situation in an Outer-Circle situation any more than in an Inner-Circle interaction. When an American and a New Zealander interact, phonological, semantic, or pragmatic variation can interfere with communicative success. Such interference is generally explained away by citing cultural differences underlying the linguistic choices each speaker has made, and this variation is accepted as legitimate for the American and the New Zealander because they are native speakers of their respective varieties.

This interdependence of context and communicative competence can also be demonstrated in instances of cross-cultural communication. Realizations of such speech acts as an apology or greeting do not necessarily convey the intended message when the participants in the interaction do not share socio-cultural norms. Thus, an African-English participant selects from his options for making meaning the greeting "I see you've put on weight," which is met with indignation by the American-English-speaking addressee, who doesn't interpret the utterance as the cultural equivalent, "You're looking well," which is considered appropriate, acceptable, and intelligible in her speech community. Her expectations of how to exchange greetings are not met; nor are the African's when she responds, by his norms, inappropriately. The issue highlighted by such encounters is identification of the facet of communicative competence leading to the misunderstanding: is it linguistic – rate of speech, choice of register, lexical items? Or is it cultural – pragmatic choices determined by the values of the speech community? In this case it is the latter; behind the observable factors of linguistic form and polite social behavior are the value systems of the speakers.

To shape the concept to suit the task at hand, Kachru drew on Firth, Hymes, and Halliday. He takes Hymes' formulation of communicative competence as sociolinguistic rules, which he relates to Firth's "means of common verbalizations of the common situational context, and of the experiential contexts of the participants" (Firth, 1930). Context of situation – the social and cultural parameters relevant to the setting in which participants find themselves – is also taken from Firth. Kachru's formulation of communicative competence integrates Halliday's focus on the interpersonal function of language and a socially constructed meaning potential. Ultimately, communicative competence becomes a cornerstone in the theoretical foundation of the new paradigm that is now known as world Englishes.

4 Communicative Competence Applied: Controversies

The applicability of Kachru's interpretation of communicative competence has been demonstrated in debates concerning the identification of the rightful guardians of the English language: whose communicative competence is to be the reference point for evaluating whether or not a use of English, wherever spoken, is appropriate and acceptable? Is the legitimacy accorded native-speaker variation available to the Englishes of non-native speakers? Are native-speaker norms, native-speaker communicative competence (or meaning potential) the only acceptable ways of speaking?

One position regards the "native speaker" as the only logical choice; two well-known proponents of this view are Clifford Prator and Randolph Quirk. The other position argues that local users can best determine what is appropriate and acceptable in their own contexts of use; Kachru subscribes to this view and has responded both to Prator and to Quirk.

Prator (1968) sparked the first of Kachru's challenges to the native-speaker argument (Kachru, 1976). For Prator, the English of all speakers of English in the Outer and Expanding Circles should be measured by Inner-Circle standards and should conform to Inner-Circle norms. This would be essential in limiting the deviations in non-native-speaker English that he attributed to the incomplete and incorrect learning of English. Curtailing deviations from the native-speaker norm would minimize "fossilization" of forms and of uses a native speaker finds unacceptable and inappropriate. Further, tolerating these deviations would lead, over time, to a total lack of intelligibility between native speakers and non-native speakers.

Prator was reacting to the suggestion that a pluralistic, rather than a monomodel, monocultural, Anglocentric orientation might be more productive when it comes to understanding the forms and functions of English in contexts beyond the Inner Circle. He referred to this position as "heresy" and to specific points of the proposition as "heretical tenets." One such tenet he took particular exception to was "the idea that it is best, in a country where English is not spoken natively but is widely used as the medium of instruction, to set up the local variety of English as the ultimate model to be imitated by those learning the language" (Prator, 1968: 459). International mutual intelligibility can be assured only when all learners of English pattern their English after that of a native speaker.

Quirk's position (1985, 1988, 1990) echoes that of Prator. In arguing against non-native norms and for the desirability of a global standard for English, Quirk claims that "the relatively narrow range of purposes for which the non-native needs to use English is arguably well catered for by a single monochrome standard form that looks as good on paper as it sounds in speech" (1985: 6). For Quirk (1990), the responsibility for maintaining respect for Standard (Inner-Circle) English falls to its native speakers, since non-native speakers do not have recourse to institutionalized standards and norms to legitimate any non-standard variety. Like Prator, Quirk is concerned with use of English in the international domain. He assumes that English teaching in schools throughout the world should not cater for local purposes, but for purposes of global communication. The pedagogical model should be the uniform competence shared among well-educated speakers whose speech and writing are based on a homogeneous Standard English.

Such assumptions conflict with those underlying Kachru's communicative competence, in particular one aspect following Hymes: if social life shapes a person's ability to use language appropriately, that is, if the context into which a child is born determines that child's later communicative competence, and if there is more than one social setting in which appropriateness in using a language can be shaped, the concept of communicative competence cannot be considered in monolithic or homogeneous and uniform terms. As English has, as a result of contact with different cultural and social systems, been adapted to the social life of the English-speaking communities in which it has come to function, the process of adaptation, or nativization, has been extended to notions of appropriateness and acceptability in form and function, to development of norms and standards, and to multiple communicative competences. In making this socially realistic assessment, Kachru negates Prator's and Quirk's puristic and prescriptivist claims, and ties communicative competence directly to choosing a variety as a standard, norm, and model through these questions: Acceptable to whom? Appropriate for whom? And intelligible to whom?

5   Communicative Competence Applied: Explorations

In the mid-1980s, several studies, among the first to consider contexts outside of the Inner-Circle contexts from a world Englishes perspective, illustrated how different cultural settings of English language use are associated with distinct communicative competences. Chishimba (1985) addressed the question of which features characterize the Africanness in indigenous varieties of English and illustrated how previous studies of English in Africa had consistently ignored the relevance of the context of situation to describe variation. Magura (1985), writing on South Africa and Zimbabwe, demonstrated that the African variety of English has developed a meaning system that is closely related to the African sociocultural context. Further, he showed that a native norm makes the African variety a distinct variety of English. Lowenberg (1984) looked at the multilingual speech fellowships of Singapore, Malaysia, and Indonesia to describe the complexity of communicative competence in such contexts because it involves not only competence in distinct languages, their diverse styles, registers, and even dialects, but also the ability to mix and switch among them in appropriate and acceptable ways. Berns (1985) looked at the Expanding-Circle settings of Germany and Japan in order to describe features, forms, and functions of English within each and explore the implications of these characteristics of their respective communicative competence for pedagogical models.

Later studies have explored issues associated with recognition of pluricentric norms of communicative competence. Topics of these studies have included the relationship between communicative competence and culture for users of English in cross-cultural interaction. Nelson (1992) and Berns (1995) ask whose culture and whose communicative competence will be the frame of reference in these situations. Rhetorical and communicative styles as socially constructed norms have also been investigated. For example, studies by Y. Kachru (1997, 2001) on both conversational and textual discourse show how cultural values are conveyed through rhetorical strategies, determinants of acceptable content, and text structure that are conventions of the local community and context.

Related research is on intelligibility, which, along with acceptability and appropriateness, is a means by which communicative competence is demonstrated. Key investigations here are those by Smith (1988, 1992) and Nelson (1984, 2001), who provide a nuanced interpretation of what is referred to as "understanding." They identify three separate levels: *intelligibility*, or recognition of the word/utterance; *comprehensibility*, or perception of the word/

utterance (referential) meaning; and *interpretability*, apprehension of the intent, purpose, or meaning behind the word/utterance. This distinction among aspects of understanding is a valuable tool in world Englishes studies for analysis of misunderstandings in cross-cultural interaction and description of differences in the participants' knowledge of the rules of speaking that apply or, in Halliday's terms, the meaning potential a speaker has available in any given context of situation. This broad interpretation of intelligibility plays a role in assessment of communicative competence in social settings as well as in pedagogical contexts.

6   Communicative Competence and Pedagogical Theory

Communicative competence is as central in pedagogical theory as it is for sociolinguistics (see Savignon, 1997 for pedagogical developments) and its impact on language teaching is parallel. Its adoption as a teaching goal has shifted the focus in language pedagogy from approaches preoccupied with grammatical correctness to those concerned with all aspects of communicative effectiveness in written as well as spoken interaction.

Until recently, native-speaker competence has been the uncontested goal for all learners, and an Inner-Circle English – predominantly an American or British variety – has been presented by the teacher and in teaching materials to learners as the model to follow. All norms and standards are to be consistent with those underlying Inner-Circle practices and behaviors. Learners are prepared for interaction with the written and spoken texts and the members of the Inner Circle regardless of the context of situation. Evidence that the status quo is no longer adequate and that native-speaker communicative competence may not be best suited as the goal in a given pedagogical setting have raised concerns. The introduction of acceptability, appropriateness, and intelligibility as relative concepts for language pedagogy has been a challenge to the status quo in classrooms around the world (see Savignon, 2002 for illustrations).

Quirk and Prator (see above) represent an Inner-Circle response to acceptance of regional variation for pedagogical purposes. Expanding-Circle representatives have also argued for maintenance of Inner-Circle norms. Görlach and Schröder's (1985) estimation of the proficiency of learners of English is illustrative. For them, as a consequence of the "liberal use" of different varieties (in this case American and British) and standards in the teaching of English, the level of proficiency achieved by young German learners is unacceptable; standards have declined and the English spoken by many learners "is an odd mixture of speech levels and an uncontrollable mid-Atlantic mishmash that is acceptable neither to the American nor British native speaker" (p. 230).

The claims and arguments presented by these scholars are based on three assumptions of particular relevance to language pedagogy: (1) everyone learning English does so in order to interact with native speakers; (2) the communicative competence learners need to develop is the native speaker's; and (3) learning English means dealing with the sociocultural realities of England or the US, that is, British or American ways of doing, thinking, and being. Kachru (1982) identifies each of these assumptions with a monomodel approach to pedagogy, which raises a number of questions in the light of the documentation of variation in the communicative competence of users of English worldwide: Although American and British varieties of English are acceptable as suitable models in their respective contexts, are they appropriate as models in non-native contexts? Is it appropriate for schoolchildren in rural West Africa, for example, to learn a variety of English based on the communicative competence of American schoolchildren? Will this ensure that the learners will achieve mutual intelligibility with other members of their local speech community? That they will be accepted as a member of the speech community although they do not follow its norms – the very norms that are markers of group identity? As an alternative, Kachru identifies a polymodel approach as more socially realistic. Responsive to the sociocultural dimensions of functional and formal diversity in speech communities requiring competence in English, this approach provides a means of addressing the questions of "which model?" or "whose communicative competence?" from a perspective which does not regard the concept of model as absolute. It considers the diversity of the social and cultural context in which the learners will be using the language as fundamental to any informed and realistic choice of a classroom model.

In pedagogical terms, the concept *model* implies a linguistic ideal that a learner and teacher keep in mind in the course of language instruction. The model represents a norm or standard for language use at all levels – from the phonological to the pragmatic. Selection of a model is a key decision in language teaching. Often the terms *norm* and *standard* are used along with *model* to identify the "correct" and "acceptable" variety of the language chosen, which is based on that used by a segment of the educated population. Choice of a particular model depends upon the communicative competence learners are to develop in order for their use of language to be acceptable, appropriate, and intelligible in a specified speech community. A learner's progress is measured against the model: How closely does pronunciation approximate the desired norm? How well do written texts follow the conventions for text construction? How well is the learner able to interpret texts? Can the learner create texts that are intelligible, comprehensible, and interpretable to other members of the speech community? Can the learner appropriately realize the functions that English serves in that community?

The logical starting point for selection of a model is a consideration of (1) the uses the learners will make of the language and (2) the users who are members of the group in which learners will become members. Questions to be posed include: Which functions does the language serve? Who are the users? Will they use it in interaction with native speakers, other non-native speakers, or both? Which culture should the language represent? The answers determine the nature of the interaction at local, national, and international levels.

If the selection of the model is not made on the basis of learners' needs for the language, the communicative competence achieved may be inappropriate for these learners. A pragmatic approach to determination of model must then include consideration of the actual forms and functions of the speech community with which learners will interact and the attitudes of members of that speech community toward the language and its speakers. A polymodel approach provides a means of addressing the question of "which model?" from a perspective that does not regard the concept of model as absolute and that provides a basis for consideration of the diversity of the social and cultural context as fundamental to any informed and realistic choice of model for learners.

Teaching for communicative competence is nothing new (see, for example, Musumeci, 1997). While some critics, most recently Bhatia (2003), may consider it passé if looking only at British interpretations, support for and interest in communicative competence as a goal continues and its currency is made more relevant and realistic through the integration of a polymodel approach into the theoretical foundation for teaching learners of English to develop the communicative competence that enables them to perform within the contexts in which they will use English. Examples of innovation along these lines are found in Berns (1990), in which she analyzed three interpretations of teaching for a communicative competence that were responses to the sociocultural contexts of their implementation, namely, Germany, Japan, and India (see Piepho, 1974 on teaching for communicative competence in Germany and Prabhu, 1987 for India). The analysis was to test approaches to teaching for communicative competence against the assumptions of a polymodel approach and explore the limits of what has come to be known as communicative language teaching.

Implementation of a polymodel approach has come to include assessment of teaching materials for linguistic tolerance, for correspondence with the sociocultural context for the use of English as well as the expressed or implied norms against which learners will be judged for the acceptability, appropriateness, and intelligibility of their linguistic performance. Put another way, do the materials reflect the sociocultural reality of the users? Teachers' communicative competence is also germane to a pluralistic approach. Do teachers in the Outer and as well as Expanding Circles perceive themselves as competent communicators in English or as incompetent when compared to a native-speaker model?

Changes in the sociolinguistic landscape of Europe with respect to English have produced a context of increasing social and professional needs for learning and using English and exposure to it through a variety of media. Continental uses, including cross-cultural, intra-European communication, just as their functional counterparts in other regions of the world, are realized in ways negotiated among the users. Communicative norms of appropriateness and standards for acceptability, and the parameters of intelligibility, if not already established, are developing among the English-using European speech community. It has been claimed that there is "the emergence of an endonormative model of lingua franca English which will increasingly derive its norms of correctness and appropriacy from its own usage" (Jenkins, Modiano, and Seidlhofer, 2001: 15; see also Deneire and Goethals, 1997). This development raises the issue of a pedagogical model for performance varieties, not only in Europe, but also in China or South America, and other contexts of increasing contact and use of English in the Expanding Circle (see Bolton and Tong, 2002; Berns and Friedrich, 2003).

7 Conclusion

The connection between communicative competence and world Englishes is firmly rooted in recognition of the social realities of the users and uses of a given variety (or varieties, in multilingual societies). The construct has proven useful in refuting claims of a uniform, ideal communicative competence for English and has motivated a growing body of research and scholarship that adopts a pluricentric approach to investigating the nature of acceptability, appropriateness, and intelligibility and implications not only for pedagogy but also literary criticism, cultural studies, and language policy, among other areas.

There is still room for further research into communicative competence, particularly with respect to the parameters of intelligibility for communication between various combinations of speakers – between Inner-Circle and Outer-Circle users. Do Expanding-Circle speakers find Inner- or Outer-Circle varieties easier to interpret and comprehend? What are the factors that contribute to misunderstandings in the various contexts of use? With the expansion in uses and contact with English in the Expanding Circle, to what extent are Expanding-Circle performance varieties being replaced by local or regional varieties with their own norms, models, and standards? We are far from in-depth insights into the communicative competence of the evolving speech communities of Africa, including South Africa. How does the communicative competence of this region relate to the sociocultural context? What are the potential meanings available to members of the speech communities, how are they realized, and how are they received by participants in the communication unfamiliar with the norms of these communities? To what extent is communicative competence as a relative notion, as varying along with the context of situation, taken into account in studies of Expanding-Circle Englishes as well as those of the Outer Circle? To what extent do views like those articulated by Prator and by Quirk about the necessity of a single norm and standard for English influence the learning, teaching, and assessment of communicative competence? What is the nature of this influence and what are its consequences for communication across cultures through English?

See also Chapters 24, World Englishes and Issues of Intelligibility; 36, Teaching World Englishes; 37, Models, Methods and Curriculum for ELT Preparation.

REFERENCES

Berns, Margie (1985) Functional Approaches and Communicative Competence: English language teaching in non-native contexts. PhD dissertation, University of Illinois at Urbana-Champaign.

Berns, Margie (1990) *Contexts of Competence: Social and Cultural Considerations in Communicative Language Teaching*. New York: Plenum Press.

Berns, Margie (1995) English in Europe: Whose language, which culture? *International Journal of Applied Linguistics*, 5(1), 21–32.

Berns, Margie and Friedrich, Patricia (eds.) (2003) English in South America: A different kind of difference. Special issue of *World Englishes*, 22(2), 83–214.

Bhatia, Vijay K. (2003) Comment 2. *World Englishes*, 22(1), 69–71.

Bolton, Kingsley and Tong, Q. S. (eds.) (2002) English in China: Interdisciplinary perspectives. Special issue of *World Englishes*, 21(2), 177–355.

Chishimba, Maurice Mulenga (1985) African Varieties of English: Text in context. PhD dissertation, University of Illinois at Urbana-Champaign.

Deneire, Marc G. and Goethals, Michaël (eds.) (1997) English in Europe. Special issue of *World Englishes*, 16(1), 1–179.

Firth, John R. (1930) *Speech*. London: Benn's Sixpenny Library.

Görlach, Manfred and Schröder, Konrad (1985) "Good usage" in an EFL context. In *The English Language*

Today. Edited by Sidney Greenbaum. Oxford: Pergamon, pp. 227–32.

Halliday, M. A. K. (1978) *Language as Social Semiotic: The Social Interpretation of Language and Meaning*. London: Edward Arnold.

Hymes, Dell (1962) The ethnography of speaking. In *Anthropology and Human Behavior*. Edited by Thomas Gladwin and William C. Sturtevant. Washington, DC: Anthropological Society of Washington, pp. 13–53.

Hymes, Dell (1972) On communicative competence. In *Sociolinguistics*. Edited by John B. Pride and Janet Holmes. Harmondsworth: Penguin, pp. 269–85.

Hymes, Dell (1980) *Language in Education: Ethnolinguistic Essays*. Washington, DC: Center for Applied Linguistics.

Jenkins, Jennifer, Modiano, Marko, and Seidlhofer, Barbara (2001) Euro-English. *English Today*, 17(4), 13–19.

Kachru, Braj B. (1976) Models of English for the Third World: White man's burden or language pragmatics?" *TESOL Quarterly*, 10(2), 221–39.

Kachru, Braj B. (1977) New Englishes and old models. *English Language Forum*, 15, 29–35.

Kachru, Braj B. (1981) Socially-realistic linguistics: The Firthian tradition. *International Journal of the Sociology of Language*, 31, 65–89.

Kachru, Braj B. (1982) Models for non-native Englishes. In *The Other Tongue: English across Cultures*. Edited by Braj B. Kachru. Urbana:

University of Illinois Press,
pp. 31–57.

Kachru, Yamuna (1997) Culture and argumentative writing in world Englishes. In *World Englishes 2000*. Edited by Larry E. Smith and Michael L. Forman. Honolulu: University of Hawai'i and the East-West Center, pp. 48–67.

Kachru, Yamuna (2001) Discourse competence in world Englishes. In *The Three Circles of English*. Edited by Edwin Thumboo. Singapore: UniPress, pp. 341–56.

Lowenberg, Peter H. (1984) English in the Malay Archipelago. PhD dissertation, University of Illinois at Urbana-Champaign.

Magura, Benjamin (1985) Style and Meaning in Southern African English. PhD dissertation, University of Illinois at Urbana-Champaign.

Musumeci, Diane (1997) *Breaking Tradition: An Exploration of the Historical Relationship between Theory and Practice in Second Language Teaching*. New York: McGraw-Hill.

Nelson, Cecil L. (1984) Intelligibility: The case of non-native varieties of English. PhD dissertation, University of Illinois at Urbana-Champaign.

Nelson, Cecil L. (1992) My language, your culture: Whose communicative competence? In *The Other Tongue: English across Cultures*. 2nd edition. Edited by Braj B. Kachru. Urbana: University of Illinois Press, pp. 327–39.

Nelson, Cecil L. (2001) Intelligibility and creativity in world English literatures. In *The Three Circles of English*. Edited by Edwin Thumboo, Singapore: UniPress, pp. 35–44.

Piepho, Hans-Eberhard (1974) *Kommunikative Kompetenz als übergeordnetes Lernziel im Englischunterricht* [Communicative competence as the overall goal in English language instruction].

Dornburg-Frickhofen, Germany: Frankonius.

Prabhu, N. S. (1987) *Second Language Pedagogy*. Oxford: Oxford University Press.

Prator, Clifford (1968) The British heresy in TESL. In *Language Problems of Developing Nations*. Edited by Joshua A. Fishman, Charles A. Ferguson, and Jyotirindra Das Gupta. New York: John Wiley, pp. 459–76.

Quirk, Randolph (1985) The English language in a global context. In *English in the World: Teaching and Learning the Language and Literatures*. Edited by Randolph Quirk and Henry G. Widdowson. Cambridge: Cambridge University Press, pp. 1–30.

Quirk, Randolph (1988) The question of standards in the international use of English. *Georgetown University Round Table in Languages and Linguistics 1987*. Washington, DC: Georgetown University Press, pp. 278–341.

Quirk, Randolph (1990) Language varieties and standard language. *English Today*, **21**, 3–10.

Savignon, Sandra J. (1997) *Communicative Competence: Theory and Classroom Practice: Texts and Contexts in Second Language Learning*. New York: McGraw-Hill.

Savignon, Sandra J. (ed.) (2002) *Interpreting Communicative Language Teaching: Contexts and Concerns in Teacher Education*. New Haven, CT: Yale University Press.

Smith, Larry E. (1988) Language spread and issues of intelligibility. In *Language Spread and Language Policy: Issues, Implications and Case Studies*. Edited by James E. Alatis. Washington, DC: Georgetown University Press, pp. 265–82.

Smith, Larry E. (1992) Spread of English and issues of intelligibility. In *The Other Tongue: English across Cultures*. Edited by Braj B. Kachru. Urbana: University of Illinois Press, pp. 75–90.

FURTHER READING

Kachru, Braj B. (1990) World Englishes and applied linguistics. *World Englishes* **9**(1), 3–20.

Kachru, Yamuna (1999) Culture, context, and writing. In *Culture in Second Language Teaching and Learning*. Edited by Eli Hinkel. Cambridge: Cambridge University Press, pp. 75–89.

Kachru, Yamuna (2003) Conventions of politeness in plural societies. In *Anglophone Cultures in Southeast Asia*. Edited by Rüdiger Ahrens, David Parker, Klaus Stierstorfer, and Kwok-Kan Tam. Heidelberg: Universitätsverlag, pp. 39–53.

Kramsch, Claire (1993) *Context and Culture in Language Teaching*. Oxford: Oxford University Press.

McNeill, R. (ed.) (2000) *Language and Gesture*. Cambridge: Cambridge University Press.

Ochs, E. (2002) Becoming a speaker of culture. In *Language Acquisition and Language Socialization: Ecological Perspectives*. Edited by Claire Kramsch. London: Continuum, pp. 99–120.

Singh, R. (ed.) (1998) *The Native Speaker: Multilingual Perspectives*. New Delhi: Sage.

Part IX   Resources on World Englishes

41 World Englishes and Corpora Studies

GERALD NELSON

1 Introduction

Kennedy (1998: 1) provides succinct definitions of both the terms "corpus" and "corpus linguistics":

> In the language sciences a corpus is a body of written text or transcribed speech which can serve as a basis for linguistic analysis and description. Over the last three decades the compilation and analysis of corpora stored in computerized databases has led to a new scholarly enterprise known as corpus linguistics.

As Kennedy's definition shows, the corpus-based method of linguistic research is a very recent development, and the use of corpora in the study of world Englishes is more recent still. McEnery and Wilson (2001: 1) provide a useful account of what they call "early" corpus linguistics, by which they refer to range of research projects undertaken from the 1950s to the 1970s, using entirely manual methods for compiling and analyzing large collections of text. Notable among these was the work of Randolph Quirk, who compiled the Survey of English Usage (SEU) corpus, beginning in 1959. SEU is a one-million-word corpus of British English, dating for the most part from the 1960s. From our perspective in the technologically sophisticated twenty-first century, it is astonishing to recall that the SEU corpus was an entirely paper-based corpus, with each instance of every word annotated on its own paper slip, and the slips stored in a vast array of metal filing cabinets (Peppé, 1995). In contrast with this, corpus linguistics today exploits the ever-increasing power of computer hardware and software, and with the aid of computer technology, linguists are compiling ever-larger collections of text. Since the 1980s, the corpus-based approach has become firmly established as a methodology for linguistic research.

Table 41.1   Composition of the Brown Corpus

Informative prose: 374 samples	Imaginative prose: 126 samples
Press: reportage	General fiction
Press: editorial	Mystery and detective fiction
Press: reviews	Science fiction
Religion	Adventure and western fiction
Skills and hobbies	Romance and love story
Popular lore	Humor
Belles lettres, biography, memoir	
Miscellaneous	
Learned	

2   Electronic Corpora

The first electronic corpus of English is generally agreed to be the Brown corpus, which was compiled by Francis and Kučera at Brown University, Rhode Island, in 1963–4. The compilers refer to the corpus as *A Standard Corpus of Present-Day Edited American English* (Francis and Kučera, 1971). It consists of just over one million words of printed English produced in the United States during the calendar year 1961. It includes 500 individual samples of 2,000 words each, selected from the range of text types shown in Table 41.1.

The Brown corpus has been, and continues to be, enormously influential, especially in terms of the methodology of corpus design and compilation. For that reason, it is worth quoting the compilers at some length here:

> Samples were chosen for their representative quality rather than for any sub-jectively determined excellence. The use of the word standard in the title of the Corpus does not in any way mean that it is put forward as "standard English"; it merely expresses the hope that this corpus will be used for comparative studies where it is important to use the same body of data. Since the preparation and input of data is a major bottleneck in computer work, the intent was to make available a carefully chosen and prepared body of material of considerable size in standardized format. The corpus may further prove to be standard in setting the pattern for the preparation and presentation of further bodies of data in English or in other languages. (Francis and Kučera, 1971)

The Brown corpus did, indeed, become a "standard" in the sense that the compilers express here. It set in motion a series of corpus-based projects around the world, in which the researchers invariably looked to Brown as their model. The Lancaster-Oslo/Bergen (LOB) corpus was begun in 1976 in order to provide a British English equivalent of the Brown corpus (Johansson, Leech, and Goodluck, 1978). To this end, the compilers followed the design of Brown closely, selecting texts printed in Great Britain in 1961, and choosing the same number and size of samples from the same text categories. The objective was, of course, to ensure that the two corpora would be directly comparable with each other, so that they could be used as the basis for comparative studies across the two dominant varieties, American and British English (AmE and BrE).

In 1978, S. V. Shastri noted that previous studies of Indian English had been largely confined to aspects of the spoken variety (Bansal, 1969), or to isolated topics in the language (Kachru, 1965). Having worked at Lancaster University with Geoffrey Leech, one of the prime movers behind the LOB corpus, Shastri recognized that "a comprehensive description [of Indian English] will have to be based on a standard corpus" (Shastri, 1986). To this end, Shastri compiled the Kolhapur corpus of written Indian English, using both Brown and LOB as his models. He declared his objectives in the following terms:

> The present corpus of Indian Written English is comparable to the Brown and the LOB corpora. It is intended to serve as source material for comparative studies of American, British and Indian English which in its turn is expected to lead to a comprehensive description of Indian English. (Shastri, 1986)

However, unlike Brown and LOB, which sampled texts from 1961, the Kolhapur corpus takes 1978 as its sampling date. Part of the rationale behind this had to do with the perceived "Indianness" of post-independence Indian English. As Shastri explained:

> it is felt that the value of the Indian corpus is immensely enhanced in general and in particular as a source for the description of Indian English . . . as the Indianness of Indian English is a post-independence phenomenon and may have reached a discernible stage in the thirty years after Independence. It is argued in theory that in the same thirty years the American and British English may not have undergone such changes. (Shastri, 1986)

This is an interesting observation, and one which, consciously or unconsciously, informs descriptions of other post-colonial Englishes as well. What Shastri was consciously attempting to construct was a corpus of distinctively Indian English, as opposed to the variety used at the time of Independence. Whether the 30-year gap to 1978 would be sufficient to allow the "Indianness" of Indian English to manifest itself is perhaps a moot point. The key issue here is that Shastri, following Kachru (1965), recognized Indian English as a distinct variety, and set about capturing it in the Kolhapur corpus.

The Australian Corpus of English (ACE) was compiled at Macquarie University, beginning in 1986. As with the Kolhapur corpus, the compilers were motivated primarily by a wish to differentiate between their own variety of English and the British and American varieties. For that reason, they followed the Brown and LOB models closely in terms of corpus design, though again there is a chronological gap: ACE samples texts from 1986.

At Victoria University of Wellington, New Zealand, researchers compiled the Wellington Corpus of Written New Zealand English (WWC; Bauer, 1993). Once again, Brown and LOB were the models, though the compilers decided to use ACE as their model in terms of sampling date. In the Wellington corpus, the majority of samples date from 1986 or 1987. The corpus of written New Zealand English was followed in 1998 by the Wellington Corpus of Spoken New Zealand English (WSC), consisting of dialogs and monologs collected in the period 1988 to 1994 (Holmes, Vine, and Johnson, 1998).

Beginning with the highly influential Brown corpus in the early 1960s, the enterprise of compiling English-language corpora has continued in highly principled and systematic ways. As a result, linguists now have five "parallel" corpora of international written English at their disposal: Brown, LOB, Kolhapur, ACE, and Wellington. In 1990, a new project was initiated which would significantly expand this collection, and more importantly, greatly increase both the linguistic and the geographical coverage of available corpora.

3   The International Corpus of English

The International Corpus of English (ICE) project was conceived in the late 1980s by Sidney Greenbaum, then Director of the Survey of English Usage, University College London. The idea was first proposed in a brief notice in *World Englishes* (Greenbaum, 1988), in which researchers were invited to collaborate on the compilation of parallel English corpora, specifically in countries where English is used as a first language, or as a second official language. The invitation was timely, and the response from linguists worldwide was both immediate and enthusiastic. The ICE project currently involves research teams working in the following countries or regions: Australia, Canada, East Africa (Kenya and Tanzania), Great Britain, Hong Kong, India, Ireland, Jamaica, Malaysia, New Zealand, Philippines, Singapore, South Africa, Sri Lanka, United States.

From its inception, ICE aimed to compile parallel corpora from two of Kachru's Three Circles of English (Kachru, 1985). The Inner Circle is represented by countries such as Britain, the United States, and Australia, while the Outer Circle is represented by countries such as India, Singapore, and the Philippines. Kachru's third circle, the Expanding Circle, is represented in an anciliary project, the International Corpus of Learner English (ICLE), which is discussed below.

Each ICE team is compiling (or has already compiled) a one-million-word corpus of their own variety of English, produced by adults (aged 18 or over) in the period after 1989. While each national or regional corpus can exist independently as a valuable resource for the study of individual varieties, the real value of the corpora lies in their being exactly compatible with each other. This compatibility lies in every area of the corpus design and annotation (Nelson, 1996a, 1996b). The design, in terms of text categories, is shown in Table 41.2.

Each corpus consists of 500 samples of approximately 2,000 words each, to give a total of one million words. The first major division is between speech

Table 41.2 Composition of the ICE corpora

WRITTEN TEXTS (200 samples)	SPOKEN TEXTS (300 SAMPLES)
Non-printed	**Dialogue**
Non-professional writing	*Private*
Student essays	Direct conversations
Examination scripts	Telephone calls
Correspondence	*Public*
Social letters	Class lessons
Business letters	Broadcast discussions
Printed	Broadcast interviews
	Parliamentary debates
Academic writing	Legal cross-examinations
Humanities	Business transactions
Social sciences	**Monologue**
Natural sciences	
Technology	*Unscripted*
	Spontaneous commentaries
Non-academic writing	Unscripted speeches
Humanities	Demonstrations
Social sciences	Legal presentations
Natural sciences	
Technology	*Scripted*
	Broadcast news
Reportage	Broadcast talks
Press news reports	Non-broadcast talks
Instructional writing	
Administrative writing	
Skills and hobbies	
Persuasive writing	
Press editorials	
Creative writing	
Novels and stories	

(300 samples) and writing (200 samples). Further subdivisions are made in a hierarchical fashion, with speech divided among dialog (180 samples) and monolog (120 samples), and writing divided among non-printed (50 samples) and printed (150 samples). The hierarchical subdivision continues to the fundamental level of the text categories, of which there are 15 in speech and 17 in writing.

The overall design was arrived at following extensive discussion (see Leitner, 1992; Schmied, 1990). While it is informally based on the design of Brown and LOB, it also reflects some important differences. Most notably, it samples spoken English, and in a greater proportion than writing. Within the spoken component, by far the greatest contribution is from face-to-face conversations (90 samples, or 180,000 words). The ICE corpora, therefore, are distinctive in the emphasis they place on the spoken medium, and in particular on informal, conversational English. They are also distinctive in that they include only those text categories which are internationally applicable. So, for example, the corpus design (Table 41.2) contains no Religion category, as Brown and LOB did, because writing on this topic is not available (in English, at least) in all the participating countries. Similarly, the subdivision of Fiction into Romance, Westerns, Detective Fiction, etc., have been dispensed with, since these subtypes simply do not apply internationally. The ICE corpora aim to be maximally representative of English in use in all the participating countries, and not in any one country.

Each of the ICE teams has had a slightly different experience in compiling their respective corpora, depending on local circumstances, and specifically on the status of English in the country concerned. Many of the teams have written informatively about these experiences, and they provide some valuable insights into the processes and rationales behind corpus building in the context of world Englishes. Schmied (1995) discusses the issue of national standards in the context of the ICE project, with special emphasis on East African varieties. Holmes (1996) discusses methodological problems in compiling the spoken component of ICE New Zealand. Bolt and Bolton (1996) discuss the Hong Kong ICE project, and their observations provide an interesting contrast with Shastri's comments on the "Indianness" of Indian English, discussed earlier. The Hong Kong component of ICE (ICE-HK) was compiled during a crucial period in the territory's history: the texts in the corpus date from both before and after the "Handover" in 1997, which saw Hong Kong reverting from British to Chinese rule. As such, the data in the corpus may be said to represent English in Hong Kong at the "end of empire," in contrast with Shastri's conception of Indian English 30 years after Independence. Indeed, the compilers of ICE-HK worked in the knowledge that this would probably be the last opportunity to sample "Hong Kong English," since they predicted (correctly, it now seems) that the status of English in Hong Kong was about to change dramatically, with both Cantonese and Putonghua (Mandarin) rising quickly to prominence (Bolt and Bolton, 1996). Thus, while conforming to an agreed international standard, each ICE corpus reflects the unique situation of English in each participating region.

At the time of writing, six ICE corpora are available for the purposes of non-profit, academic research. These are Great Britain (ICE-GB), New Zealand (ICE-NZ), Singapore (ICE-SIN), India (ICE-IND), East Africa (ICE-EA), and the Philippines (ICE-PHI). Details of availability are given at the end of this chapter. The British corpus, ICE-GB, was completed in 1998. In terms of annotation, it is the most advanced of all the ICE corpora. Every word has been tagged for part of speech, using a specially designed tagset (Greenbaum, 1993), and each sentence/utterance has been parsed at phrase and clause level. The syntactic structures are represented in the familiar form of tree diagrams, as illustrated in Figure 41.1.

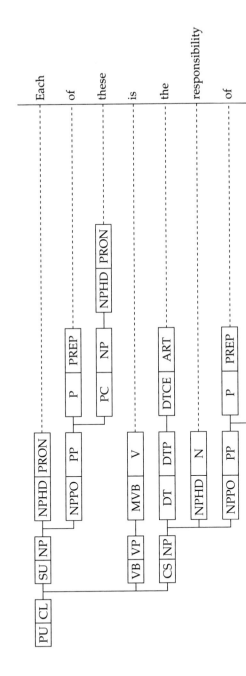

Key: ART: article; CL: clause; CS: subject complement; DT: determiner; DTP: determiner phrase; DTPS: post-determiner; N: noun; NP: noun phrase; NPHD: noun phrase head; NPPO: noun phrase postmodifier; MVB: main verb; NUM: numeral; P: prepositional; PC: prepositional complement; PP: prepositional phrase; PREP: preposition; PRON: pronoun; PU: parsing unit; V: verb

Figure 41.1   A tree diagram from the ICE-GB corpus

The ICE-GB corpus contains just over 83,000 syntactic trees, and represents the largest amount of data ever parsed to this level of detail. The grammatical terminology used in the corpus is based for the most part on the function/ form approach found in *A Comprehensive Grammar of the English Language* (Quirk et al., 1985). The annotation was carried out using software developed by the TOSCA research group at the University of Nijmegen, under the direction of Professor Jan Aarts (Van Halteren and Oostdijk, 1993). The corpus is dis-tributed with its own retrieval software, ICECUP (the ICE Corpus Utility Program), which supports complex searches of the syntactic trees (Nelson, Wallis, and Aarts, 2002).

One of the central principles underlying the ICE project is the notion that a common grammatical "core" unites all the varieties. This can be seen, perhaps, as a slight but important shift of emphasis: from concentrating on the "distinc-tiveness" of, say, Indian English or Australian English, ICE focuses primarily on what unites the varieties. The notion of the common core is described in the following terms by Quirk et al. (1985: 16):

> A common core or nucleus is present in all the varieties so that, however esoteric a variety may be, it has running through it a set of grammatical and other characteristics that are present in all the others. It is this fact that justifies the application of the name "English" to all the varieties.

Quirk et al. appear to accept the existence of the common core as an established fact, though this cannot be empirically tested without extensive study of parallel corpora such as the ICE components. Discovering whether such a core actually exists or not, and how it might be constituted, is perhaps the ultimate objective of the ICE project. In order to do this, all the ICE corpora will have to be annotated to the same level as ICE-GB. That is, they will all have to be syntactically parsed at least to the level of annotation illustrated in Figure 41.1. Once this has been achieved, linguists will be able to examine those grammatical structures that form the putative "core," and also to see which structures (if any) are present only in individual varieties. However, the other currently available corpora mentioned above are still at the "lexical" stage; that is, they contain the words only, with no part of speech tagging or syntactic analysis. Reaching the level of annotation of ICE-GB will be time-consuming and expensive, but well worth the effort. However, despite their lack of annotation at present, many of the ICE corpora have already proved invaluable as sources of data for comparative studies of English varieties.

4   Corpus-Based Studies of World Englishes

The corpora described above have been used as the basis for a very large and varied body of research, and they continue to be used in this way. The results of this research are far too numerous to cite here, though special mention should perhaps be made of the pioneering work, *Computational Analysis of Present-Day American English* (Kučera and Francis, 1967), based on the Brown corpus. This large-scale, quantitative study was later replicated using the LOB corpus of British English, in *Frequency Analysis of English Vocabulary and Grammar* (Johansson and Hofland, 1989). For comprehensive bibliographies of corpus-based studies of English, see Glauser, Schneider, and Görlach (1993), Altenberg (1998), and Fallon (2004).

The Kolhapur corpus has proved to be an especially fruitful resource for investigators of world Englishes. For an account of early work based on the corpus, see Shastri (1988). Sayder (1989) contrasts the use of the subjunctive in Indian, British, and American English, while Leitner (1992) analyzes the verbs *begin* and *start* in Indian English, in comparison with both AmE and BrE. A particularly important recent contribution in this context is Schneider (2000), which analyzes a range of grammatical phenomena in the Kolhapur corpus, including the subjunctive, case marking of *wh*-pronouns, pro-form *do*, and the indefinite pronouns in -*body* and -*one*. Comparing his findings with those from Brown and LOB, Schneider concludes that "my empirical corpus investigations have shown that no fundamental, categorical difference between Indian English and any other of the national varieties was detected, but on the other hand there is no full identity of patterns and preferences to be observed" (Schneider, 2000: 133). Schneider's conclusion is a complex one, and in particular his finding that "no full identity of patterns" may be observed is especially interesting in the light of the putative common core.

The ACE corpus of Australian English has provided data for a wide range of investigations, focusing on, for example, comparisons of Australian and British usage (Peters 1993a, 1993b), the influence of AmE and BrE on Australian verb morphology (Peters, 1994), the language of Australian newspapers (Peters et al., 1988), and the semantics of modal verbs (Collins, 1988, 1991). The two Wellington corpora – of written New Zealand English (WWC) and of spoken New Zealand English (WSC) – have supported research into a wide range of topics, including gender-based variation (Holmes, 1993), relative pronouns (Sigley, 1997), and the discourse of direct and indirect speech (Yang, 1997).

Whether researchers examine aspects of Indian English, Australian English, or New Zealand English, a comparison is usually made – explicitly or implicitly – with AmE and/or BrE. This is to be expected, because of the traditional dominance of these two varieties, and, on a more practical level, because of the availability of the Brown and LOB corpora. The corpora in the International Corpus of English offer scope for much more inclusive studies of English worldwide, taking account not only of first-language varieties, but of second-language varieties as well. ICE-GB has been extensively used in research, initially as a "snapshot" of BrE in the early 1990s, and later in comparative studies with other varieties. Most notably, ICE-GB formed the most important data source for the *Oxford English Grammar* (Greenbaum, 1996), and a subset of the corpus was used in a study of subordination in speech and writing (Greenbaum and Nelson, 1995a, 1995b, 1996; Greenbaum, Nelson, and Weitzman, 1995).

A range of "first findings" from other ICE corpora were published in a special issue of *World Englishes* in 1996 (vol. 15, no. 1). The papers in that volume deal with such topics as coordination in BrE and AmE (Meyer, 1996), the language of sports reporting (Leitner and Hesselmann, 1996), intervocalic /t/ in New Zealand English (Bauer and Holmes, 1996), and the stylistic features of East African newspaper English (Schmied and Hudson-Ettle, 1996). Since then, the task of completing the ICE corpora has continued, and researchers have continued to explore the data as it has been collected. Sand (1998) examined the structure of the verb phrase in Jamaican English, and found that while it does not deviate markedly from international Standard English norms, the preferences selected by users in given situations are markedly different. For instance, in the expression of future time, Sand found that both the *will* form (including *'ll* and *shall*) and the *going to* form (including *gonna*) are readily attested in Jamaican speech, just as they are in BrE. However, she found that the *going to* option is more frequent in Jamaican English, and that this accords with a significantly greater use of progressives generally in that variety (1998: 209). She concludes that the difference between Jamaican English and international Standard English, in this respect, is "not manifested in the presence or absence of a feature, but in different usage preference patterns" (p. 212).

Similar findings have been reported by other researchers. Nelson (2003) studied the use of modal verbs expressing obligation and necessity (*must, should, ought to, need to, have to, have got to, gotta*) in six varieties of English (British, New Zealand, East Africa, India, Hong Kong, Jamaica). In the case of these modals, the usage preference patterns were distinctly different. While the most frequent modal in all varieties was found to be *have (got) to*, the other modals exhibit very different distribution patterns in the varieties under review. For instance, *need to* was found to be unusually frequent in Jamaican English (34 instances in 40,927 tokens), and unusually rare in Indian English (only one instance in 47,212 tokens) (Nelson, 2003: 28). Just as Sand found that the difference between varieties is not one of absence or presence, but of different distributions, the study of modals leads to a similar conclusion: in these terms at least, the difference is one of degree, not of kind.

Having said that, both Sand and Nelson discovered in their data examples of English usage which had not (as far as we know) been previously attested. In the Jamaican data, Sand found several instances of *have to be* VERB + *ing* with non-epistemic meaning:

. . . and we *have to be making* some new steel couplings to attach the new piece (Sand, 1998: 209–10)

Similarly, Nelson (2003: 31) found 57 instances of the following construction in the East African ICE corpus:

there *is need to* address cultural constraints

there *is need to* work on culture family and socialisation

This construction was found in both speech and writing, and in the data from both Tanzania and Kenya. It has not been found in any of the other currently available ICE corpora. It opens up many possible avenues of research. On the syntactic level, it is an interesting construction since the status of *need* is unclear. Is *need* verbal or nominal in this existential construction? Its nominal status is certainly unclear, since it never occurs (in this construction) with a determiner (*there is a need/there is the need*). On the pragmatic level, too, it opens up the whole question of when and why speakers would use an existential construction to express obligation.

More immediately, however, the discovery of these two constructions in ICE-Jamaica and in ICE-East Africa should lead us to revise our earlier observation. Perhaps some of the grammatical difference between varieties is, after all, a difference of kind, and not simply of degree. If this were proven to be true, it would inevitably force us to reconsider the notion of the "common core" which unites varieties of English. Findings such as these, together with those of Schneider (2000), cited above, offer a glimpse of the kinds of theoretical perspectives on world Englishes that become available for exploration using corpora. As Schneider puts it: "it is likely that at some point a larger set of such corpus-based results, drawn from further corpora and varieties will allow generalizations as to prototypical paths of linguistic evolution in New Varieties of English" (2000: 134).

5   The International Corpus of Learner English

Varieties of English from the Expanding Circle are catered for in the International Corpus of Learner English (ICLE), which is coordinated by Professor Sylviane Granger, University of Louvain-la-Neuve, Belgium. The ICLE project samples learner (EFL) English from a wide range of mother-tongue backgrounds, including French, German, Dutch, Spanish, Swedish, Finnish, Czech, Japanese, Chinese, Polish, and Russian (Granger, 1996). The ICLE corpus has been extensively used in studies of learner English, focusing, for example, on the forms of questions (Virtanen, 1998), the functions of participle clauses in academic writing (Granger, 1997), and the use of adverbial connectors (Granger and Tyson, 1996; Altenberg and Tapper, 1998).

6   Conclusion

As a discipline, corpus linguistics has come of age in recent years, but comparatively speaking, the corpus-based study of world Englishes is still in its infancy. The collection and annotation of the ICE corpora has proved far more time-consuming than originally anticipated, despite the tireless efforts of researchers worldwide. A great deal of work remains to be done. On the practical side, the existing ICE corpora need to be completed. This will take place in at least two distinct phases: those corpora which have not been fully compiled in lexical form need to be completed, and then released for research. Following this, the corpora will have to be annotated to the level shown in ICE-GB, that is, with full part-of-speech tagging and syntactic analysis. There are also some major gaps in the geographical coverage that has been achieved so far. Most notably, very few African varieties are represented. Without proper

Table 41.3 An outline of the units and structures from morpheme to discourse which can be investigated using the completed ICE corpora (adapted from Kennedy, 1996: 223)

Word classes
  adjectives, adverbs, determiners, nouns, prepositions, pronouns, verbs, etc.
Word morphology and functions
  affixation, tense, number, etc.
Word types
Lemmas
Collocations
Phrases
  noun phrases, prepositional phrases, verb phrases, etc.
Clause elements
  subject, object, complement, adverbial, etc.
Clause patterns
  SV, SVO, SVOA, existential *there* constructions, etc.
Clause processes and information packaging
  extraposition, clefting, fronting, passivization, negation, etc.
Sentence types
  declarative, interrogative (*yes/no*, *wh-*), imperatives, etc.
Form and function
  interrogative versus question, etc.
Clause types
  subordinate clauses (nominal, relative, adverbial, comparative, etc.)
Clause relationships
  coordination, subordination, hypotaxis, parataxis
Discourse particles
Cohesion
Varieties and variation
  lexis, grammar, and discourse in different domains
    speech and writing
    sociolinguistic variation
    register variation
    regional variation

representation of important varieties from Nigeria, Cameroon, and Ghana – to mention just three – the ICE project will always offer only a partial picture of world Englishes.

On a more theoretical level, some consideration must be given to the methodology of comparing corpora. Previous work has been invaluable, though largely uncoordinated. Perhaps we now need a more coordinated approach, under the auspices of the ICE project. A useful starting point for such an approach is provided by Kennedy (1996), which offers an outline of the topics that can be investigated using the ICE corpora once they have been fully annotated to the same level as ICE-GB. Kennedy's outline is summarized in Table 41.3. As this table shows, the ICE corpora offer exciting possibilities for future research. This is especially true since most of the topics listed have never been systematically studied in most of the ICE varieties, and, for the most part, no comparative studies have ever been carried out on these topics. Though it is not exhaustive, Table 41.3 might be considered the starting point for a "prospectus" for future empirical research into world Englishes using the ICE corpora.

See also Chapters 20, WRITTEN LANGUAGE, STANDARD LANGUAGE, GLOBAL LANGUAGE; 35, A RECURRING DECIMAL: ENGLISH IN LANGUAGE POLICY AND PLANNING.

AVAILABILITY OF CORPORA

The corpora mentioned in this chapter are available as follows:

Brown, LOB, Kolhapur, ACE, Wellington:
  on a single CD-ROM from ICAME (International Computer Archive of Modern English), at the following address: The HIT Centre, Allegt. 27, N-5007, Bergen, Norway. Email: icame@hit.uib.no.
  Website: http://www.hd.uib.no.icame.html
  The Manuals for these corpora, cited in the references, are also available on the ICAME CD-ROM.

ICE-GB (The British component of the International Corpus of English):
  Survey of English Usage, University College London, Gower St, London WC1E 6BT, UK. Email: ucleseu@ucl.ac.uk.
  Website: http://www.ucl.ac.uk/english-usage/

ICE-New Zealand:
  Corpus Manager, Archive of New Zealand English, School of Linguistics and Applied Language Studies, Victoria University of Wellington, PO Box 600, Wellington, New Zealand.
  Website: www.vuw.ac.nz/lals/corpora/icenz.aspx

ICE-India, ICE-Singapore, ICE-East Africa, ICE-Philippines:
  Dr Gerald Nelson, Department of English Language and Literature, University College London, Gower St, London WC1E 6BT, UK. Email: g.nelson@ucl.ac.uk. Website: http://www.ucl.ac.uk/english-usage/ice/index.htm

ICLE corpora (components of the International Corpus of Learner English):
  Professor Sylviane Granger, Centre for English Corpus Linguistics (CECL), Collège Erasme, Place Blaise Pascal 1, Université Catholique de Louvain, 1348 Louvain-la-Neuve, Belgium. Email: granger@lige.ucl.ac.be. Website: http://www.fltr.ucl.ac.be/FLTR/GERM/ETAN/CECL/cecl.html

REFERENCES

Altenberg, Bengt (1998) *ICAME Bibliography 3 (1990–1998)*. http://www.hd.uib.no/icame.html.

Altenberg, Bengt and Tapper, Marie (1998) The use of adverbial connectors in advanced Swedish learners' written English. In *Learner English on Computer*. Edited by Sylviane Granger. London: Addison Wesley Longman, pp. 80–93.

Bansal, R. K. (1969) *The Intelligibility of Indian English*. Hyderabad: CIEFL.

Bauer, Laurie (1993) *Manual of Information to Accompany the Wellington Corpus of Written New Zealand English*. Wellington: Victoria University of Wellington.

Bauer, Laurie and Holmes, Janet (1996) Getting into a flap!: /t/ in New Zealand English. *World Englishes*, **15**(1), 115–24.

Bolt, Philip and Bolton, Kingsley (1996) The International Corpus of English in Hong Kong. In *Comparing English Worldwide: The International Corpus of English*. Edited by Sidney Greenbaum. Oxford: Clarendon Press, pp. 197–214.

Collins, Peter (1988) The semantics of some modals in contemporary Australian English. *Australian Journal of Linguistics*, **8**, 233–58.

Collins, Peter (1991) The modals of obligation and necessity in Australian English. In *English Corpus Linguistics: Studies in Honour of Jan Svartvik*. Edited by Karin Aijmer and Bengt Altenberg. London: Longman, pp. 145–65.

Fallon, Helen (2004) Comparing world Englishes: A research guide. *World Englishes*, **23**(2), 309–16.

Francis, W. Nelson and Kučera, Henry (1971) *Manual of Information to Accompany a Standard Corpus of Present-Day Edited American English, for Use with Digital Computers*. Revised edition. Providence: Department of Linguistics, Brown University.

Glauser, Beat, Schneider, Edgar W., and Görlach, Manfred (1993) *A New Bibliography of Writings on Varieties of English 1984–1992/3*. Amsterdam: Benjamins.

Granger, Sylviane (1996) Learner English around the world. In *Comparing English Worldwide: The International Corpus of English*. Edited by Sidney Greenbaum. Oxford: Clarendon Press, pp. 13–24.

Granger, Sylviane (1997) On identifying the syntactic and discourse features of participle clauses in academic English: Native and non-native writers compared. In *Studies in English Language and Teaching in Honour of Flor Aarts*. Edited by

Igne de Mönnink Aarts and Herman Wekker. Amsterdam: Rodopi, pp. 185–98.

Granger, Sylviane and Tyson, Stephanie (1996) Connector usage in the English essay writing of native and non-native EFL speakers of English. *World Englishes*, **15**(1), 17–27.

Greenbaum, Sidney (1988) A proposal for an International Corpus of English. *World Englishes*, **7**, 315.

Greenbaum, Sidney (1993) The tagset for the International Corpus of English. In *Corpus-Based Computational Linguistic*. Edited by Clive Souter and Eric Atwell. Amsterdam: Rodopi, pp. 11–24.

Greenbaum, Sidney (1996) *Oxford English Grammar*. Oxford: Oxford University Press.

Greenbaum, Sidney and Nelson, Gerald (1995a) Clause relationships in spoken and written English. *Functions of Language*, **2**, 1–21.

Greenbaum, Sidney and Nelson, Gerald (1995b) Nuclear and peripheral clauses in speech and writing. In *Studies in Anglistics*. Edited by Gunnel Melchers and Beatrice Warren. Stockholm: Almqvist and Wiksell, pp. 181–90.

Greenbaum, Sidney and Nelson, Gerald (1996) Positions of adverbial clauses in British English. *World Englishes*, **15**(1), 69–81.

Greenbaum, Sidney, Nelson, Gerald, and Weitzman, Michael (1995) Complement clauses in English. In *Using Corpora for Language Research: Studies in Honour of Geoffrey Leech*. Edited by Jenny Thomas and Mike Short. London: Addison Wesley Longman, pp. 76–91.

Holmes, Janet (1993) Sex-marking suffixes in written New Zealand English. *American Speech*, **68**, 357–70.

Holmes, Janet (1996) The New Zealand spoken component of ICE: Some methodological challenges. In

Comparing English Worldwide: The International Corpus of English. Edited by Sidney Greenbaum. Oxford: Clarendon Press, pp. 163–81.

Holmes, Janet, Vine, Bernadette, and Johnson, Gary (1998) *Guide to the Wellington Corpus of Spoken New Zealand English*. Victoria University of Wellington: School of Linguistics and Applied Language Studies.

Johansson, Stig and Hofland, Knut (1989) *Frequency Analysis of English Vocabulary and Grammar: Based on the LOB Corpus*. 2 vols. Oxford: Oxford University Press.

Johansson, Stig, Leech, Geoffrey, and Goodluck, Helen (1978) *Manual of Information to Accompany the Lancaster-Oslo/Bergen Corpus of British English, for Use with Digital Computers*. Oslo: University of Oslo.

Kachru, Braj B. (1965) The Indianness in Indian English. *Word*, **2**, 391–410.

Kachru, Braj B. (1985) Standards, codification and sociolinguistic realism: The English language in the outer circle. In *English in the World: Teaching and Learning the Language and Literatures*. Edited by Randolph Quirk and Henry G. Widdowson. Cambridge: Cambridge University Press, pp. 11–30.

Kennedy, Graeme (1996) The corpus as a research domain. In *Comparing English Worldwide: The International Corpus of English*. Edited by Sidney Greenbaum. Oxford: Clarendon Press, pp. 217–26.

Kennedy, Graeme (1998) *An Introduction to Corpus Linguistics*. London: Longman.

Kučera, Henry and Francis, W. Nelson (1967) *Computational Analysis of Present-Day American English*. Providence: Brown University Press.

Leitner, Gerhard (1992) *Begin* and *start* in British, American and Indian English. *Hermes*, **13**, 99–122.

Leitner, Gerhard and Hesselmann, M. (1996) "What do you do with a ball in soccer?" Medium, mode, and pluricentricity in soccer reporting. *World Englishes*, **15**(1), 83–102.

McEnery, Tony and Wilson, Andrew (2001) *Corpus Linguistics*. 2nd edition. Edinburgh: Edinburgh University Press.

Meyer, Charles F. (1996) Coordinate structures in English. *World Englishes*, **15**(1), 29–41.

Nelson, Gerald (1996a) The design of the corpus. In *Comparing English Worldwide: The International Corpus of English*. Edited by Sidney Greenbaum. Oxford: Clarendon Press, pp. 27–35.

Nelson, Gerald (1996b) Markup systems. In *Comparing English Worldwide: The International Corpus of English*. Edited by Sidney Greenbaum. Oxford: Clarendon Press, pp. 36–53.

Nelson, Gerald (2003) Modals of obligation and necessity in varieties of English. In *From Local to Global English: Proceedings of the Style Council 2001/2*. Edited by Pam H. Peters. Sydney: Dictionary Research Centre, Macquarie University, pp. 25–32.

Nelson, Gerald, Wallis, Sean, and Aarts, Bas (2002) *Exploring Natural Language: Working with the British Component of the International Corpus of English*. Amsterdam: Rodopi.

Peppé, Sue (1995) The Survey of English Usage and the London-Lund Corpus: Computerizing manual prosodic transcription. In *Spoken English on Computer: Transcription, Mark-up and Application*. Edited by Geoffrey Leech, Greeg Myers, and Jenny Thomas. London: Longman, pp. 187–202.

Peters, Pam (1993a) American and British English in Australian usage. In *Style on the Move: Proceedings of the Style Council 92*. Edited by Pam Peters. Sydney: Dictionary Research Centre, Macquarie University, pp. 20–7.

Peters, Pam (1993b) Corpus evidence on some points of usage. In *English Language Corpora: Design, Analysis and Exploitation*. Edited by Jan Aarts, Pieter de Haan, and Nelleke Oostdijk. Amsterdam: Rodopi, pp. 247–55.

Peters, Pam (1994) American and British influence in Australian verb morphology. In *Creating and Using English Language Corpora*. Edited by Udo Fries, Gunnel Tottie, and Peter Schneider. Amsterdam: Rodopi, pp. 149–58.

Peters, Pam, Collins, Peter, Blair, David, and Brierley, Alison (1988) The Australian corpus project: Findings on some functional variants in the Australian press. *Australian Review of Applied Linguistics*, **11**(1), 22–33.

Quirk, Randolph, Leech, Geoffrey, Svartvik, Jan, and Greenbaum, Sidney (1985) *A Comprehensive Grammar of the English Language*. London: Longman.

Sand, Andrea (1998) First findings from ICE-Jamaica: The verb phrase. In *Explorations in Corpus Linguistics*. Edited by Antoinette Renouf. Amsterdam: Rodopi, pp. 201–16.

Sayder, S. (1989) The subjunctive in Indian, British, and American English: A corpus-based study. In *Englische Textlinguistik und Varietätenforschung*. Edited by Gottfried Graustein and Wolfgang Thiele. Leipzig: Karl-Marx-Universität, pp. 58–66.

Schmied, Josef (1990) Corpus linguistics and non-native varieties of English. *World Englishes*, **9**(3), 255–68.

Schmied, Josef (1995) National standards and the International Corpus of English. In *New Englishes: A West African Perspective*. Edited by Ayọ Bamgbọṣe, Ayọ Banjo, and Andrew

Thomas. Ibadan, Nigeria: Mosuro, pp. 337–48.

Schmied, Josef and Hudson-Ettle, Diana (1996) Analyzing the style of East African newspapers in English. *World Englishes*, **15**(1), 103–13.

Schneider, Edgar W. (2000) Corpus linguistics in the Asian context: Exemplary analyses of the Kolhapur corpus of Indian English. In *Parangalcang Brother Andrew: Festschrift for Andrew Gonzalez on His Sixtieth Birthday*. Edited by Ma. Lourdes S. Bautista, Teodora A. Llamzon, and Bonifacio P. Sibayan. Manila: De La Salle University Press, pp. 115–37.

Shastri, S. V. (1986) *Manual of Information to Accompany the Kolhapur Corpus of Indian English, for Use with Digital Computers*. Kolhapur: Shivaji University.

Shastri, S. V. (1988) The Kolhapur corpus of Indian English and work done on its basis so far. *ICAME Journal*, **12**, 15–26.

Shastri, S. V. (1992) Opaque and transparent features of Indian English. In *New Directions in English Language Corpora: Methodology, Results, Software Developments*. Edited by Gerhard Leitner. Berlin/New York: Mouton de Gruyter, pp. 263–75.

Sigley, Robert (1997) The influence of formality and channel on relative pronoun choice in New Zealand English. *English Language and Linguistics*, **1**(2), 207–32.

Van Halteren, Hans and Oostdijk, Nelleke (1993) Towards a syntactic database: The TOSCA analysis system. In *English Language Corpora: Design, Analysis and Exploitation*. Edited by Jan Aarts, Pieter de Haan, and Nelleke Oostdijk. Amsterdam: Rodopi, pp. 145–61.

Virtanen, T. (1998) Direct questions in argumentative student writing. In *Learner English on Computer*. Edited by Sylviane Granger. London: Addison Wesley Longman, pp. 94–110.

Yang, Wen (1997) Discourse analysis of direct and indirect speech in spoken New Zealand English. *New Zealand Studies in Applied Linguistics*, **3**, 62–78.

FURTHER READING

Biber, Douglas (1993) Representativeness in corpus design. *Literary and Linguistic Computing*, **8**, 1–15.

Bolton, Kingsley (ed.) (2002) *Hong Kong English: Autonomy and Creativity*. Hong Kong: Hong Kong University Press.

Chafe, Wallace (1992) The importance of corpus linguistics to understanding the nature of language. In *Directions in Corpus Linguistics*. Edited by Jan Svartvik. Berlin: Mouton de Gruyter, pp. 79–97.

Granger, Sylviane (ed.) (1998) *Learner English on Computer*. London: Addison Wesley Longman.

Greenbaum, Sidney (1990) Standard English and the International Corpus of English. *World Englishes*, **9**(1), 79–83.

Greenbaum, Sidney (ed.) (1996) *Comparing English Worldwide: The International Corpus of English*. Oxford: Clarendon Press.

Hundt, Marianne (1998) *New Zealand English Grammar: Fact or Fiction?* Amsterdam: Benjamins.

Mair, Christian (1992) Problems in the compilation of a corpus of standard Caribbean English: A pilot study. In *New Directions in English Language Corpora: Methodology, Results, Software Developments.* Edited by Gerhard Leitner. Berlin/New York: Mouton de Gruyter, pp. 75–96.

Meyer, Charles F. (2002) *English Corpus Linguistics: An Introduction.* Cambridge: Cambridge University Press.

Oostdijk, Nelleke (1991) *Corpus Linguistics and the Automatic Analysis of English.* Amsterdam: Rodopi.

Peters, Pam (1998) In quest of international English: Mapping the levels of regional divergence.

In *Explorations in Corpus Linguistics.* Edited by Antoinette Renouf. Amsterdam: Rodopi, pp. 281–92.

Quirk, Randolph (1992) On corpus principles and design. In *Explorations in Corpus Linguistics: Directions in Corpus Linguistics. Proceedings of Nobel Symposium 82, Stockholm, 4–8 August 1991.* Edited by Jan Svartvik. Berlin: Mouton de Gruyter, pp. 457–69.

Schmied, Josef (1991) *English in Africa: An Introduction.* London/New York: Longman.

Schneider, Edgar W. (2003) Evolution(s) in global English(es). In *From Local to Global English: Proceedings of the Style Council 2001/2.* Edited by Pam H. Peters. Sydney: Dictionary Research Centre, Macquarie University, pp. 3–24.

42 Comparing World Englishes: A Research Guide

HELEN FALLON

1 Introduction

As the papers in this volume amply demonstrate, the comparison of varieties of English has become a major area of academic research. This is partly due to the pioneering work of such scholars as Manfred Görlach, Sidney Greenbaum, and Braj Kachru. The availability of electronic corpora of world Englishes has also contributed very significantly to the recent growth. In the case of the International Corpus of English (ICE), many of the component corpora represent the first ever attempt to compile a database of the national or regional variety.

The literature of world Englishes is well documented in comprehensive bibliographies such as Bolton (Chapters 15 and 17 in this volume), Glauser, Schneider, and Görlach (1993), B. Kachru (1997: 209–51), and Viereck, Schneider, and Görlach (1984). The scope of the present research guide is narrower than these general bibliographies. It is specifically concerned with *comparative* studies of varieties of English, and it includes items published in the major journals, and book chapters, during the period 1992 to 2004. This research guide is selective rather than exhaustive. It is aimed primarily at research students, though I hope that those established in the field will also find it useful.

Many of the journals included in this research guide provide tables of contents and sometimes abstracts of articles in recent issues, free of charge, via the web. Rather than listing each individual website, I would suggest that a web search by title via the name of the journal will generally retrieve the homepage of the relevant journal. While tables of contents are available free of charge, the fulltext electronic version of journals is generally available in one of two ways. For subscribers to the print version of a journal, the electronic version may be included in the price, or – more usually – for an additional charge. If the library in your institution subscribes to the printed version of a journal it is worth checking if the electronic version is also available. Depending on policy, you may be able to get a special password – generally an Athens password – which will allow you to access electronic journals and databases both on-campus and from your home or other location.

While it is important to scan individual journal titles and their contents to keep abreast of the literature, detailed subject or author searches over a period of time can be done much more effectively via a range of electronic databases. Two of the key databases consulted in the compilation of this research guide are the *MLA* (Modern Language Association) *International Bibliography* and *LLBA* (*Language and Linguistic Behavior Abstracts*). The *MLA International Bibliography* provides indexing and abstracting of critical scholarship in literature, language, linguistics, and folklore. Covering 3,500 journals and other sources, it provides abstracts of journal articles, series, books, dissertations, and conference papers. Coverage is from 1963 to the present. A range of indexes allow the user to search by author name, keyword, subject, title, journal name, year of publication, and so forth. The major journals in the field of world Englishes are covered in both databases, including *English Language and Linguistics*, *English Studies: A Journal of English Language and Literature*, *English Today: The International Review of the English Language*, and *World Englishes*.

While these two databases are key sources for the indexing and abstracting of journal articles in the field of world Englishes, coverage is quite extensive across a range of databases including *Linguistic Bibliography*, *Linguistics Abstracts*, *Education Abstracts*, *Periodicals Contents Index*, *Social Sciences Citation Index*, *Sociological Abstracts*, *Abstracts of English Studies*, *Arts and Humanities Citation Index*, *Bibliography of English Language and Literature*, and *Annual Bibliography of English Language and Literature*.

Searches of library catalogs by author, title, or subject have been greatly enhanced by the development of COPAC (http://www.copac.ac.uk), which provides free access to the merged catalogues of 22 of the largest research libraries in the UK and Ireland, including the British Library.

2   Select Bibliography of Comparative Studies of World Englishes 1992–2004

Aceto, Michael and Williams, Jeffrey P. (2003) *Contact Englishes of the Eastern Caribbean*. Amsterdam: Benjamins.

Ahulu, Samuel (1995) Variation in the use of complex verbs in international English. *English Today*, **11**, 2(42), 28–34.

Ahulu, Samuel (1998) Grammatical variation in international English. *English Today*, **14**, 4(56), 19–25.

Ahulu, Samuel (1998) Lexical variation in international English. *English Today*, **14**, 3(55), 29–34.

Baik, Martin J. (1994) Syntactic features of Englishization in Korea. *World Englishes*, **13**(2), 155–66.

Baik, Martin J. and Shim, Rosa J. (1993) Yes, we have no bananas: English negative tags in cross-linguistic communication. *Studies in the Linguistic Sciences*, **23**(1), 43–60.

Baker, Philip and Huber, Magnus (2001) Atlantic, Pacific and world-wide features in English-lexicon contact languages. *English World-Wide*, **22**(2), 157–208.

Bamgboṣe, Ayọ (1992) Standard Nigerian English: Issues of identification. In *The Other Tongue: English across Cultures*. 2nd edition. Edited by Braj B. Kachru. Urbana: University of Illinois Press, pp. 148–61.

Bamgbṣe, Ayọ (1998) Torn between the norms: Innovations in world Englishes. *World Englishes*, **17**(1), 1–14.

Bamgboṣe, Ayọ, Banjo, Ayọ, and Thomas, Andrew (eds.) (1995) *New Englishes: A West African Perspective*. Ibadan: Mosuro Publishers for the British Council. Reprinted 1997, Trenton, NJ: Africa World Press.

Bautista, Ma. Lourdes S. and Bolton, Kingsley (eds.) (2004) Philippine English: Tensions and Transitions. Special issue of *World Englishes*, **23**(1), 1–210.

Berns, Margie and Friedrich, Patricia (eds.) (2003) English in South America: A Different Kind of Difference. Special issue of *World Englishes*, **22**(2), 83–214.

Betts, Jerome (1997) In and on. *English Today*, **13**, 1(49), 49–51.

Bhatt, Rakesh M. (ed.) (1996) Symposium on Constraints on Code-Mixing. *World Englishes*, **15**(3), 359–404.

Bokamba, Eyamba G. (1992) The Africanization of English. In *The Other Tongue: English across Cultures*. Edited by Braj B. Kachru. Urbana: University of Illinois Press, pp. 126–47.

Bolton, Kingsley (ed.) (2000) Hong Kong English: Autonomy and Creativity. Special issue of *World Englishes*, **19**(3), 263–452.

Bolton, Kingsley (2005) World Englishes today. Chapter 15 (*in this volume*).

Bolton, Kingsley (2005) Varieties of World Englishes. Chapter 17 (*in this volume*).

Bolton, Kingsley and Tong, Q. S. (eds.) (2002) English in China: Interdisciplinary Perspectives. Special issue of *World Englishes*, **21**(2), 177–355.

Bradford, Barbara (1997) Upspeak in British English. *English Today*, **13**, 3(51), 29–36.

Cheng, Chin-Chuan (1992) Chinese varieties of English. In *The Other Tongue: English across Cultures*. Edited by Braj B. Kachru. Urbana: University of Illinois Press, pp. 162–77.

Chevillet, Francois (1993) English or Englishes. *English Today*, **9**(4), 29–33.

Clarke, Sandra (1997) The role of Irish English in the formation of New World Englishes: The case from Newfoundland. In *Focus on Ireland*. Edited by Jeffrey Kallen. Amsterdam: John Benjamins, pp. 207–25.

Clyne, Michael, Eisikovits, Edina, and Tollfree, Laura (2001) Ethnic varieties of Australian English. In *English in Australia*. Edited by David Blair and Peter Collins. Amsterdam: John Benjamins, pp. 223–39.

Coelho, Gail M. (1997) Anglo-Indian English: A nativised variety of Indian English. *Language in Society*, **26**(4), 561–89.

Davidson, Fred (ed.) (1993) Symposium on Testing English Across Cultures. *World Englishes*, **12**(1), 85–125.

Dissanayake, Wimal (ed.) (1993) Symposium on Power, Politics, and English. *World Englishes*, **12**(2), 143–221.

Frenck, Susan (ed.) (1998) Symposium on Linguistic Creativity in LGBT Discourse. *World Englishes*, **17**(2), 187–261.

Gordon, Elizabeth, Campbell, Lyle, Hay, Jennifer, Maclagan, Margaret, Sudbury, Andrea, and Trudgill, Peter (2004) *New Zealand English: Its Origins and Evolution*. Cambridge: Cambridge University Press.

Görlach, Manfred (1994) Innovation in New Englishes. *English World-Wide,* **15**(1), 101–26.

Görlach, Manfred (1995) *More Englishes: New Studies in Varieties of English 1988–1994.* Amsterdam: John Benjamins.

Görlach, Manfred (1996) And is it English? *English World-Wide,* **17**(2), 153–74.

Görlach, Manfred (2002) *Still More Englishes.* Amsterdam: John Benjamins.

Görlach, Manfred (2003) *English Words Abroad.* Amsterdam: John Benjamins.

Gorrell, Robert (1995) The future of past tenses. *English Today,* **11**, 4(44), 25–7.

Greenbaum, Sidney (ed.) (1996) *Comparing English Worldwide: The International Corpus of English.* Oxford: Clarendon Press.

Greenbaum, Sidney and Nelson, Gerald (eds.) (1996) Studies on International Corpus of English. Special issue of *World Englishes,* **15**(1), 1–124.

Gupta, Anthea Fraser (1997) Correct pronunciation and the millennium. *English Today,* **13**, 3(51), 23–5.

Hansen, Klaus (1997) British English and International English: Two database terms. In *Englishes around the World, I: General Studies, British Isles, North America.* Edited by Edgar W. Schneider. Amsterdam: John Benjamins, pp. 59–69.

Hartmann, Reinhard (1995) The Kachru contrasts. *English Today,* **11**, 2(42), 62–3.

Holmes, Janet (1993) Sex-marking suffixes in written New Zealand English. *American Speech,* **68**(4), 357–70.

Hsu, Jia-Ling (1994) Englishization and language change in Modern Chinese in Taiwan. *World Englishes,* **13**(2), 167–84.

Iwasaki, Yasufumi (1994) Englishization of Japanese and acculturation of English to Japanese culture. *World Englishes,* **13**(2), 261–72.

Jenkins, Jennifer (2003) *World Englishes: A Resource Book for Students.* London: Routledge.

Kachru, Braj B. (1983) *The Indianization of English: English Language in India.* Delhi: Oxford University Press.

Kachru, Braj B. (1986 [1990]) *The Alchemy of English: The Spread, Functions, and Models of Non-native Englishes.* Urbana: University of Illinois Press.

Kachru, Braj B. (ed.) (1992) *The Other Tongue: English across Cultures.* 2nd edition. Urbana: University of Illinois Press.

Kachru, Braj B. (1994) English in South Asia. In *The Cambridge History of the English Language, vol. 5: English in Britain and Overseas: Origins and Development.* Edited by Robert Burchfield. Cambridge: Cambridge University Press, pp. 497–553.

Kachru, Braj B. (1995) The alchemy of English. In *The Post-Colonial Studies Reader.* Edited by Helen Tiffin. London: Routledge, pp. 291–6.

Kachru, Braj B. (1996) South Asian English: Toward an identity in diaspora. In *South Asian English: Structure, Use, and Users.* Edited by Robert J. Baumgardner. Urbana: University of Illinois Press, pp. 9–28.

Kachru, Braj B. (1997) World Englishes 2000: Resources for research and teaching. In *World Englishes 2000.* Edited by Larry E. Smith and Michael L. Forman. Honolulu: University of Hawai'i Press, pp. 209–51.

Kachru, Braj B. (1999) Asian Englishes: Constructs, contact and convergence. Paper presented at the Twelfth World Congress of Applied Linguistics (AILA), Waseda University, Tokyo, August 1–6.

Kachru, Braj B. (2002) On nativizing *Mantra*: Identity construction in Anglophone Englishes. In *Anglophone Cultures in Southeast Asia: Appropriations, Continuities, Contexts.* Edited by Rüdiger Ahrens, David

Parker, Klaus Stierstorfer, and Kowk-Kan Tam. Heidelberg: Heidelberg University Press, pp. 55–72.

Kachru, Braj B. (2005) *Asian Englishes: Beyond the Canon*. Hong Kong: Hong Kong University Press.

Kachru, Braj B. and Nelson, Cecil L. (2001) World Englishes. In *Analysing English in a Global Context*. Edited by Anne Burns and Caroline Coffin. London: Routledge, pp. 9–25.

Kachru, Braj B. and Smith, Larry E. (eds.) (1990) Supplement on English in Japanese society and education: Four perspectives. *World Englishes*, 9(3), 317–66.

Kachru, Braj B. and Smith, Larry E. (eds.) (1993) Symposium on Linguistic Imperialism. *World Englishes*, 12(3), 335–91.

Kachru, Yamuna (1992) Social meaning and creativity in Indian English speech acts. *Georgetown University Round Table on Languages and Linguistics 1992*. Washington, DC: Georgetown University Press, pp. 378–87.

Kachru, Yamuna (1995) Contrastive rhetoric in world Englishes. *English Today*, 11, 1(41), 21–31.

Kachru, Yamuna (1996a) Kachru revisits contrasts. *English Today*, 12, 1(45), 41–4.

Kachru, Yamuna (1996b) Language and cultural meaning: Expository writing in South Asian English. In *South Asian English: Structure, Use, and Users*. Edited by Robert J. Baumgardner. Urbana: University of Illinois Press, pp. 127–40.

Kachru, Yamuna (1997) Cultural meaning and contrastive rhetoric in English education. *World Englishes*, 16(3), 337–50.

Kachru, Yamuna (1998) Culture and speech acts: Evidence from Indian and Singaporean English. *Studies in the Linguistic Sciences*, 28(1), 79–98.

Kachru, Yamuna (1999) Culture, context and writing. In *Culture in Second Language Teaching and Learning*. Edited by Eli Hinkel. Cambridge: Cambridge University Press, pp. 75–89.

Kachru, Yamuna (2001a) Discourse competence in world Englishes. In *The Three Circles of English*. Edited by Edwin Thumboo. Singapore: UniPress, pp. 341–55.

Kachru, Yamuna (2001b) World Englishes and rhetoric across cultures. *Asian Englishes: An International Journal of the Sociolinguistics of English in Asia/Pacific*, Winter, 54–71.

Kachru, Yamuna (2003) Conventions of politeness in plural societies. In *Anglophone Cultures in South-East Asia: Appropriations, Continuities, Contexts*. Edited by Rüdiger Ahrens, David Parker, Klaus Stierstorfer, and Kowk-Kan Tam. Heidelberg, Germany: Universitätsverlag Winter Heidelberg, pp. 39–53.

Kachru, Yamuna (guest ed.) (1987) Pedagogical Grammars of English: Approaches and Resources. Special issue of *World Englishes*, 6(3), 189–279.

Kachru, Yamuna (guest ed.) (1991) Symposium on Speech Acts in World Englishes. *World Englishes*, 10(3), 295–340.

Kachru, Yamuna and Nelson, Cecil L. (2006) *World Englishes in Asian Contexts*. Hong Kong: Hong Kong University Press.

Kallen, Jeffrey L. (1997) Irish Englishes and world Englishes: Lexical perspectives. In *Englishes around the World, I: General Studies, British Isles, North America*. Edited by Edgar W. Schneider. Amsterdam: John Benjamins, pp. 139–57.

Kam-Mei, Jacqueline Lam (2000) Asia's Englishes and world Englishes. *English Today*, 16, 1(61), 17–22.

Kamwangamalu, Nkonko M. (ed.) (2002) English in South Africa. Special issue of *World Englishes*, **21**(1), 1–163.

Kortmann, Bernd and Schneider, Edgar W. (2004) *A Handbook of Varieties of English*. Berlin: Mouton de Gruyter.

Kubota, Ryoko and Ward, Lori (2000) Exploring linguistic diversity through world Englishes. *English Journal*, **89**(6), 80–6.

Lilles, Jaan (2000) The myth of Canadian English. *English Today*, **16**, 2(62), 3–10.

Mair, Christian (1992) Problems in the compilation of a corpus of standard Caribbean English: Pilot study. In *New Directions in English Language Corpora: Methodology, Results, Software Developments*. Edited by Gerhard Leitner. Berlin: Mouton de Gruyter, pp. 75–96.

McArthur, Tom (1994) Models of English. *Ideologies dans le Monde Anglo Saxon*, **7**, 5–14.

McArthur, Tom (1999a) English in the world, in Africa and in South Africa. *English Today*, **15**, 1(57), 11–16.

McArthur, Tom (1999b) World or international or global English – and what is it anyway? *Georgetown University Round Table on Language and Linguistics, 1999*. Washington, DC: Georgetown University Press, pp. 396–403.

McArthur, Tom (2001) World English and world Englishes: Trends, tensions, varieties, and standards. *Language Teaching: The International Abstracting Journal for Language Teachers, Educators and Researchers*, **34**(1), 1–20.

McArthur, Tom (2003) *Oxford Guide to World English*. Oxford: Oxford University Press.

Melchers, Gunnel and Shaw, Philip (2003) *World Englishes: An Introduction*. London: Arnold.

Mesthrie, Rajend (1996) Language contact, transmission, shift: South African Indian English. In *Focus on South Africa*. Edited by Vivian De Klerk. Amsterdam: John Benjamins, pp. 79–98.

Modiano, Marko (1999) International English in the global village. *English Today*, **15**, 2(58), 22–34.

Modiano, Marko (1999) Standard English and educational practices for the world's Lingua Franca. *English Today*, **15**, 4(60), 3–13.

Mompean, Annick (1997) Pronouncing English in Brazil. *English Today*, **13**, 1(49), 28–35.

Moore, Margaret E. (1997) *Understanding British English: Bridging the Gap between the English Language and its American Counterpart*. Revised and updated edition. New Jersey: Carol Publishing Group.

Morris, Mervyn (1993) Is English we speaking. *English Today*, **9**, 4(36), 18–26.

Mufwene, Salikoko S. (2001) What is African American English? In *Sociolcultural and Historical Contexts of African American English*. Edited by Sonja L Lanehart. Amsterdam: John Benjamins, pp. 21–51.

Mufwene, Salikoko S. (ed.) (1997) Symposium on English-to-Pidgin Continua. *World Englishes*, **16**(2), 181–279.

Mufwene, Salikoko S. (ed.) (2003) Symposium on approaches to change in American English. *World Englishes*, **22**(4), 347–461.

Nelson, Cecil L. (1992) Sociocultural parameters of intelligibility. *Georgetown University Round Table on Languages and Linguistics 1992*. Washington, DC: Georgetown University Press, pp. 403–12.

Nelson, Gerald (2003) Modals of obligation and necessity in varieties of English. In *From Local to Global English: Proceedings of the Style Council 2001/2002*. Edited by Pam Peters. Sydney: Macquarie

University, Dictionary Research Centre, pp. 25–33.

Nelson, Gerald (ed.) (2004) The International Corpus of English. Special issue of *World Englishes*, **23**(2), 225–316.

Peters, Pam (2003) What is international English? In *From Local to Global English: Proceedings of the Style Council 2001/2002*. Edited by Pam Peters. Sydney: Macquarie University, Dictionary Research Centre, pp. 33–42.

Phillips, Betty (1998) British versus American -ate and -ator: Convergence, divergence and the lexicon. *American Speech*, **73**(2), 160–77.

Schmied, Josef (1993) Analysing style variation in the East African corpus of English. In *Creating and Using English Language Corpora: Papers from the Fourteenth International Conference on English Language Research on Computerized Corpora 1993*. Edited by Udo Fries, Gunnel Tottie, and Peter Schneider. Amsterdam: Rodopi, pp. 169–74.

Schmied, Josef (1996) English in Zimbabwe, Zambia and Malawi. In *Focus on South Africa*. Edited by Vivian De Klerk. Amsterdam: John Benjamins, pp. 301–21.

Schmied, Josef and Hudson-Ettle, Diana (1996) Analyzing the style of East African newspapers in English. *World Englishes*, **15**(1), 103–13.

Schneider, Edgar W. (1992) Who(m)? Case marking of wh-pronouns in written British and American English. In *New Directions in English Language Corpora: Methodology, Results, Software Developments*. Edited by Gerhard Leitner. Berlin: Mouton de Gruyter, pp. 231–45.

Schneider, Edgar W. (1995) White language contact through the centuries: Diachronic aspects of linguistic convergence or divergences in the United States of America. In *Linguistic Change under Contact Conditions*. Edited by Jacek Fisiak. Berlin: Mouton de Gruyter, pp. 127–252.

Schneider, Edgar W. (1996a) Introduction: Research trends in the study of American English. In *Focus on the USA*. Edited by Edgar W. Schneider. Amsterdam: John Benjamins, pp. 1–12.

Schneider, Edgar. W. (2000) Feature diffusion vs. contact effects in the evolution of new Englishes: A typological case study of negation patterns. *English World-Wide*, **21**(2), 201–30.

Schneider, Edgar W. (2000) From region to class to identity: "Show me how you speak, and I'll tell you who you are?" *American Speech*, **75**(4), 359–61.

Schneider, Edgar W. (2001) Global Englishes computerized. *American Speech*, **76**(3), 316–22.

Schneider, Edgar W. (2003) Evolution(s) in global English(es). In *From Local to Global English: Proceedings of the Style Council 2001/2002*. Edited by Pam Peters. Sydney: Macquarie University, Dictionary Research Centre, pp. 3–24.

Schneider, Edgar W. and Montgomery, Michael B. (2001) On the trail of early nonstandard grammar: An electronic corpus of Southern U.S. Antebellum Overseers' letters. *American Speech*, **76**(4), 388–410.

Schneider, Edgar W., Burridge, Kate, Kortman, Bernd, Mesthrie, Rajend, and Upton, Clive (eds.) (2004) *A Handbook of Varieties of English* (2 vols). Berlin: Mouton de Gruyter.

Schreider, Daniel (2002) Terra Incognita in the anglophone world: Tristan da Cunha, South Atlantic Ocean. *English World-Wide*, **23**(1), 1–29.

Shastri, S. V. (1992) Opaque and transparent features of Indian English. In *New Directions in English Language Corpora: Methodology,*

Results, Software Developments 1992. Edited by Gerhard Leitner. Berlin: Mouton de Gruyter, pp. 263–75.

Shastri, S. V. (1996) Using the computer corpora in the description of language with special reference to complementation in Indian English. In *South Asian English: Structure, Use and Users.* Edited by Robert J. Baumgardner. Urbana: University of Illinois Press, pp. 70–81.

Shim, Rosa J. (1994) Englishized Korean: Structure, status, and attitude. *World Englishes,* **13**(2), 225–44.

Shim, Rosa J. (1999) Codified Korean English: Process, characteristics and consequence. *World Englishes,* **18**(2), 247–59.

Siegel, Jeff (1997) Mixing, leveling and Pidgin/Creole development; Including selected papers from the meetings of the Society for Pidgin and Creole Linguistics. In *The Structure and Status of Pidgins and Creoles.* Edited by Arthur Spears and Donald Winford. Amsterdam: John Benjamins, pp. 111–49.

Siegel, Jeff (1997) Pidgin and English in Melanesia: Is there a continuum? *World Englishes,* **16**(2), 185–205.

Simo-Bobda, Augustin (1998) British or American English: Does it matter? *English Today,* **14**, 4(56), 13–18.

Simo-Bobda, Augustin (2000) Comparing some phonological features across African accents of English. *English Studies: A Journal of English Language and Literature,* **81**(3), 249–66.

Simo-Bobda, Augustin (2000) Research on New Englishes: A critical review of some findings so far with a focus on Cameroon English. *Arbeiten aus Anglistik und Amerikanistik,* **25**(1), 53–70.

Simo-Bobda, Augustin and Bamgbose, Ayo (1995) Aspects of Cameroon English phonology. *World Englishes,* **14**(3), 391–5.

Smith, Larry E. (1992) Spread of English and issues of intelligibility. In *The Other Tongue: English across Cultures.* 2nd edition. Edited by Braj B. Kachru. Urbana: University of Illinois Press, pp. 75–90.

Smith, Larry E. and Bisazza, John (1982) The comprehensibility of three varieties of English for college students in seven countries. *Language Learning,* **32**, 259–70.

Smith, Larry E. and Nelson, Cecil L. (1985) International intelligibility of English: Directions and resources. *World Englishes,* **4**(3), 333–42.

Smith, Larry E. and Rafiqzad, Khalilulla (1979) English for cross-cultural communication: The question of intelligibility. *TESOL Quarterly,* **13**(3), 371–80.

Smith, Larry E. and Forman, Michael L. (eds.) (1997) *World Englishes 2000.* Honolulu: University of Hawai'i Press.

Taylor, Brian (2001) Australian English in interaction with other Englishes. In *English in Australia. 2001.* Edited by David Blair and Peter Collins. Amsterdam: John Benjamins, pp. 317–40.

Tent, Jan (2000) English lexicography in Fiji. *English Today,* **16**, 3(63), 22–8.

Tent, Jan (2001) A profile of the Fiji English lexis. *English World-Wide,* **22**(2), 209–45.

Toolan, Michael (1997) Recentering English: New English and global. *English Today,* **13**, 4(52), 3–10.

Trudgill, Peter, Nevalainen, Terttu, and Wischer, Ilse (2002) Dynamic *have* in North American and British Isles English. *English Language and Linguistics,* **6**(1), 1–15.

Van der Walt, Christa (1997) Justifying their existence: South African varieties of English. In *Human Contact through Language and Linguistics.* Edited by Birgit Smieja and Meike Tasch. Frankfurt: Peter Lang, pp. 341–51.

Van der Walt, Christa (2000) The
   international comprehensibility of
   varieties of South African English.
   World Englishes, **19**(2), 139–53.
Van Horn, Stanley (ed.) (2003)
   Symposium on Ethics, Ideology and
World Englishes. *World Englishes*,
   22(3), 215–70.
Watson-Gegeo, Karen A. (ed.) (1989)
   English in the South Pacific.
   Special issue of *World Englishes*,
   8(1), 1–94.

3   Journals

American Speech
1925–. Quarterly. Duke University
Editor: **Connie C. Eble**
Address: American Dialect Society Publications, Duke University, Box 90660, Durham,
NC 27708-90660, USA
Phone: 919-684-6561
Email: amspeech@dukeupress.edu
www.dukeupress.edu/americanspeech

Arbeiten aus Anglistik und Amerikanistik
1976–. Two issues per year. Germany: Gunter Narr Verlag
Text in English and German
(not refereed)
Address: ostfach 2567, Tuebingen 72015, Germany
Phone: 49 7071 97970
Fax: 49 70071 75288
Email: info@narr.de
www.narr.de

English Journal (EJ)
1912–. Bi-monthly. Urbana, IL: National Council of Teachers of Education (NCTE)
Editor: Louann Reid
Address: English Department, 1773 Campus Delivery, Colorado State University, Fort
Collins, CO 80523-3097, USA
Email: English-journal@colostate.edu
www.ncte.org/pubs/journals/ej

English Language and Linguistics
1997–. Semi-annually. Cambridge: Cambridge University Press
Editors: Bas Aarts, David Denison, Richard Hogg, Douglas Biber
Address: English Language and Linguistics, c/o Department of English Language and
Literature, University College London, Gower Street, London WC1E 6BT, UK.
Phone: 20 76793130
Fax: 20 79162054
Email: ell@ucl.ac.uk
www.cambridge.org/uk/journals/

English Studies: A Journal of English Language and Literature
1919–. Bi-monthly. United Kingdom: Taylor and Francis
Editor-in-chief: Odin Dekkers
Address: Department of English, University of Nijmegen, PO Box 9103, Nijmegen, The Netherlands
www.tandf.co.uk/journals/

English Today: The International Review of the English Language
1985–. Quarterly. Cambridge: Cambridge University Press
Editor: Tom McArthur
Address: 22-23 Ventress Farm Court, Cherry Hinton Rd, Cambridge CB1 4HD, UK
Phone: 1223 245934
Fax: 1223 241161
Email: mailto:scotsway@aol.com
www.journals.cambridge.org/

English World-Wide: A Journal of Varieties of English
1980–. Semi-annually. Amsterdam: Benjamins
Editors: Edgar W. Schneider
Address: Institut für Anglistik, Universität Regensburg, Universitaetsstr. 31, 93040, Regensburg, Germany
Email: customer.services@benjamins.nl
www.benjamins.com

Language in Society
1972–. Five times per year. Cambridge: Cambridge University Press
Editor: Jane Hill, University of Arizona, USA
Address: The Edinburgh Building, Shaftesbury Road, Cambridge CB2 2RU, UK
Phone: 1223 326070
www.journals.cambridge.org/

Language Problems and Language Planning
1969–. 3 times per year. Amsterdam: Benjamins
Editors: Probal Dasgupta
Address: University of Hyderabad, Centre for Applied Linguistics and Translation Studies, University of Hyderabad, Hyderabad-500 046, India
Phone: 91-40-23012069
Fax: 91-40-230100003
Email: pdgalts@uohyd.ernet.in and probal53@yahoo.com
Humphrey Tonkin, University of Hartford
Address: University of Hartford, 200 Bloomfield Avenue, West Hartford, CT 06117-1599, USA
Email: tonkin@hartford.edu
www.benjamins.com

Language Teaching: The International Abstracting Journal for Language Teachers, Educators and Researchers
1968–. Quarterly. Cambridge: Cambridge University Press
Editor: Sue Wharton, University of Warwick, UK

Email: s.m.wharton@warwick.ac.uk
www.journals.cambridge.org/

Studies in the Linguistic Sciences
1974–. Two issues per year. Illinois: Department of Linguistics, University of Illinois
Editor: Peter Lasersohn
Address: Department of Linguistics, University of Illinois, 4088 Foreign Languages Building, 707 South Mathews Ave, Urbana, IL 61801, USA
Phone: 217 333-3563
Fax: 217 244-8430
Email: deptling@uiuc.edu
www.linguistics.uiuc.edu/sls/

World Englishes: Journal of English as an International and Intranational Language
1982– Four issues per year. Oxford and Malden, MA: Blackwell
Editors: Braj B. Kachru, Larry E. Smith
Address: Department of Linguistics, University of Illinois, 4088 Foreign Languages Building, 707 South Mathews Ave., Urbana, IL 61801 USA
Phone: Braj B. Kachru 217 333-3563; Larry E. Smith 808 263-7054
Fax: Braj B. Kachru 217 328 1966 and 217 333-3466; Larry E. Smith, 808 247-9084
www.blackwell-synergy.com

4 Electronic Resources

The corpora in the International Corpus of English (ICE) (Greenbaum, 1996) are available under license for non-commercial, academic research. The following ICE corpora are now available: East Africa (Kenya and Tanzania), Great Britain, India, the Philippines, New Zealand, and Singapore. The Hong Kong corpus has been collected and computerized, and will be available in the near future. For news and updates relating to the ICE corpora, readers are invited to join the ICE mailing list. To join the mailing list, go to http://www.ucl.ac.uk/english-usage/ice/mail.htm.

All the ICE corpora consist of one million words of spoken and written English dating from the 1990s. They are all lexical corpora, with the exception of the British component (ICE-GB), which has been tagged for part of speech and syntactically analyzed. ICE-GB is supplied with its own retrieval software, ICECUP (the ICE Corpus Utility Program). For details see www.ucl.ac.uk/english-usage/ice/index.html.

The International Computer Archive of Modern English (ICAME) is a major source of electronic corpora. ICAME distributes a large number of corpora on CD–ROM, including the following:

Kolhapur Corpus of Indian English
Australian Corpus of English (ACE)
Wellington Corpus of Written New Zealand English
Wellington Corpus of Spoken New Zealand English

For full details, see http://www.hd.uib.no/icame.html.

The 100 million-word British National Corpus (BNC) is accessible online via www.natcorp.ox.ac.uk.

Other sources of electronic corpora include the Linguistic Data Consortium (LDC), http://www.ldc.upenn.edu/, and the European Language Resources Association (ELRA), http://www.elra.info/. See also Chapter 41 in this volume.

REFERENCES

Glauser, Beat, Schneider, Edgar W., and Görlach, Manfred (1993) *A New Bibliography of Writings on Varieties of English, 1984–1992/93.* Amsterdam/Philadelphia: John Benjamins.

Greenbaum, Sidney (ed.) (1996) *Comparing English Worldwide: The International Corpus of English.* Oxford: Clarendon Press.

Kachru, Braj B. (1997) World Englishes 2000: Resources for research and teaching. In *World Englishes 2000.* Edited by Larry E. Smith and Michael L. Forman. Honolulu: University of Hawai'i Press, pp. 209–51.

Viereck, Wolfgang, Schneider, Edgar W., and Görlach, Manfred (1984) *A Bibliography of Writings on Varieties of English, 1965–1983.* Amsterdam: John Benjamins.

Author Index

Subject Index

Western Isles (Scotland)
44–5
White East African
English 191
White South African
English 162
"white speech" 337
Whole Language
Approach 682, 685
Whorfian hypothesis 174,
416
wider communication,
languages of 122,
139, 224, 453, 572, 623
"Wogspeak" *see* New
Australian English
women
as agents of
transmission 571–2,
574
assimilation to the
standard 519
creativity of bilingual
10, 572–6
education of 386–8
experiential and
attitudinal differences
from men 10
and grammar 485–8
and language policy
569
leaders in linguistic
change 64, 79, 571–2,
574
politeness 573
subjectivity of 551
and use of non-sexist
language 504–5
women's language 571–2
word formation, resources
for 354
word-stress
Germanic 25, 194
influence of French on
English 25
Romance 194
words
and conceptualization
496

criteria for establishing
canonical form of
694
and order 496
workplace discourse 223,
620
Works Project
Administration
(WPA) 334
World English,
McArthur's circle of
48
World Englishes 13, 241,
243, 248, 252, 258,
263, 274, 624, 661,
742, 752
world Englishes 1–16
against relativism
537–9
the challenge from
536–7
the concept of 13,
240–3, 248–9, 289,
447, 567
corpus-based studies
13, 740–3
as a discursive
construct 545–66
early contact history
277–8
historical context 2–3,
17–270, 273–88
intelligibility 428–45
non-literary written
sources 274–86
paradigm 172–3, 234,
273, 304, 305–8, 689,
720–1
and popularizers 255–7
resources on 13, 731–62
today 3, 240–69
variational contexts
4–5, 271–345
varieties of 289–312
see also New Englishes
World Standard English
45, 241, 306
World Standard Spoken
English (WSSE) 259

World Trade Organization
623
worldview, and language
expression 505
writers
female 486, 575–6
and the milieu 411–16
role as public
intellectuals in Third
World 558
writing 366–85, 405–27
black 409–10
features of non-Inner-
Circle 377–8
functions of creative
575
gendered styles 575–6
good vs. good grammar
8, 478–9
indigenous and English
554–5
introduction of 356,
358, 361
and philosophy 548
reasons for 409–10
rhetorical strategies in
374–9
systems 356
see also literature
written language 5, 274,
349–65
corpora 736, 741
syntax compared with
spoken 518

Xhosa 159, 162, 283

Yiddish language 295
Yiddish English 276
Yoruba language 177, 181,
361
youth culture, African
American 336–7

Zambia 188
Zanzibar 189, 190
Zimbabwe 188, 190, 296,
723
Zulu 159, 162, 408, 573